Advanced
Accounting

SEVENTH EDITION

Paul M. Fischer, PhD, CPA

Professor of Accounting

University of Wisconsin, Milwaukee

William J. Taylor, PhD, CPA

Assistant Professor of Accounting

University of Wisconsin, Milwaukee

Rita H. Cheng, PhD, CPA

Associate Professor of Accounting

University of Wisconsin, Milwaukee

South-Western College Publishing

an International Thomson Publishing company I(T)P®

Cincinnati • Albany • Boston • Detroit • Johannesburg • London • Madrid • Melbourne • Mexico City
New York • Pacific Grove • San Francisco • Scottsdale • Singapore • Tokyo • Toronto

Team Director:	Richard Lindgren
Developmental Editor:	Sara Wilson
Production Editor:	Marci Dechter
Production House:	Navta Associates, Inc.
Cover Designer:	Ann Small/A Small Design Studio
Cover Illustrator:	copyright/Garneau/Provost/SuperStock
Marketing Manager:	Maureen L. Riopelle
Manufacturing Coordinator:	Gordon Woodside

Library of Congress Cataloging-in-Publication Data:
Fischer, Paul M.
    Advanced accounting / Paul M. Fischer, William J. Taylor,
Rita H. Cheng. — 7th ed.
        p.   cm.
    Includes bibliographical references and index.
    ISBN 0-538-86655-1
    1. Accounting.   I. Taylor, William James.   II. Cheng, Rita H., 1952-   .
III. Title.
    HF5635.F5389 1998
657'.046—dc21   98-3027
                                                  CIP

Student Edition, Chapters 1–21   ISBN: 0-538-86655-1

4 5 6 7 8 9 D1 5 4 3 2 1
Printed in the United States of America

I(T)P®

International Thomson Publishing
South-Western College Publishing is an ITP Company.
The ITP trademark is used under license.

Preface

Follow the Leader

Clear. Conceptual. Comprehensive.

With a strong tradition of combining sound theoretical foundations with a hands-on learn-by-example approach, this book has earned itself a prominent place in advanced accounting classrooms across the country. In this Seventh Edition, we build on *Advanced Accounting's* clear writing style, comprehensive coverage, and focus on conceptual understanding. This edition expands on its time-tested and proven approach by adding new features that enhance comprehension and knowledge, as well as topics and issues that are timely.

Realizing that students reap the greatest benefits when they can visualize the application of theories, *Advanced Accounting* closely links theory and practice by providing examples that are common to real-world accounting. When students can visualize the concept being discussed and apply it directly to an example, their understanding greatly improves. This focus on conceptual understanding makes even the most complex topics approachable. Questions are used to reinforce theory, and exercises are short, focused applications of specific topics in the chapter. These exercises make great assignments to be done prior to class. The book's problems—more comprehensive than the exercises—often combine topics and are designed to work well as after-class assignments. For group projects, the cases found in the business combinations chapters provide an innovative way to blend theoretical and numerical analysis.

Ideal for student self-study and unique to *Advanced Accounting* is the *Student Companion Enrichment Manual.* With step-by-step application of the methods discussed in the text, as well as a complete study guide, the enrichment manual reinforces student understanding and helps students in their mastery of text subject matter. See page viii for more information on the Enrichment Manual.

Of importance to both instructors and students is the emphasis on accuracy in both the book and supplementary items. Through meticulous proofing and quality control, we have taken great strides to ensure its error-free content. Each author has carefully proofread the chapters, and an editor has gone over the content to ensure accuracy. In addition, all the ancillaries have been reviewed and checked by highly qualified individuals.

Comprehensive

Highlights of Changes in the Seventh Edition

Advanced Accounting, Seventh Edition, reflects changes in accounting procedures and standards while improving on those features that aid in student comprehension. The book's authorship now includes Rita Cheng of the University of Wisconsin, Milwaukee, a well-respected educator in the governmental and not-for-profit accounting arena.

New features of this edition include:

- *Expanded coverage of the pooling-of-interests method.* Chapter 1 takes a more in-depth look at the comparison of pooling versus purchase and analyzes the current increase in pooling. It also focuses on the motivation to use this method to enhance performance measures. An actual case is used to demonstrate the financial reporting advantages of pooling.
- *Changes in accounting and business combinations procedures that may take place in the coming years.* The impact of these changes on current GAAP methods used in the text is analyzed. Many of the methods used in the text, such as disclosure of the minority interest and 100% elimination of intercompany profits, are ratified by the FASB proposals.
- *Two new special appendices that focus on the existing FASB proposals for new consolidation procedures.* The first appendix, Special Appendix 1, follows Chapter 3 and focuses on the mark to market the noncontrolling interest (currently the minority interest). Following Chapter 8, Special Appendix 2 studies the possible changes in accounting for changes in the level of parent ownership and changes in the subsidiary equity structure.

- *Substantial improvements and updated coverage in accounting for the taxation of the consolidated firm.* New support schedules guide the worksheet procedures for consolidated firms, which are taxed as separate entities.

- *Enhancements of the very popular Determination and Distribution of Excess Schedule.* "Zone Analysis" is now included in the scheduling process, allowing students to determine in advance if the price will allow goodwill, be a bargain, or result in a deferred credit.

- *Simplified worksheet procedures for intercompany fixed asset sales and for intercompany inventory transactions, where the periodic inventory method is used.* Chapter 4 includes this easier approach for students.

- *Substantial revision of end-of-chapter assignments.* There is an expanded use of cases to study alternative accounting methods for business combinations. These cases build an awareness of the important issues now under consideration by the FASB.

- *A study of the specific differences between accounting procedures in the United States and selected major foreign countries.* The countries are compared by cultural classification and selected accounting principles. Chapter 9 also studies the development of international accounting standards and identifies areas which differ from existing U.S. GAAP. The material on foreign currency transactions has been revised to reflect the FASB exposure draft on derivatives.

- *Coverage of SFAS No. 131 (segmental reporting).* Financial disclosure for segments has been made less structured and more consistent with internal measurement methods. This edition includes a full discussion of the new procedures and illustrates their application.

- *Coverage of SFAS No. 128 (earnings per share).* Our traditional, unique, and simplified formula approach has been revised to insure clear explanation and illustration of the new calculations of earnings per share.

- *A discussion of recent developments in state and local government financial reporting, including the GASB's efforts to develop a new reporting model.* In addition to the reporting model, this edition also incorporates the new GASB guidance on accounting for pensions, for recognition of assets and liabilities and related disclosures arising from securities lending transactions, accounting for certain investments at fair value, and additional coverage of key issues in governmental audit, including the single audit act.

- *An appendix detailing the proposed dual-perspective financial reporting model.* At the end of Chapter 17, the unique features of the dual perspective are presented.

- *Revised coverage of FASB 116, 117, and 124 in the not-for-profit chapters.* The same transactions are used for the nonprofit organizations as for the governmental units, so that the student will clearly see the differences in the methods used.

- *Enhanced coverage throughout the government and not-for-profit chapters.* Improvements in the text, illustrations, and end-of-chapter materials are aimed at making the presentation more conceptual and less procedural. The aim is to provide students with an understanding of the unique features of the changing government and not-for-profit accounting environment.

Clear. Conceptual.

Organization of the Book

The book's flexible coverage of topics allows for professors to teach their course at their own pace and in their preferred order. There are no dependencies between major sections of the text except that coverage of consolidations should precede multinational accounting if one is to understand accounting for foreign subsidiaries. The book contains enough coverage to fill two advanced courses, but when only one semester is available, many professors find it ideal to cover the first four to six chapters in business combinations.

The text is divided into the following major topics:

BUSINESS COMBINATIONS—BASIC TOPICS
(CHAPTERS 1–6)

A unique feature of this book is the devotion of the first chapter to the basic issues of purchase and pooling-of-interests accounting in the context of direct asset acquisitions. This provides an opportunity to focus on theoretical concepts without being concerned about the mechanics of consolidations. The most difficult concept in the chapter is the combining of stockholders' equities in a pooling of interests, and this is aided by a unique "equity transfer diagram." Chapter 1 also takes an in-depth look at the comparison of pooling versus purchase and analyzes the current increase in pooling. We use a real-world case to demonstrate the financial reporting advantages of pooling.

Chapters 2 through 5 cover the basics of preparing a consolidated income statement and balance sheet.

In 1977, we introduced two schedules that have been much appreciated by students and faculty alike—the *Determination* and *Distribution of Excess Schedule* and *Income Distribution Schedule*. The determination and distribution schedule (quickly termed the D&D schedule by students) analyzes the difference between the price paid in a purchase and the underlying equity of the subsidiary. It provides a check figure for all subsequent years' worksheets, provides all information for the distribution of differences between book and market values, and provides all data for the amortization of the differences. The schedule provides rules for all types of purchase situations and for alternative consolidation theories. The income distribution schedule (known as the IDS) is a set of T accounts that distributes income between the minority and controlling interests. It also provides a useful check function to assure that all intercompany eliminations are properly accounted for. These chapters give the student all topics needed for the CPA Exam. Special Appendix 1, which follows Chapter 3, focuses on the marking to market of the noncontrolling (currently the minority) interests.

With regard to the alternative worksheet methods and why we follow the approaches we do: First, consider the method used to record the investment in the subsidiary's and the parent's books. There are two key points of general agreement. The first is that it doesn't really matter which method is used since the investment account is eliminated! Second, when the course is over, a student should know how to handle each method: simple equity, full (we call it sophisticated) equity, and cost. The real issue is which method is the easiest one to learn first. We believe the winner is simple equity since it is totally symmetric with the equity accounts of the subsidiary. It simplifies elimination of subsidiary equity against the investment account. Every change in subsidiary equity is reflected, on a pro rata basis, in the parent's investment account. Thus, the simple equity method becomes the mainline method of the text. We teach the student to convert investments maintained under the cost method to the simple equity method. In practice, most firms and the majority of the problems in the text use the cost method. This means that the simple equity method is employed to solve problems that begin as either simple equity or cost method problems.

We also cover the sophisticated equity method, which amortizes the excess of cost or book value through the investment account. This method should also adjust for intercompany profits through the investment account. The method is cumbersome because it requires the student to deal with amortizations of excess and intercompany profits in the investment account before getting to the consolidated worksheet, which is designed to handle these topics. This means teaching consolidating procedures without the benefit of a worksheet. We cover the method after the student is proficient with a worksheet and the other methods. Thorough understanding of the sophisticated method is important so that it can be applied to influential investments that are not consolidated.

The second major concern among advanced text professors has to do with the worksheet style used. There are three choices: the horizontal (trial balance) format, the vertical (stacked) method, and the balance sheet only. Again, we do cover all three, but the horizontal format is our main method. Horizontal is by far the most appealing to students. They have used it in both introductory and intermediate accounting. It is also the most likely method to be found in practice. On this basis, we use it initially to develop all topics. We do cover the vertical format, but not until the student is proficient with the horizontal format. There is no difference in the elimination entries; only the worksheet logistics differ. It takes only one problem assignment to teach the students this approach so they are prepared for its possible appearance on the CPA Exam. The balance-sheet-only format has no reason to exist other than its use as a CPA Exam testing shortcut. We cover it in an appendix.

Chapter 6 is more essential for those entering practice than it is for the CPA Exam. It contains cash flow for consolidated firms, taxation issues, and the use of the sophisticated equity method for influential investments. This edition makes substantial improvements in accounting for the taxation of the consolidated company. New support schedules guide the worksheet procedures for consolidated companies, which are taxed as separate entities. Taxation is the most difficult application of consolidation procedures. Every intercompany transaction is a tax allocation issue. Teaching the tax allocation issues with every topic as it is introduced is very confusing to students. We prefer to have the students fully understand worksheet procedures without taxes and then introduce taxes.

BUSINESS COMBINATIONS—SPECIALIZED TOPICS
(CHAPTERS 7 AND 8)

These chapters deal with topics that occasionally surface in practice and have not appeared on the

CPA Exam for over 10 years. Studying these chapters perfects the students' understanding of consolidations and stockholders' equity accounting, thus affording a valuable experience. Chapter 7 deals with piecemeal acquisitions of an investment in a subsidiary, sale of the parent's investment, and the impact of preferred stock in the subsidiary's equity structure. Chapter 8 deals with the impact of subsidiary equity transactions including stock dividends, sale of common stock shares, and subsidiary reacquisitions of shares. The chapter also considers indirect or three-tier ownership structures and reciprocal holdings where the subsidiary owns parent shares. Following Chapter 8, Special Appendix 2 studies the possible changes in accounting for changes in the level of parent ownership and changes in the subsidiary equity structure.

BUSINESS COMBINATIONS—SPECIAL APPENDICES

The Special Appendices 1 and 2 should not be dismissed from the study plan for a semester. The material on alternative consolidation theories is conceptually important. It summarizes FASB's 1995 Exposure Draft and compares alternative theories to current practice. Studying it reinforces the students' understanding and prepares them for changes that may occur. Generally, students find this material very interesting. The first one follows Chapter 3. It summarizes the Parent Company theory and explains two approaches to the Economic Unit Concept. Special Appendix 2 appears after Chapter 8. It explains additional possible changes to consolidation practice based on the FASB proposal.

Special Appendix 3 explores accounting for leveraged buyouts. This is a popular topic and is easily mastered using consolidation techniques. Students enjoy mastering it since it is a common business phenomenon that sounds difficult but really isn't. It particularly appeals to students with an interest in financial management.

MULTINATIONAL ACCOUNTING (CHAPTERS 9–11)

As business has developed beyond national boundaries, the discipline of accounting also has evolved internationally. As our global economy develops, so does the demand for reliable and comparable financial information. Chapter 9 discusses the international accounting environment and compares accounting principles among several countries. This comparison illustrates for the need for accounting standards to be in harmony with each other. Approaches to the harmonization of standards and the various organizations involved are identified.

Chapter 10 discusses accounting for foreign currency transactions. The basic mechanics of exchange rates and the business risks resulting from exchange rate changes are set forth. The use of forward contracts as a hedge against rate change fluctuations is discussed, and the accounting for such hedges is demonstrated. Chapter 11 demonstrates the remeasurement and/or translation of a foreign entity's financial statements into a U.S. investor's currency. Whenever possible, examples of footnote disclosure relating to international accounting issues are presented.

SPECIAL REPORTING CONCERNS (CHAPTERS 12 AND 13)

The usefulness of financial information naturally increases if it is communicated on a timely basis. Therefore, interim financial statements and reporting requirements are now widely accepted. In Chapter 12, the concept of an interim period as an integral part of a larger annual accounting period is set forth as a basis for explaining the specialized accounting principles of interim reporting. Particular attention is paid to the determination of the interim income tax provision including the tax implications of net operating losses. Chapter 12 also examines segmental reporting and the various disclosure requirements. A worksheet format for developing segmental data is used, and students are able to review the segmental footnote disclosure for a large public company. The section on segmental reporting has been significantly updated to reflect the new FASB Statement No. 131.

In Chapter 13, students are given a comprehensive discussion of the disclosure of earnings per share data in compliance with FASB statement No. 128. Supporting schedules are used to facilitate the calculation of per share amounts. The calculation of basic earnings per share is developed, and then, with that background, students are exposed to the calculation of diluted earnings per share. The chapter concludes with a comprehensive illustration dealing with the calculation of both basic and diluted earnings per share.

ACCOUNTING FOR PARTNERSHIPS (CHAPTERS 14 AND 15)

Chapters 14 and 15 take students through the entire life cycle of a partnership, beginning with formation and ending in liquidation. Although new forms of organization, such as the limited liability corporation, are available, partnerships continue to be a common form of organization. Practicing accountants must be aware of the characteristics of this form of organization and the unique accounting principles. The accounting aspects of profit and loss agreements, changes in the composition of partners (admissions and withdrawals), and partnership liquidations are fully illustrated. In addition to accounting principles, certain income tax principles relating to partnerships are set forth. The end-of-chapter material in this area focuses on evaluating various alternative strategies available to partners, for example, deciding whether it would be better to liquidate a partnership or admit a new partner.

GOVERNMENTAL AND NOT-FOR-PROFIT ACCOUNTING (CHAPTERS 16–19)

Chapters 16 and 17 have been updated to include recent Governmental Accounting Standards Board (GASB) pronouncements. Chapter 16 includes a complete discussion of measurement focus and basis of accounting issues for state and local governments. The deferral of GASB Statement No. 11 and the issues involved in the deliberation of a new "dual perspective" financial reporting model are outlined for the reader.

In Chapter 16, we introduce the unique accounting and financial reporting issues of state and local governments. The chapter also covers the basics of accounting and financial reporting for the general fund and the two account groups. This order emphasizes the "working capital" focus of the general fund and the resulting need to account for fixed assets and long-term liabilities elsewhere.

Chapter 17 covers the accounting and financial reporting of the specialized funds of government: those established to account for restricted operating resources, long-term construction projects or acquisition of major fixed assets, and servicing of principal and interest on long-term debt. The chapter also covers the unique accounting issues of various trust funds and proprietary (business-type) funds.

Chapters 18 and 19 include revised coverage of Financial Accounting Standards Board (FASB) 116, 117, and 124 for such organizations as private not-for-profit health care entities, private universities, and voluntary health and welfare organizations. The same transactions are used for the nonprofit organizations as for the governmental units, allowing students to clearly see the differences in the methods used. The standards define how the resources of a private not-for-profit organization are to be divided into unrestricted, temporarily restricted, or permanently restricted net asset classifications. Financial statements also are based on net asset classifications. The new standards represent a shift away from fund accounting to organi-zation-wide financial reporting. A statement of cash flows is now required. The chapters also cover the updated guidance in the 1996 industry audit guides.

In Chapter 18, we provide an overall summary of the new accounting and financial reporting standards as they apply to all not-for-profit organizations. We then offer a complete description of accounting and illustrations of the financial reports of public universities. Since the GASB has not changed accounting for the public universities, these organizations will continue to follow the "old" version of the AICPA audit guide. The next section in this chapter illustrates accounting and financial reporting for private not-for-profit organizations following the new FASB guidance. For ease of presentation, these illustrations are presented without regard to a fund structure. However, since the new FASB guidance does not preclude funds-based reporting, an appendix is included incorporating the new standards within the existing funds structure. This gives the instructor the option of teaching the material for private universities with or without funds.

Chapter 19 covers accounting and financial reporting for health care entities and voluntary health and welfare organizations. The chapter also incorporates for each type of organization the most recent FASB standards in addition to the 1996 updated AICPA audit guide. In this chapter, funds are viewed as internal control and management tools. External financial statements are illustrated without a funds structure. As in Chapter 18, however, a funds-based illustration is included in the appendix for both health care organizations and voluntary health and welfare organizations.

Throughout the government and not-for-profit chapters, improvements in the text, illustrations, and end-of-chapter materials are aimed at making the presentation more conceptual and less procedural. The aim is to provide students with an understanding of the unique features of the changing government and not-for-profit accounting environment.

FIDUCIARY ACCOUNTING (CHAPTERS 20 AND 21)

The role of estate planning and the use of trusts are important to many individuals and present some unique accounting principles. The tax implications of estate planning are discussed so that the student has a basic understanding of this area. Various accounting reports necessary for the administration of an estate or trust are illustrated in Chapter 20.

No business is immune from financial difficulty. Chapter 21 discusses various responses to such difficulties, including troubled debt restructuring, quasi-reorganizations, corporate liquidations, and corporate reorganizations.

Supplementary Materials

For the Instructor

Solutions Manual. This manual provides descriptions of all exercises, problems, and cases with their estimated completion time. You'll find answers to all end-of-chapter questions and solutions to all exercises, problems, and cases, along with the logic for the solutions when appropriate. In particular, answers to multiple-choice questions include supporting explanations and computations.

Transparencies. The set of transparencies contains blank worksheets, solutions for all of the consolidation problems, and selected solutions from the remainder of the text.

Test Bank. This resource, available in both print and electronic formats, contains multiple-choice questions and examination problems for each chapter along with the solutions. These materials may be reproduced by the instructor. The electronic test bank is Windows® based.

Excel® Templates. Both student and solutions templates for use with Excel® are available. The templates, for use with selected problems from the text, are for use with selected nonconsolidation chapters as well as the consolidation chapters. Instructors may choose from horizontal and vertical presentations for the consolidation assignments.

PowerPoint® Presentations. Author-designed electronic slides are available to enrich classroom teaching of concepts and practice.

For the Student

Student Companion Enrichment Manual. This manual greatly enhances student self-study. With step-by-step application of the methods discussed in the text, the enrichment manual helps students in their mastery of text subject matter. The manual is composed of three main sections: the Text Companion, the Enrichment, and the Study Guide. The Text Companion section contains the worksheets from Chapters 2–8 and 11 and the Special Appendices reproduced on removable pages to give students

easy reference as they study the related text narrative. Also in the Text Companion section are several supporting examples, diagrams, and illustrations to assist understanding of complex topics. The Enrichment section contains coverage of branch accounting and the SEC as background information for the students. The Study Guide section contains a detailed outline of each chapter and several learning activities, such as true/false, multiple choice, and matching questions, as well as short problems. The solutions for these activities appear at the end of the section.

Working Papers for Consolidations. The working papers for solving the consolidation problems in Chapters 2–8 and Chapter 11 contain printed trial balances as a means of saving time. The pages are bound in a single volume and are perforated for easy removal. Blank worksheets are included at the end for extra assignments.

Acknowledgments

We are grateful to the following people for their important contributions to ensure a high-quality text and ancillaries:

Bruce C. Branson, *North Carolina State University*
Arthur S. Boyett, *Francis Marion University*
Frank Cicalese, *Kean University of New Jersey*
Teresa L. Conover, *University of North Texas*
Constance J. Crawford, *Ramapo College of New Jersey*
John E. Elsea, *University of Northern Colorado*
Richard B. Griffin, *University of Tennessee at Martin*
Philip Kintzele, *Central Michigan University*
Kurtis P. Klumb, *University of Wisconsin—Milwaukee*
Robert M. Kozub, *University of Wisconsin—Milwaukee*
Susan Martin, *Grand Valley State University*
David J. Medved, *Detroit College of Business*
Dave Nichols, *University of Mississippi*
Donald Pagach, *North Carolina State University*
Heibatollah Sami, *Temple University*
Ali M. Sedaghat, *Loyola College in Maryland*
R. B. Vinson, *University of Texas at Brownsville*

We appreciate the care in preparation and proofing by our student assistants: Shelly Skrobis, Brian Sobocinski, and Alexander Wheeler.

Paul M. Fischer
William J. Taylor
Rita H. Cheng

About the Authors

Paul M. Fischer is the Jerry Leer Professor of Accounting at the University of Wisconsin, Milwaukee. He teaches intermediate and advanced financial accounting and has received both the AMOCO Outstanding Professor Award and the School of Business Administration Advisory Council Teaching Award. He also teaches CPA review classes and continuing education classes, and provides executive training courses for several large corporations. He earned his undergraduate accounting degree at Milwaukee and earned an MBA and Ph.D. at the University of Wisconsin, Madison. Dr. Fischer is a CPA and is a member of the American Institute of CPAs, the Wisconsin Institute of CPAs and the American Accounting Association. He is a past president of the Midwest Region of the American Accounting Association.

Dr. Fischer has previously authored Cost Accounting: Theory and Applications (with Frank), Financial Dimensions of Marketing Management (with Crissy and Mossman), journal articles, and computer software. He actively pursues research and consulting interests in the areas of leasing, pension accounting, and business combinations.

William J. Taylor primarily teaches financial accounting and auditing at both the undergraduate and graduate levels. In addition he is involved in teaching a CPA review course and continuing professional education seminars. He has been recognized for his teaching excellence and has received both the Amoco Outstanding Professor Award and the School of Business Administration Advisory Council Teaching Award. He earned his Ph.D. from Georgia State University and is a CPA and a CVA (Certified Valuation Analyst). His professional experience includes working for Deloitte and Touche and Arthur Andersen & Co. in their audit practices. His private consulting activities include business valuations, litigation services, and issues affecting closely- held businesses.

Dr. Taylor is actively involved in the Wisconsin Institute of Certified Public Accountants and has served as their president and as a director. He is also a member of the American Institute of CPAs and the National Association of Certified Valuation Analysts. He serves as a director and officer for a number of organizations.

Rita H. Cheng is the A.O. Smith Teaching Professor of Accounting at the University of Wisconsin-Milwaukee. She teaches government and nonprofit accounting and advanced accounting. She also teaches in a CPA review and is often asked to speak on government and nonprofit accounting topics. She has been recognized for her teaching excellence and is a recipient of the School of Business Administration Advisory Council Outstanding Teaching Award. She earned her Ph.D. in Accounting from Temple University. She is a CPA and a Certified Government Financial Manager.

Dr. Cheng is actively involved in research focusing on the quality of accounting and financial reporting by state and local governments and the influence of accounting regulation on corporate business competitiveness. She has published numerous journal articles and technical reports. She is an active member of the Government and Nonprofit Section of the American Accounting Association. She has also testified before the Governmental Accounting Standards Board and coordinated the academic response to several proposed standards.

Contents in Brief

Contents

Part 5
Governmental and Not-for-Profit Accounting

PART

1

COMBINED CORPORATE ENTITIES
AND CONSOLIDATIONS

The acquisition of one company by another has become an increasingly common transaction. Recording methods have been stable for over 20 years. We are now, however, in a period of uncertainty for the accounting methods used for these transactions. There are two accounting models available for acquisitions, the purchase and pooling of interests methods. Both of these methods are under great scrutiny; major changes in their application can be expected. These changes are studied in the first two special appendices.

There are two types of transactions that can be used to secure control of another company. The first is to acquire all the assets and liabilities of a company directly from the company by paying cash or issuing securities. This is called a *direct asset acquisition*. The theory of purchase and pooling will be developed in this context in Chapter 1.

The more popular method to establish control is to purchase a controlling interest, usually over 50%, in the common stock of another company. Accounting standards hold that when two or more companies are under common control, only one set of *consolidated statements* should be prepared for the companies under common control. Chapters 2 through 8 provide the methods for consolidating separate statements of the affiliated firms into one consolidated set of consolidated statements.

CHAPTER

1

Business Combinations: America's Most Popular Business Activity, Accounting's Biggest Controversy

"If we were to assess the amount of time spent on questions of pooling versus purchase, we'd find that this is the most costly accounting issue we have ever had in the U.S."

Arthur Wyatt, Retired Chairman of Arthur Andersen

The acquisition of one company by another has been a common business transaction since the start of commercial activity. Business acquisitions are, in essence, a group purchase of all of a company's assets for a single price. The magnitude of these transactions makes them front-page news in all major newspapers. For the most part, the general public views these combinations as a sound business practice which contributes to economies of scale. The shareholders of the acquired company delight in the premium price they typically receive from the acquiring corporation.

There have been many waves of business combination activities in the last 110 years. There were periods of increased levels of business combinations in the 1890s, the 1920s, and the 1960s as many prosperous companies attempted to achieve greater domination of their industry. There was a decline in combination activity in the 1970s caused by recession, energy shortages, and inflation. The 1990s have become an era of hyperactive combinations. Between 1991 and 1996, the number of deals increased at a rate of 14% per year and the value of the deals increased at a rate of 31% per year. Exhibit 1-1 includes the Merger Completion Record between 1987 and 1996.

The following quotation sums up the motivations of the recent wave of combinations:

Thus, as the m&a (mergers and acquisitions) market enters its fourth straight year of hyperactive dealmaking after rebounding from a brief slow down in the early 1990s, the overreaching theme continues to be the arsenal of powerful forces that are driving companies to buy and sell. Some have been cited. Others with legs widespread. Leapfrogging and converging technology punctuated by mounting expenses, abbreviated life cycles, and persistent development pressures are spark-plugging acquisitions in fields as varied as telecommunications and pharmaceuticals, computer peripherals and production machinery, aerospace and automobiles.

Exhibit 1-1
Mergers and Acquisition Completion 1996 vs. 1995[1]

MERGERS AND ACQUISITION COMPLETION

All M&A Activity	1996				1995			
	No. of Deals	% of Total No.	Value ($ bil[1])	% of Total Value	No. of Deals	% of Total No.	Value ($ bil[2])	% of Total Value
U.S. acq. U.S.	5,230	76.6%	$420.3	76.3%	4,742	76.4%	$285.0	76.0%
Non-U.S. acq. U.S.	628	9.2	69.9	12.7	571	9.2	52.0	13.9
U.S. acq. Non-U.S.	970	14.2	60.5	11.0	896	14.4	38.0	10.1
Total	6,828	100.0	550.7	100.0	6,209	100.0	375.0	100.0
Divestitures Only*	2,503	36.6	181.7	33.0	2,377	38.2	139.8	37.3
LBOs Only*	145	2.1	16.9	3.0	159	2.5	6.4	1.7

*Divestitures and LBOs are included in All M&A Activity data.
1 Based on 2,752 deals for which prices were revealed.
2 Based on 2,383 deals for which prices were revealed.

10-Year Merger Completion Record 1987 to 1996			
Year	No. of Deals	% Change	Value ($ Bil)	% Change
1987	2,517	–	$210.7	–
1988	3,011	19.6%	291.3	38.3%
1989	3,825	27.0	325.1	11.6
1990	4,312	12.7	206.8	−36.4
1991	3,580	−16.9	143.1	−30.8
1992	3,752	4.8	125.3	−12.4
1993	4,148	10.5	177.3	41.5
1994	4,962	19.6	276.5	55.9
1995	6,209	25.1	375.0	35.6
1996	6,828	9.9	550.7	46.8

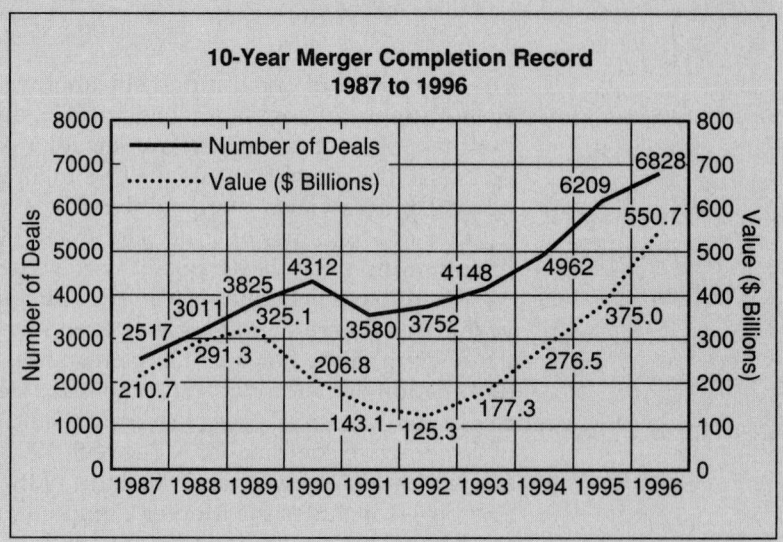

Globalization of major industries runs at a relentless pace forcing companies in food, pharmaceuticals, heavy equipment, auto and truck components, telecommunications, and many more to do business on a worldwide scale. Consolidation, cued by an elongated list of influences that are rewriting the facts of business life, have left few businesses untouched.2

The increased level of combinations has refueled major controversies which have plagued the recording of business combinations since the 1940s. The major controversies include the following:

■   Recording a combination as a pooling of interests means that all assets of the acquired company carry forward at book value. The alternative purchase method of accounting records the assets at market values and usually creates a

1 "1996 M&A Profile," *Mergers and Acquisitions Almanac,* March/April 1997.
2 "Why the M&A Boom Isn't Dying Down," *Mergers and Acquisitions,* March/April 1997.

major intangible asset, goodwill. Future periods suffer from much larger depreciation and amortization charges under the purchase method.

- "Substance over form" has always been a main theme in business combinations. When one company owns a controlling interest in another company, the financial statements of the separate companies should be combined into a single set of consolidated statements. The controversy is, what level of ownership or set of circumstances leads to a presumption of control?

- There is disagreement on what accounting procedures should be used to account for goodwill once it is recorded in a purchase. In the United States, it is amortized over a period of 40 years or less. Other countries allow either an immediate write-off or a charge to capital on the purchase date. Many manipulative practices have evolved to limit the amount of goodwill recorded.

- When a company acquires 60% of the common stock of another company in a purchase transaction, should assets be increased to 100% of market value or to just 60%, since only 60% of the company was sold? This controversy was recently mediated by the FASB which holds that all accounts, except goodwill, are recorded at 100% of market. Goodwill is limited to the percentage interest purchased.

Economic Advantages of Combinations

Business combinations are typically viewed as a way to jump start economies of scale. Savings may result from the elimination of duplicative assets. Perhaps both companies will utilize common facilities and share fixed costs. There may be economies of scale as one management team replaces two separate sets of managers. It may be possible to better coordinate production, marketing, and administrative actions. *Horizontal combinations* involve those where competitors serving similar functions hope to economize by combining similar functions. *Vertical combinations* involve companies that were at different levels in the marketing chain, such as a manufacturer acquiring a wholesaler that will market its goods. The intended benefit here is the closer coordination of the different levels of activities in a given industry.

The following comments come from a press release issued by the James River Corporation concerning its acquisition of Fort Howard Paper Company:

> *The merger is expected to generate cost savings estimated to total at least $150 million in 1998, increasing to more than $200 million over time. Fort James intends to reduce expenses and increase efficiency by combining complementary technologies, optimizing product manufacturing and logistics across the combined systems, increasing purchasing efficiencies, eliminating redundant overhead costs, consolidating work forces where duplication exists, and increasing product quality and productivity.[3]*

The press release also pointed out that the transaction would be recorded as a pooling of interests which was a signal to the financial community that future income statements would not be burdened with higher depreciation that would be caused by recording market values. Nor would there be any amortization expense for the huge amount of goodwill that would have been recorded in a purchase transaction. While stockholders rejoiced in the increase in the market value of their shares, many Wisconsin workers realized they would soon lose their jobs as the company later announced the eventual closing of many Wisconsin-based activities.

---

[3] "James River, Fort Howard Agree to Merge Creating a Preeminent Consumer Products Company," *Company Press Release, James River Corporation,* May 5, 1997.

Perhaps the most universal economic benefit in business combinations is the possible tax advantages. The owners of a small business, whether sole proprietors, partners, or shareholders, may wish to retire from the active management of their company. If they were to sell their interest for cash or accept debt instruments, they would have an immediate taxable gain. If, however, they accept common stock of another company in exchange for their interest and carefully structure the transaction as a "tax-free reorganization," they may account for the transaction as a tax-free exchange. No taxes are paid until they ultimately sell the shares received in the combination. The shares received are recorded, for tax purposes, at the book value of the interest traded for the shares. This same concept applies to large company acquisitions. The James River press release announced that the transaction was structured to qualify as a "tax-free reorganization." This assured shareholders that there would not be any tax liability connected with their exchange of Fort Howard shares for James River shares.

Further tax advantages exist when the target company has reported losses on its tax returns in prior periods. Section 172 (b) of the Internal Revenue Code provides that operating losses can be carried back two years to obtain a refund of taxes paid in previous years. Should the loss not be offset by income in the two prior years, the loss may be carried forward twenty years to offset future taxable income, thus eliminating or reducing income taxes that would otherwise be payable. These loss maneuvers have little or no value to a target company that has not had income in the two prior years and does not expect profitable operations in the near future. However, tax losses are transferable in a business combination. To an acquiring company that has a profit in the current year and/or expects profitable periods in the future, the tax losses of a target company may have real value. That value, viewed as an asset by the acquiring company, will be reflected in the price paid. However, the acquiring company must exercise caution in anticipating the benefits of tax loss carryovers. The realization of the tax benefits may be denied if it can be shown that the primary motivation for the combination was the transfer of the tax loss benefit.

There also may be a tax benefit in a subsequent period as a single consolidated tax return is filed by the single remaining corporation. The losses of one of the affiliated companies can be used to offset the net income of another affiliated company to lessen the taxes that would otherwise be paid by the profitable company. In some cases, there may be disadvantages to filing as a consolidated company. Companies with low incomes may fare better being taxed separately due to the progressive income tax rate structure. The marginal tax rate of each company may be lower than that resulting when the incomes of the two companies are combined.[4]

Obtaining Control

Control of another company may be achieved by either acquiring the assets of the target company or by acquiring a controlling interest in the target company's voting common stock. In an acquisition of assets, *all* the company's assets are acquired *directly* from the company. In most cases, existing liabilities of the acquired company also are assumed. When assets are acquired and liabilities are assumed, we refer to the transaction as an acquisition of "net assets." Payment could be made in cash, exchanged property, or issuance of either debt or equity securities. It is common to issue securities since it avoids depleting cash or other assets that may be needed in future operations. Legally, a *statutory consolidation* refers to the combining of two or more previously independent legal entities into one new legal entity. The previous companies are dissolved and are then replaced by a single continuing company. A *statutory*

4 See Chapter 6, "Taxation of Consolidated Companies," pp. 6-13 to 6-19.

merger refers to the absorption of one or more former legal entities into another company that continues as the sole surviving legal entity. The absorbed company ceases to exist as a legal entity but may continue as a division of the surviving company.

In a *stock acquisition*, a controlling interest (typically, more than 50%) of another company's voting common stock is acquired. The company making the acquisition is termed the *parent*, and the company acquired is termed a *subsidiary*. Both the parent and the subsidiary remain separate legal entities and maintain their own financial records and statements. However, for external financial reporting purposes, the companies usually will combine their individual financial statements into a single set of *consolidated statements*. Thus, a consolidation may refer to a statutory combination or, more commonly, to the consolidated statements of a parent and its subsidiary.

There may be several advantages to obtaining control by purchasing a controlling interest in stock. Most obvious is that the total cost is lower, since only a controlling interest in the assets, and not the total assets, must be acquired. In addition, control through stock ownership may be simpler to achieve since no formal negotiations or transactions with the acquired company's management are necessary. Further advantages may result from maintaining the separate legal identity of the former company. First of all, risk is lowered because the legal liability of any one corporation is limited to its own assets. Secondly, separate legal entities may be desirable when only one of the companies is subject to government control. Lastly, there may be tax advantages resulting from the preservation of the legal entities.

Stock acquisitions are said to be "friendly" when the stockholders of the target corporation, as a group, decide to sell or exchange their shares. In such a case, an offer may be made to the board of directors by the acquiring company. If the directors approve, they will recommend acceptance of the offer to the shareholders, who may approve the transaction. Often, a two-thirds vote is required. Once approval is gained, the exchange of shares will be made with the individual shareholders. If the shareholders decline the offer, or if no offer is made, the acquiring company may deal directly with individual shareholders in an attempt to secure a controlling interest. Frequently, the acquiring company may make a formal *tender offer*. The tender offer, typically, will be published in newspapers and will offer a greater than market price for shares made available by a stated date. The acquiring company may reserve the right to withdraw the offer if an insufficient number of shares are made available to it. Where management and/or a significant number of shareholders oppose the purchase of the company by the intended buyer, the acquisition is viewed as *hostile*. Unfriendly offers are so common that several standard defensive mechanisms have evolved. Following are the common terms used to describe these defensive moves:

Greenmail.   The target company may pay a premium price ("greenmail") to purchase treasury shares. It may either buy shares already owned by a potential acquiring company or purchase shares from a current owner who, it is feared, would sell to the acquiring company. The price paid for these shares in excess of their market price may not be deducted from stockholders' equity; instead, it is expensed.[5]

White Knight.   The target company locates a different company to acquire a controlling interest. This could occur when the original acquiring company is in a similar industry and it is feared that current management of the target company would be displaced. The replacement acquiring company, the "white knight," might be in a different industry and could be expected to keep current management intact.

---

5 Financial Accounting Standards Board, FASB Technical Bulletin, Nos. 85 and 86, *Accounting for a Purchase of Treasury Shares at a Price Significantly in Excess of the Current Market Price of the Shares* and the *Income Statement Classification of Costs Incurred in Defending Against a Takeover Attempt* (Norwalk, CT, 1985).

Poison Pill.   The "poison pill" involves the issuance of stock rights to existing shareholders to purchase additional shares at a price far below market value. However, the rights are exercisable only when an acquiring company purchases or makes a bid to purchase a stated number of shares. The effect of the options is to substantially raise the cost to the acquiring company. If the attempt fails, there is at least a greater gain for the original shareholders.

Selling the Crown Jewels.   This approach has the management of the target company selling vital assets (the "crown jewels") of the target company to others to make the company less attractive to the acquiring company.

Leveraged Buyouts.   The management of the existing target company attempts to purchase a controlling interest in that company. Often, substantial debt will be incurred to raise the funds needed to purchase the stock, hence the term "leveraged buyout." When bonds are sold to provide this financing, the bonds may be referred to as "junk bonds" since they are often high interest and high risk due to the high debt-to-equity ratio of the resulting corporation.

Further protection against takeovers is offered by federal and state law. The Clayton Act of 1914 (section 7) is a federal law that prohibits business combinations in which "the effect of such acquisition may be substantially to lessen competition or to tend to create a monopoly." The Williams Act of 1968 is a federal law that regulates tender offers; it is enforced by the SEC. Several states also have enacted laws to discourage hostile takeovers. These laws are motivated, in part, by the fear of losing employment and taxes.

Accounting Ramifications

When control is achieved through an asset acquisition, the acquiring company records on its books the assets and assumed liabilities of the acquired company. From the acquisition date on, all transactions of both the acquiring and acquired company are recorded in one combined set of accounts. The only new skill one needs to master is the proper recording of the acquisition when it occurs. **Once the initial acquisition is properly recorded, subsequent accounting procedures are the same as for any single accounting entity.** Combined statements of the new, larger company for periods following the combination are automatic.

Accounting procedures are more involved when control is achieved through a stock acquisition. The controlling company, the parent, will record only an investment account to reflect its interest in the controlled company, the subsidiary. Both the parent and the subsidiary remain separate legal entities with their own separate sets of accounts and separate financial statements. Accounting theory holds that where one company has effective control over another, there is only one economic entity, and there should be only one set of financial statements that combines the activities of the entities under common control. The accountant will prepare a worksheet, referred to as the *consolidated worksheet*, that starts with the separate accounts of the parent and the subsidiary. Various adjustments and eliminations will be made on this worksheet to merge the separate accounts of the two companies into a single set of financial statements, which are referred to as "consolidated statements."

This chapter will discuss business combinations resulting from asset acquisitions, since the accounting principles are more easily understood in this context. The principles developed are applied directly to business combinations resulting from stock acquisitions that are studied in the chapters that follow. Our first mission is to understand the two basic theoretical models used to record business combinations, the *pooling* and the *purchase* methods. These two models apply to all business combinations where one company achieves control over another, whether this control is achieved through an asset or a stock acquisition.

Pooling vs. Purchase

APB Opinion No. 16, *Business Combinations*, published in 1970, still provides the basic principles for accounting for business combinations. Purchases are characterized as situations where one company tends to achieve control over another, often displacing former owners and/or management. In essence, there has been a group purchase of assets which should be recorded at fair market value. In most cases, the price paid is clear; it will be the cash given or the fair market value of the equity or debt instruments issued. In a limited number of cases, the payment may be made using securities that have no clear market value. In these cases, the price will have to be inferred from the fair market value of the assets acquired. When the acquired company has liabilities that will be assumed and later paid by the purchasing company, these liabilities are recorded at their current market value based on current interest rates on the purchase date. *Goodwill* is recorded when the price paid exceeds the market value of the separate assets (minus liabilities assumed). Goodwill is, in theory, either a payment for anticipated above-average earnings and/or a premium price paid to achieve control.

It has been customary to amortize total goodwill on a straight-line basis over the maximum 40-year life. Litte consideration has been given to the true duration of goodwill. In February of 1998, the FASB agreed that straight-line amortization should be used unless another systematic method that accelerated the deductions could be demonstrated to be more appropriate. The FASB directed the staff to explore alternative methods that would amortize goodwill over the average life of its determinable elements. This approach would identify goodwill elements as attaching to various groups of assets. Total goodwill would be desegregated, and amortization would be tailored to the identified components. This approach can be expected to significantly shorten the goodwill amortization period.

According to APB Opinion No. 16 (par. 47), the only exception to the accounting for a business combination as a purchase may apply to situations where the surviving company issues only voting common stock for all the assets of an acquired company in an asset acquisition or issues only voting common stock for at least 90% of the voting common stock of the acquired company in a stock acquisition. There are also additional criteria that must be met. They are discussed shortly. The term "pooling of interests" is used to describe the fusion of two separate stockholder groups into a single accounting entity. The exchange of voting common stock and meeting other required pooling criteria support the argument that **no sale has occurred.** Instead, the stockholders of the acquired company are merely exchanging their interest in the former company for an interest in the combined corporation. The absence of a sale means there is no cause to record market values for the assets received or the securities issued. The acquiring company combines the book value of the acquired company's assets and liabilities with its own. The only exceptions to maintaining those book values occur when

- Lower market values are acknowledged according to the lower-of-cost-or-market rule, and

- Changes in accounting principles are made to afford consistency of accounting methods for the two former companies.

The total paid-in capital of the acquired company is assigned to the paid-in capital recorded for the shares issued by the acquiring company. The retained earnings of the acquired company are added to the retained earnings of the acquiring company, except in some rare cases where it is needed to meet the par value requirements of the shares issued. (Detailed coverage of pooling of interest requirements and accounting procedures is presented later in this chapter.)

Effect on Future Statements

The consequences of the purchase versus pooling methods on the accounting statements may be very pronounced. The following chart compares the impact of the two accounting methods on future balance sheets of the combined company:

Item	Purchase Method	Pooling Method
1. Assets and liabilities of acquired company	Recorded at current fair market values with a possibility of goodwill.	Recorded at book value of acquired company.* No additional goodwill acknowledged.**
2. Equity securities issued	Market value of shares issued is added to paid-in capital.	Paid-in capital of acquired company is assigned as paid-in value of shares issued.***
3. Retained earnings of acquired company.	Not acknowledged.	Added to retained earnings.***

*   Where the book values of assets exceed fair market value, the assets are recorded at the lower fair market value, and the retained earnings of the acquired company are reduced.

**   Goodwill previously recorded by the acquired company would be recorded at its remaining book value.

***   The retained earnings of the acquired company may be reduced to meet the issuer's par or stated value requirement.

Future income statements are affected by the differing values assigned to assets under the purchase and pooling methods. The purchase method will record individual assets at fair market values exceeding book values that would be recorded under the pooling method. The higher market values will lead to higher depreciation charges in future periods. The purchase method usually will require the recording of goodwill that must be amortized over a period not to exceed 40 years for financial reporting purposes. As an example, let us assume that Company P will issue 100,000 shares of its stock (market value of $10 per share) for all the assets of Company S. Company S's simplified balance sheet immediately prior to the acquisition is as follows:

Assets		Equity	
Fixed asset.	$300,000	Common stock, $10 par	$100,000
		Retained earnings	200,000
Total assets.	$300,000	Total equity	$300,000

If the acquisition is a purchase, the $10 per share market value of the shares would be recorded as the price paid, $1,000,000. If the market value of the fixed assets is $600,000, they will be recorded at $600,000 and $400,000 will be assigned to goodwill. If the acquisition is deemed to be a pooling of interests, only the $300,000 book value of the fixed assets would be recorded. Consider the following income statement comparison resulting from the use of the purchase method versus the pooling method:

	Purchase	Pooling
Revenue	$250,000	$250,000
Less:		
All expenses other than depreciation on the acquired		
company's assets and goodwill amortization	100,000	100,000
Depreciation of acquired company's fixed assets:		
Purchase, 1/10 of $600,000 market value	60,000	
Pooling, 1/10 of $300,000 book value		30,000
Goodwill amortization:		
Purchase, 1/40 of $400,000	10,000	
Pooling, no goodwill recorded		0
Net Income	$ 80,000	$120,000

The major difference in the above incomes is caused solely by the recognition of fair market values and goodwill in a purchase as opposed to book values in a pooling and the likely recording of goodwill in a purchase. Case 1 at the end of this chapter analyzes the 1997 pooling of the Fort Howard Paper Corporation with the James River Paper Corporation. Fort Howard was the acquired company. The use of the pooling method resulted in $4 billion lower asset values and increased income by a minimum of $105 million per year. If income were to continue at current levels, income would increase 50% just by using the pooling method instead of the purchase method!

The income statements of both the current and prior periods also benefit from the retroactive application of the pooling concept. If a company purchases another company midway through the year, it may add to its own income only the purchased company's income from the purchase date to year-end. In a pooling, income may be added for the entire year no matter when during the year the combination occurred. When a purchase occurs, the prior years' comparative statements of the acquiring company do not include the income of the acquired company. In a pooling, prior years' comparative statements of the acquiring company are restated to include the income of the acquired company. (Additional information on the effects of purchases and poolings on financial statements will be covered at the end of this chapter.)

Expenses to Accomplish a Combination

There may be significant expenses involved in negotiating and consummating a business combination. There are three categories of expenses:

1. *Direct acquisition costs.* These are payments made to third parties for costs such as audit and legal expenses.
2. *Indirect acquisition costs.* These are allocations of internal costs that probably would have existed without a combination but reflect management time allocated to acquisition activities.
3. *Security issuance costs.* These include bond and stock issue costs incurred by the decision to use securities rather than cash as consideration.

Purchase accounting rules add the direct acquisition costs to the price paid for the acquired company. It is a cost necessary to purchase the assets, much like legal fees incurred to buy real estate, and should be added to the cost of the assets purchased. Indirect acquisition costs are hard to attribute directly to the combination and must be expensed when incurred. The cost of issuing securities is deducted from the value assigned to the debt or equity securities issued. This is the normal procedure for issue costs, and it remains unchanged in a purchase.

Pooling rules require that all three types of costs be expensed at the time of the combination. Since no sale is considered to have occurred, there is no basis upon which to increase asset values. The stock issued is viewed as a continuation of the original shares. The likely account used for all expenses connected with a pooling would be Professional Service Expenses.

Overview

If given a choice, most companies would choose to account for combinations under the pooling method. Where assets are undervalued and/or goodwill exists, the pooling method will produce higher incomes and a higher return on assets in future years. In addition, the balance sheet of the continuing company is enhanced when the retained earnings of the acquired company are added to existing retained earnings. The only likely disadvantage of the pooling method is that acquired assets may not be shown on the balance sheet at their full value. Therefore, the total worth of the combined companies may be considerably less than would have resulted under the purchase method. There are a limited number of cases where a company may not prefer the pooling method. This may occur in acquisitions of companies with low or negative amounts of income and retained earnings.

Despite the advantages of the pooling method, it is difficult to justify its continued use. The distortions it causes, as compared to the purchase method, are disturbing to many accountants and financial analysts. It seems that the careful structuring of an acquisition to meet arbitrary criteria (see pages 1-24 to 1-29) is a shallow excuse for ignoring the true value of the assets over which control is achieved. U.S. accounting rules are at variance with those of most other countries who allow pooling only in the case of a true merger of equals. Rules adopted by the International Accounting Standards Committee make it almost impossible to pool.

Prior to the issuance of APB Opinion No. 16, companies frequently chose the pooling method even though the transactions did not have the characteristics of a pooling. As a result, APB Opinion No. 16 provided very restrictive criteria for the use of the pooling method. All combinations not meeting the criteria must be accounted for as purchases. Thus, there are no criteria for the use of the purchase method in accounting for combinations other than the failure to have the combinations qualify as poolings. If the pooling method is desired by the acquiring company, the combination must be structured carefully in order to be classified as such. Currently, very few combinations meet the criteria. In recent years, about 10% of the companies surveyed in *Accounting Trends and Techniques* used the pooling method.[6] In 1996, the FASB added reconsideration of APB Opinion No. 16 to its agenda. It will likely be 1999 or 2000 before a new pronouncement will be issued.

Coverage of the application of the more popular purchase method is presented below and is followed by coverage of the criteria and application of the pooling method.

Asset Acquisition as a Purchase

When the acquisition of an existing company's assets is being considered, the current value of the company's assets and the amount of its liabilities must be appraised carefully. Such an evaluation usually precedes negotiations. Generally, the prospective purchaser will seek permission to conduct a pre-acquisition audit to determine whether all assets and liabilities are properly recorded. The purchaser knows that, while book values may be indicative of the current value of some current assets, these values may not represent a reasonable market value for inventories, plant assets, or intangibles. Inventories valued on a LIFO basis will have little relationship

---

6 Gerard L. Yarnall and Richard Rikert, eds. *Accounting Trends and Techniques*, 50th ed. (New York: American Institute of Certified Public Accountants, 1996), p. 57.

to current market value. Inventories valued on a FIFO or average cost basis may be closer to market value but may still depart significantly when prices fluctuate quickly. Plant assets and intangibles are presented at historical cost less an arbitrary depreciation or amortization allowance, with no relationship to current market value. Even liabilities to be assumed may not be stated at their current market value in light of changes in market interest rates. For example, assume 10-year bonds were issued at par 4 years ago when the prevailing interest rate was 8%. If the current market interest rate for the bonds is 6%, the bonds would now sell at a premium.

Acknowledging the limitations of book values, the purchaser may engage an independent consultant to estimate the current market values of the assets to be acquired and the liabilities to be assumed. Market values are an estimate of the price to which a willing buyer and seller would agree. These estimates provide only a guide to establishing the price to be paid for the entire company.

Assume that Acquisitions Inc. is considering the purchase of Jacobs Company and has secured the following audited condensed balance sheet:

Jacobs Company
Balance Sheet
December 31, 19X3

Accounts receivable	$ 20,000	Current liabilities	$ 20,000
Inventory	40,000	Capital stock 1,000 shares $10 par	10,000
Land	10,000	Paid-in capital in excess of par	50,000
Buildings (net)	40,000	Retained earnings	50,000
Equipment (net	20,000		
Total assets	$130,000	Total liabilities and equity	$130,000

Aware of the deficiencies of book values, management obtains the following appraisal of market values:

Accounts receivable	$ 20,000
Inventory	45,000
Land	10,000
Buildings	50,000
Equipment	40,000
Current liabilities	(20,000)
Total market value of net assets	$145,000

If the market values are accurate, Acquisitions Inc. will expect to pay at least $145,000 for the *net assets* (total assets less liabilities assumed) of Jacobs Company. The purchase of net assets means that Acquisitions Inc. will assume the liabilities of Jacobs Company. This is common practice in most business combinations. Perhaps a deal could be struck for less than $145,000, but, very likely, more will be paid. Acquisitions may be willing to pay a premium for Jacobs' assets, since Jacobs is a functioning company with an established trade. If the assets were purchased individually from other sources, time would be required to combine them into a viable, profitable company. The payment for this advantage is considered the purchase of goodwill. The amount of the payment depends on the expected future profitability of the assets to be acquired, the desire of the acquiring company to achieve control of the target company, and the outcome of the negotiating process.

Calculating and Recording Goodwill

The purchaser may attempt to forecast the future income of the target company in order to arrive at a logical purchase price. Goodwill is often, at least in part, a payment for above-normal expected future earnings. A forecast of future income may start by projecting recent years' incomes into the future. When this is done, it is important to factor out "one time" occurrences that will not likely reoccur in the near future. Examples would include the cumulative effect of changes in accounting principles, extraordinary items, discontinued operations, or any other unusual event. Expected future income is compared to "normal" income. Normal income is the product of the appropriate industry rate of return on assets times the **fair market value of the gross assets** (no deduction for liabilities) of the acquired company. Gross assets include specifically identifiable intangible assets such as patents and copyrights but do not include goodwill. The following calculation of earnings in excess of normal might be made for Jacobs Company:

Expected average future income		$21,000
Less normal return on assets:		
Market value of total identifiable assets	$165,000	
Industry normal rate of return	10%	
Normal return on assets		16,500
Expected annual earnings in excess of normal		$ 4,500

There are several methods that use the expected annual earnings in excess of normal to estimate goodwill. A common approach is to pay for a given number of years' excess earnings. For instance, Acquisitions might offer to pay for 4 years of excess earnings, which would total $18,000. Alternatively, the excess earnings could be viewed as an annuity. The most optimistic purchaser might expect the excess earnings to continue forever. If so, the buyer might capitalize the excess earnings as a perpetuity at the normal industry rate of return according to the following formula:

$$\text{Goodwill} = \frac{\text{Annual excess earnings}}{\text{Industry normal rate of return}}$$

$$= \frac{\$4,500}{.10}$$

$$= \$45,000$$

Another estimation method views the factors that produce excess earnings to be of limited duration, such as 10 years, for example. This purchaser would calculate goodwill as follows:

Goodwill = discounted present value of a $4,500-per-year annuity for 10 years at 10%
= $4,500 × 10-year, 10% present value of annuity factor
= $4,500 × 6.145
= $27,653

Other analysts feel that the normal industry earning rate is appropriate only for tangible assets and not goodwill. Thus, they might capitalize excess earnings at a higher rate of return to reflect the higher risk inherent in goodwill.

All calculations of goodwill are only estimates used to assist in the determination of the price to be paid for a company. For example, Acquisitions might add the $27,653 estimate of goodwill to the $145,000 market value of Jacobs' other net assets to arrive at a tentative maximum price of $172,653. However, estimates of goodwill may differ from actual negotiated goodwill. If the final agreed-upon price for Jacobs' assets was $180,000, the actual negotiated goodwill would be $35,000, which is the price paid less the market value of the net assets acquired. The price in excess of $172,563 might be a "control premium" which the acquiring company is willing to pay to establish control over the target company.

Recording a Purchase

To continue the previous example, assume that the combining companies agree to a price of $180,000 for Jacobs Company's net assets, including goodwill. If Acquisitions paid $1,000 in direct legal costs, this would raise the price paid for the net assets of Jacobs to $181,000, and the following entry would be made by Acquisitions to record the net asset purchase:

Accounts Receivable (market value)	20,000	
Inventory (market value)	45,000	
Land (appraised market value)	10,000	
Buildings (appraised market value)	50,000	
Equipment (appraised market value)	40,000	
Goodwill (price minus sum of net asset market values)	36,000	
Current Liabilities (market value)		20,000
Cash (includes direct acquisition costs)		181,000

Each identifiable asset and assumed liability is recorded at its estimated fair market value. Fixed assets are recorded at net market value with no accumulated depreciation since they are beginning as "new" assets to the acquiring company. Goodwill is recorded based on the negotiated price. Goodwill is always the excess of the total consideration given for the net assets ($181,000 in the example) above the sum of the values assigned to all identifiable net assets acquired. Goodwill is amortized over a period not to exceed 40 years. Research shows that 75% of the companies with goodwill amortize over 40 years.[7] If an acquired company already has goodwill on its books, such goodwill is ignored except as it is confirmed by the purchase price. For example, if Jacobs Company had previously recorded goodwill of $25,000, Acquisitions still would assign $145,000 to the net identifiable assets and assign the extra $36,000 paid to the goodwill. In this case, $11,000 would be added to the existing goodwill (existing goodwill is confirmed and supplemented).

It should be noted that the selling company's entries do not parallel those of the purchaser. The seller records the removal of net assets at their book values. The excess of the price received for the net assets by the seller ($180,000)[8] over the sum of the net asset book values ($130,000 assets – $20,000 liabilities = $110,000) is recorded as a gain on the sale. In this case, the gain is $70,000. The entry on Jacobs' books would be

---

7 "Goodwill Accounting: Current Practices, Variation in Source, and Market Valuation," Steve Henning, Ph.D. Dissertation, University of Wisconsin, Madison, Wisconsin, 1994.

8 Remember that the $1,000 in direct acquisition costs is paid by the purchaser to a third party, not to the seller.

Cash	180,00	
Current Liabilities	20,000	
Accounts Receivable		20,000
Inventory		40,000
Land		10,000
Buildings (net)		40,000
Equipment (net)		20,000
Gain on Sale		70,000

Recording Bargain Purchases

Occasionally, a company will be purchased at a "bargain" price. A bargain price is a price that is less than the estimated market values of a company's separate identifiable net assets. When this situation occurs, any goodwill existing on the books of the seller is ignored since the price paid does not confirm it. The least reliable estimates of market values are assumed to be those applicable to long-lived assets because a ready market often does not exist for such assets. Consequently, according to APB Opinion No. 16 (par. 87), **all current assets, long-term investments in marketable securities, and liabilities assumed are recorded at their full market value, regardless of the total price paid for the company.** Any excess of the sum of the market values of the net identifiable assets over the price paid is to be deducted only from long-lived assets other than investments in marketable securities.

For example, assume that Acquisitions Inc. acquired Jacobs Company's net assets by paying $132,000 ($152,000 total asset value – $20,000 of liabilities) to the seller and $1,000 for direct acquisition costs. The excess of the market value of the net assets over cost (often referred to as *negative goodwill*) would be determined as follows:

Total estimated market value of separate net assets	$145,000
Less price paid (including direct acquisition costs)	133,000
Excess of market value over cost	$ 12,000

The excess must be deducted from the total estimated market value of the long-lived assets to arrive at the remaining cost assignable to these assets. The assignable cost then is allocated to the individual long-lived assets in proportion to their fair market values.

The total estimated market value of the long-lived assets and the percentage of the estimated market value of each of these assets to the total estimated market value are calculated first:

Asset	Estimated Market Value	Percent of Total Market Value
Land	$ 10,000	10%
Buildings	50,000	50
Equipment	40,000	40
Total market value	$100,000	100%

The cost assignable to the long-lived assets is their $100,000 total market value less the $12,000 excess of market value over cost, or $88,000. This cost is assigned to the individual assets according to their relative market values as follows:

Asset	Percent of Total Market Value		Total Cost Assignable		Assigned Value
Land	10%	×	$88,000	=	$ 8,800
Buildings	50	×	88,000	=	44,000
Equipment	40	×	88,000	=	35,200
	100%				$88,000

The entry to record the bargain purchase is

Accounts Receivable (market value)	20,000	
Inventory (market value)	45,000	
Land (assigned purchase cost)	8,800	
Buildings (assigned purchase cost)	44,000	
Equipment (assigned purchase cost)	35,200	
Cash (includes direct acquisition costs)		133,000
Current Liabilities (market value)		20,000

Occasionally, some long-lived assets are given current asset status and recorded at net realizable value, regardless of the price paid for the company. This situation occurs only when the purchaser intends to sell these assets soon after the date of the combination, as in the case of acquired assets that duplicate those already owned by the purchaser.

Though a rare occurrence, the price paid for a company could be less than the market value of the current assets and any long-term investment in marketable securities less liabilities. This would occur only where the seller is under duress to sell quickly. **This text will refer to current assets, investments in marketable securities, and all liabilities as the "Priority Accounts."** Since accounts in these three categories must be recorded at their market values, no value would remain to be assigned to long-lived assets. According to APB Opinion No. 16 (par. 91), the excess of the values assigned to the priority accounts over the price paid is to be recorded as a deferred credit. The deferred credit is to be amortized to income over a period not to exceed 40 years. To illustrate an extreme example of this situation, assume that Acquisitions Inc. paid only $30,000 for the net assets of Jacobs Company and paid $1,000 in direct acquisition costs. Since the market value of the total net assets is $145,000, there is a bargain of $114,000 ($145,000 total net assets at market – $31,000 total price for the net assets). The bargain exceeds the market value of the land, buildings, and equipment by $14,000 ($114,000 bargain – $100,000 combined market value of land, buildings, and equipment accounts). The remaining $14,000 bargain may not be subtracted from the priority accounts which must be recorded at market value. Instead, the remaining bargain becomes the deferred credit which will be amortized to income in future periods. The entry would be as follows:

Accounts Receivable (market value)	20,000	
Inventory (market value)	45,000	
Land (no value available)	0	
Buildings (no value available)	0	
Equipment (no value available)	0	
Cash (includes direct acquisition costs)		31,000
Current Liabilities (market value)		20,000
Deferred Credit		14,000

A Pre-Calculation to Aid Purchase Analysis

A "pre-calculation" can be made before you attempt to record a purchase. It will guide your entry, provide a check figure, and avoid the unnecessary use of bargain allocation procedures. The pre-calculation works as follows using the above example of the Jacobs Company:

1. Calculate the market value of the total net assets excluding goodwill; this will be called the *market value of the net assets*. For Jacobs, this is **$145,000**.
2. Calculate the market value of only the priority accounts (including a deduction for liabilities). For Jacobs, this is **$45,000**.
   Then think of the following zones:

   Goodwill zone—any price higher than the market value of the net assets, $145,000. In this zone, no allocation is needed. All accounts are at market, and goodwill is recorded.

   Super bargain zone—any price below the amount assigned to priority accounts, $45,000. Priority accounts are recorded at market; all other assets are recorded at "0." There is no goodwill, but there is a deferred credit.

   Bargain zone—a price less than the market value of the net assets but greater than the amount assigned to the priority accounts. In our example, a price between $45,000 and $145,000. There is no goodwill or deferred credit. This is the only zone where allocation procedures are needed.

Issuing Securities as Consideration

Many major business acquisitions involve the issuance of the purchaser's securities as payment. As previously stated, the use of securities preserves cash for the future operations of the buyer and may allow the transaction to qualify as a tax-free exchange for the seller. The principles for recording the purchase are not changed; only the recording of the consideration differs. The market value of the securities issued becomes the total consideration to be assigned to the acquired company. The purchaser also must add the market value of the securities issued to its debt or paid-in capital. Using an earlier example which involved a $180,000 acquisition price for the net assets of Jacobs Company, assume that Acquisitions Inc. will issue its $2 par common stock as consideration. The total market value of the shares issued to Jacobs Company must equal the agreed-upon net price of $180,000. Assuming a market value of $20 per share for its stock, Acquisitions Inc. must issue 9,000 shares ($180,000 ÷ $20). The following entry to record the purchase is identical to the entry on page 1-13, except that the addition to Acquisitions' paid-in capital accounts is substituted for the cash payment.

Accounts Receivable (market value)	20,000	
Inventory (market value)	45,000	
Land (appraised market value)	10,000	
Buildings (appraised market value)	50,000	
Equipment (appraised market value)	40,000	
Goodwill ($180,000 price minus sum of net market values		
plus $1,000 of acquisition costs)	36,000	
Current Liabilities (market value)		20,000
Common Stock (9,000 shares × $2 par)		18,000
Paid-In Capital in Excess of Par ($180,000 − $18,000		
par value)		162,000
Cash (for acquisition costs)		1,000

Another form of consideration involves the issuance of the purchasing company's bonds for the assets of the acquired company. Market values are recorded in the same manner as in the preceding entry. However, care must be taken to properly record the market value of the bonds issued. The applicable bond premium or discount must be recorded. For instance, assume that Acquisitions Inc. plans to issue $1,000, 8% bonds in exchange for the $180,000 net assets of Jacobs Company. Normally, the purchaser would exchange 180 bonds ($180,000 ÷ $1,000 per bond) for the net assets of Jacobs Company. However, on the settlement date, the bonds have a market value of $990 each. Therefore, a discount of $1,800 ($10 per bond × 180 bonds) should be recorded. If the discount is settled by cash payment to the Jacobs Company, the purchase would be recorded as follows:

Accounts Receivable	20,000	
Inventory	45,000	
Land	10,000	
Buildings	50,000	
Equipment	40,000	
Goodwill	36,000	
Discount on Bonds Payable	1,800	
Current Liabilities		20,000
Cash (acquisition cost plus discount on bonds)		2,800
Bonds Payable		180,000

The resulting discount (or premium) must be amortized over the life of the bond issue. As an alternative to the cash payment, additional bonds could have been issued to compensate for the discount.

Any costs incurred to register and issue the securities are subtracted from the value assigned to the securities and are not treated as a direct acquisition cost. Had there been a $500 bond issuance cost in this example, a $500 deferred charge or increase in the discount would have been recorded.

Assigning the Purchase Price: Special Concerns

There are several situations that may complicate the recording of a purchase. There may be long-term liabilities that need to be revalued based on market values that differ from the recorded amounts on the books of the selling company. Also, there may be lease agreements to which the seller was a party that must be recorded. In addition, tax law may require the purchasing company to use the selling company's book value for depreciation on future tax returns instead of the higher market value on the purchase date. Furthermore, the company purchased may have tax loss carryovers available to the purchasing company which become one of the assets being acquired. Lastly, there may be contingent assets, liabilities, or asset impairments that exist on the purchase date. Each of these situations is examined separately.

Revaluation of Long-Term Liabilities.   Liabilities that are assumed by the buyer in a purchase transaction must always be recorded at their current market value. When interest rates have increased since the original issue of the debt, the market value of the debt will be less than book value and a discount will be recorded. If interest rates have decreased since issuance of the debt, the debt will have a value in excess of book value and a premium will be recorded. For large corporations with publicly traded debt securities, the market value of the debt is easily secured. In those cases where quoted market prices are not available, the current value of the debt instrument is imputed using the market rate of interest for similar debt instruments. Consider the following example of imputing the current value of an existing bond. The company being acquired has outstanding a $100,000, 8% bond with 5 years remaining to maturity. Interest is paid annually each December 31. The acquisition date is January 1, 19X1. The current interest rate for a similar bond is 6%. The current value of the debt would be imputed:

Present value of interest payments at 6%
   ($8,000 annual interest × 5-year, 6% present value of annuity
      factor of 4.2124) . . . . $ 33,699
Present value of principal ($100,000 × 5-year present value factor
   of .7473)   74,730
Imputed market value of liability $108,429

The purchase entry would include the following credits:

Bonds Payable   100,000
Premium on Bonds Payable   8,429

The premium will be amortized over the remaining 5-year term using either the effective interest or straight-line amortization methods. Had the current interest rate exceeded the original face rate of 8%, the bonds would have a market value below $100,000, and a discount would result.

Lease Agreements.   Special analysis of the purchase price in a business combination is necessary when the company acquired in a purchase transaction is bound contractually by existing leases as either a lessee or lessor. Sometimes, the terms of the lease may be modified as a result of the combination. These modifications would require the consent of a third party; either the lessor, when the selling company is the lessee, or the lessee, when the selling company is the lessor. When the terms of the lease are modified to the extent that a new lease is created, the new lease is classified and recorded according to the requirements of FASB Statement No. 13.[9] It is more common, however, to find that the contractual terms of a lease are not altered as a result of the purchase. In such cases, it is necessary to record only the market value of the seller's existing rights and obligations under the lease.

When the company acquired is a lessee under an operating lease, it has recorded rent as an expense but has not recorded any asset or long-term liability. Thus, there is no existing recorded asset or liability to adjust. At acquisition, if the contractual rent under the remaining lease term is materially below fair market rental value, an asset should be recorded equal to the value of the rent savings. The asset should be amortized over the lease term as an adjustment to rent expense. If the contractual rent exceeds the market rental value, a liability should be credited, equal to the value of the excess rent, using an appropriate market interest rate. The liability should be amortized as a reduction of rent expense in future periods. Under both situations, future rent expense would reflect market rental value as of the date of the combination.[10]

When the acquired company is a lessee under a capital lease, it has recorded the asset as well as the liability under that lease. At the time of the purchase, both the asset and the liability should be analyzed independently and recorded at their separate market values.

---

9 Statement of Financial Accounting Standards No. 13, *Accounting for Leases* (Stamford, CT: Financial Accounting Standards Board, 1976,) par. 9.
10 Accounting Principles Board Opinion No. 16, *Business Combinations* (New York: American Institute of Certified Public Accountants, 1970), par. 88.

When the acquired company is a lessor under an operating lease, it has recorded the cost of the leased asset less accumulated depreciation. In the purchase transaction, the asset should be recorded at its current market value. However, the market value may be based partly on the present value of the rents due under existing leases.

When the acquired company is a lessor under a capital lease, it has recorded only a receivable due for future rents and perhaps an unguaranteed residual value. In the purchase transaction, the receivable should be recorded at its fair market value based on prevailing current interest rates. The unguaranteed residual value should be estimated and discounted to its present value, using the same current interest rate.

Research and Development Costs.   The company acquired may have incurred substantial research and development (R&D) costs in the current and prior periods. The purchasing firm may be willing to pay for these activities rather than incur the costs themselves in future periods. The values assigned to the purchased R&D costs are **not based on past, recorded expenditures.** The value of the R&D costs would be based on an appraisal of their current value. Most likely, a discounted present value model would be used to value future income projections. Once a value is arrived at for the purchased R&D, it must be expensed in the period of the purchase. The only case where R&D can be treated as an asset is when there are R&D assets with multiple future uses.[11]

A major example of this issue occurred in 1995, when IBM purchased Lotus Development Corporation. The purchase price of $2.9 billion for fixed assets included the assignment of $1.84 billion to purchased R&D, which was immediately expensed. Imagine telling stockholders that it was prudent to buy this expense! Consider the fact, that if the R&D value had not been carefully established, a major portion of the price paid for Lotus would have been recorded as goodwill. The goodwill could have been amortized over a period as long as 40 years.

Nontaxable Exchanges.   The selling company may wish to structure the purchase so as to avoid a taxable gain at the time of the combination. Section 368(a)(1) of the Tax Code authorizes seven types of reorganizations that qualify as tax-free exchanges. For asset acquisitions, the tax-free exchange status is accomplished by exchanging the common stock of the purchasing company for substantially all the assets of the selling company. After the exchange, the selling corporation liquidates by distributing the shares received to its shareholders. The shareholders of the selling company do not record a gain for tax purposes until the shares received are sold. The purchasing company in a nontaxable exchange inherits the book values of the assets purchased for use in future tax calculations. This means that only the net book value on the books of the selling company are used as the tax basis of the assets acquired when they are sold or depreciated later. This results in the recording of a deferred tax liability for the added tax burden caused by the inability of the purchasing company to deduct the excess of the value assigned to the assets over the selling company's book value.

As an example, assume that in a nontaxable exchange the tax basis of a given fixed asset is $50,000, and its fair market value at acquisition is $150,000. Depreciation on the $100,000 difference is not deductible on future tax returns. Therefore, if the purchasing company is in a 35% tax bracket, there will be a $35,000 increase in future tax payments caused by the tax-free status of the purchase transaction. The purchasing company will acknowledge this added tax burden by recording a deferred tax liability of $35,000 at the same time that it records the asset at $150,000. This tax liability will be paid off in future periods when taxable income

---

11 Financial Accounting Standards Board Interpretation No. 4, *Applicability of FASB Statement No. 2 to Purchase Business Combinations,* (Stamford, 1975).

exceeds financial ("book") income because of the lack of deductibility for the depreciation on the $100,000 excess of market over book value. The goodwill arising in a tax-free exchange is not deductible. This means that a deferred tax liability also arises applicable to the goodwill. Suppose that after recording all other assets and liabilities at market value, $65,000 of unallocated cost remains. The net of tax value of the goodwill is $65,000. Thus, the goodwill is recorded at a gross value of $100,000 ($65,000 ÷ .65) and a deferred tax liability of $35,000 is recorded.

Tax Loss Carryovers.   Tax law provides that an existing company with a tax loss may first carry the loss back to the previous two years to offset income and thus receive a refund of taxes paid in the preceding years. If the loss exceeds income available in the prior two-year period, the loss can be carried forward up to twenty years to offset future income and therefore reduce the taxes which otherwise would be paid. The selling company may have unused tax loss carryovers which it has not been able to utilize due to an absence of sufficient income in prior years. This becomes a benefit for which the purchasing company will pay. Tax provisions limit the amount of the NOL (net operating loss) available to the acquiring company to discourage business combinations that are motivated primarily by tax loss carryovers. The purchaser is allowed to use the seller's tax loss carryovers to offset its own income in the current and future periods subject to the following limitations:

1. None of the target company's NOL can be used to refund taxes paid in prior years.
2. Section 381{c} of the Tax Code restricts the use of the target company's NOL in the tax year of the acquisition. The NOL that can be used cannot exceed

$$\text{Income of acquiring company} \times \left(\frac{\text{number of days in year after the acquisition}}{\text{number of days in the tax year}} \right)$$

    Thus, if the target company was acquired on July 1, the acquiring company could not use an NOL in excess of 50% of its income for the year.
3. For years subsequent to the acquisition, Section 382 of the Tax Code restricts the use of the NOL from an acquired company to an amount not greater than the product of total market value of the acquired company's stock multiplied by the long-term tax-exempt interest rate on U.S. obligations. Thus, if the market value of the acquired company's stock was $2 million and the U.S. tax-exempt rate was 6%, the NOL used in any one year could not exceed $120,000.

The value of the expected future tax loss carryovers is recorded as *Deferred Tax Asset* on the date of the acquisition. It is, however, necessary to attempt to determine whether there will be adequate future tax liabilities to support the value of the deferred tax asset. The accountant would have to consider existing evidence to make this determination. If it is likely that some or all of the deferred tax asset will not be realized, the contra-account Allowance for Unrealizable Tax Assets would be used to reduce the deferred tax asset to an estimated amount to be realized.[12] This may have the practical effect of the contra-account's totally offsetting the deferred tax asset. The inability to record a net deferred tax asset often will result in the consideration paid for the NOL carryover being assigned to goodwill. This occurs because the price paid will exceed the value of the assets that are allowed to be recorded.

Consider an example of a purchase that includes both of the previous tax ramifications. Farlow Inc. is purchasing Granada Company, which has the following balance sheet on the purchase date:

---

12 Statement of Accounting Standards No. 109, *Accounting for Income Taxes* (Norwalk, CT: Financial Accounting Standards Board, 1992), par. 17.

Assets		Liabilities and Equity	
Inventory	$ 50,000	Liabilities	$180,000
Land	100,000	Common stock ($10 par)	100,000
Building	270,000	Retained earnings	70,000
Accum. depreciation	(70,000)		
		Total liabilities	
Total assets	$350,000	and equity	$350,000

The market values of the land and the building are $100,000 and $300,000, respectively. Granada Company has an NOL carryover totaling $200,000. Granada has not recorded the deferred tax asset, since it does not foresee adequate future tax liabilities. Farlow Inc. issued 10,000, $10 par value common stock shares with a market value of $32.50 each, for the net assets of Granada in a transaction structured as a tax-free exchange. Farlow has an effective tax rate of 30% and believes that NOL carryovers will be realized. The price paid would be compared first to market values. The market values include the deferred tax liability caused by the excess of the building's market value over its book value.

Farlow would allocate its purchase price to the accounts in the following manner:

Price paid		$325,000
Market values of net assets:		
Inventory	$ 50,000	
Land	100,000	
Building	300,000	
Deferred tax liability, 30% × ($300,000 market value of building − $200,000 book value)	(30,000)	
Recorded liabilities	(180,000)	
Deferred tax asset value of the NOL carryover (30% × $200,000)	60,000	300,000
Goodwill (Net of deferred tax liability)		$25,000

Recorded as follows:

Goodwill (gross value) ($25,000 ÷ 70%)	$ 35,714
Deferred Tax Liability (30% × $35,714)	(10,714)
Net Goodwill	$ 25,000

Inventory	50,000	
Land	100,000	
Building	300,000	
Deferred Tax Asset	60,000	
Goodwill	35,714	
Liabilities		180,000
Deferred Tax Liability ($30,000 building, $10,714 goodwill)		40,714
Common Stock, $10 par		100,000
Paid-in Capital in Excess of Par		225,000

Notice that the deferred tax asset and deferred tax liability are recorded separately, though they are offset in the statements. In future periods, the tax loss carryover realized will be credited to the deferred tax asset account.

Contingencies.   Special procedures should be followed when the seller has a contingent asset, liability, or asset impairment which exists on the date of the purchase. A contingency is "an existing condition, situation, or set of circumstances involving uncertainty as to possible gain or loss to an enterprise that will ultimately be resolved when one or more future events occur or fail to occur."[13] An example would be a lawsuit that existed before the purchase or was filed shortly after the purchase but that involved an event that occurred prior to the purchase date.

When the existence of the contingent asset, liability, or asset impairment is probable and can be reasonably estimated, it should be recorded at the estimated amount as part of the allocation of the purchase price.[14] It is not necessary that the amount be probable and estimable on the date of the purchase. The assessments may be made subsequent to the purchase date during what is called the "allocation period" which is the time period when noncontingent assets and liabilities acquired in the purchase are quantified and valued. Normally, this period should not exceed one year. Amounts not recorded during the allocation period should be included in the income calculations for the period in which the amounts are determined.[15]

Including Contingent Consideration in a Purchase Agreement

A purchase agreement may provide that the purchaser will transfer additional consideration to the seller, contingent upon the occurrence of specified future events or transactions. This consideration could involve the transfer of cash or other assets, or the issuance of additional securities. During the period preceding the date on which the contingency is resolved, the purchaser has a contingent liability that is disclosed in a footnote to the financial statements but is not recorded.[16] On the date that the contingency is resolved, the contingent liability ceases, and the purchaser records any additional consideration as an adjustment to the original purchase transaction. The method used to make the adjustment is dependent upon the nature of the contingency.

Contingent Consideration Based on Earnings.   A purchaser may agree to make a final payment contingent upon the earnings of the acquired company during a specified future time period. If, during this period, the earnings of the acquired company reach or exceed an agreed amount, further payment will be made at the end of the contingency period. In essence, the value of all or part of the goodwill is to be confirmed before full payment is made. Clearly, when an earnings contingency exists, the total price to be paid for the acquired company is not known until the end of the contingency period. As is the case for the initial payment, the purchaser must record the fair market value of the consideration given, including the market value of additional securities issued. Normally, the amount of the additional payment will result in an increased amount of goodwill.[17] Adjustments to other assets would be made only if the contingency was based on their value.

---

13 Statement of Financial Accounting Standards No. 5, *Accounting for Contingencies* (Stamford: Financial Accounting Standards Board, 1975), par. 1.
14 Statement of Financial Accounting Standards No. 38, *Accounting for Postacquisition Contingencies of Purchased Enterprises* (Stamford: Financial Accounting Standards Board, 1980), par. 5.
15 *Ibid.*, par. 6.
16 APB Opinion No. 16 (par. 78) provides that a liability is to be recorded if the amount of the contingent liability is determinable at the date of the acquisition. Of course, doing so would increase the price paid for the firm and would impact values assigned to the assets.
17 When the contingency involves the value of an asset other than goodwill, that asset's value is to be adjusted as a result of the contingent payment. For example, with a contingency involving the value of a building, the value would be adjusted at the time the contingency was resolved and the added payment made.

To illustrate, assume that Company A acquires the assets of Company B on January 1, 19X2, in exchange for Company A's common stock under conditions that require the acquisition to be recorded as a purchase. Also, Company A agrees to issue 10,000 additional common shares to the former stockholders of Company B on January 1, 19X5, if the acquired company's average annual income before taxes for the three years, 19X2 through 19X4, reaches or exceeds $50,000. During the contingency period, Company A will disclose the contingent liability in the footnotes of its financial statements. If the earnings condition is met, Company A will record the final payment on January 1, 19X5, by increasing the goodwill account. Assuming the 10,000 shares have a par value of $1 and a market value of $8 per share on January 1, 19X5, the following entry would be made:

Goodwill ($8 market value × 10,000 shares)	80,000	
Common Stock ($1 par × 10,000 shares)		10,000
Paid-In Capital in Excess of Par		70,000

Goodwill recorded as a result of a contingency payment must be amortized over the **remaining** life of the original goodwill. The period of amortization must end within 40 years of the original date of the combination. If a contingency involving goodwill is resolved 3 years after the original purchase, the added goodwill recorded can be amortized over a maximum of only 37 (40 − 3) years. No retroactive adjustment may be made for amortization applicable to prior periods.[18]

Contingent Consideration Based on Issuer's Security Prices.   In exchange for its assets, a seller may be reluctant to accept the securities of the purchasing company. This reluctance is caused by the seller's fear of a possible future decline in the market value of the securities. When a stock issuance is involved, the concern may be based, in part, on the dilutive effect of a significant increase in the number of shares outstanding. To combat this apprehension, the purchaser may guarantee the total value of the securities on a given future date. The purchaser agrees to transfer additional assets or issue additional securities on that date, for the amount by which the guaranteed value exceeds the market value on the date selected. For example, on January 1, 19X2, Company C issues 100,000 shares of its common stock, which has a $1 par value and a $12 market value per share, in exchange for the assets of Company D. The conditions of the exchange require the acquisition to be recorded as a purchase. The following summarized entry would be recorded:

Net Assets ($12 market value × 100,000 shares)	1,200,000	
Common Stock ($1 par × 100,000 shares)		100,000
Paid-In Capital in Excess of Par		1,100,000

Company C guarantees the value of the stock at $12 per share as of January 1, 19X3. If necessary, additional consideration will be paid in cash. During the contingency period, Company C must disclose the contingent liability in a footnote. Should the market price of the common stock be less than $12 per share on January 1, 19X3, additional consideration will be recorded.

Assume that on January 1, 19X3, the market value is $10 per share. Then $200,000 (100,000 shares × $2 per share deficiency) is the amount by which the guaranteed value of the shares exceeds the total market value. Company C will have to pay an additional $200,000 in cash. How should the payment be recorded? The payment is not based on a revaluation of the goodwill account, as is the case with an earnings contingency. Instead, the payment reflects the fact that the value assigned to the orig-

---

18 Accounting Principles Board Opinion No. 16, *Business Combinations* (New York: American Institute of Certified Public Accountants, 1970), par. 80.

inal security issuance was only an estimate, with the final amount to be determined later. To record the adjustment of the estimate, the original credit to Paid-In Capital should be decreased as shown by the following entry:

Paid-In Capital in Excess of Par	200,000	
Cash		200,000

In the preceding example, the value guaranteed was satisfied in cash. More often, the satisfaction will involve the issuance of additional securities. In that case, Company C would issue 20,000 additional shares ($200,000 market value deficiency ÷ $10 current market value per share). Company C will now need 120,000 shares to equal the $1,200,000 original consideration, rather than the 100,000 shares previously issued. Accordingly, the $1,200,000 originally assigned to the 100,000 shares must be reassigned to 120,000 shares. The following entry will accomplish the reassignment:

Paid-In Capital in Excess of Par	20,000	
Common Stock ($1 par × 20,000 shares)		20,000

Asset Acquisition as a Pooling of Interests

A pooling of interests is a combination that must meet very strict criteria to ensure that there is a true bonding of existing interests. Since the company being acquired must fully cooperate to assure the pooling treatment, it is unlikely that the pooling method could ever be applied to a hostile takeover. When the pooling criteria are met, it is held that there has not been a purchase or a sale and, thus, there is no cause to recognize market values. Please understand that the negotiation of the combination will consider market values of assets and liabilities; they just are not recorded.

Criteria for the Use of the Pooling Method

As previously mentioned, prior to the issuance of APB Opinion No. 16, many companies tended to ignore the then loosely defined criteria for the use of the purchase and pooling methods. A choice between the methods often was based on the impact of the methods on future financial statements. However, APB Opinion No. 16 states that the purchase and pooling methods are not alternative recording methods available for any given combination. Any combination not meeting **all of the criteria** for a pooling of interests must be designated as a purchase. Thus, the criteria seek to ensure that only a true fusion of previous stockholder interests and assets will be accorded the pooling treatment. APB Opinion No. 16 classifies the criteria according to the attributes of the combining companies, the agreement as to how interests are to be combined, and the required absence of planned subsequent transactions. The following quotation from the *Institutional Investor* summarizes the accounting profession's opinion of the pooling rules:

> *Indeed, over the past three years or so, auditors and regulators have been deluged by companies requesting clarification of the rules. "We find that 10% of the questions clients put to us relate to the purchase method, while 90% relate to poolings," notes Dennis Garmer, a partner with Arthur Andersen L.L.P. in Chicago. Securities and Exchange Commission chief accountant Michael Sutton estimates that his staff spends more than 40% of its time dealing with pooling, which he calls a "highly labor-intensive (accounting) standard."*[19]

---

19 "Goodwill Games," *Institutional Investor*, March 1997.

The Opinion also introduces special terminology for referring to companies combining under the pooling method. The acquiring company (the one that will issue the stock) that will continue in existence is termed the *issuer*, while the acquired company is termed the *combiner*. These terms will be used in subsequent discussions to avoid any connotation of a purchase's or sale's having occurred when the pooling method is appropriate.

Attributes of the Combining Companies.   APB Opinion No. 16 (par. 46) provides two criteria that establish essential attributes of the combining companies.

Criterion 1.   Each of the combining companies may not have been a subsidiary or division of another company for two years preceding the date on which a plan of combination is initiated. The initiation date is the earliest date at which the stockholders of the combining companies are informed, by a public announcement or written notification, of the terms of the combination (including the stock exchange ratio).

The intent of this condition is that a company should not be able to fragment a business enterprise and pool only part of it. For new companies created within the two years, this condition is applicable only to the company's period of existence. For the purposes of this condition, a former subsidiary that was separated from the parent by government order is considered a "new" company.

Criterion 2.   Each of the combining companies must be independent of one another. On the date of initiation of the plan and until its consummation, no combining company may own more than 10% of the voting common stock of any other combining company. Shares acquired as a part of the plan of the combination are exempted.

Agreement on How Interests Are to Be Combined.   APB Opinion No. 16 (par. 47) provides seven criteria that relate to the manner in which interests are combined.

Criterion 1. The combination must be accomplished in a single transaction or in accordance with a specific plan, in which case the plan must be executed within one year of its initiation. One exception is allowed when there is a delay that is beyond the control of the combining companies. The only delays considered uncontrollable are (1) proceedings and deliberations with a federal or state regulatory agency on whether to approve or disapprove a combination where the combination cannot be effected without approval and (2) litigation aimed at prohibiting the combination.

The intent of this condition is to prevent a piecemeal, selective displacement of stockholders on possibly different terms.

Criterion 2.   Subsequent to the initiation date, the issuer must issue its common stock for either all the assets of the combiner or at least 90% of the outstanding voting common shares of the combiner in a stock acquisition. The shares issued must have rights identical to those of the majority of the issuer's outstanding voting common shares.

In an asset acquisition, there is a minor modification of the requirement that all assets be acquired. The combining company may retain cash or other assets on a temporary basis to settle existing liabilities, contingencies, or items in dispute. Once these matters are settled, any remaining assets should be transferred to the issuer in exchange for common stock.

For poolings accomplished as a stock acquisition, the 90% requirement must be carefully analyzed. For the purposes of this requirement, the computation of combiner shares received excludes

a)   *Shares held by the issuer or its subsidiaries prior to the initiation date, and*

b)   *Shares acquired after the initiation date by giving any consideration other than the voting common shares of the issuer. Fractional shares acquired for cash cannot be considered in meeting the 90% provision.*

To illustrate, assume that Company C (combiner) has 20,000 shares of voting common stock outstanding and Company I (issuer) exchanges 8,500 shares of its voting common stock for 17,000 shares of Company C stock. Company I, prior to the date of initiation, acquired 1,000 shares of Company C stock in exchange for its own shares. In addition, Company I paid cash for 500 shares of Company C stock as a part of the combination plan. Even though Company I holds 92.5% (18,500 ÷ 20,000) of Company C shares at the consummation date, the 90% rule is not met, and the combination must be accounted for as a purchase. The computations are as follows:

Shares owned by Company I	18,500
Less disqualified shares:	
Company C shares owned prior to initiation date	1,000
Company C shares acquired for cash after initiation date	500
Shares meeting the pooling requirement	17,000

Ownership interest for pooling criteria
(17,000 shares ÷ 20,000 outstanding shares) **85%**

The application of the 90% rule becomes more complex when the combiner holds shares of the issuer. To illustrate, assume that Company I issues 9,250 shares of its stock for 18,500 of the 20,000 shares of outstanding Company C stock subsequent to the initiation date of a plan of combination. In addition, Company C previously acquired 500 shares of Company I stock. The following diagram summarizes the intercompany stock transactions:

	Company I	Company C
Prior to initiation date	500 shares of ◄————— Company I stock	Owns
Subsequent to initiation date	Issues 9,250 shares of Company I stock ————►	In exchange for 18,500 shares of Company C stock

According to the exchange ratio, 1 share of Company I stock is equal in value to 2 shares of Company C stock.[20] Thus, 1,000 (500 × 2) shares of Company C stock represent an equity in Company I. Viewed in another manner, the 1,000 shares of Company C stock support the investment in 500 shares of Company I stock. APB Opinion No. 16 would hold that on an equivalent share basis, 1,000 of the shares of Company C stock received by Company I are, in essence, a return of its own shares. Therefore, the equivalent shares must be subtracted from the total combiner shares held by the issuer on the consummation date. The 90% test is not met, and the combination must be accounted for as a purchase. The calculations are as follows:

---

20 The exchange rate used is the actual resulting ratio at the consummation date. Any cash given for fractional shares will diminish the exchange rate.

Shares owned by Company I	18,500
Less disqualified shares:	
Equivalent number of Company C shares represented by Company C	
investment in Company I (500 × 2)	1,000
Shares meeting the pooling requirement	17,500

Ownership interest for pooling criteria
(17,500 shares ÷ 20,000 outstanding shares) **87.5%**

If the combiner acquires shares of the issuer subsequent to the initiation date, these shares also are subtracted on an equivalent share basis from the total shares acquired by the issuer in determining compliance with the 90% rule.

The 90% criterion does allow partial payment using cash or other consideration for a minor portion of the shares. However, each combiner shareholder that is participating in the combination agreement must exchange all shares for those of the issuer. Cash or other consideration can be used only for fractional shares or for dissenting shareholders who will not be shareholders in the surviving company.[21]

Criterion 3.   The combining companies may not change their equity interests in contemplation of a combination for the period of time beginning two years before the initiation date and extending through the consummation date.

The intent of this provision is to prevent a combiner from purchasing and reselling common shares in an attempt to create a group of shareholders who own 90% of the shares and who agree to combine. It is also the intent of this provision that the issuer be prevented from realigning its shareholders in an attempt to create a majority group who are willing to combine. Treasury stock purchases must be defended as normal and motivated by other purposes in order to not violate this condition. "Other purposes" would include, for example, acquisition of shares to satisfy employee stock option plans.

This rule has been a major concern in recent combinations. The previously mentioned Fort Howard Paper–James River Paper Corporation deal was probably delayed to meet this rule. The *Wall Street Journal* reported:

> "Fort Howard couldn't be sold using favorable accounting treatment until March 1997, two years after the Morgan Stanley fund relinquished majority control via the March 1995 IPO [Initial Public Offering]. The transaction with James River is believed to be a tax-free swap using the so-called pooling-of-interests accounting treatment, the method precluded until recently."[22]

Criterion 4.   Dividend distributions (other than in common stock) must be no greater than normal for two years before the initiation date through the consummation date.

"Normal" is defined by reference to past dividend policy and earnings of the period. Greater-than-normal dividends would allow a company to distribute part of its assets to shareholders and to pool only the residual. Thus, shareholders would receive part assets and part equity of the pooled company, which is counter to the concept of pooling as a fusion of existing interests.

Criterion 5.   The voting common stockholders of the combiner must receive voting shares of the issuer proportionate to their holdings in the combiner.

---

21 Accounting Principles Board Opinion No. 16, *Business Combinations* (New York: American Institute of Certified Public Accountants, 1970), par. 47b; Accounting Interpretation No. 25 of APB Opinion No. 16, *Business Combinations* (New York: AICPA, 1971).
22 "James River, Fort Howard In Merger Pact," *Wall Street Journal*, May 5, 1997.

For instance, Mr. X., who owned 30% of Combiner Company voting common stock, must receive 30% of the stock issued by the Issuer Company. In this way, the proportionate stockholder interests of the combiner are preserved.

Criterion 6.   *The voting rights of the resulting ownership interests are exercisable. There may be no deprivation or restriction of these rights for any time period.*

An attempt to place the shares issued in a voting trust, for example, would violate this criterion.

Criterion 7.   *There can be no contingent consideration agreements based on events subsequent to the consummation date.*

While contingent consideration is not allowed in a pooling, contingency agreements are permitted. The most common type of agreement that is allowed is a "general management representation," which is found in most business combinations. In such an agreement, the management of the acquired company warrants that the assets exist and are worth their agreed value, and all liabilities are recorded. These contingencies involve the values assigned to assets and liabilities existing on the consummation date and do not involve subsequent events. The agreement usually calls for an adjustment of the shares issued up to about 10%, but actual adjustments are rare.[23]

Absence of Planned Subsequent Transactions.   Stipulations exist to prevent planned subsequent transactions that would counteract the conditions of a pooling of interests and allow a purchase to appear in the guise of a pooling. The pooling treatment is denied by APB Opinion No. 16 (par. 48) if any *one* of the following conditions is included explicitly or by intent in the negotiations and/or terms of the agreement to combine

1.   An agreement by which the issuer will retire or reacquire the common shares issued to effect the combination;
2.   An agreement to financially aid a faction of the stockholders of the former combiner;
3.   A plan to dispose of a significant part of the assets of the combining companies within two years of the consummation of the combination.[24]

Disposal of combining company assets is objectionable since it could allow large gains to be recorded on the sales. This would occur since only book values were recorded in the pooling.

Added SEC Requirements.   There are several added stipulations required of companies which are both desiring to pool and subject to regulation by the Securities and Exchange Commission. The major additional requirements imposed by the SEC are

1.   The companies being pooled must be viable operating companies; that is, the combination cannot be simply a pool of assets. For example, an operating lumber company was not allowed to pool with a timber company that owned timber tracts but had not actually operated in the current and preceding years.
2.   The SEC will not allow a significant sale of assets in contemplation of the combination. Any asset disposals in the six to nine months preceding the combination must be defended as being done in the ordinary course of business.[25]

---

23 *Interpretations of APB Opinion Nos. 16 and 17*, 7th Ed. (Chicago: Arthur Andersen & Co., 1988), p. 114.
24 APB Opinion No. 16 (par. 60) provides that if there is a material gain or loss on a sale of the assets of the previously separate firms within two years of a pooling, the gain or loss is shown as an extraordinary item.
25 *Interpretation of APB Opinion Nos. 16 and 17*, 7th ed., p. 77.

3.   The SEC requires that the issuer obtain at least 90% of all combiner company voting stock, including class B common and preferred stock with voting rights. The SEC also requires obtaining 90% of any securities judged to be "substantially the same" as common stock. This includes common stock options and warrants as well as convertible securities that are currently convertible and where conversion is likely to be due to the value of the common stock.

Pooling of Interests Accounting

A pooling of interests is viewed as a fusion of existing accounting entities; there has been no purchase or sale. Thus, there is no cause to record market values. Assets, liabilities, and equities are recorded at their existing book values. Adjustments to the accounts of the combiner are allowed only if they would be appropriate in the course of normal operations. An example of this would be the write-down of inventory from cost to market value or the write-down of a fixed asset that has suffered an impairment of value. Any adjustment to the accounts of the combiner will result in an adjustment to the combiner's retained earnings prior to carrying the retained earnings to the issuer's books.

The combiner may have recorded a deferred tax asset for the benefits of a tax loss carryforward. The deferred tax asset, however, may be offset by a contra-valuation account to reflect a probable lack of full realization of the benefits. The issuer may have additional future tax liabilities that will be more able to offset the deferred tax asset. This allows the existing valuation account to be reduced or eliminated. The reduction in the valuation account becomes an increase in the combiner's retained earnings prior to its transfer to the issuer. There may be some cases where the deferred tax asset may not have been recorded by the combiner. In such a case, the net amount of the deferred tax asset, the carryforward less the valuation account (if any), is an adjustment to combiner retained earnings prior to transfer to the issuer.

To illustrate the recording of a pooling of interests, the example used in an earlier purchase analysis is revised. Assume that Expansion Inc. (formerly Acquisitions Inc.) is going to pool with Jacobs Company by issuing common stock and that Expansion will be the surviving accounting entity. Expansion is the issuer, not the purchaser, and Jacobs is the combiner, not the seller. These terms emphasize that the companies are joint owners in a pooling and are not parties to an exchange. When the pooling is consummated, the **book values of Jacobs Company will be recorded** on the books of Expansion Inc. The only exception to this rule is for assets that have book values in excess of market values; in that case, the lower market values are recorded.

The fact that market values are not recorded does not mean that they are ignored during negotiations preceding the combination. Both parties to a pooling must agree on the market values of the items involved in order to arrive at the number of issuer shares to be exchanged for the combiner's net assets.

The companies agree on the following values for the net assets of Jacobs Company:

	Book Value	Market Value
Accounts receivable	$ 20,000	$ 20,000
Inventory	40,000	45,000
Land	10,000	10,000
Buildings (net)	40,000	50,000
Equipment (net)	20,000	40,000
Current liabilities	(20,000)	(20,000)
Total	$110,000	$145,000

Expansion agrees that the value of the goodwill is $35,000. To satisfy the $180,000 net asset value, Expansion will issue common stock with a par value of $2 and a market value of $20. Expansion will issue 9,000 shares ($180,000 net asset value divided by $20 per share). It is common to state the stock exchange ratio in a business combination. In this example, the ratio would be 9 to 1, or 9,000 Expansion shares for 1,000 Jacobs Company shares. **While the negotiation and settlement of the pooling are based on market values, the recording of the transaction is based on book values.** This would include the recording of goodwill that is present on the books of the combiner at the time of the pooling. The book values of Jacobs Company, including retained earnings of $50,000, are transferred to Expansion Inc. by recording the following entry:[26]

Accounts Receivable	20,000	
Inventory	40,000	
Land	10,000	
Buildings	40,000	
Equipment	20,000	
Current Liabilities		20,000
Common Stock (9,000 shares × $2 par)		18,000
Paid-In Capital in Excess of Par		42,000*
Retained Earnings		50,000

*($60,000, the total pain-in capital of Jacobs on the consummation date, less $18,000 assigned to par value.)

The difficult aspect of recording a pooling of interests is the combining of stockholders' equities. The total paid-in capital of the combiner must be carried as a unit to the total paid-in capital of the issuer. The **composition of the combiner paid-in capital is ignored** and is redistributed between the par or stated value and the additional paid-in capital of the issuer. In addition, recall that in a pooling of interests, incomes of the combiner and issuer are combined retroactively for periods prior to the combination. This means that retained earnings balances of the combiner and issuer are also combined. Normally, the retained earnings of the combiner are added directly to the retained earnings of the issuer. The following chart summarizes the equity transfer of the previous entry:

Jacobs Company (combiner) Balances		Increase in Expansion Inc. (issuer) Balances	
Capital stock ($10 par)	$ 10,000	Capital stock ($2 par)	$ 18,000
Paid-in capital in excess of par	50,000	Paid-in capital in excess of par	42,000
Total paid-in capital	$ 60,000	Total paid-in capital	$ 60,000
Retained earnings	50,000	Retained earnings	50,000
Total equity	$110,000	Total equity	$110,000

Equity transfer rules must accommodate combinations in which the par or stated value of the shares issued exceeds the total paid-in capital of the combiner. This is a rare occurrence because most companies have no par or very low par value shares. When this situation occurs, the issuer first must use its *own* paid-in capital in excess of par to cover the deficiency. Only when such an excess is depleted, or when it does not exist, may the combiner's retained earnings be reduced. This is the only exception

26 See Jacobs Company balance sheet, p. 1-11.

to the general rule that the retained earnings of the companies are combined. As an example, assume that in the previous situation Expansion was issuing $10 par stock and all the other facts were unchanged. The issuer must add $90,000 (9,000 shares × $10 par) to its par value, while the total paid-in capital of the combiner is only $60,000. If the issuer has sufficient additional paid-in capital, the $30,000 deficiency would be met by reducing that account's balance as shown in the following chart:

Jacobs Company (combiner) Balances		Increase (Decrease) in Expansion Inc. (issuer) Balances	
Capital stock ($10 par) . . .	$ 10,000	Capital stock ($10 par) . . .	$ 90,000
Paid-in capital in excess . . .		Paid-in capital in excess	
of par	50,000	of par	(30,000)
Total paid-in capital	$ 60,000 →	Total paid-in capital. . . .	$ 60,000
Retained earnings	50,000 →	Retained earnings.	50,000
Total equity.	$110,000	Total equity	$110,000

Expansion's entry to record the pooling in this case would be:

Accounts Receivable	20,000	
Inventory	40,000	
Land	10,000	
Buildings	40,000	
Equipment	20,000	
Paid-In Capital in Excess of Par (existing on Expansion's books) .	30,000	
Current Liabilities		20,000
Common Stock ($10 par)		90,000
Retained Earnings		50,000

If the issuer has no additional paid-in capital with which to meet the deficiency, the combiner's retained earnings account would be used as shown in the following chart:

Jacobs Company (combiner) Balances		Reassignment	Increase in Expansion Inc. (issuer) Balances	
Capital stock ($10 par)	$ 10,000		Capital stock ($10 par)	$ 90,000
Paid-in capital in excess of par . . .	50,000			
Total paid-in capital.	$ 60,000	+30,000	Total paid-in capital.	$ 90,000
Retained earnings.	50,000	−30,000	Retained earnings.	20,000
Total equity	$110,000		Total equity	$110,000

The entry to record the pooling, then, would be

Accounts Receivable	20,000	
Inventory	40,000	
Land	10,000	
Buildings	40,000	
Equipment	20,000	
Current Liabilities		20,000
Common Stock ($10 par)		90,000
Retained Earnings		20,000

In some cases, it may be necessary to consume all of the combiner's retained earnings and draw upon the retained earnings of the issuer.

In a pooling, shareholders of the combiner must become shareholders of the continuing issuer. To accomplish the continuity of ownership, the combiner will usually dissolve itself by distributing the shares it receives from the issuer to its shareholders.

Pooling principles require that the assets of the combiner be recorded at book values and combined assets may not be increased through the combination. Consequently, the direct costs of consummating the combination may not be capitalized as an asset. Similarly, the issuance cost of new securities may not be deducted from the value assigned to the securities. Assume that, in the previous example, Expansion paid $1,000 in direct acquisition costs. A separate entry would expense the cost as follows:

Professional Services Expense	1,000	
Cash		1,000

Another complication arises when an issuer uses previously issued and reacquired stock (treasury stock) to accomplish a pooling. In contemplation of the combination, this treasury stock may not have been acquired in the 2-year period preceding the business combination, since such an acquisition of treasury shares would defeat a pooling criterion.[27] Pooling principles require that the book value of the combiner capital be assigned to stock issued in a pooling. Clearly, the issuer would violate these principles if it could reacquire previously issued shares and use their cost as the value assigned to the shares exchanged in the pooling. The problem that arises is: How does the issuer dispose of the difference between the price paid for the treasury shares and the value that must be assigned to them in a pooling of interests? The answer is: The treasury shares are treated as though they are retired. For instance, suppose Company E reacquired 10,000 shares of its common stock for $250,000 and later exchanged these shares for the assets of Company F. The summarized balance sheets of Companies E and F immediately prior to the pooling are as follows:

Company E (Issuer)		
	Liabilities	$200,000
	Common stock (50,000 shares, $2 par)	100,000
	Retained earnings	700,000
	Less treasury stock at cost	(250,000)
Total assets .. $750,000	Total liabilities and equity	$750,000
Company F (Combiner)		
	Liabilities	$ 50,000
	Common stock (20,000 shares, $1 par)	20,000
	Paid-in capital in excess of par	40,000
	Retained earnings	40,000
Total assets .. $150,000	Total liabilities and equity	$150,000

In this case, the shares to be used in the combination were purchased for $25 each, but must carry a book value of $10 each (combiner equity of $100,000 divided

---

27 Accounting Interpretation No. 20 of Accounting Principles Board Opinion No. 16, *Business Combinations* (New York: American Institute of Certified Public Accountants, 1971).

by 10,000 shares issued). **Since shares issued to accomplish a pooling must be treated as newly issued,** APB Opinion No. 16 (par. 54) requires that previously acquired shares be accounted for as though they were first retired. Therefore, Company E should first make a retirement entry for the 10,000 treasury shares as follows:

Common Stock (10,000 shares × $2 par)	20,000	
Retained Earnings	230,000	
Treasury Stock (at cost)		250,000

Then, the shares released to accomplish the pooling are recorded as newly issued:

Assets	150,000	
Liabilities		50,000
Common Stock (10,000 shares × $2 par)		20,000
Paid-In Capital in Excess of Par		
($60,000 total paid-in − $20,000 par)		40,000
Retained Earnings		40,000

Reporting Requirements

As is true of all asset acquisitions, the purchase of another company affects the financial statements of the purchaser only for periods following the purchase date. The comparability of current statements with statements of periods prior to the purchase is provided only by footnote disclosure of the estimation of what the financial information would have been had the purchase occurred at the beginning of the earliest period presented. Poolings of interests, however, require retroactive restatement. Thus, all of the comparative financial statements are presented as they would have appeared had the pooled companies always been combined.

In a purchase or a pooling situation, the companies involved may have used different accounting principles to account for similar types of transactions. One company might use LIFO inventory valuation, while the other may use FIFO. To achieve uniformity or to improve future reporting, it might be desirable to change the accounting principles of one or both members of the combination.

The table on the following page summarizes the reporting requirements for business combinations.

Let us study two examples of the impact of business combinations on comparative financial statements. Exhibit 1-2 is a footnote from the 1995 financial statements of Carpenter Technology Corporation concerning its purchase of Certech, Inc., and Aceros Fortuna, S.A. de C.V. Notice that the terms of the purchase, the allocation of the price paid to the assets acquired, and the liabilities assumed are disclosed. Also, note that, had the purchase occurred at the first period included in the comparative statements, there would be a pro forma disclosure of the impact the purchase would have made on the 1994 and 1995 income statements. The footnote also explains that the income of acquired companies is not included in the body of the income statement prior to the purchase date.

Exhibit 1-3 on pages 1-35 to 1-36 is a footnote from the 1995 financial statements of Hughes Supply, Inc. In that year, it was the issuer in a pooling with Moore Electric Supply, Inc. and Florida Pipe and Supply Company. The footnote explains that the statements of the periods presented have been restated to account retroactively for the pooling.

Item	Purchase Method	Pooling Method
1. Change in accounting principles	Financial statements for previous periods restated retroactively. This procedure is an exception to the usual requirement to include in current income the cumulative effect of the change.[28]	Same as for a purchase.
2. Income earned in current year, prior to date of acquisition	Income of purchased company included only as of purchase date. Disclose in footnote estimated income as if purchase had occurred at beginning of year. Estimate includes adjustments for asset and liability revaluations and goodwill amortization.	Income of both companies combined for entire period. Include in footnotes each company's operating results for period prior to the combination.
3. Prior periods included in comparative statements	Only separate statements of parent shown. Disclosure in footnote the estimated results as if purchase had occurred at the beginning of the comparative periods presented. Estimate includes adjustments for asset and liability revaluations and goodwill amortization.	Statements restated as if pooling occurred at beginning of the comparative periods presented. Intercompany transactions eliminated. Must disclose that statements of previously separate companies have been combined.

Exhibit 1-2 *Purchase*
Carpenter Technology Corporation (Jun)

NOTES TO CONSOLIDATED FINANCIAL STATEMENTS

2. Acquisitions of Businesses

During fiscal 1995 and 1994, the Company acquired the entities described below, which were accounted for by the purchase method of accounting:

On July 22, 1994, the Company acquired all of the outstanding shares of Certech, Inc., and an affiliated company, for $16.7 million, including acquisition costs, comprised of $13.5 million in cash and 106,248 shares of treasury common stock. Certech manufactures a broad line of complex injection-molded ceramics parts. The excess of purchase price over the fair values of the net assets acquired was $8.2 million and has been recorded as goodwill, which is being amortized on a straight-line basis over 20 years.

On July 28, 1993, the Company acquired all of the outstanding shares of Aceros Fortuna, S.A. de C.V., a Mexican steel distribution company, and two affiliated companies for cash of $20.4 million, paid $2.5 million for agreements not to compete, and paid acquisition costs. In addition, the Company acquired equipment from an affiliated company in Mexico for $5.1 million. The excess of the purchase price over the fair values of the net assets acquired was $8.2 million and has been recorded as goodwill, which is being amortized on a straight-line basis over 20 years.

Fiscal 1995 also includes other acquisitions which are immaterial.

The purchase prices have been allocated to the assets purchased and the liabilities assumed based upon the fair values on the dates of acquisition, as follows:

---

[28] Accounting Principles Board Opinion No. 20, *Accounting Changes* (New York: American Institute of Certified Public Accountants, 1971), pars. 29 and 30.

(in thousands)	1995	1994
Working capital, other than cash	$ 1,894	$ 6,552
Property, plant, and equipment	10,200	6,634
Other assets	1,740	2,661
Goodwill	8,154	8,213
Other liabilities	(5,756)	(1,737)
Purchase price, net of cash received	$16,232	$22,323

The operating results of these acquired businesses have been included in the consolidated statement of income from the dates of acquisition. On the basis of a pro forma consolidation of the results of operations as if the acquisitions had taken place at the beginning of fiscal 1994, consolidated net sales would have been $759.0 million for fiscal 1995, and $654.0 million for fiscal 1994. Consolidated pro forma income and earnings per share, before the extraordinary charge, would not have been materially different from the reported amounts for fiscal 1995 and 1994. Such pro forma amounts are not necessarily indicative of what the actual consolidated results of operations might have been if the acquisitions had been effective at the beginning of fiscal 1994.

Exhibit 1-3 pooling
Hughes Supply, Inc. (Jan)

NOTES TO CONSOLIDATED FINANCIAL STATEMENTS
(Dollars in thousands, except per share data)

Note 2 (In Part): Business Combinations
On August 1, 1995, the Company acquired all the common stock of Moore Electric Supply, Inc. ("Moore") in exchange for 316,000 shares of the Company's common stock. Moore is a wholesale distributor of electrical products with five outlets in North Carolina and South Carolina.

On December 18, 1995, the Company acquired all the common stock of Florida Pipe & Supply Company ("FPS") in exchange for 178,000 shares of the Company's common stock. FPS is a wholesale distributor of industrial pipe, valves, and fittings with one outlet in Florida.

The above transactions have been accounted for as poolings of interests, and, accordingly, the consolidated financial statements for the periods presented have been restated to include the accounts of Moore and FPS. Moore's and FPS's fiscal year ends have been changed to the last Friday in January to conform to the Company's fiscal year end.

Net sales and net income of the separate companies for the periods preceding the acquisitions were as follows:

	Net Sales	Net Income
Six months ended July 31, 1995 (unaudited):		
Hughes, as previously reported	$494,239	$ 6,681
Moore	32,297	1,023
Combined	$526,536	$ 7,704

(continued)

Nine months ended October 31, 1995 (unaudited):		
Hughes, as previously reported	$805,575	$11,732
FPS	14,762	520
Combined	$820,337	$12,252
Fiscal year ended January 27, 1995:		
Hughes, as previously reported	$802,445	$10,328
Moore	54,115	423
FPS	18,899	734
Combined	$875,459	$11,485
Fiscal year ended January 28, 1994:		
Hughes, as previously reported	$660,938	$ 6,286
Moore	54,854	358
FPS	19,166	(120)
Combined	$734,958	$ 6,524

Questions

1. Income tax issues may be a motivation for companies to enter into a business combination. Suggest how income tax considerations may influence the desire of both parties in a combination.

2. Describe the two basic methods by which control of another company's assets might be obtained. Which method would most likely involve a lower total cost? What are the ramifications of each method on accounting procedures in future periods?

3. The management of Local Control Inc. is unhappy about a possible tender offer being made for a controlling interest in its shares by a large conglomerate. What actions might the company take to avoid the hostile takeover?

4. Compare the balance sheet ramifications of a purchase versus a pooling of interests. Include the effects on assets, liabilities, and equity. Why might a pooling of interests create a balance sheet with a more profitable appearance?

5. Explain the likely advantage the pooling method will have on income statements for periods subsequent to the combination as compared to the purchase method.

6. The company being purchased has the total market values of $150,000 and $30,000 for its assets and liabilities, respectively. The acquiring company issues 2,000 shares of common stock with a $10 par and a $60 market value per share for the net assets. What entry would be needed by the acquiring company to record this transaction under the purchase method?

7. The company being purchased has long-lived assets with a market value of $200,000. What are the accounting consequences of paying a price that is $50,000 in excess of the market value of the identifiable net assets? What happens if the price paid is $40,000 less than the value of the identifiable net assets?

8. Under the purchase method, which accounts are always recorded at full market value by the acquiring company? Why are only these accounts given this priority? What procedure is used when the price paid for the company is less than the total market value of these "priority" accounts?

9. What are the "price zones" in a purchase, and what are the basic procedures used to record assets and liabilities in each of the zones?

10. A company that has been acquired is a party to several leases, in the capacity of both a lessee and a lessor. In each of the following situations, indicate which accounts should be used and state how to arrive at an amount:

    a) The company is a lessee on a 2-year operating lease. The rent is below that which would be paid if currently negotiated.

    b) The company is a lessee under a capital lease with a 6-year remaining term.

    c) The company is a lessor under an operating lease with a remaining term of 3 years. The rents are below current rental value.

    d) The company is a lessor under a direct financing (capital) lease with a 4-year remaining term. Title to the asset passes to the lessee at the end of the term.

11. A company is contemplating the purchase of another company in a transaction that qualifies as a **tax-free** exchange for tax purposes. The market values of the assets purchased are in excess of their book values. What are the accounting ramifications of purchasing this company at a price high enough to result in the recording of goodwill?

12. The company being purchased has a tax loss carryover of $300,000 that it has not been able to utilize. The purchasing company has an effective tax rate of 30%. How will the purchasing company record the tax loss carryforward assuming that it (a) will have deferred future tax liabilities available to offset and (b) anticipates no deferred tax liabilities?

13. Company P acquired Company S at a price far in excess of the market value of its identifiable net assets. Pursuant to an earnings contingency, an additional payment is made 10 years later. How is this payment recorded, and what are the limitations concerning the allocation of the added amount to future periods?

14. An acquiring company guaranteed that if the total market value of the 2,000 shares of $10 par stock issued in an acquisition fell below $120,000 on January 1, 19XX, additional shares would be issued to make up the deficiency. What entry would be made on January 1, 19XX, if the market value of the stock dropped to $40 per share?

15. How are the voting common stockholders of the combiner assured "equality of treatment" by the pooling-of-interests criteria?

16. One of the criteria to be met in order to use the pooling method is the 90% stock acquisition rule. Specifically, how and when must the stock of the combiner be obtained if it is to be included in the qualifying 90% of the combiner outstanding stock?

17. What uses are made of market values in a business combination accomplished through a pooling of interests versus a combination accomplished through a purchase?

18. In a pooling of interests, how are the market values of the combiner used to arrive at the stock exchange ratio? Are these market values recorded?

19. Under the purchase and pooling methods, what recognition is given to previously recorded goodwill (goodwill already recorded on the books of the acquired company) by the acquiring company?

20. In a pooling of interests, how are the total paid-in capital and retained earnings of the combiner recorded on the books of the issuer? Describe the "basic equity transfer" rule.

21. How are direct acquisition costs, indirect acquisition costs, and issue costs recorded under (a) the purchase method and (b) the pooling method?

22. Assuming that a business combination occurs at midyear, contrast the reporting requirements of a purchase versus pooling concerning income earned during the year.

23. Company A is acquiring Company B on the last day of the fiscal reporting period of both companies. Company B has had substantial income in previous periods. What is the basic impact of the combination on the three years of comparative income and retained earnings statements to be provided if the combination is recorded as (a) a purchase and (b) a pooling? Include mention of related footnote disclosures.

Exercises

Exercise 1.   Green Company is considering acquiring the assets of Gold Corporation by assuming Gold's liabilities and by making a cash payment. Gold Corporation has the following balance sheet on the date negotiations occur:

Gold Corporation
Balance Sheet
December 31, 19X7

Assets		Liabilities and Equity	
Accounts receivable	100,000	Total liabilities	$200,000
Inventory	100,000	Capital stock ($10 par)	100,000
Land	100,000	Paid-in capital in excess of par	200,000
Buildings (net)	220,000	Retained earnings.	300,000
Equipment (net)	280,000		
Total assets	$800,000	Total liabilities and equity.	$800,000

under 95

Appraisals indicate that the inventory is undervalued by $25,000, the building is undervalued by $80,000, and the equipment is overstated by $30,000. Past earnings have been considered above average and were as follows:

Year	Net Income
19X3	$ 90,000
19X4	110,000
19X5	120,000
19X6	140,000*
19X7	130,000

*Includes extraordinary gain of $40,000

It is assumed that the average operating income of the past 5 years will continue. In this industry, the average return on assets is 12% on the market value of the total identifiable assets.

1. Prepare an estimate of goodwill based on each of the following assumptions:

   a) *The purchasing company paid for 5 years of excess earnings.*

   b) *Excess earnings will continue forever and are to be capitalized at the industry normal return.*

   c) *Excess earnings will continue for only 5 years and should be capitalized at a higher rate of 16%, which reflects the risk applicable to goodwill.*

2. Determine the actual goodwill recorded if Green pays $900,000 cash for the net assets of Gold Corporation and assumes all existing liabilities.

Exercise 2.   Benz Company is contemplating the purchase of the net assets of Cardinal Company for $800,000 cash. To complete the transaction, direct acquisition costs are $15,000. The balance sheet of Cardinal Company on the purchase date is as follows:

Cardinal Company
Balance Sheet
December 31, 19X1

Assets		Liabilities and Equity	
Current assets	$ 80,000	Liabilities.	$100,000
Land	50,000	Common stock	
Building	450,000	($10 par)	100,000
Accumulated depreciation,. . .		Paid-in capital in	
building	(200,000)	excess of par	150,000
Equipment.	300,000	Retained earnings.	230,000
Accumulated depreciation,			
equipment.	(100,000)		
Total assets	$580,000		$580,000

The following market values have been obtained for Cardinal's assets and liabilities:

Current assets	$100,000
Land	75,000
Building	300,000
Equipment	275,000
Liabilities	102,000

1. Record the purchase of the net assets of Cardinal Company on Benz Company's books.
2. Record the sale of the net assets on the books of Cardinal Company.
3. Record the purchase of 100% of the common stock of Cardinal Company on Benz's books. Cardinal Company will remain a separate legal entity.

Exercise 3.   Feldmen Company was acquired by Robertson International on July 1, 19X1. This combination does not meet the pooling criteria and must be accounted for as a purchase. Robertson exchanged 60,000 shares of its $5 par stock, with a market value of $20 per share, for the net assets of Feldmen Company.

Robertson incurred the following costs as a result of this transaction:

Direct acquisition costs	$25,000
Indirect acquisition costs	30,000
Stock registration and issuance costs	10,000
Total costs	$65,000

The balance sheet of Feldmen Company, on the day of the acquisition, was as follows:

(continued)

Feldmen Company
Balance Sheet
July 1, 19X1

Assets			Liabilities and Equity		
Cash..............		$ 100,000	Current liabilities........		$ 80,000
Inventory.............		300,000	Liability under capital		
Equipment under			lease.............		150,000
capital lease (net).....		200,000	Bonds payable.........		400,000
Property, plant, and			Stockholders' equity:		
equipment:.........			Common stock.........	$200,000	
Land.............	$200,000		Paid-in capital in		
Buildings (net)........	250,000	450,000	excess of par........	100,000	
			Retained earnings.......	120,000	420,000
			Total liabilities and		
Total assets...........		$1,050,000	equity.............		$1,050,000

The appraised market values as of July 1, 19X1 are:

Inventory $250,000
Equipment under capital lease 220,000
Land 180,000
Buildings 300,000
Liability under capital lease 140,000
Bonds payable 270,000

Record the purchase of Feldmen Company on the books of Robertson Corporation.

Exercise 4. Nebco Corporation has agreed to purchase net assets of Sun Corporation. Just prior to the purchase, Sun's balance sheet was as follows:

Sun Corporation
Balance Sheet
January 1, 19X1

Assets		Liabilities and Equity		
Accounts receivable............	$200,000	Current liabilities.............		$ 80,000
Inventory..................	270,000	Mortgage payable............		250,000
Equipment (net)..............	100,000	Stockholders' equity:		
		Common stock ($10 par)......	$100,000	
		Retained earnings..........	140,000	240,000
Total assets.................	$570,000	Total liabilities and equity		$570,000

Market values agree with book values except for the equipment which has an estimated market value of $40,000. Nebco Corporation paid $10,000 in direct acquisition costs and $15,000 in indirect acquisition costs to consummate the transaction.

Record the purchase on the books of Nebco Corporation assuming the cash paid to Sun Corporation was (a) $160,000 and (b) $90,000

Suggestion: Use "price zone analysis" to guide your calculations and entries.

Exercise 5.   Everett Company is purchasing the net assets of Green Company on December 31, 19X6, when Green Company has the following balance sheet:

Assets		Liabilities and Equity	
Current assets	$100,000	Liabilities.	$ 90,000
Land	50,000	Common stock ($10 par)	200,000
Buildings (net)	200,000	Retained earnings.	140,000
Equipment (net)	60,000		
Goodwill	20,000		
Total assets	$430,000	Total liabilities and equity.	$430,000

Everett has obtained the following market values for Green Company accounts:

Current assets	$120,000
Land	100,000
Buildings	250,000
Equipment	150,000
Liabilities	92,000

Direct acquisition costs are $18,000, and indirect acquisition costs are $5,000.

Prepare the entries to record the purchase of Green Company assuming the cash payment by Everett Company to Green Company is $450,000. Everett Company will assume the liabilities of Green Company. Price zone analysis is recommended.

Exercise 6.   Your client, Lewison International, has informed you that they have reached an agreement with Herro Company for the purchase of all of Herro's assets. This transaction is considered to be a purchase and will be accomplished through the issue of Lewison's common stock.

After your examination of the financial statements and the purchase agreement, you have discovered the following important facts.

The Lewison common stock issued has a market value of $800,000. The market value of Herro's assets net of all liabilities is $700,000. All asset book values equaled their market values except for one machine valued at $200,000. This machine was originally purchased two years ago by Herro for $180,000. This machine has been depreciated using the straight-line method with an assumed useful life of 10 years and no salvage value. The acquisition is to be considered a tax-free exchange for tax purposes.

Assuming a 30% tax rate, what amounts will be recorded for the machine, deferred tax liability, and goodwill?

Exercise 7.   Lake Company had the following balance sheet on December 31, 19X1, when it was purchased for $900,000 in cash by Atlantic Corporation:

Lake Company
Balance Sheet
December 31, 19X1

Assets		Liabilities and Equity		
Current assets	$100,000	Current liabilities		$ 60,000
Equipment (net)	200,000	Stockholders' equity:		
Building (net)	270,000	Common stock ($5 par)	$100,000	
		Retained earnings.	410,000	510,000
Total assets	$570,000	Total liabilities and equity.		$570,000

(continued)

All assets have market values equal to their book values. The combination is structured as a tax-free exchange. Lake Company has a tax loss carryforward of $400,000 which it has not recorded. The balance of the $400,000 tax loss carryover is considered fully realizable. Atlantic is taxed at a rate of 30%.

Record the purchase of Lake Company by Atlantic Corporation.

Exercise 8. Gonring Company purchased the net assets of Helm Company on January 1, 19X1, and made the following entry to record the purchase:

Current Assets	100,000	
Equipment	150,000	
Land	50,000	
Buildings	300,000	
Goodwill	100,000	
Liabilities		80,000
Common Stock ($1 par)		100,000
Paid-In Capital in Excess of Par		520,000

Make the required entry on January 1, 19X3, for each of the two following independent contingency agreements:

1. An additional cash payment would be made on January 1, 19X3, equal to twice the amount by which average annual earnings of the Helm Division exceed $25,000 per year, prior to January 1, 19X3. Net income was $50,000 in 19X1 and $60,000 in 19X2.
2. Added shares would be issued on January 1, 19X3, to compensate for any fall in the value of Gonring common stock below $6 per share. The settlement would be to cure the deficiency by issuing added shares based on their market value on January 1, 19X3. The market price of the shares on January 1, 19X3, was $4.

Exercise 9. Onan Company intends to engage in a pooling of interests with General Company. General Company has 50,000 shares of common stock outstanding on the initiation date. Onan will issue 1 of its shares for every 2 General shares. On the initiation date, Onan already owns 1,000 General shares and a wholly owned subsidiary of Onan owns another 1,500 shares.

By the consummation date, Onan issued 22,000 of its shares in accord with the predetermined exchange rate. Onan also purchased 1,000 General shares from dissident shareholders of General Company for cash.

Determine the number of General Company shares that are eligible to meet the 90% test which is required to record the acquisition as a pooling of interests. Has the 90% test been satisfied?

Exercise 10. Company P holds 96,000 shares of Company S common stock on December 31, 19X6. Of these shares, 92,000 were acquired after the initiation date of the business combination by issuing 1 share of Company P stock in exchange for every 5 shares of Company S stock, 2,000 shares were purchased after the initiation date using cash, and 2,000 shares were acquired prior to the initiation date on the 1-for-5 exchange basis. On the initiation date, Company S held 500 shares of Company P stock. At all times, there were 100,000 shares of Company S common stock outstanding.

Analyze the combination to see if it qualifies as a pooling of interests.

Exercise 11. After lengthy negotiations, Fischer Industries and Taylor International have decided to merge on January 1, 19X2. This transaction meets the requirements for a pooling of interests and Fischer will be the issuer.

Immediately prior to the pooling, Taylor International prepared the following balance sheet:

Taylor International
Balance Sheet
December 31, 19X1

Assets		Liabilities and Equity		
Current assets	$ 400,000	Current liabilities		$ 100,000
Property, plant, and		Bonds payable.		800,000
equipment	2,200,000	Stockholders' equity:		
Accum. depreciation	(500,000)	Common stock ($10 par) . . .	$ 200,000	
		Retained earnings.	1,000,000	1,200,000
Total assets.	$2,100,000	Total liabilities and equity.		$2,100,000

Negotiations revolved around what Taylor felt his business was worth and what Fischer was willing to pay. It was finally agreed that the value of Taylor's net assets, including company goodwill was $1,800,000 and would be paid with $5 par common stock having a market value of $50. Fischer Industries will issue the required number of previously unissued shares in exchange for all of the net assets of Taylor International.

The following independent appraisals have been made:

Property, plant, and equipment 2,000,000
Bonds payable 750,000

In consummating the transaction, Fischer Industries incurred $5,000 of direct acquisition costs and $20,000 for stock registration and issuance.

1. Determine the number of shares of stock that Fisher Industries will issue.
2. Record the pooling of interests on the books of Fischer Industries.
3. What entry would Taylor International make to record the receipt of the shares and their distribution to the shareholders in order to liquidate the company?

Exercise 12.   KC Company is issuing 110,000 shares of its common stock for the 100,000 outstanding shares of Hill Company in a pooling of interests. KC's stockholders' equity is as follows:

Common stock $1,000,000
Paid-in capital in excess of par   200,000
Retained earnings   600,000

The balance sheet of Hill Company at the time of the pooling is as follows:

Assets	
Cash	$ 50,000
Inventory	75,000
Equipment (net)	180,000
Plant (net)	215,000
Total	$520,000

(continued)

Liabilities and Equity

Accounts payable	$ 25,000
Note payable	100,000
Common stock, $1 par	100,000
Paid-in capital in excess of par	120,000
Retained earnings	175,000
Total	$520,000

Prepare the pooling entry for each of the following independent cases:

1. The par value of the KC Company Company shares is $2.
2. The par value of the KC Company shares is $5.

Suggestion: Use equity transfer diagrams.

Exercise 13. On December 31, 19X5, Lumina Company has the following balance sheet:

Assets		Liabilities and Equity	
Cash	$100,000	Liabilities	$150,000
Receivables	150,000	Common stock ($5 par)	50,000
Inventory	200,000	Paid-in capital in excess	
Land	50,000	of par	450,000
Buildings (net)	280,000	Retained earnings	210,000
Equipment (net)	80,000		
Total assets	$860,000	Total liabilities and equity	$860,000

Zeeco Company will issue its $10 par value shares on a 1-for-1 basis to accomplish a pooling of interests. There are, however, some adjustments that may need to be acknowledged before the pooling can be recorded.

The inventory of Lumina Company is recorded on a LIFO basis. Zeeco uses the FIFO method and will also convert Lumina's inventory to FIFO. This will increase the inventory cost to $250,000. The building is obsolete and has an appraised value of only $100,000. The recorded liabilities do not include accrued interest of $5,000.

1. Prepare the adjusting entries needed on the books of Lumina Company prior to the pooling of interests.
2. Prepare the entry that Zeeco Company will make to record the pooling of interests. Support the entry with an equity transfer diagram.

Exercise 14. Marcus Company is going to exchange its 10,000 of treasury shares for all 50,000 outstanding shares of Koempfer Company in a business combination to be recorded as a pooling of interests. Just prior to the pooling, the two companies had the following balance sheets:

Assets	Marcus	Koempfer
Current assets	$ 310,000	$ 200,000
Property, plant, and equipment (net)	1,400,000	800,000
Total assets	$1,710,000	$1,000,000

Liabilities and Equity		Marcus		Koempfer
Current liabilities		$ 170,000		$ 90,000
Common stock	($5 par)	500,000	($2 par)	100,000
Paid-in capital in excess of par		800,000		170,000
Retained earnings		360,000		640,000
Treasury stock at cost,				
10,000 shares		(120,000)		
Total liabilities and equity		$1,710,000		$1,000,000

Prepare the journal entries for Marcus Company to record the pooling of interests with Koempfer Company. (Prepare a retirement entry for the treasury stock prior to recording the pooling.)

Exercise 15.   Bay Company acquired the net assets of TAP Corporation on January 1, 19X1. Bay Company has agreed to issue common stock in an amount equal to the estimated market value of TAP's net assets. Compensation for goodwill arising from the acquisition will also be satisfied through the issuance of common stock. Bay's common stock has a par value of $5 and a current market value of $20.

Bay Company will capitalize any excess net income as a perpetuity at 20%. TAP's operating net income has been $60,000 per year, and the normal return is 12% of the market value of total identifiable assets.

TAP Corporation had the following balance sheet on January 1, 19X1:

TAP Corporation
Balance Sheet
January 1, 19X1

Assets		Liabilities and Equity		
Current assets	$ 50,000	Current liabilities		$ 40,000
Property, plant, and equipment:		Stockholders' equity:		
Equipment (net)	300,000	Common stock ($5 par)	$ 50,000	
		Paid-in capital in excess of par	150,000	
		Retained earnings	110,000	310,000
Total assets	$350,000	Total liabilities and equity		$350,000

Bay Company arrived at the following market values for TAP Corporation's assets:

Current assets	$ 60,000
Property, plant, and equipment	$400,000

Required:

1. a) Compute the number of shares of common stock Bay Company will have to issue to complete the acquisition.

   b) Assuming the pooling requirements are not met, record the acquisition under the purchase method.

   c) Assuming the pooling requirements are met, record the acquisition under the pooling method.

2. Assume the combined operations for 19X1 are as follows:

Sales	$300,000
Cost of Goods Sold	125,000
Other Expenses (not including depreciation of TAP's assets or goodwill)	40,000

(continued)

Depreciation on TAP Corporation's fixed assets is straight line using a 10-year life. Goodwill, if existent, is amortized over 5 years.

a) *Compute the net income under the purchase method.*

b) *Compute the net income under the pooling method.*

Problems

Problem 1-1.   Grant Corporation has been looking to expand its operations and has decided to acquire the assets of Turner Company and Murray Company. Grant will issue 25,000 shares of its $10 par common stock to acquire the net assets of Turner Company and will issue 12,000 shares to acquire the net assets of Murray Company.

Turner Company and Murray Company have the following balance sheets as of December 31, 19X1:

Assets	Turner	Murray
Accounts receivable	$200,000	$ 80,000
Inventory.	150,000	85,000
Property, plant, and equipment:		
Land.	150,000	50,000
Building	500,000	300,000
Accumulated depreciation	(150,000)	(110,000)
Total assets	$850,000	$405,000

Liabilities and Equity		
Current liabilities	$160,000	$ 55,000
Bonds payable.	100,000	100,000
Stockholders' equity:		
Common stock ($10 par).	300,000	100,000
Retained earnings.	290,000	150,000
Total liabilities and equity	$850,000	$405,000

The following market values are agreed upon by the two firms:

Assets	Turner	Murray
Inventory.	$200,000	$100,000
Bonds payable.	80,000	95,000
Land	200,000	60,000
Buildings.	400,000	350,000

Grant's stock is currently trading at $40 per share. Grant will incur $5,000 of direct acquisition costs in Turner and $4000 of direct acquisition costs in Murray. Grant also incurred $13,000 of indirect acquisition costs and $15,000 of registration and issue costs.

Grant's stockholders' equity is as follows:

Common stock	$1,200,000
Paid-in capital in excess of par	800,000
Retained earnings	750,000

Required:

Record the acquisition on the books of Grant Corporation, using purchase accounting principles. Price zone analysis is suggested to guide your work.

Problem 1-2.   Use the facts of Problem 1-1 for the acquisition of Turner and Murray by Grant. Assume that the pooling criteria are met. Use equity transfer diagrams.

Required:

Record the acquisition on the books of Grant Corporation, using pooling of interest accounting principles.

Problem 1-3.   Gantner Company is contemplating the acquisition of Mallow Inc. on January 1, 19X1. Gantner wishes to explore the consequences of recording rhe acquisition as a purchase versus as a pooling of interests. Gantner would like you to predict the pro forma income of the new, combined firms under the alternative methods.

If Gantner proceeded to acquire Mallow as a purchase, it would pay $600,000 cash to Mallow and would pay direct acquisition costs of $20,000. If Gantner were to pool with Mallow, it would issue 20,000 shares of its $10 par stock which has a market value of $30 per share. Direct acquisition costs would still be $20,000.

The January 1, 19X1, balance sheet of Mallow Inc. is anticipated to be as follows:

Mallow Inc.
Pro Forma Balance Sheet
January 1, 19X1

Assets		Liabilities and Equity	
Cash equivalents.........	$100,000	Current liabilities	$ 30,000
Accounts receivable.......	120,000	Long-term liabilities........	165,000
Inventory	50,000	Common stock ($10 par) ...	80,000
Property, plant, and		Retained earnings	115,000
equipment	200,000		
Accum. depreciation	(80,000)		
Total assets............	$390,000	Total liabilities and equity ...	$390,000

Market values agree with book values except for the inventory and the property, plant, and equipment which have a market value of $70,000 and $400,000, respectively.

Your projections of the combined operations for 19X1 are as follows:

Combined sales	$200,000
Combined cost of goods sold, including beginning inventory	
of Mallow at book value which will be sold in 19X1	120,000
Other expenses not including depreciation of Mallow assets or	
goodwill amortization	25,000

Depreciation on Mallow fixed assets is straight line using a 20-year life. Goodwill, if existent, is amortized over 10 years.

Required:

1. In good form, prepare the entry to record the acquisition of Mallow first as a purchase and then as a pooling of interests. Gantner has paid-in capital in excess of par of $200,000.

(continued)

2. Prepare a pro forma income statement for the combined firm for 19X1 under both the purchase and pooling of interests methods. Prepare support for all calculations of consolidated income. Ignore tax issues.

Problem 1-4.   Caswell Company is contemplating the purchase of LaBelle Company as of January 1, 19X8. LaBelle Company has provided the following current balance sheet:

Assets		Liabilities and Equity	
Cash and receivables	$150,000	Current liabilities	$120,000
Inventory	180,000	9% bonds payable	300,000
Land	50,000	Common stock ($5 par)	100,000
Building	600,000	Paid-in capital in excess of par	200,000
Accum. depreciation	(150,000)	Retained earnings	150,000
Goodwill	40,000		
Total assets	$870,000	Total liabilities and equity	$870,000

The following information exists relative to balance sheet accounts:

a) The inventory has a fair market value of $200,000.

b) The land is appraised at $100,000 and the building at $600,000.

c) The 9% bonds payable have 5 years to maturity and pay annual interest each December 31. The current interest rate for similar bonds is 8% per year.

d) It is likely that there will be a payment for goodwill based on projected income in excess of the industry average which is 10% on total assets. Caswell will project the average past 5 years' operating income and will pay for excess income based on an assumption of a 5-year life and a risk rate of return of 16%. The past 5 years' net incomes for LaBelle are:

19X3	$120,000
19X4	$140,000
19X5	$150,000
19X6	$200,000 (includes $40,000 extraordinary gain)
19X7	$180,000

Required:

1. Provide an estimate of fair value for the bonds and for goodwill.
2. Using the values derived in (1), record the purchase on the Caswell books.

Problem 1-5.   Kent Corp. is considering the purchase of Williams Incorporated. Kent has asked you, his accountant, to evaluate the various offers he might make to Williams Incorporated. The December 31, 19X1 balance sheet of Williams Incorporated is as follows:

Williams Incorporated
Balance Sheet
December 31, 19X1

Assets			Liabilities and Equity		
Current assets:			Accounts payable		$ 40,000
Accounts receivable	$ 50,000				
Inventory	300,000				
		$350,000	Stockholders' equity:		
Noncurrent assets:			Common stock	$ 40,000	
Land	$ 20,000		Paid-in capital in excess of par	110,000	
Buildings (net).	70,000	90,000	Retained earnings	250,000	400,000
Total assets		$440,000	Total liabilities and equity		$440,000

The following market values differ from existing book values:

Inventory	$250,000
Land	40,000
Building	120,000

Required:

Record the purchase entry for Kent Corp. that would result under each of the alternative offers. Price zone analysis is suggested.

1. Kent Corp. issues 20,000 of its $10 par common stock with a market value of $25 per share for the net assets of Williams Incorporated.
2. Kent Corp. pays $385,000 in cash.

Problem 1-6.   Sentry Inc. purchased for $2,300,000 in cash the net assets of New Equipment Leasing Company. The purchase was made on December 31, 19X1, at which time New Equipment had prepared the following balance sheet:

New Equipment Leasing Company
Balance Sheet
December 31, 19X1

Assets		Liabilities and Equity	
Current assets	$ 100,000	Current liabilities	$ 150,000
Assets under		Obligation under capital	
operating leases	520,000	lease of equipment	35,000
Net investment in direct		Common stock ($5 par) . . .	100,000
financing			
(capital leases)	730,000	Paid-in capital in excess	
Leased equipment under		of par	400,000
capital lease (net)	40,000		
Buildings (net)	200,000	Retained earnings	955,000
Land	50,000		
Total assets	$1,640,000	Total liabilities and equity . .	$1,640,000

The following information is available concerning the assets and liabilities of New Equipment:

(continued)

a) *Current assets and liabilities are stated fairly. No payments resulting from leases are included in current accounts, since all payments are due each December 31 and payment for 19X1 has been made.*

b) *Assets under operating leases have an estimated value of $580,000. This figure includes consideration of remaining rents and the value of the assets at the end of the lease terms.*

c) *The net investment in direct financing leases represents receivables at their discounted present values. All leases are written at the current market interest rate of 12%, except one equipment lease requiring payments of $50,000 per year for 5 remaining years. The $50,000 payments include interest at 8%.*

d) *The buildings and the land have appraised market values of $400,000 and $100,000, respectively.*

e) *The leased equipment under the capital lease pertains to a computer used by New Equipment. The obligation under the capital lease of equipment includes the present value of 5 remaining payments of $9,233 due at the end of each year and discounted at 10%. The current interest rate for this type of transaction is 12%. The market value of the equipment under the lease is $60,000.*

f) *New Equipment Leasing has expended $100,000 on R&D leading to new equipment applications. Sentry estimates the value of this work to be $200,000.*

g) *New Equipment has been named in a $200,000 lawsuit involving an accident by a lessee using its equipment. It is likely that New Equipment will be found liable in the amount of $50,000.*

Required:

Record the purchase of New Equipment Leasing Company by Sentry Inc. Carefully support your entry.

Problem 1-7.   Gusty Company issued 10,000 shares of $10 par common stock for the net assets of Marco Incorporated on December 31, 19X2. The stock has a market value of $60 per share. Direct acquisition costs were $10,000, and the cost of issuing the stock was $3,000. At the time of the purchase, Marco had the following summarized balance sheet:

Assets

Current assets	$150,000
Equipment (net)	200,000
Land and buildings (net)	250,000
Total assets	$600,000

Liabilities and Stockholders' Equity

Bonds payable	$200,000
Common stock, $10 par	100,000
Retained earnings	300,000
Total liabilities and equity	$600,000

The only market value differing from book value is equipment, which is worth $300,000. Marco has $120,000 in operating losses in prior years. The previous asset values are also the tax basis of the assets which, since the acquisition is a tax-free exchange, will be the tax basis for Gusty. Gusty is confident that it will recover the entire tax loss carryforward applicable to the past losses of Marco. The applicable tax rate is 30%.

Required:

Record the purchase of the net assets of Marco Incorporated by Gusty Company.

Problem 1-8. Dodd Corporation is purchasing the net assets, exclusive of cash, of Walsh Company as of January 1, 19X1, at which time Walsh Company's balance sheet is as follows:

Assets

Current assets:		
Cash	$ 30,000	
Accounts receivable	50,000	$ 80,000
Noncurrent assets:		
Investments in marketable securities	$ 120,000	
Land	600,000	
Buildings (net)	450,000	
Equipment (net)	800,000	
Goodwill	100,000	2,070,000
Total assets		$2,150,000

Liabilities and Stockholders' Equity

Current liabilities:		
Accounts payable.	$ 150,000	
Income tax payable	190,000	$ 340,000
Equity:		
Common stock, $5 par	$1,200,000	
Retained earnings	610,000	1,810,000
Total liabilities and equity		$2,150,000

Dodd Corporation feels that the following market values should be substituted for Walsh's book values:

Accounts receivable	$ 60,000
Investment in marketable securities	150,000
Land	450,000
Buildings.	450,000
Equipment.	600,000
Accounts payable.	120,000

Dodd will issue 20,000 shares of its common stock with a $2 par value and a quoted market value of $60 per share on January 1, 19X1, to Walsh Company to acquire the net assets, exclusive of cash. Dodd also agrees that two years later it will issue additional securities to compensate Walsh for any decline in value below that on the date of issue.

Required:

1. Record the purchase on the books of Dodd Corporation on January 1, 19X1. Include support for calculations used to arrive at the values assigned to the assets and liabilities. Use price zone analysis to aid your solution.

(continued)

2. Indicate the disclosure that would be necessary in the financial statements of Dodd Corporation on December 31, 19X1, assuming the quoted value of the stock is $62 per share.
3. Record payment (if any) of contingent consideration on January 1, 19X3, assuming that the quoted value of the stock is $57.50. (Round shares to nearest whole share.)

Problem 1-9.   New Company wishes to obtain total control over one of its suppliers, Thompson Corporation. New Company is offering to exchange 120,000 shares of its common stock on a 1-to-1 basis for Thompson's common stock.

Thompson Corporation has the following balance sheet on December 31, 19X1:

Thompson Corporation
Balance Sheet
December 31, 19X1

Assets			Liabilities and Equity		
Accounts receivable		$ 275,000	Accounts payable		$ 275,000
Inventory		400,000	Stockholders' equity:		
Property, plant, and			Common stock ($5 par, 120,000		
equipment:			shares outstanding)	$600,000	
Land	$125,000		Paid-in capital in exess of par	200,000	
Building	950,000		Retained earnings	494,500	1,294,500
Accum. depreciation	(180,500)	894,500			
Total assets		$1,569,500	Total liabilities and equity		$1,569,500

Thompson Corporation has been depreciating its building using the double-declining-balance method. New Company intends to use the straight-line method, which it uses for its own assets. Had the straight-line method been used by Thompson Corporation, the depreciation charges would have been $90,000.

The transaction meets all of the pooling criteria. The stockholders' equity of New Company on January 1, 19X1 is as follows:

Common stock ($2 par value, 400,000 shares
outstanding) $800,000
Paid-in capital in excess of par 100,000
Retained earnings 700,000

Required:

Support all work with equity transfer diagrams. (Ignore tax effects.)

1. Record the pooling of interests on the books of New Company.
2. Assume, instead, that New Company has 100,000 shares of $8 par value common stock outstanding. Record the pooling of interests on the books of New Company if New Company issues 100,000 new shares.
3. Assume, instead, that New Company has 50,000 shares of $16 par value common stock outstanding. Record the pooling of interests on the books of New Company if it then issues 60,000 shares to acquire Thompson. All other equity items remain unchanged.

Problem 1-10. Gazzola Company is a corporation that was organized on July 1, 19X1. The June 30, 19X6 balance sheet for Gazzola is as follows:

Assets

Investments		$ 400,500
Accounts receivable	$1,250,000	
Allowance for doubtful accounts	(300,000)	950,000
Inventory.		1,500,000
Prepaid insurance.		18,000
Land		58,000
Machinery and equipment (net)		1,473,500
Goodwill		100,000
Total assets		$4,500,000

Liabilities and Equity

Current liabilities	$1,475,000
Common stock, $10 par	1,200,000
Retained earnings.	1,825,000
Total liabilities and equity	$4,500,000

Machinery was purchased in fiscal years 19X2, 19X4, and 19X5 for $500,000, $850,000, and $660,000, respectively. The straight-line method of depreciation and a 10-year estimated life with no salvage value have been used for all machinery, with a half-year of depreciation taken in the year of acquisition. The experience of other companies over the last several years indicates that the machinery can be sold at 125% of its book value.

An analysis of the accounts receivable indicates that the allowance for doubtful accounts should be increased to $337,500. An independent appraisal made in June 19X1 valued the land at $70,000. Using the lower cost or market rule, inventory is to be restated at $1,200,000.

To be exchanged are 14,500 shares of Hayes Corporation for 120,000 Gazzola shares. During June 19X6, the market value of a share of Hayes Corporation was $265. The stockholders' equity account balances of Hayes Corporation as of June 30, 19X6, were as follows:

Common stock, $100 par	$2,000,000
Additional paid-in capital	580,000
Retained earnings	2,496,400
Total stockholders' equity	$5,076,400

Direct acquisition costs are $12,000.

Required:

Assuming the books of Hayes Corporation are to be retained, prepare the necessary journal entry (or entries) to effect the business combination on July 1, 19X6 as (1) a pooling of interests and (2) a purchase. All supporting schedules should be in good form.

Problem 1-11.   In a business combination to be accounted for as a pooling of interests, Hawk Corporation will issue on December 31, 19X6, 50,000 shares of its $5 par common stock, which has a market value of $20 per share, in exchange for the net assets, including cash, of Rogers Corporation.

The two firms decided that Rogers should change from the FIFO method of valuing inventory to the LIFO method. The board of directors of Rogers Corporation agreed that these adjustments will be made on a retroactive basis.

The following end-of-year inventory information has been supplied by Rogers:

	FIFO	LIFO
19X5	$170,000	$150,000
19X6	200,000	146,000

Income statement data for both companies before any effect of changes in principal, cumulative effects, and extraordinary items were:

	19X5		19X6	
	Hawk	Rogers	Hawk	Rogers
Sales.	$900,000	$600,000	$1,100,000	$650,000
Cost of sales.	480,000	400,000	596,000	430,000
Operating expenses.	150,000	100,000	200,000	110,000

Hawk Corporation also discovered that Rogers Corporation has been using the cash method to account for warranties. Hawk Corporation uses the accrual warranty treatment and will make the necessary adjustments to account for Rogers' warranties in this manner. A review of products sold and still under warranty suggests the following liability status:

Assets

Cash	$160,000	$80,000
Accounts receivable	420,000	200,000
Inventory.	350,000	200,000
Property, plant, and equipment (net)	1,200,000	500,000
Total assets	$2,130,000	$980,000

Liabilities and Equity

Current liabilities	$250,000	$100,000
Bonds payable.		350,000
Stockholders' equity:		
Common stock ($5 par).	500,000	100,000
Paid-in capital in excess of par.	600,000	250,000
Retained earnings.	780,000	180,000
Total liabilities and equity	$2,130,000	$980,000

Required:

1. Prepare a pro forma balance sheet to give effect to the business combination regarded as a pooling of interests.

2. Prepare a comparative income statement for the years 19X5 and 19X6 for the combined corporation. (Ignore income taxes.)

Case 1

Why was Fort Howard Paper Pooled Rather than Purchased?

Joe Hartwig manages a large investment portfolio. During 1996 and early 1997, he purchased large blocks of Fort Howard Paper Corporation common stock. The price had been increasing steadily, but it took a major jump in early May of 1997 when it was announced that James River Paper Corporation was acquiring control of Fort Howard. The news of the acquisition is conveyed in the *Wall Street Journal* article included in Exhibit A.

Joe immediately called up the 1996 financial statements of Fort Howard and James River on the World Wide Web. The balance sheets he found are included in Exhibit B for Fort Howard and Exhibit C for James River. Joe knew that Fort Howard had a negative retained earnings balance caused by major losses on environmental charges and had written off $1.98 billion in goodwill in 1993 from businesses it had purchased. Joe was surprised that James River would want to have to combine this negative balance into its retained earnings balance.

Joe assumed that the combination was structured as a pooling of interests to avoid recording an increase in property, plant, and equipment and to avoid a recording goodwill. He also knew that the transaction was considered a "tax-free exchange" for tax purposes. Joe calculated that the average age of Fort Howard's property, plant, and equipment was 8 years and that the assets had an average remaining depreciable life of 12 years. The maximum amortization period would be used for any goodwill that would be recorded.

You are going to help Joe make two analyses:

1. Pro forma balance sheets for December 31, 1996 that would result from a purchase versus a pooling on that date using the facts of the May 1997 acquisition. In other words, you are preparing a balance sheet, assuming the combination occurred on Dec. 31, 1996 rather than the actual May 1997 date.
2. Pro forma income statements for 1997 under purchase versus pooling assuming the acquisition occurred on December 31, 1996. This is done to analyze the impact of the transaction on future years.

Some factual analysis to guide the pro-forma statements:

1. Fort Howard has 74,380,921 common stock shares outstanding. The deal assumes a market price of $42.45 per share. This means that the market value of the shares acquired by James River is $3,157,470,000. Since Fort Howard shareholders receive 1.375 James River's shares for each Fort Howard share, James River will issue 102,273,766 shares with a $.10 par value.
2. The market value of Fort Howard's depreciable fixed assets is estimated to be $1,593,928,000 based on the assumptions given above. The remaining life is 12 years. The market value of the land is equal to its book value.
3. Assume the tax rate applicable to future periods is 30%. The deferred tax liability associated with any asset write-ups under the purchase method should be based on this rate.
4. The provision for tax in future periods will be based on reported income. The actual tax liability paid will consider the existence of the deferred tax liabilities that will arise in a purchase.
5. The cumulative exchange adjustment is an equity adjustment that reflects an unrealized increase in the value of existing assets based on favorable foreign exchange rates. It would be recorded at its existing value in a purchase or a pooling of interests.
6. Forecast results for 1997 are as follows:

(all numbers in thousands)	James River	Fort Howard
Sales revenue	5,690,500	1,580,771
Cost of goods sold (assume this includes all depreciation)	4,216,700	944,257
Expenses	1,206,300	422,014
Other income	21,600	

7. The following added information was available from the footnotes:

December 31, 1996 amounts (in thousands)	James River	Fort Howard
Land	168,900	45,736
Depreciable fixed assets	5,698,300	2,011,710
Accumulated depreciation	2,115,700	809,650

The above amounts do not include added depreciation or amortization that would result from the use of the purchase method.

Required:

1. Prepare the entry that would be made to record the acquisition as a purchase. Assume that the transaction is recorded as an acquisition of assets. The transaction is a tax-free exchange, which means that a deferred tax liability is recorded on any increases of assets to market value.
2. Prepare the entry that would be made to record the acquisition as a pooling of interests. Assume that the transaction is recorded as an acquisition of assets. Use an equity transfer diagram as support.
3. Prepare a pro forma balance sheet as of December 31, 1996, under the purchase method.
4. Prepare a pro forma balance sheet as of December 31, 1996, under the pooling method.
5. Prepare pro forma income statements for 1997 under the purchase and the pooling methods.
6. Prepare a short analysis of the impact of the pooling versus purchase method on future income statements and balance sheets.

Exhibit A

James River, Fort Howard In Merger Pact

BY STEVEN LIPIN

Staff Reporter of THE WALL STREET JOURNAL

James River Corp. is expected to announce a merger pact with Fort Howard Corp. valued at about $3.4 billion in stock, or $42.45 a share, for Fort Howard shareholders, plus the assumption of debt, a transaction that would create the second-largest seller of tissue products worldwide, say people familiar with the situation.

The two companies' boards approved the pact yesterday, and a transaction is expected to be announced this morning. Spokespeople for James River, based in Richmond, Va., and Fort Howard, based in Green Bay, Wis., couldn't be reached.

The combination—the new name will be Fort James Corp.—would bring together a formidable consumer-products player in James River and a major commercial and industrial player that caters to offices and other "away-from-home" markets. The move by the two companies would create a stronger rival to Kimberly-Clark Corp., which strengthened its market share with the purchase of rival Scott Paper Co. at the end of 1995. Kimberly is the world's largest maker of tissues, and a major player in both tissue markets.

With the assumption of about $2.4 billion in debt of Fort Howard—left over from its 1980s leveraged buyout—the total debt and equity of Fort Howard, the smaller of the two companies, is valued at about $5.8 billion.

Though crafted as a merger, James River appears to have the upper hand in a number of the terms being discussed. Fort Howard shareholders will obtain a slight premium and four of its directors will join James River's board. The stakes held by existing stockholders in James River and Fort Howard will be almost evenly split between the holders of James River and Fort Howard, with James River investors owning a slight majority.

Miles L. Marsh, chairman and chief executive officer of James River, is expected to be chairman and CEO of the new company, say people familiar with the situation. Michael T. Riordan, chairman, CEO and president of Fort Howard, will become president and chief operating officer of the new company, these people say. Managements will also be combined.

These people say that shareholders of Fort Howard will receive 1.375 shares of James River per share of Fort Howard, or stock currently valued at $42.45 a share. On the Nasdaq Stock Market, Fort Howard closed Friday at $36.50, up 50 cents, while James River closed at $30.875, up 87.5 cents, in composite trading on the New York Stock Exchange.

James River's brands include Brawny towels, Dixie cups and plates, Quilted Northern toilet tissues and Vanity Fair napkins. It has an annual sales rate of about $5.6 billion, after taking into account some recent divestitures.

Fort Howard has about $1.6 billion in annual sales. Its commercial products are sold under the Preference and Envision brands, and its consumer brands include Mardi Gras napkins and paper towels; Soft 'N Gentle bath and facial tissues; So-Dri paper towels; and Green Forest tissue paper, a product made from recycled paper.

For Morgan Stanley & Co. and partners in its buyout funds, which own about 35% of Fort Howard's stock, the transaction is a long time coming. Fort Howard was taken private in a $3.7 billion leveraged buyout sponsored by the unit of Morgan Stanley Group Inc. in 1988. After delays going public and industry woes such as a spike in raw-materials prices, the company was taken public in an initial public offering at $12 a share in early 1995. The returns are believed to be below many other LBO investments.

Fort Howard couldn't be sold using favorable accounting treatment until March 1997, two years after the Morgan Stanley fund relinquished majority control via the March 1995 IPO. The transaction with James River is believed to be a tax-free stock swap using so-called pooling-of-interests accounting treatment, the method precluded until recently.

The attraction the two companies apparently have to each other is that James River is a good brand-management company, but has high costs in manufacturing. Fort Howard isn't a great consumer-marketing company, but is a low-cost manufacturer and has a strong line of industrial/commercial products.

'As Good as It Gets'

"This is as good as it gets in terms of fit," said one person familiar with the talks.

In the first quarter, James River earned $47.5 million, or 38 cents a share, compared with $20.5 million, or seven cents a share, a year earlier. The company will post a second-quarter gain of $35 million on a $111 million sale of 95,000 acres of timberland.

In the first quarter, Fort Howard earned $49.85 million a share, or 67 cents a share, compared with $26.9 million, or 43 cents a share, a year earlier. The company benefited from a drop in the cost of raw materials, such as wastepaper, and a pickup in its consumer business.

James River is expected to earn $1.86 a share this year, after posting operating earnings of $1.30 a share in 1996, according to First Call. Fort Howard is expected to earn $2.69 a share, according to First Call.

James River is believed to be advised by Salomon Brothers Inc. and Merrill Lynch & Co., while Fort Howard uses Morgan Stanley.

Exhibit B
Fort Howard Corporation
Consolidated Balance Sheets (in thousands)

	December 31,	
	1996	1995
Assets		
Current assets:		
Cash and cash equivalents...............	$ 759	$ 946
Receivables, less allowances of $3,343		
in 1996 and $2,883 in 1995	63,194	97,707
Inventories...................	151,248	163,076
Deferred income taxes..................	60,000	29,000
Income taxes receivable.................	10,121	700
Total current assets	285,322	291,429
Property, plant, and equipment..............	2,057,446	1,971,641
Less: Accumulated depreciation.............	809,650	706,394
Net property, plant, and equipment	1,247,796	1,265,247
Other assets	82,262	95,761
Total assets	$1,615,380	$1,652,437
Liabilities and Shareholders' Deficit		
Current liabilities:		
Accounts payable......................	$ 131,205	$ 112,384
Interest payable	60,443	64,375
Income taxes payable	7,700	1,339
Other current liabilities	110,357	85,351
Current portion of long-term debt............	11,972	62,720
Total current liabilities	321,677	326,169
Long-term debt........................	2,451,373	2,903,299
Deferred and other long-term income taxes	247,464	225,043
Other liabilities	49,703	36,355
Shareholders' deficit:		
Common Stock........................	744	634
Additional paid-in capital.................	1,108,976	895,652
Cumulative translation adjustment	4,717	(2,844)
Retained deficit	(2,569,274)	(2,731,871)
Total shareholders' deficit...............	(1,454,837)	(1,838,429)
Total liabilities and shareholders' deficit ...	$1,615,380	$1,652,437

The accompanying notes are an integral part of these consolidated financial statements.

Exhibit C
Consolidated Balance Sheets
James River Corporation of Virginia and Subsidiaries

(in millions)	December 29, 1996	December 31, 1995
Assets		
Current assets:		
Cash and cash equivalents	$ 33.8	$ 66.1
Accounts receivable	717.9	847.3
Inventories.	650.4	821.4
Prepaid expenses and other current assets	39.1	52.3
Deferred income taxes	78.5	83.4
Total current assets	1,519.7	1,870.5
Net property, plant, and equipment.	3,751.5	4,074.1
Investments in affiliates	154.6	146.8
Other assets	385.7	395.8
Goodwill	730.0	771.7
Total assets	$6,541.5	$7,258.9
Liabilities and Shareholders' Equity		
Current liabilities:		
Accounts payable.	$ 507.8	$ 560.5
Accrued liabilities.	595.6	493.7
Current portion of long-term debt	116.9	44.8
Total current liabilities	1,220.3	1,099.0
Long-term debt.	1,853.9	2,503.0
Accrued postretirement benefits other than pensions. . .	458.0	464.7
Deferred income taxes	443.0	489.3
Other long-term liabilities.	259.9	448.7
Total liabilities	4,235.1	5,004.7
Shareholders' equity:		
Preferred stock.	738.4	740.3
Common stock, $.10 par value; shares outstanding, 1996—86.2 million and 1995—84.9 million . . .	8.6	8.5
Additional paid-in capital	1,307.6	1,294.1
Retained earnings	251.8	211.3
Total shareholders' equity.	2,306.4	2,254.2
Total liabilities and shareholders' equity	$6,541.5	$7,258.9

The accompanying notes are an integral part of these consolidated financial statements.

Case 2

Purchase or Pool

Snow Parts Inc. is a mail order retailer of snowmobile parts. The firm now has an opportunity to expand its operations into the all-terrain vehicle parts business by acquiring Off-Roaders Inc. The deal can be structured as a pooling of interests or as a purchase. While Off-Roaders would prefer a cash payment, they are willing to take Snow Parts common stock in exchange. The president of Snow Parts asks your advice on whether to purchase or pool from the standpoint of impact on future years' income. He also is concerned about the reasonableness of the price Off-Roaders is seeking.

The following balance sheet was provided by Off-Roaders for the year just ended:

Assets		Liabilities and Equity	
Accounts receivable	$ 400,000	Current liabilities	$ 300,000
Inventory	400,000	8% bonds payable	600,000
Land	400,000	Common stock ($1 par)	100,000
Building (net)	700,000	Paid-in capital in excess of par	600,000
Equipment (net)	200,000	Retained earnings	500,000
Total assets	$2,100,000	Total liabilities and equity	$2,100,000

Your research has found the following information about the above accounts:

a) The accounts receivable and all liabilities are close enough to market value so that purchase accounting would not require any adjustment.

b) The inventory has a market value of $500,000 and would clearly be sold by the end of the next year.

c) The land is close to market value, but the building is worth $1,500,000 and the equipment is worth $500,000. The building has a 20-year remaining life and the equipment a 10-year remaining life.

d) It is common to pay for 5 years of excess earnings. Normal earnings in this industry is 12% of the market value of total assets. The average annual income of Off-Roaders has been $500,000. If goodwill is to be recorded, it would be appropriate to amortize it over 10 years.

You have received pro forma income statements for both firms for the coming year. Of course, the income statement of Off-Roaders is based on existing book values. Projected results are:

	Snow Parts	Off-Roaders
Sales revenue	$3,000,000	$1,400,000
Cost of goods sold	1,500,000	600,000
General and administrative expense	300,000	200,000
Depreciation expense	200,000	55,000
Net income	$1,000,000	$ 545,000

You have the following summaries of the two proposals that are acceptable to Off-Roaders:

Deal 1   The price being asked is $3,000,000 cash. Off-Roaders agrees that Snow Parts common stock is trading at $33 but fears dilution because of the major new issue that would be used as payment. Thus, Off-Roaders is using an assumed market value per share of $30 and is asking for 100,000 shares under this option.

Deal 2   Pay $3,000,000 cash. The funds would be borrowed by issuing long-term bonds.

In either event, direct acquisition costs covering accountants' and lawyers' fees are expected to be $100,000. The president of Snow Parts feels the use of the low $30 stock price is basically a premium being charged for the pooling of interests accounting treatment. You are convinced that the pooling criteria would not be violated if Deal 1 is accomplished.

Required:

Draft a memo to the president of Snow Parts covering the fairness of the price and advising of the impact of purchase versus pooling on the following years' combined incomes of the newly merged firm. Include with the memo all needed supporting schedules.

Case 3

Booking a Bargain

The controller of one of your primary clients has called upon you for assistance in analyzing a major business acquisition that his firm is considering. The client is a firm called Your Office Inc. The firm runs a chain of unique shops in a major city. The shops derive their revenue from doing high quality copying and artwork and by selling customized office supplies. Due to their convenience to customers, they also sell some common generic supplies. Your Office Inc. has found an opportunity to purchase a 4-store chain of traditional office supply stores in a nearby city.

The chain does business as Smith Office Supplies. It has been losing money in recent years, since it has had problems competing with a large new discount office supply store in the same city. The chain is in serious enough financial trouble that it is under pressure from the bank holding its notes payable. The bank involved has brought the opportunity to your client's attention.

You have been provided the following balance sheet:

Smith Office Supply
Balance Sheet
December 31, 19X4

Assets

Current assets
Cash equivalents	$100,000	
Accounts receivable	260,000	
Inventories	220,000	$ 580,000

Property, plant, and equipment:

	Cost	Accumulated Depreciation	Net	
Property A	$ 310,000	$160,000	$150,000	
Property B	370,000	170,000	200,000	
Property C	480,000	180,000	300,000	
Property D	250,000	150,000	100,000	
	$1,410,000	$660,000		750,000
Total assets				$1,330,000

Liabilities and Stockholders' Equity

Accounts payable		$ 100,000
Notes payable		400,000
Stockholders' equity:		
Common stock, 500,000 shares authorized and		
outstanding ($1 par)	$500,000	
Paid-in capital in excess of par	100,000	
Retained earnings	230,000	830,000
Total liabilities and stockholders' equity		$1,330,000

You have also secured the following information:

a) *Aging of the accounts receivable suggests that a $50,000 allowance for bad debts is needed.*

b) *Much of the inventory is obsolete, and other inventory is not compatible with Your Office Inc.'s product line. The inventory would be sold at a special liquidation sale and has a net realizable value of $150,000.*

c) *There are four stores, shown as A through D, on the balance sheet. Three, A through C, are in good locations and would be remodeled into Your Office shops. Store D is in a poor location and would be sold as soon as possible. A reputable realtor said that you would net $120,000 for store D. The estimated values of the other stores are: Store A at $200,000, store B at $180,000, and store C at $150,000. These values for stores A through C are questionable if a fast sale were desired.*

d) *The notes payable are held by the bank, are overdue and in default. There is $40,000 of accrued interest that has not been recorded. The accounts payable are fairly stated.*

Your client has met with the owners of Smith Office Supplies and the bank. There is a tentative agreement. Your Office Inc. would assume all liabilities of Smith and would pay only $400,000 cash to the owners of the firm. Smith has no interest in taking back stock of your client, and thus pooling of interests is out of the question. Your client wants to know how the transaction would be accounted for, the major concern being the asset values recorded and the impact of the values assigned on future income statements. Your client's controller is concerned about management's possible misperceptions. Management has heard two opinions from friends. One is that since the deal is a bargain, the company could take an immediate gain at the time of the purchase. The other opinion is that "negative good will" would be recorded and allocated over 40 years.

Required:

Provide a report to your client indicating the values you would assign to all accounts if the purchase were to occur. The report should also directly address the accuracy of the two opinions management has received from friends.

Consolidated Statements: Date of Acquisition

The preceding chapter provided the accounting methods used to record business combinations that are asset acquisitions. Chapter 1 provided an important foundation for understanding purchase and pooling procedures. This chapter applies the theories, developed in Chapter 1, to stock acquisitions. These are investments where one company owns a large interest in the voting stock of another company and has effective control over that company. Legally, the controlling parent company only has an investment in another company and will only record an investment account on its accounting records. These investments are, however, more than a simple passive investment. The parent is able to control the subsidiary's operations, and the subsidiary's operations often will become integrated with those of the parent.

Consolidated statements present the financial statements of the affiliated companies as those of a single, economic entity. The consolidated worksheet is needed to transfer two or more separate, legal entities into the one economic entity. This chapter is the first of several that will attempt to build a comprehensive set of principles and methods for the preparation of consolidated statements. **This chapter considers only the procedures that would be needed to prepare consolidated statements on the very day that the controlling interest is acquired.** In reality, consolidated statements will be prepared for dates after the acquisition date and will include operating activity for the companies. The effect of operating activities complicates the preparation of consolidated statements and is deferred until Chapter 3. This chapter provides the initial foundation for your understanding of the consolidation process.

The Function of Consolidated Statements

Consolidated financial statements are designed to present the results of operations, cash flow, and the balance sheet of the parent and its subsidiaries as if they were a single company. Generally, consolidated statements are most informative to the stockholders of the controlling company. Yet, consolidated statements do have their shortcomings. The rights of minority shareholders are limited to only the subsidiary company whose shares they own. Minority stockholders get little value from consolidated statements; they need the separate statements of the subsidiary. Creditors may look only to the legal entity that is indebted to them for the satisfaction of their claims. The creditors of the subsidiary company need the statements of the subsidiary to assess their position. The creditors of the parent should be content with consolidated statements since the investment in the subsidiary is an asset that produces cash flow that may be used to service their claim.

Consolidated statements have been criticized for being too aggregated. Unprofitable subsidiaries may not be obvious, because, when consolidated, their performance is combined with that of other affiliates. However, this shortcoming is easily overcome. One option is to prepare separate statements for the subsidiaries as supplements to the consolidated statements. The second option, which may be required, is to provide disclosure for major business segments. Where subsidiaries are in businesses distinct from the parent, the definition of a segment may parallel that of a subsidiary.

Traditional Criteria for Consolidated Statements

Generally, statements are to be consolidated when a parent firm owns over 50% of the voting common stock of another company. There may be instances where consolidation is appropriate even though less than 51% of the voting common stock is owned by the parent. SEC Regulation S-X defines control in terms of power to direct or cause the direction of management and policies of a person, whether through the ownership of voting securities, by contract, or otherwise. Thus, control has been said to exist when a less than 51% ownership interest exists but where there is no other large ownership interest that can exert influence on management. The exception to consolidating when control exists is if control is only temporary or does not rest with the majority owner. Control would be presumed not to reside with the majority owner, for example, when the subsidiary is in bankruptcy or in legal reorganization, or when foreign exchange restrictions or foreign government controls cast doubt on the ability of the parent to exercise control over the subsidiary.

Prior to 1988, it was acceptable to exclude subsidiaries from consolidation when their operations were not homogeneous with those of the parent. It was common for a manufacturing-based parent to exclude from consolidations those subsidiaries involved in banking, financing, real estate, or leasing activities, but this exception for "nonhomogeneity" came under criticism. Frequently, firms diversified and excluded some types of subsidiaries from consolidation. This meant that a significant amount of assets, liabilities, and cash flows were not presented. The option of not consolidating selected subsidiaries was often considered a form of "off-balance sheet" financing. For instance, Ford, General Motors, and Chrysler did not consolidate their financing company subsidiaries; this meant that millions of dollars of debt did not appear on the consolidated balance sheets of these firms. Stockholders are interested in the total financial position of the corporation, regardless of how diversified the operations have become. Based on their concerns and the divergence in practice as to consolidation policy, the nonhomogeneity exception was eliminated by FASB Statement No. 94.[1] In addition, the Statement eliminated less commonly used exceptions for large minority interests and foreign locations. There is a concern that the combining of unlike operations will cloud the interpretation of financial statements. In response to this concern, many corporations are preparing classified balance sheets that separate the assets and liabilities of the nonhomogeneous operations. Ford Motor Company segregates their financial services subsidiaries, which in the past had not been consolidated.

Nonconsolidated subsidiaries now have become a rarity. When they do exist, they are accounted for as an investment under the equity method. The accounting methods for such an investment are discussed in Chapter 6.

Consolidation Requires Control of Another Company

It has already been noted that the SEC has suggested that where control exists without majority ownership of voting shares, consolidation may be appropriate. The

---

1 Statement of Financial Accounting Standards No. 94, *Consolidation of All Majority-Owned Subsidiaries* (Stamford: Financial Accounting Standards Board, 1987).

FASB, in Statement 94 issued in 1987, also suggested this possibility. A Discussion Memorandum (DM), "Consolidation Policies and Procedures," issued by the FASB in 1991 continued to suggest the possibility of control without majority ownership. In 1995, the FASB issued an Exposure Draft (ED), "Consolidated Financial Statements: Policy and Procedures."

The ED proposed that a parent company that has control over another company (a subsidiary) must consolidate the statements of the subsidiary into its financial statements. The only exception would be when control is temporary. Control was defined to mean the power to control the use of the subsidiary's assets. In the ED, the FASB defined control as follows:

> *"Control of an entity is an exclusionary power over its assets—power to direct the use of individual assets of another entity in essentially the same ways as the controlling entity can use its own assets. That power to direct the use of a subsidiary's individual assets enables a reporting entity, comprising a parent and affiliates, to obtain the service potential or future economic benefits inherent in those assets. Because control of an entity is an exclusionary power, if A controls B, no other entity can control B."[2]*

Exclusionary power of control is further defined as giving the parent the right or ability to

1. Establish operating policies including the purchase, financing, use, and sale of assets.
2. Hire, fire, and determine compensation of the person responsible for implementing policies and making decisions.
3. Deny access to subsidiary assets by noncontrolling shareholders, creditors, and others.

Control would be presumed to exist if one company owns over 50% of the voting interest in another company or has an unconditional right to appoint a majority of the members of another company's controlling body, usually the board of directors. This presumption of control could be overturned only if it can be shown that control does not exist. Possible examples include an acquired company that is in legal reorganization, bankruptcy, or the existence of government restrictions that block control.[3] This is the traditional definition of control. The ED added additional conditions that would presume control. Some of the conditions are more applicable to not-for-profit organizations that were included in the consolidated reporting requirement by the ED. In the absence of evidence to the contrary, one or more of the following conditions would lead to a presumption of control:

1. Ownership of a large noncontrolling interest (the example given is 40%) where no other party has a significant interest.
2. Ownership of securities or unconditional rights in the company that can be converted into securities that would cause a controlling interest to exist. Examples are convertible preferred shares or stock options.
3. The acquiring company has the unconditional right to dissolve the entity whose interest was acquired and assume control of the assets.
4. A relationship with another entity that assures control through provisions in the charter, bylaws, or trust agreement of the controlled company. This condition is particularly relevant to defining control for not-for-profit organizations. Examples include foundations created by an organization where the exclusive purpose of the foundation is to provide financial support for the creating organization.

---

2 Exposure Draft, "Consolidated Financial Statements: Policy and Procedures," Financial Accounting Standards Board, October 1995.
3 *Ibid.*

5. A legal obligation created with the controlled entity that requires substantially all cash flows and other economic benefits to flow to the controlling entity. This could be accomplished through a charter, bylaws, or trust agreement. It is an agreement that can be changed only by the controlling entity.

6. A sole general partner in a limited partnership where no other party may dissolve the partnership or remove the general partner except for violations of the law.

Consolidated statements would not be prepared where control of another entity is only temporary at the time the subsidiary is acquired. Temporary control means that the parent company will relinquish control or dissolve the subsidiary within one year. The one-year requirement is extended if added time is required, and it is caused by factors beyond management's control. A temporary investment is to be recorded at fair market value at the time of purchase, less costs of disposal.

In late 1997, the FASB continued to deliberate on the definition of control and considered also requiring consolidation of companies which provide "significant benefits" to the parent even though the parent does not control them. This would require the consolidation of "captive special purpose entities." These entities, such as certain trusts, are not controlled by the company that created them, but they continue to provide income to the creating company as a result of prior agreements. Other companies may be barred from changing the agreements that provide the continuing benefits.

Currently, the stockholders of the subsidiary company that are not a part of the control group are referred to as the *Minority Interest*. If the ED concepts were implemented, control could exist without majority ownership by the parent company. This means that the shareholders not a part of the control group could be in the majority. Thus, the ED terms them the *Noncontrolling Interest*. This text will consolidate with only over-50% ownership by the parent and will continue to use the term Minority Interest for the noncontrolling interest.

Techniques of Consolidation

This chapter builds an understanding of the techniques used to consolidate the separate balance sheets of a parent and its subsidiary immediately subsequent to the acquisition. To focus on the combining of the balance sheet accounts, without the complication of subsequent operating transactions, the consolidated balance sheet as of the acquisition date is discussed first. The impact of consolidations on operations after the acquisition date is discussed in Chapters 3 through 8.

Chapter 1 emphasized that there are two means of achieving control over the assets of another company. A company may acquire directly the assets of another company, or it may acquire a controlling interest in the other company's voting common stock. In an *asset acquisition,* the company whose assets were purchased is dissolved. The assets acquired are recorded directly on the books of the purchaser; consolidation of balance sheet amounts is automatic. Where control is achieved through a *stock acquisition,* the acquired company (the subsidiary) remains as a separate legal entity with its own financial statements. While the initial accounting for the two types of acquisitions differs significantly, a 100% stock acquisition and an asset acquisition have the same effect of creating one larger single reporting entity and should produce the same consolidated balance sheet. There is, however, a difference if the stock acquisition is less than 100%. Then, there will be a minority interest in the consolidated balance sheet which is not possible when the assets are purchased directly.

In the following discussion, the recording of an asset acquisition and a 100% stock acquisition are compared, and the balance sheets that result from each type of acquisition are studied. Then, the chapter deals with the accounting procedures needed when there is less than a 100% stock ownership and a minority equity interest exists.

Reviewing an Asset Acquisition

Illustration 2-1 demonstrates an asset acquisition of Company S by Company P for cash. Part A of the exhibit presents the balance sheets of the two companies just prior to the acquisition. Part B shows the entry to record Company P's payment of $500,000 in cash for the net assets of Company S. The book values of the assets and liabilities acquired are assumed to be representative of their market values, and no goodwill is acknowledged. The assets and liabilities of Company S are added to those of Company P to produce the balance sheet for the combined company, shown in Part C. Since account balances are combined in recording the acquisition, **statements for the single combined reporting entity are produced automatically, and no consolidation process is needed.**

Illustration 2-1
Asset Acquisition

A. Balance sheets of Companies P and S prior to acquisition:

Company P Balance Sheet

Assets		Liabilities and Equity	
Cash	$ 600,000	Current liabilities	$ 150,000
Accounts receivable	300,000	Bonds payable	300,000
Inventory	100,000	Common stock	100,000
Equipment (net)	150,000	Retained earnings	600,000
Total	$1,150,000	Total	$1,150,000

Company S Balance Sheet

Assets		Liabilities and Equity	
Accounts receivable	$ 200,000	Current liabilities	$ 100,000
Inventory	100,000	Common stock	200,000
Equipment (net)	300,000	Retained earnings	300,000
Total	$ 600,000	Total	$ 600,000

B. Entry on Company P's books to record acquisition of the net assets of Company S by Company P:

Accounts Receivable	200,000	
Inventory	100,000	
Equipment	300,000	
Current Liabilities		100,000
Cash		500,000

(continued)

C. Balance sheet of Company P subsequent to asset acquisition:

Company P Balance Sheet

Assets		Liabilities and Equity	
Cash	$ 100,000	Current liabilities	$ 250,000
Accounts receivable	500,000	Bonds payable	300,000
Inventory	200,000	Common stock	100,000
Equipment (net)	450,000	Retained earnings	600,000
Total	$1,250,000	Total	$1,250,000

Consolidating a Stock Acquisition

In a stock acquisition, the acquiring company deals only with existing stockholders, not the company itself. Assuming the same facts as those used in Illustration 2-1, except that Company P purchases all of the outstanding stock of Company S from its shareholders for $500,000, Company P would make the following entry:

Investment in Subsidiary S	500,000	
Cash		500,000

This entry does not record the individual underlying net accounts over which control is achieved. Instead, the acquisition is recorded in an investment account that represents the controlling interest in the net assets of the subsidiary. If no further action is taken, the investment in the subsidiary account would appear as a long-term investment on the balance sheet of Company P. However, this presentation is permitted only if one of the rare exceptions to the requirement for consolidated statements is met.

Assuming consolidated statements are required, the balance sheets of the separate companies must be combined into a consolidated balance sheet for the single resulting reporting entity. The consolidation process is a supplement to the existing accounting records of the companies. The process begins with the two companies' individual balance sheets from which the accounts representing the intercompany investment must be eliminated.

The consolidation process is demonstrated in Worksheet 2-1, pages 2-46 and 2-47. (Worksheets referred to in a chapter are at the end of the chapter and in the Student Companion Enrichment Manual, as indicated by the icon in the margin.) The stockholders' equity accounts of the subsidiary are eliminated against the investment in subsidiary account of the parent. **These accounts do not appear on a consolidated balance sheet.** The equity accounts of the subsidiary have no economic substance, since the only common stock owned by parties outside the consolidated company are the shares issued by the parent company. The Investment in Subsidiary account is not needed because it will be replaced by the specific assets and liabilities of the subsidiary.

After the intercompany investment accounts are eliminated, the account balances of the two companies are combined. Worksheet 2-1 leads to the following formal consolidated balance sheet of Companies P and S:

Company P and Subsidiary Company S
Consolidated Balance Sheet
December 31, 19X1

Assets			Liabilities and Equity		
Current assets:			Current liabilities.		$ 250,000
Cash.	$100,000		Bonds payable		300,000
Accounts			Stockholders' equity:		
receivable	500,000		Common stock	$100,000	
Inventory	200,000	$ 800,000	Retained earnings	600,000	700,000
Equipment (net).		450,000			
Total assets.		$1,250,000	Total liabilities and equity		$1,250,000

The accounts and amounts on this balance sheet are exactly the same as those on the balance sheet prepared for the asset acquisition in Part C of Illustration 2-1. **This result is the objective of the consolidation process.**

The format of Worksheet 2-1 should be analyzed carefully since it will be used in subsequent examples. It is acceptable to use a single line for like accounts of both companies. However, stockholders' equity accounts of the parent and the subsidiary are shown on separate lines because the subsidiary equity is partially or entirely eliminated, while the equity of the parent survives as the controlling interest in the consolidated company. Thus, separation of the equities will avoid confusion when the elimination entries are made. Single-column trial balances and consolidated balance sheets are used to save space in future worksheets. **Credit balances are shown in the trial balances and the consolidated balance sheets in parentheses.**

It must be emphasized again that the consolidated financial statements are only a supplement to the statements of the separate companies. **Eliminations are made only on the worksheet and are never recorded on the books of either company.** Since consolidation eliminations are never recorded, the consolidation process starts anew *each year* from the statements of the separate companies.

More detailed processes for preparing a consolidated balance sheet will be examined as follows in the remainder of this chapter:

■ Consolidating a purchase:
   Parent owns 100% (no minority interest exists).
   Parent owns less than 100% (a minority interest exists)
■ Consolidating a pooling of interests.

Stock Acquisition Accounted for as a Purchase

The acquisition of a controlling interest in another company must be analyzed before it can be recorded. When 90% or more of another company's voting common stock is obtained and all other pooling criteria are met, the transaction must be recorded according to pooling procedures. All stock acquisitions not meeting the pooling criteria must be recorded under purchase procedures. Because most stock acquisitions do not qualify for the pooling treatment, the purchase treatment is discussed first.

When a subsidiary stock acquisition is to be accounted for as a purchase, the investment should be recorded at fair market value. For a cash purchase, this is the price paid. Most purchases are, however, accomplished by issuing shares of the parent company as consideration. In most cases, the investment would be recorded at the fair market value of the shares issued by the purchasing company. For publicly traded companies, this should always be the case. There may be purchases by corporations whose shares do not trade publicly and, therefore, the market value of the shares is not clear. In these cases, the purchase would be recorded at the estimated fair market value of the net assets over which control is achieved.

To illustrate, assume Company P purchases a 100% interest in Company S by issuing common stock. The summarized balance sheets prepared for Company P and Company S just prior to the purchase are shown in Illustration 2-2.

Illustration 2-2
Company P
Balance Sheet
December 31, 19X1

Assets		Liabilities and Equity	
Cash	$ 210,000	Current liabilities	$ 300,000
Accounts receivable	300,000	Bonds payable	500,000
Inventory	500,000	Common stock ($10 par)	500,000
Land	100,000	Paid-in capital in	
Building (net)	900,000	excess of par	500,000
Equipment (net)	650,000	Retained earnings	860,000
Total assets	$2,660,000	Total liabilities and equity	$2,660,000

Company S
Balance Sheet
December 31, 19X1

Assets		Liabilities and Equity	
Cash	$ 150,000	Current liabilities	$ 100,000
Accounts receivable	250,000	Bonds payable	300,000
Inventory	300,000	Common stock ($5 par)	50,000
Equipment (net)	400,000	Paid-in capital in excess of par	350,000
		Retained earnings	300,000
Total assets	$1,100,000	Total liabilities and equity	$1,100,000

On December 31, 19X1, Company P issues 20,000 shares of its $10 par stock to acquire all the common stock of Company S and pays $10,000 in direct acquisition costs. Assuming Company P shares have a market value of $50 each, the investment is recorded on Company P's books by the following entry:

```
Investment in Subsidiary S (20,000 shares × $50 market value
     + $10,000 direct acquisition costs) .................... 1,010,000
     Common Stock (20,000 shares × $10 par) .............          200,000
     Paid-In Capital in Excess of Par .....................          800,000
     Cash (for acquisition costs) .........................           10,000
```

This entry must acknowledge the market value of the shares exchanged, regardless of the underlying book value of the interest acquired in the subsidiary. As in the case of an asset acquisition, direct acquisition costs are considered part of the total cost of the interest acquired. Indirect acquisition costs are expensed, and issue costs for securities used to acquire the subsidiary are a deduction from the value assigned to the securities issued. Thus, in summary, **when deemed to be a purchase, the investment is recorded at fair market value plus direct acquisition costs. In most cases, the market value recorded is that of the consideration given.**

Consolidation of the Purchase of 100% Interest

The example used for Worksheet 2-1 portrayed a stock purchase where the price paid for the investment in the subsidiary was equal to the book value of the net assets (equity) acquired. It was also assumed that assets and liabilities had book values equal to their market values. Seldom will this be the case. The price paid will be indicative of the market value of the assets and liabilities over which control is achieved. Normally, the market value of the assets and liabilities will not agree with their book values.

The rules for assigning value to assets and liabilities remain the same as in Chapter 1. Recall that there are "priority accounts," comprised of current assets, all investments in marketable securities, and all liabilities, that are always recorded at market value. Remaining fixed assets (including specific intangible assets such as patents) are raised to market value if the price allows it. Otherwise, the bargain is subtracted from these fixed assets. In the extreme case of a super bargain, there may be no value to assign to fixed assets and a deferred credit is recorded.

A "Determination and Distribution of Excess Schedule" will be used to make the assignment of the price paid to subsidiary accounts and to guide worksheet eliminations and adjustments. Tests are built into the schedule to assure allocation of price according to the above principles.

Let us return to the example used in Illustration 2-2 where Company P issued common stock with a market value of $1,000,000 and paid $10,000 in direct acquisition costs to purchase a 100% interest in the common stock of Company S. Assume that the fair market value of Company S's inventory and equipment are estimated to be $350,000 and $550,000, respectively, and the accounts receivable are fairly stated. Recall that

- A price in excess of the market value of the total net assets, **excluding existing goodwill,** means the price is high enough to record all accounts (other than existing goodwill) at market value and the excess is goodwill.
- A "bargain price" is below the market value of the total net assets but above the market value of the priority accounts. It requires allocation of the price remaining, after all priority accounts are recorded at market, to remaining nonpriority assets (excluding existing goodwill). The nonpriority accounts are the fixed assets (also called long-lived assets) of the company.
- A "super bargain" price is below the market value of the priority accounts. Priority accounts are recorded at market, but no value is assigned to the nonpriority fixed assets. A deferred credit is recorded for the excess of the market value of the priority account over the price paid.

In this example, the zones are established by calculating the following two values:

- **The market value of the total net assets (excluding goodwill).**   This is the sum of the book values shown in Illustration 2-2, augmented by the market values for the inventory and equipment, and are calculated as follows:

Cash	$150,000	
Accounts receivable	250,000	
Inventory (at market)	350,000	
Equipment (at market)	550,000	
Total assets		$1,300,000
Current liabilities	(100,000)	
Bonds payable	(300,000)	
Total liabilities		(400,000)
Market value of net assets		**$ 900,000**

- **The market value of the priority accounts.**   This is the sum of the book values shown in Illustration 2-2 for the priority accounts, augmented by the market value for the inventory, and are calculated as follows:

Cash	$150,000	
Accounts receivable	250,000	
Inventory (at market)	350,000	
Total priority assets		$ 750,000
Current liabilities	(100,000)	
Bonds payable	(300,000)	
Total liabilities		(400,000)
Market value of priority accounts		**$350,000**

Recall the zone rules. A price above $900,000 will allow all accounts to be recorded at full market value, and there will be goodwill. A price between $350,000 and $900,000 will result in nonpriority (fixed asset) accounts being recorded at less than full market value. A price below $350,000 means that no value is assigned to nonpriority (fixed asset) accounts and a deferred credit will be recorded.

The determination and distribution of excess schedule, shown below, begins with zone analysis which identifies the market values of both the total net assets (excluding existing goodwill) and the priority accounts. In this example, the price paid exceeds the market value of the total net assets and indicates that goodwill will be $110,000. The determination and distribution of excess schedule then compares the price paid to the book value of the interest acquired. The cost of the investment exceeds book value by $310,000. Note that the parentheses following the "Excess of cost over book value" indicates that the investment account will have a debit balance after the elimination of the parent portion of subsidiary equity. Refer to Worksheet 2-2, pages 2-48 and 2-49: After elimination 1 is made, $700,000 of subsidiary equity has been eliminated against an investment balance of $1,010,000, leaving an excess cost of $310,000. **Confirming the excess shown in the determination and distribution of excess schedule is a valuable check on your work.** This balance means that the net assets of Company S must be increased $310,000 to reflect the market values when the consolidated statements are prepared.

Company P and Subsidiary Company S
Determination and Distribution of Excess Schedule
December 31, 19X1

Price paid for investment including direct acquisition costs:.	$1,010,000		
Market value of total net assets:.	900,000		
Market value of priority accounts:	350,000		
Analysis of price: **Goodwill**	110,000		
Price paid for investment:		$1,010,000	
Less book value interest acquired:			
Common stock ($5 par)	$ 50,000		
Paid-in capital in excess of par	350,000		
Retained earnings	300,000		
Total stockholders' equity	$ 700,000		
Interest acquired	100%	700,000	
Excess of cost over book value (debit):		**$ 310,000**	
Adjustment of priority accounts:			
Inventory		**50,000**	**Dr.**
Available for fixed assets:.		260,000	
Equipment.		**150,000**	**Dr.**
Goodwill.		**$ 110,000**	**Dr.**

(handwritten: MV BV 350,000 – 300,000 next to Inventory)

(handwritten: MV BV 550,000 – 400,000 next to Equipment)

(handwritten: TANGIBLE ASSET)

(handwritten: intangible Asset)

The Dr. (debit) designations following the asset adjustments indicate that the assets will be debited (increased) in the process of consolidating. Refer to entry (2) in the Eliminations & Adjustment columns of Worksheet 2-2 to see these adjustments. As a result of entries (1) and (2):

1. The investment account of the parent and the underlying stockholders' equity of the subsidiary are eliminated as follows:

Common Stock ($5 par), Co. S	50,000	
Paid-In Capital in Excess of Par, Co. S	350,000	
Retained Earnings, Co. S	300,000	
Investment in Subsidiary S		700,000

2. The subsidiary's assets are restated on the consolidated balance sheet at fair market value. Goodwill also is acknowledged as follows:

Inventory	50,000	
Equipment	150,000	
Goodwill	110,000	
Investment in Subsidiary S (remaining balance)		310,000

Bargain Purchase Procedures.   A bargain purchase is a purchase at a price too low to allow nonpriority fixed assets to be adjusted to full market value. Some accountants refer to the element of the bargain as "negative goodwill." The danger of using this term is that it could imply that such an account is recorded, which is not the case. The element of the bargain is subtracted from the value assigned to the fixed assets. Let us change the preceding example by assuming that Company P issued only 16,000 of its $50 market value ($10 par) common stock to acquire a 100% interest in the common stock of Company S and paid $10,000 in direct acquisition costs. Company P's entry to record the purchase would be

Investment in Subsidiary S (16,000 shares × $50 market value + $10,000 direct acquisition costs)	810,000	
Common Stock (16,000 shares × $10 par)		160,000
Paid-in Capital in Excess of Par		640,000
Cash (for acquisition costs)		10,000

The acquisition would lead to the following trial balances of Companies P and S. Note that both the investment in subsidiary and the paid-in capital accounts of Company P reflect the above entry.

	Company P		Company S	
Cash	200,000		150,000	
Accounts Receivable	300,000		250,000	
Inventory	500,000		300,000	
Land	100,000			
Buildings (net)	900,000			
Equipment (net)	650,000		400,000	
Investment in Subsidiary S	810,000			
Current Liabilities		300,000		100,000
Bonds Payable		500,000		300,000
Common Stock ($10 par)		660,000		
Common Stock ($5 par)				50,000
Paid-In Capital in Excess of Par		1,140,000		350,000
Retained Earnings		860,000		300,000
Total	3,460,00	3,460,000	1,100,000	1,100,000

Let us again assume that the inventory and equipment have fair market values of $350,000 and $550,000, respectively. The following determination and distribution schedule would be prepared:

Company P and Subsidiary Company S
Determination and Distribution of Excess Schedule
December 31, 19X1

Price paid for investment including direct acquisition costs:.	$810,000	
Market value of total net assets:.	900,000	
Market value of priority accounts	350,000	
Analysis of price: **Bargain, fixed asset less than**		
market value by:	90,000	
Price paid for investment		$ 810,000
Less book value interest acquired:		
Common stock ($5 par)	$ 50,000	
Paid-in capital in excess of par	350,000	
Retained earnings	300,000	
Total stockholders' equity	$700,000	
Interest acquired	100%	700,000
Excess of cost over book value (debit).		**$110,000**
Adjustment of priority accounts:		
Inventory		50,000 **Dr.**
Available for fixed assets:.		$ 60,000
Equipment.		**60,000** **Dr.**
Goodwill		$ 0

 As is true in all purchases, the *priority accounts* are adjusted to market value, regardless of the price paid. After adjusting the inventory, $60,000 is available for fixed assets. A check with the zone analysis confirms this amount. The price analysis indicates that fixed assets will be recorded $90,000 below market, $550,000 – $90,000 = $460,000. The adjustment to book value is +$60,000; $60,000 + $400,000 book value = $460,000. In Worksheet 2-3, pages 2-50–2-51, entry (1) eliminates the intercompany accounts, and entry (2) distributes the excess of the cost of the investment over the book value of the subsidiary's equity according to the determination and distribution of excess schedule. After these two steps are completed, the account balances can be added to arrive at the consolidated balance sheet amounts.

Note that the preceding example has been concerned with only one subsidiary fixed asset; thus, the assignment of the $60,000 excess was straightforward. The preparation of the determination and distribution of excess schedule for a bargain purchase is complicated when there are multiple fixed assets. In such a case, the sum of the recorded book values of those assets plus the remaining excess of cost over book value attributable to the fixed assets must be apportioned to each of them, since the price paid is not sufficient to increase all of the fixed assets to their full market values. The following procedures are used:

1. The total assigned value of the subsidiary's fixed assets will be the sum of their existing book values plus the remaining excess of cost attributable to fixed assets.

2. Allocate this total assigned value to each fixed asset in proportion to its share of the total market value of the fixed assets.
3. Apportion to each fixed asset the difference betwee its allocated assigned value and its existing book value.

Be sure to note that *all* fixed assets are placed into the allocation process, including those that have equal market and book values. This is required because, when the allocation process is completed, all fixed assets must be stated at the same percentage of their market values.

As an example, assume the excess cost attributable to the fixed assets of subsidiary Company S remains at $60,000, as shown in the determination and distribution of excess schedule below, and Company S has three fixed assets with the following values:

	Book Value	Market Value
Land	$140,000	$206,250
Buildings (net)	180,000	275,000
Equipment (net)	80,000	68,750
Total	$400,000	$550,000

The determination and distribution of excess schedule below adds procedures for allocating the total amount available for subsidiary fixed assets, $460,000, to the individual assets.

Company P and Subsidiary Company S
Determination and Distribution of Excess Schedule
December 31, 19X1

Price paid for investment including direct acquisition costs:	$810,000		
Market value of total net assets:	900,000		
Market value of priority accounts	350,000		
Analysis of price: **Bargain, fixed asset less than market value by:**	90,000		
Price paid for investment		$ 810,000	
Less book value interest acquired:			
Common stock ($5 par)	$ 50,000		
Paid-in capital in excess of par	350,000		
Retained earnings	300,000		
Total stockholders' equity	$700,000		
Interest acquired	100%	700,000	
Excess of cost over book value (debit)		$110,000	
Adjustment of priority accounts:			
Inventory		50,000	Dr.
Available for fixed assets:		$ 60,000	
Land (allocation schedule)		32,500	Dr.
Building (allocation schedule)		50,000	Dr.
Equipment (allocation schedule)		(22,500)	Cr.
Goodwill		$ 0	

(continued)

Allocation Schedule:

	Total	Percent	Controlling
Book value of fixed assets:	$400,000	100%	$400,000
Excess cost available:			60,000
Amount to allocate:			$460,000

Fixed Asset	Market	Percent	Total Assigned Value	Allocated Value	Book	Adjustment to D & D Schedule above
Land	206,250	.375	460,000	172,500	140,000	32,500
Building	275,000	.500	460,000	230,000	180,000	50,000
Equipment	68,750	.125	460,000	57,500	80,000	(22,500)
Total	550,000				400,000	60,000

The following entry would be made **on the worksheet** to adjust the current asset, Inventory, to its full market value and to distribute the $60,000 excess attributable to fixed assets:

Inventory (adjust to full market value)	50,000	
Land (partial adjustment to market)	32,500	
Building (partial adjustment to market)	50,000	
Equipment (partial adjustment to market)		22,500
Investment in Subsidiary S (excess after elimination of		
subsidiary equity)		110,000

The procedure results in each fixed asset having the same percentage of its market value. For example, each fixed asset in the preceding illustration received 83.64% of its market value. It may be tempting to shorten the procedure by allocating the $60,000 excess of cost by relative market values and then adding each asset's allocated portion of the excess to its recorded book value. This shortcut, however, will not result in each asset being recorded at the same percentage of its market value unless the original book value of each asset was an equal percentage of its market value. It is highly unlikely that book values would be so aligned. Also understand that the **allocation process is used only for bargain purchases**. It is not applied to prices in excess of the market value of total net assets.

Super Bargain Purchase Procedures.   Recall that a super bargain results when the price paid for the investment is less than the market value of the priority accounts. In our example, zone analysis showed that a price below $350,000 would be a super bargain (see page 2-13). A price in the super bargain zone means that priority accounts are still recorded at market value, but no value is assigned to nonpriority assets. The excess of the value of the priority accounts over the price paid is recorded as a deferred credit, which is amortized as an increase in income over a period not to exceed 40 years. Let us change the preceding example by assuming that Company P issued only 6,000 of its $50 market value ($10 par) common stock to acquire a 100% interest in the common stock of Company S and paid $10,000 in direct acquisition costs. Company P's entry to record the purchase would be

Investment in Subsidiary S (6,000 shares × $50 market value + $10,000 acquisition costs)	310,000	
Common Stock (6,000 shares × $10 par)		60,000
Paid-In Capital in Excess of Par		240,000
Cash (for acquisition costs)		10,000

The acquisition would lead to the following trial balances of Companies P and S. Note, that both the investment in subsidiary and the paid-in capital accounts of Company P reflect the above entry.

	Company P		Company S	
Cash	200,000		150,000	
Accounts Receivable	300,000		250,000	
Inventory.....................	500,000		300,000	
Land.	100,000			
Buildings (net)	900,000			
Equipment (net)	650,000		400,000	
Investment in Subsidiary S	310,000			
Current Liabilities		300,000		100,000
Bonds Payable.................		500,000		300,000
Common Stock ($10 par)...........		560,000		
Common Stock ($5 par)				50,000
Paid-In Capital in Excess of Par......		740,000		350,000
Retained Earnings...............		860,000		300,000
Total....................	2,960,000	2,960,000	1,100,000	1,100,000

Let us again assume that the inventory and equipment have fair market values of $350,000 and $550,000, respectively. The following determination and distribution of excess schedule would be prepared as follows

Company P and Subsidiary Company S
Determination and Distribution of Excess Schedule
December 31, 19X1

Price paid for investment including direct acquisition costs:.............	$310,000		
Market value of total net assets:.....................	900,000		
Market value of priority accounts	350,000		
Analysis of price: **Super Bargain, Deferred Credit**..............	40,000		
Price paid for investment		$ 310,000	
Less book value interest acquired:			
Common stock ($5 par)	$ 50,000		
Paid-in capital in excess of par	350,000		
Retained earnings	300,000		
Total stockholders' equity .... O/E of S	$700,000		
Interest acquired	100%	700,000	
Excess of book value over cost (credit)		$(390,000)	
Adjustment of priority accounts:			
Inventory		50,000	Dr.
Available for fixed assets:.......................		$ (440,000)	
Equipment (eliminate entire book value and reduce to zero) .		(400,000)	Cr.
Deferred credit		$ (40,000)	Cr.

This example indicates that the book value of the subsidiary exceeds the price paid by $390,000. Despite the fact that total net assets are to be reduced $390,000, the priority accounts must still be increased to market value. This means that $440,000 ($390,000 excess book value plus $50,000 increase in priority accounts) is now available to reduce nonpriority fixed asset accounts. Since the total fixed assets are only $400,000, the remaining $40,000 becomes the deferred credit. In Worksheet 2-4, pages 2-52–2-53, entry (1) eliminates the intercompany accounts. Note that the investment account is "over-eliminated" by $390,000. Entry (2) distributes the excess of the book value over cost according to the determination and distribution of excess schedule. After these two steps are completed, the account balances can be added to arrive at the consolidated balance sheet amounts.

Avoid Oversimplifying: There is a tendency for accountants and financial analysts to oversimplify purchases. Some say that a price in excess of book value leads to goodwill and that a price below book value creates a deferred credit. This is not usually the case. Consider the following simple balance sheet of a potential subsidiary:

Assets		Equity	
Inventory	$200,000		
Equipment.	400,000		
Total.	$600,000	Total equity	$600,000

Assume that the price paid is $500,000, which is below book value. Assume that the inventory and equipment have market values of $120,000 and $340,000. Zone analysis indicated that any amount over $460,000, the total market value of the assets, results in goodwill. The determination and distribution of excess schedule will show excess book value but will still create goodwill as follows:

Company P and Subsidiary Company S
Determination and Distribution of Excess Schedule
December 31, 19X1

Price paid for investment including direct acquisition costs:		$500,000	
Market value of total net assets:		460,000	
Market value of priority accounts		120,000	
Analysis of price: **Goodwill**		40,000	
Price paid for investment			$ 500,000
Total stockholders' equity	$600,000		
Interest acquired	100%		600,000
Excess of book value over cost (credit)			$(100,000)
Adjustment of priority accounts:			
Inventory			(80,000) **Cr.**
Available for fixed assets:			$ (20,000)
Equipment.			(60,000) **Cr.**
Goodwill.			$ 40,000 **Dr.**

There may be other cases where the cost exceeds book value but the purchase is a bargain. Assume the same balance sheet as above. Assume the price paid is $720,000 and that the market values of the inventory and equipment are $250,000 and $600,000, respectively. Zone analysis indicated that the price is less than the total market value of the assets and that the purchase is a bargain. The determination and distribution of excess schedule is as follows:

Company P and Subsidiary Company S Determination and Distribution of Excess Schedule December 31, 19X1			
Price paid for investment including direct acquisition costs:...........	$720,000		
Market value of total net assets:......................	850,000		
Market value of priority accounts......................	250,000		
Analysis of price: **Bargain, fixed asset less than**			
market value by:	130,000		
Price paid for investment		$ 720,000	
Total stockholders' equity	$600,000		
Interest acquired	100%	600,000	
Excess of cost over book value (debit)................		**$120,000**	
Adjustment of priority accounts:			
Inventory		50,000	Dr.
Available for fixed assets:......................		$ 70,000	
Adjustment of fixed assets:			
Equipment......................		70,000	Dr.
Goodwill......................		$ 0	

The equipment is raised from $400,000 to $470,000, which is $130,000 below its market value of $600,000.

Subsidiary with Previously Recorded Goodwill

It should be recalled, from the Chapter 1 discussion of direct asset acquisitions, that goodwill on the books of an acquired company is disregarded. In the case of a stock acquisition, however, a subsidiary's recorded goodwill is included in the subsidiary's balance sheet which is to be consolidated. But **no goodwill should appear on the consolidated balance sheet until all fixed assets are stated at full market value.** Thus, the procedure will be to reassign the amount of existing goodwill, to the extent that it is needed, in order to bring fixed assets to market value. Any portion of the previously recorded goodwill, not required for the adjustment of other accounts, will be extended to the consolidated balance sheet. To illustrate, assume that Company P pays $920,000 for Company S which has the following balance sheet:

Assets		Liabilities and Equity	
Receivables	$140,000	Liabilities	$100,000
Inventory..................	150,000	Common stock ($5 par)	100,000
Land.....................	20,000	Paid-in capital in excess of par ..	200,000
Buildings..................	340,000	Retained earnings	400,000
Equipment.................	50,000		
Goodwill..................	100,000		
Total assets	$800,000	Total liabilities and equity	$800,000

Market values exceed book values for the inventory, buildings, and equipment which are worth $200,000, $490,000, and $100,000, respectively. The determination and distribution of excess schedule would be as follows:

Company P and Subsidiary Company S
Determination and Distribution of Excess Schedule
December 31, 19X1

Price paid for investment including direct acquisition costs:.	$920,000		
Market value of total net assets (excluding goodwill):	850,000		
Market value of priority accounts	240,000		
Analysis of price: **Goodwill**	70,000		
Price paid for investment		$ 920,000	
Less book value interest acquired:			
Common stock ($5 par)	$100,000		
Paid-in capital in excess of par	200,000		
Retained earnings	400,000		
Total stockholders' equity	$700,000		
Interest acquired	100%	700,000	
Excess of cost over book value (debit).		**$220,000**	
Adjustment of priority accounts:			
Inventory		**50,000**	**Dr.**
Available for fixed assets:.		$ 170,000	
Make goodwill available for fixed assets		**100,000**	**Cr.**
Adjusted amount available for fixed assets:		270,000	
Building.		**150,000**	**Dr.**
Equipment.		**50,000**	**Dr.**
Goodwill (confirmed)		**$ 70,000**	**Dr.**
Net adjustment ($100,000 decrease − $70,000 increase)			
= $30,000 net decrease			

Notice that $100,000 is deducted from goodwill and then $70,000 is returned, making the net adjustment a $30,000 decrease.

The **worksheet entry** to distribute the excess, adjust goodwill, and to adjust assets would be as follows:

Inventory	50,000	
Building	150,000	
Equipment	50,000	
Goodwill (decrease from $100,000 to $70,000)		30,000
Investment in Subsidiary S (excess cost elimination of		
subsidiary equity)		220,000

Had the price been a bargain, goodwill would have been made available for fixed assets and none of the goodwill would have been returned. There can be no goodwill on the interest purchased, unless fixed assets are at market value.

Depreciable Assets

Previous examples have used "net" values for depreciable assets to simplify explanations. In reality, the subsidiary will list original cost less accumulated depreciation. According to *purchase theory*, there is little justification for carrying to the consolidated balance sheet an amount for accumulated depreciation on a subsidiary's asset existing prior to the purchase. To do so would imply that the asset was used by the new owner prior to the purchase date. Thus, the preferable practice is to have the consolidated amounts reflect the market value, with no accumulated depreciation. Future depreciation charges on consolidated worksheets will be based on the new market value and the new estimated remaining useful life.

To illustrate, assume an acquired company has a building on its books at an original cost of $650,000 less $400,000 accumulated depreciation. Also, the building has a $300,000 market value on the purchase date. The net write-up required is $50,000. The preferable procedure is to produce a net asset value of $300,000 as shown in the following partial worksheet:

	Partial Trial Balance		Eliminations & Adjustments		Consolidated Balance Sheet
	Co. P	Co. S	Dr.	Cr.	
Building		650,000		**350,000**	300,000
Accumulated Depreciation		(400,000)	**400,000**		—
Investment in Subsidiary S				**50,000***	—

*The $50,000 is the balance remaining after the elimination of the subsidiary equity accounts.

A less theoretically correct, but common, procedure is to not eliminate all accumulated depreciation, but rather to adjust the plant asset by

1. Increasing its net book value through a reduction of the existing accumulated depreciation, or
2. Decreasing its net book value through a reduction of the original cost of the asset.

Unless otherwise stated, this practical approach will be used in this text.

Adjustment of Assumed Liabilities

Liabilities assumed in a purchase may have market values that are at variance with their recorded book values. This situation could exist as a result of failing to record accrued interest or as a result of changing interest rates. If interest rates decrease and the market value of the debt increases, the net assets of the company are reduced and the excess of cost available for fixed assets increases. The impact on the remaining excess is the same as a decrease in the value of a current asset. Another way to view this is that an increase in a liability increases the cost of the investment and makes more excess available for fixed assets. On the other hand, if interest rates increase and the market value of the debt decreases, the net assets are adjusted upwards and the excess available for fixed assets decreases.

Remember, liabilities are a priority account and are adjusted to reflect their full market values, regardless of the price paid in a business combination. For example, assume Company P pays $500,000 for all of the outstanding common stock of Company S at a time when Company S has the following balance sheet:

Assets		Liabilities and Equity	
Current assets.	$250,000	Bonds payable	$200,000
Long-lived assets	350,000	Common stock.	100,000
		Retained earnings	300,000
Total assets.	$600,000	Total liabilities and equity . . .	$600,000

Assume that the subsidiary's current assets have a book value equal to market value. However, certain equipment is undervalued by $40,000 and, due to a decrease in the interest rates, bond liability has a market value of $208,000. A determination and distribution of excess schedule would be prepared as follows:

Company P and Subsidiary Company S
Determination and Distribution of Excess Schedule
December 31, 19X1

Price paid for investment including direct acquisition costs:.	$500,000		
Market value of total net assets:.	432,000		
Market value of priority accounts	42,000		
Analysis of price: **Goodwill**	68,000		
Price paid for investment		$ 500,000	
Less book value interest acquired:			
Common stock	$100,000		
Retained earnings	300,000		
Total stockholders' equity	$400,000		
Interest acquired	100%	400,000	
Excess of cost over book value (debit).		$100,000	
Adjustment of priority accounts:			
Premium on bonds payable.		8,000	Cr.
Available for fixed assets:.		$ 108,000	
Equipment.		40,000	Dr.
Goodwill.		$ 68,000	Dr.

The **worksheet entry** to adjust the bonds to market value and to distribute the excess attributable to fixed assets would be as follows:

Equipment (to market value)	40,000	
Goodwill (balance of excess)	68,000	
Premium on Bonds Payable (to market value)		8,000
Investment in Subsidiary S (excess cost after elimination of		
subsidiary equity)		100,000

Consolidation of the Purchase of Less-Than-100% Interest

When control of a company is achieved through the purchase of common stock and consolidated statements are required, consolidation procedures are applied. Control may be secured by purchasing less than 100% of the subsidiary's voting common stock. In those cases in which a less-than-100% interest is purchased, only a portion of the subsidiary stockholders' equity is eliminated against the parent's investment in the subsidiary account. The remaining portion of the subsidiary common stock interest belongs to the minority interest, represented by stockholders of the subsidiary other than the parent. From a consolidated viewpoint, these shareholders are a special group of owners of the consolidated company. However, their ownership rights are limited to their interest in the subsidiary as a separate legal entity. For instance, minority stockholders receive only those dividends that are paid by the subsidiary. If the corporation were to liquidate, only the assets of the subsidiary would be available to minority stockholders after subsidiary creditor and preferred stockholder claims have been satisfied.

To illustrate, assume that Company P purchased an 80% interest in Company S for $400,000 in cash. The entry to record the purchase would be

Investment in Subsidiary S	400,000	
Cash		400,000

Immediately following the acquisition, the account balances of Companies P and S would be as follows:

	Company P		Company S	
Cash	200,000			
Accounts Receivable	300,000		200,000	
Inventory	100,000		100,000	
Investment in Subsidiary S	400,000			
Equipment (net)	150,000		300,000	
Current Liabilities		150,000		100,000
Bonds Payable		300,000		
Common Stock		100,000		200,000
Retained Earnings		600,000		300,000
Total	1,150,000	1,150,000	600,000	600,000

Assume that, for all accounts, market values equal book values. The determination and distribution of excess schedule has two basic modifications. The zone test is applied to only the interest purchased, and the price is compared only to the interest purchased as follows:

Company P and Subsidiary Company S
Determination and Distribution of Excess Schedule
December 31, 19X1

	Company	Control %	Controlling Interest
Price paid for investment including direct acquisition costs:			$400,000
Market value of total net assets:	$500,000	80%	400,000
Market value of priority accounts	200,000	80%	160,000
Analysis of price: **Goodwill**			0
Price paid for investment		$400,000	
Less book value interest acquired:			
Common stock	$200,000		
Retained earnings	300,000		
Total stockholders' equity	$500,000		
Interest acquired	80%	400,000	
Excess of cost over book value (debit)		$ 0	

In Worksheet 2-5, pages 2-54 and 2-55, entry (1) eliminates the intercompany balances. That portion of the subsidiary stockholders' equity not eliminated is extended to the Minority Interest column of the worksheet. The remaining balances are added to arrive at the amounts for the consolidated balance sheet.

The following balance sheet illustration summarizes the total minority interest and includes it as a component of stockholders' equity. This presentation of the minority interest, as a subdivision of stockholders' equity, is consistent with the ED on consolidations. The minority interest is shown as a separate nonitemized line item within the stockholders' equity section of the balance sheet.

Company P and Subsidiary Company S
Consolidated Balance Sheet
December 31, 19X1

Assets

Current assets:		
Cash	$200,000	
Accounts receivable	500,000	
Inventory	200,000	$ 900,000
Equipment (net)		450,000
Total assets		$1,350,000

Liabilities

Current liabilities	$250,000	
Bonds payable	300,000	$ 550,000

Stockholders' Equity

Minority interest		**100,000**
Controlling interest:		
Common stock	$100,000	
Retained earnings	600,000	700,000
Total liabilities and stockholders' equity		$1,350,000

Adjustment of Subsidiary Accounts to Reflect Market Value

The price paid for a less-than-100% interest in a subsidiary usually will differ from the underlying book value of the interest purchased. The determination and distribution of excess schedule will compare the price paid to the book value of only the interest purchased. As shown in the prior determination and distribution of excess schedule, zone analysis is performed to guide the distribution-of-excess process. The determination and distribution of excess schedule adjusts accounts as follows:

- Zone analysis compares the price paid to only the controlling ownership percentage of market value.

- All accounts are to be adjusted to only the controlling ownership percentage market value. That means that, for an 80% purchase with an asset with a market value $50,000 in excess of book value, the asset will be adjusted up $40,000 (80% interest × $50,000) on the consolidated worksheet. Limiting the adjustments to the interest purchased is termed the "pro rata market value" method.

■ Only the goodwill applicable to the controlling interest purchased is recorded on the worksheet.

The purchase example on page 2-7 that results in goodwill will be revised to apply the "pro rata market value" method to a less-than-100% purchase. Assume Company P purchases only an 80% interest in Company S and all other facts, including the market value of the subsidiary's assets, remain the same. Since Company P was willing to issue 20,000 shares of its $50 market value ($10 par) common stock for a 100% interest in Company S, assume it now issues 16,000 shares (80% × 20,000 shares) for the 80% interest and pays $10,000 in direct acquisition costs. The entry to record the acquisition would be

Investment in Subsidiary S (16,000 shares × $50 market value + $10,000 direct acquisition costs)	810,000	
Common Stock (16,000 shares × $10 par)		160,000
Paid-In Capital in Excess of Par		640,000
Cash (for acquisition costs)		10,000

The trial balance for each company immediately following the acquisition is as follows:

	Company P		Company S	
Cash	200,000		150,000	
Accounts Receivable	300,000		250,000	
Inventory.	500,000		300,000	
Land.	100,000			
Buildings (net)	900,000			
Equipment (net)	650,000		400,000	
Investment in Subsidiary S	810,000			
Current Liabilities		300,000		100,000
Bonds Payable		500,000		300,000
Common Stock ($10 par).		660,000		
Common Stock ($5 par)				50,000
Paid-In Capital in Excess of Par.		1,140,000		350,000
Retained Earnings.		860,000		300,000
Total	3,460,000	3,460,000	1,100,000	1,100,000

 The worksheet adjustments made on the basis of the following determination and distribution of excess schedule are shown in Worksheet 2-6, pages 2-56–2-57. The subsidiary's book values are assumed to be equal to market values, except for the inventory and the equipment which have market values of $350,000 and $550,000, respectively. Notice that the determination and distribution of excess schedule increases all accounts to only 80% of market value.

The following determination and distribution of excess schedule supports Worksheet 2-6. Note the following features of this worksheet for a less-than-100% purchase:

■ Entry (1) eliminates only the controlling portion (80%) of the subsidiary equity accounts. The balance of the subsidiary equity accounts becomes the minority interest shown in the Minority Interest column of the worksheet.

■ Entry (2) distributes the $250,000 excess of cost over book value to the appropriate accounts. All accounts other than goodwill are adjusted for only 80% of the market – book value difference. The goodwill adjustment is just that applicable to the controlling interest.

Company P and Subsidiary Company S
Determination and Distribution of Excess Schedule
December 31, 19X1

	Company	Control %	Controlling Interest
Price paid for investment including direct acquisition costs:			$810,000
Market value of total net assets:	$900,000	80%	720,000
Market value of priority accounts	350,000	80%	280,000
Analysis of price: **Goodwill**			90,000

	Total	Controlling	
Price paid for investment		$ 810,000	
Less book value interest acquired:			
Common stock ($5 par)	$ 50,000		
Paid-in capital in excess of par	350,000		
Retained earnings.	300,000		
Total stockholders' equity	$700,000		
Interest acquired.	80%	560,000	
Excess of cost over book value (debit)		$250,000	
Adjustment of priority accounts:			
Inventory, 80% × $50,000.		**40,000**	**Dr.**
Available for fixed assets:		$ 210,000	
Equipment, 80% × $150,000.		**120,000**	**Dr.**
Goodwill		**$ 90,000**	**Dr.**

This ← class

Be aware of the economic unit concept

The "pro rata market value" method of adjustment is a conservative method that adjusts only the portion of the subsidiary interest that was actually sold. It is consistent with the *parent company concept* of business combinations identified by the 1991 FASB DM. It is the method most often used in practice today. The DM also discussed the *economic unit concept* of business combinations which focuses on the value of the entire subsidiary company. It would increase all subsidiary accounts to 100% of market value regardless of the parent-company ownership percentage. The 1996 FASB ED endorsed this method except for goodwill. All accounts, other than goodwill, would be adjusted to 100% of market value regardless of the parent ownership percentage. Only the goodwill applicable to the parent interest would be recorded. The Special Appendix 1 following Chapter 3 provides examples of the most recently proposed FASB ED method.

Bargain Purchase Procedures

A bargain purchase may occur when a less-than-100% interest in the common stock of a subsidiary is purchased. A bargain purchase occurs when the excess available for fixed assets is not sufficient to fully adjust them to reflect the *parent's interest* in their market values.

The following determination and distribution of excess schedule uses the same facts as those used on the schedule on page 2-12, except that it applies to an 80% interest:

Company P and Subsidiary Company S
Determination and Distribution of Excess Schedule
December 31, 19X1

	Company	Control %	Controlling Interest
Price paid for investment including direct acquisition costs:			$650,000
Market value of total net assets:	$900,000	80%	720,000
Market value of priority accounts	350,000	80%	280,000
Analysis of price: **Bargain, fixed asset (parent interest) less than market value by:**.			70,000

	Total	Controlling	
Price paid for investment		$650,000	
Less book value interest acquired:			
Common stock ($5 par).	$ 50,000		
Paid-in capital in excess of par	350,000		
Retained earnings.	300,000		
Total stockholders' equity	$700,000		
Interest acquired.	80%	560,000	
Excess of cost over book value (debit)		**$ 90,000**	
Adjustment of priority accounts:			
Inventory, 80% × $50,000.		**40,000**	**Dr.**
Available for fixed assets:		$ 50,000	
Adjustment of fixed assets:			
Equipment		**50,000**	**Dr.**
Goodwill		**$ 0**	**Dr.**

Note that the zone analysis indicated that the parent's share of fixed assets will be assigned a value $70,000 less than market. This amount would be $440,000 (80% of $550,000 market) less $70,000 or $370,000. The determination and distribution of excess schedule adds $50,000 to the parent's $320,000 ($400,000 × 80%) share of book value, which totals to the $370,000.

Complications in a Bargain Purchase.   Had there been goodwill on the books of the subsidiary, 80% of the goodwill would be added back to the excess available for fixed assets. Recorded goodwill applicable to the minority interest is not adjusted. No existing goodwill is allowed for the controlling interest unless it is reconfirmed by the price paid.

Where there is a bargain purchase and more than one fixed asset, allocation procedures must be carefully applied since the minority interest does not share in the adjustments. Let us use the fact situation on page 2-13 for the case where there are three fixed assets, but assume that the parent issues stock worth $640,000 and pays $10,000 direct acquisition costs for an 80% interest in the subsidiary. The determination and distribution of excess schedule would be prepared as follows:

Company P and Subsidiary Company S
Determination and Distribution of Excess Schedule
December 31, 19X1

	Total	Control %	Controlling Interest
Price paid for investment including direct acquisition costs:			$650,000
Market value of total net assets:	$900,000	80%	720,000
Market value of priority accounts	350,000	80%	280,000
Analysis of price: **Bargain, fixed asset (parent interest) less than market value by:**			70,000

	Total	Controlling	
Price paid for investment		$650,000	
Less book value interest acquired:			
Common stock ($5 par)	$ 50,000		
Paid-in capital in excess of par	350,000		
Retained earnings.	300,000		
Total stockholders' equity	$700,000		
Interest acquired.	80%	560,000	
Excess of cost over book value (debit)		**$ 90,000**	
Adjustment of priority accounts:			
Inventory, 80% × $50,000		**40,000**	**Dr.**
Available for fixed assets:		$ 50,000	
Land (allocation schedule).		**26,750**	**Dr.**
Buildings (allocation schedule)		**41,000**	**Dr.**
Equipment (allocation schedule)		**(17,750)**	**Cr.**
Goodwill		**$ 0**	

Allocation Schedule:

	Total	Percent	Controlling
Book value of fixed assets:	$400,000	80%	$320,000
Excess cost available:			50,000
Amount to allocate:			$370,000

Fixed Asset	Market	Percent	Total Assigned Total	Allocated Value	Book	Adjustment to D & D Schedule above
Land	206,250	.375	370,000	138,750	112,000	26,750
Building	275,000	.500	370,000	185,000	144,000	41,000
Equipment	68,750	.125	370,000	46,250	64,000	(17,750)
Total	550,000				320,000	50,000

Note that the minority interest does not share in the allocation of the amount available for fixed assets. Only the parent's share of book value plus the excess applicable to the parent's interest is made available for allocation.

Push-Down Accounting

Thus far, it has been assumed that the subsidiary's statements are unaffected by the parent's purchase of subsidiary shares. No asset or liability adjustments are reflected on the subsidiary's separate records. In all preceding examples, revaluations occur only on the consolidated worksheet. This method is the most common, but it is not the only generally accepted method.

Some accountants object to the inconsistency of using book values in the subsidiary's separate statements while using market-adjusted values where the same accounts are included in the consolidated statements. These accountants advocate push-down accounting, whereby the subsidiary's records are adjusted to reflect the market value increases. In accordance with the concept of a new basis of accounting, existing retained earnings are eliminated and the balance is added to paid-in capital. Any adjustment in the accounts of the subsidiary is also carried to paid-in capital. In essence, it is argued that the purchase of a controlling interest gives rise to a new basis of accountability for the interest traded, and that the subsidiary's accounts should reflect those values.

In December 1991, the FASB issued a discussion memorandum, "New Basis Accounting," that studied the circumstances under which it might be appropriate to adjust the accounts of a company to reflect market value. The option of applying push-down accounting is considered for all instances where there has been a change in controlling interest. In addition, consideration is given to adjusting accounts to reflect market value when there is no change in control but there are significant sales of stock or borrowing transactions that provide support for market values materially different from the existing book values.

The discussion memorandum looks at the issues of when it might be appropriate to apply push-down accounting. If the push-down method is applied to the determination and distribution of excess schedule example on page 2-10, the following entry would be made by the subsidiary on its books:

Inventory	50,000	
Equipment	150,000	
Goodwill	110,000	
Retained Earnings (previous subsidiary balance)	300,000	
Paid-In Capital in Excess of Par (previous retained earnings		
plus revaluations)		610,000

This entry would raise the subsidiary total stockholders' equity to $1,010,000 and would mean a simple elimination of the $1,010,000 investment account, with no excess on the consolidated worksheet.

In the case of a less-than-100% purchase, all accounts except goodwill would be adjusted to full market value. The only goodwill recorded would be that applicable to the controlling interest.

The SEC staff has adopted a policy of requiring the push-down method in some cases, for the separately published statements of the subsidiary. The existence of any significant minority interest (usually above 5%) and/or significant publicly held debt or preferred stock generally eliminates the requirement to use push-down accounting. **Note that the consolidated statements are unaffected by this issue.** The only difference is in the placement of the adjustments from the determination and distribution of excess schedule. The conventional approach, which is used in this text, makes the adjustments on the consolidated worksheet; the push-down method makes them on the subsidiary's books. Thus, they are in place when consolidation procedures are applied. This difference affects only the presentation of the subsidiary's separate statements.

Investment in a Subsidiary Accounted for as a Pooling of Interests

When the pooling criteria are met, as discussed in Chapter 1, the acquisition of a controlling interest in the common stock of another company is recorded as a pooling of interests. Consolidated financial statements will also be required when the operations of the pooled companies are integrated.

Consolidating a 100% Interest under Pooling

The recording and consolidation of a pooling achieved through a stock acquisition can be better understood by first reviewing the recording of a pooling achieved through an asset acquisition. Assume Company C (the combiner) had the following balance sheet just prior to pooling with Company I (the issuer):

Company C				
Balance Sheet				
December 31, 19X1				
Current assets.......	$10,000	Liabilities		$10,000
Property, plant,	30,000	Stockholders' equity:		
and equipment		Common stock		
(net)	30,000	($10 par)	$10,000	
		Retained earnings ..	20,000	30,000
		Total liabilities		
Total assets.........	$40,000	and equity		$40,000

Also, Company I is willing to issue 3,000 shares of its stock for the $30,000 net assets of Company C. Company I stock has a par value of $2 and a market value of $15 per share. Since pooling principles ignore market values and combine book balances, the entry to record the pooling on Company I's books would be

Current Assets	10,000	
Property, Plant, and Equipment (net)	30,000	
Liabilities		10,000
Common Stock ($2 per share × 3,000 shares)		6,000
Paid-In Capital in Excess of Par		4,000
Retained Earnings		20,000

The original amount of the Company C total paid-in capital is preserved, although it is redistributed between the par value and paid-in capital in excess of par accounts of Company I. The full amount in the Company C retained earnings account is transferred to the Company I retained earnings account, since a reduction was not necessary to meet a par or stated value requirement of the issuer.

In this example, which portrays a pooling through an asset acquisition, the combiner was dissolved and its accounts were merged with those of the issuer. Assume now that Company I exchanges its shares for the shares of Company C by dealing with stockholders and that all other pooling criteria are met. In addition, Company I elects not to dissolve Company C but to let Company C continue as a separate legal entity with its own accounting records. In effect, a pooling through a stock acquisition occurs. Since the assets and liabilities of Company C remain on Company C's books, Company I can record only an investment in Company C. However, this investment must be recorded at the book value of the underlying net assets in order to comply with pooling principles. The market value of the securities exchanged is ignored. Normally, Company I must add, to its paid-in capital, an amount equal to the paid-in capital of Company C. The issuer must acknowledge as retained earnings its equity in the Company C retained earnings, unless it is needed to meet a par or stated value requirement and Company I has no additional paid-in capital available for redistribution. From these principles, the following entry is derived:

Investment in Subsidiary C	**30,000**	
Common Stock ($2 per share × 3,000 shares)		6,000
Paid-In Capital in Excess of Par		4,000
Retained Earnings		20,000

This entry would lead to the separate trial balances for Companies I and C shown in the first two columns of Worksheet 2-7, pages 2-58–2-59. In this worksheet, intercompany balances are eliminated and the balance sheets of the parent and subsidiary are consolidated as of the date of the pooling.

When properly recorded, the investment in the subsidiary account **will always be eliminated** against the stockholders' equity of the subsidiary, **with no excess of any type** remaining after the elimination. This procedure must be followed because the recorded value of the investment account equals the subsidiary stockholders' equity multiplied by the parent's ownership percentage (100% in this example). As a result of this equality, no determination and distribution of excess schedule is needed when pooling.

Consolidating a Less-Than-100% Interest under Pooling

Often, the issuer will not acquire 100% of the combiner stock, although it must acquire at least 90% in exchange for its voting common stock to pool. In such a case, the issuer records only the pro rata book value acquired. If Company I of the previous example exchanges only 2,700 shares ($2 par) for 90% of Company C stock, the entry to record the investment would be

Investment in Subsidiary C	27,000	
Common Stock ($2 per share × 2,700 shares)		5,400
Paid-In Capital in Excess of Par (90% × $4,000)		3,600
Retained Earnings (90% × $20,000)		18,000

Subsequent worksheet eliminations would cancel the investment in the subsidiary account against 90% of the Company C equities, with a 10% minority interest remaining. Procedures for displaying the minority interest parallel those previously discussed.

There is a lack of clarity in the accounting literature for the procedures used to account for the possible acquisition of shares not a part of the original exchange of voting common shares. There is agreement that they are not to be recorded or consolidated under pooling principles. The position of this text is that the acquisition of fractional shares for cash and/or the cash payment for the shares of dissenting minority shareholders who will not exchange for parent shares should be treated as a retirement of the shares. This would be accomplished by recording the shares at cost on the parent's books and retiring them on the consolidated worksheet. Where the cost exceeds the original issue price, there would be a decrease in parent retained earnings. Where the cost is less than the issue price, there would be an increase in parent paid-in capital in excess of par.

Recognizing and Correcting the Improperly Recorded Investment Account

Ordinarily, when a corporation issues stock, it must increase its total paid-in capital by the entire amount of consideration received. When it issues stock to acquire noncash assets, including shares of another company's stock, the consideration received is the market value of the assets received or the shares issued, whichever is more readily determinable. The only exception to these principles is an investment in a subsidiary to effect a pooling. In this case, only the net book value of the assets received should be recorded, as was previously illustrated. However, it is common to find a company that ignores this exception. Such a company will increase both its investment and paid-in capital accounts by an amount equal to the market value of the shares given or received. When this mistake is found, the issuer's accounts should be corrected prior to preparing the consolidated worksheet.

To illustrate, assume Company I made the following **incorrect** investment entry when it acquired 90% of the stock of Company C, although pooling criteria were met:

Investment in Subsidiary C ($15 per share market value		
× 2,700 shares)	40,500	
Common Stock ($2 per share × 2,700 shares)		5,400
Paid-In Capital in Excess of Par		35,100

Prior to preparing the consolidated worksheet, the *issuer's books* would be corrected by reversing the original incorrect entry and recording the investment as a pooling. The following entries would be made:

Common Stock ($2 per share × 2,700 shares)	5,400	
Paid-In Capital in Excess of Par	35,100	
Investment in Subsidiary C		40,500
Investment in Subsidiary C (90% of Company C equity)	27,000	
Common Stock ($2 per share × 2,700 shares)		5,400
Paid-In Capital in Excess of Par ($9,000 – $5,400)		3,600
Retained Earnings (90% × $20,000)		18,000

When these corrections have been made and the proper amounts have been recorded by the issuer, the subsequent worksheet eliminations would be identical to those for a less-than-100% interest pooling.

Questions

1. What are the functions of consolidated statements? What group are they oriented to, and what groups do they not serve well?
2. Define *control* as it applies to being a requisite for the preparation of consolidated statements under the FASB Exposure Draft. What rights and/or abilities does control give the parent?
3. According to the FASB Exposure Draft, control is presumed when one company owns over 50% of the voting common stock of another company. Under what conditions would the presumption of control be overturned despite over 50% ownership? Under what conditions would control be presumed without over 50% ownership?
4. Are the eliminations that are made on a consolidated worksheet really journal entries that are recorded in the journals and ledgers? If not, what purpose do they serve?
5. Describe the two accounting models that may be used to record a stock acquisition. At what value is the investment in the stock of the subsidiary recorded under each model?
6. Describe the "price zones" in which the price paid to purchase a controlling interest in a subsidiary may fall. What is the nature of the adjustments that will

be made to priority accounts, nonpriority fixed assets, and goodwill in each zone?

7. Does an excess of the price paid for the purchase of a controlling interest over book value automatically result in recording goodwill on the consolidated balance sheet?

8. Under the purchase method, several accounts always are adjusted to their market value in consolidating, regardless of the price paid for the interest in the subsidiary. What are these accounts?

9. In a bargain purchase, describe how the value assigned to long-lived assets is determined when more than one long-lived asset exists.

10. Under what conditions will a *deferred credit* be shown on the consolidated balance sheet? Is it the same thing as *negative goodwill*?

11. How is the minority interest in the equity of the subsidiary shown on the consolidated balance sheet?

12. What are the adjustments that may be made to the minority interest in the consolidation process? Relate the adjustments to the three price zones.

13. Under the pooling method, the investment in a subsidiary account should be eliminated against the parent's share of the subsidiary stockholders' equity, with no excess. If this result does not occur, what is the likely cause and how is it corrected?

14. Why is a determination and distribution of excess schedule really not needed in a pooling of interests? If one were prepared, what would it contain in terms of an excess of cost or book value?

Exercises

Exercise 1.   Red Company is thinking about acquiring Black Company. Red Company is considering two methods of accomplishing control and is wondering how the accounting treatment will differ under each method. Red Company has estimated that the market values of Black's net assets are equal to their book values, except for the equipment which is understated by $20,000.

The following balance sheets have been prepared on the date of acquisition:

Assets	Red	Black
Cash	$460,000	$ 40,000
Accounts receivable	50,000	70,000
Inventory.	50,000	100,000
Property, plant, and equipment (net)	250,000	250,000
Total assets	$810,000	$460,000

Liabilities and Equity		
Current liabilities:	$140,000	$ 80,000
Bonds payable.	250,000	100,000
Stockholders' equity:		
Common stock, ($100 par)	200,000	150,000
Retained earnings.	220,000	130,000
Total liabilities and equity	$810,000	$460,000

(continued)

1. Assume Red Company purchased the net assets directly from Black Company for $450,000.

    a) *Prepare the entry that Red Company would make to record the purchase.*

    b) *Prepare the balance sheet for Red Company immediately following the purchase.*

2. Assume that 100% of the outstanding stock of Black Company is purchased from the former stockholders for a total of $450,000.

    a) *Prepare the entry that Red Company would make to record the purchase.*

    b) *State how the investment would appear on Red's unconsolidated balance sheet prepared immediately after the purchase.*

    c) *Indicate how the consolidated balance sheet would appear.*

Exercise 2.   Roland Company is considering the cash purchase of 100% of the outstanding stock of Burton Company. The terms are not set, and alternative prices are being considered for negotiation. The balance sheet of Burton Company shows the following values:

Assets		Liabilities and Equity	
Cash equivalents	$ 60,000	Current liabilities	$ 60,000
Inventory	120,000	Common stock ($5 par)	100,000
Land	50,000	Paid-in capital in excess of par	150,000
Building (net)	200,000	Retained earnings	120,000
Total assets	$430,000	Total liabilities and equity	$430,000

Appraisals reveal that the inventory has a market value of $160,000 and that the land and building have market values of $100,000 and $300,000, respectively. The questions to be answered concern the price to be paid for Burton's common stock:

1. Above what price would goodwill be recorded?
2. Below what price would fixed assets be recorded at less-than-full market value?
3. Below what price would a deferred credit be recorded?

Exercise 3.   Wood'n Wares Inc. purchased all the outstanding stock of Pine Inc. for $950,000. Wood'n also paid $10,000 in direct acquisition costs and $3,000 for indirect acquisition costs. Just before the investment, the two companies had the following balance sheets:

Assets	Wood'n Wares Inc.	Pine Inc.
Accounts receivable	$ 900,000	$ 500,000
Inventory	600,000	200,000
Property, plant, and equipment (net)	1,500,000	600,000
Total assets	$3,000,000	$1,300,000

Liabilities and Equity		
Current liabilities	$ 950,000	$ 400,000
Bonds payable	500,000	200,000
Common stock ($10 par)	400,000	300,000
Paid-in capital in excess of par	500,000	380,000
Retained earnings	650,000	20,000
Total liabilities and equity	$3,000,000	$1,300,000

Appraisals for the assets of Pine Inc. indicate that market values differ from recorded book values for the inventory and for the property, plant, and equipment which have market values of $250,000 and $700,000, respectively.

1. Prepare the entry to record the purchase of the Pine Inc. common stock including all acquisition costs.
2. Prepare a determination and distribution of excess schedule for the investment in Pine Inc.
3. Prepare the elimination entries that would be made on a consolidated worksheet.

Exercise 4.   Elliot Company is purchasing 100% of the outstanding stock of Stafford Company which has the following balance sheet on the date of acquisition:

Assets		Liabilities and Equity	
Accounts receivable	$ 300,000	Current liabilities	$ 250,000
Inventory	$ 200,000	Bonds payable.	200,000
Property, plant, and		Common stock ($5 par)	200,000
equipment (net)	500,000	Paid-in capital in	
Goodwill	125,000	excess of par	300,000
		Retained earnings.	175,000
Total assets	$1,125,000	Total liabilities and equity.	$1,125,000

Appraisals indicate that the following market values should be acknowledged:

Inventory	$215,000
Property, plant, and equipment	700,000
Bonds payable	210,000

1. Above what price would goodwill be recorded?
2. Below what price would a deferred credit be recorded?

Prepare the determination and distribution of excess schedule and the worksheet elimination entries that would be made if

3. The price paid for the 100% interest was $950,000.
4. The price paid for the 100% interest was $700,000.

Exercise 5.   Redwin Company is purchasing 100% of the outstanding common stock of Calumet Mining Company for $400,000 plus $20,000 of direct acquisition costs. The following balance sheet was prepared for Calumet Mining on the date of the purchase:

Assets		Liabilities and Equity	
Inventory	$ 50,000	Current liabilities	$150,000
Mineral rights	250,000	Common stock ($5 par)	100,000
Equipment (net)	150,000	Paid-in capital in excess of par . . .	300,000
Goodwill	50,000	Retained earnings.	(50,000)
Total assets	$500,000	Total liabilities and equity.	$500,000

Appraisals are as follows for the assets of Calumet Mining Company

Inventory	$ 10,000
Mineral rights	700,000
Equipment	100,000

(continued)

Based on the preceding facts,

1. Prepare a determination and distribution of excess schedule.
2. Prepare the elimination entries that would be made on a consolidated worksheet prepared on the date of purchase.

Exercise 6. Quincy Company purchased 80% of the common stock of Cooker Company for $700,000 plus direct acquisition costs of $30,000. At the time of the purchase, Cooker Company had the following balance sheet:

Assets		Liabilities and Equity	
Cash equivalents	$ 120,000	Current liabilities	$ 200,000
Inventory	200,000	Bonds payable	400,000
Land	100,000	Common stock ($5 par)	100,000
Building (net)	450,000	Paid-in capital in excess of par	150,000
Equipment (net)	230,000	Retained earnings	250,000
Total assets	$1,100,000	Total liabilities and equity	$1,100,000

Market values differ from book values for all assets other than cash equivalents. The market values are

Inventory	$300,000
Land	200,000
Building	600,000
Equipment	200,000

Based on the above facts,

1. Prepare a determination and distribution of excess schedule.
2. Prepare the elimination entries that would be made on a consolidated worksheet prepared on the date of purchase.

Exercise 7. Black Company purchased 8,000 shares of Wright Company for $74 per share. Just prior to the purchase, Wright Company had the following balance sheet:

Assets		Liabilities and Equity	
Cash	$ 20,000	Current liabilities	$250,000
Inventory	280,000	Common stock ($5 par)	50,000
Property, plant, and		Paid-in capital in excess	
equipment (net)	400,000	of par	130,000
Goodwill	100,000	Retained earnings	370,000
Total assets	$800,000	Total liabilities and equity	$800,000

Black Company believes that the inventory has a market value of $400,000 and that the property, plant, and equipment is worth $500,000. Business consultants have suggested that the goodwill is worth no more than $50,000. Based on these facts,

1. Prepare a determination and distribution of excess schedule.
2. Prepare the elimination entries that would be made on a consolidated worksheet prepared on the date of acquisition.

Exercise 8.   On January 1, 19X7, Knight Corporation purchased all the outstanding shares of Craig Company for $950,000. It has been decided that Craig Company will use push-down accounting principles to account for this transaction. The current balance sheet is stated at historical cost.

The following balance sheet was prepared for Craig Company on January 1, 19X7:

Assets			Liabilities and Equity		
Current assets:			Current liabilities		$ 90,000
Cash.	$ 80,000		Long-term liabilities:		
Accounts receivable	260,000		Bonds payable.	$300,000	
			Deferred taxes	50,000	350,000
Prepaid expenses	20,000	$ 360,000	Stockholders' equity:		
Property, plant, and equipment:			Common stock ($10 par).	$300,000	
Land.	$200,000		Retained earnings	420,000	720,000
Building (net)	600,000	800,000			
Total assets		$1,160,000	Total liabilities and equity		$1,160,000

Knight Corporation received the following appraisals for Craig Company assets and liabilities:

Accounts receivable	$280,000
Land	230,000
Building (net)	700,000
Bonds payable	280,000
Deferred tax liability	40,000

1. Record the investment.
2. Record the adjustments on the books of Craig Company.
3. Prepare the entries that would be made on the consolidated worksheet to eliminate the investment.

Exercise 9.   Afram Company and Carlos Company are planning to combine their operations through a pooling of interests. Afram Company will exchange one share of its common stock for every two shares of Carlos Company stock. All of the Carlos shares will be exchanged by their owners for Afram shares. Prior to the pooling of interests, the two companies have the following balance sheets:

Assets	Afram	Carlos	Liabilities and Equity	Afram	Carlos
Current assets	$250,000	$100,000	Liabilities	$120,000	$ 80,000
Property, plant, and			Common stock ($10 par).	200,000	
equipment (net).	450,000	160,000	Common stock ($1 stated		
Goodwill.		40,000	value).		10,000
			Additional paid-in capital	50,000	90,000
			Retained earnings	330,000	120,000
Total assets	$700,000	$300,000	Total liabilities and equity	$700,000	$300,000

1. Prepare the entry to record the investment as a pooling of interests. Support your entry with an equity transfer schedule.
2. Prepare a consolidated balance sheet immediately after the investment.

Exercise 10.   Varsity Company and Top Company had the following balance sheets prior to a pooling of interests:

Assets	Varsity	Top	Liabilities and Equity	Varsity	Top
Current assets	$ 500,000	$ 300,000	Liabilities	$ 300,000	$ 500,000
Property, plant, and			Common stock ($2 par)	400,000	
equipment (net)	1,200,000	800,000			
			Common stock ($1 par)		150,000
			Paid-in capital in excess of par . .	150,000	50,000
			Retained earnings	850,000	400,000
Total assets	$1,700,000	$1,100,000	Total liabilities and equity	$1,700,000	$1,100,000

Varsity will exchange its stock for all of the outstanding stock of Top Company. On Varsity's books, record the investment for each of the following situations. Support each entry with an equity transfer schedule.

1. Varsity issues 80,000 shares.
2. Varsity issues 100,000 shares.
3. Varsity issues 150,000 shares.
4. Varsity issues 250,000 shares.

Exercise 11.   AA Airlines Corporation is considering the acquisition of Benson Company. The following balance sheet was prepared for Benson as of December 31, 19X5:

Assets		Liabilities and Equity	
Cash	$ 20,000	Current liabilities.	$120,000
Inventory.	150,000	Common stock ($5 par)	50,000
Property, plant, and		Paid-in capital in excess	
equipment (net).	500,000	of par	150,000
. . . .		Retained earnings	350,000
Total assets	$670,000	Total liabilities and equity. . . .	$670,000

Appraisals, upon which both firms agree, show the inventory to have a market value of $250,000 and the property, plant, and equipment to have a market value of $550,000.

AA Airlines has the following stockholders' equity:

Common stock ($10 par)	$200,000
Paid-in capital in excess of par	300,000
Retained earnings	450,000
Total equity	$950,000

Any acquisition that would occur would be based on the above market values and the assumption of a $50 market price per share for the AA Airlines stock.

1. Assume that AA Airlines exchanges a sufficient number of its shares to purchase an 80% interest in Benson:

   a) *Determine how many shares of AA Airlines common stock will be exchanged.*

   b) *Record the investment in the Benson shares.*

   c) *Prepare a determination and distribution of excess schedule.*

   d) *Prepare the elimination entries that would be made on a consolidated work-sheet prepared on the acquisition date.*

2. Assume that AA Airlines exchanges a sufficient number of its shares to acquire a 90% interest in Benson and that the transaction meets the criteria for a pooling of interests.

   a) *Determine how many shares of AA Airlines common stock will be exchanged.*

   b) *Record the investment in Benson shares and provide an equity transfer schedule.*

   c) *Prepare the elimination entries that would be made on a consolidated work-sheet prepared on the acquisition date.*

Exercise 12.   Subtra Inc. had the following balance sheet on December 31, 19X7:

Assets		Liabilities and Equity	
Current assets	$ 50,000	Liabilities	$150,000
Land	70,000	Common stock ($10 par)	50,000
Buildings (net)	230,000	Retained earnings	400,000
Equipment (net)	200,000		
Goodwill	50,000		
Total assets	$600,000	Total liabilities and equity	$600,000

    Prior to a pooling of interests in which Parma was the issuer, Parma had the following stockholders' equity:

Common stock ($10 par)	$ 500,000
Retained earnings	2,000,000
	$2,500,000
Less treasury stock, 5,000 shares at cost	300,000
Total stockholders' equity	$2,200,000

    Parma exchanged the 5,000 shares of treasury stock plus 5,000 new shares of common stock for 90% of the common stock of Subtra. Parma paid $10,000 in direct acquisition costs.

    Record the acquisition of Subtra as a pooling of interests. Prepare an equity transfer schedule as support.

Exercise 13.   Wright Enterprises has given you the following balance sheet on December 31, 19X5:

Wright Enterprises
Balance Sheet
December 31, 19X5

Assets		Liabilities and Equity		
Current assets	$ 856,000	Liabilities		$ 900,000
Investment in Mazurek Company	800,000	Common stock ($5 stated value)	$1,000,000	
Property, plant, and equipment		Additional paid-in capital	950,000	
(net)	2,150,000	Retained earnings	956,000	2,906,000
		Total liabilities and stockholders'		
Total assets	$3,806,000	equity		$3,806,000

(continued)

Wright Enterprises acquired a 90% interest of Mazurek Company on October 1, 19X5, by exchanging 20,000 shares of $40 market value ($5 par) common stock directly with Mazurek's stockholders. On the exchange date, Mazurek Company had the following stockholders' equity:

Common stock ($2 par)	$ 50,000
Paid-in capital in excess of par	250,000
Retained earnings	300,000
	$600,000

Initially, the transaction was erroneously recorded as a purchase. No entries have been made in the investment account since the inception of the pooling.

Prepare the necessary journal entry to correctly portray the above combination as a pooling of interests. Provide an equity transfer schedule as support.

Problems

Problem 2-1.   On July 1, 19X6, Lyons Company exchanged 18,000 of its $30 market value ($10 par value) shares for all the outstanding shares of Belfont Company. The transaction did not meet the criteria for a pooling of interests since Lyons Company was only recently divested by its parent company. Lyons paid direct acquisition costs of $20,000 and paid $5,000 in stock issuance costs. The two companies had the following balance sheets on July 1, 19X6:

Assets	Lyons	Belfont
Other current assets	$ 50,000	$ 70,000
Inventory.	120,000	60,000
Land	100,000	40,000
Buildings (net)	300,000	120,000
Equipment (net)	430,000	110,000
Total assets	$1,000,000	$400,000

Liabilities and Equity		
Current liabilities	$ 180,000	$ 60,000
Common stock ($10 par).	400,000	200,000
Retained earnings.	420,000	140,000
Total liabilities and equity	$1,000,000	$400,000

The following market values differ from book values for Belfont's assets:

Inventory	$ 65,000
Land	100,000
Building	150,000
Equipment	75,000

Required:

1. Record the investment in Belfont Company and any other entry necessitated by the purchase.
2. Prepare a determination and distribution of excess schedule.
3. Prepare a consolidated balance sheet for July 1, 19X6, immediately subsequent to the purchase.

Problem 2-2.   Using the data given in Problem 2-1, assume that Lyons Company exchanged 18,000 of its $30 market value ($10 par value) shares for 16,000 of the outstanding shares of Belfont Company.

Required:

1. Record the investment in Belfont Company and any other entry necessitated by the purchase.
2. Prepare a determination and distribution of excess schedule.
3. Prepare a consolidated balance sheet for July 1, 19X6, immediately subsequent to the purchase.

Problem 2-3.   On March 1, 19X5, Carlson Enterprises purchased a 100% interest in Express Corporation for $400,000.

Express Corporation had the following balance sheet on February 28, 19X5:

Express Corporation
Balance Sheet
For the Month Ended February 28, 19X5

Assets		Liabilities and Equity	
Accounts receivable	$ 60,000	Current liabilities	$ 50,000
Inventory	80,000	Bonds payable	100,000
Land	40,000	Common stock	50,000
Buildings	300,000	Paid-in capital in excess of par	250,000
Accum. depr.—blg	(120,000)	Retained earnings	70,000
Equipment	220,000		
Accum. depr.—equip	(60,000)		
Total assets	$520,000	Total liabilities and equity	$520,000

Carlson Enterprises received an independent appraisal on the market values of Express Corporation's assets. The controller has reviewed the figures and accepts them as reasonable.

Inventory	$100,000
Land	55,000
Building	200,000
Equipment	150,000
Bonds payable	95,000

Required:

1. Record the investment in Express Corporation.
2. Prepare a determination and distribution of excess schedule.
3. Prepare the elimination entries that would be made on a consolidated worksheet prepared on the date of acquisition.

Problem 2-4.   On March 1, 19X5, Collier Enterprises purchased a 100% interest in Robby Corporation for $480,000. It was decided that Robby Corporation will apply push-down accounting principles to account for this acquisition.

Robby Corporation had the following balance sheet on February 28, 19X5:

(continued)

Robby Corporation
Balance Sheet
For the Month Ended February 28, 19X5

Assets		Liabilities and Equity	
Accounts receivable	$ 60,000	Current liabilities	$ 50,000
Inventory	80,000	Bonds payable.	100,000
Land	40,000	Common stock	50,000
Buildings.	300,000	Paid-in capital in excess of par	250,000
Accum. depr.—blg	(120,000)	Retained earnings.	70,000
Equipment.	220,000		
Accum. depr.—equip	(60,000)		
Total assets	$520,000	Total liabilities and equity.	$520,000

Collier Enterprises received an independent appraisal on the market values of Robby Corporation's assets. The controller has reviewed the figures and accepts them as reasonable.

Inventory	$100,000
Land	55,000
Building	200,000
Equipment	150,000
Bonds payable	98,000

Required:

1. Record the investment in Robby Corporation.
2. Prepare a determination and distribution of excess schedule.
3. Give Robby Corporation's adjusting entry showing the conversion of Retained Earnings to Paid-In Capital.

Problem 2-5.   The balance sheets of Lewis Company and Ace Company are as follows on December 31, 19X4:

Assets	Lewis	Ace
Current assets	$ 250,000	$300,000
Property, plant, and equipment.	1,100,000	500,000
Accumulated depreciation	(300,000)	(200,000)
Total assets	$1,050,000	$600,000

Liabilities and Equity	Lewis	Ace
Current liabilities	$ 250,000	$200,000
Common stock ($10 par).	300,000	
Common stock ($1 par).		50,000
Paid-in capital in excess of par	200,000	100,000
Retained earnings.	300,000	250,000
Total liabilities and equity	$1,050,000	$600,000

On this date, Lewis exchanged one share of its newly issued common stock for every two shares of Ace stock. Lewis acquired all outstanding shares of Ace Company. The market value of a share of Lewis stock was $30 on the acquisition date. Ace's assets are fairly stated except for the property, plant, and equipment which has a market value of $450,000.

Required:

1. Assume the acquisition does not meet the pooling of interests criteria.
   a) *Record the investment in Ace stock.*
   b) *Prepare a determination and distribution of excess schedule.*
   c) *Prepare a consolidated balance sheet for December 31, 19X4, immediately subsequent to the purchase.*
2. Assume that the acquisition does meet the pooling of interest criteria.
   a) *Record the investment in Ace stock.*
   b) *Prepare a consolidated balance sheet for December 31, 19X4, immediately subsequent to the pooling.*

Problem 2-6. On December 31, 19X1, Gary Company purchased 100% of the common stock of Smith Company for $380,000. On this date, any excess of cost over book value was attributed to accounts with market values that differed from book value. These accounts of the Smith Company had the following market values:

Inventory	$140,000
Land	45,000
Buildings and equipment	225,000
Bonds payable	105,000

The following balance sheets were prepared for the two companies immediately after the purchase:

	Gary	Smith
Cash	$160,000	$ 50,000
Accounts receivable	70,000	30,000
Inventory	130,000	120,000
Investment in Smith Company	380,000	
Land	50,000	35,000
Building and equipment	350,000	230,000
Accumulated depreciation	(100,000)	(50,000)
Other intangibles	40,000	
Current liabilities	$192,000	$ 65,000
Bonds payable		100,000
Common stock ($10 par), Gary	100,000	
Common stock ($5 par), Smith		50,000
Paid-in capital in excess of par	250,000	70,000
Retained earnings	538,000	130,000
Total	$ 0	$ 0

Required:

1. Prepare a determination and distribution of excess schedule for the investment in Smith Company.
2. Complete a consolidated worksheet for Gary Company and its subsidiary Smith Company as of December 31, 19X1.

Problem 2-7.   Using the data given in Problem 2-6, assume that Gary Company purchased 80% of the common stock of Smith Company for $380,000.

Required:

1. Prepare a determination and distribution of excess schedule for the investment in Smith Company.
2. Complete a consolidated worksheet for Gary Company and its subsidiary Smith Company as of December 31, 19X1.

Problem 2-8.   Kippers Steel has approached the management of Gage Company and has made an offer to acquire 90% of Gage's outstanding stock on July 1, 19X6. Kippers Steel will give 20,000 shares of its previously unissued, $1 par, $35 market value, common stock in exchange for a 90% ownership interest. If this offer is accepted, it is unclear whether *all* the criteria for a pooling of interests will be met.

Out-of-pocket costs of the acquisition incurred by Kippers Steel would be as follows:

Direct acquisition costs (legal fees and finder's fees)	$27,000
Stock issuance costs	18,000

Comparative balance sheets for the two companies just prior to the combination are as follows:

	Kippers Steel	Gage
Cash	$ 200,000	$ 80,000
Other current assets	650,000	180,000
Marketable securities	180,000	50,000
Property, plant, and equipment (net)	2,500,000	800,000
Patents	240,000	60,000
Total assets	$3,770,000	$1,170,000
Current liabilities	$ 410,000	$ 320,000
Bonds payable.	1,000,000	300,000
Common stock ($1 par).	300,000	
Common stock ($25 par).		25,000
Paid-in capital in excess of par	1,200,000	275,000
Retained earnings.	860,000	250,000
Total liabilities and equity	$3,770,000	$1,170,000

On July 1, 19X6, Gage Company's book values approximate market values, except for the following:

Marketable securities	$ 60,000
Property, plant, and equipment	950,000
Patents	80,000
Bonds payable	296,000

Required:

1. Prepare the entry that Kippers Steel would make on July 1, 19X6, to record the investment in stock of Gage Company as: (a) a purchase and (b) a pooling of interests.

2. Prepare a consolidated balance sheet for July 1, 19X6, immediately subsequent to the acquisition assuming that the acquisition is regarded as (a) a purchase and (b) a pooling of interests.
3. Compare the differences on the 19X6 fiscal year income statement that would occur as a result of the purchase versus a pooling treatment.

Problem 2-9. Comparative balance sheets of Edward Corporation and its subsidiary Hinkley Corporation on June 30, 19X7, are as follows:

	Edward Corporation	Hinkley Corporation
Cash	$ 153,200	$ 40,000
Accounts receivable	416,100	110,000
Prepayments	48,000	5,500
Land	750,000	160,000
Buildings.	690,000	147,000
Accumulated depreciation	(50,000)	(12,000)
Delivery trucks	515,500	190,000
Accumulated depreciation	(35,000)	(10,000)
Investment in Hinkley Corporation	722,000	
Total assets	$3,209,800	$630,500
Accounts payable.	$ 152,210	$ 80,500
Accrued expenses	16,100	3,600
Bonds payable.	400,000	
Common stock ($2 par).	412,000	
Common stock ($10 par).		400,000
Paid-in capital in excess of par	755,000	
Retained earnings.	1,474,490	146,400
Total liabilities and equity	$3,209,800	$630,500

On June 27, 19X7, Edward exchanged 18,000 of its shares, with a market value of $35 each, for 90% of the shares of Hinkley Corporation, using a 1-for-2 exchange rate. The transaction qualified as a pooling of interests. Edward Corporation paid $20,000 in direct acquisition costs which were capitalized in the investment account. Assume the Hinkley equity at the pooling was the same as shown above.

On June 30, 19X7, Edward acquired another 5% of Hinkley stock in exchange for 2,000 shares of Edward common stock which had a per-share market value of $36 on that date.

Any payment in excess of book value is considered a payment for goodwill.

Required:

Prepare the correcting entries to be made on Edward's books and a worksheet for a June 30, 19X7, consolidated balance sheet.

Suggestion: The first acquisition is a pooling of interests and requires a correction entry for the investment account. It should be supported by an equity transfer diagram. The second acquisition does not meet the criteria for a pooling of interests and should be accounted for as a retirement of the shares. Be careful with the direct acquisition costs in the pooling.

Case 1

Consolidating a Bargain Purchase

Your client, Best Value Hardware Stores, has come to you to assist in evaluating an opportunity to purchase a controlling interest in a hardware store in a neighboring city. The store under consideration is a closely held family corporation. Owners of 60% of the shares are willing to sell you the 60% interest, 30,000 common stock shares in exchange for 7,500 of Best Value shares which have a market value of $40 each and a par value of $10 each.

Your client sees this as a good deal and a good way to enter a new market. The controller of Best Value knows, however, that all is not well with the store being considered. The store, Al's Hardware, has not kept pace with the market and has been losing money. It also has a major lawsuit against it stemming from alleged faulty electrical components it supplied which caused a fire. The store is not insured for the loss. Legal counsel advises that the store will likely pay $300,000 in damages.

The following balance sheet was provided by Al's Hardware as of December 31, 19X4:

Assets		Liabilities and Equity	
Cash.	$ 180,000	Current liabilities	$ 425,000
Accounts receivable.	460,000	8% Mortgage payable	600,000
Inventory	730,000	Common stock ($5 par) . . .	250,000
Land	120,000	Paid-in capital in	
Building.	630,000	excess of par.	750,000
Accum. depr.—bldg.	(400,000)	Retained earnings	(80,000)
Equipment	135,000		
Accum. depr.—equip.	(85,000)		
Goodwill	175,000		
Total assets.	$1,945,000		$1,945,000

Your analysis raises substantial concerns about the values shown. You have gathered the following information:

1. Aging of the accounts receivable reveals the need for a $110,000 allowance for bad debts.
2. The inventory has many obsolete items; the market value is $600,000.
3. Appraisals for long-lived assets are as follows:

   Land $100,000
   Building   300,000
   Equipment   100,000

4. The goodwill resulted from the purchase of another hardware store that has since been consolidated into the existing location. The goodwill was attributed to customer loyalty.
5. Liabilities are fairly stated except that there should be a provision for the estimated loss on the lawsuit.

On the basis of your research, you are convinced that the statements of Al's Hardware are not representative and need major restatement. Your client is not interested in being associated with statements that are not accurate.

Your client asks you to make recommendations on two concerns:

1. Does the price asked seem to be a real bargain? It is suggested that you consider the market value of the entire equity of Al's Hardware and then decide if the price is reasonable for a 60% interest.

2. If the deal were completed, what accounting methods would you recommend either on the books of Al's Hardware or in the consolidation process? Al's Hardware would remain a separate legal entity with a substantial minority interest.

Worksheet 2-1.

100% Interest; Price Equals Book Value
Company P and Subsidiary Company S
Worksheet for Consolidated Balance Sheet
December 31, 19X1

		Trial Balance	
		Company P	Company S
1	Debits:		
2	Cash	100,000	
3	Accounts Receivable	300,000	200,000
4	Inventory	100,000	100,000
5	**Investment in Subsidiary S**	**500,000**	
6	Equipment (net)	150,000	300,000
7	Total	1,150,000	600,000
8	Credits:		
9	Current Liabilities	150,000	100,000
10	Bonds Payable	300,000	
11	Common Stock, Co. P	100,000	
12	Retained Earnings, Co. P	600,000	
13	**Common Stock, Co. S**		**200,000**
14	**Retained Earnings, Co. S**		**300,000**
15	Total	1,150,000	600,000

Worksheet 2-1 (see page 2-6)

Eliminations & Adjustments		Consolidated Balance Sheet		
Dr.	Cr.	Dr.	Cr.	
				1
		100,000		2
		500,000		3
		200,000		4
	(1) 500,000			5
		450,000		6
				7
				8
			250,000	9
			300,000	10
			100,000	11
			600,000	12
(1) 200,000				13
(1) 300,000				14
500,000	500,000	1,250,000	1,250,000	15

Eliminations and Adjustments:

(1) Eliminate the investment in the subsidiary account against the subsidiary equity accounts.

Worksheet 2-2

100% Interest; Price Exceeds Market Value
Company P and Subsidiary Company S
Worksheet for Consolidated Balance Sheet
December 31, 19X1

		Trial Balance	
		Company P	Company S
1	Debits:		
2	Cash	200,000	150,000
3	Accounts Receivable	300,000	250,000
4	**Inventory**	500,000	**300,000**
5	Land	100,000	
6	Buildings (net)	900,000	
7	**Equipment (net)**	650,000	**400,000**
8	**Investment in Subsidiary S**	**1,010,000**	
9			
10	**Goodwill**		
11	Total	3,660,000	1,100,000
12	Credits:		
13	Current Liabilities	300,000	100,000
14	Bonds Payable	500,000	300,000
15	Common Stock ($10 par), Co. P	700,000	
16	Paid-In Capital in Excess of Par, Co. P	1,300,000	
17	Retained Earnings, Co. P	860,000	
18	Common Stock ($5 par), Co. S		50,000
19	Paid-In Capital in Excess of Par, Co. S		350,000
20	Retained Earnings, Co. S		300,000
21	Total	3,660,000	1,100,000

Worksheet 2-2 (see page 2-10)

Eliminations & Adjustments				Consolidated Balance Sheet				
Dr.		Cr.		Dr.		Cr.		
								1
				350,000				2
				550,000				3
(2)	50,000			850,000				4
				100,000				5
				900,000				6
(2)	150,000			1,200,000				7
		(1)	700,000					8
		(2)	310,000					9
(2)	110,000			110,000				10
								11
								12
						400,000		13
						800,000		14
						700,000		15
						1,300,000		16
						860,000		17
(1)	50,000							18
(1)	350,000							19
(1)	300,000							20
	1,010,000		1,010,000	4,060,000		4,060,000		21

Eliminations and Adjustments:

(1) Eliminate intercompany accounts. The investment in subsidiary account includes a 100% interest in the stockholders' equity of Company S. Therefore, the entire stockholders' equity of Company S is eliminated against the investment account. The balance of the investment account, $310,000, has no intercompany counterpart, but rather reflects the total undervaluation of Company S's assets. This balance is distributed in entry (2).

(2) Distribute the $310,000 undervaluation of Company S's assets to the proper asset accounts. The following information for this distribution is taken from the determination and distribution of excess schedule:

Excess of cost over book value		$310,000
Distribute to:		
Inventory	**$ 50,000**	
Equipment	**150,000**	
Goodwill	**110,000**	310,000
		$ 0

Worksheet 2-3

100% Interest; Bargain Purchase: Market Value Exceeds Price
Company P and Subsidiary Company S
Worksheet for Consolidated Balance Sheet
December 31, 19X1

		Trial Balance	
		Company P	Company S
1	Debits:		
2	Cash	200,000	150,000
3	Accounts Receivable	300,000	250,000
4	**Inventory**	500,000	**300,000**
5	Land	100,000	
6	Buildings (net)	900,000	
7	**Equipment (net)**	650,000	**400,000**
8	Investment in Subsidiary S	810,000	
9			
10	Total	3,460,000	1,100,000
11	Credits:		
12	Current Liabilities	300,000	100,000
13	Bonds Payable	500,000	300,000
14	Common Stock ($10 par), Co. P	660,000	
15	Paid-In Capital in Excess of Par, Co. P	1,140,000	
16	Retained Earnings, Co. P	860,000	
17	Common Stock ($5 par), Co. S		50,000
18	Paid-In Capital in Excess of Par, Co. S		350,000
19	Retained Earnings, Co. S		300,000
20	Total	3,460,000	1,100,000

Worksheet 2-3 (see page 2-12)

Eliminations & Adjustments				Consolidated Balance Sheet				
Dr.		Cr.		Dr.		Cr.		
								1
				350,000				2
				550,000				3
(2)	50,000			850,000				4
				100,000				5
				900,000				6
(2)	60,000			1,110,000				7
		(1)	700,000					8
		(2)	110,000					9
								10
								11
						400,000		12
						800,000		13
						660,000		14
						1,140,000		15
						860,000		16
(1)	50,000							17
(1)	350,000							18
(1)	300,000							19
	810,000		810,000		3,860,000		3,860,000	20

Eliminations and Adjustments:

(1) Eliminate intercompany accounts. The investment in subsidiary account includes a 100% interest in the stockholders' equity of Company S. Thus, the entire stockholders' equity of Company S is eliminated against the investment account.

(2) The balance of the investment account, $110,000, represents the total undervaluation of Company S's assets. Distribute the undervaluation amount to the proper asset accounts in the following manner, as prescribed by the determination and distribution of excess schedule:

Excess of cost over book value $110,000
Distribute to:
   Inventory **$50,000**
   Equipment **60,000**   110,000
                                                                               $ 0

Worksheet 2-4

100% Interest; Super Bargain Purchase: Book Value Exceeds Priority Accounts
Company P and Subsidiary Company S
Worksheet for Consolidated Balance Sheet
December 31, 19X1

	(credits are shown in parentheses)	Trial Balance	
		Company P	Company S
1	Debits:		
2	Cash	200,000	150,000
3	Accounts Receivable	300,000	250,000
4	**Inventory**	500,000	**300,000**
5	Land	100,000	
6	Buildings (net)	900,000	
7	**Equipment (net)**	650,000	**400,000**
8	**Investment in Subsidiary S**	**310,000**	
9	Total	2,960,000	1,100,000
10	Credits:		
11	**Deferred Credit**		
12	Current Liabilities	(300,000)	(100,000)
13	Bonds Payable	(500,000)	(300,000)
14	Common Stock ($10 par), Co. P	(560,000)	
15	Paid-In Capital in Excess of Par, Co. P	(740,000)	
16	Retained Earnings, Co. P	(860,000)	
17	Common Stock ($5 par), Co. S		(50,000)
18	Paid-In Capital in Excess of Par, Co. S		(350,000)
19	Retained Earnings, Co. S		(300,000)
20	Total	2,960,000	1,100,000

Worksheet 2-4 (see page 2-16)

Eliminations & Adjustments		Consolidated Balance Sheet		
Dr.	Cr.	Dr.	Cr.	
				1
		350,000		2
		550,000		3
(2) 50,000		850,000		4
		100,000		5
		900,000		6
	(2) 400,000	650,000		7
(2) 390,000	(1) 700,000			8
				9
				10
	(2) 40,000		(40,000)	11
			(400,000)	12
			(800,000)	13
			(560,000)	14
			(740,000)	15
			(860,000)	16
(1) 50,000				17
(1) 350,000				18
(1) 300,000				19
1,140,000	1,140,000	0		20

Eliminations and Adjustments:

(1) Eliminate controlling share (100%) of subsidiary equity against the investment account.

(2) Distribute the excess of book value over cost according to the determination and distribution schedule:

Excess of book value over cost		$ 390,000
Distribute to:		
Inventory	$ 50,000	
Land	**(400,000)**	(350,000)
Deferred Credit		$ 40,000

Worksheet 2-5

80% Interest; Price Equals Book Value
Company P and Subsidiary Company S
Worksheet for Consolidated Balance Sheet
December 31, 19X1

		Trial Balance	
		Company P	Company S
1	Debits:		
2	Cash	200,000	
3	Accounts Receivable	300,000	200,000
4	Inventory	100,000	100,000
5	**Investment in Subsidiary S**	**400,000**	
6	Equipment (net)	150,000	300,000
7	Total	1,150,000	600,000
8	Credits:		
9	Current Liabilities	150,000	100,000
10	Bonds Payable	300,000	
11	Retained Earnings, Co. P	100,000	
12	Retained Earnings, Co. P	600,000	
13	**Common Stock, Co. S**		**200,000**
14	**Retained Earnings, Co. S**		**300,000**
15	**Minority Interest**		
16	Total	1,150,000	600,000

Worksheet 2-5 (see page 2-22)

| Eliminations & Adjustments | | Minority Interest | Consolidated Balance Sheet | | |
Dr.	Cr.		Dr.	Cr.	
					1
			200,000		2
			500,000		3
			200,000		4
	(1) 400,000				5
			450,000		6
					7
					8
				250,000	9
				300,000	10
				100,000	11
				600,000	12
(1) 160,000		40,000			13
(1) 240,000		60,000			14
		100,000		100,000	15
400,000	400,000		1,350,000	1,350,000	16

Eliminations and Adjustments:

(1) Eliminate 80% of the subsidiary equity against the investment in subsidiary account.

Worksheet 2-6

80% Interest; Price Exceeds Market Value
Company P and Subsidiary Company S
Worksheet for Consolidated Balance Sheet
December 31, 19X1

		Trial Balance	
		Company P	Company S
1	Debits:		
2	Cash	200,000	150,000
3	Accounts Receivable	300,000	250,000
4	**Inventory**	500,000	**300,000**
5	Land	100,000	
6	Buildings (net)	900,000	
7	**Equipment (net)**	650,000	**400,000**
8	**Investment in Subsidiary S**	**810,000**	
9			
10	**Goodwill**		
11	Total	3,460,000	1,100,000
12	Credits:		
13	Current Liabilities	300,000	100,000
14	Bonds Payable	500,000	300,000
15	Common Stock ($10 par), Co. P	660,000	
16	Paid-In Capital in Excess of Par, Co. P	1,140,000	
17	Retained Earnings, Co. P	860,000	
18	**Common Stock ($5 par), Co. S**		50,000
19	**Paid-In Capital in Excess of Par, Co. S**		350,000
20	**Retained Earnings, Co. S**		300,000
21	**Minority Interest**		
22	Total	3,460,000	1,100,000

Worksheet 2-6 (see page 2-23)

Eliminations & Adjustments		Minority	Consolidated Balance Sheet		
Dr.	Cr.	Interest	Dr.	Cr.	
					1
			350,000		2
			550,000		3
(2) 40,000			840,000		4
			100,000		5
			900,000		6
(2) 120,000			1,170,000		7
	(1) 560,000				8
	(2) 250,000				9
(2) 90,000			90,000		10
					11
					12
				400,000	13
				800,000	14
				660,000	15
				1,140,000	16
				860,000	17
(1) 40,000		10,000			18
(1) 280,000		70,000			19
(1) 240,000		60,000			20
		140,000		140,000	21
810,000	810,000		4,000,000	4,000,000	22

Eliminations and Adjustments:

(1) Eliminate 80% of the subsidiary equity accounts against the investment account.

(2) Distribute the balance of the investment account, $250,000, to the specific subsidiary accounts according to the determination and distribution of excess schedule:

Excess of cost over book value		$250,000
Distribute to:		
Inventory	$ 40,000	
Equipment	120,000	
Goodwill	90,000	250,000
		$ 0

Worksheet 2-7

100% Interest; Pooling of Interests
Company I and Subsidiary Company C
Worksheet for Consolidated Balance Sheet
December 31, 19X1

		Trial Balance	
		Company I	Company C
1	Debits:		
2	Current Assets	20,000	10,000
3	Property, Plant, and Equipment (net)	70,000	30,000
4	**Investment in Subsidiary C**	**30,000**	
5	Total	120,000	40,000
6	Credits:		
7	Liabilities	15,000	10,000
8	Common Stock, Co. I	56,000	
9	Paid-In Capital in Excess of Par, Co. I	4,000	
10	Retained Earnings, Co. I	45,000	
11	**Common Stock, Co. C**		**10,000**
12	**Retained Earnings, Co. C**		**20,000**
13	Total	120,000	40,000

Worksheet 2-7 (see page 2-29)

Eliminations & Adjustments		Consolidated Balance Sheet		
Dr.	Cr.	Dr.	Cr.	
				1
		30,000		2
		100,000		3
	(1) 30,000			4
				5
				6
			25,000	7
			56,000	8
			4,000	9
			45,000	10
(1) 10,000				11
(1) 20,000			0	12
30,000	30,000	130,000	130,000	13

Eliminations and Adjustments:

(1) Eliminate the investment account against the subsidiary equity accounts

Consolidated Statements: Subsequent to Acquisition

This chapter's mission is to teach the procedures needed to prepare consolidated income statements, retained earnings statements, and balance sheets in periods subsequent to the acquisition of a subsidiary. There are a variety of worksheet models to master. This variety is caused primarily by the alternative methods available to a parent for maintaining its investment in a subsidiary account. Accounting principles do not address the method used by a parent to record its investment in a subsidiary that is to be consolidated. The method used is of no concern to standard setters since the investment account always is eliminated when consolidating. Thus, the method chosen to record the investment usually is based on convenience.

In the preceding chapter, worksheet procedures for a combination deemed to be a purchase included asset and liability adjustments to reflect market values on the date of the purchase. This chapter discusses the subsequent depreciation and amortization of these asset and liability revaluations in conjunction with its analysis of worksheet procedures for preparing consolidated financial statements. Appendix A, pages 3-25 and 3-26, explains the vertical worksheet as an alternative approach to the horizontal worksheet used in this chapter for developing consolidated statements.

This chapter does not deal with the income tax issues of the consolidated company except to the extent that they are reflected in the original acquisition price. Appendix B, pages 3-26 to 3-31, considers tax issues that arise as part of the original purchase. These include recording procedures for deferred tax liabilities arising in a tax-free exchange and tax loss carryovers. A full discussion of tax issues in consolidations is included in Chapter 6.

Accounting for the Investment in a Subsidiary

A parent may choose one of two basic methods when accounting for its investment in a subsidiary: the *equity method* or the *cost method*. The equity method records as income an ownership percentage of the reported income of the subsidiary, whether or not it was received by the parent. The cost method treats the investment in the subsidiary as a normal stock investment by recording income only when dividends are declared by the subsidiary.

Equity Method

The equity method views the earning of income by a controlled subsidiary as sufficient reason to record the parent's share of that income. The parent has the power to demand the payment of dividends. Clearly, the decision to require the payment of dividends should not be the cause to record income. The receipt of a dividend is just the conversion into cash of a claim on income that has already been recorded.

The equity method records as income the parent's ownership interest percentage times the subsidiary reported net income. The income is added to the parent's investment account. In a like manner, the parent records its share of a subsidiary loss and lowers its investment account for its share of the loss. Dividends received from the parent are viewed as a conversion of a portion of the investment account into cash; thus, dividends reduce the investment account balance. The investment account at any point in time can be summarized as follows:

Investment in Subsidiary (equity method)	
plus: Original cost Ownership interest × reported income of subsidiary since acquisition	less: Ownership interest × reported losses of subsidiary since acquisition less: Ownership interest × dividends declared by subsidiary since acquisition
equals: Equity-adjusted balance	

The *simple equity method* makes no adjustment to the parent's share of subsidiary income for any amortizations resulting from differences between the book and market values of the investment on the date of acquisition. There is no danger in omitting these amortizations from the investment account when consolidated statements are prepared since the investment account is eliminated entirely in the preparation of those statements. The real advantage of using the simple equity method when consolidating is that every dollar of change in the stockholders' equity of the subsidiary is recorded on a pro rata basis in the investment account. This method expedites the elimination of the investment account in the consolidated worksheets in future periods. It is favored in this text because of its simplicity.

For some unconsolidated investments, the sophisticated equity method is required by APB Opinion No. 18, *The Equity Method of Accounting for Investments in Common Stock*. According to this Opinion, a company's investment should be adjusted for amortizations when the investor has an "influential" investment of 20% or more of another company's voting stock. For example, assume that the price paid for an investment in a subsidiary exceeded underlying book value and that the determination and distribution of excess schedule attributed the entire excess to goodwill. Just as goodwill will decrease in value and should be amortized, so should that portion of the price paid for the investment attributed to goodwill also be amortized. If the estimated life of the goodwill is 10 years, then the portion of the investment price attributed to goodwill should be amortized over 10 years. This would be accomplished by reducing the investment income each year by the amortization, which means that the income posted to the investment account each year is also less by the amount of the amortization.

The sophisticated equity method is required for influential investments (normally 20% to 50% interests) and for those rare subsidiaries that are not consolidated. Its use for these types of investments is fully discussed in Chapter 6. The sophisticated equity method also is used by some parent companies to maintain the investment in a subsidiary that is to be consolidated. This better reflects the investment account in the parent-only statements, but such statements may not be used as the primary statements for external reporting purposes. Parent-only statements may be used as supplemental statements only when the criteria for consolidated statements are met. The use of this method for investments to be consolidated makes recording the investment income and the elimination of the investment account more difficult than under the simple equity method.

Cost Method

When the cost method is used, the investment in subsidiary account is retained at its original cost-of-acquisition balance. No adjustments are made to the account for income as it is earned by the subsidiary. Income on the investment is limited to dividends received from the subsidiary. **An exception is made for subsidiary dividends that are based on income earned prior to the acquisition date.** Such dividends are viewed as a partial liquidation of the investment and are deducted from the original investment. For example, assume that an 80%-owned subsidiary that was acquired at the start of the year earned $10,000 and paid $15,000 in dividends. The parent would record dividend income of $8,000 (80% of the income earned) and reduce its investment account by $4,000 (80% of the dividends in excess of income since acquisition). The cost method is acceptable for subsidiaries that are to be consolidated because, in the consolidation process, the investment account is eliminated entirely.

The cost method is the most common method used in practice by parent companies. It is simple to use during the accounting period and avoids the risk of incorrect adjustments. Typically, the correct income of the subsidiary is not known until after the end of the accounting period. Awaiting its determination would delay the parent company's closing procedures. Companies that use the cost method may convert to the simple equity method as part of the consolidation process. This text emphasizes the application of the simple equity method because it is the method used to convert cost method investments so that they may be eliminated in the consolidation process.

Example of the Equity and Cost Methods

The simple equity, sophisticated equity, and cost methods will be illustrated by an example covering two years. This example, which will become the foundation for several consolidated worksheets in this chapter, is based on the following facts:

1. The following determination and distribution of excess schedule was prepared on the date of purchase. This schedule is similar to that of the preceding chapter but is modified to indicate the period over which adjustments to the subsidiary book values will be allocated. This expanded format will be used in preparing all future worksheets.
2. Income during 19X1 was $30,000 for Company S; dividends declared by Company S at the end of 19X1 totaled $10,000.
3. During 19X2, Company S had a loss of $10,000 and declared dividends of $5,000.
4. The balance in Company S's retained earnings account on December 31, 19X2, is $55,000.

Company P and Subsidiary Company S
Determination and Distribution of Excess Schedule
January 1, 19X1

	Company	Controlling Percent	Controlling Interest	Amort. Periods	Controlling Amort.
Price paid for investment including direct acquisition costs:...................			$145,000		
Market value of total net assets:...............	$150,000	90%	135,000		
Market value of priority accounts..............	30,000	90	27,000		
Analysis of price: **Goodwill**.................			10,000		

(continued)

	Total	Controlling	Amort. Periods	Controlling Amort.
Price paid for investment.		$145,000		
Less book value interest acquired:				
Common stock	$100,000			
Retained earnings	50,000			
Total stockholders' equity.	$150,000			
Interest acquired	90%	135,000		
Excess of cost over book value (debit)		**$10,000**		
Goodwill		**10,000**	**Dr. 10**	**$1,000**

The journal entries and resulting investment account balances shown on the bottom of this page and the next record this information on the books of Company P using the simple equity, cost, and sophisticated equity methods. Note that the only difference between the sophisticated and simple equity methods is that the former reduces investment income each year for an amount equal to the amortization of goodwill ($1,000).

The balance in the simple-equity-adjusted investment account of a parent easily can be tested for its correctness. Under the simple equity method, every change in the retained earnings account of the subsidiary leads to an equity adjustment in the investment account for an amount equal to the change multiplied by the ownership interest. **At any time, the balance in a simple-equity-adjusted investment account can be stated as follows:**

Balance = Cost + (Ownership Interest × Change in Subsidiary Retained Earnings since Acquisition)

Event	Simple Equity Method		
19X1			
Jan. 1 Purchase of stock	Investment in Company S.	145,000	
	Cash		145,000
Dec. 31 Subsidiary income of $30,000 reported to parent	Investment in Company S.	27,000	
	Subsidiary Income.		27,000
31 Dividends of $10,000 declared by subsidiary	Dividends Receivable	9,000	
	Investment in Company S.		9,000
	Investment Balance, Dec. 31, 19X1 . .		**$163,000**
19X2			
Dec. 31 Subsidiary loss of $10,000 reported to parent	Loss on Subsidiary Operations	9,000	
	Investment in Company S.		9,000
31 Dividends of $5,000 declared by subsidiary	Dividends Receivable	4,500	
	Investment in Company S.		4,500
	Investment Balance, Dec. 31, 19X2 . .		**$149,500**

In the illustration, the December 31, 19X2 balance in the simple-equity-adjusted Investment in Company S would be verified as follows:

$$\begin{aligned}
\text{Balance} &= \text{Cost} + (.90 \times \text{change in Company S retained earnings since acquisition}) \\
&= \$145,000 + [.90 \times (\$55,000 \text{ December 31, 19X2 balance} - \$50,000 \\
&\quad \text{January 1, 19X1 balance})] \\
&= \$145,000 + (.90 \times \$5,000) \\
&= \$149,500
\end{aligned}$$

This procedure will be valuable in checking the balance in an investment account prior to consolidating. Later in the chapter, this technique becomes the basis for converting investments recorded under the cost method to the simple equity method. If it is desired, the sophisticated equity balance can be obtained by adjusting the simple equity balance for the cumulative amortizations of excess.

Most presentations of worksheet elimination procedures in subsequent chapters are based on the use of the simple equity method. Rather than mastering a separate set of procedures for investments carried at cost, such investments will be converted to the simple equity method prior to the application of elimination procedures.

Elimination Procedures

Worksheet procedures necessary to prepare consolidated income statements, retained earnings statements, and balance sheets are examined in the following section. It must be recalled that the consolidation procedure is used each year as it is applied to each period's separate parent and subsidiary accounts. **The consolidation process is performed independently each year since the worksheet eliminations of previous years are never recorded by the parent or subsidiary.**

Cost Method		Sophisticated Equity Method	
Investment in Company S 145,000		Investment in Company S 145,000	
Cash.	145,000	Cash	145,000
No entry.		Investment in Company S ...... 26,000[a]	
		Subsidiary Income	26,000
Dividends Receivable. 9,000		Dividends Receivable 9,000	
Subsidiary (Dividend) Income ..	9,000	Investment in Company S	9,000
Investment Balance, Dec. 31, 19X1	**$145,000**	**Investment Balance, Dec. 31, 19X1**	**$162,000**
No entry.		Loss on Subsidiary Operations. . . 10,000[b]	
		Investment in Company S	10,000
Dividends Receivable. 4,500		Dividends Receivable 4,500	
Subsidiary (Dividend) Income ..	4,500	Investment in Company S	4,500
Investment Balance, Dec. 31, 19X1	**$145,000**	**Investment Balance, Dec. 31, 19X1**	**$147,500**

a Parent's share of subsidiary income less amortization of excess of $1,000 per year.
b Parent's share of subsidiary loss plus amortization of excess of $1,000 per year.

The illustrations that follow are based on the facts concerning the investment in Company S, as detailed in the previous example. The procedures for consolidating an investment maintained under the simple equity method will be discussed first, followed by an explanation of how procedures would differ under the cost and sophisticated equity methods.

Effect of Simple Equity Method on Consolidation

The trial balances of Company P and Company S at the end of 19X1 appear in the first two columns of Worksheet 3-1, pages 3-60 and 3-61. The balances reflect the simple equity adjustments for 19X1, which were just illustrated. Be sure to pay close attention to entry (1). It is this elimination entry that creates what this text refers to as *date alignment*. On the trial balance, the investment account has already been adjusted to its year-end balance. However, the subsidiary retained earnings still reflect its beginning-of-the-year balance. **Remaining eliminations may not proceed until the investment account and the subsidiary equity accounts, against which the former is eliminated, are at the same point in time.** Entry (1) eliminates the current-year equity adjustments made and intercompany dividends declared during the year. This returns the investment account to its balance at **the start of the year**. Now that date alignment exists, the subsidiary equity at the start of the year can be eliminated against the investment account in entry (2), and the excess cost can be distributed and amortized for the current year in entries (3) and (4), respectively.

Let us review the worksheet eliminations in journal entry form:

1.   Create date alignment and eliminate current-year subsidiary income:

Subsidiary Income (Co. P account)	27,000	
Investment in Company S (Co. P account)		27,000
Investment in Company S (Co. P account)	9,000	
Dividend Declared (Co. S account)		9,000

2.   Eliminate investment account, now at beginning-of-the-year balance:

Common Stock, Company S	90,000	
Retained Earnings, Jan. 1, 19X1, Co. S	45,000	
Investment in Company S (Co. P account)		135,000

3.   Distribute excess of cost (goodwill):

Goodwill (created when consolidating)	10,000	
Investment in Co. S (balance of		
Co. P's investment account)		10,000

4.   Amortize goodwill for the current year:

Expenses (charged to Co. P share of consolidated income)	1,000	
Goodwill		1,000

The Consolidated Income Statement column follows the Eliminations & Adjustments columns. The adjusted nominal accounts of the constituent companies are used to calculate the *combined net income* of $69,000. This income is distributed to the controlling and minority interests. Note that the minority receives 10% of the $30,000 reported net income of the subsidiary, or $3,000. The controlling interest receives the balance of the combined net income, or $66,000, which this text terms *consolidated net income*.

The distribution of income is handled best by using *income distribution schedules* which appear at the end of Worksheet 3-1. The subsidiary income distribution schedule is a "T account" which begins with the reported net income of the subsidiary. This income is termed *internally generated net income,* which connotes the income of only the company being analyzed without consideration of income derived from other members of the affiliated group. Until Chapter 8, when the subsidiary owns an interest in the parent, the subsidiary's internally generated net income is the same as its net income. In Worksheet 3-1, the subsidiary net income is multiplied by the minority ownership percentage to calculate the minority interest in income. A similar T account is used for the parent income distribution schedule. The parent's share of subsidiary net income is added to the internally generated net income of the parent, and amortizations of excess are deducted. Goodwill amortization is borne entirely by the controlling interest. Note that this is true for *all* excess cost over book value situations. Under the parent company concept, only the portion applicable to the purchaser's interest is acknowledged; thus, the amortization of excess affects only the controlling interest. The balance in the parent T account is the controlling share of the combined net income (called consolidated net income). **The income distribution schedule is a valuable self-check procedure since the sum of the income distributions should equal the combined net income on the worksheet.**

The Minority Interest Column of the worksheet summarizes the total ownership interest of minority stockholders on the balance sheet date. The noneliminated portion of subsidiary common stock at par, additional paid-in capital in excess of par, beginning retained earnings, the minority share of income, and dividends declared is extended to this column. The total of this column is then extended to the consolidated balance sheet column as the minority interest. The formal balance sheet will typically show only the total minority interest and will not provide information on the components of this balance.

The Controlling Retained Earnings column produces the controlling retained earnings balance on the balance sheet date. The beginning parent retained earnings balance, as adjusted by eliminations and adjustments, is extended to this column. Dividends declared by the parent are also extended to this column. The controlling share of net income (consolidated net income) is extended to this column to produce the ending balance. The balance is extended to the balance sheet column as the retained earnings of the consolidated company.

The Consolidated Balance Sheet column includes the consolidated asset and liability balances. The paid-in equity balances of the parent are extended as the consolidated paid-in capital balance. As mentioned above, the aggregate balances of the Minority Interest and the Controlling Retained Earnings are also extended to the balance sheet column.

Separate debit and credit columns may be used for the consolidated balance sheet. This arrangement may minimize errors and aid analysis. Single columns are not advocated but are used to facilitate the inclusion of lengthy worksheets in a summarized fashion.

The information for the following formal statements is taken directly from Worksheet 3-1:

Company P and Subsidiary Company S	
Consolidated Income Statement	
For Year Ended December 31, 19X1	
Revenue	$180,000
Expenses (includes $1,000 goodwill amortization)	(111,000)
Combined net income	$ 69,000
Minority interest	(3,000)
Consolidated net income	$ 66,000

Company P and Subsidiary Company S
Consolidated Retained Earnings Statement
For Year Ended December 31, 19X1

	Minority	Controlling
Retained earnings, January 1, 19X1	$5,000	$123,000
Distribution of combined net income	3,000	66,000
Dividends declared.	(1,000)	
Balance, December 31, 19X1	$7,000	$189,000

Company P and Subsidiary Company S
Consolidated Balance Sheet
December 31, 19X1

Assets		Stockholders' Equity		
Net tangible assets	$397,000	Minority interest.		$ 17,000
Goodwill	9,000	Controlling interest:		
		Common stock.	$200,000	
		Retained earnings	189,000	389,000
		Total stockholders'		
Total assets.	$406,000	equity		$406,000

There are two features of these statements that deserve added attention. The first concerns the reporting procedures for consolidated net income. In theory, consolidated net income is the total income of the entity, which is available to both the minority and controlling interest. This is the approach advocated by the *Economic Unit Concept* which views consolidated net income as the income of the entity, which is merely allocated to the two ownership groups. It is this format which is included in the FASB Exposure Draft.

Despite this theory, it has become common practice to view consolidated net income as **just that portion of combined income available to the controlling interest**. Unfortunately, this presentation suggests that the minority interest in income is an expense, which it is not. Many companies imply that the minority share of combined income is an expense. This form of presentation was used in Exhibit 1, which is taken from the 1996 annual report of the MCN Energy Group Inc. Notice that the income statement shows the Minority Interest in income in the category of *Other Income and (Deductions)*. The minority share of income, while not stated to be an expense, is treated as one. It is deducted to arrive at net income. Implying that the minority share of income is an expense derives from the *Parent Company Concept*[1], which holds that the focus of the income statement should be the income available to the controlling interest. Any income not available to controlling interest is viewed as an expense by the parent company. This text follows the common practice of first calculating the combined income of the consolidated entity. The minority share of income is displayed as a distribution of combined income to arrive at the income available to the controlling interest. This presentation is included in the preceding income statement on page 3-7.

---

1 See the appendix following Chapter 8 for a comparison of consolidation concepts.

Exhibit 1
MCN Energy Group Inc. and Subsidiaries
Consolidated Statement of Income

Year Ended December 31 (in Thousands, Except Per Share Amounts)	1996	1995	1994
Operating Revenues			
Gas and oil sales	$1,827,198	$1,323,432	$1,309,192
Transportation	120,019	120,494	114,932
Other	50,051	51,306	49,509
	1,997,268	1,495,232	1,473,633
Operating Expenses			
Cost of gas	1,193,578	786,193	823,436
Operation and maintenance	371,980	342,521	341,585
Depreciation, depletion, and amortization	145,990	114,585	97,835
Property and other taxes	74,427	63,704	62,863
	1,785,975	1,307,003	1,325,719
Operating Income	211,293	188,229	147,914
Equity in Earnings of Joint Ventures (Note 3)	17, 867	5,245	6,289
Other Income and (Deductions)			
Interest income	7,234	7,741	7,628
Interest on long-term debt	(66,517)	(44,853)	(37,811)
Other interest expense	(11,264)	(12,049)	(10,899)
Dividends on preferred securities of subsidiaries (Notes 6a and 6c)	(12,374)	(9,610)	(2,018)
Gains related to DIGP (Note 2b)	6,384	—	—
Minority interest	(1,059)	(2,491)	(2,879)
Other	(2,620)	(3,713)	(6,136)
	(80,216)	(64,975)	(52,115)
Income from Continuing Operations before Income Taxes	148,944	128,499	102,088
Income Tax Provision (Note 13)	36,375	35,330	27,490
Income from Continuing Operations	112,569	93,169	74,598
Discontinued Operations, Net of Taxes (Note 2d)			
Income from operations	1,595	3,587	3,170
Gain on sale	36,176	—	—
	37,771	3,587	3,170
Net Income	$ 150,340	$ 96,756	$ 77,768
Earnings Per Share			
Continuing operations	$ 1.68	$ 1.44	$ 1.26
Discontinued operations (Note 2d)			
Income from operations	.03	.05	.05
Gain on sale	.54	—	—
	.57	.05	.05
	$ 2.25	$ 1.49	$ 1.31
Average Common Shares Outstanding (Note 6d)	66,944	64,743	59,394
Dividends Declared Per Share	$ .9400	$ .9000	$ .8675

The notes to the consolidated financial statements are an integral part of this statement.

The balance sheet on the preceding page shows the total minority interest in equity as an aggregate amount under total stockholders' equity. There is no consistency in the treatment of this item by companies. It is common to show the minority equity interest as a liability. Notice that the MCN Energy Group consolidated balance sheet in Exhibit 2 uses this approach. The minority interest is listed among *Deferred Credits and Other Liabilities*. Some companies show the minority interest between lia-

Exhibit 2
MCN Energy Group Inc. and Subsidiaries
Consolidated Statement of Financial Positions

December 31 (in Thousands)	1996	1995
Current Assets		
Cash and cash equivalents, at cost (which approximates market value)	$ 30,462	$ 19,259
Accounts receivable, less allowance for doubtful accounts of $18,487 and $13,765, respectively	362,596	317,945
Accrued unbilled revenues	108,509	92,410
Gas in inventory (Note 4)	79,161	71,763
Property taxes assessed applicable to future periods	62,966	60,633
Accrued gas cost recovery revenues	27,672	—
Other	52,862	53,486
	724,228	615,496
Deferred Charges and Other Assets		
Investment in and advances to joint ventures (Note 3)	265,388	129,026
Deferred swap losses and receivables (Note 11a)	65,051	54,807
Deferred postretirement benefit costs (Note 10b)	5,559	13,112
Deferred environmental costs (Note 7b)	31,233	35,000
Prepaid benefit costs (Note 10)	59,248	23,827
Other	100,341	90,626
	526,820	346,398
Property, Plant, and Equipment, at cost		
Gas distribution	2,689,039	2,496,711
Exploration & production	981,901	576,810
Pipelines & processing	27,895	22,324
Other	18,722	64,709
	3,717,557	3,160,554
Less—Accumulated depreciation and depletion	1,335,201	1,223,808
	2,382,356	1,936,746
	$3,633,404	$2,898,640
Current Liabilities		
Accounts payable	$ 317,922	$ 217,184
Notes payable (Note 5)	336,126	245,635
Current portion of long-term debt, capital lease obligations, and redeemable cumulative preferred securities (Notes 5 and 9)	84,747	7,000
Federal income, property, and other taxes payable	97,646	83,384
Customer deposits	12,881	11,550
Other	97,873	87,575
	947,195	652,328
Deferred Credits and Other Liabilities		
Accumulated deferred income taxes (Note 13)	149,838	125,896
Unamortized investment tax credit	34,919	36,797
Tax benefits amortizable to customers	116,496	114,668
Deferred swap gains and payables (Note 11a)	48,365	51,923
Accrued postretirement benefit costs (Note 10b)	—	15,551
Accrued environmental costs (Note 7b)	35,000	35,000
Minority interest	17,911	18,375
Other	73,263	93,470
	475,792	491,680

(continued)

Commitments and Contingencies (Notes 7 and 9)

Capitalization (See accompanying statement)

Long-term debt, including capital lease obligations	1,252,040	993,407
MCN-obligated mandatorily redeemable preferred securities of subsidiaries holding solely subordinated debentures of MCN	173,809	96,449
Common shareholders' equity	784,568	664,776
	2,210,417	1,754,632
	$3,633,404	$2,898,640

The notes to the consolidated financial statements are an integral part of this statement.

bilities and controlling stockholders' equity. This text uses the approach recommended in the FASB Exposure Draft and shows minority interest as part of total stockholders' equity.

Now consider consolidation procedures for 19X2 as they would apply to Companies P and S under the simple equity method. This will provide added practice in preparing worksheets and will emphasize that, at the end of each year, consolidation procedures are applied to the separate statements of the constituent firms. In essence, **each year's consolidation procedures begin as if there had never been a previous consolidation**. However, reference to past worksheets is used commonly to save time.

The separate trial balances of Companies P and S are displayed in the first two columns of Worksheet 3-2, pages 3-62 and 3-63. The investment in subsidiary account includes the simple-equity-adjusted investment balance as calculated on page 3-5. Note that the balances in the retained earnings accounts of Companies P and S are calculated as follows:

Company P:	January 1, 19X1 balance	$123,000
	Net income, 19X1 (including Company P's share of subsidiary income under simple equity method)	67,000
	Balance, January 1, 19X2	$190,000

Company S:	January 1, 19X1 balance	$ 50,000
	Net income, 19X1	30,000
	Dividends declared	(10,000)
	Balance, January 1, 19X2	$ 70,000

Again, entry (1) is used to create the needed date alignment. The equity adjustment made during the year and the intercompany dividends are eliminated. This returns the investment account to its balance at the start of the second year ($163,000) so that the account is at a common point in time with the subsidiary equity accounts, against which the investment account is eliminated in entry (2). Notice that entry (4) amortizes the excess for both the current and past periods.

In journal entry form, this elimination is

Retained Earnings, Jan. 1, 19X2, Co. P	1,000	
Expenses (charged to Co. P share of consolidated income)	1,000	
Goodwill (2 years of amortization)		2,000

Note, again, the amortization of goodwill for both the prior and current year is borne only by the parent, since only its interest in goodwill was recorded. Be sure to understand that the **amortization of excess done the prior year appeared only on that year's worksheet and was** *not recorded* **on either company's accounting**

records. This emphasizes that consolidation starts from the separate statements of the two companies each year and that **the statements do not reflect the prior periods' consolidation procedures.**

Note that the original determination and distribution of excess schedule prepared on the date of acquisition becomes the foundation for **all** subsequent worksheets. Once prepared, the schedule is used without modification.

Effect of Cost Method on Consolidation

Recall that parent companies most often may choose to record their investments in a subsidiary under the cost method, whereby the investments are maintained at their original costs, with income from the investments recorded when dividends are declared by the subsidiary. The use of the cost method means that the investment account does not reflect changes in subsidiary equity. Rather than develop a new set of procedures for the elimination of an investment under the cost method, **the cost method investment will be converted to its simple equity balance at the beginning of the period** to create date alignment. Then, the elimination procedures developed earlier can be applied.

Worksheet 3-3, pages 3-64 and 3-65, is a consolidated financial statements worksheet for Companies P and S for the first year of combined operations. The worksheet is based upon the entries made under the cost method, as shown on page 3-5. Reference to Company P's Trial Balance column in Worksheet 3-3 reveals that the investment in the subsidiary account at year-end still is stated at the original $145,000 cost and the income recorded by the parent as a result of subsidiary ownership is limited to $9,000, or 90% of the dividends declared by the subsidiary. When the cost method is used, the account title *Dividend Income* may be used in place of *Subsidiary Income*.

At the end of the first year of operations, there would be no need for an equity conversion entry. Date alignment exists since the Company P investment account and the Company S equity accounts already are stated as of a common point in time, January 1, 19X1. For entry (1), it is necessary to eliminate only the intercompany dividends. The remaining eliminations, entries (2) through (4), are identical to their corresponding entries in Worksheet 3-1. The last four columns of Worksheet 3-3 are also identical to their counterparts in Worksheet 3-1.

For periods subsequent to the first year of combined operations, an entry converting the investment in the subsidiary account to its simple-equity-method balance will be needed on the consolidated worksheets in order to create date alignment. To illustrate, Worksheet 3-4, pages 3-66 and 3-67, covers the second year of operations for Companies P and S. This worksheet is identical to Worksheet 3-2 except that here the cost method is used to account for the investment in Company S. Thus, the balance of the investment account is the original $145,000 cost as of the January 1, 19X1 purchase date. However, the retained earnings account of Company S carries the January 1, 19X2 balance of $70,000. Because these accounts do not share a common point in time, eliminations cannot proceed. Note that in Worksheet 3-4 the balance of the parent retained earnings account is $18,000 less than its balance in Worksheet 3-2 since it does not include the undistributed 19X1 income of the subsidiary (90% of $20,000). The conversion entry, entry (C) in Worksheet 3-4, converts the investment account to its simple-equity-method balance on January 1, 19X2, so that the account shares a common date with the subsidiary equity accounts against which the investment account now can be eliminated. In journal entry form, the conversion entry is

```
Investment in Company S (to bring account
     to equity balance on Jan. 1, 19X2) . . . . . . . . . . . . . . .   18,000
        Retained Earnings, Jan. 1, 19X2, Co. P . . . . . . . . . . . . . .         18,000
```

The conversion entry simultaneously updates the Company P retained earnings account to its simple-equity-method balance as of January 1, 19X2. The dollar amount of the conversion is calculated by multiplying the ownership interest by the change in the subsidiary retained earnings account between the date of acquisition and the beginning of the current year. In this case, the adjustment is made as follows:

$$\text{Conversion} = .90 \times (\text{Company S Retained Earnings, January 1, 19X2} -$$
$$\text{Company S Retained Earnings, January 1, 19X1)}$$
$$= .90 \times (\$70,000 - \$50,000) = .90 \times \$20,000$$
$$= \$18,000$$

The simplicity of this technique of converting from the cost to the simple equity method should be appreciated. At any future date, in order to convert to the simple equity method, it is necessary only to compare the balance of the subsidiary retained earnings account on the worksheet trial balance with the balance of that account on the original date of acquisition (included in the determination and distribution of excess schedule). Specific reference to income earned and dividends paid by the subsidiary in each intervening year is unnecessary. The only complications occur when stock dividends have been issued by the subsidiary or when the subsidiary has issued or retired stock. These complications are examined in Chapter 8.

After the conversion, the eliminations may proceed. Since the cost method is being used, the first elimination is confined to intercompany dividends. Entries (2) through (4) are identical to the corresponding entries in Worksheet 3-2. Note that entry (2) is possible only after the conversion step brings the account balances to a common point in time.

Effect of Sophisticated Equity Method on Consolidation

In some cases, a parent may desire to prepare its own separate statements as a supplement to the consolidated statements. In this situation, the investment in the subsidiary must be shown on the parent's separate statements at the sophisticated equity balance. This requirement may lead the parent to maintain its subsidiary investment account under the sophisticated equity method. Two ramifications occur when such an investment is consolidated. First, the current year's equity adjustment is net of excess amortizations; second, the investment account contains only the remaining unamortized excess applicable to the investment.

The use of the sophisticated equity method complicates the elimination of the investment account in that the worksheet distribution and amortization of the excess procedures are altered. However, there is no impact on the other consolidation procedures. To illustrate, the information given in Worksheet 3-2 will be used as the basis for an example. The trial balance of Company P will show the following changes as a result of using the sophisticated equity method:

1. The Investment in Company S will be carried at $147,500 ($149,500 simple equity balance less 2 years' amortization of excess at $1,000 per year).
2. The January 1, 19X2 balance for Company P Retained Earnings will be $189,000 ($190,000 under simple equity less 1 year's amortization of excess of $1,000).
3. The subsidiary loss account of the parent will have a balance of $10,000 ($9,000 share of the subsidiary loss plus $1,000 amortization of excess).

Based on these changes, a partial worksheet under the sophisticated equity method follows:

Company P and Subsidiary Company S
Partial Worksheet for Consolidated Financial Statements
For Year Ended December 31, 19X2

(Credit balance amounts are in parentheses.)	Trial Balance		Eliminations & Adjustments	
	Company P	Company S	Dr.	Cr.
Investment in Company S	147,500		(1) 10,000	(2) 153,000
			(1) 4,500	(3) 9,000
Goodwill			(3) 9,000	(4) 1,000
Retained Earnings, Jan. 1, 19X2, Co. P	(189,000)			
Common Stock ($10 par), Co. S		(100,000)	(2) 90,000	
Retained Earnings, Jan. 1, 19X2, Co. S		(70,000)	(2) 63,000	
Revenue	(100,000)	(50,000)		
Expenses	80,000	60,000	(4) 1,000	
Subsidiary Loss	10,000			(1) 10,000
Dividends Declared		5,000		(1) 4,500

Eliminations and Adjustments:

(1) Eliminate the current-year entries made in the investment account and the subsidiary loss account. The loss account now includes the $1,000 excess amortization.

(2) Using the balances at the beginning of the year, eliminate 90% of the Company S equity balances against the remaining investment account.

(3) Distribute the remaining unamortized excess on January 1, 19X2, ($10,000 on purchase date less $1,000 19X1 amortization) to the goodwill account.

(4) Amortize goodwill for the current year.

The sophisticated equity method essentially is a modification of simple equity procedures. The major difference in the consolidation procedures under the two methods is that, subsequent to the acquisition, the original excess calculated on the determination and distribution of excess schedule does not appear when the sophisticated equity method is used. Only the remaining unamortized excess appears. Since the investment account is eliminated in the consolidation process, the added complexities of the sophisticated method are not justified for most companies and seldom are applied to consolidated subsidiaries.

Determination of the Method Being Used

Before you attempt to prepare a consolidated worksheet, you need to know which of the three methods is being used by the parent to record its investment in the subsidiary. You cannot begin to eliminate the intercompany investment until that is determined. The most efficient approach is to

1. Test for the use of the cost method. If the cost method is used:

    a) *The investment account will be at the original cost shown on the determination and distribution of excess schedule.*

    b) *The parent will have recorded as its share of subsidiary income its ownership interest times the dividends declared by the subsidiary. In most cases, this income will be called "subsidiary dividend income," but some may call it "subsidiary income" or "dividend income."*

2. If the method used is not cost, check for the use of simple equity as follows:

   a) *The investment account will not be at the original cost.*

   b) *The parent will have recorded as subsidiary income its ownership percentage times the reported net income of the subsidiary.*

3. If the method used is neither cost nor simple equity, it must be the sophisticated equity method. Confirm that it is by noting that

   a) *The investment account will not be at the original cost.*

   b) *The parent will have recorded as subsidiary income its ownership percentage times the reported net income of the subsidiary minus the amortizations of excess for the current period.*

Complicated Purchase, Several Causes of Excess

In Worksheets 3-1 through 3-4, it was assumed that the entire excess of cost over book value was attributable to goodwill. In reality, this assumption seldom will be true. The following example illustrates a more complicated purchase.

Paulos Company paid $790,000 to obtain 8,000 shares (80% interest) of Carlos Company on January 1, 19X1. In addition, $10,000 of direct acquisition costs were paid by Paulos Company. At the time of the purchase, Carlos Company had the following summarized balance sheet:

	Carlos Company Balance Sheet January 1, 19X1			
Assets			**Liabilities and Equity**	
Inventory		$ 75,000	Current liabilities	$ 50,000
Land		150,000	Bonds payable, 6%,	
Building	$600,000		due Dec. 31, 19X4	200,000
Less accumulated depreciation	300,000	300,000	Common stock ($10 par)	100,000
			Paid-in capital in excess of par	150,000
Equipment	$150,000		Retained earnings	250,000
Less accumulated depreciation	50,000	100,000		
Goodwill		125,000		
Total assets		$750,000	Total liabilities and equity	$750,000

The market values for Carlos Company's tangible assets and long-term liabilities on January 1, 19X1, are as follows:

		Market Values
Inventory		$ 80,000
Land		200,000
Building (20-year remaining life)		500,000
Equipment (5-year remaining life)		80,000
Bonds payable based on current 8% market interest rate as follows:		
Present value of interest payment at 8% ($12,000 annual interest × 4-year, 8% present value of annuity factor of 3.31213)	$ 39,746	
Present value of principal ($200,000 × 4-year, 8% present value factor of .73503)	147,006	186,752

Based on these market values, the determination and distribution of excess schedule, below, is prepared. Zone analysis indicated that the price paid is high enough to record goodwill on the parent's interest. This also means that the parent's share of full market value for all accounts will be recorded.

This determination and distribution of excess schedule calculates an excess of cost of $400,000 on the interest acquired; $14,598 of this excess is consumed by the revaluation of the priority accounts (current assets and liabilities). This leaves $385,402 available for remaining fixed assets. Previously recorded goodwill applicable to the controlling interest is added to the total excess available for long-lived assets. This makes $485,402 available to increase fixed assets, which is more than is needed. The balance of the excess after adjustment of fixed assets is $301,402. The amount of $301,402 is the total goodwill applicable to the controlling interest.

The determination and distribution schedule includes the amortization period for adjustments and the annual amount of amortization. This procedure will expedite the preparation of the consolidated worksheet.

Company P and Subsidiary Company S
Determination and Distribution of Excess Schedule
January 1, 19X1

	Company	Controlling Percent	Controlling Interest		
Price paid for investment including direct acquisition costs:....................			$800,000		
Market value of total assets:	$623,248	80%	498,598		
Market value of priority accounts	(156,752)	80	(125,402)		
Analysis of price: **Goodwill**....................			301,402		

	Total	Controlling		Amort. Periods	Controlling Amortization
Price paid for investment........................		$ 800,000			
Less book value interest acquired:					
Common stock ($10 par)	$100,000				
Paid-in capital in excess of par	150,000				
Retained earnings	250,000				
Total stockholders' equity..................	$500,000				
Interest acquired	80%	400,000			
Excess of cost over book value (debit).............		**$400,000**			
Adjustment of priority accounts:					
Inventory, 80% × $5,000		**$ 4,000**	Dr.	1	$ 4,000
Discount on bonds payable, 80% × $13,248		**10,598**	Dr.	4	2,650
Available for fixed assets:.....................		$ 385,402			
Add: Existing goodwill, 80% × $125,000		100,000	Cr.	10	(10,000)
Adjusted available for fixed assets:..............		$ 485,402			
Land, 80% × $50,000..................		**40,000**	Dr.		
Building, 80% × $200,000		**160,000**	Dr.	20	8,000
Equipment 80% × $20,000..............		**(16,000)**	Cr.	5	(3,200)
Goodwill (confirmed)		**$301,402**	Dr.	10	30,140
Net adjustment to goodwill ($301,402 − $100,000) .	$201,402			10	20,140

For the sake of simplicity and ease of understanding, the discount on the bonds that results from revaluation is being amortized on a straight-line basis over 4 years. As an alternative, effective interest amortization could be used. The amortization schedule would be as follows:

Period	Payment	8% Interest	Amortization	Balance	Controlling Amortization (80%)
0				186,752	
1	12,000	14,940	2,940	189,692	2,352
2	12,000	15,175	3,175	192,867	2,540
3	12,000	15,429	3,429	196,296	2,743
4	12,000	15,704	3,704	200,000	2,963

Theoretically, the plant asset adjustments required by the determination and distribution of excess schedule should be made in a manner that would eliminate all accumulated depreciation applicable to the controlling interest as of the purchase date. This procedure would complicate future worksheets. As a practical alternative, when possible, the plant asset adjustments should be made in such a way as to reduce accumulated depreciation, and adjustments should never increase accumulated depreciation. Therefore, the increase in the net value of the building was accomplished by decreasing its accumulated depreciation account, not by increasing the asset account. The reduction in the equipment was accomplished by decreasing the asset account rather than increasing its accumulated depreciation account.

Additional goodwill is recorded applicable only to the controlling interest. Recall from Chapter 2 that the controlling interest's share of existing goodwill is made available for distribution to fixed assets. In the above example, $100,000 of goodwill was made available for distribution to fixed assets, but it was not needed. Total goodwill applicable to the controlling interest is $301,402, a net increase of $201,402. The $25,000 of original goodwill on the books of S Company, which applies to the minority interest, is not altered and will remain a part of goodwill on the consolidated balance sheet. That means that the total goodwill on the acquisition date is $326,402 ($25,000 minority share plus $301,402 controlling share). The amortization of goodwill adjustment on the worksheet is always based on the net change in goodwill, $201,402 ÷ 10 years in this example.

Worksheet 3-5, pages 3-68 to 3-71, is a consolidated financial statements worksheet for Paulos Company and Carlos Company one year after the acquisition. During the year, Carlos had a net income of $60,000 and declared $20,000 in dividends. Paulos Company shows the following simple-equity-adjusted balance for its investment in Carlos:

Original cost	$800,000
80% of 19X1 income of $60,000	48,000
80% of $20,000 dividends declared by Carlos	(16,000)
Investment balance, December 31, 19X1	$832,000

Carefully review Worksheet 3-5 for the procedures used the first period of consolidated reporting:

■   The excess of cost over book value is distributed in entries (3a) through (3e). Entry (3a) reflects the increase in inventory. Since the inventory was assumed to be sold during the year, the adjustment goes to the cost of goods sold.

■ The (4) series entries amortize excess adjustments for the current year. Since it is the first year of consolidation, there are no adjustments for prior periods (that occurs in Worksheet 3-6). There is no entry in (4a) since inventory is not amortized but is just charged to the cost of goods sold in the period it is sold. There is no entry (4e) since adjustments to land are not amortized because land is a nondepreciable asset.

■ The income distribution schedules require careful study. All excess amortizations are charged to the controlling interest schedule. Recall that only the controlling share of account adjustments is acknowledged. This means that all subsequent amortizations are charged only to the controlling interest.

At this point, it should be understood that the amortizations of excess cost applicable to fixed assets and goodwill could become even more complex than they are in Worksheet 3-5. The amortization adjustments found in entries (4c) and (4d) divide the applicable excess by the assets' remaining lives as shown in the determination and distribution of excess schedule. It was implicitly assumed that the amortization periods were the assets' remaining lives used by the subsidiary and the subsidiary used straight-line depreciation. If the subsidiary had used an alternative depreciation method, that method would have been applied to the excess. It may occur that the parent company does not wish to use the subsidiary's depreciation method and/or remaining life. In this case, the parent would recompute depreciation, based on its ownership interest in the asset. The recomputed amount would be compared to the parent's ownership interest in the subsidiary's recorded depreciation expense, and the difference would become the amortization adjustment for the period. It was also assumed that the period used to amortize additional goodwill, entry (4f), was the amortization period in use for existing goodwill on the subsidiary's books. The parent may use an amortization period for goodwill that differs from that being used by the subsidiary. If that is the case, the goodwill amortization adjustment on the worksheet would be calculated as follows:

> Amortization of the parent's total interest in goodwill (additional goodwill resulting from the purchase plus controlling percentage of goodwill on subsidiary books), using the parent company amortization period
>
> Minus
>
> The controlling percentage of goodwill amortization recorded by the subsidiary.

Worksheet 3-6, pages 3-72 to 3-75, is the worksheet for the second year of combined operations for the purchase that was analyzed in Worksheet 3-5. The second year is included to emphasize that **each year the consolidation starts anew from the separate trial balances of the two companies.** None of the eliminations made on the previous period's worksheet are reflected in the 19X2 separate trial balances of Paulos Company and Carlos Company.

The following information may be inferred from the trial balance figures in Worksheet 3–6:

1. Carlos reported a net income of $100,000 for 19X2 and declared $20,000 in dividends. This income is based on the asset values maintained on Carlos' books, and does not reflect revaluations caused by the 80% purchase by Paulos.

2. The investment in Carlos' account reflects:

Investment balance, December 31, 19X1	$832,000
80% of 19X2 net income of $100,000	80,000
80% of $20,000 dividends declared by Carlos	(16,000)
Balance, December 31, 19X2	$896,000

3. Paulos recorded subsidiary income of $80,000, which is 80% of Carlos' reported net income.

4. The January 1, 19X2 balance in the Paulos retained earnings account is derived as follows:

Balance, January 1, 19X1	$700,000
19X1 income generated by Paulos Company	80,000
Subsidiary income under the simple equity method . . .	48,000
Balance, January 1, 19X2	$828,000

5. The $828,000 balance in the Paulos retained earnings account reflects 80% of the reported net income of Carlos and does not include adjustments resulting from the amortizations of the excess of the price paid for the 80% interest. These amortizations appear only on the consolidated worksheet.

The only major difference between Worksheets 3-5 and 3-6 is that Worksheet 3-6 includes amortization of excess adjustments for the prior period. Notice that the inventory adjustment, (4a), is charged to controlling retained since it was sold in a prior period. Adjustments (4b), (4c), (4d), and (4f) for the prior year's amortization are also made to controlling retained. There is no entry (4e) since there is no amortization for the adjustment to land. If we were to prepare a worksheet for December 31, 19X3, there would be two years of prior amortization for the above adjustments.

Intraperiod Purchase under the Simple Equity Method

The accountant will be required to apply specialized procedures when consolidating a controlling investment in common stock that is acquired during the fiscal year. When such an acquisition is deemed to be a purchase, the determination and distribution of excess schedule must be based on the subsidiary stockholders' equity on the interim purchase date, including the subsidiary retained earnings balance on that date. A further complication under purchase accounting is that the combined net income of the consolidated company, as derived on the worksheet, is to include only subsidiary income earned subsequent to the purchase date.

There are two options available for consolidating an intraperiod purchase. The first option is to require the subsidiary to close its books as of the purchase date. This procedure would make retained earnings on the acquisition date available for use in the determination and distribution of excess schedule and would mean that the consolidated worksheet would include only the operations of the subsidiary subsequent to the purchase date. The second and more realistic option is to modify the determination and distribution of excess schedule to include the purchased share of undistributed income for the portion of the year prior to the purchase. Then, it is possible to include the operations of the subsidiary for the entire fiscal year in the consolidated worksheet.

Option 1: Subsidiary Books Closed.   Company S has the following trial balance on July 1, 19X1, the date of an 80% purchase by Company P:

Current Assets	68,000	
Equipment	80,000	
Accumulated Depreciation		30,000
Liabilities		10,000
Common Stock ($10 par)		50,000
Retained Earnings, January 1, 19X1		45,000
Dividends Declared	5,000	
Sales		90,000
Cost of Goods Sold	60,000	
Expenses	12,000	
Total	225,000	225,000

If Company P requires Company S to close its nominal accounts as of July 1, Company S would increase its retained earnings account by $13,000 with the following entries:

Sales	90,000	
Cost of Goods Sold		60,000
Expenses		12,000
Retained Earnings		18,000
Retained Earnings	5,000	
Dividends Declared		5,000

Assume Company P pays $106,400 for its 80% interest in Company S. Assume also that all assets have market values equal to book value and that any excess is attributed to goodwill with a 10-year life. The determination and distribution of excess schedule would be as follows:

	Company	Controlling Percent	Controlling Interest			
Price paid for investment including						
direct acquisition costs:			$106,400			
Market value of total net assets:	$108,000	80%	86,400			
Market value of priority accounts	58,000	80	46,400			
Analysis of price: **Goodwill**			20,000			
	Total	Controlling				
Price paid for investment		$106,400				
Less book value interest acquired:						
Common stock ($10 par)	$ 50,000					
Retained earnings, July 1, 19X1	58,000					
Total stockholders' equity	$108,000					
Interest acquired	80%	86,400			Amort.	Controlling
Excess of cost over book value (debit)		$ 20,000			Periods	Amortization
Goodwill		**$ 20,000**		**Dr.**	**10**	**$2,000**

Proceeding to the end of the year, assume that the operations of Company S for the last six months result in a net income of $20,000 and dividends of $5,000 are declared by Company S on December 31. Worksheet 3-7, pages 3-76 to 3-79, includes Company S nominal accounts for only the second six-month period since the nominal accounts were closed on July 1. Company S Retained Earnings shows the July 1, 19X1 balance. The trial balance of Company P includes operations for the entire year. The subsidiary income listed by Company P includes 80% of the subsidiary's $20,000 second six-months' income. Company P's investment account balance shows

Original cost	$106,400
80% of subsidiary's second six-months' income of $20,000	16,000
80% of $5,000 dividends declared by subsidiary on Dec. 31	(4,000)
Investment balance, December 31, 19X1	$118,400

In conformance with purchase theory, the Consolidated Income Statement column of Worksheet 3-7 includes only subsidiary income earned after the acquisition date. Likewise, only subsidiary income earned after the purchase date is distributed to the minority and controlling interests. Income earned and dividends declared prior to the purchase date by Company S are reflected in its July 1, 19X1 retained earnings balance, of which the minority is granted its share. The notes to the statements would have to disclose what the income of the consolidated company would have been had the purchase occurred at the start of the year.

Option 2: Subsidiary Books Not Closed.   Usually, a subsidiary does not close its books as a result of the parent company's securing a controlling interest in its stock. Normally, the parent company is able to ascertain the income earned by the subsidiary between the beginning of the year and the date control is achieved. If the subsidiary has already declared dividends as of the time of the acquisition, these dividends would be deducted in arriving at the total subsidiary equity interest as of that date.

Assume the parent had access to the Company S trial balance shown in Option 1, but Company S did not close its books as of July 1, 19X1. Company P would prepare its determination and distribution of excess schedule as follows:

	Company	Controlling Percent	Controlling Interest
Price paid for investment including direct acquisition costs:			$106,400
Market value of total net assets:	$108,000	80%	86,400
Market value of priority accounts	58,000	80	46,400
Analysis of price: **Goodwill**			20,000

	Total	Controlling			
Price paid for investment		$106,400			
Less book value interest acquired:					
Common stock ($10 par)	$ 50,000				
Retained earnings, July 1, 19X1	45,000				
Income of Co. S, Jan. 1 – July 1	**18,000**				
Dividends declared, Jan. 1 – July 1	**(5,000)**				
Total stockholders' equity	$108,000				
Interest acquired	80%	86,400		Amort.	Controlling
Excess of cost over book value (debit)		$ 20,000		Periods	Amortization
Goodwill		**$20,000**		**Dr. 10**	**$2,000**

 Since the subsidiary did not close its books as of July 1, 19X1, Worksheet 3-8, pages 3-80 to 3-83, includes the Company S trial balance reflecting the entire year's operations. The Company S retained earnings account is dated January 1, 19X1. The Company P investment and subsidiary income accounts are identical to those in Worksheet 3-7.

The challenge is to create date alignment. The investment account balance and the retained earnings of the subsidiary must be adjusted to the same point in time. The investment account is as of July 1, 19X1, while the retained earnings of the subsidiary are as of January 1, 19X1. This problem is solved by using a temporary account, *Purchased Income*, to record the current-year income already earned as of July 1 by the subsidiary that was purchased by the parent. This would be 80% of the $18,000 subsidiary income earned during the first six months. Purchased income is included in step (2), which can be explained in journal entry form as follows:

Common Stock, Company S	40,000	
Retained Earnings, **Jan. 1, 19X1**, Company S	36,000	
Purchased Income[1]	14,400	
Dividends declared[2]		4,000
Investment in Company S		86,400

1 Parent share of income earned in the first six months which was included in the equity interest purchased (80% × $18,000)
2 Prior to the purchase date and deducted from subsidiary equity at time of purchase (80% × $5,000)

In Worksheet 3-8, the nominal accounts of the subsidiary for the entire year are included in the consolidated income column. Since 80% of the income earned in the first half of the year belonged to outside interests (shareholders that are no longer members of the affiliated group), Purchased Income must be deleted to arrive at the combined net income that belongs to current members of the affiliated group. As with the income, 80% of the dividends declared by the subsidiary prior to the purchase also belonged to outside interests and must be eliminated. However, this elimination does **not** affect the consolidated income statement. Note that the minority interest existed for the entire year; thus, it is permitted a **20% share** of subsidiary income for the **full** year. Worksheet 3-8 leads to the following unique income statement:

Company P and Subsidiary Company S Consolidated Income Statement For Year Ended December 31, 19X1	
Sales	$682,000
Cost of goods sold	(470,000)
Gross profit	$212,000
Other expenses.	(95,000)
Total net income of Company P and Company S for year 19X1	$117,000
Income earned by outside interests existing prior to **Company P purchase**	**(14,400)**
Combined net income	$102,600
Minority interest	(7,600)
Consolidated net income	$ 95,000

The format of this income statement has the advantage of disclosing the total net income of the two companies for the year and the consolidated net income. The total net income for the year becomes the basis for a pro forma statement of what income would have been if the combination had occurred at the beginning of the year. This figure would need to be supplemented only by a disclosure that there would have been an additional $1,000 of equipment depreciation for the first six months of the year. The disclosure is required by APB Opinion No. 16 (par. 96) for intraperiod purchases.

Special care must be taken in consolidating an intraperiod purchase in subsequent periods. It is common to find that a company has made an error by taking a full year's share of equity income in the period of acquisition rather than including only income earned after the date of acquisition. When this error is found, a correcting entry should be recorded by the parent.

Intraperiod Purchase under the Cost Method

There are only two variations of the procedures discussed in the preceding section if the cost method is used by the parent company to record its investment in the subsidiary:

1. During the year of acquisition, the parent would record as income only its share of dividends declared by the subsidiary. Thus, eliminating entries would be confined to the intercompany dividends.
2. In subsequent years, the cost-to-equity conversion adjustment would be based on the change in the subsidiary retained earnings balance **from the intraperiod purchase date** to the beginning of the year for which the worksheet is being prepared.

Pooling of Interests: Subsequent to Acquisition

In a pooling of interests, worksheet procedures in subsequent periods are simple if the original acquisition is recorded properly. Since there is no excess of cost over book value in a pooling, the amortizations of the excess are not present. For example, assume that on January 1, 19X1, Company I issued 2,700 shares of its $2 par stock ($15 market value) for a 90% interest in Company C. Assume Company C had the following condensed balance sheet:

Assets		Liabilities and Equity	
Current assets	$10,000	Liabilities.	$10,000
Property, plant, and		Common stock ($10 par)	10,000
equipment (net)	30,000	Retained earnings.	20,000
Total assets	$40,000	Total liabilities and equity. . . .	$40,000

The following net income figures were reported by Company C subsequent to the acquisition date:

19X1	$20,000
19X2	15,000
19X3 (current year)	25,000

Pooling rules require the issuer to record the investment at the book value of the underlying equity. Thus, Company I would have recorded the original acquisition as follows:

Investment in Company C (90% × $30,000 total Company C equity) . . .	27,000	
Common Stock (2,700 shares × $2 par)		5,400
Paid-In Capital in Excess of Par (90% of Company C Paid-In		
Capital = $9,000, less $5,400 assigned to par)		3,600
Retained Earnings (90% × $20,000 Company C January 1, 19X1		
Retained Earnings)		18,000

 Worksheet 3-9, pages 3-84 and 3-85, is a consolidated financial statements worksheet for Companies I and C on December 31, 19X3. The balance in the investment in Company C account is the result of Company I's use of the equity method, as follows:

Original recorded value on January 1, 19X1	$27,000
90% × Company C 19X1 income of $20,000	18,000
90% × Company C 19X2 income of $15,000	13,500
90% × Company C 19X3 income of $25,000	22,500
Equity-adjusted balance, December 31, 19X3	$81,000

An investment initially might be recorded properly as a pooling and not be equity adjusted in subsequent periods. When an investment deemed to be a pooling is maintained at cost, a simple equity conversion entry may be made to update the investment account to its beginning-of-the-period balance. After the conversion, eliminations proceed as under the simple equity method, except that the elimination entry is limited to the intercompany dividends. The conversion procedures follow those used in Worksheets 3-3 and 3-4 for an investment recorded at cost. The sophisticated equity method is not used because there are no amortizations of excess.

Also, it may occur that the investment was originally recorded incorrectly at market value. This complication was discussed in Chapter 2. If this situation is encountered, it is suggested that the investment account be corrected to reflect the book value of the investment prior to proceeding to the consolidated worksheet. The investment account should be adjusted to the correct balance under either the cost or equity method, depending on the issuer's desires.

Intraperiod Pooling

Recall that under pooling theory, the incomes of the parent and the subsidiary are to be **consolidated at the beginning of the year, regardless of when control is achieved during the year.** Thus, there is no reason to close the subsidiary's books on the date control is achieved. Closing the books would, in fact, hinder the preparation of consolidated statements. Worksheets for consolidated financial statements must begin with a trial balance of the subsidiary that includes the entire year's operations and the beginning-of-the-year balance for the subsidiary retained earnings account. **Since consolidation procedures are applied retroactively to the beginning of the year,** the entire incomes of the parent and the subsidiary are distributed to the controlling and minority interests. No income is regarded as earned by outside interests. In summary, the consolidation procedures are identical to those used when the controlling investment has been made at the beginning of the year.

Summary: Worksheet Technique

At this point, it is wise to review the overall mechanical procedures used to prepare a consolidated worksheet. It will help you to have this set of procedures at your side for the first few worksheets you do. Later, the process will become automatic. The following procedures are designed to provide for both efficiency and correctness:

1. When recopying the trial balances, always sum them before you proceed with the eliminations. At this point, you want to be sure that there are no errors in transporting figures to the worksheet. An amazing number of students' consolidated balance sheets are out of balance because their trial balances did not balance to begin with.
2. Carefully key all eliminations to aid future reference. It is suggested that a symbol, such as an asterisk, a line, or a circle, be used to identify each worksheet adjustment entry that affects combined net income. This identification will make it easier to locate the adjustments that must be posted later to the income distribution schedules. Recall that any adjustment to income must be assigned to one of the company's income distribution schedules. This second

step will become particularly important in the next two chapters where there will be many adjustments to income.

3.   Sum the eliminations to be sure that they balance before you begin to extend the account totals.

4.   Now that the eliminations are completed, horizontally determine account totals and then extend them to the appropriate worksheet column. Extend each account in the order that it appears on the trial balance. Do not select just the accounts needed for a particular statement. For example, do not work only on the income statement. This can lead to errors. There may be some accounts that you will forget to extend, and you may not be aware of the errors until your balance sheet column total fails to equal zero. Extending each account in order assures that none will be overlooked and allows careful consideration of the appropriate destination of each account balance.

5.   Calculate combined net income.

6.   Prepare income distribution schedules. Verify that the sum of the distributions equals the combined net income on the worksheet. Distribute the minority interest in income to the Minority Interest column and distribute the controlling interest in income to the Controlling Retained Earnings column.

7.   Sum the Minority Interest column and extend that total to the Consolidated Balance Sheet column. Sum the Controlling Retained Earnings column and extend that total to the Consolidated Balance Sheet column as well.

8.   Verify that the Consolidated Balance Sheet column total equals zero (or that the totals are equal if two columns are used).

Appendix A: The Vertical Worksheet

This chapter has used the *horizontal format* for its worksheet examples. Columns for eliminations and adjustments, consolidated income, minority interest, controlling retained earnings, and the balance sheet are arranged horizontally in adjacent columns. This format makes it convenient to extend account balances from one column to the next. This is the format that you used for trial balance working papers in introductory and intermediate accounting. It is also the most common worksheet format used in practice. The horizontal format will be used in all nonappendix worksheets in subsequent chapters and in all worksheet problems unless otherwise stated.

The alternative format is the *vertical format*. Rather than beginning the worksheet with the trial balances of the parent and the subsidiary, this format begins with the completed income statements, statements of retained earnings, and the balance sheets of the parent and subsidiary. This method, which is seldom used in practice and harder to master, commonly is used on the CPA Exam. Its appeal to the CPA Exam probably is that it fits on a single page and eliminates the need for foldout worksheets.

The vertical format is used in Worksheet 3-10 on pages 3-86 and 3-87. This worksheet is based on the same facts used for Worksheet 3-6 (an equity method example for the second year of a purchase with a complicated distribution of excess cost). Worksheet 3-10 is based on the determination and distribution of excess schedule shown on page 3-16.

Note that the original separate statements are stacked vertically upon each other. Be sure to follow the carrydown procedure as it is applied to the separate statements. The net income from the income statement is carried down to the retained earnings statement. Then, the ending retained earnings balance is carried down to the balance sheet. Later, this same carrydown procedure is applied to the consolidated statements.

Understand that there are no differences in the elimination and adjustment procedures as a result of this alternative format. Compare the elimination entries to those in Worksheet 3-6. Even though there is no change in the eliminations, there are two areas of caution. First, the order in which the accounts appear is reversed; that is, nominal accounts precede balance sheet accounts. This difference in order will require care in making eliminations. Second, the eliminations to retained earnings must be made against the January 1 beginning balances, not the December 31 ending balances. The ending retained earnings balances are never adjusted but are derived after all eliminations have been made.

The complicated aspect of the vertical worksheet is the carrydown procedure used to create the retained earnings statement and the balance sheet. Arrows are used in Worksheet 3-10 to emphasize the carrydown procedure. Note that the net income line in the retained earnings statement and the retained earnings lines on the balance sheet are never available to receive eliminations. These balances are always carried down. The net income balances are derived from the same income distribution schedules used in Worksheet 3-6.

Appendix B: Tax-Related Adjustments

Recall from Chapter 1 that a deferred tax liability results when the market value of an asset may not be used in future depreciation calculations for tax purposes. (This occurs when the purchase is a *tax-free exchange* as to the seller.) In this situation, future depreciation charges for tax purposes must be based on the book value of the asset, and a liability should be acknowledged in the determination and distribution of excess schedule by creating a deferred tax liability account. Consider the following determination and distribution of excess schedule for a subsidiary that has a building with a book value for tax purposes of $120,000 and a market value of $200,000. Assuming a tax rate of 30%, there is a deferred tax liability of $24,000 ($80,000 excess of market value over tax basis × 30%).

As is true in all determination and distribution of excess schedules, any remaining unallocated value becomes goodwill. In the case of a tax-free exchange, the remaining unallocated value is the amount available for goodwill **less the applicable deferred tax liability.** In the example which follows, the remaining unallocated value on the determination and distribution of excess schedule is $44,000. The $44,000 excess is what is left after a 30% deferred tax liability is recorded. The goodwill to be recorded is, therefore, $44,000 divided by the net of tax rate of 70% which equals $62,857. The deferred tax liability is 30% of the goodwill recorded (30% × $62,857 = $18,857).

Price paid for investment		$ 600,000
Less interest acquired:		
Common stock	$100,000	
Retained earnings	400,000	
Total stockholders' equity	$500,000	
Interest acquired	100%	500,000
Excess of cost over book value (debit balance)		$100,000
Available for long-lived assets:		
Building		80,000 Dr.
Deferred tax liability, building		**(24,000) Cr.**
Goodwill (net of deferred tax liability)		**$ 44,000 Dr.**
Distributed as follows:		
Goodwill ($44,000 ÷ 70%)		$ 62,857
Deferred tax liability (30% × $62,857)		**(18,857)**
Net goodwill		$ 44,000

The worksheet entry to distribute the excess of cost over book value would be as follows:

Building (to market value)	80,000	
Goodwill (balance of excess)	62,857	
Deferred Tax Liability **($24,000 + $18,857)**		42,857
Investment in Subsidiary S (excess cost after elimination of		
subsidiary equity)		100,000

Worksheet eliminations will be simpler if each deferred tax liability is recorded below the asset to which it relates. It is possible that inventory could have a market value in excess of its book value used for tax purposes. This, too, would require the recognition of a deferred tax liability.

Recall the general rule that the market values of the liabilities are acknowledged in full even in a bargain purchase. There is an exception to this rule with respect to the deferred tax liability that results from recording the market value adjustments made in a purchase: **The deferred tax liability has the same priority as the asset to which it relates.** For instance, since inventory always is adjusted to full market value, the deferred tax liability related to inventory is recognized fully as well. In the case of a long-lived asset, only a portion of the difference between book and market value is recorded in a bargain purchase; thus, the deferred tax liability is limited to the portion of the market–book value disparity that is recorded.

The need to recognize the deferred tax liability may complicate the distribution of the excess. Assume we have an asset that has a market value estimated to exceed its book value by $150,000, but there is only $70,000 of excess available to distribute to the asset. Assuming a 30% tax rate, the excess would be divided by 70%, or the net-of-tax percentage, to arrive at the amount to allocate to the asset itself—in this case, $100,000 ($70,000 ÷ 70%); thus 30% of the $100,000 would be recognized as related deferred tax liability. The $70,000 excess of cost would be distributed as follows:

Excess of cost over book value available		$70,000
Adjustment of long-lived assets:		
Asset	$100,000	
Deferred tax liability	(30,000)	70,000
		$ 0

A second tax complication arises when the subsidiary has tax loss carryovers. To the extent that the tax loss carryovers are not recorded or are reduced by a valuation allowance by the subsidiary on its balance sheet, the carryovers may be an asset to be considered in the determination and distribution of excess schedule. When a tax-free exchange occurs during the accounting period, a portion of the tax loss carry-over may be used during that period.[2] The amount that may be used is the acquiring company's tax liability for the year times the percentage of the year that the companies were under common control. If, for example, the acquiring company's tax liability was $100,000 and the purchase occurred on April 1, ¾ of $100,000 or $75,000 of the tax loss carryover could be utilized. This portion of the carryover is a current asset which makes it a priority account for asset valuation purposes. The current portion of the tax loss carryover is recorded as *Current Deferred Tax Expense*. Any remaining carryover is carried forward and recorded as a noncurrent asset using the account, *Noncurrent Deferred Tax Expense*. If it is probable that the deferred tax expense will not be fully realized, a contra-valuation allowance is provided. The

---

2 Section 381 (c)(1)(B) of the Federal Tax Code.

Noncurrent Deferred Tax Expense is a nonpriority account and should not be recorded at full market value in a bargain purchase. Instead, it should be one of several possible long-lived assets that is subject to the allocation procedure.[3]

Let us consider the example of a subsidiary that has the following tax loss carryovers on the date of purchase:

Tax loss carryover to be used in current period $100,000
Tax loss carryover to be used in future periods   200,000

Assume that the parent has anticipated future tax liabilities against which the tax loss carryovers may be offset and has a 30% tax rate. A determination and distribution of excess schedule would be prepared as follows:

	Company			Amort.	Controlling
Price paid for investment including					
direct acquisition costs:	$895,000				
Market value of total net assets:	790,000				
Market value of priority accounts.	100,000				
Analysis of price: **Goodwill (net of**					
deferred tax liability)	**105,000**				
Price paid for investment		$ 895,000			
Less book value interest acquired:					
Common stock	$300,000				
Retained earnings.	400,000				
Total stockholders' equity	$700,000				
Interest acquired.	100%	700,000		Amort.	Controlling
Excess of cost over book value (debit)		**$195,000**		Periods	Amortization
Adjustment of priority accounts:					
Current Deferred Tax Expense					
(30% × $100,000)		**30,000**	Dr.	**1**	
Remaining excess:		$165,000			
Noncurrent Deferred Tax Expense					
(30% × $200,000)		**60,000**	Dr.	**Note 1**	
Goodwill (net of deferred tax liability)		$105,000			
Goodwill adjustment distributed as follows:					
Goodwill, gross ($105,000 ÷ 70%)		$150,000	Dr.	10	$15,000
Deferred tax liability (30% × $150,000)		(45,000)	Cr.	10	(4,500)
Net goodwill		$105,000			

Note 1: depends on income in future periods

---

[3] There is a limit on the annual amount of tax loss carryforward that can be utilized. It is equal to the market value of the acquired company's stock on the purchase date multiplied by the highest of the Federal long-term tax-exempt rate for the three calendar months before the exchange. Section 382 of the Federal Tax Code.

The **worksheet entry** to distribute the excess would be

Current deferred tax expense	30,000	
Noncurrent deferred tax expense	60,000	
Goodwill	150,000	
Investment in Subsidiary S (excess after elimination of subsidiary equity)		195,000
Deferred tax liability (applicable to goodwill)		45,000

Comprehensive Example.   Both of the preceding tax issues will complicate the consolidated worksheet. Our example will consider the distribution of the tax adjustments on the worksheet and the resulting amortization adjustments needed to calculate consolidated net income. We will consider a nontaxable exchange with fixed asset and goodwill adjustments in addition to a tax loss carryover.

Assume that Paro Company purchased an 80% interest in Sunstran Corporation on January 1, 19X1. Paro expects to utilize $100,000 of tax loss carryovers in the current period, and $250,000 in future periods.[4] The following determination and distribution of excess schedule was prepared:

	Company	Controlling Percent	Controlling Interest			
Price paid for investment including direct acquisition costs:			$990,000			
Market value of total net assets:	$1,045,000	80%	836,000			
Market value of priority accounts.	280,000	80	224,000			
Analysis of price: **Goodwill (net of deferred tax liability)**			154,000			

	Total	Controlling		Amort. Periods	Controlling Amortization
Price paid for investment		$990,000			
Less book value interest acquired:					
Common stock ($10 par)	$ 100,000				
Paid-in capital excess of par	300,000				
Retained earnings	400,000				
Total stockholders' equity	$ 800,000				
Interest acquired	80%	640,000			
Excess of cost over book value (debit)		$350,000			
Adjustment of priority accounts:					
Current deferred tax expense (30% × 80% interest × $100,000)		**24,000**	Dr.	1	**$24,000**
Available for nonpriority accounts		$326,000			
Building, 80% × $200,000		160,000	Dr.	20	8,000
Deferred tax liability (Building), 30% × $160,000		**(48,000)**	Cr.	**20**	**(2,400)**

---

4 Considers tax limitations and assumes full realizability of tax loss carryovers.

Noncurrent deferred tax expense

(30% × 80% interest × $250,000).	**60,000**	**Dr.**	**Note 1**	
Goodwill (net of deferred tax liability)	$154,000			

Goodwill adjustment distributed as follows:

Goodwill, gross ($154,000 ÷ 70%)	$220,000	Dr.	10	22,000
Deferred tax liability				
(30% × $220,000)	**(66,000)**	**Cr.**	**10**	**(6,600)**
Net goodwill	$154,000			

Note 1: depends on income in future periods but must be consumed in 20 years or less.

 Worksheet 3-11, pages 3-88 to 3-91, is the consolidated worksheet for Paro Company and its subsidiary, Sunstran Corporation, at the end of 19X1. Unlike previous worksheets, the nominal accounts of both firms include a 30% provision for tax on internally generated net income (Paro does not include a tax on subsidiary income recorded). The calculation of the tax liabilities for affiliated firms is discussed further in Chapter 6. It should be noted, however, that Paro has reduced its tax provision for the benefit of the current deferred tax asset of $24,000 that resulted from the purchase ($100,000 current tax loss carryover × 80% interest × 30%). Paro's income before tax is $800,000. The 30% tax provision would be $240,000. The $240,000 has been reduced $24,000 for the benefit of the tax savings attributable to the current tax loss carryover. Since the deferred tax asset had not been recorded on the separate books, the tax savings was subtracted from the current year's provision. Since the deferred tax asset results from the purchase of the subsidiary, it is first recorded on the consolidated worksheet. The tax provision recorded by the subsidiary was also calculated using depreciation based on the building's book value and did not include any amortization of goodwill.

The procedures to eliminate the investment account are the same as for previous examples using the equity method. Notice that entry (3a) distributes $24,000 of the excess to the Provision for Tax account. The deferred tax asset has already been recorded by the parent as a reduction in its tax provision. This entry increases the provision and properly accounts for the $24,000 as the consumption of the $24,000 deferred tax asset included in the purchase price. Entry (3b) debits the Accumulated Depreciation—Building account to increase the net value of the building by $160,000, and entry (3c) records the related deferred tax loss liability resulting from the inability to depreciate the $160,000 increase for tax purposes. Entry (3d) records the non-current portion of the tax loss carryover. The goodwill resulting from the purchase is recorded in entry (3e). Entry (3f) records the deferred tax liability applicable to the goodwill which is not amortizable for tax purposes when the original purchase is a nontaxable exchange.

As a result of the increase in the net value of the building, entry (4b) increases depreciation by $8,000 for the year. Given the 30% tax rate, entry (4c) reduces the provision for the tax account by $2,400 as a result of the depreciation adjustment. This entry is not a reduction of the current taxes payable; instead, it is a reduction of the deferred tax liability recorded as part of the distribution of the excess cost—entry (3c). Remember that the deferred tax liability reflects the loss of future tax deductions caused by the difference between the building's higher market value and its lower book value on the date of purchase. Thus, the net result of this entry is to record the tax provision as if the tax deductions were allowable without changing the tax payable for the year. There is no amortization of the Noncurrent Deferred Tax Asset since it is not used in the current period. It will be amortized as an increase in the provision for tax in future periods in the same manner as was done for the current deferred tax asset in this period. Entry (4e) amortizes goodwill based on a 10-year life. Entry (4f) amortizes the deferred tax liability applicable to the goodwill amortization. Again, that entry, like (4c), reduces the current year's tax provision. All amortizations of excess and all tax adjustments are carried to the parent's income distribution schedule. This is again the case, since only the controlling share of all adjustments is recorded.

Questions

1. What is the difference between the simple equity method and the cost method? How can you tell which is being used by the parent?
2. Why doesn't it matter whether the cost method or the equity method is used to account for an investment when the consolidation process is required?
3. Describe the difference between the simple and sophisticated equity methods of accounting for an investment in a subsidiary. Explain why the difference is irrelevant when consolidated statements are to be prepared.
4. A parent company acquired an 80% interest in a subsidiary on Jan. 1, 19X1. The subsidiary reported net income of $20,000 for 19X1, and paid $10,000 in dividends. How will the parent record the income from the subsidiary on its records under the simple equity method, and under the cost method?
5. Describe the worksheet elimination procedures for the second year of control, under the simple equity and under the cost methods.
6. Assume that a parent company purchased an 80% interest in a subsidiary, at a price in excess of book value, and that subsidiary buildings were understated. The price also reflected goodwill. At the end of the first year, what are the components of the minority interest shown on the balance sheet? How is the minority interest displayed on the consolidated income statement and balance sheet?
7. Where there is a minority interest, does it share in all adjustments made to increase subsidiary accounts to market value?
8. In a purchase, the parent's share of the liabilities of the subsidiary is adjusted to reflect current market values at the time of acquisition. How are an undervalued and an overvalued subsidiary liability treated on the determination and distribution of excess schedule?
9. Prepare a skeleton outline of the parent and subsidiary income distribution schedule for a parent that owns an 80% interest in the subsidiary. Assume the purchase was at a cost in excess of book value, and that the excess was attributed to subsidiary buildings and to goodwill.
10. What effect does an intraperiod purchase have on the determination and distribution of excess schedule and on the worksheet covering the period of acquisition? What special disclosure is required on the consolidated income statement due to the intraperiod purchase?
11. In an intraperiod purchase, subsidiary income is allocated to three different interest groups in the year of acquisition. What are these groups?
12. How do the problems created by an intraperiod pooling differ from those created by an intraperiod purchase?

Exercises

Exercise 1.   Chaz Company purchased an 80% interest in Dove Company common stock for $340,000 cash on January 1, 19X1. At that time, Dove Company had the following balance sheet:

Assets		Liabilities and Equity	
Current assets	$ 60,000	Accounts payable	$ 60,000
Land	100,000	Common stock ($5 par)	50,000
Equipment	350,000	Paid-in capital in excess of par	100,000
Accumulated depreciation	(150,000)	Retained earnings	150,000
Total assets	$360,000	Total liabilities and equity	$360,000

Appraisals indicated that accounts are fairly stated except for the equipment which has a fair market value of $225,000 and a remaining life of 5 years. Any goodwill that results has an estimated life of 10 years.

Dove Company experienced the following changes in retained earnings during 19X1 and 19X2:

Retained earnings, January 1, 19X1		$120,000
Net income, 19X1	$60,000	
Dividends paid in 19X1	(10,000)	50,000
Balance, December 31, 19X1		170,000
Net income, 19X2	$40,000	
Dividends paid in 19X2	(10,000)	30,000
Balance, December 31, 19X2		$200,000

Prepare a determination and distribution of excess schedule for the investment in Dove Company. Prepare journal entries that Chaz Company would make on its books to record income earned and/or dividends received on its investment in Dove Company during 19X1 and 19X2 under the following methods: a) simple equity, b) sophisticated equity, and c) cost.

Exercise 2.   Island Corporation purchased a 75% interest in the common stock of Hang Ten Surf Company on January 1, 19X4, for $412,500 cash. Hang Ten had the following balance sheet on that date:

Assets		Liabilities and Equity	
Current assets	$ 80,000	Current liabilities	$ 50,000
Inventory	40,000	Common stock ($5 par)	50,000
Land	100,000	Paid-in capital in excess of par	150,000
Buildings and equipment (net) . . .	200,000	Retained earnings	200,000
Goodwill	30,000		
Total assets	$450,000	Total liabilities and equity	$450,000

Appraisals indicated that the book values for inventory and buildings and equipment are below fair market values. The inventory had a market value of $50,000 and was sold during 19X4. The buildings and equipment have an appraised market value of $300,000 and a remaining life of 20 years. Any goodwill, existing or new, has an estimated life of 10 years.

Hang Ten Surf Company reported the following income earned and dividends paid during 19X4 and 19X5:

Retained earnings, January 1, 19X4		$200,000
Net income, 19X4	$70,000	
Dividends paid in 19X4	(20,000)	50,000
Balance, December 31, 19X4		$250,000
Net income, 19X5	$48,000	
Dividends paid in 19X5	(20,000)	28,000
Balance, December 31, 19X5		$278,000

Prepare a determination and distribution of excess schedule for the investment in Hang Ten Surf Company and determine the balance in the Investment in Hang Ten Surf Company on Island Company's books as of December 31, 19X5, under the following methods that could be used by the parent, Island Company: a) simple equity, b) sophisticated equity, and c) cost.

Exercise 3. Aron Company purchased an 80% interest in Brewer Company for $230,000 in cash on January 1, 19X1, when Brewer Company had the following balance sheet:

Assets		Liabilities and Equity	
Current assets	$100,000	Current liabilities	$ 50,000
Property, plant, and		Common stock ($10 par)	100,000
equipment (net)	200,000	Retained earnings	150,000
Total assets	$300,000	Total liabilities and equity	$300,000

Any excess of the price paid over book value is attributable only to the plant assets, which have a 10-year remaining life. Aron Company uses the simple equity method to record its investment in Brewer Company.

The following trial balances of the two companies were prepared on December 31, 19X1

	Aron	Brewer
Current Assets	80,000	130,000
Property, Plant, and Equipment	400,000	200,000
Accumulated Depreciation	(106,000)	(20,000)
Investment in Brewer Company	246,000	
Current Liabilities	(60,000)	(40,000)
Common Stock ($10 par)	(300,000)	(100,000)
Retained Earnings, January 1, 19X1	(200,000)	(150,000)
Sales	(150,000)	(100,000)
Expenses	110,000	75,000
Subsidiary Income	(20,000)	
Dividends Declared . . . . -		5,000
Total	0	0

1. Prepare a determination and distribution of excess schedule for the investment.
2. Prepare all the eliminations and adjustments that would be made on the 19X1 consolidated worksheet.

(continued)

3. Prepare the 19X1 consolidated income statement and its related income distribution schedules.
4. Prepare the 19X1 consolidated balance sheet.

Exercise 4.   The trial balances of Aron and Brewer companies of Exercise 3 for December 31, 19X2, are presented as follows:

	Aron	Brewer
Current Assets.	172,000	105,000
Property, Plant, and Equipment.	400,000	200,000
Accumulated Depreciation.	(130,000)	(40,000)
Investment in Brewer Company	242,000	
Current Liabilities.	(80,000)	
Common Stock ($10 par)	(300,000)	(100,000)
Retained Earnings, January 1, 19X2.	(260,000)	(170,000)
Sales.	(200,000)	(100,000)
Expenses	160,000	95,000
Subsidiary Income.	(4,000)	
Dividends Declared. . . . . -		10,000
Total	0	0

Aron Company continued to use the simple equity method.

1. Prepare all the eliminations and adjustments that would be made on the 19X2 consolidated worksheet.
2. Prepare the 19X2 consolidated income statement and its related income distribution schedules.

Exercise 5.   *(Note: Read carefully. This is not the same as Exercise 3.)* Aron Company purchased an 80% interest in Brewer Company for $230,000 on January 1, 19X1, when Brewer Company had the following balance sheet:

Assets		Liabilities and Equity	
Current assets	$100,000	Current liabilities	$ 50,000
Property, plant, and		Common stock ($10 par).	100,000
equipment (net)	200,000	Retained earnings.	150,000
Total assets	$300,000	Total liabilities and equity.	$300,000

Any excess of the price paid over book value is attributable only to the plant assets, which have a 10-year remaining life. Aron uses the sophisticated equity method to record the investment in Brewer Company.

The following trial balances of the two companies were prepared on December 31, 19X1:

	Aron	Brewer
Current Assets.	80,000	130,000
Property, Plant, and Equipment.	400,000	200,000
Accumulated Depreciation.	(106,000)	(20,000)
Investment in Brewer Company	243,000	
Current Liabilities.	(60,000)	(40,000)
Common Stock ($10 par)	(300,000)	(100,000)

Retained Earnings, January 1, 19X1	(200,000)	(150,000)
Sales	(150,000)	(100,000)
Expenses	110,000	75,000
Subsidiary Income (from Brewer Company)	(17,000)	
Dividends Declared . . . . -		5,000
Total	0	0

1. If you did not solve Exercise 3, prepare a determination and distribution of excess schedule for the investment.
2. Prepare all the eliminations and adjustments that would be made on the 19X1 consolidated worksheet.
3. If you did not solve Exercise 3, prepare the 19X1 consolidated income statement and its related income distribution schedule.
4. If you did not solve Exercise 3, prepare the 19X1 consolidated balance sheet.

Exercise 6.   The trial balances of Aron and Brewer companies of Exercise 5 for December 31, 19X2, are presented as follows:

	Aron	Brewer
Current Assets	172,000	105,000
Property, Plant, and Equipment	400,000	200,000
Accumulated Depreciation	(130,000)	(40,000)
Investment in Brewer Company	236,000	
Current Liabilities	(80,000)	
Common Stock ($10 par)	(300,000)	(100,000)
Retained Earnings, January 1, 19X2	(257,000)	(170,000)
Sales	(200,000)	(100,000)
Expenses	160,000	95,000
Subsidiary Income (from Brewer Company)	(1,000)	
Dividends Declared . . . . -		10,000
Total	0	0

Aron Company continued to use the sophisticated equity method.

1. Prepare all the eliminations and adjustments that would be made on the 19X2 consolidated worksheet.
2. If you did not solve Exercise 4, prepare the 19X2 consolidated income statement and its related income distribution schedules.

Exercise 7.   *(Note: Read carefully. This is not the same as Exercise 3 or 5.)* Aron Company purchased an 80% interest in Brewer Company for $230,000 in cash on January 1, 19X1, when Brewer Company had the following balance sheet:

Assets		Liabilities and Equity	
Current assets	$100,000	Current liabilities	$ 50,000
Property, plant, and		Common stock ($10 par)	100,000
equipment (net)	200,000	Retained earnings	150,000
Total assets	$300,000	Total liabilities and equity	$300,000

Any excess of the price paid over book value is attributable only to the plant assets, which have a 10-year remaining life. Aron Company uses the cost method to record its investment in Brewer Company.

(continued)

The following trial balances of the two companies were prepared on December 31, 19X1:

	Aron	Brewer
Current Assets.	80,000	130,000
Property, Plant, and Equipment.	400,000	200,000
Accumulated Depreciation.	(106,000)	(20,000)
Investment in Brewer Company	230,000	
Current Liabilities.	(60,000)	(40,000)
Common Stock ($10 par)	(300,000)	(100,000)
Retained Earnings, January 1, 19X2.	(200,000)	(150,000)
Sales.	(150,000)	(100,000)
Expenses	110,000	75,000
Dividend Income (from Brewer Company)	(4,000)	
Dividends Declared. . . . .-		5,000
Total	0	0

1. If you did not solve Exercise 3 or 5, prepare a determination and distribution of excess schedule for the investment.
2. Prepare all the eliminations and adjustments that would be made on the 19X1 consolidated worksheet.
3. If you did not solve Exercise 3 or 5, prepare the 19X1 consolidated income statement and its related income distribution schedules.
4. If you did not solve Exercise 3 or 5, prepare the 19X1 consolidated balance sheet.

Exercise 8.   The trial balances of Aron and Brewer companies of Exercise 7 for December 31, 19X2, are presented as follows:

	Aron	Brewer
Current Assets.	172,000	105,000
Property, Plant, and Equipment.	400,000	200,000
Accumulated Depreciation.	(130,000)	(40,000)
Investment in Brewer Company	230,000	
Current Liabilities.	(80,000)	
Common Stock ($10 par)	(300,000)	(100,000)
Retained Earnings, January 1, 19X2.	(244,000)	(170,000)
Sales.	(200,000)	(100,000)
Expenses	160,000	95,000
Dividend Income (from Brewer Company)	(8,000)	
Dividends Declared. . . . .-		10,000
Total	0	0

Aron Company continued to use the cost method.

1. Prepare all the eliminations and adjustments that would be made on the 19X2 consolidated worksheet.
2. If you did not solve Exercise 4 or 6, prepare the 19X2 consolidated income statement and its related income distribution schedules.

Exercise 9.   Karen Company had the following balance sheet on January 1, 19X2:

Assets		Liabilities and Equity	
Current assets	$200,000	Current liabilities	$100,000
Equipment (net)	300,000	Common stock ($10 par)	100,000
		Retained earnings.	300,000
Total assets	$500,000	Total liabilities and equity.	$500,000

Between January 1 and July 1, 19X2, Karen Company estimated its net income to be $30,000. On July 1, 19X2, Neiman Company purchased 80% of the outstanding common stock of Karen Company for $310,000. Any excess of book value over cost was attributed to the equipment which had an estimated 5-year life. Karen Company did not close its books on July 1.

On December 31, 19X2, Neiman Company and Karen Company prepared the following trial balances:

	Neiman	Karen
Current Assets.	220,000	250,000
Equipment	500,000	300,000
Accumulated Depreciation—Equipment	(140,000)	(20,000)
Investment in Karen Company	310,000	
Current Liabilities.	(200,000)	(70,000)
Common Stock ($10 par)	(200,000)	(100,000)
Retained Earnings, 1/1/X2.	(430,000)	(300,000)
Sales.	(300,000)	(200,000)
Cost of Goods Sold	180,000	90,000
General Expenses	60,000	50,000
Total	0	0

1. Prepare a determination and distribution of excess schedule for the investment.
2. Prepare all the eliminations and adjustments that would be made on the December 31, 19X2 consolidated worksheet.
3. Prepare the 19X2 consolidated income statement and its related income distribution schedules.

Exercise 10.   On January 1, 19X4, LaRusso Company issued 12,000 shares of its common stock in exchange for 9,000 shares of Preston Company in a transaction that met the pooling of interests criteria. LaRusso shares have a par value of $10 and a market value of $30 per share. On January 1, 19X4, Preston Company had the following balance sheet:

Assets		Liabilities and Equity	
Current assets	$ 95,000	Bonds payable.	$100,000
Buildings and equipment.	350,000	Common stock ($5 par).	50,000
Accumulated depreciation.	(125,000)	Paid-in capital in excess of par	70,000
Goodwill	50,000	Retained earnings	150,000
Total assets.	$370,000	Total liabilities and equity	$370,000

(continued)

The market value of the buildings and equipment is $300,000. The balance of the market value of the interest acquired is attributed to additional goodwill with a 10-year life.

LaRusso Company had the following stockholders' equity accounts on the date of the combination:

Common stock ($10 par)	$200,000
Paid-in capital in excess of par	300,000
Retained earnings	420,000

The separate income statements of LaRusso and Preston companies contained the following information for 19X4:

	LaRusso	Preston
Sales.	$140,000	$90,000
Cost of goods sold.	80,000	60,000
General expenses	30,000	18,000

Prepare a consolidated income statement for 19X4 and the stockholders' equity section of a consolidated balance sheet prepared on December 31, 19X4.

Exercise 11.   On January 1, 19X6, Pluto Inc. issued 200,000 additional shares of its voting common stock in exchange for 100,000 shares of the outstanding voting common stock of Sherry Company in a business combination appropriately accounted for by the pooling of interests method. The market value of the voting common stock of Pluto was $40 per share on the date of the business combination. Immediately prior to the acquisition, the balance sheets of Pluto and Sherry contained the following information:

Pluto Inc.

Common stock, $5 par; authorized 1,000,000 shares; issued and outstanding 600,000 shares	$ 3,000,000
Additional paid-in capital	6,000,000
Retained earnings	11,000,000
Total stockholders' equity	$20,000,000

Sherry Company

Common stock, $10 par; authorized 250,000 shares; issued and outstanding 100,000 shares	$1,000,000
Additional paid-in capital	2,000,000
Retained earnings	4,000,000
Total stockholders' equity	$7,000,000

Additional information is as follows:

a) Net income for the year ended December 31, 19X6, was $1,150,000 for Pluto and $350,000 for Sherry.

b) During 19X6, Pluto paid $900,000 in dividends to its stockholders, and Sherry paid $210,000 in dividends to Pluto.

Prepare the consolidated stockholders' equity section of the balance sheet of Pluto Inc. and its subsidiary, Sherry Company, at December 31, 19X6.

(AICPA adapted)

Appendix Exercises

Exercise B-1. Rainman Corporation is considering the acquisition of Lamb Company through the purchase of Lamb's common stock. Rainman Corporation will issue 20,000 shares of its $5 par common stock, with a market value of $25 per share, in exchange for all 10,000 outstanding shares of Lamb Company's voting common stock.

This acquisition doesn't meet all the criteria for a pooling of interests; therefore, it must be accounted for as a purchase. The acquisition does, however, meet the criteria for a tax-free exchange as to the seller. Because of this, Rainman Corporation will be limited for future tax returns to the book value of the depreciable assets. Rainman Corporation falls into the 30% tax bracket.

The appraisal of the assets of Lamb Company showed that the inventory has a market value of $120,000, and the property, plant, and equipment has a market value of $270,000. Lamb Company had the following balance sheet just before the acquisition:

Lamb Company
Balance Sheet
December 31, 19X5

Assets		Liabilities and Equity		
Cash	$ 40,000	Current liabilities		$ 70,000
Accounts receivable	150,000	Bonds payable		100,000
Inventory	100,000	Stockholders' equity:		
Property, plant, and		Common stock ($10 par)	$100,000	
equipment (net)	210,000	Retained earnings	230,000	330,000
Total assets	$500,000	Total liabilities and equity		$500,000

1. Record the acquisition of Lamb Company by Rainman Corporation.
2. Prepare a determination and distribution of excess schedule.
3. Prepare the elimination entries that would be made on the consolidated worksheet.

Exercise B-2. Fargo Company issued securities with a market value of $400,000 for a 90% interest in Dakota Company on January 1, 19X1, at which time Dakota Company had the following balance sheet:

Assets		Liabilities and Equity	
Accounts receivable	$ 50,000	Current liabilities	$ 70,000
Inventory	80,000	Common stock ($5 par)	100,000
Land	20,000	Paid-in capital in excess of par	130,000
Building (net)	200,000	Retained earnings	50,000
Total assets	$350,000	Total liabilities and equity	$350,000

It was believed that the inventory and the building were undervalued by $20,000 and $50,000, respectively. The building had a 10-year remaining life; the inventory on hand January 1, 19X1, was sold during the year. The deferred tax liability associated with the asset revaluations was to be reflected in the consolidated statements. Each company has an income tax rate of 30%. Goodwill, if any, would be amortized over 15 years.

(continued)

The separate income statements of the two companies prepared for 19X1 are shown below.

	Fargo	Dakota
Sales.	$400,000	$150,000
Cost of goods sold.	(200,000)	(90,000)
Gross profit	$200,000	$ 60,000
General expenses	(50,000)	(25,000)
Depreciation expense.	(60,000)	(15,000)
Operating income	$ 90,000	$ 20,000
Subsidiary income	18,000	
Net income before income tax.	$108,000	$ 20,000
Provision for tax (does not include tax on subsidiary income) . .	(27,000)	(6,000)
Net income.	$ 81,000	$ 14,000

1. Prepare a determination and distribution of excess schedule for the investment.
2. Prepare the 19X1 consolidated income statement and its related income distribution schedules.

Exercise B-3.   Palto issued 20,000 of its $5 par value common stock shares, with a market value of $35 each, for a 100% interest in the Sarge Company on January 1, 19X1. The balance sheet of the Sarge Company on that date was as follows:

Assets		Liabilities and Equity	
Current assets	$100.000	Current liabilities	$ 50,000
Buildings and equipment (net)	300,000	Common stock, par	250,000
		Retained earnings	100,000
Total assets	$400,000	Total liabilities and equity	$400,000

On the purchase date, the buildings and equipment were understated $50,000 and had a remaining life of 10 years. Sarge had tax loss carryovers of $200,000. They are believed to be fully realizable at a tax rate of 30%. $40,000 of the tax loss carryovers will be utilized in 19X1. The purchase is a tax-free exchange. The tax rate applicable to all transactions is 30%. Any remaining excess is attributed to goodwill with a 10-year life.

Prepare a determination and distribution of excess schedule for this investment.

Problems

Problem 3-1.   On January 1, 19X1, Polar Company purchased an 80% interest in Solar Company by issuing 10,000 of its common stock shares with a par value of $10 per share and a market value of $70 per share. The direct acquisition costs were $20,000. At the time of the purchase, Solar had the following balance sheet:

Assets		Liabilities and Equity	
Current assets	$100,000	Current liabilities	$ 80,000
Investments	150,000	Bonds payable.	250,000
Land.	120,000	Common stock ($10 par).	100,000
Building (net)	350,000	Paid-in capital in excess of par	200,000
Equipment (net)	160,000	Retained earnings	250,000
Total assets	$880,000	Total liabilities and equity	$880,000

Appraisals indicate that book values are representative of market values with the exception of land and buildings. The land has a fair market value of $190,000 and the building is appraised at $450,000. The building has an estimated remaining life of 20 years. Any goodwill arising from the purchase would be amortized over 10 years.

The following summary of Solar's retained earnings applies to 19X1 and 19X2:

Balance, January 1, 19X1	$250,000
Net income for 19X1	60,000
Dividends paid in 19X1	(10,000)
Balance, December 31, 19X1	$300,000
Net income for 19X2	45,000
Dividends paid in 19X2	(10,000)
Balance, December 31, 19X2	$335,000

Required:

1. Prepare a determination and distribution of excess schedule for the investment in Solar Company. As a part of the schedule, indicate annual amortization of excess adjustments.
2. For 19X1 and 19X2, prepare the entries that Polar would make concerning its investment in Solar under the simple equity, sophisticated equity, and cost methods. It is suggested that you set up a worksheet with side-by-side columns for each method so that you can easily compare the entries.
3. For 19X1 and 19X2, prepare the worksheet elimination that would be made on a consolidated worksheet under the simple equity, sophisticated equity, and cost methods. It is suggested that you set up a worksheet with side-by-side columns for each method so that you can easily compare the entries.

Problem 3-2.   On January 1, 19X1, Parent Company purchased 80% of the common stock of Subsidiary Company for $308,000. On this date, Subsidiary had common stock, other paid-in capital, and retained earnings of $50,000, $100,000, and $150,000, respectively. Net income dividends for 2 years for Subsidiary Company were as follows:

	19X1	19X2
Net income	$60,000	$90,000
Dividends.	20,000	30,000

On January 1, 19X1, the only tangible assets of Subsidiary that were undervalued were inventory and building. Inventory, for which FIFO is used, was worth $10,000 more than cost. The inventory was sold in 19X1. Building, which was worth $25,000

(continued)

more than book value, has a remaining life of 10 years, and straight-line depreciation is used. Goodwill, if any, is to be amortized over the maximum period permitted.

Required:

1. Using this information or the information in the following trial balances, prepare a determination and distribution of excess schedule.
2. Parent Company carries the Investment in Subsidiary Company under the simple equity method. In general journal form, record the entries that would be made to apply the equity method in 19X1 and 19X2.
3. Compute the balance that should appear in Investment in Subsidiary Company and in Subsidiary Income on December 31, 19X2 (the second year). Fill in these amounts on Parent Company's trial balance for 19X2.
4. Complete a worksheet for consolidated financial statements for 19X2. Include columns for eliminations and adjustments, consolidated income, minority interest, controlling retained earnings, and balance sheet.

	Parent Company	Subsidiary Company
Inventory, December 31	100,000	50,000
Other Current Assets	148,000	180,000
Investment in Subsidiary Company	Note 1	
Land	50,000	50,000
Buildings and Equipment.	350,000	320,000
Accumulated Depreciation.	(100,000)	(60,000)
Goodwill		
Other Intangibles.	20,000	
Current Liabilities.	(120,000)	(40,000)
Bonds Payable		(100,000)
Other Long-Term Liabilities.	(200,000)	
Common Stock, P Co.	(200,000)	
Other Paid-In Capital, P Co.	(100,000)	
Retained Earnings, P Co.	(214,000)	
Common Stock, S Co.		(50,000)
Other Paid-In Capital, S Co.		(100,000)
Retained Earnings, S Co.		(190,000)
Net Sales.	(520,000)	(450,000)
Cost of Goods Sold	300,000	260,000
Operating Expenses.	120,000	100,000
Subsidiary Income	(72,000)	
Dividends Declared, P Co.	50,000	
Dividends Declared, S Co.		30,000

Note 1: To be calculated

Problem 3-3. (This is the same as Problem 3-2, except the sophisticated equity method is used.) On January 1, 19X1, Parent Company purchased 80% of the common stock of Subsidiary Company for $308,000. On this date, Subsidiary had common stock, other paid-in capital, and retained earnings of $50,000, $100,000, and $150,000, respectively. Net income dividends for 2 years for Subsidiary Company were as follows:

	19X1	19X2
Net income	$60,000	$90,000
Dividends	20,000	30,000

On January 1, 19X1, the only tangible assets of Subsidiary that were undervalued were inventory and building. Inventory, for which FIFO is used, was worth $10,000 more than cost. The inventory was sold in 19X1. Building, which was worth $25,000 more than book value, has a remaining life of 10 years, and straight-line depreciation is used. Goodwill, if any, is to be amortized over the maximum period permitted.

Required:

1. Using this information or the information in the following trial balances, prepare a determination and distribution of excess schedule.
2. Parent Company carries the Investment in Subsidiary Company under the sophisticated equity method. In general journal form, record the entries that would be made to apply the equity method in 19X1 and 19X2.
3. Compute the balance that should appear in Investment in Subsidiary Company and in Subsidiary Income on December 31, 19X2 (the second year). Fill in these amounts on Parent Company's trial balance for 19X2.
4. Complete a worksheet for consolidated financial statements for 19X2. Include columns for eliminations and adjustments, consolidated income, minority interest, controlling retained earnings, and balance sheet.

	Parent Company	Subsidiary Company
Inventory, December 31	100,000	50,000
Other Current Assets	148,000	180,000
Investment in Subsidiary Company	Note 2	
Land	50,000	50,000
Buildings and Equipment	350,000	320,000
Accumulated Depreciation	(100,000)	(60,000)
Goodwill		
Other Intangibles	20,000	
Current Liabilities	(120,000)	(40,000)
Bonds Payable		(100,000)
Other Long-Term Liabilities	(200,000)	
Common Stock, P Co.	(200,000)	
Other Paid-In Capital, P Co.	(100,000)	
Retained Earnings, P Co.	(203,000)	
Common Stock, S Co.		(50,000)
Other Paid-In Capital, S Co.		(100,000)
Retained Earnings, S Co.		(190,000)
Net Sales	(520,000)	(450,000)
Cost of Goods Sold	300,000	260,000
Operating Expenses	120,000	100,000
Subsidiary Income	(69,000)	

(continued)

Dividends Declared, P Co.	50,000	
Dividends Declared, S Co.		30,000

Note 2: To be calculated.

Problem 3-4.   The trial balances of Dahl Company and its subsidiary, Basset Inc., are as follows on December 31, 19X3:

	Dahl Company	Basset Inc.
Current Assets.	530,000	130,000
Property, Plant, and Equipment.	1,805,000	440,000
Accumulated Depreciation.	(405,000)	(70,000)
Investment in Basset Inc.	400,000	
Liabilities	(900,000)	(225,000)
Common Stock ($1 par)	(220,000)	
Common Stock ($5 par)		(50,000)
Paid-In Capital in Excess of Par	(980,000)	(15,000)
Retained Earnings, January 1, 19X3.	(230,000)	(170,000)
Revenues	(460,000)	(210,000)
Expenses	450,000	170,000
Dividends Declared	10,000	
Total	0	0

On January 1, 19X1, Dahl Company exchanged 20,000 shares of its common stock, with a market value of $20 per share, for all the outstanding stock of Basset Inc. in a transaction that did not meet the criteria for a pooling of interests. Any excess of cost over book value was attributed to goodwill and is being amortized over a 40-year period. The stockholders' equity of Basset Inc. on the purchase date was

Common stock ($5 par)	$ 50,000
Paid-in capital in excess of par	15,000
Retained earnings	135,000
Total equity	$200,000

Required:

1.   Prepare a determination and distribution of excess schedule for the investment.
2.   Prepare the 19X3 consolidated statements, including the income statement, retained earnings statement, and balance sheet. (A worksheet is not required.)

Problem 3-5.   On January 1, 19X3, Jack Corporation exchanged 45,000 shares of newly issued common stock, with a market value of $10 per share, for all the outstanding stock of Bob Company. The combination meets the criteria for a pooling of interests. Jack Corporation maintains its investment in the subsidiary under the cost method.

The stockholders' equity of Bob Company on January 1, 19X3, was as follows:

Common stock ($10 par)	$200,000
Paid-in capital in excess of par	75,000
Retained earnings	175,000
Total stockholders' equity	$450,000

The trial balances of the two companies on December 31, 19X3, are as follows:

	Jack	Bob
Cash.	350,000	115,400
Accounts Receivable.	75,000	45,000
Inventory	80,000	55,000
Land	100,000	65,000
Buildings	750,000	275,000
Accumulated Depreciation—Buildings	(395,000)	(28,400)
Equipment	2,150,000	426,000
Accumulated Depreciation—Equipment	(750,000)	(63,000)
Investment in Subsidiary	450,000	
Accounts Payable	(740,000)	(400,000)
Common Stock	(1,000,000)	(200,000)
Paid-In Capital in Excess of Par	(560,000)	(75,000)
Retained Earnings	(495,000)	(175,000)
Sales.	(440,000)	(210,000)
Cost of Goods Sold	315,000	100,000
Other Expenses.	100,000	40,000
Subsidiary Dividend Income	(30,000)	
Dividends Declared	40,000	30,000
Total	0	0

Required:

1. Prepare the elimination entries that would be made on the consolidated worksheet.
2. Prepare the December 31, 19X3 consolidated statements, including the income statement, retained earnings statement, and balance sheet. (A worksheet is not required.)

Problem 3-6.   Bell Corporation purchased all of the outstanding stock of Stockdon Corporation for $220,000 in cash on January 1, 19X7. On the purchase date, Stockdon Corporation had the following condensed balance sheet:

Assets		Liabilities and Equity	
Cash.	$ 60,000	Liabilities	$150,000
Inventory	40,000	Common stock ($10 par).	100,000
Land	120,000	Paid-in capital in excess of par	50,000
Building (net)	180,000	Retained earnings	100,000
Total assets.	$400,000	Total liabilities and equity	$400,000

Any excess of book value over cost was attributable to the building, which is currently overstated on Stockdon's books. All other assets and liabilities have book values equal to market values. The building has an estimated 10-year life with no salvage value.

The trial balances of the two companies on December 31, 19X7, appear as follows:

(continued)

	Bell	Stockdon
Cash	180,000	143,000
Inventory	60,000	30,000
Land	120,000	120,000
Buildings (net)	600,000	162,000
Investment in Stockdon Corp	220,000	
Accounts Payable	(405,000)	(210,000)
Common Stock ($3 par)	(300,000)	
Common Stock ($10 par)		(100,000)
Paid-In Capital in Excess of Par	(180,000)	(50,000)
Retained Earnings, 1/1/X7	(255,000)	(100,000)
Sales	(210,000)	(40,000)
Cost of Goods Sold	120,000	35,000
Other Expenses	45,000	10,000
Dividends Declared	5,000	
Total	0	0

Required:

1. Prepare a determination and distribution of excess schedule for the investment.
2. Prepare the 19X7 consolidated worksheet. Include columns for the eliminations and adjustments, the consolidated income statement, the controlling retained earnings, and the consolidated balance sheet.
3. Prepare the 19X7 consolidated statements, including the income statement, retained earnings statement, and balance sheet.

Problem 3-7.   Sauer Company prepared the following balance sheet on January 1, 19X1:

Assets		Liabilities and Equity	
Current assets	$ 50,000	Liabilities	$140,000
Land	75,000	Common stock ($10 par)	100,000
Buildings	350,000	Paid-in capital in excess of par	120,000
Accumulated depreciation	390,000	Retained earnings (deficit)	(25,000)
—buildings	(140,000)		
Total assets	$335,000	Total liabilities and equity	$335,000

On this date, Roland Company purchased 8,000 shares of Sauer Company's outstanding stock for a total price of $270,000. Also on this date, the buildings were understated by $40,000 and were felt to have a 10-year remaining life. Any remaining discrepancy between the price paid and book value was attributed to goodwill and estimated to have a 20-year life. Since the purchase, Roland Company has used the cost method to record the investment and its related income.

Roland Company and Sauer Company have prepared the following separate trial balances on December 31, 19X2:

	Roland	Sauer
Current Assets	180,000	115,000
Land	150,000	75,000
Buildings	590,000	350,000
Accumulated Depreciation—Buildings	(265,000)	(182,000)
Investment in Sauer Company	270,000	
Liabilities	(175,000)	(133,000)
Common Stock ($10 par)	(200,000)	(100,000)
Paid-In Capital in Excess of Par		(120,000)
Retained Earnings, January 1, 19X2	(495,000)	15,000
Sales	(360,000)	(120,000)
Dividend Income (from Sauer Company)	(4,000)	
Cost of Goods Sold	179,000	50,000
Expenses	120,000	45,000
Dividends Declared	10,000	5,000
Total	0	0

Required:

1. Prepare a determination and distribution of excess schedule for the investment.
2. Prepare the 19X2 consolidated worksheet. Include columns for the eliminations and adjustments, the consolidated income statement, the minority interest, the controlling retained earnings, and the consolidated balance sheet. Prepare supporting income distribution schedules.
3. Prepare the 19X2 consolidated statements including the income statement, retained earnings statement, and the balance sheet.

Problem 3-8. On January 1, 19X1, Fordum Corporation exchanged 90,000 shares of its $5 par stock, with a market value of $15 per share, for 90% of the outstanding common stock of Rice Corporation in a transaction qualifying as a pooling of interests. Direct acquisition costs were $50,000 and are included in the investment account. The account Investment in Rice Corporation reflects the market value of the shares exchanged and the issuance cost related to the common stock of Fordum Corporation.

Immediately prior to the exchange, Rice Corporation had the following owners' equity:

Common stock ($2 par)	$200,000
Paid-in capital in excess of par	400,000
Retained earnings (deficit)	(50,000)
Total equity	$550,000

Since the exchange, Fordum has used the cost method to account for its investment in Rice. No intercompany transactions have ever occurred.

Fordum Corporation and Rice Corporation have the following trial balances on December 31, 19X3:

(continued)

	Fordum Corporation	Rice Corporation
Current Assets	840,000	360,000
Property, Plant, and Equipment	4,800,000	1,570,000
Accumulated Depreciation	(1,600,000)	(520,000)
Investment in Rice Corporation	1,400,000	
Liabilities	(1,830,000)	(790,000)
Common Stock ($5 par)	(1,000,000)	
Common Stock ($2 par)		(200,000)
Paid-In Capital in Excess of Par	(1,650,000)	(400,000)
Retained Earnings, January 1, 19X3	(900,000)	10,000
Sales	(1,050,000)	(440,000)
Cost of Goods Sold	600,000	250,000
Expenses	350,000	160,000
Dividends Declared	40,000	
Total	0	0

Required:

1. Prepare the journal entries that should be made to properly reflect this investment on the books of the parent company.
2. Prepare the 19X3 consolidated worksheet. Include columns for the eliminations and adjustments, the consolidated income statement, the minority interest, the controlling retained earnings, and the consolidated balance sheet. Prepare supporting income distribution schedules as well.

Problem 3-9.   Drew Corporation purchased 80% of the outstanding stock of Winters Company for $240,000 on January 1, 19X1. Winters Company had the following stockholders' equity:

Common stock ($5 par)	$150,000
Retained earnings	50,000
Total equity	$200,000

The market values of Winters' assets and liabilities agreed with the book values, except for the equipment and the building. The equipment was undervalued by $10,000 and was thought to have a 5-year life; the building was undervalued by $50,000 and was thought to have a 20-year life. Any goodwill that results is being amortized over 40 years. Drew Corporation uses the simple equity method to record its investments.

Since the purchase date, both firms have operated separately and no intercompany transactions have occurred.

The separate trial balances of the firms on December 31, 19X2, are as follows:

	Drew Corp.	Winters Co.
Cash	319,600	110,000
Land	160,000	90,000
Buildings	225,000	85 135,000
Accumulated Depreciation—Building	(100,000)	(50,000)
Equipment	450,000	150,000

Accumulated Depreciation—Equipment	(115,000)	(60,000)
Investment in Winters Co.	260,000	
Liabilities	(480,000)	(150,000)
Common Stock ($100 par)	(400,000)	
Common Stock ($5 par)		(150,000)
Paid-In Capital in Excess of Par	(40,000)	
Retained Earnings, 1/1/X2	(251,600)	(65,000)
Sales	(460,000)	(120,000)
Cost of Goods Sold	220,000	60,000
Other Expenses	210,000	50,000
Subsidiary Income	(8,000)	
Dividends Declared	10,000	
Total	0	0

Required:

1. Prepare a determination and distribution of excess schedule for the investment.
2. Prepare the 19X2 consolidated worksheet. Include columns for the eliminations and adjustments, the consolidated income statement, the minority interest, the controlling retained earnings, and the consolidated balance sheet. Prepare supporting income distribution schedules as well.
3. Prepare the 19X2 consolidated statements, including the income statement, retained earnings statement, and balance sheet.

Problem 3-10.   Dallman International purchased 80% of the outstanding stock of the Highland Company for $1,600,000 plus $8,000 of direct acquisition costs on January 1, 19X5. At the purchase date, the inventory, the equipment, and the patents of Highland Company had fair market values of $10,000, $50,000, and $100,000, respectively, in excess of their book values. The other assets and liabilities of Highland Company had book values equal to their market values. The inventory was sold during the month following the purchase. The two companies agreed that the equipment had a remaining life of 8 years and the patents, 10 years. On the purchase date, the owners' equity of Highland Company was as follows:

Common stock ($10 stated value)	$1,000,000
Additional paid-in capital	300,000
Retained earnings	400,000
Total equity	$1,700,000

During the next two years, Highland Company had income and paid dividends as follows:

	Income	Dividends
19X5	$ 90,000	$30,000
19X6	150,000	30,000

The trial balances of the two corporations as of December 31, 19X7, are as follows:

(continued)

	Dallman International	Highland Company
Current Assets	624,000	505,000
Equipment (net)	1,320,000	940,000
Patents	100,000	35,000
Other Assets	1,620,000	730,000
Investment in Highland	1,608,000	
Accounts Payable.	(658,000)	(205,000)
Common Stock ($5 par)	(2,000,000)	
Common Stock ($10 par).		(1,000,000)
Paid-In Capital in Excess of Par.	(1,200,000)	(300,000)
Retained Earnings, 1/1/X7	(1,255,000)	(580,000)
Sales	(905,000)	(425,000)
Cost of Goods Sold	470,000	170,000
Other Expenses	250,000	100,000
Dividend Income	(24,000)	
Dividends Declared.	50,000	30,000
Total	0	0

Required:

Assume that any resulting goodwill is being amortized over 40 years and no inter-company transactions occurred.

1. Prepare the original determination and distribution of excess schedule for the investment.
2. Prepare the 19X7 consolidated worksheet for December 31, 19X7. Include columns for the eliminations and adjustments, the consolidated income statement, the controlling retained earnings, and the consolidated balance sheet.

Problem 3-11.   On July 1, 19X5, Punch Inc. purchased 90% of the common stock of Sun Inc. for $1,127,000 plus $16,000 in direct acquisition costs. Sun had the following stockholders' equity on January 1, 19X5:

Common stock ($10 par value)	$200,000
Paid-in capital in excess of par	300,000
Retained earnings	300,000
Total equity	$800,000

Sun's estimated income for the first 6 months of 19X5 was $40,000, including the $30,000 depreciation on the building, $20,000 depreciation on the equipment, and $1,000 goodwill amortization. Following is a summary of the book and market values of Sun's asset and liability accounts on July 1, 19X5. Book values include the above amortizations.

Account	Book Value	Market Value	Punch's Life Assumption
Cash	$150,000	$150,000	
Accounts Receivable	200,000	200,000	Collected by year-end
Inventory.	250,000	270,000	Sold by year-end
Land.	100,000	200,000	
Building	700,000	600,000	20-year life, no salvage, straight-line*
Accumulated Depreciation—Building	(300,000)		
Equipment.	300,000	250,000	5-year life, no salvage, straight-line*
Accumulated Depreciation—Equipment.	(160,000)		
Goodwill.	50,000	?	25 years
Mortgage Payable	(450,000)	(400,000)	10-year, straight-line amortization

*Life and method do not agree with those used by Sun Inc.

Sun's books were not closed on July 1, 19X5; thus, the following December 31, 19X5 trial balances of Punch and Sun include the results from operations for all of 19X5:

	Punch	Sun
Cash	323,000	261,000
Accounts Receivable.	200,000	230,000
Inventory	400,000	220,000
Land	200,000	100,000
Building	1,000,000	700,000
Accumulated Depreciation—Building.	(500,000)	(330,000)
Equipment	400,000	300,000
Accumulated Depreciation—Equipment	(100,000)	(180,000)
Goodwill (net).		49,000
Investment in Sun Inc	1,143,000	
Mortgage Payable.		(450,000)
Common Stock	(1,800,000)	(200,000)
Paid-In Capital in Excess of Par		(300,000)
Retained Earnings, Jan. 1, 19X5	(1,066,000)	(300,000)
Sales.	(2,000,000)	(900,000)
Cost of Goods Sold	1,500,000	600,000
General Expense.	100,000	98,000
Depreciation Expense.	200,000	100,000
Goodwill Amortization. . . . . -		2,000
Total	0	0

Note that Sun's Depreciation Expense includes $60,000 on the building and $40,000 on the equipment.

(continued)

Required:

1. Prepare the original determination and distribution of excess schedule for the investment.
2. Prepare the consolidated worksheet for December 31, 19X5. Include columns for the eliminations and adjustments, the consolidated income statement, the minority interest, the controlling retained earnings, and the consolidated balance sheet. Prepare supporting income distribution schedules as well.
3. Prepare the 19X5 consolidated statements, including the income statement, retained earnings statement, and balance sheet.

Suggestion: Due to the minority interest, it is difficult to restate long-lived assets with no accumulated depreciation. It is recommended that the adjustments be made by decreasing accumulated depreciation. However, using the parent's estimates, it is first necessary to recalculate what depreciation should be. Remember that, in this example, the parent is using different life assumptions and depreciation methods from those of the subsidiary. The parent's estimate (for 90% of the asset's value) should replace 90% of the depreciation now recorded by the subsidiary. Also, remember to reduce goodwill amortization when existing goodwill is consumed and allocated to other assets.

Problem 3-12.   On January 1, 19X4, Harpoon Corporation purchased 80% of the outstanding common stock of Largo Company for $6,026,000 in cash. The book and market values for Largo Company were as follows:

	Recorded Book Value	Market Value
Cash	1,305,000	1,305,000
Inventory	790,000	850,000
Land	2,500,000	4,000,000
Buildings	2,400,000	1,200,000
Accumulated Depreciation—Building	(1,600,000)	
Equipment	2,750,000	2,000,000
Accumulated Depreciation—Equipment	(1,850,000)	
Goodwill	120,000	300,000*
Liabilities	(580,000)	(580,000)
Bonds Payable	(2,000,000)	(1,800,000)
Common Stock ($5 par)	(3,000,000)	
Retained Earnings, 1/1/X4	(835,000)	
Total	0	

*Estimate, final value dependent upon total purchase price.

By the end of 19X4, the January 1, 19X4 inventory of Largo Company had been sold. At the purchase date, the building and equipment were estimated to have remaining lives of 10 years and 5 years, respectively. It was also decided that any goodwill resulting from the purchase shall be amortized over the next 20 years. As of January 1, 19X4, the 6% bonds had 5 years remaining to maturity.

The trial balances of Harpoon Corporation and Largo Company on December 31, 19X4, are as follows:

	Harpoon Corp.	Largo Co.
Cash	1,674,000	2,137,000
Inventory.	1,600,000	800,000
Land.	4,000,000	2,500,000
Building	6,900,000	2,400,000
Accumulated Depreciation—Building	(3,400,000)	(1,680,000)
Equipment.	10,000,000	2,750,000
Accumulated Depreciation—Equipment	(5,000,000)	(2,000,000)
Investment in Largo Co.	6,482,000	
Goodwill.	200,000	108,000
Liabilities.	(1,300,000)	(610,000)
Bonds Payable.	(6,000,000)	(2,000,000)
Common Stock ($5 par)	(13,000,000)	(3,000,000)
Retained Earnings, 1/1/X4	(1,550,000)	(835,000)
Sales	(3,000,000)	(1,500,000)
Cost of Goods Sold	1,900,000	700,000
Other Expenses	900,000	200,000
Subsidiary Income	(480,000)	
Dividends Declared.	74,000	30,000
Total	0	0

Required:

1. Prepare a determination and distribution of excess schedule for the investment.
2. Prepare the 19X4 consolidated worksheet. Include columns for the eliminations and adjustments, the consolidated income statement, the minority interest, the controlling retained earnings, and the consolidated balance sheet. Prepare supporting income distribution schedules as well.

(AICPA adapted)

Suggestion: Be sure to limit your adjustment for goodwill amortization to only the net increase in goodwill (some goodwill exists already at the time of purchase and will have been amortized by the subsidiary).

Appendix Problems

Problem 3A-1.   (Same as Problem 3-2 except vertical format worksheet is used.) On January 1, 19X1, Parent Company purchased 80% of the common stock of Subsidiary Company for $308,000. On this date, Subsidiary had common stock, other paid-in capital, and retained earnings of $50,000, $100,000, and $150,000, respectively. Net income dividends for 2 years for Subsidiary Company were as follows:

	19X1	19X2
Net income	$60,000	$90,000
Dividends.	20,000	30,000

(continued)

On January 1, 19X1, the only tangible assets of Subsidiary that were undervalued were inventory and building. Inventory, for which FIFO is used, was worth $10,000 more than cost. The inventory was sold in 19X1. Building, which was worth $25,000 more than book value, has a remaining life of 10 years, and straight-line depreciation is used. Goodwill, if any, is to be amortized over the maximum period permitted.

Required:

1. Using this information or the information in the following statements, prepare a determination and distribution of excess schedule.
2. Parent Company carries the Investment in Subsidiary Company under the simple equity method. In general journal form, record the entries that would be made to apply the equity method in 19X1 and 19X2.
3. Complete the vertical worksheet for consolidated financial statements for 19X2.

Statement — Accounts	Parent Company	Subsidiary Company
Income Statement		
Net Sales.	(520,000)	(450,000)
Cost of Goods Sold	300,000	260,000
Operating Expenses.	120,000	100,000
Subsidiary Income	72,000	
Minority Interest in Income	-	
Net Income.	(172,000)	(90,000)
Retained Earnings Statement		
Balance, Jan. 1, 19X2, P Co.	(214,000)	
Balance, Jan. 1, 19X2, S Co.		(190,000)
Net Income (from above)	(172,000)	(90,000)
Dividends Declared, P Co.	50,000	
Dividends Declared, S Co.	-	30,000
Balance, December 31, 19X2	(336,000)	(250,000)
Consolidated Balance Sheet		
Inventory, December 31	100,000	50,000
Other Current Assets	148,000	180,000
Investment in Subsidiary Company	Note 1	
Land	50,000	50,000
Building and Equipment	350,000	320,000
Accumulated Depreciation.	(100,000)	(60,000)
Goodwill		
Other Intangibles.	20,000	
Current Liabilities.	(120,000)	(40,000)
Bonds Payable		(100,000)
Other Long-Term Liabilities.	(200,000)	
Common Stock, P Co.	(200,000)	
Other Paid-In Capital, P Co.	(100,000)	
Common Stock, S Co.		(50,000)
Other Paid-In Capital, S Co.		(100,000)
Retained Earnings, 12/31/X2 (from above).	(336,000)	(250,000)
Totals	0	0

Note 1: To be calculated.

Problem 3A-2. Brandt Enterprises purchased an 80% interest in Wagner International for $800,000 on January 1, 19X5. Brandt Enterprises also paid $4,000 in direct acquisition costs. On the purchase date, Wagner International had the following stockholders' equity:

Common stock ($10 par)	$150,000
Paid-in capital in excess of par	200,000
Retained earnings	400,000
	$750,000

Also, on the purchase date, it was determined that Wright International's assets were understated as follows:

Equipment, 10-year remaining life	$80,000
Land	20,000
Building, 20-year remaining life	60,000

Any remaining excess of cost over book value was attributed to goodwill which is being amortized over 20 years.

The following summarized statements of Brandt Enterprises and Wagner International are for the year ended December 31, 19X7:

	Brandt Enterprises	Wagner International
Income Statements:		
Sales	(650,000)	(320,000)
Cost of Goods Sold	260,000	240,000
Operating Expenses	170,000	70,000
Depreciation Expense	65,000	30,000
Subsidiary (Income)/Loss	16,000	
Net (Income)/Loss	(139,000)	20,000
Retained Earnings:		
Retained Earnings, Jan. 1, 19X7, Brandt	(625,000)	
Retained Earnings, Jan. 1, 19X7, Wagner		(460,000)
Net (Income)/Loss	(139,000)	20,000
Dividends Declared . . . . -		10,000
Retained Earnings, 12/31/19X7	(764,000)	(430,000)
Balance Sheets:		
Cash	334,000	170,000
Inventory.	135,000	400,000
Land	145,000	150,000
Buildings.	900,000	500,000
Accum. Depreciation—Building.	(345,000)	(360,000)
Equipment.	350,000	250,000
Accum. Depreciation—Equipment	(135,000)	(90,000)
Investment in Wagner International	828,000	
Liabilities.	(248,000)	(40,000)
Bonds Payable.		(200,000)
Common Stock, Brandt	(1,200,000)	
Common Stock, Wagner		(150,000)
Paid-In Capital in Excess of Par.		(200,000)
Retained Earnings, 12/31/X7	(764,000)	(430,000)
Balance	0	0

(continued)

Required:

Using the vertical format, prepare a consolidated worksheet for December 31, 19X7. Precede the worksheet with a determination and distribution of excess schedule. Include income distribution schedules to allocate the combined net income to the minority and controlling interests.

Suggestion: Remember that all adjustments to retained earnings are to beginning retained earnings, and it is the beginning balance of the subsidiary retained earnings account which is subject to elimination. Carefully follow the "carry-down" procedure to calculate the ending retained earnings balances.

Problem 3A-3.   Harvard Company purchased a 90% interest in Benz Company for $740,000 on January 1, 19X1. The investment has been accounted for under the cost method. At the time of the purchase, a building owned by Benz was understated by $180,000; it had a 20-year remaining life on the purchase date. Any remaining excess was attributed to goodwill with a 10-year life. The stockholders' equity of Benz Company on the purchase date was as follows:

Common stock ($10 par)	$350,000
Retained earnings	200,000
Total equity	$550,000

The following summarized statements are for the year ending December 31, 19X2:

(Credit balance amounts are in parentheses.)

	Harvard	Benz
Income Statements:		
Sales	(580,000)	(280,000)
Cost of Goods Sold	285,000	155,000
Operating Expenses	140,000	55,000
Depreciation Expense	72,000	30,000
Dividend Income	(9,000)	
Net Income	(92,000)	(40,000)
Retained Earnings Statements:		
Retained Earnings, Jan. 1, 19X2, Harvard	(484,000)	
Retained Earnings, Jan. 1, 19X2, Benz		(320,000)
Net Income	(92,000)	(40,000)
Dividends Declared.	20,000	10,000
Retained Earnings, Dec. 31, 19X2	(556,000)	(350,000)
Balance Sheets:		
Cash	310,000	170,000
Inventory.	260,000	340,000
Land.	99,000	150,000
Building	800,000	500,000
Accumulated Depreciation—Building	(380,000)	(360,000)
Equipment.	340,000	250,000
Accumulated Depreciation—Equipment	(190,000)	(90,000)
Investment in Benz Company	740,000	
Current Liabilities	(123,000)	(60,000)

Bonds Payable.		(200,000)
Common Stock, Harvard	(800,000)	
Paid-In Capital in Excess of Par, Harvard	(500,000)	
Common Stock, Benz		(350,000)
Retained Earnings, Dec. 31, 19X2	(556,000)	(350,000)
Balance	0	0

Required:

Using the vertical format, prepare a consolidated worksheet for December 31, 19X2. Precede the worksheet with a determination and distribution of excess schedule. Include income distribution schedules to allocate the combined net income to the minority and controlling interests.

Suggestion: Remember that all adjustments to retained earnings are to beginning retained earnings, and it is the beginning balance of the subsidiary retained earnings account which is subject to elimination. One of the adjustments to the parent retained earnings account is the cost-to-equity conversion entry. Be sure to follow the carrydown procedure to calculate the ending retained earnings balances.

Problem 3B-1.   On December 31, 19X5, Linen Company exchanged 10,000 of its $10 par value shares for a 90% interest in Hart Company. The transaction did not meet the criteria for a pooling of interests and, thus, was recorded at the $75 per share market value of Linen shares. Hart Company had the following balance sheet on the date of the purchase:

Assets		Liabilities and Equity	
Cash.	$ 100,000	Current liabilities	$ 130,000
Accounts receivable.	200,000	Deferred rental income	120,000
Inventory	150,000	Bonds payable.	250,000
Investment in marketable		Common stock ($10 par)	100,000
securities	150,000	Paid-in capital in excess	
Property, plant, and		of par.	150,000
equipment (net)	400,000	Retained earnings.	250,000
Total assets.	$1,000,000	Total liabilities and equity.	$1,000,000

It was determined that the following market values differed from book values for the assets of Hart Company:

Inventory	$200,000
Property, plant, and equipment (net)	500,000
Investment in marketable securities	170,000

The purchase is a tax-free exchange to the seller, which means Linen Company will use the book value of Hart's assets for tax purposes. Hart Company has $200,000 of tax loss carryovers. Linen will be able to utilize $40,000 of the losses to offset taxes to be paid in 19X6. The balance of the tax loss carryover will not be used within a year but is considered fully realizable in the future. The tax rate for both firms is 30%.

Required:

Record the investment and prepare a determination and distribution of excess schedule.

(continued)

Suggestion: The tax loss carryback is a current asset, and the tax loss carryforward is a long-lived asset. Asset adjustments should be accompanied by the appropriate deferred tax liability.

Special Challenge: Solve this problem assuming the market value per share of stock exchanged by Linen was $50 per share. Recall that the deferred tax asset (realizable after 1 year) is not a priority account.

Problem 3B-2.   The balance sheets of Tip Company and Kim Company as of December 31, 19X6, are as follows:

	Tip	Kim
Cash	$ 1,200,000	$ 50,000
Accounts receivable	2,400,000	300,000
Inventory	11,200,000	1,500,000
Prepayments	422,000	47,000
Property, plant, and equipment	18,978,000	2,100,000
Investment in Kim Co.	2,400,000	
Total assets	$36,600,000	$3,997,000
Payables	$ 7,200,000	$1,750,000
Accruals	1,615,000	400,000
Common stock ($100 par)	10,000,000	1,000,000
Retained earnings	17,785,000	847,000
Total liabilities and equity	$36,600,000	$3,997,000

An appraisal on December 31, 19X6, which was considered carefully and approved by the boards of directors of both companies, placed a total replacement value, less depreciation, of $3,000,000 on Kim's property, plant, and equipment.

Tip Company offered to purchase all the assets of Kim Company, subject to its liabilities, as of December 31, 19X6, for $3,000,000. However, 20% of the stockholders of Kim Company objected to the price because it did not include any consideration for goodwill, which they believed to be worth at least $500,000. A counterproposal was made, and a final agreement was reached. In exchange for its own shares, Tip acquired 80% of the common stock of Kim at the agreed-upon market value of $300 per share. The purchase is structured as a tax-free exchange to the seller; thus, Tip will use the book value of the assets for future tax purposes. The tax rate for both companies is 30%.

Required:

Prepare a consolidated worksheet and a consolidated balance sheet as of December 31, 19X6. Include a determination and distribution schedule.

(AICPA adapted)

Problem 3B-3.   The trial balances of Campton Corporation and Deer Corporation as of December 31, 19X1, are as follows:

	Campton Corporation	Deer Corporation
Current Assets	167,000	80,000
Land	400,000	100,000
Building and Equipment (net)	900,000	240,000

Investment in Deer Corporation.	625,600	
Current Tax Liability	(4,200)	(6,000)
Other Current Liabilities.	(130,000)	(100,000)
Common Stock ($5 par)	(500,000)	
Common Stock ($50 par)		(200,000)
Paid-In Capital in Excess of Par.	(750,000)	
Retained Earnings, January 1, 19X1	(650,000)	(100,000)
Sales.	(309,000)	(150,000)
Subsidiary Income	(12,600)	
Cost of Goods Sold	170,000	80,000
Expenses.	89,000	50,000
Provision for Tax.	4,200*	6,000
Total	0	0

*$15,000 tax liability ($50,000 income × 30%) − $10,800 tax loss carryover ($40,000 × 90% × 30%)

On January 1, 19X1, Campton purchased 90% of the outstanding stock of Deer Corporation for $600,000, plus direct acquisition costs of $13,000. The acquisition was a tax-free exchange as to the seller. At the purchase date, Deer's equipment was undervalued by $100,000 and had a remaining life of 10 years. Deer Corporation had a tax loss carryover of $200,000, of which $40,000 was utilizable in 19X1 and the balance in future periods. The tax loss carryover is expected to be fully utilized. All other assets had book values that approximated their market values. Deer Corporation had a tax loss carryover of $200,000, of which $40,000 was utilizable in 19X1 and the balance in future periods. The tax loss carryover is expected to be fully utilized. Any resulting goodwill is being amortized over 15 years. A tax rate of 30% applies to both companies.

Required:

1. Prepare a determination and distribution of excess schedule for the investment.
2. Prepare the 19X1 consolidated worksheet. Include columns for the eliminations and adjustments, the consolidated income statement, the minority interest, the controlling retained earnings, and the consolidated balance sheet. Prepare supporting income distribution schedules as well.
3. Prepare the 19X1 consolidated statements, including the income statement, retained earnings statement, and balance sheet.

Suggestion: A deferred tax liability results from the increase in the market value of the equipment. As the added depreciation is recognized on the equipment, the deferred tax liability becomes payable. Note that income distribution schedules record net-of-tax income. Therefore, be sure that any adjustments to the income distribution schedules consider tax where appropriate.

Worksheet 3-1

Simple Equity Method
Company P and Subsidiary Company S
Worksheet for Consolidated Financial Statements
For Year Ended December 31, 19X1

	(Credit balance amounts are in parentheses.)	Trial Balance	
		Company P	Company S
1	**Investment in Company S**	**163,000**	
2			
3			
4	**Goodwill**		
5	Other Assets (Net of Liabilities)	227,000	170,000
6	Common Stock ($10 par), Co. P	(200,000)	
7	Retained Earnings, Jan. 1, 19X1, Co. P	(123,000)	
8	Common Stock, ($10 par) Co. S		(100,000)
9	Retained Earnings, Jan. 1, 19X1, Co. S		(50,000)
10	Revenue	(100,000)	(80,000)
11	**Expenses**	60,000	50,000
12	**Subsidiary Income**	**(27,000)**	
13	**Dividends Declared**		**10,000**
14		0	0
15	**Combined Net Income**		
16	**To Minority Interest (see distribution schedule)**		
17	**Balance to Controlling Interest (see distribution schedule)**		
18	Total Minority Interest		
19	Retained Earnings, Controlling Interest, Dec. 31, 19X1		
20			

Eliminations and Adjustments:

(1) Eliminate the current-year entries made in the investment account and in the subsidiary income account. It should be noted that when this step is completed, the balance in the investment account is the balance *at the beginning of the year.* At this point, the investment account and the Company S equity accounts are *adjusted to a common point in time* and are ready for elimination. Only dividends paid to outside minority stockholders remain on the worksheet.

(2) Eliminate the pro rata share of Company S equity balances *at the beginning of the year* against the investment account. The elimination of the parent's share of subsidiary stockholders' equity leaves only the minority interest in each element of the equity.

(3) Distribute the $10,000 excess cost as required by the determination and distribution of excess schedule on pages 3-3 to 3-4. In this example, Goodwill is recorded for $10,000.

(4) Amortize the resulting goodwill over the 10-year period. The current portion is $1,000 per year ($10,000 ÷ 10 years).

Worksheet 3-1 (see page 3-6)

Eliminations & Adjustments				Consolidated Income Statement	Minority Interest	Controlling Retained Earnings	Consolidated Balance Sheet	
(1)	9,000	(1)	27,000					1
		(2)	135,000					2
		(3)	10,000					3
(3)	10,000	(4)	1,000				9,000	4
							397,000	5
							(200,000)	6
						(123,000)		7
(2)	90,000				(10,000)			8
(2)	45,000				(5,000)			9
				(180,000)				10
(4)	1,000			111,000				11
(1)	27,000							12
		(1)	9,000		1,000			13
	182,000		182,000					14
				(69,000)				15
				3,000	(3,000)			16
				66,000		(66,000)		17
						(17,000)	(17,000)	18
						(189,000)	(189,000)	19
							0	20

Subsidiary Company S Income Distribution

	Internally generated net income	$ 30,000
	Adjusted income	$ 30,000
	Minority share	10%
	Minority interest	**$ 3,000**

Parent Company P Income Distribution

Goodwill amortization . . . . (4) $1,000	Internally generated net income	$ 40,000
	90% × Company S adjusted income of $30,000	27,000
	Controlling interest	**$66,000**

Worksheet 3-2

Simple Equity Method, Second Year
Company P and Subsidiary Company S
Worksheet for Consolidated Financial Statements
For Year Ended December 31, 19X2

	(Credit balance amounts are in parentheses.)	Trial Balance	
		Company P	Company S
1	**Investment in Company S**	**149,500**	
2			
3	**Goodwill**		
4	Other Assets (Net of Liabilities)	251,500	155,000
5	Common Stock ($10 par), Co. P	(200,000)	
6	**Retained Earnings, Jan. 1, 19X2, Co. P**	(190,000)	
7	Common Stock ($10 par), Co. S		(100,000)
8	Retained Earnings, Jan. 1, 19X2, Co. S		(70,000)
9	Revenue	(100,000)	(50,000)
10	Expenses	80,000	60,000
11	**Subsidiary Income**	**9,000**	
12	**Dividends Declared**		**5,000**
13		0	0
14	**Combined Net Income**		
15	**To Minority Interest (see distribution schedule)**		
16	**Balance to Controlling Interest (see distribution schedule)**		
17	Total Minority Interest		
18	Retained Earnings, Controlling Interest, Dec. 31, 19X2		
19			

Eliminations and Adjustments:

(1) Eliminate the current-year entries made in the investment account and in the subsidiary loss account. This step returns the investment in Company S account to its January 1, 19X2 balance. The investment account and the subsidiary equity accounts now are *stated at a common point in time,* which will facilitate their elimination.

(2) Using balances *at the beginning of the year,* eliminate 90% of the Company S equity balances against the remaining investment account.

(3) Distribute the $10,000 excess cost as indicated by the determination and distribution of excess schedule that was prepared on the date of acquisition.

(4) Amortize the goodwill over the selected 10-year period. It is necessary to record the amortization *for current and past periods,* because asset adjustments resulting from the consolidation process do not appear on the separate statements of the constituent companies. Thus, entry (4) reduces Goodwill by $2,000 for the 19X1 and 19X2 amortization. The amount for the current year is expensed, while the cumulative amortization for prior years is deducted from the beginning controlling retained earnings account. The minority interest does not share in the adjustments because the only goodwill originally acknowledged is that which is applicable to the controlling interest.

Worksheet 3-2 (see page 3-11)

Eliminations & Adjustments				Consolidated Income Statement	Minority Interest	Controlling Retained Earnings	Consolidated Balance Sheet	
Dr.		Cr.						
(1)	9,000	(2)	153,000					1
(1)	4,500	(3)	10,000					2
(3)	10,000	(4)	2,000				8,000	3
							406,500	4
							(200,000)	5
(4)	1,000					(189,000)		6
(2)	90,000				(10,000)			7
(2)	63,000				(7,000)			8
				(150,000)				9
(4)	1,000			141,000				10
		(1)	9,000					11
		(1)	4,500		500			12
	178,500		178,500					13
				(9,000)				14
				(1,000)	1,000			15
				10,000		(10,000)		16
					(15,500)		(15,500)	17
						(199,000)	(199,000)	18
							0	19

Subsidiary Company S Income Distribution

Internally generated loss	$10,000		
Adjusted loss.	$10,000		
Minority share.	10%		
Minority interest.	**$ 1,000**		

Parent Company P Income Distribution

Goodwill amortization . . . . (4) $ 1,000		Internally generated net income	$20,000
90% × Company S adjusted income of			
$10,000 9,000			
		Controlling interest	**$10,000**

Worksheet 3-3

Cost Method
Company P and Subsidiary Company S
Worksheet for Consolidated Financial Statements
For Year Ended December 31, 19X1

	(Credit balance amounts are in parentheses.)	Trial Balance	
		Company P	Company S
1	**Investment in Company S**	**145,000**	
2			
3	Goodwill		
4	Other Assets (Net of Liabilities)	227,000	170,000
5	Common Stock ($10 par), Co. P	(200,000)	
6	Retained Earnings, Jan. 1, 19X1, Co. P	(123,000)	
7	Common Stock ($10 par), Co. S		(100,000)
8	Retained Earnings, Jan. 1, 19X1, Co. S		(50,000)
9	Revenue	(100,000)	(80,000)
10	Expenses	60,000	50,000
11	**Subsidiary (Dividend) Income**	**(9,000)**	
12	**Dividends Declared**		**10,000**
13		0	0
14	Combined Net Income		
15	To Minority Interest (see distribution schedule)		
16	Balance to Controlling Interest (see distribution schedule)		
17	Total Minority Interest		
18	Retained Earnings, Controlling Interest, Dec. 31, 19X1		
19			

Eliminations and Adjustments:

(1) Eliminate intercompany dividends.
(2) Eliminate 90% of the Company S equity balances at the beginning of the year against the investment account.
(3) Distribute the $10,000 excess cost as indicated by the determination and distribution of excess schedule on pages 3-3 and 3-4.
(4) Amortize the goodwill for the current year.

Worksheet 3-3 (see page 3-12)

Eliminations & Adjustments				Consolidated Income Statement	Minority Interest	Controlling Retained Earnings	Consolidated Balance Sheet	
Dr.		Cr.						
		(2)	135,000					1
		(3)	10,000					2
(3)	10,000	(4)	1,000				9,000	3
							397,000	4
							(200,000)	5
						(123,000)		6
(2)	90,000				(10,000)			7
(2)	45,000				(5,000)			8
				(180,000)				9
(4)	1,000			111,000				10
(1)	9,000							11
		(1)	9,000		1,000			12
	155,000		155,000					13
				(69,000)				14
				3,000	(3,000)			15
				66,000		(66,000)		16
					(17,000)		(17,000)	17
						(189,000)	(189,000)	18
							0	19

Subsidiary Company S Income Distribution

Internally generated net income	$ 30,000
Adjusted income	$ 30,000
Minority share	10%
Minority interest	**$ 3,000**

Parent Company P Income Distribution

Goodwill amortization . . . . (4) $1,000	Internally generated net income	$ 40,000
	90% × Company S adjusted income of	
	$30,000	27,000
	Controlling interest	**$66,000**

Worksheet 3-4

Cost Method, Second Year
Company P and Subsidiary Company S
Worksheet for Consolidated Financial Statements
For Year Ended December 31, 19X2

	(Credit balance amounts are in parentheses.)	Trial Balance	
		Company P	Company S
1	**Investment in Company S**	145,000	
2			
3	Goodwill		
4	Other Assets (Net of Liabilities)	251,500	155,000
5	Common Stock ($10 par), Co. P	(200,000)	
6	**Retained Earnings, Jan. 1, 19X2, Co. P**	(172,000)	
7	Common Stock ($10 par), Co. S		(100,000)
8	Retained Earnings, Jan. 1, 19X2, Co. S		(70,000)
9	Revenue	(100,000)	(50,000)
10	Expenses	80,000	60,000
11	**Subsidiary (Dividend) Income**	(4,500)	
12	**Dividends Declared**		5,000
13		0	0
14	Combined Net Income		
15	To Minority Interest (see distribution schedule)		
16	Balance to Controlling Interest (see distribution schedule)		
17	Total Minority Interest		
18	Retained Earnings, Controlling Interest, Dec. 31, 19X2		
19			

Eliminations and Adjustments:

(C) Convert to simple equity method as of January 1, 19X2.

(1) Eliminate the current-year intercompany dividends.

(2) Eliminate 90% of the Company S equity balances at the beginning of the year against the investment account.

(3) Distribute the $10,000 excess cost as indicated by the determination and distribution of excess schedule that was prepared on the date of acquisition.

(4) Amortize the goodwill for the current year and one previous year.

Worksheet 3-4 (see page 3-12)

Eliminations & Adjustments		Consolidated Income Statement	Minority Interest	Controlling Retained Earnings	Consolidated Balance Sheet	
Dr.	Cr.					
(C) 18,000	(2) 153,000					1
	(3) 10,000					2
(3) 10,000	(4) 2,000				8,000	3
					406,500	4
					(200,000)	5
(4) 1,000	(C) 18,000			(189,000)		6
(2) 90,000			(10,000)			7
(2) 63,000			(7,000)			8
		(150,000)				9
(4) 1,000		141,000				10
(1) 4,500						11
	(1) 4,500		500			12
187,500	187,500					13
		(9,000)				14
		(1,000)	1,000			15
		10,000		(10,000)		16
		(15,500)			(15,500)	17
				(199,000)	(199,000)	18
					0	19

(handwritten note at rows 6–7: "undistributed earning by subsidiary", "90% · 20,000")

Subsidiary Company S Income Distribution

Internally generated **loss**	$10,000	
Adjusted income	$10,000	
Minority share.	10%	
Minority interest.	**$ 1,000**	

Parent Company P Income Distribution

Goodwill amortization . . . . (4) $ 1,000		Internally generated net income	$ 20,000
90% × Company S adjusted income of				
$10,000 9,000				
		Controlling interest	**$10,000**

Worksheet 3-5

Simple Equity Method, First Year
Paulos Company and Subsidiary Carlos Company
Worksheet for Consolidated Financial Statements
For Year Ended December 31, 19X1

	(Credit balance amounts are in parentheses.)	Trial Balance	
		Paulos	Carlos
1	Cash	100,000	50,000
2	Inventory	226,000	62,500
3	Land	200,000	150,000
4	Building	800,000	600,000
5	**Accumulated Depreciation, Building**	(80,000)	(315,000)
6	Equipment	400,000	150,000
7	**Accumulated Depreciation, Equipment**	(50,000)	(70,000)
8	**Investment in Carlos Company**	832,000	
9			
10			
11	Goodwill		112,500
12	Current Liabilities	(100,000)	
13	Bonds Payable		(200,000)
14	**Discount/Premium**		
15	Common Stock, Paulos	(1,500,000)	
16	Retained Earnings, Jan. 1, 19X1, Paulos	(700,000)	
17	Common Stock ($10 par), Carlos		(100,000)
18	Paid-In Capital in Excess of Par, Carlos		(150,000)
19	Retained Earnings, Jan. 1, 19X1, Carlos		(250,000)
20	Sales	(350,000)	(200,000)
21	**Cost of Goods Sold**	150,000	80,000
22	**Expenses**	120,000	60,000
23			
24			
25	**Subsidiary Income**	(48,000)	
26	**Dividends Declared**		20,000
27		0	0
28	Combined Net Income		
29	To Minority Interest (see distribution schedule)		
30	Balance to Controlling Interest (see distribution schedule)		
31	Total Minority Interest		
32	Retained Earnings, Controlling Interest, Dec. 31, 19X1		
33			

Worksheet 3-5 (see page 3-17)

Eliminations & Adjustments		Consolidated Income Statement	Minority Interest	Controlling Retained Earnings	Consolidated Balance Sheet	
Dr.	Cr.					
					150,000	1
					288,500	2
(3e) 40,000					390,000	3
					1,400,000	4
(3d) 160,000	**(4d) 8,000**				(243,000)	5
	(3c) 16,000				534,000	6
(4c) 3,200					(116,800)	7
(1) 16,000	(1) 48,000					8
	(2) 400,000					9
	(3) 400,000					10
(3f) 201,402	(4f) 20,140				293,762	11
					(100,000)	12
					(200,000)	13
(3b) 10,598	**(4b) 2,650**				7,948	14
					(1,500,000)	15
				(700,000)		16
(2) 80,000			(20,000)			17
(2) 120,000			(30,000)			18
(2) 200,000			(50,000)			19
		(550,000)				20
(3a) 4,000		234,000				21
(4b) 2,650	**(4c) 3,200**	207,590				22
(4d) 8,000						23
(4f) 20,140						24
(1) 48,000						25
	(1) 16,000		**4,000**			26
913,990	913,990					27
		(108,410)				28
		12,000	(12,000)			29
		96,410		(96,410)		30
			(108,000)		(108,000)	31
				(796,410)	(796,410)	32
					0	33

(continued)

Eliminations and Adjustments:

(1) Eliminate the current-year entries made in the investment in Carlos Company account and in the subsidiary income account. The investment account now is adjusted to its January 1, 19X1 balance so that it may be eliminated.

(2) Eliminate the 80% ownership portion of the subsidiary equity accounts against the investment. A $400,000 excess cost remains.

(3) Distribute the $400,000 excess cost as follows, in accordance with the determination and distribution of excess schedule:

   a) *Increase the beginning inventory by $4,000. However, the beginning inventory has been closed to the cost of goods sold; thus, the cost of goods sold is increased by $4,000. If the inventory had not been sold, the inventory account would be adjusted. The cost of goods sold in the later period of sale then would be adjusted on a subsequent worksheet.*

   b)   *Record discount of $10,598 on the bonds payable.*

   c) *Reduce the equipment by $16,000 by reducing the asset account directly.* *

   d) *Increase the building by $160,000 by decreasing its accumulated depreciation account.* *

   e)   *Increase the land by $40,000.*

   f)   *Increase the goodwill by $201,402.*

(4) Record amortizations resulting from the asset and liability revaluations of entry (3). The adjustments are lettered (a) through (f) to correspond with the revaluations in entry (3):

   a)   *No amortization required; adjustment already charged to the cost of goods sold.*

   b) *Record annual increase in interest expense; $10,598 net increase divided by 4 years equals $2,650.*

   c) *Record annual decrease in equipment depreciation expense; $16,000 net decrease divided by 5 years equals $3,200.*

   d) *Record annual increase in building depreciation expense; $160,000 net increase divided by 20 years equals $8,000.*

   e)   *No amortization results from adjustment of the land.*

   f)   *Record additional annual amortization of the goodwill; $201,402 net increase in the goodwill divided by the 10-year life equals $20,140. It is assumed that the previously recorded goodwill of $125,000 on January 1, 19X1, also is being amortized over 10 years.*

*In accord with page 3-17, the depreciable asset account is directly adjusted only when the market value is below book value. Otherwise, the adjustment is made to the accumulated depreciation account.

Subsidiary Carlos Company Income Distribution

	Internally generated net income	$ 60,000
	Adjusted income	$ 60,000
	Minority share	20%
	Minority interest	**$12,000**

Parent Paulos Company Income Distribution

Investment adjustment . . . . (3a)	**$ 4,000**	Internally generated net income		$ 80,000
Discount amortization . . . . (4b)	**2,650**	80% × Carlos Company adjusted		
Building depreciation . . . . (4d)	**8,000**	income of $60,000		48,000
Goodwill amortization . . . . (4f)	20,140	**Equipment depreciation . . . . . . (4c)**		**3,200**
		Controlling interest		**$96,410**

Worksheet 3-6

Simple Equity Method, Second Year
Paulos Company and Subsidiary Carlos Company
Worksheet for Consolidated Financial Statements
For Year Ended December 31, 19X2

	(Credit balance amounts are in parentheses.)	Trial Balance	
		Paulos	Carlos
1	Cash	322,000	160,000
2	Inventory	210,000	120,000
3	Land	200,000	150,000
4	Building	800,000	600,000
5	Accumulated Depreciation, Building	(120,000)	(330,000)
6	Equipment	400,000	150,000
7	Accumulated Depreciation, Equipment	(100,000)	(90,000)
8	Investment in Carlos Company	896,000	
9			
10			
11	Goodwill		100,000
12	Current Liabilities	(150,000)	(40,000)
13	Bonds Payable		(200,000)
14	Discount/Premium		
15	Common Stock, Paulos	(1,500,000)	
16	**Retained Earnings, Jan. 1, 19X2, Paulos**	**(828,000)**	
17			
18			
19			
20	Common Stock, Carlos		(100,000)
21	Paid-In Capital in Excess of Par, Carlos		(150,000)
22	Retained Earnings, Jan. 1, 19X2, Carlos		(290,000)
23	Sales	(400,000)	(300,000)
24	Cost of Goods Sold	200,000	120,000
25	Expenses	150,000	80,000
26			
27			
28	**Subsidiary Income**	**(80,000)**	
29	**Dividends Declared**		**20,000**
30		0	0
31	Combined Net Income		
32	To Minority Interest (see distribution schedule)		
33	**Balance to Controlling Interest** (see distribution schedule)		
34	Total Minority Interest		
35	Retained Earnings, Controlling Interest, Dec. 31, 19X2		
36			

Worksheet 3-6 (see page 3-18)

Eliminations & Adjustments Dr.		Eliminations & Adjustments Cr.		Consolidated Income Statement	Minority Interest	Controlling Retained Earnings	Consolidated Balance Sheet	
							482,000	1
							330,000	2
(3e)	40,000						390,000	3
							1,400,000	4
(3d)	160,000	(4d)	16,000				(306,000)	5
		(3c)	16,000				534,000	6
(4c)	6,400						(183,600)	7
(1)	16,000	(1)	48,000					8
		(2)	432,000					9
		(3)	400,000					10
(3f)	201,402	(4f)	40,280				261,122	11
							(190,000)	12
							(200,000)	13
(3b)	10,598	(4b)	5,300				5,298	14
							(1,500,000)	15
(3a)	4,000	(4c)	3,200			(796,410)		16
(4b)	2,650							17
(4d)	8,000							18
(4f)	20,140							19
(2)	80,000				(20,000)			20
(2)	120,000				(30,000)			21
(2)	232,000				(58,000)			22
				(700,000)				23
				320,000				24
(4b)	2,650	(4c)	3,200	257,590				25
(4d)	8,000							26
(4f)	20,140							27
(1)	80,000							28
		(1)	16,000		4,000			29
	1,011,980		1,011,980					30
				(122,410)				31
				20,000	(20,000)			32
				102,410		(102,410)		33
					(124,000)		(124,000)	34
						(898,820)	(898,820)	35
							0	36

(continued)

Eliminations and Adjustments:

(1) Eliminate the current-year entries made in the investment in Carlos Company account and in the subsidiary income account. The investment account now is adjusted back to its January 1, 19X2 balance so that it may be eliminated.

(2) Eliminate the 80% ownership portion of the January 1, 19X2 subsidiary equity accounts against the investment. A $400,000 excess cost remains.

(3) Distribute the $400,000 excess cost as required by the determination and distribution of excess schedule. The distribution is identical to that shown in Worksheet 3-5 except for the January 1, 19X1 inventory adjustment of $4,000. The inventory adjustment now is carried to the purchaser's January 1, 19X2 retained earnings balance since it is an adjustment to 19X1 income.

(4) Record amortizations resulting from the asset and liability revaluations of entry (3). The amortizations include those for the current and previous periods because the trial balances of the separate companies do not reflect the amortizations on the December 31, 19X1 consolidated worksheet. The adjustments are lettered (a) through (f) to correspond with the revaluations in entry (3) of Worksheet 3-5:

a)   *No amortization required; adjustment already charged to January 1, 19X2 controlling retained earnings account.*

b)   *Record $2,650 annual increase in interest expense for 19X1 and 19X2. The 19X1 amount is carried to January 1, 19X2 retained earnings, while the 19X2 amount is added to current expense.*

c)   *Record $3,200 annual decrease in equipment depreciation for 19X1 and 19X2. The 19X1 portion is carried to January 1, 19X2 controlling retained earnings, while the 19X2 adjustment is reflected in current expense.*

d)   *Record $8,000 annual increase in 19X1 and 19X2 building depreciation; the 19X1 adjustment reduces the January 1, 19X2 controlling retained earnings account; the 19X2 adjustment increases current expense.*

e)   *No amortization results from adjustment of the land.*

f)   *Amortize the goodwill for the current year by increasing expenses and for the past year by reducing the January 1, 19X2 controlling retained earnings account.*

Subsidiary Carlos Company Income Distribution

	Internally generated net income . . . . $ 100,000
	Adjusted income . . . . $ 100,000
	Minority share 20%
	Minority interest . . . . **$ 20,000**

Parent Paulos Company Income Distribution

Discount amortization. . . . . (4b)	**$ 2,650**	Internally generated net income . . . . $ 50,000
Building depreciation . . . . (4d)	**8,000**	80% × Carlos Company adjusted
Goodwill amortization . . . . (4f)	20,140	income of $100,000 80,000
		Equipment depreciation . . . . . . (4c) 3,200
		Controlling interest **$102,410**

Worksheet 3-7

Intraperiod Purchase; Subsidiary Books Closed on Purchase Date
Company P and Subsidiary Company S
Worksheet for Consolidated Financial Statements
For Year Ended December 31, 19X1

	(Credit balance amounts are in parentheses.)	Trial Balance	
		Company P	Company S
1	Current Assets	187,600	87,500
2	**Investment in Company S**	**118,400**	
3			
4			
5	Goodwill		
6	Equipment	400,000	80,000
7	Accumulated Depreciation	(200,000)	(32,500)
8	Liabilities	(60,000)	(12,000)
9	Common Stock, Co. P	(250,000)	
10	Retained Earnings, **Jan. 1, 19X1, Co. P**	(100,000)	
11	Common Stock, Co. S		(50,000)
12	Retained Earnings, **July 1, 19X1, Co. S**		(58,000)
13	Sales	(500,000)	(92,000)
14	Cost of Goods Sold	350,000	60,000
15	Expenses	70,000	12,000
16	**Subsidiary Income**	**(16,000)**	
17	Dividends Declared		5,000
18			
19		0	0
20			
21	Combined Net Income		
22	To Minority Interest (see distribution schedule)		
23	Balance to Controlling Interest (see distribution schedule)		
24	Total Minority Interest		
25	Retained Earnings, Controlling Interest, Dec. 31, 19X1		
26			

Eliminations and Adjustments:

(1) Eliminate the entries made in the investment in Company S account and in the subsidiary income account to record the parent's 80% controlling interest in the subsidiary's second *six-months' income and the subsidiary dividends,* restoring the investment account to its balance as of the July 1, 19X1 investment date.

(2) Eliminate 80% of the subsidiary's *July 1, 19X1* equity balances against the *balance* of the investment account.

(3) Distribute the excess of cost over book value of $20,000 to Goodwill in accordance with the determination and distribution of excess schedule.

(4) Amortize for one-half year the excess attributable to the goodwill.

Worksheet 3-7 (see page 3-20)

Eliminations & Adjustments				Consolidated Income Statement	Minority Interest	Controlling Retained Earnings	Consolidated Balance Sheet	
Dr.		Cr.						
							275,100	1
(1)	4,000	(1)	16,000					2
		(2)	86,400					3
		(3)	20,000					4
(3)	20,000	(4)	1,000				19,000	5
							480,000	6
							(232,500)	7
							(72,000)	8
							(250,000)	9
						(100,000)		10
(2)	40,000				(10,000)			11
(2)	46,000				(11,600)			12
				(592,000)				13
				410,000				14
(4)	1,000			83,000				15
(1)	16,000							16
		(1)	4,000		1,000			17
								18
	127,400		127,400					19
								20
				(99,000)				21
				4,000	(4,000)			22
				95,000		(95,000)		23
					(24,600)		(24,600)	24
						(195,000)	(195,000)	25
							0	26

(continued)

Subsidiary Company S Income Distribution

	Internally generated net income	
	(last 6 mo.)	**$20,000**
	Adjusted income	$ 20,000
	Minority share	20%
	Minority interest	**$ 4,000**

Parent Company P Income Distribution

Goodwill amortization . . . . (4)	$1,000	Internally generated net income	$ 80,000
		80% × Company S adjusted income	
		of $20,000 **(last 6 mo.)**	**16,000**
		Controlling interest	**$95,000**

Worksheet 3-8

Intraperiod Purchase; Subsidiary Books Not Closed on Purchase Date
Company P and Subsidiary Company S
Worksheet for Consolidated Financial Statements
For Year Ended December 31, 19X1

| | (Credit balance amounts are in parentheses.) | Trial Balance | |
		Company P	Company S
1	Current Assets	187,600	87,500
2	**Investment in Company S**	**118,400**	
3			
4			
5	Goodwill		
6	Equipment	400,000	80,000
7	Accumulated Depreciation	(200,000)	(32,500)
8	Liabilities	(60,000)	(12,000)
9	Common Stock, Co. P	(250,000)	
10	Retained Earnings, **Jan. 1, 19X1, Co. P**	(100,000)	
11	Common Stock, Co. S		(50,000)
12	Retained Earnings, **July 1, 19X1, Co. S**		(45,000)
13	Sales	(500,000)	(182,000)
14	Cost of Goods Sold	350,000	120,000
15	Expenses	70,000	24,000
16	**Subsidiary Income**	**(16,000)**	
17	**Dividends Declared**		**10,000**
18			
19	**Purchased Income**		
20		0	0
21			
22	Combined Net Income		
23	To Minority Interest (see distribution schedule)		
24	Balance to Controlling Interest (see distribution schedule)		
25	Total Minority Interest		
26	Retained Earnings, Controlling Interest, Dec. 31, 19X1		
27			

Worksheet 3-8 (see page 3-21)

Eliminations & Adjustments				Consolidated Income Statement	Minority Interest	Controlling Retained Earnings	Consolidated Balance Sheet	
Dr.		Cr.						
							275,100	1
(1)	4,000	(1)	16,000					2
		(2)	86,400					3
		(3)	20,000					4
(3)	20,000	(4)	1,000				19,000	5
							480,000	6
							(232,500)	7
							(72,000)	8
							(250,000)	9
						(100,000)		10
(2)	40,000				(10,000)			11
(2)	36,000				(9,000)			12
				(682,000)				13
				470,000				14
(4)	1,000			95,000				15
(1)	16,000							16
		(1)	4,000		2,000			17
		(2)	4,000					18
(2)	14,400			14,400				19
	131,400		131,400					20
								21
				(102,600)				22
				7,600	(7,600)			23
				95,000		(95,000)		24
					(24,600)		(24,600)	25
						(195,000)	(195,000)	26
							0	27

(continued)

Eliminations and Adjustments:

(1) Eliminate the entries made in the investment account and in the subsidiary income account (same as Worksheet 3-7). Notice that Company P's share of the subsidiary dividends declared are from those declared *after* the purchase.

(2) Eliminate 80% of the subsidiary equity balances at the beginning of the year plus 80% of Company S's income earned as of July 1, 19X1, against the investment account. The share of preacquisition income is entered as *Purchased Income* to emphasize that this income was earned prior to the date of purchase by Company P. For elimination purposes, this account may be viewed as a supplement to retained earnings. Since the subsidiary also declared dividends *prior to July 1, 19X1,* the controlling percentage of those dividends should be eliminated in this entry by crediting Dividends Declared.

(3) Distribute the $20,000 excess of cost over book value (same as Worksheet 3-7).

(4) Amortize for 6 months the excess attributable to the goodwill (same as Worksheet 3-7).

Subsidiary Company S Income Distribution

	Internally generated net income **entire year**	**$38,000**
	Adjusted income	$ 38,000
	Minority share	20%
	Minority interest	**$ 7,600**

Parent Company P Income Distribution

Goodwill amortization . . . . (4) $1,000	Internally generated net income	$ 80,000
	80% × Company S adjusted income of $20,000 **(last 6 mo.)**	16,000
	Controlling interest	**$95,000**

Worksheet 3-9

Pooling of Interests
Company I and Subsidiary Company C
Worksheet for Consolidated Financial Statements
For Year Ended December 31, 19X3

	(Credit balance amounts are in parentheses.)	Trial Balance	
		Company I	Company C
1	Current Assets	46,000	35,000
2	Property, Plant, and Equipment (net)	64,500	60,000
3	Investment in Company C	81,000	
4			
5	Liabilities		(5,000)
6	Common Stock ($2 par), Co. I	(55,400)	
7	Paid-In Capital in Excess of Par, Co. I	(3,600)	
8	Retained Earnings, Jan. 1, 19X3, Co. I	(60,000)	
9	Common Stock ($10 par), Co. C		(10,000)
10	Retained Earnings, Jan. 1, 19X3, Co. C		(55,000)
11	Sales	(150,000)	(100,000)
12	Cost of Goods Sold	70,000	50,000
13	Expenses	30,000	25,000
14	Subsidiary Income	(22,500)	
15		0	0
16	Combined Net Income		
17	To Minority Interest (see distribution schedule)		
18	Balance to Controlling Interest (see distribution schedule)		
19	Total Minority Interest		
20	Retained Earnings, Controlling Interest, Dec. 31, 19X3		
21			

Eliminations and Adjustments:

(1) Eliminate the current-year entries in the investment in Company C account and in the subsidiary income account, restoring the investment account to its January 1, 19X3 balance, so that it may be eliminated.

(2) Eliminate 90% of the balances in the Company C stockholders' equity accounts against the investment account. No excess results.

Worksheet 3-9 (see page 3-23)

Eliminations & Adjustments			Consolidated Income Statement	Minority Interest	Controlling Retained Earnings	Consolidated Balance Sheet	
Dr.		Cr.					
						81,000	1
						124,500	2
	(1)	22,500					3
	(2)	58,500					4
						(5,000)	5
						(55,400)	6
						(3,600)	7
					(60,000)		8
(2)	9,000			(1,000)			9
(2)	49,500			(5,500)			10
			(250,000)				11
			120,000				12
			55,000				13
(1)	22,500						14
	81,000	81,000					15
			(75,000)				16
			2,500	(2,500)			17
			72,500		(72,500)		18
				(9,000)		(9,000)	19
					(132,500)	(132,500)	20
						0	21

Subsidiary Company C Income Distribution

Internally generated net income	$ 25,000
Adjusted income	$ 25,000
Minority share	10%
Minority interest	**$25,000**

Parent Company I Income Distribution

Internally generated net income	$ 50,000
90% × Company C adjusted income of $25,000	22,500
Controlling interest	**$72,500**

Worksheet 3-10

Vertical Format, Equity Method
Paulos Company and Subsidiary Carlos Company
Worksheet for Consolidated Financial Statements
For Year Ended December 31, 19X2

	Compare this worksheet to Worksheet 3-6. Note that eliminations and adjustments, explanations as well as the income distribution schedules, are the same for Worksheet 3-10 as for Worksheet 3-6.	Financial Statements	
		Paulos	Carlos
1	**Income Statement**		
2	Sales	(400,000)	(300,000)
3	Cost of Goods Sold	200,000	120,000
4	Expenses	150,000	80,000
5			
6			
7	Subsidiary Income	(80,000)	
8	Net Income	(130,000)	(100,000)
9			
10	Minority Interest (see income distribution schedule)		
11			
12	Controlling Interest (see income distribution schedule)		
13			
14	**Retained Earnings Statement**		
15	Retained Earnings, Jan. 1, 19X2, Paulos	(828,000)	
16			
17			
18			
19			
20	Retained Earnings, Jan. 1, 19X2, Carlos		(290,000)
21	Net income (carrydown)	(130,000)	(100,000)
22	Dividends Declared		20,000
23	Retained Earnings, Dec. 31, 19X2	(958,000)	(370,000)
24			
25	Retained Earnings, Minority Interest, Dec. 31, 19X2		
26			
27	Retained Earnings, Controlling Interest, Dec. 31, 19X2		
28			
29	**Balance Sheet**		
30	Cash	322,000	160,000
31	Inventory	210,000	120,000
32	Land	200,000	150,000
33	Building	800,000	600,000
34	Accumulated Depreciation, Building	(120,000)	(330,000)
35	Equipment	400,000	150,000
36	Accumulated Depreciation, Equipment	(100,000)	(90,000)
37	Investment in Carlos Company	896,000	
38			
39			
40	Goodwill		100,000
41	Current Liabilities	(150,000)	(40,000)
42	Bonds Payable		(200,000)
43	Discount/Premium		
44	Common Stock, Paulos	(1,500,000)	
45	Common Stock, Carlos		(100,000)
46	Paid-In Capital in Excess of Par, Carlos		(150,000)
47	Retained Earnings, Dec. 31, 19X2 (carrydown)	(958,000)	(370,000)
48	Retained Earnings, Controlling Interest, Dec. 31, 19X2		
49			
50	Retained Earnings, Minority Interest, Dec. 31, 19X2		
51	Total Minority Interest		
52	Total	0	0

Worksheet 3-10 (see page 3-25)

Eliminations & Adjustments				Minority Interest	Consolidated	
Dr.		**Cr.**				
						1
					(700,000)	2
					320,000	3
(4b)	2,650	(4c)	3,200		257,590	4
(4d)	8,000					5
(4f)	20,140					6
(1)	80,000					7
					(122,410)	8
						9
				(20,000)		10
						11
					(102,410)	12
						13
						14
					(796,410)	15
(3a)	4,000	(4c)	3,200			16
(4b)	2,650					17
(4d)	8,000					18
(4f)	20,140					19
(2)	232,000			(58,000)		20
				(20,000)	(102,410)	21
		(1)	16,000	4,000		22
						23
						24
				(74,000)		25
						26
					(898,820)	27
						28
						29
					482,000	30
					330,000	31
(3e)	40,000				390,000	32
					1,400,000	33
(3d)	160,000	(4d)	16,000		(306,000)	34
		(3c)	16,000		534,000	35
(4c)	6,400				(183,600)	36
(1)	16,000	(1)	80,000			37
		(2)	432,000			38
		(3)	400,000			39
(3f)	201,402	(4f)	40,280		261,122	40
					(190,000)	41
					(200,000)	42
(3b)	10,598	(4b)	5,300		5,298	43
					(1,500,000)	44
(2)	80,000			(20,000)		45
(2)	120,000			(30,000)		46
						47
					(898,820)	48
						49
				(74,000)		50
				(124,000)	(124,000)	51
	1,011,980		1,011,980		0	52

Worksheet 3-11

Equity Method, Tax Issues
Paro Company and Subsidiary Sunstran Corporation
Worksheet for Consolidated Financial Statements
For Year Ended December 31, 19X1

	(Credit balance amounts are in parentheses.)	Trial Balance	
		Paro	Sunstran
1	Cash	324,000	30,000
2	Accounts Receivable (net)	354,000	95,000
3	Inventory	540,000	100,000
4	Land	100,000	30,000
5	Building	1,300,000	950,000
6	Accumulated Depreciation, Building	(400,000)	(300,000)
7	**Noncurrent Deferred Tax Expense**		
8	Investment in Sunstran Company	1,058,000	
9			
10			
11	Goodwill		
12	Current Liabilities	(248,000)	(20,000)
13	**Deferred Tax Liability**		
14			
15	Common Stock, Paro	(510,000)	
16	Retained Earnings, Jan. 1, 19X1, Paro	(1,950,000)	
17			
18	Common Stock, Sunstran		(100,000)
19	Paid-In Capital in Excess of Par, Sunstran		(300,000)
20	Retained Earnings, Jan. 1, 19X1, Sunstran		(400,000)
21			
22	Sales	(3,400,000)	(900,000)
23	Cost of Goods Sold	2,070,000	600,000
24	Expenses	530,000	150,000
25			
26	Subsidiary Income	(84,000)	
27	Provision for Tax	216,000	45,000
28			
29	Dividends Declared	100,000	20,000
30		0	0
31	Combined Net Income		
32	To Minority Interest (see distribution schedule)		
33	Balance to Controlling Interest (see distribution schedule)		
34	Total Minority Interest		
35	Retained Earnings, Controlling Interest, Dec. 31, 19X2		
36			

Worksheet 3-11 (see page 3-30)

Eliminations & Adjustments			Consolidated Income Statement	Minority Interest	Controlling Retained Earnings	Consolidated Balance Sheet	
Dr.		Cr.					
						354,000	1
						449,000	2
						640,000	3
						130,000	4
						2,250,000	5
(3b)	160,000	(4b)	8,000				(548,000)	6
(3d)	60,000						60,000	7
(1)	16,000	(1)	84,000					8
		(2)	640,000					9
		(3)	350,000					10
(3e)	220,000	(4e)	22,000				198,000	11
						(268,000)	12
(4c)	2,400	(3c)	48,000				(105,000)	13
(4f)	6,600	(3f)	66,000					14
						(510,000)	15
					(1,950,000)		16
							17
(2)	80,000				(20,000)			18
(2)	240,000				(60,000)			19
(2)	320,000				(80,000)			20
							21
			(4,300,000)				22
			2,670,000				23
(4b)	8,000			710,000				24
(4e)	22,000							25
(1)	84,000							26
(3a)	24,000	(4c)	2,400	276,000				27
		(4f)	6,600					28
		(1)	16,000		4,000	100,000		29
1,227,000		1,227,000						30
				(644,000)				31
				21,000	(21,000)			32
				623,000		(623,000)		33
					(177,000)		(177,000)	34
						(2,473,000)	(2,473,000)	35
							0	36

(continued)

Eliminations and Adjustments:

(1) Eliminate the current-year entries made in the investment in Sunstran Corporation account and in the subsidiary income account. The investment account is adjusted now to its January 1, 19X1 balance so that it may be eliminated.

(2) Eliminate the 80% ownership portion of the subsidiary equity accounts against the investment. A $350,000 excess cost remains.

(3) Distribute the $350,000 excess cost as follows, in accordance with the determination and distribution of excess schedule:

    a) *Record the current portion of tax loss carryover used this period. It is assumed the parent reduced its provision for the carryover used.*

    b) *Increase the building by $160,000 by lowering accumulated depreciation.*

    c) *Record the deferred tax liability related to the building increase.*

    d) *Record the noncurrent portion of the tax loss carryover.*

    e) *Record the goodwill.*

    f) *Record the deferred tax liability applicable to goodwill.*

(4) Record amortizations resulting from the asset and liability revaluations of entry (3).

    a) *No amortization. The tax loss carryover was already debited to the provision for tax.*

    b) *Record the annual increase in building depreciation; $160,000 net increase in the building divided by its 20-year life equals $8,000.*

    c) *Reduce the provision for tax account by 30% of the increase in depreciation expense ($2,400).*

    d) *No amortization.*

    e) *Amortize the goodwill for the current year; $220,000 divided by the 10-year life equals $22,000.*

    f) *Reduce the provision for tax account by 30% of the goodwill amortization.*

Subsidiary Sunstran Company Income Distribution

	Internally generated net income	$ 105,000
	Adjusted income	$ 105,000
	Minority share	20%
	Minority interest	**$ 21,000**

Parent Paro Company Income Distribution

Building depreciation	(4b)	$ 8,000	Internally generated net income	$ 584,000
Goodwill amortization.	(4e)	22,000	80% × Sunstran Company adjusted	
Current tax carryover	(4a)	24,000	income of $105,000	84,000
			Decrease in provision for tax	
			(4c)	**2,400**
			(4f)	**6,600**
			Controlling interest	**$623,000**

SPECIAL APPENDIX

1

Possible New Consolidation Procedures—Goodwill

The FASB issued an Exposure Draft, *Consolidated Financial Statements: Policy and Procedures*, in October of 1995. In June of 1996, a working draft of a possible pronouncement was released. Both the Exposure Draft and the subsequent revised working draft may cause significant changes in the entities that must consolidate and the methods that will be used. This matter is very controversial, and at the time of publication, no final action had been taken.

Chapter 2 included a discussion of a new definition of control that would require companies that are not consolidating now to do so in the future, if the new standards are passed. If the new standards are passed, consolidation could be required with less than a 50% ownership interest. The term *minority interest* would be renamed the *noncontrolling interest.* The name change reflects the fact that the non-parent-owned interest could be 50% or more, in which case it could no longer be called a minority interest. The concern of this appendix is to study the possible changes in consolidation procedures which could occur in the future.

Summary of Current Procedure

Chapters 2 and 3 of this text have practiced the *Parent Company* theory of consolidating a subsidiary. Under this approach, only the controlling percentage of subsidiary accounts are adjusted to reflect market values. If, for example, the parent purchases an 80% interest, all accounts are adjusted to reflect only 80% of the difference between recorded book and market value. This procedure reflects current accounting practice and is used throughout this text. A review of our prior determination and distribution of excess schedules confirms that this is the approach used.

The current approach produces a mixture of account balances on the consolidated balance sheet that are hard to defend. The consolidated balance sheet contains the following balances for an 80%-owned subsidiary:

Accounts	Valuation
Parent company accounts	Historical cost
Subsidiary company accounts:	
80%-parent-owned portion	Market value on purchase date
20% noncontrolling interest	Historical cost

This mixture of values may be confusing and may not be fully understood by the users of financial statements. The proposals of the FASB would provide consistency for the subsidiary accounts. They would be recorded at 100% of market value, no matter what the parent ownership level. The possible exception, raised by the *Exposure Draft*, is goodwill.

Both the FASB *Exposure Draft* and the later *Working Draft* applied variations of the *Economic Unit Concept* to purchases of a subsidiary. Under a true *Economic Unit Concept*, all subsidiary accounts would be adjusted to 100% of market value, no matter what the level of parent company ownership. Goodwill, when implied by the purchase price, would also be recorded at its estimated full market value. If, for example, the excess price available for goodwill on an 80% purchase was $80,000, the estimated market value of total goodwill would be $100,000 ($80,000 ÷ 80% interest). The total value of goodwill would be imputed from the price paid for the 80% interest. The noncontrolling interest would receive an equity increase for its 20% share of all account adjustments, including goodwill.

The imputing of value to goodwill, beyond that actually paid for by the parent, met with great controversy. The 1995 *Exposure Draft* did not impute goodwill to the noncontrolling interest. Many accountants believe that goodwill reflects a premium paid to achieve control. They believe that the amount paid for goodwill is not proportionate to the size of the interest purchased. Others believe that goodwill is a payment for excess future earnings and that it should be proportionate with the level of ownership. The working draft issued by the FASB in June of 1996 returned to a true *Economic Unit Concept* and confirmed the 100% adjustment of all accounts, including goodwill. Under the 1996 *Working Draft*, goodwill would be implied to the noncontrolling interest as illustrated above.

Applying the Economic Unit Concept—Full Goodwill

We will illustrate the *Economic Unit Concept—full goodwill* by applying it to the facts of the Paulos and Carlos Companies used on pages 3-15–3-18 in Chapter 3. Based on the market values provided, the following determination and distribution of excess schedule would be prepared. The format of the schedule remains intact. New columns are added to display

- The total, 100%, adjustment being made to all subsidiary asset and liability accounts;
- The adjustment to the noncontrolling equity interest;
- The amortization of the adjustments that apply to the noncontrolling interest in future periods.

Notice the following features of the revised determination and distribution of excess schedule:

- Zone analysis is unchanged. It is an analysis of only the controlling interest that was purchased.
- The excess of cost or book value is still only the amount applicable to the controlling interest.
- The total adjustment for all accounts is now displayed. It is then distributed (80/20 in this example) to the controlling and noncontrolling interest.
- 100% of existing goodwill is made available to adjust fixed assets.
- The annual amortization amounts are also shown separately for the controlling and noncontrolling interest.
- The total goodwill adjustment is not a given. It is inferred from the remaining excess on the controlling interest. In this example, the remaining excess, applicable to the controlling interest, was $301,402. This is viewed as the goodwill on only the 80% parent interest. Thus, the $301,402 parent interest in goodwill is divided by 80% to infer a total goodwill value of $376,752.

Company P and Subsidiary Company S
Determination and Distribution of Excess Schedule
January 1, 19X1

	Company	Control %	Controlling Interest				
Price paid for investment including direct acquisition costs:			$800,000				
Market value of total net assets:	$623,248	80%	498,598				
Market value of priority accounts	(156,752)	80%	(125,402)				
Analysis of price: **Goodwill** . .			301,402				

	Total	Controlling	NCI				
Price paid for investment		$ 800,000					
Less book value interest acquired:							
Common stock ($10 par) . .	$ 100,000						
Paid-in capital in excess of par.	150,000						
Retained earnings.	250,000						
Total stockholders' equity .	$ 500,000						
Interest acquired	80%	400,000					
Excess of cost over book value (debit)		$ 400,000					

					Amortization Periods	Controlling Amortization	NCI Amortization
Adjustment of priority accounts:							
Inventory	**5,000**	**4,000**	**1,000**	**Dr.**	**1**	**4,000**	**1,000**
Discount on bonds payable	**13,248**	**10,598**	**2,650**	**Dr.**	**4**	**2,650**	**662**
Available for fixed assets:		$ 385,402					
Add existing goodwill . . .	**125,000**	**100,000**	**(25,000)**	**Cr.**	**10**	**(10,000)**	**(2,500)**
Adjusted excess available for fixed assets		$ 485,402					
Land	**50,000**	**40,000**	**10,000**	**Dr.**			
Building	**200,000**	**160,000**	**40,000**	**Dr.**	**20**	**8,000**	**2,000**
Equipment	**(20,000)**	**(16,000)**	**(4,000)**	**Cr.**	**5**	**(3,200)**	**(800)**
Goodwill	**376,752**	**$301,402**	**75,350**	**Dr.**	**10**	**30,140**	**7,535**
Total NCI adjustment.			$100,000				
Net adjustment to goodwill	**$251,752**				**10**	**20,140**	**5,035**

 Worksheet SA1-1, pages SA1-12 to SA1-13, is a consolidated financial statements worksheet for Paulos Company and Carlos Company one year after the acquisition. During the year, Carlos had net income of $60,000 and declared $20,000 in dividends. Paulos Company shows the simple-equity-adjusted balance for its investment in Carlos.

Carefully review Worksheet SA1-1 for the procedures used in the first period of consolidated reporting:

- Entry (3) distributes the $400,000 excess of cost on the parent investment and credits the noncontrolling interest $100,000 for its share of all asset revaluations. The account used to adjust the noncontrolling interest is *NCI (noncontrolling interest)—adjustment*. The precise account used is not important, so long as the noncontrolling interest is credited. All noncontrolling interest equity accounts are summed into a single amount, *total noncontrolling interest*, on the consolidated balance sheet.

- The $500,000 sum of the excess of cost over book value ($400,000) and the noncontrolling equity adjustment ($100,000) are distributed in entries (3a) through (3e). Each account is adjusted to 100% of market value as indicated by the determination and distribution of excess schedule. Entry (3a) reflects the increase in inventory. Since the inventory was assumed to be sold during the year, the adjustment goes to the cost of goods sold.

- The 4 series entries amortize excess adjustments for the current year. Since it is the first year of consolidation, there are no adjustments for prior periods. There is no entry (4a) because inventory is not amortized. It is just charged to the cost of goods sold in the period it is sold. There is no entry 4e because adjustments to land are not amortized. Adjustments are made as they apply to both the controlling and noncontrolling interests.

- The income distribution schedules require careful study. All excess amortizations, including goodwill, are charged to the noncontrolling interest schedule. This means that the noncontrolling and controlling interests will share (80/20) these amortizations as they share the total income of the subsidiary company.

- The worksheet uses the proposed new FASB definition of *consolidated net income.* It would become the total income of the consolidated entity. Under current practice, consolidated net income is the income allocable to only the controlling interest. The FASB proposal views the noncontolling interest (formerly, the minority interest) in income as a distribution of consolidated income, not an expense.

The consolidated income statement that would result from Worksheet SA1-1 would be presented as follows:

Sales	$ 550,000
Less cost of goods sold	235,000
Gross profit	315,000
Operating expenses	214,487
Consolidated Net Income	**$100,513**
Distributed to:	
Noncontrolling interest	4,103
Controlling interest	96,410

Worksheets in subsequent periods would record amortizations of excess adjustments for prior periods as an adjustment of both the controlling retained earnings and the noncontolling interest on an 80/20 basis.

Applying the Economic Unit Concept— *Goodwill on Only the Controlling Interest*

The original *Exposure Draft,* issued in 1995, limited the recording of goodwill to only the controlling interest. Under this proposal, only the remaining excess applicable to the controlling interest would be recorded as goodwill. No goodwill would be inferred to the noncontrolling interest. This approach views goodwill as primarily payment made to achieve control rather than a payment for excess income.

The determination and distribution of excess schedule format, displayed above, would be slightly modified. All goodwill adjustments would be limited to only the controlling interest. Specifically,

- Only the controlling portion (80%) of existing goodwill is made available for redistribution to fixed assets.
- Only new goodwill, applicable to the controlling interest, is recorded. No goodwill is inferred for the noncontrolling interest.

The newly revised determination and distribution of excess schedule would be prepared as follows:

Company P and Subsidiary Company S
Determination and Distribution of Excess Schedule
January 1, 19X1

	Company	Control %	Controlling Interest
Price paid for investment including direct acquisition costs:			$800,000
Market value of total net assets:	$623,248	80%	498,598
Market value of priority accounts	(156,752)	80%	(125,402)
Analysis of price: **Goodwill** . .			301,402

	Total	Controlling	NCI
Price paid for investment		$ 800,000	
Less book value interest acquired:			
Common stock ($10 par) . .	$100,000		
Paid-in capital in excess of par.	150,000		
Retained earnings.	250,000		
Total stockholders' equity .	$500,000		
Interest acquired	80%	400,000	
Excess of cost over book value (debit)		$ 400,000	

					Amortization Periods	Controlling Amortization	NCI Amortization
Adjustment of priority accounts:							
Inventory	**5,000**	**4,000**	**1,000**	**Dr.**	**1**	**4,000**	**1,000**
Discount on bonds payable	**13,248**	**10,598**	**2,650**	**Dr.**	**4**	**2,650**	**662**
Available for fixed assets:		$ 385,402					
Add existing goodwill 80%	**125,000**	**100,000**		**Cr.**	**10**	**(10,000)**	
Adjusted available for fixed assets		$ 485,402					
Land	**$ 50,000**	**40,000**	**10,000**	**Dr.**			

(continued)

Building	200,000	160,000	40,000	Dr.	20	8,000	2,000
Equipment	(20,000)	(16,000)	(4,000)	Cr.	5	(3,200)	(800)
Goodwill	301,402	$301,402		Dr.	10	30,140	
Total NCI adjustment.			$ 49,650				
Net adjustment to goodwill		$251,752			10	20,140	

 The Economic Unit Concept—with Goodwill Only on the Controlling Interest is applied to a consolidated worksheet in Worksheet SA1-2. The worksheet is very similar to Worksheet SA1-1. The differences, caused by the limited goodwill adjustment, are as follows:

- The NCI adjustment is limited to adjustments to all subsidiary accounts except goodwill.
- The added goodwill recorded is only the amount that applies to the controlling interest. The goodwill amortization amount is also only that amount pertaining to the controlling interest.
- Since only the controlling share goodwill is recorded and amortized, the amortization is recorded in the parent's income distribution schedule.

The consolidated income statement that would result from Worksheet SA1-2 would be presented as follows:

Sales	$ 550,000
Less cost of goods sold	235,000
Gross profit	315,000
Operating expenses (no goodwill amortization on noncontrolling interest)	209,452
Consolidated Net Income	**$105,548**
Distributed to:	
Noncontrolling interest	9,138
Controlling interest	96,410

Worksheets in subsequent periods would record amortizations of excess based on a 100% increase to market value for all accounts except goodwill. Retained earnings adjustments on all accounts except goodwill would be allocated 80%/20% to controlling and noncontrolling retained earnings. Prior-period goodwill amortizations would apply only to the controlling interest and would be allocated to only the controlling interest.

Exercises

Exercise SA1-1. Wood'n Wares Inc. purchased 80% of the outstanding stock of Pine Inc. for $810,000. Wood'n also paid $10,000 in direct acquisition costs and $3,000 for indirect acquisition costs. Just before the investment, the two companies had the following balance sheets:

Assets

	Wood'n Wares Inc.	Pine Inc.
Accounts Receivable	$ 900,000	$ 500,000
Inventory	600,000	200,000
Property, plant, and equipment (net)	1,500,000	600,000
Total assets	$3,000,000	$1,300,000

Liabilities and Equity

	Wood'n Wares Inc.	Pine Inc.
Current liabilities	$ 950,000	$ 400,000
Bonds payable	500,000	200,000
Common stock ($10 par)	400,000	300,000
Paid-in capital in excess of par	400,000	380,000
Retained earnings	650,000	20,000
Total liabilities and equity	$3,000,000	$1,300,000

Appraisals for the assets of Pine Inc. indicate that market values differ from recorded book values for the inventory and for the property, plant, and equipment which have market values of $250,000 and $700,000, respectively.

Using the Economic Unit Concept—Full Goodwill, complete the following:

1. Prepare the entry to record the purchase of the Pine Inc. common stock, including all acquisition costs.
2. Prepare a determination and distribution of excess schedule for the investment in Pine Inc.
3. Prepare the elimination entries that would be made on a consolidated worksheet.

Using the Economic Unit Concept—Goodwill Only on the Controlling Interest, complete the following:

1. Prepare the entry to record the purchase of the Pine Inc. common stock, including all acquisition costs.
2. Prepare a determination and distribution of excess schedule for the investment in Pine Inc.
3. Prepare the elimination entries that would be made on a consolidated worksheet.

Exercise SA1-2.   Copper Company purchased 80% of the common stock of Adco Company for $700,000 plus direct acquisition costs of $30,000. At the time of the purchase, Adco Company had the following balance sheet:

Assets		Liabilities and Equity	
Cash Equivalents	$ 120,000	Current liabilities	$ 200,000
Inventory	200,000	Bonds payable	400,000
Land	100,000	Common stock ($5 par) . .	100,000
Building (net)	450,000	Paid-in capital	
Equipment (net)	230,000	in excess of par	150,000
		Retained earnings	250,000
Total assets	$1,100,000	Total liabilities and equity .	$1,100,000

(continued)

Market values differ from book values for all assets other than cash equivalents. The market values are as follows:

Inventory	$300,000
Land	200,000
Building	600,000
Equipment	200,000

Using the Economic Unit Concept—Goodwill Only on the Controlling Interest, complete the following:

1. Prepare a determination and distribution of excess schedule.
2. Prepare the elimination entries that would be made on a consolidate worksheet prepared on the date of purchase.

Problems

Problem SA1-1.   Drew Corporation purchased 80% of the outstanding stock of Winters Company for $240,000 on January 1, 19X1. Winters Company had the following stockholders' equity:

Common stock ($5 par)	$150,000
Retained earning	50,000
Total equity	$200,000

The market values of Winters' assets and liabilities agreed with the book values, except for the equipment and the building. The equipment was undervalued by $10,000 and was thought to have a 5-year life; the building was undervalued by $50,000 and was thought to have a 20-year life. Any goodwill that results is being amortized over 40 years. Drew Corporation uses the simple equity method to record its investments.

Since the purchase date, both companies have operated separately and no intercompany transactions have occurred.

The separate trial balances of the companies on December 31, 19X2, are as follows:

	Drew Corp.	Winters Co.
Cash	319,000	110,000
Land	160,000	90,000
Buildings	225,000	135,000
Accumulated Depreciation—Building	(100,000)	(50,000)
Equipment	450,000	150,000
Accumulated Depreciation—Equipment	(115,000)	(60,000)
Investment in Winters Co.	260,000	
Liabilities	(480,000)	(150,000)
Common Stock ($100 par)	(400,000)	
Common Stock ($5 par)		(150,000)
Paid-In Capital in Excess of Par	(40,000)	
Retained Earnings 1/1/X2	(251,600)	(65,000)
Sales	(460,000)	(120,000)
Cost of Goods Sold	220,000	60,000

Other Expenses	210,000	50,000
Subsidiary Income	(8,000)	
Dividends Declared	10,000	
Total.	0	0

Required:

Using the Economic Unit Concept—Goodwill Only on the Controlling Interest, complete the following:

1. Prepare a determination and distribution of excess schedule for the investment.
2. Prepare the 19X2 consolidated worksheet. Include columns for the eliminations and adjustments, the consolidated income statement, the noncontrolling interest, the controlling retained earnings, and the consolidated balance sheet. Prepare supporting income distribution schedules as well.
3. Prepare the 19X2 consolidated statements, including the income statement, retained earnings statement, and balance sheet.

Problem SA1-2.   On July 1, 19X5, Pear Inc. purchased 90% of the common stock of Core Inc. for $1,127,000 plus $16,000 in direct acquisition costs. Core had the following stockholders' equity on January 1, 19X5:

Common stock ($10 par value).	$200,000
Paid-in capital in excess of par.	300,000
Retained earnings	300,000
Total equity	$800,000

Core's estimated income for the first 6 months of 19X5 was $40,000, including the $30,000 depreciation on the building, $20,000 depreciation on the equipment, and $1,000 goodwill amortization. Following is a summary of the book and market values of Core's asset and liability accounts on July 1, 19X5. Book values include the above amortizations.

Account	Book Value	Market Value	Pear's Life Assumption
Cash.	$150,000	$150,000	
Accounts Receivable	200,000	200,000	Collected by year-end
Inventory.	250,000	270,000	Sold by year-end
Land.	100,000	200,000	
Building.	700,000	600,000	20-year life, no salvage straight-line*
Accumulated Depreciation—Building	(300,000)		
Equipment	300,000	250,000	5-year life, no salvage, straight-line*
Accumulated Depreciation—Equipment.	(160,000)		
Goodwill.	50,000	?	25 years
Mortgage Payable	(450,000)	(400,000)	10-year, straight-line amortization

*Life and method do not agree with those used by Pear Inc.

(continued)

Core's books were not closed on July 1, 19X5; thus, the following December 31, 19X5 trial balances of Pear and Core include the results from operations for all of 19X5:

	Pear	Core
Cash	323,000	261,000
Accounts Receivable	200,000	230,000
Inventory	400,000	220,000
Land	200,000	100,000
Building	1,000,000	700,000
Accumulated Depreciation—Building	(500,000)	(330,000)
Equipment	400,000	300,000
Accumulated Depreciation—Equipment	(100,000)	(180,000)
Goodwill (net)		49,000
Investment in Core Inc.	1,143,000	
Mortgage Payable		(450,000)
Common Stock	(1,800,000)	(200,000)
Paid-In Capital in Excess of Par		(300,000)
Retained Earnings, Jan. 1, 19X5	(1,066,000)	(300,000)
Sales	(2,000,000)	(900,000)
Cost of Goods Sold	1,500,000	600,000
General Expense	100,000	98,000
Depreciation Expense	200,000	100,000
Goodwill Amortization		2,000
Total	0	0

Note that Core's Depreciation Expense includes $60,000 on the building and $40,000 on the equipment.

Required:

Using the Economic Unit Concept—Goodwill Only on the Controlling Interest, complete the following:

1. Prepare the original determination and distribution of excess schedule for the investment.
2. Prepare the consolidated worksheet for December 31, 19X5. Include columns for the eliminations and adjustments, the consolidated balance sheet. Prepare supporting income distribution schedules as well.
3. Prepare the 19X5 consolidated statements, including the income statement, retained earnings statement, and balance sheet.

Suggestion: It is possible to restate long-lived assets with no accumulated depreciation. It is recommended, though, that the adjustments be made by decreasing accumulated depreciation. However, using the parent's estimates, it is first necessary to recalculate what depreciation should be. Remember that, in this example, the parent is using different life assumptions and depreciation methods from those of the subsidiary. The parent's estimate should replace the depreciation now recorded by the subsidiary. Also, remember to reduce goodwill amortization when existing goodwill is consumed and allocated to other assets.

Worksheet SA-1

Economic Unit Concept—Full Goodwill
Paulos Company and Subsidiary Carlos Company
Worksheet for Consolidated Financial Statements
For Year Ended December 31, 19X1

	(Credit balance amounts are in parentheses.)	Trial Balance	
		Paulos	Carlos
1	Cash	100,000	50,000
2	Inventory	226,000	62,500
3	Land	200,000	150,000
4	Building	800,000	600,000
5	Accumulated Depreciation, Building	(80,000)	(315,000)
6	Equipment	400,000	150,000
7	Accumulated Depreciation, Equipment	(50,000)	(70,000)
8	Investment in Carlos Company	832,000	
9			
10			
11	**Goodwill**		112,500
12	Current Liabilities	(100,000)	
13	Bonds Payable		(200,000)
14	Discount/Premium		
15	Common Stock, Paulos	(1,500,000)	
16	Retained Earnings, Jan. 1, 19X1, Paulos	(700,000)	
17	Common Stock ($10 par), Carlos		(100,000)
18	Paid-In Capital in Excess of Par, Carlos		(150,000)
19	Retained Earnings, Jan. 1, 19X1, Carlos		(250,000)
20	**NCI Adjustment**		
21	Sales	(350,000)	(200,000)
22	Cost of Goods Sold	150,000	80,000
23	Expenses	120,000	60,000
24			
25			
26	Subsidiary Income	(48,000)	
27	Dividends Declared		20,000
28		0	0
29	Consolidated Net Income		
30	To noncontrolling interest (see distribution schedule)		
31	To controlling interest (see distribution schedule)		
32	Total Noncontrolling Interest		
33	Retained Earnings, Controlling Interest		
34	December 31, 19X1		

Worksheet SA1-1 (see page SA1-3)

Eliminations & Adjustments				Consolidated Income Statement	Noncontrolling Interest	Controlling Retained Earnings	Consolidated Balance Sheet	
Dr.		Cr.						
							150,000	1
							288,500	2
(3e)	50,000						400,000	3
							1,400,000	4
(3d)	200,000	(4d)	10,000				(205,000)	5
		(3c)	20,000				530,000	6
(4c)	4,000						(116,000)	7
		(1)	32,000					8
		(2)	400,000					9
		(3)	400,000					10
(3f)	**251,751**	**(4f)**	**25,175**				399,076	11
							(100,000)	12
							(200,000)	13
(3b)	13,249	(4b)	3,312				9,937	14
							(1,500,000)	15
						(700,000)		16
(2)	80,000				(20,000)			17
(2)	120,000				(30,000)			18
(2)	200,000				(50,000)			19
		(3)	**100,000**		(100,000)			20
				(550,000)				21
(3a)	5,000			235,000				22
(4b)	3,312	(4c)	4,000	214,487				23
(4d)	10,000							24
(4f)	25,175							25
(1)	48,000							26
		(1)	16,000		4,000			27
	1,010,487		1,010,487					28
				(100,513)				29
				4,103*	(4,103)			30
				96,410*		**(96,410)**		31
					(200,103)		(200,103)	32
						(796,410)	(796,410)	33
							0	34

Eliminations and Adjustments:

(c) N/A

(1) Eliminate the current-year entries made in the investment in Carlos Company account and in the subsidiary income account. The investment account now is adjusted to its January 1, 19X1 balance so that it may be eliminated.

(2) Eliminate the 80% ownership portion of the subisdiary equity accounts against the investment. A $400,000 excess cost remains.

(3) Distribute the balance of the investment account, $400,000, plus the NCI adjustment of $100,000 to the specific subsidiary accounts according to the determination and distribution schedule.

(a) Increase the beginning inventory by $5,000. However, the beginning inventory has been closed to the cost of goods sold; thus, the cost of goods sold is increased by $5,000. If the inventory had not been sold, the inventory account would be adjusted. The cost of goods sold in the later period of sale, then, would be adjusted on a subsequent worksheet.

(b) Record discount of $13,249 on the bonds payable.

(c) Reduce the equipment by $20,000 by reducing the asset account directly.

(d) Increase the building by $200,000 by decreasing its accumulated depreciation account.

(e) Increase the land by $50,000.

(f) Increase the goodwill by $251,402.

(4) Record amortizations resulting from the asset and liability revaluations of entry (3). The adjustments are lettered (a) through (f) to correspond with the revaluations in entry (3):

(a) No amortization required; adjustment already charged to the cost of goods sold.

(b) Amortize discount on bonds, straight-line method for current year.

(c) Record annual decrease in equipment depreciation expense: $20,000 net decrease divided by 5 years equals $4,000.

(d) Record annual increase in building depreciation expense; $200,000 net increase divided by 20 years equals $10,000.

(e) No amortization results from adjustment of the land.

(f) Record additional annual amortization of the goodwill; $251,751 net increase in the goodwill divided by 10-year life equals $25,175. It is assumed that the previously recorded goodwill of $125,000 on January 1, 19X1, also is being amortized over 10 years.

Subsidiary Carlos Company Income Distribution

Inventory increase . . . . (3a)	$ 5,000	Internally generated net income $60,000
Discount on bonds . . . . (4b)	3,312	Equipment depreciaiton . . . . (4c) $ 4,000
Building depreciation . . . . (4d)	10,000	
Goodwill amortization . . . . (4f)	25,175	

Adjusted income	20,513
Noncontrolling share	20%
Noncontrolling interest	**$ 4,103**

Parent Paulos Company Income Distribution

Internally generated net income	$ 80,000
80% of Carlos adjusted income of $20,513.	16,410
Controlling interest	**$96,410**

Worksheet SA-2

Economic Unit Concept—Goodwill on Only the Controlling Interest
Paulos Company and Subsidiary Carlos Company
Worksheet for Consolidated Financial Statements
For Year Ended December 31, 19X1

	(Credit balance amounts are in parentheses.)	Trial Balance	
		Paulos	Carlos
1	Cash	100,000	50,000
2	Inventory	226,000	62,500
3	Land	200,000	150,000
4	Building	800,000	600,000
5	Accumulated Depreciation, Building	(80,000)	(315,000)
6	Equipment	400,000	150,000
7	Accumulated Depreciation, Equipment	(50,000)	(70,000)
8	Investment in Carlos Company	832,000	
9			
10			
11	**Goodwill**		112,500
12	Current Liabilities	(100,000)	
13	Bonds Payable		(200,000)
14	Discount/Premium		
15	Common Stock, Paulos	(1,500,000)	
16	Retained Earnings, Jan. 1, 19X1, Paulos	(700,000)	
17	Common Stock ($10 par), Carlos		(100,000)
18	Paid-In Capital in Excess of Par, Carlos		(150,000)
19	Retained Earnings, Jan. 1, 19X1, Carlos		(250,000)
20	**NCI Adjustment**		
21	Sales	(350,000)	(200,000)
22	Cost of Goods Sold	150,000	80,000
23	Expenses	120,000	60,000
24			
25			
26	Subsidiary Income	(48,000)	
27	Dividends Declared		20,000
28		0	0
29	Consolidated Net Income		
30	To noncontrolling interest (see distribution schedule)		
31	To controlling interest (see distribution schedule)		
32	Total Noncontrolling Interest		
33	Retained Earnings, Controlling Interest		
34	December 31, 19X1		

Worksheet SA1-2 (see page SA1-5)

Eliminations & Adjustments				Consolidated Income Statement	Noncontrolling Interest	Controlling Retained Earnings	Consolidated Balance Sheet	
Dr.		Cr.						
							150,000	1
							288,500	2
(3e)	50,000						400,000	3
							1,400,000	4
(3d)	200,000	(4d)	10,000				(205,000)	5
		(3c)	20,000				530,000	6
(4c)	4,000						(116,000)	7
		(1)	32,000					8
		(2)	400,000					9
		(3)	400,000					10
(3f)	201,401	(4f)	20,140				293,761	11
							(100,000)	12
							(200,000)	13
(3b)	13,249	(4b)	3,312				9,937	14
							(1,500,000)	15
						(700,000)		16
(2)	80,000				(20,000)			17
(2)	120,000				(30,000)			18
(2)	200,000				(50,000)			19
		(3)	49,650		(49,650)			20
				(550,000)				21
(3a)	5,000			235,000				22
(4b)	3,312	(4c)	4,000	209,452				23
(4d)	10,000							24
(4f)	20,140							25
(1)	48,000							26
		(1)	16,000		4,000			27
	955,102		955,102					28
				(105,548)				29
				9,138	(9,138)			30
				96,410		(96,410)		31
					(154,788)		(154,788)	32
						(796,410)	(796,410)	33
							0	34

Eliminations and Adjustments:

(c) N/A

(1) Eliminate the current-year entries made in the investment in Carlos Company account and in the subsidiary income account. The investment account now is adjusted to its January 1, 19X1 balance so that it may be eliminated.

(2) Eliminate the 80% ownership portion of the subisdiary equity accounts against the investment. A $400,000 excess cost remains.

(3) Distribute the balance of the investment account, $400,000, plus the NCI adjustment of $49,650 to the specific subsidiary accounts according to the determination and distribution schedule.

   (a) Increase the beginning inventory by $5,000. However, the beginning inventory has been closed to the cost of goods sold; thus, the cost of goods sold is increased by $5,000. If the inventory had not been sold, the inventory account would be adjusted. The cost of goods sold in the later period of sale, then, would be adjusted on a subsequent worksheet.

   (b) Record discount of $13,249 on the bonds payable.

   (c) Reduce the equipment by $20,000 by reducing the asset account directly.

   (d) Increase the building by $200,000 by decreasing its accumulated depreciation account.

   (e) Increase the land by $50,000.

   (f) Increase the goodwill by $201,402.

(4) Record amortizations resulting from the asset and liability revaluations of entry (3). The adjustments are lettered (a) through (f) to correspond with the revaluations in entry (3):

   (a) No amortization required; adjustment already charged to the cost of goods sold.

   (b) Amortize discount on bonds, straight-line method for current year.

   (c) Record annual decrease in equipment depreciation expense: $20,000 net decrease divided by 5 years equals $4,000.

   (d) Record annual increase in building depreciation expense; $200,000 net increase divided by 20 years equals $10,000.

   (e) No amortization results from adjustment of the land.

   (f) Record additional annual amortization of the goodwill; $201,402 net increase in the goodwill divided by 10-year life equals $20,140. It is assumed that the previously recorded goodwill of $125,000 on January 1, 19X1, also is being amortized over 10 years.

Subsidiary Carlos Company Income Distribution

Inventory increase	(3a)	$ 5,000	Internally generated net income		$60,000
Discount on bonds	(4b)	3,312	Equipment depreciaiton	(4c)	$ 4,000
Building depreciation	(4d)	10,000			
			Adjusted income		45,688
			Noncontrolling share		20%
			Noncontrolling interest		**$9,138**

Parent Paulos Company Income Distribution

Goodwill amortization	(4f)	$20,140	Internally generated net income		$ 80,000
			80% of Carlos adjusted income		
			of $45,688		36,550
			Controlling interest		**$96,410**

Intercompany Transactions:
Merchandise, Plant Assets, and Notes

The elimination of the parent's investment in a subsidiary and the adjustments that may result from the elimination process are only the start of the procedures that are necessary to consolidate a parent and a subsidiary. It is common for affiliated companies to transact business with one another. The more integrated the affiliates are with respect to operations, the more common intercompany transactions become. This chapter considers the most often encountered types of intercompany transactions. These include intercompany sales of merchandise and fixed assets as well as loans between members of the consolidated group.

Transactions between the separate legal and accounting entities must be recorded on each affiliate's books. The consolidation process starts with the assumption that these transactions are recorded properly on the separate books of the parent and the subsidiary. However, consolidated statements are the set of statements that portray the parent and its subsidiary as a single economic entity. There should not be any intercompany transactions found in these consolidated statements. Only those transactions between the consolidated company and the companies outside the consolidated company should survive to the consolidated statements. Intercompany transactions must be eliminated as part of the consolidation process. For each type of intercompany transaction, sound reasoning will be developed to support the worksheet procedures. The guiding principle shall come from answering this question: **From the standpoint of a single consolidated company, what accounts and amounts should remain in the financial statements?**

The worksheet eliminations for intercompany transactions are the same no matter what method is used by the parent to maintain its investment in the subsidiary account. The examples in this chapter assume the use of the simple equity method. This is done because any investment that is maintained under the cost method is converted to the simple equity method on the consolidation worksheet. The impact of intercompany transactions on the investment account under the sophisticated equity method is considered in the appendix to this chapter. Note, however, that even where the sophisticated equity method is used, there is no change in the procedures for the individual intercompany transactions.

Intercompany Merchandise Sales

It is common to find that the goods sold by one member of an affiliated group have been purchased from another member of the group. One company may produce component parts that are assembled by its affiliate that sells the final product. In other cases, the product may be produced entirely by one member company and sold on a wholesale basis to another member company that is responsible for selling and servicing the product to the final users. Taken as a whole, these different examples of merchandise sales represent the most common type of intercompany transaction and must be understood as a basic feature of consolidated reporting.

Sales between affiliated companies will be recorded in the normal manner on the books of the separate companies. Remember that each company is a separate legal entity maintaining its own accounting records. Thus, sales to and purchases from an affiliated company are recorded as if they were transactions made with a company outside the consolidated group, and the separate financial statements of the affiliated companies will include these purchase and sale transactions. However, when the statements of the affiliates are consolidated, such sales become transfers of goods within the consolidated entity. Since these sales do not involve parties outside the consolidated group, they cannot be acknowledged in consolidated statements.

Following are the procedures for consolidating affiliated companies engaged in intercompany merchandise sales:

1. The intercompany sale must be eliminated to avoid double counting. To understand this requirement, assume that Company P sells merchandise costing $1,000 to a subsidiary, Company S, for $1,200. Company S, in turn, sells the merchandise to an outside party for $1,500. If no elimination is made, the consolidated income statement would show the following with respect to the two transactions:

Sales.	$2,700	($1,500 outside sale plus $1,200 sale to Company S)
Less cost of goods sold.	2,200	($1,000 cost to Company P plus $1,200 purchase by Company S)
Gross profit	$ 500	(18.5% gross profit rate)

While the gross profit is correct, sales and the cost of goods sold are inflated. As a result, the gross profit percentage is understated, since the $500 gross profit appears to relate to $2,700 of sales. The intercompany sale must be eliminated from the consolidated statements. All that should remain on the consolidated income statement with respect to the two transactions is

Sales.	$1,500	(only the final sale to the outside party)
Less cost of goods sold.	1,000	(only the purchase from the outside party)
Gross profit	$ 500	(33⅓% gross profit rate)

When the goods sold between the affiliated companies are manufactured by the selling affiliate, the consolidated cost of goods sold includes only those costs that can be inventoried, such as labor, materials, and overhead, and may not include any profit.

The intercompany sale, though eliminated, does have an effect on the distribution of combined net income to the controlling and minority interests. This is true because the reported net income of the subsidiary reflects the intercompany sales price, and the subsidiary's separate income statement becomes the base from which the minority share of income is calculated. In effect, the intercompany transfer price becomes an agreement as to how a portion of combined net income will be divided. For example, if Company S is an 80%-owned subsidiary, the minority interest will receive 20% of the $300 profit made on the final sale by Company S, or $60. If the intercompany transfer price is increased from $1,200 to $1,300 and the final sales price remains at $1,500, Company S would earn only $200, and the minority interest would receive 20% of $200, or $40.

2. Often, intercompany sales will be made on credit. Thus, intercompany trade balances will appear in the separate accounts of the affiliated companies. From a consolidated viewpoint, intercompany receivables and payables represent internal agreements to transfer funds. As such, **this internal debt should not appear on consolidated statements and must be eliminated.** Only debt transactions with entities **outside** the consolidated group should appear on the consolidated balance sheet.

3. **No profit on intercompany sales may be recognized until the profit is realized by a sale to an *outside* party.** This means that any profit contained in the ending inventory of intercompany goods must be eliminated and its recognition deferred until the period in which the goods are sold to outsiders. In the example described in item 1, assume that the sale by Company P to Company S was made on December 30, 19X1, and that Company S did not sell the goods until March 19X2. From a consolidated viewpoint, there can be no profit recognized until the outside sale occurs in March of 19X2. At that time, consolidation theory will acknowledge a $500 profit, of which $200 will be distributed to Company P and $300 will be distributed to Company S as part of the 19X2 combined net income. However, until that time, the $200 profit on the intercompany sale recorded by Company P must be deferred. In addition, not only must the $1,200 intercompany sale be eliminated, but the inventory on December 31, 19X1, must be reduced by $200 (the amount of the intercompany profit) to its $1,000 cost to the consolidated companies.

Care must be taken in calculating the profit applicable to inventory. It is most convenient when the gross profit rate is provided so that it can be multiplied by the inventory value to arrive at the intercompany profit. In some instances, however, the profit on sales may be stated as a percentage of cost. For example, one might be told that the cost of units is "marked up" 25% to arrive at the intercompany sales price. If the inventory value is $1,000, it cannot be multiplied by 25% to calculate the intercompany profit because the 25% applies to the cost and not the sales price, at which the inventory is stated. Instead, the gross profit rate, which is a percentage of sales price, must be calculated. The easiest method of accomplishing this is to pick the theoretical cost of $1 and mark it up by 25% (the given percentage of cost) to $1.25 and ask: "What is the gross profit percentage?" In this example, it is $.25 ÷ $1.25, or 20%. From this point, the $1,000 inventory value can be multiplied by 20% to arrive at the intercompany profit of $200.

The worksheet procedures to eliminate the effects of intercompany inventory sales are discussed in the next four sections as follows:

1. There are no intercompany goods in the beginning or ending inventories.
2. Intercompany goods remain in the ending inventory.
3. There are intercompany goods in the ending inventory, and there were intercompany goods in the beginning inventory. This is the most common situation.
4. Instead of the perpetual inventory method assumed in sections 1–3 above, the companies use the periodic inventory method. There are intercompany goods in the ending inventory, and there were intercompany goods in the beginning inventory.

No Intercompany Goods in Purchasing Company's Inventories

In the simplest case, which is illustrated in Worksheet 4-1, pages 4-46 and 4-47, all goods sold between the affiliates have been sold, in turn, to outside parties by the end of the accounting period. Worksheet 4-1 is based on the following assumptions:

1. Company S is an 80%-owned subsidiary of Company P. On January 1, 19X1, Company P purchased its interest in Company S at a price equal to its pro rata

share of Company S book value. Company P uses the equity method to record the investment. Worksheet entries (1) and (2) eliminate the investment account.

2.   Companies P and S had the following separate income statements for 19X1:

	Company P	Company S
Sales.	$700,000	$500,000
Less cost of goods sold.	510,000	350,000
Gross profit	$190,000	$150,000
Other expenses.	(90,000)	(75,000)
Subsidiary income.	60,000	
Net income	$160,000	$ 75,000

Note that under the equity method, Company P's income includes 80% of the reported income of Company S.

3.   During the year, Company S sold goods that cost it $80,000 to Company P for $100,000 (a 20% gross profit). Company P then sold all of the goods purchased from Company S to outside parties for $150,000 (a 33⅓% gross profit). Company P had not paid $25,000 of the invoices received from Company S for the goods. (Note that it is assumed in this and Worksheets 4-2 and 4-3 that a **perpetual** inventory system is used.) Consider the journal entries made by each affiliate:

Company S

Accounts Receivable (from Company P)	100,000	
Sales (to Company P)		100,000
Cost of Goods Sold (to Company P)	80,000	
Inventory		80,000
Cash	75,000	
Accounts Receivable (from Company P)		75,000

Company P

Inventory	100,000	
Accounts Payable (to Company S)		100,000
Accounts Receivable (from outside parties)	150,000	
Sales (to outside parties)		150,000
Cost of Goods Sold (to outside parties)	100,000	
Inventory		100,000
Accounts Payable (to Company S)	75,000	
Cash		75,000

Worksheet entry (3) eliminates the intercompany sale and its effects on the Company P accounts. Entry (3) is a simplified summary entry that can be further analyzed with the following entry:

Sales (to Company P)	100,000	
Cost of Goods Sold (by Company S to Company P—the intercompany sale)		80,000
Cost of Goods Sold (by Company P to outside parties—the profit recorded by Company S)		20,000

The expanded entry above removes the cost of goods sold with respect to the intercompany sale and removes the intercompany profit from the sales made by the parent to outside parties. Note that the parent recorded the cost of the goods sold to outside parties at $100,000. However, the true cost of the goods to the consolidated company is less a 20% gross profit of $20,000. Thus, the real cost was only $80,000.

Entry (4) eliminates the intercompany receivables/payables still remaining unpaid at the end of the year. Income distribution schedules are used in Worksheet 4-1 to distribute the $175,000 of combined net income to the minority and controlling interests. It should be noted that all of the above procedures remain unchanged if the parent is the seller of the intercompany goods.

Intercompany Goods in Purchasing Company's Ending Inventory

Let us now change the example in Worksheet 4-1 to assume that Company P did not resell $40,000 of the total of $100,000 of goods it purchased from Company S. This means that $40,000 of goods purchased from Company S remain in Company P's ending inventory. Consider the following revised entries for the two affiliates:

Company S

Accounts Receivable (from Company P)	100,000	
Sales (to Company P)		100,000
Cost of Goods Sold (to Company P)	80,000	
Inventory		80,000
Cash	75,000	
Accounts Receivable (from Company P)		75,000

Company P

Inventory	100,000	
Accounts Payable (to Company S)		100,000
Accounts Receivable (from outside parties)	90,000	
Sales (to outside parties)		90,000
Cost of Goods Sold (to outside parties)	60,000	
Inventory		60,000
Accounts Payable (to Company S)	75,000	
Cash		75,000

Let us now consider what has happened to the $100,000 of goods sold to Company P by Company S:

$80,000 is the original cost of the goods sold by Company S which should be removed from the cost of goods sold since it is just the intercompany sale and not the outside sale.

$12,000 is the intercompany profit on the goods sold by Company P to outside parties. The cost of these sales should be reduced by $12,000 (20% × $60,000) to arrive at the true cost of the goods to the consolidated company.

$8,000 is the intercompany profit remaining in the Company P ending inventory. This inventory, now at $40,000 should be reduced $8,000 (20% × $40,000) to $32,000. Another way to view this is that 60% of the original intercompany goods (60% × 100,000 = $60,000) have been sold to outside parties. Thus, only the profit on these sales (20% × $60,000 = $12,000) has been realized.

If we follow the above analysis to the letter, we would make the following elimination in entry form:

Sales (by Company S to Company P) 100,000
    Cost of Goods Sold (by Company S)   80,000
    Cost of Goods Sold (by Company P)   12,000
    Inventory, December 31, 19X1 (held by Company P)   8,000

    In practice, this entry is cumbersome in that it requires an analysis of the destiny of all intercompany sales. The approach used in Worksheet 4-2, pages 4-48 and 4-49, is simplified first to eliminate the intercompany sales under the assumption that all goods have been resold, and then to adjust for those goods still remaining in the inventory. This method simplifies worksheet procedures including the distribution of combined net income. In journal form, the simplified entries are

(3) Sales (by Company S to Company P) 100,000
      Cost of Goods Sold ($80,000 cost of Company S sales
        + $20,000 possible intercompany profit on goods
        sold by Company P)   100,000
(4) Cost of Goods Sold (unrealized intercompany profit)   8,000
      Inventory, December 31, 19X1
        (held by Company P)   8,000

    The $8,000 is viewed as the unrealized intercompany inventory profit that may not be realized until a later period when the goods are sold to outside parties.

    The unrealized intercompany profit is subtracted from the seller's income distribution schedule. In the income distribution schedules for Worksheet 4-2, the unrealized profit of $8,000 is deducted from the subsidiary's internally generated net income of $75,000. The adjusted net income of $67,000 is apportioned, with $13,400 (20%) distributed to the minority interest and $53,600 (80%) distributed to the controlling interest.

    There is no change in worksheet elimination procedures if the parent is the seller and the subsidiary has intercompany goods in its ending inventory. Only the distribution of combined net income changes. To illustrate, assume the parent, Company P, is the seller of the intercompany goods. The income distribution schedules would be prepared as follows:

Subsidiary Company S Income Distribution

Internally generated net income	$ 75,000
Adjusted income	$ 75,000
Minority share	20%
Minority interest	$ 15,000

Parent Company P Income Distribution

Unrealized profit in ending		Internally generated net income	$100,000
inventory. . . . . (5) **$8,000**		80% × Company S adjusted income of	
		$75,000	60,000
		Controlling interest	$152,000

Intercompany Goods in Purchasing Company's Beginning and Ending Inventories

When intercompany goods are included in the purchaser's beginning inventory, the inventory value includes the profit made by the seller. The intercompany seller of the goods has included in the prior period such sales in its separate income statement as though the transactions were consummated. Thus, the beginning retained earnings balance of the seller also includes the profit on these goods. While this profit should be reflected on the separate books of the affiliates, it should not be recognized when a consolidated view is taken. Remember: **Profit must not be recognized until it is realized in the subsequent period through the sale of goods to an outside party.** Therefore, in the consolidating process, the beginning inventory of intercompany goods must be reduced to its cost to the consolidated company. Likewise, the retained earnings of the consolidated entity must be reduced by deleting the profit that was recorded in prior periods on intercompany goods contained in the buyer's beginning inventory.

To illustrate, using the example of Company P and Company S from Worksheet 4-3 on pages 4-50 to 4-53, assume the two companies have the following individual income data for 19X2:

	Company P	Company S
Sales	$800,000	$600,000
Less cost of goods sold	610,000	440,000
Gross profit	$190,000	$160,000
Other expenses	(120,000)	(100,000)
Subsidiary income	48,000	
Net income	$118,000	$ 60,000

Assume the following additional facts:

1.   Company P's 19X2 beginning inventory includes $40,000 of the goods purchased from Company S in 19X1. The gross profit rate on the sale was 20%.
2.   Company S sold $120,000 of goods to Company P during 19X2.
3.   Company S recorded a 20% gross profit on these sales.
4.   At the end of 19X2, Company P still owed $60,000 to Company S for the purchases. Company P also had $30,000 of the intercompany purchases in its 19X2 ending inventory.

Worksheet 4-3 contains the 19X2 year-end trial balances of Company P and Company S. Entries (1) and (2) again eliminate the investment account. Entry (3) adjusts for the intercompany profit contained in the beginning inventory. At the start of 19X2, Company P included $40,000 of goods purchased from Company S in its beginning inventory. During 19X2, the inventory was debited to the cost of goods sold at $40,000. The cost of goods sold must now be reduced to cost by removing the $8,000 intercompany profit. The intercompany profit also was included in last year's income by the subsidiary. That income was closed to retained earnings. Thus, the beginning retained earnings of Company S are overstated by $8,000. That $8,000 is divided between the minority and controlling interest in retained earnings. Subsidiary retained earnings have been 80% eliminated, and only the 20% minority interest remains. The other 80% of beginning retained earnings is included in Company P's retained earnings through the use of the equity method. In entry form, the adjustment is explained:

(3)   Retained Earnings, Jan. 1, 19X2, Company P (80%
         controlling interest)   6,400
       Retained Earnings, Jan. 1, 19X2, Company S (20%
         minority interest)   1,600
         Cost of Goods Sold (by Company P to outside parties) . .   8,000

Note that once the controlling share of subsidiary retained earnings is eliminated, there is a transformation of what were **subsidiary** retained earnings into what now is **minority interest** in retained earnings. Entries (4) through (6) eliminate the

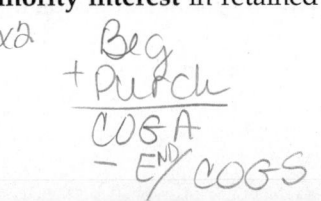

intercompany sales, ending inventory, and trade accounts in the same manner as was done in Worksheet 4-2. After all eliminations and adjustments are made, the combined net income of $132,000 is distributed as shown in the income distribution schedules. **The adjustments for intercompany inventory profits are reflected in the *selling company's schedule.***

It might appear that the intercompany goods in the beginning inventory are always assumed to be sold in the current period, since the deferred profit of the previous period is realized during the current period as reflected by the seller's income distribution schedule. That assumption need not be made, however. Even if part of the beginning inventory is unsold at year-end, it still would be a part of the $30,000 ending inventory, on which $6,000 of profit is deferred. Note that the use of the LIFO method for inventories could cause a given period's inventory profit to be deferred indefinitely. Unless otherwise stated, the examples and problems of this text will assume a FIFO flow.

Worksheet 4-3 assumed the intercompany merchandise sales were made by the subsidiary. Procedures would differ as follows if the sales were made by the parent:

1. The beginning inventory profit would be subtracted entirely from the beginning controlling retained earnings since only the parent recorded the profit.
2. The adjustments for the beginning and ending inventory profits would be included in the parent income distribution schedule and not in the subsidiary schedule.

Eliminations for Periodic Inventories

In Worksheets 4-1 through 4-3, the cost of goods sold was included in the trial balances, since both the parent and the subsidiary used a perpetual inventory system. However, in Worksheet 4-4 on pages 4-54 to 4-56, a periodic inventory system is used. In this illustration, which is based on the same facts as Worksheet 4-3, the following differences in worksheet procedures result from the use of a periodic inventory system:

1. The 19X2 beginning inventories of $70,000 and $40,000, rather than the ending inventories, appear as assets in the trial balances. The beginning inventories less the intercompany profit in Company P's beginning inventory are extended to the consolidated income statement column as a debit.
2. The purchases accounts, rather than the cost of goods sold, appear in the trial balances and, after adjustment, are extended to the consolidated income statement column.
3. Entry (3) credits the January 1 inventory to eliminate the intercompany profit.
4. Entry (4) credits the purchases account, which is still open under the periodic method, and makes the usual debit to the sales account.
5. The ending inventories of both Company P and Company S are entered in each company's trial balances as both a debit (the balance sheet amount) and a credit (the adjustment to the cost of goods sold). These inventories are recorded at the price paid for them, which, for intercompany goods, includes the intercompany sales profit. Entry (5) removes the $6,000 intercompany profit applicable to the ending inventory. The balance sheet inventory is reduced to $104,000. The $104,000 credit balance is extended to the consolidated income statement column.

Effect of Lower-of-Cost-or-Market Method on Inventory Profit

Intercompany inventory in the hands of the purchaser may have been written down by the purchaser to a market value below its intercompany transfer cost. Assume that, for $50,000, Company S purchased goods that cost its parent company $40,000.

Assume further that Company S has all the goods in its ending inventory but has written them down to $42,000, the lower market value at the end of the period. As a result of this markdown, the inventory needs to be reduced by only another $2,000 to reflect its cost to the consolidated company ($40,000). The only remaining issue is how to defer the $2,000 inventory profit in the income distribution schedules. As before, such profit is deferred by entering it as a debit on the intercompany seller's schedule. In the subsequent period, the profit will be realized by the seller.

It may seem strange that the $8,000 of profit written off is realized, in effect, by the seller, since it is not deducted in the seller's distribution schedule. This procedure is proper, however, since the loss recognized by the buyer is offset. Had the inventory been written down to $40,000 or less, there would be no need to defer the offsetting profit in the consolidated worksheet or in the income distribution schedules.

Losses on Intercompany Sales

Assume a parent sells goods to a subsidiary for $5,000 and the goods cost the parent $6,000. If the market value of the goods is $5,000 or less, the loss may be recognized in the consolidated income statement, even if the goods remain in the subsidiary's ending inventory. Such a loss can be recognized under the lower-of-cost-or-market principle that applies to inventory. However, if the intercompany sales price is below market value, the part of the loss that results from the price being below market value cannot be recognized until the subsidiary sells the goods to an outside party. Elimination procedures would be similar to but opposite in direction to those used for unrealized gains.

Intercompany Plant Asset Sales

Any plant asset may be sold between members of an affiliated group, and such a sale may result in a gain for the seller. The buyer will record the asset at a price that includes the gain, and when the sale involves a depreciable asset, the buyer will base future depreciation charges on the price paid. While these recordings are proper for the companies as separate entities, they must not be reflected in the consolidated statements. Consolidation theory views the sale as an **internal transfer of assets.** There is no basis for recognizing a gain at the time of the internal transfer. Unlike the case of merchandise sales, however, recognition of the gain on the transfer does not have to await sale of the asset to an outside party. The buyer's normal intent is to use the asset, not to resell it. Since the asset is overstated by the amount of the intercompany gain, subsequent depreciation is overstated as well. The consolidation process reduces depreciation in future years so that depreciation charges in the consolidated statements reflect the original cost of the asset to the consolidated company. While the gain is deferred in the year of sale, it is realized later through the increased combined net income resulting from the reduction in depreciation expense in subsequent periods. The decrease in depreciation expense for each and every period is equal to the difference between the depreciation based on the intercompany sales price and the depreciation based on the book value of the asset on the sale date.

Intercompany Sale of a Nondepreciable Asset

One member of an affiliated group may sell land to another affiliate and record a gain. For consolidating purposes, there has been no sale; thus, there is no cause to recognize a gain. Since the asset is not depreciable, the entire gain must be deferred until the land is sold to an outside party. This deferment may be permanent if there is no intent to sell at a later date. For example, assume that in 19X1 Company S (80% owned) sells land to its parent company, Company P. The sale price is $30,000, and the original cost of the land to Company S was $20,000. Consolidation theory would rule that, until Company P sells the land to an outside party, recognition of the profit must be deferred. The following worksheet elimination is made in the year of sale:

	Partial Trial Balance		Eliminations & Adjustments	
	Company P	Company S	Dr.	Cr.
Land	30,000			10,000
Gain on Sale of Land		(10,000)	10,000	

As usual, the selling company's income distribution schedule would reflect the deferment of the gain.

In subsequent years, assuming the land is not sold by Company P, the gain must be removed from the consolidated retained earnings. Since the sale was made by Company S, which is an 80%-owned subsidiary of Company P, the controlling interest must absorb 80% of the deferment, while the minority interest must absorb 20%. For example, the adjustments in 19X2 would be as follows:

	Partial Trial Balance		Eliminations & Adjustments	
	Company P	Company S	Dr.	Cr.
Land	30,000			10,000
Retained Earnings, Jan. 1, 19X2, Company P	(100,000)*		8,000	
Retained Earnings, Jan. 1, 19X2, Company S		(20,000)*	2,000	

*arbitrary balance

Now, assume Company P sells the land in 19X3 to an outside party for $45,000, recording a gain of $15,000. When this sale occurs, the $10,000 intercompany gain also is realized. The following elimination would remove the previously unrealized gain from the consolidated retained earnings and would add it to the gain already recorded by Company P. The retained earnings adjustment is allocated 80% to the controlling interest and 20% to the minority interest, since the original sale was made by the subsidiary.

	Partial Trial Balance		Eliminations & Adjustments	
	Company P	Company S	Dr.	Cr.
Gain on Sale of Land	(15,000)			10,000
Retained Earnings, Jan. 1, 19X3, Company P	(120,000)*		8,000	
Retained Earnings, Jan. 1, 19X3, Company S		(15,000)*	2,000	

*arbitrary balance

The income distribution schedule would add the $10,000 gain to the 19X3 internally generated net income of Company S. At this point, it should be clear that the gain on the intercompany sale was deferred, not eliminated. The original gain of $10,000 eventually is credited to the subsidiary. Thus, the gain does affect the minority share of combined net income at a future date. Any sale of a nondepreciable asset should be viewed as an agreement between the controlling and minority interests regarding the future distribution of combined net income.

When a parent sells a nondepreciable asset to a subsidiary, the worksheet procedures are the same, except that

1. The deferment of the gain in the year of the intercompany sale and the recognition of the gain in the year of the sale of the asset to an outside party flow through only the parent company income distribution schedule.
2. In the years subsequent to the intercompany sale through the year the land is sold to an external company, the related adjustment is made exclusively through the controlling retained earnings.

Intercompany Sale of a Depreciable Asset

Turning to the case where a depreciable plant asset is sold between affiliates, the following example illustrates the worksheet procedures necessary for the **deferment of a gain on the sale** *over the asset's useful life.* Assume that the parent, Company P, sells a machine to a subsidiary, Company S, for $30,000 on January 1, 19X1. Originally, the machine cost $32,000. Accumulated depreciation as of January 1, 19X1, is $12,000. Therefore, the book value of the machine is $20,000, and the reported gain on the sale is $10,000. Further assume that Company S (*the buyer*) believes the asset has a 5-year remaining life; thus, it records straight-line depreciation of $6,000 annually.

The eliminations spread the gain over the 5-year life of the asset by reducing annual depreciation charges. For consolidated reporting purposes, depreciation is based on the asset's $20,000 book value to the consolidated company. Worksheet 4-5, pages 4-58 and 4-59, is based on the following additional facts:

1. Company P owns an 80% investment in Company S. The amount paid for the investment was equal to the book value of Company S underlying equity. The simple equity method is used by Company P to record its investment. Entries (1) and (2) eliminate the investment account.
2. There were no beginning or ending inventories, and the companies had the following separate income statements for 19X1:

	Company P	Company S
Sales	$200,000	$100,000
Cost of goods sold	(150,000)	(59,000)
Gross profit	$ 50,000	$ 41,000
Depreciation expense	(30,000)	(16,000)
Gain on sale of machine	10,000	
Subsidiary income (80%)	20,000	
Net income	$ 50,000	$ 25,000

Entry (3) eliminates the $10,000 intercompany gain and restates the asset at its book value of $20,000 on the date of the intercompany sale as follows:

Gain on Sale of machinery	10,000	
Machinery		10,000

Entry (4) reduces the depreciation expense for the year by the difference between depreciation based on:

- The book value [($32,000 – $12,000 = $20,000 depreciable base) ÷ 5 years = $4,000] and
- The intercompany sales price ($30,000 depreciable base ÷ 5 years = $6,000).

The following elimination results:

Accumulated Depreciation, Machinery	2,000	
Depreciation Expense, Machinery ($6,000 – $4,000)		2,000

(handwritten left margin: prepare every year until fully depr. } correcting entry)

The allocation of combined net income of $47,000 is shown in the income distribution schedules. Note that Company S (the buyer in this example) must absorb depreciation based on the agreed sales price, and it is the controlling interest that realizes the benefit of the reduced depreciation as the asset is used. Also, note that the realizable profit for Company P (the seller) in any year is the depreciation absorbed by the buyer minus the depreciation for consolidated purposes ($6,000-$4,000). If the sale had been made by Company S, the profit deferment and recognition entries would flow through its income distribution schedule.

Worksheets for periods subsequent to the sale of the machine must correct the current-year nominal accounts and remove the unrealized profit in the beginning consolidated retained earnings. Worksheet 4-6, pages 4-60 to 4-63, portrays a consolidated worksheet for 19X2, based on the following separate income statements of Company P and Company S:

	Company P	Company S
Sales	$250,000	$120,000
Cost of goods sold	(180,000)	(80,000)
Gross profit.	$ 70,000	$ 40,000
Depreciation expense	(20,000)	(16,000)
Subsidiary income (80%)	19,200	
Net income.	$ 69,200	$ 24,000

Entry (3) in this worksheet corrects the asset's net book value, accumulated depreciation, and retained earnings as of the beginning of the year. In entry form, the adjustment is explained as follows:

Accumulated Depreciation (reduce		
19X1 depreciation recognized as profit)	2,000 *(entry 4)*	
Retained Earnings, Jan. 1, 19X2, Co. P*	8,000	
Machinery (reduce machinery to		
net book value on date of sale)		10,000

*The unrealized gain on January 1, 19X2, equals the $10,000 original gain less the $2,000 realized profit as of that date.

Since the sale was by the parent, only the controlling interest in beginning retained earnings is adjusted. Had the sale been by the subsidiary, the adjustment would have been split 20/80 to the minority and controlling interests in beginning retained earnings.

Entry (4) corrects the depreciation expense and the accumulated depreciation accounts for the current year. The resulting combined net income of $76,000 is distributed as shown in the income distribution schedules that follow Worksheet 4-6. During each year, Company S must absorb the larger depreciation expense that resulted from its purchase of the asset. Company P has the right to realize $2,000 more of the original deferred profit.

It may occur that an asset purchased from an affiliate is sold before it is fully depreciated. To illustrate this possibility, assume that Company S of the previous example sells the asset to a third party for $14,000 at the end of the second year. Since Company S's asset cost is $30,000, with $12,000 of accumulated depreciation, the loss recorded by Company S is $4,000 ($14,000 - $18,000 net book value). However, on a consolidated basis, the $4,000 loss becomes a $2,000 gain, determined as follows:

	On Books of Company S		For Consolidated Entity	
Selling price of machine sold by Company S		$14,000		$14,000
Less book value at end of second year following sale to Company S:				
Cost of machine.	$30,000		$20,000*	
Accumulated depreciation	(12,000)	18,000	(8,000)	12,000
Gain (loss)		$(4,000)		$ 2,000

*Net book value on date of intercompany sale.

Worksheet 4-7, pages 4-64 and 4-65, is a revision of the previous worksheet so that Company S's subsequent sale of the depreciable asset at the end of the second year is included. Entry (3) removes the $8,000 remaining intercompany profit on the asset sale from controlling retained earnings, adjusts current depreciation by $2,000, and converts the $4,000 loss on the sale recorded by the subsidiary into a $2,000 gain on the consolidated statements.

A loss on an intercompany sale of plant assets does not have to be deferred if the loss could have been recorded in the absence of a sale. Where there has been a permanent decline in the utility of a fixed asset, it may be written down to a lower market value. In this case, utility is defined as the benefits the asset provides the company. Where, however, the asset is sold to an affiliated company at a price below fair market value, the loss is to be deferred in the same manner as an intercompany gain. The loss would be deferred over the depreciation life of the asset. If the asset were sold to a nonaffiliated company, the remaining deferred loss would be recognized at the time of the sale.

Intercompany Long-Term Construction Contracts

One member of an affiliated group of companies may construct a plant asset for another affiliate over an extended period of time. The company constructing the asset will record progress under the completed-contract method or the percentage-of-completion method. During construction, special adjustments may be necessary when consolidating, depending on which of the two methods is used to record the contract by the constructing affiliate. From a consolidated viewpoint, such activity amounts to the self-construction of an asset to be used by the consolidated entity. Once the asset has been sold to an affiliate, consolidation procedures are similar to those used for a normal intercompany sale of a plant asset.

Completed-Contract Method.   The constructing affiliate using the completed-contract method records no profit on the asset until it is completed and transferred to the purchasing affiliate. However, costs incurred to date on the contract are capitalized in a special account, such as *Cost of Construction in Progress.* This account will appear on the trial balance of the constructing affiliate. This account should be eliminated and rerecorded as *Assets Under Construction,* which is the usual account for the cost of an asset being constructed for a company's own use.

The constructing affiliate may bill the purchasing affiliate for work done prior to the completion of the asset. When this occurs, the constructing affiliate will record billed amounts by debiting *Contracts Receivable* and crediting *Billings on Long-Term Contracts*. The billings account acts as a contra-account to Cost of Construction in Progress. The purchasing affiliate would debit *Assets Under Construction* and credit *Contracts Payable* for billings received. Consolidation procedures require that the constructing affiliate's account Billings on Long-Term Contracts be eliminated against Cost of Construction in Progress. Any excess of cost incurred over the amount of billings is closed to the purchaser's account, Assets Under Construction. In addition, it is necessary to eliminate any remaining intercompany receivable and payable amounts recorded on the long-term contract.

Percentage-of-Completion Method.   This method allows the constructing company to recognize a portion of the total estimated profit on the contract as construction progresses. During the construction period, the contracting company debits an account usually entitled *Construction in Progress* for costs that are incurred to outside companies. The contractor also debits Construction in Progress and credits *Earned Income on Long-Term Contracts* for the estimated profit earned during each accounting period. Thus, the construction in progress account includes accumulated costs and estimated earnings. When the purchaser is billed, the contractor will debit the amount billed to Contracts Receivable and credit Billings on Construction in Progress, while the purchaser will debit Assets Under Construction and credit Contracts Payable.

To illustrate the elimination procedures when the percentage-of-completion method is used, assume a subsidiary, Company S, enters into a contract to construct a building for its parent company, Company P, for $500,000 and Company S estimates the cost of the building to be $400,000. During 19X1, the building is 50% completed and $200,000 of cost has been incurred as of December 31, 19X1, but only $150,000 has been billed. The contract is completed in 19X2 at an additional cost of $200,000. The entries on the books of the separate affiliates for December 19X1 are as follows:

Company S

Construction in Progress	200,000	
Payables (to outsiders)		200,000
To record costs incurred for the long-term contract under the percentage-of-completion method.		
Construction in Progress	50,000	
Earned Income on Long-Term Contracts		50,000
To record pro rata share of estimated profit [50% × ($500,000 − $400,000)].		
Contracts Receivable	150,000	
Billings on Construction in Progress		150,000
To record billing to parent for the portion of amount due under the contract.		

Company P

Assets Under Construction	150,000	
Contracts Payable		150,000
To record billing from subsidiary for amount due.		

The subsidiary's balance sheet prepared at the end of 19X1 would list a net current asset of $100,000, as the $150,000 balance in Billings on Construction in Progress would be offset against the $250,000 balance in Construction in Progress. If billings exceed the amount recorded for construction in progress, a net current liability would be shown on the balance sheet.

The following partial consolidated worksheet for 19X1 shows the relevant accounts and the eliminations that would appear for this example. The elimination procedures are complex and involve answering this question: What should remain on the consolidated statements? From a consolidated viewpoint, a self-constructed asset is in progress and $200,000 has been spent to date. **All that should remain on the consolidated statements is a $200,000 asset under construction and a $200,000 payable to outside interests.** The income distribution schedule of the constructing affiliate would reflect the profit deferral through a debit for $50,000.

Company P and Subsidiary Company S
Partial Worksheet for Consolidated Financial Statements
For Year Ended December 31, 19X1

(Credit balance amounts are in parentheses.)	Trial Balance		Eliminations & Adjustments	
	Company P	Company S	Dr.	Cr.
Assets Under Construction	150,000		(3) 50,000	
Contracts Receivable		150,000		(1) 150,000
Billings on Construction in Progress		(150,000)	(3) 150,000	
Construction in Progress		250,000		(2) 50,000
				(3) 200,000
Earned Income on Long-Term Contracts		(50,000)	(2) 50,000	
Contracts Payable	(150,000)		(1) 150,000	
Payables (to outsiders)		(200,000)		

Eliminations and Adjustments:

(1) Eliminate the intercompany debt and receivable resulting from the long-term contract.
(2) Eliminate the income recorded on the long-term intercompany contract and remove the profit from Construction in Progress.
(3) Eliminate the balances of Construction in Progress and Billings on Construction in Progress, and increase Assets Under Construction for the unbilled costs on the long-term intercompany contract.

As is true with all intercompany sales of plant assets, any intercompany profit is deferred until realized through the subsequent sale or use of the asset. Thus, the intercompany profit resulting from a long-term construction contract should be realized as the asset is depreciated. The unrealized profit will result in an adjustment to retained earnings in subsequent years.

Intercompany Debt

Typically, a parent company is larger than any one of its subsidiaries and can secure funds under more favorable terms. Because of this, a parent company often will advance cash to a subsidiary. The parent may accept a note from the subsidiary as security for the loan, or the parent may discount a note that the subsidiary received from a customer. In most cases, the parent will charge a competitive interest rate for the funds advanced to the subsidiary.

In the examples that follow, the more common situation in which the parent is the lender is assumed. If the subsidiary were the lender, the theory and practice would be identical, with the only differences being the books on which the applicable accounts appear and the procedure for the distribution of combined net income.

Assume that on July 1, 19X1, an 80%-owned subsidiary, Company S, borrows $10,000 from its parent, Company P, signing a 1-year, 8% note, with interest payable on the due date. This intercompany loan will cause the following accounts and their balances to appear on the December 31, 19X1 trial balances of the separate affiliated companies:

Parent Company P		Subsidiary Company S	
Notes Receivable	10,000	Notes Payable	(10,000)
Interest Income	(400)	Interest Expense	400
Interest Receivable	400	Interest Payable	(400)

While this information is required on the books of the separate companies, it should not appear on the consolidated statements. The procedures needed to eliminate this intercompany note and its related interest amounts are demonstrated in Worksheet 4-8, pages 4-66 and 4-67. Entry (3) eliminates the intercompany receivable and payable for the note and the accrued interest on the note. Entry (4) eliminates the intercompany interest income and expense amounts. In this worksheet, it is assumed that the intercompany note is the only note recorded. However, it may occur that an intercompany note and its related interest expense, revenue, and accruals are commingled with notes to outside parties. Before the trial balances are entered on the worksheet and before consolidation is attempted, intercompany interest expense and revenue must be accrued properly on the books of the parent and subsidiary.

After all the necessary worksheet eliminations are made, the effect of the note on the distribution of combined net income must be considered. There might be a temptation to increase the minority share of combined net income by $400 as a result of eliminating the interest expense on the intercompany note, but it is not correct to do so. Even though the interest does not appear on the consolidated income statement, it is a legitimate expense for Company S as a separate entity and a legitimate revenue for Company P as a separate entity. In essence, Company S has agreed to transfer $400 to Company P for interest during 19X1, and the minority must respect this agreement when calculating its share of combined net income. Thus, the basis for calculating the minority share is the net income of Company S as a separate entity. The minority receives 20% of this $10,000 net income which is net of the $400 of intercompany interest expense.

A parent receiving a note from a subsidiary subsequently may discount the note at a nonaffiliated financial institution in order to receive immediate cash. This results in a note receivable discounted being recorded by the parent. From a consolidated viewpoint, there is a note payable to outside parties. Consolidation procedures should eliminate the internal note receivable against the note receivable discounted. This elimination will result in the note, now payable to an outside party, being extended to the consolidated balance sheet. Intercompany interest accrued prior to the discounting is eliminated. Interest paid by the subsidiary subsequent to the discounting is paid to the outside party and is not eliminated. The net interest expense or revenue on the discounting of the note is a transaction between the parent and the outside party and, thus, is not eliminated. When consolidated statements are prepared, however, it is desirable to net the interest expense on the note recorded by the maker subsequent to the discounting of the note against the net interest expense or revenue on the discounting transaction.

Do not do

Sophisticated Equity Method: Intercompany Transactions

Chapter 3 demonstrated the use of the sophisticated equity method for the parent's recording of its investment in a subsidiary. Recall that one major difference between the simple and sophisticated equity methods was that the latter records subsidiary income net of amortizations of excess. In contrast, the simple equity method ignores amortizations and records as income for the parent the subsidiary reported income multiplied by the parent's percentage of ownership. Some companies using the sophisticated equity method will proceed to the next level of complexity. Instead of adjusting for their share of the income reported by the subsidiary (as under the simple equity method), they will adjust for their share of subsidiary income after it is adjusted for intercompany profits. This means that, before the parent can make an equity adjustment for income of the subsidiary, it must prepare an income distribution schedule for the subsidiary company. **The adjusted net income derived in the income distribution schedule will become the income to which the parent ownership percentage is applied to arrive at equity income.**

The added complexity of the sophisticated equity method is unwarranted when statements are to be consolidated, since the subsidiary income and the investment in subsidiary accounts are eliminated entirely. However, this procedure must be used in the rare case when a subsidiary is not to be consolidated or when parent-only statements are to be prepared as a supplement to the consolidated statements.

Unrealized Profits of the Current Period

The case of intercompany profits generated only during the current period will be considered first. Although the same procedure applies to all types of subsidiary-generated unrealized intercompany profits and losses of the current period, the impact of the sophisticated equity method will be demonstrated assuming only the existence of inventory profits.

The following example is based on the information presented in Worksheet 4-2, but this time the parent is using the sophisticated equity method. Because of this fact, the parent has to prepare a subsidiary income distribution schedule before it can record its share of subsidiary income. This schedule is shown below. Note that, instead of recording **on its books** a subsidiary income of $60,000, the parent would have recorded $53,600:

Equity Income: Subsidiary Company S

Unrealized profit in ending inventory	$8,000	Internally generated net income	$ 75,000
		Adjusted income	$ 67,000
		Controlling share.	**80%**
		Controlling interest	**$53,600***

*This is the same amount that is shown in the parent's income distribution schedule for Worksheet 4-2.

The only elimination procedure in this example that differs from Worksheet 4-2 is entry (1), which eliminates the entry made by the parent to record its share of the subsidiary current period income. There is no impact on the other worksheet procedures, and the balance of Worksheet 4-2 would be unchanged. A portion of the revised worksheet is shown on page 4-18.

Unrealized Profits of Current and Prior Periods

The effect of the sophisticated equity method when there are intercompany profits from current and prior periods is demonstrated in the following example, which is based on the information given in Worksheet 4-3. The subsidiary income reported by the parent in 19X2 under the sophisticated equity method is calculated as follows:

Equity Income: Subsidiary Company S

Unrealized profit in ending inventory	$6,000	Internally generated net income	$60,000
		Realized profit in beginning inventory . . .	8,000
		Adjusted income	$62,000
		Controlling share	**80%**
		Controlling interest	**$49,600**

The elimination procedures illustrated in the following partial worksheet are applicable to all types of subsidiary-generated intercompany profits and losses of prior and current periods. The differences in the parent's trial balance are explained in the notes that follow the partial worksheet on page 4-19.

Company P and Subsidiary Company S
Partial Worksheet
For Year Ended December 31, 19X1

(Credit balance amounts are in parentheses.)	Trial Balance		Eliminations & Adjustments	
	Company P	Company S	Dr.	Cr.
Accounts Receivable	110,000	150,000		(5) 25,000
Inventory, Dec. 31, 19X1	70,000	40,000		(4) 8,000
Investment in Company S	(b) 189,600			(1) 53,600
				(2) 136,000
Other Assets	314,000	155,000		
Accounts Payable	(80,000)	(100,000)	(5) 25,000	
Common Stock ($10 par), Co. P	(200,000)			
Retained Earnings, Jan. 1, 19X1, Co. P	(250,000)			
Common Stock ($10 par), Co. S		(100,000)	(2) 80,000	
Retained Earnings, Jan. 1, 19X1, Co. S		(70,000)	(2) 56,000	
Sales	(700,000)	(500,000)	(3) 100,000	
Cost of Goods Sold	510,000	350,000	(4) 8,000	(3) 100,000
Expenses	90,000	75,000		
Subsidiary Income	(a) (53,600)		(1) 53,600	
	0	0	322,600	322,600

Notes to Trial Balance:

(a) See the previously prepared distribution schedule.

(b) $136,000 beginning-of-year balance + $53,600 sophisticated equity method income.

Eliminations and Adjustments:

(1) Eliminate the entry recording the parent's share (80%) of the subsidiary net income under the sophisticated equity method.

(2–5) Same as Worksheet 4-2.

Company P and Subsidiary Company S
Partial Worksheet
For Year Ended December 31, 19X2

(Credit balance amounts are in parentheses.)	Trial Balance		Eliminations & Adjustments	
	Company P	Company S	Dr.	Cr.
Accounts Receivable	160,000	170,000		(6) 60,000
Inventory, Dec. 31, 19X2	60,000	50,000		(5) 6,000
Investment in Company S	(c) 239,200			(1) 49,600
				(2) 189,600
Other Assets	354,000	165,000		
Accounts Payable	(90,000)	(80,000)	(6) 60,000	
Common Stock ($10 par), Co. P	(200,000)			
Retained Earnings, Jan. 1, 19X2, Co. P	(b) (403,600)			
Common Stock ($10 par), Co. S		(100,000)	(2) 80,000	
Retained Earnings, Jan. 1, 19X2, Co. S		(145,000)	(Adj) 8,000	
			(2) 109,600	
Sales	(800,000)	(600,000)	(4) 120,000	
Cost of Goods Sold	610,000	440,000	(5) 6,000	(Adj) 8,000
				(4) 120,000
Expenses	120,000	100,000		
Subsidiary Income	(a) (49,600)		(1) 49,600	
	0	0	433,200	433,200

Notes to Trial Balance:

(a)   See the previously prepared distribution schedule.
(b) $410,000 simple equity balance – (80% × $8,000 subsidiary beginning inventory profit).
(c) $136,000 original balance + $53,600 sophisticated equity method income for 19X1 + $49,600 sophisticated equity method income for 19X2.

Eliminations and Adjustments:

(Adj)   Eliminate the $8,000 beginning inventory profit from the cost of goods sold and the subsidiary beginning retained earnings accounts. This entry replaces entry (3) of Worksheet 4-3.
(1)   Eliminate the entry recording the parent's share (80%) of the subsidiary net income under the sophisticated equity method.
(2)   Eliminate 80% of the subsidiary equity balances against the investment account. The elimination of Retained Earnings is 80% of the adjusted balance of $137,000 ($145,000 – $8,000).
(4–6)   Same as Worksheet 4-3.

When the sophisticated equity method is used, the worksheet elimination of the parent's investment account against the stockholders' equity of the subsidiary is more complicated because there is an inconsistency between the parent's accounts and those of the subsidiary. In the partial worksheet illustrated, the parent's investment and retained earnings accounts do not reflect the $8,000 beginning inventory profit recorded by the subsidiary. The intercompany profit was removed in the prior period before the parent's share of the subsidiary's net income was recorded. The subsidiary's trial balance does include the $8,000 beginning inventory profit in the January 1 retained earnings balance, and the parent's beginning inventory, now in the cost of goods sold, does include the profit. The inconsistency is removed on the worksheet by making an adjustment, coded "Adj," that removes the intercompany profit from the subsidiary's beginning retained earnings and the parent's beginning inventory. This entry replaces entry (3) in Worksheet 4-3.

Entry (1) of the partial worksheet removes the subsidiary income as recorded by the parent. Entry (2) reflects the adjustment of the subsidiary's Retained Earnings. The remaining entries and worksheet procedures are identical to those in Worksheet 4-3.

Appendix: Intercompany Profit Eliminations on the Vertical Worksheet

In keeping with the overall worksheet format approach of this text, all previous examples in this chapter have been presented using the horizontal worksheet style. Worksheet 4-9, pages 4-68 to 4-71, provides the reader an opportunity to study the vertical worksheet when intercompany merchandise and plant asset transactions are involved. This worksheet is based on the following facts:

1. Company P purchased an 80% interest in Company S on January 1, 19X1. At that time, the following determination and distribution of excess schedule was prepared:

Price paid		$500,000
Less interest acquired:		
Common stock ($5 par)	$200,000	
Retained earnings, January 1, 19X1	350,000	
Total stockholders' equity	$550,000	
Interest acquired	80%	440,000
Excess of cost over book value attributed to goodwill		
(40-year life)		$ 60,000

2. Company P accounts for the investment under the simple equity method.
3. Company S sells merchandise to Company P at cost plus 25%. Sales totaled $150,000 during 19X2. There were $40,000 of such goods in Company P's beginning inventory and $50,000 of such goods in Company P's ending inventory. As of December 31, 19X2, Company P had not paid the $20,000 owed for the purchases.
4. On July 1, 19X1, Company P sold a new machine that cost $20,000 to Company S for $25,000. At that time, both companies believed that the machine had a 5-year remaining life; both companies use straight-line depreciation.
5. Company S declared and paid $20,000 in dividends during 19X2.

Notice that the eliminations in Worksheet 4-9 are identical to those required for the horizontal format. Also, when working with the vertical format, keep in mind the cautions that are stated in Appendix A of Chapter 3: a) the nominal accounts are presented above the balance sheet accounts, and b) the eliminations are made only to the **beginning** retained earnings accounts. The carrydown procedures for the vertical worksheet are the same as those presented in Appendix A of Chapter 3.

Questions

1. What types of intercompany transactions may result in a profit's being recorded by a parent or subsidiary? What is the basic theoretical approach to recognizing such profits?

2. A subsidiary sold merchandise with a cost of $30,000 to the parent company at a price equal to cost plus 50%. A perpetual inventory method is used. The parent company sold 80% of the merchandise purchased from the subsidiary to outside companies. What are the adjustments that need to be made when consolidating?

3. Explain why the intercompany sale of merchandise has an influence on the distribution of combined net income, even though the sale is eliminated on the consolidated statements.

4. A parent company sold to its subsidiary merchandise costing $80,000 for $100,000. Half of the goods were unsold at year-end and had been written down to $45,000, the lower market value. What adjusting entries are required in the consolidation process assuming the use of a perpetual inventory system and that a separate account is used for the loss?

5. Provide the worksheet entries needed to delete the unrealized profit on intercompany sales from beginning and ending inventories for the following situations, assuming the parent has a 90%-ownership interest in the subsidiary:

   a) Subsidiary's beginning inventory includes $20,000 of goods purchased from the parent company. Parent sells all merchandise at a 25% markup on cost. Subsidiary purchased goods at a price of $150,000 from parent during the year and had $45,000 of the goods in ending inventory.

   b) Parent's beginning inventory includes $36,000 of goods purchased from the subsidiary company. Subsidiary sells all merchandise at a 20% markup on cost. Parent purchased goods at a price of $280,000 from subsidiary during the year and had $25,000 of the goods in ending inventory.

6. In theory, the intercompany gain on the sale of an asset between affiliates is deferred on the date of sale. When is the intercompany gain considered to be realizable? Compare the procedures where the sale is a) the sale of merchandise to be resold, b) the sale of a depreciable fixed asset, and c) the sale of land.

7. Under what circumstances is a loss on the intercompany sale of a depreciable fixed asset deferred, and what are the procedures for its deferment?

8. Prepare parent and subsidiary income distribution schedules, and enter each of the following items in the correct column:

   a) intercompany profit on unsold ending inventory—parent seller;

   b) realized intercompany profit on beginning inventory—subsidiary seller;

   c) internally generated net income of parent;

   d) internally generated net income of subsidiary;

   e) unrealized gain on intercompany sale of depreciable asset—subsidiary seller;

   f) gain on intercompany sale of depreciable asset realized through use—subsidiary seller;

   g) realized intercompany profit on beginning inventory—parent seller; and

   h) retirement loss on bonds—bonds issued by subsidiary, purchased by parent.

9. Hiller Construction Company is a 90%-owned subsidiary of Chain O'Lakes Properties Inc. Hiller is building an office complex for Chain O'Lakes and is accounting for the contract under the percentage-of-completion method. To date, Hiller has billed but not collected $1,450,000, recorded costs of $1,200,000, and recorded earned income of $250,000.

   No adjustments or eliminations were made concerning this transaction in the process of preparing the consolidated statements. What misstatements can be found on the consolidated income statement and balance sheet?

10. Frequently, related companies will have outstanding intercompany loan balances. What effect do intercompany interest revenue and expense have on the consolidation process, including the distribution of combined net income?

Exercises

Exercise 1.   Sandal Company is a wholly owned subsidiary of Cart Enterprises. Sandal is a just-in-time supplier of goods to Cart, and, thus, Sandal maintains no inventories. Sandal consistently sells to Cart to realize a gross profit of 25%. Sandal supplies goods only to Cart. Sales for the past 3 years were as follows:

	Sandal	Cart
19X1	$250,000	$350,000
19X2	300,000	400,000
19X3	420,000	475,000

All goods sold by Cart are purchases from Sandal. Cart's inventory and purchases information is

Year	Beginning Inventory	Purchases	Ending Inventory
19X1	$ 0	$200,000	$20,000
19X2	20,000	350,000	50,000
19X3	50,000	420,000	84,000

19X1 was the first year of operations for both companies.
Prepare schedules covering 19X1 through 19X3 that calculate for each year

1. The gross profit recorded by the Sandal Company.
2. The gross profit recorded by Cart Enterprises as a separate entity.
3. The gross profit to be reported by the consolidated company.

Exercise 2.   Gander Corporation is a wholly owned subsidiary of Mountain Company. During 19X1, Gander sold all of its production to Mountain Company for $400,000, a price that includes a 20% gross profit. 19X1 is the first year that such intercompany sales were made. By year-end, Mountain sold 80% of the goods it had purchased at a markup on cost of 25%. The balance of the intercompany goods, $80,000, remained in the ending inventory and was adjusted to a lower market value $70,000. The adjustment was a charge to the cost of goods sold.

1. Determine the gross profit on sales recorded by both Gander and Mountain companies.
2. Determine the gross profit to be shown on the consolidated income statement.

Exercise 3.   Nick Company is an 80%-owned subsidiary of Van Corporation. The separate income statements of the 2 companies for 19X6 are as follows:

	Van Corporation	Nick Company
Sales	$220,000	$120,000
Cost of goods sold	(150,000)	(90,000)
Gross profit	$ 70,000	$ 30,000
Other expenses	(40,000)	(12,000)
Other income	5,000	
Operating income	$ 35,000	$ 18,000
Subsidiary income	14,400	
Net income	$ 49,400	$ 18,000

The following facts apply to 19X6:

a) Nick Company sold $70,000 of goods to Van Corporation. The gross profits on sales to Van and to unrelated companies are equal and have not changed from the previous years.

GP % = 25
30/120

b) Van Corporation held $15,000 of the goods purchased from Nick Company in its beginning inventory and $20,000 of such goods in ending inventory.

c) Van Corporation billed Nick Company $5,000 for computer services. The charge was expensed by Nick Company and treated as other income by Van Corporation.   *elim gains/losses*

Prepare the consolidated income statement for 19X6, including the distribution of the combined net income to the controlling and minority interests. The supporting income distribution schedules should be prepared as well.

Exercise 4.   On January 1, 19X2, Fan Company sold a machine to Bark Company for $25,000. The machine had an original cost of $24,000, and depreciation on the asset had accumulated to $9,000 at the time of the sale. The machine has a 5-year remaining life and will be depreciated on a straight-line basis with no salvage value. Bark Company is an 80%-owned subsidiary of Fan Company.

1. Explain the adjustments that would have to be made to arrive at combined net income for the years 19X2 through 19X6 as a result of this sale.
2. Prepare the elimination that would be required on the December 31, 19X3 consolidated worksheet as a result of this sale.
3. Assuming Bark Company was the seller of the machine and all the other facts remained constant, prepare the elimination that would be required on the December 31, 19X3 consolidated worksheet as a result of this sale.

Exercise 5.   Wavemasters Inc. owns an 80% interest in Sayner Development Company. In a prior period, Sayner Development purchased for $50,000 a parcel of land which it developed and sold to the parent company, Wavemasters Inc. Sayner agreed to sell the land for $100,000 and constructed a building on the land during 19X1 at a cost of $500,000. The building was sold to Wavemasters at the very end of 19X1 for $650,000. It is estimated that the building has a 20-year life with no salvage value.

remove gain

1. Prepare all worksheet eliminations that would be made on the 19X1 consolidated worksheet as a result of the real estate sales.
2. Prepare all worksheet eliminations that would be made on the **19X3** consolidated worksheet as a result of the 19X1 real estate sale.

Exercise 6. Hilton Corporation sold a press to its 80%-owned subsidiary, Agri Fab Inc., for $5,000 on January 1, 19X2. The press originally was purchased by Hilton on January 1, 19X1, for $20,000, and $6,000 of depreciation for 19X1 had been recorded. The fair market value of the press on January 1, 19X2, was $10,000. Agri Fab proceeded to depreciate the press on a straight-line basis, using a 5-year life and no salvage value. On December 31, 19X3, Agri Fab, having no further need for the machine, sold it for $2,000 and recorded a loss on the sale.

Explain the adjustments that would have to be made to the separate income statements of the two companies to arrive at the consolidated income statements for 19X2 and 19X3.

Exercise 7. Janis Company contracted with its 80%-owned subsidiary, Essuman Equipment Company, for the construction of 2 stamping machines. The first machine was completed and put into operation on July 1, 19X9. It cost Essuman $60,000 and has a 5-year estimated life with no salvage value. The contract price was $75,000. The machine is being depreciated on a straight-line basis. The second machine, with an estimated total cost of $90,000 and a contract price of $120,000, was 80% complete on December 31, 19X9. To date, costs on the second contract total $72,000. By the statement date, Janis had completely paid for the first machine and still owed $3,000 of the $60,000 billed to date on the second machine. Essuman uses the completed contract method to account for its long-term construction contracts.

1. Prepare the necessary eliminations for the consolidated worksheet on December 31, 19X9.
2. What are the effects of these contracts on the income distribution schedules?

Exercise 8. Donner Contractors, an 80%-owned subsidiary, is constructing a warehouse for its parent, Fast-Parts Corporation. The following information is available at December 31, 19X5:

Percent of completion	60%
Costs incurred to date	$120,000
Estimated costs to complete	80,000
Contract price	240,000
Amount billed to date (no amounts collected)	135,000

Donner uses the percentage-of-completion method to account for its long-term contracts.

Record the journal entries that each of the 2 companies would have made relative to the construction. Prepare a partial trial balance using the data from your entries, and show the eliminations relating to the contract for the December 31, 19X5 consolidated worksheet.

Exercise 9. The separate income statements of Dark Company and its 90%-owned subsidiary, Light Company, for the year ended December 31, 19X6, are as follows:

	Dark Company	Light Company
Sales	$700,000	$280,000
Cost of goods sold	(450,000)	(190,000)
Gross profit	$250,000	$ 90,000
Other expenses	(180,000)	(70,000)
Other income	20,000	
Operating income	$ 90,000	$ 20,000
Subsidiary income	18,000	
Net income	$108,000	$ 20,000

The following additional facts apply:

a) On January 1, 19X5, Light Company purchased a building, with a book value of $100,000 and an estimated 20-year life, from Dark Company for $180,000. The building was being depreciated on a straight-line basis with no salvage value.

b) On January 1, 19X6, Light Company sold a machine with a book value of $50,000 to Dark Company for $60,000. The machine had an expected life of 5 years and is being depreciated on a straight-line basis with no salvage value. Light Company is a dealer for the machine.

Prepare the December 31, 19X6 consolidated income statement and supporting income distribution schedules.

Exercise 10.   Patel Company owns an 80% controlling interest in the Sanjoy Company. Sanjoy regularly sells merchandise to Patel, which then sold to outside parties. The gross profit on all such sales is 30%. On January 1, 19X1, Patel sold land and a building to Sanjoy. Tax assessments divide the value of the parcel 20% to land and 80% to structures. Pertinent information for the companies is summarized:

	Patel	Sanjoy
Internally generated net income, 19X1	$520,000	$250,000
Internally generated net income, 19X2	340,000	235,000
Intercompany merchandise sales, 19X1		100,000
Intercompany merchandise sales, 19X2		120,000
Intercompany inventory, Dec. 31, 19X1		15,000
Intercompany inventory, Dec. 31, 19X2		20,000
Cost of real estate sold on January 1, 19X1	$500,000	
Sale price for real estate on January 1, 19X1	800,000	
Depreciable life of building		20 years

Prepare income distribution schedules for 19X1 and 19X2 for Patel and Sanjoy as they would be prepared to distribute income to the minority and controlling interests in support of consolidated worksheets.

Exercise 11.   Saratoga Company owns 80% of the outstanding common stock of Windsor Company. On May 1, 19X3, Windsor Company arranged a 1-year, $50,000 loan from Saratoga Company. The loan agreement specified that interest would accrue at the rate of 6% per annum and that all interest would be paid on the maturity date of the loan. The financial reporting period ends on December 31, 19X3, and the note originating from the loan remains outstanding.

1) Prepare the entries that both companies would have made on their separate books, including the accrual of interest.
2) Prepare the eliminations, in entry form, that would be made on a consolidated worksheet prepared as of December 31, 19X3.

Exercise 12.   Assume the same facts as in Exercise 11, but, in addition, assume that Saratoga was itself in need of cash. It discounted the note received from Windsor at the First Bank on July 1, 19X3, at a discount rate of 8% per annum.

1) Prepare the entries that both companies would make on their separate books, including interest accruals.
2) Prepare the eliminations, in entry form, that would be made on a consolidated worksheet prepared as of December 31, 19X3.

Problems

Problem 4-1. On January 1, 19X6, 100% of the outstanding stock of Sally Company was purchased by Pete Corporation for $3,200,000. At that time, the fair market value and book value of Sally's net assets equaled $2,800,000. The excess is being amortized as goodwill over a 20-year period.

The following trial balances of Pete Corporation and Sally Company were prepared on December 31, 19X6:

	Pete Corporation	Sally Company
Cash	810,000	170,000
Accounts Receivable	425,000	365,000
Inventory	600,000	275,000
Property, Plant, and Equipment (net)	4,000,000	2,300,000
Investment in Sally Company	3,410,000	
Accounts Payable	(35,000)	(100,000)
Common Stock ($10 par)	(1,000,000)	(400,000)
Paid-In Capital in Excess of Par	(1,500,000)	(200,000)
Retained Earnings 1/1/X6	(5,500,000)	(2,200,000)
Sales	(12,000,000)	(1,000,000)
Cost of Goods Sold	7,000,000	750,000
Other Expenses	4,000,000	40,000
Subsidiary Income	(210,000)	
Total	0	0

Throughout 19X6, sales to Pete Corporation made up 40% of Sally's revenue and produced a 25% gross profit rate. At year-end, Pete Corporation had sold 90% of the goods purchased from Sally Company and still owed Sally $25,000. None of the Sally products were in Pete's January 1, 19X6 beginning inventory.

Required:

Prepare the worksheet necessary to produce the consolidated income statement and balance sheet of Pete Corporation and its subsidiary for the year ended December 31, 19X6. Include the determination and distribution of excess schedule.

Problem 4-2. On April 1, 19X1, Mooney Corporation purchased 80% of the outstanding stock of Tripper Company for $425,000. A condensed balance sheet of Tripper Company at the purchase date follows:

Assets		Liabilities and Equity	
Current assets	$180,000	Liabilities	$100,000
Long-lived assets (net)	320,000	Equity	400,000
Total assets	$500,000	Total liabilities and equity	$500,000

All book values approximated market values on the purchase date. Mooney Corporation amortizes its intangibles over 20 years or their legal life, whichever is shorter.

The following information has been gathered pertaining to the first 2 years of operation since Mooney's purchase of Tripper Company stock:

a) *Intercompany merchandise sales are summarized as follows:*

Date	Transaction	Sales	Gross Profit	Merchandise Remaining in Purchaser's Ending Inventory
April 1, 19X1 to	Mooney to Tripper	$35,000	15%	$9,000
March 31, 19X2	Tripper to Mooney	20,000	20	3,500
April 1, 19X2 to	Mooney to Tripper	32,000	22	6,000
March 31, 19X3	Tripper to Mooney	30,000	25	3,000

b) On March 31, 19X3, Mooney owed Tripper $10,000, and Tripper owed Mooney $5,000 as a result of the intercompany sales.

c) Mooney paid $25,000 in cash dividends on March 20, 19X2 and 19X3. Tripper paid its first cash dividend on March 10, 19X3, giving each share of outstanding common stock a $0.15 cash dividend.

d) The trial balances of the 2 companies as of March 31, 19X3, follow:

	Mooney Corporation	Tripper Company
Cash	216,200	44,300
Accounts Receivable (net)	290,000	97,000
Inventory	310,000	80,000
Investment in Tripper Company	425,000	
Land	1,081,000	150,000
Building and Equipment	1,850,000	400,000
Accumulated Depreciation	(940,000)	(210,000)
Intangibles (net)	60,000	
Accounts Payable	(242,200)	(106,300)
Bonds Payable	(400,000)	
Common Stock ($.50 par)	(250,000)	
Common Stock ($1 par)		(200,000)
Paid-In Capital in Excess of Par	(1,250,000)	(100,000)
Retained Earnings, April 1, 19X2	(1,105,000)	(140,000)
Sales	(880,000)	(630,000)
Dividend Income (from Tripper Company)	(24,000)	
Cost of Goods Sold	704,000	504,000
Other Expenses	130,000	81,000
Dividends Declared	25,000	30,000
Total	0	0

Required:

1. Prepare the worksheet necessary to produce the consolidated financial statements of Mooney Corporation and its subsidiary for the year ended March 31, 19X3. Include the determination and distribution of excess schedule and the income distribution schedules.
2. Prepare the formal consolidated income statement for the fiscal year 19X2–19X3.

Problem 4-3.   Muskegon Corporation purchased 80% of the common stock of Shannon Ltd. on Jan. 1, 19X1, for $580,000 in order to ensure its raw material supply would be consistently available. At the time of the purchase, Shannon's net assets had a market value equal to the book value of $600,000. Also at that time, the Shannon retained earnings account had a balance of $300,000. Muskegon amortizes its intangible assets over 10 years.

Since the acquisition, 60% of Shannon's sales have been to the Muskegon Corporation. Muskegon's ending inventories on December 31, 19X1 and 19X2, contained $127,000 and $163,000, respectively, in goods purchased from Shannon. Shannon has maintained a 33⅓% markup on cost. At the end of 19X1 and 19X2, Muskegon's Accounts Payable contained $36,000 and $43,000, respectively, in liabilities to Shannon for purchases of goods.

The December 31, 19X2 total inventories were $750,000 for Muskegon and $100,000 for Shannon. The companies use the periodic inventory method.

Trial balances as of December 31, 19X2, are as follows:

	Muskegon Corporation	Shannon Limited
Cash	295,000	60,000
Accounts Receivable (net)	575,000	65,000
Inventory, Jan. 1, 19X2	720,000	90,000
Investment in Shannon Ltd	580,000	
Land	100,000	30,000
Building and Equipment (net)	1,200,000	650,000
Accounts Payable	(280,000)	(72,500)
Bonds Payable, 10%, due Jan. 1, 19X8		(100,000)
Common Stock ($15 par)	(510,000)	(180,000)
Paid-In Capital in Excess of Par	(100,000)	(120,000)
Retained Earnings, Jan. 1, 19X2	(1,750,000)	(375,140)
Sales	(3,450,000)	(750,000)
Purchases	2,100,000	572,640
Inventory, Dec. 31, 19X2		
Asset	750,000	100,000
Cost of Goods Sold	(750,000)	(100,000)
Selling and General Expenses	420,000	120,000
Interest Expense		10,000
Dividends Declared	100,000	
Total	0	0

Required:

1. Prepare the worksheet necessary to produce the consolidated financial statements of Muskegon Corporation and its subsidiary for the year ended December 31, 19X2. Include the determination and distribution of excess schedule and the income distribution schedules.
2. Prepare the formal consolidated financial statements, including the income statement, retained earnings statement, and balance sheet.

Problem 4-4.   On January 1, 19X3, Stephen Corporation exchanged on a 1-for-3 basis common stock it held in its treasury for 80% of the outstanding stock of James Company. Stephen Corporation common stock had a market price of $40 per share on the exchange date.

On the date of the acquisition, the stockholders' equity section of James Company was as follows:

Common stock ($5 par).	$ 450,000
Paid-in capital in excess of par.	180,000
Retained earnings.	370,000
Total	$1,000,000

Also on that date, James Company's book values approximated market values, except for the land, which was undervalued by $75,000. Any goodwill recognized from the acquisition is being amortized over 40 years.

Information regarding intercompany transactions for 19X5 follows:

a)   Stephen Corporation sells merchandise to James Company, realizing a 30% gross profit. Sales during 19X5 were $140,000. James had $25,000 of the 19X4 purchases in its beginning inventory for 19X5 and $35,000 of the 19X5 purchases in its ending inventory for 19X5.

b)   James signed a 12%, 4-month, $10,000 note to Stephen in order to cover the remaining balance of its payables on November 1, 19X5. No new merchandise was purchased after this date.

c)   James wrote-down to $28,000 the merchandise purchased from Stephen Corporation and remaining in its 19X5 ending inventory.

The trial balances of Stephen Corporation and James Company as of December 31, 19X5, are as follows:

	Stephen Corporation	James Company
Cash	140,000	205,200
Accounts Receivable.	285,000	110,000
Interest Receivable	1,500	
Notes Receivable	50,000	
Inventory.	470,000	160,000
Land.	350,000	300,000
Property, Plant, and Equipment	1,110,000	810,000
Accumulated Depreciation	(500,000)	(200,000)
Intangibles	60,000	
Investment in James Company	1,128,000	
Accounts Payable.	(611,500)	(175,000)
Interest Payable		(200)
Common Stock ($1 par)	(400,000)	
Common Stock ($5 par)		(450,000)
Paid-In Capital in Excess of Par.	(1,235,000)	(180,000)
Retained Earnings 1/1/X5.	(958,500)	(470,000)
Treasury Stock (at cost)	315,000	
Sales	(1,020,000)	(500,000)
Interest Income.	(1,500)	
Subsidiary Income	(88,000)	
Cost of Goods Sold	705,000	300,000
Other Expenses	200,000	90,000
Total.	0	0

(continued)

Required:

Prepare the worksheet necessary to produce the consolidated financial statements of Stephen Corporation and its subsidiary for the year ended December 31, 19X5. Include the determination and distribution of excess schedule and the income distribution schedules.

Problem 4-5. On September 1, 19X1, Gordy Corporation purchased 80% of the outstanding common stock of Sim's Corporation for $152,000. On that date, Sim's net book values equaled market values and there was no excess of cost or book value resulting from the purchase. Gordy has been maintaining its investment under the simple equity method.

Over the next 3 years, the intercompany transactions between the companies were as follows:

a) On December 1, 19X1, Sim's sold its 4-year-old delivery truck to Gordy for $14,000 in cash. At that time, Sim's had depreciated the truck, which had cost $15,000, to its $5,000 salvage value. Gordy estimated on the date of the sale that the asset had a remaining useful life of 3 years and an estimated salvage value of $200.

b) On March 1, 19X3, Gordy sold a building to Sim's for $103,000. Gordy originally paid $80,000 for the building and planned to depreciate it over 20 years, assuming a $10,000 salvage value. However, Gordy had the property for only 10 years and carried it at a net book value of $45,000 on the sale date. Sim's will use the building for 10 years, at which time Sim's expects to sell the asset for $13,000.

Both companies use straight-line depreciation for all assets. One-half year's depreciation is taken for all assets in the year they are purchased and in the year they are sold.

Trial balances of Gordy Corporation and Sim's Corporation as of the August 31, 19X3 year-end are as follows:

	Gordy Corporation	Sim's Corporation
Cash	120,000	50,000
Accounts Receivable (net)	115,000	18,000
Notes Receivable		10,000
Inventory	175,000	34,000
Investment in Sim's Corporation	217,440	
Plant and Equipment	990,700	295,000
Accumulated Depreciation	(175,000)	(85,000)
Other Assets	28,000	
Accounts Payable	(80,000)	(50,200)
Notes Payable	(25,000)	
Bonds Payable, 12%	(300,000)	
Common Stock ($10 par)	(290,000)	(70,000)
Paid-In Capital in Excess of Par	(110,000)	(62,000)
Retained Earnings, Sept. 1, 19X2	(498,850)	(118,000)
Sales	(920,000)	(240,000)
Cost of Goods Sold	598,000	132,000
Selling and General Expenses	108,000	80,000
Investment Income	(23,040)	

Interest Income.		(800)
Interest Expense	37,750	
Gain on Sale of Building	(58,000)	
Dividends Declared.	90,000	7,000
Total.	0	0

Required:

Prepare the worksheet necessary to produce the consolidated financial statements of Gordy Corporation and its subsidiary for the year ended August 31, 19X3. Include the income distribution schedules.

Problem 4-6.   Pardon Inc. purchased 100% of the common stock of Slarno Corporation for $150,000 in cash on June 30, 19X6. At that date, Slarno's stockholders' equity was as follows:

Common stock ($1 par).	$100,000
Retained earnings.	50,000
Total.	$150,000

The fair market values of the assets and liabilities did not differ materially from their book values. Slarno has made no adjustments on its books to reflect the purchase by Pardon. On December 31, 19X6, Pardon and Slarno prepared consolidated financial statements.

The transactions that occurred between Pardon and Slarno during the next year included the following:

a)   On January 3, 19X7, land with a $10,000 book value was sold by Pardon to Slarno for $15,000. Slarno made a $3,000 down payment and signed an 8% mortgage note, payable in 12 equal quarterly payments of $1,135, including interest, beginning March 31, 19X7.

b)   Slarno produced equipment for Pardon under 2 separate contracts. The first contract, which was for office equipment, was begun and completed during the year at a cost to Slarno of $17,500. Pardon paid $22,000 in cash for the equipment on April 17, 19X7. The second contract was begun on February 15, 19X7, but will not be completed until May 19X8. Slarno has incurred $45,000 of costs as of December 31, 19X7, and anticipates an additional $30,000 of costs to complete the $95,000 contract. Slarno accounts for all contracts under the percentage-of-completion method. Pardon has made no account on its books for this uncompleted contract as of December 31, 19X7.

c)   Pardon depreciates all of its equipment over a 10-year estimated economic life, with no salvage value. Pardon takes one-half-year's depreciation in the year of purchase.

d)   Pardon sells merchandise to Slarno at an average markup of 12% on cost. During the year, Pardon charged Slarno $238,000 for merchandise purchased, of which Slarno paid $211,000. Slarno has $11,200 of this merchandise on hand on December 31, 19X7.

Trial balances of Pardon Inc. and its subsidiary as of December 31, 19X7, are as follows:

	Pardon Incorporated	Slarno Corporation
Cash	45,000	31,211
Accounts Receivable	119,000	73,500
Billings on Construction in Progress		(1,201,900)
Mortgage Receivable	8,311	
Unsecured Notes Receivable	18,000	
Inventories.	217,000	117,500
Land.	34,000	42,000
Building and Equipment (net)	717,000	408,000
Investment in Slarno Corporation	150,000	
Accounts Payable.	(203,000)	(147,000)
Mortgages Payable.	(592,000)	(397,311)
Common Stock.	(250,000)	(100,000)
Retained Earnings, Jan. 1, 19X7.	(139,311)	(70,000)
Sales	(1,800,000)	
Earned Income on Long-Term Contracts		(437,000)
Cost of Goods Sold	1,155,000	
Construction in Progress.		1,289,000
Selling, General, and Administrative Expenses	497,000	360,000
Interest Income.	(20,000)	
Interest Expense	49,000	32,000
Gain on Sale of Land	(5,000)	
Total.	0	0

Required:

Prepare the worksheet necessary to produce the consolidated financial statements of Pardon Inc. and its subsidiary for the year ended December 31, 19X7. Assume both companies have made all of the adjusting entries required for separate financial statements unless an obvious discrepancy exists. Include the determination and distribution of excess schedule.

(AICPA adapted)

Problem 4-7. The December 31, 19X6 trial balances of the Pettie Corporation and its 90%-owned subsidiary Sunny Corporation are as follows:

	Pettie Corporation	Sunny Corporation
Cash	75,000	45,500
Accounts and Other Current Receivables	410,900	170,000
Inventory.	920,000	739,400
Property, Plant, and Equipment (net).	1,000,000	400,000
Investment in Sunny Corp.	1,200,000	
Accounts Payable and Other Current Liabilities	(140,000)	(305,900)
Common Stock ($10 par)	(500,000)	
Common Stock ($10 par)		(200,000)
Retained Earnings 1/1/X5.	(2,800,000)	(650,000)
Dividends Declared.		1,000
Sales	(2,000,000)	(650,000)
Dividend Income	(900)	

Interest Expense		5,000
Interest Income	(5,000)	
Cost of Goods Sold	1,500,000	400,000
Other Expenses	340,000	45,000
Totals	0	0

Pettie's investment in Sunny was purchased for $1,200,000 in cash on January 1, 19X5, and is accounted for by the cost method. On January 1, 19X5, Sunny had the following equity balances:

Common stock	$200,000
Retained earnings	600,000
Total equity	$800,000

Pettie's excess of cost over book value on Sunny's investment has been identified appropriately as goodwill and is to be amortized over 10 years.

Sunny borrowed $100,000 from Pettie on June 30, 19X6, with the note maturing on June 30, 19X7, at 10% interest. Correct accruals have been recorded by both companies.

During 19X6, Pettie sold merchandise to Sunny at an aggregate invoice price of $300,000, which included a profit of $75,000. As of December 31, 19X6, Sunny had not paid Pettie for $90,000 of these purchases, and 10% of the total merchandise purchased from Pettie still remained in Sunny's inventory.

Sunny declared a $1,000 cash dividend in December 19X6 payable in January 19X7.

Required:

Prepare the worksheet required to produce the consolidated statements of Pettie Corporation and its subsidiary, Sunny Corporation, for the year ending December 31, 19X6. Include the determination and distribution of excess schedule and the income distribution schedule.

(AICPA adapted)

Problem 4-8.   The following trial balances were prepared after completion of the examination of the December 31, 19X4 financial statements of Presidential Corporation and its subsidiaries, Sublenee Corporation and Submariner Corporation. The subsidiary investments are accounted for by the cost method.

	Presidential Corporation	Sublenee Corporation	Submariner Corporation
Cash	73,000	21,000	47,000
Accounts Receivable	104,000	31,000	123,000
Inventory	241,000	70,000	78,000
Investments (other)	185,000		
Property, Plant, and Equipment	375,000	58,000	99,000
Accumulated Depreciation	(96,000)	(7,000)	(21,000)
Investment in Sublenee Corp.	150,000		
Investment in Submariner Corp.	184,000		
Accounts Payable	(46,000)	(33,000)	(24,000)
Common Stock ($20 par)	(500,000)		
Common Stock ($20 par)		(200,000)	
Common Stock ($20 par)			(100,000)

(continued)

	Presidential Corporation	Sublenee Corporation	Submariner Corporation
Retained Earnings	(563,000)		(22,000)
Sales	(960,000)	(275,000)	(570,000)
Cost of Goods Sold.	820,000	300,000	350,000
Other Expenses	60,000	35,000	40,000
Dividend Income.	(18,000)		
Gain on Sale of Assets.	(9,000)		
Total	0	0	0

The audit working papers provided the following additional information:

a) Sublenee Corporation was formed by Presidential Corporation on January 1, 19X4. To secure additional capital, 25% of the common stock of Sublenee was sold at par value in the securities market. Presidential Corporation purchased the remaining stock at par for cash.

b) On July 1, 19X4, Presidential acquired from stockholders 4,000 shares of Submariner Corporation common stock for $184,000. Any excess paid was attributed to goodwill and is being amortized over a 10-year period. A condensed trial balance of Submariner Corporation at July 1, 19X4, was as follows:

Current Assets	165,000
Property, Plant, and Equipment (net)	60,000
Current Liabilities	(45,000)
Common Stock ($20 par)	(100,000)
Retained Earnings	(36,000)
Sales	(200,000)
Cost of Goods Sold	140,000
Operating Expenses	16,000
Total.	0

c) The following intercompany product sales were made in 19X4:

	Sales	Gross Profit on Sales	Included in Purchaser's Inventory on 12/31/X4 at LCM
Presidential to Submariner.	$50,000	30%	$20,000
Sublenee to Submariner	35,000	20	15,000
Submariner to Presidential.	60,000	30	20,000
	$145,000		$55,000

In valuing Presidential Corporation's inventory at the lower of cost or market, the portion of the inventory purchased from Submariner Corporation was written down by $2,000.

d) On January 2, 19X4, Presidential Corporation sold a punch press to Sublenee Corporation. The machine originally was purchased on January 1, 19X2, and was being depreciated by the straight-line method over a 10-year life (8 years remaining). Sublenee Corporation planned to compute *depreciation by the same method based on the remaining useful life of the press. Details of the intercompany sale are as follows:*

Sales price		$29,000
Less book value of the press:		
Cost of the press	$30,000	
Accumulated depreciation	(6,000)	24,000
Gain on sale		$ 5,000

e)   Cash dividends were paid on the following dates in 19X4:

	Presidential	Submariner
June 30	$22,000	$ 6,000
December 31.	26,000	14,000
	$48,000	$20,000

f)   Presidential Corporation billed $5,000 to each subsidiary at year-end for executive services in 19X4. Presidential treated it as sales, and the subsidiary recorded it as an operating expense. The invoices were paid in January 19X5.

Required:

Prepare the worksheet necessary to produce the consolidated financial statements of Presidential Corporation and subsidiaries for the year ended December 31, 19X4. The consolidated income statement is to contain the nominal accounts of Submariner for the entire year. Include any necessary determination and distribution of excess schedule and income distribution schedules.

(AICPA adapted)

Suggestion: Allowing amounts in the nominal accounts of Submariner for the period preceding its purchase will require the use of "purchased income" in the worksheet. Also, retained earnings of all companies should be restored to the balances on January 1 to aid elimination. This means that dividend declared accounts should be established.

Problem 4-9.   On January 1, 19X1, Peanut Company acquired 80% of the common stock of Sam Company for $200,000. On this date, Sam had total owners' equity of $200,000. During 19X1 and 19X2, Peanut has appropriately accounted for its investment in Sam using the simple equity method.

Any excess of cost over book value is attributable to inventory (worth $12,500 more than cost), to equipment (worth $25,000 more than book value), and to goodwill. FIFO is used for inventories. The equipment has a remaining life of 4 years, and straight-line depreciation is used. Goodwill is to be amortized over 10 years. On January 1, 19X2, Peanut held merchandise acquired from Sam for $20,000. During 19X2, Sam sold merchandise to Peanut for $40,000, $10,000 of which is still held by Peanut on December 31, 19X2. Sam's usual gross profit is 50%.

On December 31, 19X1, Peanut sold equipment to Sam at a gain of $15,000. During 19X2, the equipment was used by Sam. Depreciation is being computed using the straight-line method, a 5-year life, and no salvage value.

The following trial balances were prepared for the Peanut and Sam companies for December 31, 19X2.

(continued)

	Peanut Company	Sam Company
Inventory, December 31	130,000	50,000
Other Current Assets	241,000	235,000
Investment in Sam Company	308,000	
Other Long-Term Investments	20,000	
Land	140,000	80,000
Buildings and Equipment	375,000	200,000
Accumulated Depreciation	(120,000)	(30,000)
Other Intangibles		20,000
Current Liabilities	(150,000)	(70,000)
Bonds Payable		(100,000)
Other Long-Term Liabilities	(200,000)	(50,000)
Common Stock, Peanut Company	(200,000)	
Other Paid-In Capital, Peanut Company	(100,000)	
Retained Earnings, Peanut Company	(320,000)	
Common Stock, Sam Company		(50,000)
Other Paid-In Capital, Sam Company		(50,000)
Retained Earnings, Sam Company		(150,000)
Net Sales	(600,000)	(315,000)
Cost of Goods Sold	350,000	150,000
Operating Expenses	150,000	60,000
Subsidiary Income	(84,000)	
Dividends Declared, Peanut Company	60,000	
Dividends Declared, Sam Company		20,000
Totals	0	0

Required:

Complete the worksheet for consolidated financial statements for the year ended December 31, 19X2. Include any necessary determination and distribution of excess schedule and income distribution schedules.

Problem 4-10.　(This is the same as Problem 4-9 except for use of the cost method.) On January 1, 19X1, Peanut Company acquired 80% of the common stock of Sam Company for $200,000. On this date, Sam had total owners' equity of $200,000, which included retained earnings of $100,000. During 19X1 and 19X2, Peanut has accounted for its investment in Sam using the cost method.

Any excess of cost over book value is attributable to inventory (worth $12,500 more than cost), to equipment (worth $25,000 more than book value), and to goodwill. FIFO is used for inventories. The equipment has a remaining life of 4 years, and straight-line depreciation is used. Goodwill is to be amortized over 10 years.

On January 1, 19X2, Peanut held merchandise acquired from Sam for $20,000. During 19X2, Sam sold merchandise to Peanut for $40,000, $10,000 of which is still held by Peanut on December 31, 19X2. Sam's usual gross profit is 50%.

On December 31, 19X1, Peanut sold equipment to Sam at a gain of $15,000. During 19X2, the equipment was used by Sam. Depreciation is being computed using the straight-line method, a 5-year life, and no salvage value.

The following trial balances were prepared for the Peanut and Sam companies for December 31, 19X2.

	Peanut Co.	Sam Co.
Inventory, December 31	130,000	50,000
Other Current Assets	241,000	235,000
Investment in Sam Company	200,000	
Other Long-Term Investments	20,000	
Land	140,000	80,000
Buildings and Equipment	375,000	200,000
Accumulated Depreciation	(120,000)	(30,000)
Other Intangibles		20,000
Current Liabilities	(150,000)	(70,000)
Bonds Payable		(100,000)
Other Long-Term Liabilities	(200,000)	(50,000)
Common Stock, Peanut Company	(200,000)	
Other Paid-In Capital, Peanut Company	(100,000)	
Retained Earnings, Peanut Company	(280,000)	
Common Stock, Sam Company		(50,000)
Other Paid-In Capital, Sam Company		(50,000)
Retained Earnings, Sam Company		(150,000)
Net Sales	(600,000)	(315,000)
Cost of Goods Sold	350,000	150,000
Operating Expenses	150,000	60,000
Dividend Income	(16,000)	
Dividends Declared, Peanut Company	60,000	
Dividends Declared, Sam Company		20,000
Totals	0	0

Required:

Complete the worksheet for consolidated financial statements for the year ended December 31, 19X2. Include any necessary determination and distribution of excess schedule and income distribution schedules.

Problem 4-11. (This is the same as Problem 4-9 except for use of the sophisticated equity method.) On January 1, 19X1, Peanut Company acquired 80% of the common stock of Sam Company for $200,000. On this date, Sam had total owners' equity of $200,000. During 19X1 and 19X2, Peanut has appropriately accounted for its investment in Sam using the sophisticated equity method.

Any excess of cost over book value is attributable to inventory (worth $12,500 more than cost), to equipment (worth $25,000 more than book value), and to goodwill. FIFO is used for inventories. The equipment has a remaining life of 4 years, and straight-line depreciation is used. Goodwill is to be amortized over 10 years.

On January 1, 19X2, Peanut held merchandise acquired from Sam for $20,000. During 19X2, Sam sold merchandise to Peanut for $40,000, $10,000 of which is still held by Peanut on December 31, 19X2. Sam's usual gross profit is 50%.

On December 31, 19X1, Peanut sold equipment to Sam at a gain of $15,000. During 19X2, the equipment was used by Sam. Depreciation is being computed using the straight-line method, a 5-year life, and no salvage value.

The following trial balances were prepared for the Peanut and Sam companies for December 31, 19X2:

	Peanut Company	Sam Company
Inventory, December 31	130,000	50,000
Other Current Assets	241,000	235,000
Investment in Sam Company	282,000	
Other Long-Term Investments	20,000	
Land	140,000	80,000
Buildings and Equipment	375,000	200,000
Accumulated Depreciation	(120,000)	(30,000)
Other Intangibles		20,000
Current Liabilities	(150,000)	(70,000)
Bonds Payable		(100,000)
Other Long-Term Liabilities	(200,000)	(50,000)
Common Stock, Peanut Company	(200,000)	
Other Paid-In Capital, Peanut Company	(100,000)	
Retained Earnings, Peanut Company	(296,000)	
Common Stock, Sam Company		(50,000)
Other Paid-In Capital, Sam Company		(50,000)
Retained Earnings, Sam Company		(150,000)
Net Sales	(600,000)	(315,000)
Cost of Goods Sold	350,000	150,000
Operating Expenses	150,000	60,000
Subsidiary Income	(82,000)	
Dividends Declared, Peanut Company	60,000	
Dividends Declared, Sam Company		20,000
Totals	0	0

Required:

Complete the worksheet for consolidated financial statements for the year ended December 31, 19X2. Include any necessary determination and distribution of excess schedule and income distribution schedules.

Problem 4-12.   *(Review of Chapters 3 and 4)* Print Company purchased 80% of the common stock of Slow Ink Company for $368,000 on January 2, 19X1. At that time, Slow Ink had the following balance sheet:

Assets		Liabilities and Stockholders' Equity	
Cash	$ 60,000	Accounts payable	$ 50,000
Accounts receivable	65,000	Bonds payable	200,000
Inventory	125,000	Common stock ($5 par)	50,000
Land	50,000	Paid-in capital in excess of par .	100,000
Buildings (net)	250,000	Retained earnings	200,000
Goodwill (net)	50,000		
Total assets	$600,000	Total liabilities and equity . . .	$600,000

The following information was available for the accounts where market values differed from book values on the date of the acquisition:

Account	Market Value	Life at Jan. 2, 19X1
Inventory	$150,000	Sold in 19X1
Land	100,000	
Buildings	400,000	20 years of 40-year original life
Bonds payable	190,000	5 years to maturity
Goodwill	?	20 years

The bond discount is to be amortized using the straight-line method.

The following transactions have occurred since the purchase and may be of concern in preparing the 19X3 consolidated financial statements:

1. Print's 19X3 beginning inventory includes $30,000 of the goods purchased from Slow Ink. Slow Ink always sells to Print at cost plus 25%.
2. Slow Ink made sales to Print during 19X3 totaling $90,000. $10,000 still was unpaid at year-end. Print had $35,000 of such goods in its 19X3 ending inventory; however, the goods were adjusted to the lower market value of $31,000.
3. Slow Ink sold a piece of equipment to Print on January 2, 19X2, for $12,000. The equipment had a book value of $8,000 and a 5-year remaining life at the time of the sale.

The following trial balances of Print Company and its subsidiary were prepared on December 31, 19X3:

	Print Company	Slow Ink Company
Cash	72,000	100,000
Accounts Receivable	120,000	100,000
Inventory.	180,000	120,000
Investment in Slow Ink Company	368,000	
Land.	60,000	50,000
Building (net)	340,000	230,000
Equipment (net)	40,000	
Goodwill (net)		42,500
Accounts Payable	(100,000)	(60,000)
Bonds Payable		(200,000)
Common Stock.	(300,000)	(50,000)
Paid-In Capital in Excess of Par.		(100,000)
Retained Earnings, Jan. 1, 19X3	(712,000)	(222,500)
Sales	(300,000)	(120,000)
Cost of Goods Sold	200,000	80,000
Other Expenses	40,000	20,000
Dividends Declared.		10,000
Dividend Income (from Slow Ink Company)	(8,000)	
Total	0	0

Required:

Prepare the worksheet necessary to produce the consolidated financial statements of Print Company and its subsidiary for the year ended December 31, 19X3. Include the determination and distribution of excess schedule and the income distribution schedules.

(continued)

Suggestion: Print's acquisition of Slow Ink Company is a bargain purchase and will require an allocation of available market value to long-lived assets. Eighty percent of the book value plus any excess available to fixed assets should be allocated to Slow Ink Company's fixed assets. Also, this is a cost-method problem that will require a cost-to-equity conversion.

Problem 4-13.   Pine Corporation issued 200,000 shares of its $10 par common stock on March 31, 19X1, to acquire all of the outstanding $25 par value common stock of Strand Inc. The business combination meets all conditions for a pooling of interests. On March 31, 19X1, the market price of Pine's common stock was $35 per share. Both corporations continued to operate as separate businesses maintaining separate accounting records with years ending December 31.

On March 31, 19X1, immediately before the combination, the stockholders' equities were

	Pine	Strand
Common stock.	$ 5,500,000	$2,500,000
Additional paid-in capital	4,200,000	470,000
Retained earnings.	7,360,000	2,430,000
	$17,060,000	$5,400,000

Additional information is as follows:

a)   During March 19X1, Pine paid $720,000 for expenditures relating to the business combination with Strand.

b)   Pine accounts for its investment in Strand using the sophisticated equity method.

c)   On March 31, 19X1, the fair values of Strand's assets and liabilities equaled their book values, except for its long-term investment in marketable equity securities, for which the aggregate market value exceeded aggregate cost by $600,000.

d)   On March 10, 19X1, Strand paid a cash dividend totaling $250,000 on its common stock.

e)   On November 15, 19X1, Pine paid a cash dividend totaling $1,500,000 on its common stock.

f)   During August 19X1, Pine sold merchandise to Strand at a profit of $800,000. At December 31, 19X1, one-fourth of this merchandise remained in Strand's inventory.

g)   For the period April 1 through December 31, 19X1, Strand paid Pine management fees totaling $150,000.

h)   Strand's 19X1 net income was $1,450,000. Pine's 19X1 income was $2,240,000 before considering equity in Strand's net income.

i)   The balances in retained earnings at January 1, 19X1, were $6,820,000 and $2,290,000 for Pine and Strand, respectively.

Required:

1.   Prepare Pine Corporation's journal entries to record the business combination with Strand Inc. and the expenditures relating to the business combination. Provide an equity transfer schedule.

2.   Prepare a schedule to compute the investment in Strand Inc., at sophisticated equity, at December 31, 19X1.

3.   Prepare a formal consolidated statement of changes in retained earnings of Pine Corporation and its subsidiary, Strand Inc., for the year ended December 31, 19X1.

(AICPA adapted)

Appendix Problems

Problem 4A-1.   Arther Corporation acquired all of the outstanding $10 par voting common stock of Trent Inc. on January 1, 19X2, in exchange for 50,000 shares of its $10 par voting common stock. On December 31, 19X1, the common stock of Arther had a closing market price of $15 per share on a national stock exchange. The retained earnings balance of Trent Inc. was $156,000 on the date of the acquisition. The acquisition was accounted for appropriately as a purchase. Both companies continued to operate as separate business entities maintaining separate accounting records with years ending December 31.

On December 31, 19X4, after year-end adjustments but before the nominal accounts were closed, the companies had the following condensed statements:

	Arther Corporation	Trent Inc.
Income Statement:		
Sales	(1,900,000)	(1,500,000)
Dividend Income (from Trent Inc.)	(40,000)	
Cost of Goods Sold	1,180,000	870,000
Operating Expenses (includes depreciation).	550,000	440,000
Net Income	(210,000)	(190,000)
Retained Earnings:		
Retained Earnings, Jan. 1, 19X4.	(250,000)	(206,000)
Net Income	(210,000)	(190,000)
Dividends Paid.		40,000
Balance, Dec. 31, 19X4	(460,000)	(356,000)
Balance Sheet:		
Cash	285,000	150,000
Accounts Receivable (net).	430,000	350,000
Inventories.	530,000	410,000
Land, Plant, and Equipment	660,000	680,000
Accumulated Depreciation	(185,000)	(210,000)
Investment in Trent Inc. (at cost).	750,000	
Accounts Payable and Accrued Expenses	(670,000)	(544,000)
Common Stock ($10 par).	(1,200,000)	(400,000)
Additional Paid-In Capital	(140,000)	(80,000)
Retained Earnings, Dec. 31, 19X4	(460,000)	(356,000)
Total	0	0

Additional information is as follows:

a)   There have been no changes in the common stock and additional paid-in capital accounts since the one necessitated in 19X2 by Arther's acquisition of Trent Inc.

b)   At the acquisition date, the market value of Trent's machinery exceeded book value by $54,000. This excess is being amortized over the asset's estimated average remaining life of 6 years. The fair market values of Trent's other assets and liabilities were equal to book values. Any goodwill resulting from the purchase is being amortized over a 20-year period.

(continued)

c) On July 1, 19X2, Arther sold a warehouse facility to Trent for $129,000 in cash. At the date of sale, Arther's book values were $33,000 for the land and $66,000 for the undepreciated cost of the building. Trent allocated the $129,000 purchase price to the land for $43,000 and to the building for $86,000. Trent is depreciating the building over its estimated 5-year remaining useful life by the straight-line method with no salvage value.

d) During 19X4, Arther purchased merchandise from Trent at an aggregate invoice price of $180,000, which included a 100% markup on Trent's cost. At December 31, 19X4, Arther owed Trent $75,000 on these purchases, and $36,000 of the merchandise purchased remained in Arther's inventory.

Required:

Complete the vertical worksheet necessary to prepare the consolidated income statement and retained earnings statement for the year ended December 31, 19X4, and a consolidated balance sheet as of December 31, 19X4, for Arther Corporation and its subsidiary. Formal consolidated statements and journal entries are not required. Include the determination and distribution of excess schedule and the income distribution schedules.

(AICPA adapted)

Problem 4A-2.   (This is similar to Problem 4-9; it uses the simple equity method and vertical worksheet format.) On January 1, 19X1, Peanut Company acquired 80% of the common stock of Sam Company for $200,000. On this date, Sam had total owners' equity of $200,000, which included retained earnings of $100,000. During 19X1 and 19X2, Peanut has accounted for its investment in Sam using the cost method.

Any excess of cost over book value is attributable to inventory (worth $12,500 more than cost), to equipment (worth $25,000 more than book value), and to goodwill. FIFO is used for inventories. The equipment has a remaining life of 4 years, and straight-line depreciation is used. Goodwill is to be amortized over 10 years.

On January 1, 19X2, Peanut held merchandise acquired from Sam for $20,000. During 19X2, Sam sold merchandise to Peanut for $40,000, $10,000 of which is still held by Peanut on December 31, 19X2. Sam's usual gross profit is 50%.

On December 31, 19X1, Peanut sold equipment to Sam at a gain of $15,000. During 19X2, the equipment was used by Sam. Depreciation is being computed using the straight-line method, a 5-year life, and no salvage value.

The trial balances on the next page were prepared for the Peanut and Sam companies for December 31, 19X2.

	Peanut Company	Sam Company
Income Statement:		
Net Sales	(600,000)	(315,000)
Cost of Goods Sold	350,000	150,000
Operating Expenses	150,000	60,000
Subsidiary Income	(84,000)	
Net Income	(184,000)	(105,000)
Retained Earnings Statement:		
Balance, Jan. 1, 19X2, Peanut Company	(320,000)	
Balance, Jan. 1, 19X2, Sam Company		(150,000)
Net Income (from above)	(184,000)	(105,000)
Dividends Declared, Peanut Company	60,000	
Dividends Declared, Sam Company.		20,000
Balance, December 31, 19X2	(444,000)	(235,000)
Consolidated Balance Sheet:		
Inventory, December 31	130,000	50,000
Other Current Assets.	241,000	235,000
Investment in Sam Company.	308,000	
Other Long-Term Investments.	20,000	
Land.	140,000	80,000
Building and Equipment.	375,000	200,000
Accumulated Depreciation	(120,000)	(30,000)
Other Intangibles		20,000
Current Liabilities	(150,000)	(70,000)
Bonds Payable.		(100,000)
Other Long-Term Liabilities	(200,000)	(50,000)
Common Stock, Peanut Company	(200,000)	
Other Paid-In Capital, Peanut Company	(100,000)	
Common Stock, Sam Company.		(50,000)
Other Paid-In Capital, Sam Company		(50,000)
Retained Earnings, 12/31/X2	(444,000)	(235,000)
Totals	0	0

Required:

Complete the worksheet for consolidated financial statements for the year ended December 31, 19X2. Include any necessary determination and distribution of excess schedule and income distribution schedules.

<table>
<tr><td>*Case*</td></tr>
</table>

The Minority's Concern with Intercompany Transactions

Henderson Window Company was a privately held corporation until January 1, 19X4. On January 1, 19X4, Cool Glass Company purchased a 70% interest in Henderson at a price well in excess of book value. There were some minor differences between book and market values, but the bulk of the excess was attributed to goodwill. In its consolidated statements, Cool Glass is amortizing the goodwill over 10 years.

Harvey Henderson did not sell his shares to Cool Glass as a part of the January 1, 19X4 Cool Glass purchase. He wanted to remain a Henderson shareholder since he felt Henderson was a more profitable and stable company than was Cool Glass. Harvey remains an employee of Henderson Window, working in an accounting capacity.

Harvey is concerned about some accounting issues that he feels are detrimental to his ownership interest. Harvey told you that Henderson always bought most of its glass from Cool Glass. He never felt the prices charged for the glass were unreasonable. Since the purchase of Henderson by Cool Glass, he feels the price charged to Henderson by Cool Glass has risen dramatically and that it is out of step with what would be paid to other glass suppliers.

The second concern is the sale of a large Henderson warehouse to Cool Glass for less than what Harvey would consider to be the market value. Harvey agrees that the sale is reasonable since the new just-in-time order system has made the space unnecessary. He just feels the sale price is below market.

Harvey did make his concerns known to the president of Cool Glass. The president made several points. First, she said that the price charged for the glass was a little high, but Harvey should consider its high quality. She went on to say the transfer price washes out in the annual report, and it has no impact on reported net income of the corporation. She also stated that the warehouse sale was at a low price, but there was a reason. It was a good year, and a large gain wasn't needed. She would rather have lower depreciation in future years. Her last point was: "We paid a big price for Henderson, and we are stuck with big goodwill amortization expenses. We should get some benefits from it!"

Required:

Write a memo to Harvey Henderson suggesting how he might respond to the president's comments.

Worksheet 4-1

Intercompany Sales; No Intercompany Goods in Inventories
Company P and Subsidiary Company S
Worksheet for Consolidated Financial Statements
For Year Ended December 31, 19X1

	(Credit balance amounts are in parentheses.)	Trial Balance	
		Company P	Company S
1	**Accounts Receivable**	110,000	150,000
2	Inventory, Dec. 31, 19X1	70,000	40,000
3	Investment in Company S	196,000	
4			
5	Other Assets	314,000	155,000
6	**Accounts Payable**	(80,000)	(100,000)
7	Common Stock ($10 par), Co. P	(200,000)	
8	Retained Earnings, Jan. 1, 19X1, Co. P	(250,000)	
9	Common Stock ($10 par), Co. S		(100,000)
10	Retained Earnings, Jan. 1, 19X1, Co. S		(70,000)
11	**Sales**	(700,000)	(500,000)
12	**Cost of Goods Sold**	510,000	350,000
13	Expenses	90,000	75,000
14	Subsidiary Income	(60,000)	
15		0	0
16	Combined Net Income		
17	To Minority Interest (see distribution schedule)		
18	Balance to Controlling Interest (see distribution schedule)		
19	Total Minority Interest		
20	Retained Earnings, Controlling Interest, Dec. 31, 19X1		
21			

Eliminations and Adjustments:

(1) Eliminate the entry recording the parent's share of subsidiary net income.
(2) Eliminate against the investment in Company S account the pro rata portion of the subsidiary equity balances (80%) owned by the parent. To simplify the elimination, there is no discrepancy between the cost and book values of the investment in this example. Also, note that the worksheet process is expedited by always eliminating the intercompany investment first.
(3) Eliminate the intercompany sales to avoid double counting. Now only Company S's original purchase from third parties and Company P's final sale to third parties remain in the consolidated income statement.
(4) Eliminate the $25,000 intercompany trade balances resulting from the intercompany sale.

Worksheet 4-1 (see page 4-3)

Eliminations & Adjustments		Consolidated Income Statement	Minority Interest	Controlling Retained Earnings	Consolidated Balance Sheet	
Dr.	Cr.					
	(4) 25,000				235,000	1
					110,000	2
	(1) 60,000					3
	(2) 136,000					4
					469,000	5
(4) 25,000					(155,000)	6
					(200,000)	7
				(250,000)		8
(2) 80,000			(20,000)			9
(2) 56,000			(14,000)			10
(3) 100,000		(1,100,000)				11
	(3) 100,000	760,000				12
		165,000				13
(1) 60,000						14
321,000	321,000					15
		(175,000)				16
		15,000	(15,000)			17
		160,000		(160,000)		18
			(49,000)		(49,000)	19
				(410,000)	(410,000)	20
					0	21

Subsidiary Company S Income Distribution

Internally generated net income	$ 75,000
Adjusted income	$ 75,000
Minority share	20%
Minority interest	$ 15,000

Parent Company P Income Distribution

Internally generated net income	$ 100,000
80% × Company S adjusted income of	
$75,000	60,000
Controlling interest	$160,000

Worksheet 4-2

Intercompany Goods in Ending Inventory
Company P and Subsidiary Company S
Worksheet for Consolidated Financial Statements
For Year Ended December 31, 19X1

	(Credit balance amounts are in parentheses.)	Trial Balance	
		Company P	Company S
1	Accounts Receivable	110,000	150,000
2	**Inventory, Dec. 31, 19X1**	**70,000**	**40,000**
3	Investment in Company S	196,000	
4			
5	Other Assets	314,000	155,000
6	Accounts Payable	(80,000)	(100,000)
7	Common Stock ($10 par), Co. P	(200,000)	
8	Retained Earnings, Jan. 1, 19X1, Co. P	(250,000)	
9	Common Stock ($10 par), Co. S		(100,000)
10	Retained Earnings, Jan. 1, 19X1, Co. S		(70,000)
11	Sales	(700,000)	(500,000)
12	**Cost of Goods Sold**	**510,000**	**350,000**
13	Expenses	90,000	75,000
14	Subsidiary Income	(60,000)	
15		0	0
16	Combined Net Income		
17	To Minority Interest (see distribution schedule)		
18	Balance to Controlling Interest (see distribution schedule)		
19	Total Minority Interest		
20	Retained Earnings, Controlling Interest, Dec. 31, 19X1		
21			

Eliminations and Adjustments:

(1) Eliminate the entry recording the parent's share of subsidiary net income.
(2) Eliminate 80% of the subsidiary equity balances against the investment in Company S account. There is no excess of cost or book value in this example.
(3) Eliminate the intercompany sale.
(4) Eliminate the profit in the ending inventory.
(5) Eliminate the intercompany trade balances.

Worksheet 4-2 (see page 4-6)

Eliminations & Adjustments				Consolidated Income Statement	Minority Interest	Controlling Retained Earnings	Consolidated Balance Sheet	
Dr.		Cr.						
		(5)	25,000				235,000	1
		(4)	**8,000**				102,000	2
		(1)	60,000					3
		(2)	136,000					4
							469,000	5
(5)	25,000						(155,000)	6
							(200,000)	7
						(250,000)		8
(2)	80,000				(20,000)			9
(2)	56,000				(14,000)			10
(3)	100,000			(1,100,000)				11
(4)	**8,000**	(3)	100,000	768,000				12
				165,000				13
(1)	60,000							14
	329,000		329,000					15
				(167,000)				16
				13,400	(13,400)			17
				153,600		(153,600)		18
					(47,400)		(47,400)	19
						(403,600)	(403,600)	20
							0	21

Subsidiary Company S Income Distribution

Unrealized profit in ending inventory. . . . . **(4) $8,000**	Internally generated net income	$ 75,000
	Adjusted income	$ 67,000
	Minority share	20%
	Minority interest	$ 13,400

Parent Company P Income Distribution

	Internally generated net income	$ 100,000
	80% × Company S adjusted income of $67,000	53,600
	Controlling interest	$153,600

Worksheet 4-3

Intercompany Goods in Beginning and Ending Inventories
Company P and Subsidiary Company S
Worksheet for Consolidated Financial Statements
For Year Ended December 31, 19X2

	(Credit balance amounts are in parentheses.)	Trial Balance	
		Company P	Company S
1	Accounts Receivable	160,000	170,000
2	**Inventory, Dec. 31, 19X2**	**60,000**	**50,000**
3	Investment in Company S	244,000	
4			
5	Other Assets	354,000	165,000
6	Accounts Payable	(90,000)	(80,000)
7	Common Stock ($10 par), Co. P	(200,000)	
8	**Retained Earnings, Jan. 1, 19X2, Co. P**	**(410,000)**	
9	Common Stock ($10 par), Co. S		(100,000)
10	**Retained Earnings, Jan. 1, 19X2, Co. S**		**(145,000)**
11			
12	Sales	(800,000)	(600,000)
13	**Cost of Goods Sold**	**610,000**	**440,000**
14			
15	Expenses	120,000	100,000
16	Subsidiary Income	(48,000)	
17		0	0
18	Combined Net Income		
19	To Minority Interest (see distribution schedule)		
20	Balance to Controlling Interest (see distribution schedule)		
21	Total Minority Interest		
22	Retained Earnings, Controlling Interest, Dec. 31, 19X2		
23			

Eliminations and Adjustments:

(1) Eliminate the entry recording the parent's share of subsidiary net income.

(2) Eliminate 80% of the subsidiary equity balances against the investment in Company S account. There is no excess of cost or book value in this example.

(3) Eliminate the intercompany profit of $8,000 (20% × $40,000) in the beginning inventory by reducing both the cost of goods sold and the beginning retained earnings accounts. 20% of the decrease in retained earnings is shared by the minority interest, since, in this case, *the selling company was the subsidiary.* If the parent had been the seller, only the controlling interest in retained earnings would be decreased. It should be noted that the $8,000 profit is shifted from 19X1 to 19X2, since, as a result of

Worksheet 4-3 (see page 4-7)

Eliminations & Adjustments				Consolidated Income Statement	Minority Interest	Controlling Retained Earnings	Consolidated Balance Sheet	
Dr.		Cr.						
		(6)	60,000				270,000	1
		(5)	**6,000**				104,000	2
		(1)	48,000					3
		(2)	196,000					4
							519,000	5
(6)	60,000						(110,000)	6
							(200,000)	7
(3)	**6,400**					(403,600)		8
(2)	80,000				(20,000)			9
(2)	116,000							10
(3)	**1,600**				(27,400)			11
(4)	120,000			(1,280,000)				12
(5)	**6,000**	(3)	8,000					13
		(4)	120,000	928,000				14
				220,000				15
(1)	48,000							16
	438,000		438,000					17
				(132,000)				18
				12,400	(12,400)			19
				119,600		(119,600)		20
					(59,800)		(59,800)	21
						(523,200)	(523,200)	22
							0	23

the entry, the 19X2 consolidated cost of goods sold balance is reduced $8,000. This procedure emphasizes the concept that intercompany inventory profit is not eliminated but only deferred until inventory is sold to an outsider.

(4) Eliminate the intercompany sales to avoid double counting.

(5) Eliminate the intercompany profit of $6,000 (20% × $30,000) recorded by Company S for the intercompany goods contained in Company P's ending inventory, and increase the cost of goods sold balance by this same amount.

(6) Eliminate the intercompany trade balances.

(continued)

Subsidiary Company S Income Distribution

Unrealized profit in ending inventory, 20% × $30,000 . . . . . . (5) $6,000	Internally generated net income	$60,000
	Realized profit in beginning inventory, 20% × $40,000 . . . (3)	**8,000**
	Adjusted income	$62,000
	Minority share	20%
	Minority interest	$12,400

Parent Company P Income Distribution

Internally generated net income	$ 70,000
80% × Company S adjusted income of	
$62,000	49,600
Controlling interest	$119,600

Worksheet 4-4

Intercompany Goods in Beginning and Ending Inventories; Periodic Inventory
Company P and Subsidiary Company S
Worksheet for Consolidated Financial Statements
For Year Ended December 31, 19X2

	(Credit balance amounts are in parentheses.)	Trial Balance	
		Company P	Company S
1	Accounts Receivable	160,000	170,000
2	**Inventory, Jan. 1, 19X2**	**70,000**	**40,000**
3	Investment in Company S	244,000	
4			
5	Other Assets	354,000	165,000
6	Accounts Payable	(90,000)	(80,000)
7	Common Stock ($10 par), Co. P	(200,000)	
8	**Retained Earnings, Jan. 1, 19X2, Co. P**	**(410,000)**	
9	Common Stock ($10 par), Co. S		(100,000)
10	**Retained Earnings, Jan. 1, 19X2, Co. S**		**(145,000)**
11			
12	Sales	(800,000)	(600,000)
13	**Purchases**	**600,000**	**450,000**
14	**Inventory, Dec. 31, 19X2: Asset**	**60,000**	**50,000**
15	**Cost of Goods Sold**	**(60,000)**	**(50,000)**
16	Expenses	120,000	100,000
17	Subsidiary Income	(48,000)	
18		0	0
19	Combined Net Income		
20	To Minority Interest (see distribution schedule)		
21	Balance to Controlling Interest (see distribution schedule)		
22	Total Minority Interest		
23	Retained Earnings, Controlling Interest, Dec. 31, 19X2		
24			

Eliminations and Adjustments:

(1) Eliminate the entry recording the parent's share of subsidiary net income.

(2) Eliminate 80% of the subsidiary equity balances against the investment account. There is no excess of cost or book value in this example.

(3) Eliminate the intercompany profit of $8,000 (20% × $40,000) in the beginning inventory by reducing both the January 1 inventory and the beginning retained earnings balances. 20% of the decrease in retained earnings is shared by the minority interest since, in this case, *the selling company was the subsidiary*. If the parent had been the seller, only the controlling interest in retained earnings would be decreased. It should be noted that the $8,000 profit is shifted from 19X1 to 19X2 since, as a result of

Worksheet 4-4 (see page 4-8)

Eliminations & Adjustments		Consolidated Income Statement	Minority Interest	Controlling Retained Earnings	Consolidated Balance Sheet	
Dr.	Cr.					
	(6) 60,000				270,000	1
	(3) 8,000	102,000				2
	(1) 48,000					3
	(2) 196,000					4
					519,000	5
(6) 60,000					(110,000)	6
					(200,000)	7
(3) 6,400				(403,600)		8
(2) 80,000			(20,000)			9
(2) 116,000						10
(3) 1,600			(27,400)			11
(4) 120,000		(1,280,000)				12
	(4) 120,000	930,000				13
	(5) 6,000				104,000	14
(5) 6,000		(104,000)				15
		220,000				16
(1) 48,000						17
438,000	438,000					18
		(132,000)				19
		12,400	(12,400)			20
		119,600		(119,600)		21
			(59,800)		(59,800)	22
				(523,200)	(523,200)	23
					0	24

the entry, the 19X2 consolidated cost of goods sold would be reduced by $8,000. This procedure emphasizes the concept that intercompany inventory profit is not eliminated but only deferred until inventory is sold to an outsider.

(4) Eliminate the intercompany sales to avoid double counting of purchases and sales.

(5) Enter the combined ending inventories of Company P and Company S, $60,000 and $50,000, respectively, less the intercompany profit of $6,000 (20% × $30,000) recorded by Company S for the intercompany goods contained in Company P's ending inventory.

(6) Eliminate the intercompany trade balances.

(continued)

Subsidiary Company S Income Distribution

Unrealized profit in ending inventory, 20% × $30,000 . . . . . . (5) $6,000	Internally generated net income	$60,000[a]
	Realized profit in beginning inventory, 20% × $40,000 . . . (3)	**8,000**
	Adjusted income	$62,000
	Minority share	20%
	Minority interest	$12,400

a [$600,000 – ($40,000 + $450,000 – $50,000) – $100,000 = $60,000]

Parent Company P Income Distribution

Internally generated net income	$ 70,000[b]
80% × Company S adjusted income of $62,000	49,600
Controlling interest	$119,600

b [$800,000 – ($70,000 + $600,000 – $60,000) – $120,000 = $70,000]

Worksheet 4-5

Intercompany Sale of Depreciable Asset
Company P and Subsidiary Company S
Worksheet for Consolidated Financial Statements
For Year Ended December 31, 19X1

	(Credit balance amounts are in parentheses.)	Trial Balance	
		Company P	Company S
1	Current Assets	15,000	20,000
2	**Machinery**	50,000	**(a) 230,000**
3	**Accumulated Depreciation—Machinery**	(25,000)	**(b) (100,000)**
4	Investment in Company S	120,000	
5			
6	Common Stock ($10 par), Co. P	(100,000)	
7	Retained Earnings, Jan. 1, 19X1, Co. P	(10,000)	
8	Common Stock ($10 par), Co. S		(50,000)
9	Retained Earnings, Jan. 1, 19X1, Co. S		(75,000)
10	Sales	(200,000)	(100,000)
11	Cost of Goods Sold	150,000	59,000
12	**Depreciation Expense**	30,000	**(b) 16,000**
13	**Gain on Sale of Machine**	**(10,000)**	
14	Subsidiary Income	(20,000)	
15		0	0
16	Combined Net Income		
17	To Minority Interest (see distribution schedule)		
18	Balance to Controlling Interest (see distribution schedule)		
19	Total Minority Interest		
20	Retained Earnings, Controlling Interest, Dec. 31, 19X1		
21			

Notes to Trial Balance:

(a) Includes machine purchased for $30,000 *from Company P* on January 1, 19X1.
(b) Includes $6,000 depreciation on machine purchased from Company P on January 1, 19X1.

Eliminations and Adjustments:

(1) Eliminate the entry recording the parent's share of subsidiary net income for the current year.
(2) Eliminate 80% of the subsidiary equity balances against the investment account. There is no excess to be distributed.
(3) Eliminate the $10,000 gain on the intercompany sale of the machine. In addition, adjust the machine to $32,000 and restore its related accumulated depreciation to $12,000 in order to reflect the book value of the asset to the consolidated company on January 1, 19X1.
(4) Reduce the depreciation expense and accumulated depreciation accounts to reflect the depreciation ($4,000 per year) based on the consolidated book value of the machine, rather than the depreciation ($6,000 per year) based on the sales price.

Worksheet 4-5 (see page 4-11)

Eliminations & Adjustments				Consolidated Income Statement	Minority Interest	Controlling Retained Earnings	Consolidated Balance Sheet	
Dr.		Cr.						
							35,000	1
		(3)	10,000				270,000	2
(4)	2,000						(123,000)	3
		(1)	20,000					4
		(2)	100,000					5
							(100,000)	6
						(10,000)		7
(2)	40,000				(10,000)			8
(2)	60,000				(15,000)			9
				(300,000)				10
				209,000				11
		(4)	2,000	44,000				12
(3)	10,000							13
(1)	20,000							14
	132,000		132,000					15
				(47,000)				16
				5,000	(5,000)			17
				42,000		(42,000)		18
					(30,000)		(30,000)	19
						(52,000)	(52,000)	20
							0	21

Subsidiary Company S Income Distribution

Internally generated net income	$ 25,000
Adjusted income	$ 25,000
Minority share	20%
Minority interest	$ 5,000

Parent Company P Income Distribution

Unrealized gain on sale of machine . . . . (3) **$10,000**	Internally generated net income (including sale of machine) . . . . $ 30,000
	80% × Company S adjusted income of $25,000 20,000
	Gain realized through use of machine sold to subsidiary . . . (4) **2,000**
	Controlling interest $42,000

Worksheet 4-6

Intercompany Sale of Depreciable Asset
Company P and Subsidiary Company S
Worksheet for Consolidated Financial Statements
For Year Ended December 31, 19X2

	(Credit balance amounts are in parentheses.)	Trial Balance	
		Company P	Company S
1	Current Assets	85,000	60,000
2	**Machinery**	50,000	**(a) 230,000**
3	**Accumulated Depreciation—Machinery**	(45,000)	**(b) (116,000)**
4			
5	Investment in Company S	139,200	
6			
7	Common Stock ($10 par), Co. P	(100,000)	
8	**Retained Earnings, Jan. 1, 19X2, Co. P**	**(60,000)**	
9	Common Stock ($10 par), Co. S		(50,000)
10	Retained Earnings, Jan. 1, 19X2, Co. S		(100,000)
11	Sales	(250,000)	(120,000)
12	**Cost of Goods Sold**	180,000	80,000
13	**Depreciation Expense**	20,000	**(c) 16,000**
14	Subsidiary Income	(19,200)	
15		0	0
16	Combined Net Income		
17	To Minority Interest (see distribution schedule)		
18	Balance to Controlling Interest (see distribution schedule)		
19	Total Minority Interest		
20	Retained Earnings, Controlling Interest, Dec. 31, 19X2		
21			

Notes to Trial Balance:

(a) Includes machine purchased for $30,000 *from Company P* on January 1, 19X1.
(b) Includes $12,000 accumulated depreciation ($6,000 per year) on machine purchased from Company P on January 1, 19X1.
(c) Includes $6,000 depreciation on machine purchased from Company P on January 1, 19X1.

Eliminations and Adjustments:

(1) Eliminate the entry recording the parent's share of subsidiary net income for the current year.
(2) Eliminate 80% of the subsidiary equity balances against the investment account. There is no excess to be distributed.
(3) Eliminate the gain on the intercompany sale as it is reflected in beginning retained earnings on the parent's trial balance. This entry adjusts the machine account to $32,000 and restates accumulated

Worksheet 4-6 (see page 4-12)

Eliminations & Adjustments		Consolidated Income Statement	Minority Interest	Controlling Retained Earnings	Consolidated Balance Sheet	
Dr.	Cr.					
					145,000	1
	(3) 10,000				270,000	2
(3) 2,000					(157,000)	3
(4) 2,000						4
	(1) 19,200					5
	(2) 120,000					6
					(100,000)	7
(3) 8,000				(52,000)		8
(2) 40,000			(10,000)			9
(2) 80,000			(20,000)			10
		(370,000)				11
		260,000				12
	(4) 2,000	34,000				13
(1) 19,200						14
151,200	151,200					15
		(76,000)				16
		4,800	(4,800)			17
		71,200		(71,200)		18
			(34,800)		(34,800)	19
				(123,200)	(123,200)	20
					0	21

depreciation as of the *beginning* of the year. Thus, the adjustment to accumulated depreciation includes a $12,000 increase in order to acknowledge the $12,000 balance on the sale date and a $2,000 reduction for the profit element of the 19X1 depreciation. Since the sale was made by the *parent,* Company P, the entire unrealized gain at the beginning of the year (now $8,000) is removed from the controlling retained earnings beginning balance. If the sale had been made by the subsidiary, the adjustment of beginning retained earnings would be split 80% to the controlling interest and 20% to the minority interest.

(4) Reduce the depreciation expense and accumulated depreciation accounts to reflect the depreciation based on the consolidated book value of the asset on the date of sale. This entry will bring the accumulated depreciation account to its correct consolidated year-end balance.

(continued)

Subsidiary Company S Income Distribution

Internally generated net income	$24,000
Adjusted income	$24,000
Minority share	20%
Minority interest	$ 4,800

Parent Company P Income Distribution

Internally generated net income	$50,000
80% of Company S adjusted income of $24,000	19,200
Gain realized through use of machine sold to subsidiary . . . (4)	**2,000**
Controlling interest	$71,200

Worksheet 4-7

Intercompany Sale of a Depreciable Asset; Subsequent Sale of Asset to an Outside Party
Company P and Subsidiary Company S
Worksheet for Consolidated Financial Statements
For Year Ended December 31, 19X2

	(credit balance amounts are in parentheses)	Trial Balance	
		Company P	Company S
1	Current Assets	85,000	74,000
2	Machinery	50,000	200,000
3	Accumulated Depreciation—Machinery	(45,000)	(104,000)
4	Investment in Company S	136,000	
5			
6	Common Stock ($10 par), Co. P	(100,000)	
7	**Retained Earnings, Jan. 1, 19X2, Co. P**	**(60,000)**	
8	Common Stock ($10 par), Co. S		(50,000)
9	Retained Earnings, Jan. 1, 19X2, Co. S		(100,000)
10	Sales	(250,000)	(120,000)
11	Cost of Goods Sold	180,000	80,000
12	**Depreciation Expense**	20,000	**16,000**
13	**Loss on Sale of Machine**		**4,000**
14	Subsidiary Income	(16,000)	
15	**Gain on Sale of Machine**		
16		0	0
17	Combined Net Income		
18	To Minority Interest (see distribution schedule)		
19	Balance to Controlling Interest (see distribution schedule)		
20	Total Minority Interest		
21	Retained Earnings, Controlling Interest, Dec. 31, 19X2		
22			

Eliminations and Adjustments:

(1) Eliminate the entry recording the parent's share of subsidiary net income for the current year.
(2) Eliminate 80% of the subsidiary equity balances against the investment account. There is no excess to be distribut
(3) Eliminate the gain on the intercompany sale as it is reflected in the parent's beginning retained earnings account,
   adjust the current year's depreciation expense, and revise the recording of the sale of the equipment to an outside
   to reflect the net book value of the asset to the consolidated company.

Subsidiary Company S Income Distribution

Internally generated net income	$20,000
Adjusted income	$20,000
Minority share	20%
Minority interest	$ 4,000

Worksheet 4-7 (see page 4-13)

Eliminations & Adjustments		Consolidated Income Statement	Minority Interest	Controlling Retained Earnings	Consolidated Balance Sheet	
Dr.	**Cr.**					
					159,000	1
					250,000	2
					(149,000)	3
	(1) 16,000					4
	(2) 120,000					5
					(100,000)	6
(3) 8,000				(52,000)		7
(2) 40,000			(10,000)			8
(2) 80,000			(20,000)			9
		(370,000)				10
		260,000				11
	(3) 2,000	34,000				12
	(3) 4,000					13
(1) 16,000						14
	(3) 2,000	(2,000)				15
144,000	144,000					16
		(78,000)				17
		4,000	(4,000)			18
		74,000		(74,000)		19
			(34,000)		(34,000)	20
				(126,000)	(126,000)	21
					0	22

Parent Company P Income Distribution

	Internally generated net income	$50,000
	80% × Company S adjusted income of $20,000	16,000
	Gain realized on sale of machine . . . . (3)	**8,000**[a]
	Controlling interest	$74,000

[a] $10,000 original gain − $2,000 realized in 19X1

Worksheet 4-8

Intercompany Notes
Company P and Subsidiary Company S
Worksheet for Consolidated Financial Statements
For Year Ended December 31, 19X1

	(Credit balance amounts are in parentheses.)	Trial Balance	
		Company P	Company S
1	Cash	35,000	20,400
2	**Note Receivable from Company S**	**10,000**	
3	**Interest Receivable**	**400**	
4	Property, Plant, and Equipment (net)	140,000	150,000
5	Investment in Company S	128,000	
6			
7	**Note Payable to Company P**		**(10,000)**
8	**Interest Payable**		**(400)**
9	Common Stock, Co. P	(100,000)	
10	Retained Earnings, Jan. 1, 19X1, Co. P	(200,000)	
11	Common Stock, Co. S		(50,000)
12	Retained Earnings, Jan. 1, 19X1, Co. S		(100,000)
13	Sales	(120,000)	(50,000)
14	**Interest Income**	**(400)**	
15	Subsidiary Income	(8,000)	
16	Cost of Goods Sold	75,000	20,000
17	Other Expenses	40,000	19,600
18	**Interest Expense**		**400**
19		0	0
20	Combined Net Income		
21	To Minority Interest (see distribution schedule)		
22	Balance to Controlling Interest (see distribution schedule)		
23	Total Minority Interest		
24	Retained Earnings, Controlling Interest, Dec. 31, 19X5		
25			

Eliminations and Adjustments:

(1) Eliminate the parent's share (80%) of subsidiary net income.
(2) Eliminate the controlling portion (80%) of the Company S January 1, 19X1 stockholders' equity against the investment in Company S account. No excess results.

Subsidiary Company S Income Distribution

	Internally generated net income	$10,000
	Adjusted income	$10,000
	Minority share	20%
	Minority interest	$ 2,000

Worksheet 4-8 (see page 4-16)

| Eliminations & Adjustments | | Consolidated Income Statement | Minority Interest | Controlling Retained Earnings | Consolidated Balance Sheet | |
Dr.	Cr.					
					55,400	1
	(3) 10,000					2
	(3) 400					3
					290,000	4
	(1) 8,000					5
	(2) 120,000					6
(3) 10,000						7
(3) 400						8
					(100,000)	9
				(200,000)		10
(2) 40,000			(10,000)			11
(2) 80,000			(20,000)			12
		(170,000)				13
(4) 400						14
(1) 8,000						15
		95,000				16
		59,600				17
	(4) 400					18
138,800	138,800					19
		(15,400)				20
		2,000	(2,000)			21
		13,400		(13,400)		22
			(32,000)		(32,000)	23
				(213,400)	(213,400)	24
					0	25

(3) Eliminate the intercompany note and accrued interest applicable to the note. This entry removes the *internal note* from the consolidated balance sheet.

(4) Eliminate the intercompany interest expense and revenue. Since an equal amount of expense and revenue is eliminated, there is no change in the combined net income as a result of this entry.

Parent Company P Income Distribution

Internally generated net income	$5,400
80% × Company S adjusted income of $10,000	8,000
Controlling interest	$13,400

Worksheet 4-9

Vertical Worksheet Alternative
Company P and Subsidiary Company S
Worksheet for Consolidated Financial Statements
For Year Ended December 31, 19X2

	(Credit balance amounts are in parentheses.)	Financial Statements	
		Company P	Company S
1	**Income Statement**		
2	Sales	(600,000)	(530,000)
3	Cost of goods sold	400,000	280,000
4			
5	Depreciation expense	40,000	50,000
6	Other expenses	60,000	70,000
7	Subsidiary income	(104,000)	
8	**Net income**	(204,000)	(130,000)
9	Minority interest (see distribution schedule)		
10	Controlling interest (see distribution schedule)		
11			
12	**Retained Earnings Statement**		
13	Retained earnings, Jan. 1, 19X2, Co. P	(600,000)	
14			
15			
16	Retained earnings, Jan. 1, 19X2, Co. S		(400,000)
17			
18	**Net income (carrydown)**	(204,000)	(130,000)
19	Dividends declared		20,000
20	**Retained earnings, Dec. 31, 19X2**	(804,000)	(510,000)
21	Minority interest, retained earnings, Dec. 31, 19X2		
22	Controlling interest, retained earnings, Dec. 31, 19X2		
23			
24	**Balance Sheet**		
25	Inventory	300,000	250,000
26	Accounts receivable	120,000	180,000
27	Plant assets	236,000	400,000
28	Accumulated depreciation	(100,000)	(60,000)
29			
30	Investment in Company S	628,000	
31			
32			
33	Goodwill		
34	Current liabilities	(80,000)	(60,000)
35	Common stock, ($5 par), Co. S		(200,000)
36	Common stock, ($10 par), Co. P	(300,000)	
37	**Retained earnings (carrydown)**	(804,000)	(510,000)
38	Retained earnings, contolling interest, Dec. 31, 19X2		
39	Retained earnings, minority interest, Dec. 31, 19X2		
40	Total minority interest		
41	Total	0	0

Worksheet 4-9 (see page 4-20)

Eliminations & Adjustments				Minority Interest	Consolidated	
Dr.		Cr.				
						1
(6)	150,000				(980,000)	2
(7)	10,000	(6)	150,000			3
		(5)	8,000		532,000	4
		(10)	1,000		89,000	5
(4)	1,500				131,500	6
(1)	104,000					7
					(227,500)	8
				(25,600)		9
					(201,900)	10
						11
						12
(4)	1,500					13
(5)	6,400					14
(9)	4,500				(587,600)	15
(2)	320,000					16
(5)	1,600			(78,400)		17
				(25,600)	(201,900)	18
		(1)	16,000	4,000		19
						20
				(100,000)		21
					(789,500)	22
						23
						24
		(7)	10,000		540,000	25
		(8)	20,000		280,000	26
		(9)	5,000		631,000	27
(9)	500					28
(10)	1,000				(158,500)	29
		(1)	88,000			30
		(2)	480,000			31
		(3)	60,000			32
(3)	60,000	(4)	3,000		57,000	33
(8)	20,000				(120,000)	34
(2)	160,000			(40,000)		35
					(300,000)	36
						37
					(789,500)	38
				(100,000)		39
				(140,000)	(140,000)	40
	841,000		841,000		0	41

(continued)

Eliminations and Adjustments:

(1) Eliminate the current-year entries recording the parent's share (80%) of subsidiary net income and the dividends declared.

(2) Eliminate the pro rata portion of the subsidiary equity balances owned by the parent (80%) against the balance of the investment account.

(3) Distribute the excess to the goodwill account according to the determination and distribution of excess schedule.

(4) Amortize the goodwill at $1,500 per year for the past year and current year.

(5) Eliminate the intercompany profit in the beginning inventory, 20% (.25 ÷ 1.25) multiplied by $40,000. Since it was a subsidiary sale, the profit is shared 20% by the minority interest.

(6) Eliminate the intercompany sales made during 19X2.

(7) Eliminate the intercompany profit (20%) applicable to the $50,000 of intercompany goods in the ending inventory.

(8) Eliminate the intercompany trade balances.

(9) Eliminate the intercompany gain remaining on January 1, 19X2, applicable to the sale of the machine by Company P ($5,000 original gain less one-half-year's gain of $500).

(10) Reduce the depreciation expense and accumulated depreciation accounts ($1,000 for the current year) in order to reflect depreciation based on the original cost.

Subsidiary Company S Income Distribution

Unrealized profit in ending inventory (20% × $50,000). . . . . (7)	$10,000	Internally generated net income		$130,000
		Realized profit in beginning inventory (20% × $40,000). . . . . (5)		8,000
		Adjusted income		$128,000
		Minority share		20%
		Minority interest		**$25,600**

Parent Company P Income Distribution

Goodwill amortization . . . . (4)	$ 1,500	Internally generated net income		$ 100,000
		Gain realized on sale of machine . . . (10)		1,000
		80% × Company S adjusted income of $128,000.		102,400
		Controlling interest		**$201,900**

Intercompany Transactions: Bonds and Leases

This chapter focuses on intercompany transactions that create a long-term debtor–creditor relationship between the members of a consolidated group. The usual impetus for these transactions is the parent's ability to borrow larger amounts of capital at more favorable terms than would be available to the subsidiary. In addition, the parent company may desire to manage all capital needs of the consolidated company for better control of all capital sources. Intercompany leasing with the parent as the lessor also may be motivated by centralized asset management and credit control.

Intercompany bond holdings will be analyzed first. Here, one member of the consolidated group, usually the subsidiary, has issued bonds which appear on its balance sheet as long-term liabilities. Another member may purchase the bonds and list them on its balance sheet as an investment. However, when consolidated statements are prepared, the intercompany purchase, in effect, should be viewed as a retirement of the bonds. Consideration of intercompany leasing of assets will follow the bond coverage. In this case, one member of the consolidated group purchases the asset and leases it to another member. While the leasing transaction is recorded as such on the separate books of the affiliates, the lease has no substance from a consolidated viewpoint. Only a lease that involves a nonaffiliated company may appear in the consolidated statements.

Intercompany Investment in Bonds

To secure long-term funds, one member of a consolidated group may sell its bonds directly to another member of the group. Clearly, such a transaction results in intercompany debt which must be eliminated from the consolidated statements. On the worksheet, the investment in bonds recorded by one company must be eliminated against the bonds payable of the other. In addition, the applicable interest expense recorded by one affiliate must be eliminated against the applicable interest revenue recorded by the other affiliate. Interest accruals recorded on the books of the separate companies must be eliminated as well.

There are situations where one affiliate (usually the subsidiary) has outstanding bonds that have been purchased by parties that are not members of the affiliated group, and a decision is made by another affiliate (usually the parent) to obtain these bonds. The simplest way to accomplish the removal of subsidiary bonds from outsiders is for the parent to advance funds to the subsidiary so that the subsidiary may retire the bonds. From an accounting standpoint, this transaction is easy to record. The former debt is retired and a new, long-term intercompany debt originates. The only procedures required on future consolidated worksheets involve the elimination of the resulting intercompany debt.

A more complicated method is to have the parent purchase the subsidiary bonds from the outside parties and to hold them as an investment. This method creates an intercompany investment in bonds, where each affiliate continues to accrue and record interest on the bonds. While the intercompany bonds are treated as a liability on one set of books and as an investment on the other set, from a consolidated viewpoint the bonds have been retired and the debt to outside parties has been liquidated. The purchase of intercompany bonds has the following ramifications when consolidating:

1. Consolidated statements prepared for the period in which the bonds are purchased must portray the intercompany purchase as a retirement of the bonds. It is possible, but unlikely, that the bonds will be purchased at book value. There usually will be a gain or loss on retirement; this gain or loss is deemed to be **extraordinary** and is recognized on the consolidated income statement.
2. For all periods during which the intercompany investment exists, the intercompany bonds, interest accruals, and interest expense/revenue must be eliminated since the bonds no longer exist from a consolidated viewpoint.

The complexity of the elimination procedures depends on whether the bonds originally were issued at face value or at a premium or discount. Additionally, one must exercise extra care in the application of elimination procedures when only a portion of the outstanding bonds is purchased intercompany.

Bonds Originally Issued at Face Value

When bonds are sold at face value by a subsidiary to outside parties, contract (nominal) interest agrees with the effective, or market, interest, and no amortizations of issuance premiums or discounts need to be recorded. However, subsequent to the issuance, the market rate of interest most likely will deviate from the contract rate. Thus, while there is no original issuance premium or discount, there will be what could be termed an *investment premium* or *discount* resulting from the intercompany purchase of the bonds.

To illustrate the procedures required for intercompany bonds originally issued at face value, assume a subsidiary, Company S, issued 5-year, 8% bonds at face value of $100,000 to outside parties on January 1, 19X1. Interest is paid on January 1 for the preceding year. On January 2, 19X3, the parent, Company P, purchased the bonds from the outside parties for $103,600.

Company S will continue to list the $100,000 bonded debt and to record interest expense of $8,000 during 19X3, 19X4, and 19X5. However, Company P will record a bond investment of $103,600 and will amortize $1,200 per year by reducing the investment account and adjusting interest revenue. Though the interest method of amortization is preferable, the straight-line method is permitted if results are not materially different. This initial example and most others in this chapter use the straight-line method in order to simplify analysis. A summary example is used to demonstrate the interest method of amortization.

Although the investment and liability accounts continue to exist on the separate books of the affiliated companies, retirement has occurred from a consolidated viewpoint. Debt with a book value of $100,000 was retired by a payment of $103,600, and there is a $3,600 extraordinary loss on retirement. If a consolidated worksheet is prepared on the day the bonds are purchased, Bonds Payable would be eliminated against Investment in Company S Bonds, and an *extraordinary loss on retirement* would be reported on the consolidated income statement. The following abbreviated worksheet displays the procedures used to retire the bonds as part of the elimination process:

	Partial Trial Balance		Eliminations & Adjustments	
	Co. P	Co. S	Dr.	Cr.
Investment in Company S Bonds	103,600			**103,600**
Bonds Payable		(100,000)	**100,000**	
Extraordinary Loss on Bond Retirement			**3,600**	

This partial worksheet, prepared on January 2, 19X3, is only hypothetical since, in reality, there will be no consolidated worksheet prepared until December 31, 19X3, the end of the period. During 19X3, Companies P and S will record the transactions for interest as follows:

Company P			Company S		
Interest Receivable	8,000		Interest Expense	8,000	
Investment in Company S Bonds.		1,200	Interest Payable		8,000
Interest Income.		6,800	To record interest expense.		
To record interest revenue net of $1,200 per year premium amortization.					

 These entries will be reflected in the trial balances of the December 31, 19X3 consolidated worksheet, shown in Worksheet 5-1 on pages 5-40 to 5-43. Note that Investment in Company S Bonds reflects the premium amortization since the balance is $102,400 ($103,600 original cost - $1,200 amortization). In this worksheet, it is assumed that Investment in Company S Stock reflects a 90% interest purchased at a price equal to the book value of the underlying equity and the simple equity method is used by Company P to record the investment in stock.

Entries (1) and (2) eliminate the intercompany stock investment. Entry (3) eliminates the intercompany bonds at their year-end balances and the intercompany interest expense and revenue recorded during the year. In entry form, elimination entry (3) is as follows:

Bonds Payable, 8% (on Company S books)	$100,000	
Interest Income (recorded by Company P)	6,800	
Extraordinary Loss on Retirement (created in the consolidation process)	3,600	
Investment in Company S Bonds (on Company P books) . . .		102,400
Interest Expense (on Company S books)		8,000

The amount of the extraordinary gain or loss is the sum of the difference between the remaining book value of the investment on bonds compared to the debt and the difference between interest expense and debt. For this example

Investment in Bonds Balance, December 31, 19X3	$102,400	
Bonds Payable, December 31, 19X3	100,000	$2,400
Interest Expense, 19X3	8,000	
Interest Revenue, 19X3	6,800	1,200
Extraordinary Loss, January 2, 19X3		$3,600

Entry (4) of Worksheet 5-1 eliminated the intercompany interest accruals. In entry form, the elimination is

Interest Payable (recorded by Company S)   8,000
  Interest Receivable (recorded by Company P)   8,000

As a result of the elimination entries, the consolidated income statement will include the extraordinary retirement loss but will exclude intercompany interest payments and accruals. The consolidated balance sheet will not list the intercompany bonds payable or investment in bonds accounts.

The only remaining problem is the distribution of combined net income to the controlling and minority interests. The income distribution schedule shows Company S absorbing all of the retirement loss. It is most common to view the purchasing affiliate as a mere agent of the issuing affiliate. Therefore, it is the issuer, not the purchaser, that must bear the entire gain or loss on retirement. Even though the debt is retired from a consolidated viewpoint, it still exists internally. Company P has a right to collect the interest as part of its share of Company S's operations. Based on the value of the debt on January 2, 19X3, the interest expense/revenue is $6,800. The interest cost of $8,000 recorded by Company S must be corrected to reflect the internal interest expense of $6,800. The income distribution schedule increases the income of Company S to reflect the adjustment ($1,200) to interest expense. It should be noted that the retirement loss borne by Company S will entirely offset the adjustments to interest expense by the time the bonds mature. If the parent, Company P, had issued the bonds to outside parties and if the subsidiary, Company S, later had purchased them, the only change would be that the income distribution schedule of Company P would absorb the loss on retirement and the interest adjustment.

The worksheet procedures that would be needed at the end of 19X4 are shown in Worksheet 5-2 on pages 5-44 to 5-47. The interest revenue and expense have been recorded on the books of the separate companies. The investment in Company S bonds account on the parent's books reflects its book value at the end of 19X4. Entry (3) eliminates the intercompany bonds at their year-end balances and the intercompany interest expense and revenue. Recall that the original retirement loss was $3,600 when the bonds had 3 years to maturity. By the start of the second period, 19X2, $1,200 of that loss was already amortized on the separate books of the affiliates. The loss remaining is $2,400 (it is verified in the explanation to entry (3) in Worksheet 5-2). This remaining loss is debited to retained earnings since the retirement occurred in a prior period. The adjustment is allocated to minority and controlling beginning retained earnings since the bonds were issued by the subsidiary. Entry (4) eliminates intercompany interest accruals.

The 19X4 consolidated income statement will not include intercompany interest. The income distribution schedules for Worksheet 5-2 reflect the fact that the debt still existed internally during the period. However, the interest expense recorded by Company S is reduced to reflect the interest cost based on the January 2, 19X3 purchase price.

If Company S was the purchaser and Company P the issuer of the bonds, Worksheet 5-2 would differ as follows:

1. The January 1, 19X4 retained earnings adjustment would be absorbed completely by the controlling retained earnings, since the parent company would be the issuer absorbing the loss.
2. The income distribution schedule of the parent would contain the interest adjustment.

Bonds Not Originally Issued at Face Value

The principles of eliminating intercompany investments in bonds are not altered by the existence of a premium or discount stemming from original issuance. The numerical calculations just become more complex. To illustrate, assume Company S issued $100,000 of 5-year, 8% bonds on January 1, 19X1. The market interest rate approximated 9% and, as a result, the bonds sold at a discount of $3,890. Interest is paid each December 31. On each interest payment date, the discount is amortized $778 ($3,890 ÷ 5 years) by decreasing the discount and by increasing interest expense. On December 31, 19X3, the balance of the discount is $1,556 [$3,890 – (3 × $778 annual amortization)].

The parent, Company P, purchased the bonds for $103,600 on December 31, 19X3, after interest had been paid. The parent will amortize $1,800 of the investment each subsequent December 31, reducing the parent's interest income to $6,200 ($8,000 cash – $1,800 amortization) for 19X4 and 19X5.

The following abbreviated December 31, 19X3 (date of purchase) worksheet lists the investment in Company S bonds account, the bonds payable account, and the remaining issuance discount. Eliminating the $103,600 price paid for the bonds by Company P against the book value of $98,444 ($100,000 – $1,556) creates an extraordinary loss on retirement of $5,156 which is carried to combined net income. Worksheet procedures may be aided by linking the bonds payable and the related discount or premium on the worksheet. This is done on our worksheets by circling the amounts in the trial balance and in the eliminations.

	Partial Trial Balance		Eliminations & Adjustments	
	Co. P	Co. S	Dr.	Cr.
Investment in Company S Bonds	103,600			103,600
Bonds Payable, 8%		(100,000)	100,000	
Discount on Bonds Payable		1,556		1,556
Extraordinary Loss on Bond Retirement			5,156	
Interest Expense		8,778*		

*$8,000 cash + $778 straight-line amortization.

Interest expense on the books of Company S is extended to the consolidated income statement, since this interest was incurred as a result of transactions with outside parties. There would be no interest adjustment for 19X3, since the bonds were not purchased by the parent until December 31, 19X3. The income distribution schedules accompanying the worksheet would assess the retirement loss against the issuer, Company S.

The implications of these intercompany bonds on the 19X4 consolidated worksheet are reflected in Worksheet 5-3 on pages 5-48 to 5-51. Assume Company P acquired a 90% interest in the common stock of Company S at a price equal to the book value of the underlying equity. The simple equity method is used by the parent to record the investment in the stock of Company S. The trial balances include the following items:

1. The investment in Company S bonds at its amortized December 31, 19X4 balance of $101,800 ($103,600 - $1,800 amortization),
2. The interest revenue (adjusted for amortization) of $6,200 on the books of Company P,
3. The discount on bonds account at its amortized December 31, 19X4 balance of $778, and
4. The interest expense (adjusted for discount amortization) of $8,778 ($8,000 cash + $778 amortization) on the books of Company S.

Entry (3) eliminates the investment in bonds against the bonds payable and the applicable remaining discount. Entry (3) also eliminates interest expense and revenue. Be sure to understand the calculation of the adjustment to beginning retained earnings which is explained in the entry (3) information. The loss at the start of the year is the sum of the loss remaining at year-end and that amortized on the books of the separate affiliates during the year.

Again, the consolidated income statement does not include intercompany interest. However, the Company S income distribution schedule does reflect the adjustment of Company S's interest expense. The original $8,778 interest expense has been replaced by a $6,200 expense, based on the purchase price paid by Company P. The smaller interest expense compensates the subsidiary for the retirement loss absorbed in a previous period.

Purchase of Only a Portion of the Bonds

The preceding examples assume that the parent company purchases all of the outstanding bonds of the subsidiary. In such cases, all of the bonds are retired on the worksheet. There may be cases, however, where the parent purchases only a portion of the subsidiary's outstanding bonds. Suppose, for example, that the parent purchased 80% of the subsidiary's outstanding bonds. Only the 80% interest in the bonds would be eliminated on the consolidated worksheet, and only the interest expense and revenue applicable to 80% of the bonds would be eliminated on the worksheet. **The 20% interest in the subsidiary bonds owned by persons outside the control group remains as a valid debt of the consolidated company and should not be eliminated.** It is a common error for students to eliminate the 80% interest in intercompany bonds owned by a parent against 100% of the bonds issued by the subsidiary. Such a mistake improperly eliminates valid debt and greatly miscalculates the extraordinary gain or loss on retirement. It also should be noted that the interest paid to persons outside the control group should remain a part of the consolidated statements. Only the interest paid to the affiliated company is to be eliminated.

Interest Method of Amortization

The procedures used to eliminate intercompany bonds are not altered by the interest method of amortization; only the dollar values change. To illustrate the calculations, assume that Company S issued $100,000 of 5-year, 8% bonds on January 1, 19X1. The market interest rate on that date was 9%, so that the bonds sold at a discount of $3,890. Interest on the bonds is paid each December 31. The discount amortization for the term of the bonds follows:

Year	Debt Balance, January 1	Effective Interest	Nominal Interest	Discount Amortization
1	$96,110	$8,650 (.09 × $96,110)	$8,000	$ 650
2	96,760 ($96,110 + $650)	8,708 (.09 × $96,760)	8,000	608
3	97,468 ($96,760 + $708)	8,772 (.09 × $97,468)	8,000	772
4	98,240 ($97,468 + $772)	8,842 (.09 × $98,240)	8,000	842
5	98,082 ($98,240 + $842)	8,918* (.09 × $99,082)	8,000	918
*Includes $1 rounding error.				$3,890

On December 31, 19X3, after interest had been paid, the bonds were purchased by parent Company P at a price to yield 6%. Based on present value computations, $103,667 was paid for the bonds. The premium on the bonds would be amortized by Company P as follows:

Year	Investment Balance, January 1	Effective Interest	Nominal Interest	Premium Amortization
4	$103,667	$6,220 (.06 × $103,667)	$8,000	$1,780
5	101,887 ($103,667 − $1,780)	6,113 (.06 × $101,887)	8,000	1,887
				$3,667

The abbreviated December 31, 19X3 (date of purchase) worksheet below lists the investment in Company S bonds account, the bonds payable account, and the remaining issuance discount. Eliminating the $103,667 price paid by Company P against the book value of $98,240 ($100,000 - $1,760) creates an extraordinary loss on retirement of $5,427 that is carried to combined net income.

The differences in the 19X4 consolidated worksheet caused by the interest method of amortization are shown in Worksheet 5-4 on pages 5-52 to 5-55. Note particularly the change in the Company S income distribution schedule. The original 9% interest, totaling $8,842, has been replaced by the $6,220 of interest calculated using the 6% rate.

	Partial Trial Balance		Eliminations & Adjustments	
	Company P	Company S	Dr.	Cr.
Investment in Company S Bonds	103,667			103,667
Bonds Payable, 8%		(100,000)	100,000	
Discount on Bonds Payable		1,760		1,760
Extraordinary Loss on Bond Retirement			5,427	
Interest Expense		8,772*		

*See preceding discount amortization schedule for issuer

Intercompany Leases

Intercompany leases have become one of the most frequently encountered types of transactions between affiliated companies. It is particularly common for parent companies with substantial financial resources to acquire major assets and to lease the assets to their subsidiaries. This action may occur because the financially stronger parent may be able to both purchase and finance assets on more favorable terms. Also, the parent company may desire close control over plant assets and may prefer centralized ownership and management of assets. Leasing becomes a mechanism through which the parent can convey the use of centrally owned assets to subsidiaries. Some companies achieve centralized asset management by forming separate leasing subsidiaries whose major function is to lease assets to affiliated companies. When such subsidiaries exist, they are consolidated automatically with the parent regardless of the ownership percentage of the parent.[1]

Operating Leases

Consolidation procedures for intercompany leases depend on the original recording of the lease by the separate companies. When an operating lease exists, the lessor has recorded the purchase of the asset and depreciates it. The lessor records rent revenue, while the lessee records rent expense. In such cases, it is necessary to eliminate in the consolidation process the intercompany rent expense/revenue and any related rent receivable/payable. The lessor's asset and related accumulated depreciation should be reclassified as a normal productive asset rather than as property under an operating lease. As an example, assume the parent, Company P, has both productive equipment used in its own operations and equipment that is under operating lease to a subsidiary, Company S. The following partial worksheet may be used to analyze required consolidation procedures:

	Partial Trial Balance		Eliminations & Adjustments	
	Company P	Company S	Dr.	Cr.
Equipment	800,000		(3) 100,000	
Accumulated Depreciation—Equipment	(300,000)			(3) 40,000
Equipment under Operating Lease	100,000			(3) 100,000
Accumulated Depreciation—Equipment under Operating Lease	(40,000)		(3) 40,000	
Rent Receivable	1,200			(2) 1,200
Rent Payable		(1,200)	(2) 1,200	
Rent Income	(14,400)		(1) 14,400	
Rent Expense		14,400		(1) 14,400
Depreciation Expense	50,000			

Eliminations and Adjustments:

(1) Eliminate intercompany rent expense and revenue of $1,200 per month.
(2) Eliminate one month's accrued rent.
(3) Reclassify the asset under the intercompany operating lease and its related accumulated depreciation as a normal productive asset.

No adjustments are made in the income distribution schedules as a result of operating leases. The eliminations made on the worksheet do not change the amount of income or the distribution of income between the minority and controlling interests.

---

1 Statement of Financial Accounting Standards No. 13, *Accounting for Leases* (Stamford: Financial Accounting Standards Board, 1976), par. 31.

Capitalized Leases

Consolidation procedures become more complicated when the lease is recorded as a capital lease by the lessee and as a direct-financing or sales-type lease by the lessor. The lessee records both an asset and intercompany long-term debt. Generally, the criteria for determining when a lease requires such accounting treatment are the same for affiliated companies as for independent companies. However, when the terms of the lease are significantly affected by the fact that the lessee and lessor are affiliates, the usual criteria for classification of leases do not apply. Lease terms could be considered "significantly affected" when they could not reasonably be expected to occur between independent companies.[2] For example, a parent might lease to its subsidiary at a rent far below the market rate, or a parent might rent a highly specialized machine to its subsidiary on a month-to-month basis. Typically, such specialized machinery would be leased only on a long-term lease promising a full recovery of cost to the lessor, since there would be no use for the machine by other lessees if it were returned to the lessor. The month-to-month lease is possible only because the parent's control of the subsidiary assures a continued flow of rent payments. When, in the accountant's judgment, the terms of the lease are affected significantly by the parent–subsidiary relationship, the normal criteria are not used and the transaction is recorded so as to reflect its true economic substance.[3] Usually in these circumstances, the lessee is viewed as having purchased the asset using funds borrowed from the lessor.

Consolidation Procedures for Direct-Financing Leases.   A direct-financing lease is viewed as a unique type of asset transfer by the lessor, who accepts a long-term receivable from the lessee as consideration for the asset received by the lessee. There is no profit or loss to the lessor on the transfer, only future interest revenue as payments become due.

Prior to studying consolidated worksheet procedures, the entries made by the affiliated lessee and lessor will be analyzed. In its simplest form, a direct-financing lease is recorded by the lessee as an asset, and debt is recorded to recognize the lease obligation. The lessor records the lease as a receivable from the lessee. If all payments to be received by the lessor will come from or are guaranteed by the original lessee, the present value of the net receivable recorded by the lessor will equal the present value of the payable recorded by the lessee, and the interest rates used to amortize the debt will be equal.

To illustrate, assume Company S is an 80%-owned subsidiary of Company P. On January 1, 19X1, Company P purchased a machine for $5,851 and leased it to Company S. The terms of the direct-financing lease provide for rental payments of $2,000 per year at the beginning of each period and allow the lessee to exercise an option to purchase the machine for $1,000 at the end of 19X3. The $1,000 purchase option is considered a bargain purchase option that will be exercised and is included in the minimum lease payments. The implicit interest rate (which equates all payments, including the bargain purchase option, to the lessor's purchase cost) is 16%. The lessee will depreciate the capitalized cost of the machine over 5 years, using the straight-line method. The lessee may use a 5-year life, despite the 3-year lease term, because it is assumed that the bargain purchase option will be exercised and that the asset will be used for 5 years.

---

2 *Ibid.*, par. 29
3 *Ibid.*

The amortization of the debt at the implicit 16% interest rate is as follows:

Date	Payment	Interest at 16% on Previous Balance	Reduction of Principal	Principal Balance
Jan. 1, 19X1	$2,000		$2,000	$3,851*
Jan. 1, 19X2	2,000	$ 616	1,384	2,467
Jan. 1, 19X3	2,000	395	1,605	862
Dec. 31, 19X3	1,000	138	862	
Total	$7,000	$1,149	$5,851	

*Purchase price of $5,851 – $2,000 initial payment.

The journal entries for the separate companies would be as follows for the first two years:

Date	Company S (Lessee)			Company P (Lessor)		
19X1						
Jan. 1	Assets under Capital Lease	5,851		Minimum Lease Payments Receivable	5,000	
	Obligations under Capital Lease .		3,851	Cash	2,000	
	Cash		2,000	Unearned Interest Income		1,149
				Accounts Payable (for asset)		5,851
Dec. 31	Interest Expense (at 16%)	616		Unearned Interest Income	616	
	Interest Payable		616	Interest Income (at 16%)		616
	Depreciation Expense					
	(⅕ × $5,851)	1,170				
	Accumulated Depreciation—Assets					
	under Capital Lease		1,170			
19X2						
Jan. 1	Obligations under Capital Lease . . .	1,384		Cash	2,000	
	Interest Payable	616		Minimum Lease Payments		
	Cash		2,000	Receivable		2,000
Dec. 31	Interest Expense (at 16%)	395		Unearned Interest Income	395	
	Interest Payable		395	Interest Income (at 16%)		395
	Depreciation Expense	1,170				
	Accumulated Depreciation—Assets					
	under Capital Lease		1,170			

At the end of each period, consolidation procedures would be needed to eliminate the intercompany transactions. In substance, there appears on the separate records of the affiliates an intercompany transfer of a plant asset with resulting intercompany debt. The intercompany debt, related interest expense/revenue, and interest accruals must be eliminated. Also, it is necessary to reclassify the assets under capital leases as productive assets owned by the consolidated group. The adjusted partial worksheets (pages 5-11 and 5-12) illustrate consolidation procedures at the end of 19X1 and 19X2.

A review of the worksheet eliminations and adjustments reveals that **combined net income is not changed because equal amounts of interest expense and revenue were eliminated.** Therefore, no adjustments are required in the income distribution schedules.

Partial Worksheet
For Year Ended December 31, 19X1

	Trial Balance		Eliminations & Adjustments	
	Company P	Company S	Dr.	Cr.
Assets Under Capital Lease		5,851		(3) 5,851
Accumulated Depreciation—Assets Under Capital Lease		(1,170)	(3) 1,170	
Property, Plant, and Equipment	200,000	120,000	(3) 5,851	
Accumulated Depreciation—Property, Plant, and Equipment	(80,000)	(50,000)		(3) 1,170
Obligations Under Capital Lease		(3,851)	(2) 3,851	
Interest Payable		(616)	(2) 616	
Minimum Lease Payments Receivable	5,000			(2) 5,000
Unearned Interest Income	(533)		(2) 533	
Interest Expense		616		(1) 616
Interest Income	(616)		(1) 616	

Eliminations and Adjustments:

(1) Eliminate intercompany Interest Expense/Revenue of $616.

(2) Eliminate the intercompany debt recorded by the lessee (obligation under capital lease plus accrued interest payable) against the net intercompany receivable of the lessor (minimum lease payments receivable less unearned interest income).

(3) Reclassify the asset under capital lease and its related accumulated depreciation as a productive asset owned by the consolidated company.

Some capital leases will designate a portion of the annual rent as being applicable to executory costs, such as property taxes or maintenance, incurred by the lessor. Such payments for executory costs are not included in the obligation of the lessee or the minimum lease payments receivable recorded by the lessor. Instead, such payments are recorded as rent expense and revenue in each period. In the consolidation process, that portion of rent applicable to executory costs is eliminated like any other charge for intercompany services.

The preceding example has a bargain purchase option. This means that all payments to be received by the lessor would come from the original lessee. Equality of payments for both parties to a lease between affiliates is the most common case. However, there may be intercompany leases where there is an unguaranteed residual value for the lessor. This means that a portion of the total payments to be received by the lessor will come from parties outside the control group. Therefore, the stream of payments to be received by the lessor exceeds the stream of payments to be paid by the lessee. This complicates the consolidation process. (The appendix to this chapter illustrates a revised version of the preceding example that deals with an unequal stream of payments.)

Consolidation Procedures for Sales-Type Leases.   Under a sales-type lease, a lessor records a sales profit or loss at the inception of the lease. The sales profit or loss is the difference between the fair market value of the asset at the inception of the lease and the cost of an asset purchased (or the net book value of an asset previously used by the seller) for the lessor. Consolidation procedures do not allow recognition

Partial Worksheet
For Year Ended December 31, 19X2

	Trial Balance		Eliminations & Adjustments	
	Company P	Company S	Dr.	Cr.
Assets under Capital Lease		5,851		(3) 5,851
Accumulated Depreciation—Assets under Capital Lease		(2,340)	(3) 2,340	
Property, Plant, and Equipment	200,000	120,000	(3) 5,851	
Accumulated Depreciation—Property, Plant, and Equipment	(100,000)	(60,000)		(3) 2,340
Obligations under Capital Lease		(2,467)	(2) 2,467	
Interest Payable		(395)	(2) 395	
Minimum Lease Payments Receivable	3,000			(2) 3,000
Unearned Interest Income	(138)		(2) 138	
Interest Expense		395		(1) 395
Interest Income	(395)		(1) 395	

Eliminations and Adjustments:

(1) Eliminate intercompany Interest Expense/Revenue of $395.

(2) Eliminate intercompany debt and net receivable.

(3) Reclassify the asset under the capital lease and its related accumulated depreciation as a productive asset owned by the consolidated company.

of this intercompany profit or loss at the inception of the lease. Instead, the profit or loss is deferred and then amortized over the lessee's period of usage. This period will be the lease term unless there is a bargain purchase or bargain renewal option, in which case the asset's useful life would be used.

To illustrate, assume that in the previous example the asset leased to Company S had a cost to Company P of $4,951. Company P would have recorded the following entry at the inception of the sales-type lease:

Minimum Lease Payments Receivable	5,000	
Cash	2,000	
Unearned Interest Income		1,149
Asset (cost of asset leased)		4,951
Sales Profit on Leases		900

This entry differs from that of the previous example only to the extent of recording the gain and transferring an existing asset. None of the lessor's subsequent entries recording the earning of interest and the payment of the receivable would change. The lessee's entries are unaffected by the existence of the sales profit.

Consolidation procedures for a sales-type lease, however, do require added steps to those already illustrated. The sales profit is similar to a profit on the sale of a plant asset. The $900 profit in this example must be deferred over the 3-year lease term. Thus, the asset and its related depreciation accounts must be adjusted to reflect the original sales profit.

The following added adjustments on the 19X1 partial consolidated worksheet (page 5-11) would be needed for the original $900 sales profit:

Sales Profit on Leases	900	
Property, Plant, and Equipment		900
To reduce cost of asset for gain on sales-type lease.		
Accumulated Depreciation—Property, Plant, and Equipment	300	
Depreciation Expense		300
To reduce depreciation expense at the rate of $300 per year. ...		

The income distribution schedule of the parent (lessor) would reflect the deferral of the original $900 profit in the year of the sale and would recognize $300 per year during the asset's life.

For the 19X2 partial consolidated worksheet (page 5-12), the following added adjustments would be required if a sales-type lease were involved:

Retained Earnings—Controlling Interest	600	
Accumulated Depreciation—Property, Plant, and Equipment	300	
Property, Plant, and Equipment		900
To adjust the remaining sales profit at the beginning of the period.		
Accumulated Depreciation—Property, Plant, and Equipment	300	
Depreciation Expense		300
To reduce depreciation expense at the rate of $300 per year.		

Intercompany Transactions Prior to Business Combination

It is possible that the companies involved in a business combination may have had dealings with each other prior to the consummation of the acquisition. The ramifications of such dealings on the consolidation process depend on whether the combination is a purchase or a pooling of interests.

When the acquisition is a purchase, there is no need to be concerned with intercompany sales occurring prior to the acquisition. It is assumed that the sales were arm's-length transactions between unrelated parties. Even though assets containing the profit are on the balance sheet on the acquisition date, no adjustments are needed when consolidating. When one affiliate has previously purchased the other affiliate's bonds, a complication does arise. The bonds become an intercompany debt as of the purchase date and thus are viewed as retired on the purchase date when consolidating.

Acquisitions deemed to be a pooling of interests create a need for eliminating intercompany transactions occurring prior to the acquisition date. Recall that poolings are retroactive to the entire current period and to earlier periods. This means that all intercompany transactions during the period in which a pooling occurs must be eliminated, no matter when the pooling occurs. In essence, consolidated statements for the period during which a pooling occurs are the same as they would appear if the pooling had occurred at the beginning of the period. When comparative statements are prepared, pooling is retroactive for all such statements. This means that transactions between the companies during those previous periods must be eliminated. In summary, consolidation procedures are applied as they would be if the companies had been pooled from their inception.

Appendix: Intercompany Leases with Unguaranteed Residual Value

The intercompany lease may contain an unguaranteed residual value. This means that the original intercompany lessee will supply only a portion of the total cash flow to be received by the lessor. At the end of the original lease term, the lessor may lease the asset again or sell it. In either case, there is no obligation on the part of the lessee to renew the lease or to purchase the asset. Since the original lessee is contractually bound to provide only a portion of the payments to be received by the lessor, the lessee will record as its lease obligation only the present value of the minimum lease payments for which it is obligated. The present value of these minimum lease payments is computed using the lessee's incremental borrowing rate, unless the lessor's implicit interest rate in the lease is known or is reasonably estimable and is lower, in which case the lessor's implicit rate is used.[4] Usually, the lessor's implicit rate will be available since the lessee and lessor are members of the same control group. Therefore, the lessor's implicit rate will be used for leases between affiliates of the consolidated group. Leases using any other rate should be adjusted to the implicit rate prior to consolidating.

The lessor records the gross investment in the lease, which is the sum of the minimum lease payments receivable and the unguaranteed residual value. Unearned interest income is recorded as a contra-account at an amount that reduces the gross investment to the market value of the asset at the inception of the lease. Unearned interest is amortized using the implicit rate of the lessor. The implicit rate of the lessor thus equates the present value of all payments expected, including the unguaranteed residual value, to the market value of the asset.

The recording methods used by the lessee and lessor for leases with an unguaranteed residual value present a complication to the consolidation process. The amount of the asset under the capital lease recorded by the lessee will be less than the asset's market value, since the present value of the lease payments recorded by the lessee will not include the asset's unguaranteed residual value. To understand this complication, the previous example may be used with one change. Instead of the $1,000 bargain purchase option that was included in the set of minimum lease payments, assume there is a $1,000 unguaranteed residual value. Since the residual value is not guaranteed, it is not part of the minimum lease payments. The revised facts are as follows:

1. Cost of asset to lessor: $5,851.
2. Lease terms: Three annual payments of $2,000 due at the start of each year. Unguaranteed residual value of $1,000 to lessor at the end of 19X3.
3. Lessor implicit rate: 16% equates the three $2,000 payments plus the unguaranteed residual value to $5,851.
4. Lessee interest rate: 16% (lessor implicit rate) which, when applied only to the lease payments, results in a present value of $5,210.
5. Depreciation: Straight-line over the 3-year lease term, since the contractual use of the asset is for three years.
6. Amortization tables:

Lessor (16%)

Date	Payment	Interest at 16% on Previous Balance	Reduction of Principal	Principal Balance
Jan. 1, 19X1	$2,000		$2,000	$3,851*
Jan. 1, 19X2	2,000	$ 616	1,384	2,467
Jan. 1, 19X3	2,000	395	1,605	862
Dec. 31, 19X3	1,000	138	862	
Total	$7,000	$1,149	$5,851	

*Purchase price of $5,851 – $2,000 initial payment.

---

4 When the present value of the minimum lease payments using the incremental borrowing rate exceeds the market value of the asset, the asset and the obligation are recorded at the market value of the asset. The interest rate that equates the present value of the payments to the market value of the asset is used then to amortize the debt.

Lessee (16%)

Date	Payment	Interest at 16% on Previous Balance	Reduction of Principal	Principal Balance
Jan. 1, 19X1	$2,000		$2,000	$3,210**
Jan. 1, 19X2	2,000	$514	1,486	1,724
Jan. 1, 19X3	2,000	276	1,724	
Total	$6,000	$790	$5,210	

**Present value of $5,210 − $2,000 initial payment.

The journal entries for the separate companies would be as follows for the first two years:

Date	Company S (Lessee)			Company P (Lessor)		
19X1						
Jan. 1	Assets Under Capital Lease	5,210		Minimum Lease Payments Receivable	4,000	
	Cash.		2,000	Unguaranteed Residual Value.	1,000	
	Obligations Under Capital Lease .		3,210	Cash	2,000	
				Unearned Interest Income		1,149
Dec. 31	Interest Expense (at 16%)	514		Accounts Payable (for asset).		5,851
	Interest Payable.		514	Unearned Interest Income	616	
	Depreciation Expense			Interest Income (at 16%)		616
	(1/3 × $5,210)	1,737				
	Accumulated Depreciation—Assets					
	Under Capital Lease		1,737			
19X2						
Jan. 1	Obligations Under Capital Lease . . .	1,486		Cash	2,000	
	Interest Payable	514		Minimum Lease Payments		
	Cash.		2,000	Receivable		2,000
Dec. 31	Interest Expense (at 16%)	276		Unearned Interest Income	395	
	Interest Payable.		276	Interest Income (at 16%)		395
	Depreciation Expense	1,737				
	Accumulated Depreciation—Assets					
	Under Capital Lease		1,737			

A comparison of the lessor's and lessee's amortization tables shows the following difference between the lessee's interest expense and the lessor's interest income each period:

Year Ending December 31	16% Lessor Implicit Interest	16% Lessee Interest	Difference
19X1	$ 616	$514	$102
19X2	395	276	119
19X3	138		138
Total	$1,149	$790	$359

The difference is the interest on the unguaranteed residual value, which is recorded only by the lessor. This can be demonstrated as follows:

Date	16% Implicit Interest	Difference in Principal Balances
Jan. 1, 19X1		$ 641*
Dec. 31, 19X1	$102	743
Dec. 31, 19X2	119	862
Dec. 31, 19X3	138	1,000
Total	$359	

*$5,851 – $5,210.

In the consolidation process, the intercompany debt and all interest applicable to the lease are eliminated. Even the interest income recorded on the unguaranteed residual value is eliminated, since it is a ramification of a lease that, from a consolidated viewpoint, does not exist. The asset recorded by the lessee and the unguaranteed residual value recorded by the lessor are eliminated and replaced by a productive asset recorded by the consolidated company.

 Worksheet 5-5, pages 5-56 to 5-59, contains the detailed steps for the elimination of the intercompany lease at the end of 19X1. In this worksheet, it is assumed that the interest in the 80%-owned subsidiary was purchased at its book value. Entries (1) and (2) eliminate the investment. Entry (3) eliminates the $616 of interest income against the $514 of interest expense. The $102 disparity reflects the interest applicable to the unguaranteed residual value and is returned to unearned interest income. Entry (4) eliminates the intercompany debt applicable to the lease. The $359 disparity reflects the interest applicable to the unguaranteed residual value over the life of the lease. This amount is used to reduce the unguaranteed residual value to its original present value of $641. The $641, combined with the $5,210 asset under capital lease, is eliminated and replaced by an owned asset and recorded at the $5,851 original cost to the consolidated company. Entry (5) adjusts the depreciation to reflect the cost and the residual value of the asset to the consolidated company. The accumulated depreciation also is reclassified as that applicable to an owned asset.

 In Worksheet 5-6 on pages 5-60 to 5-62, the consolidation procedures for the second year of the lease term are illustrated.

Questions

1. What are the alternative methods available to affiliated companies for extinguishing debt in the hands of outside parties, and how is the consolidation process affected by each method? When the parent purchases bonds issued by the subsidiary from an outside party, why is the resulting gain or loss borne entirely by the issuer?

2. What is the effect on consolidated net income in the year of acquisition and in subsequent periods of the following parent purchases of 8% subsidiary bonds?

   a) Issued at 8.5%, purchased to yield 7%

   b) Issued at 8.5%, purchased to yield 9%

   c) Issued at 9%, purchased to yield 9.5%

   d) Issued at 9.5%, purchased to yield 9%

3. Why would the amounts of interest expense and revenue recorded by affiliated companies relative to intercompany bondholdings not agree? How is the disparity dealt with in the consolidation process?

4. Assume that a subsidiary company's outstanding bonds are purchased at a price below book value by the parent company at the start of the financial year. For the current year:

   a) Explain if and why a gain or loss on bond retirement appears on the consolidated statements even though the subsidiary has not retired the bonded debt.

   b) The income distribution schedule for the subsidiary company shows internally generated net income and adjusted income. Assuming no other intercompany transactions, compare these two income figures.

5. Company P purchased Company S's $50,000, 5-year, 8% bonds on January 1, 19X4, three years after issuance. The bonds originally were issued at face value and later purchased by Company P at a market rate of 7% for $50,904. Using the straight-line method of amortization, compute the income distribution schedule interest adjustments over the remaining term of the bonds and explain their relationship to the original consolidated gain or loss on retirement. On whose income distribution schedule do these items appear?

6. What are the benefits of leasing among affiliated companies?

7. Why are no adjustments made on the income distribution schedules of controlling and minority interests as a result of operating and direct-financing leases?

8. Distinguish between a direct-financing lease and a sales-type lease from the standpoint of the intercompany lessor. What is the impact of these two types of leases on consolidation procedures?

9. Company X is leasing several plant assets from its parent company, Company T. Which of the following items should Company X include in minimum lease payments if the lease is classified as an operating lease? As a capital lease?

   a) Annual rental payments

   b) Amounts reimbursing the lessor for executory costs, such as insurance, maintenance, and taxes

   c) Guaranteed residual value

   d) Penalties paid for failure to renew

   e) Bargain purchase option

10. Designate whether the following accounts normally are recorded on the books of the lessor or the lessee. Indicate which accounts are eliminated, reclassified, or adjusted in the consolidation process.

    a) Equipment Operating Lease

    b) Rent Expense—Executory Costs

    c) Accounts Payable (for asset)

    d) Depreciation Expense—Operating Lease

    e) Depreciation Expense—Capital Lease

    f) Unearned Interest Income

    g) Assets Under Capital Lease

11. Parent Company purchased an asset for $28,000 and has agreed to lease the asset to its subsidiary over a 5-year period starting January 1, 19X1. The fair market value of the leased asset at the inception of the lease term was $32,000. Record the adjustments pertaining to the sales profit on the lease that would be made on the consolidated worksheet for the first and final years of the lease term.

Exercises

Exercise 1.   Marcus Engineering is a large corporation with the ability to obtain financing by selling its bonds at favorable rates. Currently, it pays 7% interest on its 10-year bond issues. In the past year, Marcus purchased an 80% interest in a subsidiary, Patel Industries. Patel Industries has $1,000,000 of bonds outstanding that mature in 6 years. Interest is paid annually at a stated rate of 10%. The bonds were issued at face value. Interest rates have come down, but Patel Industries could still expect to pay 9% to 9.5% interest on a long-term issue. Patel Industries is a smaller company with a lower credit rating than Marcus.

Marcus would like to reduce interest costs on the Patel Industries debt. The company has asked your advice on whether it should purchase the bonds or loan Patel Industries the money to retire its own debt. Compare the options with a focus on the impact on consolidated statements.

Exercise 2.   Hartwig Company is an 80%-owned subsidiary of Ney Industries. Hartwig Company issued 10-year, 8% bonds in the amount of $500,000 on January 1, 19X1. The bonds were issued at face value, and interest is payable each January 1. On January, 1, 19X3, Ney Industries purchased all of the Hartwig bonds for $484,000. Ney will amortize the discount on a straight-line basis. For the years ending (a) December 31, 19X3, and (b) December 31, 19X4, determine the effects of this transaction

1.   On combined net income.
2.   On the distribution of income to the controlling and minority interests.

Exercise 3.   Karen Company is an 80%-owned subsidiary of Black Corporation. Karen Company issued $100,000 of 10%, 8-year bonds for $102,000 on January 1, 19X1. Annual interest is paid on January 1. Black Corporation purchased the bonds on January 2, 19X5, for $99,400. Both companies are using the straight-line method to amortize the premium/discount on the bonds.

1.   Prepare the eliminations and adjustments that would be made on the December 31, 19X5 consolidated worksheet as a result of this purchase.
2.   Prepare the eliminations and adjustments that would be made on the December 31, 19X6 consolidated worksheet.

Exercise 4.   On January 1, 19X4, Dunbar Corporation, an 85%-owned subsidiary of Garfield Industries, received $48,055 for $50,000 of 8%, 5-year bonds it issued when the market rate was 9%. When Garfield Industries purchased these bonds for $47,513 on January 2, 19X6, the market rate was 10%. Given the following effective interest amortization schedules for both companies, calculate the gain or loss on retirement and the interest adjustments to the issuer's income distribution schedules over the remaining term of the bonds.

Dunbar (issuer)

Date	Effective Interest (9%)	Nominal Interest	Discount Amortization	Balance
1/1/X4				$48,055
1/1/X5	$4,325	$4,000	$325	48,380
1/1/X6	4,354	4,000	354	48,734
1/1/X7	4,386	4,000	386	49,120
1/1/X8	4,421	4,000	421	49,541
1/1/X9	4,459*	4,000	459	50,000

Garfield (purchaser)

Date	Effective Interest (10%)	Nominal Interest	Discount Amortization	Balance
1/1/X6				$47,513
1/1/X7	$4,751	$4,000	$751	48,264
1/1/X8	4,826	4,000	826	49,091
1/1/X9	4,909	4,000	909	50,000

Exercise 5. Real Meat Products is an 80%-owned subsidiary of Foremost Meat Packers Inc. On January 1, 19X1, Real Meat sold $100,000 of 10-year, 7% bonds for $102,000. Interest is paid annually on January 1. The market rate for this type of bond was 9% on January 2, 19X3, when Foremost purchased 60% of the Real Meat bonds for $53,600. Discounts may be amortized on a straight-line basis.

1. Prepare the eliminations and adjustments required for this bond purchase on the December 31, 19X3 consolidated worksheet.
2. Prepare the eliminations and adjustments required on the December 31, 19X4 consolidated worksheet.

Exercise 6. Lift Industries, a 90%-owned subsidiary of Shark Incorporated, issued $100,000 of 12-year, 8% bonds on January 1, 19X5, to yield 7% interest. Interest is paid annually on January 1. The effective interest method is used to amortize the premium. Shark purchased the bonds for $94,967 on January 2, 19X8, when the market rate of interest was 9%. On the purchase date, the remaining premium on the bonds was $6,516. Lift's 19X8 net income was $500,000.

1. Prepare the eliminations and adjustments required for this purchase on the December 31, 19X8 consolidated worksheet.
2. Prepare the 19X8 income distribution schedule for the minority interest.

Exercise 7. Prince Machinery Company purchased, for cash, a $50,000 custom machine on January 1, 19X1. The machine has an estimated 5-year life and will be straight-line depreciated with no salvage value. The machine was then leased to Starlight Engineering Company, an 80%-owned subsidiary, under a 5-year operating lease for $12,400 per year, payable each January 1.

1. Record the 19X1 entries for the purchase of the machine and the lease to Starlight Engineering Company on the books of Prince Machinery Company.
2. Record the 19X1 entries for the transaction on the books of Starlight Engineering Company.
3. Provide the elimination entries that would be made on the 19X1 consolidated worksheet.

Exercise 8. On January 1, 19X1, Arnold Company, an 80%-owned subsidiary of Betty Electronics Inc., signed a 4-year direct-financing lease with its parent for the rental of electronic equipment. The lease agreement requires an $8,000 payment on January 1 of each year, and title transfers to Arnold on January 1, 19X5. The equipment originally cost $27,215 and had an estimated remaining life of 5 years at the start of the lease term. The lessor's implicit interest rate is 12%. The lessee also used the 12% rate to record the transaction.

1. Prepare the eliminations and adjustments required for this lease on the December 31, 19X1 consolidated worksheet.
2. Prepare the eliminations and adjustments for the December 31, 19X2 consolidated worksheet.

Exercise 9.   The Auto Clinic is a wholly owned subsidiary of Fast-Check Equipment Company. Fast-Check Equipment sells and leases 4-wheel alignment machines. The usual selling price of each machine is $35,000; it has a cost to Fast-Check Equipment of $25,000. On January 1, 19X1, Fast-Check Equipment leased such a machine to Auto Clinic. The lease provided for payments of $9,096 at the start of each year for 5 years. The payments include $1,000 per year for maintenance to be provided by the seller. There is a bargain purchase price of $2,000 at the end of the fifth year. The implicit interest rate in the lease is 10% per year. The equipment is being depreciated over 8 years.

The amortization schedule for the lease prepared by Fast-Check Equipment is as follows:

Date	Payment	Interest at 10% on Previous Balance	Reduction of Principal	Principal Balance
1/1/X1	$8,096		$8,096	$26,904
1/1/X2	8,096	$2,691	5,405	21,499
1/1/X3	8,096	2,150	5,946	15,553
1/1/X4	8,096	1,556	6,540	9,013
1/1/X5	8,096	901	7,195	1,818
12/31/X5	2,000	182	1,818	0

Prepare the eliminations and adjustments, in entry form, that would be required on a consolidated worksheet prepared on December 31, 19X1.

Problems

Problem 5-1.   Since its 100% acquisition of Mark Corporation stock on December 31, 19X2, Janet Corporation has maintained its investment under the equity method. However, due to Mark's earning potential, the price included a $30,000 payment for goodwill to be amortized over 10 years. At the time of the purchase, the fair market value of Mark's assets equaled their book value.

On January 2, 19X4, Mark Corporation issued 10-year, 9% bonds at a face value of $50,000. The bonds pay interest each December 31. On January 2, 19X6, Janet Corporation purchased all of Mark Corporation's outstanding bonds for $51,000. The premium is amortized on a straight-line basis. They have been included in Janet's long-term investment in bonds account. Below are the trial balances of both companies on December 31, 19X6:

	Janet Corp.	Mark Corp.
Cash.	78,500	67,500
Accounts Receivable	450,000	75,000
Inventory	200,000	65,000
Investment in Bonds	50,875	
Plant and Equipment (net)	2,420,000	196,000
Investment in Mark Corp.	340,000	
Accounts Payable	(275,000)	(18,000)
Bonds Payable (9%).		(50,000)
Common Stock, Janet ($10 par).	(1,000,000)	
Paid-in Capital in Excess of Par, Janet.	(750,000)	

Retained Earnings, Janet, 1/1/X6	(730,000)	
Common Stock, Mark ($10 par)		(100,000)
Paid-In Capital in Excess of Par, Mark.		(130,000)
Retained Earnings, Mark, 1/1/X6		(80,000)
Sales.	(2,500,000)	(540,000)
Cost of Goods Sold	1,000,000	405,000
Other Expenses.	720,000	105,000
Interest Income	(4,375)	
Interest Expense	0	4,500
Total	0	0

Required:

1. Prepare the worksheet entries needed to eliminate the intercompany debt on December 31, 19X6.
2. Prepare a consolidated income statement for the year ended December 31, 19X6.

Note: No worksheet is required.

Problem 5-2.   On January 1, 19X1, Plant Company purchased 90% of the common stock of Smart Company for $335,000. On this date, Smart had common stock, other paid-in capital, and retained earnings of $100,000, $40,000, and $210,000, respectively. Any excess of cost over book value is due to goodwill, to be amortized over 5 years. In both 19X1 and 19X2, Plant has accounted for the investment in Smart using the cost method.

On January 1, 19X1, Smart sold $100,000 par value of 10-year, 8% bonds for $94,000. The bonds pay interest semiannually on January 1 and July 1 of each year. On December 31, 19X1, Plant purchased all of Smart's bonds for $97,300. The bonds are still held on December 31, 19X2. Both companies have correctly recorded all entries relative to bonds and interest, using straight-line amortization for premium or discount.

The trial balances of Plant Company and its subsidiary were as follows on December 31, 19X2:

	Plant Company	Smart Company
Interest Receivable.	4,000	
Other Current Assets	263,300	315,200
Investment in Smart Company	335,000	
Investment in Smart Bonds.	97,600	
Land	80,000	60,000
Buildings and Equipment	400,000	280,000
Accumulated Depreciation	(120,000)	(60,000)
Interest Payable.		(4,000)
Other Current Liabilities	(98,000)	(56,000)
Bonds Payable, 8%		(100,000)
Discount on Bonds Payable.		4,800
Other Long-Term Liabilities.	(200,000)	

(continued)

	Plant Company	Smart Company
Common Stock, Plant Co.	(100,000)	
Other Paid-In Capital, Plant Co.	(200,000)	
Retained Earnings, Plant Co.	(365,000)	
Common Stock, Smart Co.		(100,000)
Other Paid-In Capital, Smart Co.		(40,000)
Retained Earnings, Smart Co.		(260,000)
Net Sales.	(640,000)	(350,000)
Cost of Goods Sold	360,000	200,000
Operating Expenses.	168,400	71,400
Interest Expense		8,600
Interest Income	(8,300)	
Dividend Income	(27,000)	
Dividends Declared	50,000	30,000
Total	0	0

Required:

Prepare the worksheet necessary to produce the consolidated financial statements of Plant and its subsidiary Smart for the year ended December 31, 19X2. Round all computations to the nearest dollar.

Problem 5-3.   On January 1, 19X3, Warehouse Outlets had the following balances in its stockholders' equity accounts: Common Stock ($10 par), $800,000; Paid-In Capital in Excess of Par, $625,000; and Retained Earnings, $450,000. General Appliances purchased 64,000 shares of Warehouse Outlets common stock for $1,700,000 on that date. Any excess of cost over book value was attributed to goodwill and given a 10-year life.

Warehouse Outlets issued $500,000 of 8-year, 11% bonds on December 31, 19X2. The bonds sold for $476,000. General Appliances purchased one-half of these bonds in the market on January 1, 19X5, for $259,000. Both companies use the straight-line method of amortization of premiums and discounts.

On July 1, 19X6, General Appliances sold to Warehouse Outlets an old building with a book value of $167,500, remaining life of 10 years, and $30,000 salvage value, for $195,000. The building is being depreciated on a straight-line basis. Warehouse Outlets paid $20,000 in cash and signed a mortgage note with its parent for the balance. Interest, at 11% of the unpaid balance, and principal payments are due annually beginning July 1, 19X7. (For convenience, the mortgage balances are not divided into current and long-term portions.)

The trial balances of the two companies at December 31, 19X6, are as follows:

	General Appliances	Warehouse Outlets
Cash.	401,986	72,625
Accounts Receivable (net)	752,500	105,000
Interest Receivable.	9,625	
Inventory	1,950,000	900,000
Investment in Warehouse Outlets	1,700,000	
Investment in 11% Bonds	256,000	
Investment in Mortgage	175,000	
Property, Plant, and Equipment	9,000,000	2,950,000

	General Appliances	Warehouse Outlets
Accumulated Depreciation	(1,695,000)	(940,000)
Accounts Payable	(670,000)	(80,000)
Interest Payable.	(18,333)	(9,625)
Bonds Payable, 11%	(2,000,000)	(500,000)
Discount on Bonds Payable.	10,470	12,000
Mortgage Payable.		(175,000)
Common Stock ($5 par)	(3,200,000)	
Common Stock ($10 par)		(800,000)
Paid-In Capital in Excess of Par	(4,550,000)	(625,000)
Retained Earnings, Jan. 1, 19X6	(1,011,123)	(770,000)
Sales.	(9,800,000)	(3,000,000)
Gain on Sale of Building	(27,500)	
Interest Income	(35,625)	
Dividend Income	(48,000)	
Cost of Goods Sold	4,940,000	1,700,000
Depreciation Expense.	717,000	95,950
Interest Expense	223,000	67,544
Other Expenses.	2,600,000	936,506
Dividends Declared	320,000	60,000
Total	0	0

Required:

Prepare the worksheet necessary to produce the consolidated financial statements of General Appliances and its subsidiary for the year ended December 31, 19X6. Include the determination and distribution of excess and income distribution schedules.

Problem 5-4.   Erin Incorporated acquired all of the outstanding $25 par value common stock of Sturm Incorporated on January 1, 19X7, in exchange for 40,000 shares of its $25 par value common stock. The business combination meets all the conditions for a pooling of interests. On June 30, 19X7, Erin's common stock closed at $65 per share on the national stock exchange. Both corporations continued to operate as separate businesses, maintaining separate accounting records with fiscal years ending December 31.

On December 31, 19X7, the companies had condensed balance sheet accounts as follows:

	Erin Incorporated	Sturm Incorporated
Cash.	925,000	326,000
Other Current Assets	2,300,000	835,000
Inventory	2,310,000	1,045,000
Land	600,000	330,000
Property, Plant, and Equipment (net)	4,525,000	1,980,000
Long-Term Investments and Other Assets	865,000	385,000
Investment in Sturm Inc.	2,010,000	
Current Liabilities.	(2,465,000)	(1,145,000)
Long-Term Debt	(1,900,000)	(1,300,000)
Common Stock ($25 par)	(3,200,000)	

(continued)

	Erin Incorporated	Sturm Incorporated
Common Stock ($25 par)		(1,000,000)
Additional Paid-In Capital.	(1,850,000)	(190,000)
Retained Earnings	(3,326,000)	(820,000)
Sales.	(2,500,000)	(2,000,000)
Cost of Goods Sold.	1,200,000	970,000
Other Expenses.	429,500	320,000
Dividend Income	(160,000)	
Dividends Declared	256,000	160,000
Interest Income	(19,500)	
Interest Expense		104,000
Total	0	0

Additional information is as follows:

a) Erin uses the cost method of accounting for its investment in Sturm.

b) On June 15, 19X7, Sturm paid a cash dividend of $4 per share on its common stock.

c) On December 10, 19X7, Erin paid a cash dividend totaling $256,000 on its common stock.

d) Sturm's long-term debt consisted of 8%, 10-year bonds issued at face value on March 31, 19X1. Interest is payable semiannually on March 31 and September 30. On March 31, 19X7, Erin purchased $300,000 of face-value Sturm bonds for $292,000. The bond discount is amortized using the straight-line method.

e) During October 19X7, Erin sold merchandise to Sturm at an aggregate invoice price of $720,000, which included profit of $180,000. On December 31, 19X7, one-half of the merchandise remained in Sturm's inventory, and Sturm had not paid Erin for the merchandise purchased.

f) Sturm's 19X7 net income was $606,000. Erin's 19X7 income before considering equity in Sturm's net income was $890,000.

g) The balances in retained earnings on December 31, 19X6, were $2,506,000 and $820,000 for Erin and Sturm, respectively.

Required:

Prepare the December 31, 19X7 consolidated worksheet for Erin Incorporated and its subsidiary, Sturm Incorporated.

(AICPA adapted)

Problem 5-5. On January 1, 19X4, Kaeppler Corporation purchased 80% of the outstanding stock of Hacker Company for $1,000,000 in cash.

A condensed January 1, 19X4 Hacker Company balance sheet follows:

Assets		Liabilities and Stockholders' Equity	
Current assets.	$ 450,000	Liabilities, net.	$ 760,000
Property, plant, and equipment (net)	1,100,000	Common stock ($8 par)	640,000
Other assets.	50,000	Retained earnings.	200,000
Total assets.	$1,600,000	Total liabilities and equity. .	$1,600,000

At the purchase date, Hacker Company's inventory and land accounts were understated by $25,000 and $100,000, respectively. Any remaining excess was attributed to goodwill and given a 40-year life. The inventory on hand January 1, 19X4, was sold during 19X4.

On January 1, 19X1, Hacker Company issued $500,000 of 20-year, 8% bonds. The bonds, which sold at a price to yield 7%, pay interest on each December 31. The premium on these bonds was $47,233 on January 1, 19X5.

On January 1, 19X5, Kaeppler Corporation purchased $200,000 (face value) of these bonds for $168,705, to yield 10%.

Trial balances of the two companies as of December 31, 19X5, are as follows:

	Kaeppler Corporation	Hacker Company
Cash.	386,024	147,789
Accounts and Notes Receivable (net)	495,000	225,000
Inventory	510,000	235,000
Investment in 8% Bonds	169,576	
Investment in Hacker Company	1,146,000	
Land	1,000,000	400,000
Building and Equipment	3,650,000	1,400,000
Accumulated Depreciation	(1,400,000)	(650,000)
Other Assets.		40,250
Accounts and Notes Payable.	(475,000)	(230,000)
Bonds Payable, 7%	(2,000,000)	
Bonds Payable, 8%		(500,000)
Premium on Bonds Payable.		(45,539)
Common Stock ($5 stated value)	(2,500,000)	
Common Stock ($8 par)		(640,000)
Retained Earnings, Jan. 1, 19X5	(705,000)	(300,000)
Sales.	(2,400,000)	(1,050,000)
Subsidiary Income.	(90,000)	
Other Income	(46,600)	(12,000)
Cost of Goods Sold	1,560,000	693,000
Other Expenses.	600,000	256,500
Dividends Declared	100,000	30,000
Total	0	0

Interest income and expense related to Hacker Company's bonds are included in the other income and other expenses accounts. Amounts included reflect amortization of premiums or discounts, using the effective interest method of amortization.

Required:

Prepare the worksheet necessary to produce the consolidated financial statements of Kaeppler Corporation and its subsidiary for the year ended December 31, 19X5. Support should be provided for amounts pertaining to interest on Hacker Company's 8% bonds. Include the determination and distribution of excess and income distribution schedules.

Problem 5-6.   (Note: This problem is designed to be worked using the vertical worksheet format introduced in the appendix to Chapter 3.) In a transaction that meets the pooling rules, Prin Company acquired 90% of the outstanding common stock of Sand

(continued)

Company on January 1, 19X0. Sand stockholders' equity on January 1, 19X0, consisted of $200,000 in Common Stock and $120,000 in Retained Earnings.

Sand issued $100,000 of 10-year, 7% bonds for $93,000 on January 1, 19X0, when the market rate was 8%.

On January 2, 19X2, Prin purchased 60% of Sand's bonds for $63,720, to yield 6%. Straight-line amortization is used for all premiums or discounts on bonds.

Prin routinely sells merchandise inventory to Sand at a price to yield a gross profit of 30%. Intercompany merchandise sales in 19X3 were $100,000. Purchases from Prin accounted for $20,000 of Sand's beginning inventory and $15,000 of its ending inventory.

Separate statements prepared by the two companies at December 31, 19X3, showed the following information:

	Prin Company	Sand Company
Income Statement:		
Sales.	(900,000)	(390,000)
Interest income	(3,735)	
Cost of goods sold	580,000	210,000
Interest expense		7,700
Other expenses.	234,850	136,802
Subsidiary income.	(31,948)	
Net income	(120,833)	(35,498)
Retained Earnings Statement:		
Retained earnings, Jan. 1, 19X3, Prin.	(265,000)	
Retained earnings, Jan. 1, 19X3, Sand.		(202,000)
Net income	(120,833)	(35,498)
Dividends declared	30,000	
Retained earnings, Dec. 31, 19X3	(355,833)	(237,498)
Balance Sheet:		
Cash.	65,495	44,100
Accounts receivable (net)	68,800	58,000
Inventory	70,000	67,000
Investment in Sand	393,748	
Investment in 7% bonds	62,790	
Property, plant, and equipment	700,000	500,000
Accumulated depreciation.	(210,000)	(92,000)
Accounts payable	(70,000)	(43,802)
Bonds payable, 7%.		(100,000)
Discount on bonds payable.		4,200
Common stock ($10 par), Prin.	(300,000)	
Common stock ($2 par), Sand.		(200,000)
Paid-in capital in excess of par, Prin	(425,000)	
Retained earnings, Dec. 31, 19X3, Prin	(355,833)	
Retained earnings, Dec. 31, 19X3, Sand	0	(237,498)
Total	0	0

Required:

Prepare the worksheet necessary to produce the consolidated financial statements of Prin Company and its subsidiary for the year ended December 31, 19X3. Use the vertical format. Include income distribution schedules.

Problem 5-7.   The problem below is an example of a question of the CPA "Other Objective Format" type as it was applied to the consolidations area. A mark-sensing answer sheet was used on the exam. You may just supply the answer which should be accompanied by calculations where appropriate.

Presented below are selected amounts from the separate unconsolidated financial statements of Poe Corporation and its 90%-owned subsidiary, Shaw Company, at December 31, 19X2. Additional information follows:

	Poe Corporation	Shaw Company
Selected income statement amounts:		
Sales.	$710,000	$530,000
Cost of goods sold.	490,000	370,000
Gain on the sale of equipment.		21,000
Earnings from investment in subsidiary		
(sophisticated equity)	61,000	
Interest expense.		16,000
Depreciation.	25,000	20,000
Selected balance sheet amounts:		
Cash.	$ 50,000	$ 15,000
Inventories	229,000	150,000
Equipment	440,000	360,000
Accumulated depreciation.	(200,000)	(120,000)
Investment in Shaw (sophisticated equity balance) . .	189,000	
Investment in bonds	100,000	
Discount on bonds.	(9,000)	
Bonds payable		(200,000)
Common stock	(100,000)	(10,000)
Additional paid-in capital	(250,000)	(40,000)
Retained earnings	(402,000)	(140,000)
Selected statement of retained earnings amounts:		
Beginning balance, Dec. 31, 19X1	$272,000	$100,000
Net income	210,000	70,000
Dividends paid	80,000	30,000

Additional information is as follows:

■ On January 2, 19X2, Poe purchased 90% of Shaw's 100,000 outstanding common stock for cash of $155,000. On that date, Shaw's stockholders' equity equaled $150,000, and the fair values of Shaw's assets and liabilities equaled their carrying amounts. Poe has accounted for the acquisition as a purchase. Poe's policy is to amortize intangibles over 10 years.

■ On September 4, 19X2, Shaw paid cash dividends of $30,000.

■ On December 31, 19X2, Poe recorded its equity in Shaw's earnings.

(continued)

Required:

1. Items (a) through (c) below represent transactions between Poe and Shaw during 19X2. Determine the dollar amount effect of the consolidating adjustment on 19X2 consolidated income before considering minority interest (combined net income). Ignore income tax considerations.

   Items to be answered:

   a) On January 3, 19X2, Shaw sold equipment with an original cost of $30,000 and a carrying value of $15,000 to Poe for $36,000. The equipment had a remaining life of 3 years and was depreciated using the straight-line method by both companies.

   b) During 19X2, Shaw sold merchandise to Poe for $60,000, which included a profit of $20,000. At December 31, 19X2, half of this merchandise remained in Poe's inventory.

   c) On December 31, 19X2, Poe paid $91,000 to purchase 50% of the outstanding bonds issued by Shaw. The bonds mature on December 31, 19X8, and were originally issued at par. The bonds pay interest annually on December 31, and the interest was paid to the prior investor immediately before Poe's purchase of the bonds.

2. Determine the amount recorded by Poe as amortization of Goodwill for 19X2.

3. Items (a) through (l) below refer to accounts that may or may not be included in Poe's and Shaw's consolidated financial statements. The list on the right refers to the various possibilities of those amounts to be reported in Poe's consolidated financial statements for the year ended December 31, 19X2. Consider all transactions stated above in determining your answer. Ignore income tax considerations.

   Items to be answered:
   - (a) Cash
   - (b) Equipment
   - (c) Investment in subsidiary
   - (d) Bonds payable
   - (e) Minority interest
   - (f) Common stock
   - (g) Beginning retained earnings
   - (h) Dividends paid
   - (i) Gain on retirement of bonds
   - (j) Cost of goods sold
   - (k) Interest expense
   - (l) Depreciation expense

   Responses to be selected:
   1. Sum of amounts on Poe's and Shaw's separate unconsolidated financial statements.
   2. Less than the sum of amounts on Poe's and Shaw's separate unconsolidated financial statements, but not the same as the amount on either.
   3. Same as amount for Poe only.
   4. Same as amount for Shaw only.
   5. Eliminated entirely in consolidation.
   6. Shown in consolidated financial statements but not in separate unconsolidated financial statements.
   7. Neither in consolidated nor in separate unconsolidated financial statements.

   (AICPA adapted)

Problem 5-8.   Paro Company acquired a 90% interest in Sandman Company on January 1, 19X1, for $660,000. Any excess of cost over book value was due to goodwill, which is being amortized over the maximum period.

Capital balances of Sandman Company on January 1, 19X1, were

Common stock ($10 par)	$200,000
Paid-in capital in excess of par	100,000
Retained earnings	300,000
Total equity	$600,000

Sandman Company sold a machine to Paro for $30,000 on January 1, 19X4. It cost Sandman $20,000 to build the machine, which had a 5-year remaining life on the date of the sale and is subject to straight-line depreciation.

Paro purchased one-half of the outstanding 9% bonds of Sandman for $89,183 (to yield 12%) on December 31, 19X5. The bonds were sold originally by Sandman to yield 10% to outside parties. The discount on the bonds was $7,586 on December 31, 19X5. The effective interest method of amortization is used.

During 19X6, Paro Company sold merchandise to Sandman for $50,000. Paro recorded a 30% gross profit on the sales price. $20,000 of the merchandise purchased from Paro remains unsold at the end of the year.

The trial balances of Paro and its subsidiary, Sandman, are as follows on December 31, 19X6:

	Paro Company	Sandman Company
Inventory	40,000	80,000
Equipment	371,193	1,522,414
Accumulated Depreciation	(200,000)	(600,000)
Investment in Sandman Stock.	660,000	
Investment in Sandman Bonds	90,885	
Bonds Payable, 9%		(200,000)
Discount on Bonds Payable.		6,345
Common Stock ($10 par)	(200,000)	(200,000)
Paid-In Capital in Excess of Par	(300,000)	(100,000)
Retained Earnings, Jan. 1, 19X6	(401,376)	(500,000)
Sales.	(300,000)	(260,000)
Cost of Goods Sold.	100,000	72,000
Interest Income	(10,702)	
Other Expenses.	150,000	160,000
Interest Expense		19,241
Total	0	0

Required:

Prepare the worksheet necessary to produce the consolidated financial statements of Paro Company and its subsidiary for the year ended December 31, 19X6. Include the determination and distribution of excess and income distribution schedules.

Problem 5-9.   Sym Corporation, a wholly owned subsidiary of Paratec Corporation, leased equipment from its parent company on August 1, 19X6. The terms of the agreement clearly do not require the lease to be accounted for as a capital lease. Both entities are accounting for the lease as an operating lease. The lease payment is $12,000 per year paid in advance each August 1.

Paratec purchased its investment in Sym on December 31, 19X1 when Sym had a retained earnings balance of $150,000. Paratec is accounting for its investment in Sym under the cost method. Included in the original purchase price was a $50,000 premium attributable to Sym's history of exceptional earnings. Intangible assets are amortized over a 10-year period.

The December 31, 19X8 trial balances of Paratec and its subsidiary are presented below:

(continued)

	Paratec Corporation	Sym Corporation
Cash.	190,000	40,000
Accounts Receivable (net)	738,350	142,000
Inventory	500,000	75,000
Prepaid Rent on Equipment		7,000
Investment in Bonds	250,000	65,000
Investment in Sym Corporation.	400,000	
Land	250,000	85,000
Plant and Equipment	1,950,000	295,000
Accumulated Depreciation—Plant and Equipment	(250,000)	(60,000)
Equipment Under Operating Lease	120,000	
Accumulated Depreciation—Assets under		
Operating Lease	(36,000)	
Accounts Payable	(385,000)	(52,000)
Deferred Rent Revenue	(7,000)	
Common Stock (no par)	(2,000,000)	(200,000)
Retained Earnings, Jan. 1, 19X8	(1,076,350)	(310,000)
Sales.	(4,720,000)	(500,000)
Rent Income	(12,000)	
Cost of Goods Sold.	3,068,000	300,000
Rent Expense		12,000
Other Expenses.	725,000	101,000
Dividends Declared	295,000	
Total	0	0

Required:

Prepare the worksheet necessary to produce the consolidated income statement and balance sheet of Paratec Corporation and its subsidiary for the year ended December 31, 19X8.

Problem 5-10.   On January 1, 19X1, Train Distributing Company acquired an 80% interest in Trac Warehousing Inc. for $1,200,000. Trac's Retained Earnings at that date were $320,000. Its book values approximated market values, and any excess was attributed to goodwill and given a 10-year life.

Train is leasing a warehouse from Trac that originally cost Trac $790,000. On July 1, 19X1, the date the lease agreement was signed, the warehouse had an estimated remaining life of 15 years, a salvage value of $50,000, and accumulated depreciation of $200,000 under the straight-line method. The terms of the 10-year lease require an $8,000 rental payment on the first of each month, including executory costs of $300 per month. Trac has other lease contracts.

In conjunction with its warehousing operations, Trac purchases and sells merchandise to distributors. Sales to Train, at the usual 25% gross profit, totaled $260,000 for 19X2. At year-end, Train owed $15,000 on these purchases. Train's beginning inventory balance included $60,000 in merchandise purchased from Trac, and its ending inventory balance included $40,000.

The following trial balances were prepared by the separate companies on December 31, 19X2:

	Train Distributing Company	Trac Warehousing Inc.
Cash.	61,000	40,000
Receivables (net)	106,600	145,000
Inventory	180,000	100,000
Investment in Trac Warehousing Inc..	1,304,000	
Property, Plant, and Equipment	2,580,000	2,000,000
Accumulated Depreciation—Property, Plant,		
and Equipment	(1,249,000)	(1,550,000)
Assets Under Operating Lease.		1,915,000
Accumulated Depreciation—Assets Under		
Operating Lease		(990,000)
Accounts Payable	(125,000)	(70,000)
Bonds Payable, 10%	(400,000)	
Common Stock ($10 par)	(1,000,000)	
Common Stock ($5 par)		(600,000)
Paid-In Capital in Excess of Par	(720,000)	(540,000)
Retained Earnings, Jan. 1, 19X2	(526,000)	(380,000)
Sales.	(2,400,000)	(1,000,000)
Rent Income		(150,000)
Cost of Goods Sold	1,390,000	600,000
Rent Expense	96,000	
Interest Expense	40,000	
Other Expenses.	662,400	450,000
Subsidiary Income.	(80,000)	
Dividends Declared	80,000	30,000
Total	0	0

Required:

Prepare the worksheet necessary to produce the consolidated financial statements of Train Distributing Company and its subsidiary for the year ended December 31, 19X2. Include the determination and distribution of excess and income distribution schedules.

Problem 5-11. Plessor Industries acquired 80% of the outstanding common stock of Slessee Company on January 1, 19X1, for $320,000. On that date, Slessee's book values approximated market values, and the balance of its retained earnings account was $80,000. Any excess was attributed to goodwill and given a 5-year life. Slessee's net income was $20,000 for 19X1 and $30,000 for 19X2. No dividends were paid in either year.

On January 1, 19X2, Slessee signed a 5-year lease with Plessor for the rental of a small factory building with a 10-year life. Payments of $25,000 are due each January 1, and Slessee is expected to exercise the $5,000 bargain purchase option at the end of the fifth year. The market value of the factory was $103,770 at the start of the lease term. Plessor's implicit rate on the lease is 12%.

A second lease agreement, for the rental of production equipment with an 8-year life, was signed by Slessee on January 1, 19X3. The terms of this 4-year lease require a payment of $15,000 each January 1. The present value of the lease payments at

(continued)

Plessor's 12% implicit rate was equal to the market value of the equipment, $52,298, when the lease was signed. The cost of the equipment to Plessor was $45,000, and there is a $2,000 bargain purchase option. Eight-year, straight-line depreciation is being used, with no salvage value.

The following trial balances were prepared by the separate companies at December 31, 19X3:

	Plessor Industries	Slessee Cormpany
Cash.	60,000	40,745
Accounts Receivable	97,778	76,000
Inventory	140,000	120,000
Minimum Lease Payments Receivable	127,000	
Unearned Interest Income	(14,417)	
Investment in Slessee Company	320,000	
Assets under Capital Lease		156,068
Accumulated Depreciation—Assets under		
Capital Lease		(27,291)
Property, Plant, and Equipment	1,900,000	310,000
Accumulated Depreciation—Property,		
Plant, and Equipment.	(1,077,000)	(72,000)
Accounts Payable	(148,000)	(45,065)
Obligations under Capital Lease		(100,520)
Common Stock ($10 par)	(700,000)	(300,000)
Paid-In Capital in Excess of Par	(325,000)	
Retained Earnings, Jan. 1, 19X3	(295,000)	(130,000)
Sales.	(1,400,000)	(600,000)
Sales Profit on Leases.	(7,298)	
Interest Income	(12,063)	
Cost of Goods Sold.	780,000	380,000
Interest Expense		12,063
Other Expenses.	510,000	165,000
Dividend Income.	(12,000)	
Dividends Declared	56,000	15,000
Total	0	0

Required:

Prepare the worksheet necessary to produce the consolidated financial statements of Plessor Industries and its subsidiary for the year ended December 31, 19X3. Include the determination and distribution of excess and income distribution schedules.

Problem 5-12. Pantro Inc. purchased an 80% interest in Simpson Company for $480,000 on January 1, 19X1, when Simpson had the following stockholders' equity:

Common stock ($10 par)	$100,000
Additional paid-in capital	300,000
Retained earnings	100,000
Total equity	$500,000

Any excess was attributed to goodwill and given a 40-year life.

The trial balances of Pantro Inc. and Simpson Company were prepared on December 31, 19X5.

	Pantro Inc.	Simpson Cormpany
Cash	91,013	26,050
Inventory	70,000	20,000
Property, Plant, and Equipment	320,000	50,000
Accumulated Depreciation—Property, Plant, and Equipment	(70,000)	(20,000)
Assets under Capital Lease	40,676	
Accumulated Depreciation—Assets under Capital Lease	(10,796)	
Assets under Operating Lease		420,000
Accumulated Depreciation—Assets under Operating Lease		(80,000)
Minimum Lease Payments Receivable		412,000
Unearned Interest Income on Leases		(4,000)
Investment in Simpson Company	480,000	
Accounts Payable	(130,000)	(180,000)
Obligations under Capital Lease	(24,560)	
Interest Payable	(4,440)	
Common Stock ($10 par)	(200,000)	(100,000)
Paid-In Capital in Excess of Par	(300,000)	(300,000)
Retained Earnings, Jan. 1, 19X5	(278,333)	(226,610)
Sales	(300,000)	(130,000)
Rent Income		(34,000)
Interest Income—Capital Lease		(4,440)
Depreciation Expense	41,000	23,000
Interest Expense	4,440	
Selling and General Expense	70,000	38,000
Cost of Goods Sold	190,000	90,000
Rent Expense	11,000	
Total	0	0

The following intercompany leases have been written by Simpson since the acquisition:

1. On January 1, 19X3, Simpson purchased for $140,000 land and a building, which it leased to Pantro Inc. under a 5-year operating lease. Payments of $11,000 per year are required at the beginning of each year. The $120,000 building cost is being depreciated over 20 years on a straight-line basis.

2. On January 1, 19X4, Simpson purchased a machine for $14,000 and leased it to Pantro Inc. The 4-year lease qualifies as a capital lease. The rentals are $5,000 per year, payable at the beginning of each year. There is a bargain purchase option whereby Pantro will purchase the machine at the end of 4 years for $2,000.

    The market value of the machine was $17,560 at the start of the lease term. The lease payments, including the purchase option, yield an implicit rate of 15% to the lessor. Pantro is depreciating the machine over 7 years on a straight-line basis with no salvage value.

3. On January 1, 19X5, Simpson purchased a truck for $23,116 and leased it to Pantro Inc. under a 3-year capital lease. Payments of $8,000 per year are

(continued)

required at the beginning of each year. There is a bargain purchase agreement for $5,000. Pantro Inc. is depreciating the truck over 4 years, straight-line with no salvage value. The lease has a lessor implicit rate of 20%.

4. Pantro Inc. has accrued interest in 19X5 on its capital lease obligations. Simpson has recognized earned interest for the year on its capital leases.

Required:

Prepare the worksheet necessary to produce the consolidated financial statements of Pantro Inc. and its subsidiary for the year ended December 31, 19X5. Include the determination and distribution of excess and income distribution schedules.

Appendix Problems

Problem 5A-1.   Steven Truck Company has been an 80%-owned subsidiary of Paulz Heavy Equipment since January 1, 19X3, when Paulz purchased 128,000 shares of Steven common stock for $832,000, an amount equal to the book value of Steven's net assets at that date. Steven's net income and dividends paid since acquisition are as follows:

Year	Net Income	Dividends
19X3	$70,000	$25,000
19X4	75,600	25,000
19X5	81,650	30,000

On January 1, 19X5, Paulz leased a truck from Steven. The 3-year financing-type lease provides for payments of $10,000 each January 1. On January 1, 19X5, the present value of the truck at Steven's 8% implicit rate, including the unguaranteed residual value of $6,000 at the end of the third year, was $32,596. Paulz also has used the 8% implicit rate to record the lease. The truck is being depreciated on a straight-line basis.

On January 1, 19X6, Steven signed a 4-year financing-type lease with Paulz for the rental of specialized production machinery with an 8-year life. There is a $7,000 purchase option at the end of the fourth year. The lease agreement requires lease payments of $30,000 each January 1 plus $1,500 for maintenance of the equipment. It also calls for contingent payments equal to 10% of Steven's cost savings through the use of this equipment, as reflected in any increase in net income (excluding gains or losses on sale of assets) above the previous growth rate of Steven's net income. The present value of the equipment on January 1, 19X6, at Paulz's 10% implicit rate was $109,388.

On October 1, 19X6, Steven sold Paulz a warehouse having a 20-year remaining life, a book value of $135,000, and an estimated salvage value of $20,000. Paulz paid $195,000 for the building, which is being depreciated on a straight-line basis.

The trial balances were prepared by the separate companies on December 31, 19X6.

	Paulz Heavy Equipment	Steven Truck Company
Cash.	90,485	123,307
Accounts Receivable (net)	228,000	120,000
Inventory	200,000	140,000
Minimum Lease Payments Receivable	97,000	10,000
Unguaranteed Residual Value		6,000
Unearned Interest Income	(9,673)	(444)
Assets Under Capital Lease.	27,833	109,388
Accumulated Depreciation—Assets Under		
Capital Lease	(18,556)	(13,674)
Property, Plant, and Equipment	2,075,000	1,145,000
Accumulated Depreciation—Property, Plant,		
and Equipment	(713,000)	(160,000)
Investment in Steven Truck Company.	1,045,800	
Accounts Payable	(100,000)	(85,000)
Interest Payable.	(740)	(7,939)
Obligations Under Capital Lease	(9,260)	(79,388)
Common Stock ($5 par)	(1,800,000)	(800,000)
Retained Earnings, Jan. 1, 19X6	(864,834)	(387,250)
Sales.	(3,200,000)	(1,400,000)
Gain on Sale of Assets.		(60,000)
Interest Income	(7,939)	(1,152)
Rent Income	(2,182)	
Cost of Goods Sold	1,882,000	770,000
Interest Expense	740	7,939
Depreciation Expense.	135,000	45,000
Other Expenses.	924,326	483,213
Subsidiary Income.	(124,000)	
Dividends Declared	144,000	35,000
Total	0	0

Required:

Prepare the worksheet necessary to produce the consolidated financial statements of Paulz Heavy Equipment and its subsidiary for the year ended December 31, 19X6. Include income distribution schedules.

Problem 5A-2. Penn Company leased a production machine to its 80%-owned subsidiary, Smith Company. The lease agreement, dated January 1, 19X1, requires Smith to pay $18,000 each January 1 for three years. There is an unguaranteed residual value of $5,000. The machine cost $50,098. The present value of the machine at Penn's 16% implicit interest rate was $50,098 on January 1, 19X1. Smith also uses the 16% lessor implicit rate to record the lease. The machine is being depreciated over 3 years on a straight-line basis with a $5,000 salvage value. Lease payment amortization schedules are as follows:

(continued)

Penn (16%)

Date	Payment	Interest at 16% on Previous Balance	Reduction of Principal	Principal Balance
Jan. 1, 19X1				$50,098
Jan. 1, 19X1	$18,000		$18,000	32,098
Jan. 1, 19X2	18,000	$5,136	12,864	19,234
Jan. 1, 19X3	18,000	3,078	14,922	4,312
Jan. 1, 19X4	5,000	688	4,312	
Total	$59,000	$8,902	$50,098	

Smith (16%)

Date	Payment	Interest at 16% on Previous Balance	Reduction of Principal	Principal Balance
Jan. 1, 19X1				$46,894
Jan. 1, 19X1	$18,000		$18,000	28,894
Jan. 1, 19X2	18,000	$4,623	13,377	15,517
Jan. 1, 19X3	18,000	2,483	15,517	
Total	$54,000	$7,106	$46,894	

Required:

1. Prepare the eliminations and adjustments required for this lease on the December 31, 19X1 consolidated worksheet.
2. Prepare the eliminations and adjustments for the December 31, 19X2 consolidated worksheet.

Case 1

Methods of Eliminating Subsidiary Debt

Power Pro Inc. is a large manufacturer of marine engines. In recent years, Power Pro, like other engine manufacturers, has purchased independent boat builders. The intent of the acquisitions is to control the engine choice of the boat builder. By including the outboard engine in the boat package, it is not necessary to sell to and finance many small dealers.

Power Pro purchased Swift-Craft during the last year. Swift-Crafts are built in California and are sold only in western states. Power Pro wants to build the boats in the Midwest as well, so as to expand sales without paying major shipping costs from the West. A new plant will cost $1,000,000 to build and another $1,500,000 to equip for production.

Currently, Swift-Craft has $800,000 in long-term debt. It has 11% annual interest bonds outstanding in the hands of local investors. Current investors have no interest in lending any more funds. The interest rate Swift-Craft pays is high due to its size and credit rating.

Power Pro has ready access to the bond market and borrows at 7.5% annual interest. Power Pro also has expertise in constructing and equipping new facilities since it has built many new plants. Power Pro also has a sophisticated fixed asset accounting system. Power Pro would prefer to build the new plant and turn it over to Swift-Craft when it is complete. It is considering either selling the building to Swift-Craft and taking back the mortgage or leasing the asset to Swift-Craft under a long-term capital lease.

Power Pro would like you to cover the options it has in using its borrowing ability and asset management experience in assisting Swift-Craft. There is a concern as to existing debt and with respect to funds needed to finance the new plant. Your discussion should consider the impact of alternatives on the consolidation process and on minority shareholders.

Case 2   Impact of Alternative Methods to Retire Subsidiary Debt

Magna Company is the parent company which owns an 80% interest in Metros Company. The interest was purchased at book value, and the simple equity method is used to record the ownership interest. The trial balances of the two companies on December 31, 19X6, are as follows:

	Magna	Metros
Cash.	258,000	100,000
Other current assets.	50,000	200,000
Investment in Metros	316,000	
Plant and equipment	800,000	500,000
Accumulated depreciation.	(300,000)	(200,000)
Current liabilities.	(40,000)	(5,000)
Bonds payable		(200,000)
Common stock, par.	(300,000)	(100,000)
Retained earnings.	(746,000)	(285,000)
Sales.	(150,000)	(170,000)
Cost of goods sold	90,000	130,000
Expenses	30,000	10,000
Interest expense		20,000
Subsidiary income.	(8,000)	
Total	0	0

As of December 31, 19X6, the Magna Company was considering acquiring the $200,000 of Metros' 10% bonds from the current owner. Based on a 12% current interest rate for bonds of this risk, the purchase price of the bonds would be $185,000. There are two possible options:

1. Magna could lend $185,000 to Metros at 8% annual interest. Metros would then use the funds to retire the bonds.
2. Magna could buy the bonds and hold them as an investment and enjoy the high interest rate.

Required:

1. Prepare a pro forma consolidated income statement and balance sheet for 19X6 assuming option 1 is used.
2. Indicate how your solution to Required (1) would change if the second option were used.

Case 3

Alternative Ways to Transfer Asset to Subsidiary

Pannier Company is the parent company which owns an 80% interest in Jodestar Company. The interest was purchased at book value, and the simple equity method is used to record the ownership interest. The trial balances of the two companies on December 31, 19X6, are as follows:

	Pannier	Jodestar
Cash.	258,000	100,000
Inventory	150,000	40,000
Other current assets.	50,000	160,000
Investment in Metros	316,000	
Plant and equipment	650,000	500,000
Accumulated depreciation.	(300,000)	(200,000)
Current liabilities.	(40,000)	(5,000)
Long-term debt		(200,000)
Common stock, par.	(300,000)	(100,000)
Retained earnings	(746,000)	(285,000)
Sales.	(150,000)	(170,000)
Cost of goods sold	90,000	130,000
Expenses	30,000	10,000
Interest expense		20,000
Subsidiary income.	(8,000)	
Total	0	0

As the year ended, Pannier was planning to transfer a major piece of equipment to Jodestar. The equipment was just purchased by Pannier and is included in its inventory account. The equipment cost Pannier $100,000 and would be transferred to Jodestar for $125,000. There are two options:

1. Sell the equipment to Jodestar for $125,000 and finance it with a 5-year 10% interest installment note.
2. Lease the equipment to Jodestar on a 5-year lease requiring payments of $29,977 in advance.

Required:

1. Make the journal entries for both companies if the intercompany sale was consummated on December 31.
2. Prepare a consolidated income statement and balance sheet for the company for 19X6.
3. Make the journal entries for both companies if the intercompany lease was executed on December 31.
4. If the lease were used, how would the consolidated statements differ from those in Required (2)?

Worksheet 5-1

Intercompany Investment in Bonds, Year of Acquisition; Straight-Line Method of Amortization
Company P and Subsidiary Company S
Worksheet for Consolidated Balance Sheet
For Year Ended December 31, 19X3

	(Credit balance amounts are in parentheses.)	Trial Balance	
		Company P	Company S
1	Other Assets	56,400	220,000
2	**Interest Receivable**	**8,000**	
3	Investment in Company S Stock (90%)	100,800	
4			
5	**Investment in Company S Bonds (100%)**	**102,400**	
6	**Interest Payable**		**(8,000)**
7	**Bonds Payable, 8%**		**(100,000)**
8	Common Stock ($10 par), Co. P	(100,000)	
9	Retained Earnings, Jan. 1, 19X3, Co. P	(120,000)	
10	Common Stock ($10 par), Co. S		(80,000)
11	Retained Earnings, Jan. 1, 19X3, Co. S		(20,000)
12	Operating Revenue	(100,000)	(80,000)
13	Operating Expense	70,000	60,000
14	**Interest Income**	**(6,800)**	
15	**Interest Expense**		**8,000**
16	Subsidiary Income	(10,800)	
17	**Extraordinary Loss on Bond Retirement**		
18		0	
19	Combined Net Income		
20	To Minority Interest (see distribution schedule)		
21	Balance to Controlling Interest (see distribution schedule)		
22	Total Minority Interest		
23	Retained Earnings, Controlling Interest, Dec. 31, 19X3		
24			

Eliminations and Adjustments:

(1) Eliminate the entry recording the parent's share of subsidiary net income for the current year. This entry returns the investment in Company S stock account to its January 1, 19X3 balance to aid the elimination process.

(2) Eliminate 90% of the subsidiary equity balances of January 1, 19X3, against the investment in stock account. No excess results.

(3) Eliminate intercompany interest revenue and expense. Eliminate the balance of the investment in bonds against the bonds payable. Note that the investment in bonds is at its end-of-the-year amortized balance. The loss on retirement at the date the bonds were purchased is calculated as follows:

Worksheet 5-1 (see page 5-3)

Eliminations & Adjustments		Consolidated Income Statement	Minority Interest	Controlling Retained Earnings	Consolidated Balance Sheet	
Dr.	Cr.					
					276,400	1
	(4) 8,000					2
	(1) 10,800					3
	(2) 90,000					4
	(3) 102,400					5
(4) 8,000						6
(3) 100,000						7
					(100,000)	8
				(120,000)		9
(2) 72,000			(8,000)			10
(2) 18,000			(2,000)			11
		(180,000)				12
		130,000				13
(3) 6,800						14
	(3) 8,000					15
(1) 10,800						16
(3) 3,600		3,600				17
219,200	219,200					18
		(46,400)				19
		960	(960)			20
		45,440		(45,440)		21
			(10,960)		(10,960)	22
				(165,440)	(165,440)	23
					0	24

Loss remaining at year-end:
Investment in bonds at Dec. 31, 19X3 . . . . $102,400
Carrying value of bonds at Dec. 31, 19X3 . . . .   100,000 $2,400

Loss amortized during year:
Interest expense eliminated   8,000
Interest revenue eliminated   6,800   1,200

Loss at Jan. 2, 19X3 . . . . $3,600

(4) Eliminate intercompany interest payable and receivable.

(continued)

Subsidiary Company S Income Distribution

Extraordinary loss on bond retirement . . . . **(3)** **$3,600**	Internally generated net income, **including interest expense** **$12,000**
	Interest adjustment
	($3,600 ÷ 3) . . . . **(3)** 1,200
	Adjusted income . . . . $ 9,600
	Minority share 10%
	Minority interest . . . . $ 960

Parent Company P Income Distribution

Internally generated net income, **including interest revenue**	**$ 36,800**
90% × Company S adjusted income of $9,600	8,640
Controlling interest	$ 45,440

Worksheet 5-2

Intercompany Investment in Bonds, Year Subsequent to Acquisition; Straight-Line Method of Amortization
Company P and Subsidiary Company S
Worksheet for Consolidated Financial Statements
For Year Ended December 31, 19X3

	(Credit balance amounts are in parentheses.)	Trial Balance	
		Company P	Company S
1	Other Assets	94,400	242,000
2	Interest Receivable	8,000	
3	Investment in Company S Stock (90%)	120,600	
4			
5	**Investment in Company S Bonds (100%)**	**101,200**	
6	Interest Payable		(8,000)
7	Bonds Payable, 8%		(100,000)
8	Common Stock ($10 par), Co. P	(100,000)	
9	**Retained Earnings, Jan. 1, 19X4, Co. P**	**(167,600)**	
10	Common Stock ($10 par), Co. S		(80,000)
11	**Retained Earnings, Jan. 1, 19X3, Co. S**		**(32,000)**
12			
13	Operating Revenue	(130,000)	(100,000)
14	Operating Expense	100,000	70,000
15	Subsidiary Income	(19,800)	
16	Interest Expense		8,000
17	Interest Income	(6,800)	
18		0	0
19	Combined Net Income		
20	To Minority Interest (see distribution schedule)		
21	Balance to Controlling Interest (see distribution schedule)		
22	Total Minority Interest		
23	Retained Earnings, Controlling Interest, Dec. 31, 19X4		
24			

Eliminations and Adjustments:

(1) Eliminate the entry recording the parent's share of subsidiary net income for the current year.

(2) Eliminate the pro rata share of subsidiary equity balances against the investment in stock account. There is no excess to be distributed.

(3) Eliminate intercompany interest revenue and expense. Eliminate the balance of the investment in bonds against the bonds payable. Note that the investment in bonds is at its end-of-the-year amortized balance. The remaining unamortized loss on retirement at the start of the year is calculated as follows:

Worksheet 5-2 (see page 5-4)

| Eliminations & Adjustments | | Consolidated Income Statement | Minority Interest | Controlling Retained Earnings | Consolidated Balance Sheet | |
Dr.	Cr.					
					336,400	1
	(4) 8,000					2
	(1) 19,800					3
	(2) 100,800					4
	(3) **102,200**					5
(4) 8,000						6
(3) 100,000						7
					(100,000)	8
(3) 2,160				(165,440)		9
(2) 72,000			(8,000)			10
(2) 28,800			(2,960)			11
(3) 240						12
		(230,000)				13
		170,000				14
(1) 19,800						15
	(3) 8,000					16
(3) 6,800						17
237,800	237,800					18
		(60,000)				19
		2,320	(2,320)			20
		57,680		(57,680)		21
			(13,280)		(13,280)	22
				(223,120)	(223,120)	23
					0	24

Loss remaining at year-end:
Investment in bonds at Dec. 31, 19X4 . . . . $101,200
Carrying value of bonds at Dec. 31, 19X4 . . . . 100,000 $1,200

Loss amortized during year:
Interest expense eliminated 8,000
Interest revenue eliminated 6,800   1,200
Remaining loss at Jan. 1, 19X4 . . . . $2,400

The remaining unamortized loss of $2,400 on January 1, 19X4, is allocated 90% to the controlling retained earnings and 10% to the minority earnings since the bonds were issued by the subsidiary.
(4) Eliminate intercompany interest payable and receivable.

(continued)

Subsidiary Company S Income Distribution

Internally generated net income, including interest expense	$22,000
Interest adjustment ($3,600 ÷ 3) . . . . **(3)**	1,200
Adjusted income	$23,200
Minority share	10%
Minority interest	$ 2,320

Parent Company P Income Distribution

Internally generated net income, including interest revenue.	$36,800
90% × Company S adjusted income of $23,200	20,880
Controlling interest	$57,680

Worksheet 5-3

Intercompany Bonds, Subsequent Period; Straight-Line Method of Amortization
Company P and Subsidiary Company S
Worksheet for Consolidated Financial Statements
For Year Ended December 31, 19X4

	(Credit balance amounts are in parentheses.)	Trial Balance	
		Company P	Company S
1	Other Assets	59,400	259,082
2	Investment in Company S Stock	143,874	
3			
4	Investment in Company S Bonds	101,800	
5	Bonds Payable		(100,000)
6	**Discount on Bonds**		**778**
7	Common Stock, Co. P	(100,000)	
8	**Retained Earnings, Jan. 1, 19X4, Co. P**	**(160,000)**	
9	Common Stock, Co. S		(40,000)
10	**Retained Earnings, Jan. 1, 19X4, Co. S**		**(110,000)**
11			
12	Sales	(80,000)	(50,000)
13	**Interest Income**	**(6,200)**	
14	Cost of Goods Sold	50,000	31,362
15	**Interest Expense**		**8,778**
16	Subsidiary Income	(8,874)	
17		0	0
18	Combined Net Income		
19	To Minority Interest (see distribution schedule)		
20	Balance to Controlling Interest (see distribution schedule)		
21	Total Minority Interest		
22	Retained Earnings, Controlling Interest, Dec. 31, 19X4		
23			

Eliminations and Adjustments:

(1) Eliminate the entry recording the parent's share of subsidiary net income for the current year.

(2) Eliminate 90% of the January 1, 19X4 subsidiary equity balances against the January 1, 19X4 investment in Company S stock balance. No excess results.

(3) Eliminate intercompany interest revenue and expense. Eliminate the balance of the investment in bonds against the bonds payable. Note that the investment in bonds and the discount on bonds are at their end-of-the-year amortized balances. The remaining unamortized loss on retirement at the start of the year is calculated as follows:

Worksheet 5-3 (see page 5-5)

Eliminations & Adjustments		Consolidated Income Statement	Minority Interest	Controlling Retained Earnings	Consolidated Balance Sheet	
Dr.	Cr.					
					318,482	1
	(1) 8,874					2
	(2) 135,000					3
	(3) 101,800					4
(3) 100,000						5
	(3) 778					6
					(100,000)	7
(3) 4,640				(155,360)		8
(2) 36,000			(4,000)			9
(2) 99,000			(10,484)			10
(3) 516						11
		(130,000)				12
(3) 6,200						13
		81,362				14
	(3) 8,778					15
(1) 8,874						16
255.230	255,230					17
		(48,638)				18
		1,244	(1,244)			19
		47,394		(47,394)		20
			(15,728)		(15,728)	21
				(202,754)	(202,754)	22
					0	23

Loss remaining at year-end:

Investment in bonds at Dec. 31, 19X4	$101,800	
Bonds payable at Dec. 31, 19X4	100,000	
Discount on bonds at Dec. 31, 19X4	(778)	$2,578

Loss amortized during year:

Interest expense eliminated	8,778	
Interest revenue eliminated	6,200	2,578
Remaining loss at Jan. 1, 19X4		$5,156

Since from the consolidated viewpoint the bonds were retired in the prior year and since the bonds were issued by the subsidiary, the remaining unamortized loss of $5,156 on January 1, 19X4, is allocated 90% to the controlling retained earnings and 10% to the minority retained earnings.

(continued)

Subsidiary Company S Income Distribution

Internally generated net income, including interest expense	$ 9,860
Interest adjustment ($8,778 – $6,200). . . . . (3)	**2,578**
Adjusted income	$12,438
Minority share	10%
Minority interest	$ 1,244

Parent Company P Income Distribution

Internally generated net income, including interest revenue.	$36,200
90% × Company S adjusted income of $12,438	11,194
Controlling interest	$47,394

Worksheet 5-4

Intercompany Bonds; Interest Method of Amortization
Company P and Subsidiary Company S
Worksheet for Consolidated Financial Statements
For Year Ended December 31, 19X4

	(Credit balance amounts are in parentheses.)	Trial Balance	
		Company P	Company S
1	Other Assets	59,333	259,082
2	Investment in Company S Stock	144,000	
3			
4	**Investment in Company S Bonds**	**101,887**	
5	**Bonds Payable**		**(100,000)**
6	**Discount on Bonds**		**918**
7	Common Stock, Co. P	(100,000)	
8	Retained Earnings, Jan. 1, 19X4, Co. P	(160,180)	
9	Common Stock, Co. S		(40,000)
10	Retained Earnings, Jan. 1, 19X4, Co. S		(110,200)
11			
12	Sales	(80,000)	(50,000)
13	**Interest Income**	**(6,220)**	
14	Cost of Goods Sold	50,000	31,358
15	**Interest Expense**		**8,842**
16			
17	Subsidiary Income	(8,820)	
18		0	0
19	Combined Net Income		
20	To Minority Interest (see distribution schedule)		
21	Balance to Controlling Interest (see distribution schedule)		
22	Total Minority Interest		
23	Retained Earnings, Controlling Interest, Dec. 31, 19X4		
24			

Eliminations and Adjustments:

(1) Eliminate the entry recording the parent's share of subsidiary net income for the current year.

(2) Eliminate 90% of the January 1, 19X4 subsidiary equity balances against the January 1, 19X4 investment in Company S stock balance. No excess results.

(3) Eliminate intercompany interest revenue and expense. Eliminate the balance of the investment in bonds against the bonds payable. Note that the investment in bonds and the discount on bonds are at their end-of-the-year amortized balances. The remaining unamortized loss on retirement at the start of the year is calculated as follows:

Worksheet 5-4 (see page 5-7)

Eliminations & Adjustments			Consolidated Income Statement	Minority Interest	Controlling Retained Earnings	Consolidated Balance Sheet	
Dr.		Cr.					
						318,415	1
	(1)	8,820					2
	(2)	135,180					3
	(3)	101,887					4
(3) 100,000							5
	(3)	918					6
						(100,000)	7
(3) 4,884					(155,296)		8
(2) 36,000				(4,000)			9
(2) 99,180				(10,477)			10
(3) 543							11
			(130,000)				12
(3) 6,220							13
			81,358				14
	(3)	8,842					15
							16
(1) 8,820							17
255,647		255,647					18
			(48,642)				19
			1,242	(1,242)			20
			47,400		(47,400)		21
				(15,719)		(15,719)	22
					(202,696)	(202,696)	23
						0	24

Loss remaining at year-end:

Investment in bonds at Dec. 31, 19X4	$101,887	
Bonds payable at Dec. 31, 19X4	100,000	
Discount on bonds at Dec. 31, 19X4	(918)	$2,805
Loss amortized during year:		
Interest expense eliminated	8,842	
Interest revenue eliminated	6,220	2,622
Remaining loss at Jan. 1, 19X4		$5,427

Since from the consolidated viewpoint the bonds were retired in the prior year and since the bonds were issued by the subsidiary, the remaining unamortized loss of $5,427 on January 1, 19X4, is allocated 90% to the controlling retained earnings and 10% to the minority retained earnings.

(continued)

Subsidiary Company S Income Distribution

Internally generated net income, including interest expense	$ 9,800
Interest adjustment **($8,842 – $6,220). . . . . (3)**	**2,622**
Adjusted income	$12,422
Minority share	10%
Minority interest	$ 1,242

Parent Company P Income Distribution

Internally generated net income, including interest revenue.	$36,220
90% × Company S adjusted income of $12,422	11,180
Controlling interest	$47,400

Worksheet 5-5

Intercompany Capital Lease
Company P and Subsidiary Company S
Worksheet for Consolidated Financial Statements
For Year Ended December 31, 19X1

	(Credit balance amounts are in parentheses.)	Trial Balance	
		Company P	Company S
1	Accounts Receivable	30,149	44,793
2	**Minimum Lease Payments Receivable**	**4,000**	
3	**Unguaranteed Residual Value**	**1,000**	
4	**Unearned Interest Income**	**(533)**	
5	**Assets under Capital Lease**		**5,210**
6	**Accumulated Depreciation—Assets under Capital Lease**		**(1,737)**
7	Property, Plant, and Equipment	200,000	120,000
8	Accumulated Depreciation—Property, Plant, and Equipment	(80,000)	(50,000)
9	Investment in Company S	87,634	
10			
11	Accounts Payable	(21,000)	(5,000)
12	**Obligations under Capital Lease**		**(3,210)**
13	**Interest Payable**		**(514)**
14	Common Stock ($10 par), Co. P	(50,000)	
15	Retained Earnings, Jan. 1, 19X1, Co. S	(120,000)	
16	Common Stock ($5 par), Co. S		(40,000)
17	Retained Earnings, Jan. 1, 19X1, Co. S		(50,000)
18	Sales	(120,000)	(70,000)
19	**Interest Income**	**(616)**	
20	Subsidiary Income	(15,634)	
21	Operating Expense	65,000	38,207
22	**Interest Expense**		**514**
23	Depreciation Expense	20,000	11,737
24		0	0
25	Combined Net Income		
26	To Minority Interest (see distribution schedule)		
27	Balance to Controlling Interest (see distribution schedule)		
28	Total Minority Interest		
29	Retained Earnings, Controlling Interest, Dec. 31, 19X1		
30			

Worksheet 5-5 (see page 5-16)

Eliminations & Adjustments Dr.		Eliminations & Adjustments Cr.		Consolidated Income Statement	Minority Interest	Controlling Retained Earnings	Consolidated Balance Sheet	
							74,942	1
		(4)	4,000					2
		(4)	1,000					3
(4)	635	(3)	102					4
		(4)	5,210					5
(5)	1,737							6
(4)	5,851						325,851	7
		(5)	1,617				(131,617)	8
		(1)	15,634					9
		(2)	72,000					10
							(26,000)	11
(4)	3,210							12
(4)	514							13
							(50,000)	14
						(120,000)		15
(2)	32,000				(8,000)			16
(2)	40,000				(10,000)			17
				(190,000)				18
(3)	616							19
(1)	15,634							20
				103,207				21
		(3)	514					22
		(5)	120	31,617				23
	100,197		100,197					24
				(55,176)				25
				3,908	(3,908)			26
				51,268		(51,268)		27
					(21,908)		(21,908)	28
						(171,268)	(171,268)	29
							0	30

(continued)

Eliminations and Adjustments:

(1) Eliminate the parent company's entry recording its share of Company S net income. This step returns the investment account to its January 1, 19X1 balance to aid the elimination process.

(2) Eliminate 80% of the January 1, 19X1 Company S equity balances against the investment in Company S balance.

(3) Eliminate the interest income recorded by the lessor, $616, and the interest expense recorded by the lessee, $514. The $102 disparity reflects the interest recorded on the unguaranteed residual value. This amount is returned to the unearned interest income.

(4) Eliminate the intercompany debt and the unguaranteed residual value. Eliminate the asset under capital lease and record the owned asset. The amounts are reconciled as follows:

Disparity in recorded debt:

Lessor balance, **$4,000 − $635** unearned interest income	$3,365
Lessee balance, **$3,210 + $514** accrued interest	3,724
Interest applicable to unguaranteed residual value	$ (359)
Unguaranteed residual value	**1,000**
Net original present value of unguaranteed residual value.	$ 641
Asset under capital lease	**5,210**
Owned asset at original cost	$5,851

(5) Reclassify accumulated depreciation and adjust the depreciation expense to acknowledge cost of asset. The adjustment to depreciation expense is determined as follows:

Capitalized cost by lessee		$5,210
Depreciable cost:		
Cost	$5,851	
Less residual (salvage) value	1,000	4,851
Decrease in depreciable cost		$ 359
Adjustment to depreciation expense ($359 ÷ 3-year lease term)		**$ 120**

Subsidiary Company S Income Distribution

	Internally generated net income, **including interest income on lease**.	$19,542
	Adjusted income	$19,542
	Minority share	20%
	Minority interest	$ 3,908

Parent Company P Income Distribution

Interest eliminated. . . . . (3) $102	Internally generated net income, **including interest income on lease**.	$35,616
	80% × Company S adjusted income of $19,542	15,634
	Decrease in depreciation . . . . . . (5)	**120**
	Controlling interest	$51,268

Worksheet 5-6

Intercompany Capital Lease, Subsequent Period
Company P and Subsidiary Company S
Worksheet for Consolidated Financial Statements
For Year Ended December 31, 19X2

	(Credit balance amounts are in parentheses.)	Trial Balance	
		Company P	Company S
1	Accounts Receivable	102,149	82,925
2	**Minimum Lease Payments Receivable**	**2,000**	
3	**Unguaranteed Residual Value**	**1,000**	
4	**Unearned Interest Income**	**(138)**	
5			
6	**Assets under Capital Lease**		**5,210**
7	**Accumulated Depreciation—Assets under Capital Lease**		**(3,474)**
8	Property, Plant, and Equipment	200,000	120,000
9	Accumulated Depreciation—Property, Plant, and Equipment	(100,000)	(60,000)
10	Investment in Company S	102,129	
11			
12	Accounts Payable	(41,000)	(15,000)
13	**Obligations under Capital Lease**		**(1,724)**
14	**Interest Payable**		**(276)**
15	Common Stock ($10 par), Co. P	(50,000)	
16	**Retained Earnings, Jan. 1, 19X2, Co. P**	**(171,250)**	
17	Common Stock ($5 par), Co. S		(40,000)
18	Retained Earnings, Jan. 1, 19X2, Co. S		(69,542)
19	Sales	(150,000)	(80,000)
20	**Interest Income**	**(395)**	
21	Subsidiary Income	(14,495)	
22	Operating Expense	100,000	49,868
23	**Interest Expense**		**276**
24	Depreciation Expense	20,000	11,737
25		0	0
26	Combined Net Income		
27	To Minority Interest (see distribution schedule)		
28	Balance to Controlling Interest (see distribution schedule)		
29	Total Minority Interest		
30	Retained Earnings, Controlling Interest, Dec. 31, 19X2		
31			

Worksheet 5-6 (see page 5-16)

Eliminations & Adjustments				Consolidated Income Statement	Minority Interest	Controlling Retained Earnings	Consolidated Balance Sheet	
Dr.		Cr.						
							185,074	1
		(5)	2,000					2
		(5)	1,000					3
(5)	359	(3)	119					4
		(4)	102					5
		(5)	5,210					6
(6)	3,474							7
(5)	5,851						325,851	8
		(6)	3,234				(163,234)	9
		(1)	14,495					10
		(2)	87,634					11
							(56,000)	12
(5)	1,724							13
(5)	276							14
							(50,000)	15
(4)	102	(6)	120			(171,268)		16
(2)	32,000				(8,000)			17
(2)	55,634				(13,908)			18
				(230,000)				19
(3)	395							20
(1)	14,495							21
				149,868				22
		(3)	276					23
		(6)	120	31,617				24
	114,310		114,310					25
				(48,515)				26
				3,624	(3,624)			27
				44,891		(44,891)		28
					(25,532)		(25,532)	29
						(216,159)	(216,159)	30
							0	31

(continued)

Eliminations and Adjustments:

(1) Eliminate the parent company's entry recording its share of Company S net income.

(2) Eliminate 80% of the January 1, 19X2 Company S equity balances against the investment in Company S balance.

(3) Eliminate the interest income recorded by the lessor, $395, and the interest expense recorded by the lessee, $276. The $119 disparity reflects the interest recorded on the unguaranteed residual value. This amount is returned to the unearned interest income.

(4) Adjust the unearned income and the parent's retained earnings for the $102 interest recorded in 19X1 on the unguaranteed residual value.

(5) Eliminate the intercompany debt and the unguaranteed residual value. Eliminate the asset under capital lease and record the owned asset. The amounts are reconciled as follows:

Disparity in recorded debt:

Lessor balance, **$2,000 – $359** unearned interest income	$1,641
Lessee balance, **$1,724 + $276** accrued interest	2,000
Interest applicable to unguaranteed residual value	$ (359)
Unguaranteed residual value	**1,000**
Net original present value of unguaranteed residual value..................	$ 641
Asset under capital lease...	**5,210**
Owned asset at original cost	$5,851

(6) Reclassify accumulated depreciation. Adjust the depreciation expense for the current year and the controlling retained earnings for the preceding year to acknowledge cost of asset. The adjustment to the depreciation expense and the retained earnings is determined as follows:

Capitalized cost by lessee		$5,210
Depreciable cost:		
Cost	$5,851	
Less residual (salvage) value	1,000	4,851
Decrease in depreciable cost		$ 359
Adjustment to depreciation expense and retained earnings ($359 ÷ 3-year lease term)		**$ 120**

Subsidiary Company S Income Distribution

Internally generated net income, **including interest on lease**....................	$18,119
Adjusted income	$18,119
Minority share...................	20%
Minority interest.................	$ 3,624

Parent Company P Income Distribution

Interest eliminated............. (3)	**$119**	Internally generated net income, **including interest income on lease**....................	$30,395
		80% × Company S adjusted income of $18,119	14,495
		Decrease in depreciation ...... (6)	**120**
		Controlling interest	$44,891

Cash Flow, EPS, Taxation, and Unconsolidated Investments

This chapter contains the remaining consolidation issues that affect the vast majority of consolidated companies and extends consolidation concepts to nonconsolidated investments that are accounted for under the sophisticated equity method.

We begin with the procedures necessary to prepare a consolidated statement of cash flows. Fortunately, this requires only minor changes in the procedures used in your prior accounting courses. Also, only minor adjustments of typical earnings per share procedures are needed for consolidated companies. The final consolidation issue is taxation of the consolidated company. Prior worksheets are now enhanced to include the provision for tax. This is quite simple when the affiliated companies are taxed as a single entity. Procedures are a bit more involved when the individual companies are taxed separately.

This chapter concludes with a discussion of the use of the sophisticated equity method for investments that are not consolidated. These investments require the use of procedures that parallel those used in consolidations. The end result is that the income reported from the investee is the same as if the investee were consolidated and the controlling interest in subsidiary income was calculated.

Consolidated Statement of Cash Flows

FASB Statement of Financial Accounting Standards No. 95 requires that a statement of cash flows accompany a company's published income statement and balance sheet. The process of preparing a consolidated statement of cash flows is similar to that which is used for a single company, a topic covered in depth in intermediate accounting texts. Since the analysis of changes in cash of a consolidated entity begins with consolidated statements, intercompany transactions will have been eliminated and, thus, will not cause any complications. However, because of the parent–subsidiary relationship, there are some situations that require special consideration. These situations are discussed in the following paragraphs.

Cash Acquisition of Controlling Interest

The cash purchase of a controlling interest in a company is considered an *investing activity* and would appear as a cash outflow in the cash flows from investing activities section of the statement of cash flows. It also is necessary to explain the total increase in consolidated assets and the addition of the minority interest to the consolidated balance sheet. This is a result of the requirement that the statement of cash flows disclose investing and *financing activities* that affect the company's financial position even though they do not impact cash.

To illustrate the disclosure required, consider an example of a cash purchase of an 80% interest in a company. Assume Company S had the following balance sheet on January 1, 19X1, when Company P acquired an 80% interest for $540,000 in cash:

Assets		Liabilities and Equity	
Cash and cash equivalents . .	$ 50,000	Long-term liabilities	$150,000
Inventory	60,000	Common stock ($10 par).	200,000
Equipment (net).	190,000	Retained earnings	350,000
Building (net)	400,000		
Total assets.	$700,000	Total liabilities and equity	$700,000

Assume the market values of the equipment and building are $250,000 and $425,000, respectively, and any remaining excess of cost is attributed to goodwill amortized over 20 years. The estimated remaining life of the equipment is 5 years and of the building is 10 years. The following determination and distribution of excess schedule would be prepared:

	Company	Controlling Percent	Controlling Interest		Amortization Periods	Controlling Amortization
Price paid for investment including						
direct acquisition costs:.			$540,000			
Market value of total net assets:.	$635,000	80%	508,000			
Market value of priority accounts:	(40,000)	80	(32,000)			
Analysis of price: **Goodwill**			32,000			
Price paid for investment		$ 540,000				
Less book value interest acquired:						
Common stock ($10 par)	$200,000					
Retained earnings	350,000					
Total stockholders' equity	$550,000					
Interest acquired	80%	440,000				
Excess of cost over book value (debit).		100,000				
Equipment, 80% × $60,000		**48,000**		Dr.	5	9,600
Buildings, 80% × $25,000		**20,000**		Dr.	10	2,000
Goodwill.		**$ 32,000**		Dr.	20	1,600

The effect of the purchase on the balance sheet accounts of the consolidated company for 19X1 would be as follows:

	Debit	Credit
Cash ($540,000 paid − $50,000 subsidiary cash)		490,000
Inventory.	60,000	
Equipment ($190,000 book value + $48,000 excess)	238,000	
Building ($400,000 book value + $20,000 excess)	420,000	
Goodwill.	32,000	
Long-term liabilities		150,000
Minority interest (20% × $550,000 subsidiary equity).		110,000
Total	750,000	750,000

The disclosure of the purchase on the statement of cash flows would be summarized as follows:

Under the heading "Cash flows from investing activities":

> Payment for purchase of Company S, net of
> cash acquired . . . . $(490,000)

In the supplemental schedule of noncash financing and investing activity:

> Company P purchased 80% of the common stock of Company S
> for $540,000. In conjunction with the acquisition, liabilities were
> assumed and a minority interest was created as follows:

Adjusted value of assets acquired ($700,000 book value + $100,000 excess)	$800,000
Cash paid for common stock	540,000
Balance (noncash)	$260,000
Liabilities assumed	$150,000
Minority interest	$110,000

Noncash Acquisition of Controlling Interest

Suppose that instead of paying cash for its controlling interest, Company P issued 10,000 shares of its $10 par stock for the controlling interest. Further assume the shares had a market value of $54 each. Since the acquisition price is the same ($540,000), the determination and distribution of excess schedule would not change. The analysis of balance sheet account changes would be as follows:

	Debit	Credit
Cash ($50,000 subsidiary cash)	50,000	
Inventory	60,000	
Equipment ($190,000 book value + $48,000 excess)	238,000	
Building ($400,000 book value + $20,000 excess)	420,000	
Goodwill	32,000	
Long-term liabilities		150,000
Minority interest (20% × $550,000 subsidiary equity)		110,000
Common stock, $10 par, Company P		100,000
Paid-in capital in excess of par, Company P		440,000
Total	800,000	800,000

The disclosure of the purchase on the statement of cash flows would be summarized as follows:

Under the heading "Cash flows from investing activities":

> Cash acquired in purchase of Company S . . . $50,000

In the supplemental schedule of noncash financing and investing activity:

> Company P acquired 80% of the common stock of Company S in
> exchange for 10,000 shares of Company P common stock valued
> at $540,000. In conjunction with the acquisition, liabilities were
> assumed and a minority interest was created as follows:

Adjusted value of assets acquired ($700,000 book value + $100,000 excess)	$800,000
Common stock issued	$540,000
Liabilities assumed	$150,000
Minority interest	$110,000

When an acquisition qualifies as a pooling of interests, all prior financial statements are consolidated retroactively which requires that cash flow analyses proceed from a comparison of the consolidated balance sheets of the current and previous periods. Due to the retroactive application of the pooling of interests, there will be no difference between the comparative statements as a result of the pooling. The impact of the pooling on the consolidated stockholders' equity is disclosed in the period the pooling is consummated.

Adjustments Resulting from Business Combinations

A business combination will have ramifications on the statements of cash flows prepared in subsequent periods. A purchase may create amortizations of excess deductions (noncash items) which need to be adjusted. In addition, there may be impact resulting from additional purchases of subsidiary shares and/or dividend payments by the subsidiary. Intercompany bonds and nonconsolidated investments also need to be considered for their impact.

Amortization of Excesses.   Income statements prepared for periods including or following a purchase of another company will include the amortization of the excesses that are shown on the determination and distribution of excess schedule as well as book value depreciation and amortization recorded by both the parent and subsidiary. These amortizations of the excesses, while reflected in consolidated net income, do not require the use of cash; thus, under the indirect method, they must be included as an adjustment to consolidated net income to arrive at cash flows from operating activities. Using the facts of the preceding examples, the following adjustments would appear on the cash flows statement for 19X1:

Cash from operating activities:	
Consolidated net income	$XXX,XXX
Add amortizations resulting from business combination:	
Depreciation on equipment ($48,000 ÷ 5)	9,600
Depreciation on building ($20,000 ÷ 10)	2,000
Goodwill amortization ($32,000 ÷ 20)	1,600

In addition, cash from operating activities would be adjusted for depreciation and amortizations of book value recorded by the constituent companies on their separate books.

Purchase of Additional Subsidiary Shares.   The purchase of additional shares directly from the subsidiary results in no added cash flowing into the consolidated company. The transfer of cash within the consolidated company would not appear in the consolidated statement of cash flows. However, the purchase of additional shares from the minority interest does result in an outflow of cash. From a consolidated viewpoint, it is the equivalent of purchasing treasury shares. Thus, it would be listed under *financing activities*.

Subsidiary Dividends.   Dividends paid by the subsidiary to the parent are a transfer of cash within the consolidated entity and, thus, would not appear in the consolidated statement of cash flows. However, dividends paid by the subsidiary to minority shareholders represent a flow of cash to parties outside the consolidated group and would appear as an outflow under the cash flows from financing activities heading of the consolidated statement of cash flows.

Purchase of Intercompany Bonds.   The purchase of intercompany bonds from parties outside the consolidated company effects a cash flow from one member of the consolidated group to parties outside the consolidated entity. Recall that the purchase of intercompany bonds is viewed as a retirement of the bonds on the consolidated worksheet. The consolidated statement of cash flows also treats the purchase of the bonds as a retirement of the consolidated company's debt and includes the cash outflow under cash flows from financing activities. Since the process of constructing a cash flows statement starts with the consolidated income statement and balance sheet, intercompany interest payments and amortizations of premiums and/or discounts already are eliminated and will not enter into the analysis of consolidated cash flows. Only cash interest payments to bondholders outside the consolidated entity are important to the analysis and should be included in cash flows from *operating* activities.

Nonconsolidated Investments.   Investments in the stock of companies not included in the consolidated group result in income to the consolidated entity. Where the investment is accounted for under the cost method, cash dividends received are included in cash flows from operating activities. However, where the equity method is applied, only that portion of the income received in cash may be included in cash from operating activities. For example, the investee may report income of $50,000 and pay dividends of $10,000. Assume further that the consolidated company paid $20,000 more than book value for its 30% interest and regards the excess as attributable to goodwill with a 40-year life. Investment income under the equity method would be calculated as follows:

30% of reported income of $50,000	$15,000
Less amortization of excess cost ($20,000 ÷ 40)	500
Equity income	$14,500

Only $3,000 (30% × $10,000) was received in the form of cash dividends; thus, the $14,500 of income would be reduced to only $3,000 of cash from operating activities. The $11,500 of undistributed income would be adjusted out of net income to arrive at cash from operating activities.

Preparation of Consolidated Statement of Cash Flows

A complete example of the process of preparing a consolidated statement of cash flows is presented in this section. Assume Company P originally purchased an 80% interest in Company S on January 1, 19X1. In addition, Company P purchased a 20% interest in Company E on January 2, 19X2, and accounted for the investment under the sophisticated equity method. The following determination and distribution of excess schedules were prepared for each investment:

Price paid for investment		$365,000
Less book value interest acquired:		
Common stock ($10 par	$ 50,000	
Paid-in capital in excess of par	150,000	
Retained earnings	100,000	
Total stockholders' equity	$300,000	
Interest acquired	80%	240,000

			Amortization Periods	Controlling Amortization
Excess of cost over book value (debit)	125,000			
Equipment, 80% × $31,250.	**25,000**	**Dr.**	**5**	**5,000**
Goodwill	**$100,000**	**Dr.**	**10**	**10,000**

For the January 2, 19X2, 20% investment in nonconsolidated Company E:

Price paid		$255,000
Less interest acquired:		
Common stock	$ 500,000	
Retained earnings	750,000	
Total equity	$1,250,000	
Interest acquired	20%	250,000
Goodwill (10-year life)		$ 5,000

Since this investment is not consolidated, there will be no recording of the goodwill. This information is used only to amortize the excess cost in future income statements. Because of this, there are no debits or credits accompanying the distribution of the excess. The following consolidated statements were prepared for Company P and its subsidiary, Company S, for 19X3:

Company P and Subsidiary Company S
Consolidated Income Statement
For Year Ended December 31, 19X3

Sales		$900,000
Less cost of goods sold		525,000
Gross profit		$375,000
Less expenses:		
General and administrative	$150,500	
Depreciation	**70,000**[a]	
Goodwill amortization	**10,000**[b]	**230,500**
Operating income		$144,500
Investment income (equity method)		**15,500**[c]
Combined net income of Companies P and S		$160,000
Less minority interest		11,200
Consolidated net income		$148,800

[a] Includes $5,000 of depreciation resulting from the excess of the subsidiary equipment's market value over book value on January 1, 19X1, the date on which the 80% interest was acquired.
[b] Consists of the $10,000 goodwill amortization on the 80% interest acquired January 1, 19X1.
[c] 20% of Company E net income of $80,000 less $500 amortization of goodwill. (Dividends received were $2,000.)

Company P and Subsidiary Company S
Consolidated Retained Earnings Statement
For Year Ended December 31, 19X3

	Minority	Controlling
Retained earnings, January 1, 19X3.	$32,000*	$420,000
Add distribution of combined net income.	11,200	148,800
Less dividends declared	(4,000)	(50,000)
Balance, December 31, 19X3.	$39,200	$518,800

* The retained earnings balance for Company S on January 1, 19X3, was $160,000; $32,000 represents the minority's 20% remaining interest.

Company P and Subsidiary Company S
Consolidated Balance Sheet
December 31, 19X2 and 19X3

Assets	19X3	19X2
Cash and cash equivalents	$ 179,000	$ 160,000
Inventory	210,000	180,000
Accounts receivable.	154,000	120,000
Property, plant, and equipment	1,330,000	1,250,000
Accumulated depreciation	(370,000)	(300,000)
Goodwill	70,000	80,000
Investment in Company E (20%)	333,500	320,000
Total assets.	$1,906,500	$1,810,000

Liabilities and Stockholders' Equity		
Accounts payable	$ 156,500	$ 166,000
Bonds payable	300,000	300,000
Minority interest	79,200	72,000
Controlling interest:		
Common stock, par	200,000	200,000
Paid-in capital in excess of par	652,000	652,000
Retained earnings	518,800	420,000
Total liabilities and stockholders' equity.	$1,906,500	$1,810,000

The following additional facts are available to aid in the preparation of a consolidated statement of cash flows:

1. Company P purchased a new piece of equipment during 19X3 for $80,000.
2. In 19X3, Company P declared and paid $50,000 in dividends and Company S declared and paid $20,000 in dividends.

Illustration 6-1 is a worksheet approach to calculating a statement of cash flows under the *indirect method.* Explanations 1 through 8 use changes in balance sheet accounts to analyze cash from operations. This information is taken from the income statement and is implied from changes in current assets and current liabilities. Explanation 9 reflects the only investing activity in this example. Explanations 10 and 11 show the financing activities. The worksheet provides the information needed to develop the statement of cash flows located on page 6-9.

If the *direct method* of disclosing cash from operating activities is used, the cash flows from operating activities section of the statement of cash flows would be prepared as follows:

Cash flows from operating activities:

Cash from customers ($900,000 sales – $34,000 increase in accounts receivable)	$866,000
Cash from investments (dividends received)	2,000
Cash to suppliers ($525,000 cost of goods sold + $30,000 inventory increase + $9,500 decrease in accounts payable)	(564,500)
Cash for general and administrative expenses	(150,500)
Net cash provided by operating activities	$153,000

Illustration 6-1
Company P and Subsidiary Company S
Worksheet for Analysis of Cash: Indirect Approach
For Year Ended December 31, 19X3

	Account Change			Explanations			
	Debit	Credit		Debit		Credit	Balance
Inventory	30,000		(6)	30,000			0
Accounts receivable	34,000		(5)	34,000			0
Property, plant, and equipment	80,000		(9)	80,000			0
Accumulated depreciation		70,000			(3)	70,000	0
Goodwill		10,000			(4)	10,000	0
Investment in Company E (20%)	13,500		(8)	13,500			0
Accounts payable	9,500		(7)	9,500			0
Bonds payable							0
Minority interest		7,200	(11)	4,000	(2)	11,200	0
Controlling interest:							
Common stock, par							0
Paid-in excess of par							0
Retained earnings		98,800	(10)	50,000	(1)	148,800	0
	167,000	186,000		221,000		240,000	
Net change in cash	19,000	0		19,000		0	
Cash from Operations:							
Consolidated net income			(1)	148,800			
Minority interest in net income			(2)	11,200			
Depreciation expense			(3)	70,000			
Amortization of goodwill			(4)	10,000			
Increase in accounts receivable					(5)	34,000	
Increase in inventory					(6)	30,000	
Decrease in accounts payable					(7)	9,500	
Equity income in excess of dividends					(8)	13,500	
Net cash provided by operating activities				153,000			
Cash from Investing:							
Purchase of equipment					(9)	80,000	
Net cash used in investing activities						80,000	
Cash from Financing:							
Dividend payment to controlling interest					(10)	50,000	
Dividend payment to minority interest					(11)	4,000	
Net cash used in investing activities						54,000	
Net cash provided				19,000			

> ### Company P and Subsidiary Company S
> ### Consolidated Statement of Cash Flows
> ### For Year Ended December 31, 19X3
>
> | | | |
> |---|---:|---:|
> | Cash flows from operating activities: | | |
> | Consolidated net income. . . . . | | $148,800 |
> | Adjustments to reconcile net income to net cash: | | |
> | Minority interest in combined net income . . . . | $11,200 | |
> | Depreciation expense . . . . | 70,000 | |
> | Amortization of goodwill . . . . | 10,000 | |
> | Increase in accounts receivable. . . . . | (34,000) | |
> | Increase in inventory. . . . . | (30,000) | |
> | Decrease in accounts payable . . . . | (9,500) | |
> | Equity income from Company E in excess of | | |
> | dividends received . . . . | (13,500) | |
> | Total adjustments . . . . | | 4,200 |
> | Net cash provided by operating activities. . . . . | | $153,000 |
> | Cash flows from investing activities: | | |
> | Purchase of equipment . . . . | | (80,000) |
> | Cash flows from financing activities: | | |
> | Dividend payments to controlling interests. . . . . | (50,000) | |
> | Dividend payments to minority interest . . . . | (4,000) | |
> | Net cash used in financing activities . . . . | | (54,000) |
> | Net increase in cash and cash equivalents . . . . | | $ 19,000 |
> | Cash and cash equivalents at beginning of year . . . . | | 160,000 |
> | Cash and cash equivalents at year-end . . . . | | $179,000 |

Consolidated Earnings Per Share

The computation of consolidated earnings per share (EPS) remains virtually the same as that for single entities (see Chapter 13). For the purpose of this discussion, all calculations will be made only on an annual basis. **Basic Earnings Per Share (BEPS) is calculated by dividing only the controlling interest in consolidated net income by parent company outstanding stock.** The calculation of Diluted Earnings Per Share (DEPS) is not complicated when applied to the consolidated company, provided that the subsidiary company has no dilutive securities. As long as no such securities exist, consolidated net income (the controlling interest's share of combined net income) is divided by the number of outstanding parent company shares. The numerator and denominator adjustments caused by parent company dilutive securities can be considered in the normal manner.

When the subsidiary has dilutive securities, the calculation of consolidated DEPS becomes a two-stage process. First, the DEPS of the subsidiary must be calculated. Then, the consolidated DEPS is calculated using as a component of the calculation the adjusted DEPS of the subsidiary. This two-stage process handles subsidiary dilutive securities which require the possible issuance of subsidiary company shares. A further complication occurs when the subsidiary has outstanding dilutive options, warrants, and/or convertible securities which may require the issuance of parent company shares.

First consider the calculation of consolidated DEPS when the subsidiary has outstanding dilutive securities which may require the issuance of subsidiary company shares only. The EPS model for a single entity is modified in two ways:

1. Only the parent's adjusted internally generated net income, the parent's income adjusters, and the parent's share adjusters enter the formula directly.
2. The parent's share of subsidiary's income is entered indirectly by multiplying the number of equivalent subsidiary shares owned by the parent times the subsidiary DEPS.

The basic model by which to compute consolidated EPS in this situation is as follows:

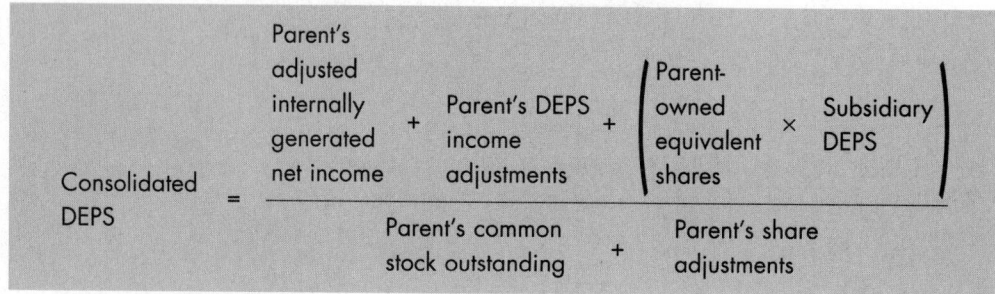

The parent's adjusted internally generated net income includes adjustments for unrealized profits recorded during the current period and for realization of profits deferred from previous periods. It is also adjusted for the amortizations of excess resulting from the original purchase of the subsidiary. **This would be all of the adjustments that appear on the parent's income distribution schedule, except for the inclusion of the parent's share of subsidiary income.** Likewise, the income used to compute the subsidiary DEPS must be adjusted for intercompany transactions (as shown in the subsidiary income distribution schedule). To illustrate the computation of consolidated DEPS, assume the following data concerning the subsidiary:

Net income (adjusted for intercompany profits). $22,000
Preferred stock dividend. . . . . $ 2,000
Interest on convertible bonds. . . . . $ 3,000
Common stock shares outstanding   5,000
Warrants to purchase one share of common stock.   1,000
   Warrants held by parent.   500
Convertible bonds outstanding (convertible into 10 shares of common stock). .   200
   Convertible bonds held by parent.   180

$$\text{Subsidiary DEPS} = \frac{\$22,000 - \overset{(1)}{\$2,000} + \overset{(2)}{\$3,000}}{\underset{(3)}{5,000} + \underset{}{2,000} + \underset{(4)}{500}} = \$3.07$$

(1) Dividend on nonconvertible preferred stock, none of which is owned by the parent.
(2) Income adjustment for convertible bonds which are dilutive.
(3) Share adjustment associated with convertible debentures, 200 bonds × 10 shares per bond.
(4) Share adjustment (treasury stock method—see Chapter 13) associated with the warrants. It is assumed that, using the average market value of the stock, 500 shares could be purchased with the proceeds of the sale and that 500 additional new shares would be issued.

Assume the parent owns 80% of the subsidiary and has an adjusted internally generated net income of $40,000 and 10,000 shares of common stock outstanding.

Also assume the parent has dilutive bonds outstanding which are convertible into 3,000 shares of common stock and the interest paid on these bonds was $5,000. The consolidated DEPS would be computed as follows:

$$\text{Consolidated DEPS} = \frac{\$40{,}000 + \overset{(1)}{\$5{,}000} + \overset{(2)}{\$18{,}574}}{10{,}000 + \underset{(3)}{3{,}000}} = \$4.89$$

(1) Income adjustment from interest on parent company convertible bonds, which are dilutive.

(2) Subsidiary common shares owned by parent
    (80% × 5,000)   4,000

    Parent-owned equivalent shares applicable to convertible
    bonds (90% × 2,000)[1]   1,800

    Parent-owned equivalent shares applicable to warrants
    (50% × 500)[2]   250

    Total parent-owned equivalent shares   6,050

    Parent's interest in subsidiary income
    (6,050 shares × $3.07 subsidiary DEPS) $18,574

(3) Shares assumed to be issued in exchange for parent company convertible bonds (a CSE).

1 Parent owns 180 (or 90%) of 200 subsidiary bonds.
2 Parent owns 500 (or 50%) of 1,000 subsidiary warrants.

If the dilutive subsidiary securities enable the holder to acquire common stock of the parent, these securities are not included in the computation of subsidiary DEPS. However, these securities must be included in the parent's share adjustment in computing consolidated DEPS. The basic model by which to compute consolidated DEPS in this situation is as follows:

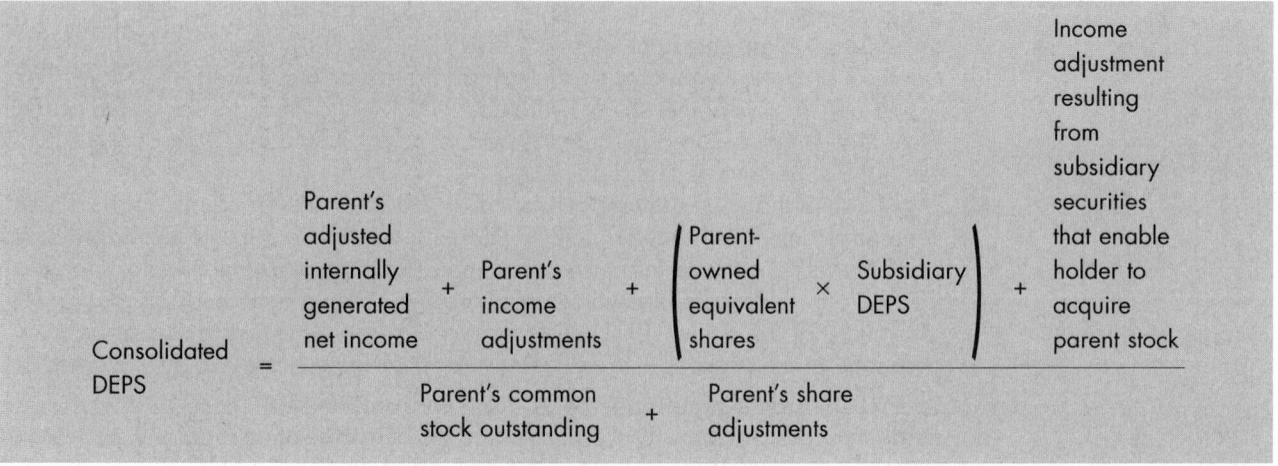

$$\text{Consolidated DEPS} = \frac{\begin{array}{c}\text{Parent's}\\\text{adjusted}\\\text{internally}\\\text{generated}\\\text{net income}\end{array} + \begin{array}{c}\text{Parent's}\\\text{income}\\\text{adjustments}\end{array} + \left(\begin{array}{c}\text{Parent-}\\\text{owned}\\\text{equivalent}\\\text{shares}\end{array} \times \begin{array}{c}\text{Subsidiary}\\\text{DEPS}\end{array}\right) + \begin{array}{c}\text{Income}\\\text{adjustment}\\\text{resulting}\\\text{from}\\\text{subsidiary}\\\text{securities}\\\text{that enable}\\\text{holder to}\\\text{acquire}\\\text{parent stock}\end{array}}{\begin{array}{c}\text{Parent's common}\\\text{stock outstanding}\end{array} + \begin{array}{c}\text{Parent's share}\\\text{adjustments}\end{array}}$$

To illustrate, assume the following facts for a parent owning 90% of the outstanding subsidiary shares:

Parent internally adjusted net income	$20,000
Parent company common stock shares outstanding	10,000
Parent company dilutive convertible bonds:	
Interest expense.	$ 1,000
Shares to be issued in conversion.	2,000
Subsidiary adjusted net income	$ 7,000
Subsidiary common stock shares outstanding	4,000
Subsidiary preferred stock convertible into parent common stock:	
Dividend requirement.	$ 1,200
Number of preferred shares	1,000
Number of parent company common shares required	2,000
Subsidiary common stock warrants to acquire 100 parent shares	100

The first step is to calculate the subsidiary's BEPS as follows:

$$\text{Subsidiary BEPS} = \frac{\$7,000 - \$1,200 \text{ preferred dividends}}{4,000 \text{ outstanding shares}} = \$1.45$$

Note that the subsidiary convertible preferred stock and stock warrants are not satisfied with subsidiary shares and, thus, are not considered converted for the purpose of calculating subsidiary EPS. The consolidated DEPS would be computed as follows:

$$\text{Consolidated DEPS} = \frac{\overset{(1)}{\$20,000 + \$1,000} + \overset{(2)}{(3,600 \times \$1.45)} + \overset{(3)}{\$1,200}}{\underset{(4)}{10,000 + (2,000 + 2,000 + 50)}} = \$1.95$$

(1) $1,000 income adjustment associated with the parent company convertible security.

(2) The parent's share of subsidiary EPS. Again, since the subsidiary's preferred stock and warrants are not convertible into subsidiary shares, the total parent-owned equivalent shares is 90% × 4,000.

(3) Income adjustment representing the dividend on subsidiary preferred shares that would not be paid if the shares were converted into common stock of the parent. Note that 100% of the adjustment is added back, even though the parent's interest in the subsidiary is less than 100%.

(4) The parent's share adjustment consisting of 2,000 shares traceable to the parent company convertible security; 2,000 shares traceable to the subsidiary preferred stock that is convertible into parent common stock; and 50 incremental shares traceable to the subsidiary warrants to acquire parent common stock. It is assumed that 50 of the 100 shares required to satisfy the warrants can be purchased with the proceeds of the exercise and 50 new shares must be issued.

Special analysis is required in computing consolidated BEPS and DEPS when an acquisition occurs during a reporting period. When the acquisition is a pooling of interests, the computations of both BEPS and DEPS include subsidiary income and securities for the entire period. However, when the acquisition is a purchase, only subsidiary income since the acquisition date is included, and the number of subsidiary shares is weighted for the partial period.

Taxation of Consolidated Companies

Consolidated companies that do not meet the requirements to be an *affiliated group*, as defined by the tax law, must pay their taxes as separate entities. The tax definition of an affiliated group is less inclusive than that used in accounting theory. Section 1504(a) of the Tax Code does not allow two or more corporations to file a consolidated return or to be considered an affiliated group for tax purposes unless the parent owns

1. 80% of the voting power of all classes of stock and
2. 80% of the fair market value of all the outstanding stock of the other corporation.

For these provisions, preferred stock is not included if it a) is not entitled to vote, b) is limited and preferred as to dividends, and c) does not have redemption rights beyond its issue price plus a reasonable redemption or liquidation premium and is not convertible into the other class of stock. Comparison of these criteria with those required for consolidated financial reporting indicates that many consolidated companies have no choice but to submit to separate taxation of the member companies.

Consolidated companies that meet the tax law requirements to be an affiliated group may elect to be taxed as a single entity or as separate entities. Once the election is made to file as a single entity, the permission of the Internal Revenue Service is required before the companies can be taxed separately again. Companies that elect to be taxed as a single entity file a consolidated tax return which may provide several tax advantages. For example, a consolidated return generally permits the offset of operating profits and losses and of capital gains and losses. Also, intercompany profits are not taxed until realized in later periods.

When companies that comprise an affiliated group elect not to file a consolidated return, each company within the group computes and pays its taxes independently. In some cases, there could be advantages in doing so. The first is that the companies do not have to use the same fiscal period or the same accounting method if separate tax returns are filed. Secondly, there may be intercompany losses that could be deducted in separate returns but not in consolidated returns. This is, however, quite rare since most intercompany losses are not deductible even when preparing separate returns.

Members of consolidated groups, when filing separate returns, must sum their incomes when applying graduated corporate tax rates. The lower tax rates available for low income levels can be used only once and cannot be applied by each of the companies individually.

Consolidated Tax Return

When an affiliated group elects to be taxed as a single entity, combined income as determined on the worksheet is the basis for the tax calculation. The affiliated companies should not record a provision for income tax based on their own separate incomes. Rather, the income tax expense is calculated as part of the consolidated worksheet process. The tax provision is based on consolidated net income; intercompany profits will have been eliminated already. Thus, no special procedures are needed to deal with intercompany transactions when computing the tax provision. Once calculated, the tax provision may be recorded on the books of the separate companies.

As an example of an affiliated group's choosing to be taxed as a single entity, assume Company P purchased an 80% interest in Company S on January 1, 19X1, at which time the following determination and distribution of excess schedule was prepared:

Price paid for investment		$795,000			
Less book value interest acquired:					
Common stock ($10 par)	$500,000				
Retained earnings	400,000				
Total stockholders' equity	$900,000			Amortization	Controlling
Interest acquired	80%	720,000		Periods	Amortization
Excess of cost over book value (debit)		75,000			
Goodwill		$ 75,000	Dr.	15	5,000

The following income statements are for Companies P and S for 19X3. Since the companies desire to file a consolidated tax return, neither company has recorded a provision for income tax. The corporate tax rate is 30%.

	Company P	Company S
Sales	$600,000	$400,000
Less cost of goods sold	350,000	200,000
Gross profit	$250,000	$200,000
Less operating expenses	100,000	100,000
Operating income	$150,000	$100,000
Subsidiary income	80,000	
Income before tax	$230,000	$100,000

On January 1, 19X2, Company P sold a piece of equipment, with a book value of $40,000, to Company S for $60,000. The equipment is depreciated by Company S on a straight-line basis over a 5-year life.

The following applies to 19X3 intercompany merchandise sales to Company P by Company S:

Intercompany sales in beginning inventory of Company P	$ 50,000
Intercompany sales in ending inventory of Company P	70,000
Sales to Company P during 19X3	100,000
Gross profit rate	50%

A 30% tax rate applies to both companies.

Worksheet 6-1, pages 6-48 to 6-57, contains the trial balances of Companies P and S on December 31, 19X3. Since the income tax is to be calculated on the worksheet, no provision exists on the separate books. If separate provisions appear in the trial balances, they should be eliminated as an initial procedure in consolidating.

The balance of the investment in Company S account results from the use of the simple equity method. All eliminations should be made prior to calculating the provision for tax. This will assure that the combined net income, upon which the provision is based, is adjusted for all intercompany transactions. **Entries (1) through (9) are identical to the procedures used in all prior worksheets; they are unchanged by taxation issues.** Combined net income before tax is calculated on the worksheet and becomes the base for the tax provision. Entry (t) is not entered until this calculation is made. In journal entry form, the entry is

| Provision for Income Tax | 71,700 | |
| Income Tax Payable | | 71,700 |

Explanation:

Combined income before tax (from the consolidated worksheet)	$239,000
Tax rate	30%
Tax provision and liability	$ 71,700

In this case, it was assumed that the purchase was a taxable exchange as to the seller and that all asset adjustments, including goodwill, are deductible. For tax purposes, goodwill is amortized over 15 years. As indicated in Chapter 1, there are some combinations that are nontaxable exchanges and amortizations of excess are, then, not deductible.[1]

The final complexity caused by a consolidated return involves the distribution of combined income. In the schedules that accompany Worksheet 6-1, the income distributions start with internally generated income before taxes. All adjustments to the worksheet are entered before tax effects. This procedure results in an adjusted income before tax for each company.

The income tax expense of the member companies, then, is calculated. The income distribution schedules allocate the income tax expense and proceed to calculate each company's adjusted net income. The subsidiary adjusted net income is distributed to the controlling and minority interests according to ownership percentages. There is no further tax on the controlling share of subsidiary income.

It will be necessary for each member company to record its share of the tax provision on its own books. The subsidiary, Company S, would record the following:

Provision for Income Tax	27,000	
Income Tax Payable		27,000
To record the allocated portion of the tax provision.		

The parent, Company P, would record the following:

Subsidiary Income (80% × $27,000 tax provision)	21,600	
Investment in Company S		21,600
To adjust Subsidiary Income for the tax expense recorded by Company S.		
Provision for Income Tax	44,700	
Income Tax Payable		44,700
To record the allocated portion of the tax provision.		

In review: Consolidated returns are consistent with consolidated reporting procedures and do not alter in any way the procedures that have been discussed in previous chapters. It is necessary to add only new procedures to the worksheet to provide for income taxes. The procedures were explained in our example assuming the use of the simple equity method. There would not be any impact on the tax entry if the cost or sophisticated equity method were used.

Separate Tax Returns

When separate returns are required or are elected to be filed, each member of the consolidated group must base its provision for tax on its own reported income. For

---

1 When there are nondeductible amortizations of excess cost, there also may be a recorded deferred tax liability. Recall that an excess of market value over cost relative to an identifiable asset requires the recording of a deferred tax liability for the amount of the tax rate times the excess. This deferred tax liability would be amortized to tax expense in proportion to the amortization of the excess.

the parent, taxable income may include dividends received from other corporations. When the members of the consolidated company meet the requirements of an affiliated company (this requires at least an 80% ownership interest), 100% of the dividends received are excluded from reported income. For ownership interests of at least 20% but less than 80%, 80% of the dividends received are excluded from reported income.[2] For ownership interests less than 20%, 70% of the dividends received are excluded from reported income. The full or partial exclusion of dividends applies only to dividends from domestic corporations and is intended to reduce multiple taxation of the same income.

A major complication arises in consolidating. **The provision for tax recorded by each company is based on its reported separate net income prior to eliminating intercompany transactions.** That means that there are timing differences that are created when consolidating. For example, suppose that the parent sells inventory to the subsidiary at a price that includes a 25% gross profit. If $40,000 of intercompany sales remains in the subsidiary's ending inventory, consolidation procedures defer $10,000 of intercompany profit. The problem is that the parent already recorded a 30% or $3,000 tax provision on the profit as a separate company. This $3,000 now becomes a deferred (prepaid) tax asset when the profit to which it attaches is deferred on the consolidated worksheet. In the following period, the intercompany profit on the inventory is realized (assuming the inventory is sold in that period). The deferred tax asset relative to the inventory profit is then expensed as part of the current year's provision for tax. The adjustments required as a result of these tax issues are examples of applying interperiod tax allocation procedures.

The use of separate tax returns for a consolidated group leads to a complicated application of interperiod tax allocation techniques. The calculations may become cumbersome when intercompany sales of plant assets and merchandise are involved. To illustrate, assume Company P purchased a 75% interest in Company S on January 1, 19X1, at which time the following determination and distribution of excess schedule was prepared:

				Amortization	Controlling
Price paid for investment		$285,000			
Less book value interest acquired:					
Common stock ($10 par)	$250,000				
Retained earnings	100,000				
Total stockholders' equity	$350,000			Amortization	Controlling
Interest acquired	75%	$262,500		Periods	Amortization
Excess of cost over book value (debit)		22,500			
Goodwill		$ 22,500	Dr.	15	1,500

On January 1, 19X3, Company S sold equipment, with a book value of $60,000, to Company P for $100,000. Company P is depreciating the asset over 5 years on a straight-line basis.

During 19X4, Companies P and S reported the following operating incomes before tax:

---

2 The exclusion rate is determined by current tax law and is subject to change.

	Company P	Company S
Sales	$430,000	$240,000
Less cost of goods sold	280,000	150,000
Gross profit	$150,000	$ 90,000
Less operating expenses	70,000	30,000
Operating income before tax	$ 80,000	$ 60,000

A 30% corporate tax rate is assumed for both companies. The following data apply to the 19X4 intercompany merchandise sales to Company S by the parent, Company P:

Intercompany sales in beginning inventory of Company S	$ 60,000
Intercompany sales in ending inventory of Company S.	40,000
Sales to Company S during 19X4	100,000
Gross profit rate	40%

Taxation of Separate Entities.   Before Companies P and S can be consolidated, it is necessary to calculate their separate tax liabilities since the 80% test of an affiliated group for tax purposes is not met. The tax provision of the subsidiary is $18,000 (30% × $60,000 Company S income before tax). Company S would record its tax provision as follows:

Provision for Income Tax	18,000	
Income Tax Payable		18,000

The tax provision for Company P requires consideration of the tax status of subsidiary income. When the conditions for an affiliated group are not met, the parent company must include in its taxable income 20% of the dividends it receives from a subsidiary. When an affiliated group *elects* separate taxation, no dividends are included and no additional tax needs to be calculated. According to APB Opinion No. 23, subsidiary income included in the pretax income of a parent leads to a temporary difference between the earning of the income and its inclusion in the tax return as dividend income.[3] It is not necessary to account for the temporary difference if the tax law provides a means by which the investment can be recovered tax free. Accordingly, Company P will provide for tax expense equal to its tax rate times 20% of its share of the total subsidiary net income. It is assumed that the parent records its tax provision based on the income it records from the subsidiary. In this example, the parent records the investment under the simple equity method. Thus, the tax accrual is based on 20% of the simple equity income without any reduction for amortization of excesses. A parent using the cost method would record the tax only on dividends received and would need to accrue tax on the worksheet based on the cost-to-equity conversion.

This tax may be viewed as a *secondary tax* since it is the second taxation of subsidiary income. For 19X4, this tax liability would be calculated as follows:

Subsidiary net income	$42,000
Controlling interest, 75% × $42,000	31,500
Provision for tax on subsidiary income, 30% × (20% × $31,500)	1,890

Company P would add this amount to the tax it has provided for its internally generated income to arrive at its total tax provision for the period:

3 Opinions of the Accounting Principles Board No. 23, *Accounting for Income Taxes—Special Areas* (New York: American Institute of Certified Public Accountants, 1971), pars. 9–12 as amended by Statement of Financial Accounting Standards No. 109, *Accounting for Income Taxes* (Stamford, CT: Financial Accounting Standards Board, 1992), Appendix D.

Tax on internally generated income, 30% × $80,000 . . . . $24,000
Secondary tax provision for subsidiary income.   1,890
    Total Company P provision for tax $25,890

Since Company P has not received its share of the income of Company S, the secondary tax is not immediately payable, and a deferred tax liability for $1,890 is created. Assuming that the tax on internally generated income is currently payable, Company P would make the following entry to record its 19X4 tax provision:

Provision for Income Tax   25,890
    Income Tax Payable   24,000
    Deferred Tax Liability   1,890

If dividends had been paid by the subsidiary, the secondary tax applicable to the dividends received by Company P would be included in the current tax liability. Note that the secondary tax applies only to consolidated companies that do not qualify as an affiliated group. Companies that do meet the requirements would calculate only a single tax on each company's adjusted net income.

Worksheet Procedures.   Worksheet 6-2, pages 6-52 to 6-55, includes the trial balances of Companies P and S. The companies do not qualify as an affiliated group for tax purposes. **Several observations should be made regarding the amounts listed in the trial balance before you study the elimination entries.**

1. The balance in Investment in Company S is computed according to the simple equity method, as follows:

Original cost $285,000
Subsidiary income, 19X1–19X3 (*after tax*):
    Company S retained earnings, Jan. 1, 19X4 . . . . $350,000
    Company S retained earnings, Jan. 1, 19X1   100,000
        Net increase $250,000
        Controlling interest 75%   187,500
Controlling interest in subsidiary net income, 19X4
    (75% × $42,000)   31,500
Equity-adjusted balance, Dec. 31, 19X4 . . . . $504,000

2. Since the parent's share of subsidiary undistributed income has been recorded from the date of acquisition, a deferred tax liability has been recorded by Company P each year to recognize the secondary tax provision. The total deferred tax liability on December 31, 19X4, is calculated as follows:

Deferred tax liability on 19X1–19X3 income
    (20% × 30% × $187,500 19X1–19X3 undistributed income) $11,250
Current year's additional deferment (20% × 30% × $31,500)   1,890
    Total deferred tax liability $13,140

3. The trial balances of both companies include their separate provisions for income tax and the current tax liabilities. **These provisions do not reflect adjustments for intercompany transactions.**

Worksheet entries (1) through (9) are identical to those that would be prepared in the absence of any consideration of taxes. The first special procedure to consider is entry (t1). Its purpose is to adjust for the tax impact of the adjustments that affect beginning retained earnings. Entry (5) reduced retained earnings for the intercompany profit on the equipment sale. Now, it is necessary to increase retained earnings for the tax expense previously recorded by the separate companies concerning this profit. Not only has a tax provision relative to this sale been recorded by the subsidiary, but the parent also has recorded the secondary tax applicable to the sale. Both sets of taxes are viewed now as a deferred tax asset. Since the taxes have been expensed previously, they also are removed from retained earnings. In addition, entry (t1) defers the tax that has been recorded by Company P relative to the intercompany inventory profit at the start of the year. Since the sale was made and the tax recorded by the parent company, there is no secondary tax. Entry (t1) also records the tax deduction for goodwill in the prior 3 years. The tax accrual for simple equity income recorded by the parent did not consider amortizations of excess. The goodwill amortization also creates a deferred tax asset.

Entry (t2) deals with the tax impact of adjustments to the current-year income. Since part of the intercompany profit on the equipment sale will be recognized this year, the deferred tax asset (including the secondary tax) now is expensed. Likewise, the deferred tax asset relative to the beginning inventory profit is expensed. It then becomes necessary to defer the tax expense applicable to the intercompany profit in the ending inventory. Again, since the inventory profit was recorded by the parent and not the subsidiary, there is no secondary tax. The tax deduction relative to the goodwill amortization is included in the adjustment.

When the entries in Worksheet 6-2 are completed, the resulting combined net income is $106,008, which is distributed to the controlling and minority interests. The distribution schedules start with internally generated net income *after tax*, since the tax expense is calculated separately by each company. Thus, **each adjustment must be on an after-tax basis when made to the internally generated net income.**

Let us revisit Worksheet 6-2 to discuss how it would be simplified if the consolidated company met the requirements of an affiliated company. The following procedures would be omitted from the worksheet:

1. Company P would not have recorded the deferred tax liability of $13,140 on its books. If the companies are an affiliated group, there is no tax due on the parent's share of subsidiary income. The parent's current-year provision for income tax would be only $24,000 since there would not be the secondary tax of $1,890 on the parent's share of subsidiary income.

2. Entry (t1) would not include the secondary tax of $1,008 applicable to the intercompany equipment sale.

3. Entry (t2) would not include the secondary tax of $252 applicable to the intercompany equipment sale.

4. The parent's income distribution schedule would not deduct the secondary tax on the parent's share of subsidiary income. Instead, the parent would just include 75% of the subsidiary's after-tax income of $47,600, or $35,700.

There are some additional minor worksheet modifications required if the cost or sophisticated equity methods are used by the parent company. If the cost method is used, there needs to be a recording of the deferred tax liability for prior years' subsidiary income. The adjustment would be to multiply the net amount of the cost-to-equity conversion adjustment by the effective tax rate, to debit the parent's retained earnings, and to credit a deferred tax liability account. If the sophisticated equity method is used, the parent company's retained earnings and current-year tax provision are correct and need no adjustment. The only entry needed in consolidating is to adjust the beginning retained earnings of the subsidiary for any intercompany profits on a net-of-tax basis. The adjustment of subsidiary retained earnings on the consolidated worksheet was covered in the partial worksheet on page 4-19. It still would be necessary to calculate the minority and controlling interest in combined net income on an after-tax basis when preparing the income distribution schedules.

Equity Method for Unconsolidated Investments

Prior to the 1971 issuance of APB Opinion No. 18, "The Equity Method of Accounting for Investments in Common Stock," investors could freely choose between the equity and cost methods to recognize income on their investments. When the equity method was used, it tended to be a simple equity method that recognized only a pro rata share of the investee's income, without any attempt to amortize an excess of cost or book value on the investment or to defer intercompany gains and losses. The choice between these two divergent methods is not significant when consolidation is required since the investment and investment income accounts are eliminated in the consolidation process. However, the accounting profession did become concerned with the use of the cost method for major investments not subject to consolidation. The APB reasoned that, in such cases, the investor may have significant influence over the investee's dividend policy and the payment of dividends often would be unrelated to the investee's income during a given period. For example, dividend payments would be level over a period of years during which income varied significantly. This reasoning led the APB to state the following:

> The equity method tends to be most appropriate if an investment enables the investor to influence the operating or financial decisions of the investee. The investor then has a degree of responsibility for the return on its investment, and it is appropriate to include in the results of operations of the investor its share of earnings or losses of the investee. Influence tends to be more effective as the investor's percent of ownership in the voting stock of the investee increases. Investments of relatively small percentages of voting stock of an investee tend to be passive in nature and enable the investor to have little or no influence on the operations of the investee.[4]

APB Opinion No. 18 requires the use of the sophisticated equity method for the following types of investments:

1. *Influential investments.* The APB defines influence as "representation on the board of directors, participation in policy-making processes, material intercompany transactions, interchange of managerial personnel, or technological dependency."[5] When the investor holds 20% or more of the voting shares of an investee, influence is assumed and the sophisticated equity method is required unless the investor takes on the burden of proof to show that influence does not exist, in which case the cost method would be used.[6] When the investment falls below 20%, the presumption is that influence does not exist, and the cost method is to be used unless the investor can show that influence does exist despite the low percentage of ownership. Since the most common use of the sophisticated equity method is for influential (20% to 50%) investments, such investments are used in subsequent illustrations.

2. *Corporate joint ventures.* A corporate joint venture is a separate, specific project organized for the benefit of several corporations. An example would be a research project undertaken jointly by several members of a given industry. The member corporations typically participate in the management of the venture and share the gains and losses. Since such an arrangement does not involve passive investors, the sophisticated equity method is required.

---

4 Opinions of the Accounting Principles Board No. 18, *The Equity Method of Accounting for Investments in Common Stock* (New York: American Institute of Certified Public Accountants, 1971), par. 12.

5 *Ibid.*, par. 17.

6 For examples of situations that may overcome the presumption of influence, see FASB Interpretation No. 35, *Criteria for Applying the Equity Method of Accounting for Investments in Common Stock* (Stamford: Financial Accounting Standards Board, 1981).

3. *Unconsolidated subsidiaries.* A parent may own over 50% of the shares of a subsidiary but may meet one of the exceptions (control is temporary or does not rest with the majority owner) to the requirement that subsidiaries be consolidated. However, if influence does exist, the sophisticated equity method would be used for the investment.

As defined by APB Opinion No. 18, the use of the equity method requires that the investment in common stock appear as a single, equity-adjusted amount on the balance sheet of the investor. The investor's income statement will include the investor's share of the investee ordinary income as a single amount in the ordinary income section. The investor's share of investee discontinued operations, extraordinary items, and cumulative effects of changes in accounting principles will appear as single amounts in the sections of the investor's income statement that correspond to the placement of these items in the investee's statement.

Calculation of Equity Income

In its basic form, the equity method requires the investor to recognize its pro rata share of investee reported income. Dividends, when received, do not constitute income, but are viewed instead as a partial liquidation of the investment. In reality, however, the price paid for the investment usually will not agree with the underlying book value of the investee, which requires that any amortization of an excess of cost or book value be treated as an adjustment of the investor's pro rata share of investee income. It is very likely that the reported income of the investee will include gains and losses on transactions with the investor. As was true in consolidations, these gains and losses cannot be recognized until they are confirmed by a transaction between the affiliated group and unrelated parties. The proper application of the sophisticated equity method will mean that the income recognized by the investor will be the same as it would be under consolidation procedures. In fact, the sophisticated equity method sometimes is referred to as "one-line consolidation."

In the next two sections, the sophisticated equity method will be presented without consideration of the tax implications. Following that, the tax effect on such an investment will be addressed.

Amortization of Excesses.   A determination and distribution of excess schedule is prepared for a sophisticated equity method investment just as it would be if the investment were to be consolidated. For example, assume the following schedule was prepared by Excel Corporation for a 25% interest in Flag Company acquired on January 1, 19X1:

Price paid		$300,000
Less interest acquired:		
Common stock ($10 par)	$200,000	
Retained earnings, January 1, 19X1	600,000	
Total stockholders' equity	$800,000	
Interest acquired	25%	200,000
Excess of cost over book value		$100,000
Less excess attributable to equipment with a 5-year remaining		
life and undervalued by $80,000, 25% × $80,000		20,000
Goodwill (40-year life).		$ 80,000

As a practical matter, APB Opinion No. 18 states that it may not be possible to relate the excess to specific assets, in which case the entire excess may be considered goodwill. However, an attempt should be made to allocate the excess in the same manner as would be done for the purchase of a controlling interest in a subsidiary.

The determination and distribution of excess schedule indicates the pattern of amortization to be followed. The required amortizations must be made directly through the investment account since the distributions shown on the schedule are not recorded in the absence of consolidation procedures. The debit and credit indicators have been dropped from the determination and distribution of excess schedule since there will not be any worksheet adjustments in the absence of consolidation. Assuming Flag Company reported net income of $50,000 for 19X1, Excel Corporation would make the following entry for 19X1:

Investment in Flag Company	6,500	
Investment Income		6,500

Income is calculated as follows:

25% × Flag reported net income of $50,000		$12,500
Less amortizations of excess cost:		
Equipment, $20,000 ÷ 5	$4,000	
Goodwill, $80,000 ÷ 40	2,000	6,000
Investment income, net of amortizations		$ 6,500

If an investment is acquired for less than book value, the excess of book value over cost would be amortized over a period not to exceed 40 years. This procedure would increase investment income in the years of amortization.

Intercompany Transactions by Investee.   The investee may sell inventory to the investor. As would be true if the investment were consolidated, the share of the investee's profit on goods still held by the investor at the end of a period cannot be included in income of that period. Instead, the profit must be deferred until the goods are sold by the investor. Since the two firms are separate reporting entities, the intercompany sales and related debt cannot be eliminated. Only the investor's share of the investee's profit on unsold goods in the hands of the investor is deferred. In a like manner, the investor may have plant assets that were purchased from the investee. The investor's share of the investee's gains and losses on these sales also must be deferred and allocated over the depreciable life of the asset. Profit deferments should be handled in an income distribution schedule similar to that used for consolidated worksheets. To illustrate, assume the following facts for the example of the 25% investment in Flag by Excel. Again, note that income tax is not being considered in this illustration:

1. Excel had the following merchandise acquired from Flag Company in its ending inventories:

Year	Amount	Gross Profit of Flag Company
19X1	$30,000	40%
19X2	40,000	45

2. Excel purchased a truck from Flag Company on January 1, 19X1, for $20,000. The truck is being depreciated over a 4-year life on a straight-line basis with no salvage value. The truck had a net book value of $16,000 when it was sold by Flag.
3. Flag Company had an income of $50,000 in 19X1 and $70,000 in 19X2.
4. Flag declared and paid $10,000 in dividends in 19X2.

Based on these facts, Excel Corporation would prepare the following income distribution schedules:

19X1 Income Distribution for Investment in Flag Company

Gain on sale of truck, to be amortized over 4 years.	$ 4,000	Reported income of Flag Company		$50,000
Profit in Excel ending inventory, 40% × $30,000	12,000	Realization of ¼ of profit on sale of truck		1,000
		Adjusted income of Flag Company		$35,000
		Ownership interest, 25%.		$ 8,750
		Less amortization of excess cost:		
		Equipment	$4,000	
		Goodwill	2,000	6,000
		Investment income, net of amortizations		$ 2,750

19X2 Income Distribution for Investment in Flag Company

Profit in Excel ending inventory, 45% × $40,000	18,000	Reported income of Flag Company		$70,000
		Profit in Excel beginning inventory, 40% × $30,000		12,000
		Realization of ¼ of profit on sale of truck		1,000
		Adjusted income of Flag Company		$65,000
		Ownership interest, 25%.		$16,250
		Less amortization of excess cost:		
		Equipment	$4,000	
		Goodwill	2,000	6,000
		Income from investment.		$10,250

The schedules would lead to the following entries to record investment income:

19X1	Investment in Flag Company	2,750	
	Investment Income		2,750
19X2	Investment in Flag Company	10,250	
	Investment Income		10,250

In addition, the following entry would be made in 19X2 to record dividends received:

Cash	2,500	
Investment in Flag Company		2,500

It should be noted that only the investor's share of intercompany gains and losses is deferred. The investee's remaining stockholders are not affected by the Excel Corporation investment.

Tax Effects of Equity Method

The investor not meeting the requirements of affiliation as defined by tax law pays income taxes on dividends received. In the case of a domestic corporation, 20% of the dividends are includable in taxable income. However, a temporary difference is created through the use of the equity method for financial reporting.[7] As a result, **the provision for tax must be based on the equity income, and a deferred tax liability must be created for undistributed investment income.** The provision may be based on the assumption that investment income will be distributed in dividends, or it will be realized via the sale of the investment. In the latter case, it is likely that the income would be taxed in the form of a capital gain. The assumption used will determine the rate to be applied to the undistributed income. The provision for tax is based on the investor's net investment income after adjustments and amortizations. However, **amortizations of excess cost are not deductible** since they have no impact on the income that could be distributed to the investor and, thus, must be added back to the net investment income to compute the tax.

The following entries are based on the previous example of Flag Company and Excel Corporation, but it is assumed that each company is subject to a 30% income tax. Excel Corporation's share of Flag Company *net* income would now be calculated as follows:

	19X1	19X2
Adjusted income of Flag Company, before tax*	$35,000	$65,000
Tax provision (30%)	10,500	19,500
Adjusted net income of Flag Company	$24,500	$45,500
Ownership interest in adjusted net income (25%)	$ 6,125	$11,375
Less amortizations of excess*	6,000	6,000
Net income from investment	$ 125	$ 5,375

*See the income distribution schedules in the previous section.

Note that the tax provision calculated by the investor will not agree with the provision for tax on the books of the investee. This is due to the adjustments made in the income distribution schedules to recognize the profit deferrals.

The 19X1 and 19X2 entries to record investment income and the applicable tax provision would be

19X1	Investment in Flag Company	125	
	Investment Income		125
	Provision for Income Tax [20% × 30% × ($125 net income + $6,000 nondeductible amortizations of excess)]	368	
	Deferred Tax Liability		368
19X2	Investment in Flag Company	5,375	
	Investment Income		5,375
	Cash	2,500	
	Investment in Flag Company		2,500

---

7 Opinions of the Accounting Principles Board No. 24, *Accounting for Income Taxes—Investments in Common Stock Accounted for by the Equity Method (Other than Subsidiaries and Corporate Joint Ventures)* (New York: American Institute of Certified Public Accountants, 1972), par. 7.

Provision for Income Tax [20% × 30% × ($5,375 net income
  + $6,000 nondeductible amortizations of excess)]. . . .   683
    Income Tax Payable (20% × 30% × $2,500 dividends) . .   150
    Deferred Tax Liability ($683 – $150)   533

Unusual Equity Adjustments

There are several unusual situations involving the investee that require special procedures for the proper recording of investment income. These situations are
described in the following paragraphs.

Investee with Preferred Stock.   In the absence of consolidation, an investment in
preferred stock does not require elimination. However, the existence of preferred
stock in the capital structure of the investee requires that the investor's equity adjustment be based on only that portion of investee income available for common stockholders. Dividends declared on preferred stock must be subtracted from income of
the investee. When the preferred stock has cumulative or participation rights, the
claim of preferred stockholders must be subtracted from the investee income each
period to arrive at the income available for common stockholders. The procedures
for calculating this income are contained in Chapter 7.

Investee Stock Transactions.   The investee corporation may engage in transactions with its common stockholders, such as issuing additional shares, retiring
shares, or engaging in treasury stock transactions. Each of these transactions affects
the investor's equity interest. A comparison is made of the investor's ownership
interest before and after the investee stock transaction. An increase in the investor's
interest is treated as a gain, while a decrease is recorded as a loss.

Write-Down to Market Value.   The investment in another company is subject to
reduction to a lower market value if it appears that a relatively permanent fall in
value has occurred. The fact that the current market value of the shares is temporarily less than the equity-adjusted cost of the shares is not sufficient cause for a write-
down. When the sophisticated equity method is used and a permanent decline in
value occurs, a reduction would be made to the equity-adjusted cost. The equity
method would continue to be applied subsequent to the write-down. There can be
no subsequent write-ups, however, other than through normal equity adjustments.

Zero Investment Balance.   It is possible that an investee will suffer losses to the
extent that the continued application of the equity method could produce a negative
balance in the investment account. Equity adjustments are to be discontinued when
the investment balance becomes zero.[8] Further losses are acknowledged only by
memo entries, which are needed to maintain the total unrecorded share of losses. If
the investee again becomes profitable, the investor must not record income on the
investment until its subsequent share of income equals the previously unrecorded
share of losses.

To illustrate these procedures, assume Grate Corporation has a 35% investment
in Dittmar Company, with a sophisticated-equity-adjusted cost of $30,000 on January
1, 19X1, and Dittmar reports the following results:

---

8 According to APB Opinion No. 18 (par. 19i), any net advance to the investee that the investor may have
  on its books also is available to offset the investor's share of investee losses until the receivable is reduced
  to a zero balance.

Period	Income (loss)
19X1	$(80,000)
19X2	(50,000)
19X3	(20,000)
19X4	90,000

The following T account summarizes entries for 19X1 through 19X4 (taxes are ignored):

Investment in Dittmar Company

Equity-adjusted balance, Jan 1, 19X1	$30,000	Equity loss for 19X1, 35% × $80,000 Dittmar loss	$28,000
		Recorded equity loss for 19X2, 35% × $50,000 Dittmar loss = $17,500; loss limited to investment balance.	2,000
Balance	$ 0		
		Memo entries:	
Memo entry:		Unrecorded 19X2 loss, $17,500 – $2,000. .	$15,500
Unrecorded share of 19X4 Dittmar income. .	22,500	Unrecorded loss for 19X3, 35% × $20,000 Dittmar loss	7,000
Actual entries resumed:			
Recorded equity income, 19X4, 35% × $90,000 Dittmar income, less amount to cover unrecorded losses ($15,500 + $7,000)	$ 9,000		
Balance, Dec. 31, 19X4.	$ 9,000		

Intercompany Transactions by Investor.   An investor may sell merchandise and/or plant assets to an investee at a gain or loss. When influence is deemed to exist, it might seem appropriate to defer the entire gain or loss until the asset is resold or depreciated by the investee. However, an interpretation of APB Opinion No. 18 requires the entire gain or loss to be deferred only when the transaction is with a controlled (over 50%-owned) investee and is not at arm's length. In all other cases, it is appropriate to defer only a gain or loss that is in proportion to the investor's ownership interest.[9]

To illustrate, assume Grant Corporation, which owns a 35% interest in Hartwig Company, sold $50,000 of merchandise to Hartwig at a gross profit of 40%. Of this merchandise, $20,000 is still in Hartwig's 19X1 ending inventory. Grant needs to defer only profit equal to the $8,000 (40% x $20,000) unrealized gross profit multiplied by its 35% interest, or $2,800. Grant would make the following entry on December 31, 19X1:

Sales   2,800
    Deferred Gross Profit on Sales to Investee   2,800

9 Accounting Interpretations, *The Equity Method of Accounting for Investments in Common Stock: Accounting Interpretations of APB Opinion No. 18* (New York: American Institute of Certified Public Accountants, 1971), par. 1.

Assuming the investor recorded the provision for income tax prior to this adjustment, the tax applicable to the unrealized gain would be deferred by the following entry, which is based on a 30% tax rate:

Deferred Tax Expense (30% x $2,800)   840
    Provision for Income Tax   840

The deferred gross profit and the related tax deferment would be realized in the period in which the goods are sold to outside parties. The deferred profit and related tax effects on plant asset sales would be realized in proportion to the depreciation recorded by the investee company.

It may occur that the investor will purchase outstanding bonds of the investee. Unlike consolidation procedures, the bonds are not assumed to be retired since the investor and investee are separate reporting entities. Similarly, a purchase of investor bonds by the investee is not a retirement of the bonds. Thus, no adjustments to income are necessary as a result of intercompany bondholdings.

Gain or Loss of Influence. An investor may own less than a 20% interest in an investee, in which case the cost method ordinarily would be used to record investment income. If the investor subsequently buys sufficient additional shares to have its total interest equal or exceed 20%, the investor must retroactively apply the sophisticated equity method to the total holding period of the investment. APB Opinion No. 18 requires an adjustment of retained earnings for the period prior to the time the 20% interest is achieved.

It is possible that an investor will own 20% or more of the voting shares of the investee but will sell a portion of the shares so that the ownership interest falls below 20%. In such a case, the sophisticated equity method is discontinued as of the sale date. However, there is no adjustment back to the cost method. The balance of the investment account remains at its equity-adjusted balance on the sale date. Should influence be attained again, a retroactive ("catch-up") equity adjustment would be made.

When all or part of an investment recorded under the sophisticated equity method is sold, the gain or loss is based on the equity-adjusted balance as of the sale date. An adjustment also would be necessary for deferred tax balances applicable to the investment.

Disclosure Requirements

Since a significant portion of the investor's income may be derived from investments, added disclosures are required in order to inform properly the readers of the financial statements. For investments of 20% or more, the investor must disclose the name of each investee, the percentage of ownership in each investee, and the disparity between the cost and underlying book value for each investment. If the sophisticated equity method is not being applied, the reasons must be given. When investments are material with respect to the investor's financial position or income, the financial statements of the investees should be included as supplemental information.

When a market value for the investment is available, it should be disclosed. However, if the investor owns a relatively large block of a subsidiary's shares, quoted market values would have little relevance because the sale of an entire controlling interest would involve different motivations and would result in a unique value.

Questions

1. During the current period, a company purchased an 80% interest in another company. What is the impact of the purchase on the consolidated statement of cash flows in the period of the purchase assuming (a) the interest was acquired for cash? (b) bonds were issued in exchange for the interest? (c) the parent company issued common stock in exchange for the interest?

2. What are the possible ramifications on the current period's consolidated statement of cash flows of a purchase of a subsidiary that occurred in a prior period?

3. Which of the following items would be included in a consolidated statement of cash flows and, if they are included, in what section would they appear?

   a) *Amortization of excesses relative to the investment.*

   b) *Parent company investment in subsidiary bonds purchased directly from the subsidiary.*

   c) *Parent company acquisition that meets the pooling criteria.*

   d) *Cash acquisition of remaining interest in a subsidiary following a pooling of interests.*

   e) *Minority interest in subsidiary equity in the year of acquisition.*

   f) *Parent company sale of a part of its interest in a subsidiary.*

   g) *Cash dividends paid by a 90%-owned subsidiary.*

4. Indicate how the computation of consolidated earnings per share is influenced by the minority interest in a subsidiary's equity.

5. Discuss the need for interperiod tax allocation as a part of the consolidation process when members of a consolidated group file separate tax returns.

6. Company S has operating income of $100,000 before tax. Company P has a 70% ownership interest in Company S. Assuming Companies P and S are taxed as separate entities, what provision for tax must P make for its share of S income? Assume a 30% tax rate for both companies.

7. Briefly describe when the APB Opinion No. 18 sophisticated equity method must be used in accounting for an investment.

8. Why is the APB Opinion No. 18 sophisticated equity method viewed as requiring a one-line consolidation?

9. Is it possible for the investment account to have a negative balance under the sophisticated equity method?

10. Hummer Corporation owns a 30% interest in Canfield Company. How much profit would you adjust for and how would you make the adjustment if (a) Hummer sold merchandise to Canfield during the year and Canfield has in its ending inventory goods purchased for $5,000 which were sold by Hummer at a 30% gross profit? (b) Canfield sold merchandise to Hummer during the year and Hummer has in its ending inventory goods purchased for $8,000 which were sold by Canfield at a 25% gross profit?

11. Discuss the use of lower-of-cost-or-market values in regard to investments carried under the APB Opinion No. 18 equity method.

12. Describe the accounting procedures for (a) an investor who owns less than a 20% interest in an investee and subsequently purchases enough stock to exceed 20%, and (b) an investor whose ownership interest exceeds 20%, but who subsequently sells a portion of the investment to cause the interest to fall below 20%.

13. What disclosures concerning material investments must be made on the financial statements?

Exercises

Exercise 1. Batton Company purchased an 80% interest in Ricky Company for $500,000 cash on January 1, 19X3. Any excess of cost over book value was attributed to goodwill with a 20-year life. To help pay for the acquisition, Batton Company issued 300, $1,000 face value, 10-year, 8% bonds. Ricky's balance sheet on the date of the purchase was as follows:

Assets		Liabilities and Equity	
Cash	$ 20,000	Current liabilities	$110,000
Inventory	140,000	Bonds payable	100,000
Property, plant,		Common stock ($10 par)	200,000
and equipment (net)	550,000	Retained earnings	300,000
Total assets	$710,000	Total liabilities and equity	$710,000

Consolidated net income for 19X3 was $140,000, net of the minority's interest of $10,000. Batton declared and paid dividends of $10,000, and Ricky declared and paid dividends of $5,000. There were no purchases or sales of property, plant, or equipment during the year. Based on the following information, prepare a statement of cash flows using the indirect method for Batton Company and its subsidiary for the year ended December 31, 19X3. Any supporting schedules should be in good form.

	Batton Company December 31, 19X2	Consolidated December 31, 19X3
Cash	$100,000	$ 104,000
Inventory	220,000	454,000
Property, plant, and equipment (net)	800,000	1,230,000
Goodwill		95,000
Current liabilities	(160,000)	(284,000)
Bonds payable	(200,000)	(600,000)
Minority interest		(109,000)
Controlling common stock, $10 par	(200,000)	(200,000)
Controlling paid-in capital in excess of par	(300,000)	(300,000)
Retained earnings	(260,000)	(390,000)
Totals	0	0

Exercise 2. Duckworth Corporation purchased an 80% interest in Poladna Corporation on January 1, 19X3, in exchange for 5,000 Duckworth shares (market value of $18) plus $155,000 cash. The appraisal showed that some of Poladna's equipment, with a 4-year estimated remaining life, was undervalued $20,000. Goodwill is to be amortized over a 10-year period. The following is Poladna Corporation's balance sheet on December 31, 19X2:

Assets	
Cash	$ 30,000
Inventory	30,000
Property, plant, and equipment	300,000
Accumulated depreciation	(90,000)
Total assets	$270,000

(continued)

Liabilities and Equity

Current liabilities.	$ 30,000
Long-term liabilities	40,000
Common stock ($10 par)	150,000
Retained earnings	50,000
Total liabilities and equity	$270,000

Comparative balance sheet data are as follows:

	December 31, 19X2 (Parent only)	December 31, 19X3 (Consolidated)
Cash	$100,000	$ 95,000
Inventory	60,000	84,200
Property, plant, and equipment.	950,000	1,342,000
Accumulated depreciation	(360,000)	(574,000)
Goodwill		62,100
Current liabilities	(80,000)	(115,000)
Long-term liabilities.	(100,000)	(130,000)
Minority interest.		(43,000)
Controlling interest:		
Common stock ($10 par).	(350,000)	(400,000)
Additional paid-in capital	(50,000)	(90,000)
Retained earnings	(170,000)	(231,300)
	0	0

The following information relates to the activities of the two companies for 19X3:

a) Poladna paid off $10,000 of its long-term debt.

b) Duckworth purchased production equipment for $76,000.

c) Combined net income was $97,300; the minority interest's share was $6,000. Depreciation expense taken by Duckworth and Poladna on their separate books was $92,000 and $28,000, respectively.

d) Duckworth paid $30,000 in dividends; Poladna paid $15,000.

Prepare the consolidated statement of cash flows for the year ended December 31, 19X3, for Duckworth Corporation and its subsidiary, Poladna Corporation.

Exercise 3.   Paridon Motors purchased an 80% interest in Super Battery Company on January 1, 19X2, for $700,000 cash. At that date, Super Battery Company had the following stockholders' equity:

Common stock ($10 par)	$100,000
Paid-in capital in excess of par.	300,000
Retained earnings	250,000
Total stockholders' equity.	$650,000

Any excess of cost over book value was attributed to goodwill with a 20-year amortization period. A statement of cash flows is being prepared for 19X5. For each of the following situations, indicate the impact on the cash flow statement for 19X5.

a) Adjustment resulting from the original purchase of the controlling interest.

b) Super Battery Company issued 2,000 shares of common stock for $90 per share on January 1, 19X5. At the time, the stockholders' equity of Super Battery was $800,000. Paridon Motors purchased 1,000 shares.

c) Paridon Motors purchased at 102, $100,000 of face value, 10% annual interest bonds issued by Super Battery Company at face value on January 1, 19X3. Paridon purchased the bonds on January 1, 19X5.

d) Super Battery purchased a production machine from Paridon Motors on July 1, 19X5, for $80,000. Paridon's cost was $60,000 and accumulated depreciation was $20,000.

Exercise 4.   On May 1, 19X6, Karn Company purchased a 70% interest in Bellow Company for $350,000. Karn also paid $30,000 in direct acquisition costs. The following determination and distribution of excess schedule was prepared:

	Company	Controlling Percent	Controlling Interest		
Price paid for investment including direct acquisition costs:.			$380,000		
Market value of total net assets:.	$400,000	70%	280,000		
Market value of priority accounts:	n/a	n/a	n/a		
Analysis of price: **Goodwill**			100,000		
Price paid for investment		$ 380,000			
Less book value of interest acquired:					
Common stock, Bellow	$300,000				
Retained earnings	100,000				
Total stockholders' equity	$400,000				
Interest acquired	70%	280,000		Amortization Periods	Controlling Amortization
Goodwill.		**$100,000**	Dr.	**20**	**5,000**

Karn Company and Bellow Company had the following separate income statements for the year ended December 31, 19X8:

	Karn Company	Bellow Company
Sales.	$750,000	$560,000
Less cost of goods sold.	440,000	350,000
Gross profit	$310,000	$210,000
Less other expenses	200,000	140,000
Income before dividends. . . .	$110,000	$ 70,000
Dividends received	17,500	
Income before tax	$127,500	$ 70,000

During 19X8, Bellow Company paid cash dividends of $25,000.

Prepare the entry to record income tax payable on each company's books. Assume a 30% corporate income tax rate.

Exercise 5. Dills Company purchased an 80% interest in the common stock of Sarada Company for $850,000 on January 1, 19X7. The price was $75,000 in excess of the book value of the underlying equity, and the excess was attributed to goodwill with a 15-year life.

During 19X9, Dills Company and Sarada Company reported the following internally generated income before taxes:

	Dills Company	Sarada Company
Sales	$300,000	$120,000
Cost of goods sold	(200,000)	(90,000)
Gain on machine	5,000	
Expenses.	(40,000)	(20,000)
Income before taxes	$ 65,000	$ 10,000

Sarada Company sold goods to Dills Company for $50,000. Dills Company had $20,000 of Sarada Company's goods in its beginning inventory and $6,000 of Sarada's goods in its ending inventory. Sarada Company sells goods to Dills Company at cost plus 25%.

Dills Company sold a new machine to Sarada Company on January 1, 19X9, for $30,000. The machine has a 5-year life, and its cost was $25,000.

The affiliated group files a consolidated tax return and is taxed at 30%.

Prepare a consolidated income statement for 19X9. Include income distribution for both companies.

Exercise 6. *(This is the same as Exercise 5, but with separate taxation.)* Dolls Company purchased an 80% interest in the common stock of Sarah Company for $850,000 on January 1, 19X7. The price was $75,000 in excess of the book value of the underlying equity, and the excess was attributed to goodwill with a 15-year life.

During 19X9, Dolls Company and Sarah Company reported the following internally generated income before taxes:

	Dolls Company	Sarah Company
Sales	$300,000	$120,000
Cost of goods sold	(200,000)	(90,000)
Gain on machine	5,000	
Expenses.	(40,000)	(20,000)
Income before taxes	$ 65,000	$ 10,000

Sarah Company sold goods to Dolls Company for $50,000. Dolls Company had $20,000 of Sarah Company's goods in its beginning inventory and $6,000 of Sarah's goods in its ending inventory. Sarah Company sells goods to Dolls Company at cost plus 25%.

Dolls Company sold a new machine to Sarah Company on January 1, 19X9, for $30,000. The machine has a 5-year life, and its cost was $25,000.

The companies file separate tax returns. Both are subject to a 30% tax rate. Dolls receives an 80% dividend deduction.

Prepare a consolidated income statement for 19X9. Include income distribution for both companies.

Exercise 7. The separate income statements of Cooper Company and its 60%-owned subsidiary, Vacant Company, for the year ended December 31, 19X7, are as follows:

	Cooper Company	Vacant Company
Sales.	$520,000	$350,000
Less cost of goods sold.	350,000	180,000
Gross profit	$170,000	$170,000
Less operating expenses	100,000	90,000
Operating income	$ 70,000	$ 80,000
Subsidiary income.	12,600	
Income before tax	$ 82,600	$ 80,000
Provision for income tax	21,756	24,000
Net income	$ 60,844	$ 56,000

The following additional information is available:

a) Cooper Company purchased its interest in Vacant Company on July 1, 19X5. The price paid was $60,000 in excess of book value. This excess was attributable to goodwill with a 20-year life.

b) Vacant Company sold a piece of equipment to Cooper Company on December 31, 19X6, for $10,000. This piece of equipment had a book value of $6,000 and an estimated future life of 4 years at the purchase date. Straight-line depreciation is assumed.

c) Cooper Company sold $15,000 worth of merchandise to Vacant Company during 19X7. Cooper sells its merchandise at a price that enables it to realize a gross profit of 30%.

d) Vacant Company had $2,000 worth of this merchandise in its ending inventory.

e) A corporate income tax rate of 30% is assumed.

Prepare the worksheet adjustments pertaining to goodwill amortization and the intercompany transactions, and prepare the interperiod tax allocations that result from the elimination of the intercompany transactions. The companies do not qualify as an affiliated group under the tax code.

Exercise 8. Trailer Corporation purchased a 25% interest in Like Company for $110,000 on January 1, 19X7. The following determination and distribution of excess schedule was prepared:

Price paid		$110,000
Less interest acquired:		
Common stock ($10 par)	$200,000	
Retained earnings.	100,000	
Total stockholders' equity	$300,000	
Interest acquired.	25%	75,000
Excess of cost over book value		$ 35,000

(continued)

Less excess attributable to equipment, 25% × $40,000

(10-year life)   10,000

Goodwill (20-year life). . . . . $ 25,000

Like Company earned income of $20,000 in 19X7 and $24,000 in 19X8. Like Company declared a 25-cent per share cash dividend on December 22, 19X8, payable January 12, 19X9, to stockholders of record on December 30, 19X8.

During 19X8, Like sold merchandise costing $10,000 to Trailer for $15,000. 20% of the merchandise was still in Trailer's ending inventory on December 31, 19X8.

Prepare the equity adjustment required by APB Opinion No. 18 on Trailer's books on December 31, 19X7, and December 31, 19X8, to account for its investment in Like Company. Assume Trailer Corporation makes no adjustment except at the end of each calendar year. Ignore income tax considerations.

Exercise 9.   Bert Company purchased a 30% interest in Mickey Company for $90,000 on January 1, 19X1, when Mickey had the following stockholders' equity:

Common stock ($10 par)	$100,000
Paid-in capital in excess of par.	20,000
Retained earnings	130,000
Total	$250,000

Any excess cost was due to goodwill that is being amortized over 10 years.

Since the investment, Bert had consistently sold goods to Mickey to realize a 30% gross profit. Such sales totaled $50,000 during 19X3. Mickey had $10,000 of such goods in its beginning inventory and $40,000 in its ending inventory.

On January 1, 19X3, Mickey sold a machine with a book value of $15,000 to Bert for $20,000. The machine has a 5-year life and is being depreciated on a straight-line basis.

Mickey reported a net income of $60,000 before taxes for 19X3. Mickey paid $5,000 in dividends in 19X3.

Prepare all entries caused by Bert's investment in Mickey for 19X3 (ignore tax ramifications). Assume that Bert has recorded the tax on its internally generated income. Bert has properly recorded the investment in previous periods.

Exercise 10.   Spancrete Corporation acquired a 30% interest in the outstanding stock of Werl Corporation on January 1, 19X5. At that time, the following determination and distribution of excess schedule was prepared:

Price paid		$125,000
Less interest acquired:		
Common stock	$150,000	
Retained earnings.	160,000	
Total stockholders' equity	$310,000	
Interest acquired.	30%	93,000
Excess of cost over book value attributable to goodwill		
(10-year life)		$ 32,000

During 19X5, Spancrete purchased $200,000 of goods from Werl. $20,000 of these purchases were in the December 31, 19X5 ending inventory. During 19X6, Spancrete purchased $250,000 of goods from Werl. $30,000 of these purchases were in the December 31, 19X6 ending inventory. Werl's gross profit rate is 30%.

Also, Spancrete purchased a machine from Werl for $15,000 on January 1, 19X6. The machine had a book value of $10,000 and a 5-year remaining life. Werl reported net income of $90,000 and paid $20,000 on dividends during 19X6.

Prepare an income distribution schedule for Werl, and record the entries to adjust the investment in Werl for 19X6.

Exercise 11. Hanson Corporation purchased a 10% interest in Novic Company on January 1, 19X6, and an additional 15% interest on January 1, 19X8. These investments cost Hanson Corporation $80,000 and $110,000, respectively.

The following stockholders' equities of Novic Company are available:

	December 31, 19X5	December 31, 19X7
Common stock ($10 par)	$500,000	$500,000
Retained earnings	250,000	300,000
Total equity	$750,000	$800,000

Any excess of cost over book value on the original investment was attributed to goodwill and given a 5-year life. Any excess on the second purchase is attributable to equipment with a 4-year life.

Novic Company had income of $30,000, $30,000, and $40,000 for 19X6, 19X7, and 19X8, respectively. Novic paid dividends of $.20 per share in 19X7 and 19X8.

Ignore income tax considerations, and assume adjusting entries are made at the end of the calendar year only.

1. Prepare the cost-to-equity conversion entry, as required by APB Opinion No. 18, on January 1, 19X8, when Hanson's investment in Novic Company first exceeded 20%. Any supporting schedules should be in good form.
2. Prepare the December 31, 19X8 equity adjustment on Hanson's books. Provide supporting calculations in good form.

Exercise 12. On January 1, 19X7, Lund Corporation purchased a 30% interest in Aluma-Boat Company for $200,000. At the time of the purchase, Aluma-Boat had total stockholders' equity of $400,000. Any excess of cost over the equity purchased was attributed in part to machinery worth $50,000 more than book value with a remaining useful life of 5 years. Any remaining excess would be allocated to goodwill with an assumed life of 10 years.

Aluma-Boat reported the following income and dividend distributions in 19X7 and 19X8:

	19X7	19X8
Income	$50,000	$45,000
Dividends declared and paid . .	10,000	10,000

Lund sold its investment in Aluma-Boat Company on January 2, 19X9, for $230,000. Record the sale of the investments. You may ignore income taxes. Carefully schedule the investment account balance at the time of the sale.

Problems

Problem 6-1.   Anton Company is an 80%-owned subsidiary of Roland Company. The interest in Anton was purchased on January 1, 19X0, for $620,000 cash. At that date, Anton had a stockholders' equity of $650,000. The excess price was attributed to equipment with a 5-year life undervalued by $25,000 and to goodwill with an estimated life of 10 years.

The following comparative consolidated trial balances apply to Roland Company and its subsidiary, Anton:

	December 31, 19X0	December 31, 19X1
Cash	$ 34,000	$ 55,500
Inventory	120,000	160,000
Accounts receivable	200,000	300,000
Property, plant, and equipment.	3,000,000	3,350,000
Accumulated depreciation	(1,080,000)	(1,280,000)
Investment in Charles Corp. (30%)		244,500
Goodwill	72,000	64,000
Accounts payable	(117,000)	(200,000)
Bonds payable	(100,000)	(400,000)
Minority interest.	(138,000)	(151,000)
Controlling interest:		
Common stock, par	(1,000,000)	(1,000,000)
Additional paid-in capital	(650,000)	(650,000)
Retained earnings	(341,000)	(493,000)
Total	$ 0	$ 0

The following 19X1 information is available for the Roland and Anton companies:

a) *Anton purchased equipment for $50,000.*

b) *Anton issued $300,000 of long-term bonds and later used the proceeds to purchase a new building*

c) *On January 1, 19X1, Roland purchased 30% of the outstanding common stock of Charles Corporation for $230,000. This is an influential investment. Charles's stockholders' equity was $700,000 on the date of the purchase. Any excess cost is attributed to goodwill with a 10-year life. Charles reported net income of $80,000 in 19X1 and paid dividends of $25,000.*

d) *Consolidated net income (controlling interest) for 19X1 was $252,000; the minority interest in combined net income was $16,000. Roland paid $100,000 in dividends in 19X1; Anton paid $15,000 in dividends in 19X1.*

Required:

Prepare the consolidated statement of cash flows for 19X1 using the indirect method. Any supporting calculations should be in good form.

Problem 6-2.   Billing Enterprises purchased a 90% interest in the common stock of Raush Corporation on January 1, 19X0, for an agreed price of $500,000. Billing issued $400,000 of bonds to Raush shareholders plus $100,000 cash as payment. Raush's balance sheet on the acquisition date was as follows:

Assets		Liabilities and Equity	
Cash	$ 60,000	Accounts payable	$ 45,000
Accounts receivable	95,000	Long-term liabilities	120,000
Plant assets (net)	460,000	Common stock ($10 par)	150,000
		Retained earnings	300,000
Total assets	$615,000	Total liabilities and equity	$615,000

Raush's equipment was understated by $20,000 and had a remaining depreciable life of 5 years. Any remaining excess was attributed to goodwill with a 10-year life.

In addition to the bonds issued as part of the purchase, Billing sold additional bonds in the amount of $100,000.

Combined net income for 19X0 was $85,000. The controlling interest was $80,000, and the minority interest was $5,000. Raush paid $10,000 in dividends to all shareholders, including Billing Enterprises.

No plant assets were purchased or sold during 19X0.

Comparative balance sheet data are as follows:

	December 31, 19W9 Parent Only	December 31, 19X0 Consolidated
Cash	$ 82,000	$ 182,700
Accounts receivable	120,000	161,000
Plant assets (net)	870,000	1,276,000
Goodwill		69,300
Accounts payable	(52,000)	(80,000)
Bonds payable		(500,000)
Long-term liabilities	(80,000)	(40,000)
Minority interest		(49,000)
Controlling interest:		
Common stock ($10 par)	(200,000)	(200,000)
Additional paid-in capital	(300,000)	(300,000)
Retained earnings	(440,000)	(520,000)
Total	$ 0	$ 0

Required:

Prepare a consolidated statement of cash flows using the indirect method for the year ended December 31, 19X0. Supporting schedules should be in good form.

Problem 6-3.   Presented below are the consolidated workpaper balances of Bush Inc. and its subsidiary, Dorr Corporation, as of December 31, 19X6 and 19X5:

Assets	19X6	19X5	Net Change Incr. (Decr.)
Cash	$ 313,000	$ 195,000	$118,000
Marketable equity securities (at cost)	175,000	175,000	
Allowance to reduce marketable equity securities to market	(13,000)	(24,000)	11,000
Accounts receivable (net)	418,000	440,000	(22,000)

(continued)

Inventories.	595,000	525,000	70,000
Land.	385,000	170,000	215,000
Plant and equipment	755,000	690,000	65,000
Accumulated depreciation	(199,000)	(145,000)	(54,000)
Goodwill (net)	57,000	60,000	(3,000)
Total assets.	$2,486,000	$2,086,000	$400,000

Liabilities and Stockholders' Equity

Current portion of long-term note	$150,000	$ 150,000	
Accounts payable and accrued liabilities . .	595,000	474,000	$121,000
Note payable, long-term	300,000	450,000	(150,000)
Deferred income taxes.	44,000	32,000	12,000
Minority interest in net assets of subsidiary .	179,000	161,000	18,000
Common stock ($10 par)	580,000	480,000	100,000
Additional paid-in capital.	303,000	180,000	123,000
Retained earnings.	335,000	195,000	140,000
Treasury stock (at cost).		(36,000)	36,000
Total liabilities and stockholders' equity .	$2,486,000	$2,086,000	$400,000

Additional information:

a) On January 20, 19X6, Bush Inc. issued 10,000 shares of its common stock for land having a fair market value of $215,000.

b) On February 5, 19X6, Bush reissued all of its treasury stock for $44,000.

c) On May 15, 19X6, Bush paid a cash dividend of $58,000 on its common stock.

d) On August 8, 19X6, equipment was purchased for $127,000.

e) On September 30, 19X6, equipment was sold for $40,000. The equipment cost $62,000 and had a net book value of $34,000 on the date of the sale.

f) On December 15, 19X6, Dorr Corporation paid a cash dividend of $50,000 on its common stock.

g) Deferred income taxes represent timing differences relating to the use of accelerated depreciation methods for income tax reporting and the straight-line method for financial reporting.

h) Net income for 19X6 was as follows:

Controlling interest in combined net income	$198,000
Dorr Corporation	110,000

i) Bush Inc. owns 70% of Dorr Corporation. There was no change in ownership interest in Dorr during 19X5 and 19X6. There were no intercompany transactions other than the dividend paid to Bush by its subsidiary.

Required:

Prepare the statement of cash flows for the consolidated company using the indirect method. A cash analysis worksheet should be prepared to aid in the development of the statement. Any other supporting schedules should be in good form.

Problem 6-4.   On January 1, 19X2, Peanut Corporation acquired an 80% interest in Sunny Corporation. Information regarding the income and equity structure of the two companies as of the year ended December 31, 19X4, is as follows:

	Peanut	Sunny
Internally generated net income.	$55,500	$56,000
Common shares outstanding during the year	20,000	12,000
Warrants to acquire Peanut stock, outstanding during the year.	2,000	1,000
5% convertible (into Sunny's shares), $100 par preferred shares, outstanding during the year		800
Nonconvertible preferred shares outstanding	1,000	

Additional information is as follows:

a)   The warrants to acquire Peanut stock were issued in 19X3. Each warrant can be exchanged for one share of Peanut common stock at an exercise price of $12 per share.

b)   Each share of convertible preferred stock can be converted into two shares of Sunny common stock. The preferred stock pays an annual dividend totaling $4,000. Peanut owns 60% of the convertible preferred stock.

c)   The nonconvertible preferred stock was issued on July 1, 19X4, and paid a 6-month dividend totaling $500.

d)   Relevant market prices per share of Peanut common stock during 19X4 are as follows:

	Average
1st Quarter	$10
2nd Quarter	12
3rd Quarter	13
4th Quarter	16

Required:

Compute the basic and diluted consolidated EPS for the year ended December 31, 19X4. Use quarterly share averaging.

Problem 6-5.   On January 1, 19X1, Delta Corporation exchanged 12,000 shares of its common stock for an 80% interest in Moore Company. The stock issued had a par value of $10 per share and a market value of $20 per share. On the date of purchase, Moore had the following balance sheet:

Common stock ($2 par)	$ 20,000
Paid-in capital in excess of par.	50,000
Retained earnings	100,000
Total equity	$170,000

On the purchase date, Moore had equipment with an 8-year remaining life that was undervalued by $20,000. Any remaining excess cost was attributed to goodwill with a 15-year remaining life.

There are intercompany merchandise sales. During 19X2, Delta sold $20,000 of merchandise to Moore. Moore sold $30,000 of merchandise to Delta. Moore had

(continued)

$2,000 of Delta goods in its beginning inventory and $4,200 of Delta goods in its ending inventory. Delta had $2,500 of Moore goods in its beginning inventory and $3,000 of Moore goods in its ending inventory. Delta's gross profit rate is 40%; Moore's is 25%.

On July 1, 19X1, Delta sold a machine to Moore for $90,000. The book value of the machine on Delta's books was $50,000 at the time of the sale. The machine has a 5-year remaining life. Depreciation on the machine is included in expenses.

The consolidated group meets the requirements of an affiliated group under the tax law and files a consolidated tax return. The original purchase was not structured as a nontaxable exchange. Assume a 30% tax rate.

Delta uses the cost method to record its investment in Moore. Since Moore has never paid dividends, Delta has not recorded any income on its investment in Moore. The two companies prepared the following income statements for 19X2:

	Delta	Moore
Sales	$1,000,000	$600,000
Less cost of goods sold	800,000	375,000
Gross profit	$ 200,000	$225,000
Less expenses	80,000	185,000
Income before tax	$ 120,000	$ 40,000

Required:

Prepare the 19X2 consolidated net income in schedule form. Include eliminations and adjustments. Provide income distribution schedules to allocate combined net income to the controlling and minority interests.

Problem 6-6. On January 1, 19X1, Pepper Company purchased 80% of the common stock of Salt Company for $270,000. On this date, Salt had total owners' equity of $300,000. Any excess of cost over book value is due to goodwill, to be amortized over 15 years.

During 19X1, Pepper has appropriately accounted for its investment in Salt using the simple equity method.

During 19X1, Pepper sold merchandise to Salt for $50,000, of which $10,000 is held by Salt on December 31, 19X1. Pepper's gross profit on sales is 40%.

During 19X1, Salt sold some land to Pepper at a gain of $10,000. Pepper still holds the land at year-end. Pepper and Salt qualify as an affiliated group for tax purposes and, thus, will file a consolidated tax return. Assume a 30% corporate income tax rate.

The following trial balances were prepared on December 31, 19X1:

	Pepper Company	Salt Company
Inventory, December 31	100,000	50,000
Other Current Assets	198,000	200,000
Investment in Salt Co.	302,000	
Land	240,000	100,000
Buildings and Equipment	300,000	200,000
Accumulated Depreciation	(80,000)	(60,000)
Current Liabilities	(150,000)	(50,000)
Long-Term Liabilities	(200,000)	(100,000)
Common Stock	(100,000)	(50,000)

Paid-In Capital in Excess of Par	(180,000)	(100,000)
Retained Earnings	(320,000)	(150,000)
Sales.	(500,000)	(300,000)
Cost of Goods Sold	300,000	180,000
Operating Expenses.	100,000	80,000
Subsidiary Income	(40,000)	
Gain on Sale of Land.		(10,000)
Dividends Declared	30,000	10,000
Totals.	$ 0	$ 0

Required:

Prepare a consolidated worksheet for Pepper Company and Subsidiary Salt Company for the year ended December 31, 19X1. Include the determination and distribution of excess schedule and the income distribution schedules.

Problem 6-7.   On January 1, 19X6, Pankow Company purchased an 80% interest in Johnson Company for $420,000. Pankow Company prepared the following determination and distribution of excess schedule for its investment:

Price paid		$420,000
Less interest acquired:		
Common stock ($10 par)	$100,000	
Paid-in capital in excess of par	150,000	
Retained earnings	200,000	
Total stockholders' equity	$450,000	
Interest acquired	80%	360,000
Excess of cost over book value		$ 60,000
Less excess attributable to building, 80% × $30,000		
undervaluation (20-year life)		24,000
Goodwill (15-year life).		$ 36,000

Additional information:

a) On July 1, 19X6, Pankow sold a machine to Johnson Company for $40,000. The machine had a net book value of $24,000 and an estimated future life of 8 years as of the sale date. Straight-line depreciation is assumed.

b) Pankow and Johnson had intercompany merchandise sales since January 1, 19X6. A summary of the 19X8 intercompany merchandise sales follows:

	Pankow to Johnson	Johnson to Pankow
Seller's merchandise in buyer's		
January 1, 19X8 inventory	$ 3,000	$ 1,000
19X8 sales.	20,000	30,000
Seller's merchandise in buyer's		
December 31, 19X8 inventory.	2,000	3,000
Outstanding intercompany payables,		
December 31, 19X8	1,500	2,000
Gross profit on sales	25%	30%

(continued)

c) *Trial balances of the two companies as of December 31, 19X8, are as follows:*

	Pankow Company	Johnson Company
Cash.	$ 112,600	$ 35,000
Accounts Receivable	180,000	84,000
Inventory	200,000	100,000
Investment in Johnson Company.	420,000	
Property, Plant, and Equipment.	1,800,000	750,000
Accumulated Depreciation.	(1,180,000)	(365,500)
Accounts Payable	(136,000)	(68,000)
Other Liabilities.	(46,000)	(6,000)
Common Stock ($10 par)	(1,000,000)	(100,000)
Paid-In Capital in Excess of Par		(150,000)
Retained Earnings, Jan. 1, 19X7	(260,000)	(250,000)
Sales.	(1,200,000)	(400,000)
Subsidiary Dividend Income	(10,000)	
Cost of Goods Sold	800,000	250,000
Other Expenses.	259,400	108,000
Dividends Declared	60,000	12,500
Total	$ 0	$ 0

d) *Neither company has provided for income tax. The companies qualify as an affiliated group and, thus, will file a consolidated tax return based on a 30% corporate tax rate. The original purchase was not a nontaxable exchange.*

Required:

1. Prepare a consolidated worksheet based on the trial balances. Include a provision for income tax and include the income distribution schedules.
2. Record the provisions for tax on the books of the separate companies.

Problem 6-8.   On January, 1, 19X1, Pikkart Company acquired 70% of the common stock of Sundee Company for $340,400 in a taxable combination. On this date, Sundee had total owners' equity of $422,000, including retained earnings of $222,000. Any excess of cost over book value is attributable to goodwill, which is to be amortized over 15 years.

During 19X1 and 19X2, Sundee Company reported the following information:

	19X1	19X2
Net income before taxes	$40,000	$40,000
Dividends.	0	30,000

During 19X1 and 19X2, Pikkart has appropriately accounted for its investment in Sundee using the simple equity method, including income tax effects.

On January 1, 19X2, Pikkart held merchandise acquired from Sundee for $10,000. During 19X2, Sundee sold merchandise to Pikkart for $60,000, of which $20,000 is held by Pikkart on December 31, 19X2. Sundee's usual gross profit on affiliated sales is 40%.

On December 31, 19X1, Pikkart sold some equipment to Sundee with a cost of $40,000 and a book value of $18,000. The sales price was $30,000. Sundee is depreciating the equipment over a 3-year life, assuming no salvage value and using the straight-line method.

Pikkart and Sundee do not qualify as an affiliated group for tax purposes and, thus, will file separate tax returns. Assume a 30% corporate tax rate and an 80% dividends-received exclusion.

The following trial balances were prepared by Pikkart and Sundee on December 31, 19X2:

	Pikkart Company	Sundee Company
Inventory, December 31.	$110,000	$ 85,000
Other Current Assets	327,176	295,000
Investment in Sundee Co.	378,200	
Land.	150,000	90,000
Buildings and Equipment	335,000	280,000
Accumulated Depreciation	(150,000)	(70,000)
Deferred Tax Liability.	(2,268)	
Income Taxes Payable	(31,260)	(24,000)
Other Current Liabilities	(120,000)	(80,000)
Long-Term Liabilities.	(200,000)	(100,000)
Common Stock.	(100,000)	(50,000)
Paid-In Capital in Excess of Par.	(200,000)	(150,000)
Retained Earnings.	(450,000)	(250,000)
Sales	(590,000)	(370,000)
Cost of Goods Sold	340,000	220,000
Operating Expenses	150,000	70,000
Subsidiary Income	(39,200)	
Provision for Income Taxes	32,352	24,000
Dividends Declared.	60,000	30,000
Totals	$ 0	$ 0

Required:

Prepare a consolidated worksheet for Pikkart Company and Subsidiary Sundee Company for the year ended December 31, 19X2. Include the determination and distribution of excess schedule and the income distribution schedules.

Problem 6-9.   Heinrich Company purchased an influential 25% interest in Fink Company on January 1, 19X6, for $320,000. At that time, Fink's stockholders' equity was $1,000,000.

Fink Company assets had market value similar to book value except for a building that was undervalued by $40,000. The building had an estimated remaining life of 20 years. Any remaining excess was attributed to goodwill with a 10-year life.

The following additional information is available:

a)   On July 1, 19X6, Heinrich sold a machine to Fink for $24,000. The carrying value of the machine to Heinrich was $16,000. The machine is being depreciated on a straight-line basis over 10 years.

b)   Heinrich provides management services to Fink at a billing rate of $15,000 per year. This arrangement started in 19X6.

(continued)

c) *Fink has sold merchandise to Heinrich since 19X7. Sales were $10,000 in 19X7 and $25,000 in 19X8. The merchandise is sold to provide a gross profit rate of 25%. Heinrich had $2,000 of these goods in its December 31, 19X7 inventory and $3,000 of such goods in its December 31, 19X8 inventory.*

d) *The income earned and dividends paid by Fink are as follows:*

Year	Income	Dividends
19X6	$48,000	$10,000
19X7	50,000	10,000
19X8	65,000	10,000

Required:

Prepare all entries necessitated by Heinrich's investment in Fink Company for 19X6 through 19X8 using the equity method for an influential investment. Supporting schedules should be in good form. Ignore taxes.

Problem 6-10.   On January 1, 19X6, Autumn Company purchased a 25% interest in Clarence Company for $180,000. Autumn Company prepared the following determination and distribution of excess schedule:

Price paid for investment:			$180,000
Less book value of interest acquired:			
Common stock ($5 par)		$100,000	
Paid-in capital in excess of par		200,000	
Retained earnings		150,000	
Total stockholders' equity.		$450,000	
Interest acquired	25%	112,500	
Excess of cost over book value (debit).			$ 67,500
Equipment, 25% × $30,000 (10-year life)			7,500 Dr.
Goodwill (20-year life)			$ 60,000 Dr.

The following additional information is available:

a) *Clarence Company sold a machine to Autumn Company for $30,000 on July 1, 19X7. At this date, the machine had a book value of $25,000 and an estimated future life of 5 years. Straight-line depreciation (to the nearest month) is being used. For income tax purposes, the gain on the sale was taxable in the year of the sale.*

b) *The following applies to Autumn Company sales to Clarence Company for 19X7 and 19X8:*

	19X7	19X8
Intercompany merchandise in beginning inventory		$ 4,000
Sales for the year	$10,000	15,000
Intercompany merchandise in ending inventory	4,000	5,000
Gross profit on sales	40%	40%

c) *Internally generated net income, (before tax) for the two companies are as follows:*

	19X6	19X7	19X8
Autumn Company	$140,000	$150,000	$155,000
Clarence Company	40,000	50,000	45,000

d) *Clarence paid dividends of $5,000, $10,000, and $10,000 in 19X6, 19X7, and 19X8, respectively.*

e) *The corporate income tax rate of 30% applies to both companies. Assume an 80% dividend exclusion.*

Required:

Prepare all adjustments to Autumn Company's investment in Clarence Company account, as required by APB Opinion No. 18, on December 31, 19X6, 19X7, and 19X8. Consider income tax implications. Supporting calculations and schedules should be in good form.

Problem 6-11.   Bastian Inc., a domestic corporation having a fiscal year ending June 30, has purchased common stock in several other domestic corporations. As of June 30, 19X8, the balance in Bastian's investment account was $870,600, the total cost of stock purchased less the cost of stock sold. Bastian Inc. wishes to restate the investment account to reflect the provisions of APB Opinion No. 18.
Data concerning the investments follow:

		Hupp Inc.	Geer Inc.	Cargo Inc.
Shares of common stock outstanding		3,000	32,000	100,000
Shares purchased by Bastian	(a)	300	8,000	30,000
	(b)	810		
Date of purchase	(a)	July 1, 19X5	June 30, 19X6	June 30, 19X7
	(b)	July 1, 19X7		
Cost of shares purchased	(a)	$ 49,400	$46,000	$670,000
	(b)	142,000		

Balance sheet at date indicated:

Assets	Hupp Inc. July 1, 19X7	Geer Inc. June 30, 19X6	Cargo Inc. June 30, 19X7
Current assets	$ 362,000	$ 39,600	$ 994,500
Property, plant, and equipment (net of depreciation)	1,638,000	716,400	3,300,000
Patent (net of amortization)			148,500
Total assets	$2,000,000	$ 756,000	$4,443,000
Liabilities and Equity			
Liabilities	$1,500,000	$ 572,000	$2,494,500
Common stock	260,000	80,000	1,400,000
Retained earnings	240,000	104,000	548,500
Total liabilities and equity	$2,000,000	$ 756,000	$4,443,000

(continued)

Additional information:

	Hupp Inc.	Geer Inc.	Cargo Inc.
Changes in common stock since July 1, 19X5	None	None	None
Average remaining life of plant assets at date of balance sheet (above)	12 years	9 years	22 years
Analysis of retained earnings:			
Balance, July 1, 19X5	$234,000		
Net income, July 1, 19X5, to June 30, 19X6	53,400		
Dividend paid—April 1, 19X6.	(51,000)		
Balance, June 30, 19X6.	$236,400	$104,000	
Net income (loss), July 1, 19X6, to June 30, 19X7	55,600	(2,000)	
Dividend paid—April 1, 19X7.	(52,000)		
Balance, June 30, 19X7.	$240,000	$102,000	$548,500
Net income, July 1, 19X7, to June 30, 19X8	25,000	18,000	330,000
Dividends paid:			
December 31, 19X7			(150,000)
June 1, 19X8		(5,600)	
Balance, June 30, 19X8.	$265,000	$114,400	$728,500

Bastian's first purchase of Hupp stock was made because of the high rate of return expected on the investment. All later purchases of stock were made to gain significant influence over the operations of the various companies.

In December, 19X7, changing market conditions caused Bastian to reevaluate its relation to Geer. On December 31, 19X7, Bastian sold 6,400 shares of Geer for $54,400.

For Hupp and Geer, the fair market values of the net assets did not differ materially from the book values shown in the balance sheets. For Cargo, fair market values exceeded book values only with respect to the patent, which had a market value of $151,500 in excess of book value and a remaining life of 15 years as of June 30, 19X7.

At June 30, 19X8, Bastian's inventory included $48,600 of items purchased from Cargo during May and June at a 20% markup over Cargo's cost.

Required:

Prepare a worksheet to calculate the balance of Bastian's investment account as of June 30, 19X8, and its investment income by year for the 3 years then ended. Transactions should be listed in chronological order, and supporting computations and schedules should be in good form. Ignore income taxes. Amortization of goodwill, if any, is to be over a 40-year period. Use the following columnar headings for the worksheet:

		Investments			Investment Income For Year Ended June 30			Other Accounts	
		Hupp	Geer	Cargo	19X6	19X7	19X8	Name	Amount
Date	Description	Dr. (Cr.)	Dr. (Cr.)	Dr. (Cr.)	Cr. (Dr.)	Cr. (Dr.)	Cr. (Dr.)		Dr. (Cr.)

(AICPA adapted)

Worksheet 6-1

Affiliates File Consolidated Income Tax Return
Company P and Subsidiary Company S
Worksheet for Consolidated Financial Statements
For Year Ended December 31, 19X3

	(Credit balance amounts are in parentheses.)	Trial Balance	
		Company P	Company S
1	Cash	205,000	380,000
2	Inventory, Dec. 31, 19X3	150,000	120,000
3	Plant and Equipment	900,000	1,100,000
4	Accumulated Depreciation	(440,000)	(150,000)
5			
6	Investment in Company S	1,115,000	
7			
8			
9	Goodwill		
10	Liabilities		(150,000)
11	Common Stock, Co. P.	(800,000)	
12	Retained Earnings, Jan. 1, 19X3, Co. P	(900,000)	
13			
14			
15	Common Stock, Co. S		(500,000)
16	Retained Earnings, Jan. 1, 19X3, Co. S		(700,000)
17			
18	Sales	(600,000)	(400,000)
19	Cost of Goods Sold	350,000	200,000
20			
21	Expenses	100,000	100,000
22	Subsidiary Income	(80,000)	
23		0	0
24	**Combined Income Before Tax**		
25	**Provision for Income Tax**		
26	**Income Tax Payable**		
27		0	0
28	Combined Net Income		
29	To Minority Interest (see distribution schedule)		
30	Balance to Controlling Interest (see distribution schedule)		
31	Total Minority Interest		
32	Retained Earnings, Controlling Interest, Dec. 31, 19X3		
33			

Worksheet 6-1 (see page 6-14)

Eliminations & Adjustments Dr.		Eliminations & Adjustments Cr.		Consolidated Income Statement	Minority Interest	Controlling Retained Earnings	Consolidated Balance Sheet	
							585,000	1
		(9)	35,000				235,000	2
		(5)	20,000				1,980,000	3
(5)	4,000						(582,000)	4
(6)	4,000							5
		(1)	80,000					6
		(2)	960,000					7
		(3)	75,000					8
(3)	75,000	(4)	15,000				60,000	9
							(150,000)	10
							(800,000)	11
(4)	10,000					(854,000)		12
(5)	16,000							13
(8)	20,000							14
(2)	400,000				(100,000)			15
(2)	560,000				(135,000)			16
(8)	5,000							17
(7)	100,000			(900,000)				18
(9)	35,000	(7)	100,000	460,000				19
		(8)	25,000					20
(4)	5,000	(6)	4,000	201,000				21
(1)	80,000							22
								23
				(239,000)				24
(10)	**71,700**			71,700				25
		(10)	**71,700**				(71,700)	26
1,385,700		1,385,700						27
				(167,300)				28
				12,600	(12,600)			29
				154,700		(154,700)		30
					(247,600)		(247,600)	31
						(1,008,700)	(1,008,700)	32
							0	33

(continued)

Eliminations and Adjustments:

(1) Eliminate the parent's entry recording its share of the current year's subsidiary income. This step returns the investment account to its balance on January 1, 19X3.

(2) Eliminate 80% of the January 1, 19X3 subsidiary equity balances against the investment in Company S.

(3) Distribute the $75,000 excess of cost to the goodwill account.

(4) Amortize the goodwill at an annual amount of $5,000 for each of the past two years and for the current year.

(5) Remove from retained earnings the undepreciated gain at the beginning of the year on the sale of the equipment. Since the sale was by the parent, the entire adjustment is removed from the controlling interest in retained earnings.

(6) Adjust accumulated depreciation and the current year's depreciation expense for the $4,000 overstatement of depreciation caused by the original $20,000 intercompany gain.

(7) Eliminate intercompany merchandise sales of $100,000 to avoid double counting.

(8) Reduce the cost of goods sold by the $25,000 of intercompany profit included in the beginning inventory. Since the sale was made by the subsidiary, the reduction to retained earnings is borne 80% by the controlling interest and 20% by the minority interest.

(9) Reduce the ending inventory to its cost to the consolidated firm by decreasing it $35,000, and increase the cost of goods sold by $35,000.

(10) Record the provision for income tax, calculated as follows: $39,000 \times .3 = $71,700.

Subsidiary Company S Income Distribution

Gross profit on ending inventory (50% × $70,000) . . . . (9) $35,000	Internally generated net income before tax . . Gross profit on beginning inventory (50% × $50,000) . . . . (8)	$100,000 25,000
	Adjusted income before tax	$ 90,000
	Company S share of taxes **(30% × $90,000)** . . . . **(10)**	**27,000**
	Company S net income	$ 63,000
	Minority share	20%
	Minority interest	$ 12,600

Parent Company P Income Distribution

Amortization of goodwill . . . . (4) $ 5,000	Internally generated income before tax . . . . . Realized profit on equipment ($20,000 × 20%) . . . . (6)	$150,000 $ 4,000
	Adjusted income before tax	$149,000
	Company P shares of taxes **(30% × $149,000)** . . . . **(10)**	**44,700**
	Company P net income	$104,300
	Share of subsidiary net income (80% × $63,000)	50,400
	Controlling interest	$154,700

Worksheet 6-2

Nonaffiliated Group for Tax Purposes
Company P and Subsidiary Company S
Worksheet for Consolidated Financial Statements
For Year Ended December 31, 19X4

	(Credit balance amounts are in parentheses.)	Trial Balance	
		Company P	Company S
1	Cash	19,200	80,000
2	Inventory, Dec. 31, 19X4	170,000	150,000
3	Plant and Equipment	600,000	550,000
4	Accumulated Depreciation	(410,000)	(120,000)
5			
6	Investment in Company S	504,000	
7			
8			
9	Goodwill		
10	Common Stock, Co. P	(250,000)	
11	Retained Earnings, Jan. 1, 19X4, Co. P	(510,450)	
12			
13			
14	Common Stock, Co. S		(250,000)
15	Retained Earnings, Jan. 1, 19X4, Co. S		(350,000)
16			
17	Sales	(430,000)	(240,000)
18	Cost of Goods Sold	280,000	150,000
19			
20	Expenses	70,000	30,000
21	**Provision for Income Tax**	**25,890**	**18,000**
22	Subsidiary Income	(31,500)	
23	**Income Tax Payable**	**(24,000)**	**(18,000)**
24	**Deferred Tax (Liability) Asset**	**(13,140)**	
25		0	0
26	Combined Net Income		
27	To Minority Interest (see distribution schedule)		
28	Balance to Controlling Interest (see distribution schedule)		
29	Total Minority Interest		
30	Retained Earnings, Controlling Interest, Dec. 31, 19X4		
31			

Worksheet 6-2 (see page 6-18)

Eliminations & Adjustments				Consolidated Income Statement	Minority Interest	Controlling Retained Earnings	Consolidated Balance Sheet	
Dr.		Cr.						
							99,200	1
		(9)	16,000				304,000	2
		(5)	40,000				1,110,000	3
(5)	8,000						(514,000)	4
(6)	8,000							5
		(1)	31,500					6
		(2)	450,000					7
		(3)	22,500					8
(3)	22,500	(4)	6,000				16,500	9
							(250,000)	10
(4)	4,500					(474,708)		11
(5)	24,000							12
(8)	24,000	(t1)	16,758					13
(2)	187,500				(62,500)			14
(2)	262,500				(81,900)			15
(5)	8,000	(t1)	2,400					16
(7)	100,000			(570,000)				17
		(7)	100,000	322,000				18
(9)	16,000	(8)	24,000					19
(4)	1,500	(6)	8,000	93,500				20
(t2)	4,602			48,492				21
(1)	31,500							22
							(42,000)	23
(t1)	19,158	(t2)	4,602				1,416	24
	721,760		721,760					25
				(106,008)				26
				11,900	(11,900)			27
				94,108		(94,108)		28
					(156,300)		(156,300)	29
						(568,816)	(568,816)	30
							0	31

(continued)

Eliminations and Adjustments:

(1) Eliminate the parent's entry recording its share of subsidiary income for the current year. The entry now includes the parent's share of the subsidiary income *after tax,* since the companies are taxed as separate entities.

(2) Eliminate 75% of the January 1, 19X4 subsidiary equity balances against the investment in Company S.

(3) Distribute the $22,500 excess of cost in the investment account to the goodwill account.

(4) Amortize the goodwill for the current year and the three previous years at $1,500 per year.

(5) Eliminate the unamortized intercompany profit on the equipment sale by Company S as of January 1, 19X4. This elimination includes a $40,000 reduction in the asset account, an $8,000 decrease in accumulated depreciation, and a $32,000 *(before-tax)* decrease in beginning retained earnings. Since the sale was by the subsidiary, the retained earnings adjustment is allocated 75% to the controlling interest and 25% to the minority interest.

(6) Adjust the current year's depreciation expense and accumulated depreciation by the $8,000 current year's portion of the intercompany profit on the equipment sale.

(7) Eliminate intercompany merchandise sales of $100,000 to avoid double counting.

(8) Remove the gross profit on intercompany sales recorded by Company P in 19X3 from its January 1, 19X4 retained earnings. The beginning inventory of Company S included $60,000 of goods sold by Company P with a gross profit of 40%, or $24,000. On a consolidated basis, the cost of goods sold is overstated, and this entry removes $24,000 from the consolidated cost of goods sold.

(9) Remove the $16,000 gross profit from the ending inventory and increase the cost of goods sold by the same amount. The Company S ending inventory includes $40,000 of goods sold by Company P with a gross profit of 40%.

(t1) Adjust the beginning retained earnings balance and create a deferred tax asset (DTA) on previous adjustments, as follows

		Deferred Tax Asset	
	Total	25% Minority Interest	75% Controlling Interest
DTA on $32,000 unamortized intercompany equipment gain of entry (5), paid by Company S (30% × $32,000)	$ 9,600	$2,400	$ 7,200
DTA on $32,000 unamortized intercompany gain of entry (5), paid by Company P (30% tax on 20% **taxable portion** of 75% share of after-tax gain of $22,400*)	1,008		1,008
DTA relating to Company P gross profit on goods in Company S beginning inventory, entry (8) (30% × $24,000)	7,200		7,200
Goodwill amortization (30% × $4,500)	1,350		1,350
Total increase in retained earnings and DTA	$19,158	$2,400	$16,758

*70% × $32,000 = $22,400

Entry (t1) increases the minority share of January 1, 19X4 retained earnings by $2,400 and increases the controlling share of January 1, 19X4 retained earnings by $16,758. The deferred tax liability is decreased by the total, $19,158.

(t2)   Adjust the current-year tax provision and adjust deferred tax expense for the tax effects of previous adjustments to the current year's income, as follows:

		Increase (decrease) in deferred tax asset	
	Total	25% Minority Interest	75% Controlling Interest
Expiration of DTA on equipment gain of entry (6), paid by Company S (30% × $8,000)	($2,400)	($600)	($1,800)
Expiration of DTA on equipment gain of entry (6), paid by Company P (30% tax on 20% **taxable portion** of 75% share of after-tax realized gain of $5,600*)	(252)		(252)
Expiration of DTA relating to gross profit on Company P goods in Company S beginning inventory, entry (8) (30% × $24,000)	(7,200)		(7,200)
DTA originating on gross profit on Company P goods in Company S ending inventory, entry (9) (30% × $16,000)	4,800		4,800
Goodwill amortization (30% × $1,500)	450		450
Total decrease in DTA.	($4,602)	($600)	($4,002)

*70% × $8,000 = $5,600

No adjustment results from the amortization of goodwill since it is not tax deductible.

Subsidiary Company S Income Distribution

Internally generated net income **after tax** (70% × $60,000)	$42,000
Realized gain on depreciable asset sale ($8,000 − $2,400 tax) . . . . . (6) **(t2)**	5,600
Adjusted net income	$47,600
Minority share	25%
Minority interest	$11,900

Parent Company P Income Distribution

Ending inventory profit ($16,000 − $4,800 tax) . . . . (9) **(t2)**	$11,200	Internally generated net income **after tax** (70% × $80,000)	$56,000
Goodwill amortization ($1,500 − $450 tax) . . . . (4) **(t2)**	$ 1,050	Beginning inventory profit ($24,000 − $7,200 tax) . . . . (8) **(t2)**	16,800
		75% of subsidiary adjusted income less tax [(75% × $47,600) − (30% tax × 20% **taxable portion** × 75% × $47,600)]	33,558
		Controlling interest	$94,108

Special Issues in Accounting for an Investment in a Subsidiary

This chapter considers several issues concerning the acquisition and sale of a parent's interest in a subsidiary. The first concern is unique purchase situations. A parent may purchase its interest directly from the subsidiary at the time of original issue. This will require special consideration when consolidating. Procedures also are developed for ownership interests that are acquired in a series of separate purchases over time.

This chapter then will consider the issues involved when a parent company sells all or a portion of its controlling interest in a subsidiary. Not only must the sale be properly recorded, special care must also be taken in accounting for any portion of the investment retained.

The final equity concern of the chapter is the procedure needed in consolidation when the subsidiary has preferred stock in its equity structure. An apportionment of retained earnings may be needed in order to properly account for the parent's interest in common stock. If the parent owns any subsidiary preferred stock, it must be treated as retired in the consolidation process.

The chapter concludes with an appendix that provides the consolidation procedures needed when a worksheet is used to produce only a consolidated balance sheet. These procedures are really only of concern when preparing for the CPA Exam. The Exam uses this approach to save time and space. It is not a worksheet that is used in practice since the accountant must prepare a consolidated income statement, a consolidated statement of retained earnings, and a consolidated balance sheet. There would be no reason to use a worksheet for only one of the three statements.

Parent Acquisition of Stock Directly from Subsidiary

A parent company may organize a new corporation and supply all of the common stock equity funds in exchange for all of the newly organized company's common stock. Since the newly formed corporation receives the funds directly, there will be no difference between the price paid for the shares and the equity in assets acquired. Thus, the determination and distribution of excess schedule will show no excess of cost over book value or excess of book value over cost.

In other cases, the parent company will allow the newly organized subsidiary to sell a portion of the shares to persons outside the consolidated group. If the shares are sold to outsiders at a price equal to the price paid by the parent, the cost and book value again will be equal. However, if a price greater or less than the price paid by the parent is charged to outside parties, an excess of cost or book value will result. This excess occurs because the total price paid by the parent will not equal its ownership interest multiplied by the total subsidiary common stockholders' equity.

Normally, the excess of cost is recorded as goodwill, and an excess of book value is recorded as a deferred credit since the only asset held by a newly organized company is cash, which is not subject to adjustment. If noncash assets are given in exchange for the subsidiary shares, these assets would be adjusted according to the normal distribution of excess procedures.

An existing corporation might sell a sufficient number of new shares to grant a controlling interest to the buying company. For example, assume Company S had the following equity balances prior to a sale of shares to Company P:

Common stock, $10 par, 10,000 shares	$100,000
Paid-in capital in excess of par	150,000
Retained earnings.	220,000
Total stockholders' equity	$470,000

Assume Company S sells 30,000 additional shares directly to Company P at $50 per share, for a total of $1,500,000. Subsequent to the sale, the equity balances of Company S appear as follows:

Common stock, $10 par, 40,000 shares	$ 400,000
Paid-in capital in excess of par	1,350,000
Retained earnings	220,000
Total stockholders' equity	$1,970,000

A determination and distribution of excess schedule must be prepared for this investment as it would be for any acquisition of a controlling interest. There is no direct connection between the price paid and the interest in subsidiary equity received. The monies paid become a part of the subsidiary's total equity. The interest purchased is a 75% interest (30,000 of 40,000 shares) in the total equity after the sale of the new shares, not a 100% interest in the funds provided by the specific sale of the new shares purchased by the parent. The following determination and distribution of excess schedule would be prepared for the interest purchased by the parent:

Price paid		$1,500,000
Less interest acquired:		
Common stock ($10 par)	$ 400,000	
Paid-in capital in excess of par	1,350,000	
Retained earnings.	220,000	
Total stockholders' equity	$1,970,000	
Interest acquired	75%	1,477,500
Excess of cost over book value		$ 22,500

The excess would be distributed using normal purchase rules. Any adjustment of existing identifiable accounts would be limited to 75% of the difference between book and market values since only a 75% interest has been purchased. Any remaining excess would be considered goodwill.

Piecemeal Acquisition of Interest in Subsidiary

Past examples of combinations in this text have involved an acquisition of a controlling interest in a subsidiary through its single purchase of stock. A parent also may acquire a controlling interest as a result of a series of purchases of subsidiary stock. Current practice follows the *parent company concept*, which views each block as a separate ownership interest with a different excess of cost or book value for each block. Each block is seen as having separate causal factors for the difference between the price paid and the underlying book value. Thus, each block requires a separate determination and distribution of excess schedule and separate elimination steps.

The Economic Entity Concept, advanced by the 1995 FASB Exposure Draft on Business Combinations, prepares only one determination and distribution schedule on the day that control is achieved. On that date, all accounts (with the possible exception of goodwill) are increased to their full market values. No adjustments are made to accounts on the day that any block, not creating control, is purchased. When control is achieved on the first block, a later block is viewed as a type of stock reacquisition which impacts only equity accounts. When control is achieved on a later purchase, the first block is added to the second and considered as if it were a single purchase at the summed price. The possible new procedures are explained in Special Appendix 2 which follows Chapter 8. This chapter will explain procedures currently in use.

Control Achieved upon Initial Investment

When control is achieved with the initial investment, consolidation procedures already are in effect when subsequent blocks are purchased. Thus, no major change in accounting methods is required. Another determination and distribution of excess schedule must be prepared for each new investment, and additions to the existing consolidated worksheet procedures must be acknowledged.

Assume Company P purchases on the open market its original 60% interest in Company S on January 1, 19X1, for $126,000, when Company S has the following balance sheet:

Assets		Liabilities and Equity	
Current assets	$ 50,000	Liabilities	$ 40,000
Equipment (net)	150,000	Common stock ($10 par).	100,000
		Retained earnings	60,000
Total assets	$200,000	Total liabilities and equity	$200,000

Further assume that the current assets require no adjustment, and the equipment has a net market value of $180,000 and a 5-year remaining life. Goodwill resulting from the purchase of the stock will be amortized over a 10-year period. The following determination and distribution of excess schedule would be prepared on *January 1, 19X1*, for the first acquisition:

Price paid		$126,000
Less interest acquired:		
Common stock	$100,000	
Retained earnings	60,000	
Total stockholders' equity.	$160,000	
Interest acquired.	**60%**	96,000
Excess of cost over book value (debit balance)		$ 30,000
Excess of cost attributable to equipment:		
60% × **$30,000** undervaluation (to be amortized		
over **5 years**)		18,000 Dr.
Goodwill (**10-year** amortization)		$ 12,000 Dr.

On January 1, 19X3, Company P purchases on the open market an additional 20% interest in Company S by paying $50,000. The following balance sheet of Company S on January 1, 19X3, reflects two years of continued operations:

Assets		Liabilities and Equity	
Current assets	$ 80,000	Liabilities	$ 50,000
Building (net).	80,000	Common stock ($10 par).	100,000
Equipment (net)	90,000	Retained earnings	100,000
Total assets	$250,000	Total liabilities and equity	$250,000

Company P's analysis on January 1, 19X3, indicates that the equipment listed on Company S's balance sheet now is undervalued by $24,000 and has a 3-year remaining life. The current assets and the building appear to have market values equal to their book values. Goodwill is assumed to have a 10-year life. Based on this analysis, the following determination and distribution of excess schedule would be prepared for the *January 1, 19X3* investment:

Price paid		$50,000	
Less interest acquired:			
Common stock	$100,000		
Retained earnings	100,000		
Total stockholders' equity.	$200,000		
Interest acquired.	**20%**	40,000	
Excess of cost over book value (debit balance)		$10,000	
Excess of cost attributable to equipment:			
20% × **$24,000** undervaluation (to be amortized over **3 years**)		4,800	Dr.
Goodwill (**10-year** amortization)		$5,200	Dr.

Note that this determination and distribution of excess schedule is *free standing;* that is, it is completely independent of the appraisals made for the January 1, 19X1 schedule.

The additional worksheet procedures that arise from this piecemeal acquisition are shown in Worksheet 7-1 on pages 7-54 to 7-57. The trial balances of Companies P and S are shown as they would appear on December 31, 19X3. The investment in the Company S account is based on the use of the simple equity method during the current and previous years. The December 31, 19X3 balance was determined as follows:

Cost of **60%** investment (January 1, 19X1)		$ 126,000
Add equity share of change in Company S retained earnings as of January 1, 19X3:		
Balance, January 1, 19X3	**$100,000**	
Balance, January 1, 19X1	**60,000**	
Increase in retained earnings.	**$ 40,000** × **60%** =	24,000
Cost of **20%** investment (January 1, 19X3)		50,000
Add equity share of Company S 19X3 net income:		
80% × $35,000		28,000
Investment account balance, December 31, 19X3 . . .		**$228,000**

The combined net income of $78,080 is distributed to the controlling and minority interests as shown in the income distribution schedules that accompany Worksheet 7-1. **Since only the parent's share of excesses of cost or book value is recorded,** all amortizations of excess resulting from parent company purchases are deducted **only** from the controlling interest.

When investment blocks are carried **at cost**, each block must be converted separately to its simple equity balance as of the **beginning** of the year. For each block, the adjustment is based on the change in subsidiary retained earnings between the date of acquisition of the individual block and the beginning of the current year.

The determination and distribution of excess schedule for the second block should consider existing unrealized intercompany profits recorded by the subsidiary. Suppose the subsidiary of the previous example sold merchandise to the parent during 19X2, and a $2,000 subsidiary profit is included in the parent's ending inventory of merchandise and in the subsidiary retained earnings. *In theory*, the determination and distribution of excess schedule prepared for the 20% investment purchased on January 1, 19X3, should reflect the unrealized gross profit on sales applicable to the 20% interest purchased. Thus, the determination and distribution of excess schedule would be revised to distribute the excess as follows:

Excess of cost over book value	$10,000
Deferred gross profit on inventory sale (**20%**)	400
Excess of cost attributable to equipment (3-year life)	(4,800)
Goodwill (10-year life)	$ 5,600

The deferred gross profit on the inventory sale means that the minority interest just acquired is overstated since the profit already is included in retained earnings. The decrease in the equity acquired increases the excess of cost over book value, thereby making more excess available to remaining assets.

The following entry would distribute the revised excess on the 19X3 worksheet:

Accumulated Depreciation—Equipment	4,800	
Goodwill	5,600	
Deferred Gross Profit on Inventory Sale		400
Investment in Company S		10,000

The following elimination for the $2,000 profit in the beginning inventory then would be made:

Retained Earnings—Controlling Interest (**60%** interest at time of		
original sale)	1,200	
Retained Earnings—Minority Interest (20%)	400	
Deferred Gross Profit on Inventory Sale	400	
Cost of Goods Sold (beginning inventory)		2,000

In practice, the concept of materiality often will prevail, and the above procedure may not be followed. The determination and distribution of excess schedule may not recognize the deferred inventory profit which will result in less excess being available to other assets. In this case, goodwill will be down by $400; this also would reduce goodwill amortization in the years that follow. Under this practical approach, worksheets for periods subsequent to the second purchase will ignore the deferred profit existing on the purchase date and will distribute the retained earnings adjustment according to the ownership percentages existing at the time the worksheet is prepared. In this example, the 20% profit applicable to the inventory on the second purchase date would be allocated to the parent with the following adjustment on the worksheet:

Retained Earnings—Controlling Interest (**80%**)	1,600	
Retained Earnings—Minority Interest (20%)	400	
Cost of Goods Sold (beginning inventory)		2,000

Notice that the practical approach eventually leads to the same result on the distribution of retained earnings as the theoretically correct approach. Under the correct theoretical approach, the parent retained earnings are reduced for 60% of the profit at the end of the first year. Eventually, it absorbs the other 20% interest through greater amortization of goodwill. Under the practical approach, the parent picks up the added 20% at the end of the first year. There is only a timing difference as to when the parent absorbs the 20% interest in the beginning inventory profit.

Control Not Achieved upon Initial Investment

Ordinarily it is improper to prepare consolidated statements when an initial investment in the stock of another company represents less than a 50% interest. Such an investment is carried under the cost or the sophisticated equity method, depending upon the percentage of interest acquired. APB Opinion No. 18 generally requires the use of the sophisticated equity method when the interest equals or exceeds 20% of the outstanding common shares of an investee corporation.[1] If a second block of stock is purchased, resulting in an interest that exceeds 50%, consolidation becomes appropriate. Current practice is derived from the parent company concept, which views each block as a separate ownership interest with independent causes of excess cost or book value. Thus, each block will have a separate determination and distribution of excess schedule and will have separate elimination procedures on the consolidated worksheet. Added complications arise because the original investment must be subjected to the consolidation process retroactively. The complexities involved depend on whether the original investment was recorded under the sophisticated equity method or the cost method. Alternative procedures, derived from the economic unit concept, will be addressed in Special Appendix 2 which follows Chapter 8.

Original Interest under the Equity Method.   The sophisticated equity method of APB Opinion No. 18 requires that the original excess of cost over book value be amortized as an adjustment of investment income in subsequent years. The amortization pattern depends on the underlying nature of the excess. The Opinion admits that it may be difficult to ascertain the nature of the excess; thus, goodwill may be assumed to be the inferred cause of the entire excess of cost over book value of an investment.

To illustrate the sophisticated equity method, assume Company P purchases on the open market a 20% interest in Company S on *January 1, 19X1*, for $48,000. The balance sheet of Company S on January 1, 19X1, is

Assets			Liabilities and Equity	
Current assets		$ 50,000	Liabilities	$ 50,000
Building and			Common stock ($10 par) . .	50,000
equipment.	$225,000		Retained earnings	100,000
Less accumulated				
depreciation	75,000	150,000		
Total assets		$200,000	Total liabilities and equity . .	$200,000

Assuming the excess of cost is attributable to goodwill, the determination and distribution of excess schedule would be prepared as follows:

1 Opinions of the Accounting Principles Board No. 18, *The Equity Method of Accounting for Investments in Common Stock* (New York: American Institute of Certified Public Accountants, 1971), par. 17.

Price paid		$48,000
Less interest acquired:		
Common stock	$ 50,000	
Retained earnings	100,000	
Total stockholders' equity	$150,000	
Interest acquired	**20%**	30,000
Goodwill (to be amortized over **20** years)		$18,000

This schedule requires that the investor reduce the investment account $900 ($18,000 ÷ 20) per year. Since goodwill cannot be recorded in the absence of consolidation and merely is buried in the investment account, the amortization required must be accomplished indirectly through the investment income account. If Company S reports income of $15,000 for 19X1, for example, Company P would record the following sophisticated equity adjustment to the $48,000 recorded investment cost:

Investment in Company S	2,100	
Investment Income		2,100
To recognize 20% of Company S reported income less		
amortization of goodwill [(20% × $15,000) – $900].		

Continuing this example, assume that on January 1, 19X2, Company P acquires an additional 60% interest in Company S on the open market for a price of $130,000. The balance sheet of Company S appears as follows on January 1, 19X2:

Assets			Liabilities and Equity	
Current assets		$ 70,000	Liabilities	$ 40,000
Building and			Common stock ($10 par) . .	50,000
equipment	$225,000		Retained earnings	115,000
Less accumulated				
depreciation	90,000	135,000		
Total assets		$205,000	Total liabilities and equity . .	$205,000

If it is assumed that the current assets have book values equal to their market values and the equipment with a 9-year remaining life is undervalued by $9,000, the determination and distribution of excess schedule for the 60% acquisition on *January 1, 19X2,* would be prepared as follows:

Price paid		$130,000	
Less interest acquired:			
Common stock	$ 50,000		
Retained earnings	115,000		
Total stockholders' equity	$165,000		
Interest acquired	**60%**	99,000	
Excess of cost over book value (debit balance)		$ 31,000	
Excess of cost attributable to equipment:			
60% × $9,000 undervaluation			
(to be amortized over 9 years)		5,400	Dr.
Goodwill (to be amortized over **20** years)		$ 25,600	Dr.

Assuming Company S reports net income of $20,000 for 19X2, Company P would make the following simple equity adjustment for its entire investment:

Investment in Company S   16,000
   Subsidiary Income   16,000
      To adjust for **80%** of Company S reported income of
      $20,000.

Since control now has been achieved, it is appropriate to use the simple equity method. It no longer is necessary to amortize the excess resulting from the January 1, 19X1 and January 1, 19X2 investments through the investment account, since the amortizations will be recorded on the consolidated worksheet as shown in Worksheet 7-2 on pages 7-58 to 7-61. The balance in the investment account results from the investments and income adjustments, which are summarized as follows:

Cost of **20%** investment (January 1, 19X1) . . . . $ 48,000
19X1 sophisticated equity adjustment   2,100
Cost of **60%** investment (January 1, 19X2)   130,000
19X2 simple equity adjustment for **80%** interest   16,000
Investment balance, December 31, 19X2 . . . .   **$196,100**

If the parent wished for consistency in the recording of the investment, it could elect to remove the previous year's amortization of excess adjustments from the investment account and restore them to the parent's retained earnings. This would mean that the worksheet could include all amortization adjustments, not just those subsequent to obtaining control.

Original Interest Under the Cost Method.   When the investment acquired prior to obtaining control is recorded under the cost method, the easiest procedure is to convert the investment account to its simple equity balance if the later investment in the subsidiary is to be recorded under the simple equity method in future periods. Conversion to the simple equity method thus will make the prior investment compatible with the later investment made to secure control. **The conversion preferably should be made directly on the parent's books.**

Assume Company P in the previous illustration originally purchased only a 10% interest for $24,000 on January 1, 19X1, and used the cost method to record its investment in Company S. The following determination and distribution of excess schedule would be prepared as of *January 1, 19X1*:

Price paid $24,000
Less interest acquired:
  Common stock . . . . $ 50,000
  Retained earnings.   100,000
    Total stockholders' equity $150,000
    Interest acquired **10%**   15,000
Goodwill (to be amortized over 20 years) . . . . $ 9,000

When Company P acquires controlling interest on January 1, 19X2, it would convert the 10% interest to the simple equity method *on its books* as follows:

Investment in Company S   1,500
   Retained Earnings   1,500
      To adjust for **10%** of the $15,000 increase in the
      subsidiary retained earnings during 19X1.

It would not be necessary to amortize the $450 ($9,000 ÷ 20 years) of goodwill through the investment account since that amortization can be done in the normal manner on the 19X2 worksheet for consolidated statements. The conversion process simplifies eliminations and adjustments because the entire original excess of cost of $9,000 will appear on the worksheet.

If the parent does not make the conversion entry on its books, a cost conversion entry should be made on the worksheet. Worksheet 7-3, pages 7-62 to 7-65, is similar to Worksheet 7-2, except that Company P used the cost method on an original *10%* investment in Company S and did not convert to the simple equity method on January 1, 19X2. Note that the balance in the investment account would be

Cost of **10%** investment (January 1, 19X1)	$ 24,000
Cost of **60%** investment (January 1, 19X2)	130,000
19X2 simple equity adjustment (**70%** × Company S income of $20,000). . . .	14,000
Investment balance, December 31, 19X2	$168,000

Alternative Procedure for Cost Method Investment.   When control is not achieved on the first purchase, ARB No. 51 permits a parent to use the date control is achieved as the date of acquisition for both blocks.[2] Thus, a parent is excused from analyzing the cause of excess for a prior-to-achieving-control investment and is allowed to let the original investment remain under the cost method up to the date control is achieved if the result of doing so is not material. In the previous case of Companies P and S, the original 10% interest purchased for $24,000 could be added to the $130,000 cost of the second investment to produce the following determination and distribution of excess schedule on January 1, 19X2:

Price paid (January 1, 19X1 plus January 1,			
19X2 investments, $24,000 + $130,000 . . .		**$154,000**	
Less interest acquired:			
Common stock	$ 50,000		
Retained earnings	115,000		
Total stockholders' equity.	$165,000		
Interest acquired.	**70%**	115,500	
Excess of cost over book value (debit balance)		$ 38,500	
Excess of cost attributable to equipment: **70%** × $9,000			
undervaluation (to be amortized over 9 years)		6,300	Dr.
Goodwill (to be amortized over 20 years)		$ 32,200	Dr.

The procedure of lumping investments together *cannot* be recommended on theoretical grounds, since the facts surrounding the separate investments are ignored. Also, when the original investment meets or exceeds 20% of the shares of the subsidiary, this procedure would be a direct violation of APB Opinion No. 18.

The parent may use the cost method for blocks that are acquired prior to achieving control and continue to use it for blocks acquired after achieving control. In this situation, each block would be *independently converted* to the equity method as of the beginning of the year, prior to making any elimination entries. The cost-to-equity conversion technique was described in Chapter 3.

2 Accounting Research Bulletin No. 51, *Consolidated Financial Statements* (New York: American Institute of Certified Public Accountants, 1959), par. 10.

Sale of Parent's Investment in Common Stock

A parent may sell all of its subsidiary interest, or sell enough shares to fall below the 50% interest generally required for consolidated reporting. When control is lost, a gain or loss on the transaction is recorded. There may be other stock sales where the parent reduces its percentage interest but still has control after the sale. Current procedures record a gain or loss on such a sale, even though the sale is an intercompany sale of shares to minority stockholders.

Sale of Entire Investment

The sale of the entire investment in a subsidiary terminates the need for consolidated financial statements. In fact, when a sale occurs during the parent's fiscal year, the results of the subsidiary operations prior to the sale date typically are not consolidated. In recording the sale of the investment in a subsidiary, the accountant's primary concern is to adjust the carrying value of the investment so that the correct gain or loss on the sale can be recorded. The results of the subsidiary's operations up to the date of sale must be reported in one of two ways: a) the net results of operations as a separate line item in the determination of income from continuing operations or b) as a disposal of a segment of a business.

The accountant must determine if the sale of the investment in a subsidiary constitutes a disposal of a segment of a business as defined by APB Opinion No. 30. The Opinion states: "... the term *segment of a business* refers to a component of an entity whose activities represent a separate major line of business or class of customer."[3] The Opinion indicates that a segment can be in the form of a subsidiary. However, an interpretation of the Opinion makes it clear that not all subsidiaries qualify as segments of a business. For example, a parent may own several subsidiaries engaged in mining coal. If one subsidiary is sold, that would not constitute a sale of a major line of business since the parent still is involved in coal mining. When the sale of a subsidiary qualifies as a disposal of a business segment, both the gain or loss on the sale and the results of operations for the period are shown net of tax in a separate discontinued-segment section of the income statement. When the sale does not qualify as a disposal of a business segment, the gain or loss and the results of operations for the period usually are shown on the income statement as a part of the normal recurring operations.

The complexities of properly recording the sale of an entire subsidiary investment are shown in the following example. Suppose Company P purchased an 80% interest in Company S on January 1, 19X1, for $250,000, and the following determination and distribution of excess schedule was prepared:

Price paid		$250,000
Less interest acquired:		
Common stock ($10 par)	$100,000	
Retained earnings, January 1, 19X1	150,000	
Total stockholders' equity	$250,000	
Interest acquired	80%	200,000
Excess of cost over book value (debit balance)		$ 50,000
Excess of cost attributable to equipment (5-year life) . . .		20,000 Dr.
Goodwill (10-year life)		$ 30,000 Dr.

---

3 Opinions of the Accounting Principles Board No. 30, *Reporting the Results of Operations* (New York: American Institute of Certified Public Accountants, 1973), par. 13.

Company S earned $40,000 in 19X1 and $25,000 in 19X2. Company P sells the entire 80% interest on January 1, 19X3, for $320,000. Assuming the use of the simple equity method, Company P's separate statements reflect the following:

Purchase price	$250,000
Share of subsidiary income, 19X1, 80% × $40,000.	32,000
Share of subsidiary income, 19X2, 80% × $25,000.	20,000
Investment in Co. S, December 31, 19X2	$302,000

The investment account and the parent's January 1, 19X3 retained earnings balance reflect a $52,000 increase as a result of subsidiary operations in 19X1 and 19X2. On this basis, it appears that there is an $18,000 gain on the sale of the investment ($320,000 selling price less $302,000 simple-equity-adjusted cost). This result does not agree, however, with the consolidated financial statements prepared for 19X1 and 19X2, which included as expenses the amortizations of excess required by the determination and distribution of excess schedule. The parent's share of subsidiary income appeared as follows in the consolidated statements:

	19X1	19X2	Total
Share of subsidiary income to Company P (80%) . .	$32,000	$20,000	$52,000
Less amortization of excess of cost of investment over book value:			
Adjustment for depreciation on equipment:			
$20,000 ÷ 5 = $4,000 per year	(4,000)	(4,000)	(8,000)
Adjustment for amortization of goodwill:			
$30,000 ÷ 10 = $3,000 per year	(3,000)	(3,000)	(6,000)
Net increase in Company P income due to ownership of Company S investment	$25,000	$13,000	$38,000

Thus, while Company P's separate books show a $52,000 share of Company S income, the consolidated statements reflect only $38,000, the difference being caused by the $14,000 of amortizations indicated by the determination and distribution of excess schedule. Clearly, the recording of the sale of the parent's interest must be based on the $38,000 share of income, since that amount of income is shown on the prior income statements of the consolidated company. Before recording the sale of the investment, Company P must adjust its books to be consistent with prior consolidated statements. The entry needed will adjust the January 1, 19X3 retained earnings account on the separate books of the parent to the December 31, 19X2 balance of the controlling interest in retained earnings shown on the consolidated statements. The adjusting entry on the books of Company P is

Retained Earnings (January 1, 19X3)	14,000	
Investment in Company S		14,000
To adjust the investment account and Company P retained earnings account for amortizations made on past consolidated statements.		

If the sophisticated equity method was used, the amortizations would be reflected already in the investment account and no adjustment would be needed. Under either equity method, the entry to record the sale then would be

Cash	320,000	
Investment in Company S ($302,000 – $14,000)		288,000
Gain on Disposal of Subsidiary		32,000
To record the gain on the sale of the 80% interest in		
Company S.		

Note that the $14,000 adjusting entry for the past years' amortizations of excess normally would have been made on the consolidated worksheet for 19X3. However, since there will be no further consolidations, the adjustment must be made directly on Company P's books. The gain (net of tax) on the disposal of the subsidiary will appear as a separate item on the income statement for 19X3 if the sale of the subsidiary meets the criteria for a disposal of a business segment.

In this example, if Company P had used the cost method, the investment account still would be shown at the original cost of $250,000. It then would be necessary to update the investment and retained earnings accounts on the separate books of Company P to include its $38,000 (net of amortizations) share of subsidiary income for 19X1 and 19X2. This adjustment would allow the accounts of the parent on January 1, 19X3, to conform to past consolidated statements. The following entries would be made on the books of Company P to record the sale of the parent's 80% interest:

Investment in Company S	38,000	
Retained Earnings (January 1, 19X3)		38,000
To record the parent's share of subsidiary income as		
shown on prior years' consolidated statements.		
Cash	320,000	
Investment in Company S ($250,000 + $38,000)		288,000
Gain on Disposal of Subsidiary		32,000

It also is necessary to adjust the investment account for any unrealized intercompany gains and losses. These profits would have been deferred in the most recent consolidated statement, but under the cost or simple equity method they are not reflected in the investment account. Again, we must adjust the investment account to reflect the income reported in past consolidated statements. Suppose the parent had on hand at the sale date inventory on which the subsidiary recorded a $1,000 profit. Since the parent owns an 80% interest, the adjusting entry on the day the investment is sold would be

| Retained Earnings . . . . | 800 | |
| Investment in Company S . . . . | | 800 |

Assume the investment in the previous example was sold for $320,000 on July 1, 19X3, and Company S reported income of $12,000 for the first six months of 19X3. Since Company S will not be a part of the consolidated group at the end of the period, the results of its operations will not be consolidated with those of the parent. Therefore, the parent must record its share of subsidiary income for the current period to the date of disposal. The parent's net share of subsidiary income would be calculated on a basis consistent with past consolidated statements, as follows:

Share of subsidiary income for first six months to Company P (80%)	$9,600
Less amortizations of excess of cost over book value that	
would have been made on consolidated statements:	
Equipment depreciation adjustment, $4,000 per year × ½ year	(2,000)
Amortization of goodwill adjustment, $3,000 per year × ½ year	(1,500)
Net share of subsidiary income	$6,100

The parent would proceed to record the July 1, 19X3 sale of its subsidiary investment as follows:

1. Assuming the past use of the simple equity method, the parent's investment account on January 1, 19X3, is adjusted to reflect the amortizations made on past consolidated statements (as calculated on pages 7-11 and 7-12).

Retained Earnings (January 1, 19X3)	14,000	
Investment in Company S		14,000

2. The parent's share of subsidiary income for the partial year is recorded. This amount is the $6,100 income net of amortizations (as calculated on page 7-12).

Investment in Company S	6,100	
Operating Income of Subsidiary Disposed of During Year . .		6,100

3. The sale of the investment for $320,000 is recorded.

Cash	320,000	
Investment in Company S		294,100
Gain on Disposal of Subsidiary		25,900

The adjusted cost of the investment is determined as follows:

Original cost (January 1, 19X1).	$250,000
Simple equity income adjustments for 19X1 and 19X2	52,000
Amortization of excess (entry 1).	(14,000)
Share of Company S income for six months (entry 2).	6,100
Net cost, July 1, 19X3	$294,100

Sale of Portion of Investment

The sale of a portion of an investment in a subsidiary requires unique treatment, depending on whether effective control is lost as a result of the sale. Special procedures must also be used when a sale of a partial interest occurs during a reporting period.

Loss of Control.   A parent may sell a portion of its investment in a subsidiary so that its remaining interest falls below 50%. This situation may occur for foreign subsidiaries when the foreign government passes a law forbidding control of its companies by nonresidents. Such a sale also may be made to avoid consolidating affiliated companies. FASB Statement No. 94 now requires the consolidation of nonhomogeneous subsidiaries that previously did not have to be consolidated.[4] Some sell-downs did occur after the issuance of that Statement to avoid adding the substantial debt of real estate and financing subsidiaries to the consolidated statements. If an interest is reduced below 50%, consolidation procedures no longer will apply. This situation would require that the parent company books be adjusted to make them consistent with prior consolidated statements. Exactly the same adjusting entries as in the immediately preceding section are needed to adjust the parent's investment account. Note that the adjustments are made for the entire interest previously owned, not just the portion sold. If, in the preceding example, Company P sells one-half instead of all of its 80% interest, the investment account should be adjusted for the entire 80%

---

4 Statement of Financial Accounting Standards No. 94, *Consolidation of All Majority-Owned Subsidiaries* (Stamford: Financial Accounting Standards Board, 1987), par 9.

interest in past and current years' subsidiary income, net of amortizations. The 40% interest sold must be adjusted to properly record the sale, and the 40% interest retained also must be adjusted, since it no longer will be consolidated. Past adjustments that would be handled as part of the annual consolidation process now must be made directly to the investment account, so that the investment remaining conforms with APB Opinion No. 18. The sophisticated equity method described in that Opinion should be applied to remaining interests of 20% or more.[5]

If one-half of Company P's investment of the preceding section is sold for $160,000 on July 1, 19X3, the following entries would be recorded:

1. Assuming the past use of the simple equity method, the parent's investment account on January 1, 19X3, is adjusted to reflect the amortizations made on past consolidated statements.

Retained Earnings (January 1, 19X3)   14,000
    Investment in Company S   14,000

2. The parent's share of subsidiary income for the partial year is recorded. This amount is the $6,100 income net of amortizations.

Investment in Company S   6,100
    Subsidiary Income   6,100

Note that this income is no longer from a "disposed-of subsidiary."

3. The sale of one-half of the investment for $160,000 is recorded. The resulting gain is always ordinary income and never a gain from a "discontinued segment."

Cash   160,000
Investment in Company S (½ of $294,100 adjusted
    cost calculated on page 7-13)   147,050
    Gain on Sale of Investment   12,950

Note that the sale of a partial interest will not qualify as a discontinued segment. Thus, the operating results on the investment to the sale date and the gain or loss on the sale would be shown as a part of ordinary income from continuing operations.

Control Retained.   A parent company may sell a portion of its investment in a subsidiary but still have an interest that exceeds 50% after the sale. For example, assume that on January 1, 19X1, a parent purchased from outside parties 8,000 of the total 10,000 shares of a subsidiary. On January 1, 19X3, the parent sold 2,000 shares and thereby lowered its percentage of ownership to 60%. Since the parent still had control, the 2,000 shares were sold, in essence, to minority shareholders. The 1995 FASB exposure draft on business combinations considers this type of sale to be the sale of additional shares to minority shareholders. Under the *economic unit concept*, the parent has chosen to sell subsidiary shares, instead of parent shares, to raise additional equity capital. Under this concept, there can be no income statement gains or losses resulting from any stock issuances by the consolidated entity. This transaction would impact only paid-in capital. The possible new procedures are contained in Special Appendix 2 which follows Chapter 8.

Current practice derives from the *parent company concept*. Sales that do not result in the loss of control result in income statement gains or losses. The transaction is viewed as the sale of a corporate asset (the investment in the subsidiary) to an out-

---

5 Opinions of the Accounting Principles Board No. 18, *The Equity Method of Accounting for Investments in Common Stock* (New York: American Institute of Certified Public Accountants, 1971), par. 17.

side party (not an existing minority stockholder at the time of the sale). The new shareholders do, of course, become part of the minority interest after the sale. The gain/loss approach is currently required by the SEC (unless the sale is part of a broader corporate reorganization). The gain/loss approach is used in the example which follows.

To illustrate the recording of such a partial sale, return to the example for which a determination and distribution of excess schedule was prepared on page 7-10. Assume that on January 1, 19X3, Company P sells 2,000 subsidiary shares to lower its total interest to 60%. Only the portion of the investment account sold is to be adjusted to the sophisticated equity method to allow the proper recording of the sale. The 60% retained need not be adjusted on Company P's books since all amortization adjustments on the 60% interest will be made on future consolidated statements. The adjustment of the 20% interest on the separate books of Company P must agree with the treatment of that interest in prior consolidated statements. Assuming the use of the simple equity method, the portion of the investment sold must be adjusted for its share of the past amortizations made on consolidated statements. Since the 19X1 and 19X2 amortizations on page 7-11 totaled $14,000 for an 80% interest, the amortizations for the 20% interest sold would be **one-fourth** of $14,000, or $3,500. The parent would make the following entry:

Retained Earnings (January 1, 19X3)	3,500	
Investment in Company S		3,500
To adjust for amortizations made on previous consolidated		
statements for the portion of the subsidiary investment sold.		

To record the sale of the investment, the parent would remove from its books **one-fourth** of the simple-equity-adjusted cost of January 1, 19X3 (calculated at $302,000 on page 7-11), which along with the previous $3,500 adjustment nets to $72,000. If the sale price is less than $72,000, a loss would be recorded. If the sale price is greater than $72,000, a gain would be recorded, as shown in the following entry to record the sale of the investment for $80,000:

Cash	80,000	
Investment in Company S [(¼ × $302,000) – $3,500		
amortization adjustment]		72,000
Gain on Sale of Subsidiary Stock		8,000

If the parent in the previous example had used the cost method, only the portion of the investment sold would be adjusted to the sophisticated equity method on the parent's books. The analysis on page 7-11 shows that the parent's 80% share of income for 19X1 and 19X2 was $38,000 on a consolidated basis, net of amortizations. The 20% interest sold must be adjusted by **one-fourth** of $38,000, or $9,500. The remaining 60% will be adjusted in future worksheets. The entry to adjust the 20% interest would be

Investment in Company S	9,500	
Retained Earnings (January 1, 19X3)		9,500
To adjust for the parent's share of past consolidated income		
pertaining to the interest sold.		

The parent then would proceed to record the sale of the investment for $80,000 as follows:

Cash	80,000	
Investment in Company S (¼ of original $250,000 cost +		
$9,500 equity income)		72,000
Gain on Sale of Subsidiary Stock		8,000

Intraperiod Sale of a Partial Interest.   When a sale of an interest during the reporting period does not result in loss of control, careful analysis is needed to ensure that the worksheet adheres to consolidation theory. Referring to the situation on page 7-15, assume Company P sells one-fourth of its 80% interest for $80,000 on July 1, 19X3, and subsidiary income for the first half of the year is $12,000. Assuming the use of the simple equity method, the parent would adjust its own investment and the beginning-of-the-year retained earnings accounts for **one-fourth** of the amortizations of excess cost recorded on the prior years' consolidated worksheets. The adjustment would be recorded as follows:

Retained Earnings (January 1, 19X3)	3,500	
Investment in Company S		3,500
To record **one-fourth** of the $14,000 amortizations		
(shown on page 7-11) for 19X1 and 19X2.		

A parent using the cost method would adjust the retained earnings for the subsidiary income, net of amortizations, for 19X1 and 19X2 (20% × $38,000 income on a consolidated basis).

Next, the parent would calculate its share of subsidiary income for the first half of 19X3 applicable to the 20% interest sold and adjusted for partial-year amortizations of excess relating to that portion of the investment as follows:

Income on 20% interest in Company S sold (20% × $12,000)	$2,400
Less amortizations of excess of cost over book value that would be necessary	
on consolidated statements:	
Equipment depreciation adjustment,	
$4,000 per year × ½ year × ¼ interest sold	(500)
Amortization of goodwill adjustment,	
$3,000 per year × ½ year × ¼ interest sold	(375)
Net share of income on interest sold	$1,525

The parent then would make a sophisticated equity method adjustment for this income and record the sale as follows:

Investment in Company S	1,525	
Subsidiary Income		1,525
To record share of first 6 months' subsidiary income		
applicable to the 20% interest sold and adjusted for		
partial-year amortizations of excess relating to that		
portion of the investment.		
Cash	80,000	
Investment in Company S [(¼ × $302,000) − $3,500		
amortizations + $1,525 income]		73,525
Gain on Sale of Subsidiary Stock		6,475
To record sale of 20% interest in subsidiary.		

The sale of a partial interest that does not result in loss of control requires special procedures on the consolidated worksheet for the period in which the sale occurs. Worksheets of later periods would not include any complications resulting from the sale. In Worksheet 7-4 on pages 7-66 to 7-69, the following should be noted:

1. The investment in Company S account reflects its simple equity balance on December 31, 19X3, for the remaining 60% interest held. The balance is computed as follows:

December 31, 19X2 balance applicable to remaining (60%) interest	
held at year-end, ¾ × $302,000	$226,500
Add **60%** of subsidiary reported income of $30,000	18,000
Simple equity balance, December 31, 19X3	$244,500

2. The balance in Gain on Sale of Subsidiary Stock is the gain resulting from the 20% interest sold.
3. The balance in Subsidiary Income includes **60%** of the subsidiary's $30,000 19X3 income, plus the $1,525 earned on the **20%** interest prior to its sale.
4. The share of income applicable to the interest sold, $2,400 is transferred to the minority interest. The share of subsidiary income purchased by the minority interest is not reduced for the amortizations of excess cost applicable to the parent's purchase. These amortizations apply only to the income recorded by the controlling interest. The amortizations are recorded and allocated to the parent for the portion of the year prior to the sale. Entry (1) on Worksheet 7-4 makes the transfer and records the partial-year amortizations. In entry form, the procedure is

Subsidiary Income (on 20% interest for first 6 months)	1,525	
Expenses (amortizations of excess for the first 6 months)	875	
Income Sold to Minority (income for the first 6 months,		
no amortization)		2,400

Carefully study the income distribution schedules for Worksheet 7-4. The minority interest receives its 40% interest in subsidiary income for the entire year, but there is a deduction for the income purchased from the parent for the first 6 months. The parent company income distribution schedule claims 60% of the subsidiary income for the entire year plus a 20% interest in the first 6 months' income.

If the parent, Company P, had used the cost method, there would be few changes in Worksheet 7-4. Entry (1) would be unchanged; however, an entry would be needed to convert the remaining 60% interest to the simple equity method at the beginning of the year. Entry (2) would not be applicable since there would be no current-year equity adjustment to reverse. Entries (3) through (6) would remain the same.

Complications Resulting from Intercompany Transactions.   When a sale of subsidiary stock results in loss of control, the parent should adjust its investment account on the date of the sale for its share of unrealized subsidiary gains and losses resulting from intercompany transactions. When control is not lost as the result of a sale of subsidiary shares, the adjustment on the consolidated worksheet for unrealized gains and losses resulting from previous intercompany transactions need be recorded only as it applies to the interest sold. The remaining controlling interest's share of these gains and losses can be adjusted on subsequent consolidated worksheets. On these worksheets, retained earnings adjustments for unrealized gains and losses would be distributed according to the relative ownership interests existing on the dates the worksheets are prepared.

Subsidiary Preferred Stock

The existence of preferred stock in the capital structure of a subsidiary complicates the calculation of a parent's claim on subsidiary retained earnings, both at the time of acquisition and in the preparation of subsequent consolidated statements. In previous examples, the subsidiary had only common stock outstanding, so that all retained earnings were associated with common stock, and the parent had a claim on subsidiary retained earnings in proportion to its ownership interest. When a subsidiary has preferred stock outstanding, however, the preferred stock also may have a claim on retained earnings. This claim may be caused by a liquidation value in excess of par value and/or by participation and cumulative dividend rights. When these conditions exist, the retained earnings must be divided between the preferred and common stockholder interests.

Once retained earnings are allocated between the common and preferred stockholders, the intercompany investments can be eliminated. The investment in subsidiary common stock account will be eliminated against the total equity claim of the common stockholders. If there is an investment in subsidiary preferred stock account, it will be eliminated against the preferred stockholders' total equity.

Determination of Preferred Shareholders' Claim on Retained Earnings

The allocation of the retained earnings to the preferred and common stockholder interests is accomplished by employing the procedures used to calculate the book value of preferred and common stock. Although typically covered in intermediate accounting, the topic will be reviewed briefly in the following paragraphs.

The preferred shareholders' claim on retained earnings equals the claim they would have if the company was dissolved. In addition to the par value of the preferred shares, there may be a stipulated liquidation value in excess of par and/or dividend preferences. In the rare case of a liquidation value in excess of par, an amount equal to the liquidation bonus (liquidation value less par value) must be segregated from retained earnings as a preferred shareholder claim. Liquidation values should not be confused with paid-in capital in excess of par which results from the sale of preferred shares. Such paid-in capital is not available to preferred shareholders in liquidation and is not part of the book value of preferred shares. Instead, it becomes part of the total paid-in capital that is available to common shareholders.

In addition to a liquidation bonus, there must be an analysis of any cumulative and/or participation clauses applicable to the preferred stock. Other than the effect of a liquidation bonus, if the preferred stock is noncumulative and nonparticipating, the preferred stockholders would have no claim and all the retained earnings attach to the common stock. However, if there are preferred shareholder claims resulting from cumulative and/or participation clauses, these claims reduce the retained earnings applicable to the common stock. For example, if the preferred stock is noncumulative but fully participating, the retained earnings are allocated pro rata according to the total par or stated values of the preferred and common stock. If the preferred stock is cumulative but nonparticipating and, for example, has two years' dividends in arrears, a claim on retained earnings equal to the two years of dividends exists, although there is no liability to pay the preferred dividends until a dividend is declared.

When preferred stock is both cumulative and fully participating, the arrearage for prior periods is met first. The remaining retained earnings are allocated pro rata according to the total par values of the preferred and common stock. When preferred stock is cumulative and participating but no dividends are in arrears, the analysis is the same as if the preferred stock were noncumulative but participating.

When preferred stock is cumulative and limited in participation to a percentage of par value, the arrearage for prior periods is met first and is excluded from the limited participation. The lesser of a pro rata share of the remaining retained earnings or the limiting percentage of the preferred stock's par value is allocated to the preferred claim. Any retained earnings remaining after this allocation are assigned to the common stock.

Apportionment of Retained Earnings

Additional procedures are required when a subsidiary with preferred stock that has liquidation and/or dividend preferences is consolidated, even if none of the preferred shares are owned by the parent. In this situation, allocation of retained earnings to the preferred and common stock is as follows:

1. The determination and distribution of excess schedule prepared as of the date of the parent's investment in common stock must include only that portion of retained earnings that is allocable to the common stock on the purchase date.
2. Periodic equity adjustments for the parent's investment in common stock are made only for the common shareholders' claim on income. The preferred shareholders' claim on the current year's income, including dividends paid or accumulated and any participation rights for the current year, must be deducted to arrive at income available to common shareholders. When the cost method is used, the worksheet simple equity conversion adjustment is made for the parent's share of change in the retained earnings applicable to common stock since the date of acquisition.
3. Subsidiary retained earnings must be allocated between preferred and common stockholders on consolidated worksheets. The parent's investment in common stock account then is eliminated against the parent's pro rata share of only the equity attaching to common stock.

To illustrate these procedures, assume Company S has the following stockholders' equity on January 1, 19X3, the date on which Company P purchases an 80% interest in the common stock for $150,000:

Preferred stock, $100 par, 6% cumulative	$100,000
Common stock, $10 par	100,000
Retained earnings.	80,000
Total equity	$280,000

The preferred stock has a liquidation value equal to par value, and dividends are 2 years in arrears as of January 1, 19X3. Company S assets have a market value equal to book value. Any excess purchase price is attributable to goodwill with a 10-year life. The determination and distribution of excess schedule would be prepared as follows:

Price paid.			$150,000
Less interest acquired:			
Common stock ($10 par).		$100,000	
Retained earnings:			
Balance, Jan. 1, 19X3.	**$80,000**		
Less preferred dividends in			
arrears (2 years × $6,000)	**12,000**	68,000	
Total equity applicable to common stock.		$168,000	
Interest acquired.		80%	134,400
Goodwill (10-year life)			$ 15,600

Assume that income is exactly $25,000 per year in future years and no dividends are paid. Each year, the following entry would be made by Company P using the simple equity method of accounting for its subsidiary investment:

Investment in Common Stock of Company S   15,200
    Subsidiary Income   15,200
        To adjust for 80% of Company S income applicable to
        common stock ($25,000 reported income – $6,000
        cumulative claim of preferred stock).

Worksheet 7-5, pages 7-70 to 7-73, is a consolidated financial statements work-sheet for the year ended *December 31, 19X5* (3 years subsequent to the purchase). The investment in common stock account includes the original cost of the investment plus 3 years (3 × $15,200 = $45,600) of simple equity adjustments for income and dividends. The worksheet is unique in that it subdivides the subsidiary retained earnings into two parts: one for the common portion and one for the preferred portion of retained earnings. Entry (1) of Worksheet 7-5 accomplishes this apportionment. In entry form, the procedure is

Retained Earnings, Jan. 1, Co. S*   24,000
    Retained Earnings, allocated to preferred stock,
      Jan. 1, Co. S   24,000

*The remaining retained earnings reflect the common stockholders' interest.

This division of retained earnings is only for worksheet purposes; the subsidiary will maintain only one retained earnings account.

After the eliminations and adjustments are completed, the resulting combined net income of $173,440 is allocated as shown in the income distribution schedules. Since none of the preferred stock is owned by controlling shareholders, the minority interest receives all applicable preferred income plus 20% of the income allocable to common stock. It should be observed that the Minority Interest column, as well as the minority interest shown on a formal balance sheet, includes the minority interest in both preferred and common shares.

The worksheet just analyzed can handle all types of subsidiary preferred stock-holder claims. Once the claim is determined, with supporting calculations, it can be isolated in a separate worksheet account, *Retained Earnings Allocated to Preferred Stock.*

When a parent uses the cost method to record its investment in a subsidiary, slightly different worksheet procedures are used. In the previous illustration, if Company P had used the cost method, the investment account still would be at the $150,000 original cost. In addition, there would be no subsidiary income shown, and the January 1, 19X5 retained earnings of Company P would not reflect the 19X3 and 19X4 simple equity adjustments. As described earlier, a conversion to the simple equity method is made on the worksheet. Since the beginning-of-the-period investment balance is needed for elimination, the equity adjustment converts the investment account to the January 1, 19X5 balance, as follows:

Retained earnings, Company S, January 1, 19X5	$130,000	
Less 4 years' arrearage of preferred dividends	24,000	
Retained earnings applicable to common stock, January 1, 19X5		**$106,000**
Retained earnings, Company S, January 1, 19X3	$ 80,000	
Less 2 years' arrearage of preferred dividends	12,000	
Retained earnings applicable to common stock, January 1, 19X3		**68,000**
Increase in common stock portion of retained earnings		$ 38,000
Controlling interest (80%).		$ 30,400

The conversion entry for $30,400 would debit the investment account and credit the Company P retained earnings account. The investment account now would be stated at its simple-equity-adjusted, January 1, 19X5 balance. Worksheet entries (1), (3), (4), and (5) would be made just as in Worksheet 7-5. Only entry (2) would be omitted, since it is not applicable to the cost method. The partial worksheet on page 7-22 includes the conversion and subsequent eliminations and adjustments under the cost method. All remaining procedures for this example would be identical to those used in Worksheet 7-5.

Subsidiary Preferred Stock, None Owned by Parent
Cost Method Used for Investment in Common Stock

	Partial Trial Balance		Eliminations & Adjustments	
	Company P	Company S	Dr.	Cr.
Investment in Common Stock of Co. S	**150,000**		**(C) 30,400**	(3) 164,800
				(4) 15,600
Goodwill			(4) 15,600	(5) 4,680
Retained Earnings, Jan. 1, 19X5, Co. P	(309,600)		(5) 3,120	**(C) 30,400**
Preferred Stock ($100 par), Co. S		(100,000)		
Retained Earnings, Allocated to Preferred Stock, Jan. 1, 19X5, Co. S				(1) 24,000
Common Stock ($10 par), Co. S		(100,000)	(3) 80,000	
Retained Earnings, Jan. 1, 19X5, Co. S		(130,000)	(1) 24,000	
			(3) 84,800	
Expenses	100,000	25,000	(5) 1,500	

Eliminations and Adjustments:

(C) The cost-to-equity conversion entry was explained prior to the partial worksheet.

(1) Distribute the beginning-of-the-period subsidiary retained earnings into the portions allocable to common and preferred stock. The typical procedure would be to consider the stated subsidiary retained earnings as applicable to common and to remove the preferred portion. This distribution reflects 4 years of arrearage (as of January 1, 19X5) at $6,000 per year.

(3) Eliminate the pro rata subsidiary common stockholders' equity at the beginning of the period against the investment account. This entry includes elimination of the 80% of subsidiary retained earnings applicable to common stock.

(4) Distribute the excess of cost according to the determination and distribution of excess schedule.

(5) Amortize the goodwill for the past two years and the current year.

Parent Investment in Subsidiary Preferred Stock

A parent may purchase all or a portion of the preferred stock of a subsidiary. Normally, preferred stock is nonvoting; therefore, it is not considered in determining whether the parent owns a controlling interest in the subsidiary. Thus, a 100% ownership of nonvoting preferred stock and a 49% interest in voting common stock normally would not require the preparation of consolidated statements.

From a consolidated viewpoint, the parent's purchase of subsidiary preferred stock usually is viewed as a retirement of the stock.[6] The amount paid is compared

---

6 It also would be possible to view the investment as treasury shares, in which case they would appear as a contra-account to the preferred stock in the minority interest section of the consolidated balance sheet. This approach, however, does not have popular support. It could be justified only if there were an intent to reissue the shares.

to the sum of the original proceeds resulting from the issuance of the shares and any claim the shares have on retained earnings, and an increase or decrease in equity as a result of the retirement is calculated. When the price paid is less than the preferred equity retired, the resulting increase in equity is credited to the controlling paid-in capital account, not the retained earnings account, because it results from a transaction with the consolidated company's shareholders. A decrease in equity, which occurs when the price paid exceeds the preferred equity, would offset against the paid-in capital applicable to the preferred stock. If not enough of the preferred stock paid-in capital exists, the remaining decrease would be taken from the controlling retained earnings and viewed as a retirement dividend.

To illustrate this type of investment, assume Company P in the previous example purchased 600 shares (60%) of Company S preferred stock on January 1, 19X3, for $65,000. The increase or decrease in equity resulting from the retirement would be calculated as follows:

Price paid		$65,000
Less **preferred** interest acquired:		
Preferred stock ($100 par)	$100,000	
Claim on dividends (2 years in arrears × $6,000 per year) . .	12,000	
Total preferred interest	$112,000	
Interest acquired	60%	67,200
Increase in equity (credit Paid-In Capital)		**$2,200**

Though viewed as retired, the preferred stock investment account will continue to exist on the books of the parent in subsequent periods. At the end of each period, the investment must be "retired" on the consolidated worksheet. The procedures used depend on whether the parent accounts for the investment in preferred stock under the equity method or the cost method. Under the equity method, the parent adjusts the investment in preferred stock account each period for any additional claim on the subsidiary retained earnings, including any continued arrearage or participation privilege. In this example, the arrearage of dividends would be recorded each year, 19X3 to 19X5, as follows:

Investment in Company S Preferred Stock	3,600	
Subsidiary Income		3,600
To acknowledge 60% of the annual increase in the		
Company S preferred stock dividend arrearage.		

Assuming the equity adjustments are properly made, any original discrepancy between the price paid for the preferred shares and their book value would be maintained. The equity method also acknowledges that, even though the shares are viewed as retired in consolidated reports, the controlling interest is entitled to its proportionate share of combined net income based on both its common and preferred stock holdings.

 Worksheet 7-6, pages 7-74 to 7-77, displays the consolidation procedures that would be used for the ownership interest in preferred stock described above. This worksheet parallels Worksheet 7-5 except that the parent owns 60% of the subsidiary preferred stock. The investment is listed at its $65,000 cost plus three years of equity adjustments to reflect the increasing dividend arrearage.

Combined net income is distributed as shown in the income distribution schedules that accompany the worksheet. The distributions respect the controlling/minority ownership of both common and preferred shares. The common and preferred equity interests of the minority again are summarized on the worksheet and for presentation on the formal balance sheet.

If a parent uses the cost method for its investment in subsidiary preferred stock, the investment should be converted to its equity balance as of the beginning of the period. In this example, if the cost method is used for the investment in preferred stock, the following conversion adjustment would be made on the worksheet:

Investment in Company S Preferred Stock   7,200
    Retained Earnings (January 1, 19X5, Co. P)   7,200

The adjustment reflects 2 years of arrearage at $6,000 per year times the 60% ownership interest. Eliminations and adjustments would proceed as in Worksheet 7-6, except that there would be no need for entry (6).

This example contains only cumulative preferred stock. However, the same principles would apply to participating preferred stock, and the allocation procedures outlined earlier in this chapter would be used. Only the subdivision of the subsidiary retained earnings and the amounts of the equity adjustments would differ.

Appendix: Worksheet for a Consolidated Balance Sheet

Previous chapters displayed procedures applicable to worksheets that produced a consolidated income statement, retained earnings statement, and balance sheet. However, there may be occasions when only consolidated balance sheets are required, and the separate balance sheets of the affiliates form the starting point for consolidation procedures. Such occasions are rare in practice but are of concern to students desiring to take the CPA Exam. Past examinations have used balance-sheet-only consolidation problems as an expedient method for testing purposes. This type of problem requires less time to solve while still testing the candidates' knowledge of consolidations.

A balance sheet worksheet requires only adjustments to balance sheet accounts. No adjustments for nominal accounts are required. Your past experience often will lead you to consider the impact of an elimination on the nominal accounts, but you must adjust your thinking to cover only the remaining impact of an elimination on the balance sheet. For example, intercompany merchandise sales no longer will require an elimination of the sales and cost of goods sold relative to the transaction. The following sections examine the simplified procedures that are used on a consolidated balance sheet worksheet.

Investment Account

When the investment account is maintained under the simple equity method, it will reflect the same point in time as do the subsidiary equity balances. There is no need to eliminate the parent's entry for its share of subsidiary income. Instead, the pro rata share of subsidiary equity balances may be eliminated directly against the investment account.

Investments maintained under the sophisticated equity method are also at a common point in time and, thus, can be eliminated directly against the underlying subsidiary equity. The distributable excess, however, will be only that which remains net of the amortizations made in the current and previous periods.

Investments maintained at cost should be converted to the simple equity method as of the **end of the year** to agree in time with the subsidiary equity balances. The entire conversion adjustment is carried to the controlling retained earnings.

Excesses are distributed according to the determination and distribution of excess schedules. Once distributed, the excesses are amortized to the balance sheet date and the entire amortization is carried to the controlling retained earnings.

Merchandise Sales

Only the intercompany profit in the ending inventory needs adjustment. The profit is eliminated from the inventory and from retained earnings. The adjustment to retained earnings is allocated according to the minority/controlling ownership percentages in effect when the subsidiary made the intercompany sale. If the parent made the sale, the adjustment is made only to the controlling retained earnings. The intercompany profit in the beginning inventory either has been realized through the subsequent sale of the merchandise to an outside party, or, if the units in the beginning inventory are still on hand at year-end, they would be included in the adjustment for intercompany profit in the ending inventory.

Plant Asset Sales

The only matter for concern in the case of intercompany plant asset sales is the adjustment of the asset and retained earnings accounts for the undepreciated portion of the intercompany gain or loss as of year-end. The asset account is adjusted to its cost to the consolidated firm; accumulated depreciation is adjusted for all periods to date; and retained earnings are adjusted for the undepreciated profit or loss that is to be deferred to future periods. If the subsidiary sold to the parent, the retained earnings adjustment is allocated to the minority and controlling interests that existed at the time of the sale.

Investment in Bonds

The amortized balance in Investment in Company S Bonds is eliminated against the bonds payable and any related discount or premium balance. The net disparity in amounts is the net retirement gain or loss remaining at year-end, which is carried to retained earnings. When the subsidiary is the issuer, the retained earnings adjustment is allocated to the minority and controlling interests.

Leases

For operating leases, it is necessary only to reclassify the asset and accumulated depreciation as owned assets rather than assets under operating leases. Where direct financing leases exist, the intercompany debt resulting from the capitalized lease must be eliminated. Also, it is necessary to reclassify the asset and accumulated depreciation as owned assets rather than assets under capital leases. An intercompany sales-type lease requires the same procedures as a direct-financing lease plus an additional adjustment to defer the remaining undepreciated intercompany profit on the lease. If the subsidiary leased the asset to the parent, the retained earnings adjustment is allocated to the minority and controlling interest that existed at the inception of the lease.

Illustration

To illustrate the procedures used for the balance sheet worksheet, assume Company P purchased an 80% interest in Company S on January 1, 19X1. Company P uses the cost method to record its investment in Company S. The determination and distribution of excess schedule prepared for this purchase is as follows:

Price paid		$750,000
Less interest acquired:		
Common stock ($10 par)	$200,000	
Retained earnings, January 1, 19X1.	600,000	
Total stockholders' equity.	$800,000	
Interest acquired	80%	640,000
Excess of cost over book value (debit balance).		$110,000
Excess of cost attributable to building (10-year		
remaining life).		30,000 Dr.
Goodwill (20-year life)		$ 80,000 Dr.

The facts pertaining to intercompany sales by Company S to Company P are as follows:

	19X3	19X4
Intercompany sales.	$80,000	$100,000
Gross profit.	30%	40%
Intercompany sales in ending inventory	20,000	40,000
Unpaid balance, end of the year	30,000	35,000

On January 1, 19X2, Company P sold a new piece of equipment that cost $10,000 to Company S for $15,000. Company S is depreciating the equipment over 5 years on a straight-line basis.

Company S has outstanding $100,000 of 20-year, 5% bonds due January 1, 19X9. Interest is payable on January 1 for the previous year. The bonds originally were sold to yield 6%. On January 1, 19X3, Company P purchased the bonds on the open market at a price to yield 8%.

Worksheet 7-7, pages 7-78 and 7-79, contains the balance sheets and eliminations and adjustments for Companies P and S on December 31, 19X4. After the worksheet entries are completed, the amounts are combined to produce the consolidated balance sheet. The time saving of the balance sheet worksheet results from the fact that there is no combined net income to calculate and distribute.

Questions

1. Under what circumstances is a determination and distribution of excess schedule needed when a parent acquires its controlling interest in stock directly from the subsidiary?
2. What is a piecemeal purchase? Describe the accounting consequences of such an acquisition as they affect the determination and distribution of excess schedules and worksheet procedures.
3. Is it possible that a piecemeal acquisition could include a transaction that qualifies as a pooling of interests? If so, explain the ramifications.
4. Explain how the equity method investment account balance generally can be recalculated to verify its correctness when an investment in a subsidiary has been acquired in more than one purchase.
5. What factors determine whether the sale of a parent's entire interest in a subsidiary qualifies as a disposal of a segment?

6. Parent Company sold its entire 75% interest in Subsidiary Company for $100,000. The interest originally was purchased at a price in excess of book value. May it be said that the parent realized a $20,000 gain on the sale (a) assuming a correct simple equity method investment account balance of $80,000? (b) assuming a correct cost method investment account balance of $80,000? Explain.

7. Describe the adjustments required when a parent sells enough of its ownership interest in a subsidiary to lose control. How do these adjustments differ when the parent sells part of its ownership interest, but not enough to lose control?

8. What special consolidation procedures are required when a subsidiary has preferred stock outstanding?

9. If a parent company owns 80% of the preferred stock and 45% of the common stock of a subsidiary, would the parent company normally have a controlling interest in the subsidiary? Explain.

10. What are the consolidation procedures required when a parent owns subsidiary preferred stock?

Exercises

Exercise 1.   Prior to January 2, 19X4, Pulse and Spark were separate corporations. Spark Corporation was contemplating a major expansion and sought to be purchased by a larger corporation with available cash. Pulse Corporation issued $1,000,000 of bonds and used the proceeds to buy 30,000 newly issued Spark shares. Just prior to the issue of the bonds and the issue and purchase of Spark stock, Pulse and Spark had the following separate balance sheets:

Assets	Pulse Corporation	Spark Corporation
Current assets	$ 600,000	$100,000
Land.	150,000	60,000
Property, plant, and equipment	700,000	400,000
Total assets	$1,450,000	$560,000
Liabilities and Stockholders' Equity		
Current liabilities	$250,000	$100,000
Common stock ($5 par).	400,000	100,000
Retained earnings.	800,000	360,000
Total liabilities and equity.	$1,450,000	$560,000

Purchasing the 30,000 new shares gave Pulse Corporation a 60% controlling interest (30,000 of a total 50,000 common shares). On the purchase date, Spark's property was undervalued by $100,000. Any remaining excess cost can be attributed only to goodwill.

Prepare a determination and distribution of excess schedule for Pulse Corporation's investment in Spark. Prepare a consolidated balance sheet for the consolidated firm immediately after the purchase by Pulse Corporation.

Exercise 2.   Barker Corporation purchased a 60% interest in Hard Knock Company on January 1, 19X1, for $150,000. On that date, Hard Knock Company had the following stockholders' equity:

Common stock ($10 par)...................	$100,000
Retained earnings	20,000
	$120,000

Any excess of cost over market value was due to equipment with a 10-year life.

Barker Corporation purchased another 20% interest for $40,000 on January 1, 19X3, when Hard Knock Company had the following stockholders' equity:

Common stock ($10 par)...................	$100,000
Retained earnings	50,000
	$150,000

Any excess of cost over market value was due to goodwill with a 20-year life. On December 31, 19X5, Barker Corporation and Hard Knock Company had the following balance sheets:

Assets	Barker Corporation	Hard Knock Company
Current assets	$ 270,000	$ 80,000
Investment in Hard Knock Company	190,000	
Property, plant, and equipment.................	740,000	240,000
Total assets	$1,200,000	$320,000
Liabilities and Stockholders' Equity		
Current liabilities	$400,000	$100,000
Stockholders' equity:		
Common stock ($10 par)...................	500,000	100,000
Retained earnings.......................	300,000	120,000
Total liabilities and stockholders' equity	$1,200,000	$320,000

Prepare the consolidated balance sheet of Barker Corporation and subsidiary Hard Knock Company on Dec. 31, 19X5, subsequent to the purchase of the additional 20% block by Barker.

Exercise 3. Golf Corporation purchased a 10% interest in Manco Company on January 1, 19X1. The following determination and distribution of excess schedule was prepared as of the purchase date:

Price paid		$35,000
Less interest acquired:		
Common stock ($10 par)	$100,000	
Retained earnings.............................	120,000	
Stockholders' equity..........................	$220,000	
Interest acquired.............................	10%	22,000
Goodwill (20-year life)............................		$13,000

From January 1, 19X1, through December 31, 19X5, Manco Company paid no dividends and reported the following net incomes:

(continued)

19X1	$ 8,000	19X4	$20,000
19X2	10,000	19X5	22,000
19X3	20,000		

On January 1, 19X6, Golf Corporation purchased 7,000 additional shares of Manco Company from existing shareholders for $275,000. This purchase raised Golf's interest to 80%. Manco Company had the following balance sheet just prior to Golf's second purchase:

Assets		Liabilities and Equity	
Current assets	$125,000	Liabilities	$ 65,000
Buildings (net)	140,000	Common stock, $10 par	100,000
Equipment (net)	100,000	Retained earnings	200,000
Total assets	$365,000	Total liabilities and equity	$365,000

At the time of the second purchase, Golf determined that Manco's equipment was understated by $50,000 and had a 5-year remaining life. All other book values approximated market values. Any remaining excess is attributed to goodwill with a 20-year life.

1. Prepare a determination and distribution of excess schedule for the second purchase.
2. Record the investment made by Golf on January 1, 19X6.
3. Since control has now been achieved, Golf will use the simple equity method for its investment in Manco. Assume that the cost method was used to account for the initial 10% interest. Convert the 10% interest to the simple equity method balance on January 1, 19X6.

Exercise 4.   Cleft Company purchased a 20% interest in Key Industries on January 1, 19X2, for $100,000 and another 60% interest on January 1, 19X4, for $360,000. Key had the following stockholders' equity balances immediately prior to each purchase:

Stockholders' Equity	Jan. 1, 19X2	Jan. 1, 19X4
Common stock ($7 par)	$350,000	$350,000
Paid-in capital in excess of par	100,000	100,000
Retained earnings	20,000	100,000
Total equity	$470,000	$550,000

Cleft's analysis on the two purchase dates revealed the following: (1) On January 1, 19X2, Key's equipment was undervalued by $10,000 and had a remaining life of 5 years. (2) On January 1, 19X4, Key's equipment was undervalued by $9,000, with a 3-year remaining life. (3) Any excess attributable to goodwill is to be amortized over 10 years.

Key had income of $30,000 in 19X4 and $50,000 in 19X5 and paid its first dividend, a $.20 per share dividend to common stock, on December 30, 19X5.

1. Prepare a determination and distribution of excess schedule for each investment.
2. Assuming the cost method is used for both investments, prepare the calculations necessary to convert the investment account to its simple-equity-adjusted balance on December 31, 19X5.

Exercise 5. Rob Company purchased a 90% interest in Venlo Company for $415,000 on January 1, 19X3. Any excess of cost over book value was attributed to goodwill, which is being amortized over 20 years. Both companies end their reporting periods on December 31. Since the investment in Venlo Company is consolidated, Rob Company has chosen to use the cost method to maintain its investment.

On December 31, 19X6, Rob Company sold 8,000 shares of Venlo Company for $700,000. The following stockholders' equity balances of Venlo Company are available:

	Jan. 1, 19X3	Jan. 1, 19X6
Common stock ($10 par).	$100,000	$100,000
Retained earnings.	250,000	420,000
Total equity	$350,000	$520,000

Venlo Company earned $70,000 during 19X6. Prepare a determination and distribution of excess schedule. Record the sale of the shares of Venlo Company and any other adjustments needed to the investment account.

Exercise 6. Doering Company has the following balance sheet on December 31, 19X5:

Assets		Liabilities and Equity		
Current assets	$160,000	Liabilities		$100,000
Investment in Brass		Equity:		
Company	150,000	Common stock		
Property, plant, and		($10 par)	$500,000	
equipment (net)	390,000	Retained earnings	100,000	600,000
Total assets	$700,000	Total liabilities and equity . . .		$700,000

The investment in Brass Company account reflects the original cost of an 80% interest (40,000 shares) purchased on January 1, 19X2. On the date of the purchase, Brass stockholders' equity had a book value of $150,000. Brass' other book values approximated market, except for a machine with a 5-year remaining life that was undervalued by $20,000. Any additional excess was attributed to goodwill and given a 10-year life.

A review of Brass' past financial statements reveals the following:

	Income	Dividends Paid
19X2.	$ 10,000	$ 3,000
19X3.	25,000	3,000
19X4.	40,000	4,000
19X5.	35,000	4,000
Total	$110,000	$14,000

Doering sold 2,000 shares of Brass common stock on January 1, 19X6, for $25,000.

Prepare the necessary entries on Doering's books to account accurately for the sale of the 2,000 Brass shares. Provide a determination and distribution of excess schedule along with all other necessary computations as support.

Exercise 7.   Dorn Inc. purchased 24,000 shares of Schmitt Corporation, which equated to an 80% interest, on January 1, 19X5. The following determination and distribution of excess schedule was prepared:

Determination and Distribution of Excess Schedule

Price paid for investment in Schmitt.		$700,000
Less interest acquired:		
Common stock ($10 par)	$300,000	
Retained earnings	400,000	
Total stockholders' equity.	$700,000	
Interest acquired	80%	560,000
Excess of cost over book (debit balance)		$140,000
Building (80% × $50,000 undervaluation with		
10-year life = 4,000 per year).		40,000 Dr.
Goodwill (40-year life = 2,500 per year)		$100,000 Dr.

Schmitt Corporation reported net income of $35,000 for the six months ended July 1, 19X8. Dorn's simple-equity-adjusted investment balance was $764,000 as of December 31, 19X7.

Prepare all entries for the sale of the Schmitt Corporation shares for each of the following situations:

a)   24,000 shares are sold for $850,000.

b)   12,000 shares are sold for $400,000.

c)   6,000 shares are sold for $200,000.

Exercise 8.   On January 1, 19X2, Boelter Company purchased 80% of the outstanding common stock of Miller Corporation for $280,000. On this date, Miller Corporation stockholders' equity was as follows:

6% preferred stock (1,000 shares, $100 par)	$100,000
Common stock (20,000 shares, $10 par)	200,000
Retained earnings	90,000
Total stockholders' equity	$390,000

Prepare a determination and distribution of excess schedule under each of the following situations (any excess of cost over book value is attributable to goodwill with a 10-year life):

a)   The preferred stock is cumulative, with dividends 1 year in arrears at January 1, 19X2, and has a liquidation value equal to par.

b)   The preferred stock is noncumulative but fully participating.

c)   The preferred stock is cumulative, with dividends 2 years in arrears as of January 1, 19X2, has a liquidation value equal to par, and is 10% (limited) participating.

Exercise 9.   Acme Construction Company had the following stockholders' equity on January 1, 19X1, the date on which Russel Company purchased an 80% interest in the common stock for $700,000:

8% cumulative preferred stock (5,000 shares, $100 par).............	$ 500,000
Common stock (40,000 shares, $20 par)........................	800,000
Retained earnings...	100,000
Total stockholders' equity................................	$1,400,000

Acme Construction Company did not pay preferred dividends in 19X0.

1. Prepare a determination and distribution of excess schedule. Assume that the preferred stock's liquidation value is equal to par and that any excess of cost is attributable to goodwill with a 20-year life.
2. Assume Acme Construction has the following net income (loss) for 19X1 and 19X2 and does not pay any dividends:

19X1........................	$60,000
19X2........................	(10,000)

Prepare the entries necessary on Russell Company's books to adjust its investment account to the simple equity balance at the end of 19X1 and 19X2.

Exercise 10. On December 31, 19X4, Zigler Corporation purchased an 80% interest in the common stock of Kip Company for $420,000. The stockholders' equity of Kip Company on December 31, 19X4, was as follows:

8% cumulative preferred stock (2,000 shares, $100 par).............	$200,000
Common stock (30,000 shares, $10 stated value)	300,000
Retained earnings	160,000
Total stockholders' equity................................	$660,000

Any excess of cost over book value was attributable to goodwill and had been given a 20-year life. The common stock investment is accounted for under the cost method.

Zigler Corporation purchased 1,000 shares of the cumulative preferred stock of Kip Company on January 1, 19X5, for $90,000. Kip Company issued a total of 2,000 preferred shares on January 1, 19X1. Dividends on preferred stock were paid in 19X1 and 19X2, but not in subsequent years. Zigler Corporation accounts for its investment using the cost method.

During 19X5 and 19X6, Kip Company paid no dividends and its retained earnings balance on December 31, 19X6, was $210,000. Kip Company income during 19X7 was $60,000.

1. Calculate the preferred and common stockholders' equity claim on Kip Company retained earnings balance at January 1, 19X7.
2. Prepare the cost-to-simple-equity conversion and the elimination that would be made on the December 31, 19X7 consolidated trial balance worksheet for the investment in preferred stock.
3. Prepare the cost-to-simple-equity conversion and the elimination that would be made on the December 31, 19X7 consolidated trial balance worksheet for the investment in common stock. Provide a determination and distribution of excess schedule as support.

Problems

Problem 7-1.   The following determination and distribution of excess schedule was prepared on January 1, 19X2, the date on which Paro Company purchased a 60% interest in Sandin Company:

Price paid.		$120,000
Less interest acquired:		
Common stock ($10 par).	$ 75,000	
Retained earnings.	60,000	
Total stockholders' equity	$135,000	
Interest acquired.	60%	81,000
Excess of cost over book value attributable to goodwill		
(20-year life)		$ 39,000

On December 31, 19X3, Paro Company purchased an additional 20% interest in Sandin Company for $60,000. Sandin's stockholders' equity was determined to be the following at that date:

Common stock.	$ 75,000
Retained earnings	85,000
Total stockholders' equity.	$160,000

Any excess of cost over book value was attributed to goodwill and given a 20-year life.

On December 31, 19X5, the following trial balances are available:

	Paro Company	Sandin Company
Current Assets	230,000	65,000
Investment in Sandin Company	239,000	
Property, Plant, and Equipment (net).	450,000	170,000
Current Liabilities	(110,000)	(20,000)
Common Stock ($10 par).	(500,000)	(75,000)
Retained Earnings, Jan. 1, 19X5.	(198,000)	(100,000)
Sales	(400,000)	(110,000)
Subsidiary Income	(36,000)	
Cost of Goods Sold	200,000	50,000
Other Expenses	100,000	15,000
Dividends Declared.	25,000	5,000
Total	0	0

Required:

1. Prepare the determination and distribution of excess schedule for the second purchase of Sandin stock by Paro Company.
2. Prepare the worksheet necessary to produce the consolidated financial statements of Paro Company and its subsidiary as of December 31, 19X5. Include income distribution schedules.

Problem 7-2.   On January 1, 19X1, James Company purchased 70% of the common stock of Chris Company for $244,000. On this date, Chris had common stock, other paid-in capital, and retained earnings of $50,000, $100,000, and $150,000, respectively.

On May 1, 19X2, James Company purchased an additional 20% of the common stock of Chris Company for $92,000.

Net income and dividends for 2 years for Chris Company were as follows:

	19X1	19X2
Net income for year	$60,000	$90,000
Dividends, declared in December	20,000	30,000

In 19X2, the net income of Chris from January 1 through April 30 was $30,000.

On January 1, 19X1, the only tangible asset of Chris that was undervalued was equipment, which was worth $20,000 more than book value. The equipment has a remaining life of 4 years, and straight-line depreciation is used. Goodwill, if any, is to be amortized over 10 years.

On May 1, 19X2, any excess of cost over book value is due to goodwill, to be amortized over 10 years.

In the last quarter of 19X2, Chris sold $50,000 in goods to James, at a gross profit rate of 30%. On December 31, 19X2, $10,000 of these goods are in James' ending inventory.

The trial balances for the companies on December 31, 19X2, are as follows:

	James Company	Chris Company
Inventory, Dec. 31	100,000	50,000
Other Current Assets	127,000	180,000
Investment in Chris Company	?	
Land	50,000	50,000
Buildings and Equipment	350,000	320,000
Accumulated Depreciation	(100,000)	(60,000)
Other Intangibles	20,000	
Current Liabilities	(120,000)	(40,000)
Bonds Payable		(100,000)
Other Long-Term Liabilities	(200,000)	
Common Stock—James	(200,000)	
Other Paid-In Capital—James	(100,000)	
Retained Earnings—James	(214,000)	
Common Stock—Chris		(50,000)
Other Paid-In Capital—Chris		(100,000)
Retained Earnings—Chris		(190,000)
Net Sales	(520,000)	(450,000)
Cost of Goods Sold	300,000	260,000
Operating Expenses	120,000	100,000
Subsidiary Income	?	
Dividends Declared	50,000	30,000
Total	0	0

(continued)

Required:

1. Using this information, prepare determination and distribution of excess schedules for the two purchases.
2. James Company carries the Investment in Chris Company under the simple equity method. In general journal form, record the entries that would be made to apply the equity method in 19X1 and 19X2.
3. Compute the balance that should appear in Investment in Chris Company and in Subsidiary Income on December 31, 19X2 (the second year). Fill in these amounts on James Company's trial balance on the worksheet for 19X2.
4. Complete the worksheet for consolidated financial statements for 19X2.

Problem 7-3.   On January 1, 19X4, Madden Company purchased a 20% interest in Clayton Company for $100,000. Two years subsequent to this purchase, Madden Company acquired an additional 45% interest in Clayton Company for $250,000.

Balance sheets of Clayton Company immediately prior to these purchases were as follows:

Assets	Jan. 1, 19X4	Jan. 1, 19X6
Current assets.	$150,000	$120,000
Land	150,000	150,000
Equipment (net).	200,000	300,000
Total assets.	$500,000	$570,000

Liabilities and Equity		
Liabilities	$100,000	$110,000
Equity:		
Common stock ($5 par)	$100,000	$100,000
Paid-in capital in excess of par	150,000	150,000
Retained earnings	150,000	210,000
Total equity.	$400,000	$460,000
Total liabilities and equity	$500,000	$570,000

On January 1, 19X4, and January 1, 19X6, Clayton's book values approximated market values, except for the land, which was undervalued by $50,000. Any resulting goodwill is being amortized over 10 years.

The original 20% investment had been maintained under the sophisticated equity method. Since it now will be necessary to prepare consolidated statements, the simple equity method is in use for 19X6.

On December 31, 19X6, Madden's investment in Clayton Company was determined as follows:

Original cost of 20% investment	$100,000
19X4–X5 equity adjustment, net of excess amortization	10,000
Original cost of 45% investment	250,000
65% of income, January 1, 19X6–December 31, 19X6.	26,000
Investment in Clayton Company	$386,000

The following trial balances were prepared on December 31, 19X6:

	Madden Company	Clayton Company
Current Assets.	250,000	225,000
Investment in Clayton Company	386,000	
Land	240,000	150,000
Building (net)	480,000	
Equipment (net)	400,000	220,000
Other Assets	20,000	5,000
Liabilities	(340,000)	(100,000)
Common Stock ($10 par)	(1,000,000)	
Common Stock ($5 par)		(100,000)
Paid-In Capital in Excess of Par		(150,000)
Retained Earnings, Jan. 1, 19X6	(350,000)	(210,000)
Sales.	(900,000)	(350,000)
Subsidiary Income.	(26,000)	
Cost of Goods Sold	540,000	180,000
Other Expenses.	250,000	130,000
Dividends Declared	50,000	
Total	0	0

Required:

Prepare the worksheet necessary to produce the consolidated financial statements of Madden Company and its subsidiary as of December 31, 19X6. Include the determination and distribution of excess and income distribution schedules.

Problem 7-4.   On January 1, 19X1, Prince Company purchased 20% of the common stock of Spud Company for $80,000. On this date, Spud had common stock, other paid-in capital, and retained earnings of $50,000, $100,000, and $150,000, respectively. On this date, any excess of cost over book value is due to goodwill, to be amortized over 10 years.

On January 1, 19X2, Prince Company purchased an additional 60% of the common stock of Spud Company for $284,000. On this date, the only tangible asset of Spud that was undervalued was land, which was worth $30,000 more than book value. Goodwill, if any, is to be amortized over 10 years.

Net income and dividends for 2 years for Spud Company were as follows:

	19X1	19X2
Net income for year	$60,000	$90,000
Dividends, declared in December	20,000	30,000

For 19X1, Prince accounted for its investment using the sophisticated equity method. For 19X2, Prince accounted for all of its investment using the simple equity method.

On July 1, 19X2, Spud purchased equipment for $40,000 and immediately sold it to Prince for $50,000. Prince is using the equipment and depreciating it over 5 years, using the straight-line method and assuming no salvage value.

The trial balances for both companies on December 31, 19X2, are as follows:

(continued)

	Prince Company	Spud Company
Inventory, Dec. 31	100,000	50,000
Other Current Assets	157,000	180,000
Investment in Spud Company	418,000	
Land	50,000	50,000
Buildings and Equipment	350,000	320,000
Accumulated Depreciation	(100,000)	(60,000)
Other Intangibles	20,000	
Current Liabilities	(120,000)	(40,000)
Bonds Payable		(100,000)
Other Long-Term Liabilities	(200,000)	
Common Stock—Prince	(200,000)	
Other Paid-In Capital—Prince	(100,000)	
Retained Earnings—Prince	(253,000)	
Common Stock—Spud		(50,000)
Other Paid-In Capital—Spud		(100,000)
Retained Earnings—Spud		(190,000)
Net Sales	(520,000)	(450,000)
Cost of Goods Sold	300,000	270,000
Operating Expenses	120,000	100,000
Gain on Sale of Equipment		(10,000)
Subsidiary Income	(72,000)	
Dividends Declared	50,000	30,000
Total	0	0

Required:

1. Using this information, prepare determination and distribution of excess schedules for the two purchases.
2. Prepare the worksheet necessary to produce the consolidated financial statements of Prince and Spud as of December 31, 19X2. Include income distribution schedules.

Problem 7-5.   On January 1, 19X1, Prug Company purchased an 80% interest (8,000 shares) directly from Bohr Company, on the day Bohr was organized, for $160,000.

On April 1, 19X5, Prug Company purchased 1,000 additional shares of Bohr Company for $38,900. Bohr had an exceptional first quarter with income of $9,000. No dividends had been paid. Any excess of cost is considered to be goodwill with a 10-year life. Unrealized gains and losses applicable to the 10% interest are ignored on the basis of materiality.

The subsidiary sells merchandise to the parent at cost plus 50%. Intercompany sales were $60,000 during 19X5; $20,000 was unpaid at year-end. There were $9,000 of such goods in the beginning inventory of Prug Company and $15,000 of such goods in the ending inventory. However, the ending inventory had been adjusted down to its market value of $12,000.

The parent sold a machine with a book value of $10,000 to the subsidiary for $15,000 on January 1, 19X4. The machine had a 5-year life as of January 1, 19X4, and is being depreciated on a straight-line basis.

Bohr Company issued $100,000 of face value, 5-year, 6% bonds on January 1, 19X3. The bonds sold at a premium of $4,500 since the market rate of interest was 5%. On January 1, 19X4, when the market rate was 8%, Prug Company purchased all of these bonds for $93,400. Straight-line amortization is being used for the bonds.

Bohr Company paid a $1 per share cash dividend on December 31, 19X5.

The following trial balances were prepared as of December 31, 19X5:

	Prug Company	Bohr Company
Cash. . . .	12,050	103,700
Accounts Receivable	80,000	40,000
Inventory . . .	43,100	63,000
Plant and Equipment	400,000	300,000
Accumulated Depreciation	(200,000)	(80,000)
Investment in Bohr Company Stock.	198,900	
Investment in Bohr Company Bonds	96,700	
Liabilities . . .	(64,100)	(40,000)
6% Bonds Payable. . .		(100,000)
Premium on Bonds Payable. . .		(1,800)
Common Stock ($10 par) . . .	(200,000)	(100,000)
Paid-In Capital in Excess of Par . . .		(100,000)
Retained Earnings, Jan. 1, 19X5 . . .	(300,000)	(80,000)
Sales. . .	(250,000)	(120,000)
Cost of Goods Sold . . .	150,000	80,000
Other Expenses. . .	50,000	20,000
Subsidiary Income. . .	(9,000)	
Interest Income . . .	(7,650)	
Interest Expense . . .		5,100
Dividends Declared . . .		10,000
Total . . .	0	0

Required:

Prepare the worksheet necessary to produce the consolidated financial statements of Prug Company and its subsidiary as of December 31, 19X5. Include the determination and distribution of excess and income distribution schedules.

Suggestion: Determine what method Prug Company is using to maintain its investment in Bohr Company stock account (i.e., cost, simple equity, or sophisticated equity) before attempting the requirements of this problem.

Problem 7-6. During 19X7, Away Company acquired a controlling interest in Stallman Inc. Trial balances of the companies at December 31, 19X7, are as follows:

	Away Company	Stallman Inc.
Cash. . .	100,000	78,000
Notes Receivable	100,000	
Accounts Receivable	200,000	100,000
Interest Receivable. . .	3,000	
Dividends Receivable. . .	4,500	

(continued)

	Away Company	Stallman Inc.
Inventories	924,000	125,000
Investment in Stallman Inc.	468,700	
Property, Plant, and Equipment	1,250,000	500,000
Accumulated Depreciation	(500,000)	(150,000)
Deferred Charges	25,000	
Patents and Licenses		50,000
Accounts Payable	(425,000)	(80,000)
Notes Payable		(75,000)
Dividends Payable		(5,000)
Capital Stock	(300,000)	(100,000)
Retained Earnings, Jan. 1, 19X7	(1,605,000)	(400,000)
Sales and Services	(1,800,000)	(750,000)
Subsidiary Income	(43,200)	
Interest Income	(3,000)	
Cost of Goods Sold	1,350,000	525,000
Administrative and Selling Expenses	251,000	174,000
Interest Expense		3,000
Dividends Declared		5,000
Total	0	0

The following information is available regarding the transactions and accounts of the two companies:

a)   An analysis of the investment in Stallman Inc. account follows:

	Description	Amount	Interest Acquired
January 1, 19X7	Investment	$325,000	70%
September 30, 19X7	Investment	105,000	20%
Total		$430,000	90%
December 31, 19X7	90% of Stallman income for 19X7	43,200	
December 31, 19X7	90% of Stallman dividends for 19X7	(4,500)	
Total		$468,700	

The net income of Stallman Inc. for the 9 months ended September 30, 19X7, was $25,000.

b)   *The price paid by the parent on January 1, 19X7, to achieve control reflects uncertainty as to the future value of the patents. The remaining amortization is 10 years.*

c)   *On September 30, 19X7, Away Company loaned its subsidiary $100,000 on a 1-year, 12% note. Interest and principal are payable in quarterly installments beginning December 31, 19X7. The December 31, 19X7 payment was made by Stallman but was not received by Away. Away Company has no other notes receivable outstanding.*

d) *Stallman Inc.'s sales principally are engineering services billed at cost plus 50%. During 19X7, Away Company was billed for $40,000, of which $16,500 was treated as a deferred charge at December 31, 19X7.*

e) *During the year, parent company sales to the subsidiary totaled $60,000, of which $10,000 remained in the inventory of Stallman Inc. at December 31, 19X7.*

f) *In 19X7, Away constructed certain tools at a cost of $15,000 and sold them to Stallman Inc. for $25,000. Stallman Inc. depreciates such tools using the straight-line method over a 5-year life. One-half year's depreciation is taken in the year of acquisition.*

Required:

Prepare the worksheet necessary to produce the consolidated financial statements of Away Company and its subsidiary for the year ended December 31, 19X7. Include the determination and distribution of excess and income distribution schedules.

(AICPA adapted)

Problem 7-7. On January 1, 19X3, Horn Corporation purchased 90% (18,000 shares) of the outstanding common stock of Norm Company for $486,000. Just prior to Horn Corporation's purchase, Norm Company had the following stockholders' equity:

Common stock ($5 par).....................	$100,000
Paid-in capital in excess of par...............	300,000
Retained earnings........................	100,000
Total stockholders' equity	$500,000

At this time, Norm Company's book values approximated market values. Any excess of cost was attributed to goodwill and given a 20-year life.

On January 1, 19X7, Norm Company's retained earnings balance amounted to $200,000. No changes had taken place in the paid-in capital accounts since the original sale of common stock on July 10, 19X0.

On July 1, 19X7, Horn Corporation sold 2,000 of its Norm Company shares to Welch Corporation for $75,000. At the time of this sale, Horn had no intention of selling the balance of its holding in Norm Company.

In an unexpected move on December 31, 19X7, Horn Corporation sold its remaining 80% interest in Norm Company to Welch Corporation for $500,000.

Norm Company reported income and dividends for 19X7 are as follows:

	Income	Dividends
January 1, 19X7–July 1, 19X7	$25,000	$.50/share
July 1, 19X7–December 31, 19X7	35,000	.50/share

Required:

Prepare the determination and distribution of excess schedule for Horn Corporation's purchase of Norm Company common stock on January 1, 19X3. Then, prepare all the entries on Horn's books needed to reflect the changes in its investment account from January 1, 19X7, to December 31, 19X7. (Assume Horn uses the cost method to report its investment in Norm Company.)

Problem 7-8. The following information is available regarding the investments of Billings Corporation in Chassel Company for the years 19X1-19X5:

Date	Transaction	Interest	Price
1/1/X1	Purchased common	10%	$ 25,000
1/1/X2	Purchased preferred	60	30,000
1/1/X3	Purchased common	50	140,000
1/1/X5	Purchased common	20	60,000
1/1/X6	Sold common	10	35,000

The stockholders' equity section of Chassel Company's balance sheet has not changed since the January 1, 19X0 original sale of preferred stock to the public, except for the balance in the retained earnings account. The stockholders' equity as of January 1, 19X5, is as follows:

6% cumulative preferred stock	
($50 par, liquidation value equals par value)	$ 50,000
Common stock ($10 par)	100,000
Paid-in capital in excess of par	20,000
Retained earnings	150,000
Total stockholders' equity	$320,000

Other relevant facts are as follows:

a) On January 1, 19X1, Chassel had a $60,000 retained earnings balance and there were no dividends in arrears on the preferred stock.

b) The excess of cost over book value on each investment in common stock was viewed as goodwill with a 10-year life.

c) The 10% interest sold on January 1, 19X6, was the interest purchased on January 1, 19X1.

d) Income and dividends were as follows for 19X1–19X5:

	Net Income	Preferred Dividends	Common Dividends
19X1	$25,000	$3,000	None
19X2	30,000	3,000	$6,000
19X3	30,000	3,000	5,000
19X4	25,000	None	None
19X5	20,000	None	None

Billings' investment account balances for its interests in Chassel Company were calculated as follows on December 31, 19X5:

Investment in preferred stock:	
Original cost	$ 30,000
Plus dividends in arrears for 19X4	1,800
Balance, December 31, 19X5	$ 31,800

Investment in common stock:

January 1, 19X1 purchase	$ 25,000
January 1, 19X3 purchase	140,000
19X3 Chassel income, $30,000 x 60%	18,000
19X3 Chassel dividends, $5,000 x 60%.	(3,000)
19X4 Chassel income, $25,000 x 60%	15,000
January 1, 19X5 purchase	60,000
19X5 Chassel income, $20,000 x 80%	16,000
December 31, 19X5 sale	(35,000)
Balance, December 31, 19X5	$236,000

Required:

Assume the investment accounts are to be properly maintained under the simple equity method. Prepare all necessary correcting entries on the books of Billings Corporation as of January 1, 19X6. (Assume nominal accounts are open.) All supporting computations and schedules should be in good form.

Problem 7-9. Marsha Corporation purchased an 80% interest in the common stock of Trans Corporation on December 31, 19X3, for $720,000, when Trans had the following condensed balance sheet:

Assets		Liabilities and Stockholders' Equity	
Current assets	$ 500,000	Liabilities	$ 600,000
Land	100,000	Preferred stock (8% cumulative, $100 par)	100,000
Building (net)	400,000	Common stock ($20 par)	750,000
Equipment (net)	500,000	Retained earnings	50,000
Total assets	$1,500,000	Total liabilities and equity	$1,500,000

On the December 31, 19X3 purchase date, the dividends on the preferred stock were 2 years in arrears. Also on this date, the book values of Trans' assets approximated market values, except for the building which was undervalued by $28,000 and had a 20-year remaining life. Any resulting goodwill is being amortized over a 10-year life.

For 19X4–19X6, earnings and dividends for Trans Corporation were as follows:

	Income	Preferred Dividends	Common Dividends
19X4	$40,000		
19X5	50,000	$16,000	
19X6	80,000	24,000	$26,750

The following trial balances of the two companies were prepared on December 31, 19X6:

	Marsha Corporation	Trans Corporation
Current Assets	806,400	463,250
Investment in Trans Corporation	720,000	
Land	400,000	210,000

(continued)

	Marsha Corporation	Trans Corporation
Building	950,000	500,000
Accumulated Depreciation—Building	(200,000)	(160,000)
Equipment	1,500,000	740,000
Accumulated Depreciation—Equipment	(400,000)	(200,000)
Liabilities	(800,000)	(550,000)
Preferred Stock, 8%		(100,000)
Common Stock ($20 par)	(2,000,000)	(750,000)
Retained Earnings, Jan. 1, 19X6	(860,000)	(124,000)
Sales	(2,100,000)	(1,000,000)
Subsidiary Dividend Income	(21,400)	
Cost of Goods Sold	1,155,000	600,000
Other Expenses	650,000	320,000
Dividends Declared	200,000	50,750
Total	0	0

On January 1, 19X5, Marsha sold production equipment to Trans for $55,000 with a 5-year remaining life. Marsha's original cost was $80,000, and accumulated depreciation on the date sold was $50,000.

Required:

Prepare the worksheet necessary to produce the consolidated financial statements of Marsha Corporation and its subsidiary as of December 31, 19X6. Include the determination and distribution of excess and income distribution schedules.

Problem 7-10. The following information pertains to Titan Corporation and its two subsidiaries, Boat Corporation and Motor Corporation:

a) The three corporations are all in the same industry and their operations are homogeneous. Titan Corporation exercises control over the boards of directors of Boat Corporation and Motor Corporation and has installed new principal officers in both.

b) Boat Corporation had a retained earnings balance of $92,000 at January 1, 19X7, and had income of $15,000 for the first 3 months of 19X7 and $20,000 for the first 6 months of 19X8.

c) Titan Corporation acquired 250 shares of fully participating Motor preferred stock for $7,000 and 14,000 shares of Motor common stock for $196,000 on January 2, 19X8. Motor Corporation had a net income of $20,000 in 19X8 and did not declare any dividends.

d) Motor Corporation's inventory includes $22,400 of merchandise acquired from Boat Corporation subsequent to July, 19X8, for which no payment has been made. Boat Corporation marked up the merchandise 40% on cost.

e) Titan Corporation acquired in the open market twenty-five $1,000, 6% bonds of Boat Corporation for $21,400 on January 1, 19X5. Boat Corporation bonds mature December 31, 19Y0. Interest is paid each June 30 and December 31. Straight-line amortization is allowed on the basis of materiality.

f) The 19X8 year-end balance in the investment in Boat Corporation stock account is composed of the items shown in the following schedule:

Date	Description	Amount
4/1/X7	Cost of 5,000 shares of Boat Corp. stock.	$ 71,400
12/31/X7	20% of the dividends declared in December 19X7 by Boat Corp.	(9,000)
12/31/X7	20% of the 19X7 annual net income of Boat Corp.	12,000
7/1/X8	Cost of 15,000 shares of Boat Corp.	226,200
12/31/X8	80% of the dividends declared in December 19X8 by Boat Corp.	(24,000)
12/31/X8	80% of the 19X8 annual net income of Boat Corp.	32,000
12/31/X8	Total.	$308,600

g) The December 31, 19X8 trial balances for the three corporations appear as follows:

	Titan Corporation	Boat Corporation	Motor Corporation
Cash.	100,000	87,000	95,000
Accounts Receivable	158,200	210,000	105,000
Inventories	290,000	90,000	115,000
Advance to Boat Corporation	17,000		
Dividends Receivable.	24,000		
Property, Plant, and Equipment	777,600	325,000	470,000
Accumulated Depreciation	(180,000)	(55,000)	(160,000)
Investment in Boat Corporation:			
6% Bonds	23,800		
Common Stock	308,600		
Investment in Motor Corporation:			
Preferred Stock	7,400		
Common Stock	207,200		
Notes Payable	(45,000)	(14,000)	(44,000)
Accounts Payable	(170,000)	(96,000)	(86,000)
Bonds Payable	(285,000)	(150,000)	(125,000)
Discount on Bonds Payable.	8,000		
Dividends Payable	(22,000)	(30,000)	
Preferred Stock ($20 par).	(400,000)		(50,000)
Common Stock ($10 par).	(600,000)	(250,000)	(200,000)
Retained Earnings, Jan. 1,19X8	(154,600)	(107,000)	(100,000)
Sales	(1,050,000)	(500,000)	(650,000)
Other Revenue	(2,100)		
Subsidiary Income:			
Common Stock (Boat).	(32,000)		
Preferred Stock (Motor).	(400)		
Common Stock (Motor).	(11,200)		
Cost of Goods Sold.	650,000	300,000	400,000
Other Expenses	358,500	160,000	230,000
Dividends Declared.	22,000	30,000	
Total	0	0	0

Required:

Prepare the worksheet necessary to produce the consolidated financial statements of Titan Corporation and its subsidiaries as of December 31, 19X8. Consolidated

(continued)

retained earnings should be allocated to Titan Corporation, and the minority interests should be shown separately in the consolidated balance sheet column. The consolidation is to be accounted for as a purchase. All supporting computations and schedules should be in good form.

(AICPA adapted)

Problem 7-11.   On January 1, 19X7, Black Jack Corporation purchased all of the preferred stock and 60% of the common stock of Zenon Company for $56,000 and $110,000, respectively. Immediately prior to the purchases, Zenon Company had the following stockholders' equity:

8% cumulative preferred stock ($100 par, 2 years in arrears)	$ 50,000
Common stock ($10 par)	100,000
Paid-in capital in excess of par (common stock)	20,000
Retained earnings	30,000
Total stockholders' equity	$200,000

The December 31, 19X8 trial balances of the two companies are as follows:

	Black Jack Corporation	Zenon Company
Cash.	31,400	10,000
Accounts Receivable (net)	80,000	76,000
Inventories	230,000	44,000
Other Current Assets	20,000	8,000
Property, Plant, and Equipment	1,450,000	122,000
Accumulated Depreciation	(420,000)	(25,000)
Investment in Zenon Preferred Stock	56,000	
Investment in Zenon Common Stock	120,200	
Liabilities	(350,000)	(18,000)
Common Stock—Black Jack.	(1,000,000)	
Retained Earnings—Black Jack.	(195,000)	
Preferred Stock—Zenon ($100 par)		(50,000)
Common Stock—Zenon		(100,000)
Paid-In Capital in Excess of Par—Zenon		(20,000)
Retained Earnings—Zenon		(41,000)
Sales.	(420,000)	(96,000)
Cost of Goods Sold	300,000	60,000
Other Expenses.	80,000	26,000
Dividends Declared	25,000	4,000
Subsidiary Income—Preferred	(4,000)	
Subsidiary Income—Common	(3,600)	
Paid-In Capital in Excess of Par—Black Jack		
Total	0	0

Additional information:

  a)   On January 1, 19X7, Zenon Company's only plant asset, equipment, had a market value of $200,000. All its other assets and liabilities had market values equal to their book values. The equipment had an estimated remaining life of 8 years and is being depreciated on a straight-line basis.

  b)   On December 30, 19X7, and December 30, 19X8, Zenon Company paid preferred stock dividends of $8 per share.

c) Zenon Company had a net income of $15,000 in 19X7 and $10,000 for 19X8.

d) Zenon Company sold a piece of equipment with a book value of $8,000 to Black Jack Corporation for $13,000 on January 2, 19X7. The machine had an estimated future life of 5 years, and straight-line depreciation is being used.

e) During 19X8, Black Jack sold $20,000 of goods to Zenon for cost plus 40%. Zenon had $2,800 of such purchases in its beginning inventory and $7,000 of such purchases in its ending inventory. Zenon owed Black Jack $2,000 for purchases at year-end. During 19X8, Zenon sold $8,000 of goods to Black Jack at cost plus 60%. $1,200 of these goods were in Black Jack's beginning inventory, and $1,600 of such goods were in its ending inventory. Black Jack owed Zenon $6,000 for purchases at year-end.

f) On January 1, 19X9, Black Jack Corporation sold its 60% interest in Zenon Company common stock for $130,000.

Required:

1. Prepare the worksheet necessary to produce the consolidated financial statements of Black Jack Corporation and its subsidiary for the year ended December 31, 19X8. Include the determination and distribution of excess and income distribution schedules.
2. Prepare the entries on Black Jack Corporation's books to reflect the sale of its investment in Zenon Company common stock on January 1, 19X9.

Problem 7-12. Condensed (unconsolidated) statements of income and retained earnings statements for the year ended December 31, 19X5, and the balance sheets as of December 31, 19X5, of Pace Company and its subsidiary, Smith Company, are as follows:

Condensed Statements of Income	Pace Company	Smith Company
Sales	$(4,000,000)	$(1,700,000)
Cost of goods sold	2,982,000	1,015,000
Operating expenses	400,000	377,200
Dividend income	(75,000)	
Subsidiary income	(232,000)	
Interest expense		7,800
Net income	$(925,000)	$(300,000)

Retained Earnings Statements		
Balance, January 1, 19X5	$(2,100,000)	$(640,000)
Net income	(925,000)	(300,000)
Dividends declared	170,000	100,000
Balance, December 31, 19X5	$(2,855,000)	$(840,000)

Balance Sheets		
Cash	$ 486,000	$249,600
Accounts receivable	235,000	185,000
Inventories	475,000	355,000
Machinery and equipment (net)	2,231,000	530,000

(continued)

Balance Sheets	Pace Company	Smith Company
Investment in stock of Smith Company	954,000	
Investment in bonds of Smith Company	58,000	
Accounts payable.	(384,000)	(62,000)
Bonds payable.		(120,000)
Unamortized discount on bonds payable		2,400
Common stock, Pace Company.	(1,200,000)	
Common stock, Smith Company		(250,000)
Paid-in capital in excess of par		(50,000)
Retained earnings (carried down)	(2,855,000)	(840,000)
Total.	0	0

Additional information:

a) On January 3, 19X3, Pace acquired from the sole stockholder of Smith Company 80% of the outstanding common stock of Smith and a patent valued at $40,000. Pace's total cost of the transaction was $440,000 in cash. The net book value of Smith stock on the date of acquisition was $500,000, and the book values of the individual assets and liabilities were equal to their fair market values. Pace charged the entire $440,000 to the account, Investment in Stock of Smith Company. The patent, for which no amortization had been charged, had a remaining legal life of 4 years as of January 3, 19X3.

b) On July 1, 19X5, Pace reduced its interest in Smith Company stock to 75% by selling shares for $70,000 to an unaffiliated company at a profit of $16,000. Pace recorded the proceeds as a credit to its investment account.

c) For the 6 months ended June 30, 19X5, Smith had a net income of $140,000. Pace recorded 80% of this amount on its books of account prior to the time of sale.

d) During 19X4, Smith sold merchandise to Pace for $130,000, which was at a markup of 30% over Smith's cost. On January 1, 19X5, $52,000 of this merchandise remained in Pace's inventory. This merchandise subsequently was sold by Pace in February 19X5 at a profit of $8,000.

e) In November 19X5, Pace sold merchandise to Smith for the first time. Pace's cost for this merchandise was $80,000, and the sale was made at 120% of cost. Smith's inventory at December 31, 19X5, contained $24,000 of the merchandise that was purchased from Pace.

f) On December 31, 19X5, there was a $45,000 payment in transit from Smith Company to Pace Company. Accounts Receivable and Accounts Payable include intercompany receivables and payables.

g) In December 19X5, Smith declared and paid cash dividends of $100,000 to its stockholders.

h) On December 31, 19X5, Pace purchased, for $58,000, 50% of the outstanding bonds issued by Smith. The bonds mature on December 31, 19X9, and originally were issued at a discount. On December 31, 19X5, the balance in Smith's account, Unamortized Discount on Bonds Payable, was $2,400. It is the intention of the management of Pace to hold these bonds until their maturity.

Required:

Prepare the worksheet in vertical format for the consolidated financial statements of Pace Company and its subsidiary as of December 31, 19X5. Include the determination and distribution of excess and income distribution schedules.

(AICPA adapted)

Appendix Problems

Problem 7A-1.   Prior to January 1, 19X7, the stockholders of East Company and West Company approved the merger of the two companies. On January 1, 19X7, 5,000 shares of East Company $10 par common stock were issued and recorded at par value to West Company stockholders in exchange for the 3,000 shares of West Company $20 par common stock outstanding. The transaction met the criteria for a pooling of interest.

The following December 31, 19X7 balance sheets have been prepared:

Assets	East Company	West Company
Cash.	$ 36,400	$ 28,200
Notes receivable.	22,000	9,000
Notes receivable discounted	(8,100)	
Accounts receivable.	20,900	21,700
Interest receivable	13,000	3,300
Dividends receivable		
Inventories	81,200	49,600
Property, plant, and equipment	83,200	43,500
Accumulated depreciation.	(12,800)	(9,300)
Investment in West Company.	50,000	
Total assets.	$285,800	$146,000

Liabilities and Stockholders' Equity		
Notes payable	$4,000	$ 12,000
Accounts payable	42,000	19,600
Dividends payable		4,500
Interest payable	2,600	2,100
Common stock—East	120,000	
Paid-in capital in excess of par—East	28,500	
Retained earnings—East.	88,700	
Common stock—West		60,000
Paid-in capital in excess of par—West		20,000
Retained earnings—West		27,800
Total liabilities and stockholders' equity	$285,800	$146,000

The following additional information is available:

a)   Net income for 19X7 (disregard income taxes):

East Company	$21,700
West Company	10,200

b)   On December 31, 19X7, West Company owed East Company $16,000 on open account and $8,000 in interest-bearing notes. East Company discounted $3,000 on the notes received from West Company with the First State Bank.

c)   On December 31, 19X7, West Company accrued interest payable of $120 on the notes payable to East Company: $40 on the note of $3,000 discounted with the bank and $80 on the remaining note of $5,000. East Company did not accrue interest receivable from West Company.

(continued)

d) During 19X7, East Company sold merchandise, which cost $30,000, to West Company for $40,000. West Company's December 31 inventory included $10,000 of this merchandise priced at West Company's cost.

e) On July 1, West Company sold equipment, which had a book value of $15,000, to East Company for $17,000. East Company recorded depreciation on the equipment in the amount of $850 for 19X7. The remaining life of the equipment at the date of sale was 10 years.

f) West Company shipped merchandise to East Company on December 31, 19X7, and recorded an account receivable of $6,000 for the sale. West Company's cost for the merchandise was $4,800. Because the merchandise was in transit, East Company did not record the transaction. The terms of the sale were f.o.b. shipping point.

g) West Company declared a dividend of $1.50 per share on December 30, 19X7, payable on January 1, 19X8. East Company made no entry for the declaration.

Required:

Using the balance-sheet-only method of consolidation, complete the December 31, 19X7 worksheet for East Company and its subsidiary.

Suggestion: The investment was improperly recorded at par value. The equity of West must be added to East following the equity transfer rules.

Problem 7A-2. The December 31, 19X9 post-closing trial balances of Encanto Corporation and its subsidiary, Norris Corporation, are as follows:

	Encanto Corporation	Norris Corporation
Cash	167,250	101,000
Accounts Receivable.	178,450	72,000
Notes Receivable.	87,500	28,000
Dividends Receivable	36,000	
Inventories	122,000	68,000
Property, Plant, and Equipment.	487,000	252,000
Accumulated Depreciation.	(117,000)	(64,000)
Investment in Norris Corporation	240,800	
Accounts Payable	(222,000)	(76,000)
Notes Payable.	(79,000)	(89,000)
Dividends Payable		(40,000)
Common Stock ($10 par)	(400,000)	(100,000)
Retained Earnings	(501,000)	(152,000)
Total	0	0

The following additional information is available:

a) Encanto initially acquired 60% of the outstanding common stock of Norris in 19X7. There was no difference between the cost and book value of the net assets acquired. As of December 31, 19X9, the percentage owned is 90%. An analysis of the investment in Norris Corporation account is as follows:

	Description	Amount
December 31, 19X7	Acquired 6,000 shares	$ 70,800
December 31, 19X8	60% of 19X8 net income of $78,000	46,800
September 1, 19X9	Acquired 3,000 shares	92,000
December 31, 19X9	Subsidiary income for 19X9	67,200*
December 31, 19X9	90% of dividends declared	(36,000)
Investment balance, December 31, 19X9		$240,800

*Subsidiary income for 19X9:

60% × $96,000	$57,600
30% × $96,000 × 33⅓%	9,600
Total	$67,200

Norris net income is earned ratably during the year. Amortization of the excess of cost over the net assets acquired is being recorded over 60 months.

b) *On December 15, 19X9, Norris declared a cash dividend of $4 per share of common stock, payable to shareholders on January 7, 19Y0.*

c) *During 19X9, Encanto sold merchandise to Norris. Encanto's cost for this merchandise was $68,000, and the sale was made at 125% of cost. Norris' inventory at December 31, 19X9, included merchandise purchased from Encanto at a cost to Norris of $35,000.*

d) *In December, 19X8, Norris sold merchandise to Encanto for $67,000, which was at a markup of 35% over Norris' cost. On January 1, 19X9, $54,000 of this merchandise remained in Encanto's inventory. This merchandise subsequently was sold by Encanto at a profit of $11,000 during 19X9.*

e) *On October 1, 19X9, Encanto sold excess equipment to Norris for $42,000. Data relating to this equipment are as follows:*

Book value on Encanto's records	$36,000
Method of depreciation	Straight-line
Estimated remaining life on October 1, 19X9	10 years

f) *Near the end of 19X9, Norris reduced the balance of its intercompany account payable to zero by transferring $8,000 to Encanto. This payment still was in transit on December 31, 19X9.*

Required:

Prepare the worksheet necessary to produce the consolidated balance sheet of Encanto Corporation and its subsidiary as of December 31, 19X9. Include the determination and distribution of excess schedule for Encanto's purchase of Norris common stock on September 1, 19X9.

(AICPA Adapted)

Problem 7A-3.   Case Inc. acquired all of the outstanding $25 par common stock of Frey Inc. on June 30, 19X4, in exchange for 40,000 shares of its $25 par common stock. The business combination meets all the criteria for a pooling of interests. On June 30, 19X4, Case Inc. common stock closed at $65 per share on a national stock exchange. Both corporations continued to operate as separate businesses, maintaining separate accounting records with years ending December 31.

(continued)

Additional information is as follows:

a) Case Inc. uses the simple equity method to account for its investment in Frey. The investment account has not been adjusted to reflect intercompany transactions.

b) On June 30, 19X4, Frey's assets and liabilities had market values equal to book values, except for the land which had a market value of $550,000.

c) On June 30, 19X4, Frey paid cash dividends of $4 per share on its common stock.

d) On December 10, 19X4, Case paid a cash dividend totaling $256,000 on its common stock.

e) On June 30, 19X4, immediately before the combination, the stockholders' equities were:

	Case Inc.	Frey Inc.
Common stock.	$2,200,000	$1,000,000
Additional paid-in capital	1,660,000	190,000
Retained earnings	3,036,000	980,000
Total.	$6,896,000	$2,170,000

f) Frey's long-term debt consisted of 10-year, 10% bonds issued at face value on March 31, 19W8. Interest is payable semiannually on March 31 and September 30. Case had purchased Frey's bonds at the face value of $320,000 in 19W8, and there has not been any change in ownership.

f) During October, 19X4, Case sold merchandise to Frey at a total invoice price of $720,000, which included a profit of $180,000. At December 31, 19X4, one-half of the merchandise remained in Frey's inventory, and Frey had not paid Case for the merchandise purchased.

h) The 19X4 net income amounts per the separate books of Case and Frey were $890,000 (exclusive of equity in Frey earnings) and $580,000, respectively.

i) The retained earnings balances at December 31, 19X3, were $2,506,000 and $820,000 for Case and Frey, respectively.

j) On December 31, 19X4, the companies had the following post-closing trial balances:

	Case Inc.	Frey Inc.
Cash	825,000	330,000
Accounts and Other Current Receivables	2,140,000	835,000
Inventories	2,310,000	1,045,000
Land	650,000	300,000
Depreciable Assets (net)	4,575,000	1,980,000
Investment in Frey Inc..	2,430,000	
Long-Term Investments and Other Assets	865,000	385,000
Accounts Payable and Other Current Liabilities .	(2,465,000)	(1,145,000)
Long-Term Debt	(1,900,000)	(1,300,000)
Common Stock ($25 par)	(3,200,000)	(1,000,000)
Additional Paid-In Capital	(1,850,000)	(190,000)
Retained Earnings	(4,380,000)	(1,240,000)
Total.	0	0

Required:

1. Prepare the worksheet necessary to produce the consolidated balance sheet of Case Inc. and its subsidiary for the year ended December 31, 19X4.
2. Prepare the formal consolidated statement of retained earnings for December 31, 19X4.

Problem 7A-4. On January 1, 19X1, Press Company acquired 90% of the common stock of Solid Company for $317,000. On this date, Solid had total owner's equity of $270,000, including retained earnings of $100,000.

On January 1, 19X1, any excess of cost over book value is attributable to the undervaluation of land, building, and goodwill. Land is worth $20,000 more than cost. Building is worth $40,000 more than book value. It has a remaining useful life of 6 years and is depreciated using the straight-line method. Goodwill is to be amortized over 10 years.

During 19X1 and 19X2, Press has appropriately accounted for its investment in Solid using the simple equity method.

During 19X2, Solid sold merchandise to Press for $40,000, of which $15,000 is held by Press on December 31, 19X2. Solid's usual gross profit on affiliated sales is 40%. On December 31, 19X2, Press still owes Solid $8,000 for merchandise acquired in December.

On October 1, 19X0, Solid sold $100,000 par value of 10-year, 10% bonds for $102,000. The bonds pay interest semiannually on April 1 and October 1. Straight-line amortization is used. On October 2, 19X1, Press repurchased $60,000 par value of the bonds for $59,100. Straight-line amortization is used.

On January 1, 19X2, Press purchased equipment for $111,332 and immediately leased the equipment to Solid on a 3-year lease. The minimum lease payments of $40,000 are to be made annually on January 1, beginning immediately, for a total of 3 payments. The implicit interest rate is 8%. The useful life of the equipment is 3 years. The lease has been capitalized by both companies. Solid is depreciating the equipment using the straight-line method and assuming a salvage value of $6,332. A lease amortization schedule, applicable to both companies, follows:

Carrying Value on	Carrying Value	Interest Rate	Interest	Payment	Principal Reduction
1/1/19X1	111,332				
	− 40,000				
1/1/19X2	71,332	8%	5,707	40,000	34,293
	− 34,293				
1/1/19X3	37,039	8%	2,961*	40,000	37,039
	− 37,039				
1/1/19X4	0				

*Adjusted for rounding error.

The balance sheet for the companies on December 31, 19X2, was as follows:

Assets	Press Company	Solid Company
Accounts receivable.	72,000	50,000
Bond interest receivable	1,500	
Minimum lease payments receivable.	80,000	

(continued)

Assets	Press Company	Solid Company
Unearned interest income	(2,961)	
Inventory	86,000	80,000
Other current assets	60,236	183,668
Investment in Solid Company	344,000	
Investment in Solid bonds	59,225	
Land	60,000	30,000
Buildings and equipment	300,000	230,000
Accumulated depreciation	(100,000)	(50,000)
Equipment under capital lease		111,332
Accumulated depreciated equipment under lease		(35,000)
Total	$960,000	$600,000

Liabilities and Equity		
Accounts payable	$ 78,000	$ 70,000
Bond interest payable		2,500
Lease interest payable		5,707
Other current liabilities	57,000	48,911
Lease obligation payable		71,332
Bonds payable	150,000	100,000
Premium on bonds		1,550
Common stock—Press	200,000	
Other paid-in capital—Press	150,000	
Retained earnings—Press	325,000	
Common stock—Solid		100,000
Other paid-in capital—Solid		70,000
Retained earnings—Solid		130,000
Total	$960,000	$600,000

Required:

Complete the worksheet for a consolidated balance sheet as of December 31, 19X2. Round all computations to the nearest dollar.

Worksheet 7-1

Investment Acquired in Blocks; Immediate Control
Company P and Subsidiary Company S
Worksheet for Consolidated Financial Statements
For Year Ended December 31, 19X3

	(Credit balance amounts are in parentheses.)	Trial Balance	
		Company P	Company S
1	Current Assets	60,000	130,000
2	Investment in Company S	228,000	
3			
4			
5			
6	Building	400,000	80,000
7	Accumulated Depreciation—Building	(100,000)	(5,000)
8	Equipment		150,000
9	**Accumulated Depreciation—Equipment**		**(90,000)**
10			
11	Goodwill		
12			
13	Liabilities	(100,000)	(30,000)
14	Common Stock, Co. P	(200,000)	
15	**Retained Earnings, Jan. 1, 19X3, Co. P**	**(210,000)**	
16			
17	Common Stock, Co. S		(100,000)
18	Retained Earnings, Jan. 1, 19X3, Co. S		(100,000)
19	Sales	(400,000)	(200,000)
20	Cost of Goods Sold	300,000	120,000
21	**Expenses**	**50,000**	**45,000**
22			
23			
24			
25	Subsidiary Income	(28,000)	
26		0	0
27	Combined Net Income		
28	To Minority Interest (see distribution schedule)		
29	Balance to Controlling Interest (see distribution schedule)		
30	Total Minority Interest		
31	Retained Earnings, Controlling Interest, Dec. 31, 19X3		
32			

Worksheet 7-1 (see page 7-4)

Eliminations & Adjustments			Consolidated Income Statement	Minority Interest	Controlling Retained Earnings	Consolidated Balance Sheet	
Dr.		**Cr.**					
						190,000	1
	(1)	28,000					2
	(2)	160,000					3
	(3a)	**30,000**					4
	(4a)	**10,000**					5
						480,000	6
						(105,000)	7
						150,000	8
(3a)	**18,000**	**(3b)**	**10,800**				(79,600)	9
(4a)	**4,800**	**(4b)**	**1,600**					10
(3a)	**12,000**	**(3c)**	**3,600**				13,080	11
(4a)	**5,200**	**(4c)**	**520**					12
						(130,000)	13
						(200,000)	14
(3b)	**7,200**				(200,400)		15
(3c)	**2,400**						16
(2)	80,000			(20,000)			17
(2)	80,000			(20,000)			18
			(600,000)				19
			420,000				20
(3b)	**3,600**		101,920				21
(3c)	**1,200**						22
(4b)	**1,600**						23
(4c)	**520**						24
(1)	28,000						25
	244,520		244,520					26
			(78,080)				27
			7,000	(7,000)			28
			71,080		(71,080)		29
				(47,000)		(47,000)	30
					(271,480)	(271,480)	31
						0	32

(continued)

Eliminations and Adjustments:

(1) Eliminate the parent's entry recognizing 80% of the subsidiary net income for the current year. This entry restores the investment account to its balance at the beginning of the year, so that it can be eliminated against Company S beginning-of-the-year equity balances.

(2) Eliminate the 80% controlling interest in beginning-of-the-year subsidiary accounts against the investment account. The 60% and 20% investments could be eliminated separately if desired.

(3a) The $30,000 excess of cost on the original 60% investment is distributed to the accumulated depreciation and goodwill accounts according to the determination and distribution of excess schedule prepared on January 1, 19X1.

(b) Since the equipment has a 5-year remaining life on January 1, 19X1, the depreciation should be increased $3,600 per year for 3 years. This entry corrects the controlling retained earnings for the past 2 years by $7,200 and corrects the current depreciation expense by $3,600.

(c) The $12,000 original goodwill is to be amortized $1,200 per year for 3 years. The controlling retained earnings must be corrected for 2 past years ($2,400), and the current year's expenses are increased by $1,200.

(4a) The $10,000 excess of cost on the 20% block is distributed to the accumulated depreciation and goodwill accounts according to the determination and distribution of excess schedule prepared on January 1, 19X3.

(b) The $4,800 excess attributable to the equipment is to be depreciated over 3 years. Therefore, current expenses are increased by $1,600.

(c) The $5,200 increase to the goodwill account is to be amortized over 10 years, requiring current expenses to be increased by $520.

Subsidiary Company S Income Distribution

	Internally generated net income	$35,000
	Adjusted income	$35,000
	Minority share	20%
	Minority interest	$ 7,000

Parent Company P Income Distribution

Equipment depreciation:			Internally generated net income	$50,000
Block 1, 60% . . . . **(3b)**	$3,600		80% × Company S adjusted income of	
Block 2, 20% . . . . **(4b)**	1,600		$35,000	28,000
Goodwill amortization:				
Block 1, 60% . . . . **(3c)**	1,200			
Block 2, 20% . . . . **(4c)**	520			
			Controlling interest	$71,080

Worksheet 7-2

Investment Acquired in Blocks; Control Achieved with Second Block
Company P and Subsidiary Company S
Worksheet for Consolidated Financial Statements
For Year Ended December 31, 19X2

	(Credit balance amounts are in parentheses.)	Trial Balance	
		Company P	Company S
1	Current Assets	69,900	85,000
2	Investment in Company S	196,100	
3			
4			
5			
6	Building and Equipment	300,000	150,000
7	**Accumulated Depreciation—Building and Equipment**	**(200,000)**	**(30,000)**
8	**Goodwill**		
9			
10	Liabilities		(20,000)
11	Common Stock, Co. P	(100,000)	
12	Retained Earnings, Jan. 1, 19X2, Co. P	(200,000)	
13	Common Stock, Co. S		(50,000)
14	Retained Earnings, Jan. 1, 19X2, Co. S		(115,000)
15	Sales	(300,000)	(100,000)
16	Cost of Goods Sold	200,000	60,000
17	**Expenses**	**50,000**	**20,000**
18			
19			
20	Subsidiary Income	(16,000)	
21		0	0
22	Combined Net Income		
23	To Minority Interest (see distribution schedule)		
24	Balance to Controlling Interest (see distribution schedule)		
25	Total Minority Interest		
26	Retained Earnings, Controlling Interest, Dec. 31, 19X2		
27			

Worksheet 7-2 (see page 7-8)

Eliminations & Adjustments				Consolidated Income Statement	Minority Interest	Controlling Retained Earnings	Consolidated Balance Sheet	
Dr.		Cr.						
							154,900	1
		(1)	16,000					2
		(2)	132,000					3
		(3a)	17,100					4
		(4a)	31,000					5
							450,000	6
(4a)	5,400	(4b)	600				(225,200)	7
(3a)	17,100	(3b)	900				40,520	8
(4a)	25,600	(4c)	1,280					9
							(20,000)	10
							(100,000)	11
						(200,000)		12
(2)	40,000				(10,000)			13
(2)	92,000				(23,000)			14
				(400,000)				15
				260,000				16
(3b)	900			72,780				17
(4b)	600							18
(4c)	1,280							19
(1)	16,000							20
	198,880		198,880					21
				(67,220)				22
				4,000	(4,000)			23
				63,220		(63,220)		24
					(37,000)		(37,000)	25
						(263,220)	(263,220)	26
							0	27

(continued)

Eliminations and Adjustments:

(1)   Eliminate the parent's entry recognizing 80% in subsidiary net income under the simple equity method. This entry restores the investment account to its balance at the beginning of the year.

(2)   Eliminate the 80% controlling interest in beginning-of-the-year subsidiary equity accounts against the investment account. If desired, the two investment blocks may be eliminated separately.

(3a) The remaining excess of cost over book value on the original 20% investment is $17,100 ($18,000 less 1 year of $900 amortization). It must be remembered that under the sophisticated equity method, amortization entries prior to securing control reduce the investment account. Always remember that *only the unamortized original excess remains.* The remaining $17,100 excess is carried to the goodwill account according to the determination and distribution of excess schedule prepared on January 1, 19X1.

(b) Goodwill amortization of $900 is recorded for the current year. Recall that no amortization is needed for periods prior to achieving control, since that amortization was recorded previously through the parent's investment account. Thus, the controlling retained earnings are already reduced.

(4a) The excess attributable to the January 1, 19X2 60% acquisition is distributed to the accumulated depreciation and goodwill accounts according to the determination and distribution of excess schedule for this second acquisition.

(b) Depreciation for the current year is increased $600 according to the January 1, 19X2 determination and distribution of excess schedule.

(c) Goodwill amortization of $1,280 increases expenses for the current year as required by the January 1, 19X2 determination and distribution of excess schedule.

Subsidiary Company S Income Distribution

	Internally generated net income	$20,000
	Adjusted income	$20,000
	Minority share	20%
	Minority interest	$ 4,000

Parent Company P Income Distribution

Equipment depreciation:			Internally generated net income	$50,000
Block 2, 20% . . . . **(4b)**	$ 600		80% × Company S adjusted income of	
Goodwill amortization:			$20,000	16,000
Block 1, 20% . . . . **(3b)**	900			
Block 2, 60% . . . . **(4c)**	1,280			
			Controlling interest	$63,220

Worksheet 7-3

Investment Acquired in Blocks; Control Achieved with Second Purchase; Cost Method on First Investment
Company P and Subsidiary Company S
Worksheet for Consolidated Financial Statements
For Year Ended December 31, 19X2

	(Credit balance amounts are in parentheses.)	Trial Balance	
		Company P	Company S
1	Current Assets	93,900	85,000
2	**Investment in Company S**	**168,000**	
3			
4			
5			
6	Building and Equipment	300,000	150,000
7	**Accumulated Depreciation—Building and Equipment**	**(200,000)**	**(30,000)**
8	**Goodwill**		
9			
10	Liabilities		(20,000)
11	Common Stock, Co. P	(100,000)	
12	**Retained Earnings, Jan. 1, 19X2, Co. P**	**(197,900)**	
13	Common Stock, Co. S		(50,000)
14	Retained Earnings, Jan. 1, 19X2, Co. S		(115,000)
15	Sales	(300,000)	(100,000)
16	Cost of Goods Sold	200,000	60,000
17	Expenses	50,000	20,000
18			
19			
20	Subsidiary Income	(14,000)	
21		0	0
22	Combined Net Income		
23	To Minority Interest (see distribution schedule)		
24	Balance to Controlling Interest (see distribution schedule)		
25	Total Minority Interest		
26	Retained Earnings, Controlling Interest, Dec. 31, 19X2		
27			

Worksheet 7-3 (see page 7-9)

Eliminations & Adjustments			Consolidated Income Statement	Minority Interest	Controlling Retained Earnings	Consolidated Balance Sheet	
Dr.		Cr.					
						178,900	1
(C)	1,500	(1) 14,000					2
		(2) 115,500					3
		(3a) 9,000					4
		(4a) 31,000					5
						450,000	6
(4a)	5,400	(4b) 600				(225,200)	7
(3a)	9,000	(3b) 900				32,420	8
(4a)	25,600	(4c) 1,280					9
						(20,000)	10
						(100,000)	11
(3b)	450	(C) 1,500			(198,950)		12
(2)	35,000			(15,000)			13
(2)	80,500			(34,500)			14
			(400,000)				15
			260,000				16
(3b)	450		72,330				17
(4b)	600						18
(4c)	1,280						19
(1)	14,000						20
	173,780	173,780					21
			(67,670)				22
			6,000	(6,000)			23
			61,670		(61,670)		24
				(55,500)		(55,500)	25
					(260,620)	(260,620)	26
						0	27

(continued)

Eliminations and Adjustments:

(C)   Convert the original 10% investment to the simple equity method: 10% × $15,000 change in Company S Retained Earnings.

(1)   Eliminate the parent's entry recognizing 70% interest in subsidiary net income under the simple equity method. This entry restores the investment account to its balance at the beginning of the year.

(2)   The 70% controlling interest in the beginning-of-the-year subsidiary equity accounts is eliminated against the investment account.

(3a) The original excess of cost on the 10% investment ($9,000) is still contained in the investment account and now can be recognized as goodwill according to the January 1, 19X1 determination and distribution of excess schedule.

(b)   Goodwill for the past year and current year is amortized at $450 per year. Note that the Company P beginning-of-the-year retained earnings are corrected for the prior year's goodwill amortization. Amortization was not recorded previously since the cost method was in use.

(4a)   The excess attributable to the January 1, 19X2 60% acquisition is distributed to the accumulated depreciation and goodwill accounts according to the determination and distribution of excess schedule for the 60% block on January 1, 19X2.

(b)   Depreciation for the current year is increased $600.

(c)   Goodwill of $1,280 is amortized for the current year.

Subsidiary Company S Income Distribution

	Internally generated net income	$20,000
	Adjusted income	$20,000
	Minority share	30%
	Minority interest	$ 6,000

Parent Company P Income Distribution

Equipment depreciation:			Internally generated net income	$50,000
Block 2, 60% . . . . (4b)	$ 600		70% × Company S adjusted income of	
Goodwill amortization:			$20,000	14,000
Block 1, 20% . . . . **(3b)**	**450**			
Block 2, 60% . . . . (4c)	1,280			
			Controlling interest	$61,670

Worksheet 7-4

Sale of Subsidiary Interest During Period; No Loss of Control
Company P and Subsidiary Company S
Worksheet for Consolidated Financial Statements
For Year Ended December 31, 19X3

	(Credit balance amounts are in parentheses.)	Trial Balance	
		Company P	Company S
1	Investment in Company S (60%)	244,500	
2			
3			
4	Equipment	600,000	100,000
5	Accumulated Depreciation—Equipment	(100,000)	(60,000)
6	Other Assets	581,500	305,000
7	Goodwill		
8	Common Stock, Co. P	(500,000)	
9	Retained Earnings, Jan. 1, 19X3, Co. P	(700,000)	
10			
11	Common Stock, Co. S		(100,000)
12	Retained Earnings, Jan. 1, 19X3, Co. S		(215,000)
13	Sales	(500,000)	(200,000)
14	Cost of Goods Sold	350,000	140,000
15	Expenses	50,000	30,000
16			
17			
18	**Gain on Sale of Subsidiary Stock, Co. P**	**(6,475)**	
19	Subsidiary Income	(19,525)	
20			
21	**Income Sold to Minority (second 20% block)**		
22		0	0
23	Combined Net Income		
24	To Minority Interest (see distribution schedule)		
25	Balance to Controlling Interest (see distribution schedule)		
26	Total Minority Interest		
27	Retained Earnings, Controlling Interest, Dec. 31, 19X3		
28			

Worksheet 7-4 (see page 7-16)

Eliminations & Adjustments				Consolidated Income Statement	Minority Interest	Controlling Retained Earnings	Consolidated Balance Sheet	
Dr.		Cr.						
		(2)	18,000					1
		(3)	189,000					2
		(4)	37,500					3
							700,000	4
(4)	15,000	(5)	9,000				(154,000)	5
							886,500	6
(4)	22,500	(6)	6,750				15,750	7
							(500,000)	8
(5)	6,000					(689,500)		9
(6)	4,500							10
(3)	60,000				(40,000)			11
(3)	129,000				(86,000)			12
				(700,000)				13
				490,000				14
(1)	875			86,125				15
(5)	3,000							16
(6)	2,250							17
				(6,475)				18
(1)	1,525							19
(2)	18,000							20
		(1)	2,400		(2,400)			21
	262,650		262,650					22
				(130,350)				23
				9,600	(9,600)			24
				120,750		(120,750)		25
					(138,000)		(138,000)	26
						(810,250)	(810,250)	27
							0	28

(continued)

Eliminations and Adjustments:

(1) The income earned by the parent on the 20% interest sold on July 1, though earned by the controlling interest, now belongs to the minority interest. The minority interest owns 20% of the reported subsidiary income for the half-year ($12,000), which is $2,400. The minority is unaffected by amortizations resulting from a previous price paid by the parent. Note that entry (1) credits the account, Income Sold to Minority, to accomplish the transfer of the income to the minority interest. The offsetting debits are explained as follows:

20% of subsidiary income for the first six months, adjusted for one-fourth of the parent's half-year amortization of excess or (20% × $12,000) − [¼ × ½ × ($4,000 + $3,000)]	$1,525
Depreciation adjustment (¼ × ½ × $4,000)	500
Goodwill amortization (¼ × ½ × $3,000)	375
Total debits	$2,400

Amortizations based on an 80% interest for the first half of the year are proper, since the consolidation involves an 80% controlling interest for the first half of the year and a 60% controlling interest for the second half of the year.

(2) Eliminate the parent's entry recording its 60% share of subsidiary net income of $30,000. This entry restores the 60% interest to its simple-equity-adjusted cost at the beginning of the year, so that the investment can be eliminated against subsidiary equity balances at the beginning of the year.

(3) Eliminate 60% of the subsidiary equity balances at the beginning of the year against the investment account. An excess cost of $37,500 remains. This amount is three-fourths (60% ÷ 80%) of the original excess shown on page 7-10, since only a 60% interest is retained, as compared to an original investment of 80%.

(4) Since only three-fourths of the original investment remains, 75% of the excesses shown in the original determination and distribution of excess schedule on page 7-10 is recorded.

(5) 75% of the original $4,000 annual depreciation adjustments is recorded for the past two years and the current year. Note that the remaining depreciation adjustments applicable to the interest sold are already recorded.

(6) 75% of the original $3,000 annual goodwill amortization is recorded for the past two years and the current year. Again, amortizations of goodwill applicable to the interest sold have already been recorded.

Subsidiary Company S Income Distribution

	Internally generated net income	$ 30,000
	Adjusted income	$ 30,000
	Minority share	40%
	Minority interest for full year.	$ 12,000
	Less income purchased (20% × **$12,000, first 6 months)**.	**2,400**
	Minority interest	$ 9,600

Parent Company P Income Distribution

Depreciation adjustment on 60% interest . . . . (5) $3,000	Internally generated net income	$100,000
Goodwill amortization on 60% interest . . . . (6) 2,250		
	Adjusted income	$ 94,750
	60% × Company S income of $30,000 . .	18,000
	20% × Company S income for **first 6 months (net of** **amortization)**.	**1,525**
	Gain on sale of subsidiary interest	**6,475**
	Controlling interest	$120,750

Worksheet 7-5

Subsidiary Preferred Stock, None Owned by Parent
Company P and Subsidiary Company S
Worksheet for Consolidated Financial Statements
For Year Ended December 31, 19X5

	(Credit balance amounts are in parentheses.)	Trial Balance	
		Company P	Company S
1	Current Assets	259,600	150,000
2	Property, Plant, and Equipment (net)	400,000	250,000
3	Investment in Common Stock of Company S	195,600	
4			
5			
6	Goodwill		
7	Liabilities	(150,000)	(45,000)
8	Common Stock, Co. P	(200,000)	
9	Retained Earnings, Jan. 1, 19X5, Co. P	(340,000)	
10	Preferred Stock ($100 par), Co. S		(100,000)
11	**Retained Earnings Allocated to Preferred Stock, Jan. 1, 19X5, Co. S**		
12	Common Stock ($10 par), Co. S		(100,000)
13	Retained Earnings, Jan. 1, 19X5, Co. S		(130,000)
14			
15	Sales	(450,000)	(200,000)
16	Cost of Goods Sold	200,000	150,000
17	Expenses	100,000	25,000
18	Subsidiary Income	(15,200)	
19		0	0
20	Combined Net Income		
21	To Minority Interest (see distribution schedule)		
22	Balance to Controlling Interest (see distribution schedule)		
23	Total Minority Interest		
24	Retained Earnings, Controlling Interest, Dec. 31, 19X5		
25			

Eliminations and Adjustments:

(1) Distribute the beginning-of-the-period subsidiary retained earnings into the portions allocable to common and preferred stock. The typical procedure would be to consider the stated subsidiary retained earnings as applicable to common and to remove the preferred portion. This distribution reflects 4 years of arrearage (as of Jan. 1, 19X5) at $6,000 per year.

Worksheet 7-5 (see page 7-20)

Eliminations & Adjustments Dr.	Eliminations & Adjustments Cr.	Consolidated Income Statement	Minority Interest	Controlling Retained Earnings	Consolidated Balance Sheet	
					409,600	1
					650,000	2
	(2) 15,200					3
	(3) 164,800					4
	(4) 15,600					5
(4) 15,600	(5) 4,680				10,920	6
					(195,000)	7
					(200,000)	8
(5) 3,120				(336,880)		9
			(100,000)			10
	(1) 24,000		(24,000)			11
(3) 80,000			(20,000)			12
(1) 24,000			(21,200)			13
(3) 84,800						14
		(650,000)				15
		(350,000)				16
(5) 1,560		(126,560)				17
(2) 15,200						18
224,280	224,280					19
		(173,440)				20
		9,800	(9,800)			21
		163,640		(163,640)		22
			(175,000)		(175,000)	23
				(500,520)	(500,520)	24
					0	25

(2) Eliminate the parent's entry recording its share of subsidiary current income.

(3) Eliminate the pro rata subsidiary common stockholders' equity at the beginning of the period against the investment account. This entry includes elimination of the 80% of subsidiary retained earnings applicable to common stock.

(4) Distribute the excess of cost according to the determination and distribution of excess schedule.

(5) Amortize the goodwill for the past 2 years and the current year.

(continued)

Subsidiary Company S Income Distribution

Internally generated net income, (no adjustments)	$ 25,000
Less preferred cumulative claim to minority	**(6,000)**
Common stock income	**$19,000**
Minority share	20%
Minority interest in common income	$ 3,800
Total minority interest (**$6,000** + $3,800)	$ 9,800

Parent Company P Income Distribution

Amortization of goodwill . . . . (5)	$1,560	Internally generated net income	$150,000
		80% × Company S adjusted income on common stock of $19,000	15,200
		Controlling interest	$163,640

Worksheet 7-6

Subsidiary Preferred Stock Owned by Parent
Company P and Subsidiary Company S
Worksheet for Consolidated Financial Statements
For Year Ended December 31, 19X5

	(Credit balance amounts are in parentheses.)	Trial Balance	
		Company P	Company S
1	Current Assets	194,600	150,000
2	Property, Plant, and Equipment (net)	400,000	250,000
3	Investment in Company S Common Stock	195,600	
4			
5			
6	**Investment in Company S Preferred Stock**	**75,800**	
7			
8	Goodwill		
9	Liabilities	(150,000)	45,000)
10	Common Stock, Co. P	(200,000)	
11	**Paid-In Capital in Excess of Par, Co. P**		
12	Retained Earnings, Jan. 1, 19X5, Co. P	(347,200)	
13	Preferred Stock ($100 par), Co. S		(100,000)
14	Retained Earnings Allocated to Preferred Stock, Jan. 1, 19X5, Co. S		
15	Common Stock ($10 par), Co. S		(100,000)
16	Retained Earnings, Jan. 1, 19X5, Co. S		(130,000)
17			
18	Sales	(450,000)	(200,000)
19	Cost of Goods Sold	200,000	150,000
20	Expenses	100,000	25,000
21	Subsidiary Income—Common	(15,200)	
22	**Subsidiary Income—Preferred**	**(3,600)**	
23		0	0
24	Combined Net Income		
25	To Minority Interest (see distribution schedule)		
26	Balance to Controlling Interest (see distribution schedule)		
27	Total Minority Interest		
28	Retained Earnings, Controlling Interest, Dec. 31, 19X5		
29			

Eliminations and Adjustments:

(1-5) Same as Worksheet 7-5; the common stock investment elimination procedures are unaffected by the investment in preferred stock.

(6) Eliminate the entry recording the parent's share of income allocable to preferred stock. If declared, intercompany preferred dividends would also have been eliminated. This adjustment restores the investment account to its beginning-of-the-period equity balance.

Worksheet 7-6 (see page 7-22)

Eliminations & Adjustments		Consolidated Income Statement	Minority Interest	Controlling Retained Earnings	Consolidated Balance Sheet	
Dr.	Cr.					
					344,600	1
					650,000	2
	(2) 15,200					3
	(3) 164,800					4
	(4) 15,600					5
	(6) 3,600					6
	(7) 72,200					7
(4) 15,600	(5) 4,680				10,920	8
					(195,000)	9
					(200,000)	10
	(7) 2,200				(2,200)	11
(5) 3,120				(344,080)		12
(7) 60,000			(40,000)			13
(7) 14,400	(1) 24,000		(9,600)			14
(3) 80,000			(20,000)			15
(1) 24,000			(21,200)			16
(3) 84,800						17
		(650,000)				18
		350,000				19
(5) 1,560		126,560				20
(2) 15,200						21
(6) 3,600						22
302,280	302,280					23
		(173,440)				24
		6,200	(6,200)			25
		167,240		(167,240)		26
			(97,000)		(97,000)	27
				(511,320)	(511,320)	28
					0	29

(7)   The parent's ownership portion of the par value and beginning-of-the-period retained earnings applicable to preferred stock is eliminated against the balance in the investment in preferred stock account. The difference in this case was an increase in equity, and it was carried to the controlling paid-in capital.

(continued)

Subsidiary Company S Income Distribution

Internally generated net income, (no adjustments)	$ 25,000
Less preferred cumulative claim:	
to minority, 40% × $6,000	(2,400)
to controlling, 60% × $6,000 . . .	**(3,600)**
Common stock income	$19,000
Minority share	20%
Minority interest in common income.	$ 3,800
Total minority interest ($2,400 + $3,800)	$ 6,200

Parent Company P Income Distribution

Amortization of goodwill . . . . (5)	$1,560	Internally generated net income	$150,000
		60% × Co. S income attributable to preferred stock	**3,600**
		80% × Co. S adjusted income on common stock of $19,000	15,200
		Controlling interest	$167,240

Worksheet 7-7

Balance Sheet Only
Company P and Subsidiary Company S
Worksheet for Consolidated Balance Sheet
December 31, 19X4

	(Credit balance amounts are in parentheses.)	Trial Balance	
		Company P	Company S
1	Cash	61,936	106,535
2	Accounts Receivable	80,000	200,000
3	Inventory, Dec. 31, 19X4	60,000	150,000
4	Land	300,000	250,000
5	Building	800,000	600,000
6	Accumulated Depreciation—Building	(400,000)	(100,000)
7	Equipment	120,000	95,000
8	Accumulated Depreciation—Equipment	(70,000)	(30,000)
9	Investment in Company S Bonds	90,064	
10	Investment in Company S Stock	750,000	
11			
12	Goodwill		
13	Accounts Payable	(92,000)	(75,000)
14	Bonds Payable		(100,000)
15	Discount on Bonds Payable		3,465
16	Common Stock, Co. P	(500,000)	
17	Retained Earnings, Dec. 31, 19X4, Co. P	(1,200,000)	
18			
19			
20			
21	Common Stock, Co. S		(200,000)
22	Retained Earnings, Dec. 31, 19X4, Co. S		(900,000)
23			
24		0	0
25	Total Minority Interest		
26			

Eliminations and Adjustments:

(C) Investment in Company S Stock is converted to the simple equity method *as of December 31, 19X4,* as follows:
$80\% \times \$300,000$ increase in retained earnings = $240,000.
(1) 80% of the subsidiary equity balances are eliminated against the investment in stock account.
(2) The $110,000 excess of cost is distributed according to the determination and distribution of excess schedule.
(3) The excess attributable to the building is amortized for 4 years at $3,000 per year.
(4) The excess attributable to goodwill is amortized for 4 years at $4,000 per year.
(5) The intercompany trade balance is eliminated.

Worksheet 7-7 (see page 7-25)

Eliminations & Adjustments				Minority Interest	Consolidated Balance Sheet	
Dr.		Cr.				
					168,471	1
		(5)	35,000		245,000	2
		(6)	16,000		194,000	3
					550,000	4
					1,400,000	5
(2)	30,000	(3)	12,000		(482,000)	6
		(7)	5,000		210,000	7
(7)	3,000				(97,000)	8
		(8)	90,064			9
(C)	240,000	(1)	880,000			10
		(2)	110,000			11
(2)	80,000	(4)	16,000		64,000	12
(5)	35,000				(132,000)	13
(8)	100,000					14
		(8)	3,465			15
					(500,000)	16
(3)	12,000	(C)	240,000		(1,402,377)	17
(4)	16,000					18
(6)	12,800	(8)	5,177			19
(7)	2,000					20
(1)	160,000			(40,000)		21
(1)	720,000	(8)	1,294	(178,094)		22
(6)	3,200					23
	1,414,000		1,414,000			24
				(218,094)	(218,094)	25
					0	26

(6) The gross profit of $16,000 (40% × $40,000) recorded by Company S and applicable to merchandise in Company P's ending inventory is deferred by reducing the inventory and retained earnings. Since the sale was made by Company S, the adjustment is allocated to the minority and controlling retained earnings.

(7) As of December 31, 19X4, $2,000 (2/5) of the profit on the equipment sale is still to be deferred. Since the sale was made by Company P, the controlling retained earnings absorb this adjustment, and the equipment and accumulated depreciation accounts are adjusted.

(8) Investment in Company S Bonds is eliminated against the net book value of the bonds. The net gain on the worksheet retirement is allocated to the minority and controlling retained earnings, since the subsidiary originally issued the bonds.

Subsidiary Equity Transactions; Indirect and Mutual Holdings

This chapter is concerned with subsidiary equity transactions and complicated parent ownership arrangements that affect the recording and consolidations of the parent's investment in a subsidiary. First, we will consider the impact of subsidiary equity transactions on the investment of the parent company. The subsidiary may issue stock dividends, sell additional shares of stock, or repurchase outstanding shares. Each of these transactions has an effect on the procedures used by the parent to record and to consolidate its investment in the subsidiary.

Second, this chapter will deal with more complex ownership structures. Accounting procedures will be developed for indirect holdings and mutual holdings. Indirect holdings are situations where a parent holds a controlling interest in a subsidiary and the subsidiary is, in turn, a parent of another company. A mutual holding exists when the subsidiary owns voting common stock of the parent company.

Subsidiary Stock Dividends

A subsidiary may issue stock dividends to convert retained earnings into paid-in capital. The minimum amount to be removed from retained earnings is the par value or stated value of the shares distributed. However, according to accounting principles, when the distribution does not exceed 20% to 25% of the previously outstanding shares, an amount equal to the market value of the shares should be removed from retained earnings and transferred to paid-in capital. The recording of stock dividends at market value is defended by the following statement from ARB No. 43:

> . . . a stock dividend does not, in fact, give rise to any change whatsoever in either the corporation's assets or its respective shareholders' proportionate interests therein. However, it cannot fail to be recognized that, merely as a consequence of the expressed purpose of the transaction and its characterization as a dividend in related notices to shareholders and the public at large, many recipients of stock dividends look upon them as distributions of corporate earnings and usually in an amount equivalent to the fair value of the additional shares received.[1]

Accounting theory, however, is not consistent when it comes to recording the receipt of dividends by an investor. Even though the false impression of the "typical" investor is sufficient reason to allow the issuing corporation to record the market value of the shares distributed, the investor is not permitted to do likewise. In fact,

---

[1] Accounting Research and Terminology Bulletin No. 43, *Restatement and Revision of Accounting Research Bulletins* (New York: American Institute of Certified Public Accountants, 1961), Ch. 7, Sec. B, par. 10.

the investor must not record income when stock dividends are received but must acknowledge the true impact of the transaction, which is that nothing of substance has been given or received. Thus, the investor merely makes a memo entry indicating that the cost of the original investment now is allocated to a greater number of shares. The revised number of shares is important in computing cost per share if there is a subsequent partial sale of the investment.

To review the recording of a stock dividend and to provide a basis for worksheets, assume Company P acquired an 80% interest in Company S on January 1, 19X1, at which time the following determination and distribution of excess schedule was prepared:

Price paid		$200,000
Less interest acquired:		
Common stock ($10 par)	$100,000	
Retained earnings	80,000	
Total stockholders' equity	$180,000	
Interest acquired	80%	144,000
Goodwill (10-year life)		$ 56,000 Dr.

On January 2, 19X3, Company S declared and distributed a 10% stock dividend. Prior to declaration of the dividend, its stockholders' equity appeared as follows:

Common stock ($10 par)	$100,000
Retained earnings	120,000
Total stockholders' equity	$220,000

In the following entry to record the stock dividend, Company S acknowledged the $25 market value of the 1,000 shares distributed:

Retained Earnings (or Stock Dividends Declared)		
($25 market value × 1,000 shares)	25,000	
Common Stock ($10 par × 1,000 shares)		10,000
Additional Paid-In Capital from Stock Dividend		
(1,000 shares × $15 excess over par)		15,000

Parent Using the Simple Equity Method

Continuing the example, on January 1, 19X3, Company P has a simple-equity-adjusted balance of $232,000, in its investment in Company S account, derived as follows:

Original cost		$200,000
Share of undistributed income:		
Company S retained earnings, January 1, 19X3	$120,000	
Company S retained earnings, January 1, 19X1	80,000	
Increase in retained earnings	$ 40,000	
Ownership interest	80%	32,000
Simple-equity-adjusted balance, January 1, 19X3		$232,000

During 19X3, Company S earned $20,000 and made no other dividend declarations. Company P would make the following entries under the simple equity method:

Receipt of stock dividend:

    Jan. 2, 19X3   Memo: Investment in Company S now includes 800 added shares for a total of 8,800 shares. The parent's interest remains at 80%.

Recording of equity income:

    Dec. 31, 19X3   Investment in Company S. 16,000
                         Subsidiary Income   16,000
                          To record the 80% interest in Company S
                          $20,000 reported net income for 19X3.

      The partial worksheet below lists the investment in Company S account at the December 31, 19X3 simple-equity-adjusted cost of $248,000. Note that the partial worksheet includes the redistributed capital structure of Company S which results from the stock dividend. It should be clear that the complications arising from stock dividends pertain primarily to their recording by the separate affiliated firms. There is only a minimal effect on the consolidated worksheet.

	Trial Balance		Eliminations & Adjustments	
	Company P	Company S	Dr.	Cr.
Investment in Co. S	248,000			(1) 16,000
				(2) 176,000
				(3) 56,000
Goodwill			(3) 56,000	(4) 16,800
Common Stock, Co. P	(500,000)			
Retained Earnings, Co. P	(420,000)		(4) 11,200	
Common Stock ($10 par), Co. S		(110,000)	**(2) 88,000**	
Additional Paid-In Capital from Stock Dividend, Co. S		(15,000)	**(2) 12,000**	
Retained Earnings, Co. S (reduced $25,000 for stock dividend)		(95,000)	**(2) 76,000**	
Subsidiary Income	(16,000)		(1) 16,000	
Expenses	30,000	18,000	(4) 5,600	

Eliminations and Adjustments:

(1) Eliminate the parent's entry recording its share of subsidiary income for the current year. There is no complication caused by the stock dividend since it does not constitute income to Company P.

(2) Eliminate 80% of Company S equity balances as restructured by the stock dividend. If the subsidiary recorded the stock dividend with a debit to Stock Dividends Declared, 80% of that account would be eliminated in this step.

(3) Distribute the excess cost to the goodwill account as required by the determination and distribution of excess schedule.

(4) Amortize the goodwill for 3 years. Amortization for the 2 prior years reduces the controlling interest in retained earnings, while the current-year amortization reduces current combined net income.

Parent Using the Sophisticated Equity Method

Using the sophisticated equity method, the parent would have a balance in its investment in Company S account of $220,800, derived as follows:

Original cost		$200,000
Share of undistributed income:		
Company S retained earnings, January 1, 19X3	$120,000	
Company S retained earnings, January 1, 19X1	80,000	
Increase in retained earnings.	$ 40,000	
Ownership interest.	80%	32,000
Goodwill amortization, 2 years × $5,600.		(11,200)
Sophisticated-equity-adjusted balance, January 1, 19X1 . .		$220,800

During 19X3, Company P would make the same memo entry as under the simple equity method to record the stock dividend. The following entry would be made to record equity income for 19X3:

Dec. 31, 19X3 Investment in Company S.	10,400	
Subsidiary Income		10,400
To record the 80% interest in Company S		
reported income for 19X3 less $5,600		
amortization of goodwill.		

The partial worksheet on page 8-5 would apply to the investment maintained under the sophisticated equity method. Note the following special features:

1. The investment is at the sophisticated equity balance of $231,200 ($220,800 balance on January 1, 19X3, plus $10,400 equity income for 19X3).
2. The retained earnings of Company P are $408,800. This is $11,200 less than under the simple equity method since there is $5,600 per year of goodwill amortization subtracted for 19X1 and 19X2.
3. Subsidiary income is the sophisticated equity amount of $10,400.
4. Only the goodwill remaining on January 1, 19X3, is entered when distributing the excess in entry (3). Recall that the prior years' amortizations have already reduced the investment account and the parent retained earnings. Note that only the current-year amortization is made in entry (4).

Parent Using the Cost Method

In the preceding example, if the parent, Company P, had used the cost method to record its investment in Company S, no adjustments would have been made to the investment account. The investment in Company S still would be carried at its original cost of $200,000 on the December 31, 19X3 worksheet.

The declaration of a stock dividend by a subsidiary requires a more difficult process for the conversion of the parent's investment account from a cost to a simple equity basis. The conversion must reflect all the changes in subsidiary retained earnings since acquisition, including the retained earnings transferred to paid-in capital as a result of a stock dividend. The correct simple equity conversion would be made as follows for the preceding example:

Retained earnings, January 2, 19X3 (after stock dividend)	$95,000
Retained earnings, January 1, 19X1.	80,000
Change in retained earnings balance.	$15,000
Retained earnings transferred to paid-in capital ($25 × 1,000 shares)	
as a result of stock dividend	25,000
Total change in retained earnings.	$40,000
Ownership interest.	80%
Simple equity conversion	$32,000

A faster approach to the simple equity conversion is to consider the change in total subsidiary stockholders' equity available to common stockholders as follows:

Subsidiary equity, January 1, 19X3	$220,000
Subsidiary equity, January 1, 19X1	180,000
Net change	$40,000
Ownership interest.	80%
Simple equity conversion	$ 32,000

	Trial Balance		Eliminations & Adjustments	
	Company P	Company S	Dr.	Cr.
Investment in Co. S	231,200			(1) 10,400
				(2) 176,000
				(3) 44,800
Goodwill			(3) 44,800	(4) 5,600
Common Stock, Co. P	(500,000)			
Retained Earnings, Co. P	(408,800)			
Common Stock ($10 par), Co. S		(110,000)	**(2) 88,000**	
Additional Paid-In Capital from Stock Dividend, Co. S		(15,000)	**(2) 12,000**	
Retained Earnings, Co. S (reduced $25,000 for stock dividend)		(95,000)	**(2) 76,000**	
Subsidiary Income	(10,400)		(1) 10,400	
Expenses	30,000	18,000	(4) 5,600	

Eliminations and Adjustments:

(1) Eliminate the parent's entry recording its share of subsidiary income for the current year. There is no complication caused by the stock dividend since it does not constitute income to Company P.

(2) Eliminate 80% of Company S equity balances as restructured by the stock dividend. If the subsidiary recorded the stock dividend with a debit to Stock Dividends Declared, 80% of that account would be eliminated in this entry.

(3) Distribute the remaining (8 years') excess cost to the goodwill account as required by the determination and distribution of excess schedule.

(4) Amortize the goodwill for the current year.

Normally, a parent will maintain a permanent file with the needed information for this adjustment. This faster method, however, could be useful in later years if facts surrounding the stock dividend were not readily available. The faster procedure will work well, provided in the interim periods there have been no other changes in subsidiary paid-in capital, such as a subsidiary sale or retirement of its shares.

The $32,000 simple equity conversion would be the first step on a worksheet when the cost method is used for the subsidiary investment. This step converts the investment in subsidiary account to its simple equity balance at the beginning of 19X3. The entry would be:

Investment in Company S	32,000	
Retained Earnings (January 1, 19X3)		32,000

The remaining worksheet procedures would not include the elimination of the current year's subsidiary income, but otherwise it would be identical to entries (2) through (4) of the partial worksheet on page 8-3.

Subsidiary Sale of Its Own Common Stock

In virtually all cases where the subsidiary issues additional shares of stock, the transaction impacts the parent's investment in the subsidiary account. Even though the parent purchases none of the newly issued shares, its share of subsidiary equity has changed and consolidation procedures must acknowledge the change. When the parent purchases some of the newly issued shares, the adjustment needed depends on whether the ownership interest after the purchase is equal to, less than, or greater than the ownership interest prior to the purchase. The adjustments resulting from a subsidiary stock sale are made at the time of the sale when the equity method is used, or they are part of the cost-to-equity conversion process when the cost method is used.

Sale of Subsidiary Stock to Minority Shareholders

A parent may allow a subsidiary to sell additional shares of stock in order to raise equity funds. A sale of stock by the subsidiary to new or existing minority shareholders results in an increase in the total stockholders' equity against which the controlling interest has a claim. However, the effect of increasing the number of subsidiary shares in the hands of minority stockholders is to lower the controlling interest ownership percentage. Thus, the controlling ownership receives a smaller portion of a larger subsidiary equity. The net effect on the value of the controlling interest depends on the price at which the shares are sold.

A subsidiary stock sale may appear to create a gain or a loss to the parent because there is an effect on the value of the controlling interest. The *parent company concept* supports this position since it focuses on the ownership of the parent. The more commonly used procedure in practice is derived from the *economic unit concept*. From the viewpoint of the single entity, how the parent's interest changes is the result of a transaction between the consolidated firm and its shareholders. Essentially, new stock has been issued. Any increase in the parent's interest is viewed as generating additional paid-in capital. A decrease in the parent's interest reduces paid-in capital in excess of par if it exists; otherwise, parent retained earnings are reduced.

In 1980, the AICPA Accounting Standards Executive Committee released an issues paper supporting the recognition of gains and losses on some of these types of transactions, and in 1983 the SEC issued Staff Bulletin 51 which endorsed the gain or loss treatment if the stock is sold in a public offering and is not part of a broader reorganization that will involve other capital transactions. The recognition of a gain or loss is supported on the grounds that it should not matter whether the parent decreases its interest by selling shares (in which case a gain or loss is recognized) or whether the parent decreases its interest by directing the subsidiary to issue additional shares. The public offering requirement assures that a gain or loss is not created arbitrarily but instead relies on a well-defined market value. This text will use the gain/loss approach only for public offerings (to comply with SEC requirements) but will retain the use of the adjustment of paid-in capital for other sales.

The FASB exposure draft and the subsequent working draft on business combinations support the economic unit concept which does not record a gain or loss on subsidiary equity transactions. Instead, all increases and decreases in equity resulting from subsidiary equity transactions would be adjustments to paid-in capital (decreases in equity would decrease retained earnings if there was insufficient paid-in capital).

Parent Using the Equity Method.   A parent company using either the simple or sophisticated equity method usually will need to make an adjustment to its investment account when its subsidiary sells additional shares of stock to minority shareholders. To illustrate, assume Company P has a 90% interest in Company S. The interest was purchased on January 1, 19X1, at which time the following determination and distribution of excess schedule was prepared:

Price paid		$140,000
Less interest acquired:		
Common stock ($10 par)	$100,000	
Retained earnings, January 1, 19X1.	50,000	
Total stockholders' equity	$150,000	
Interest acquired	90%	135,000
Goodwill (10-year life)		$ 5,000 Dr.

On January 1, 19X4, 2,000 shares of previously unissued common stock are sold to the minority interest. As a result, the parent's interest is reduced to 75% (9,000 ÷ 12,000). An analysis of the controlling interest before and after the sale of 2,000 new subsidiary shares to minority shareholders follows. The analysis shows the three possibilities: shares sold at book value (Case 1), at more than book value (Case 2), and at less than book value (Case 3).

	Case 1	Case 2	Case 3
Sale price per share	$ 24	$ 30	$ 20
Company S shareholders' equity prior to sale	$240,000	$240,000	$240,000
Add to common stock, $10 par × 2,000 shares.	20,000	20,000	20,000
Add to paid-in capital in excess of par	28,000	40,000	20,000
Company S shareholders' equity subsequent to sale . . .	$288,000	$300,000	$280,000
Controlling interest subsequent to sale (75%)	$216,000	$225,000	$210,000
Prior controlling interest (90% × $240,000).	216,000	216,000	216,000
Net increase (decrease) in controlling interest	$ 0	$ 9,000	($ 6,000)

Based on the results of the three cases within the above table, it should be noted that no change in controlling interest occurs when a subsidiary sells new stock to minority shareholders at book value. An increase occurs when the stock is sold above book value, and a decrease results when the stock is sold below book value.

Assuming the shares were not sold in a public offering, no gain or loss would be recognized. The parent would adjust its investment in subsidiary account to record the effect on controlling interest in each of the three cases as follows:

Case 1: Memo entry only to record a change from a 90% to a 75% interest.

Case 2:	Investment in Company S	9,000	
	Paid-In Capital in Excess of Par		9,000
	To record increase in ownership interest		
Case 3:	Paid-In Capital in Excess of Par	6,000	
	Investment in Company S		6,000
	To record decrease in ownership interest. It is assumed that parent additional paid-in capital exists to offset the decrease.		

Note that when the equity method is used, these entries would be made directly on the books of the parent; they are not worksheet adjustments.

To illustrate the effect of Case 2 on consolidation, assume subsidiary income for 19X4 was $40,000 and no dividends were declared. The investment account balance under the simple equity method would be determined as follows:

Original cost	$140,000
Simple equity income adjustments, 19X1 through 19X3, 90% × $90,000 increase in retained earnings	81,000
Increase from stock sale to minority on January 1, 19X4	9,000
Simple equity adjustment for 19X4 subsidiary income, 75% × $40,000 income	30,000
Balance, December 31, 19X4	$260,000

In the partial worksheet (shown on page 8-9) for the year ended December 31, 19X4, the trial balances of Company P and Company S reflect the sale of 2,000 additional shares at $30 per share (Case 2).

If the shares were sold in a public offering, a gain or loss could be recognized based on the market value of the shares sold. The gain/loss approach takes the position that the parent has indirectly sold a portion of its interest. This means that the portion of any excess of cost or book value applicable to the interest sold should be adjusted for that interest sold, just as it would be if the parent sold a portion of its interest directly. In the preceding example, the parent's ownership interest decreased from 90% to 75% as a result of the subsidiary stock sale. Of the total original goodwill of $5,000, $833 (15% interest sold divided by 90% original interest times $5,000) is applicable to the interest sold and must be removed from the investment account. Goodwill has been amortized over three years of its 10-year life; thus, $250 [($833 ÷ 10) × 3] of the goodwill applicable to the interest sold already has been amortized on the consolidated worksheets. Since the 15% interest no longer will be consolidated, it is necessary to adjust the parent's retained earnings for the $250 of amortizations. The net or remaining goodwill applicable to the interest is $583 ($833 − $250) which should be deducted from the increase or added to the decrease in controlling interest resulting from the stock sale. The same procedure would be used for any other excesses of cost or book value applicable to identifiable assets. The net impact of the subsidiary stock sale at the three alternative prices is:

	Case 1	Case 2	Case 3
Sale price per share	$ 24	$ 30	$ 20
Net increase (decrease) in controlling interest	$0	$9,000	($6,000)
Adjustment for net goodwill applicable to interest sold. . . .	(583)	(583)	(583)
Gain (loss) on interest sold	($583)	$8,417	($6,583)

Company P and Subsidiary Company S
Partial Worksheet (Simple Equity Method, No Gain or Loss Recorded)
For Year Ended December 31, 19X4

	Trial Balance		Eliminations & Adjustments	
	Company P	Company S	Dr.	Cr.
Investment in Co. S (75%)	260,000			(1) 30,000
				(2) 225,000
				(3) 5,000
Goodwill			(3) 5,000	(4) 2,000
Common Stock, Co. P	(400,000)			
Paid-In Capital in Excess of Par, Co. P	(9,000)			
Retained Earnings, Co. P	(320,000)		(4) 1,500	
Common Stock, Co. S		(120,000)	(2) 90,000	
Paid-In Capital in Excess of Par, Co. S		(40,000)	(2) 30,000	
Retained Earnings, Co. S		(140,000)	(2) 105,000	
Subsidiary Income	(30,000)		(1) 30,000	
Expenses	40,000	27,000	(4) 500	

Eliminations and Adjustments:

(1) Eliminate the parent's entry recording subsidiary income for the current year. The parent's share is now **75%** of the subsidiary undistributed net income. If the sale had occurred *during the year,* the *old* percentage of ownership would be applied to income earned prior to the sale date.

(2) Eliminate the parent's **75%** share of subsidiary equity balances at the beginning of the year against the investment account.

(3) Distribute to the goodwill account the original excess of cost over book value as required by the January 1, 19X1 determination and distribution of excess schedule.

(4) Amortize the goodwill for the past 3 years and the current year.

The parent would record the effect on the controlling interest in each case as follows:

Case 1: Retained Earnings (three years' amortization on 1/6 of
  $5,000 goodwill) 250
  Loss on Sale of Subsidiary Stock 583
    Investment in Company S (1/6 of $5,000 goodwill) . . .   833
    To record loss on subsidiary stock sale.

Case 2: Investment in Company S ($9,000 − $833 goodwill) 8,167
  Retained Earnings. 250
    Gain on Sale of Subsidiary Stock   8,417
    To record gain on subsidiary stock sale.

Case 3: Retained Earnings. 250
  Loss on Sale of Subsidiary Stock 6,583
    Investment in Company S ($6,000 + $833 goodwill) . .   6,833
    To record loss on subsidiary stock sale.

To illustrate the effect of Case 2 on consolidation, assume subsidiary income for 19X4 was $40,000 and no dividends were declared. The investment account balance under the simple equity method would be determined as follows:

Original cost	$140,000
Simple equity income adjustments, 19X1 through 19X3, 90% × $90,000	
increase in retained earnings.	81,000
Increase from stock sale to minority on January 1, 19X4	8,167
Simple equity adjustment for 19X4 subsidiary income, 75% × $40,000	
income	30,000
Balance, December 31, 19X4.	$259,167

In the Case 2 partial worksheet (shown on page 8-11) for the year ended December 31, 19X4, the trial balances of Company P and Company S reflect the sale of 2,000 additional shares at $30 per share where the gain is to be recognized.

The consolidated worksheet may require the adjustment of both the controlling and minority interests in beginning retained earnings for intercompany transactions originating in previous periods. When such adjustments are necessary, the current, not the original, ownership interest percentages are used.

Parent Using the Cost Method.   A parent using the cost method records only dividends received from a subsidiary. Usually, no adjustment is made for any other changes in the subsidiary stockholders' equity, including changes caused by sales of subsidiary stock. As a result, the entry to convert from the cost method to the equity method on future worksheets must consider not only the equity adjustments for the subsidiary undistributed income but also adjustments in the parent's ownership interest caused by subsidiary stock sales. A parent using the cost method still would list the subsidiary investment at its original cost.

The partial worksheet on page 8-12 demonstrates the consolidation procedures needed for Case 2 when the cost method is used. This example further assumes the sale of subsidiary stock was a private offering and no gain needs to be recognized.

To review this process, the cost-to-simple-equity conversion amount for Case 2 is determined as it would apply to the December 31, 19X5 worksheet:

Undistributed income:		
90% of change in retained earnings of Company S		
from January 1, 19X1, to January 1, 19X4,		
90% × $90,000		$ 81,000
75% of change in retained earnings of Company S		
from January 1, 19X4, to January 1, 19X5,		
75% × $40,000		30,000
Increase in Company P retained earnings		$111,000
Adjustment to paid-in capital:		
Controlling interest in Company S equity subsequent		
to sale on January 1, 19X4, 75% × $300,000	$225,000	
Controlling interest in Company S equity prior to sale		
on January 1, 19X4, 90% × $240,000	216,000	
Net increase in paid-in capital.		9,000
Total increase in investment account		$120,000

A dangerous shortcut might be attempted, whereby the net change in the controlling ownership interest is calculated by comparing 90% of the total subsidiary equity on January 1, 19X1, to 75% of the total subsidiary equity on January 1, 19X5. This shortcut will produce the correct adjustment to the investment in subsidiary account, but it will **not** provide the analysis needed to distribute the adjustment to the parent's paid-in capital and retained earnings.

Company P and Subsidiary Company S
Partial Worksheet (Simple Equity Method, No Gain or Loss Recorded)
For Year Ended December 31, 19X4

	Trial Balance		Eliminations & Adjustments	
	Company P	Company S	Dr.	Cr.
Investment in Co. S (75%)	259,167			(1) 30,000
				(2) 225,000
				(3) 4,167
Goodwill			(3) 4,167	(4) 1,668
Common Stock, Co. P	(400,000)			
Paid-In Capital in Excess of Par, Co. P	(9,000)			
Retained Earnings, Co. P	(320,000)		(4) 1,251	
Common Stock, Co. S		(120,000)	(2) 90,000	
Paid-In Capital in Excess of Par, Co. S		(40,000)	(2) 30,000	
Retained Earnings, Co. S		(140,000)	(2) 105,000	
Subsidiary Income	(30,000)		(1) 30,000	
Gain on Sale of Subsidiary Stock	(8,417)			
Expenses	40,000	27,000	(4) 417	

Eliminations and Adjustments:

(1) Eliminate the parent's entry recording subsidiary income for the current year. The parent's share is now 75% of the subsidiary undistributed net income. If the sale had occurred *during the year*, the *old* percentage of ownership would be applied to income earned prior to the sale date.

(2) Eliminate the parent's 75% share of subsidiary equity balances at the beginning of the year against the investment account.

(3) Distribute to the goodwill account the remaining (5/6) excess of cost over book value that was shown on the original determination and distribution of excess schedule.

(4) Amortize the remaining goodwill for the past three years and the current year (5/6 × 500 per year = $417).

A unique situation arises for a company, using the cost method, that wishes to record a gain or loss on a subsidiary stock sale. In order to record the gain or loss, the equity-adjusted cost must be calculated on the date of the transaction and the investment account must be adjusted for the gain or loss. This means that, when consolidating, the investment account is adjusted for the impact of the subsidiary stock sale but not for the parent's share of subsidiary earned income. In the previous example, it would be necessary to do a cost-to-equity adjustment based on a 90% interest prior to the subsidiary stock sale and a 75% interest subsequent to the sale. This approach does have the advantage of making the adjustment only once on the parent's books rather than repeating it on each year's worksheet.

Parent Purchase of Newly Issued Subsidiary Stock

A parent may purchase all or a portion of the newly issued stock. The general approach in such cases is to compare the change in equity before and after the sale to the price paid for the additional interest. When the ownership interest remains the same, there will be no adjustment. When the ownership interest increases, any difference between the change in equity and the price paid is the excess of cost or book

Company P and Subsidiary Company S
Partial Worksheet (Cost Method, No Gain or Loss Recorded)
For Year Ended December 31, 19X4

	Trial Balance		Eliminations & Adjustments	
	Company P	Company S	Dr.	Cr.
Investment in Co. S (75%)	140,000		**(C) 90,000**	(1) 225,000
				(2) 5,000
Goodwill			(2) 5,000	(3) 2,000
Common Stock, Co. P	(400,000)			
Paid-In Capital in Excess of Par, Co. P				**(C) 9,000**
Retained Earnings, Co. P ($81,000 less since no equity income was recorded)	(239,000)		(3) 1,500	**(C) 81,000**
Common Stock, Co. S		(120,000)	(1) 90,000	
Paid-In Capital in Excess of Par, Co. S		(40,000)	(1) 30,000	
Retained Earnings, Co. S		(140,000)	(1) 105,000	
Expenses	40,000	27,000	(3) 500	

Eliminations and Adjustments:

(C) The simple equity conversion is recorded:

Undistributed income:
   90% of change in retained earnings of Company S from
      January 1, 19X1, to January 1, 19X4, 90% × $90,000 . . . . $81,000
Adjustment to paid-in capital resulting from the subsidiary stock sale:
   Controlling interest in Company S equity subsequent to sale
      on January 1, 19X4, 75% × $300,000 . . . . $225,000
   Controlling interest in Company S equity prior to sale on
      January 1, 19X4, 90% × $240,000   216,000
        Net increase in paid-in capital.   9,000
Total increase in the investment account $90,000

(1) Eliminate 75% of the subsidiary equity balances at the beginning of the year against the investment account.
(2) Distribute the excess of cost to the goodwill account as shown by the original determination and distribution of excess schedule.
(3) Amortize the goodwill for the past 3 years and the current year.

value attributable to the new block. When the ownership interest decreases, the difference between the change in equity and the price paid is viewed as a gain or a loss on the sale of an interest for a public offering or a change in paid-in capital or retained earnings for a private offering. Let us consider these three cases based on the previous example for which the determination and distribution of excess schedule was shown on page 8-7. Recall that the subsidiary is issuing 2,000 new shares of common stock for $30 per share.

		Maintain Interest		Increase Interest		Decrease Interest
1	Shares purchased by parent	1,800		2,000		1,000
2	Total shares owned by parent after purchase	10,800		11,000		10,000
3	Total subsidiary shares outstanding after issue	12,000		12,000		12,000
4	Subsidiary equity after the sale	$300,000		$300,000		$300,000
5	Parent's ownership percent after purchase **(2 ÷ 3)**	90%		91.67%		83.33%
6	Parent's new equity interest after purchase **(4 × 5)**		$270,000		$275,000	$250,000
7	Subsidiary equity prior to the sale	$240,000		$240,000		$240,000
8	Parent's ownership percent prior to the purchase	90%		90%		90%
9	Parent's equity interest prior to purchase **(7 × 8)**		$216,000		$216,000	$216,000
10	Change in parent's equity interest due to purchase **(6 − 9)**		$ 54,000		$ 59,000	$ 34,000
11	Price paid **($30 × 1)**		54,000		60,000	30,000
12	Increase (decrease) in parent's equity interest over price paid **(10 − 11)** . . .	$ 0		$ (1,000)		$ 4,000

In the first case, the parent maintains its ownership interest by purchasing 90% of the newly issued shares. Note that there is no difference between the price paid by the parent for the new shares and the dollar change in the parent's ownership interest due to the purchase. Thus, no entry is needed other than to record the purchase of the shares as follows:

Investment in Company S (1,800 shares × $30)   54,000
    Cash   54,000

No new disparity between cost and underlying equity is created. As a result, **no additional equity adjustment is needed when the parent maintains its ownership interest, and the same price is paid by all buyers.**

In the second case, the parent has increased its ownership interest to 91.67%. The price paid in excess of the additional interest could be allocated to various assets and liabilities, based on differences between cost and market value. However, the adjustments would be limited to the size of the new interest, 1.67%, times the disparities between book and market values. Based on materiality, this new excess usually would be considered goodwill. No entry would be made at the time of the purchase other than to record the added purchase of the shares as follows:

Investment in Company S (2,000 shares × $30)   60,000
    Cash   60,000

Future eliminations would be based on the 91.67% interest; the new $1,000 of excess would require separate distribution and amortization on future worksheets.

In the final case, the parent did not buy enough shares to maintain its ownership interest. This means that there will be a decrease in its interest, which is viewed as a decrease in its investment. If the shares are sold in a public offering, a gain or loss on the decrease in interest is recorded. If there is not a public offering, the increase would be an addition to paid-in capital. A decrease would be a debit to existing paid-in capital. If there is no existing paid-in capital on the parent's books, retained earnings would be reduced. In the third example, the investment account increased

$34,000, and the price paid was only $30,000. In addition to recording the purchase of the shares, an entry should be made to record the $4,000 increase in the parent's ownership interest. The entries for the transactions discussed would be

Investment in Company S (1,000 shares × $30)	30,000	
Cash		30,000
Investment in Company S	4,000	
Paid-In Capital in Excess of Par		4,000

The above entry to record the increase assumes that the sale was not a public offering since no gain or loss was recorded. This entry is made at the time of the purchase and assumes the use of the equity method. If the cost method were used, it would be made as part of the cost-to-equity conversion process. Had the subsidiary sale been a public offering, a gain would have been recorded at the time of the issuance. Also, it would have been necessary to adjust the investment account for the amortization of goodwill applicable to the interest sold. However, it would not be a material amount since only 7.41% [(90% − 83.33%) ÷ 90%] of the original interest was sold.

The FASB exposure draft and working draft on business combinations would apply the economic unit concept, which would require that all changes in equity flow through paid-in capital (decreases in equity would decrease retained earnings if there was insufficient paid-in capital). Increases in the percentage level of ownership would not be treated as a new block. These changes would also be an adjustment to paid-in capital.

Subsidiary Purchase of Its Own Common Stock

When a subsidiary acquires some of its own shares from the minority interest, the resulting reduction of shares outstanding effectively increases the parent's ownership percentage. Thus, such an acquisition is considered to be an indirect purchase of an additional interest in the subsidiary by its parent company.[2] From a consolidated viewpoint, the subsidiary is acting as an agent of the parent which desires the additional interest in the subsidiary. This means that another block of stock has been purchased that will require a determination and distribution of excess schedule. Typically, the subsidiary would record the purchase of the shares as treasury stock at cost. On subsequent consolidated worksheets, the treasury stock account would be eliminated against the underlying equity it represents.

Some consolidated firms still may practice what could be termed the *retirement method*. This method has the subsidiary retire the minority shares purchased. The parent company then adjusts its subsidiary investment account for the impact of the retirement on its interest in the subsidiary.[3] The continued use of this method can be defended only on the basis of materiality.

---

2 *Accounting Interpretations of APB Opinion No. 16* (New York: American Institute of Certified Public Accountants, 1972), par. 26.

3 To illustrate the retirement method, consider this example. A subsidiary has 10,000 shares outstanding and has a total stockholders' equity of $240,000. The parent company owns 7,000 shares prior to the purchase of 2,000 minority shares by the subsidiary for $52,000. The purchase changes the parent's interest to 87.5%. However, as the calculation below shows, the dollar amount of the parent's interest has been reduced due to the large amount paid by the subsidiary for the minority shares. The parent's change in equity would be calculated as follows:

Parent interest prior to retirement, 70% × $24,000 equity	$168,000
Parent interest after retirement, 87.5% × ($240,000 − $52,000)	164,500
Adjustment.	$ 3,500

The adjustment in the investment is accompanied by an adjustment in the parent company paid-in capital in excess of par since the decrease in interest results from a stock transaction in which the parent did not actively participate.

Purchase of Shares as Treasury Stock

To illustrate a subsidiary treasury stock purchase, assume the parent, Company P, owned a 70% interest in Company S. On January 1, 19X1, Company S had the following stockholders' equity:

Capital stock ($10 par)	$100,000
Paid-in capital in excess of par	50,000
Retained earnings.	90,000
Total stockholders' equity	$240,000

On this date, the subsidiary purchased 2,000 of its 10,000 outstanding shares. The following entry then was recorded by Company S as a result of this purchase from minority shareholders at a cost of $26 each:

Treasury Stock (at cost)	52,000	
Cash		52,000

As a result of the purchase, Company S had the following stockholders' equity:

Capital stock ($10 par)	$100,000
Paid-in capital in excess of par	50,000
Retained earnings.	90,000
Total.	$240,000
Less treasury stock (at cost).	52,000
Total stockholders' equity	$188,000

Although the subsidiary views the investment as treasury stock, the consolidated viewpoint treats the investment as an additional interest purchased by the parent. This is the first time an investment on the books of the subsidiary should be eliminated against subsidiary equity. Assuming no assets or liabilities had market values different from book values, the parent's determination and distribution of excess schedule would be prepared as follows:

Price paid		$52,000	
Less interest acquired in Company S:			
Common stock ($10 par)	$100,000		
Paid-in capital in excess of par	50,000		
Retained earnings, January 1, 19X1	90,000		
Total stockholders' equity	$240,000		
Interest acquired	**20%**	48,000	
Excess of cost over book value attributed to goodwill			
(with a 40-year life)		$ 4,000	Dr.

The parent's additional 20% investment caused by the subsidiary treasury stock purchase will have the following ramifications on subsequent worksheets:

1. The subsidiary will maintain the investment in treasury stock at cost and would have no reason to make equity adjustments to the cost. This means that a cost-to-equity conversion entry will be required for the investment on the worksheet. The adjustment to the investment account will require an adjustment to the controlling retained earnings.

2. The treasury stock account, which is treated as an additional investment in the subsidiary on the worksheet, will be eliminated against the *subsidiary equity*

accounts like any other investment in subsidiary account. The excess will be distributed and amortized. All previous years' amortizations are, as always, adjustments only to controlling retained earnings.

3. All adjustments of intercompany profits will be based on a 90% (original 70% plus new 20%) interest as of January 1, 19X1.

4. The adjusted internally reported income of the subsidiary now will be distributed 90% to the controlling interest and 10% to the minority interest.

The above procedures, which treat the subsidiary acquisition of shares as a new block, are a strict interpretation of the *parent company concept*. This concept isolated the excess of cost or book value on each purchase. The FASB exposure draft applies the *economic unit concept* to subsidiary purchases of its own stock. The change in the parent's interest, as a result of the transaction, is an adjustment to paid-in capital (a negative adjustment could affect retained earnings if there is insufficient paid-in capital).

Resale of Shares Held in Treasury

The purchase and resale of treasury stock by a subsidiary would be handled as two separate events using the previously described methods. There may be alternative procedures which could be used if there is the intent to resell the treasury shares in the near future. When, for example, the treasury stock is purchased and resold within the consolidated company's fiscal period, a shortcut is possible. Since there would be no change in the parent's percentage of ownership by the end of the period, the parent only needs to make an adjustment equal to its ownership interest multiplied by the subsidiary's increase or decrease in equity as a result of the treasury stock transaction. This adjustment should be carried to the additional paid-in capital of the parent and is not viewed as an operating gain or loss since it results from dealings with the company's own shareholders. Using the same reasoning, a decrease in equity reduces parent retained earnings only when no additional paid-in capital is available.

This procedure also might be justified for treasury stock transactions crossing over fiscal periods. It is necessary that only the subsidiary treasury stock account be left on the consolidated worksheet at cost and eliminations be made according to the parent's ownership percentage, unadjusted for the number of treasury shares. When the treasury shares are resold, the parent would adjust its accounts in the same manner as was done for a treasury stock purchase and resale within a fiscal period.

If a parent is using the cost method and did not adjust for subsidiary treasury stock transactions, an adjustment can be made as part of the cost-to-equity conversion process.

Indirect Holdings

A parent company may own a controlling interest in a subsidiary which, in turn, owns a controlling interest in another company. For example, Company A may own a 75% interest in Company B which, in turn, owns an 80% interest in Company C. Thus, A has indirect holdings in C. This situation could be diagrammed as follows:

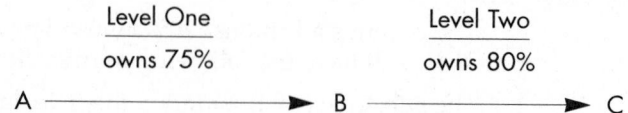

The treatment of the *level one* investment in B and the *level two* investment in C can be mastered with the theory that has been discussed, but the procedures must be applied carefully. The procedures are applied easily to indirect holdings when the level one investment already exists at the time of the level two purchase. Complications arise in preparing the determination and distribution of excess schedule for the new investment when the level two investment exists prior to the time that the parent achieves control over the subsidiary (level one investment). These complications result because the level two investment held by the subsidiary represents one of the subsidiary's assets that may require adjustment to market value on the determination and distribution of excess schedule prepared at the time of the parent's level one acquisition. The use of separate and distinct determination and distribution of excess schedules for each level of investment should facilitate the maintaining of proper accounting when two or more levels are involved.

Level One Holding Acquired First

Assume Company A purchased a 75% interest in Company B on January 1, 19X1, at which time the following determination and distribution of excess schedule was prepared:

Price paid		$400,000
Less interest acquired in Company B:		
Common stock ($10 par)	$200,000	
Retained earnings, January 1, 19X1	100,000	
Total stockholders' equity	$300,000	
Interest acquired	75%	225,000
Excess of cost over book value attributed to building and		
equipment (10-year life)		$175,000 Dr.

On January 1, 19X2, the subsidiary, Company B, purchased an 80% interest in Company C, and the following schedule was prepared:

Price paid		$270,000
Less Company B's interest acquired in Company C:		
Common stock ($10 par)	$100,000	
Retained earnings, January 1, 19X2	120,000	
Total stockholders' equity	$220,000	
Interest acquired	80%	176,000
Excess of cost over book value attributed to goodwill		
(20-year life)		$ 94,000 Dr.

Equity adjustments must be made carefully. Company A must be sure that Company B has included its equity income from Company C in its net income before Company A records its percentage share of Company B income.

Assume the following internally generated net incomes:

	Company A	Company B	Company C
19X1	$100,000	$100,000	$20,000
19X2	70,000	76,000	30,000
19X3	90,000	100,000	30,000

On this basis, the following simple equity adjustments would be required:

Date	Company B's Books		Company A's Books		
19X1 Dec. 31	None (interest in Company C not yet acquired).		Investment in Company B .... 75,000 　Subsidiary Income .... 　　To adjust for 75% of Company B 　　reported income.		75,000
19X2 Dec. 31	Investment in Company C ..... 24,000 　Subsidiary Income .... 　　To adjust for 80% of Company 　　C reported income.	24,000	Investment in Company B .... 75,000 　Subsidiary Income .... 　　To adjust for 75% of Company B 　　total income ($76,000 plus 　　$24,000 sbusidiary income).		75,000
19X3 Dec. 31	Investment in Company C ..... 24,000 　Subsidiary Income .... 　　To adjust for 80% of Company 　　C reported income.	24,000	Investment in Company B .... 93,000 　Subsidiary Income .... 　　To adjust for 75% of Company B 　　total income ($100,000 plus 　　$24,000 subsidiary income).		93,000

Worksheet 8-1, pages 8-46 to 8-49, is based on the trial balances of the three separate companies on December 31, 19X3. The investment account balances reflect the equity adjustments previously shown. The following additional information for 19X3 is assumed:

	Intercompany Sales by B to A	Intercompany Sales by C to B
Selling company goods in buyer's 　January 1, 19X3 inventory	$ 8,000	$ 6,000
Sales during 19X3	50,000	40,000
Selling company goods in buyer's 　December 31, 19X3 inventory	10,000	10,000
Gross profit on all sales	25%	30%

The investment accounts must be handled carefully when any eliminations are made in order to ensure that the minority interest accounts are available to receive amortizations of excesses. It is suggested that the level one investment be eliminated first, thereby reducing Company B retained earnings to the minority interest. Then, it will be possible to allocate the amortizations of excess resulting from the level two (Company C) holding to the controlling interest (Company A) and the Company B minority interest. Since Company B owns the interest in Company C, the Company B minority interest must share in the amortizations of excess resulting from the investment in Company C.

In Worksheet 8-1, the combined net income is $196,100, which must be distributed to the two minority interests and to the controlling interest. Distribution must proceed from the lowest level (level two) to ensure proper distribution. Company B adjusted income includes 80% of Company C adjusted income. Thus, the Company C income distribution schedule must be completed first, followed by the distribution schedules for Companies B and A. These schedules accompany Worksheet 8-1.

If the cost method was used in the previous example, the investment account balances still would contain the January 1, 19X1, $400,000 cost of the Company B investment and the January 1, 19X2, $270,000 cost of the Company C investment. Conversion entries would be made on the consolidated worksheet to update both investment accounts to their January 1, 19X3 simple equity balances. It is advisable to make equity adjustments at the lowest level of investment first, because the retained earnings of the midlevel firm must be adjusted for its share of investment income before the parent can adjust for the change in its subsidiary's retained earnings. The following simple equity conversion entry would be made first for Company B's investment in Company C:

Investment in Company C 24,000
    Retained Earnings (Company B)   24,000
        80% of $30,000 increase in Company C retained earnings
        between January 1, 19X2, and January 1, 19X3.

The following conversion entry then would be made for Company A's investment in Company B:

Investment in Company B 150,000
    Retained Earnings (Company A)   150,000
        75% of $200,000 increase in Company B retained earnings
        (including previous equity adjustment for Company B)
        between January 1, 19X1, and January 1, 19X3.

Eliminations and adjustments would be made as on Worksheet 8-1, except that there would be no need to eliminate the current year's equity adjustment.

Level Two Holding Exists at Time of Parent's Purchase

When a parent acquires a controlling interest in another parent company, the determination and distribution of excess schedule must be **based on the acquired company's consolidated balance sheet.** For example, assume Company Y purchased an 80% interest in Company Z on January 1, 19X1, and Company X purchased a 70% interest in Company Y on January 1, 19X3. Also assume that on January 1, 19X3, Company Y owns equipment which is undervalued by $40,000 and Company Z (the subsidiary) has equipment which is undervalued by $100,000. Company X would prepare the determination and distribution of excess schedule below based on the controlling interest in Company Y.

Note the following features of the schedule:

1. Company Y consolidated equity is multiplied by the parent's (Company X) ownership interest to arrive at the excess of cost over book value.
2. When a Company Y (level one investment) asset is to be adjusted, it should be adjusted for the parent's ownership portion (70%) of the value discrepancy.
3. When a Company Z (level two investment) asset is to be adjusted, it should be adjusted for only the Company X ownership share of the Company Y share (70% × 80%, or 56%) of the value discrepancy.
4. Resulting goodwill is based on the consolidated asset values for Companies Y and Z.

Price paid		$700,000
Less interest acquired:		
Company Y common stock	$400,000	
Company Y controlling interest in consolidated		
retained earnings	320,000	
Total Company Y stockholders' equity	$720,000	
Interest acquired	70%	504,000
Excess of cost over book value (debit balance).		$196,000
Excess of cost attributable to Company Y		
equipment: 70% × $40,000 undervaluation. .		**28,000** Dr.
Excess of cost attributable to Company Z		
equipment: 70% × 80% × $100,000		
undervaluation		**56,000** Dr.
Goodwill (20-year life)		$112,000 Dr.

When the simple equity method is used for the investments, the procedures illustrated in Worksheet 8-1 apply without modification. When the cost method is used, simple equity conversion adjustments again proceed from the lowest level. Be sure to note, however, that in this example Company X would convert to the equity basis for the change in Company Y retained earnings after January 1, 19X3.

Connecting Affiliates

A business combination involving connecting affiliates exists when a parent company has a direct (level one) investment in a company and an indirect (level two) investment in the same company sufficient to result in control. For example, the following diagram illustrates a connecting affiliate structure:

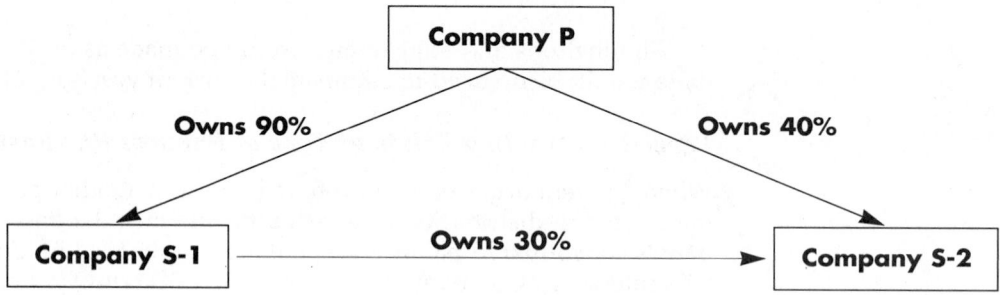

Not only does Company P have a 90% interest in Company S-1, but it also has, in effect, a 67% interest in Company S-2, calculated as follows:

Direct	40%
Indirect (90% × 30%)	27%
Total	67%

This type of structure is consolidated more readily once the determination and distribution of excess schedule has been prepared. Caution must be used in the schedule preparation because of differing dates for each investment. Referring to the diagram, the special concerns in consolidating connecting affiliates are as follows:

1. Company S-2 generally is not included in the consolidation process until the total percentage of S-2 shares held by the parent and its subsidiaries (70% in this example) exceeds 50%. Prior to that time, an investment of 20% or more is treated according to APB Opinion No. 18 and a less-than-20% investment is accounted for under the cost method.
2. Any amortizations of excess resulting from the 30% investment of Company S-1 in Company S-2 are distributed to the controlling and S-1 minority interests in retained earnings on a 90/10 basis.
3. Any adjustments to retained earnings caused by Company S-2–generated transactions are distributed 30% to minority S-2, 3% (10% × 30%) to minority S-1, and 67% [40% + (90% × 30%)] to the controlling interest.
4. Income distributions would begin with Company S-2: 30% of its income would go to minority S-2, 30% would flow to the Company S-1 distribution schedule, and 40% would flow to the Company P schedule. Company P will receive 90% of the Company S-1 adjusted income (including the 30% share of Company S-2).

5. When either equity method is used, Companies P and S-1 each must adjust for its interest in Company S-2, even though neither company's interest by itself would merit consolidation techniques.

6. When the cost method is used, each investment is converted to the simple equity method from the purchase date forward. Again, equity conversions must begin at the lowest level. For example, the Company S-1 investment in Company S-2 must be converted first, so that Company S-1 retained earnings are updated before the Company P investment in Company S-1 is converted to the simple equity method.

Mutual Holdings

A mutual holding structure exists when the subsidiary owns any percentage of the parent company common stock. Such an investment must be eliminated in the consolidation process. There are two methods through which such holdings may be consolidated. The first and more popular method is called the *treasury stock method*. From a consolidated viewpoint, the subsidiary acquisition of parent shares is viewed as a retirement of the shares or as a temporary treasury stock purchase where there is an intent to resell the shares. Under both approaches to the treasury stock method, the shares are **off the market** and have **no claim to income.** The other method is termed the *reciprocal method*, which allocates to the minority interest a percentage of the parent income. This method requires simultaneous equations and becomes even more complicated when there are excesses of cost or book value applicable to each set of investments and/or intercompany profit transactions. The method will be explained in its simplest state, but it is considered to be obsolete and theoretically unsound in that it views parent shares held by the subsidiary as being alive and entitled to a share of combined net income.

The reciprocal method would no longer be allowed under the proposed FASB exposure draft on business combinations.

Treasury Stock Method

The treasury stock method does not view parent shares held by the subsidiary as outstanding. When it is intended that the shares are to be reissued, they are viewed as treasury shares and are recorded at cost. When resold, an excess received over cost is carried to additional paid-in capital. If cost exceeds proceeds on resale, the difference is offset against existing paid-in capital. If there is no paid-in capital, retained earnings are reduced. When it is not intended that the shares be reissued, the stock is retired on the worksheet using the original investment cost as the retirement price. Regardless of the approach used, the resulting capital account adjustments fall entirely upon the parent. The subsidiary is viewed as an agent accomplishing the transaction. An important requirement of either of the treasury stock approaches is that the subsidiary investment in the parent be **maintained at its original cost.** Since the stock is not to be viewed as outstanding, it has no claim on income. If equity adjustments have been made in error, they must be reversed on the consolidated worksheet.

To illustrate the treasury stock method, consider the following example. Suppose Company P acquired an 80% interest in Company S on January 1, 19X1, at which time the following determination and distribution of excess schedule was prepared:

Price paid		$200,000
Less interest acquired:		
Common stock ($10 par)	$100,000	
Retained earnings	50,000	
Total stockholders' equity	$150,000	
Interest acquired	80%	120,000
Excess of cost over book value attributed to equipment (20-year remaining life)		$ 80,000 Dr.

Further assume that on January 1, 19X3, Company S purchases a 10% interest in the parent for $80,000. There would be no need for a determination and distribution of excess schedule for the subsidiary investment, since no excess of cost or book value is acknowledged or distributed. For 19X3, the parent will make the normal simple equity adjustment to acknowledge its 80% interest in subsidiary income of $20,000:

Investment in Company S	16,000	
Subsidiary Income		16,000
To record 80% of subsidiary reported income of $20,000.		

There is no equity adjustment for the Company S investment in the parent since it must remain at cost.

The trial balances of the two companies on December 31, 19X3, are contained in the first two columns of Worksheet 8-2 on pages 8-50–8-53. The investment in Company S account on Worksheet 8-2 is computed as follows:

Original cost	$200,000
80% × 19X1 and 19X2 undistributed income of $40,000	32,000
19X3 simple equity adjustment	16,000
Balance, December 31, 19X3	$248,000

Examination of the formal statements of the consolidated company reveals that the treasury shares are held by the consolidated company and no income accrues to them. These statements, based on Worksheet 8-2, are as follows:

Company P and Subsidiary Company S
Consolidated Income Statement
For Year Ended December 31, 19X3

Sales	$500,000
Less cost of goods sold	300,000
Gross profit	$200,000
Less expenses	144,000
Combined net income	$ 56,000
Minority interest of Company S	4,000
Consolidated net income	$ 52,000

Company P and Subsidiary Company S
Retained Earnings Statement
For Year Ended December 31, 19X3

	Minority Interest	Controlling Interest
Balance, January 1, 19X3	$18,000	$192,000
Net income	4,000	52,000
Balance, December 31, 19X3	$22,000	$244,000

Company P and Subsidiary Company S
Consolidated Balance Sheet
December 31, 19X3

Assets		Stockholders' Equity		
Equipment	$868,000	Minority interest		$ 42,000
Less accumulated		Controlling interest:		
depreciation	162,000	Common stock	$500,000	
		Retained earnings	244,000	744,000
		Total		$786,000
		Less treasury stock (at cost) . .		80,000
Total assets	$706,000	Net stockholders' equity		$706,000

Reciprocal Method

To understand the objections to the reciprocal method, it is necessary to examine the procedures required by the method. This will be done using the same example as was used for the treasury stock method. The same determination and distribution of excess schedule would be prepared for the parent company investment in the subsidiary. But, unlike the treasury stock method, a separate determination and distribution of excess schedule must be prepared for the subsidiary investment in the parent company.

On January 1, 19X3, Company S purchases a 10% interest in Company P. The determination and distribution of excess schedule for this investment is prepared as follows:

Price paid		$80,000
Less interest acquired:		
Common stock	$500,000	
Retained earnings	200,000	
Total stockholders' equity	$700,000	
Ownership interest.	**10%**	70,000
Excess of cost over book value attributed to goodwill		
(10-year life).	$10,000	Dr.

 Typically, the determination and distribution of excess schedule will be based only on Company P equity and not on the total controlling interest. The excess could be distributed to the separate assets of Company P (including the investment in Company S), but based on materiality, it usually would be distributed only to goodwill. The parent and the subsidiary may use either the cost method or the equity method to account for intercompany investments. In Worksheet 8-3 on pages 8-54–8-57, both companies are assumed to be using the simple equity method. Company P has recorded subsidiary income of $16,000 (80% × Company S reported income of $20,000), and Company S has recorded investment income of $4,000 (10% × Company P internal income of $40,000).

In Worksheet 8-3, the combined net income is distributed to Company P and Company S by simultaneously solving the following equations which are based on each company's **adjusted internally generated income:**

Let P = Company P income

Let S = Company S income

$$P = \$36{,}000 + .8S$$
$$S = \$19{,}000 + .1P$$

Solution:
$$P - .8S = \$36{,}000$$
$$-.1P + S = \$19{,}000$$

Multiply the first solution equation by .1 and then add the equations:

$$.1P - .08S = \$ 3{,}600$$
$$+ (-.1P + 1.00S = \$19{,}000)$$

$$.92S = \$22{,}600$$
$$S = \$24{,}565$$

Substitute for S in the first equation:

$$P = \$36{,}000 + .8(\$24{,}565)$$
$$P = \$55{,}652$$

To minority interest: 20% × Company S income of $24,565 = $4,913

To controlling interest: 90% × Company P income of $55,652 = $50,087

The treasury stock method usually is more practical to use than the reciprocal method and is supported by ARB No. 51, which states, "Shares of the parent held by a subsidiary should not be treated as outstanding stock in the consolidated balance sheet."[4] Further support comes from an American Accounting Association publication, which states:

> Shares of the controlling company's capital stock owned by a subsidiary before the date of acquisition of control should be treated in consolidation as treasury stock. Any subsequent acquisition or sale by a subsidiary should likewise be treated in the consolidated statements as though it had been the act of the controlling company.[5]

Questions

1. What effect does a subsidiary stock dividend have on consolidation procedures a) when the equity method is used? (b) when the cost method is used?
2. Indicate how one calculates the dollar impact on the parent company's investment account of a sale of additional common stock by a subsidiary to minority shareholders only.
3. Assume a subsidiary issues additional shares of common stock, but the parent

---

4 Accounting Research Bulletin No. 51, *Consolidated Financial Statements* (New York: American Institute of Certified Public Accountants, 1959), par. 13.

5 *Accounting and Reporting Standards for Corporate Financial Statements and Preceding Statements and Supplements* (Columbus, OH: American Accounting Association, 1957), 44.

buys none of these shares. Further assume the parent's interest (in dollars) increases as a result of the transaction. What are the alternative theories of dealing with the increase and under what circumstances might each be appropriate?

4. Assume the parent company owns an 80% interest in a subsidiary just prior to the issuance of additional shares by the subsidiary. Indicate the type of adjustment you would make to the investment account if

   a) The parent purchased 80% of the new shares.

   b) The parent purchased all the newly issued shares.

   c) The parent purchased 50% of the new shares.

5. What is the applicable general accounting theory for the purchase of treasury shares by a subsidiary? How should the investment be recorded on the subsidiary's books, and what are the consolidated worksheet procedures for the treasury stock?

6. What special procedures are necessary when making equity adjustments to record subsidiary income when an indirect holding situation exists?

7. What new procedures are needed on the determination and distribution of excess schedule when a parent acquires a controlling interest in a subsidiary company which, at the time of the acquisition, also owns a controlling interest in another company?

8. What is a connecting affiliate, and how is income distributed to the parent calculated?

9. Describe a mutual holding and the alternative methods used to consolidate such holdings.

10. Why might the reciprocal method of accounting for mutual holdings be considered theoretically unsound?

11. Under the treasury stock method of accounting for mutual holdings, intent determines the exact treatment of the parent shares owned by the subsidiary. Explain the different treatments available under the treasury stock method.

Exercises

Exercise 1. On January 1, 19X7, Bear Company purchased 90% of the outstanding stock of Cub Company for $720,000. At the time of the acquisition, Cub Company had the following stockholders' equity:

Common stock ($10 par)	$300,000
Paid-in capital in excess of par	150,000
Retained earnings	200,000
Total stockholders' equity	$650,000

It was determined that Cub Company's book values approximated market as of the purchase date. Any excess of cost over book value was attributed to goodwill and given a 20-year life.

On July 1, 19X7, Cub Company distributed a 10% stock dividend when the market value of its common stock was $30 per share. A cash dividend of $.50 per share was distributed on December 31, 19X7. Cub Company net income for 19X7 amounted to $120,000 and was earned evenly throughout the year.

(continued)

1. Prepare the entry required on Cub Company books to reflect the stock dividend distributed on July 1, 19X7. Prepare the stockholders' equity section of the Cub Company balance sheet as of December 31, 19X7.
2. Prepare the simple equity method entries that Bear Company would make during 19X7 to record its investment in Cub Company.
3. Prepare the eliminations that would be made on the December 31, 19X7 consolidated worksheet. (Assume the use of the simple equity method.)

Exercise 2.   Farm Company owned a 90% interest in Field Company on January 1, 19X6, when Field had the following stockholders' equity:

Common stock ($10 par).	$100,000
Paid-in capital in excess of par	250,000
Retained earnings.	200,000
Total stockholders' equity	$550,000

On July 1, 19X6, Field sold 2,000 additional shares to minority shareholders in a private offering for $70 per share. Field's net income for 19X6 was $50,000, and the income was earned evenly during the year.

Farm uses the simple equity method to record the investment in Field. Summary entries are made each December 31 to record the year's activity.

Prepare Farm's equity adjustments for 19X6 that result from the above activities of Field Company during 19X6. Assume Farm has $500,000 of paid-in capital in excess of par.

Exercise 3.   On January 1, 19X8, Tom Company purchased an 80% interest in Car Company for $400,000. On the purchase date, Car Company had the following stockholders' equity:

Common stock ($10 par).	$200,000
Paid-in capital in excess of par	100,000
Retained earnings.	150,000
Total stockholders' equity	$450,000

Assets and liabilities have market values equal to book values. Any excess is due to goodwill and is to be amortized over a 20-year life.

Car Company had net income of $50,000 for 19X8. No dividends were paid or declared during 19X8.

On January 1, 19X9, Car Company sold 10,000 shares of common stock at $40 per share in a public offering.

Assuming the parent uses the simple equity method, prepare all parent company entries required for the issuance of the shares. Also prepare a new determination and distribution of excess schedule for the investment if it is needed. Assume the following alternative situations:

1. Tom Company purchased 8,000 shares.
2. Tom Company purchased 9,000 shares.
3. Tom Company purchased 5,000 shares.

Suggestion: It is helpful to use a 3-column table which, for each case, organizes the changes in ownership interest. See the schedule on page 8-13.

Exercise 4.   The following comparative statements of stockholders' equity were prepared for Nolte Corporation:

	Jan. 1, 19X3	Jan. 1, 19X5	Jan. 1, 19X8
Common stock ($10 par)	$300,000	$300,000	$300,000
Paid-in capital in excess of par.	60,000	60,000	60,000
Retained earnings		42,000	120,000
Total	$360,000	$402,000	$480,000
Less treasury stock (at cost)		(75,000)	(75,000)
Total stockholders' equity.	$360,000	$327,000	$405,000

Tarman Corporation purchased 60% of Nolte Corporation common stock for $12 per share on January 1, 19X3, when the latter corporation was formed.

On December 31, 19X4, Nolte Corporation purchased 5,000 shares of its own common stock from minority interests for $15 per share. These shares were accounted for as treasury stock at cost.

Nolte had $50,000 of net income in 19X8 and has never declared a cash dividend.

Assuming Tarman Corporation uses the cost method to record its investment in Nolte Corporation, prepare the necessary cost-to-simple-equity conversion and the eliminations and adjustments required on the consolidated worksheet as of December 31, 19X8. Include all pertinent supporting calculations in good form. Any excess of cost over book value is considered to be goodwill with a 10-year life.

Exercise 5.   You have secured the following information for Companies A, B, and C concerning their internally generated net incomes (excluding subsidiary income) and dividends paid:

		A	B	C
19X5	Internally generated net income.	$30,000	$20,000	$10,000
	Dividends declared and paid	10,000	5,000	
19X6	Internally generated net income.	50,000	30,000	25,000
	Dividends declared and paid	10,000	5,000	5,000
19X7	Internally generated net income.	40,000	40,000	30,000
	Dividends declared and paid	10,000	5,000	5,000

1. Assume Company A purchased an 80% interest in Company B on January 1, 19X5, and Company B purchased a 60% interest in Company C on January 1, 19X6. Prepare the simple equity method adjusting entries made by Companies A and B for subsidiary investments for the years 19X5 through 19X7.
2. Assume Company B acquired a 70% interest in Company C on January 1, 19X5, and Company A acquired a 90% interest in Company B on January 1, 19X7. Prepare the simple equity method adjusting entries made by Companies A and B for subsidiary investments for the years 19X5 through 19X7.

Exercise 6.   Company SP purchased an 80% interest in the common stock of Company S for $580,000 on January 1, 19X1. Any excess of cost is attributable to goodwill with a 20-year life. Company SP maintains its investment in Company S under the cost method.

(continued)

Company P purchased a 60% interest in the common stock of Company SP on January 1, 19X5, for $2,600,000. Any excess of cost is attributable to Company S equipment, which is understated by $80,000, and a Company SP building, which is understated by $200,000. Any remaining excess is considered goodwill. Relevant stockholders' equities are as follows:

	Company SP	Company S	
	1/1/X5	1/1/X1	1/1/X5
Common stock.	$ 400,000	$100,000	$100,000
Paid-in capital in excess of par	1,100,000	150,000	150,000
Retained earnings.	2,000,000	300,000	450,000

1. Prepare a determination and distribution of excess schedule for the investment in Company SP.
2. On January 1, 19X6, Company S sold a machine with a net book value of $35,000 to Company P for $50,000. The machine has a 5-year life. Prepare the eliminations and adjustments needed on the December 31, 19X7 trial balance worksheet that relate to this intercompany sale.

Exercise 7.   Companies A, B, and C produced the following separate internally generated net incomes during 19X9:

	A	B	C
Sales.	$300,000	$400,000	$100,000
Less cost of goods sold.	200,000	300,000	60,000
Gross profit	$100,000	$100,000	$ 40,000
Expenses	60,000	30,000	10,000
Internally generated net income	$ 40,000	$ 70,000	$ 30,000

Company A purchased an 80% interest in Company B on January 1, 19X6, and Company B purchased a 60% interest in Company C on January 1, 19X7. Each investment was acquired at a price equal to the book value of the stock purchased.
Additional information:

   a) Company A purchased goods billed at $30,000 from Company C during 19X9. The price includes a 66⅔% markup on cost. One-half of the goods are held in Company A's year-end inventory.
   b) Company B purchased goods billed at $30,000 from Company A during 19X9. Company A always bills Company B for cost plus 50%. Company B had $6,000 of Company A goods in its beginning inventory and $2,400 of Company A goods in its ending inventory.
   c) Company C purchased goods billed at $15,000 from Company B during 19X9. Company B bills Company C at cost plus 25%. At year end, $7,500 of the goods remain unsold. The goods were inventoried at $5,000, under the lower-of-cost-or-market procedure.
   d) Company B sold a machine to Company C on January 1, 19X8, for $50,000. Company B's cost was $70,000, and accumulated depreciation on the date of sale was $40,000. The machine is being depreciated on a straight-line basis over 5 years.

Prepare the consolidated income statement for 19X9, including the distribution of combined net income supported by distribution schedules.

Exercise 8.   On January 1, 19X6, Hartland Company purchased an 80% interest in Fort Company for $120,000. The purchase price represented a $20,000 excess over book value, which was attributed to goodwill and given a 10-year life. The investment is recorded under the simple equity method.

On January 1, 19X8, Oconto Company purchased a 60% interest in Hartland Company for $380,000. Oconto Company believes that the goodwill remaining on the investment by Hartland in Fort is stated correctly. Comparative equities of Hartland Company and Fort Company immediately prior to the purchase revealed:

Stockholders' Equity	Hartland Company	Fort Company
Common stock ($5 par)	$200,000	
Common stock ($10 par)		$100,000
Paid-in capital in excess of par	100,000	20,000
Retained earnings.	150,000	80,000
Total stockholders' equity	$450,000	$200,000

An analysis of the separate accounts of Hartland and Fort on January 1, 19X8, revealed that Fort's inventory was undervalued by $20,000 and that Hartland's equipment with a 5-year future life was undervalued by $30,000. All other book values approximated market values for Hartland and Fort.

Prepare the determination and distribution of excess schedule for Oconto's purchase of Hartland Company on January 1, 19X8.

Exercise 9.   The following diagram depicts the investment affiliations between Companies M, N, and O:

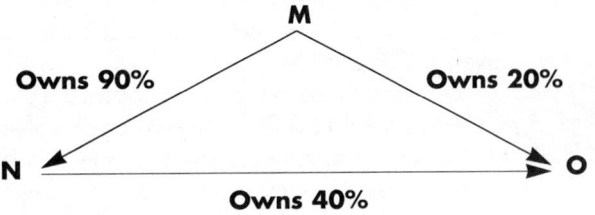

The following facts apply to 19X3 operations:

	M	N	O
Internally generated net income	$200,000	$90,000	$40,000
Dividends declared and paid	40,000	10,000	5,000

All investments were made at a price equal to book value.

1. Prepare the simple equity method adjustments that would be made for the investments owned by Companies M and N during the year 19X3.
2. Intercompany inventory transactions affecting 19X3 were as follows:

	Sold by N to O	Sold by O to M
Profit on sales.	25%	30%
Beginning inventory of intercompany goods.	$10,000	$15,000
19X3 sales.	50,000	75,000
Ending inventory of intercompany goods.	12,000	20,000

(continued)

Using the facts given, determine the combined income of the consolidated company, the minority interest, and the consolidated net income. Income distribution schedules may be used for support.

Exercise 10. Myles Corporation and its subsidiary, Dowling Corporation, had the following trial balances as of December 31, 19X8:

	Myles Corporation	Dowling Corporation
Current Assets.	400,000	182,000
Investment in Dowling Corporation.	398,000	
Investment in Myles Corporation		150,000
Property, Plant, and Equipment (net)	850,000	400,000
Liabilities	(200,000)	(100,000)
Common Stock ($10 par)	(1,000,000)	(500,000)
Retained Earnings, Jan. 1, 19X8	(400,000)	(100,000)
Sales.	(800,000)	(350,000)
Dividend Income		(2,000)
Subsidiary Income.	(18,000)	
Cost of Goods Sold	600,000	240,000
Expenses	150,000	80,000
Dividends Declared	20,000	
Total	0	0

Myles Corporation purchased its 60% interest in Dowling Corporation for $350,000 on January 1, 19X6. At that time, Dowling's retained earnings balance was $50,000. Any excess of cost over book value was attributed to goodwill and given a 20-year life.

Dowling Corporation purchased a 10% interest in Myles Corporation on January 1, 19X8, for $150,000. Myles' book values approximated market values at the time of the purchase. Any resulting goodwill is being amortized over 20 years.

No intercompany transactions occurred during 19X8.

1. Prepare determination and distribution of excess schedules for the intercompany investments.
2. Prepare the 19X8 consolidated income statement, including the combined net income distribution, using the reciprocal method for mutual holdings.
3. Prepare the 19X8 consolidated income statement, including the combined net income distribution, using the treasury stock method for mutual holdings. Prepare the supporting income distribution schedules.
4. State how the investment in Myles stock will appear on the consolidated balance sheet under the two alternative methods of accounting for mutual holdings.

Problems

Problem 8-1. On January 1, 19X7, Zee Corporation purchased 8,000 shares of Thomas Company stock and 18,000 shares of Sand Company stock for $196,000 and $270,000, respectively. The excess of cost over book value on each investment was attributed to goodwill and given a 10-year life.

Thomas Company and Sand Company had the following stockholders' equities immediately prior to Zee's purchases:

	Thomas Company	Sand Company
Common stock ($5 par)	$ 50,000	
Common stock ($10 par)		$300,000
Paid-in capital in excess of par	100,000	
Retained earnings	70,000	100,000
Total stockholders' equity	$220,000	$400,000

Additional information:

a) Net income for Thomas Company and Sand Company for 19X7 and 19X8 follows (income is assumed to be earned evenly throughout the year):

	19X7	19X8
Thomas Company	$25,000	$30,000
Sand Company	30,000	40,000

b) No cash dividends were paid or declared by Thomas or Sand during 19X7 and 19X8.

c) Thomas Company distributed a 10% stock dividend on December 31, 19X7. Thomas stock was selling at $25 per share when the stock dividend was declared.

d) On July 1, 19X8, Thomas Company sold 2,750 shares of stock at $32 per share in a private offering. Zee Corporation purchased none of these shares. The sale was not a public offering; therefore, no gain or loss is recognized.

e) Sand Company sold 5,000 shares of stock on July 1, 19X7, in a private offering at $20 per share. Zee Corporation purchased 3,700 of these shares.

f) On January 1, 19X8, Sand Company purchased 5,000 shares of its common stock from minority interests at $14 per share.

Required:

Assume Zee Corporation uses the simple equity method. For 19X7 and 19X8, record each of the adjustments to the investment accounts. Provide all supporting calculations in good form.

Problem 8-2. On January 1, 19X6, Bear Corporation acquired a 60% interest in Keller Company and an 80% interest in Samco Company. The purchase prices were $225,000 and $250,000, respectively. The excess of cost over book value for each investment was considered to be goodwill with a 10-year life. Neither subsidiary is trading its stock publicly.

Immediately prior to the purchases, Keller Company and Samco Company had the following stockholders' equities:

(continued)

	Keller Company	Samco Company
Common stock ($10 par)	$200,000	
Common stock ($20 par)		$200,000
Paid-in capital in excess of par	50,000	
Retained earnings	100,000	100,000
Total stockholders' equity	$350,000	$300,000

Additional information:

a) Keller Company and Samco Company had the following net incomes for 19X6 through 19X8 (incomes were earned evenly throughout the year):

	19X6	19X7	19X8
Keller Company	$50,000	$60,000	$60,000
Samco Company	40,000	30,000	55,000

b) Keller Company had the following equity-related transactions for the first three years after it became a subsidiary of Bear Corporation:

July 1, 19X6	Sold 5,000 shares of its own stock at $20 per share. Bear purchased 3,000 of these shares.
December 31, 19X7	Paid a cash dividend of $1 per share.
July 1, 19X8	Purchased 5,000 shares of minority-owned stock as treasury shares at $27 per share.

c) Samco Company had the following equity-related transactions for the first three years after it became a subsidiary of Bear Corporation:

December 31, 19X6	Issued a 10% stock dividend. The estimated market value of Samco common stock was $30 per share on the declaration date.
October 1, 19X7	Sold 4,000 shares of its own stock at $30 per share. Of these shares, 200 were purchased by Bear.

d) Bear Corporation has $200,000 of additional paid-in capital on December 31, 19X8.

Required:

Bear Corporation uses the cost method to account for its investments in subsidiaries. Convert its investments to the simple equity method as of December 31, 19X8, and provide adequate support for the entries. Assume that the 19X8 nominal accounts are closed.

Suggestion: Since the stock sales were not public offerings, no gain or loss is recognized; instead, the adjustment is to the paid-in capital of the parent company.

Problem 8-3.   On January 1, 19X6, Parson Company purchased 80% of the outstanding common stock of Schell Company for $650,000.

On January 1, 19X8, Schell Company sold 25,000 shares of common stock to the public at $9 per share. Parson Company did not purchase any of these shares. It is considered appropriate for the parent to record a gain or loss on the subsidiary stock sale; however, no entry has been made by the parent. Schell Company had the following stockholders' equity at the end of 19X5 and 19X7:

	December 31	
	19X5	19X7
Common stock ($2 par)	$200,000	$200,000
Paid-in capital in excess of par	400,000	400,000
Retained earnings	100,000	180,000
Total stockholders' equity	$700,000	$780,000

On the January 1, 19X6 acquisition date, Schell Company's book values approximated market values, except for a building that was undervalued by $60,000. The building had an estimated future life of 20 years. Any additional excess was attributed to goodwill and given a 10-year life.

Trial balances of the two companies as of December 31, 19X8, are as follows:

	Parson Company	Schell Company
Cash	229,040	30,000
Accounts Receivable (net)	280,000	190,000
Inventory	325,000	175,000
Investment in Schell Company	650,000	
Property, Plant, and Equipment	2,450,000	1,400,000
Accumulated Depreciation	(1,256,000)	(536,000)
Liabilities	(750,000)	(210,000)
Common Stock ($10 par)	(1,500,000)	
Common Stock ($2 par)		(250,000)
Paid-In Capital in Excess of Par		(575,000)
Retained Earnings, Jan. 1, 19X8	(375,000)	(180,000)
Sales	(1,600,000)	(750,000)
Subsidiary Dividend Income	(23,040)	
Cost of Goods Sold	1,120,000	450,000
Other Expenses	405,000	220,000
Dividends Declared	45,000	36,000
Total	0	0

During 19X8, Schell Company sold $200,000 of merchandise to Parson Company at cost plus 25%. This was the first intercompany sale between the two companies. $50,000 of the goods remain in Parson's ending inventory.

Required:

Prepare the worksheet necessary to produce the consolidated financial statements of Parson Company and its subsidiary as of December 31, 19X8. Include the determination and distribution of excess and income distribution schedules.

Problem 8-4.   On January 1, 19X7, Mitta Corporation purchased a 60% interest (12,000 shares) in Trainer Company for $158,000. Trainer stockholders' equity on the purchase date was as follows:

Common stock ($5 par)	$100,000
Paid-in capital in excess of par	50,000
Retained earnings	80,000
Total stockholders' equity	$230,000

(continued)

At the purchase date, Trainer's book values for assets and liabilities closely approximate market values. Any excess of cost over book value is attributed to goodwill with a 10-year life.

On January 1, 19X8, Trainer Company sold 5,000 shares of common stock in a public offering at $20 per share. Mitta Corporation purchased 4,000 shares. Any excess of cost over book value on the additional interest was attributed to goodwill and given a 10-year life.

During 19X8, Mitta sold $30,000 of goods to Trainer at a gross profit of 25%. There were $6,000 of Mitta goods in Trainer's beginning inventory, and $8,000 of Mitta goods in Trainer's ending inventory.

Merchandise sales by Trainer to Mitta were $20,000 during 19X8 at a gross profit of 30%. There were $6,000 of Trainer goods in Mitta's beginning inventory and $2,000 of Trainer goods in Mitta's ending inventory.

Intercompany gross profit rates have been constant for many years. There are no intercompany payables/receivables.

Mitta's investment in Trainer Company balance was determined as follows:

Original cost	$158,000
60% of Trainer 19X7 income ($40,000 × 60%)	24,000
Subtotal	$182,000
Less 60% of Trainer dividends declared in 19X7 (60% × $8,000)	(4,800)
Subtotal	$177,200
Cost to acquire additional shares (new issue)	80,000
64% of Trainer 19X8 income ($50,000 × 64%)	32,000
Subtotal	$289,200
Less 64% of Trainer dividends declared in 19X8 (64% × $10,000)	(6,400)
Investment balance, December 31, 19X8	$282,800

Trainer has paid a quarterly $.10 dividend per outstanding common share since the second quarter of 19X6.

The trial balances of the two companies as of December 31, 19X8, are as follows:

	Mitta	Trainer
Cash	104,200	63,500
Accounts Receivable.	113,600	60,000
Inventory	350,000	80,000
Investment in Trainer Company.	282,800	
Property, Plant, and Equipment.	1,800,000	360,000
Accumulated Depreciation.	(600,000)	(89,500)
Accounts Payable	(180,000)	(64,000)
Other Current Liabilities	(26,000)	(8,000)
Bonds Payable	(500,000)	
Common Stock ($10 par)	(1,000,000)	
Common Stock ($5 par)		(125,000)
Paid-In Capital in Excess of Par		(125,000)
Retained Earnings, Jan. 1, 19X8	(212,600)	(112,000)
Sales	(1,950,000)	(600,000)
Subsidiary Income	(32,000)	
Cost of Goods Sold	1,170,000	420,000
Other Expenses	630,000	130,000
Dividends Declared	50,000	10,000
Total	0	0

Required:

Prepare the worksheet necessary to produce the consolidated financial statements of Mitta Corporation and its subsidiary as of December 31, 19X8. Include the determination and distribution of excess and income distribution schedules.

Problem 8-5.   The audit of Barns Company and its subsidiaries for the year ended December 31, 19X2, was completed. The working papers contain the following information:

a)   Barns Company acquired 4,000 shares of Webb Company common stock for $320,000 on January 1, 19X1. Webb Company purchased 500 shares of its own stock as treasury shares for $48,000 on January 1, 19X2.

b)   Barns Company acquired all 8,000 outstanding shares of Elcho Company stock on January 1, 19X1, for $600,000. On January 1, 19X2, Elcho Company issued through a private sale 2,000 additional shares to new minority shareholders at $85 per share. Barns has no investments other than the stock of Webb and Elcho.

c)   Elcho Company originally issued $200,000 of 10-year, 8% mortgage bonds at 98, due on January 1, 19X5. On January 1, 19X2, Webb Company purchased $150,000 of these bonds in the open market at 98. Interest on the bonds is paid each June 30 and December 31.

d)   Condensed balance sheets of Webb and Elcho on January 1, 19X1, and January 1, 19X2, are as follows:

	Webb Company		Elcho Company	
	1/1/X1	1/1/X2	1/1/X1	1/1/X2
Current assets	$195,000	$225,000	$280,400	$205,000
Property, plant, and equipment.	305,000	350,000	613,000	623,800
Unamortized bond discount.			1,600	1,200
Total	$500,000	$575,000	$895,000	$830,000
Current liabilities	$100,000	$125,000	$95,000	$105,000
Bonds payable			200,000	200,000
Capital stock ($50 par).	250,000	250,000	400,000	400,000
Retained earnings	150,000	200,000	200,000	125,000
Total	$500,000	$575,000	$895,000	$830,000

e)   Total dividends declared and paid during 19X2 were as follows:

Barns Company $24,000
Webb Company   25,000
Elcho Company   10,000

In addition to the dividend payments, Barns Company and Webb Company each had declared dividends of $1 per share payable in January 19X3.

f)   On June 30, 19X2, Barns sold equipment with a book value of $8,000 to Webb for $10,000. Webb depreciates equipment by the straight-line method based on a 10-year life.

g)   Barns Company consistently sells to its subsidiaries at prices that realize a gross profit of 25% on sales. Webb and Elcho Companies sell to each other

(continued)

and to Barns Company at cost. Prior to 19X2, intercompany sales were negligible, but the following sales were made during 19X2:

	Total Sales	Included in Purchaser's Inventory at December 31, 19X2
Barns Company to Webb Company	$172,000	$20,000
Barns Company to Elcho Company	160,000	40,000
Webb Company to Elcho Company	25,000	5,000
Webb Company to Barns Company	28,000	8,000
	$385,000	$73,000

h) *At December 31, 19X2:*

Barns Company owed Webb Company	$24,000
Webb Company owed Elcho Company	16,000
Elcho Company owed Barns Company	12,000
Total	$52,000

i)   *The following trial balances as of December 31, 19X2, were prepared:*

	Barns	Webb	Elcho
Cash	110,000	23,500	165,200
Accounts Receivable	85,000	73,500	105,000
Inventories	138,000	163,000	150,000
Investment in Webb Company Stock	320,000		
Investment in Elcho Company Stock	600,000		
Investment in Elcho Company Bonds		148,000	
Property, Plant, and Equipment	700,000	525,000	834,000
Accumulated Depreciation	(402,000)	(325,000)	(240,000)
Accounts Payable	(202,000)	(150,500)	(86,900)
Dividends Payable	(12,000)	(5,000)	
Bonds Payable	(400,000)		(200,000)
Unamortized Bond Discount			800
Capital Stock ($50 par)	(600,000)	(250,000)	(500,000)
Paid-In Capital in Excess of Par			(70,000)
Retained Earnings, Jan. 1, 19X2*	(278,200)	(170,000)	(115,000)
Treasury Stock (at cost)		48,000	
Gain on Sale of Equipment	(2,000)		
Sales	(2,950,000)	(1,550,000)	(1,750,000)
Interest Income on Bonds		(13,000)	
Dividend Income	(28,000)		
Cost of Goods Sold	2,500,000	1,200,000	1,400,000
Operating Expenses	405,000	280,000	290,500
Interest Expense	16,200	2,500	16,400
Total	0	0	0

*Reduced directly for dividends declared.

Required:

Prepare the worksheet necessary to produce the consolidated financial statements of Barns Company and its subsidiaries for the year ended December 31, 19X2. Include the determination and distribution of excess and income distribution schedules. Any excess of cost over book value is attributable to goodwill with a 10-year life. All bond discounts are assumed to be amortized on a straight-line basis.

(AICPA adapted)

Suggestion: The treasury stock represents a separate block of stock to be eliminated. The impact of the subsidiary sale of shares should not be reflected as an income statement gain or loss.

Problem 8-6.   The following diagram depicts the relationships between Mary Company, Jack Company, and Jill Company on December 31, 19X8:

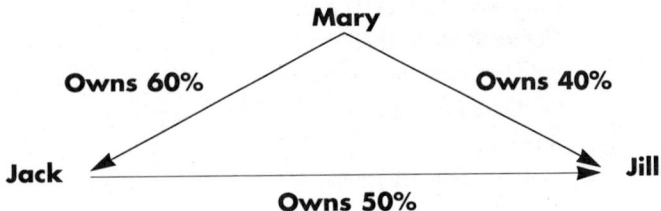

Mary Company purchased its interest in Jack Company on January 1, 19X6, for $200,000. Jack Company purchased its interest in Jill Company on January 1, 19X7, for $75,000. Mary Company purchased its interest in Jill Company on January 1, 19X8, for $72,000.

The following stockholders' equities are available:

	Jack Company December 31, 19X5	Jill Company December 31, 19X6	Jill Company December 31, 19X7
Common stock ($10 par)	$150,000		
Common stock ($20 par)		$100,000	$100,000
Paid-in capital in excess of par.	75,000		
Retained earnings	75,000	50,000	80,000
Total equity.	$300,000	$150,000	$180,000

On January 2, 19X8, Jill Company sold a machine to Mary Company for $20,000. The machine had a book value of $10,000, with an estimated life of 5 years and is being depreciated on a straight-line basis.

Jack Company sold $20,000 of merchandise to Jill Company during 19X8 to realize a gross profit of 30%. Of this merchandise, $5,000 remained in Jill Company's December 31, 19X8 inventory. Jill owes Jack $3,000 on December 31, 19X8, for merchandise delivered during 19X8.

Trial balances of the three companies prepared from general ledger account balances on December 31, 19X8, are as follows:

(continued)

	Mary Company	Jack Company	Jill Company
Cash	66,500	60,000	30,000
Accounts Receivable	200,000	55,000	30,000
Inventory	360,000	80,000	50,000
Investment in Jack Company	266,000		
Investment in Jill Company	86,000	107,500	
Property, Plant, and Equipment	2,250,000	850,000	350,000
Accumulated Depreciation	(938,000)	(377,500)	(121,800)
Intangibles	15,000		
Accounts Payable	(215,500)	(61,000)	(22,000)
Accrued Expenses	(12,000)	(4,000)	(1,200)
Bonds Payable	(500,000)	(300,000)	(100,000)
Common Stock ($5 par)	(500,000)		
Common Stock ($10 par)		(150,000)	
Common Stock ($20 par)			(100,000)
Paid-In Capital in Excess of Par	(700,000)	(75,000)	
Retained Earnings, Jan. 1, 19X8	(290,000)	(130,000)	(80,000)
Sales	(1,800,000)	(500,000)	(300,000)
Gain on Sale of Equipment			(10,000)
Subsidiary Income	(58,000)	(20,000)	
Cost of Goods Sold	1,170,000	350,000	180,000
Other Expenses	525,000	100,000	90,000
Dividends Declared	75,000	15,000	5,000
Total	0	0	0

Required:

Prepare the worksheet necessary to produce the consolidated financial statements of Mary Company and its subsidiaries as of December 31, 19X8. Include the determination and distribution of excess and income distribution schedules. Any excess of cost is assumed to be attributable to goodwill with a 20-year life.

Problem 8-7.   Shelby Corporation purchased 90% of the outstanding stock of Boehm Company on January 1, 19X4, for $600,000 cash. At that time, Boehm Company had the following stockholders' equity balances. Common Stock: $200,000; Paid-In Capital: $80,000; and Retained Earnings: $300,000.

All book values approximated market values except for the plant assets (undervalued by $50,000 and with an estimated remaining life of 10 years). Any goodwill was amortized over 20 years.

DeNoma Company acquired a 60% interest in Shelby on January 1, 19X6, for $750,000. At this time, Shelby had consolidated shareholders' equity of Common Stock: $500,000; Paid-In Capital: $150,000; and Controlling Retained Earnings: $500,000 (not including amortization of excess price applicable to investment in Boehm).

At that time, it was also determined that Shelby's plant assets were undervalued by $50,000 and had a 10-year remaining life. Boehm's plant assets were undervalued by $18,519. Any goodwill is to be amortized over 20 years.

Intercompany merchandise sales from Boehm to Shelby for 19X7 were (1) seller's goods in buyer's beginning inventory, $7,500; (2) sales during 19X7, $125,000; (3) seller's goods in buyer's ending inventory, $10,000; and (4) gross profit on intercompany sales, 80%.

On July 1, 19X6, Shelby sold plant assets with a cost of $80,000 and accumulated depreciation of $45,000 to DeNoma for $50,000. Remaining life on the date of sale was estimated to be 5 years.

Shelby and DeNoma use the simple equity method to account for their investments. The trial balances on December 31, 19X7, were as follows:

	DeNoma Company	Shelby Corporation	Boehm Company
Inventory	75,000	60,000	40,000
Other Current Assets	900,000	5,000	390,000
Plant Assets	1,200,000	800,000	600,000
Accumulated Depreciation	(450,000)	(300,000)	(200,000)
Investment in Shelby Corporation	894,000		
Investment in Boehm Company		825,000	
Common Stock	(1,500,000)	(500,000)	(200,000)
Paid-In Capital in Excess of Par		(150,000)	(80,000)
Retained Earnings	(922,000)	(620,000)	(500,000)
Sales	(900,000)	(700,000)	(600,000)
Cost of Goods Sold	570,000	425,000	400,000
Expenses	205,000	200,000	150,000
Subsidiary Income	(72,000)	(45,000)	
Total	0	0	0

Required:

Prepare the determination and distribution of excess schedule for Shelby's investment in Boehm and DeNoma's investment in Shelby. Prepare the December 31, 19X7 consolidated worksheet and income distribution schedules.

Suggestion: The determination and distribution of excess schedule must show an adjustment to Shelby's retained earnings for the amortization of excess applicable to Shelby's investment in Boehm. (Hint for consolidated balance sheet: The reduced retained earnings in the determination and distribution of excess schedule must be adjusted before eliminating the pro rata share of equity balances.)

Problem 8-8. The following diagram depicts the relationships between Ackley Company, Biernat Company, and Cromwell Company on December 31, 19X7:

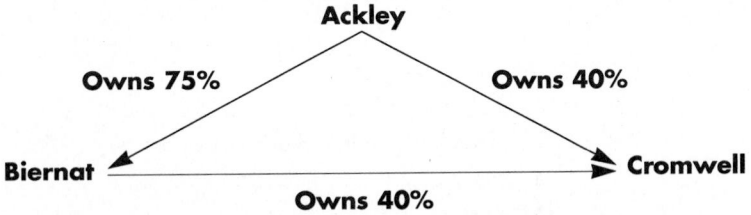

Information regarding the preceding investments follows:

a) *Ackley Company purchased its 40% interest in Cromwell Company on December 31, 19X3, for $50,000. On that date, Cromwell Company's book values approximated market values. Cromwell's plant assets consisted of several pieces of equipment that were being depreciated on a straight-line basis with estimated future lives of 10 years.*

(continued)

b) On January 1, 19X6, Ackley Company purchased a 75% interest in Biernat Company for $400,000. The following determination and distribution of excess schedule was prepared at that time:

Price paid		$400,000
Less interest acquired:		
Common stock ($5 par)	$300,000	
Paid-in capital in excess of par	100,000	
Retained earnings	30,000	
Total stockholders' equity	$430,000	
Interest acquired	75%	322,500
Excess of cost over book value		$ 77,500
Excess of cost attributable to building (20-year life),		
75% × $40,000		30,000
Goodwill (10-year life)		$ 47,500

c) On January 1, 19X7, Biernat Company acquired a 40% interest in Cromwell Company for $92,000. Cromwell's book values approximated market values at this date.

d) The following stockholders' equities have been made available:

	Cromwell Company December 31		Biernat Company December 31
	19X3	19X6	19X5
Noncumulative $6 preferred stock			
($100 par and liquidating value) . . .			$ 50,000
Common stock ($5 par)			300,000
Common stock ($10 par)	$200,000	$200,000	
Paid-in capital in excess of par.			100,000
Retained earnings (deficit)	(50,000)	30,000	30,000
Total equity	$150,000	$230,000	$480,000

e) The following is information regarding intercompany merchandise sales in 19X7:

	Ackley to Cromwell	Cromwell to Biernet
Seller's merchandise in buyer's December 31, 19X6		
inventory	$ 2,000	
19X7 sales.	16,000	$5,000
Seller's merchandise in buyer's December 31, 19X7		
inventory	1,000	1,000
Intercompany receivable/payable on December 31, 19X7 . . .	3,000	500
Gross profit on sales	30%	40%

Trial balances of the three companies as of December 31, 19X7, are as follows:

	Ackley Company	Biernat Company	Cromwell Company
Cash	117,800	49,300	20,000
Accounts Receivable (net)	200,000	100,000	44,000
Inventory	277,000	206,000	58,000
Investment in Cromwell Company	50,000	92,000	
Investment in Biernat Company	400,000		
Property, Plant, and Equipment	2,800,000	1,500,000	220,000
Accumulated Depreciation	(1,120,000)	(593,000)	(90,000)
Accounts Payable	(206,000)	(112,000)	(4,000)
Bonds Payable	(1,000,000)	(700,000)	
Preferred Stock		(50,000)	
Common Stock ($5 par)	(500,000)	(300,000)	
Common Stock ($10 par)			(200,000)
Paid-In Capital in Excess of Par	(700,000)	(100,000)	
Retained Earnings, Jan. 1, 19X7	(270,000)	(61,000)	(30,000)
Sales	(1,500,000)	(850,000)	(400,000)
Subsidiary Dividend Income	(18,800)	(800)	
Cost of Goods Sold	1,050,000	552,500	240,000
Other Expenses	350,000	240,000	140,000
Preferred Dividends Declared		3,000	
Common Dividends Declared	70,000	24,000	2,000
Total	0	0	0

Required:

Prepare the worksheet necessary to produce the consolidated financial statements of Ackley Company and its subsidiaries as of December 31, 19X7. Include the determination and distribution of excess and income distribution schedules.

Problem 8-9.   On January 1, 19X1, Paro Company purchased 80% of the common stock of Salger Company for $368,000. On this date, Salger had common stock, other paid-in capital, and retained earnings of $50,000, $140,000, and $220,000, respectively.

Any excess of cost over book value is due to goodwill, to be amortized over the maximum period permitted.

In both 19X1 and 19X2, Paro has accounted for the investment in Salger using the cost method.

On January 1, 19X2, Salger purchased 500 shares (5%) of the common stock of Paro Company from outside investors for $37,500. It is expected that the shares may be resold later. Salger uses the cost method in accounting for the investment. Any excess is attributed to goodwill with a 5-year life.

During the last quarter of 19X2, Paro sold merchandise to Salger for $40,000, one-fourth of which is still held by Salger on December 31, 19X2. Paro's usual gross profit on intercompany sales is 40%.

(continued)

The trial balances for Paro and Salger on December 31, 19X2, are as follows:

	Paro Company	Salger Company
Inventory.	170,000	120,000
Other Current Assets	248,000	258,500
Investment in Salger Company	368,000	
Investment in Paro Company.		37,500
Land.	80,000	70,000
Buildings and Equipment	400,000	280,000
Accumulated Depreciation	(180,000)	(90,000)
Current Liabilities	(98,000)	(74,000)
Long-Term Liabilities.	(250,000)	(100,000)
Common Stock—Paro Company	(100,000)	
Other Paid-In Capital—Paro Company	(200,000)	
Retained Earnings—Paro Company	(350,000)	
Common Stock—Salger Company.		(50,000)
Other Paid-In Capital—Salger Company.		(140,000)
Retained Earnings—Salger Company.		(260,000)
Net Sales	(640,000)	(350,000)
Cost of Goods Sold	360,000	200,000
Operating Expenses	160,000	90,000
Dividend Income.	(8,000)	(2,000)
Dividends Declared.	40,000	10,000
Total	0	0

Required:

Complete the worksheet for consolidated financial statements for the year ended December 31, 19X2. Use the treasury stock method for the investment in Paro Company. Round all computations to the nearest dollar. Include a determination and distribution of excess schedule and income distribution schedule.

Problem 8-10.   Using the data of Problem 8-9, prepare the 19X2 consolidated worksheet of Paro Company and its subsidiary using the reciprocal method. The distribution of combined net income should be determined by solving simultaneous equations. Include a determination and distribution of excess schedule and income distribution schedule.

Problem 8-11.   On January 1, 19X6, Heckert Company purchased a controlling interest in Allen Company. The following information is available:

a) Heckert Company purchased 1,600 shares of Allen Company outstanding stock on January 1, 19X5, for $48,000 and purchased an additional 1,400 shares on January 1, 19X6, for $52,000.

b) An analysis of the stockholders' equity accounts at December 31, 19X5, and 19X4, follows:

	Heckert Company December 31		Allen Company December 31	
	19X5	19X4	19X5	19X4
Common stock ($10 par)	$150,000	$150,000		
Common stock ($5 par)			$ 20,000	$ 20,000
Paid-in capital in excess of par	36,000	36,000	10,000	10,000
Retained earnings	378,000	285,000	112,000	82,000
Total	$564,000	$471,000	$142,000	$112,000

c) Allen Company's marketable securities consist of 1,500 shares of Heckert Company stock purchased on June 15, 19X6, in the open market for $18,000. The securities were purchased as a temporary investment and were sold on January 15, 19X7, for $25,000.

d) On December 10, 19X6, Heckert Company declared a cash dividend of $.50 per share, payable January 10, 19X7, to stockholders of record on December 20, 19X6. Allen Company paid a cash dividend of $1 per share on June 30, 19X6, and distributed a 10% stock dividend on September 30, 19X6. The stock was selling for $15 per share ex-dividend on September 30, 19X6. Allen Company paid no dividends in 19X5.

e) Allen Company sold machinery, with a book value of $4,000 and a remaining life of 5 years, to Heckert Company for $4,800 on December 31, 19X6. The gain on the sale was credited to the other income account.

f) Allen Company includes all intercompany receivables and payables in its trade accounts receivable and trade accounts payable accounts.

g) During 19X6, the following intercompany sales were made:

	Net Sales	Included in Purchaser's Inventory at December 31, 19X6
Heckert Company to Allen Company.	$ 78,000	$24,300
Allen Company to Heckert Company.	104,000	18,000
	$182,000	$42,300

Heckert Company sells merchandise to Allen Company at cost. Allen Company sells merchandise to Heckert at the regular selling price to make a normal profit margin of 30%. There were no intercompany sales in prior years.

The trial balances of the two companies at December 31, 19X6, are as follows:

	Heckert Company	Allen Company
Cash	37,900	29,050
Marketable Securities	33,000	18,000
Trade Accounts Receivable	210,000	88,000
Allowance for Doubtful Accounts	(6,800)	(2,300)
Intercompany Receivables	24,000	
Inventories	275,000	135,000
Machinery and Equipment	514,000	279,000

(continued)

	Heckert Company	Allen Company
Accumulated Depreciation.	(298,200)	(196,700)
Investment in Allen Company (at cost)	100,000	
Patents.	35,000	
Dividends Payable.	(7,500)	
Trade Accounts Payable	(195,500)	(174,050)
Intercompany Payables.	(8,000)	
Common Stock ($10 par)	(150,000)	
Common Stock ($5 par)		(22,000)
Paid-In Capital in Excess of Par	(36,000)	(14,000)
Retained Earnings	(370,500)	(102,000)
Sales and Services.	(850,000)	(530,000)
Dividend Income	(3,000)	
Other Income	(9,000)	(3,700)
Cost of Goods Sold	510,000	374,000
Depreciation Expense.	65,600	11,200
Administrative and Selling Expenses	130,000	110,500
Total	0	0

Required:

Prepare the worksheet necessary to produce the consolidated financial statements of Heckert Company and its subsidiary for the year ended December 31, 19X6. Include the determination and distribution of excess and income distribution schedules. Assume any excess of cost over book value is attributable to goodwill with a 20-year life. For any mutual holdings, use the treasury stock method.

(AICPA adapted)

Worksheet 8-1

Indirect Holdings; Intercompany Sales
Company A and Subsidiary Companies B and C
Worksheet for Consolidated Financial Statements
For Year Ended December 31, 19X3

	(Credit balance amounts are in parentheses.)	Trial Balance		
		Company A	Company B	Company C
1	Inventory, Dec. 31, 19X3	80,000	20,000	30,000
2				
3	Other Assets	60,000	146,000	130,000
4	Building and Equipment	300,000	200,000	150,000
5	Accumulated Depreciation	(100,000)	(60,000)	(30,000)
6	Investment in Company B	643,000		
7				
8				
9	Investment in Company C		318,000	
10				
11				
12	Goodwill			
13	Common Stock ($10 par), Co. A	(300,000)		
14	**Retained Earnings, Jan. 1, 19X3, Co. A**	**(500,000)**		
15				
16				
17				
18	Common Stock ($10 par), Co. B		(200,000)	
19	**Retained Earnings, Jan. 1, 19X3, Co. B**		**(300,000)**	
20				
21				
22				
23	Common Stock ($10 par), Co. C			(100,000)
24	**Retained Earnings, Jan. 1, 19X3, Co. C**			**(150,000)**
25				
26	Sales	(400,000)	(300,000)	(150,000)
27	Cost of Goods Sold	250,000	160,000	80,000
28				
29				
30	Expenses	60,000	40,000	40,000
31				
32	Subsidiary Income	(93,000)	(24,000)	
33				
34		0	0	0
35	Combined Net Income			
36	To Minority Interest, Company C (see distribution schedule)			
37	To Minority Interest, Company B (see distribution schedule)			
38	To Controlling Interest (see distribution schedule)			
39	Total Minority Interest			
40	Retained Earnings, Controlling Interest, Dec. 31, 19X3			
41				

Worksheet 8-1 (see page 8-18)

Eliminations & Adjustments		Consolidated Income Statement	Minority Interest	Controlling Retained Earnings	Consolidated Balance Sheet	
Dr.	Cr.					
	(11) 2,500				124,500	1
	(13) 3,000					2
					336,000	3
(3) 175,000					825,000	4
	(4) 52,500				(242,500)	5
	(1) 93,000					6
	(2) 375,000					7
	(3) 175,000					8
	(5) 24,000					9
	(6) 200,000					10
	(7) 94,000					11
(7) 94,000	(8) **9,400**				84,600	12
					(300,000)	13
(4) 35,000				(458,895)		14
(8) **3,525**						15
(10) 1,500						16
(12) **1,080**						17
(2) 150,000			(50,000)			18
(2) 225,000			(72,965)			19
(8) **1,175**						20
(10) 500						21
(12) **360**						22
(6) 80,000			(20,000)			23
(6) 120,000			(29,640)			24
(12) **360**						25
(9) 90,000		(760,000)				26
(11) 2,500	(9) 90,000	401,700				27
(13) 3,000	(10) 2,000					28
	(12) **1,800**					29
(4) 17,500		162,200				30
(8) **4,700**						31
(1) 93,000						32
(5) 24,000						33
1,122,200	1,122,200					34
		(196,100)				35
		5,760	(5,760)			36
		29,460	(29,460)			37
		160,880		(160,880)		38
			(207,825)		(207,825)	39
				(619,775)	(619,775)	40
					0	41

(continued)

Eliminations and Adjustments:

(1) Eliminate the entry made by Company A to record its share of Company B income. This step returns the investment in Company B account to its January 1, 19X3 balance to aid the elimination process.

(2) Eliminate 75% of the January 1, 19X3 Company B equity balances against the investment in Company B.

(3) Distribute the $175,000 excess of cost to the building and equipment account according to the determination and distribution of excess schedule applicable to the level one investment.

(4) Amortize the excess (added depreciation) according to the determination and distribution of excess schedule. This step requires adjustment of Company A retained earnings for 19X1 and 19X2, plus adjustment of 19X3 expenses.

(5) Eliminate the entry made by Company B to record its share of Company C income. This returns the investment in Company C account to its January 1, 19X3 balance to aid elimination.

(6) Eliminate 80% of the January 1, 19X3 Company C equity balances against the investment in Company C.

(7) Distribute the $94,000 excess of cost to goodwill according to the determination and distribution of excess schedule applicable to the level two investment.

(8) Amortize the excess (goodwill amortization) according to the determination and distribution of excess schedule. Since it is created by actions of subsidiary Company B, the 19X2 amortization must be prorated 25% ($1,175) to the Company B minority interest and 75% ($3,525) to the controlling interest. Note that the Company B minority interest appears on the worksheet only after the first-level investment has been eliminated, again pointing to the need to eliminate the level one investment first.

(9) Eliminate intercompany sales to prevent double counting in the consolidated sales and cost of goods sold.

(10) Eliminate the Company B profit contained in the beginning inventory. Since Company B generated the sale, the correction of beginning retained earnings is split 75% to the controlling interest and 25% to the minority interest. The cost of goods sold is decreased since the beginning inventory was overstated.

(11) The cost of goods sold is adjusted and the ending inventory is reduced by the $2,500 of Company B profit contained in the ending inventory.

(12) Eliminate the Company C profit contained in the beginning inventory. Since Company C generated the retained earnings adjustment, it is apportioned as follows:

To minority interest in Company C (20%)	$ 360
To minority interest in Company B (25% of 80%)	360
To controlling interest (75% of 80%)	1,080
Total	$1,800

(13) The cost of goods sold is adjusted and the ending inventory is reduced by the $3,000 of Company C profit contained in the ending inventory.

Company C Income Distribution

Ending inventory profit . . . . (13)	$ 3,000	Internally generated income	$ 30,000
		Beginning inventory profit . . . . **(12)**	**1,800**
		Adjusted income	$ 28,800
		Company B share, 80%	23,040
		Company C minority interest, 20%	$5,760

Company B Income Distribution

Ending inventory profit . . . . (11)	$ 2,500	Internally generated income	$100,000
Amortization of goodwill resulting		Beginning inventory profit . . . . (10)	2,000
from purchase of investment in		80% of Company C adjusted income . . .	23,040
Company C . . . . **(8)**	**4,700**		
		Adjusted income	$117,840
		Company A share, 75%	88,380
		Company B minority interest, 25%	$ 29,460

Company A Income Distribution

Building and equipment depreciation		Internally generated income	$ 90,000
resulting from investment in		75% of Company B adjusted income. . . .	88,380
Company B. . . . . (4)	$17,500		
		Controlling interest	$160,880

Worksheet 8-2

Mutual Holdings, Treasury Stock Method
Company P and Subsidiary Company S
Worksheet for Consolidated Financial Statements
For Year Ended December 31, 19X1

	(Credit balance amounts are in parentheses.)	Trial Balance	
		Company P	Company S
1	Investment in Company S (80%)	248,000	
2			
3			
4	**Investment in Company P (10%), at cost**		**80,000**
5	Equipment	608,000	180,000
6	Accumulated Depreciation	(100,000)	(50,000)
7	Common Stock, Co. P	(500,000)	
8	Retained Earnings, Jan. 1, 19X3, Co. P	(200,000)	
9	Common Stock, Co. S		(100,000)
10	Retained Earnings, Jan 1, 19X3, Co. S		(90,000)
11	Sales	(300,000)	(200,000)
12	Cost of Goods Sold	180,000	120,000
13	Expenses	80,000	60,000
14	Subsidiary Income	(16,000)	
15	**Treasury Stock (at cost)**		
16		0	0
17	Combined Net Income		
18	To Minority Interest (see distribution schedule)		
19	Balance to Controlling Interest (see distribution schedule)		
20	Total Minority Interest		
21	Retained Earnings, Controlling Interest, Dec. 31, 19X3		
22			

Eliminations and Adjustments

(1) Eliminate the entry made by the parent during the current year to record its share of Company S income.
(2) Eliminate 80% of the January 1, 19X3 subsidiary equity balances against the investment in Company S account.
(3) Distribute the excess of cost over book value to the equipment account as specified by the determination and distribution of excess schedule applicable to the level one investment.
(4) Amortize the excess of $80,000 for the past two years and the current year.
(5) The investment in Company P must be at cost. If any equity adjustments have been made, they must be reversed and the investment in the parent returned to cost. If the shares are to be reissued, as is the case in this example, the investment is then transferred to the treasury stock account, a contra-account to total consolidated stockholders' equity.

Worksheet 8-2 (see page 8-22)

| Eliminations & Adjustments | | Consolidated Income Statement | Minority Interest | Controlling Retained Earnings | Consolidated Balance Sheet | |
Dr.	Cr.					
	(1) 16,000					1
	(2) 152,000					2
	(3) 80,000					3
	(5) 80,000					4
(3) 80,000					868,000	5
	(4) 12,000				(162,000)	6
					(500,000)	7
(4) 8,000				(192,000)		8
(2) 80,000			(20,000)			9
(2) 72,000			(18,000)			10
		(500,000)				11
		300,000				12
(4) 4,000		144,000				13
(1) 16,000						14
(5) 80,000					80,000	15
340,000	340,000					16
		(56,000)				17
		4,000	(4,000)			18
		52,000		(52,000)		19
			(42,000)		(42,000)	20
				(244,000)	(244,000)	21
					0	22

As an alternative to entry (5), the cost of the treasury shares could be used to retire them on the worksheet as follows:

Common Stock, Company P   50,000
Retained Earnings, Company P   30,000
   Investment in Company P   80,000

(continued)

Subsidiary Company S Income Distribution

Internally generated net income	$20,000
Adjusted income	$20,800
Minority share	20%
Minority interest	$ 4,000

Parent Company P Income Distribution

Amortization of excess cost— Depreciation . . . . (4)	$4,000	Internally generated net income	$40,000
		80% × Company S adjusted income of $20,000	16,000
		Controlling interest	$52,000

Worksheet 8-3

Mutual Holdings, Reciprocal Method
Company P and Subsidiary Company S
Worksheet for Consolidated Financial Statements
For Year Ended December 31, 19X3

	(Credit balance amounts are in parentheses.)	Trial Balance	
		Company P	Company S
1	Investment in Company S (80%)	248,000	
2			
3			
4	**Investment in Company P (10%)**		**84,000**
5			
6			
7	Equipment	608,000	180,000
8	Accumulated Depreciation	(100,000)	(50,000)
9	Goodwill		
10	**Common Stock, Co. P**	**(500,000)**	
11	**Retained Earnings, Jan. 1, 19X3, Co. P**	**(200,000)**	
12			
13	Common Stock, Co. S		(100,000)
14	Retained Earnings, Jan. 1, 19X3, Co. S		(90,000)
15	Sales	(300,000)	(200,000)
16	Cost of Goods Sold	180,000	120,000
17	Expenses	80,000	60,000
18			
19	**Subsidiary (or Investment) Income**	**(16,000)**	**(4,000)**
20			
21		0	0
22	Combined Net Income		
23	**To Minority Interest (see solution to simultaneous equations, page 8-24)**		
24	**Balance to Controlling Interest (see solution to simultaneous equations)**		
25	Total Minority Interest		
26	Retained Earnings, Controlling Interest, Dec. 31, 19X3		
27			

Eliminations and Adjustments

(1–4) Same as entries 1–4 of Worksheet 8-2.
(5) Eliminate the entry made by Company S to record its share of Company P income.
(6) Eliminate 10% of the January 1, 19X3 parent equity balances against the investment in Company P account. Note that 10% of the original January 1, 19X3 Company P retained earnings is eliminated without regard to the $8,000 amortization of excess adjustment since this adjustment was not included in the original determination and distribution of excess schedule.

Worksheet 8-3 (see page 8-24)

Eliminations & Adjustments Dr.	Eliminations & Adjustments Cr.	Consolidated Income Statement	Minority Interest	Controlling Retained Earnings	Consolidated Balance Sheet	
	(1) 16,000					1
	(2) 152,000					2
	(3) 80,000					3
	(5) 4,000					4
	(6) 70,000					5
	(7) 10,000					6
(3) 80,000					868,000	7
	(4) 12,000				(162,000)	8
(7) 10,000	(8) 1,000				9,000	9
(6) 50,000					(450,000)	10
(4) 8,000				(172,000)		11
(6) 20,000						12
(2) 80,000			(20,000)			13
(2) 72,000			(18,000)			14
		(500,000)				15
		300,000				16
(4) 4,000						17
(8) 1,000		145,000				18
(1) 16,000						19
(5) 4,000						20
345,000	345,000					21
		(55,000)				22
		4,913	(4,913)			23
		50,087		(50,087)		24
			(42,913)		(42,913)	25
				(222,087)	(222,087)	26
					0	27

(7) Distribute the excess of cost over book value to the goodwill account as specified by the determination and distribution of excess schedule.

(8) Amortize the excess for the current year.

(continued)

Company S Adjusted Internally Generated Income (see page 8-24)

Amortization of excess cost—goodwill amortizaton. . . . . (8)	$1,000	Unadjusted internally generated income. .	$20,000
		Adjusted.	$19,000

Company P Adjusted Internally Generated Income (see page 8-24)

Amortization of excess cost— depreciation . . . . (4)	$4,000	Unadjusted internally generated income. .	$40,000
		Adjusted.	$36,000

Note: If intercompany profit adjustments existed, they would be entered in the income distribution schedule.

SPECIAL APPENDIX

2

Possible New Consolidation Procedures— Changes in Parent's Interest and Subsidiary Equity

The 1995 FASB Exposure Draft on Consolidated Financial Statements and the revisions contained in the 1996 Working Draft of the Consolidations Statement would change several of the procedures currently found in Chapters 7 and 8. There would no longer be separate accounting for each block in step purchases. There would be only one adjustment to market value and only one determination and distribution of excess schedule prepared on the date control is achieved.

There would no longer be a gain recorded when the parent sells a part of its interest but retains control. This transaction, and any change in the parent's equity caused by subsidiary stock transactions, would be considered to be an adjustment to paid-in capital. These transactions would no longer result in an income statement gain or loss.

The specific effects of possible changes contained in the FASB proposals are discussed below, as they apply to major topic areas in Chapters 7 and 8.

Chapter 7 Topics

Piecemeal Acquisitions

This area is simplified. There will no longer be separate purchase blocks with separate determination and distribution of excess schedules. A determination and distribution schedule is prepared only once, on the date control is achieved. Assets and liabilities are also adjusted only once, on the date control is achieved. When control is achieved with the first block, there will be no adjustments to any asset or liability accounts when the second block is purchased. The difference between the price paid for the second block and the equity purchased (using the values as adjusted by the purchase that established control) is an adjustment to controlling paid-in capital (a price in excess of the equity purchased may require a reduction of retained earnings when no paid-in excess exists). When control is achieved with a later block, the carrying value of the former block will be added to the price paid for the later block. A single determination and distribution of excess schedule will be prepared based on this summed price.

Control Achieved with First Block

When control is achieved with the initial investment, consolidation procedures already are in effect when subsequent blocks are purchased. The accounts of the subsidiary were adjusted to market value on the date control was achieved. These values are not revised when the later block is purchased. Therefore, no change in accounting methods is required. At the time that a later block is purchased, the price paid for it will be compared to the adjusted carrying value of the noncontrolling interest (NCI) purchased. The carrying value of the NCI reflects the market values assigned on the day control was achieved less subsequent amortizations. A difference between the price paid and the carrying value of the NCI will be an adjustment to the parent's paid-in capital. If the carrying value of the NCI exceeds the price paid and parent's paid-in capital is insufficient to absorb the adjustments, retained earnings would be reduced.

Assume Company P purchases its original controlling 60% interest in Company S on January 1, 19X1, for $126,000, when Company S has the following balance sheet:

Assets		Liabilities and Equity	
Current assets.	$ 50,000	Liabilities	$ 40,000
Equipment (net).	150,000	Common stock ($10 par)	100,000
		Retained earnings	60,000
Total assets.	$200,000	Total liabilities and equity	$200,000

Further, assume that the current assets require no adjustment, and the equipment has a net market value of $180,000 and a 5-year remaining life. Goodwill resulting from the purchase of the stock will be amortized over a 10-year period. The example which follows records only the goodwill applicable to the controlling interest. The following determination and distribution of excess schedule would be prepared on January 1, 19X1, for the purchase of the first 60% interest:

	Company	Controlling Percent	Controlling Interest
Price paid for investment including direct acquisition costs:			$126,000
Market value of total net assets:	$190,000	60%	114,000
Market value of priority accounts:.	10,000	60	6,000
Analysis of price: **Goodwill**.			12,000

	Total	Controlling	NCI		Amort-ization Periods	Controlling Amort-ization	NCI Amort-ization
Price paid for investment		$126,000					
Less book value interest acquired:							
Common stock ($10 par)	$100,000						
Retained earnings	60,000						
Total stockholders' equity.	$160,000						
Interest acquired	60%	96,000					
Excess of cost over book value (debit) . .		30,000					
Equipment	30,000	18,000	12,000	Dr.	5	3,600	2,400
Goodwill	$ 12,000	$ 12,000		Dr.	10	1,200	
Total NCI adjustment			$ 12,000				

On January 1, 19X3, Company P purchases another 20% interest for $50,000. At that date, Company S's retained earnings are $100,000. The price paid for the 20% interest would be compared to the adjusted book value of the noncontrolling interest purchased. The schedule would be prepared as follows:

Price paid for 20% interest on January 1, 19X3		$50,000
Book value of 40% noncontrolling interest:		
Common stock, $10 par, 40% of $100,000.	$40,000	
Retained earnings (January 1, 19X3),		
40% of $100,000	40,000	
Remaining unamortized adjustment to market value		
made on January 1, 19X1, 3/5 of $12,000.	7,200	
Adjusted noncontrolling interest.	87,200	
Portion of noncontrolling interest purchased		
20% purchased of total 40% noncontrolling interest . .	.5	
Adjusted carrying value of interest purchased		43,600
Decrease in equity		$ 6,400

It is recommended that the parent company make this adjustment at the time the later interest is purchased. The entry to record the investment would then be

Investment in Company S ($50,000 cost − $6,400 adjustment) . . .	43,600	
Paid-in capital in excess of par, Company P	6,400	
Cash		50,000

If this adjustment to record the investment account at the noncontrolling adjusted book value was not made at the time of purchase, it would have to be made each year as an adjustment on the consolidated worksheet. This would be done prior to making eliminations, as is the case with a cost-to-equity conversion entry.

Future consolidated worksheets would eliminate an 80% controlling interest and would continue to adjust all accounts based on market values on the date that control was achieved (January 1, 19X1 with a 60% purchase). The subsequent 20% interest does create some complications for the consolidation process. Worksheet SA2-1, on pages SA2-12 to SA2-15, is prepared on December 31, 19X3, the end of the year during which the added 20% interest was purchased. Notice the following amounts in the trial balance of Company P:

1.   The investment account balance is derived as follows:

Cost of 60% interest on January 1, 19X1	$126,000
Equity adjustments for 19X1 and 19X2,	
60% × $40,000 increase in retained earnings.	24,000
Cost of 20% interest on January 1, 19X3	50,000
Adjustment to paid-in excess at time of 20% purchase.	(6,400)
Equity adjustment for 19X3, 80% × $35,000 Company S income. . .	28,000
Balance, December 31, 19X3.	$221,600

2.   Company P's paid-in excess is $100,000 at the time of the 20% purchase on January 1, 19X3, less the $6,400 adjustment applicable to the 20% investment.

Eliminations are slightly affected by the two-block purchase. Entry (1) eliminates the current-year equity adjustment on the total 80% interest, and entry (2) eliminates 80% of the subsidiary equity and the $3,600 (½ of $7,200 balance) NCI adjustment applicable to the interest purchased on January 1, 19X3. Entry (3) distributes the original $30,000 excess and $12,000 NCI adjustment according to the determination and distribution of excess schedule prepared when control was achieved on January 1,

19X1. Entries (3a) and (3b) distribute the excess to Equipment and Goodwill, using the information on the original determination and distribution of excess schedule. The amortization of excess for the building is amortized to the controlling retained earnings and NCI adjustment accounts using the 60/40 investment ratio that existed during the amortization periods. The income distribution schedules allocate the subsidiary income 80/20, based on the controlling/noncontrolling ownership interests at year-end.

Recall from Special Appendix 1 that, under the *economic unit concept*, all accounts except goodwill are adjusted to 100% of market value on the determination and distribution of excess schedule. The NCI shares in the adjustment and shares the subsequent amortizations of the excess. Notice that the amortization of the excess attributed to the building is debited to the subsidiary income distribution schedule. This assures that the adjustment, along with all other subsidiary income items, is split 20/80 to the minority and controlling interests.

If the investments were carried under the cost method, it would be necessary to do a cost-to-equity conversion **separately for each block.** This is the case since each block would be adjusted only for the increase in retained earnings of the subsidiary during the period of ownership for each block.

Control Not Achieved upon Initial Investment

There will no longer be separate determination and distribution of excess schedules for each block. There will be only one schedule and only one adjustment of subsidiary values on the date control is achieved. The carrying value of the prior purchase will be "rolled into" the price paid for the later interest, to arrive at one combined price, which will be used to prepare the determination and distribution of excess schedule. If, for example, the parent company owned a 10% interest and later purchased a 60% interest, a single determination and distribution of excess schedule would be prepared for the combined 70% interest.

The early block is added to the later block at the following values:

- Influential investment is added at its equity-adjusted cost. The investment should be equity adjusted for any partial period, prior to the purchase of the controlling interest.
- An *available for sale* category investment is added at its original cost. Any existing market value adjustment is reversed out of the Market Value Adjustment account and the Other Comprehensive Income (equity adjustment) account.
- A *trading* category security is added at its adjusted market value, on the date the controlling interest is purchased.

Sale of Parent Interest

There is no change in procedures when control is lost. There is a change in recording when there is not a loss of control. The difference between the equity-adjusted cost (including amortizations of excess) and the price paid is no longer a gain or loss; it is now an adjustment of controlling paid-in capital (unless there is a decrease in equity and there is no controlling paid-in capital, in which case retained earnings are reduced).

A special procedure has been added when there is a later sale which results in the loss of control. The prior adjustment to paid-in capital (or retained earnings for some decreases) is reversed and is added to (or deducted from) the gain or loss on the later sale.

Chapter 8 Topics

Subsidiary Sale of Its Own Common Stock

The impact on the controlling equity will continue to be calculated as is shown on pages 8-6 to 8-16. Any adjustment needed will always be recorded as an adjustment of controlling paid-in capital. There will no longer be a gain or loss recorded (even if the offering is public). If the parent purchases additional shares, the net adjustments calculated on page 8-13 will always be an adjustment of controlling paid-in capital. There will no longer be a "new block" if the controlling ownership percentage increases.

Subsidiary Purchase of Its Own Shares

There will no longer be a "new block" for the increase in parent percentage ownership. Instead, the net impact of the transaction on the controlling interest will be calculated, and it becomes an adjustment of controlling paid-in capital.

Indirect Holdings

In general, procedures do not change. As in the case of any purchase, the noncontrolling share of liability and tangible asset adjustments is now acknowledged.

Mutual Holdings

The reciprocal method is dead. Shares of the parent, held by the subsidiary, may not be treated as outstanding. The most common method to handle the shares is to treat them as treasury shares. An alternative would be to treat them as retired, with an adjustment to controlling paid-in capital.

Exercises

Exercise SA2-1 (Chapter 7). McKay Corporation purchased a 60% interest in Rocket Company on January 1, 19X1, for $150,000. On that date, Rocket Company had the following stockholders' equity:

Common stock ($10 par)	$100,000
Retained earnings	20,000
	$120,000

Any excess of cost over market value was due to equipment with a 10-year life.

McKay Corporation purchased another 20% interest for $40,000 on January 1, 19X3, when Rocket Company had the following stockholders' equity:

Common stock ($10 par)	$100,000
Retained earnings	50,000
	$150,000

On December 31, 19X5, McKay Corporation and Rocket Company had the following balance sheets:

(continued)

Assets	McKay Corporation	Rocket Company
Current assets	$ 270,000	$ 80,000
Investment in Rocket Company	190,000	
Property, plant, and equipment	740,000	240,000
Total assets	$1,200,000	$320,000

Liabilities and Stockholders Equity		
Current liabilities	$400,000	$100,000
Stockholders' equity:		
Common stock ($10 par)	500,000	100,000
Retained earnings	300,000	120,000
Total liabilities and stockholders' equity	$1,200,000	$320,000

Prepare the consolidated balance sheet of McKay Corporation and subsidiary Rocket Company on December 31, 19X5, subsequent to the purchase of the additional 20% block by McKay. The NCI is not adjusted for goodwill.

Exercise SA2-2 (Chapter 7).   Bridge Corporation purchased a 10% interest in Martin Company on January 1, 19X1, for $35,000. The investment was classified as a trading security.

On January 1, 19X6, Bridge Corporation purchased 7,000 additional shares of Martin Company from existing shareholders for $266,000. This purchase raised Bridge's interest to 80%. Martin Company had the following balance sheet just prior to Bridge's second purchase:

Assets		Liabilities and Equity	
Current assets	$125,000	Liabilities	$ 65,000
Building (net)	140,000	Common stock ($10 par) . . .	100,000
Equipment (net)	100,000	Retained earnings	200,000
Total assets	$365,000	Total liabilities and equity . . .	$365,000

At the time of the second purchase, Bridge determined that Martin's equipment was understated by $50,000 and had a 5-year remaining life. All other book values approximated market values. Any remaining excess was attributed to goodwill with a 20-year life. The NCI was not adjusted for goodwill.

1. Record any adjustment to the original 10% interest as a result of achieving control.
2. Prepare a determination and distribution of excess schedule for the second purchase.
3. Record the investment made by Bridge on January 1, 19X6.

Exercise SA2-3 (Chapter 8).   Phoenix Company owned a 90% interest in Willow Company on January 1, 19X6, when Willow had the following stockholders' equity:

Common stock ($10 par)	$100,000
Paid-in capital in excess of par	250,000
Retained earnings	200,000
Total stockholders' equity	$550,000

On July 1, 19X6, Willow sold 2,000 additional shares to noncontrolling share-holders in a public offering for $48 per share. Willow's net income for 19X6 was $50,000, and the income was earned evenly during the year.

Phoenix uses the simple equity method to record the investment in Willow. Summary entries are made each December 31 to record the year's activity.

Prepare Phoenix's equity adjustments for 19X6 that result from the above activities of Willow Company during 19X6. Assume Phoenix has $500,000 of paid-in capital in excess of par.

Exercise SA2-4 (Chapter 8).   On January 1, 19X8, Sam Company purchased an 80% interest in GT Company for $400,000. On the purchase date, GT Company had the following stockholders' equity:

Common stock ($10 par)	$200,000
Paid-in capital in excess of par	100,000
Retained earnings	150,000
Total stockholders' equity	$450,000

Assets and liabilities have market value equal to book values. Any excess is due to goodwill and is to be amortized over a 20-year life.

GT Company had net income of $50,000 for 19X8. No dividends were paid or declared during 19X8.

On January 1, 19X9, GT Company sold 10,000 shares of common stock at $40 per share in a public offering.

Assuming the parent uses the simple equity method, prepare all parent company entries required for the issuance of the shares.

Assume the following alternative situations:

1. Sam Company purchased 8,000 shares.
2. Sam Company purchased 9,000 shares.
3. Sam Company purchased 5,000 shares.

Suggestion: It is helpful to use a 3-column table which, for each case, organizes the changes in ownership interest. See the schedule on page 8-13.

Problems

Problem SA2-1 (Chapter 7).   On January 1, 19X4, Rogers Company purchased a 20% interest in Tilman Company for $100,000. Two years subsequent to this purchase, Rogers Company acquired an additional 45% interest in Tilman Company for $247,500.

Balance sheets of Tilman Company immediately prior to these purchases were as follows:

Assets	Jan. 1, 19X4	Jan. 1, 19X6
Current assets	$150,000	$120,000
Land.	150,000	150,000
Equipment (net)	200,000	300,000
Total assets	$500,000	$570,000

(continued)

Liabilities and Equity		
Liabilities.	$100,000	$110,000
Equity:		
Common stock ($5 par).	100,000	100,000
Paid-in capital in excess of par	150,000	150,000
Retained earnings.	150,000	210,000
Total equity	$400,000	$460,000
Total liabilities and stockholders' equity	$500,000	$570,000

On January 1, 19X4, and January 1, 19X6, Tilman's book values approximated market values, except for the land, which was undervalued by $50,000. Any resulting goodwill is being amortized over 10 years.

The original 20% investment had been maintained under the sophisticated equity method. Since it now will be necessary to prepare consolidated statements, the simple equity method is in use for 19X6.

On December 31, 19X6, Rogers' investment in Tilman Company was determined as follows:

Original cost of 20% investment	$100,000
19X4–X5 equity adjustment, net of excess amortization	10,000
Original cost of 45% investment	247,500
65% of income, January 1, 19X6–December 31, 19X6.	26,000
Investment in Tilman Company.	$383,500

The following trial balances were prepared on December 31, 19X6:

	Rogers Company	Tilman Company
Current assets	252,500	225,000
Investment in Tilman Company.	383,500	
Land	240,000	150,000
Building (net)	480,000	
Equipment (net)	400,000	220,000
Other assets	20,000	5,000
Liabilities	(340,000)	(100,000)
Common stock ($10 par)	(1,000,000)	
Common stock ($5 par)		(100,000)
Paid-in capital in excess of par		(150,000)
Retained earnings, January 1, 19X6.	(350,000)	(210,000)
Sales.	(900,000)	(350,000)
Subsidiary income.	(26,000)	
Cost of goods sold.	540,000	180,000
Other expenses.	250,000	130,000
Dividends declared	50,000	
Total	0	0

Required:

Prepare the worksheet necessary to produce the consolidated financial statements of Rogers Company and its subsidiary as of December 31, 19X6. Include the determination and distribution of excess and income distribution schedules. The NCI is not adjusted for goodwill.

Problem SA2-2 (Comprehensive).   On January 1, 19X1, Croy Company purchased for $160,000 an 80% interest (8,000 shares) directly from Heath Company on the day Heath was organized.

On April 1, 19X5, Croy Company purchased 1,000 additional shares of Heath Company for $38,900. Heath had an exceptional first quarter with income of $9,000. No dividends had been paid. Any excess of cost is considered to be goodwill with a 10-year life. Unrealized intercompany gains and losses applicable to the 10% interest are ignored on the basis of materiality.

The subsidiary sells merchandise to the parent at cost plus 50%. Intercompany sales were $60,000 during 19X5; $20,000 was unpaid at year-end. There were $9,000 of such goods in the beginning inventory of Croy Company and $15,000 of such goods in the ending inventory. However, the ending inventory had been adjusted down to its market value of $12,000.

The parent sold a machine with a book value of $10,000 to the subsidiary for $15,000 on January 1, 19X4. The machine had a 5-year life as of January 1, 19X4, and is being depreciated on a straight-line basis.

Heath Company issued $100,000 of face value, 5-year, 6% bonds on January 1, 19X3. The bonds sold at a premium of $4,500 since the market rate of interest was 5%. On January 1, 19X4, when the market rate was 8%, Croy Company purchased all of these bonds for $93,400. Straight-line amortization is being used for the bonds.

Heath Company paid a $1 per share cash dividend on December 31, 19X5.

The following trial balances were prepared as of December 31, 19X5:

	Croy Company	Heath Company
Cash	12,050	103,700
Accounts receivable	80,000	40,000
Inventory	43,100	63,000
Plant and equipment	400,000	300,000
Accumulated depreciation	(200,000)	(80,000)
Investment in Heath Company stock	198,900	
Investment in Heath Company bonds	96,700	
Liabilities	(64,100)	(40,000)
6% bonds payable		(100,000)
Premium on bonds payable		(1,800)
Common stock ($10 par)	(200,000)	(100,000)
Paid-in capital in excess of par		(100,000)
Retained earnings, January 1, 19X5	(300,000)	(80,000)
Sales	(250,000)	(120,000)
Cost of goods sold	150,000	80,000
Other expenses	50,000	20,000
Subsidiary income	(9,000)	
Interest income	(7,650)	
Interest expense		5,100
Dividends declared		10,000
Total	0	0

Required:

Prepare the worksheet necessary to produce the consolidated financial statements of Croy Company and its subsidiary as of December 31, 19X5. Include the determination and distribution of excess and income distribution schedules.

Suggestion: Determine what method Croy Company is using to maintain its investment in Heath Company stock account (i.e., cost, simple equity, or sophisticated equity) before attempting the requirements of this problem.

Worksheet SA2-1

Investment Acquired in Blocks; Immediate Control
Company P and Subsidiary Company S
Worksheet for Consolidated Financial Statements
For Year Ended December 31, 19X3

	(Credit balance amounts are in parentheses.)	Trial Balance	
		Company P	Company S
1	Current Assets	60,000	130,000
2	Investment in Company S	221,600	
3			
4			
5	Building	400,000	80,000
6	Accumulated Depreciation—Building	(100,000)	(5,000)
7	Equipment		150,000
8	Accumulated Depreciation—Equipment		(90,000)
9	Goodwill		
10	Liabilities	(100,000)	(30,000)
11	Common Stock, Co. P	(100,000)	
12	Paid-In Capital in Excess of Par, Co. P	(93,600)	
13	Retained Earnings, Co. P	(210,000)	
14			
15	Common Stock, Co. S		(100,000)
16			
17	Retained Earnings, Company S		(100,000)
18			
19	Paid-in Capital, Market Adjustment, Co. S		
20			
21	Sales	(400,000)	(200,000)
22	Cost of Goods Sold	300,000	120,000
23	Expenses	50,000	45,000
24			
25	Subsidiary Income	(28,000)	
26	Totals	0	0
27	Consolidated Net Income		
28	To Noncontrolling Interest (see income distribution schedule)		
29	To Controlling Interest (see income distribution schedule)		
30	Total Noncontrolling Interest		
31	Controlling Retained Earnings		
32			

Worksheet SA2-1 (see page SA2-3)

Eliminations & Adjustments				Consolidated Income Statement	Noncontrolling Interest	Controlling Retained Earnings	Consolidated Balance Sheet	
Dr.		Cr.						
							190,000	1
		(1)	28,000					2
		(2)	163,600					3
		(3)	30,000					4
							480,000	5
							(105,000)	6
							150,000	7
(3a)	30,000	(4a)	18,000				(78,000)	8
(3b)	12,000	(4b)	3,600				8,400	9
							(130,000)	10
							(100,000)	11
							(93,600)	12
(4a)	7,200					(200,400)		13
(4b)	2,400							14
(2)	80,000				(20,000)			15
								16
(2)	80,000				(20,000)			17
								18
(2)	3,600	(3)	12,000		(3,600)			19
(4a)	4,800							20
				(600,000)				21
				420,000				22
(4a)	6,000			102,200				23
(4b)	1,200							24
(1)	28,000							25
	255,200		255,200					26
				(77,800)				27
				5,800	(5,800)			28
				72,000		(72,000)		29
					(49,400)		(49,400)	30
						(272,400)	(272,400)	31
							0	32

(continued)

Worksheet SA2-1 Eliminations and adjustments:

(1) Eliminate the $28,000 simple equity adjustment for the current year.

(2) Eliminate the total 80% ownership interest against the sum of the subsidiary equity accounts on January 1 of the current year and ½ the NCI adjustment balance on January 1 of the current year.

(3) Distribute the $30,000 original excess applicable to the controlling interest and the original $12,000 NCI adjustment to

 (3a) Equipment—accumulated depreciation, $30,000

 (3b) Goodwill, $12,000

(4) Amortize excess as follows:

 (4a) Equipment, $6,000 ($30,000 ÷ 5 years) per year for 2 prior and the current years. The $12,000 of prior-year amortization is allocated 60/40 to controlling retained earnings and the NCI account based on the ownership interests in effect during the prior periods.

 (4b) Goodwill is amortized $1,200 per year for 2 prior and the current years. The goodwill applies only to the controlling interest. It is amortized only to controlling retained earnings.

Income Distribution Schedule, Company S

Equipment amortization . . . . (4)	$6,000	Internally generated net income	$35,000
		Adjusted income.	$29,000
		Noncontrolling share.	20%
		Noncontrolling interest.	$ 5,800

Income Distribution Schedule, Company P

Goodwill amortization . . . . (5)	$1,200	Internally generated net income	$50,000
		80% × Company S adjusted income of $29,000	23,200
		Adjusted income.	$72,000

SPECIAL APPENDIX

3

Leveraged Buyouts

It has become a common occurrence to form a skeleton corporation for the sole purpose of acquiring a controlling interest in an existing corporation. Frequently, the management of the corporation to be acquired are the instigators of the acquisition. Some leveraged buyouts are financed in part by funds supplied by investment partnerships. Investors are expected to have supplied over $10 billion to these partnerships in 1994, which would equal investments made in these funds in the record year of 1987. It is anticipated that the increased funds coupled with rising prices paid in leveraged buyouts will lead to lower returns on these investments than have existed in the past.[1] A successful example of a leveraged buyout is offered by Harley Davidson Corporation, the only American manufacturer of motorcycles. Once a separate corporation, Harley Davidson was acquired by AMF Corporation. After several years of being a subsidiary, the Harley Davidson division was purchased by new investors, including employees, and again became a separate corporation.

When structured properly, a leveraged buyout follows purchase accounting principles. With only minor exceptions, the market values of the assets and liabilities of the company subject to the leveraged buyout are recorded. In order to record assets and liabilities at market value, there must be a change in control. The new control group does not have to be a single individual; it is sufficient to have a group of investors with a common interest act as a control group. The requirements for what constitutes a control group were issued by the Emerging Issues Task Force of the FASB in 1989[2].

The most difficult accounting task in a leveraged buyout is to determine the total value available for assignment to the company's assets and liabilities. The total value is the sum of the value assigned to outstanding shares of common stock. Where there may be three blocks of stock, the three blocks are the market value block, the equity-adjusted cost block, and the book value block. The number of shares included in each block is determined as follows.

Market Value Block

The block includes the shares owned by shareholders of the new control group *who were not owners* of the shares of the prior company. This block also may include the shares of some shareholders who owned shares of the prior company. In order to include a former shareholder's shares in the market value block, one of two conditions must be met:

1. The shareholder's new residual ownership interest must be greater than the residual ownership interest in the prior company. The shareholder's new resid-

---

1 Greg Steinmetz, "LBO Funds Lure Investors, But Returns Worry Some," *Wall Street Journal*, 29 June 1994.
2 Highlights of Financial Reporting Issues, *Leveraged Buyouts: Emerging Issues Task Force Consensus Issue No. 88-16* (Norwalk: Financial Accounting Standards Board, May 1989).

ual ownership interest cannot, however, exceed 5%. The residual ownership interest includes all outstanding common and preferred shares except those shares that have liquidation or redemption features. This is different from the definition of ownership interest that includes only common shares.

2. If the former shareholder's residual interest percentage decreased, all of the following requirements must be met to record the shares at market value.

   a) *The shareholder's voting interest in common stock must be under 20%.*

   b) *The individual must have supplied less than 20% of the new company's total capital including debt.*[3]

   c) *The shareholder's new residual ownership interest must be less than 5%, and all former owners whose residual ownership interest decreased must have a new residual interest of less than 20%.*

There is a limitation on the number of shares included in the market value block; it is based on the amount of monetary consideration given to owners of the former company. Monetary consideration includes cash, debt, and debt-type securities such as mandatory redeemable preferred stock. If at least 80% of the consideration given to all shareholders (including continuing shareholders) is monetary, there is no limitation on the market value block. If monetary consideration is under 80% of the total, the market value block is limited to the monetary consideration percentage times the total common shares outstanding. Thus, for example, if the percentage of shares that would otherwise qualify was 90%, but monetary consideration given for common shares was 70%, the market value block would be limited to 70% of the outstanding shares. The nonqualifying 20% interest would be assigned book value.

Equity-Adjusted Cost Block

Shares of continuing shareholders who owned shares of the former company are recorded at their simple-equity-adjusted cost unless they meet the above requirements to be included in the market value block. The shareholders whose interest does not qualify for inclusion in the market value block are termed "continuing shareholders."

Book Value Block

These are the shares that would otherwise be included in the market value block but are excluded because of the 80% monetary consideration test. Recall the prior example where 90% of the shares otherwise qualified for the market value block, but only 70% of the consideration was monetary. The excluded 20% of the shares would be valued at current book value.

Acquisition Meeting the 80% Monetary Consideration Test

As an example of a leveraged buyout's meeting the 80% monetary consideration test, assume Former Company had the following balance sheet on the date it is acquired by a new ownership group, New Company:

---

3 This test is applied in steps starting with common stock and proceeding to each lesser risk security. The test may be passed at any level. See Highlights of Financial Reporting Issues, *Leveraged Buyouts: Emerging Issues Task Force Consensus Issue No. 88-16.*

Assets		Liabilities and Equity	
Current assets	$100,000	Liabilities	$ 80,000
Land and buildings (net)	200,000	Common stock (10,000 shares, $2 par)	20,000
Equipment (net)	50,000	Paid-in capital in excess of par	70,000
		Retained earnings	180,000
Total assets	$350,000	Total liabilities and equity	$350,000

The market values of Former Company's assets and liabilities equal book value, except for the land and buildings which have a fair market value of $300,000. The market value of Former Company shares is $40 each. 10,000 shares of Former Company are acquired as follows:

1. 2,000 New Company shares are exchanged for 1,000 Former Company shares. These 1,000 shares are owned by continuing shareholders who are members of the new control group. These shares do not meet the tests required to be included in the market value block and must be recorded at simple-equity-adjusted cost. Their equity-adjusted cost for Former Company shares is $38. The shares originally were purchased for $30 when the retained earnings of Former Company were $100,000.
2. 500 Former Company shares are received in exchange for 1,000 New Company shares from parties that are former owners but that are not members of the new control group. The shares do meet the criteria to be included in the market value block.
3. The remaining 8,500 Former Company shares are purchased for $340,000 cash from shareholders that are not owners of the new company.

Monetary consideration was used to acquire 85% of Former Company shares. Since this exceeds the required 80% level, the entire interest acquired from shareholders who are not considered continuing members is recorded at market value. The value to be assigned to the net assets is calculated as follows:

Market Value Block:

8,500	shares acquired for cash at $40 market value	$340,000
500	shares acquired in exchange for 1,000 New Company shares from parties that are not continuing members at $40 market value	20,000
	Total Market Value	$360,000

Equity-Adjusted Cost Block:

1,000	shares acquired in exchange for 2,000 New Company shares from continuing shareholders at $38 simple-equity-adjusted cost	38,000
	Total	$398,000

The determination and distribution of excess schedule would be prepared as follows for the 90% interest acquired from former shareholders that are not continuing members:

Price paid, 9,000 × $40		$360,000
Interest acquired:		
Stockholders' equity	$270,000	
Percentage	90%	243,000
Excess of cost over book value		$117,000
Land and buildings, 90% × $100,000		90,000
Goodwill		$ 27,000

The determination and distribution of excess schedule would be prepared as follows for the 10% interest acquired from continuing shareholders:

Simple-equity-adjusted cost, 1,000 × $38		$38,000
Interest acquired:		
Stockholders' equity	$270,000	
Percentage	10%	27,000
Excess of cost over book value		$11,000
Land and buildings, 10% x $100,000		10,000
Goodwill.		$ 1,000

Separate determination and distribution of excess schedules are recommended for each block since it is possible to have one of the schedules indicate a bargain purchase that would not allow full recognition of market values for long-term fixed assets. If the two blocks were combined into a single determination and distribution of excess schedule, goodwill from one block could offset a bargain on another.

The entries to record the formation of New Company and to acquire Former Company are as follows:

Formation of New Company

Cash	40,000	
Common Stock, No Par (2,000 shares × $20).		40,000

Borrowing of $300,000 . . . .

Cash	300,000	
Long-Term Debt.		300,000

Acquisition of Former Company

Current Assets	100,000	
Land and Buildings ($200,000 + $90,000 + $10,000)	300,000	
Equipment	50,000	
Goodwill ($27,000 + $1,000)	28,000	
Liabilities.		80,000
Cash		340,000
Common Stock, No Par (3,000 shares in exchange for 500		
Former shares × $40 and 1,000 Former shares × $38). .		58,000

Acquisition Not Meeting the 80% Monetary Consideration Test

Let us revise the previous example slightly:

1.   Instead of borrowing $300,000, only $240,000 is borrowed.
2.   Instead of acquiring 8,500 shares for cash from parties that are not members of the new control group, assume 6,500 shares are acquired for cash at $40 each and a total of 2,500 shares is acquired by exchanging 5,00 shares of New Company common stock; 2,000 New Company shares are still being issued to former shareholders that are part of the new control group in exchange for 1,000 Former Company shares.

Now only 65% (6,500 for cash ÷ 10,000 total shares acquired) of the shares are acquired in exchange for cash and can be recorded at market value. The remaining 2,000 shares acquired from parties that were not continuing members of Former Company are recorded at book value. The value assigned to the net assets is calculated as follows:

Market Value Block:

6,500 shares acquired for cash at $40 market value $260,000

Equity-Adjusted Cost Block:

1,000 shares acquired in exchange for 2,000 New Company shares from
continuing members of Former Company; at $38 simple-equity-
adjusted cost   38,000

Book Value Block:

2,500 shares acquired in exchange for 5,000 New Company shares from
Former Company shareholders who are not a part of the new
control group at book value of $27 per share ($270,000 total
equity ÷ 10,000 shares)   67,500

Total $365,500

A determination and distribution of excess schedule would be prepared for the
65% interest acquired for cash as follows:

Price paid, 6,500 x $40		$260,000
Interest acquired:		
Stockholders' equity	$270,000	
Percentage	65%	175,500
Excess of cost over book value		$ 84,500
Land and buildings, 65% x $100,000		65,000
Goodwill		$ 19,500

The determination and distribution of excess schedule for the 1,000 shares
acquired from continuing shareholders is unchanged.

Simple-equity-adjusted cost 1,000 x $38		$38,000
Interest acquired:		
Stockholders' equity	$270,000	
Percentage	10%	27,000
Excess of cost over book value		$11,000
Land and buildings, 10% x 100,000		10,000
Goodwill		$ 1,000

There would be no adjustment to market value for the 2,000 shares acquired
from noncontinuing shareholders in exchange for New Company shares.

The entries to record the formation of New Company and acquire Former
Company are as follows:

Formation of New Company		
Cash	40,000	
Common Stock, No Par (2,000 shares)		40,000

Borrowing of $240,000		
Cash	240,000	
Long-Term Debt		240,000

(continued)

Acquisition of Former Company

Current Assets	100,000	
Land and Buildings ($200,000 + $65,000 + $10,000)	275,000	
Equipment.	50,000	
Goodwill ($19,500 + $1,000).	20,500	
Liabilities.		80,000
Cash (6,500 × 40)		260,000
Common Stock, No Par (7,000 shares in exchange for 2,500		
Former shares × $27 and 1,000 Former shares × $38). .		105,000

Special Appendix 3 Questions

1. A leveraged buyout that meets the 80% monetary consideration test may not allow the recognition of market values for the interest acquired from shareholders of the predecessor company. Under what conditions is the interest of former company shareholders recorded at market value? If market value is not allowed, at what value are the shares recorded?

2. Some of the interest acquired in a leveraged buyout may have to be recorded at the underlying book value of the former company. Under what conditions does this occur?

3. Lever Company was formed to purchase all of the outstanding shares of Ancient Company in a leveraged buyout. 85% of the outstanding Ancient shares were purchased for cash from persons not part of the new control group. The remaining shares were purchased from individuals that would qualify as continuing shareholders who are members of the new control group. What procedures would you follow to assign values to the assets of Ancient Company?

Special Appendix 3 Exercises

Exercise SA3-1.   Modum Corporation was formed on January 1, 19X1, by issuing 4,000 shares of $10 par stock for $20 per share. Modum Corporation is going to engage in a leveraged buyout of Antique Company. Antique Company had the following stockholders' equity on January 1, 19X1:

Common stock ($10 par, 10,000 shares outstanding)	$100,000
Paid-in capital in excess of par	150,000
Retained earnings	80,000
Total equity.	$330,000

The market value of Antique Company shares is $40 each. 1,000 Antique shares will be acquired from continuing members of Antique Company's control group in exchange for 2,000 Modum Corporation shares. The equity-adjusted cost of the control group's shares is $25 per share. Calculate the total cost of Antique Company under each of the following assumptions:

1. Modum Corporation borrows $280,000 and purchases for $40 each the remaining 9,000 shares held by parties outside the control group of Antique Company.

2. Modum Corporation borrows $240,000 and purchases 8,000 noncontrol group

shares for $40 each. Modum issues 2,000 of its shares in exchange for 1,000 Antique Company shares held by noncontrol group members.

3. Modum Corporation borrows $200,000 and purchases 7,000 noncontrol group shares for $40 each. Modum issues 4,000 of its shares in exchange for 2,000 Antique Company shares held by noncontrol group members.

Exercise SA3-2.   Old Time Company has the following balance sheet on January 1, 19X1, when it is the target of a leveraged buyout by Hercules Corporation:

Assets		Stockholders' Equity	
Cash.	$ 50,000	Common stock ($5 par, 10,000 shares).	$ 50,000
Inventory	100,000	Paid-in capital in excess of par .	160,000
Property and plant.	200,000	Retained earnings	140,000
Total assets.	$350,000	Total equity.	$350,000

The property and plant have a market value of $230,000.

Hercules Corporation incorporated by issuing 3,000 shares of $10 par common stock for $40 each. The company also borrowed $160,000 from long-term lenders. The leveraged buyout was accomplished as follows:

1,000   shares exchanged on a 1-to-1 basis with continuing members of the old control group. The equity-adjusted cost per share for these shares was $38. These shares do not need the criteria to be included in the market value block.

2,000   shares exchanged on a 1-to-1 basis with noncontrol group members.

7,000   shares of Old Time purchased from noncontrol group members for $40 per share.

Prepare the balance sheet of Hercules Corporation immediately after the leveraged buyout. Provide supporting calculations in good form.

Special Appendix 3 Problem

Problem SA3-1.   Newtone Company was formed on January 1, 19X5. The shareholder group issued 4,000 shares of $10 par common stock for $25 per share. The company was formed by an employee group to purchase Oldtime (a subsidiary of Gigantic Corporation) which had the following balance sheet on the January 3, 19X5 acquisition date:

Assets		Liabilities and Stockholders' Equity	
Cash.	$ 60,000	Bonds payable	$150,000
Inventory	130,000	Common stock ($10 par)	100,000
Accounts receivable.	40,000	Paid-in capital in excess	
Equipment	75,000	of par	120,000
Building (net)	120,000	Retained earning.	85,000
Land	30,000	Total liabilities and	
Total assets.	$455,000	stockholders' equity	$455,000

The market values differed from book values in the case of the inventory, equipment, and building which were appraised at $150,000, $100,000, and $200,000, respectively.

(continued)

The market value of Newtone stock is $25 per share. 2,000 Newtone shares were exchanged for 1,000 Oldtime shares with parties who were continuing members of the control group of Oldtime. These shares do not qualify for inclusion in the market value block. The equity-adjusted cost of the shares held by Oldtime's control group was $45 per share. These individuals also will be part of the control group of Newtone. The 9,000 remaining shares of Oldtime were acquired from parties that are not part of Newtone's control group.

Required:

1. Assume Newtone borrowed $250,000 on a long-term note. Newtone then paid $50 per share for 7,000 shares of Oldtime and issued 4,000 of its shares in exchange for 2,000 Oldtime shares. Prepare all entries to record the formation of Newtone Corporation, the borrowing, and the buyout of Oldtime. Include a support schedule for the values assigned to the accounts.
2. Assume Newtone borrowed $300,000 on a long-term note. Newtone then paid $50 per share for 8,000 shares of Oldtime and issued 2,000 of its shares in exchange for 1,000 Oldtime shares. Prepare all entries to record the formation of Newtone Corporation, the borrowing, and the buyout of Oldtime. Include a support schedule for the values assigned to the accounts.

Suggestion: Be sure to determine if the 80% test is met in each case before proceeding to assign values to the accounts.

PART

2

MULTINATIONAL ACCOUNTING

We are part of a truly global economy. More and more companies are engaging in activities which bring their products, services, and resources to markets which lie beyond our national boundaries. In response to these growing opportunities, accounting has also had to evolve. Accounting principles around the world differ, and it has become increasingly evident that these principles must be made more comparable or harmonious in order to serve the needs of a global economy. It is unlikely that differences between accounting principles will ever be fully eliminated. However, as harmonization proceeds, it is important to understand the various influences which shape accounting principles throughout the world. Many companies begin their involvement in the global economy by engaging in transactions with foreign parties. Often, these transactions are denominated in a foreign currency even though they must be measured in a company's domestic currency. If a transaction is denominated in a foreign currency, changes in the exchange rate between the foreign currency and the domestic currency may expose the domestic company to either an economic gain or loss. Many domestic companies have acquired equity interests in foreign companies. These investments must be measured in the domestic currency even though the financial statements of the foreign investee are measured in a foreign currency. The foreign financial statements must be translated or remeasured into the domestic currency according to specialized accounting procedures.

The International Accounting Environment

The Jacob Corporation (a fictitious company) began with a small facility in central Wisconsin, where it manufactured precision measuring devices to be used primarily in the food industry. As the company began to grow, its sales extended throughout the continental United States. While attending a trade show in Atlanta, Georgia, the company had the opportunity to arrange a sale to a foreign customer in Germany, and that was the beginning of the company's venture into export sales. The sales to the German company were collected in U.S. dollars, and the company began to expand its sales to other foreign customers. However, as these sales increased, a number of customers settled their accounts by payment in foreign currencies rather than U.S. dollars. The company quickly realized that this could be good news or bad news, depending on how the U.S. dollar performed against the respective foreign currencies. For example, if the dollar strengthened against the foreign currency, the foreign currency collected by the company when the company paid its account was actually worth fewer dollars than its value at the time of sale. To help reduce the risks that it encountered because its sales contracts were often settled in foreign currencies, Jacob Corporation retained outside consultants.

As the company grew and attempted to increase profit margins, it began to purchase sub-assemblies from a foreign vendor. Years later, the company established a foreign sales office in Frankfurt, Germany, which allowed the company to qualify for certain tax benefits associated with such sales offices as provided by the Internal Revenue Service. However, the income associated with the sales office was subject to the tax laws of Germany.

As sales continued to grow, the company decided to open another manufacturing facility. This new facility was to be built in France. The facility was established as a separate French company subject to the laws of France but owned 90% by the U.S. company. The social, language, legal, taxation, and cultural differences of operating in a foreign country were just a few of the challenges that the company was now dealing with. Shortly after opening the French facility, a national strike resulted in a shutdown of the plant for two months. The French facility has resumed production and ships approximately 40% of its production to a Brazilian company that is a wholly-owned subsidiary of the U.S. company. The transfer pricing between the French and Brazilian companies is designed to take advantage of the higher tax rate in France without violating any tax laws that discourage the manipulation of taxable income through transfer-pricing policies.

When developing business policies such as strategic planning, budgeting, inventory control, and internal control, companies have had to take into consideration the differences between the various parties involved in the operation of domestic and foreign entities. For example, the just-in-time inventory system used in the U.S. manufacturing facility may not work in a foreign manufacturing facility because of less-developed transportation systems or because of instabilities in the countries where major vendors operate.

Today, we find our U.S. company constructing its sixth manufacturing facility; this one, on the African continent. As part of its agreement with the government of the African country, the U.S. company will be constructing a health clinic and school in the community and guaranteeing a minimum employment level for the next five years. Thus, Jacob Corporation has come a long way from central Wisconsin. It may be a fictitious company, but the scenario described is a common happening in companies today. Welcome to international business and the global economy. All of this is possible when a commercial activity transcends national boundaries or borders.

In this and the following two chapters, several issues relating to international accounting will be explored, including the following:

- Factors influencing international accounting standards;
- The international standard-setting process;
- Accounting for transactions denominated in foreign currencies; and
- The translation and remeasurement of financial statements prepared in a foreign currency.

The Scope of International Business Activities

An entity's involvement in international business can range from export or import activity to that of a multinational enterprise with a global approach to manufacturing, distribution, and sales. Trade between different nations certainly is not new. It has existed since biblical times and has provided the means by which certain nations have evolved into world powers. England and the Netherlands are just two examples of countries that have been active in international trade for centuries. However, it has been since World War II that international trade has increased significantly, and many more goods and services are becoming part of a global economy.

Dramatic changes occurring in recent times have allowed a global economy to become a reality for an increasing number of entities. The restructuring of eastern Europe and the former Soviet Union has opened the door for free enterprise. The growth of the European Union has been responsible for reducing the economic barriers between nations by forming a single market which, ultimately, is intended to have its own common currency. In 1993, the United States, Mexico, and Canada agreed to a comprehensive free trade agreement known as the North American Free Trade Agreement (NAFTA). The World Trade Organization, formerly the General Agreement on Tariffs and Trade (GATT), is committed to reducing trade barriers through multilateral agreements.

As the barriers to world trade are reduced, the world becomes smaller in a number of senses. For example, modern communications technology makes it much easier to transact business between countries. The credit card purchase you made today may be processed in a center located in Ireland, and tomorrow you will be able to inquire about your account balance which will include your recent purchase. The Internet also is proving to be a significant way in which entities are making their goods and services available to consumers on an international scale.

Not only are goods and services trading in international markets, but also the securities of the companies involved. International securities trading has increased rapidly due to a number of forces. As companies expand into different international markets, they need to acquire the factors of production in those markets and, thus, need to raise additional capital. For example, the construction of a new manufacturing facility in France requires French francs to pay for the construction and other operating costs. International securities trading also offers investors the opportunity to diversify their portfolios against loss from currency fluctuations, political instabilities, and economic downturns.

The Emerging Needs for International Accounting

Multinational companies must have comparable accounting standards with which to measure the effectiveness and efficiency of their various international subsidiaries, branches, and/or other equity investments. Also, in order to efficiently allocate and regulate the exchange of capital, international capital markets need to evaluate the adequacy of financial statements and disclosures made by those companies seeking to raise capital. Comparable standards of accounting and financial disclosure for companies competing for capital on an international scale are critical to the functioning of such markets. Finally, individual investors exposed to opportunities on an international scale need comparable financial information upon which to base their decisions. Evaluating the profitability or financial position of two competing investment opportunities will have meaning only if comparable accounting standards are in place. The international growth of business and investing naturally creates a need for the international development of accounting. Thus, the development of international accounting standards must be based on an understanding of international business and markets and the factors that affect accounting in various countries.

The Focus of International Accounting

With all of the economic developments in the world occurring at such a rapid rate, it is not surprising that international accounting is also rapidly developing. Professional organizations have special interest groups focusing on the area, and a number of organizations concerned with the process of establishing international accounting standards have emerged.

The development of a global economy has drastically changed the environment in which a growing number of entities operate. It is only logical, then, to expect that financial information and accounting systems will evolve to better serve the changing environment. If goods and services are exchanged on an international scale, financial information will also need to be exchanged on a similar scale. International accounting has developed in response to these changes and is primarily focused on several major areas of interest. The primary areas of interest are as follows:

1. The identification and understanding of principles of financial accounting, managerial accounting, and taxation used in different nations, especially as to how they differ from nation to nation.
2. The identification of the various organizations and interests involved in the process of establishing international accounting and auditing principles and standards.
3. The special accounting valuation and recognition principles associated with accounting for transactions that are recorded in one nation's currency and settled in another nation's currency. These transactions are referred to as *foreign currency transactions*.
4. The translation of financial statements that are measured in one nation's currency into another nation's currency.

Due to the expanding nature of international trade and capital markets, today's accounting professional must have some knowledge of international accounting. The balance of this chapter, therefore, will focus on the various environmental factors affecting the development of accounting principles used in certain nations and the establishment of international accounting principles and standards.

The development of accounting principles and standards is an extremely complex process involving various special interest groups and varying degrees of due process. By studying the standard-setting process in the United States, one realizes how complex the process can be. This complexity holds true in the development of accounting principles and standards in other nations, too. However, it is the factors influencing the process that vary from nation to nation.

Factors Influencing the Development of Accounting

Accounting is not defined by nature but, rather, is man-made. It evolves from the environment in which man exists and defines itself in a way which serves the needs of that environment. Given the differences in various environments, it is not surprising that accounting differs between nations. A number of environmental factors such as the following may explain these differences to varying degrees:

- Social/cultural values
- Political and legal systems
- Types of business activities and economic conditions
- Standard-setting processes
- Forms of ownership and capital markets
- Cooperative efforts between nations

Social and Cultural Values.   Social and cultural differences between nations and regions of the world are well documented, and they have had a significant influence on how accounting has developed. For example, if one society places a higher value on privacy than another, it would follow that the financial statement disclosures between the two societies would reflect their respective views toward privacy as well. If a society places emphasis on the individual and his or her immediate family unit over that of a larger group of individuals, it would not be a surprise to see accounting principles being developed in a more independent manner by a professional group rather than a regulatory body. For example, since the United States has emphasized individualism and personal freedoms, the establishment of accounting principles is more the result of private influences rather than regulatory influences.

Political and Legal Systems.   A major factor influencing the development of accounting principles has been the political environment in which a nation has developed. For example, nations that previously were ruled or colonized by another country tend to have developed principles similar to those of the ruling nation. Nations such as the United States, Canada, and the Bahamas have accounting principles that historically were patterned after those found in the United Kingdom. Those nations that have more democratic political environments tend to develop principles more through private standard-setting groups than through government decree or regulation. The tax laws and legal requirements of a country also may influence the development of accounting to the extent that differences between accounting income and tax income are rare or nonexistent.

Business Activities and Economic Conditions.   The type and pace of economic development also have influenced the development of accounting. Economies which are more agrarian usually are made up of smaller family-business entities and have not experienced the need for sophisticated accounting practices, such as consolidated financial statements and capitalized lease accounting. On the other hand, those nations which have experienced more rapid economic growth have realized the need for higher-level systems of accounting. Furthermore, as businesses have grown, in most instances in a corporate form, widening investor bases and greater capital needs have led to more emphasis on financial disclosure and the need for audited financial statements.

Standard-Setting Processes.   The accounting standard-setting process and the respective views of the standard setters have certainly had an influence on how accounting has developed. The standard-setting process is in response to cultural, political, legal, and other influences. Therefore, it has become a major force through which a number of factors influence accounting. For example, as a country's economy grows, generally the standard-setting process also expands.

Forms of Ownership and Capital Markets.   In many countries, most business is still conducted by small, closely held, family businesses. As these economies move toward the corporate form of organization with an increase in equity ownership, the complexity and focus of accounting will change. When a separation of ownership from management occurs, the focus and complexity of accounting also changes. As nations move toward privatization of their infrastructure, encourage free enterprise, and strive to raise the standard of living of their people, their need to attract capital increases. Capital demands, in these instances, are often so great that domestic security markets alone are unable to satisfy them. Providers of capital are fundamentally interested in identifying investment alternatives, evaluating associated risks, and monitoring performance of their investments. Obviously, comparability is a desirable characteristic of accounting information which is sought by providers of capital. As a nation's demand for outside capital increases, there will be pressures to improve the quality of financial measurements and disclosures.

Cooperative Efforts.   As nations engage in cooperative trade efforts, their need for comparable financial information also increases. For example, the standard-setting bodies in the United States, Canada, and Mexico have conducted a joint study of the differences and similarities between their respective accounting standards and concepts. This cooperative effort is an outgrowth of NAFTA and promises to improve the comparability of accounting among these nations.[1] The similarities or differences between accounting principles in various countries may be partially explained by the extent to which cooperative efforts have occurred.

International Accounting Classification Systems

Once the factors influencing the development of accounting have been identified, it is possible to categorize nations according to one or more of those factors. For example, countries could be categorized as those reflecting more of a macroeconomic or national economic approach to financial reporting compared to those reflecting more of a microeconomic approach with emphasis on the individual entity and maintenance of stakeholder value. The application of these classification systems has resulted in certain countries being grouped together and raises the question of whether social and cultural factors could serve as a useful method of classifying various accounting systems. Using the research performed by S. J. Gray, Radebaugh and Gray have used cultural classification to identify the following categories:[2]

- Anglo-Saxon accounting
- Germanic accounting
- Nordic accounting
- Latin accounting
- Asian accounting

Anglo-Saxon accounting is most closely identified with the United States and the United Kingdom. However, it is also easily traceable to countries (Bermuda, Australia, Canada, Kenya, and Singapore) which were heavily influenced or colonized by major Anglo-Saxon countries. This category is characterized by more independent private standard setting rather than government control and is less constrained by tax laws. The reporting environment is less conservative and less secretive, so there is more disclosure. Germanic accounting has been heavily influenced by a legal system, based on Roman law. As a result, it has a higher level of uni-

1 *Financial Reporting in North American—Highlights of a Joint Study* (Norwalk, CT: Financial Accounting Standards Board, 1994).
2 Lee H. Radebaugh and Sidney J. Gray, *International Accounting and Multinational Enterprises* (New York: John Wiley & Sons, Inc., 1997), p. 87.

formity in accounting. Differences between accounting income and tax income are uncommon, thus leading to a conservative approach to accounting measurement. As one might expect, the standard setting at the private level is not significant. Germany, Austria, Switzerland, and Israel are included in this category.

Nordic accounting lies somewhere between Anglo-Saxon and Germanic accounting in that it is less conservative than Germanic and yet more secretive than Anglo-Saxon. The use of replacement-value accounting has been most common among this group. Included in this group are Sweden, Denmark, Norway, Netherlands, and Finland. Latin accounting is descriptive of the accounting in France, Italy, Belgium, Spain, Portugal, much of South America, Mexico, and certain African nations. Company (corporate) law and taxation are important influences and result in very conservative measurement practices. The high rates of inflation experienced in certain Latin American countries has led to the use of inflation-adjusted financial statements. The accounting profession in these nations does not tend to be well developed. Asian accounting has been influenced by several of the other categories due to the colonial history of the area. For example, accounting in Japan reflects the influences of both the U.S. and Germany. As discussed earlier, the accounting in China has been influenced heavily by the former Soviet Union. The government has a major influence over accounting in these countries, and financial reporting adheres to tax law. Accounting tends to be conservative, and yet, in response to the capital markets which have developed, it is becoming more open regarding disclosure.

The classification systems help explain why accounting practices differ among countries. In some areas, the differences are quite significant. A summary of accounting practices for several countries is presented in Exhibit 9-1 in order to illustrate how principles differ. The characteristics of a particular cultural classification are reflected in some of the principles identified according to country in that exhibit. As one begins to explore the area of international accounting, the classification of accounting systems serves several purposes. Obviously, any progress toward harmonization of accounting systems must begin with an understanding of how various systems differ from each other. Knowledge of these differences and the factors which have influenced them will also help in assessing to what extent harmonization may be achieved. It is very difficult to imagine that differences will not always exist to some extent. Given this observation, comparability can still be achieved indirectly if the differences are well understood.

Harmonization of Accounting Systems

In a perfect world, it would seem that identical transactions occurring in different nations should receive identical accounting treatment. It doesn't seem that different currencies or languages should make a difference. However, it is apparent that there are many more factors which explain why similar transactions receive different accounting treatments. Classification systems, such as the cultural classifications previously discussed, are of further use in understanding and analyzing the differences between countries. Such differences have a significant impact on the measurement and presentation of accounting information. Nevertheless, there are a number of parties who are interested in making accounting information as comparable as possible. Although comparability is their main desire, they may seek it for different reasons. For example, an international labor union may want to have comparable information for collective bargaining and policy decisions. If a governmental body is assessing a multinational enterprise's performance for purposes of determining taxable income, it would be interested in achieving comparability in terms of expense and revenue recognition in each country where the enterprise operates. The government of each country in which it operates would want to know how the enterprise prices goods transferred from one country to another.

Exhibit 9-1
Summary of Selected Accounting Practices By Country

	United States	**United Kingdom**	**Japan**	**Germany**	**Mexico**
Cultural Classification:					
Category	Anglo-Saxon	Anglo-Saxon	Asian	Germanic	Latin
Standard Setting	Private versus government. Less constrained by tax laws.	Private versus government. Less constrained by tax laws.	Heavily influenced by government and tax laws	Influenced by legal systems versus private standard setting. Constrained by tax laws.	Influenced by legal systems versus private standard setting. Constrained by tax laws.
Measurements	Less conservative.	Less conservative.	Conservative.	Conservative.	Conservative.
Accounting Principles:					
Disclosure of Related Party Transactions	Related party transactions are not accounted for differently. However, the substance of the transaction must be disclosed.	There are no general requirements for disclosure. However, disclosure requirements are set forth in various legal and stock exchange requirements. Most of the focus is on transactions with directors and persons connected to them.	Related party transactions are not accounted for differently. However, the substance of the transaction must be disclosed.	Related parties are defined by commercial code as affiliated enterprises. Transactions with these enterprises are not accounted for differently. However, the substance of the transaction must be disclosed.	Related parties are defined in terms of whether they can exert significant influence over the other party. The substance of the transaction must be disclosed.
Valuation of Property, Plant, and Equipment	Assets are valued at historical cost. Writeup of asset values to fair market value is not allowed. However, impairment in the value of assets is recognized.	Assets other than goodwill can be revalued to current cost. The effect of revaluations is not included in the profit or loss account but is reflected in equity.	Assets are carried at historical cost. Devaluations are permitted in certain special situations.	Assets are carried at historical cost, and adjustments to market value are not allowed.	Fixed assets are restated to current value using either indices or replacement value. The adjustment to current values is recorded in equity.
Classification of Leases	Leases are classified as either operating or capitalized. Several criteria are used to determine the classification.	Leases are classified as either operating or capitalized. Only one criterion regarding the present value of lease payments is used to determine the classification of a lease.	Most lease transactions are accounted for as operating leases. However, in certain specific instances, leases may be capitalized.	Leases are classified as either operating or capitalized. Tax rules are used to determine the classification.	Leases are classified as either operating or capitalized. Several criteria are used to determine the classification.

(continued)

	United States	**United Kingdom**	**Japan**	**Germany**	**Mexico**
Valuation of Investments	Trading securities and securities available for sale are valued at market value. The change in market value for trading securities is included in income. The change in market value for securities which are available for sale is included in other comprehensive income. Securities held to maturity are valued at amortized cost. Valuation is generally applied on a total portfolio basis.	Current asset investments are normally valued at lower of cost or market. However, they may be marked to market value. Noncurrent investments are generally measured at cost. However, they too may be marked to market. Valuation is applied to individual investments rather than on a total portfolio basis.	Marketable securities are carried either at cost or lower of cost or market. Investment securities are carried at acquisition cost. Lower of cost or market may be adopted for these securities. Bonds are valued at amortized cost.	Current investments are carried at lower of cost or market. Noncurrent investments are carried at cost although permanent declines in value may be recognized.	Marketable securities are carried at net realizable value (estimated market value less sales/transaction costs), and changes in value are recognized as income. Other securities are measured at the lower of cost or net realizable value.
Use of the Equity Method	The method is used for investments which represent an equity interest of significant influence but less than a controlling interest. Significant influence is generally presumed by an interest of 20% or more.	Similar to the U.S. However, in addition to the 20% test, a number of factors may indicate significant influence.	The equity method is required for companies in which a voting interest of between 20% and 50% is held.	The equity method is required for companies in which a voting interest of between 20% and 50% is held. In addition to the percentage guidelines, the investment must be established for the purpose of creating a long-term connection with the investee.	The equity method is used when an investor can exercise significant influence. Such influence is normally evidenced when the investor has acquired more than 10% of the voting stock. If influence can be exercised, the equity method may be used if stock participation is less than or equal to 10%.
Valuation of Inventory	Inventory is stated at lower of cost or market. Cost is determined based on a number of acceptable methods, including LIFO.	Inventory is stated at lower of cost or market. Cost is determined based on a number of acceptable methods. However LIFO is not acceptable for tax purposes and is seldom used.	Inventory is stated at lower of cost or market. Cost is determined based on a number of acceptable methods, including LIFO.	Inventory is stated at lower of cost or market. Cost is generally determined using specific identification or the moving-average method. FIFO and LIFO are permitted.	Inventory is valued at current value using either indices or replacement costs. If realizable value is lower, it should be used. Cost is determined by several acceptable methods, including LIFO, last purchase price, and standard costing.

(continued)

	United States	**United Kingdom**	**Japan**	**Germany**	**Mexico**
Accounting for Research and Development (R & D) Costs	Such costs are generally expensed as incurred. Certain exceptions exist regarding software and those costs which have alternative future uses.	Research costs are expensed when incurred. However, development costs may be capitalized in certain instances.	R & D incurred in the ordinary course of business is expensed. however, R & D for certain purposes may be capitalized and amortized over five years.	R & D is expensed as incurred.	R & D is expensed as incurred.
Accounting for Business Combinations	The purchase method is most commonly used, although the pooling method is used in certain circumstances. Goodwill is measured based on the fair market value of net assets acquired.	Accounting for business combinations is very similar to that used in the U.S. with the exception of its treatment of goodwill.	Purchase accounting is most common with the pooling method not usually allowed. The measurement of goodwill is not based on fair market values.	Purchase accounting is most common with the pooling method being used only in rare circumstances. Goodwill may be measured by using either fair market values or a special allocation process using both book values and market values.	Control is the principal criteria for determining whether entities should be consolidated. Both the purchase and the pooling method are allowed with very little firm guidance on when to use which method.
Accounting for Goodwill	Goodwill is capitalized and amortized over its useful life, which is not to exceed 40 years.	Under the preferred treatment, goodwill can be charged directly to equity rather than being capitalized and amortized.	Goodwill is normally amortized over a period not to exceed 5 years. If not significant, goodwill may be immediately charged against income.	Goodwill may either be immediately charged against equity or amortized over a period of 4 years or over its useful life.	Goodwill is to be capitalized and amortized over its useful life, which is not to exceed 20 years.
Foreign Currency Translation Method	Generally, the functional currency method is used for translation. In certain instances, the temporal method is used. (See Chapter 11.)	The closing rate/net investment method is used. Profit and loss accounts are translated at the average exchange rates. Balance sheet accounts are translated at the closing rate (year-end rate) of exchange. The change in the translated value of the net investment is a recognized gain or loss.	A modified temporal method is most common.	Various methods are used, and there is no one required method. Gains or losses on translation can be recognized in income or equity. The temporal method is most common.	There are no prescribed methods. However, U.S. standards are generally followed.

Investors seeking to provide capital have a wide range of investment opportunities. In order to achieve the most effective allocation of capital among competing parties, investors are logically seeking as much disclosure of financial information as possible. Furthermore, they are seeking information which is comparable between entities. The International Organization of Securities Commissions (IOSCO) is committed to encouraging international securities trading dependent on providing investors with comparable information which can be used for investment decisions.

The Reconciliation of Accounting Principles

In the United States, the Securities and Exchange Commission (SEC) requires foreign entities that wish to sell securities on U.S. stock exchanges to meet special requirements. These companies may use accounting principles other than U.S. GAAP in the preparation of their financial statements if they are based on a comprehensive body of accounting principles such as that set forth by a professional accounting body in the foreign country. However, these companies must present a reconciliation to U.S. GAAP as set forth in Form 20-F of the 1934 SEC Act. The reconciliation highlights the major differences between GAAP as used by the foreign registrant and U.S. GAAP and reconciles earnings of the foreign entity to the earnings which would have been reported had U.S. GAAP been employed. Exhibit 9-2 contains excerpts from the reconciliations of two foreign registrants, Advanced Gravis Computer Technology Ltd., a Canadian company, and SmithKline Beecham, a British company.

A review of Exhibit 9-2 reveals that there may be significant differences between GAAP used by a foreign registrant and U.S. GAAP and that the reconciliation represents a major effort. It is possible that the filing requirements of the SEC and the requirement to conform by either using U.S. GAAP or reconciling to U.S. GAAP have made the U.S. capital markets less competitive.

However, companies seeking capital through international sources should not be advantaged or disadvantaged as a result of the accounting principles and disclosures that they may or may not employ. The development of comparable accounting and auditing standards would be in the best interest of a properly functioning global economy.

Approaches to Harmonization

The above discussion identifies some of the parties which are interested in increasing comparability among various reporting countries. Harmonization of accounting systems is designed to achieve this goal. Rather than moving toward a strict pattern of uniformity in accounting, harmonization is a flexible approach designed to improve comparability without necessarily requiring a strict system of uniformity in accounting. It is possible to improve comparability through a combination of changes in accounting valuation, presentation, and supplemental disclosures.

Bilateral Agreements.   The harmonization of accounting standards may take several approaches and is a combination of an evolutionary process and a standard-setting process. One approach to harmonization involves bilateral agreements among two or more countries. This is often a more expedient and efficient method of reducing differences in standards among significant trading partners. For example, Canada, Mexico, and the United States have conducted a joint study to assess the similarities and differences in accounting standards among these nations. The significant trading relationships which exist among them due to the North American Free Trade Agreement (NAFTA) provided the impetus for the joint study. This effort has as a primary objective the harmonization of accounting standards and the improvement of comparability among reporting entities in the three countries.[3]

---

3 Op. cit.

Exhibit 9-2
Reconciliation of Foreign GAAP to U.S. GAAP
Excerpts for Advanced Gravis Computer Technology Ltd., a Canadian
company and SmithKline Beecham, a British company

ADVANCED GRAVIS COMPUTER TECHNOLOGY LTD.

SUMMARY OF OPERATIONS – PREPARED IN ACCORDANCE WITH CANADIAN GAAP

	Fiscal Year Ended January 31,		
	1996	1995	1994
(In Canadian dollars)	<C>	<C>	<C>
Sales	$42,570,941	$43,572,279	$23,675,496
Net Earnings (Loss)	(8,551,043)	(956,150)	(776,941)
Earnings (Loss) Per Share	(0.46)	(0.05)	(0.05)

SUMMARY OF OPERATIONS – PREPARED IN ACCORDANCE WITH U.S. GAAP

	Fiscal Year Ending January 31,		
	1996	1995	1994
	<C>	<C>	<C>
Sales	$ 42,570,941	$43,572,279	$23,675,496
Net Earnings (Loss)	(7,272,713)	(2,319,158)	(2,185,463)
Earnings (Loss) Per Share	(0.39)	(0.13)	(0.15)

DIFFERENCES BETWEEN GENERALLY ACCEPTED ACCOUNTING PRINCIPLES IN CANADA AND THOSE IN THE UNITED STATES (continued)

(b) Loss and deficit as determined under U.S. generally accepted accounting principles are as follows:

	1996	1995	1994
	<C>	<C>	<C>
Deficit retained earnings— beginning of year as determined under U.S. accounting principles	$ (8,962,890	$ (6,643,732)	$ (4,458,269)
Loss for the year determined under Canadian accounting principles	(8,551,043)	(956,150)	(776,941)
Adjustments to GAAP:			
Compensation expense due to release of shares from escrow	Nil	(1,057,030)	(859,375)
Adjustment due to write-off of development costs	Nil	((955,250)	(1,047,932)
Amortization of deferred development costs	892,830	649,272	498,785
Restructuring provision	385,000		
Loss for the year as determined under U.S. accounting principles	(7,272,713	(2,319,158)	(2,185,463)
Deficit—end of year as determined under U.S. accounting principles	$(16,235,603)	$ (8,962,890)	$ (6,643,732)
Primary loss per share (Note 15)	$(0.39)	$(0.13)	$(0.15)

SMITHKLINE BEECHAM

ADDITIONAL INFORMATION FOR U.S. INVESTORS
(Annual Report, 1996)

The Group prepares its consolidated financial statements in accordance with generally accepted accounting principles (GAAP) in the U.K.

The terms and principles used in the U.K. and U.S. are explained on pages 88 and 89. U.K. GAAP differs in certain respects from U.S. GAAP. The effect of such differences of a material natureis set out below. There is a fundamental difference between U.K. and U.S. GAAP in the accounting for the merger in 1989 of SmithKline and Beecham to create SmithKline Beecham plc. Under U.K. GAAP the combination is accounted for using merger accounting principles, whereas under U.S. GAAP the transaction is accounted for using the purchase accounting method. For the purposes of this reconciliation to U.S. GAAP, it has been assumed that SmithKline is the acquiree.

Income Statement Data	Notes	1996 £m	1995 £m	1994 £m
Net income per U.K. GAAP		1,035	970	72
U.S. GAAP adjustments (net of taxation)				
Purchase accounting and goodwill				
Amortisation [*sic*[of goodwill	(a)	(97)	(94)	(82)
Amortisation of intangible and other assets	(a)	(68)	(76)	(97)
Exceptional items (refer to *Segment Information*)	(a)	—	—	458
taken	(h)			
to goodwill				
Intangible assets	(b)	(22)	15	(39)
Deferred taxation	(c)	21	(23)	(24)
Foreign currency hedging	(f)	17	(13)	32
Post-retirement benefits	(g)	—	(7)	(15)
Restructuring costs	(h)	(104)	(122)	305
Disposal of Animal Health	(l)	—	(206)	—
Other, net		18	2	(10)
Net income per U.S. GAAP		800	446	600
Represented by				
Income from continuing operations before taxes on income		1,174	717	890
Taxes on income		(374)	(360)	(344)
Income from continuing operations		800	357	546
Income from discontinued operations (net of taxes)	(j)	—	89	54
Net income per U.S. GAAP		800	446	600
Per share data				
Average number of Ordinary Shares in issue (restated)		2,733m	2,730m	2,729m
U. S. GAAP net income per Ordinary Share				
Income from continuing operations		29.3p	13.1p	20.0p
Net income		29.3p	16.3p	22.0p
U.S. GAAP net income per Ordinary Share ADR				
Income from continuing operations		146.5p	65.5p	100.0p
Net income		146.5p	81.5p	110.0p

Balance Sheet Data	Notes	**1996** **£m**	1995 £m
Shareholders' funds—equity interests per U.K. GAAP		1,369	**1,223**
U.S. GAAP adjustments			
Purchase accounting and goodwill	(a)		
Goodwill		3,252	**3,302**
Intangible and other assets		192	**277**
Intangible assets	(b)	(81)	**(64)**
ESOT shares	(k)	**(126)**	—
Deferred taxation	(c)	(39)	**(59)**
Dividends.	(d)	160	**141**
Revaluation reserve	(e)	(56)	**(70)**
Foreign currency hedging	(f)	12	**(5)**
Post-retirement benefits	(g)	(59)	**(66)**
Restructuring costs	(h)	79	**183**
Other, net		32	**39**
Shareholders' funds—equity interests per U.S. GAAP		4,735	**4,901**

(a) Purchase accounting and goodwill

Under U.K. GAAP, the Group either eliminates goodwill against reserves or it is capitalised and amortised over an appropriate period, depending on the circumstances of each acquisition. Under U.S. GAAP, all goodwill is capitalised and amortised by charges against income over the period which, it is estimated, is to be benefited. Goodwill eliminated directly against reserves in the U.K. accounts has been reinstated and amortised over a 40-year period, which is the estimated useful life for the purpose of U.S. GAAP.

Under U.S. GAAP, certain separately identifiable intangible assets such as customer lists are included as part of the fair value of acquired businesses and are separately capitalised and amortised over their useful economic lives, but no longer than 20 years. Under U.K. GAAP such intangibles are not separately identified on acquisition but are included in the goodwill arising.

Under U.K. GAAP, brands may be independently valued and capitalised as part of the fair value of the businesses acquired from third parties, where the brand has a value which is substantial and long term and where the brands can be sold separately from the rest of the business acquired. These brands are not amortised but are reviewed annually for any permanent diminution invalue. Where provision is required it is charged to the profit and loss account in the year concerned. Under U.S. GAAP the brands are included as part of the fair value of the acquired businesses but are amortised over a 40-year period, which is the estimated useful life over which benefit is expected to arise.

Under U.K. GAAP, Financial Reporting Standard 7, 'Fair Values in Acquisition Accounting' no longer permits provisions for future losses or for the reorganisation costs expected to be incurred as a result of an acquisition to be included as part of the fair value adjustments. U.S. GAAP requires the costs of reorganising the acquiree, which do not benefit future operations, to be included as fair value adjustments.

Under U.K. GAAP, the combination of SmithKline and Beecham to create SmithKline Beecham plc was accounted for using merger accounting principles, pursuant to which the assets and liabilities of the Group are the sum of the his-

(continued)

torical net assets of Beecham and SmithKline. Under U.S. GAAP, the combination has been accounted for using the purchase method. For the purposes of this reconciliation, SmithKline has been treated as the acquiree. Under the purchase method, the aggregate purchase price was allocated to the assets and liabilities of SmithKline based upon their independently appraised fair values, with the remainder allocated to goodwill and amortised over 40 years.

(b) Intangible assets

Under U.K. GAAP, the costs of acquiring separately identifiable intangible assets (such as patents, licences and marketing rights) to develop specific compounds or products for commercial application, have been capitalised separately from goodwill and are amortised over their estimated useful lives, but no longer than 20 years. Under U.S. GAAP, payments made for purchased intangible assets which are still in development are charged directly to the profit and loss account.

...

(e) Property revaluation

Under U.K. GAAP, properties are carried either at original cost or a subsequent valuation, less related depreciation reserve, calculated on the revalued amount where applicable. Any surplus or deficit (to the extent that the revaluation reserve is in surplus) on the revaluation of a property is taken directly to shareholders' equity. Under U.S. GAAP, revaluations of properties are not permitted. Accordingly, these assets are restated to historical cost and the depreciation charge is adjusted.

(f) Foreign currency hedging

The Group enters into forward exchange contracts and other financial instruments which, under U.K. GAAP, are treated as hedges of future income. The matching principle is used to match the gain or loss under these hedging contracts to the foreign currency transaction or profits to which they relate. Under U.S. GAAP, these instruments are not regarded as hedges and any unrealised gain or loss on hedges of future profits of transactions must be valued at the year-end at market rates and recognised in the net income of the current year.

...

Initiatives of the European Union.   Even further developed are the initiatives of the European Union (EU) to harmonize accounting standards among trading nations. As of 1997, the EU consists of 15 member nations (Austria, Belgium, Denmark, Finland, France, Germany, Greece, Ireland, Italy, Luxembourg, the Netherlands, Portugal, Spain, Sweden, United Kingdom of Great Britain and Northern Ireland).[4] The EU has attempted to create a common economic environment in which member nations can trade. In order to reduce the competitive differences which may exist among member nations, Directives on Company Law have been issued which reduce legal differences and promote the comparability of accounting information. To further enhance trade, an Economic and Monetary Union (EMU) that calls for a common currency among the member nations has been established. Although this is an ambitious goal, it is hoped that the currency, which will be known as the "euro," will take effect in 1999.

The above-mentioned Directives on Company Law, in part, establish legally binding accounting directives to be used among its members. Of particular impor-

---

4 In 1992, the Maastricht Treaty changed the name of the European Community to the European Union. The European Community was formed in 1967 by the merger of the European Economic Community (Common Market), the European Coal and Steel Community, and Euratom.

tance is the fourth directive, which is concerned with the form and content of financial statements and valuation issues. Consolidated financial statements are addressed by the seventh directive, which emphasizes economic versus legal aspects of control. The directive calls for the use of fair value with respect to assets acquired through an acquisition and the disclosure of selected segmental information by line of business and geographical area. The eighth directive addresses the audit function and sets minimum educational standards for auditors. The accounting directives of the EU have increased the level of disclosure among EU nations and have served to set forth the differences in accounting among these nations. In addition to the EU, the United Nations (UN) and the Organization for Economic Cooperation and Development (OECD) are also involved in promoting comparability, improved disclosure, and harmonization of accounting information.

International Standard-Setting Process.   A final approach to the harmonization of accounting standards involves an international standard-setting process on a worldwide basis. The goal is to involve professional accounting organizations from different countries in the development of accounting standards that will be accepted by all countries. This obviously represents a monumental task. The leaders of this movement must be sensitive to the variety of cultural, ethical, and economic differences that exist among countries. For example, as discussed in Chapter 13 of this text, the FASB has recently revised its earnings per share (EPS) standard in order to become more in harmony with other international efforts regarding EPS. This approach to harmonization is gaining recognition, and major forces behind the effort have been the International Accounting Standards Committee (IASC) and the International Federation of Accountants (IFAC). The International Accounting Standards Committee is concerned with the promulgation and harmonization of international accounting standards. The International Federation of Accountants is concerned primarily with addressing issues affecting the practice of accounting rather than the establishment of accounting standards.

The International Accounting Standards Committee

The International Accounting Standards Committee (IASC), which is based in London, was formed as an independent private organization in 1973 and has the following major objectives:

1. to formulate and publish standards on financial accounting and reporting and to promote their worldwide acceptance and
2. to work for the harmonization of accounting standards and procedures relating to the presentation of financial statements.

These objectives are aimed at allowing a company to raise capital anywhere in the world. Rather than each nation establishing its own rules regarding the accounting information which must be presented in order to access capital markets, the IASC is taking a global approach toward standard setting. Because of the organization's private nature, international accounting standards (IAS) issued by the IASC are not legally enforceable; rather, compliance is voluntary.

Membership and Organizational Structure.   As of mid-1997, membership in the IASC consisted of 120 national accounting bodies representing 89 countries. Business of the IASC is carried on by a board consisting of a) representatives of accounting bodies from 13 countries (or combinations of countries) which are appointed by the Council of the International Federation of Accountants (IFAC) and b) up to four other organizations, that have an interest in financial reporting and are appointed by the IASC board itself. Although the Financial Accounting Standards

Board (FASB) is not a member of the IASC board, it has the right to be heard at IASC board meetings. Within the structure of the IASC is the Consultative Group which advises the IASC board as to policies and practical/conceptual issues affecting the acceptance of international accounting standards. The Consultative Group is comprised of representatives from a range of users, preparers of financial statements, and standard-setting bodies.

In 1982, an important mutual commitment was reached between the IASC and the IFAC[5] whereby the IFAC recognizes the IASC as the sole body having the authority to promulgate accounting standards and to negotiate for their acceptance. Such cooperative efforts and the initiatives by the IASC have led to the recognition of the IASC as the leader in establishing financial accounting standards on a worldwide basis, including developing and newly industrialized nations. A number of nations (for example, Germany, Singapore, Hong Kong) are accepting IASC standards for domestic use, and the European Union (EU) is also considering the use of IASC standards. The International Organization of Securities Commission (IOSCO) has recognized the importance of the IASs, and it is working with the IASC to insure that new or revised IASs will be acceptable to the IOSCO. Recognition by the national securities regulators, such as the SEC, would be the next difficult step. If successful, this could result in the recognition that compliance with IAS will allow the listing of a complying company's securities on all of the world's stock exchanges. The work of the IASC is also being recognized as a major benchmark against which the development of a nation's accounting standards should be assessed. Although some critics feel that the IASC leans too much toward Anglo-Saxon accounting, countries which are based on the Anglo-Saxon accounting models still have significant principles that are not consistent with IASC standards. For example, in contrast to IASC recommendations, accounting in the United Kingdom allows for the immediate write-off of goodwill. As all countries are encouraged to embrace IASs, there will obviously be discontent. However, the accounting standard-setting bodies are recognizing the importance of involvement in the IASC and the benefits associated with the harmonization of accounting standards.

International Accounting Standards.   The IASC has issued 33 International Accounting Standards (IASs) of which 31 are still operative. In addition, the IASC has published the "Framework for the Preparation and Presentation of Financial Statements." The framework sets forth the concepts that underlie the preparation and presentation of financial statements for external users. In 1997, the IASC began publishing a series of interpretations of IASs. The IASC also has a number of current projects underway including exposure drafts dealing with the impairment of assets, leases, and employee benefits. By the year 1999, it is expected that 15 new or revised standards will be issued. Standards on income tax allocation and accounting for intangibles are expected shortly. Exhibit 9-3 briefly summarizes several of the IASs, which represent an important effort to harmonize accounting standards. The IASC is strongly encouraging standard setters in separate countries to establish principles that are consistent with IASC standards. The IASC has adopted a uniformity approach by identifying the required or benchmark treatment in a number of areas. In some instances, an alternative treatment would be allowed, but reconciliation with the benchmark method is encouraged. However, in a number of areas, a previously acceptable accounting treatment was eliminated. For example, in the area of accounting for the income on construction contracts, the percentage of completion method is the "benchmark" and the completed-contract method is eliminated.

---

5 See pages 9–17 for a discussion of the IFAC.

Exhibit 9-3
Highlights of Selected IASs

IAS 2, Inventories—Inventories should be valued at lower of cost or net realizable value. Cost should be based on specific cost if determinable; otherwise, the benchmark treatment is FIFO or weighted average. LIFO is currently an allowed alternative with the disclosure of the lower of a) net realizable value or b) FIFO, weighted average or current cost.

U.S. GAAP: Does not require the same disclosures with respect to the use of LIFO. Lower of cost or market allows for the use of other measures than net realizable value.

IAS 11, Construction Contracts—The percentage of completion method is the benchmark method, assuming necessary values can be reliably estimated. If such reliable estimates are not possible, the cost recovery method should be used. In all cases, expected losses on contracts should be recognized immediately.

U.S. GAAP: Allows for the use of the completed contract method as the alternative to the percentage of completion method.

IAS 12, Taxes on Income—Deferred tax liabilities should be recognized for nearly all temporary differences. Deferred tax assets will be recognized if it is probable that a tax benefit will be realized. The deferred tax asset associated with net operating loss carryforwards and/or unused tax credits will also be recognized if future benefit is probable. Deferred tax liabilities and assets will be measured at the tax rates expected at the time of realization.

U.S. GAAP: An asset and liability approach is used to account for income taxes. Deferred tax amounts are recognized for virtually all temporary differences. The deferred tax liabilities and assets are measured based on provisions of the current enacted tax law, and possible changes in future tax rates are not recognized. The criteria for the recognition of deferred tax assets are based on criteria that are different from those used in the IAS.

IAS 16, Property, Plant and Equipment—Such assets should initially and subsequently be measured at cost. However, an allowed alternative is to use a current fair value. Increases in value are generally recognized as a credit to equity unless reversing a previous charge to income. Decreases in value are charged to income unless reversing a previous credit to equity.

U.S. GAAP: The impairment in the value of long-lived assets, held for either resale or use, is recognized and included as a component of income.

IAS 22, Business Combinations—The standard provides for the purchase method of accounting for a combination. Assets and liabilities are measured at fair market value. Any excess of acquisition cost over fair market values is recognized as goodwill which is amortized. Amortization of goodwill should not exceed 5 years unless a longer period (not to exceed 20 years) can be justified. Procedures for the recognition and measurement of negative goodwill are set forth. The pooling-of-interests method is allowed for those rare situations in a uniting of interests when an acquirer cannot be identified.

(continued)

U.S. GAAP: The purchase method is to be used unless specific criteria for the pooling-of-interests method are satisfied. Pooling would be more common under U.S. GAAP than under the International Accounting Standard. Goodwill recorded in a purchase is to be amortized over its useful life, which should not exceed 40 years.

IAS 25, Investments—Current investments (those which are immediately realizable and intended to be held for up to one year) should be valued at market or at lower of cost or market. If market is employed, unrealized gains or losses on individual securities may be accounted for under one of two alternatives. One alternative allows for all gains or losses to be recorded as a component of income. The other alternative allows for individual net gains to be recorded as a component of equity and individual net losses to be included in income. Long-term investments that are marketable equity securities may be measured at cost, lower of cost or market, or revalued amounts. When revaluation is used, individual securities are valued at market with net unrealized losses being included in income and unrealized gains being reported in an additional equity account. Other long-term investments should be valued at cost or at revalued amounts. Permanent declines in value should be recognized on an individual basis.

U.S. GAAP: The valuation of investments is dependent on whether the securities are considered as held-to-maturity securities, trading securities, or available-for-sale securities. Trading securities and available-for-sale securities are reported at fair value. The unrealized gains and losses are included in earnings for trading securities and in shareholders' equity for available-for-sale securities. Held-to-maturity securities are debt securities which are reported at amortized cost. Permanent declines in value should be recognized in earnings.

IAS 33, Earnings Per Share—The standard applies only to public companies and calls for the presentation of basic and diluted per share amounts.

U.S. GAAP: As discussed in Chapter 13 of this textbook, the treatment is virtually identical to the treatment required by the IAS.

The establishment of international accounting standards is a major undertaking toward the harmonization of accounting. In establishing comparability, many standard setters, government/regulatory bodies, reporting companies, and users of financial information are being asked to make some major adjustments and sacrifices in the name of harmonization. For example, the IASC is proposing the elimination or "blacklisting" of principles such as LIFO and pooling of interests. These are major areas whose proposed elimination is generating tremendous reaction.

The IASC's accomplishments to date are impressive; yet there certainly will be new challenges facing it in the future. Professional bodies that are members of the IASC have pledged their support to bring domestic accounting standards into conformity with IASC standards. In the United States, the AICPA and several other professional bodies, as members of the IASC, will be affected by this cooperative movement. Although the FASB is not a member of the IASC, it undoubtedly will have to be responsive to these pressures.

The International Federation of Accountants

Organized in 1977 with headquarters in New York, the International Federation of Accountants (IFAC) is a private standard-setting body whose membership consists of the same professional bodies as those belonging to the IASC. The IFAC is concerned primarily with aspects of the professional practice of accountancy. It is involved, not with establishing principles per se, but, rather, with becoming the leading organization for the international accounting profession. Therefore, the IFAC is more appropriately compared to the AICPA than the FASB, which is more akin to the IASC.

The IFAC consists of an assembly of national bodies and a governing council which is made up of individuals from more than 18 countries. The governing council sets policy and oversees the work of technical groups. Currently, the technical groups focus on international auditing practices, education, ethics, financial and management accounting, information technology, membership, and public-sector issues. International Auditing Guidelines have been issued dealing with a variety of auditing topics similar to those dealt with by the Auditing Standards Board of the AICPA in the United States. The Education Committee and the Ethics Committee have both issued a number of guidelines regarding the competence and ethical qualities of international accountants. The other committees of the IFAC also have issued a number of statements and guidelines.

The success of the organizations discussed above is dependent on a variety of factors. Harmonization of accounting standards may be flawed until greater attention is focused on a conceptual framework of accounting from which to build. Certainly, the experiences of the U.S. accounting environment suggest the importance and struggles associated with such a framework. Standards generally cannot be imposed; rather, they must be acceptable after appropriate due process. This process must recognize the environmental similarities and, perhaps more important, the dissimilarities between nations. A bridging of the factors separating nations must be accomplished subject to significant time and funding constraints. However, as national economies develop into global economies, the harmonization of accounting standards and the professional practice of accountancy will become more of a natural process.

Other Issues of International Importance

In addition to the identification of differences in accounting standards and the harmonization efforts regarding accounting standards and the practice of accounting, there are a number of other issues which are of international importance.

Transfer-Pricing Issues

Goods or services transferred or conveyed between units of a multinational enterprise are priced using a variety of methods. These methods of transfer pricing may serve a variety of purposes, many of which relate to taxation and/or the imposition of other trade duties. For example, if the corporate income tax rate is lower in a subsidiary's home country than in the parent's home country, taxes may be minimized by setting a higher transfer price on sales from the subsidiary to the parent. The parent company would then have a resulting higher cost of sales and a lower amount of taxable income. Import duties could be reduced if the value of a foreign company's shipments to its manufacturing facility in another country were made at a lower transfer price. Furthermore, the savings in duties result in a lower unit cost which may then allow the final product to be sold at lower prices, thereby creating a further competitive advantage. Clearly, the profit measures that are critical to agreements with employees and business partners could be manipulated in order to achieve a desired goal. At any one time, a multinational enterprise may be confronted with a number of factors that suggest both lower and higher transfer prices. However, in order to address some of the manipulation in transfer-pricing decisions, countries have set out to regulate transfer pricing. The Internal Revenue Code regulates transfer pricing in the United States by encouraging the use of a transfer price that reflects what the prices would have been if the underlying transactions had taken place on an arm's-length basis between unrelated parties. It is important to note that, once again, comparability between multinationals may be affected by differences in transfer-pricing methods.

Differences in Tax Systems

Another issue of international importance relates to the differences in tax systems. These systems vary regarding the definition of allowable revenues and expenses and the type of tax to be imposed. For example, one country may require the use of depreciation methods that are the same for financial reporting and tax reporting purposes, while another country may allow accelerated methods for tax purposes and a different method for financial reporting. Some countries may include only revenue from domestic sources, while others include income from foreign sources as well. It is recognized that countries will establish their own systems of taxation to best serve their fiscal, social, and political agendas. There has been little progress in developing a uniform system of taxation among countries, although the EU recognizes this as a logical part of a common trading environment. Currently, the important issue is to recognize the differences that do exist and understand how they may affect decisions.

The types of taxes imposed also differ among countries, with tax generally being based either on income or some other measure of value. The corporate income tax is common among most major trading nations and may, in some instances, include provisions to reduce the effect of double taxation resulting from distributions to shareholders. Furthermore, many domestic corporate income tax systems also include foreign-source income that already may have been taxed in the foreign country. In order to avoid double taxation, generally, a credit is allowed as a reduction of the domestic tax liability, based on the extent of foreign income taxes incurred. One of the most common methods of taxation is the value-added tax (VAT) which is common throughout Europe. This tax is applied to the amount of value added at each stage or level, from initial production to final sale to the individual consumer. The VAT incurred by a previous level reduces the cost of sales of the current level in order to determine the value added. For example, if a manufacturer produced a good with a value of 100 and a retailer added 70 to the value, the VAT tax would be calculated on the total value added of 170. Assuming the VAT rate is 20%, the tax would be incurred at each level as follows:

	Level		
	Manufacturer	Retailer	Consumer
Input cost of goods	N/A	120	204
VAT included	N/A	20	
Selling price excluding VAT	100	170	
VAT @ 20%	20	34	
Selling price including VAT	120	204	
VAT collected from next level	20	34	
VAT previously remitted to government	0	(20)	
Net VAT due government	20	14	

Certainly, international taxation is very complex and is affected by specific regulations and tax treaties that are beyond the scope of this text.

Questions

1. What are the primary areas that are dealt with in the area of international accounting?
2. In what way do capital markets influence the harmonization of accounting standards?
3. What are the various categories which may be used to classify differing accounting principles along cultural lines, and which of these is most appropriate for classifying principles in Canada?
4. What is the accounting measurement issue that results from a U.S. company's acquiring inventory on account from a foreign vendor and having to settle or pay for the transaction with foreign currency?
5. Identify several environmental factors that may explain why accounting principles differ between countries.
6. What are the primary areas of international accounting that a multinational corporation should be aware of?
7. How might the independence and autonomy of accounting professionals in a particular country influence accounting standard setting?
8. With respect to construction contracts, how do the International Accounting Standards (IAS) differ from the U.S. accounting principles?
9. To what extent is the European Union involved in the harmonization of accounting principles?
10. How might a multinational company use transfer pricing to reduce taxes and duties?
11. What are the major objectives of the International Accounting Standards Committee?
12. What are the two primary approaches to the harmonization of accounting standards?

Exercises

Exercise 1.   The single market created by the European Union (EU) will eliminate trade barriers among its member nations. Most U.S. businesses see the EU as an opportunity for growth.

1. Discuss some of the apparent opportunities presented by the EU.
2. Discuss why harmonization of accounting standards among members of the EU is important to the success of the EU.

Exercise 2.   The level of a country's technological development is a factor influencing the development of accounting principles. A small agrarian economy is interested in developing a presence as an exporter of high-technology products. Discuss how this new focus may affect the development of accounting.

Exercise 3.   Both the IASC and the IFAC have home pages on the Internet (www.iasc.org.uk and www.ifac.org, respectively). Using these sites, identify some current projects of these organizations. Using the site for the IASC, identify (a) the current members of the IASC Board and (b) several U.S. companies which are using IAS in their annual reports.

Exercise 4. Assuming that a 10% value-added tax is in effect, prepare a schedule to indicate how it would be calculated, assuming also that a manufacturer produces a product which is sold to a wholesaler who, in turn, sells the product to a retailer who then sells the product to a final consumer.

Exercise 5. Harmonization of accounting standards through a private standard-setting process will have both advantages and disadvantages to American investors and businesses.

1. Discuss the advantages of harmonization to American investors.
2. Discuss why differences in accounting principles and disclosure requirements may place American businesses at a competitive disadvantage.
3. Discuss how the U.S. accounting profession can influence the process of harmonization.

Exercise 6. SEC Form 20-F provides a reconciliation between the accounting principles used by a foreign registrant and those required by the SEC. Given the excerpts presented in the chapter as Exhibit 9-2, respond to the following questions:

a) *In Canada, development costs are deferred to the extent that their recovery can be reasonably regarded to be assured. At the point of commercial production, they are amortized over the estimated period of production. Discuss how development costs are accounted for in the United States and to what extent this difference affected the net income of Advanced Gravis Computer Technology for fiscal 1996.*

b) *Given the information for SmithKline Beecham, discuss how accounting principles regarding the treatment of goodwill and the valuation of property differ between the United Kingdom and the United States*

c) *Given the information for SmithKline Beecham, calculate the percentage change in net income and shareholders' equity for the years 1995 and 1996 as a result of employing U.S. GAAP versus United Kingdom GAAP.*

CHAPTER

10

Foreign Currency Transactions

As discussed in the previous chapter, modern businesses often find themselves affected by a global economy that presents a variety of challenges and opportunities. This chapter focuses on how a domestic entity should account for transactions which are denominated or settled in a foreign currency. For example, a U.S. company purchases raw materials from a French vendor and pays for the goods with French francs. Such transactions may expose the U.S. entity to risks or opportunities depending on how exchange rates change over time. Strategies to manage the exposure to exchange rate changes are also discussed in this chapter. The following chapter discusses the issues associated with a domestic entity having an investment interest in a foreign entity. The primary focus is on the translation and/or remeasurement of foreign financial statements so that they may be consolidated with the domestic parent's financial statements.

Companies in the United States realize the importance of international trade and are expanding their market share into a number of foreign nations. In turn, other nations are expanding their market share into the United States as more companies acquire factors of production on an international scale. This exporting and importing activity has increased significantly in recent years as evidenced by the following measures, in billions of dollars, of activity:

U.S. Exports and Imports, 1950–95
Source: Office of Trade and Economic Analysis, U.S. Dept. of Commerce
(millions of dollars)

Year	Exports	Imports	Year	Exports	Imports	Year	Exports	Imports
1950	$ 9,997	$ 8,954	1975	$107,652	$ 98,503	1992	$448,164	$532,665
1955	14,298	11,566	1980	220,626	244,871	1993	465,091	580,659
1960	19,659	15,073	1985	213,133	345,276	1994	512,626	663,256
1965	26,742	21,520	1990	394,030	495,042	1995	584,742	743,445
1970	42,681	40,356	1991	421,730	485,453			

When two parties from different nations transact business, each normally would like to carry out the transaction by using its own national currency. However, it is possible to use only one currency as the medium of exchange in the transaction. Therefore, a decision must be made as to which currency to use, and rates of exchange must be established between the two competing currencies.

For example, if a U.S. manufacturer of footwear purchases leather from a German supplier, a decision must be made as to whether the transaction will be settled in U.S. dollars or German marks. If German marks are used as the medium of exchange, a rate of exchange between the U.S. dollar and the German mark must be determined in order to record the transaction on the American company's books in dollars. Given that rates of exchange vary over time, the number of U.S. dollars needed to acquire the necessary German marks also could change between the time the order is placed and when the goods are paid for. If, during this time, more dollars are needed to acquire the necessary marks to pay for the leather, the U.S. purchaser is exposed to an additional business risk. The more volatility there is in exchange rates, the more risk to which the party is exposed. Similarly, if the dollar is used as the medium of exchange, this risk would still exist but it would be transferred to the German vendor.

It becomes readily apparent that the decision as to which currency will be used for settlement purposes becomes an important factor in negotiating such transactions. Due to the volatility of currency exchange rates, companies transacting business in foreign markets should aggressively control and measure exchange risk. Management should develop a model that enables them to forecast the direction, magnitude, and timing of exchange rate changes. This model, in turn, can be used to develop a strategy to minimize foreign exchange losses and maximize foreign exchange gains.

Business transactions that are settled in a currency other than that of the domestic (home country) currency are referred to, in this text, as *foreign currency transactions* and require the use of special terminology. One of the transacting parties will settle the transaction in its own domestic currency and also measure the transaction in its domestic currency. For example, a British company sells inventory to a U.S. company and requires payment in British pounds. The currency used to settle the transaction is referred to as the *denominated currency* and would be the British pound in this case. The other transacting party will settle the transaction in a foreign currency but will need to measure the transaction in its domestic currency. For example, the U.S. company that purchased inventory from a British company must settle the resulting accounts payable in British pounds and yet must measure the purchase of inventory and the accounts payable in terms of U.S. dollars. This measurement process involves the use of exchange rates and is referred to as *foreign currency translation.*

The International Monetary System

Denominating a transaction in a currency other than the entity's domestic currency requires the establishment of a *rate of exchange* between the currencies. The international monetary system establishes rates of exchanges between currencies through the use of a variety of systems. The selection of a particular monetary system and the resulting exchange rates have a significant effect on international business and the risk associated with such business.

Alternative International Monetary Systems

Several major international monetary systems have been employed over time, and occasionally there are suggestions that previous systems be reestablished. Prior to 1944, the monetary system was the *gold system,* which provided a strict apolitical system based on gold. The currencies of nations were backed by or equivalent to some physical measure of gold. For example, Nation A has 1 million currency units backed by 1,000 ounces of gold, and Nation B has 2 million currency units also backed by 1,000 ounces of gold. With gold as the common denominator, exchange rates between currencies could be established. In the above example, 1 unit of Nation A's currency could be exchanged for 2 units of Nation B's currency. A nation's supply of gold, therefore, influences its money supply, rates of exchange, prices, and international trading levels (imports and exports).

In 1944, the *Bretton Woods Agreement*, which created the International Monetary Fund (IMF) and a *fixed rate exchange system*, was signed. The fixed rate system was a gold/U.S. dollar system which required each nation to set a par value for its currency in terms of gold or the U.S. dollar. In turn, the U.S. dollar's value was defined in terms of gold. Modest variations from a currency's par value were allowed, and each nation could adjust its money supply in order to maintain its par value. The IMF could provide support to a nation in order to maintain its par value. Changes in a currency's par value were referred to as *devaluations* and *revaluations*.

As pressures to maintain the par values established by the fixed rate system increased, pressure was placed on the U.S. dollar. The ability of the dollar to support the system became questionable, and there were fears that countries with dollar sur-pluses might seek to convert these dollars into gold. In 1971, the U.S. government, for all practical purposes, terminated the Bretton Woods Agreement by suspending the convertibility of the dollar into gold.

Currencies temporarily became part of a *floating system* where rates of exchange were in response to the supply and demand factors affecting a currency. Shortly thereafter, the *Smithsonian Agreement* was accepted by the IMF. This agreement deval-uated the U.S. dollar and did not allow for the convertibility of the dollar into gold. Par values of currencies were established along with a wider margin of acceptable values around the par value. The Smithsonian Agreement was short-lived, and in response to increasing pressures on the U.S. dollar, the fixed rate system was aban-doned in 1973.

Today, the international monetary system is a floating system whereby the fac-tors of supply and demand primarily define currency exchange rates. Each nation's central bank may intervene in order to move its currency toward a target rate of exchange. This intervention results in a managed, or "dirty," float versus an unman-aged, or "clean," float. Supply and demand factors along with possible central bank intervention result in an exchange system with much more uncertainty and risk than experienced in a fixed rate system. Unfortunately, a myriad of factors beyond supply and demand affect exchange rates in a floating system. Some of these factors are[1]

- The speed of recovery from a recession.
- A nation's vulnerability to an energy crisis.
- A nation's trade and payment balances.
- The supply of and growth in the domestic money supply.
- Stability in the national economy, including a stable inflation rate, political sta-bility, national prosperity, labor costs, and unemployment rates.
- A currency's vulnerability to rumors.
- Domestic interest rates and changes in these rates. (If interest rates are relatively high, others will want to obtain that currency and invest it in the securities of that nation and earn high yields.)
- The strength or weakness of the domestic GNP as a major gauge of a nation's underlying economic strength.
- Confidence and expectations, especially during uncertainty and crisis.
- In a dirty float, the amount of governmental intervention in the market.

Although the present international monetary system is best described as a float-ing system, there are a number of special variations within the system. Some nations still maintain a fixed system whereby the rate of exchange is established by their cen-tral bank. However, because these fixed rates are changed frequently, sometimes daily, they may be viewed as a controlled or "dirty" float. A currency that is fre-quently adjusted downward, such as those in less developed nations, is referred to

---

1 Thomas G. Evans, Martin E. Taylor, and Oscar Holzmann, *International Accounting and Reporting* (Boston: PWS-Kent Publishing Company, 1988), pp. 134–135.

as a "crawling peg" currency. Tiered systems also exist whereby special rates are established for certain types of transactions, such as import and export sales and dividend payments, to accomplish desired political and economic objectives. For example, to encourage exports and to discourage capital withdrawal, a foreign government may establish favorable official rates for export sales and less favorable exchange rates for the payment of dividends to investors in other countries. The forces of supply and demand, however, occasionally make it difficult for a government to maintain an official exchange rate. In response, the government either devalues or revalues its currency.

The Mechanics of Exchange Rates

An exchange rate is a measure of how much of one currency may be exchanged for another currency. These rates may be in the form of either *direct or indirect quotes* made by a foreign currency trader who usually is employed by a large commercial bank. A direct quote measures how much of the domestic currency must be exchanged to receive 1 unit of the foreign currency (1 FC). Direct quotes allow the party using the quote to understand the price of the foreign currency in terms of its own "base" or domestic currency. This method is frequently used in the United States, and direct quotes are published daily in financial papers such as the *Wall Street Journal*. Indirect quotes, also known as European terms, measure how many units of foreign currency will be received for 1 unit of the domestic currency. Thus, if the direct quote for French francs (FF) is $0.25, this means that 1 FF would cost $0.25. The indirect quote would be the reciprocal of the direct quote, or 4 FF per dollar ($1.00 divided by $0.25).

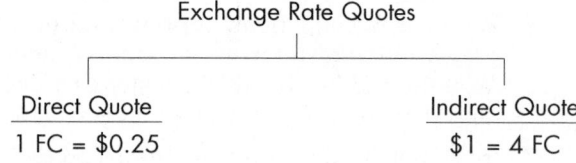

Exchange Rate Quotes

Direct Quote	Indirect Quote
1 FC = $0.25	$1 = 4 FC

Exhibit 10-1 is a currency table from the Internet and shows various foreign currency rates of exchange. For each country listed, the first two columns represent direct quotes and the last two quotes represent indirect quotes. Using Canada as an example, as of February 16, 1998, the direct quote is $0.69180 and the indirect quote is $1 = 1.4455 Canadian dollars.

Exhibit 10-1
The Interactive Currency Table*

This table was generated via the form at http://www.xe.net/currency/table.htm

Rates as of February 16, 1998 at 12:00 EST (UTC-5)
Base currency is USD American Dollars.

Currency Unit		USD/Unit	Units/USD
DZD	Algerian Dinars	0.0169	59.0
USD	American Dollars	1.0000	1.0000
ARP	Argentinian Pesos	1.0002	0.99979
AUD	Australian Dollars	0.6644	1.505
ATS	Austrian Schillings	0.078284	12.774
BSD	Bahamian Dollars	1.0000	1.0000
BBD	Barbados Dollars	0.4972	2.011
BEF	Belgian Francs	0.02669	37.47
BMD	Bermudian Dollars	1.0000	1.0000
BRR	Brazilian Real	0.88737	1.1269

GBP	British Pounds	1.6383	0.61038
BGL	Bulgarian Lev	0.000553	1810
CAD	Canadian Dollars	0.69180	1.4455
CLP	Chilean Pesos	0.002264	441.6
CNY	Chinese Renmimbi	0.1208	8.279
CYP	Cyprus Pounds	1.8733	0.53381
CSK	Czech Koruna	0.0288	34.7
DKK	Danish Kroner	0.1446	6.916
NLG	Dutch Guilders	0.4883	2.048
XEG	Eastern Caribbean Units	0.3704	2.700
EGP	Egyptian Pounds	0.2946	3.395
XEU	European Currency Units	1.0887	0.91854
FJD	Fijian Dollars	0.5280	1.894
FIM	Finnish Markka	0.1817	5.505
FRF	French Francs	0.1642	6.091
DEM	German Marks	0.5508	1.815
XAU	Gold Ounces (New York)	299.15	0.0033428
GRD	Greek Drachmas	0.003493	286.3
HKD	Hong Kong Dollars	0.1292	7.738
HUF	Hungarian Forint	0.00481	208
ISK	Icelandic Krona	0.01392	71.84
INR	Indian Rupees	0.02576	38.82
IDR	Indonesian Rupiah	0.000103	9700
IEP	Irish Punt	1.3721	0.72880
ILS	Israeli New Shekels	0.2782	3.594
TRL	Turkish Lira	0.000044	230000
VEB	Venezuelan Bolivar	0.001938	515.9
ZMK	Zambian Kwacha	0.000641	1560
ITL	Italian Lira	0.000558	1790
JMD	Jamaican Dollars	0.02809	35.60
JPY	Japanese Yen	0.0079488	125.81
JOD	Jordanian Dinar	1.4104	0.70900
LBP	Lebanese Pounds	0.000658	1520
LUF	Luxembourg Francs	0.02669	37.47
MYR	Malaysian Ringgit	0.2544	3.930
MXP	Mexican New Pesos	0.1182	8.458
NZD	New Zealand Dollars	0.5772	1.733
NOK	Norwegian Kroner	0.1323	7.556
PKR	Pakistani Rupees	0.02273	44.00
PHP	Philippines Peses	0.02500	40.00
XPT	Platinum Ounces (New York)	387.90	0.0025780
PLZ	Polish Zloty	0.2816	3.551
PTE	Portugese Escudo	0.00538	186
ROL	Romanian Leu	0.000122	8170
SUR	Russian Rubles	0.16541	6.0455
SAR	Saudi Arabian Riyal	0.2666	3.751
XAG	Silver Ounces (New York)	7.0301	0.14225
SGD	Singapore Dollars	0.5938	1.684
SKK	Slovakian Koruna	0.0283	35.3
ZAR	South African Rand	0.2028	4.930
KRW	South Korean Won	0.000603	1660
ESP	Spanish Pesetas	0.00650	154
XDR	Special Drawing Right	1.3471	0.74235
SDD	Sudanese Dinar	0.00578	173
SEK	Swedish Krona	0.1235	8.098
CHF	Swiss Francs	0.6859	1.458
TWD	Taiwan Dollars	0.03043	32.86
THB	Thai Baht	0.0212	47.2
TTD	Trinidad and Tobago Dollars	0.1613	6.201

The business news often reports that a currency has strengthened (gained) or weakened (lost) relative to another currency. Assuming a direct quote system, such changes measure the difference between the new rate and the old rate as a percentage of the old rate. For example, if the dollar strengthened or gained 20% against the French franc from its previous rate of $0.25, the dollar would now command more francs. To be exact, the new exchange rate would be $0.20 [$0.25 − (20% × 0.25)]. Therefore, **the strengthening currency would be evidenced by a reduction in the directly quoted amount and an increase in the indirectly quoted amount.** The opposite would be true for a weakening of the domestic currency. The reaction to a strengthening or weakening of a currency depends on what type of transaction is contemplated. For example, an American exporter would want a weaker dollar because the foreign importer would need fewer of its currency units to acquire a dollar's worth of U.S. goods. Thus, U.S. goods would cost less in terms of the foreign currency. If the dollar strengthened so that one could acquire more foreign currency units for a dollar, importers would benefit. Therefore, people and companies in the United States would have to spend fewer U.S. dollars to buy the imported goods.

Changes Relative to Another Currency

A Strengthening U.S. Currency	A Weakening U.S. Currency
BEFORE: 1 FC = $0.25	BEFORE: 1 FC = $0.25
AFTER: 1 FC = $0.20	AFTER: 1 FC = $0.30
RESULT: The dollar gained 20% ($0.25 − $0.20 = $0.05; $0.05 ÷ $0.25 = 20%)	RESULT: The dollar lost 20% ($0.25 − $0.30 = −$0.05; −$0.05 ÷ $0.25 = −20%)

Exchange rates often are quoted in terms of a *buying rate* (the bid price) and a *selling rate* (the offered price). The buying and selling rates represent what the currency broker (normally a large commercial bank) is willing to pay to acquire or sell a currency. The difference or spread between these two rates represents the broker's commission and is often referred to as *the points*. The spread is influenced by several factors, including the supply of and demand for the currency, the number of transactions taking place, currency risk, and the overall volatility of the market. For example, assume a currency broker agrees to pay $0.20 to a holder of a foreign currency and agrees to sell that currency to a buyer of foreign currency for $0.22. In this case, the broker will receive a commission of $0.02 ($0.22 − $0.20). In the United States, rates generally are quoted between the U.S. dollar and a foreign currency. However, rates between two foreign currencies are also quoted and are referred to as *cross rates*.

In addition to all of the above exchange rate terms, there are two primary types of exchange rates. A *spot rate* is the rate of exchange for a currency with delivery, selling, or buying of the currency normally occurring within 2 business days. In addition to exchange rates governing the immediate delivery of currency, *forward rates* apply to the exchange of different currencies at a future point in time, such as in 30 or 180 days. Although not all currencies are quoted in forward rates, virtually all major trading nations have forward rates.

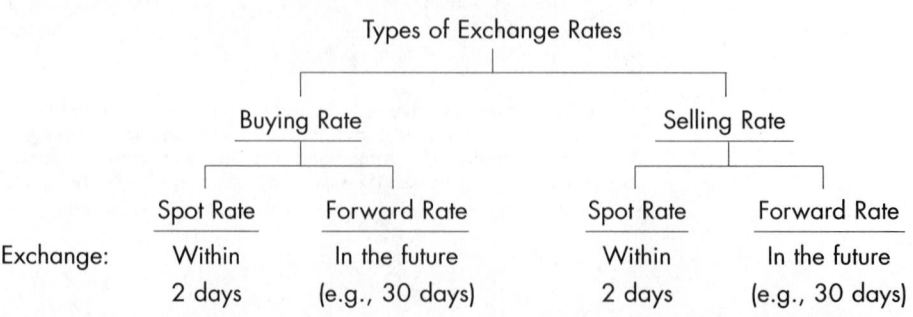

Types of Exchange Rates

	Buying Rate		Selling Rate	
	Spot Rate	Forward Rate	Spot Rate	Forward Rate
Exchange:	Within 2 days	In the future (e.g., 30 days)	Within 2 days	In the future (e.g., 30 days)

The agreement to exchange currencies at a future date is contained in a *forward exchange contract* which is designed to protect against future changes in spot rates. The forward exchange contract specifies the future exchange date and the forward rate of exchange. Although future exchange dates typically are quoted in 30-day intervals, contracts can be written covering any number of days. To illustrate a forward contract, assume the forward rate on a British pound to be delivered in 90 days is $1.6501. This means that, after the specified time from the inception of the contract date (90 days), one pound will be exchanged for $1.6501 regardless of what the spot rate is at that time.

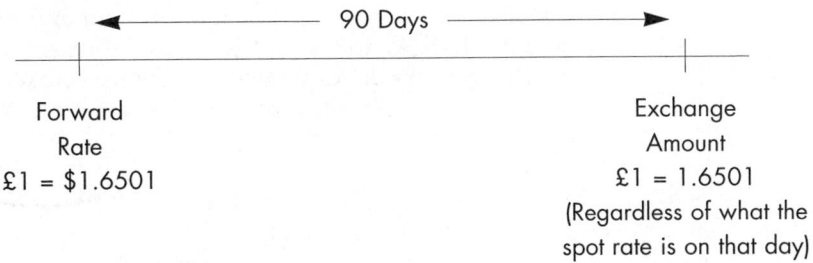

If the forward rate is greater than the spot rate at inception of the contract, the contract is said to be at a *premium*. The opposite situation results in a *discount*. Quoting premiums or discounts (known as forward differentials), rather than forward rates, is common industry practice.

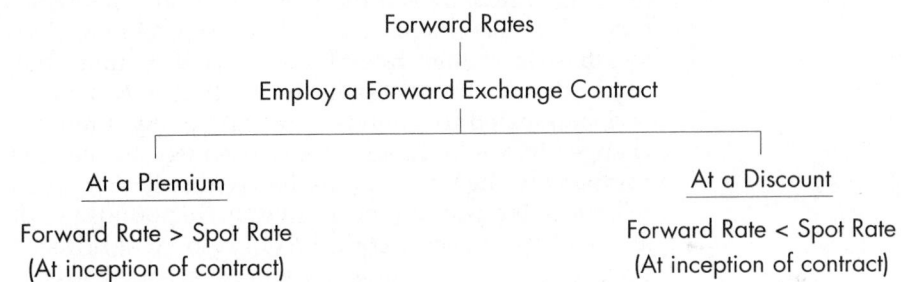

The difference between the forward and spot rates represents a contract expense or income to the purchaser of the forward contract. There are a number of factors that influence forward rates and, thus, account for the difference between a forward rate and a spot rate. A primary factor is the interest rate differential between holding an investment in foreign currency and holding an investment in domestic currency. For example, if a broker sold a contract to deliver foreign currency in 30 days, the interest differential would be the difference between

1.   The interest earned on investing foreign currency for the 30 days prior to delivery date and
2.   The 30 days of interest lost on the domestic currency that was not invested but was used to acquire the foreign currency needed for delivery.

Assume that the spot rate is 1 FC = $0.60 and that you want to determine a 6-month forward rate. Furthermore, assume that the dollar could be invested at 4.5% and the FC could be invested at 7.25%. The forward rate would be calculated as follows:

	U.S. $s	Foreign Currency (FC)
Value today	$600	1,000 FC
Interest rate.	4.5%	7.25%
6 months of interest	$13.50	36.25 FC
Value in 6 months	$613.50	1036.25 FC

6-month forward rate = $613.50 ÷ 1036.25 FC = 1 FC = $0.592

If the interest yield on the FC is greater than the yield on the U.S. dollar, the forward rate will be less than the spot rate (contract sells at a discount). The forward contract will sell at a premium if the opposite is true. The forward rate based on interest differentials will be slightly different than the quoted forward rate because the quoted rate includes a commission to the foreign currency broker. Furthermore, other factors in addition to interest differentials could also be incorporated into the forward rate. These other factors include movements in spot rates, the time period covered by the contract, expectations of future exchange rate movements, and the political and economic environments for a given country.

It is important that the student of international accounting have an understanding of the international monetary system and exchange rates. As previously mentioned, changes in exchange rates represent an additional business risk when transactions are denominated in a foreign currency. The accounting for foreign currency transactions measures this risk and demonstrates the use of both spot and forward rates.

Accounting for Foreign Currency Transactions

Assume a U.S. company sells mining equipment to a British company and the equipment must be paid for in 30 days with U.S. dollars. This transaction is denominated in dollars and will be measured by the U.S. company in dollars. Changes in the exchange rate between the U.S. dollar and the British pound from the transaction date to the settlement date will not expose the U.S. company to any risk of gain or loss from exchange rate changes. Now assume that the same transaction occurs except that the transaction is to be settled in British pounds. Because this transaction is denominated in pounds and will be measured by the U.S. company in dollars, changes in the exchange rate subsequent to the transaction date expose the U.S. company to the risk of an exchange rate loss or gain. If the U.S. dollar strengthens relative to the pound (one receives more pounds per dollar), settlement of the receivable will result in collecting a fixed amount of British pounds which are worth fewer dollars, and the U.S. company will experience a loss due to exchange rate changes. If the dollar weakens, the opposite effect would be experienced, as the U.S. company would have a gain due to exchange rate changes. Whether a transaction is settled in dollars versus a foreign currency is a matter which is negotiated between the transacting parties and is influenced by a number of factors. A bank wire transfer is generally used to transfer currency between parties in different countries. For one of the parties, the currency will be a foreign currency; for the other party, the currency will be its domestic currency.

To summarize, **changes in exchange rates do not affect transactions that are both denominated and measured in the reporting entity's currency.** Therefore, these transactions require no special accounting treatment. However, **if a transaction is denominated in a foreign currency and measured in the reporting entity's currency, changes in the exchange rate between the transaction date and settlement date result in a gain or loss to the reporting entity.** These gains or losses are referred to as exchange gains or losses, and their recognition requires special accounting treatment.

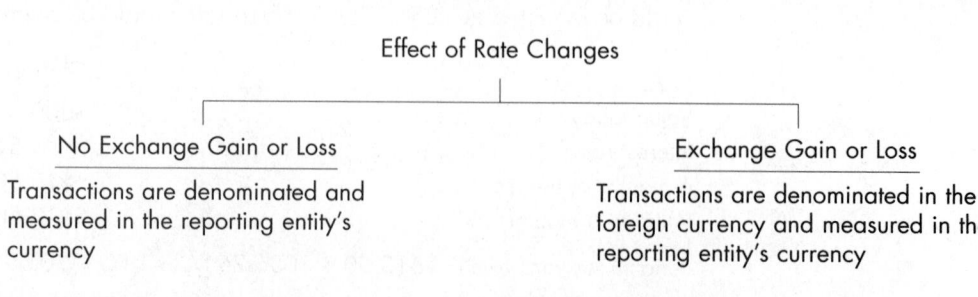

Effect of Rate Changes

No Exchange Gain or Loss

Transactions are denominated and measured in the reporting entity's currency

Exchange Gain or Loss

Transactions are denominated in the foreign currency and measured in the reporting entity's currency

Originally, two methods were proposed for the treatment of exchange gains or losses arising from foreign currency transactions. After considering the merits of these two methods, the FASB adopted what is referred to as the "two-transactions method." This method views the initial foreign currency transaction as one transaction. The effect of any subsequent changes in the exchange rates and the resulting exchange gain or loss is viewed as a second transaction. Therefore, the initial transaction is recorded independently of the settlement transaction. This method is consistent with accepted accounting techniques, which normally account for the financing of a transaction as a separate and distinct event. (The required two-transactions method is used in all instances with one exception. The exception relates to a hedge on a foreign currency commitment that is discussed later in this chapter. Therefore, unless otherwise stated, the two-transactions method will be used throughout the chapter.)

In order to illustrate the two-transactions method, assume that a U.S. company sells mining equipment on June 1, 20X4, with the corresponding receivable to be paid or settled on July 1, 20X4. The equipment has a selling price of $306,000 and a cost of $250,000. On June 1, 20X4, the British pound is worth $1.70, and on July 1, 20X4, the pound is worth $1.60. Illustrations 10-1 and 10-2 present the entries to record the sale of the mining equipment, assuming that the transaction is denominated in dollars and then in pounds. It is important to note in Illustration 10-1 that, when the transaction is denominated in dollars, the U.S. company does not experience an exchange gain or loss. However, because the British company measures the transaction in pounds but denominates the transaction in dollars, it experiences an exchange loss. In substance, the value of the British company's accounts payable changed because it was denominated in a foreign currency (dollars, in this case), that is a currency other than its own. In order to emphasize that the value of certain account balances is not fixed and will change over time, these changing accounts are identified in **bold italics** throughout the text.

When the transaction is denominated in pounds, as in Illustration 10-2, the U.S. company experiences an exchange loss (or gain). The exchange loss (or gain) is accounted for separately from the sales transaction and does not affect the U.S. company's gross profit on the sale. This separately recognized exchange gain or loss is not viewed as an extraordinary item, but should be included in determining income from continuing operations for the period and, if material, should be disclosed in the financial statements or in a note to the statements. Finally, it is important to note in Illustration 10-2 that the British company does not experience an exchange gain or loss. This is because the British company both measured and denominated the transaction in pounds.

Illustration 10-1
Transaction Denominated in **Dollars:** Two-Transactions Method

U.S. Company (dollars)			British Company (pounds)		
June 1, 20X4					
Accounts Receivable	306,000		Equipment	180,000*	
Sales Revenue.		306,000	Accounts Payable (Denominated in FC)		180,000
Cost of Goods Sold	250,000				
Inventory		250,000			
July 1, 20X4					
Cash.	306,000		Accounts Payable (Denominated in FC)	180,000	
Accounts Receivable . .		306,000	**Exchange Loss**	**11,250**	
			Cash.		191,250**

Note: The U.S. company experienced no exchange gain or loss because its transaction was *both* denominated and measured in dollars. However, under the two-transactions method, the British company did experience an exchange loss since its transaction was measured in pounds and denominated in dollars. The decrease in the value of the British pound relative to the U.S. dollar means more pounds must be paid to cover the liability.

*($306,000 ÷ $1.70 = $180,000)   **($306,000 ÷ $1.60 = $191,250)

Illustration 10-2
Transaction Denominated in **Pounds:** Two-Transactions Method

U.S. Company (dollars)			British Company (pounds)		
June 1, 20X4					
Accounts Receivable			Equipment	180,000	
(Denominated in FC)	306,000		Accounts Payable.		180,000
Sales Revenue		306,000			
Cost of Goods Sold	250,000				
Inventory.		250,000			
July 1, 20X4					
Cash	288,000*		Accounts Payable.	180,000	
Exchange Loss	**18,000****		Cash		180,000
Accounts Receivable					
(Denominated in FC)		306,000			

Note: The loss is considered to be part of a separate financing decision and unrelated to the original sales transaction.

*Normally, the company would not physically receive pounds but would have the dollar equivalent wired to its bank account. Through the use of a bank wire transfer, the British company's account would be debited for the number of pounds and the U.S. company's bank account would be credited for the applicable number of dollars, given the exchange rate.

**The *decrease* in the value of the British pound from $1.70 to $1.60 results in an *exchange loss* to the U.S. company since the pounds it *received* are less valuable than they were at the transaction date. [180,000 × ($1.60 – $1.70) = –$18,000]

Unsettled Foreign Currency Transactions

If a foreign currency transaction is unsettled at year-end, an *unrealized* gain or loss should be recognized to reflect the change in the exchange rate occurring between the transaction date and year-end. This treatment focuses on accrual accounting and the fact that exchange gains and losses occur over time rather than only at the date of settlement or payment.

To illustrate the accounting for unsettled transactions, assume a U.S. company purchases goods from a foreign company on November 1, 20X1. The purchase in the amount of 1,000 foreign currencies (FC) is to be paid for on February 1, 20X2, in foreign currency. To record or measure the transaction, the domestic company would make the following entry, assuming an exchange rate of 1 FC = $0.50:

Inventory	500	
Accounts Payable		500
Purchase of inventory for 1,000 FC when the exchange rate is 1 FC = $0.50.		

Assuming the exchange rate on the December 31, 20X1 year-end is 1 FC = $0.52, the following entry would be necessary:

Exchange Loss * [1,000 × ($0.52 – $0.50)]	20	
Accounts Payable		20
To accrue the exchange loss on the unperformed portion of the foreign currency transaction when 1FC = $0.52.		

*The *increase* in the value of each FC from $0.50 to $0.52 results in a *loss* to the domestic company since, as of year-end, the company would have to *pay out* more dollars than originally recorded in order to eliminate the liability.

Assuming an exchange rate of 1 FC = $0.55 on the settlement date (February 1, 20X2), the domestic entity would make the following entry to record the settlement:

Accounts Payable ($500 + $20)   520
Exchange Loss [1,000 × ($0.55 − $0.52)]   30
  Cash   550
        To record payment of liability for 1,000 FC when 1 FC = $0.55.

The December 31 entry implies that, if the transaction had been settled at year-end, the domestic company would have had to expend $520 to acquire 1,000 FC. Therefore, a loss of $20 is traceable to the unperformed portion of the transaction. Some theorists have suggested that an exchange gain or loss should not be recognized prior to settlement because the gain or loss has not been "realized" through settlement. This position fails to recognize the merits of accrual accounting and is in conflict with the position of the FASB, which calls for the recognition of exchange gains and losses in the period in which exchange rates change.

Hedging against Foreign Currency Exchange Risk

The previous discussion illustrates that foreign currency transactions may expose a transacting party to exchange gains or losses if exchange rates change between the transaction date and settlement date. It is the exchange losses which one would want to hedge against. For example, if a U.S. company has a receivable (payable) denominated in FC, and the FC weakens (strengthens), the U.S. company will experience an exchange loss.

In addition to foreign currency transactions, there are a number of other situations in which a company may want to manage its exposure to exchange rate changes. One situation involves when an entity commits to enter into a future foreign currency transaction for some predetermined fixed amount of foreign currency; a domestic company becomes exposed to foreign currency risk in that exchange rates may change between the commitment date and the transaction date. Hedging against the risk associated with a foreign currency commitment is discussed in a subsequent section. In another situation, a domestic parent is exposed to foreign currency risk to the extent of its net investment in a foreign subsidiary. If the exchange rate between the parent's and the foreign subsidiary's currency changes, the value of the parent's investment in the subsidiary will, in turn, change as well.

Entities also may manage their exposure to exchange rate changes in connection with forecasted transactions which will be denominated in FC. For example, a domestic company may forecast sales, associated with long-term contracts, in foreign currency over the next 24 months. Even though no sales have occurred, the company may currently want to hedge against the future possibility that the foreign currency weakens relative to the dollar. For example, a company may have a policy to acquire forward contracts to sell foreign currency equal to approximately 50% of certain qualifying forecasted sales amounts. Potential changes between exchange rates also complicate the bidding/quoting process associated with forecasted transactions. Assume a U.S. company builds large turbines and the typical construction period is 30 months. Progress payments are generally expected from the customer at 6-month intervals. Bidding such a project in foreign currency must attempt to incorporate the risk that exchange rates may move negatively over the commitment and construction period. Although the company would prefer to bid the project in dollars, a failure to transact in foreign currency may place the company in a competitive disadvantage relative to other parties who bid in foreign currency.

There are a number of financial instruments which may be used to hedge against the risks associated with transacting in foreign currency. Many of these instruments are derivatives in that they derive their value from a related or underlying commodity (e.g., foreign currency) or instrument. A *derivative instrument* is defined by the FASB as *a financial instrument or other contract with two distinguishing characteristics—one or more underlyings and one or more notional amounts. An underlying is an interest rate, a per-share price, a commodity price, a foreign exchange rate, an index of prices, or another variable that is applied to the notional amount to determine the cash flows or other exchanges required by the contract. A notional amount is an amount of currency, a number of shares, or a number of bushels, pounds, or other units specified in the contract.*[2]

For purposes of applying the FASB standards for accounting for derivatives, an instrument must, at inception or upon the occurrence of a specified event, meet two conditions. First, the value of the instrument changes by direct reference to the underlying. For example, the value of an instrument to sell foreign currencies (FC) at some future date is directly affected by the rate of exchange between the FC and the domestic currency ($). Second, the instrument can actually or in substance be settled net. For example, an instrument to sell FC can be settled by paying the net difference between the selling price of the FC per the instrument and the current exchange rate between the FC and the domestic currency ($).

Foreign Currency Options.   Foreign currency options may also be used to hedge against foreign currency risk. An option is a contract which gives the holder the right, but not the obligation (unlike a forward contract), to buy *(a call option)* or sell *(a put option)* foreign currency at a fixed exercise or *strike* price during a specified period. In exchange for this right, the holder pays the writer of the option a nonrefundable fee or premium. In addition to the premium, a brokerage fee is charged for writing the option. If the option is actually exercised, an additional brokerage fee is also charged. For a holder of an option, the total risk is limited to the premium paid and applicable brokerage fees, whereas the writer of the option has unlimited risk associated with the exchange rate fluctuations which are not offset by the premium charged. If an option can be exercised at any time during the option period (e.g., at any time during the next 30 days), it is referred to as an "American option." This term refers to when an option can be exercised and does not have anything to do with the use of U.S. dollars or whether the option involved American parties. If an option can be exercised only at the option's expiration date (e.g., one can exercise the option 30 days from now), it is referred to as a "European option." Such options are generally less expensive than an American option. A European option has to do with the date of exercise and not the use of European currency and/or European parties. The following terms are used to describe the relationship between the exercise price (strike price) and the current rate:

	Exercise Price Is Equal to Current Rate	Exercise Price Is Greater Than Current Rate	Exercise Price Is Less Than Current Rate
American:			
Buy (Call) Option	At-the-Money	Out-of-the-Money	In-the-Money
Sell (Put) Option	At-the-Money	In-the-Money	Out-of-the-Money

At any point in time, if an option is in-the-money, the option is said to have intrinsic value represented by the difference between the exercise price and the current rate. The difference between the premium paid for an option and its intrinsic value is referred to as the time value of the option. For example, if one pays $2,000

2 Task Force Draft, *Accounting for Derivative Instruments and for Hedging Activities* (Norwalk, CT: Financial Accounting Standards Board, 1997), par. 6. At the time of this writing, the FASB had not yet issued its final Statement on Derivatives. References in this text to derivatives and hedge accounting are based on the conclusions set forth in the Task Force Draft.

for a put option to sell foreign currency (FC) for $20,000 when the FC is currently worth $18,500, the values are:

Intrinsic value ($20,000 – $18,500)	$1,500
Premium paid	2,000
Time value	$ 500

If at inception an option is out-of-the-money or at-the-money, the entire premium represents the time value because there is no intrinsic vale. Although options are generally used less frequently than forward contracts, in part due to their cost, there may be instances in which the use of an option is well suited. For example, if a company is bidding a major contract and realizes that the contract may not be awarded, an option is very flexible because the holder is not obligated, unlike a forward contract, to exercise the option. If the company were to receive foreign currency, it could acquire a sell (put) option. The only cost to the company if the contract were not awarded would be the premium and relevant brokerage fees paid. However, if the contract were awarded, the put would serve as a hedge against the resulting receivable denominated in foreign currency. If the exact size of the foreign currency exposure is unknown, the flexibility of an option may be desirable.

Foreign Currency Swaps.   A foreign currency swap is also used when two parties need each other's domestic currency. The swap is a contractual obligation, arranged by an intermediary, between two parties to deliver a sum of money in one currency in exchange for a sum of money in another currency. Assume a U.S. company has an opportunity to invest in a French joint venture which is anticipated to last for 6 months. However, the investment must be made in French francs. At the end of the 6-month period, the investment would be liquidated and French francs would be returned to the U.S. company. One alternative would be for the U.S. company to contract with a French company which needs U.S. dollars for 6 months. The U.S. company would borrow dollars, and the French company would borrow francs. The U.S. company would then exchange or swap the dollars for francs. Interest on the U.S. borrowing would be paid by the French company, and interest on the French borrowing would be paid by the U.S. company. At the end of the 6 months, the French company would return the dollars to the U.S. company and the U.S. company would return the francs to the French company. If a swap had not been employed, the U.S. company could have purchased francs at the spot rate and then simultaneously purchased a forward contract to sell francs in 6 months.

Hedging with Forward Exchange Contracts

The value of an asset or liability denominated in foreign currency can certainly be affected, either positively or negatively, by changes in exchange rates. As discussed, there are various instruments which may be employed to manage the exposure to exchange rate changes. The extent and conditions under which such instruments are employed are a function of management policy and perceived risks. Some companies, as a matter of policy, hedge all foreign currency transactions over a specified amount. This approach recognizes the uncertainties regarding whether exchange rate changes will affect a company in a positive or negative manner. Rather than trying to assess those probabilities, management elects to hedge all qualifying transactions and/or commitments. As an alternative strategy, hedging may be employed only in those instances when losses from exchange rate changes are anticipated.

Whenever the value of an asset or liability denominated in a foreign currency would be adversely affected due to fluctuating exchange rates, management would prefer to eliminate or reduce such adverse effects. Amounts adversely affected may be a receivable from a foreign customer, a liability to a foreign vendor, or a foreign bank loan. Management could eliminate the risk associated with exchange rate fluctuations by settling the related transaction immediately. Rather than paying a balance due to a foreign vendor in the future, it could pay the obligation using currently available cash balances. However, this would deprive the company of the opportunity of using the cash amounts for other purposes. Alternatively, the company could currently borrow the necessary funds from an outside source and settle the transaction. However, this alternative would result in incurring additional interest expense. Obviously, the costs associated with using available cash or borrowing necessary cash must be evaluated against the potential exchange loss which might be incurred if neither course of action were taken.

Another way that management could reduce the risk of exchange losses would be to engage in a hedging transaction using a forward exchange contract. *Hedging* is a form of risk-reduction management in response to fluctuating currency exchange rates. To avoid exposure to changes in future exchange rates when a transaction is denominated in a foreign currency, it is possible to agree currently to buy or sell the foreign currency at a preestablished, rather than an uncertain, future rate of exchange. This would be accomplished through the use of a *forward exchange contract*. The forward contract allows an entity to hedge against exchange losses that may arise since the contract fixes the future rate of exchange. The goal of hedging is to offset the change in value of a hedged item (e.g., an accounts payable denominated in FC) with the change in value of a hedge instrument (e.g., a forward contract to buy FC). In essence, the hedged item and the hedge instrument are linked to each other.

In the earlier example of a foreign currency transaction discussed under the topic of "Unsettled Foreign Currency Transactions," the U.S. company experienced a $50 exchange loss because it had to settle a liability denominated in 1,000 FC at a settlement date exchange rate of 1 FC = $0.55 rather than at the original transaction date exchange rate of 1 FC = $0.50. However, if a forward contract had provided for the delivery of the needed foreign currency at a forward rate of 1 FC = $0.52, the exchange loss would have been reduced to $20 since the transaction could have been settled with currency acquired at a rate of 1 FC = $0.52 rather than 1 FC = $0.55. The FC transaction, the hedged transaction, was effectively linked to the hedge instrument in order to reduce the risks associated with exchange rate fluctuations.

Forward exchange contracts are used in connection with foreign currency transactions in several ways. A forward contract may be used to hedge against either the exposed position created by a single transaction or the net exposed position created by several transactions. An e*xposed net asset position* exists when a foreign currency transaction, or a series of such transactions, results in foreign-currency-denominated assets exceeding foreign-currency-denominated liabilities. Another use of a forward contract with respect to foreign currency transactions is in response to an *identifiable foreign currency commitment*. In this instance, the forward contract is acquired as a hedge because there is an existing commitment that will result in a future transaction denominated in a foreign currency. For example, an entity could commit to purchase raw materials to be delivered and paid for, in FC, at a future date. This hedge is in response to an exposed position that will arise via the commitment rather than an exposed position that has already arisen via existing foreign currency transactions. Although less certain than a commitment, a projected or forecasted transaction could also result in exposure to a company and, therefore, be hedged by a forward contract.

Hedge on Exposed Position.   Forward exchange contracts are similar to purchase commitments in that both are forms of executory contracts in which future exchange rates have been established. Typically, executory contracts are not recorded until at least partial performance has taken place by one of the parties to the contract. The fact that forward contracts may be sold after inception indicates that they are economic resources and is the basis for suggestions that unperformed forward contracts should be recorded as assets stated at market price. The FASB requires that an entity recognize its derivatives as assets (liabilities) depending on the rights (obligations) under the derivative contract and that such derivatives be measured at fair value. In the case of a hedge on an exposed position, changes in the value of the forward contract would be recognized as a gain or loss and be recognized currently in earnings. At a given measurement date, the gain or loss on the forward contract will be computed by multiplying the contract's foreign currency amount by the difference between the current forward rate for the remaining length of the contract and the forward rate at the date of inception of the contract (or the forward rate last used to measure the gain or loss). It is important to note that, at the expiration date of the forward contract, the market value of the contract is suggested by the spot rate.

To illustrate, assume the following:

1. On November 1, 20X1, a U.S. company buys inventory from a foreign company payable on February 1, 20X2, in the amount of 1,000 FC.
2. On November 1, 20X1, the U.S. company purchases a forward contract to buy 1,000 FC on February 1, 20X2, at a forward rate of 1 FC = $0.506.
3. Spot rates on selected dates are as follows:

Date	Rate
November 1, 20X1	1 FC = $0.50
December 31, 20X1	1 FC = 0.52
February 1, 20X2	1 FC = 0.55

4. On December 31, 20X1, the forward rate for a contract to buy FC on February 1, 20X2, was 1 FC = $0.53.

Illustration 10-3 presents the following entries on the books of the U.S. company that reflect the proper accounting for these facts. The entries have been separated between those relating to the purchase of inventory and those relating to the forward contract. This emphasizes that the company is entering into two separate but related transactions. One relates to a transaction with a foreign party that is denominated in foreign currency (or FC transaction). This transaction is exposed to risk resulting from exchange rate changes. The other transaction accounts for a forward contract between the company and a broker and is designed to hedge against the exchange risk related to the FC transaction. The exchange gains (losses) on the forward contract are intended to offset the exchange losses (gains) on the FC transaction. Accounting for a forward contract requires that the value of the foreign currency due to or from the broker be periodically adjusted to its market value based on forward rates for the remaining length of the contract. Once again, in order to emphasize that the value of certain account balances is not fixed and will change over time, these accounts are identified in **bold italics**.

Because a forward contract is an executory contract, technically there is no need to record the contract at inception. In reality, most companies follow this practice of not recording the contract at inception but do keep supporting schedules detailing the contracts. Even if this practice is followed, the forward contract is marked to market in order to reflect changes in the value of the underlying foreign currency. These changes in market value are recorded by the company. For instructional purposes, forward contracts will be recorded at inception. This allows for a better understanding of the concepts underlying the use of a forward contract.

Changes in the spot exchange rate affecting the hedging transaction are reflected in the account Foreign Currency Due from [to] Broker only. Notice that the account representing dollars due to (from) the broker is fixed in amount and does not change

Illustration 10-3
Hedging an Exposed Liability Position

Relating to Purchase of Inventory[1]			Relating to Purchase of Forward Contract		

November 1, 20X1

Inventory	500*		**Foreign Currency Due from Broker** . .	506	
Accounts Payable			Dollars Due to Broker.		506*
(denominated in FC)		500	Purchase of 1,000 FC to be delivered		
Purchase of inventory for			in 90 days when forward rate is		
1,000 FC when 1 FC = $0.50.			1 FC = $0.506.[2]		
*Not affected by change in			*Not affected by change in exchange		
exchange rate.			rate.		

December 31, 20X1

Exchange Loss	20		**Foreign Currency Due from Broker** . .	24	
Accounts Payable			Exchange Gain.		24
(denominated in FC)		20	To record the gain on the forward		
To accrue the exchange loss			contract when the remaining forward		
on the unperformed portion			rate is 1 FC = $0.53.[3]		
of the foreign currency transaction					
when 1 FC = $0.52.					

February 1, 20X2

			Dollars Due to Broker.	506	
			Cash.		506
			To record payment of cash due to		
			broker.		
Accounts Payable.	520		Investment in Foreign Currency[4]	550	
Exchange Loss	30		**Foreign Currency Due from Broker** . .		530
Investment in Foreign Currency		540[4]	Exchange Gain.		20
To record settlement of the			To record receipt of foreign currency		
liability when 1 FC = $0.55.			from broker when 1 FC = $0.55.		

1 Note that the first two entries are identical to those on page 10-10 when no forward exchange contract was purchased.

2 Noting the offsetting nature of the two accounts, an alternative for this entry would be a memo entry to describe the commitment resulting from the contract. Such treatment emphasizes the executory nature of the contract and is most common in practice. However, recognizing the forward contract with entries helps students to understand the relationships in using forward contracts. It should be noted that no separate accounting is given to the contract premium or discount. In substance the premium or discount is recognized over the life of the contract.

3 If the contract is not recorded initially, exchange gains or losses would be recognized and an allowance for exchange gains or losses would be employed. For example, in the illustration the entry would be

       Allowance for Exchange Gains or Losses. 24
          Exchange Gain 24

4 Generally the company would not physically receive the foreign currency. Instead, a bank wire transfer would be used to settle the transaction. The currency broker would debit the domestic company's bank account for the necessary number of dollars and credit the foreign company's bank account for the necessary number of foreign currencies.

given exchange rate fluctuations. The entries shown in Illustration 10-3 reflect the objective of a forward contract, which is to hedge against exchange losses. The exchange loss that would have been experienced without the hedge was effectively offset as on the following page:

	Without the Hedge	With the Hedge
Exchange gain (loss) on foreign currency transaction		
[1,000 FC × ($0.55 – $0.50)]	$(50)	$(50)
Exchange gain (loss) on the forward contract		
[1,000 FC × ($0.55 – $0.506)]		44
Effect on net income.	$(50)	$ (6)

Unfortunately, not all hedging transactions are as effective in reducing foreign currency transaction exchange losses. For instance, when a forward contract establishes a forward rate, it is possible that changes in the spot rate may not move in the same direction or not move as much as had been expected. Considering the previous transactions, assume the same facts except that the spot rates are as follows:

Date	Spot Rate
November 1, 20X1	1 FC = $0.50
December 31, 20X1	1 FC = 0.49
February 1, 20X2	1 FC = 0.48

In addition, on December 31, 20X1, the forward rate for a contract to buy foreign currency on February 1, 20X2, was 1 FC = $0.482.

In effect, the hedge eliminated potential exchange gains as follows:

	Without the Hedge	With the Hedge
Exchange gain (loss) on foreign currency transaction		
[1,000 FC × ($0.48 – $0.50)]	$20	$20
Exchange gain (loss) on the forward contract		
[1,000 FC × ($0.48 – $0.506)]		(26)
Effect on net income.	$20	$ (6)

It is important to note that forward contracts also may be used to sell foreign currencies at a more favorable rate than the spot rate existing at the settlement date. To illustrate, assume the following:

1. On December 1, 20X3, a U.S. company sells inventory for 20,000 FC to a foreign buyer. The account receivable is due on January 30, 20X4. The inventory had a cost of $8,000.
2. On December 1, 20X3, the U.S. company purchases a forward contract to sell 20,000 FC on January 30, 20X4, at a forward rate of 1 FC = $0.498.
3. Spot rates on selected dates are as follows:

Date	Rate
December 1, 20X3	1 FC = $0.4983
December 31, 20X3	1 FC = $0.497
January 30, 20X4	1 FC = $0.496

4. On December 31, 20X3, the forward rate for a contract to sell FC on January 30, 20X4, was 1 FC = $0.4968.

Illustration 10-4 presents the entries on the books of the U.S. company that reflect the proper accounting for these facts.

Illustration 10-4
Hedging an Exposed Asset Position

Relating to Sale of Inventory			Relating to Purchase of Forward Contract		

December 1, 20X3

Accounts Receivable	9,966		Dollars Due from Broker	9,960	
Sales		9,966	**Foreign Currency Due to Broker**		9,960
Sale of inventory for 20,000			Sale of 20,000 FC to be delivered in		
FC when 1 FC = $0.4983			60 days when the forward rate is		
			1 FC = $0.498.		

Cost of Sales	8,000	
Inventory		8,000
To record cost of sales.		

December 31, 20X3

Exchange Loss	26		**Foreign Currency Due to Broker**	24	
Accounts Receivable		26	Exchange Gain		24
To accrue the exchange			To record the gain on the forward		
loss at year-end when			contract when the forward rate is		
1 FC = $0.497			1 FC = $0.4968		

January 30, 20X4

Investment in Foreign Currency	9,920		Cash	9,960	
Exchange Loss	20		Dollars Due from Broker		9,960
Accounts Receivable		9,940	To record receipt of cash from		
To record settlement of			broker.		
the receivable when					
1 FC = $0.496.					

			Foreign Currency Due to Broker	9,936	
			Exchange Gain		16
			Investment in Foreign Currency		9,920
			To record payment of foreign currency		
			to broker when 1 FC = $0.496.		

Special Hedging Complications.   The previous examples assumed that a forward contract covered the same period of time as the settlement period, which is defined as the period of time between the transaction date and the settlement date. However, it is possible that a forward contract could cover a period of time different from the settlement period. The previous examples also assumed that the forward contract was for the same number of foreign currency units as required by the foreign currency transaction. It also is possible that a forward contract could be for a number of foreign currency units different from the number of units required by the transaction.

Forward Contract Expires Before Settlement Date.   If a forward contract expires before the settlement date, the gain or loss on the hedge or contract is given the same accounting treatment as previously discussed; the gain or loss on the hedge will partially offset the gain or loss on the foreign currency transaction. Obviously, the expiration of a forward contract before the settlement date may present unexpected alternatives. For example, assuming that a contract to sell foreign currency expires before the customer remits the foreign currency, the seller may wonder where the necessary foreign currencies are going to come from. Several alternatives may be available, including a) a rollover of the forward contract, b) purchasing the necessary foreign currency to satisfy the contract and acquiring a forward contract to sell the foreign currency when the customer pays, or c) purchasing the necessary foreign currency to satisfy the contract and not acquiring a forward contract to sell the currency when the customer pays. It is very common that transactions do not settle on the same date that a forward contract settles. Some currency brokers will extend a forward contract for a short time at the original forward rate as a courtesy to their clients. However, if settlement is not expected soon, the original contract will be rolled over into a new contract. If foreign currency is not currently available to settle a contract to sell foreign currency, the currency broker will be asked to roll the contract forward to a future anticipated date. To illustrate, assume the facts from Illustration 10-4 except that the customer is not able to pay the receivable until February 15, 20X4, even though the forward contract expired on January 30, 20X4. If the broker agrees to roll forward the contract until February 15, 20X4, at a forward rate of 1 FC = $0.4956, the necessary entries on January 30, 20X4, and February 15, 20X4, when the spot rate is assumed to be 1 FC = $0.495, would be as shown in Illustration 10-5. In summary, the customer's failure to pay on time cost the seller an additional $8 in that the seller received $9,952 ($40 + $9,912) rather than the originally anticipated amount of $9,960.

The cost of $8 associated with the delay could be evaluated against an alternative strategy which would have been to buy the necessary FC to settle the original forward contract and sell the FC ultimately received by the customer at the then spot rate. This alternative exposes the seller to the exchange rate risk associated with exchange rate changes between January 30, 20X4, and February 15, 20X4, because a new forward contract has not been acquired. Furthermore, a broker may not be interested in a rollover or issuance of a new forward contract because of other uncertainties, beyond interest rate differentials, affecting the market. If this alternative were selected, the company would have to use $9,920 of cash, forgoing other uses for the cash, to acquire the necessary FC to settle the original forward contract. Unfortunately, the value of the FC received on February 15 would have been worth only $9,900. Note that this loss of $20 was not covered by a forward contract.

The two possible alternatives discussed above are summarized as follows:

	Contract Date and Settlement Coincide (as in Illustration 10-4)	Dates Do Not Coincide	
		Alternative #1 Rollover Contract	**Alternative #2** Buy Necessary FC and and Do Not Acquire a New Forward Contract
Exchange gain (loss) on FC transaction	$(46)	$(66)	$(66)
Original forward contract: Exchange gain (loss)	40	40	40
Subsequent forward contract: Exchange gain (loss)	Not applicable	12	Not applicable
Total gain (loss)	$(6)	$(14)	$(26)

Illustration 10-5
Special Hedging Complications

Alternative #1—Rollover of Contract

Relating to Sale of Inventory   Relating to Purchase of Forward Contract

December 1, 20X3

Accounts Receivable.   9,966   Dollars Due from Broker   9,960
   Sales.   9,966   **Foreign Currency Due to Broker** . .   9,960
      Sale of inventory for 20,000   Sale of 20,000 FC to be delivered in
      FC when 1 FC = $0.4983   60 days when the forward rate is
                                                               1 FC = $0.498.

Cost of Sales   8,000
   Inventory   8,000
      To record cost of sales.

December 31, 20X3

Exchange Loss   26   **Foreign Currency Due to Broker**   24
   Accounts Receivable.   26   Exchange Gain.   24
      To accrue the exchange . . . .   To record the gain on the forward
      loss at year-end when. . . . .   contract when the forward rate is
      1 FC = $0.497. . . . .   1 FC = $0.4968

Note that all of the above entries are the same as those for Illustration 10-4 through December 31, 20X3.

January 30, 20X4

Exchange Loss   20   **Foreign Currency Due to Broker**   16
   Accounts Receivable.   20   Exchange Gain.   16
      To accrue the exchange loss when   To record the gain on the forward
      1 FC = $0.496.   contract when the spot rate is
                                                               1 FC = $0.496.

                                                         Foreign Currency Due to Broker   9,920
                                                         Dollars Due from Broker (See 2/15 entry) . .   40
                                                            Dollars Due from Broker   9,960
                                                               To close out original forward contract.
                                                         Dollars Due from Broker   9,912
                                                            Foreign Currency Due to Broker . .   9,912
                                                               To record new contract to sell
                                                               20,000 FC at a forward rate of
                                                               1 FC = $0.4956.

February 15, 20X4

Investment in Foreign Currency   9,900   **Foreign Currency Due to Broker**   9,912
Exchange Loss   20   Exchange Gain.   12
   Accounts Receivable.   9,920   Investment in Foreign Currency   9,900
      To record settlement of   To record payment of foreign
      the receivable when   currency to broker when
      1 FC = $0.495.   1 FC = $0.495.

                                                         Cash.   9,952
                                                            Dollars Due from Broker   9,952
                                                               To record receipt of cash from broker.

Forward Contract Expires After Settlement Date.   A forward contract could also expire after the settlement date. For example, a customer, paying in foreign currency, accelerates the payment date in order to improve his/her current ratio. The seller once again has several options. He/she could hold the foreign currency until the date of the original forward contract to sell foreign currency or he/she could roll the contract back and sell foreign currency immediately. Another option would be to convert the FC to U.S. dollars and sell the forward contract to another party. A much more speculative alternative would be to sell the foreign currency at the spot rate for U.S. dollars, temporarily invest the dollars, and then subsequently liquidate the investment and use the dollars to acquire foreign currency when the forward contract comes due. Such speculative alternatives are discouraged by many company policy statements. If a forward contract expires after the settlement date, the gain or loss on the hedge accruing after the settlement date is recognized as a component of current operating income.

Forward Contract Amount Different Than Transaction Amount.   If a forward contract is for a fewer number of foreign currency units than the foreign currency transaction, the contract gain or loss is still recognized as a partial hedge on the exposed position. However, if the forward contract is for a greater number of foreign currency units than the exposed asset or liability position, special treatment is required. The gain or loss on that portion of the contract which exceeds the exposed position is accounted for as a *speculative hedge*. Accounting for speculative hedges is discussed in a later section of this chapter.

Hedge on Identifiable Foreign Currency Commitment.   In Illustration 10-3, the company purchased inventory for 1,000 FC which was recorded at $500 when the exchange rate was 1 FC = $0.50. This inventory basis will subsequently be used to determine the cost of sales and subsequent gross profit arising from the sale of inventory. Assuming the company would sell the inventory for $800, it would experience a gross profit of $300 ($800 − $500). To change the example slightly, assume that the company committed to purchase this inventory with delivery in two months followed by a subsequent sale to a customer for $800. At the time of the purchase commitment, the exchange rate is 1 FC = $0.46, and at delivery date the exchange rate remains at $0.50. If the company could have recorded the inventory at a basis of $460 (1,000 FC × $0.46) by using the spot exchange rate at the commitment date, the gross profit on the subsequent sale would have been $340 ($800 − $460) rather than the previous $300. In other words, it may be desirable for a company to establish the dollar basis of an item at the commitment date rather than the later transaction date. This would be the case if the company anticipates exchange rate changes between the commitment date and the transaction date, which would adversely affect the company.

Fortunately, there is a solution to this dilemma. A company could fix or establish the basis of an item at the commitment date by hedging, at that date, the subsequent transaction. For example, the company discussed above could hedge the commitment by acquiring a forward exchange contract. This type of hedge is referred to as a fair value hedge. The gain or loss on a forward contract (derivative) designated and qualifying as a fair value hedge shall be recognized currently in earnings. An equal amount of offsetting loss or gain on the firm commitment should also be recognized in earnings, and the carrying amount of the hedged item should also be adjusted. This accounting treatment is appropriate if specific criteria are satisfied. Significant criteria include the following:[3]

---

3 *Ibid.*, pars. 16–17.

1. At inception of the hedge, there is formal documentation of the hedging rela-
    tionship and the entity's risk-management objective and strategy for undertak-
    ing the hedge.
2. Both at the inception of the hedge and on an ongoing basis, the hedging rela-
    tionship is expected to be highly effective in achieving offsetting changes in fair
    value attributable to the hedged risk.
3. The hedged item is specifically identified as either all or a specific portion of a
    recognized asset or liability of a firm commitment.
4. The hedged item is a single asset or liability or is a portfolio of similar assets or
    liabilities.
5. The hedged item presents an exposure to changes in fair value for the hedged
    risk that could affect reported earnings.

    The accounting treatment given a fair value hedge should continue unless

- The criteria identified above are no longer satisfied,
- The derivative expires or is sold, or
- The entity no longer designates the derivative as a fair value hedge.

It is important to note that the treatment given a fair value hedge does not continue beyond the transaction date of the commitment. For example, if the commitment to purchase inventory occurs on June 1 and delivery of the inventory occurs on
August 1, the transaction date, the hedge on the commitment ends. If the derivative
does not expire on the transaction date, the hedge is subsequently considered to be
a hedge of an exposed position.

Foreign currency commitments are frequently hedged through the use of forward exchange contracts. However, it is important to note that other forms of hedging are also acceptable, such as options or foreign currency loans. For example, in the
case of purchasing inventory and trying to fix the basis at the commitment date, a
loan could have been used to hedge the commitment. If the company had made a
loan to another party and required repayment in foreign currency, this could effectively hedge the commitment and provide the necessary foreign currency to pay for
the inventory. In conclusion, it is possible to hedge an identifiable foreign currency
commitment in several ways. In any case, the goal is to fix or establish the basis of an
item. Although the previous examples have focused on fixing the basis of inventory
and the resulting cost of sales in order to preserve a desired gross profit, a company
may also want to fix the basis of sales. For example, if a customer commits to buying
a product for delivery in two months, the company may want to fix the basis of sales
at the commitment date rather than wait until the transaction date. This would be
true if the company expects to experience exchange losses due to the dollar's
strengthening relative to the foreign currency.

To illustrate a hedge on an identifiable foreign currency commitment coupled
with a hedge on an exposed position, assume the following:

1. The criteria necessary for treatment as a fair value hedge prior to the transac-
    tion date have been satisfied.
2. On January 1, 20X1, a domestic company agrees to sell goods to a foreign cus-
    tomer, with delivery to be made on March 1, 20X1. The goods, valued at 10,000
    FC and having a cost of $4,000, are to be paid for on June 1, 20X1.
3. On January 1, 20X1, the domestic company purchased a forward contract to
    sell 10,000 FC on June 1, 20X1, at a forward rate of 1 FC = $0.4998. Note that
    the contract not only hedges the commitment period but also the time through
    the settlement date (i.e., the exposed position).
4. Spot rates on selected dates are as follows:

January 1, 20X1	1 FC = $0.50
March 1, 20X1	1 FC = 0.49
June 1, 20X1	1 FC = 0.485

5. On March 1, 20X1, the forward rate to sell FC on June 1, 20X1, is 1 FC = $0.4898.

In Illustration 10-6, the entries on the books of the U.S. company reflect the proper accounting for these facts.

Illustration 10-6
Hedging on an Identifiable Foreign Currency Commitment

Relating to Sale of Inventory			Relating to Purchase of Forward Contract		
January 1, 20X1			Dollars Due from Broker	4,998	
			Foreign Currency Due to Broker . .		4,998
			Purchase of contract to sell 10,000 FC on June 1, 20X1, at a forward rate of 1 FC = $0.4998.		
March 1, 20X1					
Commitment Loss.	100		**Foreign Currency Due to Broker**	100	
Firm Commitment		100	Exchange Gain.		100
To record the loss on the financial instrument component of the commitment.			To record the gain on the forward contract prior to the transaction date when the forward rate is 1 FC = $0.4898.		
Accounts Receivable.	4,900				
Firm Commitment	100				
Sales		5,000			
To record the sale when 1 FC = $0.49 and to recognize the sale.					
Cost of Sales	4,000				
Inventory		4,000			
To record cost of sales.					
June 1, 20X1					
Investment in Foreign Currency	4,850		**Foreign Currency Due to Broker**	4,898	
Exchange Loss	50		Exchange Gain.		48
Accounts Receivable.		4,900	Investment in Foreign Currency		4,850
To record the collection of the receivable when the spot rate is 1 FC = $0.485.			To record payment of foreign currency to broker when 1 FC = $0.485.		
			Cash.	4,998	
			Dollars Due from Broker		4,998
			To record recipt of cash from broker.		

At the commitment date, the seller wanted to fix the basis of sales because of an expected strengthening of the dollar relative to the foreign currency. This would allow the seller to achieve the anticipated gross profit of $1,000, which is the difference between the $4,000 inventory cost and the sales value of $5,000. The hedge on the commitment was employed to preserve this anticipated gross profit on the sale. Note that the account "firm commitment" serves the purpose of fixing the basis of the sales by the amount of the loss recognized during the commitment period. Extending the hedge past the transaction date was done to reduce the risk of exchange fluctuations' affecting the collection value of the account receivable. The effect of the hedge on the foreign currency commitment and the exposed asset position is illustrated below:

	Desired Position	Without Hedge	With Hedge
Sales price	$5,000	$4,900*	$5,000
Cost of sales	(4,000)	(4,000)	(4,000)
Gross profit	$1,000	$ 900	$1,000
Loss on commitment			(100)
Exchange gain (loss) on foreign currency transaction		(50)**	(50)
Exchange gain (loss) on hedge			148
Income effect	$1,000	$ 850	$ 998

*This represents the 10,000 FC at the March 1, 20X1 exchange rate of 1 FC = $0.49.

**This represents the 10,000 FC receivable originally recorded at $4,900 but collected for $4,850 when the exchange rate was 1 FC = $0.485.

If the risk of adverse exchange rate changes during the commitment period had not been hedged, the actual gross profit on the sale would have been reduced to $900 ($4,900 − $4,000) because sales would have been recorded at the spot exchange rate on March 1 (10,000 FC × $0.49 = $4,900 of sales). However, the hedge was effective in maintaining the originally anticipated dollar basis of the transaction and allowed for the recognition of a $100 gross profit. This was accomplished by hedging the commitment and adjusting the carrying amount of the hedged sale by the amount of the gain on the forward contract prior to the transaction date. Furthermore, extending the hedge beyond the transaction date resulted in offsetting the subsequent exchange rate loss. The direct cost to manage these risks was $2 which represented the difference between the value of the 10,000 FC at the original spot rate versus the forward rate [10,000 × ($0.50 − $0.4998)].

Although the illustration ignored the tax impact of the transactions, the FASB provides for hedging on an after-tax basis. A hedge on an after-tax basis recognizes that there may be a tax impact associated with the foreign currency commitment itself and a separate tax impact associated with the gain or loss on the forward contract. In the illustration, for example, there is a tax impact associated with the sale of inventory and a tax impact associated with the gain on the forward contract to hedge the foreign currency commitment. The desired objective is for the gain (loss) on such a hedge less the net related tax impact to equal the exchange loss (gain) associated with the settlement of the foreign currency commitment.

In order to provide an after-tax hedge, a hedging transaction would exceed the related foreign currency commitment. In these situations, the gain or loss on the transaction should be accounted for as follows:[4]

1. The gain or loss on the portion of the hedging transaction in excess of the commitment should be recognized to the extent that the transaction provides an after-tax hedge. The gain or loss offsets the related tax effects in the period such tax effects are recognized.

---

4 FASB Statement No. 52, *Foreign Currency Translation* (Stamford: Financial Accounting Standards Board, 1981), par. 21.

2. That portion of a gain or loss on a hedging transaction in excess of the amount that provides a hedge on an after-tax basis should not be accounted for as a fair value hedge.

Companies engaged in material hedging transactions frequently disclose the extent of this activity in the notes to their financial statements. An example of the hedging on foreign currency commitments and transactions is disclosed as shown in Exhibit 10-2.

Exhibit 10-2
Xerox Corporation
Excerpt from Form 10-K
(000 omitted)

Forward Exchange Contracts. We utilize forward exchange contracts to hedge against the potentially adverse impacts of foreign currency fluctuations on foreign currency denominated receivables and payables; firm foreign currency commitments; and investments in foreign operations. Firm foreign currency commitments generally represent committed purchase orders for foreign sourced inventory. These contracts generally mature in six months or less. At December 31, 1996 and 1995, we had outstanding forward exchange contracts of $2,259 and $1,474, respectively. Of the outstanding contracts at December 31, 1996, the largest single currency represented was the Japanese yen. Contracts denominated in Japanese yen, Brazilian reais, U.S. dollars, French francs, Italian lira, and Swiss francs accounted for over 75 percent of our forward exchange contracts. On contracts that hedge foreign currency denominated receivables and payables, gains or losses are reported currently in income and premiums or discounts are amortized to income and included in Other, net in the consolidated statements of income. Gains or losses, as well as premiums or discounts, on contracts that hedge firm commitments are deferred and subsequently recognized as part of the underlying transaction. At December 31, 1996, we had a net deferred loss of $26. Gains or losses on contracts that hedge an investment in a foreign operation are reported currently in the balance sheet as a component of cumulative translation adjustments. The premium or discount on contracts that hedge an investment in a foreign operation are amortized to income and included in Other, net in the consolidated statements of income. During 1996, the average notional amount of a forward exchange contract amounted to $8.

Foreign Currency Swap Agreements. During 1996, we entered into cross currency interest rate swap agreements, whereby we issued foreign currency denominated debt and swapped the proceeds with a counterparty. In return, we received and effectively denominated the debt in local currencies. Currency swaps are utilized as hedges of the underlying foreign currency borrowings, and exchange gains or losses are recognized currently in Other, net in the consolidated statements of income. At December 31, 1996, cross currency interest rate swap agreements with an aggregate notional amount of $511 remained outstanding.

http://www.sec.gov/Archives/edgar/data/108772/0000108772-97-000009.txt

---

Forward Contracts as Means of Speculation.   In addition to employing forward contracts as a means of hedging an exposed position or a foreign currency commitment, they may be employed as a means of speculating in foreign currencies. Foreign currencies are actively traded as commodities, thus providing opportunities for speculation. An investor attempts to make a profit by predicting changes in exchange rates. For example, a U.S. investor might purchase a forward contract to sell foreign currency at a given forward rate. The investor hopes that the forward rate will be greater than the spot rate which exists at the expiration of the contract. The investor may not even possess the foreign currency but, subsequently, will attempt to sell the contract at a gain. The investment in the speculative contract is initially recorded at the forward rate. A gain or loss on a contract held in speculation should be determined by multiplying the foreign currency amount of the forward contract by the difference between the forward rate available for the remaining maturity of the contract and the contracted forward rate (or the forward rate last used to measure a gain or loss on that contract for an earlier period).

The initial accounting treatment for speculative contracts is similar to that used for other investments. First, upon acquisition, the investment is initially recorded at its fair market value. For a speculative contract, its initial fair market value is the forward rate for the contract. The subsequent accounting for gains or losses on the speculative contract results in the basis of the investment being adjusted to fair market value. This process is consistent with current requirements to measure investments at fair value.

In order to illustrate the accounting for a speculative contract, assume the following:

1. On November 1, 20X2, a calendar-year investor purchased a 90-day forward contract to buy 1,000 FC at a forward rate of 1 FC = $0.505.
2. On December 31, 20X2, the forward rate for a 30-day forward contract was 1 FC = $0.51.
3. On February 1, 20X3, the investor paid the broker and received the foreign currency. The spot rate was 1 FC = $0.515.

The following entries reflect the proper accounting for these facts:

20X2

Nov. 1 **Foreign Currency Due from Broker**   505
        Dollars Due to Broker   505
            To record the purchase of the forward contract
            when the forward rate is 1 FC = $0.505.

Dec. 31 **Foreign Currency Due from Broker**   5
        Exchange Gain   5
            To recognize the speculation gain based on the
            difference between the forward rate available for
            the remaining maturity and the original forward
            rate [1,000 FC × ($0.51 − $0.505)].

20X3

Feb. 1 Dollars Due to Broker   505
        Cash   505
            To record the payment to the broker at the agreed
            rate of 1 FC = $0.505.

        Foreign Currency   515
        Foreign Currency Due from Broker   510
        Exchange Gain   5
            To record the receipt of 1,000 FC when the spot
            rate was 1 FC = $0.515.

Note that the investor's exchange gain prior to maturity was measured by the difference between forward rates. The total exchange gain of $10 is based on the difference between the spot rate at the maturity of the contract and the original forward rate [1,000 FC × ($0.515 − $0.505)].

The illustration assumed the investor took delivery of the foreign currency. The investor may use the foreign currency for some other purpose (for example, a foreign investment) or may sell the currency at the spot rate for U.S. dollars. However, in a more typical situation, an investor would not hold a forward contract to maturity but would sell the contract to another party. Assuming the same facts except that the investor sold the contract for $5 on December 31, 20X2, the following entry would have been made on December 31, in addition to the other November 1 and December 31 entries:

20X2
Dec. 31   Cash   5
           Dollars Due to Broker   505
                Foreign Currency Due from Broker.   510

As mentioned previously, the special treatment given forward contracts held for speculation also is required for other forward contracts to the extent they exceed

1. That amount required to cover an exposed net asset or liability position, and/or
2. That amount needed to hedge on an after-tax basis an identifiable foreign currency commitment.

Hedging a Foreign-Denominated Forecasted Transaction

A forecasted transaction is one which is expected to occur in the future at market prices that will be in existence at the time of the transaction. This is in contrast to a foreign currency commitment, which typically involves market prices that have been previously determined at the time of the commitment. If a forecasted transaction is denominated in foreign currency, exchange rate fluctuations could affect the values associated with the forecasted transaction. For example, a U.S. manufacturing company may forecast sales of goods to a foreign customer with payment for the goods to be received in foreign currency. In order to reduce the risk due to exchange rate fluctuations which could result in a decrease in the U.S. dollar equivalent associated with the forecasted sale, the company could hedge the forecasted transaction with a derivative instrument. Such hedging is referred to as a *cash flow hedge* and will qualify for special accounting treatment if specific criteria are satisfied. Some of the more significant criteria are as follows:[5]

1. At inception of the hedge, there is formal documentation of the hedging relationship and the entity's risk-management objective and strategy for undertaking the hedge.
2. Both at the inception of the hedge and on an ongoing basis, the hedging relationship is expected to be highly effective in achieving offsetting cash flows attributable to the hedged risk.
3. The forecasted transaction is a single transaction or a series of individual transactions.
4. The forecasted transaction is probable, and there is a positive expectation that the forecasted transaction(s) will occur within an insignificant variance from the initially projected date of the forecasted transaction.

If the above criteria are satisfied, the gain or loss on the hedging derivative shall be recognized as a component of other comprehensive income (outside of earnings). The cumulative gain or loss included in other comprehensive income shall then be recognized in earnings in the same period(s) in which the hedged forecasted

---

5 *Op.cit.,* pars. 24–25.

transaction affects earnings. For example, if a derivative instrument is acquired in June to hedge a forecasted purchase of inventory in August which is sold in September, the gain or loss on the derivative prior to the September sale is included in other comprehensive income. However, when the sale of inventory affects earnings in September, the gain or loss previously included in other comprehensive income is reclassified and recognized as a component of earnings in September. It is important to note that it is possible that deferred losses in other comprehensive income may not be offset by expected earnings associated with the forecasted transaction. If this is the case, the losses which will not be offset should be recognized immediately in earnings.

The accounting treatment given cash flow hedges will discontinue if

- The previously discussed criteria for a cash flow hedge are no longer met;
- The derivative instrument expires, is sold, or is exercised; or
- The entity no longer designates the derivative as a hedge on a forecasted transaction.

Once the forecasted transaction occurs, it is possible at that time to designate the original derivative, if not expired, or a new derivative as a hedge on any exposed asset or liability resulting from the transaction. If it is probable that the forecasted transaction will not occur and the cash flow hedge will be discontinued, the gain or loss accumulated in other comprehensive income should be recognized immediately in earnings.

In order to illustrate the accounting treatment for a cash flow hedge, assume the following:

1. On October 1, 20X1, a calendar-year company forecasted highly probable sales of goods to a customer in February of 20X2.
2. The sales are estimated to be in the amount of 100,000 FC with payment due at the time of delivery. The costs associated with the sale are estimated to be $100,000.
3. On October 1, 20X1, the company purchased a European put option to sell FC for U.S. dollars at a strike price of 1 FC = $1.35 at the end of February, 20X2. A premium of $3,000 was paid for the option.
4. The value of the option on December 31, 20X1, is $5,000.
5. The spot rate at the end of February 20X2 is 1 FC = $1.26.

Illustration 10-7 presents the necessary entries to account for the cash flow hedge of the forecasted transaction.

The use of the put option in Illustration 10-7 provided a hedge against the adverse effects that changes in the foreign exchange rate had on the forecasted transaction. The effect the cash flow hedge had on the forecasted transaction is summarized as follows:

	Without the Put Option	With the Put Option
Sales price	$126,000	$126,000
Cost of sales.	(100,000)	(100,000)
Gross profit	$ 26,000	$ 26,000
Gain on option		6,000
Total effect on earnings.	$ 26,000	$ 32,000

The total effect on earnings resulting from the use of the put option is the same as what would have resulted if there were no risk of exchange rate fluctuation (the spot rate at the forecast date does not change) less the cost of the option (sales of $135,000 less cost of sales of $100,000 less the cost of the option of $3,000 equals $32,000).

Illustration 10-7
Cash Flow Hedge of a Forecasted Transaction

October 1, 20X1

Investment in Put Option	3,000	
Cash		3,000
To record purchase of put option.		

December 31, 20X1 ....

Investment in Put Option	2,000	
Other Comprehensive Income		2,000
To recognize gain in the value of the option.		

February 28, 20X2

Investment in Put Option	4,000	
Other Comprehensive Income		4,000
To recognize gain in the value of the option prior to the transaction date. The value of the option at February 28 is the difference between the strike price of \$1.35 and the spot rate of \$1.26 for the 100,000 FC.		
Foreign Currency	126,000	
Sales		126,000
To record actual sale of 100,000 FC when the spot rate is 1 FC = \$1.26.		
Cost of Sales	100,000	
Inventory		100,000
To record cost of sales.		
Cash	135,000	
Investment in Put Option		9,000
Foreign Currency		126,000
To record exercise of put option.		
Other Comprehensive Income	6,000	
Gain on Options		6,000
To recognize in earnings the net gain on the put option when the forecasted transaction affects earnings.		

Summary of Hedging Transactions

When transactions are denominated in one currency and measured in another, changes in currency exchange rates can expose the transacting party to potential exchange gains or losses. In order to reduce the uncertainty associated with exchange rate changes, forward contracts and other derivatives are often used to hedge against this exposure. Forward contracts and options may also provide speculative opportunities. The following table summarizes some of the details relating to these risk-management techniques.

	Hedge of an Exposed Position	Hedge of an Identifiable Commitment	Speculative Hedge	Hedge of a Forecasted Transaction
Basic purpose for using the hedging instrument.	Hedge the exchange rate risk between the transaction date and the settlement date.	Hedge the risk between the commitment date and the transaction date, and maintain the dollar basis of the transaction as of the commitment date.	Speculate on the changing values of foreign currencies over time.	Hedge exchange rate risk which is anticipated to affect forecasted transactions
Time period covered.	From the transaction date to the expiration of the instrument used to hedge.	From the date of commitment to the date of the transaction or life of the instrument, whichever is earlier.	The life of the instrument.	From the inception of the hedge to the date the forecasted transaction actually occurs.
Calculation of the gain or loss on the forward contract used as a hedge.	Measured as the difference between the forward rate at the date of the hedge and the spot rate at termination of the contract.	Measured as the difference between the forward rate at the commitment date and the forward rate at the date of the transaction.	Measured as the difference between the forward rates over the life of the instrument.	Measured as the difference between the forward rate at the time of the hedge and the forward rate when the forecasted transaction actually occurs.
Calculation of the gain or loss on an option used as a hedge.	Measured as the difference between the premium paid for the option and the fair market value of the option at the time the option is exercised or expires.	Measured as the difference between the premium paid for the option and the fair market value of the option at the time the transaction, which was committed to, occurs.	Measured as the difference between the premium paid for the option and the fair market value of the option at the time the option is traded, is exercised, or expires.	Measured as the difference between the premium paid for the option and the fair market value of the option at the date the forecasted transaction actually occurs.
Recognition of gain or loss.	Recognized on an accrual basis in earnings currently, along with the gain or loss on the hedged item attributable to the risk being hedged.	Recognized on an accrual basis as a gain or loss until the date of the transaction. In addition, an offsetting gain or loss on the commitment is also recognized as a component of earnings prior to the transaction date. At the date of the transaction, the dollar basis of the transaction is adjusted by the amount of the gain or loss on the commitment.	Recognized on an accrual basis as a component of current earnings.	Recognized as a component of other comprehensive income prior to the time the forecasted transaction actually occurs. When the forecasted transaction occurs and affects earnings, the gain or loss included in other comprehensive income is recognized as a component of earnings.

(continued)

	Hedge of an Exposed Position	Hedge of an Identifiable Commitment	Speculative Hedge	Hedge of a Forecasted Transaction
Treatment if the life of the instrument extends beyond the settlement date of an exposed position.	The gain or loss accruing after the settlement date is recognized as a component of current income.	Not applicable.	Not applicable.	Not applicable.
Early expiration of the hedging instrument.	If the instrument expires prior to the settlement date of the exposed position, gains or losses are measured through that point in time and recognized as previously stated.	If the instrument expires prior to the transaction date, gains or losses are measured through that point in time and recognized as previously stated.	Not applicable.	If the instrument expires prior to the date of the forecasted transaction, gains or losses are measured through that point in time and recognized as previously stated.
Treatment if the instrument is for more than the amount of the hedged item.	The excessive portion of the instrument should be accounted for as a speculative hedge.	The excessive portion of the instrument should be accounted for as a speculative hedge.	Not applicable.	The excessive portion of the instrument should be accounted for as a speculative hedge.
Treatment if the instrument is for less than the amount at risk (the hedge is not totally effective).	Gains or losses are recognized as a partial offset against the losses or gains on the hedged item.	Gains or losses are accounted for as before and are, therefore, recognized as a partial adjustment to the basis of the transaction.	Not applicable.	Gains and losses are recognized as before.

Disclosures Regarding Financial Instruments and Hedging Activity

The discussion in this chapter has identified foreign currency forward contracts, currency swaps, and options as ways that a company might manage its foreign currency risks. These are just a few of the instruments which an entity might use to manage its financial risks associated with a broad range of business activities. For example, a producer of foodstuffs might use commodity options on various agricultural goods to manage the risk of changing prices. A financial institution might use interest rate swaps to manage the spread between interest rates on dollars loaned and dollars received. There has been explosive growth in the number of financial instruments that are designated to help entities manage a variety of financial risks.

In order to better understand how an entity employs derivatives as foreign currency hedges, the FASB requires the following disclosures:[6]

1.   The objectives of using hedging instruments and the strategies for achieving the objective.
2.   A description of the various types of hedges, such as fair value hedges and cash flow hedges.
3.   A description of the entity's risk-management policy for hedging types along with a description of the types of transactions which are hedged.

---

6 *Ibid.*, pars. 40–41.

4. Detailed information regarding the amount of gains/losses on hedges, how such amounts are recognized in earnings or other comprehensive income, when gains/losses in other comprehensive income will be recognized in earnings, where gains/losses recognized in earnings are reported in the income statement, and gains/losses recognized due to a hedge no longer qualifying for hedge accounting.

FASB Statement No. 107 applies to all entities and calls for the disclosure of the fair value of all financial instruments (with certain exceptions) including those associated with foreign currencies. All derivatives are to be measured at fair market value and should be recorded as assets or liabilities on the balance sheet.[7] Fair values are to be provided where practical, and the methods and significant assumptions used to determine fair values are to be disclosed. Fair value is the amount at which a financial instrument would be exchanged between a willing buyer and a willing seller in an orderly transaction versus a forced sale or liquidation. The actual disclosures should be either in the body of the financial statements or in the accompanying notes.

Exhibit 10-3 presents a sample of the disclosures regarding financial instruments. It is important to note that the footnote in Exhibit 10-2 does not yet include all of the disclosure requirements for derivatives discussed above. This is because the effective date for implementing these disclosure requirements has not yet been established. However, the footnote does provide an explanation of how various financial instruments are employed. The complete set of disclosures for financial instruments is quite significant and can consist of several pages of information for many companies.

Exhibit 10-3
Schering-Plough Corporation: Notes to Consolidated Financial Statements

Financial Instruments
The table below presents the carrying values and estimated fair values for the Company's financial instruments, including derivative financial instruments. Estimated fair values were determined based on market prices, where available, or dealer quotes.

	December 31, 1996		December 31, 1995	
	Carrying Value	Estimated Fair Value	Carrying Value	Estimated Fair Value
ASSETS:				
Cash and cash equivalents	$535.1	$535.1	$321.4	$321.4
Debt and equity investments	148.0	148.0	142.6	142.6
LIABILITIES:				
Short-term borrowings	855.1	855.1	841.3	842.0
Long-term debt	46.4	46.4	87.1	88.9
Derivative Financial Instruments:				
Interest rate swap contracts	–	–	1.5	1.5
Foreign currency swap contracts	47.9	64.5	64.5	81.3

Credit and Market Risk
Most financial instruments expose the holder to credit risk for non-performance and to market risk for changes in interest and currency rates. The

---

7 FASB Statement No. 107, *Disclosures about the Fair Value of Financial Instruments* (Norwalk, CT: Financial Accounting Standards Board, 1991).

Company mitigates credit risk by dealing only with financially sound counterparties. Accordingly, the Company does not anticipate loss for non-performance. The Company manages market risk primarily by investing in short-term, highly liquid investments and, in the case of derivatives, by limiting the use of derivatives to hedging activities or by limiting potential exposure to amounts that are not material to results of operations or cash flow. The Company does not enter into derivative instruments to generate trading profits.

Derivatives

The Company has not used derivative financial instruments to manage overall interest rate or exchange rate risk. Further, the Company has not used derivative financial instruments to speculate. The use of derivative financial instruments has been limited to:

- Hedging selected foreign exchange exposures that arise from international operations, and
- International cash management.

Hedging Selected Foreign Exchange Exposures

The profitability of the Company's foreign operations, as measured in U.S. dollars, is subject to exchange rate risk. If the U.S. dollar weakens, the profitability of foreign operations benefits. However, if the U.S. dollar strengthens, the profitability of foreign operations can be adversely affected. Historically, the level of pre-tax operating profitability subject to this kind of exchange risk has been as follows:

	1996	1995	1994
Europe, Middle East, and Africa	$287.9	$264.1	$235.5
Latin America	107.5	104.5	101.8
Canada, Pacific Area, and Asia	132.0	128.5	138.8

To date, management has not deemed it cost-effective to engage in a formula-based program of hedging the profitability of these operations using derivative financial instruments. Because the Company's foreign subsidiaries purchase significant quantities of inventory payable in U.S. dollars, managing the level of inventory and related payables and the rate of inventory turnover provides a level of protection against adverse changes in exchange rates.

Questions

1. Explain how a direct exchange rate differs from an indirect one and what would happen to each if the U.S. dollar weakened.
2. Explain how interest differentials would explain why a foreign currency's spot rate is greater than its 90-day forward rate relative to the U.S. dollar.
3. If the U.S. dollar was expected to strengthen relative to a foreign currency, what effect might this have on a U.S. exporter and an investor who has a speculative hedge to sell foreign currency?
4. Assume that a U.S. company secured a 2-year bank loan from a foreign bank which is to be repaid in foreign currency. Explain how exchange rate gains and/or losses would be measured on this transaction.
5. A U.S. company imports foreign goods from France and Japan, and all transactions are denominated in the respective foreign currencies. The U.S. dollar is expected to strengthen relative to the French currency and weaken relative to the Japanese currency. Explain how hedging might be employed in these circumstances.

6. Why might a U.S. company which is forecasting sales in foreign currency have more flexibility with an option to sell foreign currency rather than with a forward contract to sell foreign currency?

7. Under what conditions would a hedge on an exposed asset position result in off-setting exchange gains?

8. A U.S. importer has hedged a foreign currency (FC) receivable with a forward contract to sell FC. Assuming that the FC is collected prior to the contract's forward date, what options are available to the U.S. company?

9. Explain how an exporter's gross profit can be maintained if the U.S. dollar begins to strengthen relative to the currency used to settle the transaction.

10. A U.S. company has a forward contract to buy 1,000 foreign currency units as a hedge against a payable of 800 foreign currency units. Explain the accounting for the excess hedge.

11. A U.S. company has sold inventory to a French customer, and the transaction is denominated in German marks. Explain how taking out a loan from a German bank might serve as a hedge against the sale.

Exercises

Exercise 1. Booker, Inc., manufactures printing presses and acquires some of its component parts from a German fabricator. On December 15, 20X4, when 1 mark (M) = $0.60, it purchased components costing 300,000 M from a German company. The resulting account payable is due in 30 days when 1 M = $0.59. Booker has a calendar year-end, and the spot rate at that time was 1 M = $0.58.

1. Prepare the journal entries to record the above transactions.
2. How might borrowing the necessary funds to pay the vendor affect net income, assuming a German bank loan is employed?

Exercise 2. Given the facts of Exercise 1, assume Booker, Inc., secured a loan from a German bank on December 31, 20X4. The principal amount of the loan is 300,000 M, bears interest at 12%, and is payable in 30 days when 1 M = $0.56. Calculate the effect on net income from the original transaction described in Exercise 1 and from the bank loan for the years 20X4 and 20X5.

Turn-in
10/02

Exercise 3. Jahnke Controls, Inc., manufactures special control devices used in the mixing of various liquids. On November 1, 20X8, a foreign customer ordered devices to be delivered on December 15, 20X8, with terms of 2/10 net 60. The devices with a U.S. cost of $90,000 were sold for 600,000 foreign currency (FC). On December 15, 20X8, Jahnke purchased a forward contract to sell FC in 60 days. Various spot and forward rates are as follows:

Date	Spot Rates	Forward Rates
November 1, 20X8	1 FC = $0.20	Forward to 2/15/20X9 1 FC = $0.198
December 15, 20X8	1 FC = $0.19	Forward to 2/15/20X9 1 FC = $0.187
December 31, 20X8	1 FC = $0.18	Forward to 2/15/20X9 1 FC = $0.179
January 31, 20X9	1 FC = $0.17	Forward to 2/15/20X9 1 FC = $0.168
February 15, 20X9	1 FC = $0.16	Forward to 3/1/20X9 1 FC = $0.159
March 1, 20X9	1 FC = $0.15	

Prepare a schedule to calculate the net income effect of the above for the years 20X8 and 20X9, assuming that the foreign customer settled the transaction on

February 15, 20X9. Separate the net income effect between that which is traceable to the FC transaction and that related to the forward contract.

Exercise 4.   Given the facts presented in Exercise 3, prepare a schedule to calculate the net income effect for the years 20X8 and 20X9, assuming each of the following situations:

1. The U.S. company decided to hedge the FC commitment by purchasing on November 1, 20X8, a forward contract to sell FC on February 15, 20X9.
2. The commitment was hedged as in 1) above, however, the foreign customer did not pay until March 1, 20X9. On February 15, 20X9, the forward contract was rolled forward to March 1, 20X9, at a forward rate of 1 FC = $0.159.

Exercise 5.   Cortez Electronics buys subassemblies from a foreign vendor. On June 1, 20X9, the company committed to acquire subassemblies costing 400,000 foreign currency units (FC). The parts will be shipped, f.o.b. shipping point, on June 15, 20X9, with payment due on July 31, 20X9. Cortez is considering two alternative forms of hedging its exposed liability position. One alternative would involve acquiring a forward contract on June 1 to buy 400,000 FC for delivery on July 31, 20X9. The forward rate would be 1 FC = $0.62, and the spot rate on June 1 is 1 FC = $0.60. As an alternative, the company has an opportunity to lend $240,000 to another party with payment due in FC and interest at the rate of 8%. The loan would be dated June 1, 20X9, and would be due on July 31, 20X9.

Determine under what conditions the company would favor one alternative over the other.

Exercise 6.   A U.S. importer purchased subassemblies, which are to be paid for in foreign currency (FC), from a foreign vendor. The importer purchased a forward contract to buy FC. Due to production delays, the FC necessary to pay the foreign vendor was not needed until 20 days after originally anticipated. Discuss the various options which would be available to the importer given the unanticipated delay.

Exercise 7.   Grande Manufacturing Company purchased equipment from a foreign vendor. The equipment, which cost 1,200,000 FC, was delivered on June 1, 20X8, and was to be paid for by July 31, 20X8. On June 1, 20X8, Grande also anticipated needing 200,000 FC on July 31, 20X8, in order to pay for additional forecasted purchases of raw materials. On June 1, 20X8, the company purchased a forward contract to buy 1,400,000 FC on July 31, 20X8. On July 31, the company purchased materials for 200,000 FC. The company has a June 30 fiscal year-end, and relevant spot and forward rates are as follows:

Forward Rate

Date in 20X8	Spot Rate	for delivery on July 31, 20X8
June 1	1 FC = $1.10	1 FC = $1.108
June 30	1 FC = 1.15	1 FC = $1.146
July 31	1 FC = 1.14	

Prepare the journal entries necessary to record the above transactions.

Exercise 8.   Maxwell Enterprises purchases forward exchange contracts for a variety of reasons. Determine the effect on 20X8 net income of each of the following hedging transactions.

(continued)

1. Forward Contract A was purchased on November 1, 20X8, for speculative purposes at a forward rate of 1 FC = $1.45 when the spot rate was $1.50. This 90-day contract to buy 100,000 FC has a forward rate of $1.43 on December 31, 20X8.
2. Forward Contract B was purchased on September 1, 20X8, as a hedge against a commitment to take delivery of equipment on December 1, 20X8. The equipment will be used by Maxwell in its manufacturing division and has a cost of 100,000 FC. Maxwell must settle the transaction in foreign currency on February 1, 20X9. The 150-day forward contract to buy 80,000 FC had a forward rate of $1.47 on September 1, 20X8. Forward rates to buy FC on February 1, 20X9, are as follows: on December 1, 20X8—$1.48; on December 31, 20X8—$1.475.
3. Forward Contract C was purchased on October 1, 20X8, to cover an exposed asset position when the spot and forward rates were $1.48 and $1.49, respectively. The contract to sell 30,000 FC expired on December 1, 20X8, when the spot rate was $1.48.
4. Forward Contract D was purchased for speculation and had terms identical to Contract C. Maxwell sold the contract on November 1, 20X8, for $250 net of commissions.

Exercise 9.   Stratco Manufacturing engages in a number of foreign currency transactions which have resulted in the following current balances:

Cash	400,000	Canadian dollars
Cash	300,000	French francs
Accounts receivable	1,200,000	French francs
Accounts receivable	850,000	Canadian dollars
Accounts payable	500,000	French francs
Accounts payable	700,000	German marks
Notes payable—line of credit	300,000	French francs

Management anticipates that the following exchange rate changes will occur in the near future:

The French franc will weaken against the dollar by 10%.
The Canadian dollar will strengthen by 5%, relative to the dollar.
The German mark will strengthen against the dollar by 15%.

Develop a strategy that will minimize Stratco's foreign currency exchange loss.

Problems

Problem 10-1.   People Power Inc. (PPI) is an international temporary service that provides contract help throughout the world. Selected transactions occurring during its calendar business year 20X5 are as follows:

Transaction A: On October 1, 20X5, PPI paid a European advertising agency 200,000 foreign currency units (FC) for an advertising campaign. In anticipation of this transaction, on September 1, 20X5, PPI purchased a 30-day contract to buy 200,000 FC at a forward rate of $1.26.

Transaction B: On December 20, 20X5, a European customer contracted for a temporary work force to begin working on March 1, 20X6, for a 3-week project. The contract fee is 100,000 FC and, at the commitment date, PPI purchased a 60-day forward contract to sell 120,000 FC at a forward rate of $1.285. At December 31, 20X5, a 49-day contract to sell FC had a forward rate of $1.31.

Transaction C: On December 15, 20X5, PPI forecasted a purchase of supplies from a European vendor. The 100,000 FC forecasted purchase would occur in approximately 30 days. At the same time, the company purchased a 30-day forward contract to buy 100,000 FC at a forward rate of $1.29. The contract's forward rate on December 31, 20X5, is $1.292.

Transaction D: PPI purchased 3 speculative forward contracts during 20X5. One contract was purchased on October 1, 20X5, and was a 90-day contract to buy 50,000 FC at a forward rate of $1.31. Sixty days later, the contract was sold at a forward rate of $1.32. Another contract to sell 40,000 FC in 60 days was acquired on December 1, 20X5, when the forward rate was $1.29. The contract is still held at year-end. The forward rate for a 30-day contract to sell is $1.30 on December 31, 20X5.

A final contract to sell 100,000 FC in 180 days was acquired on November 1, 20X5, at a forward rate of $1.33. On December 1, 20X5, this contract was designated as a hedge on a firm foreign currency commitment when the forward rate for the remaining 150 days was $1.34.

Relevant spot exchange rates are as follows:

Date	1 FC =
September 1, 20X5	$1.25
October 1, 20X5	1.30
December 1, 20X5	1.31
December 15, 20X5	1.30
December 20, 20X5	1.29
December 31, 20X5	1.28
March 1, 20X6	1.32

Required:

1. With respect to transaction A, calculate the effect of the transaction on net income and what the effect would have been had a forward contract not been employed.
2. With respect to transaction B, calculate the net income effect of the forward contract as of December 31, 20X5.
3. With respect to transaction C, calculate the net income effect of the transaction as of December 31, 20X5.
4. With respect to transaction D, calculate the 20X5 income effect of the various speculative hedges.

Problem 10-2.   Master Industries manufactures large hydroelectric turbines. On February 1, 20X8, the company committed to deliver a turbine to a Canadian customer with delivery on or about May 1, 20X9. The turbine is to be constructed over a 12-month period as detailed below:

Date	Event
April 1, 20X8	Begin construction. The completed contract method is used versus percent of completion.
July 31, 20X8	Progress payment of 500,000 Canadian dollars (C$) received.
October 1, 20X8	Received construction components from German vendor—300,000 German marks (DM) payable November 30, 20X8.
November 30, 20X8	Progress payment of 500,000 C$ received.
December 31, 20X8	Master Industries' year-end.

(continued)

Date	Event
March 31, 20X9	Construction completed at an additional cost of $700,000. This amount does not include the components purchased on October 1, 20X8.
May 1, 20X9	Turbine is shipped to customer f.o.b. shipping point.
June 30, 20X9	Final payment of 500,000 C$ received.

On February 1, 20X8, Master purchased 3 forward contracts. Each contract was to sell 500,000 C$ on July 31, 20X8; November 30, 20X8; and June 30, 20X9, with forward rates of 1 C$ = $0.712, 1 C$ = $0.69, and 1 C$ = $0.705, respectively. Various spot rates are as follows:

February 1, 20X8	1 C$ = $0.70	December 31, 20X8	1 C$ = $0.61
July 31, 20X8	1 C$ = 0.65	March 31, 20X9	1 C$ = 0.63
October 1, 20X8	1 DM = 0.55	May 1, 20X9	1 C$ = 0.64
November 30, 20X8	1 C$ = 0.63	June 30, 20X9	1 C$ = 0.63
November 30, 20X8	1 DM = 0.58		

On December 31, 20X8, the forward rate for the contract to sell FC on June 30, 20X9, is $0.632.

Required:

1. Prepare the necessary journal entries to account for Master's activities related to the above construction project through December 31, 20X8. Divide your entries between those that relate to the construction project and those that relate to the forward contracts.
2. Based on the above information, calculate the amount of gross profit which would be reported for this construction project.

Problem 10-3.   Equipment Reconditioners Inc. (ERI) specializes in reconditioning equipment used in the blow-molding process. In recent years, an increasing number of sales have been made to Mexican companies. On March 1, 20X8, a Mexican customer committed to acquire a reconditioned machine for a sale price of 2,500,000 pesos. The cost to recondition the machine was $250,000. The equipment would be shipped on April 15, 20X8, f.o.b. shipping point. Allowing for installation and setup time, payment for the equipment is due on May 31, 20X8.

Also on March 1, 20X8, the Mexican customer indicated a very strong interest in taking delivery of a second machine sometime in early July 20X8. It is anticipated that the second machine would have a similar cost and sales value as the first machine.

On March 1, 20X8, ERI purchased a forward contract to sell 2,500,000 pesos on May 31, 20X8, in order to hedge the commitment regarding the first machine. The contract had a forward rate of 1 peso = $0.129. Although there was no firm commitment regarding the potential sale of a second machine, the forecasted sale seemed very likely, and on April 1, 20X8, ERI purchased a put option to sell 2,500,000 pesos on July 15, 20X8. The option fee was $3,000 and had a strike price of $0.1295. On June 1, 20X8, a second machine was shipped to the Mexican customer. This sale had identical terms and values as the first sale except that payment was due on July 15, 20X8. The value of the option was $3,750 as of June 1, 20X8.

Relevant 20X8 spot rates are as follows:

March 1	1 peso = $0.130	May 31	1 peso = $0.132
April 1	1 peso = 0.131	June 1	1 peso = 0.128
April 15	1 peso = 0.128	July 15	1 peso = 0.126

On April 15, 20X8, the forward rate on a contract to sell pesos on May 31, 20X8, is $0.1285.

Required:

1. Prepare all necessary entries suggested by the above facts.
2. Prepare a schedule which calculates the income effect the use of an option had on the sale of equipment.

Problem 10-4.   Jenner Corporation recently has begun to expand its international markets and has engaged in several foreign currency transactions. In one particular series of transactions, the company purchased components from a French manufacturer on October 1, 20X8. The components cost 800,000 French francs (FF), and Jenner anticipated that the components could be assembled at its Kentucky plant for an additional cost of $40,000. Upon receipt of the goods on October 20, 20X8, Jenner entered into an agreement with a British company to purchase the finished goods for $224,900, to be settled in British pounds (£). The goods will be shipped on November 30, 20X8, with payment to be received on January 20, 20X9.

Required:

1. Assuming the liability to the French vendor becomes due before the payment from the British company is received, how can Jenner protect itself against fluctuations in the respective foreign currencies?
2. Assuming the payment to the French vendor is due subsequent to the receipt of pounds from the British company, how can Jenner guard against foreign currency fluctuations relative to the dollar?
3. Assume that on October 20, 20X8, Jenner purchases a forward contract to sell British pounds for 800,000 French francs (FF) on January 20, 20X9. Assume that the payment to the French vendor may be paid on or after January 20, 20X9. Given the following rates, calculate the contract premium or discount on the forward contract.

   Spot rates as of October 20, 20X8:

$$£1 \quad = \quad \$1.73$$
$$£1 \quad = \quad 17.3 \text{ FF}$$
$$1 \text{ FF} = \quad £0.058$$
$$1 \text{ FF} = \quad \$0.10$$

   Forward rate as of October 20, 20X8, for delivery on January 20, 20X9:

$$£1 \quad = \quad 16 \text{ FF}$$

4. Assume the same spot and forward rates as given in (3) and that the following additional forward rates are available:

   Forward rates as of October 20, 20X8, for delivery on January 20, 20X9:

$$£1 \quad = \quad \$1.72$$
$$\$1 \quad = \quad 9.5 \text{ FF}$$

   Calculate whether Jenner is better off (a) using one forward contract of £50,000 for 800,000 FF to settle the amount due the French vendor or (b) buying two contracts: one to sell £50,000 for dollars and the other to sell dollars for 800,000 FF.

Problem 10-5. Wagner Corporation transacts business in a number of foreign currencies and had the following activities during the current year. On July 1, the company signed a 60-day, 400,000 foreign currency A (FC-A) note with a foreign bank. The note is to be repaid in FC-A and bears simple interest at the rate of 7.2%. The company used the proceeds of the note to purchase manufacturing equipment. The equipment will be depreciated by the straight-line method over a useful life of 15 years (salvage value is to be ignored).

On July 15, the company committed to purchase inventory from a foreign vendor with a delivery date of August 15. Payment of 250,000 foreign currency B (FC-B) is due on October 15. In order to limit their exposure on this transaction, the company hedged the commitment by acquiring a contract to buy 250,000 FC-B for delivery on October 15. Forward rates for a contract to buy FC = B on October 15 are as follows:

On July 15	$1.06
On July 31	1.061
On August 31	1.068
On September 30	0.071

On August 1, the company acquired a forward contract to buy 404,800 FC-A on August 31, in order to repay the loan taken out on July 1. The contract was at the forward rate of 1 FC-A = $0.66.

On September 1, the company shipped (f.o.b. shipping point) finished goods to a foreign vendor with payment due on October 15. These items were the inventory that the company ordered on July 15, as discussed above. The sales price was 600,000 foreign currency C (FC-C).

Selected spot rates are as follows:

	1 FC-A =	1 FC-B =	1 FC-C =
July 1	$0.62		
July 15		$1.04	
July 31	0.66	1.05	
August 1	0.65		
August 31	0.64		
September 1		1.06	$0.56
September 30	0.67	1.07	0.62

Required:

Prepare a schedule by month that details the effect on net income of the above transactions for the months of July, August, and September.

Problem 10-6. Boyd Enterprises has begun to purchase certain component parts from a foreign vendor. These purchases will be denominated in foreign currency units (FC), and the company is trying to evaluate various alternative methods of paying for the purchases. The company does not expect to order from the foreign vendor more than twice a year and with the following terms:

Commitment (order date)	30 days before delivery
Delivery	f.o.b. destination
Payment date	60 days after receipt
Late payments	Charged interest at the rate of ½% per month.

Various alternative methods of payment are as follows:

Option A   Do not hedge the exposed liability position.
Option B   Hedge the commitment with a forward contract due on payment date.

Option C   Hedge the transaction at delivery date versus commitment date.

Option D   Borrow foreign currency on the payment date with repayment of the note in 30 days. The note bears interest at 6% and is denominated in foreign currency units.

The company wants to evaluate the options under two alternative assumptions regarding spot and forward rates. The assumptions are as follows:

	Assumption 1	Assumption 2
Spot rate at commitment date	$1.200	$1.20
Spot rate at delivery date	1.224	1.17
Spot rate on payment date	1.289	1.12
Spot rate 30 days after payment date	1.320	1.10
90-day forward rate at commitment date	1.210	1.18
120-day forward rate at commitment date.	1.220	1.17
60-day forward rate at delivery date	1.230	1.19

Required:

Prepare a schedule that shows the effect on net income for each of the payment options given the assumptions regarding exchange rates. Assume that the average purchase is for 100,000 FC.

Problem 10-7.   Global Distributing, Inc., is building a new warehouse facility in Germany. The facility is expected to cost 2,000,000 German marks (DM), and construction will take place over a 6-month period beginning March 1, 20X8.

Construction payments will occur as follows:

March 1	20% down payment due
May 31	30% progress payment due
August 31	40% progress payment due
September 30	10% final holdback payment due

Global will finance the construction as follows:

Down payment—financed with a 90-day note due May 31 from a German bank with interest at 8%.

May 31 progress payment—financed by a swap of U.S. $426,000 for marks. The swap requires Global to exchange 600,000 marks for $426,000 on September 30, 20X8, plus 12,000 marks for interest.

August 31 progress payment—financed by a forward contract to buy marks. The contract was acquired on March 1 and had a forward rate of 1 DM = $0.687.

September 30 holdback payment—financed by purchasing marks at the spot rate.

Various 20X8 spot rates are as follows:

| March 1 | 1 DM = $0.70 | August 31 | 1 DM = $0.69 |
| May 31 | 1 DM = $0.71 | September 30 | 1 DM = $0.68 |

Required:

Assuming Global has no other debt or borrowings:

1. Calculate the dollar basis of the new warehouse, including capitalized interest/finance costs.
2. Calculate what the dollar basis would have been if no derivatives or financial instruments had been employed.

Translation of Foreign Financial Statements

The magnitude of U.S. investment abroad has increased significantly in response to a more global economy, reduction in trade barriers, and the growth of international capital markets. Similarly, these same factors have encouraged an increase in foreign investment in the United States. The size and growth of these investment patterns are suggested by the following statistics:

U.S. Investment Position Abroad

	1992	1993	1994	1995	1996
In millions of dollars	502,063	564,283	640,320	717,554	796,494

U.S. Business Acquired or Established by Foreign Direct Investors

	1992	1993	1994	1995	1996
Number of investments	941	980	1,036	1,124	1,158
Investment outlays in millions of dollars	15,333	26,229	45,626	57,195	80,537

Source: Department of Commerce.

The previous chapter identified a variety of transactions that may occur between a domestic (U.S.) company and a foreign entity. These transactions were not dependent on the domestic company's having any type of ownership interest in the foreign entity. However, as the above statistics suggest, many domestic companies do have an ownership interest in or control of foreign companies, and accounting for these interests presents special problems. The accounting treatments of domestic and foreign entity relationships that involve some degree of control are summarized as follows:

Domestic Entity	Foreign Entity	Accounting Treatment
Home Office	Branch	Branch accounting
Parent	Subsidiary	Consolidated financial statements or separate financial statements
Investor	Investee	Investment in foreign entity at cost or equity

The above relationships suggest the need to combine or consolidate the foreign entity's financial statements with those of the domestic entity. The financial statements of a foreign entity typically are measured in the currency of that foreign country. This currency usually is different from the reporting currency of the domestic entity. Therefore, a methodology must be developed to express the foreign entity's financial statements in the reporting currency of the domestic entity. The process of expressing amounts denominated or measured in foreign currencies into amounts measured in the reporting currency (dollars) of the domestic entity (U.S.) is referred to as *foreign currency translation*.

In addition to establishing a methodology for translation, the process is complicated by the reality that the foreign financial statements may have been prepared using accounting principles that are different from those of the domestic reporting entity. As discussed in Chapter 9, there are a number of differences between generally accepted accounting principles (GAAP) employed in the United States and principles employed in financial statements of certain foreign entities. Therefore, prior to translation, the statements of a foreign entity must be adjusted to reflect the principles (GAAP) employed by the domestic reporting entity. For example, a foreign subsidiary may not be required to capitalize leases although the lease would be capitalized if GAAP followed by the parent company were employed. Before proceeding with translation, the accounting for these leases must be adjusted to conform with the principles employed by the reporting entity. The international efforts to harmonize accounting principles are slowly eliminating the need for such adjustments.

Statement of Financial Accounting Standards No. 52

In late 1981, after considering two exposure drafts, the FASB issued Statement of Financial Accounting Standards No. 52, *Foreign Currency Translation*. FASB Statement No. 52 adopted a *functional currency* approach which focuses on whether the domestic reporting entity's cash flows will be indirectly or directly affected by changes in the exchange rates of the foreign entity's currency. Assume a foreign entity operates exclusively in its own country using only its currency. It is questionable whether changes in the exchange rate between its currency and that of the parent entity would directly affect the parent's cash flows. After all, how could changes in the rate of exchange between the British pound and the dollar affect you if your transactions were primarily denominated in pounds? However, if a foreign entity operates or functions in a currency other than its own currency, exchange rate changes between these currencies presumably will directly affect cash flows of the parent. In this instance, the resulting effect should be the same as if transactions were denominated in a foreign currency.

Functional Currency Identification

In order to achieve the objectives of the translation process, it is critical to identify the foreign entity's functional currency. The functional currency is the currency of the primary economic environment in which the entity generates and expends cash. For example, assume a French company that is a subsidiary of a U.S. company purchases labor and materials and pays for these items with French francs. The finished product of the company is sold, and payment is received in francs. In this situation, changes in the exchange rate between the French franc and the dollar of the U.S. parent do not generally have an economic impact on the French company or its U.S. parent. Because of this, the French company's day-to-day operations are not dependent on the economic environment of the U.S. parent's currency (dollars). Therefore, the French franc would be considered the functional currency of the French company.

The identification of the functional currency is not always easily arrived at. Assume the French company discussed above received most of its debt capital in the form of dollars from an American bank and that its products were sold primarily in the United States with payment being received in dollars. In this case, changes in the exchange rate between the franc and the dollar would affect the parent company's cash flows. The French company's day-to-day operations are dependent on the economic environment of the U.S. parent's currency (dollars). Changes in the foreign entity's assets and liabilities will, or will have the potential to, immediately impact the cash flows of the U.S. parent. It is important to note that a foreign entity may have a functional currency which is not its domestic currency or that of the parent entity. Thus, the French company could have the German mark as its functional currency, rather than the franc or the dollar, if the mark is the currency that primarily influences the company's cash flows. This might be the case if the French company's financing, sales, and purchases of goods and services are denominated in marks.

Identification of the functional currency is not subject to definitive criteria. However, certain basic economic factors should be considered in making this identification.[1] Some of these factors are summarized in Exhibit 11-1.

Exhibit 11-1
Factors Suggesting the Functional Currency

Indicator	Foreign Currency as Functional Currency	Parent's Currency as Functional Currency
Cash flows	Cash flows are primarily in the foreign currency. Such flows do not impact the parent's cash flows.	Cash flows directly impact the parent's cash flows and are readily available to the parent.
Sales price	Sales prices are influenced by local factors rather than exchange rates.	Sales prices are influenced by international factors and exchange rate changes.
Sales market	There is an active and primarily local market.	The sales market is primarily in the parent's country.
Expenses	Goods and services are acquired locally and denominated in local currencies.	Goods and services are acquired from the parent's country.
Financing	Financing is secured locally and denominated in local currencies. Debt is serviced through local operations.	Financing is secured primarily from the parent or is denominated in the parent's currency.
Intercompany transactions and arrangements	Intercompany transaction volume is low. Major interrelationships between foreign and parent operations do not exist.	Intercompany transaction volume is high. There are major interrelationships between entities. A foreign entity holds major assets and obligations of the parent.

Although these factors focus on the parent's currency as a possible functional currency, it is important to remember that the functional currency may be one other than that of the foreign entity or the parent.

These factors should be considered both individually and collectively in order to identify the functional currency. The selection of a functional currency should be applied consistently over time, unless significant changes suggest that the functional currency has changed. Changes should not be accounted for on a retroactive basis or as a cumulative effect.

Objectives of the Translation Process

The focus of FASB Statement No. 52 is critical to achieving the objectives of translation. The compatibility resulting from translating various financial statements into a common reporting currency is a practical necessity. However, this process should not alter the significance of the results and relationships experienced by the individual

---

1 Statement of Financial Accounting Standards No. 52, *Foreign Currency Translation* (Stamford: Financial Accounting Standards Board, 1981), par. 42.

entities comprising the consolidated entity. Consistent with this underlying concern, the translation process should accomplish the following objectives:

   a)   *Provide information that is generally compatible with the expected economic effects of a rate change on an enterprise's cash flows and equity.*

   b)   *Reflect in consolidated statements the financial results and relationships of the individual consolidated entities as measured in their functional currencies in conformity with U.S. generally accepted accounting principles.*[2]

The first objective recognizes that exchange rate changes may or may not have any substantial or direct effect on the cash flows and economic well-being of the constituent entities. Assume that a foreign entity's operations are not dependent upon the economic environment of the parent's functional currency. In this case, changes in exchange rates between the foreign entity and the parent are not expected to have an immediate or potentially immediate effect on the cash flows and well-being of the parent company. Therefore, the parent has not experienced a gain or loss due to exchange rate changes, and current period net income should not be affected. For example, assume that a foreign subsidiary borrows 1,000 foreign currencies (FC) from a bank in order to purchase a tract of land for 1,000 FC when the rate of exchange is 1 FC = $1. If the land were to be sold for 1,000 FC when the rate of exchange is 1 FC = $0.80, 1,000 FC would be available to repay the loan. Neither the foreign entity's nor the parent's cash flows, nor their economic well-being, would have been adversely affected by the change in exchange rates.

However, if exchange rates changes are expected to, or have the potential to, immediately affect the parent company's cash flows or economic well-being, the effect of such changes should be included in current-period income. To illustrate, assume the same facts as in the above example except that the funds necessary to purchase the land were borrowed from the U.S. parent and that the funds were to be repaid in dollars. If the land were to be sold for 1,000 FC and the proceeds converted to U.S. dollars when 1 FC = $0.80, only $800 would be available to repay the loan. Therefore, the change in exchange rates would have an effect on both the potential cash flows available to the parent and the parent's economic well-being. This adverse effect of the exchange rate changes should be reflected in the current-period net income.

The expected economic effects of rate changes must be properly reflected in financial statements and may be analyzed as follows:

Expected Economic Effect of Rate Changes	Accounting Response to Effect of Rate Changes
Cash inflows increase, and/or cash outflows decrease. Economic well-being is affected.	Translation gains should be included in net income.
Cash inflows decrease, and/or cash outflows increase. Economic well-being is affected.	Translation losses should be included in net income.
Cash inflows and/or outflows are not affected. Economic well-being is not affected	No translation gain or loss should be included in net income. The effect of rate changes will not be realized until the parent's investment in the foreign entity is disposed of or liquidated. Therefore, the effect of translation does not affect current net income and is shown as a separate component of other comprehensive income.

2 *Ibid.,* par. 4.

Expected Economic Effects of Rate Changes When the Functional Currency Is Not the Foreign Currency.   The first objective of translation seeks to provide accounting information that is consistent or compatible with the expected economic effects of rate changes. This objective is satisfied by focusing on the functional currency and may be demonstrated by consideration of the following example. Assume that a foreign subsidiary is formed on January 1, 20X2, when the rate of exchange is 1 foreign currency (FC) = $1.50. At the date of formation, the subsidiary

1. Received a $30,000 equity investment in dollars from the parent company's sale of stock.
2. Received a $120,000 loan in dollars from a U.S. bank.
3. Purchased a parcel of land for 100,000 FC payable in dollars.

At the end of 20X2 when the rate of exchange is 1 FC = $2.00, the parcel of land is sold for 100,000 FC collectible in dollars. Shortly thereafter, dollars will be remitted to the U.S. bank and the parent.

When evaluating the factors used to identify the functional currency, it would appear that the dollar, not the foreign currency, is the functional currency, because financing is denominated in dollars, acquisitions of goods and services are paid for in dollars, and sales are receivable in dollars. Furthermore, the substance of these transactions suggests that the foreign subsidiary is merely a conduit through which the U.S. parent conducts business and experiences dollar cash flows. Therefore, if the translation process is sound, it should provide information that is compatible with the expected economic effects of rate changes. In this particular example, the translated dollar amounts for the subsidiary should be identical to the dollar balances that would have resulted had the U.S. parent engaged in these transactions without the foreign subsidiary serving as a conduit. In that case, the following analysis would have been appropriate:

Parent's entries to record the transactions—measured in U.S. dollars:

1/1/X2	Cash		150,000	
		Owners' Equity		30,000
		Loans Payable		120,000
		To record receipt of $30,000 from stock sale and $120,000 from loan proceeds.		
	Land		150,000	
		Cash		150,000
		To record purchase of land.		
12/31/X2	Cash		200,000	
		Land		150,000
		Gain on Sale		50,000
		To record sale of land.		

Resulting financial statements at year-end—measured in U.S. dollars:

Balance Sheet

Cash	200,000
Loan Payable	120,000
Owners' Equity:	
Original Amount	30,000
Net Income	50,000
	200,000

Income Statement

Gain on Sale	50,000

If the U.S. parent engaged in the transactions through a foreign subsidiary, the following analysis would be appropriate:

Foreign subsidiary's entries to record the transactions—measured in FC:

1/1/X2	Cash	100,000	
	Owners' Equity		20,000
	Loans Payable		80,000
	To record receipt of $30,000 equity investment and $120,000 loan, both of which are denominated in U.S. dollars.		
	Land	100,000	
	Cash		100,000
	To record purchase of land for 100,000 FC.		
12/31/X2	Loan Payable	20,000	
	Exchange Gain on Loan		20,000
	To adjust $120,000 loan payable, which is denominated in dollars, to an equivalent amount of FC due to change in rate from 1 FC = $1.50 to 1 FC = $2.00.		
	Cash	100,000	
	Land		100,000
	To record sale of land for 100,000 FC.		

Resulting financial statements at year-end—measured in FC and translated into U.S. dollars:

Balance Sheet

	FC	Relevant Exchange Rate	$
Cash	100,000	2.00	200,000
Loan Payable	60,000	2.00	120,000
Owners' Equity:.....................			
Original Amount	20,000	1.50	30,000
Net Income......................	20,000	see below	50,000
	100,000		200,000

Income Statement

	FC	Relevant Exchange Rate	$
Exchange Gain on Loan	20,000	2.00	40,000
Translation Adjustment		**to Balance**	**10,000**
	20,000	20000 x .5 (2.00-1.50)	50,000

plus

When comparing the above resulting financial statements to those presented earlier, assuming the transactions occurred without the foreign subsidiary, it is important to note that the statements are identical. The first objective of the translation process has been satisfied, and the results confirm that

1. The foreign subsidiary merely acted as a conduit through which the U.S. parent operated.
2. If the dollar is the functional currency, the foreign subsidiary's translated financial statements are identical to those statements that would have resulted had the transactions been originally recorded in the dollar functional currency.

3. The transactions of the foreign entity had an immediate or potentially immediate impact on the dollar cash flows and, therefore, the impact was included in net income.

If the proceeds from the sale of the land were subsequently remitted to the U.S. bank and the parent, the proceeds of 100,000 FC collectible in dollars would result in $200,000 being available. The U.S. bank would receive $120,000 (ignoring interest for purposes of discussion). The remaining $80,000 would be distributed to the parent which is $50,000 more than their original investment of $30,000. Therefore, the exchange rate change did have a potentially immediate effect on the cash flows and economic well-being of the parent and should be included in net income of the period in which exchange rates change. Furthermore, if the rate had not changed, the proceeds of 100,000 FC collectible in dollars would have resulted in $150,000 (the rate remains at 1 FC = $1.50) of which $120,000 would have been remitted to the U.S. bank. The remaining $30,000 is the same as the parent's original investment and clearly the absence of an exchange rate change had no effect on the parent's potentially immediate cash flows and/or economic well-being.

Expected Economic Effects of Rate Changes When the Functional Currency Is the Foreign Currency.   If the foreign currency (FC) is the functional currency, rate changes are not expected to have an immediate impact on the parent's cash flows. Therefore, in response to rate changes, the accounting information should not include any translation adjustment in the determination of current net income. Instead, translation adjustments should be classified as a separate component of other comprehensive income. This component would be recognized as a component of net income when realized through the liquidation or disposition of the foreign entity. In order to demonstrate these concepts, consider the following example.

Assume a foreign subsidiary is formed on January 1, 20X2, when the rate of exchange is 1 FC = $1.50. At the date of formation, the subsidiary

1. Received 20,000 FC from the U.S. parent,
2. Received an 80,000 FC loan from a local bank, and
3. Purchased a parcel of land from a local party for 100,000 FC.

At the end of 20X2 when the rate of exchange is 1 FC = $2.00, the parcel of land is sold to a local party for 100,000 FC.

When evaluating the factors used to identify a functional currency, it would appear that the FC is the functional currency because financing is denominated in FC, acquisitions of goods and services are paid for in FC, and sales prices are based on local economics and are collected in FC. Furthermore, the substance of these transactions suggests that the foreign subsidiary operates independently of the U.S. parent, and its day-to-day operations are not dependent on the economic environment of the U.S. parent's currency but on that of the foreign country. An analysis of the foreign entity's activities is as follows:

Foreign subsidiary's entries to record the transactions—measured in FC:

1/1/X2	Cash	100,000	
	Owners' Equity		20,000
	Loans Payable		80,000
	To record receipt of 20,000 FC from		
	equity investment and 80,000 FC from		
	loan proceeds.		
	Land	100,000	
	Cash		100,000
	To record purchase of land for 100,000 FC.		
12/31/X2	Cash	100,000	
	Land		100,000
	To record sale of land for 100,000 FC.		

Resulting financial statements at year-end—measured in FC and translated into U.S. dollars (using the functional method):

Balance Sheet

	FC	Relevant Exchange Rate	$
Cash	100,000	2.00	200,000
Loan Payable	80,000	2.00	160,000
Owners' Equity			
Original Amount	20,000	1.50	30,000
Net Income.	0		0
Translation Adjustment—			
Other Comprehensive Income . . .		**to Balance**	**10,000**
	100,000		200,000

In comparing the results of the above example to that of the prior example, where the foreign entity was merely a conduit and the functional currency was the dollar, several important differences surface. Notice that the exchange rate change required an adjustment to the loan payable when the dollar was the functional currency but did not require this adjustment when the foreign currency was the functional currency. When the FC is the functional currency, changes in the exchange rate did not produce a gain with respect to the loan because the loan is denominated in FC and rate changes have no impact on the settlement value of the loan. There is no indication that the exchange rate changes will impact immediately the parent's cash flows. Therefore, to include the translation adjustment as a component of net income would not be compatible with the economic effects of the rate change. It is quite likely that the foreign entity will redeploy available cash by buying more goods and services and/or by repaying the loan. In either case, cash flows are not being remitted to the parent. Because the impact on the parent's cash flows is unclear, the translation adjustment is included as a separate component of other comprehensive income rather than as net income. It is important to note that the translation adjustment amount may be temporary and, in fact, either increase or decrease over time. For example, if the trial balance of the subsidiary at year-end 20X3 is the same as it was at year-end 20X2 and the rate of exchange returns to 1 FC = $1.50, then the balance of the cumulative translation adjustment will be zero. However, if the exchange rate at year-end 20X3 had been 1 FC = $2.20, the balance of the cumulative translation adjustment would have increased.

If there is a balance in the cumulative translation adjustment, its impact on the parent's cash flows and/or economic well-being is normally not considered to be immediate or potentially immediate. However, the potential impact on cash flows will become apparent if the parent liquidates or disposes of its investment in the foreign subsidiary. At that time, the separate component of other comprehensive income may be transferred to the income statement and be recognized as a component of net income. To illustrate, assume that in the above example the foreign subsidiary is liquidated after having sold the land. Keeping in mind that the FC is the functional currency, 80,000 FC of cash would be used to repay the loan (ignoring interest for purposes of discussion), and this would leave 20,000 FC of cash. In the final liquidation transaction, the 20,000 FC of cash is remitted to the parent in exchange for its equity investment. The 20,000 FC received by the parent has a value of $40,000 (assuming the exchange rate remains at 1 FC = $2.00). When compared to the historical basis of the parent's $30,000, equity in the subsidiary represents a $10,000 realized gain which may now be recognized in net income.

In reviewing the subsidiary's balance sheet presented above, it becomes apparent that another objective of the translation process has been satisfied. The FASB stated that the translation process should produce (consolidated) financial statements that reflect the financial results and relationships of the individual entities as measured in their functional currency. This objective can be achieved when the foreign entity's currency is the functional currency and when the same exchange rates are employed to translate accounts. In our example where the FC was the functional currency, the current exchange rate was used to translate all assets and liabilities. Therefore, this preserved the relationship between these accounts which existed prior to translation. Prior to translation, the FC statements reflected that 80% of assets were financed by debt capital, the debt-to-equity ratio was 4:1, and the current ratio was 1.25:1 (assuming that the loan is a current liability). After the FC statements have been translated into dollars, the above results and relationships are retained. The current ratio is still 1.25:1, and debt capital is still 4 times greater than equity capital.

The above illustrations emphasize the importance of properly identifying the functional currency. The expected economic effects of rate changes vary, and the foreign subsidiary's financial statements differ significantly, depending upon the identification of the functional currency. The translation process set forth by the FASB does achieve its objectives when the functional currency is properly identified.

Relative to a parent/subsidiary relationship, a summary of the critical implications associated with the identification of the functional currency is as follows:

	When the Functional Currency	
	Is Not the Foreign Currency	Is the Foreign Currency
Nature of the subsidiary entity	Operates as a conduit through which transactions occur in the parent's functional currency.	Operates as an independent entity through which transactions occur in the subsidiary's functional currency.
Exchange rate changes	Affect the economic well-being of the parent.	Do not affect the economic well-being of the parent.
Effect of exchange rate changes on net income	The effect is a gain or loss which is recognized as a component of net income.	The effect is not currently recognized as a component of net income but rather as a component of other comprehensive income.
Effect of exchange rate changes on the parent's cash flows.	Changes have an immediate or potentially immediate impact on cash flows.	Changes do not have an immediate or potentially immediate impact on cash flows. The impact on cash flows is currently unclear.
Financial relationships between accounts.	Relationships subsequent to translation are different than they were prior to translation, therefore, reflecting the economic effect of exchange rate changes.	Relationships subsequent to translation retain the same values as they had prior to translation. Exchange rate changes do not have an economic effect on the parent.

Adoption of a translation method that fails to properly reflect the economic effects of rate changes may produce misleading results. Prior to FASB Statement No. 52, earlier statements were subject to the major criticism that they resulted in the recognition of major translation losses that distorted earnings and had no effect on cash flows. The FASB No. 52 functional currency approach does not remeasure foreign operations as though they originally had been conducted in the domestic reporting currency. Rather, this approach retains the financial results and relationships that were influenced by the economic environment in which the foreign entity operates.

Basic Translation Process: Functional Currency to Reporting Currency

Before beginning the translation process, the financial statements of the foreign entity must be adjusted to conform with generally accepted accounting principles. This is an important step in light of the differences in accounting principles that currently exist among nations. The next step in the translation process is to identify the functional currency. The discussion that follows assumes that the foreign entity's currency is the functional currency.

Once a foreign entity's functional currency has been identified, it must be translated into the domestic entity's reporting currency (dollars for U.S. companies) using an appropriate exchange rate. In studying the problems associated with foreign currency translation, the FASB concluded that the results and relationships presented in functional currency financial statements would be retained if the translation is based exclusively on the current rate of exchange between the functional currency and the reporting currency. Generally, this *current rate* method is governed by the following procedures:

1. All assets and liabilities are translated at the current exchange rate at the date of translation.
2. Elements of income are translated at the current exchange rates that existed at the time that the revenues and expense were recognized. As a practical consideration, income elements normally are translated at a weighted average exchange rate for the period.
3. Equity accounts other than retained earnings are translated at historical exchange rates. If the domestic parent's investment in a foreign company has been acquired as a purchase (versus pooling of interests), the historical rate on the date of acquisition is used to translate equity accounts. If a pooling of interests has occurred, the original historical rate in effect when the foreign company experienced the equity transaction is used for translation purposes.
4. Translated retained earnings generally are equal to:

    a) *The translated retained earnings at the end of the prior period, plus*

    b) *The translated income (see item 2), less*

    c) *The value of dividends translated at the appropriate historical exchange rates at the date of declaration.*

    If the domestic company has acquired an interest in a foreign company during the current period, the retained earnings balance at the date of acquisition should be translated using the rate at that time. Only after the year of acquisition will retained earnings be translated as the sum of items (a) through (c).

5. Components of the statement of cash flows are translated at the exchange rates in effect at the time of the cash flows. Operations are translated at the rate used for income elements (see 2. above). The reconciliation of the change in cash and cash equivalents during the period should include the effect of exchange rate changes on cash balances.

In all translations that follow, it will be assumed that purchase accounting, rather than pooling-of-interests accounting, is appropriate unless otherwise stated.

Demonstrating the Translation Process

The basic translation process just discussed is applied to a company's trial balance prior to its inclusion in consolidated financial statements, home and branch combined statements, and the computation of equity income for influential foreign investments.

With respect to consolidated financial statements, one of the primary criteria to determine if consolidation is appropriate deals with the extent of control the parent entity exercises over the subsidiary. For foreign subsidiaries, effective control is determined, in part, by currency restrictions and the possibility of nationalization of the operations by foreign governments. Assuming consolidation is appropriate, the financial statements of the foreign entity must be translated into dollars according to the principles expressed in FASB Statement No. 52. Then intercompany eliminations are made, and the statements are consolidated according to the principles of consolidation discussed earlier in this text.

Illustration 11-1 demonstrates the translation of a subsidiary's financial statements for the purpose of preparing consolidated financial statements and is based on the following facts:

1. Fori Corporation began operations on January 1, 20X0. On January 1, 20X1, when net assets totaled 100,000 foreign currency units (FC), 90% of Fori stock was acquired by Dome Corporation. Fori's functional currency is the foreign currency, and it maintains its records in the functional currency.

2. Sales to Dome are billed in the foreign currency, and all receivables from Dome have been collected except for the amount shown in the account Due from Dome. All other sales are billed in the foreign currency as well. The level of sales and purchases was constant over the year. None of the inventory purchased from Fori remains in Dome's ending inventory.

3. Selected exchange rates between the functional currency and the dollar are as follows:

Date	Rate
January 1, 20X0	1 FC = $0.98
January 1, 20X1	1 FC = 1.00
December 31, 20X1	1 FC = 1.05
20X1 average	1 FC = 1.03

Accounting for Translation Adjustment.   Translation adjustments result from the process of translating foreign financial statements *from their functional currency into the domestic entity's reporting currency*. Because various exchange rates (current, historical, and weighted average) are used in the translation process, the basic equality of the balance sheet equation is not preserved. Therefore, from a mechanical viewpoint, the translation adjustment is an amount necessary to balance a translated entity's trial balance. Translation adjustments do not exist in terms of the functional currency and have no immediate effect on the cash flows of the foreign or domestic entity. At the time of the translation, the effect that exchange rate fluctuations may have on the reporting (parent) entity is uncertain and remote. Therefore, it would be improper to include the translation adjustment in current reported net income. However, the translation adjustment must be reported somewhere. Rather than being included as a component of reported earnings, the translation should be included as a component of other comprehensive income.

Illustration 11-1
Fori Corporation
Trial Balance Translation
December 31, 20X1

Account	Balance in Functional Currency		Relevant Exchange Rate ($/FC)	Balance in Dollars
Cash	10,000	FC	1.05	$ 10,500
Accounts Receivable	21,000		1.05	22,050
Allowance for Doubtful Accounts	(1,000)		1.05	(1,050)
Due from Dome	14,000		1.05	14,700
Inventory (at Market, Cost = 32,000)	30,000		1.05	31,500
Prepaid Insurance	3,000		1.05	3,150
Land	18,000		1.05	18,900
Depreciable Assets	120,000		1.05	126,000
Accumulated Depreciation	(15,000)		1.05	(15,750)
Cost of Goods Sold	180,000		1.03	185,400
Depreciation Expense	10,000		1.03	10,300
Income Tax Expense	30,000		1.03	30,900
Other Expenses	23,000		1.03	23,690
Total	443,000	FC		$460,290
Accounts Payable	20,000	FC	1.05	$ 21,000
Taxes Payable	30,000		1.05	31,500
Accrued Interest Payable	1,000		1.05	1,050
Mortgage Payable—Land	10,000		1.05	10,500
Common Stock	80,000		1.00	80,000
Retained Earnings	20,000		Note A	20,000
Sales—Dome	80,000		1.03	82,400
Sales—Other	200,000		1.03	206,000
Gain on Sale of Depreciable Assets	2,000		1.03	2,060
Cumulative Translation Adjustment (to Balance)				5,780
Total	443,000	FC		$460,290

Note A—The beginning balance of retained earnings normally is equal to the translated value of the previous period's ending retained earnings. However, since 20X1 is the first year Dome has owned Fori, the beginning balance is set equal to the January 1, 20X1 (acquisition date) balance of retained earnings in foreign currency translated at the January 1, 20X1 spot rate (in this case, 1.00). The balance sheet for 20X1 would show a translated value for retained earnings equal to the translated beginning balance of retained earnings plus the translated value of net income less dividends translated at the rate existing on the declaration date.

Direct Calculation of the Translation Adjustment.   Although the translation adjustment is a balancing amount necessary to satisfy the balance sheet equation, the current period's adjustment may be calculated directly as follows:

1.   The change in exchange rates during the period multiplied by the amount of net assets (i.e., owners' equity) held by the domestic investor at the beginning of the period, plus

2. The difference between the weighted average exchange rate used in translating income elements and the end-of-period exchange rate multiplied by the increase or decrease in net assets for the period, excluding capital transactions, plus (minus)

3. The increase (decrease) in net assets as a result of capital transactions, including investments by the domestic investor during the period (e.g., stock issuances, retirements, and dividends), multiplied by the difference between the end-of-period exchange rate and the exchange rate at the time of the transaction.

Based on the information given in Illustration 11-1, the direct calculation of the translation adjustment is as follows:

Reconciliation of Annual Translation Adjustment

Net assets at beginning of period multiplied by the change in exchange rates during the period [0* × ($1.05 − $1.00)]	$ 0
Increase in net assets (excluding capital transactions) multiplied by the difference between the current rate and the average rate used to translate income [39,000 FC** × ($1.05 − $1.03)]	780
Increase in net assets due to capital transactions (including investments by the domestic investor) multiplied by the difference between the current rate and the rate at the time of the capital transaction [100,000 FC*** × ($1.05 − $1.00)]	5,000
Translation adjustment	$5,780

*Although Fori Corporation began operations in 20X0, the parent company, Dome Corporation, had not acquired an interest until 20X1. Therefore, Dome had no investment in Fori as of the beginning of 20X1.
**This is the net income for the period (80,000 + 200,000 + 2,000 − 180,000 − 10,000 − 30,000 − 23,000).
***This is the original capital balance as of the date of the parent's acquisition.

The above reconciliation is not a required disclosure but may help in understanding the factors which contribute to the translation adjustment. Note that the reconciliation explains only the $5,780 translation adjustment traceable to 20X1. After the first year of operation, the annual translation adjustments will be accumulated and presented as a component of other comprehensive income. For example, if Fori Corporation has a translation adjustment of $4,400 traceable to 20X2, the accumulated other comprehensive income portion of equity on the balance sheet at the end of 20X2 will show a cumulative adjustment of $10,180 ($5,780 + $4,400).

Accomplishing the Objectives of Translation.   The translation demonstrated in Illustration 11-1 has accomplished the objectives of translation as presented in FASB Statement No. 52. The economic effect of the exchange rate change (i.e., translation adjustment) has been presented as an increase in stockholders' equity. The spot rate had increased from a beginning-of-the-year rate of 1 FC = $1.00 to an end-of-period rate of 1 FC = $1.05. This change indicates that the foreign currency strengthened relative to the dollar. Therefore, the domestic company's investment in the net assets of the foreign subsidiary has increased in accounting value as evidenced by the increase in stockholders' equity. In addition, the translated financial statements reflect the same financial results and relationships of the foreign company as originally measured in its functional currency. For instance, the following ratios indicate that the original relationships have been preserved after translation.

Ratio	Before Translation	After Translation
Current	1.51 (77,000 ÷ 51,000)	1.51 (80,850 ÷ 53,550)
Debt-to-equity	0.44 (61,000 ÷ 139,000)*	0.44 (64,050 ÷ 145,950)**
Gross profit %	36% (100,000 ÷ 280,000)	36% (103,000 ÷ 288,400)

*(80,000 + 20,000 + 80,000 + 200,000 + 2,000 − 180,000 − 10,000 − 30,000 − 23,000)
**(80,000 + 20,000 + 82,400 + 206,000 + 2,060 + 5,780 − 185,400 − 10,300 − 30,900 − 23,690)

Subsequent Recognition of the Translation Adjustment. Although translation adjustments have no immediate effect on reported earnings, they may ultimately affect income when there is a *partial or complete sale or complete or substantially complete liquidation of the investment in the foreign entity.*[3] Unfortunately, the FASB has not defined what constitutes a substantially complete liquidation. Given such a sale or liquidation, some or all of the accumulated translation adjustment included in equity would be removed and included as part of the gain or loss on disposition of the investment. For example, assume a company owns 100% of a foreign entity and its investment account has a balance of $4,200,000 and its owners' equity includes accumulated other comprehensive income containing a debit of $320,000 representing the accumulated translation adjustment. If the entire investment in the subsidiary is sold for $4,750,000, the translation adjustment does affect the gain on sale as follows:

Proceeds from sale of investment.	$4,750,000
Basis of investment account	(4,200,000)
	550,000
Balance in accumulated translation adjustment	(320,000)
Gain on sale of investment.	$ 230,000

It is important to note that if only a portion of the investment in the subsidiary were sold, then only a pro rata portion of the translation adjustment would have been allocated to the sale.

Gains and Losses Excluded from Income

The accumulated other comprehensive income section of equity in which cumulative translation adjustments are reported also should include gains and losses attributable to

1. Foreign currency transactions that are designated and effective as economic hedges of a net investment in a foreign entity, commencing as of the designation date.
2. Intercompany foreign currency transactions that are of a long-term investment nature (i.e., settlement is not planned or anticipated in the foreseeable future) when the entities to the transaction are consolidated, combined, or accounted for by the equity method in the reporting enterprise's financial statements.[4]

In order to illustrate a foreign currency translation that is a hedge on a net investment in a foreign entity, assume a U.S. company has a wholly owned French company in which the French franc is the functional currency. If the franc weakens

---

3 See FASB Interpretation No. 37, *Accounting for Translation Adjustments upon Sale of Part of an Investment in a Foreign Entity* (Norwalk, CT: Financial Accounting Standards Board, 1983) and Statement of Financial Accounting Standards No. 52, *op. cit.*, pars. 110 and 119.
4 Statement of Financial Accounting Standards No. 52, *op. cit.*, par. 20.

relative to the dollar, a translation adjustment with a debit balance will reduce equity due to the effect of the rate change on the net investment. The U.S. parent can hedge against this decline in owners' equity, for example, by securing a loan payable in francs and identifying the transaction as a hedge on the net investment in the French subsidiary. As the franc weakens, the basis of the franc-denominated liability will decrease (it will take fewer dollars to settle the debt), and an exchange gain will occur. Because the foreign currency transaction (securing a loan payable in francs) has been designated and is effective as a hedge of the net investment, the exchange gain or loss should be recognized as an offset to the translation adjustment associated with the net investment. In substance, the effect of the exchange rate changes on the net investment and the related hedge (foreign currency transaction) is viewed as one combined effect rather than two separate and distinct effects. If, after tax effects, the gain (loss) on the hedge is greater than the corresponding translation loss (gain), the excess transaction gain (loss) must be included in the determination of the period's net income.

The second example of an exchange gain or loss that may be excluded from income and be included as a component of equity relates to certain long-term investment transactions between a domestic company and its foreign subsidiary. For example, assume a U.S. parent borrows funds from a French subsidiary with the loan being denominated in francs. If the settlement of the loan is not planned or anticipated in the foreseeable future, the effect of rate changes on the loan also would not have a foreseeable effect on the income of the U.S. parent. Therefore, the effect of rate changes on long-term investment transactions should be reflected in owners' equity as other comprehensive income, not current net income.

Consolidating the Foreign Subsidiary

Once a foreign subsidiary's financial statements have been translated into the reporting currency, certain eliminations and adjustments due to intercompany transactions generally will be required. With regard to the exchange rate that should be used to translate such transactions, the FASB concluded that all intercompany balances, except for intercompany profits and losses, should be translated at the rates used for all other accounts. Intercompany profits and losses should be translated using the exchange rate that existed at the date of the sale or transfer. As a practical matter, however, average rates or approximations may be used to translate such profits and losses.

In order to demonstrate the consolidation process, the facts of Illustration 11-1 will be discussed further. Assume Dome Corporation paid 105,000 FC for its 90% interest in Fori Corporation, and recall that, at the time of acquisition (January 1, 20X1), Fori equity consisted of 80,000 FC of common stock and 20,000 FC of retained earnings. Upon acquisition of Fori, Dome recorded its investment as follows:

Investment in Fori	105,000	
Cash (105,000 × $1.00)		105,000

Assuming that any excess is traceable to goodwill with a 10-year useful life, the excess of cost over book value is determined as follows:

Price paid		105,000 FC
Equity purchased:		
Common Stock	80,000 FC	
Retained Earnings	20,000 FC	
Total	100,000 FC	
90% Interest Acquired		90,000 FC
Excess cost		15,000 FC
Goodwill		15,000 FC

Notice that the determination of excess is calculated in the foreign currency (FC) not the parent's currency because the acquisition price was paid in FC. However, the excess will be translated into the parent's currency using the rate of exchange at the date of the acquisition.

Because the foreign subsidiary is to be consolidated, the cost or simple equity method would be used by the parent. Assuming the simple equity method is used, the parent would record its interest in the current-period income and declared dividends (none in this example) of the foreign subsidiary. However, Dome, under the simple equity method, would not recognize the current-period amortization of the excess of cost over book value component of its investment. The 20X1 income for Fori and Dome's equity share is calculated as follows:

Account	Balance in Functional Currency	Relevant Exchange Rate ($/FC)	Balance in Dollars
Sales—Dome.	80,000	1.03	$ 82,400
Sales—Other.	200,000	1.03	206,000
Gain on Sale of Depreciable Assets.	2,000	1.03	2,060
Cost of Goods Sold	(180,000)	1.03	(185,400)
Depreciation Expense	(10,000)	1.03	(10,300)
Income Tax Expense	(30,000)	1.03	(30,900)
Other Expenses (including interest)	(23,000)	1.03	(23,690)
Net Income	39,000		$ 40,170
Dome's share.			90%
Dome's interest in Fori net income (in dollars)			$ 36,153

The parent's entry to record its interest in the foreign subsidiary's undistributed income would be as follows:

Investment in Fori	36,153	
Subsidiary Income		36,153

Worksheet 11-1, pages 11-50 to 11-53, shows the consolidated financial statements of the Dome and Fori corporations. The trial balance amounts for Dome are assumed, and Fori's balances are based on Illustration 11-1. Steps (1) and (2) of the worksheet follow the usual procedures of eliminating the current-period entry recording the parent's share of the subsidiary net income and its share of the subsidiary equity accounts as of the beginning of the period. Step (3) allocates 90% of Fori's cumulative adjustment to the controlling interest.

Step (4) recognizes that the excess of cost over book value of 15,000 FC must be translated at the exchange rate existing at year-end. However, the amortization of this excess must be translated at the average exchange rate for the period. These rates result in the following translated amounts for the worksheet entry:

Depreciable assets and goodwill (15,000 FC × $1.05)	$15,750
Accumulated depreciation and amortization (15,000 FC ÷ 10 × $1.05)	1,575
Depreciation and amortization expense (15,000 FC ÷ 10 × $1.03)	1,545

The cumulative adjustment included in step (4) results from changes in exchange rates which have occurred

1. Since the excess at the beginning of the period was translated ($750 credit adjustment),
2. Since the accumulated amortization at the beginning of the period was translated ($75 debit adjustment), and

3. Since the current period's amortization of the excess was translated ($45 credit adjustment).

Because the excess of cost over book value is not recorded by the foreign subsidiary (assuming push-down accounting is not applied), the effect of such rate changes on this excess has not been included previously in the cumulative translation adjustment. The $720 additional cumulative adjustment traceable to the excess of cost over book value is determined as follows:

	Exchange Rate Used		
	Beginning or Average	End of Period	Difference
1. Excess at beginning of period	$15,000	$15,750	$750
2. Less accumulated amortization at beginning of period	0	0	0
3. Less current amortization expense	(1,545)	(1,575)	(30)
Net balance	$13,455	$14,175	$720

Steps (5) and (6) follow the usual worksheet eliminations and adjustments for intercompany transactions.

The consolidation procedures just discussed also are applicable to periods subsequent to the first year of acquisition. Although the methodology is the same, the following should be noted:

1. The parent must continue to recognize its interest in the amortization of any original excess of cost over book value.
2. Any additional cumulative adjustment traceable to the excess of cost over book value should continue to be recognized.

When consolidating a foreign subsidiary, special attention must be paid to the elimination of intercompany profits. This is true only when the foreign entity's currency is the functional currency. The problem arises because the exchange rates used to translate receivables and payables resulting from intercompany transactions are different than the rates which existed at the date of the intercompany transaction. In order to illustrate this point, assume that a U.S. parent sold inventory to a foreign subsidiary and that none of the inventory had been sold by the subsidiary as of the end of the period. In the consolidation process, it would be appropriate to eliminate the parent's receivable and the subsidiary's corresponding payable. Furthermore, the unrealized intercompany profit on the unsold inventory must also be eliminated. For purposes of discussion, assume that the intercompany transaction is denominated in foreign currencies (FC) in the amount of 1,000 FC and that relevant exchange rates are as follows:

Date of sale   1 FC = $1.00   End of period   1 FC = $1.20

Relevant balances at the end of the period would be as follows:

	Value in FC	Value in U.S. $	Calculation of dollar value
Parent's Accounts			
Accounts Receivable		1,200	(1,000 FC × $1.20)
Sales Revenue		1,000	(1,000 FC × $1.00)
Cost of Sales (assume 80%)		800	Assumed amount
Subsidiary's Accounts			
Accounts Payable	1,000	1,200	(1,000 FC × $1.20)
Inventory	1,000	1,200	(1,000 FC × $1.20)

It is clear from the preceding schedule of account balances that the dollar values of the parent's accounts receivable and the subsidiary's accounts payable equal and could be eliminated against each other. However, the problem arises with the elimination of the unrealized intercompany profit included in the ending inventory of the subsidiary. If the profit of 20% were eliminated using the translated value of the inventory, then $240 (20% × $1,200) of profit would be eliminated, which does not agree with the $200 of intercompany profit which actually existed at the date of the transaction. However, if the intercompany profit is eliminated using the rate of exchange which existed at the date of the transaction, no inconsistency exists. At the date of the transaction, the inventory had a dollar equivalent of $1,000 (1,000 FC × $1), and the 20% unrealized profit of $200 (20% × $1,000) would be the appropriate amount of profit to eliminate against the parent's gross profit of $200 (sales revenue of $1,000 versus the cost of sales of $800). Therefore, the exchange rate at the date of the original transaction must *always* be used to determine the amount of unrealized profit to be eliminated. Once again, this complication will be encountered only when translating from the functional currency into the parent's reporting currency.

Unconsolidated Investments:
Translation for the Cost or Equity Method

Unconsolidated foreign investments are accounted for by either the cost method or the sophisticated equity method. Under the cost method, a complete translation of the foreign financial statements is not necessary. The parent company must record the cost basis of its investment in dollars. If the cost is incurred in foreign currency, the exchange rate at the date of acquisition should be used. Investment income is translated at the exchange rate at the date dividends are declared. If factors existing in the foreign environment suggest a permanent impairment in the value of the investment, the basis of the investment should be reduced accordingly.

If the parent's interest in the foreign subsidiary is considered influential, the subsidiary will not be consolidated and the sophisticated equity method should be employed. This method requires the adjustment of subsidiary income or loss for the amortization of differences between book and market values of the investment and any intercompany profits or losses. Application of this method to an investment in a foreign entity will be demonstrated using the facts of Illustration 11-1.

Assume Dome Corporation paid 35,000 FC ($35,000) for a 30% interest in Fori Corporation on January 1, 20X1. Furthermore, assuming that any excess is traceable to goodwill with a 10-year useful life, the excess of cost over book value is determined as follows:

Price paid		35,000 FC
Equity purchased:		
Common Stock	80,000 FC	
Retained Earnings	20,000 FC	
Total	100,000 FC	
30% Interest Acquired		30,000 FC
Excess cost		5,000 FC
Goodwill		5,000 FC

Dome's interest in the adjusted net income of Fori is calculated as follows:

Fori net income translated into dollars.	$40,170
Dome's share	30%
Dome's interest in Fori net income	$12,051
Amortization of excess related to the goodwill	
[5,000 FC ÷ 10 years × $1.03 average rate]	(515)
Dome's equity share of Fori net income adjusted for amortization of excess. . . .	$11,536

The investor also must recognize its interest in the cumulative translation adjustment for 20X1, calculated as follows:

Cumulative translation adjustment (from Illustration 11-1)	$5,780
Dome's share	30%
Dome's interest in the cumulative translation adjustment	$1,734

The following entries are to record Dome's interest in the foreign entity under the sophisticated equity method:

20X1
Jan. 1   Investment in Fori Corporation   35,000
                  Cash   35,000
                       To record the initial investment of 35,000 FC
                       when the spot rate was 1 FC = $1.00.

Dec. 31   Investment in Fori Corporation   13,270
                  Subsidiary Income   11,536
                  Cumulative Translation Adjustment   1,734
                       To record share of net income adjusted for
                       the amortization of excess and share of
                       cumulative translation adjustment.

Notice that under the sophisticated equity method the investor recorded both the amortization of the excess of cost over book value and its share of the current year's translation adjustment.

Remeasured Financial Statements: Foreign Currency to Functional Currency

The previous illustrations of the translation process assumed that the currency of the foreign entity was the functional currency. However, there are certain instances when the functional currency is not the currency of the foreign entity. In these instances, the financial statements of the foreign entity must be remeasured into the functional currency before the financial statements can be translated. The remeasurement process is intended to produce financial statements that are the same as if the entity's transactions had been originally recorded in the functional currency. Generally speaking, the remeasurement process is based on the *temporal method.* The temporal method was originally adopted by FASB Statement No. 8, which has been superseded by Statement No. 52. In essence, the historical exchange rates between the functional currency and the foreign currency are used to remeasure certain accounts. The adjustment resulting from the remeasurement process is referred to as a remeasurement gain or loss and is included as a component of net income. The remeasurement process is encountered in two situations. One situation arises when the entity's financial statements are prepared in a currency that is not the functional currency. Another situation arises when the foreign entity is in a highly inflationary economy. In that case, the functional currency is the domestic entity's reporting currency (dollars for U.S. parent companies).

Books of Record Not Maintained in Functional Currency

Perhaps one of the most common situations in which the books of record are not maintained in the functional currency is when the functional currency is the parent/investor's currency. For example, assume that a U.S. company has a Mexican subsidiary. That parent invested dollars in that subsidiary, and dollar-denominated loans were arranged on behalf of the subsidiary. The Mexican company acquires raw materials from Japan which are paid for in dollars and sells the manufactured products throughout Central and North America. The subsidiary's sales are denominated in dollars, and distributions of earnings are remitted to the parent in dollars. Based on the above information, it is clear that the Mexican company's functional currency is the U.S. dollar even though it maintains its books of record in Mexican pesos.

It is also possible that a foreign entity which maintains its books of record in its domestic currency may have a functional currency that is not the parent/investor's currency. For instance, assume a French subsidiary of an American company purchases materials from British vendors with amounts due payable in British pounds. The materials are assembled in France and then returned to England for resale. Sales revenues are collected in pounds. Considering the factors used to identify the functional currency, the pound would be the French company's functional currency. However, the French company maintains its books of record (accounting records) in French francs although its functional currency is the British pound. In this example, a two-step process is involved. First, the financial statements prepared in francs would have to be remeasured into pounds, the functional currency. Then, second, the remeasured financial statements would have to be translated into dollars.

If the books of record are not maintained in the functional currency, a remeasurement process, which differs significantly from that functional currency approach of FASB Statement No. 52, is employed in order to express trial balance amounts in the functional currency. Furthermore, the adjustment resulting from the remeasurement is included as a component of net income rather than as a component of other comprehensive income. It is important to remember that once the trial balance is remeasured into the functional currency, further translation may or may not be necessary. Possible scenarios are as follows:

1. Books of record currency (not U.S. dollars) remeasured to U.S. dollar functional currency. Therefore, no further translation is necessary.

2. Books of record currency (not U. S. currency) remeasured into functional currency (not U.S. dollars). Therefore, further translation is necessary in order to translate the functional currency (not U.S. dollars) into U.S. dollars.

Exhibit 11-2 compares the methodologies applicable to the remeasurement and translation processes. The following factors regarding Exhibit 11-2 should be noted:

1. When remeasuring, the exchange rates represent the relationship between the books of record currency and the functional currency. When translating, the exchange rates represent the relationship between the functional currency and the parent/investor currency.

2. Examples of accounts that should be remeasured at historical rates include the following:

- Marketable securities carried at cost
- Inventories carried at cost
- Prepaid expenses such as insurance, advertising, and rent
- Property, plant, and equipment
- Accumulated depreciation on property, plant, and equipment
- Patents, trademarks, licenses, and formulas
- Goodwill
- Other intangible assets
- Deferred charges and credits except deferred income taxes and policy acquisition costs for life insurance companies
- Deferred income
- Common stock
- Preferred stock carried at issuance price
- Examples of revenues and expenses related to nonmonetary items:
    Cost of goods sold
    Depreciation of property, plant, and equipment

Amortization of intangible items such as goodwill, patents, licenses, etc. Amortization of deferred charges or credits except deferred income taxes and policy acquisition costs for life insurance companies[5]

3. If amounts to be remeasured at historical exchange rates are traceable to transactions occurring prior to the parent's date of acquisition, the historical exchange rate existing at the date of acquisition should be used. This assumes that the acquisition is accounted for as a purchase.

Exhibit 11-2
Remeasurement and Translation Methodologies

	Remeasurement	Translation
	Investee's books of record remeasured into functional currency—**temporal method**	Functional currency translated into parent/investor's reporting currency—**functional currency method**
Assets and Liabilities:		
Monetary items* or measured at current values	Remeasure using current exchange rate	Translate using current exchange rate
Not monetary items or not measured at current values	Remeasure using historical exchange rates	Translate using current exchange rate
Revenues and Expenses:		
Representing amortization of historical accounts	Remeasure using historical exchange rates	Translate using weighted average rate for the period
Not representing amortization of historical accounts	Remeasure using weighted average exchange rate for the period	Translate using weighted average rate for the period
Equity accounts (excluding retained earnings)	Remeasure using historical exchange rates**	Translate using historical exchange rates**
Retained earnings	Beginning balance plus remeasured net income less dividends (remeasured using historical rates)	Beginning balance plus translated net income less dividends (translated using historical rates)
Recognition of:		
Measurement gain/loss	As a component of net income	As a component of net income translated at the weighted average rate for the period
Translation adjustment	Not applicable	Recognize as a component of other comprehensive income

*Monetary items represent rights to receive or pay an amount of money which is (a) fixed in amount or (b) determinable without reference to future prices of specific goods/services; that is, its value does not change according to changes in price levels.

**If amounts are to be remeasured or translated at historical exchange rates which are traceable to transactions occurring prior to the parent's date of acquisition, they should be remeasured/translated at the historical exchange rate existing at the parent's date of acquisition. This special treatment is appropriate if the acquisition is accounted for as a purchase.

5 *Ibid.*, par. 48.

4. The remeasurement gain or loss is included as a component of net income expressed in the functional currency, whereas the translation adjustment is not included as a component of net income but rather as a component of other comprehensive income.

A special remeasurement rule is necessary for inventory when the rule of cost or market, whichever is lower, is applied. Before the rule is applied, the inventory cost and market amounts must be expressed in the functional currency. A possible result is for an inventory write-down to occur in the functional currency, even if no write-down is suggested in the books of record currency. It also is possible for a write-down in the books of record currency to no longer be appropriate in the functional currency. This special rule is demonstrated in Illustration 11-2.

Illustration 11-2 demonstrates the remeasurement process and is based on the same facts as Illustration 11-1 with the following additional information:

1. The dollar, rather than the books of record (BR), is determined to be the functional currency.
2. Inventory is recorded at its market value of 30,000 FC even though its historical cost is 32,000 FC. The historical cost of sales is based on the FIFO method of costing. Ending inventory consists of the following:

    10,000 FC acquired October 1, 20X1

    22,000 FC acquired November 1, 20X1

3. The prepaid insurance represents amounts that were incurred on October 1, 20X1.
4. The depreciable assets were acquired as follows:

    80,000 FC acquired on January 1, 20X0

    60,000 FC acquired on July 1, 20X1

5. The cost of sales consists of the following purchases:

    20,000 FC acquired December 1, 20X0

    60,000 FC acquired March 1, 20X1

    80,000 FC acquired July 1, 20X1

    20,000 FC acquired October 1, 20X1

6. The other expenses include 3,000 FC of insurance expense that was originally prepaid on October 1, 20X1. The balance of other expenses was incurred uniformly throughout the year.
7. The land and the related mortgage were acquired on March 1, 20X1.
8. Selected exchange rates between the FC and the U.S. dollar functional currency are as follows:

1/1/X0	1 FC = $0.98	7/1/X1	1 FC = $1.04
7/1/X0	1 FC = 1.01	10/1/X1	1 FC = 1.045
12/1/X0	1 FC = 0.99	11/1/X1	1 FC = 1.043
1/1/X1	1 FC = 1.00	12/31/X1	1 FC = 1.05
3/1/X1	1 FC = 1.015	20X1 average	1 FC = 1.03

Illustration 11-2
Fori Corporation
Trial Balance Remeasurement
December 31, 20X1

Account	Balance in Books of Record (BR) Currency		Relevant Exchange Rate ($/FC)	Balance in Functional Currency ($)
Cash	10,000	BR	1.050	$ 10,500
Accounts Receivable	21,000		1.050	22,050
Allowance for Doubtful Accounts	(1,000)		1.050	(1,050)
Due from Dome	14,000		1.050	14,700
Inventory (at Market, Cost = 32,000)	30,000		Note A	31,500
Prepaid Insurance	3,000		1.045	3,135
Land	18,000		1.015	18,270
Depreciable Assets	120,000		Sch. A	122,400
Accumulated Depreciation	(15,000)		Sch. A	(15,120)
Cost of Goods Sold	180,000		Note B	185,000
Depreciation Expense	10,000		Sch. A	10,120
Income Tax Expense	30,000		1.030	30,900
Other Expenses	23,000		Note C	23,735
Total	443,000	BR		$456,140
Accounts Payable	20,000	BR	1.050	$ 21,000
Taxes Payable	30,000		1.050	31,500
Accrued Interest Payable	1,000		1.050	1,050
Mortgage Payable—Land	10,000		1.015	10,150
Common Stock	80,000		1.000	80,000
Retained Earnings	20,000		Note D	20,000
Sales—Dome	80,000		1.030	82,400
Sales—Other	200,000		1.030	206,000
Gain on Sale of Depreciable Assets	2,000		Note E	2,760
Remeasurement Gain (to Balance)				1,280
Total	443,000	BR		$456,140

Note A—The historical cost and market value of the ending inventory must be remeasured into the functional currency before the rule of cost or market, whichever is lower, may be applied.

Historical cost	(10,000 × 1.045)		$10,450
	(22,000 × 1.043)		22,946
			$33,396
Market value	(30,000 × 1.05)		$31,500

Because the market value in functional currency is still less than the historical cost in functional currency, market value will be the carrying basis.

(continued)

Note B— Cost of sales is remeasured as follows:

	Balance in BR	Exchange Rate ($/FC)	Functional Currency ($)
December 1, 20X1 acquisition	20,000	1.000**	20,000
March 1, 20X1	60,000	1.015	60,900
July 1, 20X1	80,000	1.040	83,200
October 1, 20X1	20,000	1.045	20,900
Total	180,000		185,000

**Note that the exchange rate on the parent's date of acquisition is used rather than any earlier historical exchange rates.

Note C—Other expenses are remeasured as follows:

	Balance in BR	Exchange Rate ($/FC)	Functional Currency ($)
Insurance expense.	3,000	1.045	3,135
Balance of expense	20,000	1.030	20,600
			23,735

Note D—The beginning balance of retained earnings normally is equal to the remeasured value of the previous period's ending retained earnings. However, since 20X1 is the first year Dome has owned Fori, the beginning balance is set equal to the January 1, 20X1 (acquisition date) balance of retained earnings in foreign currency remeasured at the January 1, 20X1 spot rate. The balance sheet for 20X1 would show a remeasured value for retained earnings equal to the remeasured beginning balance of retained earnings plus the remeasured value of net income less dividends remeasured at the rate existing on the declaration date.

Note E— The remeasured value of the gain must be inferred, based on the following entry to record the sale of the asset:

```
Cash (19,000 × 1.04) . . . . . . . . . . . . . . . . . . . . . . . . .        19,760
Accumulated Depreciation (3,000 × 1.00) . . . . . . . . . . . .         3,000
    Depreciable Assets (20,000 × 1.00). . . . . . . . . . . . . . .                  20,000
    Gain on Sale of Depreciable Assets . . . . . . . . . . . . . .                   2,760
```

Schedule A
Remeasurement of Depreciable Assets, Depreciation Expenses, and Accumulated Depreciation

	Balance in Books of Record Currency		Relevant Exchange Rate ($/FC)		Balance in Functional Currency ($)
Depreciable Assets:					
January 1, 20X0 acquisition	80,000	BR	1.00	**	80,000
July 1, 20X1 acquisition	60,000		1.04		62,400
July 1, 20X1 disposition	(20,000)		1.00	**	(20,000)
	120,000				122,400
Depreciation Expense:					
January 1, 20X0 acquisition	6,000		1.00	**	6,000
	1,000		1.00	**	1,000
July 1, 20X1 acquisition	3,000		1.04		3,120
	10,000				10,120

Accumulated Depreciation:				
January 1, 20X0 acquisition	6,000	1.00	**	6,000
	6,000	1.00	**	6,000
July 1, 20X1 acquisition	3,000	1.04		3,120
	15,000			15,120

**Note that the exchange rate on the parent's date of acquisition is used rather than any earlier historical exchange rates.

In reviewing Illustration 11-2, it is important to note the following:

1. If amounts are to be remeasured at historical exchange rates that are traceable to transactions occurring prior to the parent's date of acquisition, they should be remeasured at the historical exchange rate existing at the parent's date of acquisition. This special treatment is appropriate if the acquisition is accounted for as a purchase.

2. The remeasurement gain or loss is recognized as a component of income rather than a direct component of stockholders' equity. Remeasurement gains or losses from prior years would be included in the remeasured amount of retained earnings at the beginning of the current year.

3. Because in Illustration 11-2 the functional currency is the dollar, the remeasurement process resulted in amounts that needed no further translation. However, it is important to note that in certain instances the remeasurement process results in amounts expressed in the functional currency that must still be translated into the currency of the parent/investor (e.g., French francs—the books of record currency to British pounds—the functional currency to U.S. dollars—the parent's reporting currency).

4. The remeasurement process resulted in a gain that favorably affects net income. This is because the FC strengthened against the dollar and made the parent's net investment in the subsidiary more valuable. If the FC had weakened, a remeasurement loss would have likely occurred and the parent may have employed some type of financial instrument to hedge against this loss.

5. If the investor is using the equity method of accounting for its investment in the investee, income from the investment should include the investor's share of the remeasurement gain or loss. Therefore, the investment account must be adjusted to reflect the investor's interest in the remeasurement gain or loss. For example, if an investor has a 60% interest in an investee and there is a current remeasurement gain of $50,000, the following entry would be made under the equity method:

Investment in investee	30,000	
Investment income		30,000

Worksheet 11-2, pages 11-54 to 11-56, shows the consolidated financial statements of the Dome and Fori Corporations. The trial balance for Fori has been remeasured into dollars based on Illustration 11-2. Note that the excess cost over book value and related amortization is measured at the original historical exchange rates that existed at the date of acquisition. The remeasurement gain is allocated entirely to the controlling interest.

Illustration 11-3 demonstrates the remeasurement of a subsidiary's trial balance into the functional currency and the subsequent translation into the parent's reporting currency. This might be the case if, by way of example, the subsidiary records in French francs, functions in German marks, and has a U.S. parent. Illustration 11-3 is based on the following information:

1. Clancy Corporation began operations on January 1, 20X1, as a wholly owned foreign subsidiary of Drake Inc., a U.S. company.
2. Inventory in the books of record currency (BR) is carried at market even though its historical cost is 16,000 BR. Inventory was acquired uniformly throughout the year. The weighted average cost method is used to determine the cost of sales.
3. Depreciable assets were acquired (sold) on the following dates:

Date	Cost
January 1, 20X1	100,000 BR
May 1, 20X1	30,000 BR
July 1, 20X1	(10,000) BR

The asset sold was acquired on January 1, 20X1. The selling price of this asset was 11,000 BR.

4. Depreciation is based on the straight-line method and a 10-year useful life.
5. Relevant direct exchange rates are as follows:

Date	FC/BR	$/FC
January 1, 20X1	1 BR = 2.0 FC	1 FC = $1.40
May 1, 20X1	1 BR = 2.1 FC	1 FC = 1.30
July 1, 20X1	1 BR = 2.4 FC	1 FC = 1.10
December 31, 20X1	1 BR = 2.8 FC	1 FC = 1.00
20X1 average	1 BR = 2.5 FC	1 FC = 1.25

Illustration 11-3
Clancy Corporation
Trial Balance Translation
December 31, 20X1

Account	Balance in BR	Relevant Exchange Rate (FC/BR)	Balance in FC	Relevant Exchange Rate ($/FC)	Balance in Dollars
Cash	10,000 BR	2.80	28,000 FC	1.00	$ 28,000
Accounts Receivable	28,000	2.80	78,400	1.00	78,400
Inventory (at Market)*	15,000	Note A	40,000	1.00	40,000
Prepaid Expenses	5,000	2.50	12,500	1.00	12,500
Depreciable Assets	120,000	Sch. A	243,000	1.00	243,000
Cost of Goods Sold	145,000	2.50	362,500	1.25	453,125
Depreciation Expense	11,500	Sch. A	23,200	1.25	29,000
Other Expenses	27,000	2.50	67,500	1.25	84,375
Income Tax Expense	16,500	2.50	41,250	1.25	51,562
Remeasurement Loss			58,650	1.25	73,313
Total Debits	378,000 BR		$955,000 FC		$1,093,275
Accounts Payable	7,500 BR	2.80	21,000 FC	1.00	$ 21,000
Accrued Expenses	12,000	2.80	33,600	1.00	33,600
Notes Payable	84,000	2.80	235,200	1.00	235,200
Common Stock	40,000	2.00	80,000	1.40	112,000

Cumulative Transaction					
Adjustment.	0		0		(33,075)
Retained Earnings	0	Note B	0		0
Sales	220,000	2.50	550,000	1.25	687,500
Gain on Sale of Depreciable Assets . . .	1,500	Note C	7,400	1.25	9,250
Allowance for Doubtful Accounts.	2,000	2.80	5,600	1.00	5,600
Accumulated Depreciation	11,000	Sch. A	22,200	1.00	22,200
Total Credits	378,000 BR		955,000 FC		$1,093,275

*In more complex instances, the remeasurement of ending inventory and cost of sales will depend on the inventory valuation method used. LIFO ending inventory will consist of the (1) beginning inventory multiplied by the applicable exchange rate(s) plus (2) unsold current purchases multiplied by the applicable exchange rate(s).

Note A—The historical cost and market value of the ending inventory must be remeasured into the functional currency before the rule of cost or market, whichever is lower, may be applied.

        Historical cost (16,000 × 2.50)   40,000
        Market value (15,000 × 2.80)   42,000

Because the historical cost in functional currency is less than the market value in functional currency, historical cost will be the carrying basis.

Note B—The remeasured value of zero for retained earnings represents the beginning-of-the-period value. The balance sheet for 20X1 would show a remeasured value for retained earnings equal to the remeasured value of undistributed net income. This value also would represent the remeasured value for beginning retained earnings in the 20X2 trial balance.

Note C—The remeasured value of the gain must be inferred, based on the following entry to record the sale of the asset:

        Cash (11,000 × 2.40)   26,400
        Accumulated Depreciation (500 × 2.00)   1,000
            Depreciable Assets (10,000 × 2.00)   20,000
            Gain on Sale of Depreciable Asset   7,400

Schedule A
Remeasurement of Depreciable Assets, Depreciation Expenses, and Accumulated Depreciation

	Balance in BR	Exchange Rate (FC/BR)	Balance in FC
Depreciable Assets:			
January 1, 20X1 acquisition.	100,000 BR	2.00	200,000 FC
May 1, 20X1 acquisition	30,000	2.10	63,000
July 1, 20X1 disposition	(10,000)	2.00	(20,000)
. . . .	120,000 BR		243,000 FC
Depreciation Expense:			
January 1, 20X1 acquisition.	9,000 BR	2.00	18,000 FC
. . . .	500	2.00	1,000
May 1, 20X1 acquisition	2,000	2.10	4,200
. . . .	11,500 BR		23,200 FC
Accumulated Depreciation:			
Annual expense	11,500 BR	see above	23,200 FC
Asset disposed	(500)	2.00	(1,000)
. . . .	11,000 BR		22,200 FC

Highly Inflationary Economies.   When an entity's financial statements are expressed in the functional currency, the statements are translated directly into the parent's reporting currency. However, this procedure is not followed for a foreign entity with a functional currency of a country that has a highly inflationary economy. The FASB defines such an economy as one that has a cumulative inflation rate of approximately 100% or more over a 3-year period. Other factors, such as the trend of inflation, also may suggest a highly inflationary economy.[6]

If a foreign entity's currency has lost its utility as a measure of a store of value and lacks stability, it probably would not serve as a useful functional currency. To ignore this situation in subsequent translations might produce misleading results. The translation of noncurrent assets of a foreign company in a highly inflationary economy at current rates of exchange produces curious results. The translated amounts may not represent reasonable dollar-equivalent measures of such assets' historical costs.

Suppose a foreign company acquires a fixed asset for a cost of 100,000 FC when the exchange rate is 1 FC = $1.00. Since that time, the foreign country has experienced a cumulative rate of inflation of 270%, and the current rate of exchange is 1 FC = $0.40. If the fixed asset was translated using the current-rate method, the translated value of the asset would be $40,000 versus its original translated cost of $100,000. One proposed solution to this curious result would be to adjust the foreign financial statements for inflation rates since acquisition and then apply the current-rate method. The inflation-adjusted value of the fixed asset would be 270,000 FC (100,000 FC × 270%), and its translated value at current rates would be $108,000 (270,000 FC × $0.40). This translated amount is more meaningful than the $40,000 value previously determined. The FASB decided against adjusting foreign amounts for inflationary effects and instead decided that the domestic currency (dollars) should serve as the foreign entity's functional currency. Thus, the foreign entity's statements should be remeasured into the functional currency (U.S. dollars). Applying this to the fixed asset example would require the use of the original historical rate of exchange and results in a remeasured value of $100,000 (100,000 FC × $1.00). This value is more meaningful than the $40,000 value previously determined, and it does not commingle historical and inflation-adjusted values into the same set of financial statements. It is important to note that (a) this will result in the remeasurement of the statements into dollars, making any further translation unnecessary, and (b) the remeasurement gain or loss should be included in the net income for the period.

Summary of Translation and Remeasurement Methodologies

This chapter has discussed the translation and/or remeasurement of foreign financial statements into the reporting currency (dollars) of the domestic parent/investor entity. Translation of foreign financial statements is employed when a foreign entity's financial statements are measured in their functional currency and then expressed in the reporting currency of the domestic parent/investor entity. The remeasurement of foreign financial statements is appropriate when

1.   A foreign entity's books of record are not maintained in the functional currency and/or
2.   A foreign entity's functional currency is that of a highly inflationary economy.

It is important to note that a domestic parent/investor entity may have a number of subsidiary/investee entities that require translation and/or remeasurement. For example, a U.S. parent may have

---

6 *Ibid.*, par. 11.

1. A subsidiary whose financial statements are measured in their functional currency and then are *translated* into dollars,

2. Another subsidiary whose financial statements are measured in a currency other than the *foreign* functional currency, in which case the statements must be *remeasured* into the foreign functional currency and then translated into dollars,

3. Another subsidiary whose financial statements are measured in a currency other than the *dollar* functional currency, in which case the statements must be *remeasured* into dollars, and

4. Another subsidiary whose financial statements are measured in a functional currency of a country that has a *highly inflationary economy*, in which case the statements must be remeasured into dollars.

The accounting policies footnote (Exhibit 11-3) to the financial statements of Ford Motor Company illustrates how both translation and remeasurement are applied to the foreign subsidiaries of the company.

Exhibit 11-3
Ford Motor Company

ACCOUNTING POLICIES—FOREIGN CURRENCY TRANSLATION

Revenues, costs, and expenses of foreign subsidiaries are translated to U.S. dollars at average-period exchange rates. The effect of changes in exchange rates on revenues and costs was generally unfavorable in 1996, 1995, and 1994.

Assets and liabilities of foreign subsidiaries are translated to U.S. dollars at end-of-period exchange rates. The effects of this translation for most foreign subsidiaries and certain other foreign currency transactions are reported in a separate component of stockholders' equity. Translation gains and losses for foreign subsidiaries that are located in highly inflationary countries or conduct a major portion of their business with the company's U.S. operations are included in income. Also included in income are gains and losses arising from transactions denominated in a currency other than the functional currency of the subsidiary involved.

The effect of changes in exchange rates on assets and liabilities, as described above, decreased net income by $156 million in 1996, and increased net income by $13 million in 1995 and $376 million in 1994. These amounts included a pre-tax net transaction and translation loss of $300 million in 1996, and gains of $37 million in 1995 and $574 million in 1994.

Source: Ford Motor Company, SEC Form 10-K, for fiscal year-end December 31, 1996.

The situations requiring the use of a particular translation and/or remeasurement methodology are summarized in a flowchart and matrix that follow:

Translation/Remeasurement Flowchart

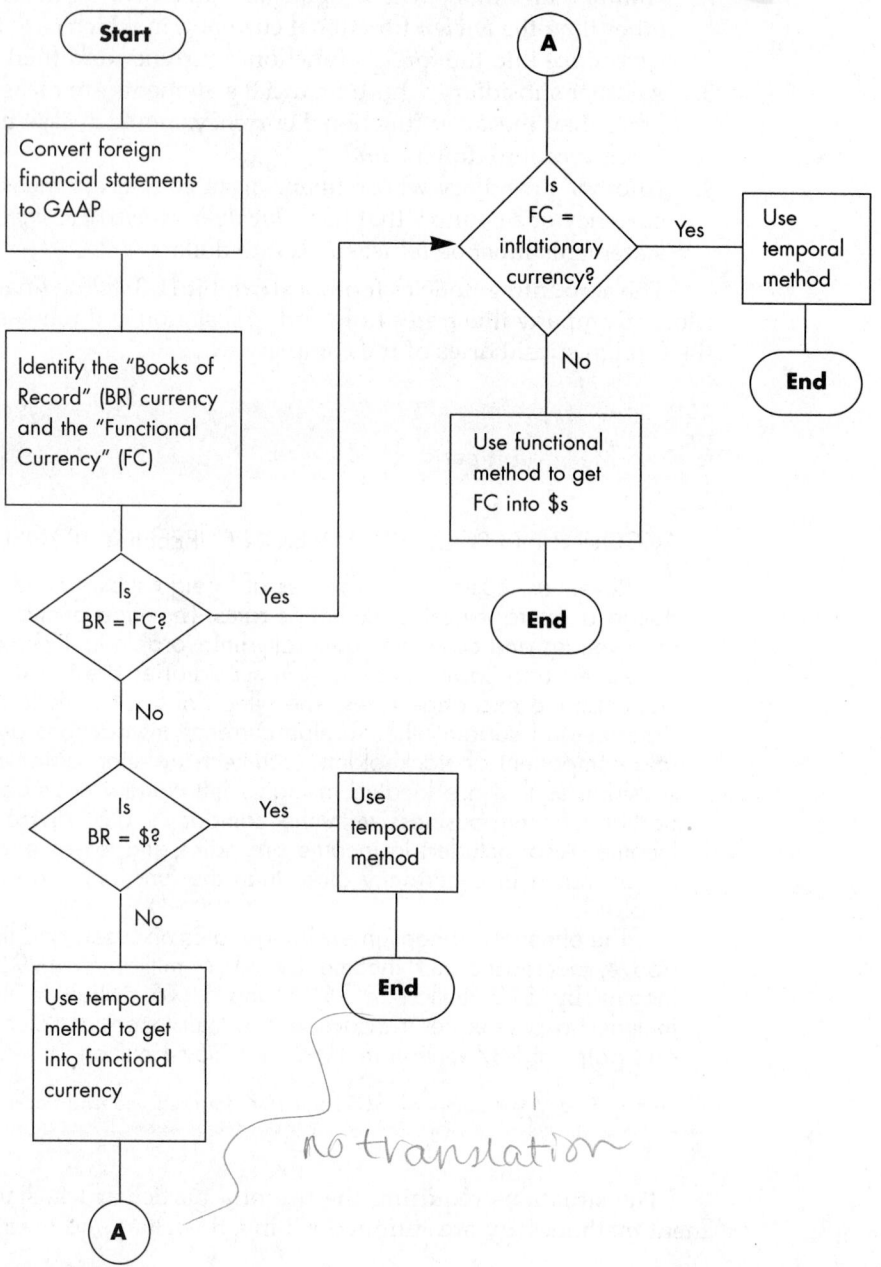

No translation

Account	Method	
	Temporal (SFAS #8)	**Functional (SFAS #52)**
Assets & Liabilities:		
At current values or monetary items*	Current	Current
Not at current values or monetary items*	Historical	Current
Revenues & Expenses:		
Representing amortization of historical amounts	Historical	Weighted Average
Not representing amortization of historical amounts	Weighted Average	Weighted Average
Equity Accounts (excluding retained earnings)	Historical	Historical
Retained Earnings	Beginning balance plus remeasured net income less remeasured dividends	Beginning balance plus translated net income less translated dividends
Translation/Remeasurement Adjustment:		
Record as a component of	Net income	Other comprehensive income

*Monetary items—rights to receive or pay an amount of money which is (a) FIXED or (b) determinable without reference to future prices of specific goods/services; that is, its value does not change according to changes in price levels.

Tax Allocation and Disclosure Requirements

Interperiod tax allocation is appropriate when temporary differences exist due to differences in the timing or recognition of items for financial statement purposes and for tax purposes. To the extent that remeasurement gains or losses and/or translation adjustments are recognized in different periods for financial and tax purposes, tax allocation is required. In addition, the principles of intraperiod tax allocation require that the income taxes related to items recorded as components of other comprehensive income should also be allocated to equity. Therefore, this would be applicable to translation adjustments and certain gains or losses excluded from income that are recorded as other comprehensive income.

FASB Statement No. 52 requires that foreign currency transaction and hedging gains or losses included in the determination of net income be disclosed in the financial statements or the accompanying notes. An analysis of the separate component of other comprehensive income affected by certain foreign currency transactions and hedges and translation adjustments should be presented. The analysis may be in a separate statement, in a note to the financial statements, or as part of the statement of changes in equity. At a minimum, the analysis should disclose

1. Beginning and ending amount of cumulative translation adjustments.

2. The aggregate adjustment for the period resulting from translation adjustments and gains and losses from certain hedges and intercompany balances.
3. The amount of income taxes for the period allocated to translation adjustments.
4. The amounts transferred from cumulative translation adjustments and included in determining net income for the period as a result of the sale or complete or substantially complete liquidation of an investment in a foreign entity.[7]

Although the various effects of rate changes subsequent to the end of the period normally are not disclosed, their effects on unsettled balances arising from foreign currency transactions should be disclosed if significant.

Questions

1. A foreign corporation maintains its books and records in the British pound. What types of cash outflows might suggest that the pound is not the corporation's functional currency?
2. Specify the basic objectives in translating foreign currency financial statements.
3. Assume a U.S. company has a French subsidiary whose functional currency is the French franc. Explain why the translation adjustment is not included as a component of net income on the consolidated income statement.
4. Explain why a sale on account during the year by a subsidiary would contribute to the amount of the adjustment resulting from the translation of the subsidiary's financial statements.
5. Assume a foreign company had been in existence several years before a U.S. company acquired an interest in it. Explain what rates of exchange should be used to translate the common stock account of the subsidiary.
6. A U.S. company acquired an 80% interest in a French company whose functional currency is the French franc. The transaction was accounted for as a purchase, and the price paid exceeded the underlying book value due to appreciated equipment. Explain why the recognition and amortization of this excess results in a translation adjustment.
7. Assume that the U.S. dollar is strengthening relative to the German mark. Explain whether this would be a desirable situation for a U.S. company with an equity interest in a German company.
8. Explain how the negative effects of a foreign subsidiary's translation adjustment may be negated by a parent company.
9. If a foreign subsidiary employs the LIFO method of inventory and has an inventory turnover of 3 times per year, explain how the dollar value of cost of sales would be determined assuming a remeasurement as compared to a translation.
10. Under what circumstances might the cumulative translation adjustment be removed from stockholders' equity (other comprehensive income)?

---

7 *Op. cit.*, par. 31.

Exercises

Exercise 1.   At the beginning of 20X8, the rate of exchange between the foreign currency (FC) and the U.S. dollar was 1 FC = $0.80. A foreign company had net assets at the beginning of 20X8 in the amount of 200,000 FC and was wholly owned by a U.S. company. During 20X8, the foreign company had net income of 60,000 FC and sold additional common stock to the parent company. The common stock had a par value of 40,000 FC and was sold for 50,000 FC when the exchange rate was 1 FC = $0.78. The average exchange rate during 20X8 was 1 FC = $0.76, and at the end of 20X8 the rate was 1 FC = $0.70.

1. Assuming that FC is the functional currency, calculate the amount of the translation adjustment which would be traceable to 20X8.
2. Explain how a bank loan involving foreign currency could have been used by the parent company to reduce the effect of the translation adjustment on owners' equity.

Exercise 2.   Hughes Consulting formed a French company to market its climate control devices in Western Europe. Hughes contributed $200,000 of cash and $320,000 of inventory upon formation of the company. The French company paid, in dollars, general and administrative expenses of $110,000 at the end of the first 3 months of operation. Sales on account and cost of sales for the first 3 months were $440,000 and $280,000, respectively, and were denominated in U.S. dollars. The sales occurred uniformly throughout the 3-month period. Spot exchange rates between the French franc (FF) and the dollar during the first 3 months were as follows: beginning, 1 FF = $0.20; average, 1 FF = $0.22; and ending, 1 FF = $0.24.

Prepare the French company's trial balance at the end of the first 3 months both in French francs and U.S. dollars. Discuss how the objectives of the translation process have been achieved in this example.

Exercise 3.   Grant Company is a German subsidiary of Tri-Coast, a U.S.-based manufacturer. The majority of Grant's cash flows are in the British pound, which has been determined to be the functional currency. Grant's condensed trial balance in German marks (M) as of December 31, 20X5, is as follows:

	Debit	Credit
Cash and Receivables	1,100,000	
Inventory	1,500,000	
Property, Plant, and Equipment (net)	1,985,000	
Accounts Payable		900,000
Long-Term Debt		1,300,000
Dividends Payable		100,000
Stockholders' Equity		1,200,000
Sales Revenue		7,500,000
Expenses	6,415,000	
	11,000,000	11,000,000

The company employs the FIFO inventory method. The most recent purchase of inventory occurred on August 1, 20X5, and November 1, 20X5, in the amounts of 800,000 M and 1,100,000 M, respectively. Depreciable assets consist of the following acquisitions:

(continued)

	Cost Measured
Acquisition Date	in Marks
February 1, 20X3	1,800,000
October 5, 20X4.	300,000
April 1, 20X5	400,000

Depreciation is based on the straight-line method with a 10-year useful life and no salvage value. One-half year of depreciation is taken in the year of acquisition and the year of disposition.

The long-term debt was incurred to finance the February 1, 20X3 acquisition of equipment. The current-year dividend was declared on November 1, payable on January 10, 20X6, to shareholders of record on December 15, 20X5.

The following exchange rates existed:

Date	1 Mark =	1 £ =
February 1, 20X3	£0.27	$1.50
October 5, 20X4.	0.30	1.55
March 1, 20X5	0.32	1.53
April 1, 20X5	0.31	1.52
August 1, 20X5	0.33	1.54
November 1, 20X5	0.34	1.57
December 15, 20X5.	0.35	1.58
December 31, 20X5.	0.36	1.60
20X5 Average.	0.33	1.55
January 10, 20X6	0.37	1.61

1. Calculate the dollar value of the following accounts as of December 31, 20X5:

   a) Inventory
   b) Depreciation Expense
   c) Accounts Payable
   d) Long-Term Debt
   e) Dividends Payable

2. Discuss how the effect of remeasuring the trial balance into the functional currency would be accounted for.

3. Discuss whether a hedge on the net investment would have been beneficial and what form it might have taken.

Exercise 4.   On June 1, 20X8, the Auburn Company (a U.S. company) acquired a 30% interest in a foreign company which was formed on November 1, 20X7. Auburn accounted for the investment using the sophisticated equity method. At the date of acquisition, the net assets of the foreign company were 800,000 foreign currencies (FC) and Auburn paid $600,000 for their interest. Appreciated land accounted for approximately 20% of the excess paid by Auburn, and the balance was traceable to depreciable assets. On average, depreciable assets have a remaining useful life of 12 years and are depreciated using the straight-line method of depreciation. The foreign company's net income for the last 7 months of 20X8 was 140,000 FC. The functional currency is the FC, and the translation adjustment at year-end is a credit of $13,000. Selected exchange rates are as follows:

November 1, 20X7	1 FC = $2.10
Weighted average (June 1 to December 31, 20X8)	1 FC = 2.24
June 1, 20X8................................	1 FC = 2.20
December 31, 20X8........................	1 FC = 2.27

Determine the U.S. dollar balance of Auburn's investment in the foreign company as of December 31, 20X8.

Turn in 10/24

Exercise 5.   Asti Importers Inc. (Asti) has an 80% interest in Boutica, a foreign subsidiary which produces leather goods for sale in the United States. Asti acquired their interest in Boutica on June 1, 20X5, for $850,000 when the net equity of Boutica was 1,200,000 foreign currencies (FC). Any excess paid over book value is deemed to be attributable to undervalued depreciable assets which are deemed to have a remaining useful live of 6 years. At that time, Boutica had depreciable assets and related accumulated depreciation of 800,000 FC and 320,000 FC, respectively. The accumulated depreciation is based on the assets having a 10-year useful life, no salvage value, and the use of the straight-line method of depreciation. Since June 1, 20X5, additional depreciable assets have been acquired as follows:

| July 1, 20X6............. | 400,000 FC | January 1, 20X7......... | 200,000 FC |
| July 1, 20X7............. | 300,000 FC | | |

The assets use the same depreciation variables as the original equipment, and all purchases were paid for in U.S. dollars and were financed with equipment loans in dollars.

The ending inventory of Boutica on December 31, 20X7, consisted of the following:

500,000 FC which existed on June 1, 20X5
200,000 FC which was produced uniformly throughout 20X6
300,000 FC which was produced uniformly throughout 20X7
The cost of sales is based on use of the LIFO inventory method.

As of December 31, 20X7, Asti's ending inventory consisted of $200,000 of goods which were purchased from Boutica on December 1, 20X7. The transfer price for sales from Boutica to Asti is 125% of Boutica's cost.

Various exchange rates between the FC and the U.S. dollars are as follows:

June 1, 20X5	1 FC = $0.75	July 1, 20X7...........	1 FC = $0.65
July 1, 20X6............	1 FC = 0.72	20X7 average	1 FC = 0.64
20X6 average	1 FC = 0.71	December 31, 20X7	1 FC = 0.62
January 1, 20X7.........	1 FC = 0.69		

Assuming the dollar is Boutica's functional currency, determine the following:

1. The 20X7 translated value of depreciation expense.
2. The 20X7 translated value of ending inventory.
3. The 20X7 consolidating entry to record the excess of cost over book value and record the appropriate amortization.
4. The 20X7 consolidating entry to eliminate profit on intercompany sales.

A+C
Turn IN
10/24

Exercise 6.   For each of the following independent cases, determine the translated value of the relevant accounts.

Case A: A foreign subsidiary has inventory accounted for by the lower-of-cost-or-market rule. The 20X7 ending inventory, with a cost of 180,000 FC, was written down to a market value of 176,000 FC. The cost of the inventory is traceable to an October 1, 20X7 purchase of 150,000 FC and a December 15, 20X7 purchase of 30,000 FC. The foreign company's functional currency is the U.S. dollar. Relevant exchange rates on October 1, 20X7, December 15, 20X7, and December 31, 20X7, are 1 FC = $1.76; 1 FC = $1.72; and 1 FC = $1.82, respectively. Calculate the translated value of the December 31, 20X7 ending inventory.

Case B: A foreign subsidiary purchased inventory for 380,000 FC from its U.S. parent on November 1, 20X7. The parent's cost of the inventory sold was $500,000. As of December 31, 20X7, the subsidiary has 60% of the inventory on hand. The subsidiary's functional currency is the foreign currency. Relevant exchange rates on November 1, 20X7, and December 31, 20X7, are 1 FC = $2.00 and 1 FC = $2.10, respectively. Calculate the translated value of the subsidiary's December 31, 20X7 inventory after eliminating the intercompany profit.

Case C: A foreign subsidiary acquired depreciable assets measured in foreign currency A (FCA) over several years. The subsidiary's functional currency is foreign currency B (FCB). All assets are depreciable on a straight-line basis over a 10-year useful life. Relevant asset costs and exchange rates are as follows:

	Asset Cost	1 FCA =	1 FCB =
January 1, 20X6	380,000	2.10 FCB	$1.10
March 1, 20X6	710,000	1.98	1.08
July 1, 20X6	216,000	1.92	1.06
December 1, 20X6	30,000	2.01	1.04
20X6 average		2.03	1.05

Calculate the translated value of the 20X6 depreciation expense.

Exercise 7.   Paco Industries is a foreign corporation which was formed in 20X5. An analysis of activity affecting equity accounts reveals the following through December 31, 20X7:

Date	Activity/Event	Amount in Foreign Currency (FC)	Exchange Rate × 1 FC =
3/1/20X5	Initial sale of common stock (1,400,000 par value)	2,000,000	$1.20
3/1 – 12/31/20X5	Net income	200,000	1.25 weighted ave.
3/1/20X6	Dividend declared	30,000	1.27
10/1/20X6	Second offering of common stock (1,500,000 par value)	3,000,000	1.32
20X6	Net income	450,000	1.30 weighted ave.
4/1/20X7	Acquisition of treasury stock (210,000 par value)	300,000	1.28
7/1/20X7	Dividend declared	90,000	1.25
20X7	Net income	550,000	1.22 weighted ave.

1. Assuming that the foreign currency is the functional currency, prepare the translated equity section for Paco as of December 31, 20X7, noting that the year-end exchange rates were as follows: 20X5, 1 FC = $1.29; 20X6, 1 FC = $1.32; 20X7, 1 FC = $1.21.
2. Calculate what amount of the December 31, 20X7 translation adjustment balance was traceable to 20X7.

Exercise 8. Fuente Enterprises is a foreign company that was acquired by a U.S. company on January 1, 20X7. At that time, Fuente had 2,000,000 units of inventory at a cost of 800,000 foreign currency units (FC) and acquired additional inventory during the year as follows:

	Units	Cost in FC
February 15 purchase.	1,200,000	600,000
July 1 purchase	2,150,000	1,840,000
September 20 purchase.	1,650,000	2,940,000

During the year, Fuente sold 5,900,000 units. Fuente's currency is that of a highly inflationary economy, and spot exchange rates during the year were as follows:

January 1	1 FC = $5.10	September 20.	1 FC = $2.80
February 15.	1 FC = 4.20	December 31	1 FC = 2.10
July 1	1 FC = 3.15	20X7 average	1 FC = 3.58

The ending inventory had a market value of 2,200,000 FC.

Assuming Fuente uses the FIFO inventory method and applies lower of cost or market, calculate the 20X7 cost of sales and ending inventory.

Problems

Problem 11-1. On October 1, 20X5, Codensco acquired a 100% interest in the net assets of Fabrico (a foreign company) for $10,000,000. At that time, the net assets of Fabrico were 8,300,000 foreign currency (FC) units as measured in conformity with GAAP. A condensed trial balance for Fabrico as of December 31, 20X7, is as follows:

	Debit	Credit
Working Capital.	2,840,000 FC	
Property, Plant, and Equipment (net)	15,690,000	
Other Assets.	1,340,000	
Long-Term Debt.		7,800,000 FC
Common Stock (issued on 1/1/X4)		2,000,000
Paid-In Capital in Excess of Par		5,000,000
Retained Earnings		3,420,000
20X7 Net Income		1,650,000
. . . .	19,870,000 FC	19,870,000 FC

The trial balance is based, in part, on certain national accounting principles that are accepted in the country in which Fabrico operates. However, these principles do not conform to U.S. GAAP. These differences are summarized as follows:

(continued)

Tax allocation—The trial balance includes a tax expense equal to the current year's tax liability. If tax allocation were employed, the tax expense and deferred tax liability would increase by 300,000 FC and 1,200,000 FC, respectively.

Land appreciation—Appreciation on a parcel of land was recognized in 20X7 as resulting in an increase in land and retained earnings of 200,000 FC.

Building appreciation—Appreciation was also recognized on certain buildings. The effect is that buildings and accumulated depreciation at the beginning of the year are overstated by 1,200,000 FC and 160,000 FC, respectively. The current depreciation is overstated by 50,000 FC. Because such appreciation is not recognized for tax purposes, the tax provision and liability are not affected by the item.

A dividend of 200,000 FC was declared on February 1, 20X7, and was paid on March 1, 20X7.

The long-term debt of Fabrico includes a loan from Codensco which was made on July 1, 20X7. The loan bears interest at the rate of 10% and has a principal amount payable in dollars of $670,000. Both Fabrico and Codensco have made all 20X7 adjusting entries applicable to the loan including recognition of appropriate transaction gains or losses.

Relevant exchange rates are as follows:

January 1, 20X4............	$1.05	March 1, 20X7.............	$1.31
October 1, 20X5	1.12	July 1, 20X7...............	1.34
January 1, 20X7............	1.28	December 31, 20X7	1.37
February 1, 20X7	1.30	20X7 Average	1.33

Required:

1. Calculate the 20X7 translation adjustment assuming the foreign currency is the functional currency.
2. Prepare all the necessary eliminating and adjusting entries upon consolidation for the year 20X7 assuming use of the cost method. Any excess of cost over book value is traceable to goodwill with a 10-year useful life.

Problem 11-2. Keltner Enterprises has acquired an 80% interest in Jacklandia (a foreign company). The acquisition was accounted for as a purchase and occurred on January 1, 20X6, as follows:

Purchase price of 7,200,000 FC for net assets with a book value of
   $5,600,000 FC (7,000,000 FC × 80%)
Allocation of excess paid:
   Goodwill (10-year remaining life, straight-line amortization)   1,600,000 FC

A condensed trial balance for both Keltner and Jacklandia as of December 31, 20X8, is as follows:

	Keltner (in $s)	Jacklandia (in FC)
Working Capital	$32,160,800 FC	9,550,000
Due from Jacklandia	800,000	
Investment in Jacklandia	14,221,200	
Land	5,120,000	1,000,000
Depreciable Assets	54,000,000	6,000,000
Accumulated Depreciation	(27,000,000)	(2,000,000)
Other Assets......................	5,978,800	1,500,000
Due to Keltner.......................		(620,155)
Other Long-Term Debt...............	(31,320,800)	(4,679,845)

Common Stock (issued July 1, 20X5)	(30,000,000)	(5,000,000)
Paid-In Capital in Excess of Par	(6,000,000)	(1,000,000)
Retained Earnings	(15,000,000)	(3,450,000)
20X8 Net Income	(2,920,000)	(1,300,000)

Jacklandia had net income expressed in foreign currency (FC) in the following amounts for 20X6 and 20X7 of 1,400,000 FC and 2,250,000 FC, respectively. Furthermore, Jacklandia declared a dividend of 1,200,000 FC on February 1, 20X8.

The FC is Jacklandia's functional currency, and various exchange rates are as follows:

July 1, 20X5.	1 FC = $1.39	December 31, 20X7	1 FC = $1.32
January 1, 20X6.	1 FC = 1.40	20X8 Average	1 FC = 1.27
20X6 Average	1 FC = 1.42	February 1, 20X8	1 FC = 1.25
20X7 Average	1 FC = 1.35	December 31, 20X8	1 FC = 1.29

Required: Prepare a columnar worksheet to present the combined income statement and balance sheet of Keltner and its foreign subsidiary, Jacklandia, with all amounts stated in U.S. dollars. Key and explain worksheet eliminations and adjustments, and show supporting computations in good form. Ignore income taxes, and assume use of the simple equity method. (You may want to prepare a translated trial balance for Jacklandia first and then prepare a consolidated worksheet.)

Problem 11-3.   Divall is a French company whose functional currency is the French franc (FF). The company was founded on July 1, 20X7, with the sale of stock for 11,880,000 FF, of which 10,000,000 FF represented par value. On January 1, 20X9, a U. S. company purchased for cash all of the stock of Divall for 14,000,000 FF when the retained earnings balance of Divall was 1,200,000 FF. The excess paid over book value is attributable to undervalued depreciable property which had a remaining useful life of 12 years at the date of acquisition.

Divall's unadjusted trial balance in FF on December 31, 20X9, is as follows:

	Debit	Credit
Cash and Receivables.	2,210,000	
Inventory.	5,700,000	
Prepaid Assets	122,000	
Property, Plant, and Equipment	7,533,000	
Accumulated Depreciation		817,000
Other Assets	1,200,000	
Accounts and Notes Payable		2,984,000
Dividends Payable (declared on December 1, 20X9) . . .		320,000
Common Stock.		10,000,000
Paid-In Capital in Excess of Par.		1,880,000
Dividends Declared.	320,000	
Retained Earnings, 1/1/X9		1,200,000
Sales Revenue		8,954,000
Cost of Goods Sold	6,060,000	
Selling, General, and Administrative Expenses	3,010,000	
Total.	26,155,000	26,155,000

(continued)

The trial balance has not been adjusted to reflect gains and losses on the following transactions:

a) Inventory includes materials purchased from a German company in the amount of 230,000 FF. At the date of purchase, 1 FF = 0.35 M (German Marks) and at December 31, 20X9, 1 FF = 0.38 M. The purchase which is denominated in M is payable in early January of the next year.

b) Notes payable includes a loan from a U.S. bank in the amount of 700,000 FF. The loan was received on August 1, 20X9, and is denominated in dollars.

The December 31, 20X9 ending inventory includes 430,000 FF of goods, which is a portion of the amount purchased from the U.S. parent on October 1, 20X9. The original purchase, which was denominated in FF, had a value of $130,000 and a cost to the parent of $104,000.

Relevant direct exchange rates ($/FF) are as follows:

July 1, 20X7	$0.140
January 1, 20X9	0.170
August 1, 20X9	0.173
October 1, 20X9	0.180
December 1, 20X9	0.179
December 31, 20X9	0.178
20X9 Average	0.174

Required:

1. Prepare for Divall the December 31, 20X9 adjusted trial balance in FF and the translated value of the account balances in dollars. Supporting schedules should be in good form.
2. Prepare the parent's journal entries related to the investment in the foreign subsidiary and all necessary eliminating and adjusting entries upon consolidation assuming use of the simple equity method. Supporting schedules should be in good form.

Problem 11-4.   In an attempt to expand their sales internationally, Autocare (a U.S. company) acquired a 30% interest in Eurocar, which is a British company. Eurocar distributes a variety of car-repair equipment throughout Europe and will be acquiring inventory from Autocare for subsequent sale in its markets. Eurocar's functional currency is the British pound, and even its purchases from Autocare are denominated in British pounds.

Autocare acquired its interest in Eurocar on July 1, 20X6, for a purchase price of $8,000,000 when the book value of net assets was represented by the following:

Common Stock	5,000,000 Pounds
Paid-In Capital in Excess of Par Value	2,000,000
Retained Earnings	2,000,000

Any excess of cost over related book value is attributable to undervalued depreciable assets, and such excess should be amortized over 10 years using a straight-line method.

Since the date of acquisition, the underlying equity of Eurocar has been affected by the following:

Second half of 20X6 net income.	440,000 pounds
Declaration of dividend on March 1, 20X7	100,000
20X7 net income	830,000
Declaration of dividend on March 1, 20X8	100,000
20X8 net income	950,000

On April 1, 20X8, Autocare lent Eurocar $4,000,000 which calls for the interest to be paid annually but settlement of the principal amount is payable on demand. However, settlement of the loan is not anticipated in the foreseeable future. The loan is denominated in British pounds.

As of December 31, 20X8, Autocare has in its inventory goods acquired from Eurocar at a cost of 120,000 pounds on December 15, 20X8. This inventory was sold by Autocare at a profit margin of 20% of cost.

Relevant exchange rates are as follows:

July 1, 20X6 . . . . 1 Pound = $1.65		March 1, 20X8 . . . . 1 Pound = $1.58	
Second half of 20X6. . . . . 1 Pound = 1.63		20X8 Average. . . . . 1 Pound = 1.55	
December 31, 20X6. . . . . 1 Pound = 1.62		April 1, 20X8 . . . . 1 Pound = 1.59	
March 1, 20X7 . . . . 1 Pound = 1.60		December 15, 20X8. . . . . 1 Pound = 1.53	
20X7 Average. . . . . 1 Pound = 1.57		December 31, 20X8. . . . . 1 Pound = 1.52	
December 31, 20X7. . . . . 1 Pound = 1.56			

Required:

1. Calculate the cumulative translation adjustment resulting from translation of Eurocar's trial balance as of December 31, 20X8, and that portion which is traceable to 20X8.
2. Calculate the book value of Autocare's investment in Eurocar as of December 31, 20X8, assuming use of the sophisticated equity method.
3. Provide an analysis of the separate component of Autocare's other comprehensive income in which translation adjustments and other related matters are recorded.

Problem 11-5.   Reslin Corporation is a New York-based manufacturer of photographic supplies. On August 1, 20X3, Reslin expanded its network of operations by opening a branch office in Great Britain. The following information is available regarding accounts of the home office and branch for the year ended December 31, 20X5:

a) On December 22, 20X5, the home office shipped merchandise billed at $12,600 to the branch office. The merchandise was received in January 20X6.

b) The branch office received all of its beginning inventory and 40% of its ending inventory from the home office. The home office bills the goods at cost plus a markup of 12% of cost. Purchases are made uniformly throughout the year, and branch inventory is accounted for by the FIFO method. The 20X5 beginning inventory of the branch office is £86,000. The current cost of ending inventories at December 31, 20X5, excludes the shipment in transit.

c) A photographer on location in Great Britain purchased film on account from the branch office. Upon returning to the United States, however, the photographer erroneously paid the account to the New York office on December 30, 20X5. The bookkeeper recorded the $1,300 payment on the books of the home office but did not notify the branch office.

d) On December 30, the branch office authorized a remittance of £4,400 to be made to the home office. Payment was received by the home office on January 2, 20X6.

e) On December 31, the branch office recorded the December allocated general and administrative expense from the home office as £570 instead of £750.

f) The annual insurance premium is paid by the branch office on March 31 of each year.

g) As of May 1, 20X5, the rate of exchange is £1 = $1.60. The previous rate, which had been in effect since 20X2, was £1 = $1.75. The average annual rate of exchange was £1 = $1.65.

Trial balances at December 31, 20X5, for the home office and its branch are as follows. No adjustments required by home office accounting procedures have been recorded.

	Branch Office Trial Balance (£)	Home Office Trial Balance ($)
Cash	65,000	140,000
Accounts Receivable	100,000	205,000
Inventory, Dec. 31, 20X5	131,250	650,000
Prepaid Insurance.	1,500	
Customer Deposits (refundable).	680	2,300
Property, Plant, and Equipment	950,000	2,710,000
Investment in Branch		23,940
Cost of Goods Sold	1,424,750	3,780,000
Selling Expenses.	41,000	113,000
General and Administrative Expense	92,500	366,000
Depreciation Expense	120,000	250,000
Accounts Payable.	(130,000)	(290,000)
Customer Deposits (refundable).	(680)	(2,300)
Mortgage Payable on Building	(203,000)	(512,000)
Accumulated Depreciation	(380,000)	(995,000)
Home Office Equity	(3,320)	
Capital Stock ($2 par).		(320,000)
Retained Earnings, Jan. 1, 20X5.		(510,000)
Sales	(2,209,680)	(4,750,940)
Shipments to Branch (at retail)		(860,000)
Total	0	0

Required:

Prepare a columnar worksheet to present the combined income statement and combined balance sheet of Reslin Corporation and its foreign branch office with all amounts stated in U.S. dollars. Key and explain worksheet eliminations and adjustments, and show supporting computations in good form. Ignore income taxes.

Problem 11-6. On July 1, 20X6, Spencer International acquired an 80% interest in the net assets of Quatro, which is a foreign company, for $6,260,000. At that time the net assets of Quatro in foreign currency (FC) were as follows:

Common Stock	8,000,000 FC
Paid-In Capital in Excess of Par	1,000,000
Retained Earnings	3,000,000

Any excess paid over book value was attributed to the fair market value of certain licensing agreements which were held by Quatro. The agreements had an original useful life of 10 years and have a remaining life of 5 years and are amortized using a straight-line method.

Spencer's investment in Quatro was designed to provide Spencer with additional manufacturing capacity for its product line and a distribution system which would allow for expanded sales in foreign markets. In order to implement these goals, Spencer lent Quatro $5,940,000 in 20X6 for the purpose of improving the manufacturing capacity. For the next 5 years, only interest payments at the rate of 8% would be made on a monthly basis. The loan originated on October 1, 20X6, and the proceeds were disbursed at that time as follows:

Purchase of additional machinery	$3,410,000
Purchase of additional tooling	992,000
Purchase of additional inventory	1,538,000

All depreciable assets are depreciated using the straight-line method, and salvage values are ignored. Machinery is depreciated over a 10-year useful life, and tooling is depreciated over 10 years. No other additions or dispositions of depreciable assets have occurred since Spencer's acquisition of Quatro.

The manufacturing lead time for Quatro's products is such that the inventory typically turns over approximately 4 times a year; however, production costs are incurred fairly uniformly throughout the year. Virtually all material costs are denominated in U.S. dollars although labor costs are denominated in FCs. The company employs the FIFO inventory method, and 20X7 ending inventory and cost of sales detail is as follows:

Ending Inventory

2,200,000 FC acquired in the last quarter of 20X7 when on average	1 FC = $0.55
1,500,000 FC acquired in the third quarter of 20X7 when on average	1 FC = 0.56

Cost of Sales

800,000 FC acquired in the third quarter of 20X6 when on average	1 FC = $0.61
1,200,000 FC acquired in the fourth quarter of 20X6 when on average . . .	1 FC = 0.62
3,200,000 FC acquired in the first quarter of 20X7 when on average	1 FC = 0.60
4,100,000 FC acquired in the second quarter of 20X7 when on average . .	1 FC = 0.57
3,400,000 FC acquired in the third quarter of 20X7 when on average	1 FC = 0.56

The December 31, 20X7 trial balance for Quatro is as follows:

	Debit	Credit
Cash and Receivables	2,200,000 FC	FC
Inventory	3,700,000	
Machinery and Equipment	22,950,000	
Accumulated Depreciation—		
Machinery and Equipment		5,922,500
Tooling	6,000,000	
Accumulated Depreciation—Tooling		1,520,000

(continued)

	Debit	Credit
Licensing Agreements.	500,000	
Accumulated Amortization—		
Licensing Agreements.		325,000
Accounts and Notes Payable		2,000,000
Due to Spencer.		11,000,000
Common Stock		8,000,000
Paid-In Capital in Excess of Par		1,000,000
Retained Earnings.		3,700,000
Sales Revenue		20,527,500
Cost of Sales (excluding depreciation)	12,700,000	
Depreciation Expense	2,895,000	
Amortization Expense	50,000	
Other Expenses.	3,000,000	
	53,995,000 FC	53,995,000 FC

The retained earnings balance as of December 31, 20X7, reflects net income for the last half of 20X6 of 1,300,000 FC (which had a translated value of $806,000) and dividend declarations in the amount of 300,000 FC each on both August 1, 20X6, and August 1, 20X7.

Additional exchange rates are as follows:

July 1, 20X6.	1 FC = $0.60	20X7 Average	1 FC = $0.57
October 1, 20X6	1 FC = 0.62	August 1, 20X7	1 FC = 0.55
August 1, 20X6	1 FC = 0.61	December 31, 20X7	1 FC = 0.54
Last half of 20X6 Average . .	1 FC = 0.62		

Required:

1. Prepare a remeasured trial balance in dollars as of December 31, 20X7, assuming that Quatro's functional currency is the dollar.
2. Prepare all of the necessary elimination entries to account for the acquisition price being in excess of the book value of net assets.

Problem 11-7.   On January 1, 20X8, Hadley Corporation paid 34,000,000 FC to acquire an 80% interest in Greco Manufacturing, a foreign company. At that time, Greco's owners' equity, in foreign currency (FC), was as follows:

Common Stock	17,000,000 FC
Paid-In Capital in Excess of Par	8,000,000
Retained Earnings	12,480,000

During 20X8, Greco purchased inventory from local suppliers with the exception of the following amounts which were purchased from Hadley, the parent company:

June 15 purchase.	$5,400,000
December 1 purchase.	2,380,000

Hadley's cost on the above sales is 70% of the sales value. Invoice amounts were due the parent, payable in dollars, 45 days after receipt. Of the December 1 purchase, 40% remains unsold as of year-end.

Sales during the year were all denominated in FC with the exception of the following sales which were denominated in U.S. dollars:

July 31 (payment due 8/31/X8) $12,450,000
December 15 (payment due 1/15/X9)   4,800,000

The sales proceeds were immediately converted into FC.

On December 1, Greco secured financing for a planned addition to their manufacturing facility. The total amount borrowed of 30,000,000 FC was loaned by the following sources:

A German bank. . . . .   20,000,000 FC
The parent company.   10,000,000

The loan from the German bank bears interest at the rate of 12%, and the principal amount of 8,000,0000 M is to be repaid in German marks in 36 months. Relevant rates of exchange between FC and the German mark are as follows: December 1, 1 FC = 0.40 M, and December 31, 1 FC = 0.41 M. The $15,400,000 loan from the parent bears interest at the rate of 7% and is payable in dollars on December 1, 20X9.

On December 31, 20X8, Greco's condensed trial balance in FC was as follows:

	Debit	Credit
Current Assets	34,200,000	
Depreciable Assets	121,320,000	
Accumulated Depreciation		24,570,000
Other Assets	20,670,000	
Cost of Sales	125,850,000	
Selling, General, and Administrative Expenses	32,340,000	
Income Tax Expense	12,740,000	
Current Liabilities		15,880,000
Noncurrent Liabilities.		72,000,000
Common Stock.		17,000,000
Paid-In Capital in Excess of Par.		8,000,000
Retained Earnings.		12,480,000
Sales		197,190,000
Totals	347,120,000	347,120,000

Relevant spot exchange rates for the year 20X8 are as follows:

January 1	1 FC = $1.50	December 1	1 FC = $1.54
June 15	1 FC = 1.46	December 15	1 FC = 1.56
July 31	1 FC = 1.48	December 31	1 FC = 1.58
August 31	1 FC = 1.45	Average	1 FC = 1.53

Required:

1. Prepare an analysis of Greco's exchange gains or losses, in FC, that resulted from the foreign currency transactions detailed above.
2. Calculate the total translation adjustment including that which is traceable to the excess of cost over book value. Assume the excess is amortized over 10 years on a straight-line basis.
3. Prepare all of the eliminating and adjusting entries that would be necessary in order to prepare consolidated financial statements.
4. Prepare a schedule to calculate the minority interest amount that would appear on the consolidated balance sheet.

Problem 11-8.   Mirronics Corporation has been the original owner of LeBec, a French company that manufactures alternative energy systems for a number of German customers. Although LeBec maintains its books and records in French francs (FF), its functional currency is the German mark (M). LeBec's forecasted trial balance, in francs, as of December 31, 20X8, is expected to be as follows:

	Debit	Credit
Cash and Receivables	1,388,000	
Inventory	2,230,000	
Depreciable Assets	2,470,000	
Accumulated Depreciation		1,235,000
Other Assets	300,000	
Cost of Sales	3,980,000	
Depreciation Expense	247,000	
Other Expenses	1,280,000	
Current Liabilities		1,870,000
Noncurrent Liabilities		1,300,000
Common Stock		1,200,000
Retained Earnings		860,000
Sales		5,430,000
Totals	11,895,000	11,895,000

The inventory represents costs that were incurred evenly over the last quarter of 20X8, and the cost of sales represents costs that were incurred evenly over the first 6 months of 20X8. The depreciable assets were acquired during the first quarter of 20X3. The other assets represent deposits and prepaid items that were incurred during the last quarter of 20X8. Other expenses and sales occurred evenly throughout the year. The common stock was issued on January 1, 20X3, and February 1, 20X8, in the amounts of 1,100,000 FF and 100,000 FF, respectively. The remeasured value of retained earnings as of January 1, 20X8, was 560,000 M.

Mirronics has experienced a weakening U.S. market and is under extreme pressure to maximize reported earnings. In response, Mirronics wants to hedge against remeasurement losses and current-year translation adjustments. It is anticipated that the necessary hedges will require Mirronics to secure a long-term loan from a German bank. Such a loan could be taken out at the beginning of the fourth quarter of 20X8 and would bear interest at the rate of 9%.

Various actual and expected exchange rates are as follows:

	1 FF =	1 M =
January 1, 20X3	0.50 M	$0.40
1st quarter average, 20X3	0.50	0.41
January 1, 20X8	0.46	0.55
February 1, 20X8	0.43	0.57
1st 6 months' average, 20X8	0.41	0.56
20X8 average	0.39	0.53
October 1, 20X8	0.37	0.54
4th quarter average, 20X8	0.36	0.52
December 31, 20X8	0.35	0.51

Required:

1. Prepare a remeasured forecasted trial balance for LeBec as of December 31, 20X8.
2. Prepare a schedule to calculate the expected translation adjustment traceable to 20X8.
3. Identify the amount of a German bank loan that would be necessary to minimize the adverse effects of remeasurement and translation on Mirronics' equity.

Problem 11-9.   Balfour Corporation acquired 100% of Tobac, Inc., a foreign corporation, for 33,000,000 foreign currency units (FC). The acquisition, which was accounted for as a purchase, occurred on July 1, 20X5, when Tobac's equity, in foreign currency units, was as follows:

Common Stock	19,000,000 FC
Paid-In Capital in Excess of Par	8,480,000
Retained Earnings	2,520,000

Any excess of cost over book value is traceable to goodwill which is to be amortized over 10 years. Balfour uses the simple equity method to account for its investment in Tobac.

On April 1, 20X7, Tobac acquired additional equipment costing 4,000,000 FC. Equipment is depreciated by the straight-line method over 10 years. No other equipment had been acquired or disposed of since 20X4. Tobac employs the LIFO inventory method. Ending inventory on December 31, 20X7, consists of

Acquired in the 1st quarter of 20X4	1,000,000 FC
Acquired in the 1st quarter of 20X5	500,000
Acquired in the 1st quarter of 20X7	6,500,000

The cost of sales is traceable to goods purchased during 20X7 as follows:

Acquired uniformly over the last 9 months	23,400,000
Acquired in the 1st quarter	4,200,000

Other expenses were incurred evenly over the year.

On April 1, 20X7, Tobac borrowed $1,280,000 from the parent company in order to help finance the purchase of equipment. The note is due in 1 year and bears interest at the rate of 8%. Principal and interest amounts are due to the parent in dollars.

Various spot rates are as follows:

	1 FC =		1 FC =
1st quarter, 20X4 Average	$0.46	December 31, 20X6	$0.60
20X4 Average	0.49	1st quarter, 20X7 Average	0.62
January 1, 20X5	0.51	April 1, 20X7	0.64
1st quarter, 20X5 Average	0.53	20X7 Average	0.67
July 1, 20X5	0.55	Last 9 months, 20X7 Average	0.66
December 31, 20X5	0.58	December 31, 20X7	0.65
Last 6 months, 20X5 Average	0.57		
20X6 Average	0.58		

The December 31, 20X7 trial balances for Tobac and Balfour are as follows:

	Tobac		Balfour
Cash	3,087,385	FC	$ 4,463,200
Net Accounts Receivable	12,000,000		15,350,000
Inventory	8,000,000		16,300,000
Due from Tobac			1,356,800
Investment in Tobac—See Note A			23,712,363
Depreciable Assets	34,000,000		68,000,000
Accumulated Depreciation	(12,300,000)		(42,000,000)
Due to Balfour	(2,087,385)		
Other Liabilities	(3,700,000)		(27,000,000)
Common Stock	(19,000,000)		(35,000,000)
Paid-In Capital in Excess of Par	(8,480,000)		(2,000,000)
Retained Earnings, 1/1/X7	(7,520,000)		(4,500,000)
Sales	(40,000,000)		(98,000,000)
Cost of Sales	27,600,000		64,000,000
Depreciation Expense	3,300,000		8,076,800
Interest Expense on Balfour Loan (accrued on 12/31/X7) —See Note B	118,154		
Exchange Gain on Balfour Loan—See Note B	(30,769)		
Other Expenses	5,012,615		10,000,000
Interest Income			(76,800)
Subsidiary Income			(2,682,363)
Totals	0		0

Note A—Balfour's Investment in Tobac consists of the following:

Initial investment (33,000,000 FC × 0.55)	$18,150,000
Last 6 months, 20X5 income (2,000,000 FC × 0.57)	1,140,000
20X6 income (3,000,000 FC × 0.58)	1,740,000
20X7 income	2,682,363
Balance	$23,712,363

Note B—The original loan from Balfour was 2,000,000 FC or $1,280,000 (2,000,000 FC × 0.64). On December 31, 20X7, it would require 1,969,231 FC ($1,280,000 ÷ 0.65) to settle the loan. This represents an exchange gain of 30,769 FC (2,000,000 FC − 1,969,231 FC).

The year-end balance due to Balfour is determined as follows:

Principal balance	1,969,231	FC
Accrued interest ($1,280,000 × 8% × ⁶/₁₂ ÷ 0.65)	118,154	
Balance	2,087,385	FC

The interest is accrued at year-end and, therefore, interest expense should be translated at the year-end rate.

Required:

Assuming the FC is Tobac's functional currency, translate Tobac's trial balance and prepare a consolidating worksheet using the format of Worksheet 11-1.

turn-in
10/24

Problem 11-10. Assume the same facts as Problem 11-9 with the following exceptions:

   a) Tobac's functional currency is the U.S. dollar.

   b) Balfour's investment in Tobac consists of the following:

Initial investment (33,000,000 FC × 0.55)	$18,150,000
Last 6 months, 20X5 income (including the remeasurement gain or loss)	1,610,000
20X6 income (including the remeasurement gain or loss)	1,860,000
20X7 income (excluding the remeasurement gain or loss).	3,495,363
Balance.	$25,115,363

Note that the balance has not yet been adjusted for the 20X7 remeasurement gain or loss.

   c) The trial balances for Tobac and Balfour are the same as in Problem 11-9 with the following exceptions:

	Balfour
Investment in Tobac	$25,115,363
Retained Earnings, 1/1/X7.	(5,090,000)
Subsidiary Income	(3,495,363)

Required:

Remembering that Tobac's functional currency is the U.S. dollar, translate Tobac's trial balance and prepare a consolidating worksheet using the format of Worksheet 11-1.

Remember that transactions traceable to pre-7/1/X5 should be remeasured at the rate in effect on 7/1/X5. This is because on 7/1/X5 Balfour acquired its interest in Tobac and established the dollar basis of net assets existing at that time.

Worksheet 11-1

Consolidating the Foreign Subsidiary
Dome Corporation and Subsidiary Fori Corporation
Worksheet for Consolidated Financial Statements (in dollars)
For Year Ended December 31, 20X1

	(Credit balance amounts are in parentheses.) In U.S. dollars	Trial Balance Dome Corp.	Fori Corp.
1	Cash	56,800	10,500
2	Accounts Receivable	112,000	22,050
3	Allowance for Doubtful Accounts	(5,600)	(1,050)
4	Due from Dome		14,700
5	Inventory, Dec. 31, 20X1	154,700	31,500
6	Prepaid Insurance	9,050	3,150
7	Investment in Fori Corporation	141,153	
8			
9			
10	Land	125,000	18,900
11	Depreciable Assets and Goodwill	500,000	126,000
12	Accumulated Depreciation and Amortization	(100,000)	(15,750)
13	Accounts Payable	(112,000)	(21,000)
14	Taxes Payable	(150,000)	(31,500)
15	Accrued Interest Payable	(16,000)	(1,050)
16	Mortgage Payable—Land	(105,000)	(10,500)
17	Common Stock	(350,000)	(80,000)
18	Paid-In Capital in Excess of Par	(100,000)	
19	Retained Earnings, Jan. 1, 20X1	(116,000)	(20,000)
20	**Cumulative Translation Adjustment—Fori**		**(5,780)**
21	**Cumulative Translation Adjustment—Dome**		
22			
23	Sales—Dome		(82,400)
24	Sales—Other	(908,600)	(206,000)
25	Gain on Sale of Depreciable Assets	(8,600)	(2,060)
26	Cost of Goods Sold	703,850	185,400
27	Depreciation and Amortization Expense	45,600	10,300
28	Income Tax Expense	108,000	30,900
29	Other Expenses (including interest)	51,800	23,690
30	Subsidiary Income	(36,153)	
31		0	0
32	Combined Net Income		
33	To Minority Interest		
34	Balance to Controlling Interest		
35	Total Minority Interest		
36	Retained Earnings, Controlling Interest, Dec. 31, 20X1		
37			

Worksheet 11-1 (see page 11-16)

Eliminations & Adjustments Dr.	Eliminations & Adjustments Cr.	Consolidated Income Statement	Minority Interest	Controlling Retained Earnings	Consolidated Balance Sheet	
					67,300	1
					134,050	2
					(6,650)	3
	(5) 14,700					4
					186,200	5
					12,200	6
	(1) 36,153					7
	(2) 90,000					8
	(4) 15,000					9
					143,900	10
(4) 15,750					641,750	11
	(4) 1,575				(117,325)	12
(5) 14,700					(118,300)	13
					(181,500)	14
					(17,050)	15
					(115,500)	16
(2) 72,000			(8,000)		(350,000)	17
					(100,000)	18
(2) 18,000			(2,000)	(116,000)		19
(3) 5,202			(578)			20
	(3) 5,202				(5,922)	21
	(4) 720					22
(6) 82,400						23
		(1,114,600)				24
		(10,660)				25
	(6) 82,400	806,850				26
(4) 1,545		57,445				27
		138,900				28
		75,490				29
(1) 36,153						30
245,750	245,750					31
		(46,575)				32
		4,017	(4,017)			33
		42,558		(42,558)		34
			(14,595)		(14,595)	35
				(158,558)	(158,558)	36
					0	37

(continued)

Eliminations and Adjustments:

(1) Eliminate the entries in the subsidiary income account against the investment in Fori account to record the parent's 90% controlling interest in the subsidiary.

(2) Eliminate 90% of the subsidiary's January 1, 20X1 equity balances against the balance of the investment account.

(3) Distribute the cumulative translation adjustment between controlling and minority interests.

(4) Distribute the excess of cost over book value of 15,000 FC to goodwill, and record appropriate amortization.

(5) Eliminate the intercompany trade balances.

(6) Eliminate the intercompany sales assuming that none of the goods purchased from Fori remain in Dome's ending inventory.

Subsidiary Fori Corp. Income Distribution

	Internally generated net income	$40,170
	Adjusted income	$40,170
	Minority share	10%
	Minority interest	$ 4,017

Parent Dome Corp. Income Distribution

Goodwill amortization	$1,545	Internally generated net income	$ 7,950
		Share of subsidiary income	
		(90% × $40,170)	$36,153
		Controlling interest	$42,558

Worksheet 11-2

Consolidating the Foreign Subsidiary
Dome Corporation and Subsidiary Fori Corporation
Worksheet for Consolidated Financial Statements (in dollars)
For Year Ended December 31, 20X1

	(Credit balance amounts are in parentheses.)	Trial Balance	
		Dome Corp.	Fori Corp.
1	Cash	56,800	10,500
2	Accounts Receivable	112,000	22,050
3	Allowance for Doubtful Accounts	(5,600)	(1,050)
4	Due from Dome		14,700
5	Inventory, Dec. 31, 20X1	154,700	31,500
6	Prepaid Insurance	9,050	3,135
7	Investment in Fori Corporation	141,153	
8			
9			
10	Land	125,000	18,270
11	Depreciable Assets and Goodwill	500,000	122,400
12	Accumulated Depreciation and Amortization	(100,000)	(15,120)
13	Accounts Payable	(112,000)	(21,000)
14	Taxes Payable	(150,000)	(31,500)
15	Accrued Interest Payable	(16,000)	(1,050)
16	Mortgage Payable—Land	(105,000)	(10,150)
17	Common Stock	(350,000)	(80,000)
18	Paid-In Capital in Excess of Par	(100,000)	
19	Retained Earnings, Jan. 1, 20X1	(116,000)	(20,000)
20	Remeasurement Gain		(1,280)
21			
22			
23	Sales—Dome		(82,400)
24	Sales—Other	(908,600)	(206,000)
25	Gain on Sale of Depreciable Assets	(8,600)	(2,760)
26	Cost of Goods Sold	703,850	185,000
27	Depreciation and Amortization Expense	45,600	10,120
28	Income Tax Expense	108,000	30,900
29	Other Expenses (including interest)	51,800	23,735
30	Subsidiary Income	(36,153)	
31		0	0
32	Combined Net Income		
33	To Minority Interest		
34	Balance to Controlling Interest		
35	Total Minority Interest		
36	Retained Earnings, Controlling Interest, Dec. 31, 20X1		
37			

Worksheet 11-2 (see page 11-25)

Eliminations & Adjustments Dr.	Eliminations & Adjustments Cr.	Consolidated Income Statement	Minority Interest	Controlling Retained Earnings	Consolidated Balance Sheet	
					67,300	1
					134,050	2
					(6,650)	3
	(4) 14,700					4
					186,200	5
					12,185	6
	(1) 36,153					7
	(2) 90,000					8
	(3) 15,000					9
					143,270	10
(3) 15,000					637,400	11
	(3) 1,500				(116,620)	12
(4) 14,700					(118,300)	13
					(181,500)	14
					(17,050)	15
					(115,150)	16
(2) 72,000			(8,000)		(350,000)	17
					(100,000)	18
(2) 18,000			(2,000)	(116,000)		19
		(1,280)				20
						21
						22
(5) 82,400						23
		(1,114,600)				24
		(11,360)				25
	(5) 82,400	806,450				26
(3) 1,500		57,220				27
		138,900				28
		75,535				29
(1) 36,153						30
239,753	239,753					31
		(49,135)				32
		4,141	(4,141)			33
		44,994		(44,994)		34
			(14,141)		(14,141)	35
				(160,994)	(160,994)	36
					0	37

(continued)

Eliminations and Adjustments:

(1) Eliminate the entries in the subsidiary income account against the investment in Fori account to record the parent's 90% controlling interest in the subsidiary.
(2) Eliminate 90% of the subsidiary's January 1, 20X1 equity balances against the balance of the investment account.
(3) Distribute the excess of cost over book value of 15,000 FC, and record appropriate amortization.
(4) Eliminate the intercompany trade balances.
(5) Eliminate the intercompany sales assuming that none of the goods purchased from Fori remain in Dome's ending inventory.

Subsidiary Fori Corp. Income Distribution

	Internally generated net income	$42,685*
	Adjusted income	$42,685
	Minority share	10%
	Minority interest.	$ 4,269

Parent Dome Corp. Income Distribution

Goodwill amortization	$1,500	Internally generated net income	$ 7,950
		Share of subsidiary income (90% × $42,685).	$38,416
		Controlling interest	$44,866

*This amount includes the remeasurement gain of $1,280.

PART 3

SPECIAL REPORTING CONCERNS

Most of the principles discussed in this part of the text are required of public companies as governed by the Securities and Exchange Commission. However, all these principles are also of benefit to nonpublic companies. In order to best serve the needs of users, accounting information should be timely. It is common practice for companies to disclose financial statements on a more frequent basis than annually. These interim reporting periods are viewed as an integral part of a larger annual reporting period. In order to be reflective of the larger annual reporting period, special accounting principles have been developed for interim reporting. A growing number of companies are diversifying their business operations although financial statements for the company as a whole may not reflect the diversity of their operations. In order to provide users with information regarding various segments of business, special disclosures providing key information regarding the operations of business segments are required.

Equity investors are interested in knowing what portion of a company's earnings accrue to the benefit of the investor. Such information is most conveniently reported on a per share basis for common shareholders through the measurement of Basic Earnings Per Share. These investors are also interested in knowing whether there are other outstanding securities that have the potential of becoming common stock. The possible dilutive effect on earnings of such potential common shares is measured by Diluted Earnings Per Share. Information about potential common shares and other types of securities must be disclosed so that a user has a complete understanding of the various securities which make up a company's capital structure.

Interim Reporting and Disclosures about Segments of an Enterprise

This chapter focuses on two areas of significance to most large, publicly held enterprises: interim reporting and segmental disclosure. The relevance of financial information is enhanced if the information is provided on a timely basis. Interim financial reporting addresses the need for timely information and provides users with relevant data which may be used to evaluate the present and help to project future results. The division of an annual reporting period into shorter interim periods results in some unique accounting problems which are addressed in this chapter. Disclosure about segments of an enterprise is designed to provide relevant information about the various business activities in which an enterprise is involved. Such disclosures also provide information about the economic environments in which enterprises operate. Many enterprises consist of operating segments that differ significantly from each other in terms of products, economic environments, markets served, and manufacturing methods. The disclosure of segmental information follows a management approach which emphasizes how management organizes the segments of the enterprise for decision-making purposes and evaluation of performance. This approach will allow users of such information to better understand the activities and environments which affect an enterprise's performance, cash flows, and business risks. The disclosures called for by this approach for both annual and interim reporting purposes are discussed in this chapter.

Interim Reporting

To satisfy the need for timely financial information, many business enterprises have developed interim reporting models that provide financial information on a monthly or quarterly basis or at other defined intervals. These interim data may consist of statements of financial position and retained earnings, income statements, and statements of cash flows. However, primary emphasis is placed on the public disclosure of interim income data.

A substantial amount of empirical research has been devoted to an examination of the utility of publicly disclosed interim financial reports. This research has identified significant stock market reaction to the issuance of interim reports and has noted the influence of interim reports on actual investment decisions. Interim reports provide such an important basis for the prediction of annual income that the demand for these reports nearly parallels the demand for annual reports.

The established utility of interim data emphasizes the importance of applying generally accepted accounting principles, including the principle of adequate disclosure, to interim reports. Therefore, the American Institute of Certified Public Accountants, the National Association of Accountants, the Financial Executives Institute, the Financial Analysts Federation, the Securities and Exchange

Commission, and the principal stock exchanges have directed efforts toward the development and improvement of interim financial reporting.

Approaches to Reporting Interim Data

Earlier forms of interim reporting provided the user of such data with various disclosures other than the computation of net income. However, as the importance of interim income statements became more apparent, different views of the interim period developed. One view of the interim period is that it represents a distinct, independent accounting period, separate from the annual accounting period. Therefore, interim net income should be determined by using the same principles and estimations as would be used if the interim period were an annual accounting period. For example, annual research and development incurred during the interim period should be expensed in that period rather than deferred to future interim periods.

Another view of the interim period is that it is an integral part of the annual period and does not stand as a distinct, independent period. Therefore, interim data should include appropriate adjustments and estimates so that they can be used to predict annual amounts. For example, assume annual income normally includes a year-end accrual for executive bonuses in the amount of $120,000. If the interim statements are to serve as a predictor of annual values, it would seem appropriate that quarterly income statements should include a proportionate amount of this year-end adjustment. Including a $30,000 adjustment for bonuses in the quarterly income statement would allow one to predict annual bonuses in the amount of $120,000. If this interim adjustment were not made, bonuses would be reflected only in the fourth quarter, and previous quarters would not have provided the user with a basis for predicting this annual amount. From this example, one can see that an interim period is viewed as an integral part of a larger annual period. This view of the interim period has been adopted as the underlying theory used to formulate interim accounting principles and practices.

Accounting Principles Board Opinion No. 28

In 1973, the Accounting Principles Board issued APB Opinion No. 28, *Interim Financial Reporting*, which applies to both internally and externally issued reports. This Opinion was in response to the growing interest in the credibility of interim data and to the apparent need for an authoritative statement from the accounting profession regarding generally accepted accounting principles for such data. The Opinion also may have been influenced by the interim reporting requirements of the SEC.

APB Opinion No. 28 is based on the conclusion that an interim period should be viewed as an *integral part of the annual period*, not as a distinct, independent period. The Opinion reflects the APB's concern for the consistent application of principles by stating that financial statements for each interim period should be based on the *same accounting principles and practices* that are used for the preparation of annual financial statements. However, certain modifications of these principles and practices that relate to costs and expenses may be necessary so that the reported results of an interim period are more indicative of anticipated annual income statement amounts. Modifications of accounting principles and practices also are necessary in order to provide timely information.

Modifications for Costs and Expenses.   Those costs that are directly related or allocated to products sold or to services rendered for annual reporting purposes should be given similar treatment for interim reporting purposes. However, the following modifications are acceptable in the area of inventory costing:

1. The gross profit method or other estimation methods that are not acceptable for annual purposes may be used for interim purposes in those instances where taking an interim physical inventory would be too costly or where perpetual inventory records are lacking or unreliable. Furthermore, use of the gross profit method provides a timely measurement which may not be the case if other methods of inventory accounting were employed. The inventory method used for interim purposes should be disclosed. Significant differences between estimates of the perpetual annual inventory and the annual physical inventory also should be recorded in interim statements on a proportionate basis.

2. Use of the LIFO method for interim purposes may result in inventory liquidations that will be replaced by year-end. To compensate for these interim liquidations, the interim cost of goods sold should include the *replacement cost* of temporarily liquidated inventory rather than its historical cost.

3. The use of lower of cost or market may suggest inventory losses for the interim period. Recoveries of these losses in subsequent periods should be recognized as gains to the extent of the losses previously recognized in interim periods within the same fiscal year. An exception to this rule is that temporary market declines that can reasonably be expected to be restored in the fiscal year need not be recognized for the interim period.

4. The use of standard costs for determining inventory generally should be applied on the same basis as is required for annual purposes. Price variances and volume variances that are planned and expected to be absorbed by year-end should be deferred at interim reporting dates.[1] However, unplanned or unanticipated variances should be reported at the end of an interim period.

Illustration of an Interim Liquidation of Inventory.   In order to illustrate the special treatment given interim liquidations, assume a company's LIFO inventory available for sale during the third quarter consisted of beginning inventory of 1,200 units at a cost of $20 each and current purchases of 2,000 units at a cost of $30 each. Assume 2,500 units were sold during the quarter with the expectation that they would be replaced for $32 a unit. Management anticipates that the annual ending inventory will be 1,100 units. Therefore, although the beginning inventory has been liquidated by 500 units, management expects to replenish 400 of these units by year-end. Assuming the company anticipates paying $32 each to replenish the inventory, the third-quarter cost of sales would be calculated as follows:

Current purchases (2,000 units @ $30)............	$60,000
Prior inventory (500 units @ $20 original cost).......	10,000
Excess replacement cost (400 units @ $12).........	4,800
	$74,800

The entry to record the third-quarter cost of sales would be as follows:

Cost of Sales	74,800	
Inventory		70,000
Excess of Replacement Cost for Temporary Liquidation		4,800
To record cost of sales with a historical cost of $70,000		
and an excess of additional replacement cost equal to		
$4,800 ($12 × 400 units).		

1 Accounting Principles Board Opinion No. 28, *Interim Financial Reporting* (New York: American Institute of Certified Public Accountants, 1973), par. 14.

The Excess of Replacement Cost for Temporary Liquidation is classified as a current liability on the interim financial statements. When the 400 units are replenished in the fourth quarter at an assumed cost of $32, the following entry is made:

Inventory	8,000	
Excess of Replacement Cost for Temporary Liquidation	4,800	
Accounts Payable (Cash)		12,800
To record replenishment of inventory previously liquidated.		

Notice that the 400 units replenish the inventory account at a cost of $20 each as though no liquidation had occurred. That is, the inventory now consists of 1,100 units (700 at the end of the third quarter plus the 400 replenished) at a cost of $20 each.

Illustration of Cost or Market for Interim Inventory.   Assume at the end of the second quarter, ending inventory has a cost of $380,000 and a market value of $350,000. The use of lower of cost or market would require a $30,000 loss due to market declines to be recognized in the second quarter. At the end of the third quarter, the company has ending inventory with a cost of $520,000 and a market value of $560,000. Of the $40,000 excess of market value over cost, the company can recognize $30,000 of this amount as a recovery of the second-quarter loss. Therefore, the third-quarter financial statements would include a $30,000 gain due to market recoveries.

Reporting of Costs Unrelated to Inventory.   In reporting costs and expenses that are not allocated to products sold or to services rendered but are charged against income in the interim period, the following standards apply:

a)   *Costs and expenses other than product costs should be charged to income in interim periods as incurred, or be allocated among interim periods based on an estimate of time expired, benefit received, or activity associated with the periods. Procedures adopted for assigning specific cost and expense items to an interim period should be consistent with the bases followed by the company in reporting results of operations at annual reporting dates. However, when a specific cost or expense item charged to expense for annual reporting purposes benefits more than one interim period, the cost or expense item may be allocated to those interim periods.*

b)   *Some costs and expenses incurred in an interim period, however, cannot be readily identified with the activities or benefits of other interim periods and should be charged to the interim period in which incurred. Disclosure should be made as to the nature and amount of such costs unless items of a comparable nature are included in both the current interim period and in the corresponding interim period of the preceding year.*

c)   *Arbitrary assignment of the amount of such costs to an interim period should not be made.*

d)   *Gains and losses that arise in any interim period similar to those that would not be deferred at year-end should not be deferred to later interim periods within the same fiscal year.[2]*

To illustrate the above concepts, assume the following expenditures have occurred at the beginning of the second quarter:

---

2 *Ibid.,* par. 15.

1.   A 12-month insurance premium was paid in the amount of $1,200.
2.   Research costs in the amount of $18,000 were paid and are expected to benefit the company over the next 18 months.
3.   A contribution in the amount of $1,000 was made, although the benefits to subsequent quarters are uncertain.

The expenses to be recognized in the second quarter are as follows:

Insurance expense ($1,200 ÷ 12 × 3 months)	$ 300
Research costs ($18,000 ÷ 3 quarters—not to be deferred beyond year-end)	6,000
Contribution expense	1,000
	$7,300

Certain costs and expenses of an entity are subject to year-end adjustments, such as inventory shrinkage, allowance for uncollectible accounts, and year-end bonuses. These adjustments should not be recognized totally in the final interim period if they relate to activities of other interim periods. Therefore, to generate interim financial reports that contain a reasonable portion of annual expenses, a portion of estimated year-end adjustments should be allocated to each interim period on the basis of a revenue or a cost relationship. For example, a company that estimates an expected material year-end adjustment to its perpetual inventory, based on a physical inventory, should allocate a portion of that estimated adjustment to each interim period. In this case, a portion of the annual estimated inventory shrinkage could be allocated to the quarter using a ratio of current quarter cost of sales to annual estimated cost of sales. Changes in earlier quarters' estimates should be accounted for in the current quarter.

The costs and expenses as well as revenues of some businesses are subject to seasonal variations. Since interim reports for such businesses must be considered as representative of the annual period, APB Opinion No. 28 states that

> . . . such businesses should disclose the seasonal nature of their activities, and consider supplementing their interim reports with information for twelve-month periods ended at the interim date for the current and preceding years.3

Adjustments Related to Prior Interim Periods.   By the definitions set forth in FASB Statement No. 16, *Prior Period Adjustments*, many items that were viewed previously as prior-period adjustments became elements of current operating income. However, certain items are treated as adjustments related to prior interim periods of the current fiscal year. These items include an adjustment or settlement of: litigation or similar claims, income taxes, renegotiation proceedings, or utility revenue under rate-making processes. Treating these items as prior-period adjustments is appropriate if all of the following criteria are met:

a)   The effect of the adjustment or settlement is material in relation to income from continuing operations of the current fiscal year or in relation to the trend of income from continuing operations or is material by other appropriate criteria, and

b)   All or part of the adjustment or settlement can be specifically identified with and is directly related to business activities of specific prior interim periods of the current fiscal year, and

c)   The amount of the adjustment or settlement could not be reasonably estimated prior to the current interim period but becomes reasonably estimable in the current interim period.[4]

---

3 *Ibid.,* par. 13.
4 Statement of Financial Accounting Standards No. 16, *Prior Period Adjustments* (Stamford: Financial Accounting Standards Board, 1977), par. 13.

If such an item occurs in other than the first interim period of the current fiscal year and if all or part of the item is an adjustment related to prior interim periods of the current fiscal year, it should be reported as follows:

a) *The portion of the item that is directly related to business activities of the enterprise during the current interim period, if any, shall be included in the determination of net income for that period.*

b) *Prior interim periods of the current fiscal year shall be restated to include the portion of the item that is directly related to business activities of the enterprise during each prior interim period in the determination of net income for that period.*

c) *The portion of the item that is directly related to business activities of the enterprise during prior fiscal years, if any, shall be included in the determination of net income of the first interim period of the current fiscal year.*[5]

Disclosure also is required regarding adjustments related to prior interim periods of the current year in the period in which the adjustment occurs. Disclosures should be made for each prior period of the current year setting forth both the effect on and actual adjusted amount of income from continuing operations, net income, and related per share amounts.

Finally, it is important to note that those adjustments that are related to prior interim periods do not include normal recurring corrections and adjustments that result from the use of estimates. For example, in the current interim period, the revision of estimates used to measure uncollectible accounts is not accounted for as an adjustment related to prior interim periods. Instead, this correction is accounted for in the current interim period and prospectively, as is the case with other changes in estimates.

Accounting for Income Taxes in Interim Statements

Keeping in mind that the interim period is viewed as an integral part of a larger annual period, interim financial statements should reflect a proportionate amount of the estimated annual income taxes. Each interim period will not be viewed as a separate tax period; therefore, estimates of annual tax amounts and rates become critical. The basic objective of accounting for income taxes in interim periods is to estimate the annual effective tax rate and apply that rate to the interim periods' pretax net incomes.

Accounting for income taxes in interim financial statements is based on the application of principles established in APB Opinion Nos. 23 and 24, FASB Interpretation No. 18, and FASB Statement No. 109. In addition, the following guidelines are applicable to the determination of an effective tax rate for interim purposes that is representative of the estimated annual effective tax rate:

1. The effective tax rate for the annual fiscal period must be estimated at the end of each interim period and applied to year-to-date interim income from ordinary continuing operations. The current interim period's tax expense or benefit is the difference between a) the year-to-date tax expense or benefit and b) the amounts of tax reported in previous interim periods of the current year.

2. The estimated effective tax rate should reflect tax planning alternatives, such as capital gains rates, permanent differences, and tax credits.

3. Nonordinary items of income or loss (unusual or infrequently occurring items, extraordinary items, discontinued operations, and the cumulative effect of changes in accounting principles) are not included in the computation of the estimated annual effective tax rate, nor are these items prorated over the

---

5 *Ibid.,* par. 14.

balance of the fiscal period. The tax effect on these items is determined incrementally.

4. Changes in tax legislation are to be accounted for in interim periods subsequent to the effective date of the legislation.[6]

The first guideline is designed to ensure that the interim income tax rate is representative of the tax rate applicable to the entire fiscal period. For example, if income from continuing operations during the first interim period is $25,000, under a graduated taxing system the effective tax rate at this level of income might be 15%. However, if the annual ordinary income is expected to be $335,000, the effective annual tax rate might be approximately 34%. Therefore, the latter rate should be used as the interim tax rate. If this estimated annual effective tax rate were not used, a reader of the first interim period's financial statements might conclude that income is taxed at only 15%.

Mechanically speaking, the first guideline also provides an effective way of accounting for changes in the estimated annual effective tax rate. As mentioned earlier, normal recurring corrections and adjustments that result from the use of estimates are accounted for in the current interim period. Applying the estimated annual effective tax rate to the year-to-date income and then subtracting (adding) the tax expenses (benefits) traceable to prior interim periods of the current year results in a difference that represents

1. The tax on the current interim period's pretax income at the present estimated annual effective tax rate and

2. Corrections of previous interim periods' tax expenses or benefits resulting from a change in the estimated annual effective tax rate.

To illustrate, assume that the first quarter's pretax income of $40,000 was taxed at a tax rate of 30%, resulting in a $12,000 tax expense. At the end of the second quarter, the estimated annual effective tax rate is 32% and the second quarter's pretax income is $50,000. The tax on the year-to-date pretax income of $90,000 ($40,000 + $50,000) is $28,800 (32% × $90,000). Subtracting from this year-to-date amount the first-quarter tax expense of $12,000 results in a current second-quarter tax expense of $16,800. The $16,800 consists of

1. The tax on the second quarter's pretax income at the present estimated annual effective tax rate (50,000 × 32%) $16,000

2. Corrections of prior interim period's tax expense resulting from a change in the estimated annual effective tax rate [$40,000 × (32% – 30%)] . . . . <u>800</u>

$16,800

If necessary, the estimated effective annual tax rate should be revised each interim period in order to reflect changed expectations. The guidelines indirectly emphasize that changes in the estimated annual effective tax rate should be accounted for as a change in estimate. Therefore, such changes in the tax rate from period to period should be reflected in the tax expense or benefit of the current period in which the change occurs. The second guideline emphasizes that tax planning alternatives should be reflected in the determination of the estimated effective annual tax rate. For example, if it is estimated that pretax operating income will include some tax-exempt income (a permanent difference), this should be reflected in a lower estimated tax rate. Tax credits and/or lower capital gains tax rates will also have the effect of lowering the estimated rate. Tax allocation principles resulting from the existence of timing differences would be factored into the calculation of the estimated effective annual tax rate as well.

---

6 Accounting Principles Board Opinion No. 28, *op. cit.*, pars. 19–20.

The third guideline recognizes that nonordinary items of income or loss may have a distortive effect on estimated annual effective tax rates; therefore, they are excluded from such calculations. This guideline also recognizes that such items are not allocated to other interim periods of the current year. Thus, such items are accounted for entirely in the interim period in which they occur, and the resulting tax impact must be separately determined. The separate determination of the tax employs an incremental approach which is demonstrated in a later section of this chapter.

The fourth guideline echoes the underlying theory of the first guideline in that changes in estimated tax rates are to be accounted for currently and prospectively. Changes in tax legislation are just one possible explanation for a change in estimated annual effective tax rates.

The computation of the estimated effective tax rate is presented in Cases A and B of Illustration 12-1. Case C demonstrates the determination of the tax expense traceable to interim income and the handling of a change in the estimated effective tax rate.

Illustration 12-1
Case A
Income in All Interim Periods—Tax Credit; No Permanent Differences

Year-to-date (YTD) pretax income is $170,000, and projected pretax income for the balance of the fiscal year is $30,000. No permanent differences exist, and it is anticipated that an annual tax credit of $13,250 will be available. Corporate income is taxed as follows: first $50,000 at 15%, next $25,000 at 25%, next $25,000 at 34%, amounts over $100,000 up to $335,000 at 39%. The effective tax rate is computed as follows:

	Pretax Income (Pretax Loss)	
YTD Income	$170,000	
Projected income	30,000	
Annual income	$200,000	
Permanent differences.	-0-	
Adjusted income	$200,000	
Tax on adjusted income	$ 61,250*	
Tax credits	(13,250)	
Net tax (Note A)	$ 48,000	
Effective tax rate	(24%)	(48,000 × 200,000)

*[($50,000 × 15%) + ($25,000 × 25%) + ($25,000 × 34%) + ($100,000 × 39%)]

Note A: A general business tax credit that cannot be used in the current period may be carried back to the prior year. If tax credits still remain after the carryback, they may be carried forward 20 years.

Case B
Income in All Interim Periods—Tax Credit; Permanent Difference; No Tax Credit

Year-to-date (YTD) pretax income is $30,000, and projected pretax income for the balance of the fiscal year is $90,000. Annual income includes $10,000 of expense which is never deductible for tax purposes (i.e., a permanent difference). Assume that corporate income is taxed at the rates set forth in Case A above. The effective tax rate is computed as follows:

	Pretax Income (Pretax Loss)
YTD Income	$ 30,000
Projected income	90,000
Annual income	$120,000
Permanent differences	10,000
Adjusted income	$130,000
Tax on adjusted income	$ 33,950*
Tax credits	-0-
Net tax	$ 33,950
Effective tax rate	(28%) (33,950 ÷ 120,000)**

* [($50,000 × 15%) + ($25,000 × 25%) + ($25,000 × 34%) + ($30,000 × 39%)]

**Note that the rate always is based on estimated annual pretax income versus adjusted income.

Case C
Income in All Interim Periods—Change in Effective Tax Rate

Interim Period (Quarter)	Ordinary Pretax Income Loss			Tax Expense (Benefit)		
	Current Period	Year-to-Date	Effective Tax Rate	Year-to-Date	Previously Reported	Current Period
First	$30,000	$ 30,000	28%	$ 8,400	—	$ 8,400
Second	40,000	70,000	28	19,600	$ 8,400	11,200
Third	20,000	90,000	32	28,800	19,600	9,200
Fourth	50,000	140,000	32	44,800	28,800	16,000

Year-to-Date Operating Losses.   In some instances, an interim year-to-date (YTD) operating loss may be present. Given this loss, a question arises as to the potential tax benefit associated with the loss. The potential tax benefit is a function of several factors.

The YTD loss first must be combined with the projected income or loss for the remaining interim periods of the current fiscal year. If the YTD loss is offset by the projected income, a tax benefit traceable to the YTD loss may be recognized. However, if it is more likely than not that some portion of the projected income will not be recognized, then the recognized tax benefit traceable to the loss will be reduced accordingly. The concept of "more likely than not" means a level of likelihood at least more than 50% and requires the consideration of many sources of evidence, both positive and negative.[7] For example, a backlog of unfilled orders and/or a strong earnings history exclusive of the YTD loss would suggest that, more likely than not, losses may be offset by projected income. A history of operating losses or unsettled circumstances or economic conditions may suggest that, more likely than not, losses will not be offset totally by projected income.

---

7 Further discussion of the phrase "more likely than not" can be found in *Statement of Financial Accounting Standards No. 109, Accounting for Income Taxes* (Norwalk, CT: Financial Accounting Standards Board, 1992).

After considering the projected income or loss for the balance of the current year, an estimated annual operating loss may exist. The potential tax benefit traceable to this estimated annual operating loss is a function of the following factors:

1. The extent to which the operating loss may be offset by income of the prior two fiscal years included in the carryback period and/or
2. The extent to which the operating loss may be offset by subsequent years' annual income which is more likely than not to be recognized in the 20-year carryforward period.

The basic concern addressed by these factors is whether the operating loss is able to be offset against operating income and, therefore, result in a tax benefit. If the facts suggest that such a benefit is more likely than not, the benefit should be recognized in the calculation of the effective annual tax rate.

Offsetting YTD Operating Losses against Subsequent Interim Income. The benefit associated with a YTD operating loss should be recognized if the loss will be offset against income in later interim periods of the fiscal year. This offset against income may be recognized if it is more likely than not that such income will be recognized. Although "more likely than not" is a subjective concept, knowledge of a company's past performance, existing commitments relating to the future, and seasonal patterns must be considered. APB Opinion No. 28 states that

> *An established seasonal pattern of loss in early interim periods offset by income in later interim periods should constitute evidence that realization is assured beyond reasonable doubt, unless other evidence indicates the established seasonal pattern will not prevail. The tax effects of losses incurred in early interim periods may be recognized in a later interim period of a fiscal year if their realization, although initially uncertain, later becomes assured beyond reasonable doubt. When the tax effects of losses that arise in the early portions of a fiscal year are not recognized in that interim period, no tax provision should be made for income that arises in later interim periods until the tax effects of the previous interim losses are utilized.8*

The offset of an established seasonal loss by subsequent interim income is demonstrated in Case A of Illustration 12-2 on page 12-12. Case B of the same illustration demonstrates a YTD loss whose tax benefit is not initially certain but later becomes recognizable. It is important to note that, in both Cases A and B, it is assumed that no pretax income is available in prior and/or subsequent years to absorb the current year's operating losses.

Offsetting YTD or Annual Operating Losses against Income of Prior Fiscal Years. In certain instances, a current YTD interim loss may not be offset entirely by income in later interim periods of the current fiscal year. However, as suggested by the first factor discussed above, the tax benefit of the YTD should be recognized to the extent that the loss may be carried back against the prior two years of income. Loss carrybacks must begin with the earliest of the prior two years and then proceed to the next earlier year. The tax benefit traceable to the loss, therefore, is a function of the tax rate applied to a prior year's income. Case C of Illustration 12-2 involves the carryback of a YTD loss. Note that, in this case, the loss is not offset completely against prior income. However, the tax benefit is recognized to whatever extent possible.

The same carryback principles apply if an annual loss is anticipated. For example, if a company has a YTD loss of $40,000 and an anticipated annual loss of

---

8 Accounting Principles Board Opinion No. 28, *op. cit.*, par. 20.

$100,000, the amount of tax benefit would be dependent upon the extent to which the $100,000 loss may be carried back. If a company has a year-to-date income of $60,000 and an anticipated annual loss of $20,000, the estimated annual effective tax rate would be dependent upon the tax benefit associated with the annual loss of $20,000. These principles are demonstrated in Case D of Illustration 12-2.

Offsetting Annual Operating Losses against Future Annual Income.   To the extent that losses are not absorbed by income in later interim periods of the current fiscal year and/or the prior two years of income, tax benefits still may be recognized currently. Losses not already offset may be carried forward against future annual income which more likely than not will be recognized in the 20-year carryforward period. Estimating whether future annual income will more likely than not be recognized is one of the most difficult aspects of determining the estimated annual effective tax rate associated with operating losses. Certain amounts of future annual income may have a low level of likelihood that they will be recognized. For example, if an entity has a history of operating losses and is in an industry experiencing a significant number of bankruptcies, a low level of likelihood would seem reasonable. Alternatively, certain amounts of future annual income have a high level of likelihood. For example, the future taxable amounts represented by deferred tax liabilities are considered to have a very high level of likelihood. Therefore, such future taxable amounts will more likely than not be recognized and serve as a basis for offsetting a current annual operating loss. The principles of offsetting current annual operating losses against likely future annual income are demonstrated in Case E of Illustration 12-2.

Operating Losses That Are Not Offset.   If present net operating losses cannot be offset totally by any of the options discussed (subsequent interim income of the current fiscal year, carrybacks, or carryforwards), the potential tax benefit is reduced accordingly. However, those losses that are not offset may be offset subsequently against future years' recognized income or additional deferred tax liabilities which may arise in the carryforward period. When the tax benefit associated with these remaining losses is recognized, it is classified the same as the item against which the losses were offset. For example, if the remaining losses were offset against subsequent income from continuing operations, the benefit would become a component of income from continuing operations. However, if the remaining losses were offset against a subsequent extraordinary item, the tax benefit would be classified as extraordinary. To demonstrate these principles, consider the facts of Case E in Illustration 12-2. In this instance, the annual anticipated loss of $80,000 was used to offset $10,000 of prior years' income and $50,000 of likely future income in the carryforward period taxed at 40%. Therefore, the equivalent of $60,000 ($10,000 + $50,000) of the loss was offset in order to generate the $24,000 tax benefit. The remaining loss of $20,000 (original $80,000 – $60,000 offset) may offset future income or deferred tax liabilities arising in the 20-year carryforward period. Assuming the subsequent year has a recognized pretax income from continuing operations of $25,000 which would be taxed at 40%, a tax benefit of $8,000 ($20,000 × 40%), representing the offsetting of the remaining $20,000 loss against the income from continuing operations, would be recognized. The subsequent year's net tax expense on the continuing income would be $2,000, for an effective tax rate of 8% ($2,000 ÷ $25,000). The net tax expense results from the tax expense of $10,000 on the $25,000 of income reduced by the $8,000 tax benefit.

Case F of Illustration 12-2 demonstrates a special limitation of the tax benefits associated with operating losses. This special limitation arises when a YTD operating loss exceeds the annual operating loss.

Illustration 12-2

(Note that the effective tax rates are not based on the actual corporate tax rates but, rather, are only for illustrative purposes.)

Case A
Seasonal YTD Loss Offset by Subsequent Interim Income
Which Is "More Likely Than Not"

Interim Period (Quarter)	Ordinary Pretax Income (Loss)		Effective Tax Rate	Tax Expense (Benefit)		
	Current Period	Year-to-Date		Year-to-Date	Previously Reported	Current Period
First	$(30,000)	$(30,000)	40%	$(12,000)		$(12,000)
Second	40,000	(10,000)	40	(4,000)	$(12,000)	8,000
Third	40,000	30,000	40	12,000	(4,000)	16,000
Fourth	40,000	70,000	40	28,000	12,000	16,000

Case B
YTD Loss Where Tax Benefit Is Initially Uncertain

Interim Period (Quarter)	Ordinary Pretax Income (Loss)		Effective Tax Rate	Tax Expense (Benefit)		
	Current Period	Year-to-Date		Year-to-Date	Previously Reported	Current Period
First	$(30,000)	$(30,000)	0%			
Second	20,000	(10,000)	0			
Third	40,000	30,000	40	12,000		$12,000
Fourth	40,000	70,000	40	28,000	12,000	16,000

Case C
YTD Loss with No Assurance of Subsequent Interim Income;
$30,000 of Prior Two Years' Income Taxed at 50%

Interim Period (Quarter)	Ordinary Pretax Income (Loss)		Effective Tax Rate	Tax Expense (Benefit)		
	Current Period	Year-to-Date		Year-to-Date	Previously Reported	Current Period
First	$(40,000)	$(40,000)	38%	$(15,000)[a]		$(15,000)
Second	10,000	(30,000)	50	(15,000)	$(15,000)	
Third	35,000	5,000	40[b]	2,000	(15,000)	17,000
Fourth	30,000	35,000	40	14,000	2,000	12,000

a Only $30,000 of the $40,000 loss can be offset against the prior years' income, resulting in a tax benefit of $15,000.
b The current-year statutory tax rate is assumed to be 40%.

Case D
YTD and Anticipated Annual Loss (of $100,000) with $60,000 of Prior Two Years' Income Taxed at 50%

Interim Period (Quarter)	Ordinary Pretax Income (Loss)		Effective Tax Rate	Tax Expense (Benefit)		
	Current Period	Year-to-Date		Year-to-Date	Previously Reported	Current Period
First	$(40,000)	$ (40,000)	30%[c]	$(12,000)		$(12,000)
Second	(30,000)	(70,000)	30	(21,000)	$(12,000)	(9,000)
Third	5,000	(65,000)	30	(19,500)	(21,000)	1,500
Fourth	(35,000)	(100,000)	30	(30,000)	(19,500)	(10,500)

c The effective tax rate of 30% is based on a $30,000 tax benefit of ($60,000 × 50%) expressed as a percentage of the $100,000 anticipated annual loss.

Case E
YTD and Anticipated Annual Loss (of $80,000) with Carrybacks and Carryforwards Available

Interim Period (Quarter)	Ordinary Pretax Income (Loss)		Effective Tax Rate	Tax Expense (Benefit)		
	Current Period	Year-to-Date		Year-to-Date	Previously Reported	Current Period
First	$(20,000)	$(20,000)	30%[d]	$ (6,000)		$ (6,000)
Second	15,000	(5,000)	30	(1,500)	$ (6,000)	4,500
Third	(35,000)	(40,000)	30	(12,000)	(1,500)	(10,500)
Fourth	(40,000)	(80,000)	30	(24,000)	(12,000)	(12,000)

d The calculation of the effective tax rate is based on the following:

Prior 2 years of income of $10,000 taxed at a prior rate of 40%. . . . . $ 4,000
Deferred tax liability reversing the next 20 years based on the current tax rate
of 40% ($50,000 of temporary differences) 20,000
Total tax benefit $24,000

$24,000 ÷ $80,000 anticipated annual loss = 30%

Note: If likely future income in the carryforward period had been at least $70,000, then a tax benefit would have been recognized on the entire current operating loss of $80,000. The $80,000 of loss would have been carried back in the amount of $10,000 and carried forward in the amount of $70,000.

Case F
YTD and Anticipated Annual Loss (of $48,000) with a $40,000 Carryback at 30% Available

Interim Period (Quarter)	Ordinary Pretax Income (Loss)		Effective Tax Rate	Tax Expense (Benefit)		
	Current Period	Year-to-Date		Year-to-Date	Previously Reported	Current Period
First	$(10,000)	$(10,000)	25%[e]	$(2,500)	—	$(2,500)
Second	(20,000)	(30,000)	25	(7,500)	$(2,500)	(5,000)
Third	(30,000)	(60,000)	Note	(12,000)	(7,500)	(4,500)
Fourth	12,000	(48,000)	25	(12,000)	(12,000)	

(continued)

e The calculation of the effective tax rate is based on the following:

Prior 2 years of income of $40,000 taxed at a prior rate of 30%. $12,000

The effective tax rate of 25% is based on the $12,000 total tax benefit expressed as a percentage of the $48,000 anticipated annual pretax loss.

Note: If the rate of 25% were used, a YTD tax benefit of $15,000 would be suggested. However, a YTD loss of $60,000 could receive a benefit of only $12,000 (30% × $40,000 prior year's income). Therefore the YTD benefit is limited to $12,000. This special rule arises when a YTD operating loss exceeds the annual anticipated operating loss. Notice that both YTD and annual amounts must be losses. In this case, the YTD tax benefit is limited to the amount that would be recognized if the YTD loss were the expected loss for the entire fiscal year.

Nonordinary Items of Income or Loss.   Certain elements making up an entity's net income are reported separately and/or shown net of tax. These elements include unusual or infrequently occurring items, discontinued operations, extraordinary items, and cumulative effects of changes in accounting principles. For purposes of discussion, these items are referred to as nonordinary items.

There also are interim gains or losses that are directly accounted for as a component of owners' equity. The tax impact on these items should be determined by the same methodology as is used for nonordinary items. As previously stated, these items are not included in the determination of the estimated effective tax rate applied to ordinary income. The estimated effective tax rate applied to ordinary income may not be appropriate for nonordinary items of income for a variety of reasons, including the following:

1. Nonordinary items may be taxed at different statutory tax rates, such as capital gains tax rates, than ordinary items.
2. Nonordinary items, when combined with ordinary items, may cause the total income to increase (decrease), and a higher (lower) progressive tax rate will then become applicable.
3. Nonordinary items may, in total, represent a loss whose tax benefit is limited because there are not adequate sources of other income which can be offset by the loss.
4. Nonordinary items may, in total, represent income that provides a source against which ordinary losses may find tax benefit.

Therefore, the tax effect of these nonordinary items must be determined independently on an incremental basis.

If *one* nonordinary item exists, the incremental income tax is the *difference* between

1. The income tax expense (benefit) traceable to the estimated annual pretax *ordinary* income (loss), and
2. The income tax expense (benefit) traceable to the *total pretax income* (loss) [the sum of the estimated annual pretax ordinary income or loss and the nonordinary income or loss].

When several nonordinary items exist, the calculation of their individual tax impact becomes more complex. This complexity usually occurs because of differences in tax rates for nonordinary items, surtax charges, and tax credit limitations. If several nonordinary items exist, the incremental tax traceable to each nonordinary item or category is determined as follows:

1. The incremental income tax expense (benefit) traceable to *all* nonordinary categories is the difference between

    a) *The income tax expense (benefit) traceable to the estimated annual pretax ordinary income (loss) and*

    b) *The income tax expense (benefit) traceable to the* total *of all sources of pretax income (loss).*

2. The incremental income tax benefit traceable to *all* nonordinary loss categories is the difference between

    a) *The income tax (benefit) traceable to the* total *of all sources of pretax income (loss) (step 1b) and*

    b) *The income tax expense (benefit) traceable to the* total *of all sources of pretax income (loss) excluding all nonordinary losses.*

3. The incremental income tax expense traceable to *all* nonordinary *gain* categories is the difference between

    a) *The incremental income tax expense (benefit) traceable to* all *nonordinary items (step 1) and*

    b) *The incremental income tax benefit traceable to* all *nonordinary* loss *categories (step 2).*

    Note that the incremental tax expense or benefit traceable to all nonordinary items from step 1 has been allocated between nonordinary losses (step 2) and nonordinary gains (step 3).

4. Next, the incremental income tax benefit traceable to each *individual* nonordinary *loss* category is the difference between

    a) *The income tax expense (benefit) traceable to the* total *of all sources of pretax income (loss) (step 1b) and*

    b) *The income tax expense (benefit) traceable to the* total *of all sources of pretax income (loss) excluding the* individual *nonordinary* loss *category.*

    Note that this step is repeated for *each* nonordinary loss category. Furthermore, it is likely that the sum of each of the incremental tax benefits will not equal the total tax benefit associated with all nonordinary losses as calculated in step 2, above.

5. Then, the incremental income tax benefit traceable to *all* nonordinary *loss* categories (step 2) is *apportioned ratably* to each individual loss category based on the incremental income tax benefit of each *individual* nonordinary *loss* category (step 4).

6. The incremental income tax expense traceable to each *individual* nonordinary *gain* category is the difference between

    a) *The income tax expense (benefit) traceable to the* total *of all sources of pretax income (loss) (step 1b) and*

    b) *The income tax expense (benefit) traceable to the* total *of all sources of pretax income (loss) excluding the* individual *nonordinary gain category.*

    Note that this step is repeated for *each* nonordinary gain category. Furthermore, it is likely that the sum of each of the incremental tax expenses will not equal the total tax expense associated with all nonordinary gains as calculated in step 3, above.

7. Finally, the incremental income tax expense traceable to *all* nonordinary *gain* categories (step 3) is *apportioned ratably* to each individual gain category based on the incremental income tax expense traceable to each *individual* nonordinary *gain* category (step 6).

The tax impact of nonordinary gains and losses based on the above steps is demonstrated in Illustration 12-3. It is important to remember that the principles discussed earlier regarding offsetting YTD losses also are applicable to nonordinary loss categories.

Illustration 12-3
Tax Impact on Nonordinary Gains and Losses

Facts:

Ordinary income of		$180,000
Nonordinary losses consist of:		
Loss (Category #1)	$(30,000)	
Loss (Category #2)	(20,000)	(50,000)
Nonordinary gains consist of:		
Gain (Category #3)	$ 20,000	
Gain (Category #4)	10,000	30,000
Total pretax income of		$160,000
Tax information:		
Tax rate on income.	30%	
Surtax on income between $100,000 and $170,000	5%	
Tax credit	10,000	
Tax rate on Gain (Category #3) which is also exempt		
from the surtax	20%	

Calculation of Total Incremental Tax Impact (steps 1, 2, and 3):

	Ordinary Income	Total Income	Total Income Excluding Nonordinary Losses	Total Income Excluding Nonordinary Gains
Pretax income	$180,000	$160,000	$210,000 ($160,000 + $50,000)	$130,000 ($160,000 − $30,000)
Tax expense (benefit)*	**A** $47,500 (step 1a)	**B** $38,000 (step 1b)	**C** $54,500 (step 2b)	

*Tax on income: $180,000 × 30% = $54,000 $160,000

             { $140,000 × 30% = $42,000
                 20,000 × 20% =   4,000
                 $ 40,000 × 5% =   2,000 } $210,000

{ $190,000 × 30% = $57,000
   20,000 × 20% =   4,000
$ 70,000 × 5% =   3,500

Surtax: $ 70,000 × 5% =   3,500

Tax credit: (10,000)   (10,000)   (10,000)

Tax expense: **A** $47,500   **B** $38,000   **C** $54,500

Incremental tax expense (benefit) traceable to:

D   All nonordinary items   ($38,000 − $47,500) . . . . $ (9,500)
                              (step 1: **B − A**)

E   All nonordinary losses   ($38,000 − $54,500) . . . . $(16,500)
                              (step 2: **B − C**)

F   All nonordinary gains   [$(9,500) − $(16,500)] . . . . $ 7,000**
                              (step 3: **D − E**)

**If the incremental tax associated with all nonordinary items is a $9,500 benefit and the incremental tax associated with all nonordinary losses is a benefit of $16,500, the incremental tax expense associated with all nonordinary gains must be $7,000 [($9,500) = ($16,500) +$7,000]. Obviously, the incremental tax associated with all nonordinary items must be allocated to either nonordinary losses or gains. Furthermore, the amounts allocated to nonordinary losses and gains must equal the amount traceable to all nonordinary items.

Calculation of Incremental Tax Benefit Traceable to Each Individual Loss Category: (step 4):

	Total Income	Total Income Excluding Nonordinary Losses	Total Income Excluding Loss (Category 1)	Total Income Excluding Loss (Category 2)
Pretax income	$160,000	$210,000	$190,000	$180,000
Tax expense (benefit)***	B $38,000	C $54,500	G $48,500 (step 4b)	H $45,000 (step 4b)

***Tax on income $190,000 $\left\{\begin{array}{l}\$170,000 \times 30\% = \$51,000 \\ 20,000 \times 20\% = 4,000\end{array}\right.$

Surtax: $\quad\$ 70,000 \times 5\% = 3,500$

Tax credit: $\qquad$ (10,000)

Tax expense: $\qquad$ **G** $48,500

$180,000 $\left\{\begin{array}{l}\$160,000 \times 30\% = \$48,000 \\ 20,000 \times 20\% = 4,000\end{array}\right.$

Surtax: $\quad\$ 60,000 \times 5\% = 3,000$

Tax credit: (10,000)

Tax expense: **H** $45,000

Incremental tax expense (benefit) traceable to:

E   All nonordinary losses   ($38,000 – $54,500) . . . . $(16,500)
(step 2: **B – C**)

I   Nonordinary loss   (Category #1) ($38,000 – $48,500) . . . . $(10,500)
(step 4, first loss category: **B – G**)

J   Nonordinary loss   (Category #2) ($38,000 – $45,000) . . . . $ (7,000)****
(step 4: second loss category: **B – H**)

****Notice that the sum of the incremental tax benefit on categories 1 and 2 of $17,500 [($10,500) + ($7,000)] does not equal the incremental tax benefit of $16,500 on all losses. It is for this very reason that an apportionment of the tax impact of individual categories is necessary.

Apportionment of Tax Benefit Traceable to Nonordinary Losses (step 5):

The $16,500 incremental tax benefit traceable to all nonordinary losses is ratably apportioned to each individual loss category as follows:

		Each Loss Category		
		Incremental Benefit	Percent	Apportioned Amount
Loss (Category #1)	**I**	$(10,500)	60%	$ (9,900) = (60% × $16,500)
Loss (Category #2)	**J**	(7,000)	40	$ (6,600) = (40% × $16,500)
		$(17,500)	100%	**E** $(16,500)****

Calculation of Incremental Tax Expense Traceable to Each Individual Gain Category: (step 6):

	Total Income	Total Income Excluding Gain (Category #3)	Total Income Excluding Gain (Category #4)
Pretax income	$160,000	$140,000	$150,000
Tax expense (benefit)*****	B $38,000	K $34,000 (step 6b)	L $34,500 (step 6b)

*****Tax on income $140,000 × 30% = $42,000

Surtax: $\quad\$ 40,000 \times 5\% = 2,000$

Tax credit: (10,000)

Tax expense: **K** $34,000

$150,000 $\left\{\begin{array}{l}\$130,000 \times 30\% = \$39,000 \\ 20,000 \times 20\% = 4,000\end{array}\right.$

$\quad\$ 3,000 \times 5\% = 1,500$

(10,000)

L $34,500

(continued)

Incremental tax expense (benefit) traceable to:

F	All nonordinary gains	[$(9,500) – $(16,500)]		$7,000
		(step 3: **D – E**)		
M	Nonordinary gain	(Category #3) ($38,000 – $34,000)		4,000
		(step 6, first gain category: **B – K**)		
N	Nonordinary gain	(Category #4) ($38,000 – $34,500)		3,500
		(step 6, second gain category: **B – L**)		

Apportionment of Tax Expense Traceable to Nonordinary Gains (step 7):

The $7,000 incremental tax expense traceable to all nonordinary gains is ratably apportioned to each individual gain category as follows:

		Each Gain Category		
		Incremental Benefit	Percent	Apportioned Amount
Gain (Category #3)	**M**	$4,000	53%	$3,710 = (53% × $7,000)
Gain (Category #4)	**N**	3,500	47	3,290 = (47% × $7,000)
		$7,500	100%	**F** $7,000

Summary of Tax Impact Associated with Ordinary and Nonordinary Items:

	Pretax Income (Loss)	Tax Expense (Benefit)
Ordinary Income.	$180,000	**A** $47,500
Loss (Category #1)	(30,000)	(9,900)
Loss (Category #2)	(20,000)	(6,600)
Gain (Category #3).	20,000	3,710
Gain (Category #4).	10,000	3,290
Totals	$160,000	**B** $38,000

If there is a nonordinary loss, the tax benefit of the loss should be recognized if it can be offset by other existing YTD elements of income and projected income for the balance of the year, which is likely. If the nonordinary loss category cannot be offset by elements of income in the current fiscal year, the principles discussed previously regarding carrybacks against prior years' income and carryforwards against likely future income would be applicable. Illustration 12-4, demonstrates the offsetting of a nonordinary (an extraordinary item) loss under various situations.

Illustration 12-4
Case A
Offsetting a Nonordinary Loss against Ordinary Income

Interim Period (Quarter)	Type of Income	Pretax Income (Loss)			Tax Expense (Benefit)		
		Current Period	Year-to-Date	Effective Tax Rate	Year-to-Date	Previously Reported	Current Period
First	Continuing Op.	$40,000	$40,000	26%	$10,400	—	$10,400
Second	Continuing Op.	30,000	70,000	28	19,600	$ 10,400	9,200

Third	Continuing Op.	20,000	90,000	28	25,200	19,600	5,600
Third	Extraordinary	(50,000)	(50,000)	Note A	(14,000)	—	(14,000)
Fourth	Continuing Op.	40,000	130,000	30	39,000	25,200	13,800
Fourth	Extraordinary	—	(50,000)	Note B	(15,000)	(14,000)	(1,000)

Note A: The entire extraordinary loss can be offset against ordinary income which has an effective tax rate of 28%.

Note B: Due to a change in the estimated effective tax rate, the benefit associated with the extraordinary loss has increased.

Case B
Offsetting a Nonordinary Loss—Assuming Future Interim Income Is Not "More Likely Than Not," and Carrybacks and Carryforwards Are Not Available

Interim Period (Quarter)	Type of Income	Pretax Income (Loss)			Tax Expense (Benefit)		
		Current Period	Year-to-Date	Effective Tax Rate	Year-to-Date	Previously Reported	Current Period
First	Continuing Op.	$40,000	$40,000	26%	$10,400	—	$10,400
Second	Continuing Op.	30,000	70,000	28	19,600	$10,400	9,200
Third	Continuing Op.	20,000	90,000	28	25,200	19,600	5,600
Third	Extraordinary	(110,000)	(110,000)	Note C	(25,200)	—	(25,200)
Fourth	Continuing Op.	40,000	130,000	30	39,000	25,200	13,800
Fourth	Extraordinary	—	(110,000)	Note D	(33,000)	(25,200)	(7,800)

Note C: Because future income is not "more likely than not," and carrybacks/carryforwards are not available, the extraordinary loss can be offset only against YTD income.

Note D: Because additional income is available in the fourth quarter, an additional amount of tax benefit traceable to the extraordinary loss can be recognized. Additional benefit also is recognized because of the change in the effective tax rate.

Case C
Offsetting a Nonordinary Loss—Assuming Future Interim Income of $40,000 Is "More Likely Than Not," and a Carryback Is Available against Prior Income of $30,000 Taxed at 30%

Interim Period (Quarter)	Type of Income	Pretax Income (Loss)			Tax Expense (Benefit)		
		Current Period	Year-to-Date	Effective Tax Rate	Year-to-Date	Previously Reported	Current Period
First	Continuing Op.	$ 40,000	$40,000	26%	$10,400	—	$10,400
Second	Continuing Op.	30,000	70,000	28	19,600	$10,400	9,200
Third	Continuing Op.	20,000	90,000	28	25,200	19,600	5,600
Third	Extraordinary	(180,000)	(180,000)	Note E	(45,400)	—	(45,400)
Fourth	Continuing Op.	40,000	130,000	28	36,400	25,200	11,200
Fourth	Extraordinary	—	(180,000)	Note F	(45,400)	(45,400)	—

Note E: Because future income of $40,000 is assured, the extraordinary loss can be offset against $130,000 of current-year income at an estimated effective tax rate of 28%. This results in a tax benefit of $36,400. In addition, another $30,000 of the extraordinary loss can be offset against prior income of $30,000. This results in an additional tax benefit of $9,000 for a total benefit of $45,400 ($36,400 + $9,000). If future interim income had not been more likely than not, the total benefit would have consisted of $25,200 resulting from an offset of YTD income plus the $9,000 resulting from the carryback against prior years' income.

Note F: Of the $180,000 extraordinary loss, $160,000 has been offset ($130,000 against current income and $30,000 against prior years'). The tax benefit on the remaining $20,000 of loss not offset may be recognized in the future, as subsequent annual income becomes recognized. If $20,000 of future income was more likely than not to be recognized in the carryforward period, the tax benefit on the entire extraordinary loss could have been recognized in the current year.

Accounting for Discontinued Operations

The accounting effects of a discontinued operation should be reflected in an income statement as two distinct components: a) income or loss from operations of the discontinued operation prior to the measurement date and b) income or loss on disposal of the discontinued operation. Both of these items should be presented net of tax. When interim statements are prepared, a problem arises in that income or loss from operations of the discontinued operation, recognized in the interim period(s) prior to the measurement date, will have been included in income from continuing operations of the prior period(s) and in the determination of the effective tax rate of the prior period(s). Once the measurement date has been established, the total taxes of the prior periods must be allocated between ordinary income (loss) traceable to continuing operations and ordinary income (loss) traceable to the now-discontinued operations. This allocation of previously reported information is necessary in order to achieve comparability between prior and subsequent interim periods. Users of financial information would naturally want to know what portion of prior interim pretax income and related tax expense was traceable to the now discontinued operation. The allocation of the previously reported pretax income and related tax involves the following steps:

1.   The original YTD and balance-of-the-year projections used to calculate the estimated effective tax rate are allocated between the now presently defined continuing and discontinued operations.
2.   The original tax planning alternatives, permanent differences, and tax credits used to calculate the tax rate are allocated between the continuing and discontinued operations.
3.   The projected items being allocated in (1) and (2) are the originally reported amounts. That is, the projections relating to the balance of the year are not changed or revised but remain the same as in the prior interim periods. To permit the revision of an earlier projection would have the effect of accounting for a change in estimate on a retroactive basis, which is not acceptable.
4.   The amounts now allocated to continuing operations are used to calculate a new effective tax rate traceable to continuing operations. The tax on the continuing operations of the prior interim period(s) also is recalculated.
5.   The new tax on the continuing operations of the prior interim period(s) is compared to the originally reported tax (which included both the continuing and discontinued operations), with the difference representing the tax traceable to the discontinued operations.

From the measurement date forward, the discontinued operations will not be commingled with the continuing operations. Thus, the tax effect of the discontinued operations is calculated on an incremental basis, as is the case with other nonordinary items of income. The interim effect of a discontinued operation is demonstrated in Illustration 12-5.

Illustration 12-5
Discontinued Operation

Facts:

After issuing first-quarter interim data, the company adopted in the second quarter a formal plan calling for the disposal of one of its operations. Ordinary income reported in the first quarter included a $10,000 loss traceable to the operation being discontinued. It is assumed that any loss traceable to the discontinued operation will have tax benefits and that the estimated effective tax rate of 40% on income from continuing operations, used in the first quarter, is to be revised to 45% and applied to the remaining continuing operations.

Analysis:

The following schedule illustrates the retroactive restatement of previously issued interim data in order to disclose separately both continuing and discontinued operations.

Interim Period (Quarter)	Type of Income	Pretax Income (Loss)			Tax Expense (Benefit)		
		Current Period	Year-to-Date	Effective Tax Rate	Year-to-Date	Previously Reported	Current Period
First	Continuing Op.	$40,000	$40,000	40%	$16,000	—	$16,000
First—Restated	Continuing Op.	50,000	50,000	45	22,500	—	22,500
First—Restated	Discontinued—Operating Inc. (D-OI)*	(10,000)	(10,000)	Note A	(6,500)	—	(6,500)
Second	Continuing Op.	30,000	80,000	45	36,000	$22,500	13,500
Second	D-OI	5,000	(5,000)	Note B	(2,250)	(6,500)	4,250
Second	Discontinued Loss on Disposal (D-LD)	(60,000)	(60,000)	Note B	(27,000)	—	(27,000)
Third	Continuing Op.	50,000	130,000	45	58,500	36,000	22,500
Third	D-OI	—	(5,000)	Note B	(2,250)	(2,250)	—
Third	D-LD	—	(60,000)	Note B	(27,000)	(27,000)	—
Fourth	Continuing Op.	55,000	185,000	45	83,250	58,500	24,750
Fourth	D-OI	—	(5,000)	Note B	(2,250)	(2,250)	—
Fourth	D-LD	(10,000)	(70,000)	Note C	(31,500)	(27,000)	(4,500)

*This amount is entirely traceable to pre-measurement-date operations of the discontinued operation. None of this amount is traceable to the gain or loss on disposal of the discontinued operation.

Note A: The $6,500 tax benefit traceable to the discontinued operation is the result of comparing the tax of $22,500 traceable to continuing operations with the $16,000 of tax previously recognized on the continuing operations. Therefore, the difference between the two tax amounts relates to the exclusion and inclusion, respectively, of the results traceable to the discontinued operation. Notice that the total tax expense presented for the first period, restated, totals $16,000, which is the tax originally reported for the first quarter.

Note B: The YTD tax benefit of $2,250 traceable to the YTD pretax D-OI is the *assumed* incremental tax benefit traceable to this item. When the YTD tax benefit of $2,250 is compared to the previous first-quarter restated tax benefit of $6,500, a current-period tax expense of $4,250 is suggested. The $60,000 D-LD represents the estimated loss from the measurement date through the disposal date. The YTD tax benefit of $27,000 traceable to the YTD pretax D-LD is the *assumed* incremental tax benefit traceable to this item.

Note C: The fourth-quarter current-period D-LD of a $10,000 loss represents an adjustment to the original estimated loss traceable to the D-LD of $60,000. The $31,500 YTD tax benefit is the *assumed* incremental tax benefit associated with the D-LD loss of $70,000.

Accounting for a Change in Accounting Principle

APB Opinion No. 28 indicates that, in general, a change in accounting principle during an interim period should be accounted for in accordance with APB Opinion No. 20, *Accounting Changes*. To simplify the accounting for such changes, the APB encouraged management to adopt accounting changes in the first interim period of the current fiscal year. Nevertheless, the APB recognized that changes would continue to be made in other than the first interim period and, therefore, prescribed special procedures. However, these procedures were amended in 1974 by FASB Statement No. 3, *Reporting Accounting Changes in Interim Financial Statements*. When interim reports are prepared, the proper accounting for a change in an accounting principle depends on a) whether the change requires the determination of a cumulative effect or retroactive restatement and b) whether the change takes place in the first interim period of the fiscal year.

A Change Requiring Retroactive Restatement.   A change requiring retroactive restatement of previously issued annual financial statements, rather than the determination of the cumulative effect, will require the restatement of previously issued interim financial information. If such a change occurs in other than the first interim period, such restatement will also involve the restatement of taxes to reflect the estimated effective tax rate, which is based on annual income (or loss) from continuing operations as determined in accordance with the newly adopted accounting principle. The restatement of the previous tax rate is affected by only the change in principle and, therefore, does not allow for any revisions of projected data that were used to calculate the earlier tax rate. This treatment is consistent with the principle that changes in estimates should not be accounted for on a retroactive basis.

A Change Requiring a Cumulative Effect.   If a cumulative-effect-type change takes place in the first interim period of the fiscal year, the cumulative effect of the change on retained earnings as of the beginning of the year should be included in net income of the first interim period. However, if the cumulative-effect-type change is made in other than the first interim period, it is assumed for accounting purposes that it took place in the first interim period. Therefore, the change should be accounted for as follows:

1. Financial statements for all interim periods in the current fiscal year should be restated to reflect the adoption of the new principle, and
2. The cumulative effect of the change on retained earnings as of the beginning of the current fiscal year should be included in the restated net income of the first interim period rather than in the interim period in which the change was adopted.[9]

Accounting for the cumulative effect of a change in principle may result in a restated tax rate for the interim periods prior to the change. As is the case with all other restatements of earlier tax rates, only the effect of the *nonordinary* income items should be considered. Therefore, the tax on the cumulative effect should be computed on an *incremental* basis, as previously illustrated for nonordinary items of income or loss, and the tax previously reported for ordinary income of the prechange interim periods should be restated as follows:

> *The restated tax (or benefit) shall reflect the year-to-date amounts and annual estimates originally used for the prechange interim periods, modified only for the effect of the change in accounting principle on those year-to-date and estimated annual amounts.*[10]

The principle described above for a cumulative-effect-type change is demonstrated in Illustration 12-6.

Illustration 12-6
Change in Accounting Principle: Cumulative Effect

Facts:

During the third quarter, management decided to change depreciation methods. The effect of the change is to decrease the pretax income of quarters one and two by $30,000 and $20,000, respectively. The effect on prior years is to decrease pretax income by $40,000.

---

9 Statement of Financial Accounting Standards No. 3, *Reporting Accounting Changes in Interim Financial Statements* (Norwalk, CT: Financial Standards Board, 1974), par. 10.
10 FASB Interpretation No. 18, *Accounting for Income Taxes in Interim Periods* (Stamford: Financial Accounting Standards Board, 1977), par. 64.

Analysis:

The following schedule illustrates the restatement of previously issued interim data in order to reflect the cumulative effect of the change.

Interim Period (Quarter)	Type of Income	Pretax Income (Loss)		Effective Tax Rate	Tax Expense (Benefit)		
		Current Period	Year-to-Date		Year-to-Date	Previously Reported	Current Period
First	Continuing Op.	$80,000	$ 80,000	40%	$32,000	—	$32,000
Second	Continuing Op.	50,000	130,000	40	52,000	$32,000	20,000
First—Restated	Continuing Op.	50,000	50,000	42*	21,000	—	21,000
First—Restated	Cum. Effect	(40,000)	(40,000)	Note A	(16,800)	—	(16,800)
Second—Restated	Continuing Op.	30,000	80,000	42	33,600	21,000	12,600
Second—Restated	Cum. Effect	—	(40,000)	Note A	(16,800)	(16,800)	—
Third & Fourth	Continuing Op.	70,000	150,000	42	63,000	33,600	29,400
Third & Fourth	Cum. Effect	—	(40,000)	Note A	(16,800)	(16,800)	—

*Note that a new effective tax rate of 42% has been calculated as a result of modifications relating to only the change in accounting principle.

Note A: It is assumed that the cumulative effect of a $40,000 loss will offset annual income taxed at an effective rate of 42%. This results in a tax benefit of $16,800 (40,000 × 42%).

A cumulative-effect-type change in principle also requires the following disclosures:

1. For the interim period in which the new accounting principle is adopted:

   a) *Income from continuing operations, net income, and related per share amounts computed on a pro forma basis for (i) the interim period in which the change is made and (ii) any interim periods of prior fiscal years for which financial information is being presented;*

   b) *The nature of and justification for the change and the effect of the change on income from continuing operations, net income, and related per share amounts for that interim period;*

   c) *When that period occurs after the first period (i) the effect of the change on income from continuing operations, net income, and related per share amounts for each current fiscal year interim period prior to the change and (ii) income from continuing operations, net income, and related per share amounts for each restated current-fiscal-year interim period prior to the change.*

2. In the period of change, if no financial information for interim periods of prior fiscal years is being presented

   a) *the actual and pro forma amounts of income from continuing operations, net income, and related per share amounts for the interim period of the immediately preceding fiscal year that corresponds to the interim period of change.*

3. For year-to-date and last-12-months-to-date financial reports through the interim period of the adoption:

   a) *the effect of the change on income from continuing operations, net income, and related per share amounts and their pro forma bases.*

4. For a subsequent (post-change) interim period of the fiscal year in which the new accounting principle is adopted

   a) *the effect of the change on income from continuing operations, net income, and related per share amounts for that post-change interim period.*[11]

---

11 Statement of Financial Accounting Standards No. 3, *op. cit.*, par. 11.

In a change to the LIFO inventory method, the disclosures for a cumulative-effect-type change are required except that the cumulative effect of the change on retained earnings and pro forma amounts should not be determined. If the change is made in other than the first interim period, all prechange interim statements must be restated to reflect the adoption of the new accounting principle. The beginning inventory computed by the previous inventory method is assumed to be the beginning measure of base stock for purposes of applying LIFO.

Disclosures of Summarized Interim Data

To maintain the timeliness of interim data, companies frequently report summarized interim data rather than complete financial statements. When publicly traded companies report summarized interim data, the following disclosures are required, at a minimum:

1. Sales or gross revenues, provision for income taxes, extraordinary items (including related income tax effects), cumulative effect of a change in accounting principles or practices, and net income.
2. Basic and diluted earnings per share data for each period presented, determined in accordance with the provisions of FASB Statement No. 128, *Earnings per Share.*
3. Seasonal revenue, costs or expenses.
4. Significant changes in estimates or provisions for income taxes.
5. Disposal of a segment of a business and extraordinary, unusual, or infrequently occurring items.
6. Contingent items.
7. Changes in accounting principles or estimates.
8. Significant changes in financial position.
9. Information about reportable operating segments determined according to the provisions of FASB Statement No. 131, *Disclosures about Segments of an Enterprise and Related Information,* including provisions related to restatement of segment information in previously issued financial statements.[12]

The information in (9) above is more fully discussed in the following section of this chapter dealing with disclosures about segments of an enterprise.

In addition to providing this data for the current quarter, such data should be provided for the current year-to-date or the last 12 months-to-date, plus comparable data for the preceding year.

Frequently, companies do not issue separate fourth-quarter reports or provide fourth-quarter disclosure of summarized data because annual audited statements will be forthcoming. In such cases, a note to the annual financial statements should disclose the effect of the following items for the fourth quarter: disposals of a segment, extraordinary items, unusual or infrequently occurring items, and changes in accounting principles. Disclosure in the annual financial statements should also include the aggregate effect of year-end adjustments that are material to the fourth-quarter results.

Disclosures about Segments of an Enterprise

For various reasons, enterprises may develop a strategy which allows them to become involved in a variety of activities, some of which may be similar or related. For example, an enterprise in the entertainment/recreation industry may have business activities in film, theme parks, hotels, and restaurants. Enterprises with such

---

12 Accounting Principles Board Opinion No. 28, *op. cit.*, par. 30 (as amended).

activities are referred to as being *horizontally integrated*. In other instances, the activities may be *vertically integrated*, which suggests that they relate to the sales and distribution of a final good or service. For example, a manufacturer of modular housing may also be involved in activities such as the growing and harvesting of timber, the manufacture of windows, and the development of land for housing subdivisions. Enterprises may also become involved in activities which do not necessarily have a close relationship to their original core business but, rather, allow them to diversify their business. Such businesses are referred to as *conglomerates* or *diversified companies*. For example, a single enterprise may be involved in such diverse activities as radio and television broadcasting, managed care facilities, development of software for engineering applications, and the manufacture of fluid metering devices.

The traditional consolidated financial statements of a truly diversified enterprise would provide the user of these statements with limited information regarding the diversity of the enterprise's activities and the economic environments in which those activities function. For example, unless separate disclosures were present, it would not be possible to tell what portion of consolidated sales was traceable to various business activities. Certainly, the uncertainties affecting potential cash flows can be better understood if information related to an enterprise's products and services, as well as geographical areas of operation, is provided. Fortunately, special disclosures regarding the segments or activities of an enterprise are required and provide users with fundamental information through which they can better understand operating performance and prospects for future cash flows for both individual segments and the enterprise as a whole. Furthermore, such information will provide users with an improved basis for making comparisons between enterprises that are not diversified with those that are.

There is a strong body of empirical research that supports the position that segmental data have utility. This research and the prominence of diversified companies have effectively established the importance of segmental data for maintaining an efficient capital market. For example, studies have suggested that segmental data can lead to more accurate predictions of enterprise earnings and changes in earnings levels. In addition, surveys have shown that sophisticated users, such as financial analysts, find the use of segmental data to be a significant factor in the area of security valuation.

A number of professional groups, including the American Institute of Certified Public Accountants, the Financial Executives Institute, the Financial Analysts Federation, the International Accounting Standards Committee, the Association for Investment Management and Research, and the FASB, have consistently emphasized the importance of segmental disclosures. In 1976, the FASB had issued Statement of Financial Accounting Standards No. 14, which also dealt with the topic of segmental disclosures. However, that statement had come under criticism from both reporting enterprises and users of the information. A major criticism was that the definition of a segment resulted in the reporting of information which did not necessarily represent the information which the top management of an enterprise actually used for making internal operating decisions and assessing performance. It became obvious that an external reporting requirement that did not align with internal reporting, which was used for decision-making purposes, was not serving the needs of external users of segmental information. Why provide external users information which they will use to make assessments of an enterprise if the information is not what is being used by enterprise management to make decisions? Furthermore, the segmental disclosures called for were not consistent with how management discussed and analyzed segmental data in other sections of annual reports. Segmental reporting standards were also criticized for not requiring more information about a greater number of segments. **Aligning external reporting of segmental information with internal reporting helps users view an enterprise in a way that will allow them to better anticipate and understand the actions of management.**

The importance of segmental reporting, coupled with the criticisms directed toward earlier authoritative pronouncements, has resulted in a renewed interest, both nationally and globally, in establishing standards for segmental reporting. Of recent importance is the joint effort of FASB and the Accounting Standards Board of the Canadian Institute of Chartered Accountants (CICA). This cooperative effort to develop disclosure standards for segmental reporting is an excellent example of the emphasis which is being placed on the harmonization of accounting principles both regionally and globally. The FASB and the CICA reached the same conclusions regarding appropriate standards and have each issued new authoritative standards regarding segmental disclosures. In the case of the FASB, the authoritative standard is Statement of Financial Accounting Standards No. 131, *Disclosures about Segments of an Enterprise and Related Information.*[13]

Statement of Financial Accounting Standards No. 131

FASB Statement No. 131, which replaces the earlier Statement No. 14, is applicable to public business enterprises. A company is considered to be a public enterprise if it a) has issued debt or equity securities that are traded in a public market, b) is required to file financial statements with the Securities and Exchange Commission (SEC), or c) provides financial statements for the purpose of issuing securities in a public market. Although the statement does not apply to nonpublic enterprises or not-for-profit organizations, such enterprises or organizations are encouraged to adopt the requirements of the standard.

Definition of an Operating Segment.   The FASB chose to define operating segments by emphasizing a "management approach" which focuses on how management organizes information for purposes of making operating decisions and assessing performance. For example, assume that a public company, which manufactures circuit boards for a variety of applications, organizes information by sales-market area for decision-making purposes. Therefore, the segments of the company might logically be defined as sales-market areas such as North America, South America, etc. Also, consider a public company that is involved in a number of diverse industries such as banking, retail brokerage services, and real estate development. If this company organizes information for decision-making purposes according to the types of products or services it offers, such as life insurance, then its segments would be defined accordingly. The segments should be evident from the structure of the organization in terms of how information is organized for internal decision-making purposes. Furthermore, if this information is already being generated internally, then management should be able to disclose certain relevant portions of this information to external users without incurring significant incremental costs.

The segments which emerge from an analysis of how management organizes information for decision-making purposes are called *operating segments* and are defined as a component of an enterprise

1.   That engages in business activities from which it may earn revenues and incur expenses (including revenues and expenses relating to transactions with other components of the same enterprise),
2.   Whose operating results are regularly reviewed by the enterprise's chief operating decision maker to make decisions about resources to be allocated to the segment and assess its performance, and
3.   For which discrete financial information is available.[14]

It is important to note that not all parts of an enterprise will necessarily qualify

---

13 Statement of Financial Accounting Standards No. 131, *Disclosures about Segments of an Enterprise and Related Information* (Stamford, CT: Financial Accounting Standards Board, 1997).
14 *Ibid.*, par. 10

as an operating segment. For example, some parts may not earn revenues of an operating nature, such as is the case with corporate headquarters. The chief operating decision maker who reviews a segment is one who assesses performance and allocates resources. This is a function which could be held by one individual, such as a chief executive officer (CEO) or chief operating officer (COO), or a group of individuals. One or more individuals typically have responsibility to account and report to the chief operating decision maker. This function is carried out by segment managers whose identification may also help identify operating segments.

Once operating segments have been identified, it is possible that some of the segments will appear to be similar due to similar economic characteristics. These segments may have virtually the same future prospects, and separate reporting of them may provide users with additional data of limited utility. Therefore, it may be possible to combine two or more of these segments into a single segment, if they are similar in each of the following areas:

- The nature of the products or services
- The nature of the production processes
- The type or class of customer for their products and services
- The methods used to distribute their products or provide their services
- The nature of the regulatory environment (if applicable), for example, banking, insurance, or public utilities.[15]

Once segments have been identified and aggregated, if necessary, information should be disclosed about those segments which are deemed to be reportable. That is, even though there may be an operating segment, it may not be significant enough to require disclosure. A *reportable segment* is one which is deemed to be significant because of any of the following:

- Its reported revenue, including both sales to external customers and intersegment sales or transfers, is 10% or more of the combined revenue, internal and external, of all reported operating segments.
- The absolute amount of its reported profit or loss is 10% or more of the greater, in absolute amount, of a) the combined profit of all operating segments that did not report a loss, or b) the combined reported loss of all operating segments that did report a loss.
- Its assets are 10% or more of the combined assets of all operating segments.[16]

It is important to note that, even if a segment does not satisfy the above criteria, management may report information about that individual segment if they believe it to be material.

For those operating segments which do not meet the above criteria, they will constitute a separate "all other" category for reporting purposes. It is possible that those segments which qualify as reportable do not represent a significant enough portion of the enterprise's operating activities. The total of **external revenues** for reportable segments must constitute at least 75% of the total consolidated revenue. If this is not the case, then additional operating segments must be designated as reportable even though they did not initially qualify as such. The goal of these guidelines is to reach a balance between providing users with information about a reasonable number of segments and yet not be excessive. In the latter regard, if the number of reportable segments exceeds 10 in number, consideration should be given to whether this number should be reduced by aggregating certain segments. The above criteria used to identify reportable segments and analyze the appropriate number of reportable segments are shown in Illustration 12-7.

---

15 *Ibid.*, par. 17.
16 *Ibid.*, par. 18.

Illustration 12-7
Reportable Segments: Demonstration of Criteria

Facts:

Whalen Corporation has classified its operations into segments and has provided the following data for each segment:

| | Revenues | | | | |
	Unaffiliated Customers	Intersegment Sales	Total	Operating Profit (Loss)	Assets
Segment					
A	$100,000	$15,000	$115,000	$ 45,000	$ 280,000
B	20,000		20,000	(10,000)	80,000
C	230,000	40,000	270,000	130,000	1,100,000
D	45,000	5,000	50,000	(60,000)	320,000
E	37,000	8,000	45,000	25,000	295,000
F	140,000	14,000	154,000	85,000	760,000
	$572,000	$82,000	$654,000	$215,000	$2,835,000
Corporate level	60,000		60,000	20,000	705,000
Total	$632,000	$82,000	$714,000	$235,000	$3,540,000

Analysis:

The determination of which segments are reportable requires the following evaluation, in which only combined data relating to the segments (not including corporate-level activity) are employed:

1. Total sales to unaffiliated customers $572,000
   Total intersegment sales 82,000
   Combined revenue $654,000

   Segment revenue required to satisfy criterion (a): $654,000 × 10% = $65,400

2. | Segment | Operating Profit | Operating Loss |
   |---|---|---|
   | A | $ 45,000 | — |
   | B | — | $10,000 |
   | C | 130,000 | — |
   | D | — | 60,000 |
   | E | 25,000 | — |
   | F | 85,000 | — |
   | Total | $285,000 | $70,000 |

   Portion of absolute amount of the greater of the operating profit or the operating loss to satisfy criterion (b):

   $285,000 × 10% = $28,500

3. Segment assets required to satisfy criterion (c): $2,835,000 × 10% = $283,500

Whether the criteria are satisfied is summarized as follows:

		Criterion Satisfied		
Segment	Revenue	Operating Profit (Loss)	Identifiable Assets	Segment Reportable
A	Yes ($115,000 > $65,400)	Yes ($ 45,000 > $28,500)	No ($ 280,000 < $283,500)	Yes
B	No ($ 20,000 < $65,400)	No ($ 10,000 < $28,500)	No ($ 80,000 < $283,500)	No
C	Yes ($270,000 > $65,400)	Yes ($130,000 > $28,500)	Yes ($1,100,000 > $283,500)	Yes
D	No ($ 50,000 < $65,400)	Yes ($ 60,000 > $28,500)	Yes ($ 320,000 > $283,500)	Yes
E	No ($ 45,000 < $65,400)	No ($ 25,000 < $28,500)	Yes ($ 295,000 > $283,500)	Yes
F	Yes ($154,000 > $65,400)	Yes ($ 85,000 > $28,500)	Yes ($ 760,000 > $283,500)	Yes

All of the segments are reportable except for Segment B.

4. Significance of the reportable segments:

Consolidated revenue.	$632,000
Percentage requirement	75%
Dollar requirement.	$474,000
External revenue of reportable segments (all segments except Segment B)	$552,000

The reportable segments represent a significant portion of the enterprise.

5. Reasonableness of the number of reportable segments:

The 5 reportable segments do not exceed the guideline number of 10.

Comparability of Segmental Information. Another issue which arises deals with comparability of segmental information over time. For example, it is possible for a segment to meet the criteria as being reportable in one fiscal period and not in another, resulting, therefore, in a lack of compatibility. In order to ensure comparability, the following guidelines are appropriate for both interim and annual periods:

1. If a segment is deemed to be reportable in the current period, prior-period segmental data should also include the segment for comparative purposes.
2. If a segment was deemed to be reportable in prior-period segmental data presented, the segment should continue to be deemed reportable if it is considered to be of continuing significance.
3. If an enterprise's structure changes such that the composition or makeup of segments changes, then prior-period segmental data presented should be restated, if practical, to reflect the new composition of segments. It should be disclosed as to whether or not prior-period information has been restated. If such information has not been restated, segment information for the current period should be presented on both the current and previous basis of segmentation. This dual presentation is appropriate only in the current period of change and if practical.

Content of Segmental Disclosures. Once the identification of reportable segments and the proper guidelines regarding the number of segments have been satisfied, various general and financial information regarding segments is required to be disclosed as a part of a complete set of financial statements. The factors used to identify reportable segments must be disclosed along with a discussion of how the segments are organized. For example, segments could be organized around products or services, geographical areas, marketing areas, or products within geographical areas.

For each reportable segment, the type of products and/or services from which they derive their revenues should be disclosed. Certain information about profit or loss and assets must also be disclosed for each reportable segment, and then these amounts must be reconciled to corresponding enterprise consolidated amounts.

Information about Profit or Loss and Assets.   The measure of profit or loss which is disclosed is a function of what information is reviewed by the chief operating decision maker of the enterprise. For example, the measure could exclude items relating to the cost of capital, or the measure could include an allocation of general corporate overhead. It is important to note that the measure of profit or loss follows a management approach focusing on internal decision making rather than any strict definition of profit used by the enterprise for general purpose external reporting. Therefore, it is possible that segmental profit or loss may not necessarily incorporate the same generally accepted accounting principles (GAAP) as are employed at the consolidated level. For example, segment profit or loss may not include the effects of tax allocation or pension expense. The following items regarding profit or loss should be disclosed **only if** the items are included in the values reviewed by the chief operating decision maker: revenues from external customers, revenues from other operating segments, interest revenue, interest expense, depreciation, depletion, and amortization expense, unusual items, equity in net income of investees accounted for under the equity method, income tax expense/benefit, extraordinary items, and other significant noncash items such as deferred tax expense. If a majority of a segment's revenues are from interest, such as those of a financial segment, and the decision-making process focuses on net interest (interest revenue less interest expense), then interest revenue may be reported net of interest expense.

In order to better evaluate a segment, it would be useful to disclose the assets which were employed to generate the profit or loss traceable to that segment. Therefore, those segment assets which are evaluated by the chief operating decision maker are also to be disclosed. The following items regarding assets should be disclosed **only if** the items are included in the values reviewed by the chief operating decision maker: the carrying basis of investments in investees measured under the equity method and total expenditures for additions to long-lived assets (other than financial instruments, long-term customer relationships of a financial institution, mortgage and other servicing rights, deferred policy acquisition costs, and deferred tax assets).

Because the measurement of segment profit or loss and assets follows a management approach, additional disclosures are necessary in order to assist users in understanding how these values are measured. For example, segment profit may not include the allocation of certain corporate-level expenses or it may measure cost of sales using a method different than that used for consolidated purposes. Therefore, an enterprise should disclose, at a minimum, the following:

1. The basis of accounting for any transactions between reportable segments.
2. The nature of any differences between the measurements of the reportable segments' profits or losses and the enterprise's consolidated income before income taxes, extraordinary items, discontinued operations, and the cumulative effect of changes in accounting principles (if not apparent from the reconciliations). Those differences could include accounting policies and policies for allocation of centrally incurred costs that are necessary for an understanding of the reported segment information.
3. The nature of any differences between the measurements of the reportable segments' assets and the enterprise's consolidated assets (if not apparent from the reconciliations). Those differences could include accounting policies and policies for allocation of jointly used assets that are necessary for an understanding of the reported segment information.

4. The nature of any changes from prior periods in the measurement methods used to determine reported segment profit or loss and the effect, if any, of those changes on the measure of segment profit or loss.

5. The nature and effect of any asymmetrical allocations to segments. For example, an enterprise might allocate depreciation expense to a segment without allocating the related depreciable assets to that segment.[17]

The various dollar amounts disclosed for reportable segments represent a significant portion of the respective consolidated dollar amounts. For example, the sum of profit or loss for all reportable segments will naturally represent a significant portion of consolidated profit or loss. However, all of the consolidated profit or loss will not be traceable to the reportable segments. The difference between the sum of the reportable segment values and the respective consolidated value is most often due to the following:

1. Not all segments are considered to be reportable. Therefore, some values are allocated to the category of segments known as "all other."

2. Segment revenues, profits, and assets include the effect of intersegment transactions that are eliminated from consolidated amounts. Note that intersegment transactions which have *not been realized* through an exchange with an outside entity must be eliminated from consolidated amounts.

3. Certain values are not allocated to segments because they are not part of the information which is used by the chief operating decision maker as a basis for evaluating performance and allocating resources.

4. Certain values cannot be allocated to segments on a reasonable basis.

5. The accounting methods used to determine values for a reportable segment may be different than those used to prepare consolidated values. This is due to the focus on the management approach and the information used for internal rather than external reporting purposes.

A requirement of segmental reporting is that the revenue, profit or loss, and asset amounts presented for reportable segments must be reconciled to the respective consolidated amounts for the enterprise as a whole. A reconciliation must also be made for other significant items presented by reportable segments. The reconciliation should be described in sufficient detail. Illustration 12-8 contains an example of the required segmental disclosures and the reconciliation to consolidated enterprise values.

Illustration 12-8
Presentation of Segmental Values

	Auto Parts	Motor Vessels	Software	Electronics	Finance	All Other	Totals
Revenues from external customers	$3,000	$5,000	$9,500	$12,000	$5,000	$1,000[a]	$35,500
Intersegment revenues	—	—	3,000	1,500	—	—	4,500
Interest revenue	450	800	1,000	1,500	—	—	3,750
Interest expense	350	600	700	1,100	—	—	2,750
Net interest revenue[b]	—	—	—	—	1,000	—	1,000
Depreciation and amortization	200	100	50	1,500	1,100	—	2,950
Segment profit	200	70	900	2,300	500	100	4,070
Other significant noncash items:							
Cost in excess of billings on long-term contracts	—	200	—	—	—	—	200

(continued)

17 *Ibid.*, par. 31.

	Auto Parts	Motor Vessels	Software	Electronics	Finance	All Other	Totals
Segment assets	2,000	5,000	3,000	12,000	57,000	2,000	81,000
Expenditures for segment assets	300	700	500	800	600	—	2,900

a Revenue from segments below the quantitative thresholds are attributable to 4 operating segments of Diversified Company. Those segments include a small real estate business, an electronics equipment rental business, a software consulting practice, and a warehouse leasing operation. None of those segments has ever met any of the quantitative thresholds for determining reportable segments.

b The finance segment derives a majority of its revenue from interest. In addition, management relies primarily on net interest revenue, not the gross revenue and expense amounts, in managing that segment. Therefore, only the net amount is disclosed.

Reconciliation of Segmental Values to Enterprise Consolidated Values

Revenues

Total revenues for reportable segments	$34,500
Other revenues	1,000
Elimination of intersegment revenues.	(4,500)
Total consolidated revenues.	$31,000

Profit or Loss

Total profit or loss for reportable segments.	$ 3,970
Other profit or loss	100
Elimination of intersegment profits	(500)
Unallocated amounts:	
Litigation settlement received	500
Other corporate expenses.	(750)
Adjustment to pension expense in consolidation	(250)
Income before income taxes and extraordinary items.	$ 3,070

Assets

Total assets for reportable segments	$79,000
Other assets.	2,000
Elimination of receivables from corporate headquarters	(1,000)
Goodwill not allocated to segments	4,000
Other unallocated amounts.	1,000
Consolidated total.	$85,000

Other Significant Items

	Segment Totals	Adjustments	Consolidated Totals
Interest revenue	$3,750	$ 75	$3,825
Interest expense	2,750	(50)	2,700
Net interest revenue (finance segment only)	1,000	—	1,000
Expenditures for assets	2,900	$1,000	3,900
Depreciation and amortization	2,950	—	2,950
Cost in excess of billing on long-term contracts	200	—	200

The reconciling item to adjust expenditures for assets is the amount of expenses incurred for the corporate headquarters building, which is not included in segment information. None of the other adjustments are significant.

Source: Statement of Financial Accounting Standards No. 131, *Disclosures about Segments of an Enterprise and Related Information.*

Interim Period Disclosures.   The current standard on segmental reporting addresses a criticism of the previous standard regarding interim reporting disclosures. The previous standard was criticized for not requiring segmental disclosures in interim reports. Interim information has become increasingly important, and users would find it even more useful if it included information regarding segments. Therefore, the new standard requires that *condensed* financial statements for interim periods include the following for each reportable segment: revenues from both external customers and intersegment sales, profit or loss, a reconciliation of reportable segments' profit or loss to enterprise pretax net income from continuing operations, total assets which have materially changed from the values reported in the most recent annual report, and disclosure of any differences from the last annual report in terms of whether the basis for segmentation and/or measurement of segment profit or loss have changed. It is important to note that these disclosures are appropriate for only condensed financial statements of an interim period. If a complete set of financial statements is presented, then the more comprehensive disclosures discussed earlier would be appropriate.

Enterprise-Wide Disclosures.   Because of the use of the management approach to defining segments, it is possible that segments may not necessarily be defined around product/service groups or geographical areas. For example, a segment may consist of several unrelated products because that is how information is structured for decision-making purposes. A company which produces beverages, produces snack foods, operates a chain of restaurants, and operates amusement parks may decide to include all but the amusement parks in a single segment. Segments may also be defined in such a way that a given segment includes activities which are occurring in more than one foreign geographical area. If information regarding product/service groups and/or geographical areas is not provided as part of the segmental disclosures, such information must be provided as an additional disclosure. These additional disclosures must be presented if practical; if it is not practical, that fact must be disclosed. These additional disclosures are presented on an enterprise-wide basis, not on a segmental basis. Furthermore, the disclosures are required even if there is only one reportable segment. The enterprise is required to[18]

1.   Report revenues from **external** customers for each product or service or each group of related products or services. The revenues are based on the information used for general purpose financial statements.

2.   Report revenues from **external** customers for the enterprise's country of domicile and all foreign countries in total. The revenues are based on the information used for general purpose financial statements. If material, revenues from separate foreign countries should be disclosed. Subtotals of revenue may also be disclosed by groups of foreign countries (e.g., South America). The basis used to allocate revenues to separate foreign countries must be disclosed. For example, revenues may be allocated based on where products are shipped or based on the location of customers.

3.   Report **long-lived** assets located in the enterprise's country of domicile and all foreign countries in total. The measurement of assets is based on the information used for general purpose financial statements. If material, assets traceable to separate foreign countries should be disclosed. Subtotals of assets may also be disclosed by groups of foreign countries (e.g., South America).

Disclosures Regarding Major Customers.   Enterprises are also required to disclose information about major customers if revenues traceable to a single customer repre-

_____
18 *Ibid.*, par. 37 – 39.

sent 10% or more of total enterprise revenues. For each such customer, the enterprise must disclose the total amount of revenues and identify the segment or segments to which the revenues are traceable. The specific identity by name of the major customer need not be disclosed. For purposes of this disclosure, a group of entities under common control is considered to be a single customer. Federal, state, local, and foreign governments or agencies should each be considered as a single customer.

Questions

1. Explain why interim statements may be more useful if an interim period is viewed as an integral part of a larger annual period.
2. A company has increased its shipment of goods to customers in the second quarter in anticipation of a strike occurring in the third quarter. Would it be appropriate for management to defer some of the sales revenues to the third quarter so that users of the statements do not think that second-quarter sales will be indicative of third-quarter sales?
3. Explain how a temporary liquidation of LIFO inventory is accounted for in an interim period.
4. If a change in accounting principle occurs in the third quarter of the year, how should it be disclosed in the interim statement?
5. If the estimated annual effective tax rate is different from an earlier interim estimate, how is the change in rate accounted for?
6. If a company typically accrues bonuses for officers at year-end, how should such bonuses be reflected in interim statements?
7. If a company is projecting an operating loss for the current year, and income in subsequent years is not "more likely than not," how is the estimated effective annual tax rate determined?
8. Explain how the management approach, which is used to define segments, may not result in segments being defined along product lines.
9. Once a segment has been defined, what criteria must be satisfied in order for that segment to be considered reportable?
10. The total operating profit of reportable segments must be reconciled to enterprise operating profit before taxes. Identify the nature of several reconciling items.
11. If an international company defines its segments along product lines, what information will be provided regarding its international sales activities?
12. What guidelines exist to help answer the question of whether the reportable segments are too few or too great in number?
13. An enterprise incurs significant costs to operate its customer information center. What alternatives are available regarding the allocation of those costs to the reportable segments, assuming segments are defined in terms of product groups?
14. A U.S. public company has engaged in sales to foreign companies and governments. Some of the foreign companies are affiliates of the U.S. company. Under what conditions must these sales be separately disclosed?

Exercises

Exercise 1. The following data represent the accounting results and projections of 4 separate cases for the year ended September 30, 20X9, with YTD totals as of May 31, 20X9.

	Case A	Case B	Case C	Case D
Statutory tax rate	34%	34%	28%	28%
Year-to-date realized pretax income (loss).	$100,000	$(260,000)	$(120,000)	$ 160,000
Pretax income (loss) projected for the remainder of the year	85,000	(320,000)	180,000	(245,000)
Annual tax credit available	6,000	21,000	3,000	3,000

The following additional information is available:

Case B: Pretax income was $335,000 in 20X7 and $110,000 in 20X8. The effective tax rate was 30% in each of these years.

Case C: A total deduction of $15,000 is included in the 20X9 figures. Such deduction is not allowed for income tax purposes. Established seasonal patterns assure the realization of the tax benefit associated with the YTD loss and the $3,000 available tax credit.

Case D: YTD income includes interest income of $18,000 on tax-free municipal bonds. Pretax income (loss) was $60,000 in 20X7 and $60,000 in 20X8. The effective tax rate was 35% in each of these years.

Calculate the effective annual tax rate for each case.

Exercise 2.   The Wheeler Corporation experienced an extraordinary pretax gain of $15,000 in the second quarter of the current fiscal year. At the end of the second quarter, *annual pretax* amounts were as follows:

Estimated income from continuing operations	$10,000
Cumulative effect of a change in accounting principle	30,000
Estimated loss on discontinued operation	(22,000)
Extraordinary gain	15,000
Total estimated annual pretax income	$33,000

Statutory tax rates were as follows: 15% on the first $25,000 of taxable income, 20% on the next $25,000 of taxable income, and 30% on taxable income in excess of $50,000. Taxable income of $18,000 was reported in the prior year and is available for purposes of a net operating loss carryback.

Given the above information, determine the year-to-date tax expense traceable to the extraordinary gain.

Exercise 3.   The statutory tax rate for 20X7 is 30%. For each of the following cases, determine the YTD tax benefit traceable to the YTD operating loss.

	Case A	Case B	Case C	Case D
YTD operating (loss)	$(80,000)	$(80,000)	$(80,000)	$(20,000)
Projected interim income (loss) for balance of year:				
More likely than not	120,000		50,000	(40,000)
Not more likely than not		30,000		
Carryback income (tax rate):				
Second prior year (25%)		20,000	40,000	34,000
First prior year (25%)		10,000	10,000	24,000
Likely future income in carryforward period				30,000

Exercise 4.   Wert Company has sought assistance in preparing its second-quarter income statement for 20X2. Figures for sales revenue, selling expenses, and general and administrative expenses are $860,000, $68,000, and $117,000, respectively.

For each of the following situations, determine the cost of goods sold and prepare an interim income statement in good form for the 3 months ended June 30, 20X2.

1.   Wert uses a standard cost accounting system for inventory and product costs. Net unfavorable cost variances for the second quarter total $2,600 and represent the difference between actual and standard production costs. Management considers such variances as a manufacturing cost and includes them in the income statement above the gross profit line. It is expected that an unfavorable purchase price variance of $900 will be absorbed by December 31, 20X2. Production for the second quarter at standard cost was $600,000. Beginning and ending finished goods inventories (standard cost) were $71,000 and $98,000, respectively.

2.   The LIFO cost of goods sold was $596,000 and includes sales of 15,000 units costed out at their 20X1 base layer cost of $7 per unit. The current replacement cost of these units is $11 per unit. It is expected that the 20X2 year-end inventory will be 2,000 units less than the 20X1 year-end inventory.

3.   Beginning inventory of $52,000 reflects a first-quarter write-down of $2,200 due to the application of the lower-of-cost-or-market rule. Through a market price recovery in the second quarter, inventory increased in value by $3,750. Wert purchased 18,000 units of inventory ($28 per unit) in the second quarter. Ending inventory (FIFO basis) was $60,500.

Exercise 5.   The Merlot Corporation reported a net operating loss before taxes for the first quarter of 20X3 in the amount of $80,000 (which included $4,000 of tax-exempt income) and a projected loss for the balance of the year in the amount of $50,000 (which included $2,000 of tax-exempt income). The company also had a first-quarter tax credit in the amount of $4,000 and anticipated tax credits of $6,000 for the balance of the year. Pretax income and effective rates for the prior 2 years are as follows:

	20X1	20X2
Pretax income	$35,000	$30,000
Effective tax rate	25%	22%

The statutory tax rate in 20X3 is 30%, and it is estimated that, more likely than not, pretax income in 20X4 will be $50,000.

Late in the second quarter of 20X3, the company decided to discontinue an operation. The effect of the decision on the previous year-to-date (YTD) and projected information which was used in quarter one was as follows:

	YTD Income (Loss)	Projected Income (Loss)	Annual Tax Credit	Annual Tax-Exempt Income
Continuing Operations.	$ 30,000	$ 90,000	$ 7,000	$5,000
Discontinued Operations	(110,000)	(140,000)	3,000	1,000
Total	$ (80,000)	$ (50,000)	$10,000	$6,000

Given the above information, calculate the estimated effective annual tax rate which would have been used to prepare the original first-quarter, 20X3 statements. Also, calculate how the original first-quarter tax benefit would be restated and allocated between the continuing and discontinued operation as a result of the second-quarter decision to discontinue an operation.

Exercise 6.   Tripper Industries, Inc., decided to change accounting principles in the third quarter of the current year. Originally, the first 6 months had a YTD pretax income of $40,000, a projected pretax income for the balance of the year of $60,000, and an estimated annual effective tax rate of 20%. The rate is based on statutory rates of 15% on the first $50,000 of income, 25% on the next $50,000 of income, and 35% on amounts in excess of $100,000. Had the new principle been adopted at the beginning of the year, the first 6 months' pretax income would have been $30,000 and projected pretax income for the balance of the year would have been $30,000. The effect of the change in principle on prior years is to decrease net income by $50,000.

The third-quarter pretax income, based on the new accounting principle, is $50,000, and the projected pretax income for the balance of the year is $40,000.

Calculate the pretax income and related tax expense (benefit) for the first 3 quarters of the current year.

Exercise 7.   Williams Inc. is in its fifth year of operations and has had prior pretax income and taxes as follows:

	Pretax Income	Effective Tax Rate	Tax Expense
20X1	$30,000	26%	$ 7,800
20X2	42,000	29	12,180
20X3	40,000	28	11,200
20X4	30,000	25	7,500

In the first quarter of 20X5, the company experienced a pretax loss of $50,000, and projected income for the balance of the year was zero.

In the second quarter of 20X5, the company once again incurred a pretax loss of $20,000. However, income of $30,000 was projected for the balance of the year and is more likely than not to be recognized. In the third quarter, the company recognized an extraordinary gain of $50,000 and reported a modest pretax operating income of $20,000. Income of $25,000 was projected for the balance of the year and is more likely than not to be recognized. A pretax income of $15,000 was recognized in the final quarter along with $2,000 of tax credits. The final quarter included a penalty expense of $4,000, which is not deductible for tax purposes.

Calculate the tax expense (benefit) for each quarter of the current year, assuming the 20X5 statutory tax rate is 25%.

Exercise 8.   The chief operating decision maker of a publicly traded company has defined segments around 4 product/service groups. Various revenues, profits or losses, and assets associated with the segments are as follows:

	Film Studios	Software Development	Leisure Clothing	Office Design Group	Total Enterprise Values
Revenues:					
External	$82,000,000	$12,000,000	$45,000,000	$22,000,000	$177,000,000
Intersegment	0	3,400,000	0	2,700,000	0
Expenses	93,000,000	18,000,000	22,000,000	18,000,000	166,000,000
Assets	38,000,000	5,400,000	13,000,000	5,000,000	70,000,000

Determine which segments are considered to be reportable and whether the reportable segments represent a significant portion of enterprise consolidated revenues.

Exercise 9. Assume the facts as presented in Exercise 8. The total enterprise revenues and expenses include the following:

Corporate-level revenues	$16,000,000
Corporate-level expenses	9,000,000
Unallocated noncorporate expenses	6,000,000

The intersegment sales made by the software development segment had a cost of sales of $2,040,000. Of these goods sold, only 80% were, in turn, sold to outside customers.

Prepare a reconciliation of reportable revenues and profits or losses to enterprise consolidated revenues and profit.

Exercise 10. The following information is given for the 7 segments of Staven Supplies:

Segment	Revenues	Operating Profit (Loss)	Assets
1.	$1,540,000	$ 602,000	$1,600,000
2.	805,000	(208,000)	870,000
3.	1,948,000	530,000	1,250,000
4.	1,070,000	375,000	1,800,000
5.	760,000	220,000	965,000
6.	980,000	402,000	1,400,000
7.	1,071,000	(106,000)	1,380,000
Corporate-level items	820,000	170,000	560,000
	$8,994,000	$1,985,000	$9,825,000
Intercompany adjustments and eliminations.	(278,300)	(75,000)	(305,000)
Consolidated total	$8,715,700	$1,910,000	$9,520,000

10% of the revenues of segments 2, 4, and 5 are traceable to intersegment sales.
1.   Determine which segments are reportable.
2.   Determine whether a substantial portion of Staven's total operations is represented by reportable segments.
3.   Discuss how information traceable to nonreportable segments should be presented.
4.   Assume that segment 3 has revenues in the amount of $1,230,000 which result from sales to the U.S. government. Prepare the necessary disclosure which is required due to this assumption.

Exercise 11. Norfo International is a large company with extremely diversified activities. These activities include

a)   *Food-processing operations in California, Spain, and Italy. Processed foods are sold throughout Europe, South America, and the United States. Cans and containers for the processed foods are manufactured by Canco Industries, a wholly owned subsidiary of Norfo. Canco has manufacturing facilities in Arizona, Germany, and Spain.*

b)   *Seven citrus groves in central Florida. Approximately 70% of a harvest is trucked to the company's Louisville food-processing operation; the balance of the harvest is processed, on location, into frozen juice concentrates.*

    c)   *A Chicago operation that manufactures packaging for perishable food products and cardboard packaging for transporting equipment components, such as engines and transmissions.*

    d)   *Four large resort hotels, three of which are located along the eastern seaboard, and one of which is located in the Bahamas.*

    e)   *A chain of travel agencies in the New York and Boston areas.*

    f)   *A paper products division located in Maine that manufactures napkins, paper plates, paper towels, and greeting cards. These products are sold to grocery stores and variety stores.*

Given the management approach, discuss various ways in which the segments of Norfo might be structured.

Problems

Problem 12-1.   Prior to the second quarter of 20X9, Portico, Inc. had depreciated its assets by the straight-line method. However, during the second quarter of 20X9, the company changed to an accelerated method of depreciation. The effect of the change on the first quarter of 120X9 was an increase in pretax income of $5,000. The effect of the change in prior years was to decrease pretax income by $84,000. The first quarter of 20X9 had originally reported a pretax income of $30,000 and a tax expense of $5,832. The projected income for the balance of the year was originally estimated to be $60,000 at the end of the first quarter. However, due to the change in depreciation methods, the projection should have been $75,000. Pretax income, based on the new depreciation method for the second quarter of 20X9 and the balance of the year, is $25,000 and $80,000, respectively. At this time, anticipated annual tax credits were $4,000.

During the third quarter of 20X9, the company experienced a pretax income of $40,000 and projected $20,000 of pretax income for the balance of the year. Annual tax credits were anticipated to be $3,000. Also during the quarter, the company experienced an extraordinary gain of $20,000, which is taxed at 20%.

The statutory tax rate is 15% on the first $50,000 of income, 25% on the next $50,000, and 35% on all additional income.

Required:

Calculate the pretax income and related tax expense for the first three quarters of 20X9.

Problem 12-2.   The following schedule relates to interim reporting for the Hughes Corporation:

Quarter	Type of Income (Loss)	Current Income (Loss)	YTD Income (Loss)	Effective Tax Rate	YTD Tax Expense (Benefit)
2	Continuing operations	$40,000	$60,000	30%	$18,000
2	Extraordinary.	(10,000)	(10,000)	—	3,000
2 restated	Continuing operations	-A-	-B-	28%	-C-
	Discontinued operations—Pre-measurement date	-D-	—	—	-E-
	Extraordinary.	(10,000)	(10,000)	—	3,000
3	Continuing operations	20,000	95,000	-F-	-G-

(continued)

Discontinued operations—Pre-measurement date	—	12,000	—	-H-
Discontinued operations—Post-measurement date.	(80,000)	(80,000)	—	-I-
Extraordinary.	(10,000)	(10,000)	—	-J-
4 Discontinued operations—Post-measurement date	-K-	—	—	—

A decision was made in the third quarter to discontinue an operation. Information relating to the income (loss) traceable to the discontinued operation is as follows:

Pre-measurement-date amounts:		Post-measurement-date amounts:	
Quarter 1	$ 0	Quarter 3	$(45,000)
Quarter 2	(15,000)	Quarter 4	(10,000)
Quarter 3	27,000	Subsequent year:	
		Loss on disposal	(30,000)
		Gain on disposal	5,000

The statutory tax rate was 30% for the year.

At the end of the third quarter, the company projected a loss from continuing operations of $30,000 for the balance of the year. At that time, the company also projected annual tax credits of $6,000. The prior 2 years had reported taxable income of $10,000 ($2,000 in the second prior year and $8,000 in the first prior year) in total which was taxed at 30%.

During the fourth quarter, the company actually experienced a loss of $14,000 from the discontinued operation and revised its projection of subsequent-year results traceable to the discontinued operation as follows: loss on disposal of $18,000 and a gain on disposal of $20,000.

Required:

Calculate the value for items A through K above.

Problem 12-3.   Mikelson Company, a California corporation listed on the pacific Coast Stock Exchange, budgeted activities for 20X5 as follows:

	Amount	Units
Net sales	$6,000,000	1,000,000
Cost of goods sold	3,600,000	1,000,000
Gross profit	$2,400,000	
Selling, general, and administrative expenses	1,400,000	
Operating income	$1,000,000	
Nonoperating revenue and expenses		
Income before income taxes	$1,000,000	
Estimated income taxes (current and deferred)	550,000	
Net income	$450,000	
Earnings per share of common stock	$4.50	

Mikelson has operated profitably for many years and has experienced a season pattern of sales volume and production. For 20X5, sales volume is expected to follow a quarterly pattern of 10%, 20%, 35%, and 35%, respectively, because of the seasonality of the industry. Also, due to production and storage capacity limitations, it is expected that production will follow a pattern of 20%, 25%, 30%, and 25% per quarter, respectively.

At the end of the first quarter of 20X5, the controller of Mikelson prepared and issued the following interim report for public release:

	Amount	Units
Net sales	$ 600,000	100,000
Cost of goods sold	360,000	100,000
Gross profit	$ 240,000	
Selling, general, and administrative expenses	275,000	
Operating loss	$ (35,000)	
Loss from warehouse fire	(175,000)	
Loss before income taxes	$(210,000)	
Estimated income taxes		
Net loss	$(210,000)	
Loss per share of common stock	$(2.10)	

The following additional information is available for the first quarter but was not included in the public information released:

a) The company uses a standard cost system in which standards are set at currently attainable levels on an annual basis. At the end of the first quarter, there was an underapplied fixed factory overhead (volume variance) of $50,000 that was treated as an asset at the end of the quarter. Production during the quarter was 200,000 units, of which 100,000 were sold.

b) The selling, general, and administrative expenses were budgeted on a basis of $900,000 fixed expenses for the year plus $0.50 variable expenses per unit of sales.

c) Assume the warehouse fire loss met the conditions of an extraordinary loss. The warehouse had an undepreciated cost of $320,000; $145,000 was recovered from insurance on the warehouse. No other gains or losses are anticipated this year from similar events or transactions, nor has Mikelson had any similar losses in preceding years; thus, the full loss will be deductible as an ordinary loss for income tax.

d) The effective income tax rate, for federal and state taxes combined, is expected to average 55% of income before income taxes during 20X5. There are no permanent differences between pretax accounting income and taxable income.

Required:

1. Without reference to the specific situations described in this problem, what are the standards of disclosure for interim financial data (published interim financial reports) for publicly traded companies? Explain.

2. Identify the weakness in form and content of Mikelson's interim report without reference to the additional information.

3. For each of the four items of additional information, indicate the preferable treatment for interim reporting purposes and explain why that treatment is preferable.

Problem 12-4.   During 20X8, Midway Corporation reported first 6 months' pretax income of $120,000 from continuing operations and a year-to-date tax expense of $37,668. The tax expense reflects projected pretax income for the balance of the year of $100,000 and the following statutory tax rates:

Tax on first $50,000 . . . . .15%

Tax on next $25,000 . . . . .25%

Tax on next $25,000 . . . . .34%

Tax on next $235,000 . . . . .39%

Tax on remaining income 34%

The first 6 months also included the following nonordinary items:

A.	Extraordinary gain	$10,000
B.	Loss on noncurrent marketable securities recorded as a component of owners' equity	(85,000)
C.	Loss on discontinued operations	(80,000)

Required:

Calculate the incremental tax impact traceable to each of the nonordinary items directly affecting income or owners' equity.

Problem 12-5.   The following information relates to 3 independent cases:

	Case A	Case B	Case C
Pretax net income (loss) from continuing operations:			
Year-to-date	$(80,000)	$ 30,000	$20,000
Projected	60,000	20,000	40,000
Tax-exempt income included in above net income:			
Year-to-date	0	3,000	0
Projected	3,000	3,000	0
Statutory tax rate	30%	30%	30%
Tax credits:			
Year-to-date	0	4,000	2,000
Projected	2,000	2,200	2,000
Information regarding prior 2 years:			
Taxable income	50,000	100,000	20,000*
Effective tax rate	30%	40%	25%

*The $20,000 is equally divided between the 2 prior years.

Required:

1. For Case A, calculate the year-to-date tax expense or benefit.
2. Assume that the YTD tax expense was originally calculated using the facts of Case B. Furthermore, assume that the original amounts are to be restated because of a subsequent decision to discontinue an operation. Calculate the year-to-date restated tax expense or benefit traceable to the discontinued operation assuming the following allocation of year-to-date and projected amounts.

	Total	Continuing Operations	Discontinued Operations
Pretax income (loss)			
Year-to-date	$30,000	$50,000	$(20,000)
Projected	20,000	90,000	(70,000)
Tax-exempt income included in above net income:			
Year-to-date	3,000	3,000	0
Projected	3,000	2,000	1,000
Tax credits:			
Year-to-date	4,000	3,500	500
Projected	2,200	2,000	200

3. For Case C, calculate the year-to-date tax expense or benefit associated with, in addition to the continuing income, a $50,000 extraordinary loss and a $20,000 loss due to a change in accounting principle.

Problem 12-6.   Niemoth Inc. has retained you to prepare interim data. The following information is available.

a) *During the third quarter of 20X4, it was discovered that the second quarter contained the effect of a LIFO liquidation, which was expected to be offset by year-end. The liquidation of 2,000 units was recorded at their base cost of $12 per unit even though the year-end liquidation was estimated to be only 500 units. Units purchased during the last half of 20X4 are expected to have an average cost of $16 per unit. Prior to the detection of this error, the income for the first 6 months of 20X4 was $38,000.*

b) *During the third quarter of 20X4, the company decided to change its method of accounting for depreciable assets. The effect of the change was to decrease prior years' income by $65,000, increase the first 6 months' income by $7,000, and increase the third-quarter income to $32,000.*

c) *During the fourth quarter of 20X4, the company decided to discontinue an operation with the following realized and unrealized income (loss):*

> Pre-measurement date:
>> Prior years (20X3 and 20X2) . . . . $(27,000)
>> First 6 months of 20X4 0
>> Third quarter of 20X4 . . . . (8,000)
>> Fourth quarter of 20X4 . . . . (7,000)
> Post-measurement date:
>> Fourth quarter of 20X4 . . . . (6,000)
>> 20X5 operations . . . . (22,000)
>> 20X5 disposal of assets 26,000

Fourth-quarter income from continuing operations was $16,000, and annual tax credits were actually $2,000.

d) *During the first quarter of 20X5, the continuing operations generated income of $28,000. The discontinued operation reported operating losses of $24,000 with projected gains on disposal of assets of $20,000. These latter amounts are in lieu of the earlier post-measurement-date estimates for 20X5 generated in the fourth quarter of 20X4.*

e) *The statutory tax rate is 30%, and income and tax credit projections were as follows:*

Quarter	Balance of Year Projected Income (Loss)	Projected Annual Tax Credits
First 6 months, 20X4:		
Originally	$(70,000)	$5,000
After change in depreciation.	(52,000)	5,000
After eliminating discontinued operations . . .	(52,000)	5,000
Third quarter, 20X4:		
Originally	(30,000)	1,000
After eliminating discontinued operations . . .	11,000	1,000
First quarter of 20X5	82,000	6,000

> f) Income as originally reported in the prior 2 years was $18,000 in the second prior year and $16,000 in the first prior year and was taxed at a rate of 25%. Future income in the carryforward period is not considered likely.

Required:

Calculate the interim income and tax expense for all the quarters of 20X4 and the first quarter of 20X5.

Problem 12-7.   At the end of the first quarter of 20X9, Interco reported pretax income from continuing operations of $30,000 and projected another $60,000 of income for the balance of the year. It was estimated that certain tax credits totaling $6,000 would be available during the year.

Midway through the second quarter, the company decided to change its method of computing depreciation. The change had the following effects:

	Incremental Impact on Pretax Income
Prior years	$25,000
First quarter	7,000
First half of second quarter	4,000
First-quarter projection for the balance of the year	22,000

The second quarter resulted in a pretax loss of $80,000, which was based on the newly adopted depreciation method. Unfortunately, a loss of $2,000 was projected for the balance of the year. The estimated amount of annual tax credits was reduced to zero.

Due to the poor results in the first half of the year, a decision was made in the third quarter to discontinue an operation. The discontinued operation had the following profits and losses:

	Income (Loss)
Pre-measurement-date realized effects traceable to the discontinued operation:	
First quarter	$(20,000)
Second quarter	(60,000)
Third quarter	(10,000)
Portion of earlier projections traceable to the discontinued operation:	
First-quarter projection	(15,000)
Second-quarter projection	(62,000)

Post-measurement-date effects traceable to the discontinued operation:

Third quarter	(8,000)
Fourth-quarter estimate	(50,000)
Subsequent-year estimate	70,000

The third-quarter pretax income from continuing operations was $30,000 with a projected income of $20,000 for the balance of the year. It was estimated that annual tax credits of $2,000 would be available to the company in the fourth quarter.

Pretax income from continuing operations in the prior 2 years totaled $10,000, as originally reported. The statutory tax rate for the prior and current years is 30%. The likely income estimated for next year is $100,000 from continuing operations.

Required:

Prepare in good form the calculation of the income (loss) and tax expense (benefit) for the first 3 quarters of 20X9. Include restated quarters as needed, and prepare a schedule showing the calculation of the effective tax rates.

Problem 12-8.   Tress Corporation is a rapidly growing company that has diversified into a number of different segments. The following partial trial balance, which includes the effect of intercompany transactions, is for the year ended December 31, 20X9:

Net Sales	$(14,332,250)
Cost of Goods Sold	7,180,000
General and Administrative Expenses	1,620,000
Gain on Sale of Fixed Asset	(100,000)
Investment Income	(315,000)
Interest Income	(162,000)

Tress Corp. has five distinct segments (A-E) in addition to corporate operations. Net sales are allocated to the segments as follows:

Segment	Net Sales
A	$ 4,023,500
B	2,749,000
C	574,500
D	6,185,250
E	800,000
Total	$14,332,250

Ten percent of D's sales are made to A, and 7% of B's sales are made to C. The cost of the goods sold to A by D is $200,000, and the cost of the goods sold to C by B is $144,000. The total cost of goods sold is allocated to the segments by the following percentages: A 30%, B 29%, C 6%, D 24%, and E 11%. Of the items C purchased from B, 25% are included in C's ending inventory.

Of general and administrative expenses, 20% are traceable to corporate operations. The balance is allocated in proportion to the segment revenues, including interest income and the gain on the sale of the fixed asset.

Investment income is traceable to corporate operations.

(continued)

Interest income is traceable directly to the segments and the corporate level as follows:

Segment A	$48,000
Segment B	10,000
Segment C	0
Segment D	60,000
Segment E	12,000
Corporate level	32,000

Unconsolidated assets are identifiable as follows:

	A	B	C	D	E	Corporate
Current assets	$ 912,000	$ 681,000	$ 305,000	$ 309,000	$ 389,000	$ 115,000
Property, plant, and equipment (net)	7,136,000	4,643,000	1,480,000	4,181,000	1,543,000	1,737,000

Included in B's property, plant, and equipment is a machine that B purchased at the beginning of the year from A for $300,000. Segment A originally purchased the machine for $250,000, two years prior to the sale. Accumulated depreciation (straight-line method) on the machine was $50,000 at the time of the sale. Segment B recorded $30,000 of depreciation on the machine for the year based on the straight-line method. The gain on the sale of equipment is included in A's revenue.

Required:

1. Assuming that segments A, B, and D are reportable, prepare a schedule that discloses the revenues, operating profits or losses, and assets for each of the reportable segments and all "all other" segments.
2. Prepare a schedule which reconciles the above amounts to the respective enterprise consolidated amounts.

Problem 12-9.   Autoplus International is a publicly traded company which manufactures and distributes a number of products for use within the automobile industry. Major products are categorized as follows:

A. Automobile collision repair equipment
B. Automobile battery and starter parts
C. Automobile seating and safety belts
D. Automobile paints and trim parts
E. Automobile tire retreading equipment
F. Miscellaneous automobile products

The chief operating decision maker for the enterprise uses information organized by product groups for purposes of evaluating performance and allocating resources. Intersegment transactions can be summarized as follows:

Selling Segment	Buying Segment	Cost of Sales	Selling Price	Amount Included in Ending Inventory of Buying Segment
Miscellaneous Products	Battery and Starter Parts	$2,540,000	$ 3,556,000	$420,000
Paint and Trim Parts	Collision Repair Equipment	4,500,000	5,400,000	720,000
Seating and Safety	Collision Repair Equipment	1,650,000	2,200,000	440,000

For the year ended December 31, 20X7, amounts allocated to the segments are as follows:

Segment	Revenues (including inter-segment activity)	Cost of Sales	General and Administrative Expenses	Total Assets	Long-Lived Assets
A	$24,840,000	$17,560,000	$ 2,480,000	$ 45,720,000	$ 34,250,000
B	6,470,000	4,250,000	1,120,000	14,780,000	10,100,000
C	13,850,000	7,560,000	1,840,000	37,500,000	21,500,000
D	25,500,000	18,650,000	4,570,000	47,800,000	32,000,000
E	4,780,000	3,100,000	980,000	13,950,000	8,540,000
F	8,650,000	4,320,000	2,130,000	16,570,000	9,870,000
Corporate	6,750,000	0	4,730,000	29,860,000	15,500,000
	$90,840,000	$55,440,000	$17,850,000	$206,180,000	$131,760,000

The products of the enterprise are sold throughout the world. The percentage of revenues from external customers (excluding corporate revenues) and long-lived assets (including corporate assets) traceable to various geographic areas are, respectively, as follows:

Percentage of	United States	United Kingdom	Italy	Germany	Mexico	All Other Foreign
External sales traceable to:	51%	20%	10%	5%	9%	5%
Long-lived assets traceable to:	54	21	8	4	10	3

Required:

1. Determine which of the segments are considered to be reportable and whether the guidelines regarding the number of reportable segments have been satisfied.
2. Given the available information, prepare all of the necessary schedules and disclosures regarding the enterprise's segments, geographical areas and reconciliations to consolidated amounts.

The Disclosure of Earnings Per Share and Information about Capital Structure

The measurement of the earnings of a corporation is affected by a variety of complex revenue and expense recognition concepts. Corporate earnings are significant with respect to the evaluation of an entity's past and future operations. These earnings are useful in predicting future dividend yields and capital appreciation. Shareholders are obviously interested in knowing how much of the total corporate earnings accrue to them, individually. Therefore, earnings are reported on a per share basis in order to facilitate analysis by individual shareholders. The importance of earnings per share information has been demonstrated by both theoretical analysis and empirical research dealing with security valuation and dividend policy.

The Importance of Earnings Per Share Information

Although the prediction of future earnings is extremely important, earnings per share data is designed to measure the performance of a corporation over a given historical reporting period. This information, although of a historical nature, may be a useful input into a predictive process. To the extent that there are securities outstanding during the current period which have the potential of becoming common stock, consideration should be given to the potential effect such securities may have on earnings per share. Furthermore, given the global nature of capital markets, it is desirable that the measurement of earnings per share data be consistent between companies operating in various countries in order to achieve international comparability. Although the determination of earnings varies among countries, the methodology for calculating Earnings Per Share (EPS) discussed in this chapter is compatible with standards of other countries and that of the International Accounting Standards Committee (IASC).

Merely reporting earnings per common share is not adequate to meet the needs of users because of the existence of potentially dilutive shares. Potentially dilutive shares, or potential common shares, are represented by securities which do not currently have the right to participate fully in earnings of the corporation but may have the right to do so at some future point in time. The right to such future participation is by virtue of the security's option or conversion rights which will result in the security becoming common shares. Certainly, this potential dilution is important to users in that it may reduce the per share amounts of dividends to be distributed and increase the number of shares over which capital appreciation is to be allocated. A major objective of per share information is to present users with a range of earnings per share possibilities ranging from no potential dilution to maximum dilution. Notice that the focus is on providing a conservative measure of potential dilution. Securities which would have an antidilutive affect on earnings are not included in this information.

In order to meet the needs of users, two measures of EPS are required to be presented by public companies. Public companies are those entities whose securities trade in a public market, either in a stock exchange or over-the-counter market, or where a filing has been made or is in the process of being made with a regulatory agency in preparation for the sale of securities in a public market. Public companies will be reporting EPS data for each quarter and the respective year to date. Although not required, nonpublic companies may provide EPS data. The two measures of earnings per share data are referred to as basic and diluted earnings per share.[1]

Basic Earnings Per Share

Basic earnings per share is a measure which reflects the performance of the entity over the reporting period and does not reflect possible dilution traceable to potential common shares. Basic earnings per share (BEPS) is computed by dividing the earnings traceable or attributable to common shareholders (the numerator) by the weighted average number of common shares outstanding during the reporting period (the denominator). Earnings traceable to common shareholders are initially measured as net income from continuing operations[2] less dividends declared during the period on preferred stock and/or current period dividends in arrears on cumulative preferred stock. The same procedure is also applied to net income. However, if there is a loss from continuing operations or a net loss, the loss is increased by the amount of the above preferred dividends. The weighted average number of common shares outstanding is the arithmetical mean average of shares outstanding during the period. Although weighting the shares on a daily basis would be most precise, less precise averaging methods, such as weighting on a monthly basis, may be used as long as they produce reasonable results.

It is important to note that the calculation of the weighted average number of shares should include contingently issuable shares if all necessary conditions required by such shares have been satisfied[3] by the end of the reporting period (i.e., issuance of such shares is no longer contingent). To summarize, BEPS is calculated as follows:

$$\text{Basic Earnings Per Share} = \frac{\text{Adjusted Net Income (ANI)}}{\text{Weighted Average Number of Shares Outstanding during the Period (S)}}$$

Where: ANI = Net income from continuing operations reduced by applicable preferred dividends

S = The weighted average number of common shares outstanding during the period, including contingently issuable shares where the necessary conditions have been satisfied

---

1 Statement of Financial Accounting Standards No. 128, *Earnings per Share* (Norwalk, CT: Financial Accounting Standards Board, 1997).

2 If an entity does not have a discontinued operation but does have an extraordinary item or cumulative effect of a change in accounting principle, net income before such items should be used in lieu of net income from continuing operations; for example, net income before extraordinary items.

3 Such shares are considered to be outstanding common stock as of the date that all necessary conditions have been satisfied. At that point, the issuance of the shares is no longer contingent and Basic Earnings Per Share (BEPS) should reflect the certainty that these shares will be issued. For example, assume a contingent share agreement calls for the issuance of 10,000 shares for each new location established. If a new location is established on June 1, 20X3, the resulting shares will be considered to be outstanding for $\frac{7}{12}$ of a year for purposes of calculating 20X3 BEPS.

Computation Guidelines for Basic Earnings Per Share (BEPS)

Illustration 13-1 provides an example for the computation of BEPS. A careful analysis of the illustration reveals the following computational guidelines which must be considered:

1. The per share amounts are initially calculated using the measure of net income from continuing operations. This per share amount is referred to as the "control number" and is used to determine whether potential common shares considered in the calculation of diluted earnings per share are dilutive or antidilutive.

2. The net income from continuing operations is adjusted to reflect current-period dividends declared (whether or not they are paid) on preferred stock or current-period arrearages on cumulative preferred stock. Note that, even though the cumulative preferred stock was in arrears for both 20X1 and 20X2, the net income for 20X2 was reduced only by the 20X2 arrearage. The 20X1 arrearage was used to reduce the net income for 20X1. Reducing the 20X2 net income for both years of arrearage would result in double counting the effect of the 20X1 arrearage.

3. The weighted average number of shares outstanding during the period included the common shares which would be issued due to the satisfaction of all necessary conditions required by contingently issuable shares. Note that, in the illustration, only Contingent Share Agreement A is considered, because it was the only one to have satisfied all necessary conditions as of year-end.

4. The weighted average number of shares outstanding during the period which is used to calculate BEPS for net income from continuing operations is also used to calculate BEPS for other categories of income such as extraordinary items and the cumulative effect of a change in accounting principle.

5. If a stock dividend or stock split (including a reverse stock split) occurs during the reporting period, the number of common shares outstanding prior to that time must be restated to reflect the change in capital structure.

6. If a stock dividend or stock split (including a reverse stock split) occurs subsequent to the end of the reporting period but before issuance of the financial statements, the per share computations for the current and all prior periods presented must be based on the revised number of shares in order to reflect the change in capital structure.

Illustration 13-1
Computation of Basic Earnings Per Share

a. Net income for the current year ended December 31, 20X2 is as follows:

Income from continuing operations before cumulative effect of changes in accounting principles	$840,000
Cumulative effect of changes in accounting principles	120,000
Net income	$960,000

b. 20X2 dividends on preferred stock are as follows:

Annual dividend declared on Class A preferred stock	$ 40,000
Annual arrearage on Class B cumulative preferred stock	20,000

The Class B preferred stock is also in arrears for 20X1 in the amount of $20,000.

(continued)

c.   An analysis of the common stock account reveals the following changes in the number of shares considered outstanding during the current year:

Date	Item	No. of Shares
1/1	Beginning balance	100,000
5/1	Purchase of treasury stock	(10,000)
7/1	2-for-1 stock split	90,000
10/1	Contingent issuance of stock	30,000

The weighted average of shares outstanding is as follows:

Time Span	No. of Shares	Weight (in months)	Share-Months
1/1–4/30	100,000 × 2	4	800,000
5/1–6/30	90,000 × 2	2	360,000
7/1–9/30	180,000	3	540,000
10/1–12/31	210,000	3	630,000
Total		12	2,330,000

Weighted average number of shares: 2,330,000 divided by 12 = 194,167

d.   On December 1, 20X1, management approved the following contingent share agreements:

Contingent Share Agreement A—30,000 shares (adjusted for the stock split) of common stock will be issued in early 20X3 if 20X2 year-to-date net income from continuing operations exceeds $700,000. The contingency was satisfied at the end of the third quarter of 20X2.

Contingent Share Agreement B—30,000 shares (adjusted for the stock split) of common stock will be issued in the first quarter of 20X4 if net income from continuing operations for the year 20X3 exceeds $950,000.

Note that the weighted average number of shares calculated in item c above includes the 30,000 shares of stock from Contingent Share Agreement A that has been satisfied. These shares have been weighted for $\frac{3}{12}$ of a year since the agreement was satisfied as of October 1, 20X2.

e.   The calculation of BEPS for the year 20X2 is as follows:

	Income (numerator)	Shares (denominator)	Per Share Amount
Income from continuing operations	$840,000		
Less: Preferred stock dividend—Class A	(40,000)		
Preferred stock dividend—Class B	(20,000)		
Income available to common stockholders	$780,000	194,167	$4.02
Cumulative effect of change in accounting principle	120,000	194,167	0.62
Net income available to common stockholders	$900,000	194,167	$4.64

Diluted Earnings Per Share (DEPS)

Diluted Earnings Per Share (DEPS) is a measure designed to show the dilutive effect of potential common shares which were outstanding during the reporting period. Although such shares do not have a current right to participate in earnings, potential common shares may have a right to do so in the future. Generally, potential common shares are represented by options, warrants, convertible securities, and/or contingently issuable shares which, through their exercise, conversion, or subsequent satisfaction of certain conditions, may result in the issuance of additional common shares. Once again, it is important to note that this calculation includes only potential common shares which will have a dilutive effect on earnings per share. Antidilutive securities would either increase earnings per share or decrease the loss per share. An antidilutive effect will always result if either

1. There is a loss from continuing operations, or
2. A loss to common shareholders as a result of net income from continuing operations being less than the relevant preferred dividends.

In order to provide a measure of maximum dilution, the most advantageous (lowest) exercise price per share, in the case of options or warrants, or the most advantageous (highest) conversion rate, in the case of convertible securities, from the standpoint of the security holder should be used.

The numerator in the calculation of DEPS is the same as that for basic earnings per share increased by the after-tax effect on earnings from the assumed transition of potential common shares into outstanding common shares. For example, if a convertible bond were assumed to be converted, then net earnings would be increased by the after-tax interest expense which would not have been incurred during the period had the bond been converted. Any other nondiscretionary expenses which would be affected by the assumed conversion, such as bonuses or profit-sharing expenses, would also have to be included in the calculation of the income effect. The denominator in the calculation of DEPS is the same as that for BEPS increased by the weighted average number of additional shares that would have been outstanding had the potential common shares been issued. For example, if a convertible bond was in existence for the last half of a 12-month reporting period and could have been converted into 10 common shares, the numerator would have been increased by 5 shares per bond (10 shares times $\frac{6}{12}$ of a year). To summarize, DEPS is calculated as follows:

$$\text{Diluted Earnings Per Share} = \frac{\text{Adjusted Net Income (ANI)} + \text{Income Adjustment (IA)}}{\substack{\text{Weighted Average Number of Shares} \\ \text{Outstanding during the Period (S)} + \\ \text{Share Adjustment (SA)}}}$$

Where: IA = The income adjustment traceable to each dilutive potential common share

SA = The share adjustment traceable to each dilutive potential common share

Options and Warrants

Call options and warrants represent rights to acquire shares of common stock in exchange for a cash exercise price in accordance with underlying agreements. The following securities are also considered the equivalent of options and warrants: convertible securities allowing or requiring the payment of cash at conversion, stock purchase contracts, stock subscriptions not fully paid, and compensation plans providing for the issuance of common stock. However, if stock options are performance based in that they are contingent upon satisfying conditions in addition to the mere passage of time, they are not considered to be options but, rather, contingently issuable shares.

Options and warrants will not be included in DEPS unless their effect is dilutive. Their effect will be antidilutive if, during the reporting period, the average market price of the common stock obtainable upon exercise is less than the exercise price per share.

Dilutive options and warrants are assumed to be exercised at the beginning of the period or at their issuance date, if later. The assumed exercise of the options and warrants would result in the generation of cash in an amount equal to the exercise price per share multiplied by the number of shares obtainable. If the exercise price per share varies over time, the price most favorable (lowest) to the holder should be used. The hypothetical funds generated by the assumed exercise of the securities could be used, hypothetically speaking, in a variety of ways. For example, the funds could be used to reduce debt and, thereby, reduce interest expense, to purchase short-term securities as an investment, or to expand the business and, thereby, earn the corporation's return on investment. Recognizing that some use of the exercise proceeds must be assumed, even though there is no certainty that the assumed use will coincide with the actual use of the proceeds, it is important to adopt a solution which is consistent between entities, is not extremely complex, and deals with the dilutive effect of options or warrants in a practical manner. The solution, which is also consistent with international accounting standards, is to use the *treasury stock method*.

The treasury stock method assumes that shares of common stock are issued upon exercise of the option or warrant and that the exercise proceeds will, in turn, be used to acquire treasury stock at the average market price for the reporting period. Therefore, the net difference between the assumed issuance of shares and the assumed repurchase of shares represents an incremental share adjustment which will increase the denominator used in the calculation of DEPS. This method most often does not require an income adjustment. However, if a warrant allows or requires the tendering or retiring of debt, an income adjustment would be necessary. This adjustment would be equal to the net-of-tax interest on debt.

For each option or warrant, the share adjustment under the treasury stock method is determined by using the following formula:

$$\text{Share Adjustment (SA)} = \text{Total Shares Obtainable upon Exercise of Security} - \frac{\text{Exercise Proceeds}}{\text{Average Market Price of Shares}}$$

The share adjustment will always be a positive number because options or warrants cannot influence DEPS unless the effect is dilutive, i.e., unless the average market price is greater than the exercise price. When the market price per share is greater than the exercise price, the option or warrant is said to be "in the money." The share adjustment must be converted into a weighted average in those instances where the security was not outstanding during the entire period.

For example, if an option which exists at the beginning of the year is actually exercised at the beginning of the fourth quarter, the incremental shares assumed to be issued under the treasury stock method will be weighted for that portion of the reporting period during which the option was outstanding (i.e., ¾ of a year) and the actual shares actually issued upon exercise will be weighted for that portion of the period during which they were actually outstanding (i.e., ¼ of a year). It is important to note that the assumed repurchase of treasury stock is based on the use of the average market price of common stock for the period during which the option or warrant was outstanding. For example, if an option is actually exercised during the reporting period, the treasury stock method will use the average market price of the shares prior to exercise. The average market price used should be a meaningful average and usually is based on the average of weekly or monthly closing prices of the common stock.

To demonstrate the treasury stock method, assume that options to acquire 4,000 shares of common stock were granted on January 1, 20X2, and still are outstanding as of December 31, 20X2. The options expire 2 years from the date of the grant and can be exercised at a price of $12 per share. BEPS prior to considering the options is $2, based on 25,000 shares. Assuming an average annual market price of $13.25, DEPS would be computed as follows:

Income adjustment (IA): Not applicable

Share adjustment (SA):

$$
(SA) = \frac{\text{Total Shares Obtainable}}{\text{upon Exercise of Security}} - \left[\frac{\text{Exercise Proceeds}}{\frac{\text{Average Market}}{\text{Price of Shares}}}\right]^{*}
$$

$$
= 4,000 - \frac{(\$12 \times 4,000)}{\$13.25} = 4,000 - 3,623
$$

$$
= 377 \text{ shares}
$$

*The maximum number of treasury shares that could be acquired assuming all options are exercised and all treasury shares are purchased at the average market price.

DEPS considering option

$$
DEPS = \frac{ANI + IA}{S + SA}
$$

$$
= \frac{\$50,000 + 0}{25,000 + 377} = \$1.97
$$

When the reporting period is longer than three months, a *quarterly averaging technique* should by used in applying the treasury stock method. However, if market prices are relatively stable during the year, the treasury stock method may be applied on an annual basis using the annual average market price, as was done in the previous example. The quarterly averaging technique as well as the concepts affecting the application of the treasury stock method for options and warrants to be considered in the computation of DEPS are demonstrated in Illustration 13-2.

Illustration 13-2
DEPS Computations: Options and Warrants

1. At the beginning of 20X2, 250,000 shares of common stock were outstanding. The weighted average number of shares outstanding for the year was 250,500. The income from continuing operations for 20X2 was $400,000.

2. During 20X2, the following stock warrants existed:

    Warrant X—10,000 warrants were issued in 20X0, giving the holder of each warrant the right to purchase 1 share of common stock for $40. 1,000 warrants were exercised on June 30, 20X2.

    Warrant Y—5,000 warrants were issued in 20X0, giving the holder of each warrant the right to purchase 1 share of common stock for $55 anytime after December 31, 20X5.

(continued)

3.   Relevant market price information for 20X2 was as follows:

Quarter	Average Market Price
1	$41
2	43
3	49
4	39

Calculation of Income and Share Adjustments for DEPS

Stock Warrant X

Income adjustment: Not applicable
Share adjustment:

Using the Quarterly Averaging Technique

Quarter	Shares Obtainable	Treasury Shares Acquired	SA
1	10,000	$\dfrac{\$400,000}{\$41} = 9,756$	244
2	10,000	$\dfrac{\$400,000}{\$43} = 9,302$	698
3	9,000	$\dfrac{\$360,000}{\$49} = 7,347$	1,653
4	9,000	$\dfrac{\$360,000}{\$39} = 9,231$	0*
			2,595

Weighted average SA: 2,595 ÷ 4 = 649 shares

*The option is antidilutive in the fourth quarter because the exercise price per share is greater than the average market price.

Stock Warrant Y

This warrant is not considered in the calculation of DEPS because it has an antidilutive effect in all quarters due to the exercise price of $55 per share exceeding the average market prices.

The calculation of diluted earnings per share for the year 20X2 is as follows:

	Income (numerator)	Shares (denominator)	Per Share Amount
Income from continuing operations	$400,000		
Less: Preferred stock dividend	0		
Basic earnings per share			
Income available to common stockholders	$400,000	250,500	$1.60
Warrants		649	
Diluted earnings per share			
Net income available to common stockholders + assumed conversions	$400,000	251,149	$1.59

Note that the share adjustments for a given period are not retroactively adjusted for subsequent changes in the average market price of the common stock.

Stock-based compensation arrangements with employees are also considered the same as options. They are viewed as being outstanding as of the date of grant even if the employees' right to such shares has not yet vested. Furthermore, if dilutive, such shares should be included in the calculation of DEPS even if the employee is not yet able to receive or sell the shares. The treasury stock method is applied to stock-based compensation arrangements; however, the assumed proceeds used to purchase treasury shares are calculated differently. The assumed proceeds consist of a) any cash amounts the employee must pay at exercise, b) the amount of measured compensation cost which has not yet been recognized (as compared to compensation cost traceable to past services and already recognized), and c) the tax benefit traceable to the excess amount of deduction taken for tax purposes over the amount of compensation expense recognized for financial reporting purposes.

If a stock-based compensation arrangement may be paid either in common stock or cash, a decision must be made as to whether the arrangement should be considered for purposes of calculating DEPS. The decision will be based on facts available each reporting period. However, it is generally assumed to be settled in common stock if the effect is more dilutive.

The reverse of a call option may exist if the reporting entity has a written put option or forward purchase contract. Such contracts obligate the reporting entity to repurchase common stock at an exercise price. If the exercise price is more than the average market price, there will be a dilutive effect as calculated by the "reverse" treasury stock method. This reverse method assumes the following:

1. The issuance of common stock at the average market price in order to generate enough proceeds to repurchase the stock at the obligated exercise price (e.g., if the exercise price is $30 per share and the average market price is $20, 1.5 shares are assumed to be issued in order to generate the needed exercise price of $30).
2. The assumed proceeds from item 1 above are used to repurchase stock at the exercise price.
3. The difference between the number of shares assumed to be issued in item 1 above and the number of shares assumed to be repurchased in item 2 above represents the incremental number of shares. Note that, in order to be dilutive, the exercise price must exceed the market price (item 1 above is greater than item 2 above).

If a reporting entity has purchased a call option or put option on its own stock, the options are not included in the calculation of DEPS. The effect of including the purchased options would be antidilutive.

Contingently Issuable Shares.   Contingently issuable shares are shares whose issuance is contingent upon the satisfaction of certain specified conditions. Generally, the conditions involve one or more of the following:

1. The mere passage of time.
2. The passage of time, along with other conditions.
3. The maintenance of some level of earnings.
4. The attainment of some level of earnings.
5. Changes in the market price of shares.
6. The occurrence of events unrelated to earnings or market prices.

At the end of the reporting period, contingently issuable shares fall into one of two broad categories: a) the necessary conditions have been satisfied or b) the necessary conditions have not been satisfied. In the case of the former, these contingently issuable shares would have been considered as outstanding common shares upon satisfaction of the necessary conditions. As a result, they would be included in the calculation of BEPS.

If the conditions called for by contingently issuable shares have been satisfied by the end of the reporting period, the resulting shares will also be included in the calculation of DEPS. It is important to note that, for DEPS, the shares will be included as of the beginning of the period in which the condition is satisfied or as of the date of the agreement, if later. For year-to-date computations, contingent shares are included on a weighted average basis similar to the approach employed for quarterly averaging under the treasury stock method. To illustrate this concept, assume that a contingent share agreement (dated at the beginning of the year) calls for the issuance of an additional 4,000 shares of common stock if quarterly net income from continuing operations exceeds $300,000. Quarterly net income from continuing operations for quarters 1 through 4 is $250,000, $325,000, $400,000, and $275,000, respectively. The resulting share adjustments for each quarter and for the year are as follows:

BEPS Share Adjustment:	Quarter				
	1	2	3	4	Fiscal Year
Quarter 1 contingency[1]	0	0	0	0	0
Quarter 2 contingency[2]		0	4,000	4,000	2,000[5]
Quarter 3 contingency[3]			0	4,000	1,000[6]
Quarter 4 contingency[4]				0	0

DEPS Share Adjustment:	Quarter				
	1	2	3	4	Fiscal Year
Quarter 1 contingency[1]	0	0	0	0	0
Quarter 2 contingency[7]		4,000	4,000	4,000	3,000[9]
Quarter 3 contingency[8]			4,000	4,000	2,000[10]
Quarter 4 contingency[4]				0	0

1 The condition was not satisfied at the end of the quarter.
2 The condition was satisfied at the end of the quarter and, therefore, the 4,000 shares will be considered to be outstanding for quarters 3 and 4.
3 The condition was satisfied at the end of the quarter and, therefore, the 4,000 shares will be considered to be outstanding for quarter 4.
4 The condition was not satisfied at the end of the quarter.
5 4,000 shares $\times \%_2$ = 2,000 shares.
6 4,000 shares $\times \%_2$ = 1,000 shares.
7 Since the condition was satisfied by the end of quarter 2, the shares will be included as of the beginning of the period in which the condition was satisfied.
8 Since the condition was satisfied by the end of quarter 3, the shares will be included as of the beginning of the period in which the condition was satisfied.
9 (0 + 4,000 + 4,000 + 4,000) ÷ 4 = 3,000 shares
10 (0 + 0 + 4,000 + 4,000) ÷ 4 = 2,000 shares

If the necessary conditions associated with a contingent share agreement have not been satisfied by the end of the reporting period, the calculation of the DEPS share adjustment is more complex. In order to calculate the share adjustment, the actual conditions that exist at the end of the reporting period will be assumed to be the conditions which would exist at the end of the contingency period. Therefore, the need to make projections about future conditions is eliminated, and this allows the user to focus on the historical perspective of earnings per share information. For example, assume that at the beginning of 20X1 a contingent share agreement exists which will result in the issuance of 10,000 common shares if 20X2 net income from continuing operations is in excess of $4,200,000. The net income from continuing operations during 20X1 is as follows:

	Year-to-Date at End of Quarter			
	1	2	3	4
	$1,000,000	$2,800,000	$3,500,000	$4,300,000

The 20X1 BEPS will not include a share adjustment for this contingent share agreement because the necessary condition has not actually been satisfied as of the end of 20X1 (the condition relates to 20X2 income, not 20X1 income). Assuming that the current period values (20X1 values) were the same as those at the end of the contingency period, a share adjustment will exist for DEPS if the condition would have been satisfied given this assumption. The contingently issuable shares will be included as a share adjustment as of the beginning of the period (or the date of the agreement, if later) calculated as follows:

	Quarter				
	1	2	3	4	Fiscal Year
DEPS share adjustment	0[1]	0[1]	0[1]	10,000[2]	2,500[3]

[1] The year-to-date income is assumed to be the income at the end of the contingency period (December 31, 20X2), and it is less than the required condition. Contingency is not satisfied.
[2] The year-end net income of $4,300,000 is assumed to be the income at the end of the contingency period (December 31, 20X2), and it satisfies the condition. The shares will be included as of the beginning of the period in which the condition is assumed to be satisfied.
[3] (0 + 0 + 0 + 10,000) ÷ 4 = 2,500 shares.

If the conditions called for by a contingent share agreement are not actually satisfied at a later date, previously reported DEPS data is not retroactively restated. Furthermore, earlier periods are not retroactively restated if a contingent share agreement which was not previously considered is subsequently satisfied.

Those agreements that call for the issuance of additional shares if certain market price changes occur present a special situation. If market prices at the end of the current period would result in the issuance of additional shares, the calculation of DEPS will include a share adjustment. Assume that a company issued 100,000 shares to a party on January 1, 20X2, when the market price of a common share was $10, for a total market value of $1,000,000 (100,000 × $10). An existing contingent agreement states that, if the market value for these shares is less than $1,000,000 at the end of 20X3, additional shares will be issued so that a total market value of $1,000,000 is achieved. If the market value per share at the end of the first quarter of 20X2 is $9.50, it will require a total of 105,263 shares ($1,000,000 ÷ $9.50) to equal the required total value. Therefore, the first-quarter 20X2 calculation of DEPS would include a share adjustment for the additional 5,263 shares to be issued per the contingent share agreement. Earlier reported amounts would not be retroactively restated if the number of shares ultimately required by the agreement changes.

Convertible Securities

A convertible security allows the holder to convert the security into some number of common shares. For example, a bond or preferred stock may be convertible into common stock. Therefore, a portion of the security's value is generally traceable to the conversion feature. This conversion feature means that the security represents potential common shares which may dilute the basic earnings per share of the issuing company. In order to determine the potential dilutive effect, an income and share adjustment must be calculated for the convertible security using the "if converted" method.

The "If Converted" Method.   For each outstanding convertible security, it is assumed that the security was converted into common stock as of the beginning of the period or the issuance date, if later. Therefore, both a share adjustment and an income adjustment are necessary. The share adjustment is determined by calculating the weighted average number of common shares that would have been outstanding if conversion had taken place. The conversion rate most favorable to the holder should be used. The income adjustment is equal to the net-of-tax interest expense or the preferred stock dividend that would not have been paid or accumulated if the conversion had taken place. Furthermore, the after-tax effect of a premium or discount amortization must be eliminated from income. In the case of convertible bonds, the income adjustment should include *nondiscretionary* adjustments that were based on some measure of net income, e.g., bonus expense or royalty expense. It is important to note that preferred dividends are distributions of net income, not components of net income. Therefore, the income adjustment for convertible preferred stock is not tax effected.

To illustrate, assume that $100,000, 4%, 20-year bonds were issued on July 1, 20X2, at a price of 98. Each $1,000 bond is convertible into 10 shares of common stock, beginning July 1, 20X3. Assuming that the effective tax rate is 40%, the income adjustment and share adjustment for 20X2 would be computed as follows:

Income adjustment:
$$\text{Interest} = [(4\% \times \$100{,}000) + (\$2{,}000 \text{ discount} \div 20 \text{ years})] \times \tfrac{1}{2} \text{ year}$$
$$= \$2{,}050$$
$$\text{Interest after tax} = \$2{,}050 \times (1 - 40\% \text{ tax rate}) = \$1{,}230$$

Share adjustment:
$$\text{Number of shares} = 100 \text{ bonds} \times 10 \text{ shares} = 1{,}000 \text{ shares}$$
$$\text{Weighted average shares} = 1{,}000 \times \tfrac{1}{2} \text{ year} = 500 \text{ shares}$$

Dilutive Effect.   Convertible securities are included in DEPS only if their effect is dilutive. However, it is important to note that an individual convertible security may be dilutive but may be antidilutive or not as dilutive when included with other potential common shares in the calculation of DEPS. In order to ensure that the maximum amount of dilution is shown, an "earnings per incremental share" approach must be developed as follows:

1. For each convertible security, calculate the earnings per incremental share by dividing the relevant income adjustment by the relevant share adjustment.
2. Arrange the convertible securities in the order of increasing earnings per incremental share.
3. Beginning with the security which has the lowest measure of earnings per incremental share, individually include each security in the calculation of DEPS and determine if the effect is dilutive relative to the previous measure of DEPS.
4. If an individually considered security is antidilutive, it will not be included in the calculation of DEPS.

To demonstrate this approach for determining whether convertible securities are dilutive, assume the following:

1.

	Income Adjustment	Share Adjustment	Earnings per Incremental Share
Security A	$9,700	1,000	$9.70
Security B	4,000	1,500	2.67

2. DEPS before considering the above convertible securities is $10, based on 10,000 shares.

If the convertible securities are included in the calculation of DEPS in the order presented above, final DEPS would be as follows:

	Income Available	Common Shares	Per Share	
Before convertibles	$100,000	10,000	$10.00	
Security A	9,700	1,000		
	$109,700	11,000	$ 9.97	Dilutive
Security B	4,000	1,500		
	$113,700	12,500	$ 9.10	Dilutive

Conclusion: Final DEPS is $9.10.

However, if the convertible securities are included in the calculation of DEPS in the order of increasing earnings per incremental share, final DEPS would be as follows:

	Income Available	Common Shares	Per Share	
Before convertibles	$100,000	10,000	$10.00	
Security B	4,000	1,500		
	$104,000	11,500	$ 9.04	Dilutive
Security A	9,700	1,000		
	$113,700	12,500	$ 9.10	Antidilutive

Conclusion: Final DEPS is $9.04.

The above example illustrates that convertible securities will have the maximum dilutive effect on the calculation of DEPS if they are considered in the order of increasing earnings per incremental share.

Earnings Per Share Presentation and Disclosure Requirements

Earnings per share information is required to be presented as follows:

1. For entities that do not have securities representing potential common shares (i.e., a simple versus complex capital structure), basic earnings per share amounts for income from continuing operations and net income should be disclosed on the face of the income statement.
2. For entities that have securities representing potential common shares, basic and diluted earnings per share for income from continuing operations and net income should be shown, with equal prominence, on the face of the income statement.
3. Respective per share amounts for discontinued operations, extraordinary items, and/or cumulative effects of changes in accounting principles may be shown either on the face of the income statement or in the notes to the financial statements. These BEPS and DEPS amounts are based on the number of shares used in the denominator to calculate the per share amounts in item 2 above. It is possible that the DEPS amounts for these items may be antidilutive. However, they are to be reported because a security's dilutive effect is measured only against the control number (BEPS for net income from continuing operations).

4. With respect to comparative financial statements, respective per share amounts should be presented for all periods for which an income statement or summary of earnings is presented.

5. With respect to comparative financial statements, if diluted earnings per share is presented for at least one period, it should be presented for all periods, even if DEPS is the same as BEPS.

6. The above presentation requirements are applicable to interim as well as annual data.

In addition to the above presentation requirements, reporting entities are also required to disclose the following for each period in which an income statement is presented:

1. A reconciliation of the numerators and the denominators of the basic and diluted per share computations for income from continuing operations. The reconciliation shall include the individual income and share amount effects of all securities that affect earnings per share.

2. The effect that has been given to preferred dividends in arriving at income available to common stockholders in computing BEPS.

3. Securities (including those issuable pursuant to contingent stock agreements) that could potentially dilute basic EPS in the future that were not included in the computation of diluted EPS because to do so would have been antidilutive for the period(s) presented.[4]

Accompanying the most recent income statement, an entity must provide a description of any transactions occurring subsequent to the end of the period but prior to issuance that would have materially changed the number of shares used to calculate BEPS and/or DEPS if such transactions had occurred before the end of the period. Such transactions might include the issuance of common stock or convertible securities, the satisfaction of a contingent share agreement, or the exercise of an option.

A comprehensive illustration of the computation of basic and diluted earnings per share and the related disclosure requirements appears in Illustration 13-3.

Illustration 13-3
Comprehensive Illustration of BEPS and DEPS Calculations and Disclosures

1. The Hughes Corporation has income for 20X2 as follows:

Income from continuing operations.	$811,900
Extraordinary loss	(70,000)
Cumulative effect of change in accounting principle	50,000
Net income	$791,900

2. As of January 1, 20X2, 200,000 shares of common stock were outstanding. On May 1, 20X2, the company issued an additional 48,000 common shares. Other changes in the number of shares outstanding have occurred due to the securities in item 3 below.

3. The following potential common shares were present during the year:

Security A— consisting of 4,000 stock options which were granted in 20X0. Each option entitles the holder to 1 share of common stock at an exercise price of $13 through the third quarter of 20X2 and a price of $14 thereafter. One-half of the options were exercised on July 1, 20X2.

Security B— consisting of 1,000 warrants, each exchangeable for 2 shares of common stock at an exercise price per option of $30. The warrants were issued on July 1, 20X2.

---

4 *Op. cit.*, par. 40.

Security C—consisting of 5,000 contingently issuable shares which will be issued if the company opens 20 new store locations by the end of 20X3. As of the end of 20X2, the company had opened 12 new stores. The contingent agreement was dated December 31, 20X1.

Security D—consisting of 20,000 contingently issuable shares which will be issued if the annual net income from continuing operations for 20X3 is at least $800,000. The contingent agreement was dated July 1, 20X2. Prior to the fourth quarter of 20X2, the year-to-date income amounts had never exceeded $650,000.

Security E—consisting of 10-year, 5%, $100,000 convertible bonds, issued on April 1, 20X2, at a price of 102. Each $100 bond is convertible into 8 shares of common stock before 20X3 and 10 shares thereafter.

Security F—consisting of 2,000 shares of 6% cumulative, $10, convertible preferred stock issued in 20X0. Each share of preferred stock is convertible into 1 share of common stock. All of the preferred shares were converted into common stock on October 1, 20X2, and dividends were paid up to the conversion date.

4. The corporate tax rate is 40%.
5. Average market prices per share of common stock during 20X2 are as follows:

First quarter.	$12.00	Third quarter.	$14.50
Second quarter	$15.00	Fourth quarter	$15.50

6. An analysis of the common stock account reveals the following changes in the number of shares outstanding during 20X2:

Date	Item	No. of Shares
1/1	Beginning balance	200,000
5/1	Sale of additional shares	48,000
7/1	Exercise of Security A	2,000
10/1	Conversion of Security F	2,000

The weighted average of shares outstanding is as follows:

Time Span	No. of Shares	Weight (in months)	Share-Months
1/1–4/30	200,000	4	800,000
5/1–6/30	248,000	2	496,000
7/1–9/30	250,000	3	750,000
10/1–12/31	252,000	3	756,000
Total		12	2,802,000

Weighted average number of shares: 2,802,000 ÷ 12 = 233,500

7. The calculation of basic earnings per share for the year 20X2 is as follows:

	Income (numerator)	Shares (denominator)	Per Share Amount
Income from continuing operations	$811,900		
Less: Preferred stock dividend	(900)		
Income available to common stockholders	$811,000	233,500	$3.47
Extraordinary loss	(70,000)	233,500	(0.30)
Cumulative effect of change in accounting principle	50,000	233,500	0.21
Net income available to common stockholders	$791,000	233,500	$3.38

(continued)

8. The calculation of diluted earnings per share for the year 20X2 is as follows:

	Income (numerator)	Shares (denominator)	Per Share Amount
Income from continuing operations	$811,900		
Less: Preferred stock dividend	(900)		
Basic earnings per share			
Income available to common stockholders	$811,000	233,500	$3.47
Options—Security A (see Note A)		234	
Warrants—Security B (see Note B)		16	
Contingently issuable shares— Security C (see Note C)			
Contingently issuable shares— Security D (see Note D)		5,000	
Convertible bonds— Security E (see Note E)	2,160	7,500	
Convertible preferred stock— Security F (see Note F)	900	1,500	
Diluted earnings per share			
Net income available to common stockholders + assumed conversions	$814,060	247,750	$3.29

Note A: Calculation of the share adjustment for the stock options—Security A

Quarter	Dilutive*	Shares Obtainable	Treasury Shares Acquired	SA
1	No			—
2	Yes	4,000	$\dfrac{\$52,000}{\$15} = 3,466$	534
3	Yes	2,000	$\dfrac{\$26,000}{\$14.50} = 1,793$	207
4	Yes	2,000	$\dfrac{\$28,000}{\$15.50} = 1,806$	194
				935

Weighted average SA: 935 ÷ 4 = 234

* Dilutive if average market price is greater than exercise price.

Note B: Calculation of the share adjustment for the stock warrants—Security B

Quarter	Dilutive*	Shares Obtainable	Treasury Shares Acquired	SA
1	Not issued			—
2	Not issued			—
3	No			—
4	Yes	2,000	$\dfrac{\$30,000}{\$15.50} = 1,935$	65
				65

Weighted average SA: 65 ÷ 4 = 16

(continued)

Note C: The contingency is not assumed to be satisfied. The actual conditions existing at the end of the reporting period are assumed to exist at the end of the contingency period. The 12 new stores which actually exist do not satisfy the required 20 stores.

Note D: Because the level of net income at the end of 20X2 is assumed to be the value of income at the end of the contingency period, the desired level of maintained income is assumed to have been attained. The condition is assumed to have been satisfied in the fourth quarter of 20X2. Therefore, the contingently issuable shares will be included as a share adjustment as of the beginning of the fourth quarter $(20,000 \times \frac{3}{12} = 5,000)$.

Note E: The income adjustment for the convertible bonds is calculated as follows:

$$IA = [(5\% \times \$100,000) - (\$2,000 \text{ premium} \div 10 \text{ years})] \times \\ \frac{9}{12} \text{ year} \times (1 - 40\% \text{ tax rate}) = \$2,160$$

The share adjustment is 1,000 bonds $\times$ 10 shares $\times \frac{9}{12}$ year = 7,500

Note F: The income adjustment for the convertible preferred stock is calculated as follows:

$$IA = 2,000 \text{ shares} \times \$0.60 \times \frac{9}{12} \text{ year} = \$900$$

The share adjustment is 2,000 shares $\times$ 1 share $\times \frac{9}{12}$ year = 1,500

9. The following is an example of how the earnings per share data might be presented on the face of the income statement:

For the Year Ended 20X2	Basic Earnings Per Share	Diluted Earnings Per Share
Income from continuing operations	$3.47	$3.29
Extraordinary loss	(0.30)	(0.28)
Cumulative effect of change in accounting principle	0.21	0.20
Net income	$3.38	$3.21

10. An example of the disclosure regarding securities that could potentially dilute BEPS but which were not included in the calculation of DEPS is as follows: A contingent share agreement calling for the issuance of 5,000 common shares was outstanding during 20X2. These shares were not included in the computation of diluted earnings per share. The agreement expires at the end of 20X3.

Disclosure of Information about Capital Structure

The presentation and disclosure of information regarding earnings per share may provide a reader of financial statements with a considerable amount of information regarding securities of the subject company. However, not all securities issued may have an effect on earnings per share. Therefore, all entities, whether public or non-public, are required to explain in summary form the pertinent rights and privileges of the various securities outstanding. Such information could include dividend and liquidation preferences, exercise prices for options and warrants, and rates at which securities may be converted into common stock. In addition, the entity must disclose the number of shares which were issued as a result of exercise, conversion, or satisfaction of required conditions during the past fiscal year and any subsequent interim period presented. Information regarding preferred stock liquidation preferences, redemption/call privileges, and cumulative dividend arrearages must also be disclosed. Redemption requirements for any issue of capital stock which is redeemable within the next 5 years must be disclosed.[5]

---

5 Statement of Financial Accounting Standards No. 129, *Disclosure of Information about Capital Structure* (Norwalk, CT: Financial Accounting Standards Board, 1997).

Questions

1. What are potentially dilutive shares, and why is it important for users of financial statements to know about them?
2. How are potentially dilutive shares included in the calculation of basic earnings per share?
3. What is the control number for determining whether a security is dilutive, and how do dividends on preferred stock affect this number for purposes of computing earnings per share?
4. How do stock dividends and/or splits which occur either before or after the end of the reporting period affect the calculation of the weighted average number of shares outstanding?
5. Explain when an option would be considered antidilutive for purposes of computing diluted earnings per share.
6. What effect does vesting have on a stock option plan which is part of an employee's compensation, and when might such an option be treated as a contingently issuable share for purposes of calculating diluted earnings per share?
7. If an option has several exercise prices available in the future, which exercise price is used for the calculation of diluted earnings per share, and why?
8. When is the quarterly averaging technique appropriate for calculating the share adjustment traceable to options or warrants?
9. In the calculation of diluted earnings per share, why is it not necessary to determine an income adjustment for contingently issuable shares which require the attainment of some future level of net income?
10. How do income taxes and an unamortized discount on convertible bonds affect the income adjustment when calculating diluted earnings per share?
11. Why does the income adjustment for a convertible preferred stock not include an income tax adjustment?
12. If a security has an antidilutive effect on earnings per share, how would a user of the financial statements know about the potential future effect such securities could have on earnings per share?
13. Explain what a put option is and how the reverse treasury stock method relates to a put option.
14. If a contingent share agreement is actually satisfied during the reporting period, why is the share adjustment used for BEPS different than that for DEPS?

Exercises

Exercise 1.   Sharp Products has various convertible securities which are summarized as follows:

Security A: 10,000, 10% convertible, 10-year bonds, issued on June 1, 20X4, at 97. Each of the $100 bonds may be converted into 3 shares of common stock after June 1, 20X7.

Security B: 2,000, 7% convertible, 15-year bonds with a $100 face value. These bonds were issued on January 1, 20X3, at 102 and are convertible into common stock as follows:

4 shares per bond after January 1, 20X4
5 shares per bond after January 1, 20X5
6 shares per bond after January 1, 20X7

On August 1, 20X6, 40% of the bonds were converted.

Security C: 5,000 shares of $2.50 preferred stock, $50 par, issued January 1, 20X5, each convertible into 2 shares of common stock after January 1, 20X6.

Calculate the 20X6 annual income and share adjustments for each convertible security. Assume all premiums and discounts are amortized by the straight-line method. The effective tax rate is 40%.

Exercise 2.   Westcor Corporation had the following stock transactions during the year 20X2:

January 1, 20X7	Beginning balance, 1,800,000 shares of common stock.
February 1, 20X7	The corporation purchased 150,000 shares of treasury stock.
April 1, 20X7	The corporation issued a 20% stock dividend.
July 1, 20X7	Preferred stock was converted into 55,000 shares of common stock.
November 1, 20X7	An additional 700,000 shares of common stock were issued.

Calculate the weighted average number of shares for 20X7.

Exercise 3.   At the beginning of 20X5, Webco Company had 200,000 shares of common stock outstanding from continuing operations.

In 20X3, the company issued 25,000 options exercisable into 25,000 shares of common stock with an exercise price of $38 beginning January 1, 20X4. On July 1, 20X5, 4,000 options were exercised when the market price was $44.

Common stock market data are given as follows:

	Average Market Price
First quarter	$36
Second quarter	44
Third quarter	36
Fourth quarter	41

Calculate the 20X5 share adjustments for DEPS.

Exercise 4.   Invesco International has provided key members of management with agreements allowing them to receive additional shares of common stock if certain conditions are satisfied. For each of the following agreements, indicate the share adjustment which would be required for both basic and diluted earnings per share. Assume that the reporting period is the 9-month period ending September 30, 20X4. Pre-tax income from continuing operations for quarters 1 through 3 of 20X4 is $500,000, $850,000, and $700,000, respectively. The effective tax rate is estimated to be 40%.

a) *Agreement A was entered into in 20X3 and calls for the issuance of 10,000 shares of common stock in 20X5.*

b) *Agreement B was entered into on April 1, 20X4, and calls for the issuance of 12,000 shares of common stock if 20X5 pre-tax income from continuing operations is at least $2,800,000.*

c) *Agreement C was entered into on January 1, 20X4, and calls for the issuance of 3,000 shares of common stock for each new retail outlet opened in 20X4. Two outlets were opened in both the first and second quarter of 20X4. One outlet was opened on September 30, 20X4.*

(continued)

d) Agreement D was entered into on July 1, 20X4, and calls for the issuance of additional common shares if 20X5 pre-tax income from continuing operations exceeds $2,000,000. For each $10,000 of pre-tax income in excess of $2,000,000 management will receive 2,000 shares of common stock. However, the total number of shares to be received cannot exceed 25,000.

e) Agreement E was entered into in 20X3 as part of an acquisition of a subsidiary company. The management/owners of the subsidiary received 50,000 shares of common stock as part of the transaction when the shares were trading at $20 per share. The agreement states that, if the aggregate value of the subject shares on August 1, 20X5, has decreased from its original value, additional shares of common stock will be issued to the owners of the shares. The market value per common share at the end of each quarter was $22, $21, and $18 for quarters 1, 2, and 3, respectively.

Exercise 5. Chaplin Industries had net income from continuing operations of $2,597,000 for the year ended December 31, 20X8. As of January 1, 20X8, Chaplin had 550,000 shares of outstanding common stock. An additional 15,000 shares were issued on April 1, 20X8. Chaplin also had 200, 7%, 10-year, $1,000 convertible bonds outstanding which were issued on March 1, 20X7, to be converted after September 1, 20X7. On July 1, 20X8, 25 of these bonds were converted into 1,500 shares of common stock.

On September 15, 20X8, the board of directors declared a 2:1 stock split to be effective October 1, 20X8. The corporate tax rate is 34%.

Calculate basic and diluted EPS for the year ended December 31, 20X8.

Exercise 6. On June 1, 20X4, the Childers Corporation purchased some common stock from the Telluride Corporation. As part of the agreement, Childers agreed to issue 12,000 shares of its common stock to the Telluride Corporation if Childers' net income from continuing operations for the second quarter of 20X4 exceeded $500,000. The second-quarter income was $570,000. On March 1, 20X3, 30,000 options were issued by Childers. Each option was exercisable into 4 shares of common stock at an exercise price of $60 per option. No options were exercised in 20X4, and the average market prices of common stock for quarters 1, 2, 3, and 4 of 20X4 were $16, $13, $18, and $20, respectively.

On August 1, 20X4, Childers sold 10,000, $100 face value, 10-year, 7% convertible bonds at a price of 98. Each bond is convertible into 5 shares of common stock. The company reported net income from continuing operations of $1,300,000 for the year 20X4. The effective tax rate was 40%, and the company had 1,859,000 common shares outstanding throughout 20X4, excluding the shares associated with the contingent share agreement. The basic and diluted earnings per share were $0.697 and $0.691, respectively.

Prepare the necessary disclosures which must accompany the 20X4 income statement.

Exercise 7. Craig Manufacturing has various stock options outstanding during 20X9. All of the options were issued on January 1, 20X9, and are summarized as follows:

Option	Number of Options	Number of Shares Per Option	Exercise Price Per Option
W	2,000	1	$39
X	4,000	1	34
Y	2,000	2	70

At the beginning of 20X9, there were 50,000 common shares outstanding. However, on July 1, 20X9, one-half of the X options were exercised when the market price per share was $36. Income from continuing operations for 20X9 is $250,000. Average market prices for quarters 1 through 4 were $37, $36, $35, and $38, respectively.

Calculate the 20X9 basic and diluted EPS.

Exercise 8.   Dunphry Company had net income from continuing operations of $815,000 for the fiscal year ending March 31, 20X9. Dunphry had 150,000 shares of common stock outstanding as of April 1, 20X8. The company issued 500, $200, 7%, 10-year convertible bonds on January 1, 20X7, at 103. The premium is being amortized by the straight-line method over a 10-year period. Each bond is convertible into 2 shares of common stock. Dunphry also had 10,000 convertible preferred stock shares outstanding on April 1, 20X8. Each preferred share has a quarterly dividend of $1.00 per share and is convertible into 1 share of common stock. All quarterly dividends were declared; however, after March 31, 20Y2, each preferred share may be converted into 1½ shares. In addition, at the beginning of the fiscal year, the company had a contingent share agreement with its officers to issue 30,000 shares of common stock if the net income from continuing operations were to exceed $800,000 in either the current or subsequent year. Quarterly income had never exceeded $250,000 during the fiscal year. The market price of the common stock was $102 at year-end, and the average market price for the year was $80. The applicable tax rate is 38%.

Calculate the basic EPS and diluted EPS for the year ended March 31, 20X9.

Exercise 9.   Earth Corporation has net income of $750,000 for the fiscal year ending September 30, 20X9, including a net extraordinary loss of $200,000 and a net tax gain of $70,000 due to a change in accounting principle. The common stock account on October 1, 20X8, showed 240,000 shares outstanding. The company issued $2,000,000 of 6%, 10-year convertible bonds on June 1, 20X9, at 98. The bonds were dated June 1, 20X9, with interest payable on June 1 and December 1. The bond discount is amortized semiannually on a straight-line basis. Each $100 bond is convertible into 1 share of common stock. On August 1, 20X9, $500,000 of these bonds were converted. The only other securities that the company had outstanding on October 1, 20X8, were 14,000 shares of convertible preferred stock, which return a yearly dividend of $2.25 per share and are convertible into 1 share of common stock for each share of preferred. On December 1, 20X8, an additional 6,000 shares of the same convertible preferred stock were issued at a price of $60 per share. All shares of preferred stock received the full annual cash dividend. The tax rate applicable to Earth Corporation is 48%.

Calculate EPS amounts for all levels of income. Show all schedules and computations in good form.

Problems

Problem 13-1.   Young Industries reported $985,000 of net income from operations before dividends for 20X8. Young had 205,000 shares of common stock outstanding as of January 1, 20X8, purchased 10,000 shares of treasury stock on June 1, 20X8, and declared a 10% stock dividend on August 1, 20X8. In addition, Young had the following securities:

   a)   Class A options with a 1:1 common stock conversion and an exercise price of $30. 40,000 options were issued on January 1, 20X6, and could be exercised after January 1, 20X7.

(continued)

b)   Class B options issued on January 1, 20X5, with an exercise price of $26. Each option is convertible into 1 share of common stock after January 1, 20X8. 30,000 options were issued, and all options were exercised on March 1, 20X8, when the market price was $32.

c)   25,000, 9%, 15-year, $100 convertible bonds issued on January 1, 20X2, at a price of $2,550,000. Each bond is convertible into 3 shares of common stock. The premium is being amortized using the straight-line method.

d)   10,000, 8%, 10-year, $100 convertible bonds issued on January 1, 20X6, at 103. Each of the bonds is convertible into 3 shares of common stock until 20X9, at which time the conversion rate changes to 4 shares. The premium is being amortized using the straight-line method.

e)   40,000 shares of cumulative 5% preferred stock, $50 par value. Dividends are in arrears for both 20X7 and 20X8.

Common stock market price data are given as follows:

	Average Market Price
First quarter	$31
Second quarter	36
Third quarter	34
Fourth quarter	34

The effective tax rate for Young is 25%.

Required:

Calculate basic and diluted EPS for 20X8.

Problem 13-2.   Boyd Manufacturing Company reported net income from operations for the year 20X5 in the amount of $1,140,000 after recognizing income tax expense of $760,000. The weighted average number of shares *actually* outstanding during the period was 560,000. In addition to common shares, the following securities or agreements exist:

Preferred stock: 20,000 shares of preferred stock were issued on June 1, 20X4. Each share has a par value of $50 and has a cumulative dividend of $2.

Stock option A: 5,000 options were issued on March 1, 20X5, for a price of $2 per option. Each option has an exercise price of $23 per option and may be exchanged for common stock as follows:
    1 share per option beginning in 20X5
    1.5 shares per option beginning in 20X7
On September 30, 20X5, 2,000 options were exercised.

5,000, 8% convertible bonds: These 10-year bonds were issued on June 1, 20X5, at a price of 98. Each bond has a face value of $100, pays interest semiannually, and is convertible into 4.5 shares of common stock beginning in 20X6.

12,000, 7% convertible bonds: These 15-year bonds were issued on March 1, 20X3, at a price of 103. Each bond has a face value of $100, pays interest semiannually, and is convertible into common stock as follows:

    4 shares per bond beginning in 20X5
    5 shares per bond beginning in 20X7
    6 shares per bond beginning in 20X9

On November 1, 20X5, 2,000 bonds were converted into common stock.

On June 1, 20X5, the company established a contingent share agreement that would entitle certain employees of the company to receive 55,000 shares of common stock if 20X5 net income before taxes from operations increased 10% over the 20X4 level. The 20X4 pre-tax income from operations was $1,720,000. Quarterly pre-tax income from operations never exceeded $600,000 in any given quarter of 20X5.

	Average Market Price Per Share
20X5:	
First quarter	$24
Second quarter	25
Third quarter	26
Fourth quarter	23

Required:

Compute basic and diluted EPS for the year 20X5.

Problem 13-3.   Tall Tales Publications Inc. is considering several contingent share agreements as part of its purchase of Real Romance Books Corporation. Tall Tales is concerned about the impact on EPS for 20X5. As chief accountant, you must determine the expected share adjustments for each agreement and report to the board of directors. The agreement to purchase Real Romance is expected to go into effect on April 1, 20X5. The contingent share agreements are as follows:

   a) *Real Romance shareholders of record on December 31, 20X6, will receive 40,000 shares of Tall Tales voting common stock on May 1, 20X8.*

   b) *Tall Tales will issue 500 shares of its voting common stock to Real Romance shareholders for every $10,000 of net income over $4,250,000 in 20X5.*

   c) *When annual net income reaches $4,750,000, Real Romance shareholders will receive 40,000 shares of Tall Tales voting common stock. This agreement expires December 31, 20X8.*

   d) *When year-to-date net income reaches $4,300,000, Real Romance shareholders will receive 40,000 shares of Tall Tales voting common stock. This agreement expires December 31, 20X8.*

   e) *The market value of Tall Tales stock on April 1, 20X5, is expected to be $35 per share. Tall Tales will issue 24,000 shares at that time and guarantees the original total stock value ($35 × 24,000) on December 31 of every year through 20X8. If the total value is not maintained, additional shares will be issued each year as necessary.*

Required:

Calculate the share adjustments for both basic and diluted EPS for each of the above agreements, assuming the following 20X5 values:

	Quarter			
	1	2	3	4
Net Income	$2,500,000	$2,100,000	($500,000)	$1,500,000
Common Stock Market Price at End of Period . .	N/A	$ 37.00	$ 32.00	$ 30.00

Problem 13-4. Ward Industries reported third-quarter and year-to-date, 20X7 net income from continuing operations of $620,000 and $2,100,000, respectively. The effective tax rate is 28%. On January 1, 20X7, the company had 800,000 common shares outstanding. The company has had no transactions affecting the number of common shares outstanding during the year to date except for the exercise of certain Class A stock options.

In 20X6, the company issued 50,000 Class A stock options that allow the holder to receive 2 shares of common stock in exchange for an exercise price of $25 per option. On August 1, 20X7, 30,000 of the options were exercised. On July 1, 20X7, the company issued 20,000 Class B stock options that allow the holder to receive 1 share of common stock in exchange for an exercise price per share of $18 during 20X7 and $20 thereafter. Average market prices per common share for quarters 1, 2, and 3 of 20X7 are $13, $15, and $17, respectively.

On August 1, 20X7, the company issued convertible debt with the following features: 10,000 bonds, $100 face value, stated interest rate of 8%, 10-year life, and a conversion rate of 9 shares per bond beginning after 20X8. The bonds sold at 102. On January 1, 20X7, the company agreed to issue 30,000 shares to key management for each new manufacturing facility opened during 20X7. One new facility was opened on September 30, 20X7.

Required:

Compute the basic and diluted EPS for third-quarter and year-to-date 20X7.

Problem 13-5. The following financial statements and additional information relate to Quin Industries:

Quin Industries
Partial Balance Sheet
June 30, 20X8

Current liabilities	
Accounts payable	$ 70,000
15% note payable	75,000
Total current liabilities	$ 145,000
Long-term debt:	
15% note payable, net current portion	$ 150,000
12% convertible $100 bonds, net of $4,800 premium,	
due 6/30/Y8 (in 10 years)	84,800
Total long-term debt	$ 234,800
Stockholders' equity:	
$4 cumulative preferred stock, $100 par, 25,000	
authorized, 10,000 shares issued and outstanding	$1,000,000
Additional paid-in capital—preferred	100,000
Common stock, $10 par, 150,000 shares authorized,	
50,000 shares issued and outstanding	500,000
Additional paid-in capital—common	30,000
Total paid-in capital	$1,630,000
Retained earnings	4,000,000
Total stockholders' equity	$5,630,000
Total liabilities and stockholders' equity	$6,009,800

Quin Industries
Partial Income Statement
For Year Ended June 30, 20X8

Income from continuing operations before extraordinary loss $1,000,000
Extraordinary loss, net of $50,000 tax benefit . . . .   (50,000)

Net income . . . . $ 950,000

The following additional information applies:

a) The 20X8 weighted average number of shares of common stock is
    490,000.

b) On January 1, 20X8, 200 of the $100 bonds were converted into common
    stock.

c) The bond conversion schedule is as follows:

Year of Conversion	Number of Shares per $100 Bond
20X8	10
20X9	12
20Y0	15

All bonds and notes were issued prior to July 1, 20X7. The premium on the 15-year bonds is being amortized on a straight-line basis.

d) On May 1, 20X8, dividends of $1.25 per share were paid to common
    stockholders.

e) Options and warrants—At the 20X8 year-end, the following were
    outstanding:

    Option #1: Issued January 1, 20X6; exercise price, $25; 20,000 options
                exercisable into 20,000 shares of common stock.

    Option #2: Issued July 1, 20X6; exercise price, $30; 8,000 options exer-
                cisable into 8,000 shares of common stock.

    Warrant: Issued December 31, 20X7; exercise price, $50 per warrant;
                30,000 warrants exercisable at 2 common stock shares per
                warrant.

All options and warrants currently are exercisable. None were exercised in the current year.

f) The fiscal year 20X8 average market prices of the common stock were as
    follows:

    First quarter $26
    Second quarter   27
    Third quarter   30
    Fourth quarter   35

g) The tax rate is 50%.

Required:

Using the above information, calculate basic and diluted EPS for the year ending June 30, 20X8. Show EPS amounts for all categories of income.

Problem 13-6.   Nexton Industries has the following securities outstanding as of June 30, 20X9:

Option A: Issued November 1, 20X6; exercise price, $32. The 2,500 options are exercisable into 2,500 shares of common stock beginning September 1, 20X8.

Option B: Issued January 30, 20X7; exercise price of $32 through March 31, 20X9, then $33. The 4,000 options are exercisable into 4,000 shares of common stock. On March 31, 20X9, 2,000 options were exercised when the market price was $35.

7% convertible preferred stock: $40 par, 5,000 shares issued and outstanding for 6 months. Each preferred share is convertible into 1 common share. The stock is not cumulative, and no dividends were declared in the current year.

8% convertible bonds: Issued on May 1, 20X6, at par. Each of the 2,000, $100 bonds was issued with a 1:3 conversion ratio, to be convertible after May 1, 20Y3.

Contingent share agreement, dated January 1, 20X9: Nexton has agreed to issue its officers 10,000 shares of common stock if current-year net earnings exceed $600,000 and will issue an additional 15,000 shares if net earnings exceed $700,000.

Nexton reported net income from continuing operations of $280,000 and $400,000, respectively, for the first 2 quarters of 20X9. Common shares outstanding as of January 1, 20X9, were 250,000. The applicable tax rate is 35%. Common stock average market prices for the current fiscal year are as follows:

First quarter	$33
Second quarter	34

Required:

Calculate basic and diluted EPS for the second quarter and year-to-date ended June 30, 20X9.

PART

4

PARTNERSHIPS

A business may be organized in a variety of ways: as a sole proprietorship, a commercial corporation, a limited liability company, a limited liability partnership, or a regular partnership. Partnerships continue to be a common form of organization, and even the recent limited liability entities have many of the characteristics of a partnership. Assisting business owners in the proper selection of an organizational form is a necessary, yet complex, part of serving the needs of business. A partnership is governed by a partnership agreement or, in some instances, by the Uniform Partnership Act. The partnership agreement must be carefully drafted to cover a variety of topics, including the purpose of the partnership, the responsibilities of the partners, the allocation of profits and losses, the admission or withdrawal of a partner, and the valuation of the partnership given changes in the ownership structure. Changes in the ownership structure provide insight into some of the basic factors which must be considered in valuing a business, whether it be a partnership or not. In addition to special financial accounting principles governing partnerships, such entities are also required to follow different rules for determining income and basis for tax purposes. If a decision is made to terminate a partnership, several legal doctrines and special accounting procedures must be applied in order to produce an equitable distribution of partnership assets.

Partnerships: Characteristics, Formation, and Accounting for Activities

A partnership is an association of two or more people for the purpose of carrying on a trade or business as co-owners. Partnerships continue to be a popular form of organization for many smaller businesses as well as certain larger businesses. Common examples of partnerships include professional services, such as the practice of accounting or law, real estate investment/development companies, and a variety of smaller manufacturing concerns.

In a majority of states, the legal nature and functioning of a partnership is governed by the Uniform Partnership Act (UPA). The UPA deals with such topics as the rights of partners, relations with persons dealing with the partnership, and the dissolution and termination of a partnership.

Characteristics of a Partnership

Practicing accountants frequently are asked to advise clients regarding the formation of a business and the accounting for the business activities. Often, a choice must be made between a partnership and a corporate form of organization. Therefore, it is important for accounting students to understand the basic characteristics of a partnership and the related accounting implications.

Relationship of Partners

A partnership represents a voluntary association of individuals carrying out a business purpose. In this association, a *fiduciary relationship* exists among the partners, requiring them to exercise good faith, loyalty to the partnership, and sound business judgment in conducting the partnership's business. An individual partner is viewed as a co-owner of partnership property, creating a *tenancy in partnership*. When specific assets are contributed by a partner, they lose their identity as to source and become the shared property of the partnership. Without the consent of all partners, such property cannot be utilized by any partner for personal purposes.

The relationship between partners also is characterized as one of *mutual agency*, which means that each partner is an agent for the other partners and the partnership when transacting partnership business. Therefore, in carrying on the business of the partnership, the acts of every partner bind the partnership itself, even when a partner commits a wrongful act or a breach of trust. However, if a partner has no authority to act for the partnership and the party with whom the partner is dealing knows this, the partnership is not bound by the partner's actions.

Legal Liability of a Partnership

Partnerships are classified as either general or limited regarding liability of the partners. In a *general partnership*, the partners act publicly on behalf of the partnership and are personally liable, jointly and severally, for the unsatisfied obligations of the partnership. This unlimited liability is in sharp contrast to the limited liability of a corporation and its shareholders. Thus, if a partnership were insolvent, the unsatisfied creditors could seek to recover against the net personal assets of individual partners. Newly admitted partners, who are personally liable for partnership debts incurred subsequent to this admission, are liable for debts of the previous partnership only to the extent of their capital interest in the partnership.

In contrast, a *limited partnership* consists of one or more general partners and one or more limited partners who contribute capital but do not participate in the management of the company. The one or more general partners have unlimited liability as in the case of a general partnership. However, the limited partners' liability for partnership obligations is restricted to a stated amount, usually equal to their capital interest in the partnership.

The legal liability of partners is obviously a serious factor to consider when assessing whether a partnership is the appropriate form of organization. One could argue that unlimited liability, as a matter of social policy, is a good thing. Society has a right to be protected from the consequences of serious errors in judgment whether they be unintentional or intentional. However, without proper limits, such exposure to liability may also impair an entity's ability to provide useful goods or services. Virtually every product or service industry, from cigarette manufacturers to the medical profession, has been affected by liability issues. For example, the public accounting profession has had to operate in such a litigious environment that major initiatives have been undertaken in response to the legal liability crisis.

In response to this growing concern, two new forms of organization have been created, a *limited liability company* (LLC) and a *limited liability partnership* (LLP). The LLC is a hybrid form of organization which has many of the advantages of both a partnership and a corporation, but few of the disadvantages of either. Similar to a corporation, shareholders of an LLC do not have personal legal liability for actions undertaken by the entity. This limited liability does not necessarily protect an individual shareholder from personal liability for his/her own wrongs. This is consistent with common law doctrine which views each individual as being responsible for the consequences of his/her own negligence and the ability of courts to "pierce the corporate veil" in order to seek recovery for wrongdoings.

An LLP is a sub-category of general partnerships. The LLP compares favorably to limited or general partnerships with respect to liability. All partners in an LLP may participate in management (unlike limited partners) and still have limited liability. Partners in an LLP are **not personally** jointly and/or severally liable for obligations of the partnership arising from the omissions, negligence, wrongful acts, misconduct, or malpractice of other partners. However, a partner does remain personally responsible for liabilities arising from his/her own actions and the actions of those who are acting under the partner's actual supervision and control in the specific activity in which the action occurred.

Underlying Equity Theories

Equity theories relate to how an entity is viewed from an accounting and legal viewpoint. These theories deal with the question of who is the entity. For example, an entity may be viewed as being providers of capital, individual owners (partners/shareholders), management, or a separate, distinct legal entity. Partnerships have been primarily affected by the *proprietary theory*, which looks at the entity through the eyes of the owners. Characteristics of a partnership that emphasize that the entity is viewed as the individual owners include the following:

■   Salaries to partners are viewed as distributions of income rather than a component of income.

■   Unlimited liability of general partners extends beyond the entity to the individual partners.

■   Income of the partnership is not taxed at the partnership level but, rather, is included as part of the partners' individual taxable income.

■   An original partnership is dissolved upon the admission or withdrawal of a partner.

Partnerships also have been influenced by the *entity theory* which views the business unit as a separate and distinct entity possessing its own existence apart from the individual partners. This theory is characteristic of corporations; yet, it is the basis for certain partnership characteristics. For example, a partnership may enter into contracts in its own name. Also, property contributed to a partnership by individual partners becomes the property of the partnership, and the contributing partner no longer retains a claim to the specific assets contributed.

Formation and Agreements

A partnership may come into existence without having to receive formal, legal, or state approval and may result simply from the actions of the parties involved. This lack of formality may be viewed as an advantage of a partnership. However, it is still necessary to carefully plan and evaluate various factors affecting the partnership. Forward and formal thinking when organizing a partnership will benefit both the business and its partners.

In order to properly capture the intent of the partners involved, it is advisable to develop a written partnership agreement. Critical issues that must be addressed include: admission of partners, withdrawal of partners, and the allocation of profits and losses. Such an agreement is referred to as the *articles of partnership* and, at minimum, should include the following provisions:

1. Partnership name and address.
2. Partners' names and addresses.
3. Effective date of partnership.
4. A description of the general business purpose and the limited duration of such purpose, if applicable.
5. Powers and duties of partners.
6. Procedures governing the valuation of assets invested.
7. Procedures governing the admission of a new partner(s).
8. Procedures governing the distribution of profits and losses.
9. Procedures governing the payment or receipt of interest on loans (versus capital contributions) among partners.
10. Salaries to be accrued to partners.
11. Withdrawals of capital to be allowed each partner and the determination of what constitutes excess withdrawals.
12. Procedures governing the voluntary withdrawal, disability, death, or divorce of a partner and the determination of the procedures for valuing the partner's interest in the partnership.
13. Matters requiring the consent of all partners.
14. The date when the profits and losses are divided and the partnership books are closed.
15. The basis of accounting (e.g., accrual or cash).

As the accounting for a partnership is developed more fully in this text, it will become apparent that the articles of partnership provide crucial guidance. Even though the UPA covers certain topics found in the articles of partnership, it is important to note that **many sections of the UPA are applicable only in the absence of a**

partnership agreement. Legal and accounting issues affecting a partnership are often best resolved by evaluating the intent of the partners as set forth in a partnership agreement, rather than looking to the UPA.

Acceptable Accounting Principles

There is a general presumption that an entity's financial position and results of operations should be accounted for in conformity with generally accepted accounting principles (GAAP). As GAAP have developed and become more complex, many have questioned the applicability of such principles to smaller business organizations, a large number of which are organized as partnerships. In response to this concern, it is recognized that, in some circumstances, a basis or method of accounting other than GAAP may be appropriate and may not adversely affect the fairness of the financial statements.

The Auditing Standards Board of the American Institute of Certified Public Accountants (AICPA) recognizes several other comprehensive bases of accounting (OCBOA) other than GAAP, including

- The cash (receipts and disbursements) basis of accounting and modifications of the basis, such as a modified accrual basis.
- The tax basis of accounting based on taxation principles that are used to file an income tax return.

Tax-basis accounting generally consists of a cash-basis format or an accrual-basis format with certain exceptions primarily resulting from tax regulations differing from GAAP. The tax basis of accounting is a frequent choice of many partnerships. Depreciation accounting can be used to illustrate the focus of tax-basis accounting. Assume a depreciable asset has an economic useful life of six years and is consumed uniformly over its life. If accrual accounting were used, it would seem that the asset should be depreciated over six years using the straight-line method of depreciation. However, adoption of the tax basis of accounting could involve the use of a shorter life and an accelerated depreciation method. Furthermore, in some instances tax-basis accounting would allow the immediate expensing of depreciable assets even though such treatment would not be justified by accrual accounting.

The recognition of these other comprehensive bases provides many smaller and more specialized entities, many of which may be partnerships, with an acceptable alternative to GAAP. The use of OCBOA will not impair the fairness of their financial statements as evaluated by outside independent accountants. In practice, it is very common to find partnerships using a comprehensive basis of accounting other than GAAP. Due to the special tax aspects of a partnership, many such entities use the tax basis of accounting rather than GAAP

Partnership Dissolution

Although a partnership is easily formed and does not need state approval, its life is limited and it may be dissolved much more easily than a corporation. *Dissolution* is defined in Section 29 of the UPA as "the change in the relation of the partners caused by any partner ceasing to be associated in the carrying on as distinguished from the winding up of the business." Generally, a partnership is dissolved upon the death, withdrawal, or bankruptcy of an individual partner (owner). The admission of a new partner also results in the dissolution of the former partnership. Thus, any change in the association of the individual partners is termed a dissolution.

Although dissolution occurs when there is a change in a partner's association with the other partners, it does not necessarily result in the termination of the basic business function. Therefore, a change in the ownership structure dissolves the former partnership, but often this change results in the formation of a new partnership to carry on the business purpose of the original partnership. The dissolution of a partnership resulting from the admission or withdrawal of a partner is more fully discussed in Chapter 15 of this text.

Tax Considerations

Unlike corporations, a partnership is not a separate taxable entity but a conduit through which taxable income or operating losses pass to the tax returns of the individual partners. The partnership must file an information return (Federal Form 1065) detailing the partnership revenues and expenses which pass through to the individual partners.

Even though a partnership is not a taxable entity, accounting for partnerships for tax-reporting purposes can become extremely complex. The tax code does not view a partnership as a separate, distinct entity but focuses, rather, on the individual partners. Therefore, activities of the partnership must be evaluated from a tax standpoint based on their impact on individual partners. This viewpoint results in special rules which must be understood by practicing accountants. Furthermore, the unique tax-related aspects of a partnership must be understood in order to advise clients as to whether the partnership form of organization is appropriate. The appendix to this chapter discusses in greater detail the tax-related aspects of a partnership.

Accounting for Partnership Activities

The activities of a partnership consist of several phases, including the initial contribution of capital to the partnership. This initial phase provides the capital necessary to begin operating activities. The remainder of this chapter discusses accounting for the partners' capital investments and the allocation of operating profits and losses among the partners. Although partners' capital investments may be subsequently influenced by partners entering or exiting the partnership and the liquidation of a partnership, these topics are discussed in the next chapter.

Contributions and Distributions of Capital

The capital contributed by shareholders to a corporation is accounted for in several accounts including capital stock, paid-in capital in excess of par, and retained earnings. Unlike a corporation, the capital investment in a partnership generally is accounted for through two accounts for each partner, a temporary account referred to as the **drawing account** and a permanent account referred to as the **capital account.**

It is not unusual for a partner to withdraw available assets (typically cash) from a partnership throughout the year. Preferably, the amount and timing of a partner's withdrawal of assets should be addressed in the articles of partnership. Practically speaking, however, withdrawals are often informal and are not easily projected due to cash flow constraints. In some instances, withdrawals in excess of some amount are considered to be direct reductions of a partner's capital account rather than a withdrawal. Some partnerships view any withdrawal as a direct reduction of a capital account. However, in some partnerships a separate account referred to as a drawing account is used to record a partner's withdrawal of capital. Withdrawals of assets, regardless of how accounted for, reduce the overall net capital of individual partners and the partnership.

A partner's withdrawals also include payments that are made by the partnership on behalf of an individual partner. For example, if a partnership pays off an individual partner's automobile loan, this is no different than if the partner had withdrawn the cash from the partnership and then paid off the loan personally.

The drawing account is a temporary account and is periodically closed to the partner's capital accounts. The balance sheet of a partnership, therefore, will present only the capital account balances of the partners. To summarize, the drawing account established for each partner is debited and credited for the following transactions:

Drawing Account

Debit	Credit
Periodic withdrawals of partnership assets up to a specified amount	Closing of balance to partner's capital account

Each partner's interest in the net assets of the partnership is measured at book value in the capital account established for that partner. This account indicates the destination of capital (claims to net assets) upon dissolution of the partnership. It is important to note that the capital balance does not normally reflect the fair market value or tax basis of the partner's interest in the net assets of the partnership.

To summarize, the partner's capital account is debited and credited for the following transactions:

Capital Account

Debit	Credit
Withdrawals in excess of a specified amount	Initial and subsequent investments of capital
Closing of a net debit balance in the partner's drawing account	Partner's share of partnership profits
Partner's share of partnership losses	

As is the case with all entities, the investment of capital in a partnership should initially be measured at the fair market value of all tangible and intangible assets contributed. An individual partner's liabilities that have been assumed by the partnership also should be recorded at fair market value.

The exception to this would be in the case where a partnership has adopted the tax basis of accounting. The appendix to this chapter discusses how a partner's interest in capital is measured for tax purposes. The proper valuation of each partner's net investment of capital is extremely important. For example, if an asset invested by a partner is initially undervalued by the partnership and is sold immediately for a gain, all the partners share in the realized gain, which properly should have accrued to the original investing partner.

The post-closing balances in the capital accounts of the various partners represent each partner's interest in the net assets of the partnership at a point in time. A partner's interest in the partnership is different from the partner's interest in the profits and losses of the partnership. To illustrate, assume partners A and B have capital balances of $8,000 and $32,000, respectively. Also assume that profits and losses are allocated to partners A and B in the amount of 40% and 60%, respectively. These profit and loss ratios should not be confused with the partners' capital ratios which are 20% ($8,000 divided by $40,000) and 80% ($32,000 divided by $40,000) for A and B, respectively.

Occasionally, partners will loan assets to the partnership, or the partnership will loan assets to partners. It is important from a legal standpoint to differentiate between a loan and an additional investment of capital, especially when the liquidation of a partnership occurs. The nature of such transactions should be made clear by examining the intent of the individual partner or the partnership. If the contribution by a partner is really an additional investment of capital, it should be accounted for in the partner's capital account. However, if the transaction is truly a loan, it should be accounted for in a separate loan account for the partner, and provision for the payment of interest on the loan should be made.

Illustration 14-1 demonstrates the use of various partnership accounts in order to record partnership activity.

Illustration 14-1
Examples of Accounting for Partnership Activity

Event	Entry		

Partner A contributes cash to the partnership. Partner B contributes inventory and office equipment, and the partnership assumes the liability associated with the equipment. The equipment was recorded by B at a book value of $6,000. However, the equipment's fair market value is $4,000.	Cash. . . . .
	Inventory . . . .
	Office Equipment . . . .
	    Note Payable . . . .
	    Partner A, Capital . . . . .
	    Partner B, Capital . . . . .
		10,000
		5,000
		4,000
			
			2,000
			10,000
			7,000

Partner B loans the partnership $3,000 to be repaid in one year at a stated annual interest rate of 6%.	Cash. . . . . Partner B, Loan	3,000	 3,000
A personal debt owed by Partner A is paid by the partnership.	Partner A, Drawing . . . . . . Cash.	500	 500
Partners A and B withdraw cash of $500 and $1,200, respectively. Drawings in excess of $1,000 are viewed as excessive withdrawals and are charged against capital.	Partner A, Drawing . . . . . . Partner B, Drawing . . . . . . Partner B, Capital . . . . Cash.	500 1,000 200	 1,700

The net income of the partnership is divided equally between the partners.	Income Summary. . . . .
	    Partner A, Capital . . . . .
	    Partner B, Capital . . . . .
		10,000	
			5,000
			5,000

The partners' drawing accounts are closed to their respective capital accounts.	Partner A, Capital . . . .
	Partner B, Capital . . . .
	    Partner A, Drawing . . . .
	    Partner B, Drawing . . . .
		1,000
		1,000
			
			1,000
			1,000

The Allocation or Division of Profits and Losses

An important process to be outlined in the articles of partnership is the manner in which profits and losses are to be divided among the partners. There are several alternative methods of allocating profits and losses. However, if the articles of partnership are silent on this point, Section 18 of the UPA states that profits and losses are to be divided equally among the partners. The division of partnership income should be based on an analysis of the correlation between the capital and labor committed to the firm by individual partners and the income that subsequently is generated. As a result, profits might be divided in one or more of the following ways:

1. According to a ratio.
2. According to the capital investments of the partners.
3. According to the labor (or service) rendered by the partners.

Profit and Loss Ratios.   Partnership agreements frequently call for the allocation or division of profits and losses according to some ratio. Normally, the ratio set forth for the division of profits also is used for the division of losses, unless a specific provision to the contrary exists. This method obviously provides a simplified way of dividing profits and, if approached properly, may provide an equitable division as well. Theoretically, the ratio should attempt to combine into one base the capital and service contributions made by the respective partners. Again, it is important to note that a partner's interest in profits and losses is often different from the partner's interest in total partnership capital (net assets).

To illustrate this method, assume the articles of partnership state that partnership profits and losses should be divided between Partners A and B in the ratio of 60:40. Partnership income of $20,000 would be divided as follows:

	Partner A	Partner B
Income to partners:		
A: 20,000 × 60%	$12,000	
B: 20,000 × 40%		$8,000

Capital Investment of Partners. The capital investments of the partners, represented by the balances in their respective capital accounts, may be employed as a basis for dividing a portion of the profits. The division is accomplished by imputing interest on the invested capital at some specified rate. This interest is not viewed as a partnership expense but, rather, as a means of allocating profits and losses among the partners. Typically, the balance of profits not allocated on the basis of invested capital is allocated according to some profit and loss ratio.

When the partners' capital investments are to be used as the basis for allocating profits, the partnership agreement should specify the following:

1. Whether the respective partners' capital balances are to be determined before or after the partners' year-to-date withdrawals recorded in their drawing accounts are offset against their capital accounts.
2. Whether the amount of capital investment for allocation purposes is to be:

    a) *capital at the beginning of the accounting period,*

    b) *capital at the end of the accounting period, or*

    c) *weighted-average capital during the accounting period.*

3. The rate of interest to be imputed on the invested capital.

With respect to the first point, it is important that the partnership agreement clearly establish how invested capital is to be determined. Since each partner's equity is really a combination of capital and drawing account balances, partners' drawings may be offset against the balances in their respective capital accounts for purposes of allocating income based on invested capital. However, a partnership agreement may state that only withdrawals above a certain limit are to be viewed as offsets against capital balances. It is possible for a partnership agreement to call for interest to be imputed only if the amount of invested capital exceeds some prescribed limit or average amount.

To illustrate the use of invested capital as a basis for allocating partnership profits, assume that

1. Partnership profit is $20,000.
2. Interest on invested capital is to be imputed at the rate of 10%. (Capital is determined before considering withdrawals.)
3. Profits not allocated on the basis of invested capital are to be allocated equally among the partners.
4. The capital accounts of Partners A and B, just prior to the closing of their drawing accounts, are as follows:

Partner A, Capital

10/1/X1	30,000	1/1/X1	100,000
		7/1/X1	10,000

Partner B, Capital

4/1/X1	10,000	1/1/X1	60,000

If interest is to be imputed on the partners' invested capital at the beginning of the period (1/1/X1), the partnership profit of $20,000 would be allocated as follows:

	Partner A	Partner B	Total
Interest on beginning capital:			
A: 10% × $100,000	$10,000		$10,000
B: 10% x $60,000		$6,000	6,000
			$16,000
Balance per ratio (equally).	2,000	2,000	4,000
Allocation of profit	$12,000	$8,000	$20,000

If interest is to be imputed on the partners' invested capital at the end of the period (12/31/X1), the partnership profit of $20,000 would be allocated as follows:

	Partner A	Partner B	Total
Interest on ending capital:			
A: 10% × $80,000	$ 8,000		$ 8,000
B: 10% × $50,000		$5,000	5,000
			$13,000
Balance per ratio (equally).	3,500	3,500	7,000
Allocation of profit	$11,500	$8,500	$20,000

If interest is to be imputed on the partners' weighted average invested capital during the period, the partnership profit of $20,000 would be allocated as follows:

	Partner A	Partner B	Total
Interest on weighted average capital:			
A: 10% × $97,500 (Schedule A)	$ 9,750		$ 9,750
B: 10% × $52,500 (Schedule B)		$5,250	5,250
			$15,000
Balance per ratio (equally).	2,500	2,500	5,000
Allocation of profit	$12,250	$7,750	$20,000

Schedule A
Weighted Average Capital of Partner A

(1) Amount Invested	(2) Number of Months Invested	(1 × 2) Weighted Dollars
$100,000	6	$ 600,000
110,000	3	330,000
80,000	3	240,000
	12	$1,170,000

Weighted average capital: $1,170,000 ÷ 12 = $ 97,500

Schedule B
Weighted Average Capital of Partner B

(1) Amount Invested	(2) Number of Months Invested	(1 × 2) Weighted Dollars
$60,000	3	$180,000
50,000	9	450,000
	12	$630,000

Weighted average capital: $630,000 ÷ 12 = $ 52,500

Services Rendered by Partners.   A partner's labor or service to the partnership may be a primary force in the generation of revenue. Normally, the profit and loss agreement recognizes variations in effort by calling for a portion of income to be allocated to partners as salary. Such salaries, like interest on capital investments, are viewed as a means of allocating income rather than as an expense. It is important to note that this treatment of partners' salaries differs from the treatment of employee/shareholder salaries in a corporation, and the difference should be considered when the performance of a partnership is compared with that of a competing corporation.

When dealing with a profit and loss agreement that employs salaries as a means of allocating income, it is important not to confuse such salaries with partners' drawings. For example, a partner's withdrawal of $1,000 a month from the partnership may suggest that $12,000 of partnership income is being distributed to the partner as an annual salary or that these withdrawals may be ignored for purposes of dividing profits. Generally, a partner's drawing is not viewed as a salary but as a withdrawal of assets that reduces the partner's equity. For clarification purposes, the partnership agreement should state whether regular withdrawals of specific amounts should be viewed as salary for purposes of allocating income among the partners.

Bonuses to partners also may be used as a means of recognizing a partner's service to the partnership. Such bonuses are most often stated as a percentage of partnership income either before or after certain other components of the allocation process. Bonuses may be stated in reference to a variety of variables such as sales, gross profit, or a particular component of net income. In its most simple form, the bonus is a percentage of net income. However, if the bonus is to reward service beyond that already recognized by salaries and/or interest, the bonus may be expressed as a percentage of partnership net income after salaries and interest. In some instances, the bonus may be expressed as a percentage of net income after the bonus. To illustrate the calculation of a bonus, assume a partnership has net income of $120,000 of which $60,000 and $5,000 have already been allocated as salaries and interest, respectively. The bonus is defined in the partnership agreement as 10% of partnership net income after salaries and interest. The bonus is calculated as follows:

Bonus = X% (Net Income − Salaries − Interest)
Bonus = 10% ($120,000 − $60,000 − $5,000)
Bonus = 10% ($55,000)
Bonus = $5,500

If the agreement had stated that the bonus would be calculated based on net income after salaries, interest, and bonus, the calculation would be as follows:

$$\text{Bonus} = X\% \text{ (Net Income} - \text{Salaries} - \text{Interest} - \text{Bonus)}$$
$$\text{Bonus} = 10\% \text{ (\$120,000} - \text{\$60,000} - \text{\$5,000} - \text{Bonus)}$$
$$110\% \text{ Bonus} = 10\% \text{ (\$120,000} - \text{\$60,000} - \text{\$5,000)}$$
$$110\% \text{ Bonus} = 10\% \text{ (\$55,000)}$$
$$110\% \text{ Bonus} = \$5,500$$
$$\text{Bonus} = \$5,000$$

Multiple Bases of Allocation.   In many cases, income is allocated to the respective partners by combining several allocation techniques. To illustrate, assume a profit and loss agreement of the ABC Partnership contains the following provisions:

1.   Interest of 6% is to be allocated on that portion of a partner's ending capital balance in excess of $100,000.
2.   Partner C is to be allocated a bonus equal to 10% of partnership income after the bonus.
3.   Salaries of $13,000 and $12,000 are to be allocated to Partners A and C, respectively.
4.   The balance of income is to be allocated in the ratio of 2:1:1 to A, B, and C, respectively.

Notice that these provisions govern the allocation of profit and not the actual distribution of assets.

Assuming a partnership income of $33,000 and ending capital balances of $80,000, $150,000, and $110,000 for Partners A, B, and C, respectively, income is allocated to the partners as shown in Illustration 14-2.

Illustration 14-2
Profit Allocation: Multiple Bases

	Partner A	Partner B	Partner C	Total
Interest on excess capital balance		$3,000	$ 600	$ 3,600
Bonus.			3,000*	3,000
Salaries	$13,000		12,000	25,000
Subtotal	$13,000	$3,000	$15,600	$31,600
Remaining profit.	700	350	350	1,400
Income allocation	$13,700	$3,350	$15,950	$33,000

$$* \text{Bonus} = 10\% \text{ (Net income} - \text{Bonus)}$$
$$\text{Bonus} = 10\% \text{ (\$33,000} - \text{Bonus)}$$
$$(110\%) \text{ Bonus} = \$3,300$$
$$\text{Bonus} = \$3,000$$

Allocation of Profit Deficiencies and Losses.   In the previous examples of profit allocations, the partnership income was large enough to satisfy all of the provisions of the profit and loss agreement. However, if the income is not sufficient or an operating loss exists, one of the two following alternatives may be employed assuming that the agreement governs both the allocation of profits or losses:

1.   Completely satisfy all provisions of the profit and loss agreement and use the profit and loss ratios to absorb any deficiency or additional loss caused by such action.
2.   Satisfy each of the provisions to whatever extent is possible. For example, the allocation of salaries would be satisfied to whatever extent possible before the allocation of interest is begun.

To illustrate these alternatives, assume the same information used in Illustration 14-2 for the ABC Partnership, except that the partnership income is $22,000. In Illustration 14-3, the income of $22,000 is divided by using the first alternative. When studying Illustration 14-3, it is important to note that the allocation of interest, bonus, and salaries results in an excessive allocation or deficiency of $8,600 (subtotal of $30,600 less the income of $22,000), which must be subtracted from the partners' previously allocated amounts. This deficiency is allocated among the partners according to their profit and loss ratios just like a remaining profit, except that the deficiency is subtracted rather than added.

Illustration 14-3
Profit Allocation: Deficiency Allocated in Profit and Loss Ratio

	Partner A	Partner B	Partner C	Total
Interest on excess capital balance		$3,000	$ 600	$ 3,600
Bonus.			2,000*	2,000
Salaries	$13,000		12,000	25,000
Subtotal	$13,000	$3,000	$14,600	$30,600
Deficiency.	(4,300)	(2,150)	(2,150)	(8,600)
Income allocation	$ 8,700	$ 850	$12,450	$22,000

*Bonus = 10% (Net income − Bonus)
Bonus = 10% ($22,000 − Bonus)
(110%) Bonus = $2,200
Bonus = $2,000

Normally, the first method also is used when the partnership has an overall loss. For example, given a partnership loss of $2,400, the methodology in Illustration 14-3 would be employed, except that a bonus would not be recognized.

However, it is possible that a separate provision governs those situations in which a net loss exists. The allocation of the assumed loss of $2,400 is shown in Illustration 14-4. In this case, the allocation of the interest and salaries results in allocating $28,600 of income even though there is a loss of $2,400. This results in a deficiency of $31,000 (subtotal of $28,600 plus the loss of $2,400) which must be allocated among the partners according to their profit and loss ratios.

Illustration 14-4
Loss Allocation: Deficiency Allocated in Profit and Loss Ratio

	Partner A	Partner B	Partner C	Total
Interest on excess capital balance		$3,000	$ 600	$ 3,600
Bonus (not applicable).				
Salaries	$13,000		12,000	25,000
Subtotal	$13,000	$3,000	$12,600	$28,600
Deficiency.	(15,500)	(7,750)	(7,750)	(31,000)
Loss allocation	$(2,500)	$(4,750)	$ 4,850	$(2,400)

The second alternative, which is used less frequently, requires that the provisions of the profit and loss agreement be ranked by order of priority. Assuming the components listed in Illustration 14-3 are already in order of priority, a partnership income of $22,000 would be distributed as shown in Illustration 14-5.

Illustration 14-5
Profit Allocation: Deficiency Allocated by Order of Priority

	Partner A	Partner B	Partner C	Total
Interest on excess capital balance		$3,000	$ 600	$ 3,600
Bonus.			2,000*	2,000
Salaries	$8,528		7,872	16,400
Income allocation	$8,528	$3,000	$10,472	$22,000

$$*\text{Bonus} = 10\% \text{ (Net income} - \text{Bonus)}$$
$$\text{Bonus} = 10\% \text{ (\$22,000} - \text{Bonus)}$$
$$(110\%)\text{Bonus} = \$2,200$$
$$\text{Bonus} = \$2,000$$

The salaries of $16,400 would be allocated to Partners A and C according to the ratio suggested by their normal salaries of $13,000 and $12,000, respectively. Therefore, A would receive 13/25 of the $16,400, or $8,528, while C would receive 12/25, or $7,872.

Special Allocation Procedures.   A partnership profit and loss agreement may include special provisions for handling items that represent (1) corrections of prior years' income or (2) current-period, nonoperating gains or losses. Even though a correction of prior years' income may not satisfy the criteria for a prior-period adjustment, as defined by the Financial Accounting Standards Board, it may be more equitable to allocate the item among the partners according to the profit and loss agreement for the relevant prior period rather than the current period. For example, assume that Partners A, B, and C, who previously shared profits equally, currently share profits in the ratio of 2:2:1. Also assume that, in the current year, the partnership incurs a loss of $10,000 due to the settlement of litigation involving a matter arising in a prior period. Rather than allocating the loss according to the current profit ratios, it may be more equitable to base the allocation on the prior ratios.

A similar procedure may be adopted for the current-period recognition of nonoperating gains or losses. Rather than allocating a gain on the sale of a plant asset according to the partners' current profit-sharing ratios, it may be more equitable to use the ratios that existed during the period when unrealized appreciation actually took place.

To illustrate, assume that land with a basis of $40,000 has been held for three years and is sold for $60,000 in the current period. Based on the assumed profit-sharing ratios of prior periods and amounts of annual appreciation, the $20,000 gain would be allocated to Partners A, B, and C as follows:

| | | | Profit Allocation | | |
Year	Profit Ratio	Appreciation	A	B	C
1	1:1:2	$ 4,000	$1,000	$1,000	$2,000
2	2:1:2	10,000	4,000	2,000	4,000
3	2:2:2	6,000	2,000	2,000	2,000
		$20,000	$7,000	$5,000	$8,000

If the partnership had not established special provisions for handling such items, the gain of $20,000 would have been allocated equally among the partners according to their current profit ratio of 2:2:2.

Appendix: Tax-Related Aspects of a Partnership

As pointed out earlier in this chapter, a partnership is not a separate taxable entity. However, the tax impact of partnership activities must be allocated to the partners and reported by them on their individual tax returns. This process is referred to as the *flowthrough of tax items*. Because the partnership is a conduit for tax purposes, certain elements of revenue and expense maintain their identity on the individual partner's tax return. For example, a partner's share of partnership investment income also will be classified as investment income on the individual return. It is important that certain items maintain their identity on the individual return because they are subject to special limitations and rules. Therefore, accounting for partnership income requires that certain items of revenue and expense be separately reported on the partnership informational tax return.

Tax Basis of a Partner's Interest

Because the partnership is not viewed for tax purposes as a separate distinct entity but, rather, as consisting of separate distinct individuals, the individual partner's interest in the partnership must be measured for tax purposes. This individual interest is referred to as the *partner's tax basis*. The tax basis is primarily used to measure the tax gain or loss resulting from a partner's sale of his/her interest in the partnership. In the most simple of cases, the partner's tax basis is equal to cash contributed plus his/her personal tax basis in other property transferred to the partnership. This personal tax basis would represent the tax basis of the asset before transfer to the partnership.

To illustrate, assume a partner contributes $10,000 cash and equipment with a fair market value of $70,000. The original cost of the equipment less depreciation taken for tax purposes resulted in a personal tax basis of $50,000. The tax and GAAP (book) basis of the partner's interest is calculated as follows:

	Tax Basis	GAAP (Book) Basis
Cash contributed	$10,000	$10,000
Equipment	50,000	70,000
Basis for partner's interest	$60,000	$80,000

Notice that the partner's tax basis in assets prior to transfer is not changed subsequent to transfer. In other words, the individual partner receives no increase (step-up) or decrease (step-down) in basis.

The calculation of a partner's tax basis becomes more complex when personal liabilities are transferred to and assumed by the partnership. A partner's tax basis is decreased by the value of the liabilities assumed by other partners. When the other partners assume a portion of the debt, it is as though that amount of debt has been forgiven. Forgiveness of debt represents income to a taxpayer. This income is eventually recognized upon the sale of a partnership interest because the tax basis has been reduced by this amount; therefore, the gain on the sale is increased by this amount. Alternatively, a partner's tax basis is increased by the value of other partners' liabilities assumed by them. The allocation among partners of liabilities transferred to a partnership is based on the partners' respective profit and loss ratios.

To illustrate, assume Partners A and B contribute assets with personal tax bases of $80,000 and $110,000, respectively. Liabilities associated with these assets are $30,000 and $60,000, respectively for A and B. Profits and losses are allocated 40% to Partner A and 60% to Partner B. The tax basis of the partners is determined as follows:

	Partner A	Partner B
Tax basis of assets contributed	$80,000	$110,000
Tax basis of other partner's liabilities assumed		
(40% of $60,000 for A and 60% of $30,000 for B) . . .	24,000	18,000
Tax basis of liabilities assumed by other partners		
(60% of $30,000 for A and 40% of $60,000 for B) . . .	(18,000)	(24,000)
Tax basis of partner's interest	$86,000	$104,000

It is important to note that the sum of the tax bases of partners' interests ($86,000 plus $104,000 in the above example) must always equal the sum of the tax basis of assets contributed by the partners ($80,000 plus $110,000 in the above example).

The initial tax basis of a partner subsequently changes due to the ongoing activities of the partnership. The basis will be increased by the following:

1. Additional contributions of individual assets.
2. The partner's share (based on profit and loss ratios) of increases in partnership liabilities resulting from:

    a) *Assuming partners' personal liabilities.*

    b) *Direct liabilities of the partnership.*

3. The partner's share of partnership income measured on a tax basis.
4. The partner's share of separately identified items of income not included in tax income (loss).

A partner's basis will be decreased by the following:

1. Distributions of partnership assets.
2. The portion of the partner's additional personal liabilities assumed by the other partners.
3. The partner's share of partnership losses measured on a tax basis.
4. The partner's share of separately identified items of loss not included in taxable income (loss).

A partner's tax basis may not be decreased below zero. If operating losses would decrease the basis below zero, they are carried forward by the partners and used to offset subsequent increases in basis.

Avoidance of Double Taxation

Major differences exist between partnerships and corporations in the area of taxation. These differences result from the fact that corporations, unlike partnerships, are viewed as separate and distinct taxable entities. The primary result of this difference is that a corporation is taxed when the income is earned (assuming an accrual tax basis), and the individual shareholders are taxed when the income is distributed as dividends. This characteristic is referred to as *double taxation*, and its significance depends on the extent to which dividends are distributed and on the tax rates to which the shareholders are subject. The effect of double taxation may be minimized if employee-shareholders do not receive dividends but are rewarded in the form of salaries, which are deductible expenses. However, the Internal Revenue Service must be satisfied that the amount of such salaries is reasonable. A corporation also may attempt to avoid double taxation by accumulating earnings or by electing to be taxed as a partnership through a Subchapter S election.

Rather than distributing taxable dividends, the corporation may retain income so that the shareholders are not currently taxed on that income. However, if the shareholders sell their stock in the corporation and if the stock sells at a price that exceeds its tax basis, the gain on the sale would be taxed at the rate applied to capital gains. In effect, the accumulated earnings then become taxed.

It should be noted, however, that the retention of income may not be practical because of the accumulated earnings tax. This tax is a penalty imposed on a corporation that accumulates its earnings to avoid the income tax that would have been incurred by the shareholders if dividends had been distributed. The intent to avoid taxes may be established by demonstrating that the corporation has accumulated earnings in excess of the reasonable needs of the business. Reasonable needs of the business would include such items as plant expansion, asset replacement, debt retirement, stock retirement, customer-supplier loans, and working capital.

The disadvantage associated with double taxation may be eliminated if a corporation elects to be taxed as a Subchapter S corporation. Under this election, the corporation is treated as a partnership for tax purposes. The corporate entity itself pays no tax, and the shareholders pay tax on their share of corporate income, whether or not it is distributed to them. This special treatment is based on the view that certain corporations, in substance, are the same as a partnership. This analogy is appropriate for nonpublic corporations, in which major shareholders act in the same capacity as partners in a partnership.

The corporation electing to be taxed as a Subchapter S corporation must meet certain requirements. For example, the corporation must have only one class of stock owned by 75 or fewer stockholders. Certain technical procedures also are employed with respect to the determination and classification of taxable income.

A limited liability company (LLC), if properly structured, will be treated as a partnership for federal tax purposes. Most LLCs are formed with the intent of being classified as a partnership for tax purposes and, therefore, must avoid having a majority of its attributes or characteristics suggest a corporate form of organization. The tax code will classify an entity as a corporation rather than a partnership if it has more corporate, versus noncorporate, characteristics or attributes. These characteristics are associates, an objective to carry on business and divide the gains, continuity of life, centralization of management, limited liability, and free transferability of interests. Most LLC agreements are structured to avoid the attributes of continuity of life and free transferability of interests in order to receive tax treatment as a partnership rather than a corporation.

Some of the more significant tax-related differences between a partnership and a corporation are summarized in Exhibit 14-1 on page 14-17.

Exhibit 14-1
Significant Tax-Related Differences
Between a Partnership and a Corporation

	Partnership	Corporation
Level(s) of Taxation	Not a separate taxable entity, but, rather, a conduit through which taxable items are passed on to the owners (partners). The individual partners are taxed on their shares of partnership income, whether distributed or not, at the progressive tax rates applicable to individuals.	A separate, distinct taxable entity apart from the shareholder. Therefore, income is taxed once at the corporate level and again at the shareholder level when such income is distributed, i.e., double taxation.
Maintaining the Identity of Various Elements of Taxable Income	Elements making up a partnership's income maintain their special tax status on the returns of the individual partners; e.g., if a partnership has tax-exempt income, it retains its identity in the preparation of the individual partners' tax returns as tax-exempt income.	Elements making up corporate income do not maintain their special status when distributed to shareholders in the form of a dividend; e.g., if corporate income includes some tax-exempt income, that income will be taxed to the shareholders when distributed in the form of a dividend.

Other Tax   The tax advantages associated with certain fringe benefits are much greater for employee-shareholders than they would be if the employees were partners in a partnership. Such fringe benefits may involve profit-sharing plans, pension plans, medical reimbursement and insurance plans, group life insurance, and death benefits.

Questions

1. With respect to responsibility for the unsatisfied obligations of a partnership, how does a limited partner compare to a general partner?
2. With respect to the allocation of profits among partners, what is the significance of classifying cash received from a partner as a loan rather than contributed capital?
3. Discuss how salaries of partners should be viewed as compared to salaries accruing to shareholders who are also employees of a corporation.
4. Although corporations are generally characterized as being exposed to double taxation, what are some alternatives available to avoid this situation and yet remain a corporation?
5. If a partnership agreement does not specifically identify how profits or losses are to be allocated among the partners, how should they be allocated?
6. Discuss what special allocation procedures might be addressed in a partnership's profit and loss agreement.
7. Under what circumstances might a salary or bonus be more appropriate than interest on capital balances as a means of allocating profits?
8. With respect to the allocation of profits among partners, what is the logic underlying the accounting for "withdrawals in excess of a specified amount" as a direct reduction of the capital account?

9. If a partnership profit and loss agreement involves salaries, interest on capital, and bonuses based on income, how are losses of the partnership generally allocated to the partners?

10. When employing a bonus as a means of allocating profits, why is net income after the bonus, rather than before the bonus, generally used to calculate the bonus?

11. When assets are contributed to a partnership by an individual partner, the partnership's tax basis of the assets is generally not the fair market value at date of transfer. What is the logic underlying this treatment?

Exercises

Exercise 1.   In 20X1, a new partnership purchased land on the edge of the town of Otisville. The partners erected a building and opened a furniture and appliance store under the name of Otisville Furniture Fair. The partnership agreement specified that profits or losses should be shared equally after the allocation of partners' salary allowances and interest on average capital balances.

Otisville has grown considerably, and the store is now one of the most prominent stores in a fashionable suburban area. Good management, imaginative merchandising, and the general growth in the economy have made Otisville Furniture Fair the leading and most profitable company of its type in the Otisville trade area.

Now, the partners wish to admit another investor and incorporate the business. The original partners will purchase at par an amount of preferred stock equal to the book value of their interest in the partnership and common stock equal to that portion of fair market value that exceeds their book value. The new investor will purchase, at a 10% premium over par value, common and preferred stock equal to one-third of the total number of shares purchased by the original partners. The corporation will then purchase the Otisville Furniture Fair partnership at its fair market value from the partners. After the consummation of the partners' plan, the corporation will acquire the partnership assets, assume the liabilities, and employ the partners to manage the corporation.

1. List and explain the differences in terms and valuations that would be expected in comparing the assets that appear on the balance sheet of the proposed corporation and the assets that appear on the partnership balance sheet.

2. List and explain the differences that would be expected in a comparison of an income statement prepared for the proposed corporation and an income statement prepared for the partnership.

(AICPA adapted)

Exercise 2.   A client of yours is forming a partnership and has asked you to review a draft of the partnership agreement. In particular, the client is interested in your thoughts regarding the section dealing with the withdrawal of a partner. Your client also anticipates that the individual partners will make major withdrawals of capital after the fiscal year-end. These withdrawals will be based on a percentage of production fees generated by each of the partners. Selected excerpts from that section are as follows:

A withdrawing partner must notify the partnership of his/her intent to withdraw by registered mail. The partnership has the first right to acquire the withdrawing partner's interest in the partnership and must exercise its right within 60 days. If the partnership is not interested in acquiring the withdrawing partner's interest, then the interest may be sold to an individual partner or another individual. However, any sale to another individual requires the approval of the existing partners. If the partnership exercises its right to acquire the withdrawing partner's interest, consideration paid for the interest will be equal to 60% of the partner's interest in the capital of the partnership as of the end of the fiscal quarter preceding notification to withdraw. Capital balances will be measured in conformity with generally accepted accounting principles. The consideration due will be paid to the withdrawing partner as follows: one-third upon withdrawal and the balance to be paid in equal installments over the next 24 months.

Prepare a memo to your client which communicates your thoughts regarding the agreement.

Exercise 3.   You are asked to provide guidance as to how to allocate profits and losses for the following two partnerships:

1. Riley, Scott, and Thompson are partners in a law firm that practices in several different areas of law including patent law, family law, and corporate law. Each of the partners practices in a different area of law.
2. Norman and Manning is a partnership specializing in tool and die making. The partnership has several major contracts, and the partners work closely with each other on each contract.

Discuss what combinations of bonus, salary, and interest on capital would provide for the most equitable allocation of profit and losses for each of the partnerships described above.

Exercise 4.   Medina, Harris, and Anderson are partners in Entertainment Systems. The partnership earned a modest profit of $30,000 in 20X3. The partnership agreement includes the following regarding the allocation of profits or losses:

a) Interest of 8% is to be paid on the portion of a partner's ending capital balance in excess of $75,000.

b) Medina and Harris receive salaries of $20,000 and $30,000, respectively. Both individuals are actively involved with day-to-day operations.

c) The balance of income is to be distributed in the ratio of 2:1:1 to Medina, Harris, and Anderson, respectively.

Assume ending capital balances of $60,000, $80,000, and $100,000 for partners Medina, Harris, and Anderson, respectively.

1. Allocate the profit among the partners, assuming the following:

a) The profit and loss ratios are used to absorb any deficiency or additional loss.

b) Each of the provisions of the profit and loss agreement is satisfied to whatever extent possible. The priority order is interest, salaries, and then remaining amounts per the profit and loss ratios.

2. Discuss which method would be best suited for this partnership.

Exercise 5.   A client of yours has been offered an attractive position with another company in the specialized tooling and machining industry. As an employee, this position would consist of a salary of $65,000 and a bonus which is estimated to be approximately another $10,000. The client's current employer, a partnership, would prefer that your client not accept this other position and has offered her an ownership interest in the partnership. The partnership agreement would be modified to provide for an allocation of profits and losses as follows:

(continued)

Component	Original Partner A	Original Partner B	New Partner (your client)
Salary.	$50,000	$60,000	$45,000
Bonus as a % of net income after the bonus. . .	5%		
Interest on weighted average capital	10%	10%	0%
Remaining profit or loss %	35%	35%	30%

It is estimated that Partner A's and Partner B's weighted average capital balances would be $185,000 and $115,000, respectively.

Identify the factors your client should consider in deciding whether to take the other position or accept admission into the partnership.

Exercise 6.   Gabriel and Hall are partners in a manufacturing business located in Portland, Oregon. Their profit and loss agreement contains the following provisions:

1. Salaries of $35,000 and $40,000 for Gabriel and Hall, respectively.
2. A bonus to Gabriel equal to 10% of net income after the bonus.
3. Interest on weighted average capital at the rate of 8%. Annual drawings in excess of $20,000 are considered to be a reduction of capital for purposes of this calculation.
4. Profit and loss percentages of 40% and 60% for Gabriel and Hall, respectively.

Capital and drawing activity of the partners for the year 20X5 are as follows:

	Gabriel Capital	Gabriel Drawing	Hall Capital	Hall Drawing
Beginning balance	$120,000	0	$ 60,000	0
April 1	20,000			
June 1		$15,000		$20,000
September 1	30,000			
November 1		15,000	40,000	
Ending balance	$170,000	$30,000	$100,000	$20,000

Assuming net income for 20X5 of $132,000, determine how much profit should be allocated to each partner.

Exercise 7.   Xavier, Yates, and Zale are partners in a dry cleaning business. Their partnership agreement provides that the partners shall receive interest on their respective average yearly capital balances at the rate of 8%. Any residual profits or losses shall be divided equally among the partners. The following information is available for the second year of operations:

a) Partners' capital balances as of January 1, 20X2:

Xavier	$24,000
Yates	17,500
Zale.	13,000

b) Additional investments were made during the year as follows:

Xavier	$4,500 on April 1, 20X2
Zale	$2,000 on July 1, 20X2
	$15,000 on September 1, 20X2

c) The drawing accounts of the partners have the following debit balances at the end of 20X2:

Xavier	$1,000
Yates	1,000
Zale	500

d) Partnership income for the year is $21,100.

1. Discuss the advantages and disadvantages of using the weighted average capital balance as the base for determining interest on capital contributed.
2. Determine the interest on weighted average capital balances that partners Xavier, Yates, and Zale should receive for the year 20X2. Assume that the partners' withdrawals are not to influence the capital balances for purposes of computing interest.
3. Determine the capital account balances for Xavier, Yates, and Zale after all closing entries have been journalized and posted at the end of 20X2. Supporting schedules should be in good form.

Exercise 8.   Powers, Scott, and Riley intend to start a business together that will be organized as a partnership. The partners are considering adopting one of the following two alternative profit-sharing agreements:

		Agreement #1	Agreement #2
Salaries:	Powers	$ 70,000	$ 29,200
	Scott.	30,000	30,000
	Riley.		
Bonus to Powers as a percentage of profit after the bonus		5%	15%
Interest on average capital		8%	10%
Estimated average capital balances:.			
	Powers	$ 50,000	$ 50,000
	Scott.	100,000	100,000
	Riley.	150,000	150,000
Remaining profit percentage			
	Powers	40%	50%
	Scott.	40	35
	Riley.	20	15

Powers seeks your advice as to which agreement would be best for him to accept.

1. Discuss the issues involved in determining the correct choice.
2. Calculate the level of income at which Powers is indifferent between the choices.

Appendix Exercises

Exercise A-1.   Thomas is considering joining Baker and Nap in a partnership. Baker and Nap will each contribute cash of $39,000 to the new partnership. The partners will share profits and losses equally, and all partners have individual tax rates of 30%. Thomas is considering contributing to the partnership a parcel of land that has a fair market value of $99,000 and an individual tax basis of $39,000. If the parcel is contributed to the partnership, the partnership would sell the parcel and distribute $6,000 to each partner in order to pay the resulting individual taxes on the sale. Thomas wants to know if he or she would be better off to personally sell the parcel and contribute the after-tax proceeds to the partnership. How would you advise Thomas?

Exercise A-2.   Berkshire Investments is a partnership consisting of three partners: Pearson, Ellis, and Parker. Pearson and Ellis each have a 40% interest in capital prior to withdrawals and the allocation of profits. Ellis and Parker are considering selling their interest in the partnership and want to estimate the personal tax impact of this sale. The activity of the partnership is summarized as follows:

	Fair Market Value/GAAP Basis	Tax Basis
Contributions of cash:		
Pearson	$ 80,000	$80,000
Ellis	25,000	25,000
Contributions of noncash assets.		
Ellis	100,000	70,000
Parker	60,000	68,000
Liabilities transferred to the partnership.		
Ellis	45,000	45,000
Parker	20,000	20,000
Withdrawals of cash.		
Pearson	30,000	30,000
Ellis	20,000	20,000
Parker	15,000	15,000
Allocation of profits.		
Pearson	30,000	28,000
Ellis	30,000	28,000
Parker	30,000	28,000

1. Calculate the book and tax basis of Ellis' and Parker's interest in the partnership.
2. Discuss why a partner's percentage interest in capital may change over time.

Problems

Problem 14-1.   Durand, Price, and Russell are partners in a business which manufactures garden tools. Their profit and loss agreement has the following provisions:

> Salaries of $40,000, $20,000, and $45,000 for Durand, Price, and Russell, respectively.
>
> Price will receive a bonus equal to 5% of sales in excess of $1,000,000.
>
> All partners will receive a bonus of 10% of net income in excess of $150,000 after the bonus.
>
> Partners will be allocated interest on their weighted average capital balance to the extent that it exceeds $50,000. Drawings in excess of annual salaries will be considered a reduction in capital. Interest is computed at the rate of 10%.
>
> Remaining profits or losses will be allocated 35%, 25%, and 40% to Durand, Price, and Russell, respectively.
>
> Gains or losses from the sale of depreciable assets will be *excluded* from the above provisions and will be equally allocated among the partners.

Activity in the partners' capital and drawing accounts during the year was as follows:

	Durand Capital	Durand Drawing	Price Capital	Price Drawing	Russell Capital	Russell Drawing
Beginning balance	$75,000	$ 0	$125,000	$ 0	$40,000	$ 0
February 1		15,000		25,000	30,000	
March 31		10,000		5,000		15,000
June 1	10,000					
June 30		10,000		5,000		15,000
August 1						
September 30		10,000				15,000
Ending balance	$85,000	$45,000	$125,000	$35,000	$70,000	$45,000

Required:

Determine how annual net income of $200,000 (including a gain on the sale of equipment of $15,000) should be allocated among the partners. Annual sales revenue was $1,100,000.

Problem 14-2.   Nichols, James, and Wilson are environmental consultants who agree to consolidate their individual practices into a partnership as of January 1, 20X4. Each partner is contributing the following assets and related liabilities:

	Nichols	James	Wilson
Fair value of:			
Cash	$20,000	$ 5,000	$20,000
Accounts receivable	24,000	15,000	35,000
Supplies	5,000	2,000	3,000
Equipment	28,000	24,200	34,000
Equipment notes payable	(18,000)	(10,000)	(24,000)
	$59,000	$36,200	$68,000
Tax basis of equipment	$20,000	$24,000	$22,000

The partnership agreement provides for the allocation of profits as follows:

a)   All partners will receive 6% interest on their weighted average capital balances as defined. Capital balances will be reduced by amounts withdrawn in excess of partners' salaries. The resulting weighted average will then be reduced by salaries. Partners with deficit balances will have their profits reduced by the interest on such amounts.

b)   Salaries for Nichols, James, and Wilson are $40,000, $32,000, and $50,000, respectively. All salaries are withdrawn during the year.

c)   Each partner will receive a bonus equal to 20% of individual gross billings in excess of $100,000.

d)   James will receive an extra 10% bonus of net income reduced by the value of items (a) to (c) above.

e)   Remaining profits will be allocated equally among partners.

During the year 20X4, the partnership recognized the following net income components:

(continued)

Gross billings:

Nichols	$120,000
James	80,000
Wilson	180,000

Depreciation expenses:

Book amount	6,120
Tax return amount	20,144
Other operating expenses	203,880

During the year, the partners had the following drawings in excess of their salaries:

	Nichols	James	Wilson
March 1	$10,000		
June 1		$ 4,000	
September 1		12,000	$20,000

Required:

1. Determine how the 20X4 accounting income of $170,000 would be allocated among the partners.
2. Determine the net capital balances for each partner as of December 31, 20X4.
3. Perform the same requirements as for items (1) and (2), but assume the calculations are being made for tax purposes.

Problem 14-3.   A client is seeking your advice on how to organize a new business. The client is proposing to acquire several single-story residences and convert them into group homes for the elderly. Each home would house eight elderly individuals, and the home would be staffed 24 hours a day. Residents would receive housing, food, and daily planned activities for a monthly fee. Group homes are licensed by the state and are closely monitored. Such homes do not provide any direct health care to the residents. The client plans to have an active role in the organization and management of the homes and is seeking another individual or two to provide necessary capital as passive investors. It is anticipated that the homes will operate at a loss for the first twelve to eighteen months. The client hopes to open two group homes for each of the next four years and then sell his interest in the business. Your client is interested in organizing the company as a partnership and wants to know how that might affect him and other potential partners.

Required:

Identify and discuss some of the characteristics of a partnership of which your client should be aware.

Problem 14-4.   Jacobsen, Matthews, and Glorioso are partners in a law firm which specializes in personal injury and medical malpractice litigation. Their fees from clients are contingent upon whether their client receives an award or settlement. Normally, the firm incurs substantial costs, such as expert fees, discovery work, etc., before a case is settled. Furthermore, some cases do not settle in favor of the firm's clients, and then the firm receives no fees from their client. Because of this environment, the partners have agreed to begin each calendar year with each of them retaining at least $150,000 of capital in the business after their respective drawing accounts have been closed. During the year, the three partners each receive a monthly draw of $10,000. At year-end, the net income of the partnership is allocated among the partners, and partners either withdraw capital in excess of $150,000 or make an investment of capital to achieve a balance of $150,000.

Profits are allocated among the partners according to the following terms:

Each partner is allocated a salary of $120,000.

Each partner is allocated 20% of his/her fees collected in excess of $250,000.

Each partner's share of income is *reduced* by the interest on any draws in excess of $10,000 per month. Simple interest is computed at the rate of 10%.

Remaining profits are allocated 35%, 35%, and 30% between Jacobsen, Matthews, and Glorioso, respectively.

Shortly after the beginning of the current year, all three partners had capital balances of $150,000 each. In addition to their normal draws, Matthews and Glorioso had additional draws as follows:

	Matthews	Glorioso
First additional draw:	$30,000	$20,000
Date of draw	April 1	April 1
Date of repayment	June 30	May 31
Second additional draw:		$30,000
Date of draw		August 1
Date of repayment		Not repaid by year-end

Required:

Assuming that net income for the year is $680,000 and fees collected by Jacobsen, Matthews, and Glorioso are $1,200,000, $800,000, and $380,000, respectively, calculate each partner's responsibility with respect to the required year-end capital balance.

Problem 14-5.   Thomas and Purnell are general partners in a partnership along with four limited partners. Ten percent of partnership profit is allocated to each of the limited partners, and the balance of the profits is allocated to Thomas and Purnell as follows:

Salaries of $40,000 and $60,000 to Thomas and Purnell, respectively.

A bonus to Thomas of 10% of sales in excess of $1,200,000.

A bonus to Purnell of 5% of net income after the bonus.

Remaining profits to be allocated 60% and 40%, respectively, to Thomas and Purnell.

The general partners have been approached by Wiggins, who has significant experience in the area of foreign sales and is seeking admission to the partnership. Wiggins is confident that she can generate significant increases in sales and that any capital needed to finance the expansion will be raised and guaranteed by her. Furthermore, Wiggins is proposing that the existing profit agreement be modified as follows:

Wiggins will be allocated a salary of $40,000.

A bonus to Wiggins of 15% of all international sales in excess of $500,000.

Thomas' bonus will be limited to domestic sales only.

Remaining profits to be allocated 40%, 40%, and 20% to Thomas, Purnell, and Wiggins, respectively.

The limited partners are in favor of admitting Wiggins, noting that their opportunities for increased profits would be improved. However, Thomas and Purnell are concerned that unless sales and profits grow significantly, they will receive a smaller allocation of profits than they did before Wiggins. Without Wiggins, the partnership

(continued)

is projecting domestic sales and profits of $1,450,000 and $280,000, respectively, for the next year. Thomas and Purnell feel that if their interest in profits increases $16,000 and $24,000, respectively, they will be inclined to admit Wiggins as a partner.

Required:

Assume that Wiggins is able to generate $700,000 of additional foreign sales which include a 40% gross profit margin and that the general and administrative expenses associated with this increase are 15% of such sales. Prepare an analysis for Thomas and Purnell that summarizes their profit allocation with and without Wiggins.

Problem 14-6.   Carson, Dowman, and Evans own an office automation and consulting business organized as a partnership. Evans is considering retirement from the partnership. In order to more fairly measure Evans' interest in capital, an audit of the company's first two years of operations was performed in early 20X9. The original partnership agreement called for Carson to receive a 10% bonus on income after the bonus, with the remaining profits or losses to be divided as follows: Carson, 30%; Dowman, 30%; and Evans, 40%. Reported income for 20X7 was $44,000. In the second year of operations, the agreement was modified to reflect Evans' decision to become less involved in the business. The new agreement called for Carson still to receive a 10% bonus on income after the bonus, but it altered the allocation of remaining amounts as follows: Carson, 35%; Dowman, 35%; and Evans, 30%. Reported income for 20X8 was $42,000. The partners always had agreed that any adjustment to reported amounts would be allocated based on the profit and loss agreement in effect during the period to which the adjustment relates. The audit indicated that the following items were not properly accounted for:

a)   *20X7:*

   (i)   *Failed to amortize the business name contributed by Carson. The fair market value of the intangible was $50,000 and should have been amortized over a 10-year life using straight-line amortization.*

   (ii)   *Failed to defer prepaid 20X8 insurance premiums of $3,000.*

   (iii)   *A capital withdrawal of $5,000 made by Carson on July 1, 20X7, was classified incorrectly as a Note Receivable.*

   (iv)   *Failed to accrue $2,000 of employee wages on December 31, 20X7.*

   (v)   *Failed to record consulting fees of $8,400 earned in 20X7 but billed in 20X8.*

b)   *20X8:*

   (i)   *Purchases of inventory included a computer invoiced on December 31, 20X8, for $4,000 but not yet received. Terms were f.o.b. destination. The item was not included in the year-end physical inventory.*

   (ii)   *Failed to accrue $8,600 of rent expense on December 31, 20X8.*

   (iii)   *Failed to reverse $3,000 of interest income properly accrued at the end of 20X7, resulting in income recognition in both years.*

Required:

Assume the following unadjusted December 31, 20X8 capital account balances: Carson, $25,000; Dowman, $30,000; and Evans, $28,000. Prepare a schedule to reflect the adjusted capital balances as of December 31, 20X8. Supporting calculations should be in good form.

Appendix Problems

Problem 14A-1.   Fandek and Franklin formed a partnership on January 1, 20X7, and contributed assets and liabilities to the partnership as follows:

	Fandek		Franklin	
	Market Value	Tax Basis	Market Value	Tax Basis
Net assets contributed				
Cash	$ 60,000	$60,000	$10,000	$10,000
Securities			15,000	10,000
Goodwill	12,000	0		
Equipment			65,000	40,000
Equipment loan			(42,000)	(42,000)

Fandek and Franklin will have initial interests in capital of 60% and 40%, respectively, and will equally share profits and losses. The partners also agreed that they would receive monthly withdrawals in the amounts of $2,000 and $3,000, respectively, for Fandek and Franklin. During the year, the company recognized sales of $240,000 and a corresponding cost of sales equal to $144,000 (60% of sales). Of the total sales, $60,000 is uncollected at year-end. These sales are being recognized for tax purposes by the installment method. For accounting purposes only, the goodwill is being amortized over a 3-year period on a straight-line basis. Equipment also is being amortized on a straight-line basis, assuming a 10-year useful life and a $5,000 residual value. For tax purposes, the equipment is depreciated by the Modified Accelerated Cost Recovery System (MACRS) and has a 20X7 depreciation rate of 25%. Of the original securities contributed, securities with a book value and tax basis of $6,000 and $2,000, respectively, were sold for $8,000. The remaining securities have a fair market value of $5,000.

Required:

1. Assuming the partnership reports 20X7 net income of $54,000 in conformity with GAAP, prepare a schedule to reconcile this amount to the tax-basis measure of net income.
2. Calculate the tax basis for each of the partners at the end of 20X7.

CHAPTER

15

Partnerships: Ownership Changes and Liquidation

In theory, a partnership may be viewed as a conduit or entity through which individual partners carry on a common business purpose. It is natural that the circumstances surrounding the individual partners' lives may change and affect their involvement in the partnership. Individual partners may increase or decrease their interest in the partnership or withdraw entirely from the partnership. In turn, new partners may become involved in the partnership. Such ownership changes are common in a partnership just as they are in other forms of organizations, such as a corporation. However, unlike a corporation, which is recognized as a separate and distinct entity having an infinite life, changes in the ownership structure of a partnership result in the dissolution of the previous partnership.

The Uniform Partnership Act (UPA) defines *dissolution* as "the change in the relation of the partners caused by any partner ceasing to be associated in the carrying on as distinguished from the winding up of the business." Sections 31 and 32 of the UPA identify the various causes of dissolution and suggest that the admission or withdrawal of a partner results in dissolution. Although dissolution ends the association of partners for their original purpose, it does not result necessarily in the termination of the partnership's basic business function. The remaining partners may continue to operate the business, or they may decide to terminate, or *liquidate*, the business.

The previous chapter stressed the importance of a well-conceived partnership agreement. Changes in the ownership structure of a partnership are one of the most important areas that should be addressed. Often, the initial concerns of a new partnership are such that the partners overlook the certain reality that, someday, there will be a change in the ownership. Accountants can be of significant help to their clients in advising them in the structuring of buy/sell agreements for the partnership. Proper planning for such changes will help to ensure smooth and equitable transitions.

In certain instances, a partnership may elect not to continue but, rather, liquidate and distribute its net assets to the partners. For example, a partnership may be organized to develop and manage a real estate investment for a designated period of time. At the end of the designated period of time, the partnership will be liquidated. It is important to note that, unlike a dissolution where the partnership purpose continues, a liquidation results in the termination or winding up of the business purpose.

Ownership Changes

Changes in the ownership structure of a corporation are everyday occurrences, as evidenced by the activity of security exchanges. These changes typically involve transactions between existing and prospective shareholders and, therefore, create no special accounting problems for the corporate entity other than updating its listings of stockholders. In the case of a partnership, however, changes in ownership structure are events that require special accounting treatment.

Accounting for changes in the ownership of a partnership is influenced heavily by the legal concept of dissolution. When there is a change in the ownership structure, the original partnership is dissolved and, most often, a new partnership is created. This dissolution and subsequent creation of a partnership indicate that a new legal entity has been created, and accounting should properly measure the initial contributions of capital being made to the new partnership.

Accounting for a partnership is influenced by the *propriety theory*, which views a partnership not as a distinct entity but, rather, as a group of individual investors. Measuring changes in the equity of the individual partners is a major aspect of partnership accounting. Because ownership changes result in the dissolution of the partnership, this provides an excellent opportunity for accounting to measure the current wealth or equity of the partners. Changes in the ownership structure of the partnership are presumed to be arm's-length transactions which reflect the current value of the partnership. Therefore, such changes may indicate that

1. The existing assets of the original partnership should be revalued;
2. Previously unrecorded intangible assets exist that are traceable to the original partnership; *and/or*
3. Intangible assets, such as goodwill, exist that are traceable to a new partner.

In practice, a change in ownership normally suggests the need to both revalue net assets and recognize intangible assets.

Admission of a New Partner

The admission of a new partner requires the approval of the existing partners, although a partner's interest may be assigned to someone outside the partnership without the consent of the other partners. However, **assigning an interest does not dissolve the partnership,** and it does not allow the assignee to participate in the management of the partnership or to review transactions and records of the partnership. The assignee receives only the agreed-upon portion of the assigning partner's profit or loss.

Assuming a new partner has been approved by the existing partners, the new partner, normally, will experience the same general risks and rights of ownership as do the other existing partners. However, creditors presenting claims against the partnership that were incurred prior to admission of the new partner cannot attach the personal assets of the new partner for settlement of their claims. Therefore, the level of liability of a new partner is less than that of an existing partner. Section 17 of the UPA states:

> *A person admitted as a partner into an existing partnership is liable for all the obligations of the partnership arising before his admission as though he had been a partner when such obligations were incurred, except that this liability shall be satisfied only out of partnership property.*

Contribution of Assets to Existing Partnership.   One method of gaining admission to an existing partnership involves contributing assets directly to the partnership entity itself. In this case, the exchange represents an arm's-length transaction between the entity and the incoming partner. If the book value of the original partnership's net assets approximates fair market value, the incoming partner's contribution would be expected to be equal to his/her percentage interest in the capital of the new partnership. For example, if an incoming partner is to acquire a one-fourth interest in a partnership that has a book value and a fair market value of $60,000, the original $60,000 would now represent a three-fourths interest in the new partnership. Therefore, the total partnership capital must be $80,000, of which $60,000 is traceable to the original partners and $20,000 is traceable to the assets contributed by the new partner.

An incoming partner may acquire an interest in the partnership for a price **in excess of** that indicated by the book value of the original partnership's net assets. This situation would suggest the existence of

1.   Unrecognized appreciation on the recorded net assets of the original partnership, and/or
2.   Unrecognized goodwill that also is traceable to the original partnership.

However, it is possible that an incoming partner may acquire an interest in the partnership at a price *less than* that indicated by the book value. This situation would suggest the existence of

1.   Unrecognized depreciation or write-downs on the recorded net assets of the original partnership, and/or
2.   A contribution by the incoming partner of some intangible asset (goodwill) in addition to a measured contribution.

When an incoming partner's contribution is different from that indicated by the book values of the original partnership, the admission of the partner, typically, is recorded by either the *bonus method* or the *goodwill method*. These two methods are mutually exclusive of each other. Both methods comprehend the possibility of adjusting the value of existing assets and/or the existence of goodwill. However, they differ in how these conditions are recognized.

Bonus Method.   The bonus method generally follows a *book-value approach*. That is, existing book values should not be adjusted to current values unless such adjustments would have otherwise been allowed by generally accepted accounting principles (GAAP). More specifically, increases in the value of assets as suggested by the admission of a new partner should not be recognized until they are realized through an actual subsequent exchange transaction. However, following the principle of conservatism, decreases or write-downs in the value of assets, which are suggested by the admission of a new partner, may be recognized even though they are not realized. Recognition of unrealized losses is not unique to partnership accounting and is not in conflict with GAAP. Even if no new partner were being admitted, unrealized losses suggested by economic events should be recognized. For example, if inventory has a cost in excess of market, or if long-lived assets are impaired, these losses should be recognized regardless of whether a new partner is being admitted. Therefore, use of the bonus method should not preclude a partnership from recognizing losses which would otherwise be recognized through the application of GAAP. However, the bonus method does preclude the recognition of asset appreciation which would otherwise not be allowed per GAAP.

Therefore, when a new partner is admitted to an existing partnership, the total capital of the new partnership consists of the following:

1.   The book value of the previous partnership *less*
2.   Any write-downs in the value of the previous partnership's assets as recognized by GAAP *plus*
3.   The value of the consideration paid to the partnership by the incoming partner.

The book-value approach of the bonus method does not directly recognize increases in asset values suggested by the consideration that the incoming partner pays. However, the method does indirectly recognize such increases by reallocating or adjusting the capital balances of the partners. For example, if increases in net asset values are suggested as being traceable to the original partners, this suggests that their equity or capital has increased. This increase in capital, or *bonus*, is accomplished by increasing their capital balances. If increases in asset values are not directly recognized, the indirect recognition through the capital balances of original partners must be offset by decreasing the capital of the incoming partner. Therefore, **the incoming partner's new capital balance is equal to the value of the consideration paid by the incoming partner less the bonus or increase in capital recorded for the original partners.** These adjustments result in the new incoming partner's capital balance always being equal to

1. The book value (BV) of the new partnership (book value of the previous partnership less asset write-downs plus the fair market value ((FMV) of consideration received from the incoming partner) times
2. The interest in capital being acquired by the incoming partner.

$$\begin{bmatrix} \text{BV of original} \\ \text{partnership} - \text{Asset write-} \\ \text{downs} \\ + \\ \text{FMV of new partnership} \\ \text{contribution} \end{bmatrix} \times \begin{matrix} \text{New partner's} \\ \text{interest \%} \end{matrix} = \begin{matrix} \text{New partner's} \\ \text{capital balance} \end{matrix}$$

The difference between the value of the consideration received from the incoming partner and his/her capital balance represents the bonus traceable to the original partners. This bonus is allocated to the original partners according to their profit and loss ratios in existence prior to the new partner's admission.

It is important to note that the profit and loss ratios of the original partners are used for this allocation rather than their percentage interest in capital. If the increases in the value of assets, as suggested by the admission of a new partner(s), are traceable to the original partners, such increases could have been alternatively realized by a sale of appreciated assets to an outside party. If this were the case, the realized gains would have become a component of net income. This net income would have, in turn, been allocated to the original partners according to their profit and loss ratios.

If the gain on such appreciated assets were realized subsequent to the admission of a new partner(s), a portion of this gain would be allocated to the new partner based on his/her profit ratio. Keeping in mind that this original appreciation in value should not accrue to the benefit of the new partner, the reduction of his/her capital balance (equal to the bonus granted to the original partners) compensates for any subsequent allocation of gains resulting from the realization of such appreciated assets.

Bonus to the Original Partners. When an incoming partner's contribution indicates the existence of unrecorded asset appreciation and/or unrecorded goodwill, the bonus method does not record these previously unrecorded items but, rather, grants a "bonus" to the original partners. The bonus, which increases the capital accounts of the original partners and reduces the capital balance of the new partner(s), is made possible by recording in the new partner's capital account only a portion of the actual contribution to the partnership.

To illustrate this method, assume the following:

Existing Partners	Capital Balance	Percentage Interest in	
		Capital	Profit
Partner A	$30,000	40%	50%
Partner B	45,000	60	50

Then assume that C invests $27,000 in the partnership in exchange for a 20% interest in capital and a 20% interest in profits. The $27,000 of consideration invested by Partner C in exchange for a 20% interest in capital suggests that the total value of the new partnership is $135,000 ($27,000 ÷ 20%). The $135,000 of value is comprised of the following:

Book value of original partners	$ 75,000
Investment of new partner	27,000
	$102,000
Asset appreciation traceable to original partners	33,000
Total suggested value	$135,000

Partners A and B will each have a 40% interest in the profits of the new partnership. Since the total capital of the new partnership equals $102,000 ($30,000 + $45,000 + $27,000) and the new partner is acquiring a 20% interest in capital, it seems reasonable that the incoming partner's capital account initially should reflect 20% of the total capital, or $20,400. The $6,600 difference between C's contribution and the interest recorded for C indicates the existence of unrecorded intangibles (goodwill) or unrecorded appreciation on existing assets. Regardless of the identity of the $6,600, the value must be allocated to the appropriate parties. If the unrecorded value had been realized through a sale, the resulting profit would have been divided between the original partners in accordance with their profit and loss agreement. Therefore, assuming the $6,600 is identified as a bonus to the original partners and is divided between them according to their profit and loss ratio prior to admission of the new partner, the entry to record C's investment is as follows:

Assets	27,000	
A, Capital		3,300
B, Capital		3,300
C, Capital		20,400

If the suggested appreciation in value of $33,000 were subsequently realized, it would be allocated among Partners A, B, and C according to their profit and loss percentages of 40%, 40%, and 20%, respectively. Therefore, Partner C will be allocated $6,600 (20% × $33,000) of the gain. The $6,600 reduction in Partner C's initial capital balance, represented by the bonus to the original partners, compensates for or negates the subsequent allocation of the realized gain to Partner C. In substance, none of the $33,000 gain should accrue to the benefit of the new partner. The bonus of $6,600 to the original partners is, in substance, the re-allocation to them of the subsequently realized gain which would be allocated to Partner C.

Bonus to the New Partner.   When the new partner invests some intangible asset, such as business acumen or an established clientele, it is possible to have a bonus credited to the new partner. For example, given the same basic facts as in the previous illustration, assume that C invests $10,000 for a 20% interest in capital and a 20% interest in profits. Total capital of the partnership would be $85,000 ($30,000 + $45,000 + $10,000), and C's share of the total capital would be 20%, or $17,000. Partner C is acquiring a $17,000 interest in capital in exchange for an investment of $10,000, and the original partners are transferring $7,000 of their capital to C in exchange for unrecorded intangible assets invested by C. Partner C's admission is recorded by the following entry:

Assets	10,000	
A, Capital	3,500	
B, Capital	3,500	
C, Capital		17,000

Partner C's bonus may be viewed as a cost incurred to acquire C's goodwill. Since all costs to acquire assets eventually affect income and are allocated among the partners, C's bonus is allocated to A and B according to their profit and loss ratio.

Overvaluation of the Original Partnership.   The recording of a bonus traceable to the incoming partner was based on the assumption that the new partner was contributing an intangible asset in addition to other assets valued at $10,000. However, the substance of the transaction may indicate that no intangibles are being contributed and the existing assets of the old partnership are overvalued. For example, in the previous illustration, C invested $10,000 in return for a 20% interest in the new partnership's total capital. Therefore, the total capital of the new partnership may be interpreted from C's investment to be equal to $50,000 ($10,000 ÷ 20%). Of this total, $10,000 is traceable to the new partner, and the balance of $40,000 represents the fair market value of the original partners' capital. Assuming this is a proper interpretation of the substance of the transaction between the new partner and the partnership, it suggests that the assets of the original partnership are overvalued by $35,000 ($75,000 less $40,000). C's admission to the partnership is recorded as follows:

A, Capital	17,500	
B, Capital	17,500	
Assets		35,000

To record the write-down of the original partners' capital from a book value of $75,000 ($30,000 + $45,000) to its implied fair market value of $40,000.

Assets	10,000	
C, Capital		10,000

To record C's contribution of assets to the partnership.

After these entries are posted, the total capital of the new partnership is $50,000 ($30,000 + $45,000 − $35,000 + $10,000), of which C's share is $10,000 (20% × $50,000), as initially represented by the balance in C's capital account.

Goodwill Method.   The goodwill method emphasizes the legal significance of a change in the ownership structure of a partnership. From a legal viewpoint, the entrance of a new partner results in the dissolution of the previous partnership and the creation of a new legal entity. Since a new entity has resulted, the assets transferred to this entity should be recorded at their **current fair market value.** After a complete analysis, both tangible and intangible assets acquired by the new entity, including goodwill created by the previous partnership, should be recorded. Therefore, the total capital of the new partnership will consist of the following values:

1.   The book value of the net assets of the previous partnership *plus*
2.   Unrecognized appreciation or less unrecognized depreciation on the recorded net assets of the previous partnership *plus*
3.   Unrecognized goodwill (GW) traceable to the previous partnership *plus*
4.   The value of the consideration, both tangible and intangible, received from the new incoming partner.

BV of original partnership	+	Unrecognized appreciation (or − unrecognized depreciation)	+	Unrecognized GW of original partnership	+	FMV of new partner's contribution including GW	=	Total capital of new partnership

When the bonus method is used to account for the admission of a new partner, the total capital of the new entity equals the book value of the previous partners' capital adjusted for asset write-downs, if appropriate, plus the incoming partner's investment. When the goodwill method is employed, however, the total capital of the new partnership must approximate the fair market value of the entity.

To illustrate the goodwill method, assume the following:

Existing Partners	Capital Balance	Percentage Interest in Capital	Percentage Interest in Profit
Partner A	$30,000	40%	50%
Partner B	45,000	60	50

If C invests $27,000 in the partnership in exchange for a 20% interest in capital and a 20% interest in profit, such an investment implies that the entity has a fair market value of $135,000 ($27,000 ÷ 20%). However, the book value of the new partnership equals only $102,000 when the former partners' capital balances of $75,000 are added to C's $27,000 investment. Thus, $33,000 must be added to the existing book value.

Another interpretation of the transaction would be that, given the $102,000 book value of the new partnership, a 20% interest should have cost $20,400 ($102,000 × 20%). The new partner paid an extra $6,600 ($27,000 – $20,400) for a 20% interest in the difference between the implied fair market value and the book value of the new entity. Therefore, the total difference must be $33,000 ($6,600 ÷ 20%).

Asset Appreciation.   The difference between the higher fair market value and the book value of the new entity, as previously discussed, may be traceable to unrecognized appreciation and/or unrecognized goodwill. Each of these possible explanations should be thoroughly analyzed to properly account for a change in the ownership structure of a partnership. If differences between the fair market value and the book value of recorded assets are identifiable, appropriate adjustments to asset balances should be considered. Since a change in ownership structure creates a new, distinct legal entity, every attempt should be made to identify differences between fair market and book values, whether such differences represent appreciation or write-downs in value. However, the absence of objective and independent valuations often prevents such an analysis. For example, fair market values are not readily available for certain specialized assets, and the alternative of engaging an independent appraiser could become an expensive option. Furthermore, estimating fair market values with the use of specific price-level indexes is often difficult because of the absence of relevant indexes. Another reason for not recording changes in market values is that the resulting differences between the bases for tax purposes and the bases for book purposes would require more complex records.

Assuming objective measures of unrecorded appreciation are available, the appreciation would be recognized and allocated to the previous partners according to their old profit and loss ratios. To illustrate, assume that the $33,000 difference in values from our previous example is entirely traceable to the unrecognized net appreciation of the recorded net assets of the previous partnership as follows:

Land appreciation	$43,000
Inventory write-down	(10,000)
Net appreciation	$33,000

This appreciation and the investment by C would be recorded as follows:

Assets (from C)	27,000	
Land	43,000	
Inventory		10,000
A, Capital		16,500
B, Capital		16,500
C, Capital		27,000

Goodwill Traceable to the Original Partners.   Unrecorded goodwill also may be identifiable. In the previous example, assuming there are no differences between the fair market value and book value of recorded assets, the new partner's willingness to pay more than the proportionate book value of the new entity indicates that goodwill existed prior to the new partner's admission. If this intangible asset could have been sold prior to the admission of the partner, the realized profit would have been allocated to the original partners. Therefore, the goodwill is recorded and allocated to the original partners according to their profit and loss ratio. The investment by C is recorded under the goodwill method as follows:

Assets (from C)	27,000	
Goodwill	33,000	
A, Capital		16,500
B, Capital		16,500
C, Capital		27,000

It is important to note that the new partner's capital account balance represents a 20% interest in the total capital of the new partnership, as verified by the following computation:

Original capital	$ 75,000
C's investment	27,000
Goodwill	33,000
	$135,000
C's interest	× 20%
C's capital balance	$ 27,000

In comparing the assumption that the $33,000 difference was traceable to net appreciation of assets versus goodwill, it should be noted that

1.   In one case, the net appreciation is allocated to specific assets versus goodwill, yet the amount is the same.
2.   Some combination of appreciated assets and goodwill could account for the $33,000 difference.
3.   The adjusted capital balances of the partners are the same regardless of whether asset appreciation and/or goodwill is recognized.

The recognition of goodwill traceable to the previous partners is criticized by some accountants. If the concept of a new legal entity is cast aside, some would argue that the goodwill is self-created and, therefore, should not be recognized. APB Opinion No. 17, *Intangible Assets*, prohibits the recognition of goodwill unless it has been purchased from another entity. To argue that the new partnership is, in substance, a continuation of the previous partnership would prevent the recognition of goodwill traceable to the original partnership. Furthermore, viewing the new partnership as a continuation of the previous partnership would prevent the recognition of appreciation on other assets as well.

It also may be argued that the difficulties associated with the measurement of the fair market value of existing assets unjustifiably forces the recognition of goodwill for lack of a more precise analysis. However, the argument that the fair market value of a new partnership, as indicated by the new partner's investment, is not objectively or independently determined overlooks the basic nature of the transaction. Negotiations between previous partners and a new partner would be described as arm's length, since both parties involved are independently seeking a fair price.

Asset Write-downs.   Given the same basic facts as in the previous illustrations, assume that C invests $10,000 to acquire a 20% interest in the partnership of A and B. C's investment implies a fair market value of the new entity equal to $50,000 ($10,000 ÷ 20%). However, the book value of the new partnership equals $85,000, consisting of the original partners' capital balances of $75,000 plus C's investment of $10,000. This difference between the fair market value and the higher book value indicates the existence of unrecorded net write-downs and/or goodwill contributed by the incoming partner.

If objective evidence supports the write-down of existing assets, the previous partners' capital balances would be reduced accordingly in proportion to their profit and loss ratios. The amount of the suggested write-down is calculated by comparing the implied market value of $50,000 to the $85,000 representing the book value of the previous partnership plus the new partner's investment. Therefore, the difference of $35,000 is equal to the necessary net write-down. Assuming the net write-down is represented by land appreciation of $20,000 and a write-down of $55,000 to inventory, the net write-down would be recorded as follows:

A, Capital	17,500	
B, Capital	17,500	
Land	20,000	
Inventory		55,000

This reduces the net assets of the previous partnership to $40,000, and the new partner's investment of $10,000 would then represent 20% of the new partnership's total capital of $50,000 ($40,000 + $10,000).

Goodwill Traceable to the New Partner.   Assuming net assets of the original partnership are properly valued and should not be written down, it is possible that goodwill may be traceable to the incoming partner. The amount of this contributed goodwill may be computed as the difference between

1.   The amount that should have been paid by the new partner, as indicated by the book value of the previous partnership (calculated by dividing the original book value of the partnership by the total percentage interest of the original partners in the new partnership, and subtracting the original book value),

$$\left[\begin{array}{ccc} \text{book value of} & & \text{original partners'} \\ \text{original} & \div & \text{interest in } \textbf{new} \\ \text{partnership} & & \text{partnership} \end{array} \right] - \begin{array}{c} \text{book value of} \\ \text{original} \\ \text{partnership} \end{array} = \begin{array}{c} \text{New partner's} \\ \text{capital balance} \end{array}$$

and

2.   The amount of consideration, excluding any goodwill, contributed by the new partner.

Using the previous example, the $75,000 original book value would represent 80% of the new partnership capital, or $93,750 ($75,000 ÷ 80%). Therefore, it appears that the new partner should have paid $18,750 ($93,750 less the original $75,000 book value) for a 20% interest in the partnership; however, the partner actually paid only

$10,000 cash. The difference between what should have been paid ($18,750) and the amount actually paid ($10,000) represents the goodwill traceable to the incoming partner. The investment by C would be recorded under the goodwill method as follows:

Assets	10,000	
Goodwill	8,750	
C, Capital		18,750

Note that the new partner's capital account balance represents a 20% interest in the total capital of the new partnership, as shown by the following computation:

Original capital	$75,000
C's investment of cash	10,000
Goodwill	8,750
	$93,750
C's interest	× 20%
C's capital balance	$18,750

The fact that a new legal entity is created supports the recognition of goodwill and other contributed assets at their fair market value. If the concept of a new entity is set aside, the goodwill may be viewed as being purchased by the previous partnership in exchange for partnership equity. Accounting theory and current practice support the recording of goodwill acquired or purchased from other entities.

Revaluation of Assets and Goodwill.   The previous examples of accounting for a new partner's investment assumed that either asset revaluations or goodwill recognition were appropriate as mutually exclusive choices. In reality, some combination of the two may be appropriate. Continuing with the previous example, assume that the $75,000 book value of the previous partnership has a market value of $64,000 and new partner C's investment remains at $10,000. The first step to be taken is to recognize the write-down of the previous partnership's net assets as follows:

A, Capital	5,500	
B, Capital	5,500	
Assets		11,000

The adjusted value of the previous partnership, then, is used to determine the goodwill traceable to the new partner. In this example, the $64,000 market value of the previous partnership would represent 80% of the new partnership capital, or $80,000 ($64,000 ÷ 80%). Therefore, it appears that the new partner should have paid $16,000 ($80,000 less the market value of the previous partnership) for a 20% interest in the partnership. The difference between what should have been paid ($16,000) and the amount actually paid ($10,000) represents the goodwill traceable to the incoming partner. The entry to record C's investment is as follows:

Assets	10,000	
Goodwill	6,000	
C, Capital		16,000

Methodology for Determining Goodwill.   An analysis of the previous examples reveals that goodwill may be traceable to either the original partners or the incoming partner. To properly apply the goodwill method, the following methodology may be helpful in identifying the origin of the goodwill and its amount:

1. Determine the entity's fair market value, as indicated by the new partner's investment (new partner's investment divided by the percentage interest acquired in the partnership).

2. If the fair market value determined is

    a) *Greater than the book value of the new partnership adjusted for net appreciation or net write-downs, implied goodwill is traceable to the original partners and is allocated among them according to their original profit ratios. The amount of goodwill is equal to the difference between 1) the fair market value indicated by the new partner's investment and 2) the adjusted book value of the new partnership.*

    b) *Less than the adjusted book value of the new partnership, implied goodwill is traceable to the new partner. The amount of goodwill is equal to the difference between 1) the amount that should have been paid by the new partner to acquire an interest in the adjusted book value of the previous partnership and 2) the actual amount paid.*

3. The initial capital balance of the new partner always is equal to the new partner's interest in the total capital of the new partnership after goodwill is recognized.

Comparison of Bonus and Goodwill Methods.   The bonus method adheres to the historical cost concept and is often used in accounting practice. It is objective in that it establishes total capital of the new partnership at an amount based on actual consideration received from the new partner. The bonus method indirectly acknowledges the existence of appreciation of assets and/or goodwill by giving a bonus to either original or new partners.

The goodwill method results in the recognition of an asset implied by a transaction rather than recognizing an asset actually purchased. Historically, goodwill has been recognized only when purchased so that a more objective measure of its value is established. Therefore, opponents of the goodwill method contend that goodwill is not determined objectively and other factors may have influenced the amount of investment required from the new partner. Also, certain recipients of partnership financial statements may question the valuation of goodwill, since increasing total assets may result in an understatement of the return on total assets or equity. However, in defense of the goodwill method, the current value of net assets, whether tangible or intangible, is reflected on the financial statements resulting in a more relevant measure of invested capital.

Use of the goodwill method could produce inequitable results if either of the following conditions exist:

1. The new partner's interest in profits does not equal the new partner's initial interest in capital.

2. After the formation of the new partnership, the former partners do not share profits and losses in the same relationship to each other as they did before the admission of a new partner.

The importance of these concepts can be illustrated using the following facts:

	Original Partners		New Partner
	A	B	C
Original capital.	$30,000	$45,000	
Original profit and loss percentage.	50%	50%	
New partner's capital.			$27,000
New profit and loss percentage	33⅓%	33⅓%	33⅓%
New partner's interest in capital.			20%

The new capital balances that result from using the goodwill method and the bonus method are as follows:

	Original Partners		New Partner
	A	B	C
Goodwill method:			
Goodwill allocation	$16,500	$16,500	
New capital balances.	46,500	61,500	$27,000
Bonus method:			
Bonus allocation	3,300	3,300	
New capital balances.	33,300	48,300	20,400

Assuming the recorded goodwill proves to be worthless (or assuming that goodwill is amortized in total), the decline in asset value would reduce the partners' capital balances according to their profit and loss ratio as follows:

	Partners			
	A	B	C	Total
Capital balances if goodwill method used	$46,500	$61,500	$27,000	$135,000
Goodwill write-off (amortization)	(11,000)	(11,000)	(11,000)	(33,000)
Capital balances after write-off	$35,500	$50,500	$16,000	$102,000
Capital balances if bonus method is used	33,300	48,300	20,400	102,000
Differences	$ 2,200	$ 2,200	$ (4,400)	0

The capital balances that result from using the two methods are different because the new partner's interest in profits and interest in capital are not equal. In this illustration, C acquired a 20% capital interest and a 33⅓% interest in profits. Therefore, C paid for 20% of the implied goodwill but had to absorb 33⅓% of the goodwill amortization.

To further illustrate these concepts, assume the same facts, except that the new profit and loss percentages are 50%, 30%, and 20% for Partners A, B, and C, respectively. If the recorded goodwill proves to be worthless, the decline in asset value would affect the partners' capital balances as follows:

	Partners			
	A	B	C	Total
Capital balances if goodwill method used	$46,500	$61,500	$27,000	$135,000
Goodwill write-off (amortization)	(16,500)	(9,900)	(6,600)	(33,000)
Capital balances after write-off	$30,000	$51,600	$20,400	$102,000
Capital balances if bonus method is used	33,300	48,300	20,400	102,000
Differences	$ (3,300)	$ 3,300	0	0

In this case, Partners A and B shared equally in the initial recording of goodwill but unequally in the subsequent amortization of goodwill.

Now, assume the same facts, except that the new profit and loss percentages are 40%, 40%, and 20% for Partners A, B, and C, respectively. After the amortization of goodwill, the capital balances would be identical to those achieved under the bonus method, as indicated in the following table:

	Partners			
	A	B	C	Total
Capital balances if goodwill method used	$46,500	$61,500	$27,000	$135,000
Goodwill write-off (amortization)	(13,200)	(13,200)	(6,600)	(33,000)
Capital balances after write-off	$33,300	$48,300	$20,400	$102,000
Capital balances if bonus method is used	33,300	48,300	20,400	102,000
Differences	$ 0	0	0	0

The equality between the capital balances is achieved because neither of the two conditions that produce inequities exists. If these conditions do exist, preference is given, typically, to the bonus method because of the possible inequities that may result from the write-off of goodwill.

Contribution of Assets to Existing Partners.   A new partner also may be admitted to the partnership by acquiring all or part of the capital interest of one or more existing partners in exchange for some consideration (assets). In this case, **the new partner deals directly with an existing partner or partners** rather than with the partnership entity. Therefore, the acquisition price is paid to the selling partner(s) and not to the partnership itself. The partnership records the redistribution of capital interests by transferring all or a portion of the seller's capital to the new partner's capital account but does not record the transfer of any assets.

To illustrate, assume the following facts:

		Percentage Interest in	
Existing Partners	Capital Balance	Capital	Profit
Partner A	$30,000	40%	50%
Partner B	45,000	60	50

Now, assume new Partner C purchased 50% of A's interest in capital and 50% of B's interest in capital in exchange for $50,000. This purchase resulted in C's having a 50% interest in the total partnership capital.

There are several alternative ways of recording the contribution of assets by C to the existing partners. If the consideration paid by the incoming partner is not used to impute the fair market value of the partnership, the transaction would be recorded by the partnership entity as follows:

A, Capital (50% × $30,000)	15,000	
B, Capital (50% × $45,000)	22,500	
C, Capital		37,500

The $50,000 actually paid by C was not used as a basis for the entry because it represents consideration paid to the individual partners personally rather than to the partnership entity. This accounting treatment frequently is compared to that of a corporation when a stockholder sells shares or an interest in corporate capital to another investor in the corporation. The corporation does not record the transaction or use it as a basis for revaluing corporate assets but merely acknowledges the changing identity of its shareholders. The preceding entry would also be appropriate if the existing partners had sold their interests for less than book value. Even though depreciation of existing assets is suggested, such depreciation is not recorded because the transaction did not involve the partnership entity itself.

An alternative but less frequently used method of recording this transaction would be to impute the fair market value of the partnership entity from the consideration paid by the new partner. For example, if C paid $50,000 to acquire a 50% interest in the capital of the partnership vis-à-vis the individual partners, the total implied current value of the original partnership would be $100,000 ($50,000 ÷ 50%). The difference between the imputed value of $100,000 and the partnership's previous book value of $75,000 ($30,000 + $45,000) is interpreted to represent undervalued existing assets and/or goodwill traceable to the original partnership. This alternative interpretation would result in recording the transaction as follows:

Assets and/or Goodwill	25,000	
A, Capital		12,500
B, Capital		12,500
To record the previously unrecognized		
increase in value of the partnership.		
A, Capital [50% × ($30,000 + $12,500)]	21,250	
B, Capital [50% × ($45,000 + $12,500)]	28,750	
C, Capital		50,000
To record the transfer of the original		
partners' adjusted capital to incoming Partner C.		

Normally, this alternative method is not employed because a) the transaction was not between the partnership and the incoming partner but, rather, between individual partners and b) the consideration paid by the incoming partner may not provide a reliable indicator of the partnership entity's current value. However, the method may provide useful information for deciding how to allocate the acquisition price between the selling partners. The selling partners' original capital plus their share of any imputed value increments may indicate the current values for which the incoming partner was paying. For example, the purchase price of $50,000 may be allocated to Partners A and B as follows:

	Partners		
	A	B	Total
Original capital	$30,000	$45,000	$ 75,000
Share of value increment	12,500	12,500	25,000
Total imputed value	$42,500	$57,500	$100,000
Percentage acquired by new partner	50%	50%	50%
Total purchase price	$21,250	$28,750	$ 50,000

Withdrawal of a Partner

When a partner withdraws, the partnership agreement should be consulted to determine whether any guidelines have been established that would influence the procedure. The withdrawal of a partner requires a determination of the fair market value of the partnership entity and a measurement of partnership income to the date of withdrawal. Also, in many cases, the equity of the retiring partner may not be equal to the partner's capital balance as a result of a) the existence of accounting errors, b) differences between the fair market value and the recorded book value of assets, and/or c) unrecorded assets such as goodwill.

If accounting errors are discovered, they should be treated as prior-period adjustments and corrected by adjusting the capital balances of the partners. Theoretically, an error should be allocated to partners' capital balances according to the profit and loss ratio that existed when the error was committed. Therefore, it is necessary to identify the period to which the error is traceable. This practice can become complicated, and a well-designed partnership agreement should include procedures for dealing with the correction of errors.

Recognizing differences between book value and fair market value may be as appropriate when an individual withdraws from the partnership as when an individual is admitted. If accounting recognition of such differences is not desired, however, these differences nevertheless should influence the amount to be paid to the withdrawing partner.

The Selling of an Interest to Existing Partners.   As is the case with the admission of a partner, the withdrawal of a partner may involve a) a transaction with existing partners or a new partner or b) a transaction with the partnership entity itself. In the first case, the equity of the withdrawing partner will be purchased with the personal assets of existing or new partners rather than with the assets of the partnership.

To illustrate, assume the following:

	Partners		
	A	B	C
Capital balance	$30,000	$50,000	$20,000
Profit and loss percentage	40%	40%	20%
Percentage interest in capital	30%	50%	20%

Now assume Partner A withdraws from the partnership and C uses personal funds to purchase A's interest at its current value of $36,000. If the price paid by C is not used to impute the value of the entity, the transaction would be recorded as follows:

A, Capital	30,000	
C, Capital		30,000

The above entry also may be appropriate if the existing partners sold their interests for less than book value. Even though depreciation of existing assets is suggested, such depreciation is not recorded because the transaction did not involve the partnership entity itself. As previously discussed, an alternative treatment would be to recognize any suggested appreciation or write-downs indicated by the transaction and then transfer the adjusted capital balances.

The Selling of an Interest to the Partnership.   When a withdrawing partner sells an interest to the partnership rather than to an individual partner, the bonus or goodwill methods may be employed. The bonus method is used most frequently, but the choice between methods should be based on a thorough analysis of the transaction. Using the same facts as in the previous illustration and assuming the use of the bonus method, the purchase of A's equity by the partnership would be recorded as follows:

A, Capital	30,000	
B, Capital	4,000	
C, Capital	2,000	
Cash		36,000

The entry indicates that the remaining partners granted a bonus to A, measured by the difference between the recorded capital and the fair market value of A's equity. The bonus is charged to the remaining partners according to their proportionate profit and loss ratio.

The goodwill method focuses on the payment to the withdrawing partner as an indication of the fair market value of the partnership. If the imputed goodwill or undervalued assets were disposed of, the partners would divide the gain according to their profit and loss ratio. Assuming existing assets are properly valued, the $36,000 payment to A consists of A's capital balance of $30,000 plus a $6,000 share of the unrecorded goodwill. Therefore, the $6,000 represents A's 40% interest in total goodwill of $15,000 ($6,000 ÷ 40%). Notice that the $6,000 represents A's interest in the gain which would be realized if the unrecorded goodwill were sold. Therefore, A's profit percentage is used to suggest the total value of the goodwill.

Two alternatives are now available: a) recognize only the goodwill that is traceable to the retiring partner or b) recognize the amount of goodwill traceable to the entire entity. The first alternative stresses the importance of recognizing only the amount of goodwill that actually is purchased from the withdrawing partner. Using this alternative, A's withdrawal would be recorded as follows:

Goodwill	6,000	
A, Capital		6,000
A, Capital	36,000	
Cash		36,000

If the amount of goodwill traceable to the entire entity is recognized, the goodwill would be allocated to the partners according to their profit and loss ratio, as reflected in the following entries to record A's withdrawal:

Goodwill	15,000	
A, Capital		6,000
B, Capital		6,000
C, Capital		3,000
A, Capital	36,000	
Cash		36,000

Whether part or all of the goodwill is recognized, opponents of this procedure contend that transactions between partners should not be viewed as arm's length; therefore, the measure of goodwill may not be determined objectively. Also, inequitable results may be produced if the remaining partners subsequently change their profit and loss ratio.

It is important to note that a withdrawing partner could sell his/her interest in a partnership for less than book value. If that interest is sold to the partnership, the following recognition would take place depending on whether the bonus or goodwill method is employed:

1. Bonus method: A bonus traceable to the remaining partners would be recognized. The bonus would be measured as the difference between the withdrawing partner's capital balance and the consideration paid for the partner's interest.

2. Goodwill method: Paying less than the withholding partner's capital balance (book value) would suggest that existing assets are overvalued. A write-down of existing assets would be recognized as the difference between the withdrawing partner's capital balance and the consideration paid for the partner's interest. As an alternative, the asset write-down traceable to the entire entity could be recognized based on the amount suggested by the transaction with the withholding partner. The write-down traceable to the withdrawing partner represents his/her percentage interest (based on profit and loss ratios) in the asset write-down traceable to the entire entity.

Effects of a Partner's Withdrawal.   When the interest of a withdrawing partner is acquired by the remaining partners or the partnership, serious demands upon the liquidity of the partners and the partnership may result. If withdrawal is due to the death of the partner, funds may be provided from the proceeds of life insurance policies taken out by the partnership itself or by individual partners. For example, if Partner A takes out a life insurance policy on Partner B, and B subsequently dies, the proceeds payable to A may be used to acquire B's interest.

The UPA, in Section 42, states that a retiring or deceased partner's estate may receive interest as an ordinary creditor on that portion of the withdrawing partner's capital interest that remains in the partnership (i.e., has not yet been disbursed). In lieu of interest, the UPA states that the profits attributable to the use of the withdrawing partner's capital still retained in the partnership may be received. Once again, a partnership agreement that addresses the valuation of a withdrawing partner's interest and the means of payment is a valuable aid in properly accounting for the withdrawal of a partner.

Partnership Liquidation

Unlike a dissolution where the partnership continues its business purpose, a liquidation results in the partnership's ending or terminating its business. The process of liquidation consists of the conversion of partnership assets into a distributable form and the distribution of these assets to creditors and owners. To achieve an orderly and legally sound liquidation, some fundamental guidelines need to be identified.

Liquidation Guidelines

The underlying theme in accounting for partnership liquidation is the equitable distribution of the assets. To be equitable, a distribution should recognize the legal rights of the partnership creditors and individual partners. All liquidation expenses and gains or losses from conversion of partnership assets also must be allocated to the partners before assets actually are distributed to the individual partners. Failure to consider these factors may result in the premature or incorrect distribution of assets to a partner. If a premature or incorrect distribution of assets cannot be recovered, the partnership fiduciary who authorized the distribution may be held liable.

The Ranking of Partnership Liabilities.   The UPA establishes rules governing the priority in which partnership assets are distributed to creditors and partners. Subject to any agreement to the contrary, the following sequence of payments should be observed:

1. Amounts owed to creditors other than partners.
2. Amounts owed to partners other than for capital and profits, i.e., partners' loans to the partnership.
3. Amounts owed to partners as capital.
4. Amounts owed to partners as profits not currently closed to partners' capital accounts.

Although loans from partners have a higher legal priority than amounts owed as capital and profits, the doctrine of *right of offset* sets aside this ranking in favor of procedural and economic considerations that facilitate the actual liquidation process. The effect of this doctrine is that loans due to partners, which have a credit balance, are combined with the respective partners' capital balances. Without the right of offset, it would be possible to distribute assets to a partner in payment of the loan balance while at the same time the partner has a debit capital account balance. In order to eliminate the debit capital balance, the partnership would have to recover personal assets from the partner. Therefore, it is possible for the partnership to distribute assets to the partner and then try to recover assets from the partner, hoping that such assets are still available. The doctrine of right of offset eliminates this problem by combining the loan and capital balances.

Amounts owed to partners as capital and profits are typically viewed as one element rather than two separate priority levels. Therefore, items 2, 3, and 4 may be combined without destroying the fairness of a distribution.

Liability for Debit Capital Balances.   The UPA, in Section 40, states that partners should contribute assets to the partnership to the extent of their debit balances. However, if such a contribution is not possible because of special personal or legal considerations, the debit balance will be viewed as a realization loss and allocated according to the remaining partners' profit and loss ratio. For example, assume Partners A, B, and C share in profits and losses in the ratio of 1:2:1, respectively. If C is unable to contribute any asset to eliminate a debit capital balance, that balance would be allocated to A and B in the ratio of 1:2. Partners who absorb other partners' debit capital balances have a legal claim against the deficient partners. However, the collectibility of such a claim depends on the personal wealth of the deficient partners.

The Marshaling of Assets.   The provisions that call for the contribution of personal assets to a liquidating partnership illustrate the characteristics of unlimited liability discussed in the previous chapter. However, such personal liability depends on the legal doctrine of *marshaling of assets*. This doctrine, which is applied when the partnership and/or one or more of the partners are insolvent, states that

1. Partnership assets are first available for the payment of partnership debts. Any excess assets are available for payment of the individual partner's debts, but only to the extent of the partner's interest in the capital of the partnership.
2. Personal assets of a partner are applied against personal debts, ranked in order of priority as follows:

    a) *Amounts owed to personal creditors.*

    b) *Amounts owed to partnership creditors.*

    c) *Amounts owed to partners by way of contribution.*

"Amounts owed to partners by way of contribution" refers to amounts owed the partnership as represented by the partner's debit capital balance. This amount is viewed by the UPA as separate from the amounts owed to personal creditors. For example, if a partner has personal assets of $12,000, personal liabilities of $8,000, and a debit capital balance of $16,000, personal assets would be distributed as follows:

Payable to personal creditors	$ 8,000
Payable to partnership for debit capital balance	4,000
Total personal assets	$12,000

Under common law and federal bankruptcy law, which may be applicable when the UPA has not been adopted, amounts owed to partners by way of contribution are on an equal basis (*pari passu*) with personal creditors of the partner. According to this rule, the $12,000 of personal assets would be distributed as follows:

Payable to personal liabilities [($8,000 ÷ $24,000) x $12,000]	$ 4,000
Payable to partnership for debit capital balance	
[($16,000 ÷ $24,000) × $12,000]	8,000
Total personal assets	$12,000

The legal doctrine of marshaling of assets is demonstrated by the following cases:

Case A—Insolvent Partners

The partnership is solvent, with total assets of $16,000 and total liabilities of $9,000. Information relating to the individual partners is as follows:

	Partner A	Partner B
Total personal assets	$10,000	$15,000
Total personal liabilities	13,000	18,000
Partnership capital balances	5,000	2,000

Analysis: Unsatisfied personal creditors may attach a partner's interest in the solvent partnership, but only to the extent of the partner's capital balance. Thus, unsatisfied personal creditors could seek recourse as follows:

	Partner A	Partner B
Unsatisfied personal creditors	$3,000	$3,000
Interest in partnership capital available to personal creditors . .	(3,000)	(2,000)
Personal liabilities not satisfied	0	$1,000

Case B—Insolvent Partnership

The partnership is insolvent, with total assets of $23,000 and total liabilities of $25,000. Information relating to individual partners is as follows:

	Partner A	Partner B
Total personal assets	$10,000	$8,000
Total personal liabilities	6,000	7,000
Partnership capital balances	500	(2,500)

Analysis: Unsatisfied partnership creditors may seek recourse from the individual partners in accordance with a proper marshaling of assets, as reflected in Illustration 15-1.

Illustration 15-1
Distribution of Assets—Insolvent Partnership

	Partner A		Partner B		AB Partnership			
	Assets	Liab.	Assets	Liab.	Assets	Liab.	A, Capital	B, Capital
Beginning balances[1]	$10,000	$6,000	$8,000	$7,000	$23,000	$25,000	$ 500	$(2,500)
Payment of liabilities	(6,000)	(6,000)	(7,000)	(7,000)	(23,000)	(23,000)		
	$ 4,000	0	$1,000	0	0	$ 2,000	$ 500	$(2,500)
Payment of partnership creditors[2]	(2,000)					(2,000)	2,000	
	$ 2,000	0	$1,000	0	0	0	$2,500	$(2,500)
Payment toward debit capital balance[3]			(1,000)		$ 1,000			1,000
	$ 2,000	0	0	0	$ 1,000	0	$2,500	$(1,500)
Capital distribution to A	1,000				(1,000)		(1,000)	
Balances[4]	$ 3,000	0	0	0	0	0	$1,500	$(1,500)

1 Beginning asset balances represent realizable values.

2 Unsatisfied partnership creditors may claim the net personal assets of any solvent partner, regardless of the amount of the partner's interest in the capital of the partnership. A's capital interest is increased by the payment of partnership liabilities.

3 If the payment toward the debit capital balance had preceded B's payment of personal liabilities, a proper marshaling of assets would not have been achieved and B's personal creditors would not have been satisfied.

4 If B later pays the debit capital balance, the funds would be distributed to A. However, if B cannot pay, the loss will be borne by A.

Case C—Insolvent Partner and Partnership

The partnership is insolvent, with total assets of $20,000 and total liabilities of $25,000. Information relating to individual partners is as follows:

	Partner A	Partner B
Total personal assets.	$13,000	$12,000
Total personal liabilities.	10,000	15,000
Partnership capital balances	(7,000)	2,000

Analysis: Partner B is insolvent, and the recourse B's personal creditors have against the partnership depends upon A's future contribution to the partnership. Illustration 15-2 reflects the distribution of assets in accordance with the marshaling concept.

Illustration 15-2
Distribution of Assets—Insolvent Partner and Partnership

	Partner A		Partner B		AB Partnership			
	Assets	Liab.	Assets	Liab.	Assets	Liab.	A, Capital	B, Capital
Beginning balances[1]	$13,000	$10,000	$12,000	$15,000	$20,000	$25,000	$(7,000)	$2,000
Payment of liabilities	(10,000)	(10,000)	(12,000)	(12,000)	(20,000)	(20,000)		.
	$ 3,000	0	0	$ 3,000	0	$ 5,000	$(7,000)	$2,000
Payment of partnership creditors	(3,000)					(3,000)	3,000	
Balances[2]	0	0	0	$ 3,000[3]	0	$ 2,000	$(4,000)	$2,000

1 Beginning asset balances represent realizable values.

2 If A later pays $4,000 to the partnership to eliminate the debit capital balance, the payment will be allocated first to the partnership liabilities and then to B. However, if A is not able to make a payment, claims against the partnership by the creditors and B will be totally uncollectible.

3 The unsatisfied personal creditors of B are unable to seek recovery against the credit capital balance of B because the partnership itself is not solvent.

Lump-Sum Liquidations

The guidelines discussed in the preceding section are important factors influencing the procedural and legal aspects of a partnership liquidation. Upon liquidation of a partnership, the amount of assets ultimately to be distributed to the individual partners is determined through the use of either a lump-sum liquidation schedule or an installment liquidation schedule. A lump-sum liquidation requires that all assets be realized before a distribution is made to partners, thus avoiding the possibility of a premature distribution. To illustrate a lump-sum liquidation, assume the following:

1. Asset, liability, loan, and capital balances are as shown in Illustration 15-3, after books for the final operational period are closed.
2. Profit and loss percentages for Partners A, B, and C are 40%, 40%, and 20%, respectively.
3. Personal assets and debts of the partners are as follows:

	A	B	C
Total personal assets	$30,000	$40,000	$20,000
Total personal liabilities	10,000	37,200	24,000

4. Sales of assets are as follows:

Date	Book Value	Selling Price	Gain (Loss)
February 15	$50,000	$60,000	$10,000
March 2	30,000	10,000	(20,000)
March 7	40,000	20,000	(20,000)

5. Total liquidation expenses of $2,000 are paid on March 4.

Illustration 15-3
Lump-Sum Liquidation Statement

	Cash	Noncash Assets	Liabilities	Loan from A	Capital Balances A	B	C
Beginning balances	$10,000	$120,000	$80,000	$ 9,000	$25,000	$10,000	$6,000
February 15, sale of assets at a gain	60,000	(50,000)			4,000	4,000	2,000
March 2, sale of assets at a loss	10,000	(30,000)			(8,000)	(8,000)	(4,000)
Payment of liquidation expenses.	(2,000)				(800)	(800)	(400)
March 7, sale of assets at a loss	20,000	(40,000)			(8,000)	(8,000)	(4,000)
Balances.	$98,000	0	$80,000	$ 9,000	$12,200	$ (2,800)	$ (400)
Payment of liabilities.	(80,000)		(80,000)				
Balances.	$18,000	0	0	$ 9,000	$12,200	$ (2,800)	$ (400)
B's contribution	2,800					2,800	
Balances.	$20,800	0	0	$ 9,000	$12,200	0	$ (400)
Absorption of C's balance . . .					(400)		400
Balances.	$20,800	0	0	$ 9,000	$11,800	0	0
Payment to A.	(20,800)			(9,000)	(11,800)		
Final balances	0	0	0	0	0	0	0

Illustration 15-3 presents the lump-sum distribution and demonstrates the following concepts that were discussed previously:

1. Gains and losses on realization are allocated according to the partners' profit and loss ratio.
2. Claims against the partnership are paid in the proper order.
3. The marshaling-of-assets doctrine is followed to determine the disposition of B's and C's debit balances in their capital accounts. That is, a partner's personal assets first are used to satisfy personal liabilities. Then, to the extent possible, remaining assets are contributed to the partnership to eliminate debit capital balances.
4. C's debit capital balance is charged against A, the only personally solvent partner.
5. Partner A will have a claim against C's future personal assets for the debit balance that was absorbed.

Installment Liquidations

The complete liquidation process might extend over several months or longer, and it may not be possible to postpone payments to creditors and partners until all assets have been realized. Therefore, payments may be made on an installment basis to creditors and partners during the liquidation process. To avoid the problem associated with premature payments, installment payments may be made to partners only after anticipating all liabilities, possible losses, and liquidation expenses. To provide a proper solution to installment liquidations, either a *schedule of safe payments* is prepared as amounts become available for distribution or a *predistribution plan* is used to direct the distribution of any available sum.

Schedule of Safe Payments.   The possibility of premature payments to partners is reduced by using a schedule of safe payments, which reflects a conservative approach to liquidation. The schedule indicates how available funds should be distributed to partners. It is based on the anticipation of all possible liabilities and expenses, including those expected to be incurred in the process of liquidation. The effect of these items on partnership capital is allocated among the partners according to their profit and loss agreement.

In keeping with the conservative approach, the schedule also is based on the assumption that all noncash assets will be worthless; therefore, the assumed loss is allocated among the partners according to their profit and loss ratio. The allocation of the assumed loss could produce debit balances in partners' capital accounts, and these balances are treated as being uncollectible. Therefore, the assumed debit capital balances are allocated to those partners with credit balances according to their profit and loss ratio. When the allocation of estimated liabilities, expenses, liquidation losses, and debit balances is completed, assets may be distributed safely to the partners in amounts equal to the resulting credit capital balances.

A new schedule of safe payments is prepared each time a distribution to partners is scheduled. These schedules support an installment liquidation statement, which summarizes changes in real account balances as the liquidation proceeds. When the partners' capital balances are in the profit and loss ratio, all partners will share in a given distribution. All future distributions to partners will be allocated automatically according to their profit ratio, thus eliminating the need for another schedule of safe payments.

To illustrate the use of schedules of safe payments in conjunction with an installment liquidation, assume the following:

1. Asset, liability, loan, and capital balances are shown, in Illustration 15-4, after books for the final operational period are closed.
2. Profit and loss percentages for Partners A, B, and C are 40%, 40%, and 20%, respectively.
3. Sales of assets are as follows:

Date	Book Value	Selling Price	Gain (Loss)
February 15	$60,000	$40,000	$(20,000)
March 2	30,000	15,000	(15,000)
March 17	10,000	20,000	10,000
April 1	20,000	24,000	4,000

4. Liquidation expenses are estimated to be $10,000. Cash is to be restricted in that amount until expenses are paid.
5. Installment distributions of unrestricted cash are made on February 17, March 5, March 18, and April 2.
6. Total liquidation expenses of $8,000 are paid on March 4.

Illustration 15-4
Installment Liquidation Statement

	Cash	Noncash Assets	Liabilities	Loan from A	A	B	C
					Capital Balances		
Beginning balances	$10,000	$120,000	$30,000	$5,000	$25,000	$55,000	$15,000
February 15, sale of assets . .	40,000	(60,000)			(8,000)	(8,000)	(4,000)
Balances.	$50,000	$60,000	$30,000	$5,000	$17,000	$47,000	$11,000
Payment of liabilities.	(30,000)		(30,000)				
February 17, distribution							
(Schedule A)	(10,000)					(10,000)	
Balances.	$10,000	$60,000	0	$5,000	$17,000	$37,000	$11,000
March 2, sale of assets	15,000	(30,000)			(6,000)	(6,000)	(3,000)
Payment of liquidation							
expenses.	(8,000)				(3,200)	(3,200)	(1,600)
Balances.	$17,000	$30,000	0	$5,000	$ 7,800	$27,800	$ 6,400
March 5, distribution							
(Schedule A)	(17,000)			(800)		(15,800)	(400)
Balances.	0	$30,000	0	$4,200	$ 7,800	$12,000	$ 6,000
March 17, sale of assets	20,000	(10,000)			4,000	4,000	2,000
Balances.	$20,000	$20,000	0	$4,200	$11,800	$ 16,000	$ 8,000
March 18, distribution							
(Schedule A)	(20,000)			(4,200)	(3,800)	(8,000)	(4,000)
Balances.	0	$20,000	0	0	$ 8,000	$ 8,000	$ 4,000
April 1, sale of assets	24,000	(20,000)	0	0	1,600	1,600	800
Balances.	$24,000	0			$ 9,600	$ 9,600	$ 4,800
Final distribution	(24,000)				(9,600)	(9,600)	(4,800)
Balances.	0	0	0	0	0	0	0

Schedule A—Schedule of Safe Payments

	A	B	C	Total
Profit and loss percentage	40%	40%	20%	100%
February 17 Distribution				
Combined capital and loan balances before distribution.	$22,000	$47,000	$11,000	$80,000
Estimated liquidation expenses	(4,000)	(4,000)	(2,000)	(10,000)
Balances	$18,000	$43,000	$9,000	$70,000
Maximum loss possible	(24,000)	(24,000)	(12,000)	(60,000)
Balances	$ (6,000)	$19,000	$ (3,000)	$10,000
Allocation of debit capital balances	6,000	(9,000)	3,000	0
Safe payment	0	$10,000	0	$10,000
March 5 Distribution				
Combined capital and loan balances before distribution.	$12,800	$27,800	$ 6,400	$47,000
Maximum loss possible	(12,000)	(12,000)	(6,000)	(30,000)
Safe payments	$ 800	$15,800	$ 400	$17,000
March 18 Distribution (schedule not required)				
Combined capital and loan balances before distribution.	$16,000	$16,000	$ 8,000	$40,000
Maximum loss possible	(8,000)	(8,000)	(4,000)	(20,000)
Safe payments	$ 8,000	$ 8,000	$ 4,000	$20,000

Illustration 15-4 is based on these facts and demonstrates the following concepts:

1. Gains and losses on realization are allocated according to the partners' profit and loss ratio.

2. Unsold noncash assets are assumed to be worthless for purposes of determining the safe payments to partners.

3. Loan balances are combined with capital balances according to the right-of-offset doctrine. This offset can result in partners receiving distributions of capital before other partners' loan accounts have been paid (as in the February 17 distribution in Illustration 15-4). However, such distributions may be placed in escrow until it is certain that debit balances will not develop in these partners' capital accounts.

4. Distributions are applied to a partner's loan balance before they are applied to the partner's capital balance.

5. Typically, the doctrine of marshaling of assets is ignored until all assets have been realized, at which time debit balances in partners' capital accounts may be satisfied through contributions of personal assets.

6. A schedule of safe payments is an iterative process that will cease when the schedule indicates that a given distribution will be shared among all partners. Further distributions will be allocated among the partners according to their profit and loss ratio. For example, when the March 5 distribution in Schedule A indicates that all partners will receive a portion of the distribution, the distribution on March 18 would be made in the profit and loss ratio, with results identical to those that would be indicated by continuing the schedule of safe payments:

Partner	(1) Total Distribution to All Partners	(2) Partners' Profit and Loss Percentage	(1) × (2) Amount to be Distributed	Amount to Be Distributed Per Schedule of Safe Payments
A	$20,000	40%	$ 8,000	$ 8,000
B	20,000	40	8,000	8,000
C	20,000	20	4,000	4,000
			$20,000	$20,000

7. The partner with the greatest ability to absorb anticipated losses (i.e., to preserve a credit capital balance after allocating anticipated losses) will be the first to receive a safe payment.

Predistribution Plan.   Schedules of safe payments provide a means of guaranteeing the propriety of installment distributions to partners, especially in complex situations. However, a predistribution plan provides a less tedious means of determining distributions to partners. The predistribution plan is prepared in advance of actual distributions and provides the user with information regarding the order and amount of all future distributions. As was the case with schedules of safe payments, the predistribution plan a) combines partners' loan balances with their capital balances, b) anticipates all possible liabilities, losses on realization, and liquidation expenses, and c) recognizes that the partner with the greatest ability to absorb anticipated losses will be the first partner to receive safe payments.

To prepare the predistribution plan, all anticipated but unrecorded liabilities and liquidation expenses are allocated to the various partners' capital balances according to their profit and loss ratio. The resulting capital balances then are evaluated to determine the maximum loss from realization that could be absorbed by the partners before a debit balance is created in each of their capital accounts. As suggested by the schedule of safe payments, the partner who maintains a credit capital balance after assuming that all noncash assets are worthless is the partner with the greatest ability to absorb realization losses. Therefore, that partner will be the first to receive an actual distribution of assets.

The maximum loss a partner could absorb (*maximum loss absorbable*) before a debit balance in the partner's capital account is created, is determined by the following calculation:

$$\text{Maximum Loss Absorbable (MLA)} = \frac{\text{Partner's Capital Balance}}{\text{Partner's Profit and Loss Percentage}}$$

Since the partner with the largest MLA will be the first to receive an actual distribution, the MLAs are used to indicate the order in which partners will receive distributions. However, it should be noted that the MLAs do not indicate the amounts of the distributions. To illustrate, assume a partnership consists of three partners (A, B, and C) who have capital balances, before the realization of noncash assets, of $70,000, $60,000, and $40,000, respectively, and profit and loss percentages of 35%, 25%, and 40%, respectively. The maximum losses absorbable by Partners A, B, and C are determined as follows:

Partner	(1) Capital Balance	(2) Profit and Loss Percentage	(1) ÷ (2) Maximum Loss Absorbable	Rank
A	$70,000	35%	$200,000	Second
B	60,000	25	240,000	First
C	40,000	40	100,000	Third

If all partners had identical MLAs, all partners would share in any given distribution. Therefore, the amount of any distribution to be paid to a particular partner can be determined by calculating the distributions needed ultimately to give all partners the same MLA. In the present example, Partner B should receive distributions first, until his/her MLA is equal to the next highest MLA of $200,000. If B's capital balance was reduced to $50,000 (next highest MLA multiplied by the partner's profit and loss percentage, $200,000 × 25%) as the result of an actual distribution of $10,000, B's new MLA would be equal to A's original MLA as follows:

Partner	(1) Capital Balance	(2) Profit and Loss Percentage	(1)/(2) Maximum Loss Absorbable
A	$70,000	35%	$200,000
B	50,000	25	200,000
C	40,000	40	100,000

Therefore, the first $10,000, or any portion thereof, that is available for distribution to partners should be paid entirely to Partner B.

Partners A and B should now receive distributions until their MLAs of $200,000 are reduced to the next highest MLA of $100,000, traceable to Partner C. If A's capital balance was reduced to $35,000 ($100,000 × 35%) and B's capital balance was reduced to $25,000 ($100,000 × 25%) as the result of actual distributions of $35,000 and $25,000, respectively, to these partners, all partners would then have equivalent MLAs. Thus, the predistribution plan suggests that the next $60,000 ($35,000 + $25,000), or any portion thereof, that is available for distribution to partners should be paid to Partners A and B according to the profit ratio of 35:25 and all further distributions should be divided among all partners according to their respective profit ratio.

The process of preparing the predistribution plan is summarized as follows:

1. Calculate each partner's MLA.
2. Rank partners in descending order according to the amounts of their MLAs.
3. Determine what amount must be paid to the partner ranked first to achieve equality between the MLAs of that partner and the second-ranked partner. This amount represents the safe payment that can be paid to the first-ranked partner.
4. Determine what amount must be paid in total to those partners having equivalent MLAs so that their new MLAs would be equal to those of the next-highest-ranked partner. This amount would be divided among the partners receiving the distribution according to the relationship that their profit percentages have to each other.
5. Continue step 4 until all partners have equivalent MLAs.
6. When all partners have equal MLAs, distributions would be allocated according to the partners' profit ratio.

To demonstrate this entire process, the following facts are used as the basis for the predistribution plan in Illustration 15-5.

	Partners		
	A	B	C
Profit and loss percentage	30%	50%	20%
Combined capital and loan balance	$33,000	$45,000	$14,000
Total liabilities of the partnership equal $20,000.			
Total liquidation expenses are expected to be $10,000.			

To relate the predistribution plan in Illustration 15-5 to an actual distribution, assume that distributions are made as follows:

Date	Amount	Purpose
February 15	$20,000	Pay liabilities
March 1	5,000	Pay partners
March 15	8,000	Pay liquidation expenses
March 27	9,000	Pay partners
April 4	30,000	Pay partners

Illustration 15-5
Predistribution Plan
Computation of Payments to Partners

		Capital Balances			Maximum Loss Absorbable		
		A	B	C	A	B	C
(1)	Profit and loss percentage...	30%	50%	20%			
	Capital and loan balance...	$33,000	$45,000	$14,000			
	Allocate expected liquidation expenses	(3,000)	(5,000)	(2,000)			
(2)	Balances	$30,000	$40,000	$12,000			
	Maximum loss absorbable (MLA) [(2) ÷ (1)]				$100,000	$80,000	$60,000
(3)	Amount needed to reduce highest-ranked MLA to next-highest-ranked MLA ..				(20,000)		
	New MLAs.............				$ 80,000	$80,000	$60,000
(4)	Reduction in capital (payment) needed to achieve reduction in MLA [(3) × (1)]	(6,000)					
(5)	New capital balance [(2) – (4)]	$24,000	$40,000	$12,000			
(6)	Amount needed to reduce highest-ranked MLAs to next-highest-ranked MLA ..				(20,000)	(20,000)	
	New MLAs.............				$ 60,000	$60,000	$60,000
(7)	Reduction in capital (payment) needed to achieve reduction in MLA [(6) × (1)]	(6,000)	(10,000)				
(8)	New capital balance [(5) – (7)]	$18,000	$30,000	$12,000			

When MLAs are equal, future distributions are allocated to all partners according to their profit and loss percentages.

			Payable to			
Level	Amount	Liabilities	Estimated Liquidation Expenses	A	B	C
I	First $20,000	$20,000				
II	Next $10,000		$10,000			
III	Next $6,000			100%		
IV	Next $16,000			37.5% (⅜)	62.5% (⅝)	
V	Any additional payments			30%	50%	20%

Rather than constructing numerous schedules of safe payments to determine the recipients of these distributions, the predistribution plan indicates the following distribution:

Date	Amount	Liabilities	Liquidation Expenses	A	B	C	Level Per Plan (Illus. 15-5)
February 15	$20,000	$20,000					I
March 1	5,000			$ 5,000			III
March 15	8,000		$8,000				II
March 27	9,000			1,000			III
				3,000	$ 5,000		IV
April 4	30,000			3,000	5,000		IV
				6,600	11,000	$4,400	V
	$72,000	$20,000	$8,000	$18,600	$21,000	$4,400	

Several aspects of this distribution need to be emphasized. First, notice that actual payments to partners precede the payment of the liquidation expenses. This action is acceptable because the computations in Illustration 15-5 already had allowed for liquidation expenses of $10,000. However, if liquidation expenses exceed the estimated amount of $10,000, previous payments to partners could prove to be premature and, ultimately, could require repayments from partners to the partnership. Another important feature is that all payments required by a specific level of the plan shown in Illustration 15-5 must be satisfied before another level of the plan is entered. Finally, when a particular distribution is divided among several partners, the amount is allocated to the sharing partners according to their respective proportionate profit ratios.

Questions

1. Assuming that specific assets of a partnership have appreciated, discuss how the bonus method recognizes such appreciation as compared to the goodwill method.
2. If the existing net assets of a partnership are overvalued, discuss how both the bonus and the goodwill methods address this situation upon the admission of a new partner.
3. What is the logic supporting the allocation of asset appreciation under the goodwill method according to the profit and loss percentages of the original partners rather than according to their percentage interest in capital?
4. Assume a CPA is acquiring a capital interest in an existing partnership of CPAs. Identify several examples of intangibles the incoming partner is contributing that may suggest goodwill traceable to that partner.
5. Why is the bonus method of accounting for ownership changes more widely used in practice?
6. If a new partner acquires an interest from an existing partner at a price in excess of the book value of the selling partner's capital balance, explain how this excess amount is accounted for by the partnership and the selling partner.
7. Under what conditions might the use of the goodwill method prove to be inequitable as compared to the bonus method?
8. If goodwill is suggested by the withdrawal of a partner, what arguments support recognizing only that portion of the goodwill traceable to the withdrawing partner?

9. If an individual partner is insolvent, discuss the rights his/her unsatisfied personal creditors have against the partnership assuming that the Uniform Partnership Act is applicable.

10. If a partnership is insolvent, discuss the procedures that govern how unsatisfied partnership creditors may recover from individual partners.

11. Why is the right of offset regarding loans from partners to the partnership followed in an installment liquidation?

12. In an installment liquidation, what might the calculation of the partners' maximum loss absorbable (MLA) suggest in determining which partner will receive a distribution based on the schedule of safe payments?

13. Given a partnership liquidation, what circumstances would explain a partner's contributing personal assets even though he/she does not have a deficit capital balance?

Exercises

Exercise 1.   Riley and Smith are partners with present capital balances (book values) of $500,000 and $400,000, respectively. The partners share profits and losses according to the following percentages: 60% for Riley and 40% for Smith. Tyler is to join the original partnership upon contribution of $250,000 to the partnership in exchange for a 20% interest in capital and a 15% interest in profits and losses. Tyler's contribution consists of $170,000 of cash and equipment having a fair market value of $80,000 (the tax basis of equipment is $42,000). The assets of the original partnership have a book value equal to their fair market value except that the land has a book value of $15,000 and a market value of $55,000. The tax bases for Riley and Smith's capital balances before Tyler's entry are $425,000 and $330,000, respectively.

1. Calculate the capital balances for each individual in the new partnership, assuming use of both the bonus and goodwill methods. All implied goodwill is traceable to the original partners.

2. Calculate the tax basis of the partners' capital balances after admitting the new partner.

Exercise 2.   Rainbow Properties is a partnership consisting of three partners: Ross, Gilmore, and Bates. The partnership's primary business is the acquisition and development of land into homesites. Projects require a significant amount of capital, which often is borrowed from area banks. The three partners share profits and losses equally and have the following capital balances: $160,000 for Ross, $120,000 for Gilmore, and $200,000 for Bates. Recently, Ross was approached to sell her personal interest in the partnership to William Lane for $210,000.

1. What advantages would there be to the partnership if Lane acquired an interest directly from the partnership rather than directly from Ross?

2. What amount would Lane have to contribute to the partnership in order to have the same interest in capital as would have been acquired had Lane purchased an interest directly from Ross?

3. Assume Lane purchased a one-fourth interest in the partnership by contributing $210,000 to the partnership. Prepare the entry to record the contribution noting that existing land has a fair market value of $330,000 and a book value of $300,000 and goodwill is recognized.

Exercise 3.   Baxter and Murphy are partners whose profits and loss percentages are 60% and 40%, respectively. The book values of the partners' capital balances are $78,000 and $52,000 for Baxter and Murphy, respectively. The partners have agreed to admit Tuttle as a partner in exchange for a contribution to the partnership of cash, equipment, and land with market values of $25,000, $30,000, and $35,000, respectively. In exchange for their investment, Tuttle will receive a 30% interest in capital and a 20% interest in profits and losses. Baxter and Murphy have agreed to revise their profit and loss percentages to 48% and 32%, respectively. An analysis of existing assets held by the original partnership indicates the following book values and current values:

	Book Value	Current Value
Accounts Receivable	$120,000	$110,000
Inventory	200,000	240,000
Equipment	354,000	374,000

Prepare the entries to record the admission of Tuttle under both the bonus and goodwill methods.

Exercise 4.   After serious consideration, Bolger had decided to sell her interest in a partnership. Prior to the sale, the partnership had the following capital balances and profit and loss percentages:

Partner	Capital Balance	Profit & Loss %
Bolger	$60,000	35
Grossman	55,000	45
Swenson	35,000	20

The book values of partnership assets and liabilities reflect current values with the following exceptions:

Asset	Book Value	Current Value
Inventory	$180,000	$170,000
Equipment	200,000	210,000
Land	75,000	100,000

1. Assuming Bolger sold her interest in capital to Grossman for $80,000, what would Grossman's capital balance be after the transaction?
2. Assuming Bolger sold her interest to the partnership for $80,000 using the bonus method, what would be Grossman's capital balance after the transaction?
3. Assuming Bolger sold her interest to the partnership for $80,000 using the goodwill method, what would be Grossman's capital balance after the transaction?
4. What might be some advantages associated with the partnership acquiring Bolger's interest rather than Grossman?

Exercise 5. The following information relates to Pfarr and Williams, who are partners in a business being liquidated:

	Pfarr	Williams
Partnership balances:		
Loan payable—Williams		$ 5,000
Capital balance (deficit)	$20,000	(14,000)
Personal assets (including partnership loan payable)	30,000	22,000
Personal liabilities	15,000	21,000
Profit and loss percentage	70%	30%

1. After applying the right-of-offset doctrine, indicate how each partner's personal assets would be distributed, assuming the Uniform Partnership Act is applicable.
2. Determine the effect on the calculations in item 1 if the right-of-offset doctrine was ignored.
3. After applying the right-of-offset doctrine, indicate how each partner's personal assets would be distributed assuming common law is applicable.

Exercise 6. JKL Construction Company, a partnership, has total assets of $149,000 and total liabilities of $165,000. The following information relates to the individual partners:

	Jason	Kelly	Linden
Total personal assets	$52,000	$41,500	$28,000
Total personal liabilities	47,000	33,500	34,000
Partnership capital balance (deficit)	7,000	3,000	(26,000)
Profit and loss percentage	50%	30%	20%

If Linden inherits $16,000 after liquidation of the JKL partnership, what will be the priority and amount of claims existing against the $16,000? What claims (who and how much) will remain unsatisfied?

Exercise 7. A real estate partnership had the following condensed balance sheet prior to liquidation:

Cash	$ 12,000	Liabilities (to outsiders)	$ 35,000
Noncash Assets	180,000	Loan Payable to A	15,000
		A, Capital (50%)	45,000
		B, Capital (30%)	70,000
		C, Capital (20%)	27,000
Total Assets	$192,000	Total Liabilities and Capital	$192,000

The percentages in parentheses after the partners' capital balances represent their respective interest in profits and losses. Each of the following is independent of each other unless otherwise stated:

1. If assets with a book value of $30,000 were sold for $20,000, how much of the available cash could be distributed to Partner A?
2. If assets with a book value of $60,000 were sold for $70,000, how much of the available cash could be distributed to Partner A?
3. Assume assets with a book value of $70,000 were sold for $50,000 and that all available cash was distributed. For what amount would the remaining assets have to be sold in order for Partner B to receive a **total** of $79,000 cash from all liquidation activities?

Exercise 8.   Coleman, Moore, and Ramsey are partners in a business being liquidated. The partnership has cash of $8,000, noncash assets with a book value of $96,000, and liabilities of $63,000. The following information relates to the individual partners as of June 1, 20X7.

	Coleman	Moore	Ramsey
Loan payable to partners........		$ 5,000	
Capital balance (deficit)........	$47,000	(14,000)	$ 3,000
Personal assets..................	10,000	15,000	25,000
Personal liabilities.............	5,000	6,000	15,000
Profit and loss percentage	60%	20%	20%

On June 15, 20X7, assets with a book value of $30,000 were sold for $20,000 cash. The proceeds were used to pay off liabilities of the partnership. During the balance of June, no additional assets were liquidated, and outside creditors began to pressure the partnership for payment. On July 1, the partners agreed to contribute personal assets, to whatever extent possible, in order to eliminate their respective capital deficits. Shortly thereafter, assets with a book value of $20,000 and a market value of $23,000 were distributed to Coleman.

Assuming additional noncash assets with a book value of $40,000 are sold in July for $54,000, determine how available cash would be distributed.

Exercise 9.   Delaney, Gray, and Sullivan are considering the liquidation of their partnership, which has assets of $110,000 and liabilities, including a $10,000 loan from Sullivan, of $30,000. Delaney and Gray each have capital balances of $33,000. Profits and losses are shared 30%, 30%, and 40% for Delaney, Gray, and Sullivan, respectively.

Prepare a predistribution plan to govern the possible liquidation, assuming liquidation expenses of $10,000.

Problems

Problem 15-1.   Buckner and Pressey are partners in a dry cleaning business in which profits and losses are shared equally. Buckner and Pressey have capital balances of $40,000 and $60,000, respectively.

Required:

For each of the 6 situations presented, prepare the necessary journal entries for the partnership records.

	Situations		
	(1)	(2)	(3)
Admission of new partner:			
Entering partner	Nelson	Nelson	Nelson
Purchase price	$60,000	$30,000	$40,000
Interest in capital acquired	30%	20%	30%
Paid to..................	Partnership	Partnership	Pressey
Method used..............	Bonus	Goodwill	N/A

(continued)

	Situations		
	(4)	(5)	(6)
Withdrawal of previous partner:			
Exiting partner.	Buckner	Buckner	Buckner
Selling price	$48,000	$25,000	$39,000
Interest in capital sold.	40%	20%	30%
Paid by	Partnership	Partnership	Partnership
Method used.	Bonus	Goodwill traceable to exiting partner	Goodwill traceable to all partners

Problem 15-2.   A partnership had the following condensed balance sheet:

Cash	$ 25,000	Liabilities.	$ 95,000
Noncash Assets	185,000	A, Capital (50%)	70,000
		B, Capital (30%).	30,000
		C, Capital (20%)	15,000
Total Assets	$210,000	Total Liabilities and Capital. . . .	$210,000

The percentages in parentheses after the partners' capital balances represent their respective interest in profits and losses.

Given the above information, respond to each of the following independent fact situations:

1. Assuming new Partner D acquires 30% of Partner B's interest from B for consideration of $15,000, what is Partner B's capital balance after this transaction?
2. If new Partner D were to acquire a 30% interest in the partnership by making a contribution of assets to the partnership, what would be the suggested value of the consideration?
3. If the above assets were overstated by $24,000, what amount of consideration should new Partner D convey to the partnership in exchange for a 25% interest in capital, keeping in mind that D would also be acquiring a 30% interest in profits?
4. If new Partner D conveyed assets with a fair market value of $70,000 to the partnership in exchange for a one-third interest in capital and a 25% interest in profits, what would be B's capital balance after the transaction, assuming use of the bonus method?
5. Same facts as item 4 above, but assume that the goodwill method is employed.
6. If the tangible assets of the original partnership were understated by $25,000 and new Partner D conveyed assets with a fair market value of $70,000 to the partnership in exchange for a 30% interest in capital and a 25% interest in profits, what would be A's capital balance after the transaction, assuming use of the bonus method?
7. Same facts as item 6 above, but assume that the goodwill method is employed.
8. If the tangible assets of the original partnership were overstated by $25,000 and new Partner D conveyed tangible assets with a fair market value of $22,000 to the partnership in exchange for a 25% interest in capital and a 20% interest in profits, what would be A's capital balance after the transaction, assuming use of the bonus method?
9. Same facts as item 8 above, but assume that the goodwill method is employed.

Problem 15-3.   Andrews and Block are partners in an engineering consulting company sharing profits and losses 40% and 60%, respectively, and their capital balances are $110,000 and $150,000, respectively. The recorded net assets of the company are as follows:

	Book Value	Market Value
Working capital.	$240,000	$220,000
Net property and equipment	80,000	108,000
Noncurrent liabilities.	60,000	60,000

In addition to the recorded assets, the partners feel that the company has goodwill valued at $40,000 because the company enjoys a strong client base and has earnings that are consistently above industry averages.

Carver is interested in merging his environmental consulting company with Andrews and Block. Carver's net assets to be conveyed to the partnership include the following:

	Book Value	Market Value
Working capital.	$50,000	$40,000
Net equipment.	60,000	50,000

In addition to the above-recorded net assets, Carver feels that his business contacts and expertise will add value to the existing partnership. Carver has valued these intangibles at $20,000.

Required:

1. If Carver were to acquire a 30% interest in the new partnership, how much additional cash would Carver have to contribute to the partnership?
2. If Carver were admitted to the partnership, all partners would share equally in profits and losses. All parties are somewhat uncertain about the values placed on intangible assets. Andrews and Block favor using the goodwill method to record Carver's investment in the partnership. Calculate the amount of risk to all partners this method would entail should the intangible assets not have value.
3. Discuss how a profit and loss agreement might be used to reward a new partner for intangible assets, while not recording the intangibles on the financial statements.

Problem 15-4.   The balance sheet of Alamo Trucking as of December 31, 20X8, is as follows:

Assets		Liabilities and Capital	
Cash	$ 15,000	Accounts payable.	$ 32,000
Accounts receivable, net	85,000	Loans payable	240,000
Equipment, net.	210,000	Duke, capital	16,000
Land.	60,000	Johnson, capital	22,000
Securities, at cost	20,000	Olsen, capital	80,000
Total assets	$390,000	Total liabilities and capital	$390,000

Earnings for the first quarter of 20X9 were $32,000. The partnership agreement calls for a monthly salary of $2,000 each for Duke and Johnson. Olsen is to receive interest of 20% on her quarterly beginning capital balance. Remaining profits or losses are to be allocated equally among the partners.

(continued)

At the beginning of the second quarter, Meyers acquired a one-fourth interest in the partnership for $45,000. The partnership agreed to record the investment by the goodwill method and to modify the profit and loss agreement as follows:

	Duke	Johnson	Olsen	Meyers
Monthly salary	$2,000	$2,000		$1,000
Bonus as a percentage of earnings after the bonus				10%
Interest on beginning quarterly capital			20%	
Profit and loss percentage	30%	20%	40%	10%

Second-quarter earnings were $22,000.

At the beginning of the third quarter, Olsen's interest in capital and profits was sold to Zeller for $92,000. The third quarter had reported earnings of $44,000.

At the beginning of the fourth quarter, Duke's interest in capital and profits was sold to the partnership for $30,000. This transaction was to be recorded by the goodwill method, recognizing goodwill traceable only to the exiting partner. The remaining partners retained their proportionate profit and loss ratio.

After Duke's retirement, Mitchell agreed to purchase a 50% interest in the partnership for $225,000. The recording of this investment was to be made using the goodwill method and was to reflect the differences between the book value and market value of certain assets as of the transaction date. Their values as of October 1, 20X9, were as follows:

	Book Value	Market Value
Accounts receivable (net)	$92,000	$73,000
Land	60,000	72,000

Required:

Prepare a schedule analyzing the changes in partners' capital balances since December 31, 20X8. Supporting calculations should be in good form.

Problem 15-5.   Book value information and market value information for the public accounting firm of Davis, Baker, and Winslow as of December 31, 20X9, are as follows:

	Book Value	Market Value
Cash	$ 78,000	$ 78,000
Receivables, net	43,000	32,000
Furniture and fixtures, net	22,000	18,000
Technical library, net	14,000	17,000
Securities, at cost	16,000	21,000
Other assets	2,000	
Total	$175,000	$166,000
Accounts payable	$4,500	
Wages and salaries payable	5,400	
Notes payable	20,100	
Loans payable, Davis	12,000	
Davis, capital	64,000	
Baker, capital	80,000	
Winslow, capital	(11,000)	
Total	$175,000	

In recent years, the partnership experienced serious disagreement over a variety of business issues. Liquidating the partnership has become a very real but rather lengthy alternative. Baker is impatient with the process of liquidation and offers to sell his interest in the partnership to Davis and Winslow for $70,000. The remaining partners would use the bonus method to record the transaction and then proceed with the liquidation. Winslow is anxious to proceed with the liquidation because her personal assets of $80,000 barely cover personal liabilities of $72,000.

Required:

Assuming liquidation expenses are estimated to be $6,000, would Davis and Winslow be well advised to accept Baker's offer or to just proceed directly with the liquidation of the company? Supporting calculations should be in good form.

Problem 15-6.   Partners Schmidt, Janis, and Glomski have operated a fuel oil business which has provided fuel oil to both residential and commercial customers. Due to existing soil contamination and new federal environmental laws, the operation is being required to spend approximately $90,000 to correct present conditions and acquire new equipment. Rather than incurring this expense, the partners are considering liquidating the company.

A summary of the net assets of the operation is as follows:

Net Assets	Book Value	Current Value
Cash	$ 25,000	$ 25,000
Receivables & prepaids.	42,000	35,000
Inventory	27,000	22,000
Equipment.	125,000	75,000
Real estate	210,000	140,000
Accounts payable.	(40,000)	(40,000)
Mortgage payable	(54,000)	(54,000)
Note payable to previous partner	(100,000)	(90,000)
Equipment note	(80,000)	(80,000)
Total.	$155,000	$ 33,000

It is estimated that, in order to realize the above current values, approximately $10,000 in expenses will have to be incurred for brokerage fees, commissions, and other liquidation costs.

Partnership and personal information relating to the partners is as follows:

	Schmidt	Janis	Glomski
Partnership capital balance	$ 85,000	$ 47,000	$ 23,000
Partnership profit & loss percentage.	30%	35%	35%
Personal assets.	225,000	167,000	140,000
Personal creditors	165,000	170,000	130,000

Schmidt had hoped to retire in 3 to 5 years and would welcome the opportunity to retire early. However, he is concerned that with the low liquidating values for the net assets of the company, it is possible that some of his net personal assets may have to be contributed to the partnership as part of the liquidation. Schmidt is also uncomfortable because he believes that his partners, especially Glomski, may not have adequate net personal assets to meet their partnership responsibilities. Schmidt's nephew has just returned from an extended stay in the Navy and had worked for the fuel company prior to his Navy career. The nephew has some net assets, is energetic, and is not adverse to working in the fuel business. Even though the cost to comply with the new federal standards is high, Schmidt feels that he could secure the necessary capital and persuade his nephew to join the business with an opportunity to ultimately own the company.

Required:

Schmidt has come to you seeking your advice. He is considering purchasing each of his partner's interests in the partnership rather than liquidating the company. Prepare an analysis which would suggest what Schmidt might offer to pay each of his partners, and summarize your findings in a memo to Schmidt.

Problem 15-7.   Baker, Tubbs, and Knapp have decided to liquidate their partnership due to competitive pressures. At this time, the partnership has cash of $21,000, noncash assets of $140,000, and liabilities of $130,000. The partners' capital balances, loan balances, and profit/loss percentages are as follows:

	Baker	Tubbs	Knapp
Capital balances	$12,000		$10,000
Loan balances	2,000	$3,000	4,000
Profit and loss percentage	60%	20%	20%

Liquidation expenses are estimated to be $4,000.

Required:

1.   Prepare a predistribution plan that may be used to determine how liquidation proceeds would be distributed to the partners.
2.   Given the predistribution plan, indicate the order in which the following alternative distributions would be allocated: Distribution A: Cash of $175,000. Distribution B: Cash of $156,500 and Equipment with a value of $17,000 given to Baker.
3.   Assume that the noncash assets of the partnership are liquidated as follows:

	Book Value	Proceeds
First sale	$40,000	$60,000
Second sale	70,000	82,000
Third sale	30,000	12,000

Determine how the cash available after each sale would be distributed using an installment liquidation schedule.
4.   Compare the result of required part 2 Distribution A to required part 3, and comment on the comparison.

Problem 15-8.   In light of major downturns in the economy, Barker Manufacturing experienced declining profits and defaults on several loans. In a recent meeting, the three partners in the business agreed to continue operations another 6 months if the partners would make personal loans to the company. These loans were made; yet no significant favorable changes occurred, and the partners agreed to liquidate the partnership. The trial balance prior to liquidation is as follows:

	Debit	Credit
Cash		$ 2,000
Other Assets	$141,000	
Loans from Barker		50,000
Loans from Dunton		24,000
Other Liabilities		82,000
Capital, Barker		16,000
Capital, Dunton	18,000	
Capital, Jacoby	15,000	
	$174,000	$174,000

Following the decision to liquidate, the partners agreed that available funds will be distributed at the end of each month. Furthermore, if necessary, the partners will contribute available personal assets to satisfy capital deficits. However, they agreed that the right of offset, with respect to partnership loans, would be observed.

During the first month of liquidation, assets with a book value of $32,000 were sold for $26,000. Actual liquidation expenses of $4,000 occurred, and future liquidation expenses of $3,000 were estimated. Personal assets and liabilities were as follows:

	Barker	Dunton	Jacoby
Personal assets (including loans to partnership)	$160,000	$48,000	$50,000
Personal liabilities	100,000	30,000	21,000

During the second month of liquidation, assets with a book value of $68,000 were sold for $30,000. Actual liquidation expenses of $5,000 were incurred during the month, and no future liquidation expenses were anticipated. Personal assets and liabilities were as follows:

	Barker	Dunton	Jacoby
Personal assets (including loans to partnership)	$130,000	$40,000	$28,000
Personal liabilities	110,000	20,000	24,000

During the third and final month of liquidation, the balance of the other assets was sold for $11,000. Personal assets and liabilities were as follows:

	Barker	Dunton	Jacoby
Personal assets (including loans to partnership)	$108,000	$36,000	$20,000
Personal liabilities	90,000	18,000	26,000

Required:

Assume the profit and loss percentages are 50%, 30%, and 20% for Barker, Dunton, and Jacoby, respectively. Prepare a schedule that details monthly cash distributions for the liquidation.

Problem 15-9.   Ziegler, Nolan, and Petersen are partners in a residential construction business which has operated for the last 32 years in the Los Angeles area. The partners have decided to leave the business and focus on other pursuits. Initially, they had hoped to sell the business to an employee or other construction company. However, the weak housing market in the area has made liquidation of the company a more likely scenario.

You have been retained to account for the liquidation and to advise the partners as to how available assets of the company should be distributed. Events surrounding the liquidation during 20X8 are as follows:

- On June 1, the company's balance sheet reflected the following: cash—$12,000; noncash assets—$228,000; liabilities to nonpartners—$120,000; loan payable to Nolan—$15,000; Ziegler capital—$20,000; Nolan capital—$35,000; and Petersen capital—$50,000. Ziegler, Nolan, and Petersen share profits and losses of 30%, 30%, and 40%, respectively.

- A review of the financial statements reveals that additional adjustments may be in order. The company has a contingent liability associated with a previous building contract dispute. It is probable that the company will incur $13,000 of cost in connection with this matter. Final wages and related payroll tax liabilities totaling $4,400 have not been accrued.

- On June 15, vehicles with a current value of $23,000 and a book value of $14,000 were conveyed to Ziegler. Other assets with a book value of $90,000 were sold for $70,000 to a competing contractor. All available cash was distributed.

- On June 30, inventory, tools, and other equipment were sold to various employees for a total of $92,000. The items had a book value of $80,000.

- On July 10, a subcontractor was paid $15,000 to complete work on a final construction project which had not been finished prior to the liquidation. The customer was billed $20,000 for the work performed, and final payment was expected by late July.

- On July 15, available cash was distributed. However, in addition to the $13,000 of cash retained to satisfy the contingent liability, another $5,000 of cash was retained as a precaution.

- On July 25, title to a vehicle with a market value of $12,000 and a book value of $8,000 was transferred to Petersen.

- At the end of July, the contingent liability was settled for $10,000, and $20,000 was received from the last customer in payment for services performed in July.

- On August 1, all available cash was distributed.

- At mid August, all the remaining assets were disposed of for $24,000. Attorney and accounting fees associated with the liquidation were paid in the amount of $6,000. All available cash was distributed.

After all of the above events, the personal financial statements of the partners reveal the following:

	Ziegler	Nolan	Petersen
Personal assets	$185,000	$187,000	$240,000
Personal creditors	165,000	140,000	120,000

Required:

Prepare an installment liquidation schedule with all necessary supporting schedules. The schedule should also reflect the marshaling-of-assets doctrine where appropriate.

Problem 15-10. Part I: The partnership of Aikens, Barnes, and Clinton is winding up its affairs. The following information has been gathered:

a) The trial balance of the partnership at June 30, 20X7, is as follows:

Cash	6,000	
Accounts Receivable	22,000	
Inventory	14,000	
Property, Plant, and Equipment (net)	99,000	
Aikens, Loan	12,000	
Clinton, Loan	7,500	
Accounts Payable		17,000
Aikens, Capital		67,000
Barnes, Capital		45,000
Clinton, Capital		31,500
Total	160,500	160,500

b) The partners share profits and losses as follows: Aikens, 50%; Barnes, 30%; and Clinton, 20%.

c) The partners are considering an offer of $100,000 for the accounts receivable, inventory, and plant assets as of June 30. The $100,000 would be paid to the partners in installments, but the number and amounts are to be negotiated.

Required:

Prepare a predistribution plan schedule as of June 30, 20X7, showing how the $100,000 would be distributed as it becomes available.

Part II: Assume the same facts as in Part I, except that the partners have decided to liquidate their partnership instead of accepting the offer of $100,000. Cash is distributed to the partners at the end of each month. A summary of liquidation transactions follows:

July:

$16,500—collected on accounts receivable; balance is uncollectible

$10,000—received from sale of entire inventory

$ 1,000—liquidation expenses paid

$ 8,000—cash retained in the business at the end of month

August:

$ 1,500—liquidation expenses paid; Clinton's capital was reduced when Clinton accepted a piece of special equipment that had a book value of $4,000. The partners agreed that a value of $10,000 should be placed on the machine for liquidation purposes.

$2,500—cash retained in the business at the end of the month

September:

$75,000—received on sale of remaining plant assets

$ 1,000—liquidation expenses paid

No cash was retained in the business.

(continued)

Required:

Prepare a schedule of cash payments as of September 30, 20X7, showing how the cash actually was distributed. Supporting calculations should be in good form.

(AICPA adapted)

Turn-in 10/31

Problem 15-11.   The partnership agreement of Smith, Bailey, Davis, Williams, and Perry contained a buy/sell agreement, among numerous other provisions, which would become operative in case of the death of any partner. Some provisions contained in the buy/sell agreement were as follows:

1. Purposes of the buy/sell agreement:

    a) *The partners mutually desire that the business shall be continued by the survivors without interruption or liquidation upon the death of one of the partners.*

    b) *The partners also mutually desire that the deceased partner's estate shall receive the full value of the partner's interest in the partnership, and the estate shall share in the earnings of the partnership until the deceased partner's interest is fully purchased by the surviving partners.*

2. Purchase and sale of deceased partner's interest:

    a) *Upon the death of a partner, the partnership shall continue to operate.*

    b) *Upon the partner's death, the survivors shall purchase, and the executor or administrator of the deceased partner's estate shall sell to the surviving partners, the deceased partner's interest in the partnership for the price and upon the terms and conditions hereinafter set forth.*

    c) *The deceased partner's estate shall retain the deceased partner's interest until the amount specified in the next paragraph is paid in full by the surviving partners.*

    d) *The partners agree that the purchase price for the partnership interest shall be an amount equal to the deceased partner's capital account at the date of death. Said amount shall be paid to the legal representative of decedent as follows:*

        1) *The first installment of 30% of said capital account shall be paid within 60 days from the date of death of the partner, or within 30 days from the date on which the personal representative of decedent becomes qualified by law, whichever date is later, and*

        2) *The balance shall be due in four equal installments, which shall be payable annually on the anniversary date of said death.*

3. Deceased partner's estate's share of the earnings:

    a) *The partners mutually desire that the deceased partner's estate shall be guaranteed a share in the earnings of the partnership over the period said estate retains an interest in the partnership. Said estate shall not be deemed to have an interest in the partnership after the final installment for the deceased partner's capital account is paid, even though a portion of the guaranteed payments specified below may be unpaid and may be due and owing.*

    b) *The deceased partner's estate's guaranteed share of the earnings of the partnership shall be determined from two items and shall be paid at different times, as follows:*

        1) *First, interest shall be paid on the unpaid balance of the deceased partner's capital account at the same date that the installment on the purchase price is paid. The amount to be paid shall be an amount equal to*

accrued interest at the rate of 6% per annum on the unpaid balance of the purchase price for the deceased partner's capital account.

2) Second, the partners agree that the balance of the guaranteed payment from the partnership earnings shall be an amount equal to 25% of the deceased partner's share of the aggregate gross receipts of the partnership for the full 36 months preceding the month of the partner's death. Said amount shall be payable in 48 equal monthly installments without interest, and the first payment shall be made within 60 days following the death of the partner or within 30 days from the date on which the personal representative of the deceased becomes qualified, whichever date is later, provided, however, that the payment so made under this provision during any 12-month period shall not exceed the highest annual salary on a calendar-year basis received by the partner for the 3 calendar years immediately preceding the date of the partner's death. In the event that said payment would exceed said salary, then an amount per month shall be paid that does not so exceed said highest monthly salary, and the term over which payment shall be paid to the beneficiary shall be lengthened beyond the said 48 months in order to complete said payment.

Smith and Perry were killed simultaneously in an automobile accident on January 10, 20X7. The surviving partners notified the executors of both estates that the first payment due under the buy/sell agreement would be paid on March 10, 20X7, and subsequent payments would be paid on the tenth day of each month as due.

The following information was determined from the partnership records:

Partner	Profit and Loss Percentage	Capital Accounts on 1/10/X7	Annual Salaries to Partners 20X4	20X5	20X6
Smith	30%	$25,140	$16,500	$17,000	$17,400
Bailey	25	21,970	15,000	15,750	16,500
Davis	20	4,780	12,000	13,000	14,000
Williams	15	5,860	9,600	10,800	12,000
Perry	10	2,540	8,400	9,600	10,800

The partnership gross receipts for the 3 prior years were:

20X4	$296,470
20X5	325,310
20X6	363,220

985,000

Required:

Prepare a schedule of the amount to be paid to the Smith Estate and to the Perry Estate in March 20X7, December 20X7, and January 20X8. The schedule should identify the amounts attributable to earnings, to interest in the guaranteed payments, and to capital. Supporting calculations should be in good form.

(AICPA adapted)

PART

5

GOVERNMENTAL AND NOT-FOR-PROFIT ACCOUNTING

Government and not-for-profit organizations are a major force in our society, comprising one-third of the United States expenditures and employing a substantial work force.

There are approximately 87,000 local governments in the United States. These include villages, towns, cities, counties, states, school districts, universities, public authorities, or special districts. There are close to a million not-for-profits in the United States. These include schools; hospitals; social service, advocacy, cultural, and civic organizations; churches; synagogues, and mosques; and foundations.

The primary objective of external financial reporting for governmental units and not-for-profit organizations is accountability. However, there is no "bottom-line" amount or earnings per share figure to judge success. Instead, there is the elusive factor of service. To control activities and measure service, variations in the accounting and reporting process are introduced. Budgets have far greater power for control, particularly when they are entered formally into the accounting records in order to provide close comparisons with actual results. With financial resources being derived from many different sources, some with specific restrictions as to their consumption, fund accounting has traditionally been used to display proper use for intended purposes. More recently, standards setters have moved away from fund accounting for private not-for-profit organizations to an organization-wide reporting of unrestricted and donor-restricted assets and liabilities. Similarly, the government standards setters are deliberating changes to the current standards to include entity-wide financial statements.

Governmental Accounting: The General Fund and the Account Groups

This chapter, the first of two that address accounting procedures used by governmental bodies, deals with the general fund. This fund accounts for most of the ordinary transactions of a governmental body. Also explained are the unique methods used to record fixed assets and long-term debt in separate accounting records called "groups." The presentation is applicable to state and local governments. The governmental accounting procedures of this and the following chapter provide a general understanding of "fund" accounting and current governmental accounting standards issued by the Governmental Accounting Standards Board (GASB). Also included is a discussion of the proposed changes to the existing government financial reporting model. The presentation in Chapters 18 and 19 incorporates the most recent Financial Accounting Standards Board (FASB) standards issued specifically for not-for-profits.

Accounting and financial reporting for governmental and not-for-profit (also called nonprofit) entities has become more important because of the increasing portion of our national economy devoted to this sector. Decision makers, such as legislators, citizens, managers, and contributors, need better information about governmental and not-for-profit organizations if they are to make optimal resource allocations to those entities and manage them efficiently and effectively. In addition, many accounting students will hold governmental and not-for-profit accounting jobs, perform audits on such organizations, and take the CPA examination, which contains questions on governmental and not-for-profit accounting.

Commercial and Governmental Accounting: A Comparison

Illustration 16-1A is a summary of the flow of resources in a profit-seeking business enterprise. *Demand for goods and services* made by customers in the commercial sector of the economy is satisfied by business enterprises. Assets of a business enterprise are supplied voluntarily by *proprietors, stockholders, bondholders, and other creditors.* The assets are consumed during *operating processes* which produce *goods and services* sold to customers who choose to deal with the company. The sales generate *revenue* for the company. The objective of the entity is to generate net income. The income statement measures the attainment of this goal by matching revenues earned with expenses incurred using accrual accounting.

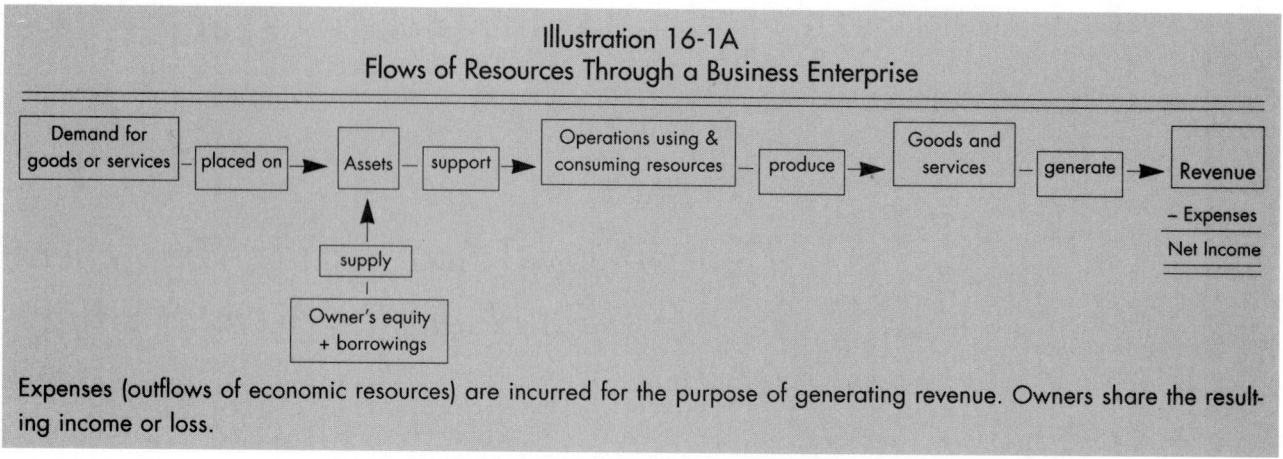

Illustration 16-1A
Flows of Resources Through a Business Enterprise

Expenses (outflows of economic resources) are incurred for the purpose of generating revenue. Owners share the resulting income or loss.

A separate cash flow statement is prepared to show the cash consequences of the period's operating, financing, and investing activities.

Illustration 16-1B is a summary of the flow of resources for a governmental entity. Residents and businesses within a government's jurisdiction *demand goods and services* from the governmental unit. *Assets* of a government are supplied primarily through the involuntary payment of *taxes* by taxpayers. Typical taxes are those levied on property, income, and sales of goods and services. There also may be some financing provided by *creditors*. The assets are consumed during *operating processes*, which produce *goods and services* dispensed to those who are legally entitled to receive them. The operations performed to provide services are not intended to generate a profit. Leftover resources at the end of a fiscal period merely lessen the need for revenue in the next period. The results of operations for an accounting period are summarized in a statement called the Statement of Revenues, Expenditures, and Changes in the Fund Balance.

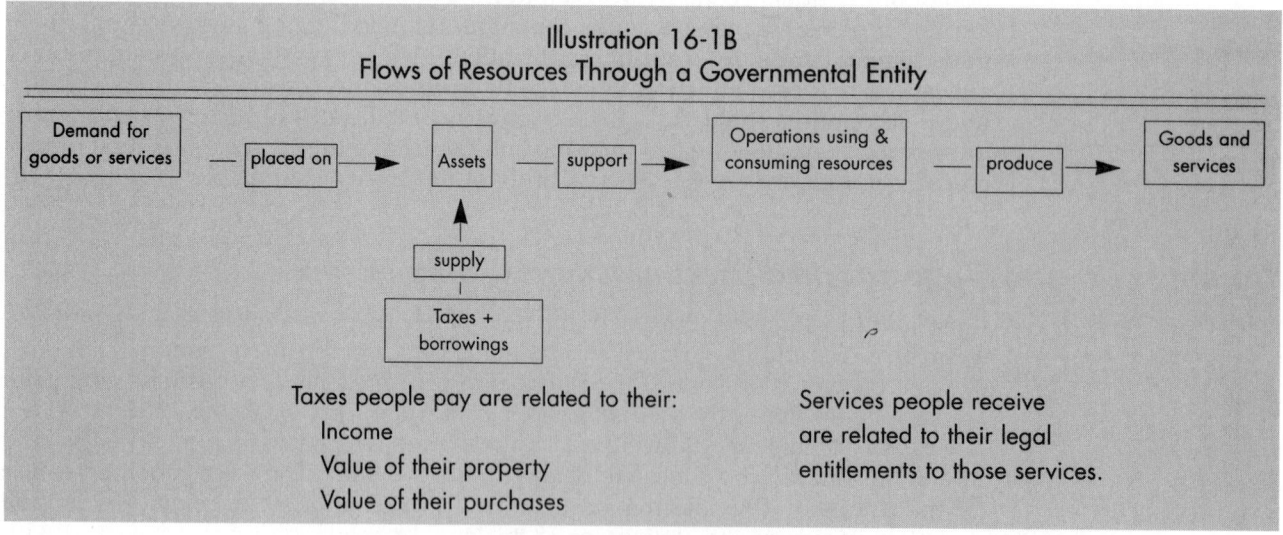

Illustration 16-1B
Flows of Resources Through a Governmental Entity

Taxes people pay are related to their:

Income
Value of their property
Value of their purchases

Services people receive
are related to their legal
entitlements to those services.

To finance general governmental activities, revenues are raised according to laws and are increases in financial resources that flow from outside the governmental unit—for example, taxes based on incomes or property values. Expenditures, such as salary payments, debt principal and interest payments, and fixed assets purchases, are incurred according to budget appropriations and are decreases in financial resources that flow to entities outside the governmental unit. The expenditures usually are not related to the amounts of taxes people pay. For example, a 7-year-old child who pays no taxes may receive a public education. Other increases in financial resources for general governmental purposes are termed "other financing sources." These include transfers from other funds within the same governmental unit and resources from several other sources including proceeds from bond issues and resources from the sale of fixed assets. Other decreases in financial resources for general governmental activities come from "other financing uses," which are typified by a transfer of financial resources to another fund within the same governmental unit. In addition, many governments engage in business activities that provide goods or services to users and finance these activities through user charges.

An important focus of governmental financial reporting is demonstrating *fiscal compliance*. Operating statements report whether or not *financial resources* received during a period are sufficient to cover expenditures of a period. Furthermore, in addition to total expenditures, whether or not spending in particular areas was in compliance with approved budgets is reported. Consequently, division of resources into *funds*, each of which is a self-balancing set of accounts, is used to keep track of the flows of financial resources dedicated to specific activities. Financial reporting on fund activities should reveal whether uses of financial resources were within restrictions imposed by law or by third parties.

A further environmental distinction between business enterprises and governmental units is *ownership versus jurisdiction*. The balance sheet residual of a business enterprise is owners' equity, denoting the ownership interest in the company. The balance sheet residual of a governmental unit, however, is *fund balance*, merely denoting the difference between assets and liabilities.

History of Governmental Financial Reporting

Three prominent periods of development in modern governmental financial reporting followed crises. In the late 1800s, large cities were rocked by misuses of funds, and accounting and financial reporting recommendations developed by the National Municipal League were adopted by some cities. In 1904, the State of New York was first to require standardized financial reporting by cities.

In the 1930s, new demands were being placed on governments while available resources were reduced by the Great Depression. The Municipal Finance Officers of America (MFOA)[1] formed its National Committee on Municipal Accounting (NCMA)[2] to promulgate accounting and financial reporting standards. The NCMA Bulletin No. 1, *Principles of Municipal Accounting*, was issued in 1934. Governmental accounting standards evolved through the actions of the NCMA and its successors. The National Committee on Governmental Accounting issued *Governmental Accounting, Auditing and Financial Reporting* (GAAFR), also called the "Blue Book," in 1968. The National Council on Governmental Accounting (NCGA) was organized in 1974, independent of the MFOA. Consequently, subsequent revisions of GAAFR codified and explained governmental financial reporting principles, but they did not have the status of "authoritative pronouncements."

In the 1970s, many cities faced fiscal stress and near-bankruptcy. Many people believed that governmental accounting and financial reporting methods were responsible in part for these fiscal problems and believed those problems were not being addressed adequately by the NCGA. Lack of confidence in the ability of the NCGA to address financial reporting issues effectively led to the formation of the Governmental Accounting Standards Board (GASB) in 1984.

---

1 Now, the Government Finance Officers Association (GFOA).
2 Renamed National Committee on Governmental Accounting in 1951 and reorganized as the National Council on Governmental Accounting (NCGA) in 1974. The NCGA was superseded by the GASB in 1984.

GASB Statement No. 1 gave authoritative status to all NCGA statements and interpretations, as well as accounting and financial reporting guidance contained in the Industry Audit Guide, *Audits of State and Local Governmental Units,* issued by the American Institute of Certified Public Accountants (AICPA) until superseded by subsequent GASB pronouncements.[3] A summary of the basic governmental accounting principles included in GASB Statement No. 1 is provided in the Appendix to this chapter.

Financial reporting standard setting for governmental units has a long history and has been a focus of numerous standard-setting boards. Illustration 16-2 presents an abridged history of financial reporting standards applicable to governments issued by major standard setters.

Illustration 16-2
Major Contributions of Governmental Accounting Standard Setters

Year	MFOA/GFOA Committees	AICPA	GASB
1934 to 1941	NCMA—*Principles of Municipal Accounting and* twelve later standards		
1951 to 1968	NCGA—four publications including 1968 Governmental *Accounting, Auditing, and Financial Reporting* (GAAFR)		
1974		*Audits of State and Local Governmental Units*	
1979 to 1982	NCGA—Four statements including the 1980 GAAFR, six interpretations, and one Concepts Statement, *Objectives of Accounting and Financial Reporting for Governmental Units*		
1980		Statement of Position 80-2 declared that financial statements presented in accordance with NCGA Statement No. 1 are in conformity with generally accepted accounting principles	
1984 to 1994			GASB, organized in 1984, has issued 32 standards and 2 concepts statements, *Objectives of Financial Reporting and Accounting for Service Efforts and Accomplishment Reporting.* Numerous projects are under way, including one which proposes sweeping changes in the way financial reports are presented. *Codification of Governmental Accounting and Financial Reporting Standards* contains generally accepted accounting principles for governmental units and is issued annually.

3 GASB Statement No. 1 *Authoritative Status of NCGA Pronouncements and AICPA Industry Audit Guide* (Norwalk, CT: Governmental Accounting Standards Board, July 1984).

Organization and Processes of the FASB and the GASB

The GASB is a sister board to the Financial Accounting Standards Board (FASB). The Financial Accounting Foundation (FAF), which appoints both boards, is responsible for their funding and the determination of their respective jurisdictions and resolves disputes which may arise between the boards.

Both the FASB and the GASB subscribe to a due process of standard setting to ensure that preparers, attestors, and users of financial statements affected by standards have a voice in the establishment of those standards. Due process includes a) issuing discussion memoranda setting forth financial reporting issues and arguments for and against possible alternative standards; b) issuing exposure drafts proposing financial reporting standards regarding issues; and c) issuing standards after considering written comments, testimony from public hearings, and research conducted by FASB and GASB staff and others throughout the due process period.

Jurisdictions of the FASB and the GASB

The authority to set external financial reporting standards for business and nonbusiness organizations rests with several standard-setting bodies. The identity of an entity's primary standard setter depends upon the nature of the operating activities of the entity issuing financial reports. Illustration 16-3 shows the primary standard setters for commercial, governmental, and not-for-profit entities.

Illustration 16-3
Authorities for Commercial, Governmental, and
Not-for-Profit Accounting Reporting Standards

Type of Entity	Primary Financial Reporting Standard Setter(s)
Business enterprises	Financial Accounting Standards Board (FASB) and Securities and Exchange Commission (SEC)
Federal government	General Accounting Office (GAO), Comptroller General, Department of the Treasury, Office of Management and Budget (OMB), and Federal Accounting Standards Advisory Board (FASAB)
State/local governments	Governmental Accounting Standards Board (GASB)
Colleges and universities	Public—GASB Private—FASB
Hospitals	Public—GASB Private—FASB
Voluntary health and welfare organizations	FASB
Certain not-for-profit organizations	FASB

Accountants and auditors of a reporting entity often rely on financial reporting standards issued by bodies of expert accountants, such as AICPA committees, that are not the entity's primary financial reporting standard setter. In addition, accountants sometimes rely on widely recognized industry practices and other relevant accounting literature, such as accounting textbooks and AICPA issues papers, in preparing financial reports in accordance with generally accepted accounting principles (GAAP). In order for accountants to know which financial reporting standards have primacy when there are multiple possibilities, the AICPA has published a hierarchy of applicable accounting principles referred to as the "GAAP hierarchy."[4] The GAAP hierarchy is directed at nongovernmental entities that look primarily to the FASB for financial reporting standards and at governmental entities that look primarily to the GASB for financial reporting standards. Generally, nongovernmental entities follow FASB pronouncements, APB Opinions, and AICPA Accounting Research Bulletins, while state and local governments follow GASB pronouncements and AICPA and FASB pronouncements if they are made applicable to state and local governments by GASB action.

GASB Objectives of Financial Reporting

We have seen differences in environments and purposes of financial reporting between business enterprises and governmental entities. These differences have led to the creation of separate financial reporting standard-setting boards for business enterprises and governments, and each board has examined and defined the objectives of financial reporting by its respective constituency. *Objectives of Financial Reporting by Business Enterprises*, Concept Statement No. 1, was issued by the FASB in 1978. *Objectives of Financial Reporting*, Concept Statement No. 1, was issued by the GASB in 1987.

In its Concept Statement No. 1, the GASB stated that "accountability is the cornerstone of all financial reporting in government."[5] A closely related concept referred to by the GASB in the concept statement is interperiod equity. Both concepts are described below.

The GASB believes that financial reporting helps a government fulfill its duty to be publicly accountable to its citizenry. They believe that taxpayers have a "right to know"; that is, a right to receive information about government activities that may lead to public debates. At a minimum, accountability through financial reporting means "providing information to assist in evaluating whether the government was operated within the legal constraints imposed by the citizenry."[6]

A significant part of accountability is *interperiod equity*, which may be demonstrated by showing "whether current-year revenues are sufficient to pay for current-year services or whether future taxpayers will be required to assume burdens for services previously provided."[7] State and local government financial reports should possess the characteristics of understandability, reliability, relevance, timeliness, consistency, and comparability.

Measurement Focus and Basis of Accounting

Measurement focus refers to which resources are being measured. *Basis of accounting* refers to when the effects of transactions or events should be recognized for financial

---

4 Statement on Auditing Standards No. 69, *The Meaning of "Present Fairly in Conformity with Generally Accepted Accounting Principles" in the Independent Auditor's Report* (New York: American Institute of Certified Public Accountants, Jan. 1992).
5 GASB Concept Statement No. 1, *Objectives of Financial Reporting* (Norwalk, CT: Governmental Accounting Standards Board, 1987), par. 58.
6 *Ibid.*
7 *Ibid.*, par. 61.

reporting purposes. In May 1990, the GASB issued a standard, GASB Statement No. 11, *Measurement Focus and Basis of Accounting—Governmental Fund Operating Statements,* which changed some basic recognition and measurement guidance for governments.[8] This new measurement focus is called the "flow of financial resources." The GASB also chose the accrual basis of accounting to accompany the flow of financial resources. The application of Statement No. 11 is, however, prohibited until its effective date—which the GASB has moved to delay. The originally scheduled effective date for Statement No. 11 was for fiscal years ending on or after June 15, 1995. In August 1993, the GASB issued Statement No. 17 which delays the effective date of Statement No. 11 indefinitely. Reasons for this delay center on the GASB project on the financial reporting model.[9]

It is conceivable that the GASB conclusions on the financial reporting project and on related issues will necessitate some Statement No. 11 provisions' being modified and, therefore, never being applicable in practice or being applicable only for some financial statements. Hence, this chapter emphasizes the currently effective accounting and reporting model of state and local governments. The Appendix to Chapter 17 details the proposed "dual-perspective" financial reporting model being deliberated by the GASB.

Governmental Accounting Structure of Funds

Governmental units use individual funds to account for financial resources used for specific purposes. Each fund is an accounting entity containing a self-balancing set of accounts for which financial statements can be prepared. Business enterprises, on the other hand, report all of their profit-making activity on a single income statement and summarize their financial position on a single balance sheet.

Currently, general purpose financial statements for governments aggregate financial information by fund type as shown in the combined balance sheet for the city of Milwaukee on page 17-40. The combined balance sheet is not subjected to the rules of consolidation to eliminate the effects of interfund transactions and interfund balances. Consolidated financial statements restricted to summarizing the effects of transactions between a governmental unit and external parties are not presented. Many argue that governmental activity does not reduce well to a single statement about profit or loss. Rather, demonstrating accountability (i.e., compliance with laws governing numerous activities) is the purpose of current governmental financial reporting.

Three fund types and two account groups are used in government financial reporting:

1. *Governmental funds* account for activities that provide citizens with services financed primarily by taxes and intergovernmental grants. These funds have a "working capital" focus and include only current assets and current liabilities.

2. *Proprietary funds* account for business-type activities that derive their revenue from charges to users for goods or services. They follow the commercial accounting model in measuring net income. An example would be a publicly owned utility.

3. *Fiduciary funds* account for resources for which the governmental unit acts as a trustee or agent.

4. *Account groups* account for and serve as a record of general fixed assets and general long-term liabilities. Financial resources and current amounts do not appear in account groups.

---

8 GASB Statement No. 11, *Measurement Focus and Basis of Accounting—Governmental Fund Operating Statements* (Norwalk, CT: Governmental Accounting Standards Board, May 1990).

9 GASB Exposure Draft, *Basic Financial Statements—and Management's Discussion and Analysis—for State and Local Governments* (Norwalk, CT: Governmental Accounting Standards Board, January 1997).

The GASB specifies different methods of applying the accrual concept in accounting for governmental funds and proprietary funds. The modified accrual basis, a hybrid system that includes some aspects of accrual accounting and some aspects of cash-basis accounting, is used for recognition of revenues and expenditures of governmental funds and similar (governmental-type) fiduciary funds. The accrual basis refers to recognition of revenues and expenses of proprietary funds and similar (proprietary-type) fiduciary funds as in business accounting.

Governmental Funds

All governments have a general fund and may have other governmental funds as well, depending on the types of activities of the government. The four governmental funds are

1. *The general fund* that accounts for resources that have no specific restrictions and are available for operational expenditures not relegated to one of the other governmental funds. Since it accounts for general operations, it is the most essential fund. Every governmental unit has a general fund.
2. *Special revenue funds* that account for resources that legally are restricted to expenditure for specific operational purposes, such as a toll tax levied to be used for road maintenance.
3. *Capital projects funds* that account for resources to be used for the construction or acquisition of major capital facilities.
4. *Debt service funds* that account for resources to be used for payment of general long-term debt and interest.

The remainder of this chapter will discuss the basic categories of transactions affecting governmental funds followed by accounting for the general fund and the account groups. The next chapter will deal with the remaining governmental funds, the proprietary funds, and the fiduciary funds.

Accounting for Transactions of Governmental Funds

The modified accrual method of accounting is used for governmental funds to measure the flow of working capital. Under the modified accrual method of accounting, *revenue* is recorded in the accounting period in which it is both measurable and available to finance expenditures made during the current fiscal period (this includes resources expected to be available within 60 days of year-end). *Expenditures* are recognized in the period in which the liabilities are both measurable and incurred.

Revenues.   These are increases in financial resources from transactions with external parties that do not have to be repaid. Revenues may come from nonexchange or exchange transactions. Nonexchange transactions are those in which people and companies pay amounts to governments but governments give nothing directly to the payors in return. Exchange transactions are those in which the government provides goods or services for fees. Under modified accrual, some revenues are recognized on the accrual basis and some revenues are recognized on the cash basis. Revenue from property taxes, intergovernmental grants, entitlements, and shared revenues; interest on investments and delinquent taxes; and billed charges for services are normally recognized under the accrual basis if funds will be "collectible within the current period or soon enough thereafter to be used to pay liabilities of the current period."[10]

---

10 GASB Interpretation No. 5, *Property Tax Revenue Recognition in Governmental Funds* (Norwalk, CT: Governmental Accounting Standards Board, November 1997).

Property taxes are recorded as revenue at the time taxes are levied on property owners provided the taxes will be collected during the current period or soon enough after year-end to pay the liabilities of the current period. Taxes levied in one year but not available until the following year are recognized as deferred revenue. Governments are conservative in recognizing property tax revenue. Only the net amount estimated to be collected is recognized.

Resources to be received from federal, state, or local governmental units (intergovernmental grants, entitlements, and shared revenues for operational purposes) should be recognized as revenue in the year for which the resources are available to finance expenditures. If resources are received prior to the period they may be used, or if the receivable is not expected to be collected soon enough to be used for the current fiscal period, Deferred Revenues are credited. Some grants to a governmental unit may carry strong restrictions on their use. For example, the federal government may be willing to give a locality a grant providing it builds a bridge over a river and connects its main road to the federal highway. In this case, the restricted grant should be recognized as revenue only to the extent that expenditures have been made, with the remainder of the grant revenue recorded as deferred. This type of restricted grant sometimes is called an *expenditure-driven* grant.

Revenues from donations of financial resources should be recognized in governmental funds when the assets are received. Donations of capital assets are not recognized in the governmental funds. Rather, donations of capital assets are recognized in the general fixed assets account group discussed later in this chapter.

Revenue for charges for services should be recognized when billed and expected to be received within 60 days of year-end. Such revenues may be from goods or services provided for fees, such as golf course fees, garbage removal fees, inspection fees, and sales of maps and other publications.

Interest and dividend revenue from investments should be recognized when earned. Investment gains and losses should be recognized when an investment is sold.

Revenues normally recognized under the cash basis method include fees for licenses and permits, fines and forfeits, and parking meter receipts. These resources are recognized when received in cash because the amount is usually not known prior to collection. In addition, these items are often not an important source of a governmental unit's income.

Taxes levied directly on taxpayers are accounted for in the same modified accrual basis of accounting that already applies to most other revenue sources.[11] Examples are taxes on income, inheritance, gasoline, general sales, and tobacco. Revenue from these taxpayer-assessed taxes, net of estimated refunds, is recognized in the accounting period in which they become susceptible to accrual, e.g., are measurable and will be collected within the current period or soon enough after year-end to finance expenditures for the period. (Note: Prior to 1993, these taxpayer-assessed taxes were accounted for on a cash basis.)

Other Financing Sources.   These inflows of financial resources arise from issuing general long-term debt, recording the present value of capital lease obligations, selling capital assets, and receiving interfund operating transfers in. Use of the other financing sources classification avoids multiple countings of inflows as revenues. Proceeds from issuing general long-term debt represent inflows of financial resources that must be repaid to lenders from later tax revenues. Tax revenue recorded in the general fund would be counted as revenue twice if amounts transferred to another governmental fund were recorded in the second fund as revenue

---

11 GASB Statement No. 22, *Accounting for Taxpayer-Assessed Tax Revenues in Governmental Funds* (Norwalk, CT: Governmental Accounting Standards Board, December 1993).

rather than as other financing sources. The same is true for proceeds from the sale of a fixed asset. Financial resources raised by tax revenues are used to purchase fixed assets. Their sale later is a conversion of fixed assets into financial resources, not a raising of new financial resources from entities outside the governmental unit.

Expenditures.   Most *expenditures* are decreases in financial resources as a result of transactions with external parties. Some expenditures, however, result from consumption of previously purchased financial resources, such as inventories and prepaid items. In certain situations, transactions with external parties that result in decreases in financial resources are classified as other financing uses. Expenditures are recognized in the period the fund liability is both measurable and incurred. This usually means that an expenditure is recognized if the related liability is expected to be liquidated through the use of expendable available financial resources. Expenditures result from operating activities, acquiring capital assets, and servicing debt. In many cases, expenditures will be recorded simultaneously with cash payments. Consider the following examples:

Expenditures (Control)	50,000	
Cash		50,000
The payment of current maintenance expenses.		

Expenditures (Control)	100,000	
Cash		100,000
Acquisition of a new capital asset for cash.		

Accounting for interest on general long-term debt is an exception to the accrual basis approach. Such expenditures are recorded on a cash basis to match them with the tax revenue raised for the interest payment.

Expenditures (Control)	42,000	
Cash		42,000
Payment of $12,000 of interest and $30,000 principal on existing general obligation debt.		

Other expenditures will be recorded if the amount is to be paid with existing resources. Consider the following entries to record wages:

Expenditures (Control)	16,500	
Cash		10,500
Liability for State and Federal Withholdings		6,000

While the liability for withholdings is current, the liability for future payment of compensated absences (such as for vacations and holidays) is considered to be long-term. Under the modified accrual basis of governmental accounting, such long-term liabilities would not be recorded in the general fund. Rather, they will be recorded in the general long-term debt account group as follows:

Amount to be Provided in Future Periods	1,500	
Liability for Compensated Absences		1,500

The compensated absences liability to be included in the fund is the amount reasonably expected to be paid from the existing governmental fund financial resources. The noncurrent liability is recognized in the general long-term debt account group. Interest on long-term debt is recorded when due.

New GASB standards for recording pension expenditures require a calculation of the "actuarial required contribution" (ARC).[12] This calculation can be made using acceptable actuarial methods and assumptions. As in the preceding example for compensated absences, the portion of the ARC that will be paid from current resources will be recorded as an expenditure in the fund.

Expenditures (Control)	5,000	
Current Pension Liability		5,000

The portion to be funded from future resources is recorded as general long-term debt in the account group as follows:

Amount to be Provided in Future Periods	2,000	
Unfunded Pension Liability		2,000

The GASB requires that a liability for claims and judgments outstanding be recognized in the accounts if it is probable that the liability has been incurred and the amount can be reasonably estimated. During the year, the government will record the amounts paid or vouchered as payable as expenditures in the fund. The noncurrent liability for claims and judgments is recorded directly in the general long-term debt account group.

In many cases, cash will be paid or a liability recorded to purchase goods and services in advance of their use. These items are recorded as financial resources (assets) as follows:

Prepaid Rent	12,000	
Prepaid Insurance	18,000	
Supplies Inventory	40,000	
Cash		70,000
Acquiring goods and services to be consumed in the future.		

Under the consumption method, expenditures are recorded when the financial resources are consumed:

Expenditures (Control)	45,000	
Prepaid Rent		10,000
Prepaid Insurance		15,000
Supplies Inventory		20,000
Receiving services and consuming supplies acquired previously.		

Notice that expenditures show the consumption of only those assets defined as financial resources. This is a narrower definition than that used in the private sector for expenses where the measurement focus is flows of economic resources. Expenses are the expirations of economic resources which include not only the use of current assets but also the amortization of long-term assets such as buildings and equipment. Examples of the differences between recording expenditures and expenses are as follows:

---

12 GASB Statement No. 27, *Accounting for Pensions by State and Local Governmental Employers* (Norwalk, CT: Governmental Accounting Standards Board; November 1994).

A Governmental Fund Using the Flows of Financial Resources Measurement Focus		A Business Entity Using the Flows of Economic Resources Measurement Focus	
Expenditures	10,000	Salary Expense	10,000
Cash	10,000	Cash	10,000
Payment of salaries; expiration of financial resource.		Payment of salaries; expiration of economic resource.	
Expenditures	90,000	Equipment	90,000
Cash	90,000	Cash	90,000
Purchase of truck; expiration of financial resource.		Purchase of truck.	
		Depreciation Expense	15,000
		Accumulated Depreciation	15,000
		Expiration of economic resource.	

An alternative method of accounting for prepaid items and supplies is the *purchases method*, which results in recording an expenditure upon acquisition, regardless of when actually consumed. Under this method, prepaid items are not recorded on the balance sheet. Significant amounts of inventory at year-end are recorded by a debit to Supplies Inventory and a credit to the Fund Balance—Reserved for Supplies. Unlike the consumption method, however, no adjustments are made to the expenditures account or the unreserved fund balance. Although both the consumption and purchase methods are recognized as acceptable alternatives, the purchases method is outdated and will no longer be acceptable under the proposed financial reporting standard.

Other Financing Uses.   The greatest use of this account classification is for operating transfers-out to other governmental funds. Using this classification for such funds outflows prevents double counting of expenditures. For example, if an amount transferred from the general fund to the debt service fund were debited to expenditures and then debited to expenditures again in the debt service fund when interest and long-term debt principal were liquidated, a double counting of expenditures would occur. Also classified as Other Financing Uses are claims incurred against financial resources from refunding general long-term debt (using proceeds from issuing new debt to pay old debt).

The following summary shows the debit and credit effects of flows of financial resources through a governmental fund. Notice that governmental funds operating statements report expenditures rather than expenses.

Governmental Funds Actual Transactions

Debits	Credits
Expenditures	Revenues
Other Financing Uses	Other Financing Sources

Operating Debt.   Governments may issue short- and long-term debt to finance their operating activities. The financing is treated as *operating debt* when the debt is not incurred to acquire capital assets or other long-term economic benefits for the government. Examples of short-term operating debt include accounts payable to vendors and tax anticipation notes. Examples of long-term operating debt include certain bonds or notes payable and long-term vendor financing. Also recognized as long-term operating debt are those obligations that a government incurs but does not pay for in a particular year, e.g., liabilities for compensated absences, claims and judgments, and unfunded pensions.

Proper recording of operating debt by government accountants is to classify the debt as short term or long term. Reporting of short-term debt is in the fund as a liability. Inflows from issuing bonds or notes are recorded as "other financing sources" in the fund. Long-term debt is reported as a liability in the general long-term debt account group.

Tax anticipation notes are an example of short-term operating debt. Cash inflows from property tax or income tax collections peak near the due dates for payment. Prior to their receipt, a governmental unit may have obligations that must be paid. Local banks usually provide short-term financing, using as security the taxing power of the government, which is required to sign an instrument referred to as a tax anticipation note. Receipt of cash from such notes would be recorded in the general fund with the following entry:

Cash	150,000	
Tax Anticipation Notes Payable		150,000

Later, as cash inflows from taxes provide resources, the following entry would record the payment of the notes and the interest:

Tax Anticipation Notes Payable	150,000	
Expenditures (Control) (for interest)	1,875	
Cash		151,875

Interest costs associated with short-term and long-term operating debt are recognized when due. Interest is not accrued.

General Long-Term Capital Debt.   Debt financing incurred to acquire capital assets or other long-term economic benefits through governmental funds is termed *general long-term capital debt*. The majority of the proceeds acquired from issuing this debt is accounted for in capital projects funds, as an other financing source, which are discussed in Chapter 17. The face amount of capital debt is accounted for in the general long-term debt account group discussed later in this chapter. Debt service (principal and interest payments) on all general long-term debt is accounted for in the debt service funds discussed in Chapter 17.

Use of Budgetary Accounting

Generally, finance personnel work with operating department personnel to develop a proposed expenditures budget for a fiscal year. The governmental unit's legislative body deliberates and acts on the budget which authorizes a certain level of expenditures for operating activities, capital acquisitions, and debt service. Authorized expenditures are termed *appropriations*. An authorization to raise revenue and, perhaps, long-term debt is approved. Estimates for other financing sources and other financing uses are also budgeted. An executive head, such as a governor or mayor, may be responsible for approving the budget or sending it back to the legislative body for further action. The budget, as finally approved, is recorded in the general ledger in summarized control accounts and in the subsidiary ledgers in detail accounts.

General Ledger Entries

Budgetary totals for appropriations (which are authorized expenditures), estimated revenues, other financing sources, and other financing uses are recorded in the general ledger as control accounts over more detailed budgetary entries in subsidiary ledgers. The following summary shows the debit and credit effects of budgetary entries:

Governmental Fund Budgetary Entries

Debit	Credit
Estimated Revenues (Control)	Appropriations (Control)
Estimated Other Financing	Estimated Other Financing
Sources (Control)	Uses (Control)

If estimated inflows do not equal estimated outflows, the difference is either a debit or credit to the budgetary fund balance—unreserved. A budgetary entry is made to the appropriate fund as follows:

Estimated Revenues (Control)	10,000,000	
Estimated Other Financing Sources (Control)	1,000,000	
Appropriations (Control)		9,300,000
Estimated Other Financing Uses (Control)		1,500,000
Budgetary Fund Balance—Unreserved		200,000
To *record* an approved annual budget.		

Actual transactions occurring during the budget year are recorded in separate general ledger accounts. This simplifies the closing process. To close the budgetary accounts, merely reverse the entry made to record the budget. Amounts may include amendments to the original budget recorded during the year. The closing entry must be entered in the same fund:

Appropriations (Control)	9,300,000	
Estimated Other Financing Uses (Control)	1,500,000	
Budgetary Fund Balance—Unreserved	200,000	
Estimated Revenues (Control)		10,000,000
Estimated Other Financing Sources (Control)		1,000,000
To *close* an annual budget as amended.		

Subsidiary Ledger Entries

Illustration 16-4, on page 16-16, will be used to show the relationship between the general ledger control accounts and the subsidiary ledgers' detail accounts. Usually, budgets are prepared according to object of expenditure. These are, for example, salaries, employee benefits, utilities, and supplies. Each object of expenditure is a line item in the budget or a classification of authorized spending by a department or function of the government. The appropriation for each line item is recorded in an expenditures subsidiary ledger account as a credit. During the accounting period, such credits will be offset by debits recording actual expenditure transactions. The credit balance in the subsidiary ledger account tells managers how much money they have remaining to spend for that line item purpose. Budgetary amounts of estimated other financing uses and actual other financing uses are recorded in the same manner. The detailed information recorded in the subsidiary ledgers is recorded at least at the level of budgetary control. That is, the accounting records should show whether authorized spending for a line item was exceeded.

A subsidiary ledger for revenues also is maintained. The budgetary amount of each revenue source is recorded in a revenues subsidiary ledger account as a debit. During the accounting period, such debits will be offset by credits recording actual revenue recognition. Budgetary amounts of estimated other financing sources and actual other financing sources are recorded in the same manner.

To emphasize accounting techniques and conserve space, this book will use only general ledger control accounts in its examples for budgetary and actual accounts.

Overview of General Fund Procedures

Illustration 16-4 is designed to be a simple example of general fund procedures that is not burdened by the complexities that follow in this chapter. It is meant to acquaint you with the mechanics of governmental accounting. There are three important features of this example you should understand:

1. There are three types of accounts in the general ledger. *Permanent balance sheet accounts* contain financial resources, liabilities, and fund balances. *Budgetary accounts* are used to record the budget. Budget amounts are entered at the start of the period, possibly amended during the period, and closed at the end of the period. There are no actual transactions recorded in these accounts during the period. *Operating accounts* record the expenditures, other financing uses, revenues, and other financing sources that occur during the period.
2. There are three types of journal entries made during the accounting period. The *budgetary entry* enters the budget into the accounting records. The *operating entries* record actual events. The *closing entries* close the budgetary accounts in one entry and the actual accounts in a second closing entry.
3. For every entry in the general ledger, there are detailed entries in the subsidiary ledgers.

Let us now follow these summary entries in Illustration 16-4. Each entry is explained as follows:

1. The budget is entered into the general ledger budgetary accounts. An excess of estimated revenues, estimated other financing sources over appropriations, and estimated other financing uses would create a credit to the budgetary fund balance. In this case, appropriations (there are no estimated other financing uses) exceed revenues and estimated other financing sources; thus, there is a debit to the budgetary fund balance. The debit entry to the budgetary fund balance anticipates a decrease in the fund balance during the period. Budgetary amounts may be amended during the year by legislative action, but are otherwise left unchanged during the period and are reversed at the end of the period as part of the closing procedure so they never actually impact the fund balance.[13] The budgetary entry is

Estimated Revenues (Control)	97,000	
Estimated Other Financing Sources (Control)	5,000	
Budgetary Fund Balance	3,000	
Appropriations (Control)		105,000

This entry is supported by detailed entries in subsidiary ledger revenue accounts, other financing sources accounts, and expenditure accounts. See entries marked "1" in the subsidiary ledger accounts. The real control feature of the budget entry is found in the subsidiary ledgers. Consider the subsidiary

---

13 Some governments do not maintain separate budgetary accounts. These governments enter the budget into the actual accounts. Since the budget is reversed at year-end, the net effect is to increase or decrease the fund balance by the difference between actual revenues and expenditures—the same impact as would have been recorded had the budgetary entries not been made.

Illustration 16-4
Simple Example of Governmental Accounts—General Ledger and Subsidiary Ledger Entries

GENERAL LEDGER ACCOUNTS:

Permanent Balance Sheet Accounts:

Cash

1/1/X2 Balance	8,000	(7) Pay vouchers	110,000
(5) Tax collection	90,500		
(3) Cash revenues	14,500		
(4) Asset sale	4,800		
12/31/X2 Balance	7,800		

Property Tax Receivable

1/1/X2 Balance	12,000	(5) Tax collection	90,500
(2) Tax Levy	85,000		
12/31/X2 Balance	6,500		

Vouchers Payable

(7) Vouchers paid	110,000	1/1/X2 Balance	13,000
		(6) Expenditures	106,800
		12/31/X2 Balance	9,800

Fund Balance

(9) Close 19X2	2,500	1/1/X2 Balance	7,000
		12/31/X2	4,500

Budgetary Accounts:

Estimated Revenues (Control)

(1) Budget entry	97,000	(8) Close budget	97,000

Estimated Other Financing Sources (Control)

(1) Budget entry	5,000	(8) Close budget	5,000

Appropriations (Control)

(8) Close budget	105,000	(1) Budget entry	105,000

Budgetary Fund Balance

(1) Budget entry	3,000	(8) Close budget	3,000

Operating Accounts:

Revenues (Control)

(9) Close actual	99,500	(2) Tax levy	85,000
		(3) Cash revenues	14,500

Other Financing Sources (Control)

(9) Close actual	4,800	(4) Asset sale	4,800

Expenditures (Control)

(6) Expenditures	106,800	(9) Close actual	106,800

ledger revenue and other financing sources accounts. Budgeted amounts are entered in the accounts as debits so that they can be compared to the actual credits as they actually occur. At any time during the year, a fast comparison of budget versus year-to-date actual is possible. At the end of the year, actual amounts are compared to budgeted to arrive at a variance. Appropriations (budgeted expenditures) are entered as credits so that they can be compared to actual debits as they occur. Again, there can be a comparison of budget versus year-to-date actual for variance analysis at the end of the period.

2. Property taxes are recorded as receivables at the time taxes are levied on property owners. Revenue is credited in the period for which the taxes are levied (that is, in the period the money will be spent) provided the taxes are due by the end of the period. Not shown are the individual receivables for each property recorded in a receivables subsidiary ledger.

Property Taxes Receivable	85,000	
Revenues (Control)		85,000

SUBSIDIARY LEDGER ACCOUNTS:

Expenditures—Salary				Revenues—Property Tax			
(6) Expenditures	57,000	(1) Enter budget	55,000	(1) Enter budget	82,000	(2) Tax Levy	85,000
Balance	2,000					Balance	3,000

Expenditures—Supplies				Revenues—Fines			
(6) Expenditures	22,000	(1) Enter budget	23,000	(1) Enter budget	12,000	(3) Cash collected	11,500
		Balance	1,000	Balance	500		

Expenditures—Repairs				Revenues—Licenses			
(6) Expenditures	9,600	(1) Enter budget	9,000	(1) Enter budget	3,000	(3) Cash collected	3,000
Balance	600						

Expenditures—Capital				Other Financing Sources—Asset Sale			
(6) Expenditures	11,500	(1) Enter budget	11,000	(1) Enter budget	5,000	(4) Cash collected	4,800
Balance	500			Balance	200		

Expenditures—Miscellaneous			
(6) Expenditures	6,700	(1) Enter budget	7,000
Balance	300		

3. Revenues from fines and licenses are recorded when cash is received because these amounts cannot be predicted accurately. The detailed source of each revenue is recorded in the subsidiary ledger.

Cash	14,500	
Revenues (Control)		14,500

4. Proceeds from the sale of used fixed assets are recorded in the general and subsidiary ledgers.

Cash	4,800	
Other Financing Sources (Control)		4,800

5. Property taxes are collected, including amounts from previous periods.

Cash	90,500	
Property Taxes Receivables		90,500

6. Expenditures are recorded when the liability is incurred and formal vouchers are prepared. Vouchers are documents attached to vendor invoices that contain information about the payables. They must be signed to authorize payments of the liabilities. Details of the expenditures are recorded in the subsidiary ledger.

Expenditures (Control)	106,800	
Vouchers Payable		106,800

7. Vouchers are paid.

Vouchers Payable	110,000	
Cash		110,000

8. The budgetary entry is closed by reversing the original budgetary entry. This "zeros out" the budgetary accounts.

Appropriations (Control)	105,000	
Estimated Revenues (Control)		97,000
Estimated Other Financing Sources (Control)		5,000
Budgetary Fund Balance		3,000

This entry is made only in the general ledger. The amounts in the subsidiary ledgers are not removed, but remain so that the budget can be compared to actual amounts.

9. Actual revenues and actual other financing sources are closed against actual expenditures to arrive at the change in the actual fund balance for the year. Again, this entry is made only in the general ledger. Detailed amounts are left in the subsidiary ledger so that variance analysis may be performed.

Revenues (Control)	99,500	
Other Financing Sources (Control)	4,800	
Fund Balance	2,500	
Expenditures (Control)		106,800

Each subsidiary ledger revenue, other financing sources, and expenditures account now may be analyzed as to the cause of variances. Finally, the balances are closed to allow for the recording of the next period's activity.

Accounting for the General Fund—An Expanded Example

To visualize the accounting process of the general fund and the flow of information that produces the financial reports, the activities of the city of Middletown will be examined for the fiscal year ended September 30, 20X7. The general fund trial balance on September 30, 20X6, is as follows:

City of Middletown General Fund Trial Balance September 30, 20X6		
Cash	$ 82,000	
Investments	153,000	
Taxes Receivable—Delinquent	30,000	
Allowance for Uncollectible Delinquent Taxes		$ 20,000
Tax Liens Receivable	24,000	
Allowance for Uncollectible Tax Liens		8,000
Supplies Inventory	10,000	
Vouchers Payable		170,000
Fund Balance—Reserved for Inventory		10,000
Fund Balance—Unreserved, Designated for Public Safety		16,000
Fund Balance—Unreserved, Undesignated		75,000
Totals	$299,000	$299,000

The city has $271,000 in financial resources (cash, net receivables, and inventory). The liability Vouchers Payable offsets $170,000 of the resources with the fund balances offsetting the remaining $101,000. The fund balance may be reserved to show obligations of a fund or legal restrictions on financial resources. The fund balance also may be *reserved* if amounts are committed and not available as cash, such as outstanding purchase orders, petty cash, receivables that are long term advances to other funds, or supplies inventory. The reserves are adjusted at year-end.

The second classification of fund balances is *unreserved*, which may be divided between *designated* and *undesignated*. The $16,000 designated for equipment may show the city council's intent to purchase a new police car. Only the $75,000 is unreserved and undesignated and, thus, available for unrestricted use in 20X7.

Uncollected property taxes may appear in three accounts. Taxes Receivable—Current is debited when property taxes are levied and Revenue is credited. When uncollected property taxes are past due and interest revenue begins to accrue, the account balance is transferred to Taxes Receivable—Delinquent. When tax liens (a claim to take property for unpaid taxes) are placed on properties for uncollected taxes, the remaining amount of uncollected property taxes is transferred to Tax Liens Receivable. In the Middletown September 30, 20X6 general fund trial balance, all property taxes receivable are past due. An allowance account for estimated uncollectibles is established for each receivable.

Recording the Budget.   The city council and the mayor have approved the budget for the following fiscal year, with estimated revenues of $1,350,000, appropriations of $1,300,000, and an estimated transfer of $30,000 to be made during the year to the debt service fund. Again, transfers to other funds are not expenditures and are segregated in the budgetary entry into a budgetary account labeled Estimated Other Financing Uses (Control). The October 1, 20X6 entry to record Middletown's fiscal year 20X7 budget for its general fund is

B1. Estimated Revenues (Control)	1,350,000	
Appropriations (Control)		1,300,000
Estimated Other Financing Uses (Control)		30,000
Budgetary Fund Balance—Unreserved		20,000

To support total estimated revenues of $1,350,000, a breakdown of sources should be provided in the explanation of the budget entry or in a separate schedule. In practice, there could be as many as one hundred or more revenue items. For purposes of illustration, however, the number of revenue items is condensed, as shown in the following schedule of estimated revenues:

City of Middletown General Fund Estimated Revenues For Year Ending September 30, 20X7	
General property taxes	$ 882,500
Fines.	75,500
Licenses and permits	50,000
Revenue from federal grants	200,000
Other revenues.	142,000
Total estimated revenues.	$1,350,000

Just as the total projected income is debited to Estimated Revenues (Control) in the general ledger, so each of the detailed estimated sources is debited to its own account in the subsidiary revenue ledger. The following subsidiary account for general property taxes illustrates the procedure of posting to subsidiary records:

Revenue Ledger

ACCOUNT General Property Taxes				ACCOUNT NO.
DATE	ITEM	DEBIT (Estimate)	CREDIT (Actual)	BALANCE (DR.) CR.
Oct. 1	Budget estimate	882,500		(882,500)

Not only must the accounting system provide for control of revenues, but it also must accommodate expenditures. To provide a basis for comparison between expected and actual expenditures, budgetary as well as actual expenditures accounts are an integral part of the accounting system. In the entry to record Middletown's budget for its general fund, the credit to Appropriations (Control) represents the estimate of the expenditures of $1,300,000 for the coming year. In support of the appropriations total, a summary of approved estimated expenditures by departments or activities might appear as follows:

City of Middletown
Department or Activity Appropriations
For Year Ending September 30, 20X7

General government: legislative, judicial, and executive	$ 129,000
Public safety.	277,300
Education	591,450
Highways and streets.	94,500
Sanitation and health.	97,750
Welfare.	51,000
Culture and recreation	59,000
Total appropriations.	$1,300,000

Each of these departments or activities must submit detailed appropriation requests on the basis of subfunctions and object of expenditure. The Education Division, for example, might present the following estimate of expenditures:

Middletown City
Education Division
Request for Appropriation
For Year Ending September 30, 20X7

Supplies	**$160,000**
Salaries.	350,000
Equipment	60,000
Professional fees	21,450
Total	$ 591,450

A further modification to controlling expenditures is to establish subsidiary accounts by division or department. If this approach is followed by Middletown City, each of the expenditure items for the Education Division would have its own subsidiary account, such as the one that follows for supplies. Each expenditure account would be designed to show the original appropriation, the encumbrances (amounts committed), the expenditures (amounts spent), and the remaining unobligated (i.e., neither encumbered nor expended) balance.

Education Division Expenditure Ledger

ACCOUNT Supplies							ACCOUNT NO.
		ENCUMBRANCES			EXPENDITURES		UNOBLIGATED BALANCE
DATE	ITEM	DEBIT	CREDIT	BALANCE	ITEM	TOTAL	
Oct. 1	Budget appropriation						**160,000**

Recording Actual Revenues and Transfers.   Property taxes are a major source of revenue for Middletown's general fund and should be recognized in the fiscal period for which the taxes are levied. The property tax roll provides information about property owners, legal descriptions, and amounts of gross tax levies. The following journal entry shows that the total tax levy against property owners is debited to Taxes Receivable—Current in a general ledger entry. The amount of allowance for uncollectible taxes is credited in the same journal entry, and the net amount (the amount the government expects to receive) is credited to Revenues (Control):

1. Taxes Receivable—Current 919,000
       Revenues (Control)   881,300
       Allowance for Uncollectible Current Taxes   37,700

Recording the revenue for the expected amount to be received is different from the accounting we would see for a business enterprise. A business enterprise would credit revenue for the entire amount of sales. In a separate entry, bad debt expense would be debited for the amount of receivables expected to be uncollectible. In a business enterprise, bad debt expense is viewed as a cost of doing business. The costs of doing business for a period (expenses) are matched on the income statement with revenues for the same period to determine net income. In governmental funds, however, property tax revenues are generated by levying taxes rather than by earning them through the production and sale of goods and services. Consequently, uncollected taxes are viewed as reductions of revenue, not as costs of doing business. If allowance amounts prove eventually to be overstated, they are written down with an offsetting credit entry to revenue. If understated, they are increased with an offsetting debit to revenue.

The general property taxes account in the subsidiary revenue ledger is credited for the actual revenue. After the preceding entry is posted, General Property Taxes appear as follows:

Revenue Ledger

ACCOUNT General Property Taxes				ACCOUNT NO.
DATE	ITEM	DEBIT (Estimate)	CREDIT (Actual)	BALANCE (DR.) CR.
Oct. 1	Budget estimate	882,500		(882,500)
1	Tax levy		**881,300**	(1,200)

During the fiscal period, a debit balance in a subsidiary revenue account usually represents additional revenue expected in the future. At the end of the fiscal period, a debit balance indicates a deficiency of actual revenue as compared to estimated revenue, while a credit balance shows an excess of actual over estimated revenues.

During the year, the following additional events related to revenue are recorded in the general fund of Middletown, whose beginning trial balance is shown on page 16-18.

Event	Entry in the General Fund		

2. Of the total delinquent taxes of $30,000 carried over from the prior period, $14,000 is collected. The balance is uncollectible.

Cash.		14,000	
Allowance for Uncollectible Delinquent Taxes		16,000	
Taxes Receivable—Delinquent			30,000

3. The excess allowance for uncollectible delinquent taxes is transferred to Revenues (Control). This transaction is viewed as a change in an accounting estimate made in a prior period.

Allowance for Uncollectible Delinquent Taxes		4,000	
Revenues (Control)			4,000

4. Of $24,000 total tax liens carried over from the prior period, $11,000 is collected. The balance is uncollectible.

Cash.		11,000	
Allowance for Uncollectible Tax Liens		8,000	
Tax Liens Receivable.			19,000

5. The remaining Tax Liens Receivable are charged against Revenues (Control). This transaction is viewed as a change in an accounting estimate made in a prior period.

Revenues (Control)		5,000	
Tax Liens Receivable.			5,000

6. Of current taxes receivable (due on or before the end of the fiscal period), $850,000 is collected during the year and $12,700 is written off as uncollectible.

Cash.		850,000	
Allowance for Uncollectible Current Taxes		12,700	
Taxes Receivable—Current.			862,700

7. A 1% sales tax on restaurant food and beverages beginning on the first day of the last quarter is adopted by Middletown. The annual budget is amended to reflect the impact of this new legislation.

Estimated Revenues (Control)		9,000	
Budgetary Fund Balance			9,000

8. Restaurant food and beverage sales for the last quarter of the year are estimated at $950,000.

Sales Tax Receivable		9,500	
Revenues (Control)			9,500

9. Police fines of $79,000 are imposed and collected during the year.

Cash.		79,000	
Revenues (Control)			79,000

10. Pet licenses are sold for 2-year periods. Half of the pet license fees collected during the current year apply to the current year. The other half apply to next year. None of the fees are refundable.

Cash.		12,000	
Revenues (Control)			6,000
Deferred Revenues			6,000

11. Revenues from other licenses and permits apply only to the current period and are not refundable.

Cash.		35,000	
Revenues (Control)			35,000

12. Interest revenue earned on investment of idle cash during the year.

Cash.		17,000	
Revenues (Control)			17,000

13. A contribution by a business to entice the city to extend a storm sewer to its property along a city street.

Cash.		130,000	
Revenues (Control)			130,000

14. City Council decided that the city's Fund Balance—Unreserved, Undesignated was too lean and rescinded its plan to buy a new police car.

Fund Balance—Unreserved, Designated for			
Public Safety.		16,000	
Fund Balance—Unreserved, Undesignated			16,000

15. At year-end, property taxes not collected are classified as delinquent, as are the estimated uncollectible allowances.

Taxes Receivable—Delinquent		56,300	
Taxes Receivable—Current			
($919,000 – $862,700)			56,300

Event	Entry in the General Fund		
	Allowance for Uncollectible Current Taxes	25,000	
	Allowance for Uncollectible Delinquent Taxes		
	($37,700 – $12,700)		25,000
16. Middletown receives a $150,000 check from the federal government for the current fiscal year to assist in the operation of its child-care program and documentation promising an additional $50,000, half of which is for the current fiscal year and half for the next fiscal year.	Cash	150,000	
	Due from Federal Government	50,000	
	Revenues (Control)		175,000
	Deferred Revenue		25,000

As indicated in the second and fourth entries, a revision of the estimated amount of uncollectible current and delinquent taxes and tax liens is treated as a change in accounting estimate through Revenues (Control). Only adjustments of confirmed errors of prior periods are recorded directly in the account Fund Balance—Unreserved, Undesignated.

Recording Encumbrances and Actual Expenditures.   To prevent overexpenditure, the Middletown general fund uses an encumbrance system. An encumbrance can be viewed as an "expected expenditure" and assists the administration to avoid overspending and to plan for payment of the "expected liability" on a timely basis. It can also be viewed as a contra-account to the fund balance to reflect the ultimate decrease that will occur. Under this system, whenever a purchase order or other commitment is approved, an entry is made to record the estimated cost of the commitment. For example, an approved purchase order for school supplies, estimated to cost $10,000, is recorded as follows:

17. Encumbrances (Control)	10,000	
Fund Balance—Reserved for Encumbrances		10,000

The entry is posted to the general ledger, where Encumbrances (Control) is a quasi-expenditure account and where Fund Balance—Reserved for Encumbrances is a form of restriction of the fund balance. The entry also is entered in the encumbrances section of the supplies account of the subsidiary expenditure ledger for the Education Division, reducing the unobligated balance, as follows:

Education Division Expenditure Ledger

ACCOUNT Supplies							ACCOUNT NO.	
		ENCUMBRANCES			EXPENDITURES		UNOBLIGATED BALANCE	
DATE	ITEM	DEBIT	CREDIT	BALANCE	ITEM	TOTAL		
Oct. 1	Budget appropriation						160,000	
4	Purchase order	**10,000**		10,000			150,000	

When the invoice is received for the purchase of items or services, the encumbrance entry is reversed, and the encumbrance is lifted to permit the deduction of the actual amount. The contra-account to the fund balance is no longer needed since the expenditure recorded will directly reduce the fund balance in the closing procedure. Note that it is always the amount of the original estimate and not the actual cost that is used in the reversing entry. Assuming that the invoice for supplies amounts to $10,200, the two entries to record the receipt of the supplies invoice are

18. Fund Balance—Reserved for Encumbrances   10,000
        Encumbrances (Control)   10,000
            To reverse entry for encumbrance at estimated cost.

19. Expenditures (Control)   10,200
        Vouchers Payable   10,200
            To record invoice at actual cost.

The supplies account in the subsidiary expenditure ledger appears as follows:

Education Division Expenditure Ledger

ACCOUNT Supplies							ACCOUNT NO.
		ENCUMBRANCES			EXPENDITURES		UNOBLIGATED
DATE	ITEM	DEBIT	CREDIT	BALANCE	ITEM	TOTAL	BALANCE
Oct. 1	Budget appropriation						160,000
4	Purchase order	10,000		10,000			150,000
Nov. 7	Invoice received		**10,000**	-0-	**10,200**	10,200	149,800

When the encumbrance and the actual amount are identical, the unobligated balance is not changed. However, when the amounts are not identical, the net effect is an adjustment of the unobligated balance to reflect the amount of the actual expenditure. Thus, at any time, the subsidiary ledgers provide a continuing record of the unobligated balances and of how closely the actual expenditures match encumbrances. The following equation is derived from an examination of the supplies account:

Unobligated balance
= Appropriations − Expenditures total − Encumbrances balance

The encumbrances account can appear as a contra to the Fund Balance—Unreserved, Undesignated at year-end as shown in the following example:

Fund balances:
    Reserved for Encumbrances   XXX
    Unreserved, Undesignated   XXX
        —Encumbrances   XXX   XXX
        Total Fund Balance   XXX

It is, however, preferable to close it against the fund balance at year-end to make it clear what amount of the fund balance is available for the future. At year-end, the remaining balance in the encumbrance account may be closed against the Fund Balance—Unreserved, Undesignated.

Fund Balance—Unreserved, Undesignated   XXX
    Encumbrances   XXX

This will leave the amount of the outstanding encumbrances in the Fund Balance—Reserved for Encumbrances, which is reported in the fund balances section of the balance sheet. Such treatment demonstrates the commitment of the government to provide for outstanding purchase orders and serves to reduce the amount of expendable available financial resources for new expenditures indicated in the Fund Balance—Unreserved, Undesignated. Encumbrances are not reported in the Statement of Revenues, Expenditures, and Changes in Fund Balances since the actual transaction with outside parties has not yet occurred.

For expenditures such as salaries, which are subject to little variation and to additional internal controls, it is not customary to involve the encumbrance accounts. When salaries are paid, they are recorded directly as expenditures and reduce the unobligated balance of the salaries account in the subsidiary expenditure ledger.

Encumbrances of a Prior Period.   When encumbrances are carried over from the prior year to the current year, the encumbrance closing entry of the prior year is reversed in order to reinstate the past commitments that will be honored in the current year.

Encumbrances	XXX	
Fund Balance—Unreserved, Undesignated		XXX

Included in the current-year budgetary entry for appropriations should be an amount equal to that prior year-end encumbrance. The encumbrances will be disposed of in the manner described earlier. The unreserved fund balance will ultimately be reduced by the current year's actual expenditures.

The following events relate to Middletown's expenditures and transfers during the year.

Event	Entry in the General Fund		
20. Throughout the year, encumbrances totaling $738,000 were recorded; there were no prior-year encumbrances.	Encumbrances (Control) . . . . Fund Balance—Reserved for Encumbrances	738,000	738,000

21. Vouchers were approved, liquidating $700,000 of encumbrances for:
   Supplies $300,000
   Building. 200,000*
   Other expenditures 272,000
       Total $772,000
	Fund Balance—Reserved for Encumbrances . . . .
	   Encumbrances (Control) . . . .
	
	Inventory of Supplies . . . .
	Expenditures (Control) . . . .
	   Vouchers Payable . . . .
		700,000
		
		300,000
		472,000
			700,000
			
			772,000

*This also requires an entry in the general fixed asset account group.			

22. Vouchers were approved for the following nonencumbered items:
   Salaries. $490,000
   Other expenditures 28,000
       Total $518,000
	Expenditures (Control) . . . .
	   Vouchers Payable . . . .
		518,000	518,000

23. Vouchers totaling $1,300,000 were paid.	Vouchers Payable . . . . Cash	1,300,000	1,300,000
24. Transfer of $30,000 is made to the debt service fund.	Other Financing Uses (Control) . . . . Cash	30,000	30,000
25. Supplies totaling $260,000 were consumed.	Expenditures (Control) . . . . Inventory of Supplies	260,000	260,000
26. Adjust Fund Balance—Reserved for Inventory of Supplies to equal inventory. (See following discussion.)	Fund Balance—Unreserved, Undesignated. . . . . Fund Balance—Reserved for Inventory of Supplies .	40,000	40,000

Fund Balance Reserves.   The amount of unreserved fund balance represents expendable, available financial resources. Any resources not available to finance expenditures of the current or future years must be removed from the unreserved fund balance. The reserve for encumbrances has already been discussed. Another asset for Middletown is the inventory of supplies, which will not be converted into cash and will not be available to meet future commitments. Therefore, the unreserved fund balance must be restricted by an amount equal to the inventory on the financial statement date. In this case, the amount of the inventory at year-end is $50,000 ($10,000 + $300,000 − $260,000). The account Fund Balance—Reserved for Inventory of Supplies is kept equal to the inventory amount by periodic adjustment through the unreserved fund balance account. Similarly, fund balance reserves may be established for petty cash and advances to other funds.

Corrections of Prior Years' Errors.   Corrections of previous years' errors in nominal accounts are made directly through the account Fund Balance—Unreserved, Undesignated. For example, Middletown failed to record invoiced expenditures for last year of $30,600 that were not encumbered. Of this amount, $10,100 was paid this year and incorrectly debited to Expenditures (Control). The unpaid portion of $20,500 was to be vouchered. The entry would be

27. Fund Balance—Unreserved, Undesignated   30,600
          Expenditures (Control)   10,100
          Vouchers Payable   20,500
              To correct error for failure to record expenditures
              chargeable to last year.

Reimbursement for Expenditure.   When expenditures are made from the general fund on behalf of other funds, a transfer is made to reimburse the general fund. The reimbursement is recorded as an expenditure by the reimbursing fund and as a reduction in expenditures by the recipient fund. For example, $3,000 is received from the Special Revenue Fund to reimburse the General Fund for payroll expenditures.

28. Cash   3,000
          Expenditures (Control)   3,000

Investments in Marketable Securities and Other Financial Instruments. Governmental entities frequently have cash available for short-, intermediate-, and long-term investment. For example, the general fund may have cash available for short periods of time pending disbursement for operating needs, the capital projects funds may have bond proceeds available for intermediate-term investment pending disbursement for construction costs, and fiduciary funds may have cash available for long-term investment. Investment pools used by several funds within a single government or by several governments may have cash available for investment for varying terms.

Governments usually make deposits with financial institutions (such as demand deposit accounts and certificates of deposit) and direct investments in U.S. government obligations. Governmental entities also invest in commercial paper, bankers' acceptances, mutual funds, pooled investment funds managed by a state treasurer, and repurchase agreements with broker–dealers. All investments, except for money market investments and participating interest-earning investment contracts with a remaining maturity of one year or less, are to be reported at *fair value* on the balance sheet. Fair value is defined as the amount at which an investment could be exchanged in a current transaction between willing parties, other than in a forced or liquidation sale.[14] The change in fair value of investments is reported as *net increase (decrease) in the fair value of investments* and recognized as revenue in the operating statement. For example, if general fund investments increased in value during the period, the following entry would be made to reflect the change in fair value:

29. Investments	4,500	
Net increase in the fair value of investments		4,500

To meet cash flow requirements for operating or capital purposes, or to earn a higher return on investment, many governments enter into *reverse repurchase agreements* and/or *securities lending transactions*. In a reverse repurchase agreement, the government temporarily converts securities in their portfolios to cash by *selling* securities to a broker–dealer for cash, with a promise to repay cash plus interest in exchange for the return of the same securities.[15] In securities lending transactions, governments *lend* out their portfolio securities in return for collateral—which may be cash, securities, or letters of credit—and simultaneously agree to return the collateral for the same securities in the future.[16]

The investments must remain on the balance sheet of the government in both cases—whether selling securities with a promise to repurchase or lending them for a period of time. The agreements to repurchase (or return) are reported as fund liabilities. Any cash received as collateral is reported as an asset. Interest costs and broker fees are reported as expenditures and are not netted with any interest earned.

Extensive note disclosures on all investments and deposits with banks and other financial institutions are required. Governments must disclose their relevant accounting policies as to investments. They must also disclose credit risk, market risk, and legal risk for all investments, including derivatives.

The preclosing year-end trial balance for Middletown is as follows:

City of Middletown General Fund Trial Balance September 30, 20X7		
Cash	$ 50,000	
Investments	157,500	
Property Taxes Receivable—Delinquent.	56,300	
Allowance for Uncollectible Delinquent Taxes		$ 25,000
Deferred Revenue.		31,000
Inventory of Supplies.	50,000	
Vouchers Payable.		190,700
Sales Taxes Receivable	9,500	
Due from Federal Government	50,000	
Fund Balance—Reserved for Inventory of Supplies		50,000
Fund Balance—Unreserved, Undesignated		20,400
Revenues (Control)		1,336,300
		(continued)

---

14 GASB Statement No. 31, *Accounting and Financial Reporting for Certain Investments and for External Investment Pools* (Norwalk, CT: Governmental Accounting Standards Board, March 1997).

15 GASB Statement No. 3, *Deposits with Financial Institutions, Investments (including Repurchase Agreements, and Reverse Repurchase Agreements)* (Norwalk, CT: Governmental Accounting Standards Board, April 1986).

16 GASB Technical Bulletin No. 94-1, *Disclosure about Derivatives and Similar Debt and Investment Transactions* (Norwalk, CT: Governmental Accounting Standards Board, December 1994).

City of Middletown General Fund Trial Balance September 30, 20X7		
Expenditures (Control)	1,250,100	
Other Financing Uses (Control)	30,000	
Encumbrances (Control)	38,000	
Fund Balance—Reserved for Encumbrances		38,000
Estimated Revenues (Control)	1,359,000	
Appropriations (Control)		1,300,000
Estimated Other Financing Uses (Control)		30,000
Budgetary Fund Balance—Unreserved		29,000
	$3,050,400	$3,050,400

Closing the General Fund

The simplest closing process is, first, to reverse the budgetary entries and then to close the actual revenue and expenditure accounts, including the other financing sources and uses accounts, into the Fund Balance—Unreserved, Undesignated account. The outstanding balance in the encumbrances account is also temporarily closed. Closing entries for Middletown would appear as follows:

B2.	Appropriations (Control)	1,300,000	
	Estimated Other Financing Uses (Control)	30,000	
	Budgetary Fund Balance—Unreserved	29,000	
	Estimated Revenues (Control)		1,359,000
	To reverse entry recording budget (including amendment).		

The final closing entry would be

30.	Revenues (Control)	1,336,300	
	Expenditures (Control)		1,250,100
	Other Financing Uses (Control)		30,000
	Fund Balance—Unreserved, Undesignated		56,200
	To close the actual accounts.		

31.	Fund Balance—Unreserved, Undesignated	38,000	
	Encumbrances (Control)		38,000
	To close outstanding encumbrances.		

Financial Reports of the General Fund

Financial statements of state and local governments are presented in columnar form for all fund types and account groups, with a combined total column, permitting an overview of the total governmental unit's operation. Existing standards require a governmental unit to issue annual combined financial statements covering all of its funds and account groups as its minimum general purpose financial statements for compliance with generally accepted accounting principles. Greater detail, including comparative data, may be provided by supplemental reports for individual funds and account groups. Both combined and individual fund and account group reports will be illustrated when appropriate.

To illustrate the recommended form of the financial statements, the year-end reports of Middletown's general fund are developed from the year-end trial balance shown on pages 16-27 to 16-28. These reports consist of a balance sheet and a statement of revenues, expenditures, and changes in fund balances.

Balance Sheet

The general fund year-end balance sheet for Middletown City, shown in Illustration 16-5, differs substantially from its private business counterpart. First, it deals primarily with current assets and current liabilities, and the difference between these two amounts appears as the fund balance—either reserved (committed) or unreserved. Second, the long-term classifications of assets and liabilities are excluded, since the general fixed assets are included in the general fixed assets account group, and the general long-term debt is carried in the general long-term debt account group.

Illustration 16-5
City of Middletown
General Fund Balance Sheet
September 30, 20X7

Assets

Cash		$ 50,000
Investments		157,500
Property taxes receivable—delinquent	$ 56,300	
Less allowance for uncollectible delinquent taxes	25,000	31,300
Sales tax receivable		9,500
Due from federal government		50,000
Inventory of supplies		50,000
Total assets		$348,300

Liabilities and Fund Equity

Liabilities:		
Vouchers payable	$190,700	
Deferred revenue	31,000	
Total liabilities		221,700
Fund balances:		
Reserved for encumbrances	$ 38,000	
Reserved for inventory of supplies	50,000	
Unreserved, undesignated	38,600	
Total fund equity		126,600
Total liabilities and fund equity		$348,300

Statement of Revenues, Expenditures, and Changes in Fund Balances

The Statement of Revenues, Expenditures, and Changes in Fund Balances is to be interpreted as an operating statement and is prepared on an all-inclusive basis, disclosing all elements that contributed to the change in fund balances. The statement contains details on the major revenue sources and on expenditures by function or program. Other financing sources or uses and any corrections that altered the fund balance also are presented. The detailed source of each revenue and purpose for each expenditure is obtained from the subsidiary ledger, not the control entries of the previous example.

For governmental funds for which an annual budget legally is adopted, a separate Statement of Revenues, Expenditures, and Changes in Fund Balances—Budget and Actual is required.[17] This statement must show both budgeted and actual amounts in order to be in compliance with generally accepted accounting principles. A variance column showing the difference between budgeted and actual amounts is advisable.

The Statement of Revenues, Expenditures, and Changes in Fund Balances—Budget and Actual for Middletown, shown in Illustration 16-6, omits the comparative figures for the preceding period, although normally they would be useful in a financial evaluation. The statement reflects estimated and actual amounts of revenues, expenditures, and other changes that relate to this year. The beginning fund balance and ending fund balance amounts are the total of unreserved and reserved fund balances. The final actual fund balances amount ($126,600) must agree with the total fund equity shown on the balance sheet.

Illustration 16-6
City of Middletown General Fund
Statement of Revenues, Expenditures, and Changes in Fund Balances—
Budget and Actual
For the Fiscal Year Ended September 30, 20X7

	Budget	Actual	Variance Favorable (Unfavorable)
Revenues:			
General property taxes	$ 882,500	$ 880,300	$ (2,200)
Fines	75,500	79,000	3,500
Licenses and permits	50,000	41,000	(9,000)
Intergovernmental revenues	200,000	175,000	(25,000)
Sales tax	9,000	9,500	500
Other revenues	142,000	151,500	9,500
Total revenues	$1,359,000	$1,336,300	$(22,700)
Expenditures:			
General government	$ 129,000	$ 120,305	$ 8,695
Public safety	277,300	252,795	24,505
Highways and streets	94,500	86,100	8,400
Sanitation and health	97,750	87,750	10,000
Welfare	51,000	46,000	5,000

---

17 The budgetary statement is prepared with the same basis of accounting used to prepare the budget. So, in practice, these numbers may be different than the Statement of Revenue, Expenditures, and Changes in Fund Balance. For simplicity, we assume in Illustration 16-6 that the budget is prepared according to generally accepted government accounting principles.

Culture and recreation	59,000	53,400	5,600
Education	591,450	603,750	(12,300)
Total expenditures.	$1,300,000	$1,250,100	$49,900
Excess of revenues over expenditures . . .	$ 59,000	$86,200	$27,200
Other financing sources (uses)	(30,000)	(30,000)	0
Excess of revenues and other sources over expenditures and other uses	$ 29,000	$ 56,200	$27,200
Fund balances, October 1, 19X3	101,000	101,000	0
Correction of prior year's expenditures . .	0	(30,600)	(30,600)
Fund balances, September 30, 20X7 . . .	$ 130,000	$ 126,600	$ (3,400)

Introduction to the Account Groups

Accounting control over general fixed assets and general long-term capital debt is maintained in the general fixed assets account group (GFAAG) and the general long-term debt account group (GLTDAG). Notice that the titles of these self-balancing sets of accounts end with the term "account group" rather than "fund." This difference in terminology from other funds removes any implication of accounting for monies. No current amounts are contained in the account groups.[18] They are used only to keep accounting control of general fixed assets and general long-term debt of the governmental unit.

Accounting and Financial Reporting for General Fixed Assets

Fixed assets of a proprietary fund or a fiduciary fund are accounted for within those funds and often are referred to as *fund capital assets*. All other fixed assets are considered *general fixed assets* and are accounted for in the general fixed assets account group. This account group, which was created to report fixed assets that are not resources of any specific fund, may be thought of as an inventory record of fixed assets for the purpose of assigning responsibility for custody and proper use. Five fixed asset categories are recommended: land, buildings, improvements other than buildings, machinery and equipment, and construction in progress. Each category should have a control account in the ledger and should be substantiated by supporting detailed records.

There is one class of fixed assets that governmental units currently may omit from their general fixed assets account group. These assets are the public domain or *infrastructure* fixed assets, such as sidewalks, streets, curbs, and bridges. Their inclusion in formal reports is recommended but not required. Whatever policy is adopted, however, must be consistently applied and disclosed in the notes to the financial statements. If infrastructure assets are formally included in the general fixed assets account group, they should be recorded as Improvements Other than Buildings. Most governmental units do not record infrastructure assets but maintain separate descriptive records on costs and financing sources.

The acquisition of a general fixed asset is recorded in the general fixed assets account group by a debit to one of the five specific asset accounts. The credit indicates the original funding source of the asset, selected from the following recommended titles:

---

[18] General long-term debt will be shown as a governmental fund liability "when due." Also, a portion should be shown as a governmental fund liability if it is expected to be paid with expendable available financial resources. These portions are removed from the GLTDAG. Examples of reclassification of long-term debt to current debt are included in the next chapter.

Investment in General Fixed Assets
—Capital Projects Funds   —Special Revenue Funds
—General Fund Revenues   —Donations

To illustrate this procedure, a building acquired with general fund revenues would require the following entries:

Fund or Group in which Entry Is Recorded	Entry		
32. General fund	Expenditures (Control)	200,000	
	Vouchers Payable.		200,000
	(This entry is part of the entry on page 16-25, which records vouchers of $772,000.)		
33. General fixed assets account group	Buildings	200,000	
	Investment in General Fixed Assets— General Fund Revenues.		200,000
	To record the fixed asset.		

The basis of a fixed asset is cost or, if the asset is donated, estimated fair market value at time of receipt. Subsequent to the acquisition of a fixed asset, capital outlay and maintenance expenditures must be accounted for separately, as they are in commercial accounting, since maintenance expenditures should not increase the book values of fixed assets.

When a governmental unit disposes of a general fixed asset, the original cost of the asset is removed from the general fixed assets account group. In the general fund, proceeds from the sale are recorded with a credit to Other Financing Sources (Control). For example, if a governmental unit sells equipment for $90,000, carried in the general fixed assets account group at $100,000, the following entries would be made:

Fund or Group in which Entry Is Recorded	Entry		
34. General fund	Cash.	90,000	
	Other Financing Sources (Control)		90,000
	To record the proceeds from the sale.		
35. General fixed assets account group	Investment in General Fixed Assets— General Fund Revenues	100,000	
	Machinery and Equipment.		100,000
	To remove the fixed asset.		

Instead of selling the equipment, assume the governmental unit traded it for a larger model costing $235,000, with an allowance of $90,000 for the smaller unit. The new asset is recorded at its total cost, with the trade-in value merely functioning as a reduction in the amount to be paid. The entries then would be

Fund or Group in which Entry Is Recorded	Entry		
36. General fund	Expenditures (Control)	145,000	
	Vouchers Payable.		145,000
	To record the outflow of cash.		
37. General fixed assets account group	Investment in General Fixed Assets— General Fund Revenues.	100,000	
	Machinery and Equipment.		100,000
	To remove the old asset.		
	Machinery and Equipment	235,000	
	Investment in General Fixed Assets— General Fund Revenues.		235,000
	To record the new fixed asset.		

Notice that there is no accumulated depreciation involved in the typical recording of the sale or exchange of a general fixed asset. When net income is determined, as in proprietary funds (or when capital maintenance is important, as in some fiduciary funds), depreciation expense must be recognized in operating statements. But governmental funds are not concerned with either of these elements.

> *To record depreciation expense in governmental funds would inappropriately mix two fundamentally different measurements, expenses and expenditures. General fixed asset acquisitions require the use of governmental fund financial resources and are recorded as expenditures. General fixed asset sale proceeds provide governmental fund financial resources. Depreciation expense is neither a source nor a use of governmental fund financial resources, and thus is not properly recorded in the accounts of such funds.19*

If a government chooses to record accumulated depreciation (not a common practice), the entry is made in the general fixed assets account group by debiting the appropriate investment in the general fixed asset account and crediting the accumulated depreciation account. Entries for the disposition of a general fixed asset would remove the related accumulated depreciation.

The general fixed asset account group is included in the combined balance sheet. A listing of general fixed assets balanced by the source of funds for the assets is a required presentation. A Statement of Changes in General Fixed Assets should be a part of the financial section of a comprehensive annual financial report (CAFR), which is discussed in Chapter 17, if that information is not included in the notes. Typical presentations include a) a Schedule of Changes in Fixed Assets by Major Class (such as Land, Buildings) in the notes to the financial statements; b) a Schedule of Changes in General Fixed Assets by Function and Activity (such as General Government, Public Safety, Highways) in the financial section of the CAFR; and c) a Comparative Statement of General Fixed Assets by Source in the financial section of the CAFR. The latter statements for Middletown are shown as follows. The statements include the transactions used as examples in this section.

		City of Middletown Comparative Statement of General Fixed Assets by Source September 30, 20X7 and 20X6	
	20X7	20X6
General fixed assets:		
Land.	$12,595,000	$12,595,000
Buildings.	28,555,000	28,355,000
Improvements other than buildings.	10,367,500	10,367,500
Machinery and equipment	4,525,000	4,390,000
Construction in progress.	17,222,500	17,222,500
Total general fixed assets	$73,265,000	$72,930,000
Investment in general fixed assets by source:		
Capital projects funds	$58,791,000	$58,791,000
General fund revenues.	5,624,000	5,289,000
Special revenue funds	3,095,000	3,095,000
Donations	5,755,000	5,755,000
Total investment in general fixed assets	$73,265,000	$72,930,000

---

19 Statement 1, *Government Accounting and Financial Reporting Principles* (Chicago: Municipal Finance Officers Association of the United States and Canada, March 1979), p. 10.

Governmental units generally comply with legal regulations in accounting for fixed assets. However, supporting records in a governmental unit often are incomplete and fail to provide the data that should be the output of a properly functioning system of asset control. The GASB is currently examining whether accounting for and financial reporting of capital assets can be changed to improve the quality of information provided to managers, citizens, legislators, and other users of governmental financial reporting.

Accounting and Financial Reporting for General Long-Term Debt

When long-term debt is related to and will be paid from proprietary or fiduciary funds, it is accounted for in those funds and is termed a *specific fund liability*. When long-term debt is related to and will be paid from governmental funds, the balance sheet reporting is in the general long-term debt account group.

The general long-term debt account group, which was designed to monitor long-term debt that is not the responsibility of any particular fund, furnishes a record of the unmatured principal of all general long-term obligations of the governmental unit. Referring to a long-term obligation as "general" indicates that the community can use its taxing power to pay debt principal and interest. General long-term debt is classified as term bonds, serial bonds, and other general long-term liabilities. Balancing debits are to Amounts Available in Debt Service Fund or to Amounts to Be Provided. The general long-term debt account group is not limited to liabilities arising from debt issuance and may include numerous types of unmatured general government liabilities, for example, claims and judgments, accumulated sick leave and other compensated absences, underfunded pension contributions, unfunded postretirement benefits other than pensions, and capital lease obligations, as well as unmatured bonds and notes. Interest is not accounted for in the general long-term debt account group. To maintain the self-balancing nature of the account group, the incurrence of long-term obligations is recorded by debiting Amount to Be Provided for Payment of [properly identified] Debt and crediting a liability account.

To illustrate the entries for the general long-term debt account group, assume that a unit incurs a general long-term obligation in the form of term bonds of $1,000,000 to acquire property.[20] Regardless of whether the bonds are issued at a premium or discount, the bond issue is recorded at its face amount in the general long-term debt account group. As shown in the following entry, the bonds are recorded in the general long-term debt account group at the face value to be redeemed at maturity.

38. Amount to Be Provided for Payment of Term Bonds   1,000,000
     Term Bonds Payable   1,000,000

Payment of both principal and interest is handled by the debt service fund, where "service" is synonymous with "payment," but the general long-term debt account group records only amounts that become available in the debt service fund for retirement of general long-term debt principal. Assuming the debt service fund receives an annual appropriation of $80,000 to provide for the eventual retirement of the term bonds, the following entry is recorded in the general long-term debt account group.

39. Amount Available in Debt Service Funds—Term Bonds   80,000
     Amount to Be Provided for Payment of Term Bonds   80,000

---

20 A term bond is one in which the entire principal is due on one date, a serial bond issue is redeemed in periodic payments. Term bonds are rare, but better illustrate entries in the general long-term debt account group.

In the combined balance sheet of a governmental unit, balances in the accounts, Amount Available and Amount to Be Provided, are shown as debits.

If sound actuarial practices have been employed, the debt service fund will retire the obligation at the appropriate time and the general long-term debt account group will make the following entry:

40.	Term Bonds Payable	1,000,000	
	Amount Available in Debt Service Funds—		
	Term Bonds		1,000,000

A comparative Statement of General Long-Term Debt for Middletown is shown below. The statement includes the transactions used as examples in this section to issue term bonds and to adjust the Amount Available in Debt Service Funds—Term Bonds and Amounts to Be Provided for Payment of Term Bonds accounts. Retirement of the term bonds would occur in a later period.

The general long-term debt account group is part of the combined balance sheet; additional information about long-term debt may appear in the notes and later in the financial section of the CAFR. Information about significant contingent liabilities, pension plan obligations, accumulated sick leave and other compensated absences, debt service requirements to maturity, commitments under noncapitalized leases, and changes in general long-term debt are required disclosures. A Statement of Changes in General Long-Term Debt is required in the CAFR unless such information is disclosed in the notes.

City of Middletown
General Long-Term Debt Account Group
Statement of General Long-Term Debt
For the Year Ended December 31, 20X7
(with comparative totals for 20X6)

Amounts available and to be provided for the retirement of general long-term debt:	20X7	20X6
Amount available in debt service fund	$ 2,102,100	$ 2,022,100
Amount to be provided for:		
Retirement of general obligation debt	20,859,950	19,939,950
Retirement of special assessment debt	2,000,000	2,000,000
Pension contribution payable from subsequent year's budget.	141,123	139,000
Capital lease purchases	135,894	99,950
Unfunded compensated absences.	163,758	160,325
Unfunded claims and judgments.	592,145	412,222
Total amounts available and to be provided.	$25,994,970	$24,773,547
General long-term debt payable:		
General obligation debt	$22,962,050	$21,962,050
Special assessment debt with governmental commitment.	2,000,000	2,000,000
Unfunded pension costs	141,123	139,000
Capital lease payable	135,894	99,950
Unfunded compensated absences.	163,758	160,325
Unfunded claims and judgment	592,145	412,222
Total general long-term debt payable	$25,994,970	$24,773,547

Leasing of equipment has become common practice among governments. When leases qualify as operating, the rent expenditures are recorded in the fund and no entry is made in the account group. However, if a lease qualifies as a capital lease (using the criteria of FASB No. 13) then the substance of the transaction is similar to the purchase of a fixed asset with long-term debt proceeds. Therefore, entries are as follows:

Event and Fund or Group in which Entry Is Recorded		Entry		
41. At inception of the lease, the present value of the lease payments is recorded in the fund as expenditures and other financing sources.	General fund	Expenditures. . . . . Other Financing Sources.	50,000	50,000
42. In the account group, the leased asset is recorded at its present value.	General Fixed Asset Account Group	Leased Asset . . . . Investment in GFA— General Funds	50,000	50,000
43. In the account group, the long-term lease obligation is recorded.	General Long-Term Debt Account Group	Amount to be Provided. . . . . Lease Obligation.	50,000	50,000

Subsequent lease payments are made from the Debt Service Fund as will be presented in Chapter 17.

Review of Entries for the General Fund and Account Groups

The following example will provide a comprehensive review of the general fund, the general fixed assets account group, and the general long-term debt account group. The general fund balance sheet for Junction City, as of December 31, 20X6, is as follows:

Junction City
General Fund Balance Sheet
December 31, 20X6

Assets

Cash.		$100,000
Taxes receivable, delinquent, 20X6	$50,000	
Less allowance for uncollectible delinquent taxes, 20X6 . .	20,000	30,000
Tax liens receivable, 20X5	$25,000	
Less allowance for uncollectible tax liens, 20X5	5,000	20,000
Inventory of supplies		20,000
Total assets		$170,000

Liabilities and Fund Equity

Liabilities:		
Vouchers payable		$ 30,000
Fund balances:		
Reserved for encumbrances	$40,000	
Reserved for inventory of supplies	20,000	
Unreserved, undesignated	80,000	
Total fund equity		140,000
Total liabilities and fund equity		$170,000

During 20X7, the following entries are recorded in the general fund of Junction City. If an event also requires that an entry be made in one of the account groups, the necessary entry is indicated as part of the event.

Event	Entry in the General Fund		

The budget is approved.

Estimated inflows are from:

Revenues	$600,000	Estimated Revenues (Control)	600,000	
General long-term debt issuance	200,000	Estimated Other Financing Sources (Control)	284,000	
Transfers from other funds	60,000	Budgetary Fund Balance—Unreserved	26,000	
Sales of fixed assets carried at		Appropriations (Control)		860,000
$100,000	24,000	Estimated Other Financing Uses (Control)		50,000

Estimated outflows are for:

Expenditures [Includes 20X6 hold-over encumbrances ($40,000) and use of supplies ($20,000)]	860,000	
Transfers to other funds	50,000	

The amount of the Fund Balance—Reserved for Encumbrances was reinstated in Encumbrances.	Encumbrances (Control)	40,000	
	Fund Balance—Unreserved, Undesignated		40,000
Property taxes of $500,000 are levied, of which $30,000 is estimated to be uncollectible.	Taxes Receivable—Current	500,000	
	Allowance for Uncollectible Current Taxes		30,000
	Revenues (Control)		470,000
Cash obtained from local banks to finance government operations in advance of collection of first property tax installment.	Cash	200,000	
	Tax Anticipation Note Payable		200,000

Collection of taxes and related interest for the year:

Current taxes	$450,000	Cash	495,000	
Delinquent taxes, 20X6	32,000	Taxes Receivable—Current		450,000
Interest on delinquent taxes	2,000	Taxes Receivable—Delinquent, 20X6		32,000
Tax liens, 20X5	10,000	Tax Liens Receivable, 20X5		10,000
Interest on tax liens, 20X5	1,000	Revenues (Control)		3,000
Total	$495,000			

Repayment of tax anticipation note payable plus interest upon collection of property taxes.	Tax Anticipation Notes Payable	200,000	
	Expenditures (Control)	3,000	
	Cash		203,000
Property against which there are unpaid tax liens for 20X5 is sold for $7,000. (The loss is an adjustment of current revenue, since it represents a change in estimate.)	Cash	7,000	
	Allowance for Uncollectible Tax Liens, 20X5	5,000	
	Revenues (Control)	3,000	
	Tax Liens Receivable, 20X5		15,000
Tax liens totaling $18,000 are issued against 20X6 delinquent taxpayers.	Tax Liens Receivable, 20X6	18,000	
	Taxes Receivable—Delinquent, 20X6		18,000
Allowance for Uncollectible Delinquent Taxes is reclassified and reduced, so as not to exceed the related receivable of $18,000. As a change in estimate, the credit is made to Revenues (Control).	Allowance for Uncollectible Delinquent Taxes, 20X6	20,000	
	Allowance for Uncollectible Tax Liens, 20X6		18,000
	Revenues (Control)		2,000

(continued)

Event	Entry in the General Fund		
Uncollected current taxes are declared delinquent and the related allowance is reclassified.	Taxes Receivable—Delinquent, 20X7	50,000	
	Taxes Receivable—Current		50,000
	Allowance for Uncollectible Current Taxes	30,000	
	Allowance for Uncollectible Delinquent Taxes, 20X7		30,000
Revenue for licenses, fees, and fines is recognized.	Fines Receivable	3,000	
	Cash	67,000	
	Revenues (Control)		70,000
To acquire land, a general long-term $200,000 serial bond issue is sold for 102.	Cash	204,000	
	Other Financing Sources (Control)		204,000
The premium is transferred to the debt service fund.	Other Financing Uses (Control)	4,000	
	Cash		4,000

This event requires an entry in the general long-term debt account group:

Amount to Be Provided for Payment of Serial
Bonds   200,000
   Serial Bonds Payable . .   200,000

Event	Entry in the General Fund		
Other funds transfer $60,000 to the general fund.	Cash	60,000	
	Other Financing Sources (Control)		60,000
Additional amount encumbered for approved purchase orders was $600,000.	Encumbrances (Control)	600,000	
	Fund Balance—Reserved for Encumbrances . . .		600,000
Compensated absences earned by employees amounted to $75,000.	No entry in the General Fund		

This event requires an entry in the general
long-term debt account group:

Amount to Be Provided for Payment of
Compensated Absences   75,000
   Unfunded Compensated Absences 75,000

Event	Entry in the General Fund		
The actuarial required contribution (ARC) of the government was calculated by the actuary to be $50,000. $20,000 was paid. The remaining $30,000 will not be funded this year.	Expenditures (Control)	20,000	
	Cash		20,000

This event requires an entry in the general
long-term debt account group:
Amount to Be Provided for payment of
Pension Obligation . . .   30,000
   Unfunded Pension
     Obligation   30,000

Event	Entry in the General Fund		

The following vouchers were approved:		Expenditures (Control)	800,000	
General expenditures	$760,000	Inventory of Supplies	70,000	
Purchase of equipment	40,000	Vouchers Payable.....................		870,000
Purchase of supplies (a perpetual				
inventory system is used)	70,000			
Total	$870,000			

Of this total, $630,000 was encumbered.	Fund Balance—Reserved for Encumbrances	630,000	
	Encumbrances (Control)		630,000

The following entry is required in the general
fixed assets account group:
Machinery and
   Equipment   40,000
   Investment in General Fixed Assets—
   General Fund   40,000

A lease agreement was signed for equipment.	Expenditures (Control)	30,000	
The present value of the lease payments is $30,000.	Other Financing Sources (Control)		30,000

This event requires an entry in the general
long-term debt account group:

Amount to Be
   Provided   30,000
   Lease Payable   30,000

This event also requires an entry in the general
fixed asset account group:

Leased Asset   30,000
   Investment in General Fixed Assets—
   Capital Lease   30,000

$50,000 was transferred from the general fund to	Other Financing Uses (Control)	50,000	
other funds.	Cash		50,000
Vouchers totaling $880,000 were paid.	Vouchers Payable	880,000	
	Cash		880,000
The year-end supplies inventory amounted to $26,000.	Expenditures (Control)	64,000	
	Inventory of Supplies ($20,000 + $70,000 −		
	$26,000)		64,000
Fund Balance—Reserved for Inventory of Supplies	Fund Balance—Unreserved, Undesignated......	6,000	
is adjusted to agree with the inventory of supplies.	Fund Balance—Reserved for Inventory of		
	Supplies ($26,000 - $20,000)..........		6,000

(continued)

Event	Entry in the General Fund		
Equipment carried at $100,000 in the general fixed assets account group is sold for $24,000.			
The following entry is required in the general fixed assets account group: Investment in General Fixed Assets— General Fund . . . . . 100,000 Machinery and Equipment 100,000	Cash . . . . Other Financing Sources (Control)	24,000	24,000
Closing entries.	Appropriations (Control)	860,000	
	Estimated Other Financing Uses (Control).	50,000	
	Estimated Revenues (Control)		600,000
	Estimated Other Financing Sources (Control). . .		284,000
	Budgetary Fund Balance—Unreserved		26,000
	Revenues (Control)	542,000	
	Other Financing Sources (Control)	318,000	
	Fund Balance—Unreserved, Undesignated	111,000	
	Expenditures (Control).		917,000
	Other Financing Uses (Control).		54,000
	Fund Balance—Unreserved, Undesignated	10,000	
	Encumbrances (Control)		10,000

Appendix

There are 12 basic governmental accounting principles included in GASB Statement No. 1 and in *Codification of Governmental Accounting and Financial Reporting Standards*. These principles form a model of fund accounting theory and are summarized below:

Principle 1—Accounting and Reporting Capabilities

A governmental accounting system must make it possible both a) to present fairly and with full disclosure the financial position and results of financial operation of the funds and account groups of the governmental unit in conformity with generally accepted accounting principles and b) to determine and demonstrate compliance with finance-related legal and contractual provisions.

Principle 2—Fund Accounting System

Governmental accounting systems should be organized and operated on a fund basis. A fund is defined as a fiscal and accounting entity with a self-balancing set of accounts recording cash and other financial resources, together with all related liabilities and residual equities or balances, and changes therein, which are segregated for the purpose of carrying on specific activities or attaining certain objectives in accordance with special regulations, restrictions, or limitations.

Principle 3—Types of Funds

The following types of funds should be used by state and local governments:

Governmental Funds:

1.   The General Fund—to account for all financial resources except those required to be accounted for in another fund.

2. Special Revenue Funds—to account for the proceeds of specific revenue sources (other than expendable trusts or for major capital projects) that are legally restricted to expenditure for specified purposes.

3. Capital Projects Funds—to account for financial resources to be used for the acquisition or construction of major capital facilities (other than those financed by proprietary funds and trust funds).

4. Debt Service Funds—to account for the accumulation of resources for, and the payment of, general long-term debt principal and interest.

Proprietary Funds:

5. Enterprise Funds—to account for operations a) that are financed and operated in a manner similar to private business enterprises where the intent of the governing body is that the costs (expenses, including depreciation) of providing goods or services to the general public on a continuing basis be financed or recovered primarily through user charges or b) where the governing body had decided that periodic determination of revenues earned, expenses incurred, and/or net income is appropriate for capital maintenance, public policy, management control, accountability, or other purposes.

6. Internal Service Funds—to account for financing of goods or services provided by one department or agency to other departments or agencies of the governmental unit, or to other governmental units, on a cost-reimbursement basis.

Fiduciary Funds:

7. Trust and Agency Funds—to account for assets held by a governmental unit in a trustee capacity or as an agent for individuals, private organizations, other governmental units, and/or other funds. These include a) expendable trust funds, b) nonexpendable trust funds, c) pension trust funds, and d) agency funds.

Principle 4—Number of Funds
Governmental units should establish and maintain those funds required by law and sound financial administration. Only the minimum number of funds consistent with legal and operating requirements should be established, however, because unnecessary funds result in inflexibility, undue complexity, and inefficient financial administration.

Principle 5—Accounting for Fixed Assets and Long-Term Liabilities
A clear distinction should be made between a) fund fixed assets and general fixed assets and b) fund long-term liabilities and general long-term debt. Fixed assets related to specific proprietary funds or trust funds should be accounted for through those funds. All other fixed assets of a governmental unit should be accounted for through the general fixed assets account group. Long-term liabilities of proprietary funds and trust funds should be accounted for through those funds. All other unmatured general long-term liabilities of a governmental unit, including special assessment debt for which the government is obligated in some manner, should be accounted for through the general long-term debt account group.

Principle 6—Valuation of Fixed Assets
Fixed assets should be accounted for at cost or, if the cost is not practicably determinable, at estimated cost. Donated fixed assets should be recorded at their estimated fair value at the time received.

Principle 7—Depreciation of Fixed Assets
Depreciation of general fixed assets should not be recorded in the accounts of governmental funds. Depreciation of general fixed assets may be recorded in cost accounting systems or calculated for cost-finding analyses, and accumulated depre-

ciation may be recorded in the general fixed assets account group. Depreciation of fixed assets accounted for in a proprietary fund should be recorded in the accounts of that fund. Depreciation is also recognized in those trust funds where expenses, net income, and/or capital maintenance are measured.

Principle 8—Accrual Basis in Governmental Accounting

The modified accrual or accrual basis of accounting, as appropriate, should be utilized in measuring financial position and operating results. Governmental fund revenues and expenditures should be recognized on the modified accrual basis. Revenues should be recognized in the accounting period in which they become available and measurable. Expenditures should be recognized in the accounting period in which the fund liability is incurred, if measurable, except for unmatured interest on general long-term debt, which should be recognized when due. Proprietary fund revenues and expenses should be recognized on the accrual basis. Revenues should be recognized in the accounting period in which they are earned and become measurable; expenses should be recognized in the period incurred, if measurable. Fiduciary fund revenues and expenses or expenditures (as appropriate) should be recognized on the basis consistent with the fund's accounting measurement objective. Nonexpendable trust and pension trust funds should be accounted for on the accrual basis; expendable trust funds should be accounted for on the modified accrual basis. Agency fund assets and liabilities should be accounted for on the modified accrual basis. Transfers should be recognized in the accounting period in which the interfund receivable and payable arise.

Principle 9—Budgeting, Budgetary Control, and Budgetary Reporting

An annual budget(s) should be adopted by every governmental unit. The accounting system should provide the basis for appropriate budgetary control. Budgetary comparisons should be included in the appropriate financial statements and schedules for governmental funds for which an annual budget has been adopted.

Principle 10—Transfer, Revenue, Expenditure, and Expense Account Classification

Interfund transfers and proceeds of general long-term debt issues should be classified separately from fund revenues and expenditures or expenses. Governmental fund revenues should be classified by fund and source. Expenditures should be classified by fund, function (or program), organization unit, activity, character, and principal classes of objects. Proprietary fund revenues and expenses should be classified in essentially the same manner as those of similar business organizations, functions, or activities.

Principle 11—Common Terminology and Classification

A common terminology and classification should be used consistently throughout the budget, the accounts, and the financial reports of each fund.

Principle 12—Interim and Annual Financial Reports

Appropriate interim financial statements and reports of financial position, operating results, and other pertinent information should be prepared to facilitate management control of financial operations, legislative oversight, and where necessary or desired, for external reporting purposes.

A comprehensive annual financial report should be prepared and published, covering all funds and account groups of the primary government (including its blended component units) and providing an overview of all discretely presented component units of the reporting entity—including an introductory section; appropriate combined, combining, and individual fund statements; notes to the financial statements; required supplementary information; schedules; narrative explanations; and statistical tables.

General purpose financial statements of the reporting entity may be issued separately from the comprehensive annual financial report. Such statements should include the basic financial statements and notes to the financial statements that are essential to fair presentation of financial position and results of operations (and cash flows of those fund types and discretely presented component units that use proprietary fund accounting). Those statements may also be required to be accompanied by required supplementary information essential to financial reporting of certain entities.

. . . the financial reporting entity consists of a) the primary government, b) organizations for which the primary government is financially accountable, and c) other organizations for which the nature and significance of their relationship with the primary government are such that exclusion would cause the reporting entity's financial statements to be misleading or incomplete. The reporting entity's financial statements should present the fund types and account groups of the primary government (including its blended component units, which are, in substance, part of the primary government) and provide an overview of the discretely presented component units.

The nucleus of a financial reporting entity usually is a primary government. However, a governmental organization other than a primary government (such as a component unit, joint venture, jointly governed organization, or other stand-alone government) serves as the nucleus for its own reporting entity when it issues separate financial statements. For all of these entities, the GASB financial reporting entity provisions should be applied in layers "from the bottom up." At each layer, the definition and display provisions should be applied before the layer is included in the financial statements of the next level of the reporting government.

Questions

1. The objective of a business enterprise is to generate _____. The objective of a government is to produce _____ _____. What entitles a recipient to receive what is produced by a government?

2. Describe four environmental differences between governmental activities of a government and the activities of a business enterprise.

3. What is the oversight body, or parent organization, of the Financial Accounting Standards Board (FASB) and the Governmental Accounting Standards Board (GASB)? Over which entities does each board have primary financial reporting standard-setting authority?

4. When the FASB and GASB have not issued financial reporting standards covering matters within their respective standard-setting jurisdictions, where else in the "GAAP hierarchy" may an accountant or auditor look for authoritative guidance?

5. What is meant by the measurement focus in accounting? What is the measurement focus for governmental funds?

6. Why is interperiod equity measurement important in governmental fund accounting?

7. Define a fund as the term is used in governmental accounting in contrast to how the term is used in commercial accounting.

8. The use of four governmental funds has been recommended. Identify the fund described in each of the following cases:

   a) *The fund that accounts for charges levied against properties directly benefited by a major capital improvement.*

b) The fund that accounts for revenues from a city sales tax legally restricted to finance new construction.

c) The fund that accounts for payment of principal and interest on general long-term debt.

d) The fund that accounts for proceeds from a bond issue to be used to construct a central library.

e) Every governmental unit should have this fund to account for day-to-day operations.

9. Define revenues and expenditures as the terms apply to governmental funds. When is each recognized in the governmental funds?

10. Distinguish between operating debt and capital debt.

11. List the advantages of introducing budgetary accounts into the accounting system.

12. What are encumbrances, and how do encumbrance accounting practices help control expenditures?

13. For what purpose does the general fixed assets account group exist?

14. Discuss the purpose of the general long-term debt account group.

15. Why does the GASB consider the recording of depreciation inappropriate in the general fund?

16. Why aren't fixed assets recorded in the accounts of a general fund? Explain.

Exercises

Exercise 1.   Select the best answer for each of the following multiple-choice questions. (Nos. 3, 5, 8, and 9–11 are AICPA adapted.)

1. In a governmental fund, which one of the following constitutes revenue?
   a) Cash received from another fund of the same unit.
   b) Bond proceeds.
   c) Property taxes.
   d) Refund on an invoice for fuel.

2. In a governmental fund, which of the following is considered an expenditure?
   a) The purchase of a capital asset.
   b) The consumption of supplies.
   c) Salaries earned by employees.
   d) All of the above.

3. Fixed assets donated to a governmental unit should be recorded
   a) At estimated fair value when received.
   b) At the lower of donor's carrying amount or estimated fair value when received.
   c) At the donor's carrying amount.
   d) As a memorandum entry only.

4. In the recording of a city's budget, which one of the following accounts is debited?
   a) Appropriations (Control).
   b) Estimated Revenues (Control).
   c) Estimated Other Financing Uses (Control).
   d) Encumbrances (Control).

5. Which of the following accounts of a governmental unit is credited when taxpayers are billed for property taxes?

    a)   Appropriations (Control).

    b)   Taxes Receivable—Current.

    c)   Estimated Revenues (Control).

    d)   Revenues (Control).

6. When a portion of property tax proceeds recorded in the general fund is transferred to another fund, the account to be debited in the general fund is

    a)   Expenditures (Control).

    b)   Revenues (Control).

    c)   Estimated Revenues (Control).

    d)   Other Financing Uses (Control).

7. The general long-term debt account group includes

    a)   All long-term debt of a governmental unit.

    b)   General long-term capital debt applicable to governmental funds.

    c)   Long-term capital debt and all long-term operating debt applicable to governmental funds.

    d)   All general long-term capital debt plus accrued interest thereon.

8. When equipment was purchased with general fund resources, an appropriate entry was made in the general fixed asset account group. What accounts would have been increased in the general fund?

    a)   Due from the general fixed asset account group.

    b)   Expenditures (Control).

    c)   Appropriations (Control).

    d)   No entry should be made in the general fund.

9. Which of the following accounts should Moon City close at the end of its fiscal year?

    a)   Vouchers Payable.

    b)   Expenditures (Control).

    c)   Fund Balance.

    d)   Fund Balance—Reserved for Encumbrances.

10. Which of the following accounts of a governmental unit is debited when a purchase order is approved?

    a)   Appropriations (Control)

    b)   Vouchers Payable

    c)   Fund Balance—Reserved for Encumbrances

    d)   Encumbrances (Control)

11. Elgar City recorded a 20-year building rental agreement as a capital lease. An asset for the building lease was recorded in the general fixed assets account group. Where should the lease liability be reported?

    a)   In the general long-term debt account group.

    b)   In the debt service fund.

    c)   In the general fund.

    d)   A lease liability should not be reported.

12. The amount available in the debt service fund is an account of a government unit that is included
    a) In the liability section of the general long-term debt account group.
    b) In the liability section of the debt service fund.
    c) In the asset section of the general long-term debt account group.
    d) In the asset section of the debt service fund.

Turn-in
11/19

Exercise 2.   Indicate the part of the general fund statement of revenues, expenditures, and changes in fund balance affected by the following transactions:
    a) *Revenues.*
    b) *Expenditures.*
    c) *Other financing sources and uses.*
    d) *Residual equity transfers.*
    e) *Statement of revenues, expenditures, and changes in fund balance is not affected.*

1. An unrestricted state grant is received.
2. The general fund paid pension fund contributions that were recoverable (reimbursed) from an internal service fund.
3. The general fund paid $60,000 for electricity supplied by the electric utility enterprise fund.
4. General fund resources were used to subsidize the swimming pool enterprise fund.
5. $90,000 of general fund resources were lent to an internal service fund.
6. A motor pool internal service fund was established by a transfer of $80,000 from the general fund. This amount will not be repaid unless the motor pool is disbanded.
7. General fund resources were used to pay amounts due on an operating lease.

(AICPA adapted)

Exercise 3.   Given the following information, you have been asked to record the budget for the general fund of the city of Monroe:

1. Inflows for 20X4 are expected to total $552,000 and include property tax revenue of $355,000, fines of $7,000, state grants of $90,000, and bond issue proceeds of $100,000.
2. Expenditures for general operations and equipment purchases for the year are estimated to be $500,000.
3. Authorized transfers include $30,000 to the debt service fund to pay interest on bond indebtedness and $15,000 to the capital projects fund to pay for cost overruns on construction of a new civic center.
4. Additional estimated receipts include $15,000 operating transfer from the special revenue fund and a $50,000 payment from the Electric Utility Enterprise Fund for property taxes.

Exercise 4.   The following information concerns tax revenues for the city of Cedar Crest. The balances concerning property taxes on January 1, 20X3 were

Delinquent property taxes receivable	$135,000
Allowance for uncollectible delinquent taxes . . .	(40,000)
Tax liens receivable	45,000
Allowance for uncollectible tax liens	(23,000)

Prepare entries in the general fund for the following 20X3 events:

Jan.   Since current property taxes would not be collected for several months, $275,000 was borrowed using tax anticipation notes.

Feb.   Tax liens of $12,000 were collected; in addition, $2,000 of interest was collected that had not been accrued. The balance of tax liens was settled by receiving $16,000 for the property subject to the tax liens.

Apr.   Collections on delinquent property taxes were $100,000, and interest of $4,500 was collected. The interest had not been accrued. The balance of the account was converted into tax liens.

July   Current property taxes were levied for $422,000 with a 5% allowance for uncollectible amounts.

Sept.   Collection of current property taxes totaled $365,000. The tax anticipation notes were paid off with interest of $18,000.

Exercise 5.   Prepare journal entries in the general fund for the following 20X4 transactions that represent inflows of financial resources to Bork City:

1. To pay the wages of part-time city maintenance employees, the Cemetery Expendable Trust Fund transfers $45,000 to the general fund.
2. A resident donates land worth $75,000 for a park.
3. The city is notified by the state that it will receive $30,000 in road assistance grants this year.
4. A fire truck with an original cost of $36,000 is sold for $9,000.
5. Sales of license stickers for park use total $5,000. The fees cover this year and next year. Patrolmen are paid from these fees to check for cars in the park without stickers.

Exercise 6.   Prepare entries in the general fund for the following transactions that represent outflows of financial resources to the city of Greene in 20X4:

1. Vouchers are prepared for the following items and amounts:

Salaries	$120,000
Repairs and maintenance	60,000
Inventory of supplies	45,000
Capital equipment	125,000
Tax anticipation notes:	
Principal	200,000
Interest	13,000

2. A transfer of $57,000 is made to the debt service fund.
3. There was no inventory of supplies at the start of the year. The inventory of supplies at year-end is $2,500.

Exercise 7.   Laster City had the following balance sheet accounts and amounts as of January 1, 20X4:

Inventory of supplies	$31,000
Fund balance, reserved for inventory	(31,000)
Fund balance, reserved for encumbrances	(18,000)
Fund balance, unreserved, undesignated	(40,000)

Prepare general fund journal entries for the following 20X4 transactions:

(continued)

1. Prior-period supplies encumbrances are reinstated in 20X4. These are included in the 20X4 budget.
2. Orders are placed for supplies inventory at an estimated cost of $70,000.
3. All inventory ordered (including amounts encumbered last year) is received; actual invoices are for $87,000.
4. The physical inventory of supplies at year-end is $35,000.

Turn-in

11/14

Exercise 8. You are maintaining a subsidiary ledger account for Police-Training Expenditures for 20X3. The following columns are used:

Date	Item	Encumbrances			Expenditures	Unobligated
		Dr.	Cr.	Bal.		Balance

Inventory purchases are initially recorded as expenditures.

Record the following 20X3 transactions in the Police Training Expenditures subsidiary ledger account:

Jan. 1   The budget includes $23,000 for police-training expenditures.
Jan. 15   Equipment and supplies, estimated at $14,000 cost, are ordered.
Feb. 1   Vouchers for $5,000 are approved for items not encumbered.
Feb. 15   Items encumbered for $12,000 on January 15 are received with invoices totaling $12,300. Supplies are expended when purchased; however, an inventory is taken at year-end, and expenditures are adjusted at that time.
June 3   The remaining encumbered expenditures arrive. The invoice totals $4,300 including items not included in the encumbered amount.
Dec. 31   An inventory of training supplies is taken and recorded at $1,500.

Turn-in

10/14

Exercise 9. Prepare the entries to record the following general fund transactions for the village of Spring Valley for the year ended September 30, 20X4:

a) Revenues are estimated at $520,000; expenditures are estimated at $515,000.
b) A tax levy is set at $378,788, of which 1% will likely be uncollectible.
c) Purchase orders amounting to $240,000 are authorized.
d) Tax receipts total $280,000.
e) Invoices totaling $225,000 are received and vouchered for orders originally estimated at $223,000.
f) Salaries amounting to $135,000 are approved for payment.
g) A state grant-in-aid of $100,000 is received.
h) Fines and penalties of $10,000 are collected.
i) Property for a village park is purchased, costing $120,000. No encumbrance had been made for this item.
j) Additional recreational property valued at $88,000 is donated.
k) Amounts of $12,000 due to other village funds are approved for payment. (Note: To establish the liability to other funds, credit Due to Other Funds.)
l) The village's share of sales tax due from the state is $30,000. Payment will be received in 30 days.
m) Vouchers totaling $175,000 are paid.
n) Accounts are closed at year-end.

Exercise 10.   The preclosing trial balance of the general fund of Marshal Village for fiscal year ended June 30, 20X5, is as follows:

	Debit	Credit
Cash	$ 210,000	
Receivables (net)	134,000	
Vouchers Payable		$ 125,000
Fund Balance—Reserved for Encumbrances		60,000
Fund Balance—Unreserved, Undesignated		92,000
Budgetary Fund Balance		50,000
Estimated Revenues (Control)	600,000	
Estimated Other Financing Sources (Control)	150,000	
Appropriations (Control)		650,000
Estimated Other Financing Uses (Control)		50,000
Expenditures (Control)	598,000	
Encumbrances (Control)	60,000	
Revenue (Control)		605,000
Other Financing Sources (Control)		166,500
Other Financing Uses (Control)	46,500	
Total	$1,798,500	$1,798,500

1. Prepare closing entries.
2. Prepare a Statement of Revenues, Expenditures, and Changes in Fund Balance—Budget and Actual for the fiscal year ended June 30, 20X5. (Include amounts with variances and the total fund equity.)
3. Prepare a balance sheet as of June 30, 20X5.

Exercise 11.   A city purchased land costing $75,000 for park development. The amount had been encumbered at $80,000. Ten years later, because of a population shift, the park is no longer practical. The city sells the land for $117,000. Prepare journal entries to record the purchase and subsequent sale of the land, indicating in what fund or group each entry would be made. Use this format:

Event	Fund or Group	Entry

Exercise 12.   For the following transactions, prepare the entries that would be recorded in the general fixed assets account group for the city of Evert:

a) From special revenue funds resources, the city purchased property costing $1,300,000, with three-fourths of the cost allocated to a building.

b) A mansion belonging to the great-granddaughter of the city's founder was donated to the city. The land cost the original owner $600, and the house was built for an additional $50,000. At the time of donation, the property had an estimated market value of $550,000, of which $330,000 was allocable to the land. The property was accepted and is to be used as a park and as a museum.

c) A central fire station, financed by general obligation bonds, was two-thirds complete at year-end with costs to date of $800,000 that were recorded in the capital project fund.

(continued)

d) A new fire engine was purchased for $165,000. The city traded a used fire engine originally purchased for $100,000. The trade-in value was $25,000. Both engines were purchased from general property tax revenues.

e) A new street was completed at a cost of $250,000, which is to be charged, through the capital projects fund's special assessments, against property owners in the vicinity. The city follows GASB recommendations and records infrastructure assets.

Exercise 13.   The following transactions directly affected a Rose City's general fund and other governmental funds. Prepare journal entries to reflect their impact upon the general long-term debt account group.

1. Rose City employees earned $8.8 million in vacation pay during the year, of which they took only $6.6 million. They may take the balance in the following 3 years.
2. The employees took $.4 million of vacation pay that they had earned in previous years.
3. Rose City settled a claim brought against it during the year by a building contractor. The city agreed to pay $7.5 million immediately and $11 million at the end of the following year.
4. Rose City issued $100 million in general obligation bonds at a price of $99.8 million—i.e., a discount of $.2 million.
5. Rose City transferred $5 million from the general fund to the debt service fund. Of this, $4 million was for the first payment of interest; the balance was for repayment of principal.
6. Rose City earned $.3 million in interest on investments held in the debt service fund. These investments have a market value $4.5 million greater than at the end of last period. The funds are available for the repayment of debt principal.

Exercise 14.   Prepare the entries that would be made in the general long-term debt account group for the following events:

a) To finance the construction of an art center, $13,000,000 of general obligation term bonds were sold for $12,500,000.

b) The general fund allocated $1,300,000 to a debt service fund to begin to provide for retirement of the bonds in item 1 at maturity.

c) To help finance an addition to the community health center, $6,000,000 of 6%, 10-year serial bonds were sold at 101. $960,000 was transferred from the general fund to the debt service fund to cover the annual interest and the first serial redemption.

d) Serial bonds of $600,000 matured and were retired through the debt service fund.

Problems

Problem 16-1.   Select the best answer for each of the following multiple-choice questions. (Nos. 5 and 6 are AICPA adapted.)

1. The measurement focus for governmental funds is the

a) Flow of cash.   c) Amount of gross revenue.

b) Flow of financial resources.   d) Matching of revenues and expenditures.

2. Interperiod equity measurement for governmental funds determines whether
    a) There is a positive cash flow.
    b) There is a profit.
    c) Current-year revenues are sufficient to pay for current-year services.
    d) Actual amounts exceed budgeted amounts.

3. The proceeds of a long-term bond issue were used by a county to acquire general fixed assets. The long-term liability is recorded
    a) Only in the general long-term debt account group.
    b) Only in the general fund.
    c) Both in the general fund and in the general long-term debt account group.
    d) In the appropriate governmental fund, depending on the nature of the asset involved.

4. What is the underlying reason a governmental unit uses separate funds to account for its transactions?
    a) Governmental units are so large that it would be unduly cumbersome to account for all transactions as a single unit.
    b) Because of the diverse nature of the services offered and legal provisions regarding activities of a governmental unit, it is necessary to segregate activities by functional nature.
    c) Generally accepted accounting principles require that not-for-profit entities report on a funds basis.
    d) Many activities carried on by governmental units are short-lived, and their inclusion in a general set of accounts could cause undue probability of error and omission.

5. The primary authoritative body for determining the measurement focus and basis of accounting standards for governmental fund operating statements is the
    a) Governmental Accounting Standards Board (GASB).
    b) National Council on Governmental Accounting (NCGA).
    c) Government Accounting and Auditing Committee of the AICPA (GAAC).
    d) Financial Accounting Standards Board (FASB).

6. Encumbrances outstanding at year-end in a state's general fund should be reported as a
    a) Liability in the general fund.
    b) Fund balance reserve in the general fund.
    c) Liability in the general long-term debt account group.
    d) Fund balance designation in the general fund.

7. An expenditure for general obligation long-term debt is always recorded at year end in the governmental funds for:

	Accrued Interest	Accrued Principal
a)	Yes	Yes
b)	No	Yes
c)	Yes	No
d)	No	No

Problem 16-2.   Select the best answer for each of the following multiple-choice questions. (Nos. 3, 6-10 are AICPA adapted.)

1. Lacking sufficient cash for operations, a city borrows money from a bank, using as collateral the expected receipts from levied property taxes. Upon receipt of cash from the bank, the general fund would credit

    a) *Revenues (Control).*   c)   *Tax Anticipation Notes Payable.*
    b) *Other Financing Sources (Control).* d)   *Taxes Receivable—Delinquent.*

2. The recorded amount for uncollectible taxes was overstated. To revise the estimate during the same fiscal period, the journal entry would credit

    a) *Expenditures (Control).*
    b) *Revenues (Control).*
    c) *Allowance for Uncollectible Delinquent Taxes.*
    d) *Fund Balance—Unreserved, Undesignated.*

3. The encumbrances control account of a governmental unit is increased when

	A voucher payable is recorded.	The budgetary accounts are closed.
a)	no	no
b)	no	yes
c)	yes	yes
d)	yes	no

4. If not expenditure driven, a grant approved by the federal government to assist in a city's welfare program during the current year should be credited to

    a) *Revenues (Control).*
    b) *Fund Balance—Reserved for Welfare Programs.*
    c) *Fund Balance—Unreserved, Undesignated.*
    d) *Other Financing Sources (Control).*

5. Which one of the following equations will yield the appropriations available balance in an expenditure subsidiary ledger account?

    a) *Appropriations—expenditures total.*
    b) *Appropriations—encumbrances balance.*
    c) *Appropriations—expenditures total – encumbrances balance.*
    d) *Appropriations—expenditures total + encumbrances balance.*

6. Elm City issued a purchase order for supplies with an estimated cost of $5,000. When the supplies were received, the accompanying invoice indicated an actual price of $4,950. What amount should Elm debit (credit) to the reserve for encumbrances after the supplies and invoice were received?

    a) $ (50)   c) $4,950
    b) $ 50   d) $5,000

7. The following are Boa City's fixed assets:

    Fixed assets used in proprietary fund activities $1,000,000
    Fixed assets used in expendable trust funds 1,800,000
    All other fixed assets 9,000,000

    What aggregate amount should Boa account for in the general fixed assets account group?

    a) $9,000,000   c) $10,800,000
    b) $10,000,000   d) $11,800,000

8. Power City's year-end is June 30. Power levies property taxes in January of each year for the calendar year. One-half of the levy is due in May, and one-half is due in October. Property tax revenue is budgeted for the period in which payment is due. The following information pertains to Power's property taxes for the period from July 1, 20X0, to June 30, 20X1:

	Calendar Year	
	20X0	20X1
Levy	$2,000,000	$2,400,000
Collected in:		
May	950,000	1,100,000
July	50,000	60,000
October	920,000	
December	80,000	

The $40,000 balance due for the May 20X1 installments was expected to be collected in August 20X1. What amount should Power recognize for property tax revenue for the year ended June 30, 20X1?

a) $2,160,000

c) 2,360,000

b) 2,200,000

d) 2,400,000

9. Dodd Village received a gift of a new fire engine from a local civic group. The fair value of this fire engine was $400,000. The entry to be made in the general fixed assets account group for this gift is

		Debit	Credit
a)	Memorandum entry only		
b)	General fund assets	$400,000	
	Private gifts		$400,000
c)	Investment in general fixed assets	$400,000	
	Gift revenue.		$400,000
d)	Machinery and equipment	$400,000	
	Investment in general fixed assets from private gifts . .		$400,000

10. The following information pertains to Spruce City's liability for claims and judgments:

Current liability at January 1, 20X2	$100,000
Claims paid during 20X2	800,000
Current liability at December 31, 20X2	140,000
Noncurrent liability at December 31, 20X2	200,000

What amount should Spruce report for 20X2 claims and judgment expenditures?

a) $1,040,000

b) 940,000

c) 840,000

d) 800,000

Problem 16-3. Omitting amounts, prepare journal entries in the general fund to record the following selected events:

a) The budget is approved. The city will float a bond issue to finance fixed assets. Inflows of resources are expected to exceed outflows.

b) Property taxes are levied, of which some percentage will be uncollectible.

c) Some of the delinquent property taxes from last year are collected. Others are written off as uncollectible, using the available allowance account.

d) Purchase orders are approved.

e) Payroll for the month is vouchered. Ignore payroll deductions.

f) An invoice is vouchered for an amount less than its encumbrance.

g) Bonds are sold at face value to finance the acquisition of new fixed assets.

h) Fixed assets are purchased.

i) Short-term tax anticipation notes are issued.

Problem 16-4. Sauk City leases a fleet of garbage trucks. The term of the lease is 10 years, approximately the useful life of the equipment. Based on a sales price of $800,000 and an interest rate of 6%, the city agrees to make annual payments of $108,694. Upon the expiration of the lease, the trucks will revert to the city.

1. Prepare appropriate journal entries in the general fund, the general fixed assets account group, and the general long-term debt account group to record the signing of the lease.

2. Prepare appropriate journal entries in the same funds and account groups to record the first payment on the lease. The city records depreciation on garbage trucks using the straight-line method.

Turn-in
11/19

Problem 16-5. On July 1, 20X0, the beginning of its fiscal year, the trial balance of the general fund of the city of Elsworth was as follows:

	Debit	Credit
Cash	$ 20,000	
Tax Receivable—Delinquent	120,000	
Allowances for Uncollectible Delinquent Taxes		$ 12,000
Interest and Penalties Receivable on Taxes	8,000	
Allowance for Uncollectible Interest and Penalties		800
Due from Other Funds	28,000	
Vouchers Payable		87,200
Fund Balance Reserved for Encumbrances		16,000
Fund Balance—Unreserved, Undesignated		60,000
	$176,000	$176,000

The following events occurred:

a) The budget shows estimated general fund revenues of $450,000 and estimated expenditures (including $16,000 encumbered in the prior year) of $392,000.

b) In July, the item ordered in the previous year was received at an invoice cost of $16,400. A voucher is prepared.

c) Property taxes amounting to $300,000 were levied, with 4% estimated to be uncollectible.

d) Cash collections during the year were as follows:

Current taxes	$270,000
Delinquent taxes (in full settlement)	104,000
Interest and penalties on last year's taxes (in full settlement)	7,600
Due from other funds	28,000
	$409,600

The controller wishes variations in estimates to be recorded in the appropriate revenue or expenditure account.

e) *Purchase orders totaling $276,000 were placed. Later, invoices for $260,000 were received and vouchered; supplies inventory purchases were $16,000 of the total. The purchase covered $254,000 of the encumbrances.*

f) *Payrolls of $50,000 were paid. (Ignore payroll taxes and other deductions.) In addition, vouchers totaling $280,000 were paid. (Supplies inventory purchases were $16,000 of the total.)*

g) *An automobile was purchased for the fire department. It cost $16,000 and was not previously encumbered. The invoice is vouchered.*

h) *At year-end, $6,000 in supplies was on hand. There were no supplies on hand a year ago. The city wishes to show the inventory and to establish a proper reserve.*

Required:

1. Prepare journal entries that would be made in the general fund for the following events.
2. Prepare closing entries.
3. Prepare a Statement of Revenues, Expenditures, and Changes in Fund.

Problem 16-6.   A summary of the general fund transactions for the city of Wautoma for the year ended December 31, 20X7, is as follows:

a) *A budget was approved, showing estimated revenues of $900,000, appropriations of $875,000, transfers-in of $27,000 from other funds, and required transfers of $20,000 to other funds.*

b) *The reserve for encumbrance at the end of 20X6 was $15,000. Amounts encumbered in the prior period are included in appropriations for 20X7.*

c) *Property taxes for $650,000 were levied. In past years, 1% of the property taxes levied proved uncollectible.*

d) *Encumbrances for $25,000 had not been liquidated by the end of 20X6. Invoices for all these items were received in 20X7 and totaled $24,000.*

e) *Collections from property taxes totaled $544,000, of which $20,000 represented collections on delinquent taxes. Delinquent taxes of $8,000 remain uncollected, on which a $3,000 allowance is carried. Remaining taxes receivable—current and taxes receivable—delinquent were converted into taxes receivable—delinquent and tax liens receivable, respectively.*

f) *Purchase orders totaling $700,000 were issued. Subsequently, invoices were received amounting to $685,000 for items estimated to cost $680,000. Included were supplies for $10,000.*

g) *An ending inventory of supplies amounted to $2,000, for which the fund balance should be reserved.*

(continued)

h) A tract of land was purchased for $250,000. Payment was made from the general fund, in whose appropriations the item had been included. The amount had not been encumbered. The purchase was made with the intent of reselling the land to a suitable developer.

i) Wautoma received $300,000 as its part of federal revenue-sharing programs. Grants-in-aid of $60,000 due from the state government are recorded. None of the grants is expenditure-driven.

j) Required transfers of $20,000 are made to other funds.

k) A $50,000 payment is made on a mortgage payable. The payment includes $21,000 of interest and a principal payment of $29,000.

l) An offer was received from a land developer who will pay $380,000 for the land acquired by the city in item h). The sale is approved. The developer remits $100,000 with a note due in 90 days, bearing 8% interest. Any gain is to be considered revenue.

m) Transfers received from other funds amount to $23,000.

n) The developer in item l) remits payment for the note plus interest.

Required:

1. Prepare journal entries to record the general fund transactions.
2. Prepare closing entries for the general fund.
3. Prepare a Statement of Revenues, Expenditures, and Changes in Fund Balances—Budget and Actual. On January 1, 20X7, the unreserved fund balance showed a debit balance (deficit) of $180,000.

Problem 16-7. Harth City maintains a defined benefit pension plan for its employees. In a recent year, the city contributed $4 million to its pension fund. However, its annual required contribution as calculated by its actuary was $6 million. The city accounts for the pension contributions in the general fund.

1. Record the pension expenditure and related liability in the general fund and account group.
2. Suppose that in the following year the city contributed $6 million to its pension fund, but its annual required contribution per its actuary was only $5 million. Prepare the appropriate journal entries.

Problem 16-8. The general fund trial balance of the city of Oakwood at December 31, 20X3, was as follows:

	Debit	Credit
Cash	$ 62,000	
Taxes Receivable—Delinquent	46,000	
Allowance for Uncollectible Delinquent Taxes		$ 8,000
Stores Inventory	18,000	
Vouchers Payable		28,000
Fund Balance—Reserved for Stores		18,000
Fund Balance—Reserved for Encumbrances		12,000
Fund Balance—Unreserved, Undesignated		60,000
	$126,000	$126,000

The following data pertain to 20X4 general fund operations:

a) *Budget adopted:*

Revenues and other financing sources:

Taxes	$220,000
Fines, forfeits, and penalties	80,000
Miscellaneous revenues	100,000
Share of bond issue proceeds	200,000
	$600,000

Expenditures and other financing uses:

Program operations	$300,000
General administration	120,000
Stores	60,000
Capital outlay	80,000
Transfer to debt service fund	20,000
	$580,000

Encumbrances from 20X3 are included in the budget.

b) *Taxes were assessed at an amount that would result in revenues of $220,800, after deduction of 4% of the tax levy as uncollectible.*

c) *Orders placed for:*

Program operations	$176,000
General administration	80,000
Capital outlay	60,000
	$316,000

d) *The city council designated $20,000 of the unreserved fund balance for possible appropriation for capital outlay.*

e) *Cash collections and transfer:*

Delinquent taxes (balance is uncollectible)	$ 38,000
Current taxes	226,000
Refund of overpayment on equipment invoice in 20X3	4,000
Fines, forfeits, and penalties	88,000
Miscellaneous revenues	90,000
Share of bond issue proceeds	200,000
Operating transfer from capital projects fund	18,000
	$664,000

f) *Vouchers approved for payment (all previously encumbered):*

	Estimated	Actual
Applicable to prior year but rebudgeted	$ 12,000	$ 12,000
Program operations	144,000	154,000
General administration	84,000	80,000
Capital outlay	62,000	62,000
	$302,000	$308,000

(continued)

g) *Additional vouchers approved, not previously encumbered:*

Program operations	$148,000
Store supplies	40,000
General administration	38,000
Capital outlay	18,000
Transfer to debt service fund	20,000
	$264,000

h) *A taxpayer overpaid 20X4 taxes by $2,000. (The taxes were credited to miscellaneous revenue upon receipt.) The taxpayer applied for a $2,000 credit against 20X5 taxes. The city council granted the request. The council instructed the city controller to adjust the estimated uncollectible current taxes to cover the remaining uncollected balance.*

i) *Vouchers paid amounted to $580,000.*

j) *Stores inventory on December 31, 20X4, amounted to $12,000.*

Required:

Using control accounts, prepare journal entries to record the foregoing data. Omit explanations.

(AICPA adapted)

Problem 16-9.   Brock County has acquired equipment through a noncancelable lease-purchase agreement dated December 31, 20X7. This agreement requires no down payment and the following minimum lease payments:

December	Principal	Interest	Total
20X8	$50,000	$15,000	$65,000
20X9	50,000	10,000	60,000
20W0	50,000	5,000	55,000

1. What account should be debited for $150,000 in the general fund at inception of the lease if the equipment is a general fixed asset and Brock does not use a capital projects fund?
2. What account should be credited for $150,000 in the general fixed assets account group at inception of the lease if the equipment is a general fixed asset?
3. What journal entry is required for $150,000 in the general long-term debt account group at inception of the lease if the lease payments are to be financed with general government resources?

(AICPA adapted)

Problem 16-10.   Prepare journal entries to record the following events using the general fund and the general fixed assets account group:

a) *The general fund vouchered the purchase of trucks for $75,000. The purchase had been encumbered earlier in the year at $70,000.*

b) *Several years ago, equipment costing $15,000 was acquired with general fund revenues. It was sold for $5,000, with proceeds belonging to the general fund.*

c) *Early in the year, a citizen donated to the city land appraised at $100,000. She submitted plans for a new library and agreed to cover the total cost of construction, paying the company directly as work proceeded. At year-end, the building was two-thirds finished, with costs to date of $300,000. The expenditures are recorded in a capital projects fund.*

   d) *A snow plow was purchased with general fund cash for $68,000, which represented a cost of $80,000 less trade-in of $12,000 for an old snow plow originally purchased for $35,000 from special revenue funds. As an emergency purchase, the acquisition of the new snow plow had not been encumbered.*

Problem 16-11.   Prepare the necessary journal entries to record the following transaction for the city of Maineville during 20X7, in the general fund and account groups, and specify the account group used. Entries in the Debt Service Fund and Capital Projects Funds should be ignored.

   a) *General obligation term bonds with a face value of $2,700,000 were sold for $2,705,000. The proceeds from the bond issue were to be used to construct a new library and were received by the capital projects fund.*

   b) *$200,000 was transferred from the general fund to the debt service fund to begin saving for the retirement of the bonds in transaction a) at maturity.*

   c) *$135,000 was transferred from the general fund to the debt service fund to retire a portion of a serial bond due in 20X9.*

   d) *A police car was purchased for $22,000 plus the trade-in of an old police car with a market value of $3,000 originally purchased for $15,000 from the general fund.*

   e) *The serial bonds funded in transaction c) were retired on their maturity date.*

   f) *By year-end, $450,000 of the work had been completed on the new library.*

Problem 16-12.   The following schedule of general fixed assets was obtained from the records of the city of Elmwood:

City of Elmwood
Schedule of General Fixed Assets
December 31, 20X6

General fixed assets:

Land	$1,000,000
Buildings	2,150,000
Improvements other than buildings	1,400,000
Machinery and equipment	800,000
Construction in progress	250,000
Total general fixed assets	$5,600,000

Investments in general fixed assets from:
  Capital projects funds:

Serial bonds	$1,900,000
Federal grants	800,000
State grants	450,000
General fund	1,250,000
Special revenue funds	1,200,000
Total investment in general fixed assets	$5,600,000

(continued)

A summary of fixed asset transactions for 20X7 follows:

a) Construction on the new school, a capital project started during 20X6, was completed at a total cost of $850,000, which was financed by a serial bond issue. No other construction was in progress at the beginning of 20X7.

b) A citizen donated 400 acres of land to the city to be used as a park. The land had a fair market value of $140,000 when donated.

c) The municipal waterworks constructed a new pumping plant at a cost of $120,000. The plant was financed from the water utility revenues. The water utility is accounted for in a proprietary fund.

d) The fire department traded in an old fire engine and $105,000 cash for a new model. The old equipment originally had cost $65,000, and $15,000 was allowed on the trade-in.

(e) The city hall was refurbished at a cost of $40,000, which was paid from general fund revenues. The refurbishing constituted a capital improvement.

(f) Road-use taxes of $30,000 were collected by a special revenue fund, of which $20,000 has been used for improvements other than buildings.

Required:

1. Prepare journal entries only for those transactions that are to be accounted for in the general fixed assets account group. Use the city's account titles.
2. Prepare a schedule of general fixed assets as of December 31, 20X7.

Problem 16-13.   The city of Chester was incorporated on January 1, 20X2. On December 31, 20X7, a careful study of the city's records revealed the following information regarding long-term debt:

a) General obligation bonds in the amount of $1,500,000 were authorized and issued at face value on July 1, 20X2, to finance the construction of a school. The 6% bonds pay interest semiannually on January 1 and July 1 and mature 10 years from the issuance date.

b) Serial bonds of $1,000,000 were sold at 99 on January 1, 20X4, to help finance a new city hall and cultural center. An additional $750,000 was received from an anonymous benefactor. The 5% serial bonds were to be redeemed in annual amounts of $100,000, beginning on January 1, 20X7. A sinking fund was established on January 2, 20X4, to provide for the retirement of the serial bonds. Deposits of $70,000 were to be made on January 2 of each year, beginning in 20X4. All amounts deposited were invested immediately at a net yield of 8%.

c) Property owners were assessed $750,000, to be paid in five equal annual installments, to finance construction of a storm sewer system and repaving of the affected roadways. To have cash when needed to pay for the construction, $600,000 of 5%, 5-year bonds were issued at face value by the Storm Sewer Proprietary Fund.

d) Term bonds totaling $400,000 were sold at face value on January 1, 20X5, to finance construction. The 5%, 10-year bonds pay interest semiannually on January 1 and July 1. Each year, starting with January 1, 20X5, $40,000 was to be set aside in a sinking fund to provide for retirement of the bonds at maturity. Any income earned by the sinking fund was to be applied to the semiannual interest payments.

Required:

1. Prepare only the journal entries for the transactions that would be recorded in the general long-term debt account group through December 31, 20X7.
2. Prepare a schedule of general long-term debt for the city of Chester as of December 31, 20X7.

Problem 16-14. The following selected information was taken from Sun City's general fund statement of revenues, expenditures, and changes in fund balance for the year ended December 31, 20X7:

Revenues		
Property taxes—20X7		$ 825,000
. . . .		
Expenditures		
Current services		
Public safety		428,000
. . . .		
Capital outlay (police vehicles)		100,000
Debt service		74,000
Expenditures—20X7		1,349,000
Expenditures—20X6		56,000
Expenditures		$1,405,000
Excess of revenues over expenditures		$ 153,000
Other financing uses		(125,000)
Excess of revenues over expenditures and other financing uses		$ 28,000
Decrease in reserve for encumbrances during 20X7		15,000
Residual equity transfers-out		(190,000)
Decrease in unreserved fund balance during 20X7		$ (147,000)
Unreserved fund balance January 1, 20X7		304,000
Unreserved fund balance December 31, 20X7		$ 157,000

The following information was taken from Sun's December 31, 20X7 general fund balance sheet:

Property taxes receivable—delinquent—20X7		$ 34,000
Less: Allowances for estimated uncollectible taxes—delinquent		20,000
Vouchers payable		89,000
Fund balance—		
Reserved for encumbrances—20X7		43,000
Reserved for supplies inventory		38,000
Unreserved		157,000

Additional information:

- Debt service was for bonds used to finance a library building and included interest of $22,000.
- $8,000 of 20X7 property taxes receivable was written off; otherwise, the allowance for uncollectible taxes balance is unchanged from the initial entry at the time of the original tax levy at the beginning of the year.
- Sun reported supplies inventory of $21,000 at December 31, 20X6.

(continued)

For items 1 through 7, provide the best answer to the question in the space provided:

1. What recording method did Sun use for its general fund supplies inventory? _____

2. What was the reserved fund balance of the 20X6 general fund? _____

3. What amount was collected from 20X7 tax assessments? _____

4. What amount is Sun's liability to general fund vendors and contractors at December 31, 20X7? _____

5. What amount should be included in the general fixed assets account group for the cost of assets acquired in 20X7 through the general fund? _____

6. What amount arising from 20X7 transactions decreased liabilities reported in the general long-term debt account group? _____

7. What amount of total actual expenditures should Sun report in its 20X7 general fund statement of revenues, expenditures, and changes in fund balance—budget and actual? _____

(AICPA adapted)

Problem 16-15.   The January 2, 20X8, trial balance of Croix Township follows:

	Dr.	Cr.
Cash	$45,000	
Taxes Receivable—Delinquent	20,000	
Allowance for Uncollectible Delinquent Taxes		$ 2,000
Tax Liens Receivable	4,000	
Allowance for Uncollectible Tax Liens		1,000
Due from Parks Fund	12,000	
Inventory of Supplies	5,000	
Vouchers Payable		43,000
Due to Utility Fund		4,000
Fund Balance—Reserved for Supplies Inventory		5,000
Fund Balance—Unreserved, Undesignated		31,000
	$86,000	$86,000

The following events occurred during the first 6 months of 20X8:

a) The adopted budget showed

Estimated expenditures	$620,000
Transfers to other funds	27,000
Estimated revenues	655,000

b) Six-month tax anticipation notes were issued in the amount of $120,000.

c) Property taxes of $430,000 were levied, with 2% of the gross levy considered uncollectible.

d) Tax liens proved uncollectible. The property was foreclosed and sold for $4,000.

e) Amounts encumbered totaled $250,000.

f)   *Cash collected:*

All delinquent property taxes	$ 20,000
Current taxes	290,000
Due from Parks Fund	11,000
Fines and penalties	23,000
	$344,000

g)   *Items vouchered totaled $186,000, representing $183,000 of encumbrances. Included in both were $26,000 for supplies, for which a perpetual inventory system is maintained.*

h)   *Cash payments:*

Vouchered items	$151,000
Nonvouchered items that were not encumbered	49,000
Due to Utility Fund	4,000
	$204,000

i)   *Supplies inventory on June 30 was $21,000.*

Required:

1.   Using the format below, complete the general fund worksheet for the 6 months ended June 30, 20X8. Ignore entries for any other fund or group. Label entries on the worksheet according to their corresponding events. Formal journal entries are not required.

2.   Prepare a balance sheet as of June 30, 20X8.

	Trial Balance		Operating Entries		Revenue and Expenditures		Balance Sheet	
Accounts	Dr.	Cr.	Dr.	Cr.	Dr.	Cr.	Dr.	Cr.

Problem 16-16.   You have been engaged by the town of Rock Elm to examine its June 30, 20X8 balance sheet. You are the first CPA to be engaged by the town, and you find that acceptable methods of municipal accounting have not been employed. The town clerk stated that the books had not been closed and presented the following trial balance of the general fund as of June 30, 20X8:

Cash	$150,000	
Taxes Receivable—Current Year	59,200	
Allowance for Uncollectible Current Taxes		$ 18,000
Taxes Receivable—Delinquent	8,000	
Allowance for Uncollectible Delinquent Taxes		10,200
Estimated Revenues	310,000	
Appropriations		348,000
Donated Land	27,000	
Expenditures—Building Addition Constructed	50,000	
Expenditures—Serial Bonds Paid	16,000	
Other Expenditures	280,000	
Revenues		354,000
Accounts Payable		126,000
Fund Balance—Unreserved, Undesignated		82,000
Budgetary Fund Balance	38,000	
	$938,200	$938,200

(continued)

Additional information:

a) The estimated uncollectible taxes of $18,000 for Taxes Receivable—Current
    Year were determined to be reasonably estimated, but for the prior year
    they should not exceed 100% of Taxes Receivable Delinquent.

b) Included in the revenues account is a credit of $27,000 representing the
    value of land donated by the state for construction of a municipal park.

c) The Expenditures—Building Addition Constructed balance is the cost of an
    addition to the town hall building. This addition was constructed and com-
    pleted in June, 20X8. The general fund recorded the payment as authorized.

d) The Expenditures—Serial Bonds Paid balance reflects the transfer to the debt
    service fund for serial bond retirement. A transfer of $7,000 for interest pay-
    ments on this bond issue is included in Other Expenditures.

e) Operating supplies ordered in the prior fiscal year and chargeable to that
    year were received and consumed in June, 20X7. The vendors' invoices
    amounting to $8,800 for these supplies were incorrectly charged to Other
    Expenditures when paid in July of 20X7.

f) Outstanding purchase orders at June 30, 20X8, for operating supplies
    totaled $2,100. These purchase orders were not recorded on the books.

g) The balance in Revenues includes credits for $20,000 for a note issued to a
    bank to obtain cash in anticipation of tax collections and for $1,000 for the
    sale of scrap iron from the town's water plant. The note was still outstanding
    at June 30, 20X8. Operations of the water plant are accounted for in the
    Water Fund (a proprietary fund), which is to receive the proceeds from the
    scrap sale.

h) At year-end, current taxes are to be reclassified as delinquent.

Required:

1. Prepare the adjusting entries for the general fund for the fiscal year ended June
    30, 20X8. Account titles should be respected if acceptable, even though differ-
    ent. Closing entries are not required.

2. Prepare formal adjusting journal entries for the general fixed assets account
    group and for the general long-term debt account group.

                                                                    (AICPA adapted)

Governmental Accounting: Other Governmental Funds, Proprietary Funds, and Fiduciary Funds

A variety of funds may be used to record events and to exhibit results for a specific area of responsibility. In a small town, there may not be enough activity to warrant more than a general fund, but the larger the governmental unit and the more diverse the activities with which it is involved, the greater the necessity to introduce special funds. While the Governmental Accounting Standards Board (GASB) recognizes the need for funds to manage and demonstrate accountability, it cautions against too many funds that unnecessarily fragment financial reporting. GASB Statement No. 1 suggests that a governmental unit establish only the *minimum* number of funds consistent with legal and operating requirements.

Special Revenue Funds

When revenue obtained from specified sources is restricted by law or donor for a specified current operating purpose or to the acquisition of a relatively minor fixed asset, accounting is accomplished through a *special revenue fund*. Although the government will have only one general fund, it could have many special revenue funds, or none at all. Examples of activities that are accounted for in special revenue funds are nonexchange transactions such as the levy of a hotel room tax to pay for expenditures that promote tourism, federal and state grant proceeds restricted to financing community development expenditures, gasoline tax revenues for highway maintenance, specific federal and/or state funds for education, resources for food stamp programs administered by state governments, other pass-through grants and on-behalf payment programs for fringe benefits and salaries,[1] and exchange transactions such as golf fees charged at a city golf course to cover a portion of the cost of course maintenance. These revenues are recognized under the modified accrual method of accounting.[2] The following are examples of revenues recorded in the special revenue funds.

---

1 GASB Statement No. 24, *Accounting and Financial Reporting for Certain Grants and Other Financial Assistance* (Norwalk, CT: Governmental Accounting Standards Board, June 1994). Pass-through grants are defined in GASB No. 24 as grants received by a government to transfer to or spend on behalf of a secondary recipient. Generally, these transactions are to be accounted for in a special revenue fund or a general fund.

2 When revenue raised for activities is on a fee basis for goods or services provided and the operations are intended to be self-supporting, the flows of resources are accounted for in proprietary funds discussed later in this chapter.

Event	Entry in the Special Revenue Funds		

During the year, local hotels/motels paid to the city a room tax totaling $98,000. The remittance included $6,000 payable from last year and $92,000 expected to be available in the current year.	Cash ....
	   Taxes Receivable. ....
	   Revenues (Control). ....
	      To record the current year's receipt
	      of hotel/motel room fees including
	      $6,000 accrued in the prior year.
		98,000	6,000
			92,000

In addition, the city estimates a $9,000 receivable from December rentals. In this city, the hotels/motels are allowed a one-month administrative lead time and are not required to pay the December tax until January 31 of the following year.	Taxes Receivable. ....
	   Revenues (Control). ....
	      To recognize hotel/motel room fees
	      applicable to December.
		9,000	9,000

Federal food stamp coupons of $10,000 are received by the state government.	Food Stamp Coupons .... Deferred Revenues	10,000	10,000

$9,000 of coupons are distributed.	Expenditures (Control) ....
	   Food Stamp Coupons ....
	
	Deferred Revenues ....
	   Revenues (Control). ....
		9,000
		
		9,000
			9,000
			
			9,000

Charges for services from exchange transactions for the year are as follows:

	Earned	Collected
Golf fees (collected at time of use)	$ 35,000	$ 35,000
Garbage fees .... (collected in advance of providing service)	240,000	260,000
Snow removal fees (collected after service is provided).	85,000	75,000
Total.	$360,000	$370,000

Entry:

	Cash	370,000	
	Accounts Receivable	10,000	
	Revenues (Control).		360,000
	Deferred Revenue		20,000
	To record current year's revenues earned and deferred that arose from exchange transactions.		

A $100,000 federal grant is received for economic development. An additional $50,000 is due prior to year-end. Revenue is recognized when expenditures are incurred for the grant program.	Cash .... Due from Federal Government. .... Deferred Revenue	100,000 50,000	150,000

In a special revenue fund, the accounting must be designed to permit close scrutiny of activities. If resources are greater than anticipated, the project is not permitted to expand beyond the original authorization, nor is money permitted to accumulate beyond reasonable needs. However, sufficient resources should be generated to permit the activity. The desired control may be accomplished by using the same accounting procedures as those used by the general fund. Annual budgets are prepared for each special revenue fund and are required to be integrated into the accounting system by using the appropriate budgetary control accounts and their related subsidiary records. Commitments are recorded by using an encumbrance and expenditure system. Since both the accounting procedures and the financial statements for special revenue funds parallel so closely those of the general fund, they will not be illustrated beyond the revenue recognition examples shown above.

When a governmental unit has more than one special revenue fund, generally accepted accounting principles require that these funds be presented in *combining* balance sheets, revenue and expenditure statements, and budget and actual statements. Combining statements provide information on each special revenue fund plus a total column of all the special revenue funds. Illustration 17-1 presents a Combining Balance Sheet, and Illustration 17-2 presents a Combining Statement of

Revenues, Expenditures, and Changes in Fund Balances. In addition, a Combining Statement of Revenues, Expenditures, and Changes in Fund Balances—Budget and Actual would also be required.

Illustration 17-1
City of Berryville—Special Revenue Funds
Combining Balance Sheet
December 31, 20X7

Assets	Federal Food Stamp Program	Community Development Block Grant	Tourism Promotion Projects	Charges for City Golf Course	Total
Cash.		$100,000	$ 98,000	$370,000	$568,000
Taxes receivable.			9,000	10,000	19,000
Due from other governmental agencies		50,000	40,000		90,000
Food Stamp Coupons	1,000				1,000
Total Assets	$1,000	$150,000	$147,000	$380,000	$678,000

Liabilities and Fund Balances					
Liabilities:					
Vouchers payable			$ 15,000	$105,000	$120,000
Due to other funds.			10,000	55,000	65,000
Deferred revenue.	$1,000	$150,000		20,000	171,000
Total liabilities.	$1,000	$150,000	$ 25,000	$180,000	$356,000
Fund balances:					
Reserved for encumbrances.			$ 95,000	$175,000	$270,000
Unreserved, designated			27,000	25,000	52,000
Total fund balances	0	0	$122,000	$200,000	$322,000
Total liabilities and fund balances	$1,000	$150,000	$147,000	$380,000	$678,000

Illustration 17-2
City of Berryville
Special Revenue Funds
Combining Statement of Revenues, Expenditures, and Changes in Fund Balances
For Year Ended December 31, 20X7

	Federal Food Stamp Program	Community Development Block Grant	Tourism Promotion Projects	Charges for City Golf Course	Total
Revenues.	$9,000	$40,000	$101,000	$360,000	$510,000
Expenditures	9,000	40,000	40,000	200,000	289,000
Excess of revenues over (under) expenditures.	0	0	$ 61,000	$160,000	$221,000
Other financing sources (uses):					
Operating transfers-out.			10,000	55,000	65,000
Total other financing sources (uses).	0	0	$ 10,000	$ 55,000	$ 65,000
Excess of revenues and other financing sources over (under) expenditures and other financing uses			$ 51,000	$105,000	$156,000
Fund balances—January 1.			71,000	95,000	166,000
Fund balances—December 31	0	0	$122,000	$200,000	$322,000

Along with the other fund types, the total of the special revenue funds is included in the Combined Balance Sheet and the Combined Statement of Revenues, Expenditures, and Changes in Fund Balances. In addition, a government having both a general fund and special revenue funds prepares a Combined Statement of Revenues, Expenditures, and Changes in Fund Balances—Budget and Actual for the two fund types. The columnar format is similar to that illustrated below and includes the general fund and totals of the special revenue funds.

General Fund			Special Revenue Funds			Total		
		Variance— Favorable			Variance— Favorable			Variance— Favorable
Budget	Actual	(Unfavorable)	Budget	Actual	(Unfavorable)	Budget	Actual	(Unfavorable)

Capital Projects Funds

Capital projects funds account for the purchase, construction, or capital lease of major *general* fixed assets, which excludes construction of capital facilities by proprietary funds that account for their own construction activities. Each project should be accounted for separately in subsidiary records to demonstrate compliance with legal and contractual provisions.

Resources for capital projects result from transfers received from the general fund or some other fund, proceeds of general obligation bonds, grants from another governmental unit, or special assessments levied against property owners who benefit from the project. Grants from another governmental unit and special assessments levied are recorded as revenues. Bond proceeds (because they must be repaid) and transfers from other funds (because they were previously recognized as revenue) are accounted for as other financing sources.

NCGA Statement 1, *Governmental Accounting and Financial Reporting Principles*, coordinated the accounting and financial reporting treatments for all governmental funds. As a result, it shifted emphasis for capital projects funds from a project-reporting basis to an annual or other budget-period basis. When the capital projects are expected to take several years to complete and will involve large amounts of money, budgetary control is advisable. The operating budget is prepared on an *annual* basis; therefore, it includes the expected revenues, estimated other financing sources, and estimated expenditures for only the current fiscal year. Adopting the annual reporting period permits the accounting for many events to be the same as for the general fund and the special revenue funds.[4] The following entry records the annual budget:

Estimated Other Financing Sources (Control)*	XXX	
Estimated Revenues (Control)**	XXX	
Appropriations (Control)***		XXX
Budgetary Fund Balance—Unreserved (either		
debited or credited)		XXX

*Resources from the general fund or other funds and the sale of general obligation bonds.
**Resources from county, state, or federal grants, interest income on temporary investments, and from special assessments.
***Estimated expenditures for current year.

The full amount of the bond issue proceeds, including the premium and net of any discount and issuance costs incurred, is recorded as an Other Financing Source in the fund that will use the resources. Since bond premiums and discounts arise because of adjustments to the interest rate, the premium and any payment received

---

4 Authoritative literature endorses the use of an encumbrance system for those funds, Many governments also use an encumbrance system in their capital projects funds.

for accrued interest are transferred to the debt service fund to cover future *interest* payments. If bonds are sold at a discount, a project authorization must be reduced by the bond discount amount and/or issuance costs unless additional resources are transferred from the general fund or other funds.

Governments issue short-term *bond anticipation notes* after obtaining necessary voter and legislative authorization to issue long-term bonds. Since these short-term notes are expected to be replaced by long-term bonds, they are, in essence, long term and are accounted for in the General Long-Term Debt Account Group. Proceeds of the bond anticipation notes are recorded in the governmental funds (often a Capital Project Fund) as other financing sources—proceeds from bond anticipation notes.[3]

Proceeds of bond issues not immediately needed for project expenditures are often temporarily invested to earn interest. These temporary investments are limited to securities whose yield does not exceed that of the new debt. Interest earned on temporary investments is recognized as revenue in the capital projects fund. It is often required to be transferred to the debt service fund to help finance bond interest expenditures.

Capital projects funds have the authority through annually approved budgets to continue expenditures within prescribed limits until a project is completed. Although a project may not be completed at the end of a fiscal period, typical closing entries are recorded. Annual closing permits the actual activity to be compared with the legally adopted annual operating budget. Also, in the closing process, the credit to Expenditures (Control) provides the amount of capitalizable expenditures to be recorded in the general fixed assets account group for Construction in Progress.

The actual cost of a capital project probably will differ from its estimated cost. A deficiency usually is covered by a transfer from the general fund. If an excess of resources exists upon completion of the project, it generally is returned to the general fund or to the debt service fund. Such a transfer is called a *residual equity transfer* and, because it is nonrecurring and nonroutine, it is reported as an adjustment to the beginning fund balances of both governmental funds involved. Upon completion of the project, it is customary to withhold part of the payment until final inspection and approval. The liability is recorded in Contracts Payable—Retained Percentage.

To illustrate accounting for capital projects funds, assume the city of Berryville plans to build a $300,000 addition to its municipal auditorium. The project will begin in 20X7 and is to be completed in 20X8. The following entries record the events that occur during construction:

Event	Entry in the Capital Projects Fund		
The project budget is $300,000, to be financed by a general bond issue. The 20X7 operating budget is based on ⅓ of the work's being completed that year. The city uses an other financing sources (control) account.	Estimated Other Financing Sources (Control)	300,000	
	Appropriations (Control)		100,000
	Budgetary Fund Balance—Unreserved		200,000
A $300,000, 8% general obligation bond issue is floated at 101	Cash	303,000	
	Other Financing Sources (Control) . . .		303,000
An entry also is made in the general long-term debt account group: Amount to Be Provided . . . . 300,000 　　Serial Bonds Payable . . . . 　　　　300,000			

(continued)

---

3 GASB states that a government may recognize bond anticipation notes as long-term obligations if, by the date the financial statements are issued, "all legal steps have been taken to refinance the bond anticipation notes and the intent is supported by an ability to consummate refinancing of the short-term note on a long-term basis." *Codification of Government Accounting and Reporting Standards* (Norwalk, CT: Governmental Accounting Standards Board, 1996, Section B50.101).

Event	Entry in the Capital Projects Fund		

The bond premium is transferred to the debt service fund to be used for interest.

Other Financing Uses (Control)	3,000	
Cash.		3,000

An entry also is made in the debt service fund

Cash.	3,000	
Other Financing Sources.		3,000

(Note: Since bond premium is assumed to be used for interest payments, no entry is made in the GLTDAG.)

A contract is signed for the auditorium construction at an estimated cost of $270,000.

Encumbrances (Control)	270,000	
Fund Balance—Reserved for Encumbrances		270,000

The architect's bill for $10,650 is received, of which $7,650 is paid. Upon final building approval, the balance is due. The item was not encumbered.

Expenditures (Control)	10,650	
Cash.		7,650
Contracts Payable—Retained Percentage.		3,000

A partial billing is received from the contractor for $60,000, equal to the amount encumbered for these items. The Contracts Payable account is credited for the liability to the principal contractor. (If the amount of equivalent encumbrance is not specified, the encumbrance entry is reversed for the amount of the billing.)

Fund Balance—Reserved for Encumbrances	60,000	
Encumbrances (Control)		60,000
Expenditures (Control)	60,000	
Contracts Payable		60,000

The contractor is paid $60,000.

Contracts Payable	60,000	
Cash.		60,000

Books for 20X7 are closed.

Budgetary Fund Balance—Unreserved . .	200,000	
Appropriations (Control).	100,000	
Estimated Other Financing Sources (Control)		300,000

The credit to Expenditures (Control) is the basis for the following entry in the general fixed assets account group:

Construction in Progress.	70,650	
Investment in General Fixed Assets—Capital Project Funds		70,650

Other Financing Sources (Control)	303,000	
Expenditures (Control)		70,650
Other Financing Uses (Control)		3,000
Fund Balance—Unreserved, Undesignated		229,350

Encumbrances are closed at year-end.

Fund Balance—Unreserved, Undesignated	210,000	
Encumbrances (Control).		210,000

20X8

The operating budget for 20X8 is recorded; completion is estimated to cost an additional $215,000, including the amount encumbered in the previous year.

Budgetary Fund Balance—Unreserved . .	215,000	
Appropriations (Control).		215,000

The encumbrances are reinstated at the beginning of 20X8.

Encumbrances (Control)	210,000	
Fund Balance—Unreserved, Undesignated		210,000

Event	Entry in the Capital Projects Fund		
	Fund Balance—Reserved for		
	Encumbrances	210,000	
	Encumbrances (Control)		210,000
The contract is completed in 20X8. Additional cost is $227,000, of which $10,000 is withheld in a separate account until final inspection and approval.	Expenditures (Control)	227,000	
	Contracts Payable...............		217,000
	Contracts Payable—		
	Retained Percentage		10,000
The construction is accepted, and the contractor and architect are paid.	Contracts Payable................	217,000	
	Contracts Payable—Retained		
	Percentage..................	13,000	
	Cash......................		230,000
Books for 20X8 are closed.	Appropriations (Control)............	215,000	
	Budgetary Fund Balance—		
	Unreserved.................		215,000
	Fund Balance—Unreserved,		
The credit to Expenditures (Control) is the basis for the following entry in the general fixed assets account group:	Undesignated...............	227,000	
	Expenditures (Control)		227,000

> The credit to Expenditures (Control) is the basis for the
> following entry in the general fixed assets account
> group:
>
> Buildings 297,650
> Construction in Progress 70,650
> Investment in General Fixed
>   Assets—Capital Projects
>   Funds............... 227,000

| The residual balance is transferred to the debt service fund. | Residual Equity Transfer-Out .... | 2,350 | |
| | Cash...................... | | 2,350 |

> An entry also is made in the debt service fund:
> Cash.................. 2,350
> Residual Equity Transfer-In ... 2,350
> Residual Equity Transfer-In 2,350
> Fund Balance—Reserved for
>   Debt Service 2,350
> (Note: Since the project was financed with general
> obligation debt, an additional entry in the GLTDAG
> indicating availability of funds to repay the debt is
> required.)
> Amount Available in the
> Debt Service Fund 2,350
> Amount to Be Provided 2,350

The Municipal Auditorium Capital Fund Project Fund is closed.	Fund Balance—Unreserved,		
	Undesignated..............	2,350	
	Residual Equity Transfer-Out		2,350

When a governmental unit has more than one capital project in progress during the year, generally accepted accounting principles require that combining financial statements be presented. Illustration 17-3 presents a combining balance sheet for the city of Berryville's capital projects funds. The 20X7 year-end balance sheet for the auditorium project, for which the accounting entries are shown, and the 20X7 year-end balance sheet for a bridge construction capital project, for which the accounting entries are *not* shown, are included in the combining balance sheet. The total column also is reported in a Capital Projects Fund column in the combined balance sheet. Cities often have many more than two capital projects in progress during a year, and each project is reported in the combining financial statements.

The combining statement of revenues, expenditures, and changes in fund balances will show as revenues those resources obtained by special assessment, by grant, or from some other governmental unit. Transfers from other funds within the same governmental unit or proceeds of a bond issue are presented as other financing sources. The form used in Illustration 17-4 on page 17-9 is the one currently preferred, with the final amount representing the total of both reserved and unreserved fund balances.

Illustration 17-3
City of Berryville
Capital Projects Funds
Combining Balance Sheet
December 31, 20X7

Assets	Municipal Auditorium	Bridge Construction Project	Total
Cash	$232,350	$102,000	$334,350
Special assessments receivable.		160,000	160,000
Investments		40,000	40,000
Total assets	$232,350	$302,000	$534,350
Liabilities and Fund Balance			
Vouchers payable		$157,000	$157,000
Contracts payable—retained percentage .	$ 3,000	50,000	53,000
Total liabilities	$ 3,000	$207,000	$210,000
Fund balances:			
Reserved for encumbrances	$210,000	$ 90,000	$300,000
Unreserved, undesignated	19,350	5,000	24,350
Total fund balances	$229,350	$ 95,000	$324,350
Total liabilities and fund balances	$232,350	$302,000	$534,350

Debt Service Funds

As discussed in Chapter 16, the function of the general long-term debt account group is to provide a record of the unredeemed principal of long-term liabilities incurred to acquire general fixed assets. Closely related to this account group are *debt service funds*, whose primary function is to account for financial resources accumulated to cover the payment of principal and interest on those obligations shown in the general long-term debt account group.

As in other governmental funds, the modified accrual basis is used for recognizing revenues, other financing sources, and expenditures in debt service funds. Interest and principal on general long-term debt are items for which the accrual basis is modified. For example, assume a governmental unit has a fiscal year ending June 30, with interest and principal on long-term debt to be paid on July 31. Since expenditures are authorized by appropriations, it is essential that expenditures be recorded in the same period as the appropriations. Thus, the interest and principal will not be accrued on June 30, because the appropriation to cover the principal and interest will not be provided until the budget for the next period is recorded on July 1. This method recognizes expenditures for interest and principal when they are "due."

Illustration 17-4
City of Berryville
Capital Projects Funds
Combining Statement of Revenues, Expenditures, and Changes in Fund Balances
For Year Ended December 31, 20X7

	Municipal Auditorium	Bridge Construction Project	Total
Revenues		$118,000	$ 118,000
Expenditures	$ 70,650	157,000	227,650
Excess (deficiency) of revenues over expenditures	$ (70,650)	$ (39,000)	$(109,650)
Other financing sources (uses):			
Proceeds of bonds	$303,000	$196,000	$ 499,000
Payments to Debt Service	(3,000)	(62,000)	(65,000)
Total other financing sources (uses) . . .	$300,000	$134,000	$ 434,000
Excess (deficiency) of revenues and other sources over expenditures and other uses	$229,350	$ 95,000	$ 324,350
Fund balances at beginning of year	0	0	0
Fund balances at end of year	$229,350	$ 95,000	$ 324,250

The most popular method of raising long-term resources is by the issuance of serial bonds, which are redeemed in a series of installments. Term bonds, whose total face value becomes due at one time, are now extremely rare. When serial bonds are issued, there is no substantial accumulation of cash in a sinking fund for redemption of the principal, unless the first series will not mature for several fiscal periods and contributions for retirement are to begin immediately. Instead, the budget for the year of payment provides for interest and principal redemption. In debt service funds, an entry to record the budget seldom is used because expenditures for principal and interest are known and there is no need to compare them with budgetary amounts.

Resources to cover expenditures may come from several sources. A portion of a property tax levy may be authorized to be recorded directly in a debt service fund. The entries would be similar to those made in the general fund to record a tax levy. The net amount of taxes estimated to be collected is credited to Revenues (Control) since the resources are received from outsiders. Transfers received by the debt service fund from funds that have already recorded the resources as revenues are credited to Other Financing Sources (Control). As discussed in Chapter 16, this procedure prevents Revenues (Control) from being credited in two funds for the same resources—once in the originating fund (in this case, the general fund) and again in the recipient fund (in this case, a debt service fund).

Prior to redemption, the bond liability for unmatured general obligation debt is not recorded in a debt service fund but is entered in the general long-term debt account group. However, when a serial bond matures and payment of interest is due, the following entry is recorded in a debt service fund:

Expenditures (Control)	XXX	
Matured Bonds Payable		XXX
Matured Interest Payable		XXX

An entry to record payment of these matured items would then be made. Simultaneously, an entry to record reduction of the bond principal is made in the general long-term debt account group. Many governmental units employ the services of financial institutions to conduct actual payments for interest and serial redemptions. When cash is released to such a fiscal agent, the account debited is Cash with Fiscal Agent. Upon notification by the agent that actual payments have been made, the debt service fund entry is

Matured Bonds Payable	XXX	
Matured Interest Payable	XXX	
Cash with Fiscal Agent		XXX

The following entries would be made in a debt service fund for the indicated events that relate to a serial bond issue. As demonstrated by these entries, the interaction between funds and groups is especially prevalent in accounting for general obligation bond issues.

Event	Entry in the Debt Service Fund
An 8%, $300,000 general obligation serial bond issue for bridge construction is sold at 101. The premium is transferred from the capital projects fund to the debt service fund.	Cash . . . . 3,000 Other Financing Sources (Control) . . . 3,000

Entries are also made in the capital projects fund:
Cash.	303,000	
Other Financing Sources . . .		303,000
Other Financing Uses	3,000	
Cash.		3,000

and in the general long-term debt account group:
Amount to Be Provided	300,000	
Serial Bonds Payable.		300,000

Event	Entry in the Debt Service Fund

Of the property taxes, $50,000 is levied specifically to cover debt service on these bonds; the levy, less 1% of the taxes estimated to be uncollectible, is recorded in the debt service fund.	Taxes Receivable—Current 50,000
	  Allowance for Uncollectible Current
	    Taxes 500
	  Revenues (Control). 49,500

All property taxes are collected except for $400 that is written off. The difference between estimated and actual uncollectible taxes is recorded in Revenues (Control).	Cash 49,600
	Allowance for Uncollectible Current
	    Taxes 400
	  Taxes Receivable—Current 50,000
	
	Allowance for Uncollectible Current
	    Taxes 100
	  Revenues (Control). 100

Assuming $30,000 is to be used toward the first installment on the principal payment an additional entry is made in the general long-term debt account group:
Amount Available in the Debt Service Fund	30,000	
Amount to Be Provided.		30,000

Event	Entry in the Debt Service Fund		
The fund receives $7,000 of its $9,000 share of state gasoline taxes. The city is not entitled to the balance until the next fiscal period.	Cash . . . . Due from State . . . . Revenues (Control). . . . . Deferred Revenues	7,000 2,000	7,000 2,000
A transfer of $30,000 is received from the general fund.	Cash . . . . Other Financing Sources (Control) . . .	30,000	30,000

Since the $30,000 is for payment of principal, an additional entry is made in the general long-term account group debt:

Amount Available in the Debt Service Fund	30,000	
Amount to Be Provided.		30,000

Event	Entry in the Debt Service Fund		
Cash is transmitted to a fiscal agent for payment of the first $60,000 of maturing bonds and $24,000 of interest due on the last day of the fiscal period.	Cash with Fiscal Agent . . . . Cash.	84,000	84,000
The matured bonds and interest are recorded.	Expenditures (Control) . . . . Matured Bonds Payable. . . . . Matured Interest Payable	84,000	60,000 24,000

$60,000 of principal is matured and no longer long term. The entry to reclassify the debt in the general long-term account group debt:

Serial Bonds Payable.	60,000	
Amount Available in the Debt Service Fund		60,000

Event	Entry in the Debt Service Fund		
The fiscal agent reports that all payments have been made except for $1,000 of interest.	Matured Bonds Payable. . . . . Matured Interest Payable . . . . Cash with Fiscal Agent.	60,000 23,000	83,000
Books are closed at year-end.	Revenues (Control) . . . . Other Financing Sources (Control) . . . . . Expenditures (Control) . . . . Fund Balance—Reserved for Debt Service.	56,600 33,000	84,000 5,600

Assets transferred to a debt service fund must be used to redeem bonds or to pay interest. There are no unreserved assets. Any excess of assets over liabilities is reserved for debt service. Therefore, at year-end, the accounts are closed to Fund Balance—Reserved for Debt Service rather than to an unreserved fund balance.

In addition to term bonds and serial bonds, debt service funds may be used to service debt arising from notes or warrants having a maturity of more than one year after date of issue, and to make periodic payments on capital leases. Although each issue of long-term debt is a separate obligation with unique legal restrictions and servicing requirements, GASB standards provide that, if legally permissible, a single debt service fund may be used to account for the service of all issues of tax-supported and special-assessment debt. If legal restrictions do not allow the servicing of all issues to be accounted for by a single debt service fund, the number of debt service funds should be held to a minimum.

Sometimes, governments will defease existing debt accounted for in the general long-term debt account group. Through advanced refunding, new debt is issued to provide resources to pay interest on old, outstanding debt as it becomes due and to pay the principal on the old debt either as it matures or for an earlier call date. As demonstrated by the following entries, when advanced refunding results in defeasance of debt (either legally or in substance), the proceeds of the new debt are reported as *other financing sources—proceeds of refunding bonds* in the debt service fund.[5] Subsequent payments to the escrow agent from resources provided by the new debt are *other financing uses*, not expenditures. The old debt is removed from the general long-term debt account group, and the new debt is reported as a long-term liability.

Event	Entry in the Debt Service Fund		

A $100,000 bond was issued, proceeds from which are to be used to pay principal and interest of an $85,000 old bond issue. The criteria for in-substance defeasance is met.	Cash . . . .
	    Other Financing Sources—Proceeds of
	        Refunding Bonds . . . .
		100,000	100,000

Cash is transmitted to an escrow agent to administer the payment of principal and interest on the old debt.	Other Financing Uses—Payment to
	    Escrow Agent . . . .
	    Cash . . . .
		100,000	100,000

The entries in the general long-term debt account group to remove the old debt:

Bonds Payable	85,000	
Amount to Be Provided		85,000

The entries in the general long-term debt account group to record the new debt:

Amount to Be Provided	100,000	
Bonds Payable		100,000

Debt service funds employ two financial statements for reporting purposes: a balance sheet and a statement of revenues, expenditures, and changes in fund balances. If two or more debt service funds are used, they are presented in *combining* statements. Illustration 17-5 is a combining balance sheet for Vernon Town. This balance sheet has a column for general obligation debt, for which the entries were shown, and a column for special assessment debt explained later in this chapter, for which the entries were *not* shown.

Illustration 17-5
Vernon Town
Debt Service Funds
Combining Balance Sheet
December 31, 20X7

Assets	General Obligation Debt	Special Assessment Debt	Total
Cash	$5,600	$ 20,000	$ 25,600
Cash with fiscal agents	1,000		1,000
Due from state	2,000		2,000
Special assessment receivable		20,000	20,000
Special assessment receivable—deferred .		160,000	160,000
Total assets	$8,600	$200,000	$208,600

---

5 GASB Statement No. 7, *Advanced Refunding Resulting in Defeasance of Debt* (Norwalk, CT: Governmental Accounting Standards Board, March 1987).

Liabilities and Fund Balance			
Liabilities:			
Matured interest payable.	$1,000		$ 1,000
Deferred revenue	2,000	$160,000	162,000
Fund balance:			
Reserved for debt service	5,600	40,000	45,600
Total liabilities and fund balance.	$8,600	$200,000	$208,600

The combining statement of revenues, expenditures, and changes in fund balances for Vernon Town's debt service funds is shown in Illustration 17-6 below. This statement itemizes revenues by source and expenditures by nature, and it summarizes the causes of changes in fund balances during the period.

Illustration 17-6
Vernon Town
Debt Service Funds
Combining Statement of Revenues, Expenditures, and Changes in Fund Balances
For Year Ended December 31, 20X7

	General Obligation Debt	Special Assessment Debt	Total
Revenues:			
Taxes.	$ 49,600	$20,000	$ 69,600
Intergovernmental.	7,000		7,000
Total revenues	$ 56,600	$20,000	$ 76,600
Expenditures:			
Principal retirement.	$ 60,000		$ 60,000
Interest charges	24,000		24,000
Total expenditures.	$ 84,000	0	$ 84,000
Excess (deficiency) of revenues over expenditures	$(27,400)	$20,000	$ (7,400)
Other financing sources (uses):			
Proceeds of Refunding Bonds.	100,000		100,000
Operating transfers-in	33,000		33,000
Payment to Escrow Agent	(100,000)		$(100,000)
Total other finance sources (uses) . .	33,000	0	33,000
Excess (deficiency) of revenues and other financing sources over expenditures . .	$ 5,600	$20,000	$ 25,600
Fund balances at beginning of year	0	20,000	20,000
Fund balances at end of year	$ 5,600	$40,000	$ 45,600

Special Assessments

Local governments may provide capital improvements and services, for the primary benefit of particular groups of property owners, which will be paid partially or totally by the same property owners. Such arrangements are called *special assessment projects* and are accounted for through the local government.

Service-type special assessments cover operating activities, such as snow plowing, that do not result in increases in fixed assets. Payment for service special assessments seldom is arranged on an installment basis. A single charge is added to the property tax bill. Service assessments are accounted for in the fund type (usually the general fund, a special revenue fund, or an enterprise fund) that best reflects the nature of the transaction.

Capital-improvement special assessments result in additions or improvements to a government's fixed assets. If an improvement provides capital assets that become part of an enterprise activity, such as water main construction for a utility, accounting would be done in an enterprise fund. If the improvement results in a general fixed asset, such as streets, gutters, or sidewalks, the asset would be recorded in the general fixed asset account group (if the government records infrastructure assets), in which case the accounting is divided into two phases.

The *first phase* consists of financing and constructing the project and usually will be accounted for through a capital projects fund. The initiative for such projects is often taken by the property owners who request the improvement. However, authorization must be approved through appropriate channels. Special assessment projects typically are financed through issues of long-term debt but may be financed with existing government resources. Once the project is approved, the estimates for the budget period (not the total project budget) are recorded in a capital projects fund.

Proper recordings of inflows of financial resources into the capital projects fund depend upon the source of financing. Illustration 17-7 presents proper recording of

Illustration 17-7   Accounting for Special Assessment Projects under Three Methods of Financing*

Debt Issued	Flows of Financial Resources through the Capital Projects Fund		
Government obligated in some manner	Cash	200,000	
	Other Financing Sources—		
	Bond Proceeds		200,000
Government not obligated in any manner	Cash	200,000	
	Contributions from Property		
	Owners		200,000
Debt not issued	Cash	200,000	
	Other Financing Sources—		
	Transfers from Other Funds . . .		200,000

Expenditures incurred during construction are recorded in the same manner as expenditures recorded for other capital projects.

*Note that budgetary entries have been omitted from this illustration.

inflows under three possible sources of financing. When the capital improvements are financed by special-assessment-related debt for which the government is obligated in some manner, such as accounting for resources raised and for the expenditure of funds during construction, accounting procedures are the same as for other capital projects, assuming secondary liability in the event of default by property owners.[6]

When the capital improvements are financed by debt for which the government is not obligated in any manner, proceeds from issuing the debt are credited by the governmental unit to Contributions from Property Owners, in the capital projects fund.

When the capital improvements are financed by existing governmental resources and debt is not issued, transfers from other funds are credited to Other Financing Sources, in the capital projects fund.

Expenditures are recorded in the capital projects fund as costs are incurred for the special assessment project. At year-end, the capitalizable costs of an unfinished special assessment project are entered in the general fixed assets account group.

Capital Projects Fund	Expenditures (Control).	80,000	
	Cash		80,000
General Fixed Assets Account Group	Construction in Progress	80,000	
	Investment in General Fixed Assets—		
	Capital Projects Funds		
	(Special Assessments)		80,000

---

6 GASB Statement No. 6, *Accounting and Financial Reporting for Special Assessments* (Norwalk, CT: Governmental Accounting Standards Board, January 1987), states that a government is obligated in some manner if a) it is legally obligated to assume all or part of the debt in the event of default or b) the government may take certain actions to assume secondary liability for all or part of the debt—and the government takes, or has given indications that it will take, these actions.

Eventual Recording of Constructed Asset in the General Fixed Assets Account Group			Recording of Special Assessment Debt in the General Long-Term Debt Account Group		
Fixed Asset Account.	200,000		Amount to Be Provided for		
Construction in Progress		80,000	Payment of Special		
Investment in General Fixed			Assessment Debt	200,000	
Assets		120,000	Special Assessment Bonds		
			Payable		200,000
Fixed Asset Account.	200,000		Long-term debt is not recorded because the government is not obligated for the debt. Debt service is accounted for through an agency fund.		
Construction in Progress		80,000			
Investment in General Fixed					
Assets		120,000			
Fixed Asset Account.	200,000		Long-term debt is not issued.		
Construction in Progress		80,000			
Investment in General Fixed					
Assets		120,000			
			Liquidation of the special assessment debt is described in the text		

Completion of the special assessment project in the second year is recorded with the following entries:

Capital Projects Fund	Expenditures (Control)................	120,000	
	Cash		120,000
General Fixed Assets Account Group	(Proper Fixed Asset Account)	200,000	
(This entry also is shown in Illustration 17-7.)	Construction in Progress		80,000
	Investment in General Fixed Assets—		
	Capital Projects Funds		
	(Special Assessments)		120,000

The *second phase* of accounting for special assessment projects consists of collecting the special assessments on an installment basis from benefited property owners and repaying the cost of financing the project. When the government is obligated in some manner for the special assessment debt, the liability should be recorded in the general long-term debt account group, as shown in this entry:

Amount to Be Provided for Payment of		
Special Assessment Debt	200,000	
Special Assessment Debt with Governmental Commitment ...		200,000

In some cases, the governmental unit has the primary responsibility for repayment of the bonds. In these situations, they are recorded, as follows, in the general long-term debt account group with the same type of entry used to record any other general obligation debt.

Amount to Be Provided for Payment of		
Special Assessment Debt	200,000	
Special Assessment Bonds Payable		200,000

(This entry is also used as an example in Illustration 17-7.)

The Special Assessment Receivable and Special Assessment Revenue are divided between current and deferred portions in the debt service fund. Amounts levied and demanded to service-related debt in the current period are credited to Revenues (Control) as shown below. The remainder to be collected and used for debt service in future periods is credited to Deferred Revenues.

Special Assessments Receivable—Current	20,000	
Special Assessments Receivable—Deferred	180,000	
Revenues (Control)		20,000
Deferred Revenues		180,000

Through the term of the debt, the amount to be collected from property owners for a period is levied and demanded by the governmental unit; consequently, that portion of deferred revenue should be recognized as revenue in that period. Recognition of the receivable from the levy and the revenue is shown below. Details of the assessments are entered in a subsidiary ledger, where the levy against each property owner and collections from the owner are indicated.

Special Assessments Receivable—Current	20,000	
Special Assessments Receivable—Deferred		20,000
Deferred Revenues	20,000	
Revenues (Control)		20,000

The general long-term debt account group is updated to reflect the amount available in the debt service fund. The debt is liquidated in the same manner as other governmental-fund debt.

When the government is not obligated in any manner, collection of the special assessment and debt service payments should be accounted for through an agency fund (discussed on pages 17-31 to 17-33 in the Agency Funds section) since the government is acting merely as an agent for the property owners and bondholders. In that case, the debt is not shown in the general long-term debt account group; it should appear, however, in the notes to the financial statements.

When no debt is issued, Revenues (Control) is credited in the recipient fund for the current levy of the special assessment. Amounts to be levied and collected in future periods are credited to Deferred Revenues.

Proprietary Funds

The funds discussed to this point have been governmental funds. The second category of funds—*proprietary funds*—now will be discussed. By definition, the term "proprietary" means pertaining to a proprietor and implies that users of goods or services will be charged on the basis of consumption, similar to the practice in private industries. Usually, charges are set to recover as much as possible of the total cost, including depreciation. Whatever is not recovered must be subsidized.

Governments account for their business-type activities in two types of proprietary funds. Enterprise funds account for operations in which goods or services are provided to the general public. Internal service funds account for operations in which goods or services are provided by one government department to other departments within the same government or to other governments.

Proprietary funds focus on capital maintenance to measure whether revenues were sufficient to cover expenses (including the amortization of noncurrent items) of the fiscal period. This is consistent with a flows of economic resources measurement focus coupled with the accrual basis of accounting. Financial reporting for proprietary funds is similar to financial reporting for business enterprises in that income statements show revenues, expenses, and net income for a fiscal period, and balance sheets include both current and noncurrent assets and liabilities of the entity. The proprietary fund balance sheet residual is comprised of contributed capital and retained earnings.

In recent pronouncements, the GASB concluded that proprietary funds *must* follow all accounting standards set forth by the FASB prior to November 30, 1989, unless they specifically conflict with a GASB pronouncement. In addition, a proprietary activity may apply all FASB pronouncements developed for business enterprises issued after that date unless they conflict with or contradict GASB standards.[7] Governments may not apply FASB standards and interpretations limited to not-for-profit organizations (such as FASB Statement Nos. 116 and 117 issued in 1993).[8]

One of the rare times that amounts transferred from another fund are treated as revenue is in the case of proprietary funds furnishing goods or services to other funds. For example, a computer center accounted for in an internal service fund may provide service to the general fund. This transaction is *quasi-external* because the item would have been treated as revenue if it had been billed to an outsider. Therefore, the billing represents revenue to the internal service fund and an expenditure to the general fund. Entries in each fund are as follows:

7 GASB Statement No. 20, *Accounting and Financial Reporting for Proprietary Funds and Other Governmental Entities That Use Proprietary Fund Accounting* (Norwalk, CT: Governmental Accounting Standards Board, September 1993).

8 GASB Statement No. 29, *The Use of Not-for-Profit Accounting and Financial Reporting Principles by Governmental Entitities* (Norwalk, CT: Governmental Accounting Standards Board, August 1995).

Internal Service Fund	Due from the General Fund	XXX	
	Revenue		XXX
General Fund	Expenditure	XXX	
	Due to the Internal Service Fund . .		XXX

Conversely, if a proprietary fund pays the general fund for services, the proprietary fund records expenses and the general fund records revenue. For example, the general government may bill an enterprise fund for payments in lieu of property taxes. Entries in each fund are

General Fund	Due from the Enterprise Fund	XXX	
	Revenue		XXX
Enterprise Fund	Expenses	XXX	
	Due to the General Fund		XXX

Such treatment is necessary for the proper determination of a proprietary fund's operation and for rate setting.

Enterprise Funds

Enterprise funds account for goods or services provided by a governmental unit to the general public. The user is charged for these goods or services, based on consumption. For example, the operations of utilities, public housing, public parking, municipal solid waste landfills, economic development corporations, cultural activities, and airports would be covered by enterprise funds. These funds continue indefinitely and are self-supporting, depending upon the amounts charged to cover part or all of the costs of operation, debt service, and maintenance of capital facilities. Net income is accumulated in an account labeled Unreserved Retained Earnings. To remain self-sustaining, the fund must deduct depreciation expense in the determination of net income. Losses eventually would require either an increase in charges or a contribution from some other source.

At the inception of an enterprise fund (or internal service fund), capital must be provided either by issuance of long-term debt or by transfer from some other source, such as a municipality's general fund. In the latter case, the amount received is credited to an account labeled *Residual Equity Transfer* from the general fund. At the end of the year, the residual equity transfer is closed into Contributed Capital—from Municipality. Note the similarity of this account to the paid-in capital account of a corporation. As a measure of original asset sources, the contribution remains in the fund indefinitely or until the fund is terminated. If operations are profitable and arrangements specify that profits shall be shared with the general fund, an amount analogous to a dividend is charged against Unreserved Retained Earnings. Financing may also be provided from loans or advances by the municipality. In such cases, the loans or advances are recorded as payables in the proprietary funds and as receivables in the general fund.

Contributed capital also is increased when capital assets financed by special assessments are acquired by an enterprise fund. When special assessments are levied, instead of crediting Revenues (Control) as is done in governmental funds, Contributed Capital from Special Assessments is credited. Upon acquisition or completion of the capital asset, its cost is capitalized in the enterprise fund.

An enterprise fund's operational efficiency may be monitored in part by the net income or net loss figure. As in commercial operations, budgets are prepared. However, budgets are not recorded formally in the accounts, perhaps because the fund's self-supporting nature requires a high degree of operational freedom, but more likely because fixed budgetary amounts would be of much less value when there is a variable demand by the public for goods and services.

Control accounts for revenues and expenses commonly are used, with details in supporting records. In accounting for revenues, two control accounts are used: Operating Revenues (Control) for charges for services and Nonoperating Revenues (Control) for grants received, interest and rent earned, or other miscellaneous financial revenues. A similar breakdown is used to account for expenses: Operating Expenses (Control) for expenses directly related to goods or services produced, such as salaries, depreciation, heat, light, materials, and taxes, and Nonoperating Expenses (Control) for financial expenses, such as bond interest. Except for the use of these four nominal control accounts, journal entries for revenues and expenses, including adjustments, are much the same as in private enterprise accounting.

One of the unusual features of accounting for enterprise funds is the introduction of restricted assets and the current liabilities to be paid therewith. *Restricted assets* are assets (cash and investments) upon which some limitation has been imposed that makes them available only for designated purposes. Examples of restricted assets are amounts of customer deposits subject to refund, proceeds from long-term debt for construction, and monies set aside for bond interest or principal redemption.

Restricted assets and their related current liabilities must be recorded in specially designated accounts so that the segregation of these items is ensured. For example, if a water utility receives deposits covering meter installations for customers and these deposits are refundable, they would be recorded as follows:

Restricted Assets—Customers' Deposits Cash	XXX	
Customers' Deposits Payable from Restricted Assets		XXX

If the deposits are invested, the entry to record the investment would be:

Restricted Assets—Customers' Deposits Investments	XXX	
Restricted Assets—Customers' Deposits Cash		XXX

The existence of restricted assets and their related current liabilities is especially common when an enterprise fund is used to account for a public utility. A major source of funding for utilities is the sale of revenue bonds, which are floated to permit the construction of, or an addition to, a facility. Since payments for these bonds depend on the existence of operating income, the bond indenture usually includes several restrictions. For example, it may require that the bond proceeds be expended only for construction, making the proceeds a restricted asset. The following entry would be required:

Restricted Assets—Revenue Bond Construction Cash	XXX	
Revenue Bonds Payable		XXX

As amounts are committed, the liability would be identified as payable from a restricted asset.

Construction in Process	XXX	
Construction Contracts Payable from Restricted Assets		XXX

Payment of the liability would be recorded with the following entry:

Construction Contracts Payable from Restricted Assets	XXX	
Restricted Assets—Revenue Bond Construction Cash		XXX

If a municipality received approval to expand its utility facilities by issuing a combination of special assessment bonds and revenue bonds, the following entry would be required in an enterprise fund:

Restricted Assets—Construction Cash	XXX	
Special Assessment Bonds Payable		XXX
Revenue Bonds Payable		XXX

Note that the redemption and servicing of both the revenue bonds and the special assessment bonds are the financial responsibility of the utility enterprise fund. Therefore, the liability appears in the enterprise fund balance sheet rather than the general long-term debt account group.

Illustration 17-8
Clermont County
Water and Sewer Fund
Balance Sheet
December 31, 20X7

Assets

Current assets:			
Cash.		$ 257,036	
Receivables (net)		33,480	
Inventories and prepaid expenses		24,230	
Total current assets			$ 314,746
Restricted assets:			
Cash with fiscal agent for bond service.		$ 80,444	
Revenue bond construction cash		17,760	
Revenue bond debt service cash		5,000	
Revenue bond fund:			
Cash.	$ 10,355		
Investments.	113,800	124,155	
Customers' deposits:			
Investments.	$ 63,000		
Interest receivable on investments.	650	63,650	
Total restricted assets			291,009
Property, plant, and equipment:			
Land		$ 211,100	
Buildings	$ 447,700		
Less accumulated depreciation.	90,718	356,982	
Improvements other than buildings	$3,887,901		
Less accumulated depreciation.	348,944	3,538,957	
Machinery and equipment	$1,841,145		
Less accumulated depreciation.	201,138	1,640,007	
Construction in process		22,713	
Total property, plant, and equipment.			5,769,759
Total assets			$6,375,514

The balance sheet of a commercial utility may begin with its fixed assets because they are extremely important. However, the combining of the balance sheet of a government-owned utility with the balance sheets of other governmental funds is simplified if the conventional sequence is followed. The balance sheet for the Clermont County Water and Sewer Fund, in Illustration 17-8 on this page and the next, adheres to such a presentation, with restricted assets following the regular current assets and preceding the fixed assets. Note also that current liabilities are segregated to show amounts payable from regular current assets and amounts payable from restricted assets.

Most revenue bonds for enterprise funds are serial bonds that require the earmarking of monies for the payment of interest and for the establishment of a fund for principal redemption. These resources are labeled restricted assets. The current interest and serial installment payables are recorded as current liabilities payable from restricted assets. To further protect the bondholder, at least psychologically, many

Liabilities and Fund Equity

Liabilities:			
Current liabilities (payable from current assets):			
Vouchers payable	$	195,071	
Accrued wages and taxes payable		2,870	
Construction contracts payable		8,347	$ 206,288
Current liabilities (payable from restricted assets):			
Construction contracts payable	$	17,760	
Accrued revenue bond interest payable		32,444	
Matured revenue bonds payable		48,000	
Customer deposits		63,000	161,204
Total current liabilities			$ 367,492
Long-term liabilities:			
Revenue bonds payable			2,448,000
Total liabilities			$2,815,492
Fund equity:			
Contributed capital:			
Contribution from municipality			$1,392,666
Retained earnings:			
Reserved for bond debt service	$	5,000	
Reserved for bond retirement		124,155	
Total reserved	$	129,155	
Unreserved		2,038,201	
Total retained earnings			2,167,356
Total fund equity			$3,560,022
Total liabilities and fund equity			$6,375,514

serial revenue bonds require that unreserved retained earnings be restricted in an amount equal to the excess of restricted assets related to debt service of the bond issue over the current liability for interest and principal. If the amounts in the Water and Sewer Fund balance sheet (Illustration 17-8) are compared with assumed amounts at the end of the previous year, the additional amount to be reserved would be determined as follows:

	Dec. 31 20X7	Dec. 31 20X6 (assumed)
Restricted assets related to revenue bonds:		
Cash with fiscal agent for bond service	$ 80,444	$ 87,200
Revenue bond debt service cash	5,000	3,000
Revenue bond fund	124,155	93,975
Total	$209,599	$184,175
Current liabilities related to revenue bonds:		
Accrued revenue bond interest payable	$ 32,444	$ 37,200
Matured revenue bonds payable	48,000	50,000
Total	$ 80,444	$ 87,200
Excess of bond-related restricted assets over bond-related current liabilities	$129,155	$ 96,975

If the bond indenture requires that the reserves be increased to equal the bond-related restricted assets that are not offset by bond-related current liabilities, the following entry becomes necessary:

Retained Earnings—Unreserved ($129,155 – $96,975)	32,180	
Retained Earnings—Reserved for Bond Debt Service ($5,000 – $3,000)		2,000
Retained Earnings—Reserved for Bond Retirement ($124,155 – $93,975)		30,180

The statement of revenues, expenses (not expenditures), and changes in retained earnings for an enterprise fund, as shown in the *GASB Codification of Governmental Accounting and Financial Reporting*, focuses on total retained earnings, both reserved and unreserved. Such a statement for the Clermont County Water and Sewer Fund is shown in Illustration 17-9.

In 1989, the GASB issued Statement No. 9, *Reporting Cash Flows of Proprietary and Nonexpendable Trust Funds and Governmental Entities That Use Proprietary Fund Accounting*. It stipulated that a statement of cash flows for such funds should show movements of combined unrestricted and restricted cash and cash equivalents for the reported period, segregated into four categories:

1. Cash flows from *operating* activities, which would include cash received from sales of goods or services and cash paid to suppliers, employees, and providers of services.
2. Cash flows from *noncapital financing activities*, which would include proceeds from borrowings not related to capital asset acquisition and repayments thereon, as well as operating grants or transfers not related to capital asset acquisition.
3. Cash flows from *capital and related financing activities* to acquire or dispose of capital assets, which would include grants or transfers related to capital asset acquisition.
4. Cash flows from *investing* activities.

Illustration 17-9
Enterprise Fund
Clermont County
Water and Sewer Fund
Statement of Revenues, Expenses, and Changes in Retained Earnings
For Year Ended December 31, 20X7

Operating revenues:		
Charges for services		$ 727,150
Operating expenses:		
Personnel services (salaries and fees)	$306,100	
Materials and supplies.	106,580	
Depreciation	103,600	
Heat, light, power, and taxes	47,900	
Total operating expenses		564,180
Operating income		$ 162,970
Nonoperating revenues (expenses):		
Operating grants	$5,000	
Interest revenue	2,830	
Rental income	1,000	
Interest expense	(92,988)	
Total nonoperating revenues (expenses)		(84,158)
Net income		$ 78,812
Retained earnings at beginning of year		
(reserved and unreserved)		2,088,544
Retained earnings at end of year		
(reserved and unreserved)		$2,167,356

The statement of cash flows should report net cash provided or used for each of the four categories. This objective can be accomplished by using the direct method, as shown in Illustration 17-10A for a hypothetical electric utility. The GASB recommends the use of this method. In addition, a reconciliation of net operating income to net cash flow from operating activities (Category 1) must be provided in a separate schedule to accompany the cash flows statement or in the notes to the financial statements. Such a reconciliation is presented in Illustration 17-10B on page 17-25.

Illustration 17-10A
Zenith City
Electric Utility Fund
Statement of Cash Flows
Increase (Decrease) in Cash and Cash Equivalents
For Year Ended June 30, 20X7

Cash flows from operating activities:		
Cash received from customers.	$456,000	
Cash paid to suppliers and employees	(400,300)	
Other operating revenues.	7,500	
Net cash provided by operating activities		$ 63,200

(continued)

Cash flows from noncapital financing activities:		
Net repayments under revolving loan arrangement. . . .	$ (10,700)	
Operating grants received	50,000	
Operating transfers-out to other funds.	(37,500)	
Net cash provided by noncapital financing activities		1,800
Cash flows from capital and related financing activities:		
Proceeds from sale of capital bonds.	$125,000	
Principal and interest paid on capital bonds	(100,000)	
Acquisition and construction of capital assets.	(75,000)	
Proceeds from sale of equipment.	70,000	
Net cash provided by capital and related financing activities.		20,000
Cash flows from investing activities:		
Purchases of investment securities	$ (62,500)	
Proceeds from sale and maturities of securities.	36,500	
Interest and dividends received on investments.	3,000	
Net cash used in investing activities.		(23,000)
Net increase in cash and cash equivalents		$ 62,000
Cash and cash equivalents at beginning of year		100,000
Cash and cash equivalents at end of year		$162,000

Many governments account for landfill operations in enterprise funds. GASB standards require closure and post-closure costs be recognized in the years in which the landfill is in operation rather than when they are to be paid.[9] Therefore, in each year of the landfill's useful life, the government recognizes as both an expense and an increase in a liability a portion of the estimated costs for closure and post-closure care. The estimated total current cost of landfill closure and post-closure care include

1. The cost of equipment expected to be installed and facilities expected to be constructed (e.g., ground-water monitoring wells, storm-water management systems, gas monitoring systems, etc.) near or after the date that the landfill stops accepting waste.
2. The cost of final cover.
3. The cost of monitoring and maintaining the landfill during the post-closure period.

The current expense (and liability) is based on the percentage of landfill actually used up during the period multiplied by the total estimated cost of closure and post-closure care. For example, suppose a government uses 90,000 cubic feet of a landfill in one year. Total capacity is estimated at 4.5 million cubic feet. Closure and post-closure care costs are estimated at $18,000,000. The entry to record the expense and liability for the year [based on $18,000,000 \times (90,000 \div 4,500,000)$] is

9 GASB Statement No. 18, *Accounting for Municipal Solid Waste Landfill Closure and Post-closure Care Costs* (Norwalk, CT: Governmental Accounting Standards Board, August 1993). Landfills accounted for in governmental funds will calculate the accrued liability the same as in the above example. These landfills will recognize expenditures and fund liabilities using the modified accrual basis of accounting. The long-term portion of the liability will be reported in the general long-term debt account group.

| Landfill expense | 360,000 | |
| Liability for landfill costs | | 360,000 |

In year 2, closure and post-closure cost estimates are adjusted to $18,500,000. Landfill used during the year totaled 120,000 cubic feet. Landfill capacity has decreased to 4,250,000. The entry to record the expense and liability for year 2 [$18,500,000 × (210,000 ÷ 4,500,000)] less $360,000 recognized in year 1 is

| Landfill expense | 554,118 | |
| Liability for landfill costs | | 554,118 |

Landfill capital assets excluded from the calculation of the estimated total cost of landfill closure and post-closure care should be fully depreciated by the date that the landfill stops accepting solid waste.

Illustration 17-10B
Zenith City
Electric Utility Fund
Reconciliation of Net Operating Income to Net Cash Provided by Operating Activities
For Year Ended June 30, 20X7

Net operating income (loss)		($49,800)
Adjustments to reconcile net operating income to		
net cash provided by operating activities:		
Depreciation	$122,000	
Provision for uncollectible accounts	1,000	
Changes in assets and liabilities:		
Increase in accounts receivable	(15,000)	
Decrease in inventory	2,000	
Decrease in prepaid expenses	500	
Increase in accounts payable	2,500	
Total adjustments		113,000
Net cash provided by operating activities		$ 63,200

If a municipality operates more than one enterprise fund, combining statements are required in order to disclose the details of each fund. GASB standards also require that segment information for major nonhomogeneous enterprise funds be presented to prevent misleading financial statements. Presentation of segment information in the notes to the financial statements is preferable, but some information may be in the combining statements. Examples of segments include utility operations, parking operations, cultural activities, and economic developments. Disclosures include material operating subsidies and material enterprise fund tax revenues, operating income (loss), and net income (loss).

Internal Service Funds

Internal service funds are similar to enterprise funds in that they are self-sustaining, depend on amounts charged for services rendered, and receive start-up resources. The difference is that users of their services are other departments of the same governmental unit or other governmental units. A computer center, a printing department, a central purchasing department, a central garage, and risk financing and self-insurance activities are accounted for in internal service funds.

Since internal service funds do not deal with the general public and usually do not issue bonds that result in restrictions, they do not have restricted assets. Their accounting procedures resemble those for a commercial business. Internal service funds must recover their costs, including depreciation, or be subsidized. Therefore, they maintain records of fixed assets and use the accrual basis of accounting. Budgetary accounts are not used, although budget forecasts facilitate the calculation of overhead rates to be applied in determining charges.

As discussed for enterprise funds, the establishment of an internal service fund may be by a contribution or an advance from the municipality. Charges to customer departments are considered quasi-external transactions and appear as expenditures in the governmental funds, expenses in the other proprietary funds, and revenue to the internal service fund.[10]

The financial statements of internal service funds consist of the balance sheet, the statement of revenues, expenses, and changes in retained earnings, and the statement of cash flows. When more than one internal service fund exists, combining statements are prepared. These statements closely resemble commercial financial statements and will not be illustrated.

Fiduciary Funds: Trust and Agency Funds

As mentioned in Chapter 16, fiduciary funds account for resources for which a governmental unit is acting as a trustee or agent. This category of funds includes expendable trust funds, nonexpendable trust funds, pension trust funds, and agency funds.

Trust Funds

Assets held by a governmental unit that functions as a trustee may be donated by a corporation or by an individual for the educational or cultural benefit of the community. The accounting for these assets and the operation of the trust fund depend on the document that created the fund. If both the assets contributed (the principal) and the earnings may be expended, the fund is an *expendable trust fund*, which is accounted for on a modified accrual basis, in much the same manner as a governmental fund. In addition to donated assets, governments with Internal Revenue Code Section 457 deferred compensation plans are required to report their assets held in trust for participants in an expendable trust.[11]

Escheat property is also reported in an expendable trust. GASB Statement No. 21 defines an escheat as ". . . the reversion of property to a government entity in the absence of legal claimants or heirs."[12] Since the rightful owner or heir can reclaim escheat property at any time, the receipt of escheat property is recorded in the trust fund offset with a liability representing the best estimate of the amount ultimately expected to be reclaimed and paid. Revenue is recognized for the amount not expected to be reclaimed. When transferred to another fund that will ultimately use the property, usually the general fund, the government records an operating transfer.

---

10 GASB Statement No. 10, *Accounting and Financial Reporting for Risk Financing and Related Insurance Issues* (Norwalk, CT: Governmental Accounting Standards Board, November 1989) allows governments to use either the general fund or internal service fund for all risk financing and self-insurance activities. Many governments choose an internal service fund to charge other funds of the government entity for claims liabilities, including future catastrophe losses based on actuarial estimates.

11 GASB No. 32, *Accounting and Financial Reporting Internal Revenue Code Section 457, Deferred Compensation Plans* (Norwalk, CT: Governmental Accounting Standards Board, October 1997).

12 GASB No. 21, *Accounting for Escheat Property* (Norwalk, CT: Governmental Accounting Standards Board, October 1993).

If earnings but not principal may be expended, the fund is a *nonexpendable trust fund*. These funds are accounted for in much the same manner as proprietary funds. Nonexpendable trust funds result from the acceptance of assets that are invested to produce earnings for a designated purpose. For example, a donor might contribute real property and investments, designating that earnings be used to enhance a city's art collection. Depreciation on real property included in the principal of the trust would be recognized in order to protect that principal. It also would be essential to differentiate between principal items and revenue items. The most complete segregation will result if two endowment funds are established—one to record principal items and another to account for the earnings. The procedure becomes especially useful if bonds are purchased at a premium as part of the trust fund. Cash flows and available revenue are not identical because of the amortization of the premium. The segregation process protects the principal.

When donors establish a nonexpendable trust, the assets donated are credited to Fund Balance in the endowment principal trust fund. Later, revenues earned are credited to Revenues (Control). A liability to the endowment earnings fund for the period's interest earnings is established, and a debit is made to recognize the operating transfer.

The only source of assets for the endowment earnings fund is the net earnings transferred from the endowment principal fund. These earnings are credited to Other Financing Sources (Control). Distributions of such revenues are recorded as expenditures. In the year-end closing process of the endowment earnings fund, any difference between the amounts received from the principal fund and total expenditures is closed to Fund Balance—Reserved for Endowments, which indicates that the undistributed assets are restricted.

The procedures for both the endowment principal trust fund and the endowment earnings fund for Cedar City are illustrated by the events and entries shown on page 17-28.

The financial statements for the endowment principle trust fund (a nonexpendable trust fund) are a balance sheet, a statement of revenues, expenses, and changes in fund balances, and a statement of cash flows. The financial statements of the endowment earnings trust fund (an expendable trust) are a balance sheet and a statement of revenues, expenditures, and changes in fund balances. These statements isolate principal and earnings components. Balance sheets for Cedar City's Governmental Accounting Scholarship Fund are shown in Illustration 17-11.

Illustration 17-11
Cedar City
Endowment Principal Trust Fund
Balance Sheet
For Period Ended December 31, 20X7

Assets

Cash	$10,640
Investments	40,000
Unamortized premiums on investments	360
	$51,000

Liabilities and Fund Balance

Due to Endowment Earnings Fund	$ 1,000
Fund Balance—Nonexpendable	50,000
	$51,000

(continued)

Cedar City
Endowment Earnings Trust Fund
Balance Sheet
For Period Ended December 31, 20X7

Assets	
Cash..	$ 560
Due from Endowment Principal Fund............................	1,000
	$ 1,560
Fund Balance	
Fund Balance—Reserved for Endowments.........................	$ 1,560

Pension Trust Funds

Public employees retirement system funds are accounted for in *pension trust funds*. In no other area of accounting is actuarial assistance so vital. Abiding by the requirements of the retirement plan and considering the employee population as to age, gender, marital status, and the myriad of other variables that affect working lives and retirement, actuaries must estimate the amount of resources necessary as of a given date to meet retirement commitments. To protect the employees' interests, pension trust funds should use a full accrual basis of accounting.

Contributions to a retirement plan may be from both employer and employees (a contributory plan) or from employer only (a noncontributory plan). Employees

Event
Cedar City receives an endowment of $50,000 to establish a nonexpendable trust fund whose revenue is to be used to encourage students to study governmental accounting.
9% bonds with a face value of $40,000 are purchased at 101, maturing in 10 years. The premium will be amortized using the straight-line method.
Bond interest of $3,600 is received.
The liability to endowment revenues fund for net revenue is recorded.
Cash due is remitted.
A grant of $3,000 is given to a student.
Books are closed at year-end.

who resign usually have the option to withdraw their own contributions (but not the employer's contributions) or to leave them in the plan as vested amounts, providing certain requirements are met. The amounts belong to the employee, who will have access to them upon meeting prescribed retirement conditions.

Increases in the resources of pension trust funds result from employee and employer contributions, investment earnings, and net appreciation (depreciation) in plan assets. Decreases in resources result from payments to retired employees, refunds to contributors, and administrative costs.

All assets of a pension trust belong to the employees, and claims against these assets are reflected in either the liabilities or the restricted net asset balance.

To demonstrate the accounting process for a pension trust fund, the journal entries recording each event for Desert City's pension trust fund for employees' retirement are shown on page 17-30. All entries illustrated are made in one trust fund and represent amounts for the entire year. The journal entries for the original events record asset inflows and outflows and are similar to entries shown previously for other funds. The additions and deductions are closed to the Plan Net Assets account. A Statement of Changes in Plan Net Assets[13] is shown in Illustration 17-12 on page 17-30.

The Statement of Changes in Plan Net Assets reports *additions* to net assets rather than revenues, and *deductions* from net assets rather than expenses. The Statement of Plan Net Assets for Desert City's pension trust fund as of December 31, 20X7, is shown in Illustration 17-13 on page 17-3. The fund has been operating for several years and has significant investments.

---

13 GASB No. 25, *Financial Reporting for Defined Benefit Pension Plans and Note Disclosures for Defined Contribution Plans* (Norwalk, CT: Governmental Accounting Standards Board, November 1994).

Entries in Endowment Principal Trust Fund (Nonexpendable Trust)			Entries in Endowment Earnings Trust Fund (Expendable Trust)		
Cash	50,000		No entry.		
Fund Balance		50,000			
Investments	40,000		No entry.		
Unamortized Premium	400				
Cash		40,400			
Cash	3,600		No entry.		
Unamortized Premium		40			
Revenues (Control)		3,560			
Operating Transfer-Out (Control)	3,560		Due from Endowment Principal Fund	3,560	
Due to Endowment Earning Fund		3,560	Other Financing Sources (Control)		3,560
Due to Endowment Revenues Fund	3,560		Cash	3,560	
Cash		3,560	Due from Endowment Principal Fund		3,560
No entry.			Expenditures (Control)	3,000	
			Cash		3,000
Revenues (Control)	3,560		Other Financing Sources (Control)	3,560	
Operating Transfer-Out		3,560	Expenditures (Control)		3,000
			Fund Balance—Reserved for Endowments		560

Event	Entry for Original Event		

Actuarial required contributions are as follows:	Cash	210,500	
Employees 90,000	Receivable from Employer	16,500	
Employers 137,000	Contributions		227,000
At year-end, $16,500 of the employer contribution is not received.			

Earnings of $291,600 are earned, including interest of $157,000; dividends of $123,900; and real estate operating income of $10,700.	Cash	258,100	
	Interest and Dividends Receivable . .	33,500	
	Investment Income		291,600

Investments depreciated in value by $241,400.	Investment Income	241,400	
	Net depreciation in fair value		
	of investments		241,400

| Payments of $170,434 were made to retired employees. | Benefits . . . . | 170,434 | |
| | Cash . . . . | | 170,434 |

Refunds of $11,550 were made, and $4,200 is due to employees who resigned and withdrew their contributions.	Refunds of contributions	15,750	
	Cash		11,550
	Refunds payable		4,200

| Investment expenses for the year are $54,000. | Investment expense . . . . | 54,000 | |
| | Cash . . . . | | 54,000 |

| Costs of administering the pension plan are $5,000. | Administrative expense . . . . | 5,000 | |
| | Cash . . . . | | 5,000 |

Illustration 17-12
Desert City's Retirement Plan
Statement of Changes in Plan Net Assets
For Year Ended June 30, 20X7

Additions:

Contributions

Employer	$ 137,000
Plan member	90,000
Total contributions	227,000

Investment income

Net appreciation (depreciation) in fair value	(241,400)
Interest	157,000
Dividends	123,900
Real estate operating income, net	10,700
Less investment expense	(54,000)
Net investment income	(3,800)
Total additions	223,200

Deductions:

Benefits	170,434
Refunds of contributions	15,750
Administrative expense	5,000
Total deductions	191,184
Net increase	32,016

Net assets held in trust for pension benefits

Beginning of year	$3,651,964
End of year	$3,683,980

The liability shown on the statement of plan net assets (Illustration 17-13) is the current benefits payable. The long-term actuarily determined projected benefit obligation is disclosed in the footnotes.

The statement of plan net assets adheres to the all-inclusive approach, whereby the net increase (decrease) is added to the total of plan assets at the beginning of the period to yield their total at the end of the period. A statement of cash flows is not required. Governments must also include in the notes to the financial statements as Required Supplementary Information a) a schedule of funding progress, b) a schedule of employer contributions for at least six plan years, and c) information on actuarial methods and assumptions.

Issued in 1994, GASB No. 26 states that when a defined benefit pension plan administers a postemployment health care plan, the financial report of the defined benefit pension plan should include a) a statement of postemployment health care plan net assets, b) a statement of changes in postemployment health care plan net assets, and c) notes to the financial statements, all prepared in accordance with the pension plan reporting standards.[14]

Accounting for postretirement benefits other than pensions (GASB Statement No. 12) also provides disclosure, not accounting guidance, for state and local government employers who provide these benefits. Accounting guidance for postretirement benefits is forthcoming from the GASB.

Illustration 17-13
Desert City's Retirement Plan
Statement of Plan Net Assets
as of June 30, 20X7

Assets	
Cash and short-term investments	$ 66,000
Receivables	
Employer	16,500
Interest and dividends	33,500
Total receivables	50,000
Investments, at fair value	
U.S. Government obligations	541,300
Municipal bonds	33,585
Domestic corporate bonds	892,300
Domestic stocks	1,276,500
International stocks	461,350
Mortgages	149,100
Real estate	184,900
Venture capital	26,795
Total investments	3,565,830
Properties, at cost, net of accumulated depreciation	6,350
Total assets	3,688,180
Liabilities	
Refunds payable	4,200
Net assets held in trust for pension benefits	$3,683,980

14 GASB No. 26, *Financial Reporting for Postemployment Healthcare Plans Administered by Defined Benefit Pension Plans* (Norwalk, CT: Governmental Accounting Standards Board, November 1994).

Agency Funds

An *agency fund* is required when money collected or withheld, such as deductions from government employees' salaries for social security or for hospitalization premiums, must be forwarded to the proper destination. Agency funds frequently have no end-of-period balances because money is transferred prior to the end of the period. When the money has not been forwarded, a liability to the ultimate recipient is shown. There is no fund balance, and the only financial statement would be a balance sheet listing the assets held and the related liabilities, supported by a statement of changes in assets and liabilities. The latter statement shows for each asset and liability its beginning balance, any additions or deletions, and the final balance. If the agency fund is to receive a fee for its services, the amount usually is recorded as a liability to the general fund of the governmental unit. The general fund records a receivable and revenue if the amount is to be collected within the current period. For example, state law may give a county the responsibility for collecting property taxes levied within its boundaries, with the county receiving a fee to cover its administration of the plan. The county, as well as each political subdivision, would record its share of taxes receivable in its general fund. The tax agency fund of Zee County would make the following series of entries for the events described:

Event	Entry in Tax Agency Fund		
Gross taxes receivable to be collected for all units are as follows:	Taxes Receivable for All Units	1,000,000	
	Due to Other Governmental		
Zee County . . . . $ 300,000	Units		1,000,000
X City 600,000			
T Town 100,000			
Total $1,000,000			

Entry in Zee County general fund:		
Taxes Receivable	300,000	
Revenue		300,000

Event	Entry in Tax Agency Fund		
Taxes are collected.	Cash	1,000,000	
	Taxes Receivable for All Units . . .		1,000,000
The liability to each unit is recorded, net of 2% fee earned by the county for collection and processing for other units. (The county would not charge itself a fee.) The fee is to be remitted to the county general fund.	Due to Other Governmental Units . .	1,000,000	
	Due to Zee County General Fund		314,000
	Due to X City		588,000
	Due to T Town		98,000

Entry in Zee County general fund:		
Due from Agency Fund . . .	314,000	
Taxes Receivable		300,000
Revenue		14,000

Event	Entry in Tax Agency Fund		
Cash is released to each governmental unit.	Due to Zee County General Fund . .	314,000	
	Due to X City	588,000	
	Due to T Town	98,000	
	Cash		1,000,000

Entry in Zee County general fund:		
Cash	314,000	
Due from Agency Fund .		314,000

The general fund of X City records the receipt of cash from the tax agency fund, net of the fee, as follows:

Cash (for net proceeds)	588,000	
Expenditures (Control) (for fee charged)	12,000	
Taxes Receivable—Current		600,000

Agency funds also are used in the case of a capital project undertaken by a government in which special assessment bonds were issued, but for which it has no financial responsibility in case of nonpayment. The government functions as an agent, a financial conduit between the bondholders and the owners of the assessed property. When property owners are assessed, an entry is recorded in the agency fund:

Special Assessments Receivable—Current	XXX	
Special Assessments Receivable—Deferred	XXX	
Due to Special Assessment Bond Creditors		XXX

When collections from assessed property owners are received by the agency fund, this entry is made:

Cash	XXX	
Special Assessments Receivable—Current		XXX
Due to Special Assessment Bond Creditors (Interest)		XXX

Upon payment to the bondholders, the entry is:

Due to Special Assessment Bond Creditors	XXX	
Due to Special Assessment Bond Creditors (interest)	XXX	
Cash		XXX

Neither the liability for principal repayment nor the debt service expenditures are recorded in any other fund or group because the governmental unit was not obligated in any manner.

Finally, a government may account for the proceeds and disbursement of a pass-through grant in an agency fund only when it serves as a cash conduit, e.g., merely transmitting funds to the recipient without having any administrative involvement in the grant.[15]

Governmental Accounting—Interactions among Funds

In governmental accounting, each fund or group is a separate accounting entity, entrusted to record only a limited phase of an event. Complete recording, as shown in Chapters 16 and 17, often involves more than one fund or group. In addition, transactions among funds are frequent. Throughout this and the previous chapter, interfund transactions have been defined. They include a) operating transfers, b) residual equity transfers, and c) quasi-external transactions. Another interfund transaction is a reimbursement. One fund may reimburse another for supplies or other items paid on its behalf. For example, the general fund might pay the entire rental of a facility even though the facility is to be used for both the general government and activities of a special revenue fund. When the expenditure is made by the general fund, the entry is

Expenditures	XXX	
Cash		XXX

When the reimbursement is received from the special revenue fund for its share of the rent, the entries in each fund are

General fund:	Cash	XXX	
	Expenditures		XXX
Special revenue fund:	Expenditures	XXX	
	Cash		XXX

15 GASB Statement No. 24, *Accounting and Financial Reporting for Certain Grants and Other Financial Assistance* (Norwalk, CT: Governmental Accounting Standards Board, June 1994).

To serve as a reference and to review governmental accounting, Illustration 17-14 below is a matrix of selected events that are recorded in more than one fund or group. Used in the matrix are the four governmental funds (general, special revenue, debt service, and capital projects), the two types of proprietary funds (enterprise and internal service), a trust and agency fund, and the two account groups for general fixed assets and general long-term debt.

The entries to record the events related to the 14 events in the matrix are as follows:

Journal Entries for Transactions Affecting More than One Fund

Event	Funds	Accounts		
1. Purchase of equipment with general fund resources for $40,000.	General Fund	Expenditures (Control) . . . . Vouchers Payable	40,000	40,000
	General Fixed Assets Account Group	Equipment . . . . Investment in General Fixed Assets— General Fund Revenues	40,000	40,000
2. Issuance of $500,000 of general obligation serial bonds at an $8,000 premium for city hall construction.	Capital Projects Fund	Cash . . . . Other Financing Sources (Control)	508,000	508,000
		Other Financing Uses (Control) . . . . Cash	8,000	8,000
	Debt Service Fund	Cash . . . . Other Financing Sources (Control)	8,000	8,000

Illustration 17-14
Matrix of Selected Events Requiring Entry in More Than One Fund or Account Group

Events to Be Recorded

1. Purchase of equipment with general fund resources for $40,000.
2. Issuance of $500,000 of general obligation serial bonds at an $8,000 premium for city hall construction.
3. Transfer by general fund to meet $100,000 matured serial bond and $50,000 interest payments.

4. Payment of $50,000 bond interest and $100,000 matured serial bonds. Fiscal agent is used for payment.
5. Completion of special assessment construction project. $150,000 paid to date; $50,000 final payment.
6. Levy of $5,000 property taxes by general fund against city's utility (quasi-external).

7. Billing of general and special revenue funds for central computer service ($12,000 and $20,000) (quasi-external).
8. Contribution made by city to establish a nonexpendable trust fund of $98,500.
9. Remittance of the city's $16,000 share of self-insurance costs for current period to an internal service fund.

10. Reimbursement of $15,000 by the special revenue fund to the general fund for general government supplies expenditures initially made in the general fund properly charged to a community development project.
11. Recording of depreciation, $6,000 enterprise fund, $13,000 internal service fund.
12. Redemption of final $100,000 serial of general obligation bonds, with $3,000 deficiency covered by general fund. Fiscal agent is used for payment.

13. Closing entry for capital projects fund involving a partially completed project. Cost to date is $130,000; revenues during the period are $300,000.
14. Payroll expenditures totaled $5,000 and included $1,000 payroll withholdings for taxes and insurance plus employer's share of these costs. $1,000 is transferred to an agency fund for remittance as follows: Private insurance company, $200; federal government, $600; and state government, $150. The agency fund makes the remittances.
15. A 5-year lease agreement was signed for equipment. The present value of the lease payments is $50,000.

16. The actuarial required contribution for pensions was $4,500. Of this $3,000 was transferred to the pension trust. $1,500 will be transferred in the future.
17. Claims and judgments against the city were estimated at $15,000. The city attorney determined that it was probable that the claims would be settled against the city. Of the $15,000, $3,000 was estimated to be paid out this fiscal year.
18. Closure and post-closure costs of local landfill were estimated at $600,000. Landfill used this period was estimated at 1,000 cubic yards, and total landfill is 100,000 cubic yards. Landfill operations are accounted for in enterprise funds.

19. Debt was refunded. The refunding met the criteria for in-substance defeasance. Proceeds of the new debt issue were placed in trust with an escrow agent.
20. Investments carried at $5,500 have a fair value of $5,750 in the general fund. Pension investments carried at $102,000 have a fair value of $101,000.

Event	Funds	Accounts		
	General Long-Term Debt Account Group	Amount to Be Provided for Payment of Serial Bonds	500,000	
		Serial Bonds Payable		500,000
3. Transfer by general fund to meet $100,000 matured serial bonds and $50,000 interest payment.	General Fund	Other Financing Uses (Control)	150,000	
		Cash		150,000
	Debt Service Fund	Cash	150,000	
		Other Financing Sources (Control)		150,000
	General Long-Term Debt Account Group	Amount Available in Debt Service Fund— Serial Bonds	100,000	
		Amount to Be Provided for Payment of Serial Bonds		100,000
4. Payment of $50,000 bond interest and $100,000 matured serial bonds. Fiscal agent is used for payment.	Debt Service Fund	Expenditures (Control)	150,000	
		Matured Bonds Payable		100,000
		Matured Interest Payable		50,000
		Cash with Fiscal Agent	150,000	
		Cash		150,000

(continued)

Governmental Funds				Proprietary Funds		Fiduciary Fund	Account Groups		
General	Special Revenue	Debt Service	Capital Projects	Enter-prise	Internal Service	Trust and Agency	General Fixed Assets	General Long-Term Debt	
X	—	—	—	—	—	—	X	—	1.
—	—	X	X	—	—	—	—	X	2.
X	—	X	—	—	—	—	—	X	3.
—	—	X	—	—	—	—	—	X	4.
—	—	—	X	—	—	—	X	—	5.
X	—	—	—	X	—	—	—	—	6.
X	X	—	—	—	X	—	—	—	7.
X	—	—	—	—	—	X	—	—	8.
X	—	—	—	—	X	—	—	—	9.
X	X	—	—	—	—	—	—	—	10.
—	—	—	—	X	X	—	—	—	11.
X	—	X	—	—	—	—	—	X	12.
—	—	—	X	—	—	—	X	—	13.
X	—	—	—	—	—	X	—	—	14.
X	—	—	—	—	—	—	X	X	15.
X	—	—	—	—	—	X	—	X	16.
X	—	—	—	—	—	—	—	X	17.
—	—	—	—	X	—	—	—	—	18.
—	—	X	—	—	—	—	—	X	19.
X	—	—	—	—	—	X	—	—	20.

Event	Funds	Accounts		
	Debt Service Fund	Matured Bonds Payable.............	100,000	
		Matured Interest Payable	50,000	
		Cash with Fiscal Agent...........		150,000
	General Long-Term Debt Account Group	Serial Bonds Payable..............	100,000	
		Amount Available in Debt Service Fund—Serial Bonds...........		100,000
5. Completion of special assessment construction project. $150,000 paid to date; $50,000 final payment.	Capital Projects Fund	Expenditures (Control)	50,000	
		Cash..........................		50,000
	General Fixed Assets Account Group	Improvements Other than Buildings......	200,000	
		Construction in Progress		150,000
		Investments in General Fixed Assets—Capital Projects Funds (Special Assessments)...........		50,000
6. Levy of $5,000 property taxes by general fund against city's utility (quasi-external).	General Fund	Due from Enterprise Fund	5,000	
		Revenues (Control)...............		5,000
	Enterprise Fund	Property Tax Expense..............	5,000	
		Due to General Fund		5,000
7. Billing of general and special revenue funds for central computer service ($12,000 and $20,000) (quasi-external).	Internal Service Fund	Due from General Fund	12,000	
		Due from Special Revenue Fund........	20,000	
		Revenues (Control)...............		32,000
	General Fund	Expenditures (Control)	12,000	
		Due to Internal Service Fund		12,000
	Special Revenue Fund	Expenditures (Control)	20,000	
		Due to Internal Service Fund		20,000
8. Contribution made by city to establish a nonexpendable trust fund of $98,500.	General Fund	Residual Equity Transfer to Nonexpendable Trust Fund..................	98,500	
		Cash..........................		98,500
	Nonexpendable Trust Fund	Cash..........................	98,500	
		Residual Equity Transfer from General Fund (Contributed Capital)		98,500
9. Remittance of the city's $16,000 share of self-insurance costs for current period to an internal service fund.	General Fund	Expenditures (Control)	16,000	
		Cash..........................		16,000
	Internal Service Fund	Cash..........................	16,000	
		Revenues (Control)...............		16,000
10. Reimbursement of $15,000 by the special revenue fund to the general fund for general government supplies expenditures initially made in the general fund properly charged to a community development project.	Special Revenue Fund	Expenditures (Control)	15,000	
		Cash..........................		15,000
	General Fund	Cash..........................	15,000	
		Expenditures (Control)		15,000
11. Recording of depreciation, $6,000 enterprise fund, $13,000 internal service fund.	Enterprise Fund	Depreciation Expense	6,000	
		Accumulated Depreciation		6,000
	Internal Service Fund	Depreciation Expense	13,000	
		Accumulated Depreciation		13,000
12. Redemption of final $100,000 serial of general obligation bonds, with $3,000 deficiency covered by general fund. Fiscal agent is used for payment.	General Fund	Other Financing Uses (Control)	3,000	
		Cash..........................		3,000
	Debt Service Fund	Cash..........................	3,000	
		Other Financing Sources (Control)		3,000
		Cash with Fiscal Agent.............	100,000	
		Cash..........................		100,000
		Expenditures (Control)	100,000	
		Matured Bonds Payable		100,000
		Matured Bonds Payable.............	100,000	
		Cash with Fiscal Agent...........		100,000

Event	Funds	Accounts		
	General Long-Term Debt Account Group	Amounts Available in Debt Service Fund . . Amount to Be Provided for Payment of Serial Bonds	100,000	100,000
		Serial Bonds Payable . . . . Amounts Available in Debt Service Fund	100,000	100,000
13. Closing entry for capital projects fund involving a partially completed project. Cost to date is $130,000; revenues during the period are $300,000.	Capital Projects Fund	Revenues (Control) . . . . Expenditure (Control) . . . . Fund Balance—Unreserved, Undesignated	300,000	130,000 170,000
	General Fixed Assets Account Group	Construction in Progress . . . . Investment in General Fixed Assets— Capital Projects Fund	130,000	130,000
14. Payroll expenditures totaled $5,000 and included $1,000 payroll withholdings for taxes and insurance plus employer's share of these costs. $1,000 is transferred to an agency fund for remittance as follows: Private insurance company, $200; federal government, $600; and state government, $150. The agency fund makes the remittances.	General Fund	Expenditures (Control) . . . . Due to Agency Fund . . . . Cash	5,000	1,000 4,000
	Agency Fund	Due from General Fund . . . . Due to Insurance Company . . . . Due to Federal Government . . . . Due to State	1,000	200 650 150
	General Fund	Due to Agency Fund . . . . Cash	1,000	1,000
	Agency Fund	Cash . . . . Due from General Fund	1,000	1,000
		Due to Insurance Company . . . . Due to Federal Government . . . . Due to State . . . . Cash	200 650 150	1,000
15. A 5-year lease agreement was signed for equipment. The present value of the lease payments is $50,000.	General Fund	Expenditures (Control) . . . . Other Financing Source	50,000	50,000
	General Long-Term Debt Account Group	Amount to be Provided . . . . Lease Payable	50,000	50,000
	General Fixed Asset Account Group	Leased Asset . . . . Investment in General Fixed Assets— Capital Lease	50,000	50,000
16. The actuarial required contribution for pensions was $4,500. Of this, $3,000 was transferred to the pension trust. $1,500 will be transferred in the future.	General Fund	Expenditures (Control) . . . . Cash	3,000	3,000
	General Long-Term Debt Account Group	Amount to be Provided . . . . Unfunded Pension Obligation	1,500	1,500
	Pension Trust Fund	Cash . . . . Receivable from Employer . . . . Contributions—Employer	3,000 1,500	4,500
17. Claims and judgments against the city were estimated at $15,000. The city attorney determined that it was probable that the claims would be settled against the city. Of the $15,000, $3,000 was estimated to be paid out this fiscal year.	General Fund	Expenditures (Control) . . . . Claims and Judgments Payable	3,000	3,000
	General Long-Term Debt Account Group	Amount to be Provided . . . . Claims and Judgments Payable	12,000	12,000
18. Closure and post-closure costs of local landfill were estimated at $600,000. Landfill used this period was estimated at 1,000 cubic yards, and total landfill is 100,000 cubic yards. Landfill operations are accounted for in enterprise funds.	Enterprise Fund	Landfill expense . . . . Liability for Landfill Costs	6,000	6,000

(continued)

Event	Funds	Accounts		
19. Debt was refunded. The refunding met the criteria for in-substance defeasance. Proceeds of the new debt issue were placed in trust with an escrow agent.	Debt Service Fund	Cash.	100,000	
		Other Financing Sources.		100,000
		Other Financing Uses.	100,000	
		Cash.		100,000
	General Long-Term Debt Account Group	Bonds Payable	100,000	
		Amount to be Provided.		100,000
		Amount to be Provided.	100,000	
		Bonds Payable		100,000
20. Investments carried at $5,500 have a fair value of $5,750 in the general fund. Pension invest- ments carried at $102,000 have a fair value of $101,000.	General Fund	Investments.	250	
		Net Appreciation in Fair Value of Investments		250
	Pension Trust Fund	Net depreciation in Fair Value of Investments	1,000	
		Investments.		1,000

Illustration 17-15 on the next page provides a summary of governmental accounting and financial reporting principles.

Annual Financial Reporting

The principal role of financial reporting is to provide information. A Comprehensive Annual Financial Report should be prepared by every governmental unit in order to demonstrate that it has complied with the provisions of the law. The comprehensive annual financial report includes at least two sets of financial statements, along with their notes and any additional data that may be considered necessary. These two sets are a) the general purpose combined financial statements and b) combining statements by fund type. General purpose combined financial statements furnish in columnar form an overview of the financial position of all funds and account groups and the operating results of all funds.

A complete set of general purpose combined financial statements would include the following:

1. A combined balance sheet for all fund types and account groups.
2. A combined statement of revenues, expenditures, and changes in fund balances for all governmental funds and expendable trust funds.
3. A combined statement of revenues, expenditures, and changes in fund balances—budget and actual for the general and special revenue funds. This statement is prepared on a *budgetary basis* of accounting (often cash basis) which may be different than generally accepted accounting practices.
4. A combined statement of revenues, expenditures or expenses, and changes in retained earnings or fund balances for all proprietary funds, non-expendable trust funds, and pension trust funds.
5. A combined statement of cash flows for all proprietary funds and nonexpendable trust funds.
6. Notes to the financial statements including segment information for major nonhomogeneous enterprise funds, schedules of long-term debt, disclosure about the risk of investments (including the nature of derivatives), and significant policies.
7. Required supplementary information (e.g., possibly some pension-related information and risk-financing and self-insurance activity).

Examples of the general purpose financial statements presented in Illustrations 17-16 through 17-20 are taken from the 1996 Comprehensive Annual Financial Report of the City of Milwaukee, Wisconsin.

Illustration 17-15
Summary of Governmental Accounting

	Governmental Funds				Expendable Trust Funds	Nonexpendable Trust Funds		Proprietary Funds		Account Groups	
	General Fund	Special Revenue Funds	Capital Project Funds	Debt Service Funds	Expendable Trust and Agency Funds	Pension Trust Funds	Endowment Principal Funds	Internal Service Funds	Enterprise Funds	General Long-Term Debt Account Group	General Fixed Asset Account Group
Basis of accounting	Modified Accrual	Modified Accrual	Modified Accrual	Modified Accrual	Modified Accrual	Accrual	Accrual	Accrual	Accrual	n/a	n/a
Measurement focus	Flow of Resources	Flow of Resources	Flow of Resources	Flow of Resources	Flow of Resources	Economic Resources	Economic Resources	Economic Resources	Economic Resources	n/a	n/a
Formal recording of budget	Yes	Yes	Optional	No	No	No	No	No	No	n/a	n/a
Encumbrance accounting	Yes	Yes	Optional	No	Optional	No	No	No	No	n/a	n/a
Maintains records of fixed assets	No	No	No	No	No	Yes	Yes	Yes	Yes	n/a	Yes
Maintains records of long-term debt	No	No	No	No	No	Yes	Yes	Yes	Yes	Yes	n/a
Balance Sheet	Yes	Yes	Yes	Yes	Yes	Yes	Yes	Yes	Yes	Yes	Yes
Statement of Revenues, Expenditures, and Changes in Fund Balance	Yes	Yes	Yes	Yes	Yes	No	No	No	No	No	No
Statement of Revenues, Expenditures, and Changes in Fund Balance—Budget and Actual	Yes	Yes	No	No	No	No	No	No	No	No	No
Statement of Revenues, Expenses, and Changes in Retained Earnings	No	No	No	No	No	Yes	Yes	Yes	Yes	No	No
Statement of Cash Flows	No	No	No	No	No	No	Yes	Yes	Yes	No	No

Illustration 17-16
City of Milwaukee
Combined Balance Sheet—
All Fund Types, Account Groups, and Discretely Presented Component Units
December 31, 1996
(Thousands of Dollars)

| | Governmental Fund Types | | | |
| | | Special | Debt | Capital |
Assets and Other Debts	General	Revenue	Service	Projects
Assets:				
Cash and cash equivalents	$ 55,644	$17,006	$ 16,220	$35,648
Investments			84,736	
Receivables (net):				
Taxes	20,259	7,505		
Accounts	4,318	959	117	209
Unbilled accounts	506			
Special assessments				12,231
Notes and loans	1,429	14,743	19,941	
Accrued interest	1,871	3	623	
Due from other funds	17,438		1,749	
Due from primary government				
Due from component units			2,531	
Due from other governmental agencies	6	7,389	1,968	1,918
Advances to other funds	10,597			
Inventory of materials and supplies	5,947			187
Inventory of property for resale	37			
Prepaid items	659	7		10
Other assets				
Restricted Assets:				
Cash and cash equivalents				
Investments	264			
Receivables				
Land				
Buildings				
Improvements other than buildings				
Machinery and equipment				
Furniture and furnishings				
Construction work in progress				
Nonutility property				
Accumulated depreciation				
Net investment in long-term leases				
Other Debits:				
Resources available in Debt Service Funds				
Resources to be Provided for:				
Retirement of general obligation debt				
Contracts payable				
Pension contribution payable from subsequent year's budget				
Unfunded compensated absences				
Unfunded claims and judgment				
Total Assets and Other Debits	$118,975	$47,612	$127,885	$50,203

| Proprietary Fund Types | | Fiduciary Fund Type | Account Groups | | Totals (Memorandum Only) | | Totals (Memorandum Only) |
Enterprise	Internal Service	Trust and Agency	General Fixed Assets	General Long-Term Obligations	Primary Government	Component Units	Reporting Entity 1996
$ 28,073	$ 965	$293,100	$	$	$ 446,656	$ 30,975	$ 477,631
42,000		1,719			128,455	2,044	130,499
		94,074			121,838		121,838
18,914	10	12			24,539	1,213	25,752
8,440					8,946		8,946
					12,231		12,231
		516			36,629	32,345	68,974
414		1			2,912	288	3,200
1,465					20,652	1,226	21,878
						23	23
					2,531		2,531
19					11,300	14,319	25,619
					10,597		10,597
2,229	8				8,371	653	9,024
2,074					2,111	7,675	9,786
201	1				878	518	1,396
364					364	811	1,175
						1,198	1,198
		247,690			247,954	38,180	286,134
						184	184
20,729			37,207		57,936	23,447	81,383
65,723			111,512		177,235	220,677	397,912
240,067					240,067		240,067
99,856	5,544		87,817		193,217	10,689	203,906
65	271				336	90	426
9,711			35,244		44,955	53,998	98,953
564					564		564
(119,384)	(5,124)				(124,508)	(92,456)	(216,964)
						179	179
				102,120	102,120		102,120
				268,397	268,397		268,397
				268	268		268
				175	175		175
				24,414	24,414		24,414
				50,812	50,812		50,812
$421,524	$1,675	$637,112	$271,780	$446,186	$2,122,952	$348,276	$2,471,228

City of Milwaukee
Combined Balance Sheet—
All Fund Types, Account Groups, and Discretely Presented Component Units
December 31, 1996
(Thousands of Dollars)

	Governmental Fund Types			
Liabilities, Fund Equity and Other Credits	General	Special Revenue	Debt Service	Capital Projects
Liabilities:				
Accounts payable	$ 9,854	$ 3,286	$	$ 9,614
Accrued wages	21,660	380		305
Accrued expenses				
Due to other funds	925	3,071	1,318	6,296
Due to primary government				
Due to component units				23
Due to other governmental agencies		1,621		
General obligation debt payable—current				
Payable from Restricted Assets:				
Deferred compensation				
Deferred revenue	672	16,337	24,441	12,357
Bonds and notes payable				
General obligation debt				
Contracts payable				
Unfunded pension costs				
Unfunded compensated absences				
Unfunded claims and judgments				
Revenue bonds payable				
Advances from other funds				10,597
Advances from other governmental agencies				
Obligations under capital lease				
Other liabilities			6	
Total Liabilities	$ 33,111	$24,695	$25,765	$39,192
Fund Equity and Other Credits:				
Contributed capital	$	$	$	$
Investment in general fixed assets				
Retained Earnings:				
Reserved for debt retirement				
Reserved for mortgage trust				
Unreserved (deficit)				
Fund Balances:				
Reserved for debt service—1997 (1996)		11,586	24,963	
Reserved for future retirement of general obligation debt		3,733	77,157	
Reserved for delinquent taxes receivable		7,505		
Reserved for encumbrances, prepaids, and carryovers	19,281	93		22,623
Reserved for inventory	5,984			187
Reserved for mortgage trust	264			
Reserved for tax stabilization—1997 (1996)	16,326			
Reserved for tax stabilization—1998 (1997) and subsequent years' budgets	44,009			
Unreserved:				
Special assessment (deficit)				(11,799)
Undesignated				
Total Fund Equity and Other Credits	$ 85,864	$22,917	$102,120	$11,011
Total Liabilities, Fund Equity, and Other Credits	$118,975	$47,612	$127,885	$50,203

The notes to the financial statements are an integral part of this statement.

| Proprietary Fund Types | | Fiduciary Fund Type | Account Groups | | Totals (Memorandum Only) | | Totals (Memorandum Only) |
Enterprise	Internal Service	Trust and Agency	General Fixed Assets	General Long-Term Obligations	Primary Government	Component Units	Reporting Entity 1996
$ 15,886	$ 505	$ 1,493	$	$	$ 40,638	$ 8,784	$ 49,422
1,709	304				24,358	11	24,369
					3,338		3,338
9,038	4				20,652	1,226	21,878
						2,531	2,531
					23		23
		133,615			135,236	12,648	147,884
3,035					3,035	3,739	6,774
		247,690			247,690		247,690
52		157,778			211,637	236	211,873
		89,500			89,500	18,412	107,912
55,410				370,517	425,927		425,927
				268	268		268
				175	175		175
				24,414	24,414		24,414
				50,812	50,812		50,812
						37,445	37,445
					10,597		10,597
						4,630	4,630
	217				217		217
					6	3,943	3,949
$ 85,130	$1,030	$630,076	$	$446,186	$1,285,185	$ 96,943	$1,382,128
$115,803	$ 508	$	$	$	$ 116,311	$193,567	$ 309,878
			271,780		271,780		271,780
						12,694	12,694
220,591	137				220,728	45,072	265,800
					36,549		36,549
					80,890		80,890
					7,505		7,505
					41,997		41,997
					6,171		6,171
					264		264
					16,326		16,326
					44,009		44,009
					(11,799)		(11,799)
		7,036			7,036		7,036
$336,394	$ 645	$ 7,036	$271,780	$	$ 837,767	$251,333	$1,089,100
$421,524	$1,675	$637,112	$271,780	$446,186	$2,122,952	$348,276	$2,471,228

Illustration 17-17
City of Milwaukee
Combined Statement of Revenues, Expenditures, and Changes in Fund Balances—
All Governmental Fund Types and Expendable Trust Funds
For the Year Ended December 31, 1996
(Thousands of Dollars)

	General	Special Revenue
Revenues:		
Property taxes	$ 84,280	$
Other taxes	11,112	1,070
Special assessments		
Licenses and permits	7,086	
Intergovernmental	268,095	56,504
Charges for services	24,907	
Fines and forfeits	13,472	
Other	18,566	13,982
Total Revenues	$427,518	$71,556
Expenditures:		
Current:		
General government	$54,473	$ 4,076
Public safety	244,428	10,266
Public works	103,226	10,007
Health	17,037	12,643
Culture and recreation	18,180	1,368
Conservation and development	6,515	33,134
Other		
Capital outlay		
Debt Service:		
Principal retirement		
Interest		
Total Expenditures	$443,859	$71,494
Excess of Revenues over (under) Expenditures	$ (16,341)	$ 62
Other Financing Sources (Uses):		
Proceeds of bonds and notes	$	$ 9,575
Payment to refunded bond escrow agent		
Operating transfers-in	12,000	50
Operating transfers-out	(5,986)	(12,301)
Operating transfers to component units	(167)	
Total Other Financing Sources (Uses)	$ 5,847	$ (2,676)
Excess of Revenues and Other Sources over (under) Expenditures and Other Uses	$ (10,494)	$ (2,614)
Fund Balances—January 1	94,007	25,974
Residual Equity Transfers from Other Funds	15,157	
Residual Equity Transfers to Other Funds	(12,806)	(443)
Fund Balances—December 31	$ 85,864	$22,917

The notes to the financial statements are an integral part of this statement.

	Governmental Fund Types		Fiduciary Fund Type	Totals (Memorandum Only) Reporting Entity
	Debt Service	Capital Projects	Expendable Trust	1996
	$ 49,467	$ 18,927	$	$152,674
	785			12,967
		4,579		4,579
				7,086
		4,695	616	329,910
				24,907
				13,472
	19,699	1,090	8,598	61,935
	$ 69,951	$ 29,291	$9,214	$607,530
	$ 2	$	$	$ 58,551
				254,694
				113,233
				29,680
				19,548
				39,649
			8,964	8,964
		88,084		88,084
	64,272			64,272
	17,671			17,671
	$ 81,945	$ 88,084	$8,964	$694,346
	$ (11,994)	$(58,793)	$ 250	$ (86,816)
	$ 67,367	$ 54,245	$	$131,187
	(67,367)			(67,367)
	23,116	4,655		39,821
	(8,869)	(6,994)		(34,150)
				(167)
	$ 14,247	$ 51,906	$	$ 69,324
	$ 2,253	$ (6,887)	$ 250	$ (17,492)
	101,262	18,944	6,707	246,894
	1,104	2	79	16,342
	(2,499)	(1,048)		(16,796)
	$102,120	$ 11,011	$7,036	$228,948

Illustration 17-18
City of Milwaukee
Combined Statement of Revenues, Expenditures, and Changes in Fund Balances
Budget and Actual—General and Budgeted Special Revenue Fund Types
For the Year Ended December 31, 1996
(Thousands of Dollars)

	Amended Budget	Actual on Budgetary Basis	General Fund Variance— Favorable (Unfavorable)
Revenues:			
Property taxes	$ 84,280	$ 84,280	$
Other taxes	10,243	11,112	869
Licenses and permits	6,978	7,086	108
Intergovernmental	267,661	268,095	434
Charges for services	23,361	24,907	1,546
Fines and forfeits	13,035	13,472	437
Other	15,832	18,566	2,734
Total Revenues	$421,390	$427,518	$ 6,128
Expenditures:			
Current:			
General government	$ 58,684	$ 54,473	$ 4,211
Public safety	244,493	244,428	65
Public works	103,236	103,226	10
Health	17,240	17,037	203
Culture and recreation	18,184	18,180	4
Conservation and development	6,556	6,515	41
Total Expenditures	$448,393	$443,859	$ 4,534
Excess of Revenues over (under) Expenditures	$ (27,003)	$ (16,341)	$10,662
Other Financing Sources (Uses):			
Operating transfers-in	$ 11,296	$ 12,000	$ 704
Operating transfers-out	(5,742)	(5,986)	(244)
Operating transfers to component units	(167)	(167)	
Use of fund balance—reserved for tax stabilization	18,900	18,900	
Total Other Financing Sources (Uses)	$ 24,287	$ 24,747	$ 460
Excess of Revenues and Other Sources over (under) Expenditures and Other Uses	$ (2,716)	$ 8,406	$11,122
Fund Balances—January 1 (Excludes Reserved for Tax Stabilization)	75,107	75,107	
Residual Equity Transfers from Other Funds	316	15,157	14,841
Residual Equity Transfers to Other Funds	(266)	(12,806)	(12,540)
Fund Balances—December 31	$ 72,441	$ 85,864	$13,423

The notes to the financial statements are an integral part of this statement.

| | Special Revenue Funds | | | Totals (Memorandum Only) Reporting Entity | |
Amended Budget	Actual on Budgetary Basis	Variance—Favorable (Unfavorable)	Amended Budget	Actual on Budgetary Basis	Variance—Favorable (Unfavorable)
$	$	$	$ 84,280	$ 84,280	$
			10,243	11,112	869
			6,978	7,086	108
57,174	56,504	(670)	324,835	324,599	(236)
			23,361	24,907	1,546
			13,035	13,472	437
16,151	13,982	(2,169)	31,983	32,548	565
$73,325	$70,486	$(2,839)	$494,715	$498,004	$ 3,289
$ 2,727	$ 2,727	$	$ 61,411	$ 57,200	$ 4,211
10,668	10,266	402	255,161	254,694	467
11,707	10,007	1,700	114,943	113,233	1,710
13,665	12,643	1,022	30,905	29,680	1,225
1,379	1,368	11	19,563	19,548	15
33,219	33,134	85	39,775	39,649	126
$73,365	$70,145	$ 3,220	$521,758	$514,004	$ 7,754
$ (40)	$ 341	$ 381	$ (27,043)	$ (16,000)	$11,043
$ 50	$ 50	$	$ 11,346	$ 12,050	$704
			(5,742)	(5,986)	(244)
			(167)	(167)	
			18,900	18,900	
$ 50	$ 50	$	$ 24,337	$ 24,797	$ 460
$ 10	$ 391	$ 381	$ (2,706)	$8,797	$11,503
145	145		75,252	75,252	
			316	15,157	14,841
(62)	(443)	(381)	(328)	(13,249)	(12,921)
$ 93	$ 93	$	$ 72,534	$ 85,957	$13,423

Illustration 17-19
City of Milwaukee
Combined Statement of Revenues, Expenses, and
Changes in Retained Earnings (Deficit)—
All Proprietary Fund Types and Discretely Presented Component Units
For the Year Ended December 31, 1996
(Thousands of Dollars)

	Enterprise
Operating Revenues:	
Charges for services	$107,861
Operating Expenses:	
Milwaukee Metropolitan Sewerage District Charges	$ 34,354
Employee services	2,614
Administrative and general	4,921
Housing assistance payments	
Depreciation	7,426
Transmission and distribution	17,100
Maintenance and utilities	
Services	7,515
Payment in lieu of taxes	8,202
Water treatment	7,016
Water pumping	4,633
Supplies and materials	274
Billing and collection	3,488
Bad debts	
Interest expense and subsidies	
Vehicle liability claims	
Cost of goods disbursed	
Rehabilitation costs (cost recoveries)	
Show expense	
Other operating expenses	
Total Operating Expenses	$ 97,543
Operating Income (Loss)	$ 10,318
Nonoperating Revenues (Expenses):	
Federal grants and subsidies	$
Interest income	2,388
Interest expense	(1,467)
Net gain (loss) on sale of fixed assets	(407)
Contributions	
Other	149
Total Nonoperating Revenues (Expenses)	$ 663
Income (Loss) before Operating Transfers	$ 10,981
Operating Transfers-In	3,448
Operating Transfers-Out	(9,119)
Operating Transfers from Primary Government	
Net Income (Loss)	$ 5,310
Retained Earnings (Deficit)—January 1	215,934
Residual Equity Transfer to Other Funds	(653)
Prior-Period Adjustments	
Transfer to Wisconsin Center District	
Retained Earnings (Deficit)—December 31	$220,591

The notes to the financial statements are an integral part of this statement.

Internal Service	Totals (Memorandum Only) Primary Government	Component Units	Totals (Memorandum Only) Reporting Entity 1996
$7,120	$114,981	$ 23,998	$138,979
$	$ 34,354	$	$ 34,354
3,998	6,612	422	7,034
	4,921	19,239	24,160
		19,111	19,111
319	7,745	4,043	11,788
	17,100		17,100
		9,755	9,755
2,410	9,925	354	10,279
	8,202		8,202
	7,016		7,016
	4,633		4,633
410	684		684
	3,488		3,488
		762	762
		104	104
10	10		10
		1,379	1,379
		278	278
		348	348
$7,147	$104,690	$ 55,795	$160,485
$ (27)	$ 10,291	$(31,797)	$ (21,506)
$	$	$ 34,033	$ 34,033
	2,388	2,208	4,596
	(1,467)	(2,130)	(3,597)
(56)	(463)	(160)	(623)
(30)	(30)	1,309	1,279
	149	582	731
$ (86)	$ 577	$35,842	$ 36,419
$ (113)	$ 10,868	$ 4,045	$ 14,913
	3,448		3,448
	(9,119)		(9,119)
		167	167
$ (113)	$ 5,197	$ 4,212	$ 9,409
250	216,184	53,554	269,738
	(653)		(653)
$ 137	$220,728	$57,766	$278,494

Illustration 17-20
City of Milwaukee
Combined Statement of Cash Flows—
All Proprietary Fund Types and Discretely Presented Component Units
For the Year Ended December 31, 1996
(Thousands of Dollars)

	Enterprise
Cash Flows from Operating Activities:	
Operating income (loss)	$10,318
Adjustments to Reconcile Operating Income (Loss) to Cash	
Provided by (Used for) Operating Activities:	
Depreciation.	7,426
Bad debt expense	
Other nonoperating revenues (expenses)	110
(Increase) decrease in receivables	1,033
(Increase) decrease in due from other funds	(60)
(Increase) decrease in due from primary government	
(Increase) decrease in due from other governmental agencies	
(Increase) decrease in inventory of materials and supplies	128
(Increase) decrease in inventory of property for resale	107
(Increase) decrease in prepaid items.	248
(Increase) decrease in other assets	140
(Increase) decrease in net investment in long-term lease	
Increase (decrease) in accounts payable	(97)
Increase (decrease) in accrued wages.	159
Increase (decrease) in accrued expenses	
Increase (decrease) in due to other funds.	2,112
Increase (decrease) in deferred revenue.	(347)
Increase (decrease) in other liabilities	
Net Cash Provided by (Used for) Operating Activities	$21,277
Cash Flows from Noncapital Financing Activities:	
Operating transfers (to) from other funds	$ (2,894)
Other nonoperating revenues	61
Other nonoperating expenses	(22)
Interest paid	
Increase (decrease) in due to other funds.	(398)
(Return of) Contributions	(149)
Proceeds from bonds and notes payable	
Retirement of general obligation debt	
Retirement of bonds and notes payable.	
Repayments to primary government	
Net decrease (increase) in due to other governmental units.	
Operating transfer to (from) primary government	
Net Cash Provided by (Used for) Noncapital Financing Activities..	$ (3,402)

Internal Service	Totals (Memorandum Only) Primary Government	Component Units	Totals (Memorandum Only) Reporting Entity 1996
$ (27)	$10,291	$(31,797)	$(21,506)
319	7,745	4,043	11,788
		625	625
	110		110
27	1,060	(2,531)	(1,471)
	(60)	(365)	(425)
		33	33
		(5)	(5)
53	181	(137)	44
	107	76	183
(1)	247	(115)	132
	140	(544)	(404)
		(126)	(126)
58	(39)	2,601	2,562
(3)	156	(6)	150
		(333)	(333)
(12)	2,100	447	2,547
	(347)	(148)	(495)
		2,642	2,642
$414	$21,691	$(25,640)	$ (3,949)
$	$ (2,894)	$	$ (2,894)
	61	1,072	1,133
	(22)		(22)
	(398)		(398)
	(149)	34,542	34,393
		27	27
		(234)	(234)
		1,388	1,388
		(1,151)	(1,151)
		167	167
$	$ (3,402)	$ 35,811	$ 32,409

Illustration 17-20
City of Milwaukee
Combined Statement of Cash Flows—
All Proprietary Fund Types and Discretely Presented Component Units
For the Year Ended December 31, 1996
(Thousands of Dollars)

	Enterprise
Cash Flows from Capital and Related Financing Activities:	
Capital contributions	$ 2,876
Proceeds from sale of bonds and notes	30,950
Acquisition of property, plant, and equipment	(31,228)
Retirement of revenue bonds payable	
Retirement of bonds and notes payable	
Retirement of general obligation debt	(3,573)
Payment to refunded bond escrow agent	(8,093)
Interest paid	(1,467)
Sale of land and other assets	1,135
Payment of obligation for capital lease	
Return of contributions	(2)
Operating transfers (to) from other funds	(2,777)
Repairs and restorations	(343)
Net advances to other funds	
(Increase) decrease in fiscal agent funds	
Proceeds from notes receivable	
Cash transferred to Wisconsin Center District	
Payment of notes receivable	
Net Cash Provided by (Used for) Capital and Related Financing Activities	$(12,522)
Cash Flows from Investing Activities:	
Interest income	$ 2,657
Purchases of investment	(42,000)
Proceeds from the sale and maturity of investments	24,462
Net Cash Provided by (Used for) Investing Activities	$(14,881)
Net Increase (Decrease) in Cash and Cash Equivalents	$ (9,528)
Cash and Cash Equivalents at December 31, 1995 (1996)	$ 37,601
Adjustments	
Cash and Cash Equivalents at January 1	$ 37,601
Cash and Cash Equivalents at December 31	$ 28,073
Cash and Cash Equivalents at December 31 Consist of:	
Unrestricted cash	$ 28,073
Restricted cash	
Noncash Activities:	$ 28,073

Enterprise Funds:
Low Interest Mortgage Program transferred loans receivable of $1,429 and other noncash assets of $304 with the offsetting liabilities and fund equity to the General Fund
Assets with a net book value of $3 were disposed of from Port of Milwaukee.
Water mains and related property installed by others were deeded to the Water Works in the amount of $868.
Internal Service Funds:
During 1996, the Central Reproduction Services Fund disposed assets having a net book value of $1.

The notes to the financial statements are an integral part of this statement.

Internal Service	Totals (Memorandum Only) Primary Government	Component Units	Totals (Memorandum Only) Reporting Entity 1996
$ 174	$ 3,050	$ 28,173	$ 31,223
	30,950	7,785	38,735
(205)	(31,433)	(36,088)	(67,521)
		(12,174)	(12,174)
		(1,428)	(1,428)
	(3,573)		(3,573)
	(8,093)		(8,093)
(30)	(1,497)	(1,655)	(3,152)
	1,135		1,135
(35)	(35)		(35)
(336)	(338)		(338)
	(2,777)		(2,777)
	(343)		(343)
		1,146	1,146
		3,928	3,928
		(886)	(886)
		501	501
$(432)	$(12,954)	$(10,698)	$(23,652)
$	$ 2,657	$ 2,207	$ 4,864
	(42,000)	(205)	(42,205)
	24,462	1,159	25,621
$	$(14,881)	$ 3,161	$(11,720)
$ (18)	$ (9,546)	$ 2,634	$ (6,912)
$ 983	$ 38,584	$ 29,539	$ 68,123
$ 983	$ 38,584	$ 29,539	$ 68,123
$ 965	$ 29,038	$ 32,173	$ 61,211
$ 965	$ 29,038	$ 30,975	$ 60,013
		1,198	1,198
$ 965	$ 29,038	$ 32,173	$ 61,211

The general purpose financial statements (GPFS) constitute the minimum financial reporting necessary for a fair presentation in accordance with generally accepted accounting principles. The GPFS are part of the *financial section* of a Comprehensive Annual Financial Report (CAFR) along with the auditor's report and combining, individual fund, and account group statements and/or schedules, which provide more detailed financial information than the combined statements. For example, Milwaukee's combined balance sheet shows that capital projects funds have a cash balance of $38,974,000. A breakdown of this amount is shown in the following combining balance sheet for all capital projects funds:

City of Milwaukee
Capital Projects Funds
Combining Balance Sheet
December 31, 1995
With Comparative Totals for December 31, 1994
(Thousands of Dollars)

Assets	Bridges	Buildings and Grounds	Sewers	Urban Renewal	Streets	Tax Incremental Districts	Special Assessments	1995
Cash and cash equivalents	$ 865	$9,380	$13,029	$2,668	$10,339	$2,693	$	$38,974
Receivables (net):								
Accounts		126	13	3	138	4		284
Special Assessments							12,641	12,641
Due from other governmental agencies .	411		200	59	2,199			2,869
Inventory of materials and supplies. . . .			143					143
Prepaid items					7			7
Total Assets.	$1,276	$9,506	$13,385	$2,737	$12,676	$2,697	$12,641	$54,918

Two sections of the CAFR, which are in addition to the financial section, are the *introductory section* and the *statistical section*. The introductory section of the CAFR includes a table of contents, a letter of transmittal from the chief executive or finance officer to the mayor (or the mayor and legislative body), and other information. The letter of transmittal tells about the contents of the CAFR, management's view of the economic condition of the governmental unit, and the community and management's summary of governmental operating activity. The statistical section reports numerous statistics about the governmental unit and the community, such as general governmental expenditures by function and community demographic statistics.

The GASB Codification of Governmental Accounting and Financial Reporting provides an excellent pyramid of financial reporting, as shown in Illustration 17-21. The top of the pyramid represents highly aggregated consolidated financial statements while the bottom represents details of transactions. Current government financial reporting is in the mid-levels of the pyramid. As GASB continues to deliberate its financial reporting model, the level of detail provided on the financial statements will be discussed. Rather than providing top-of-the-pyramid data, the GASB is proposing a dual model. The appendix to this chapter summarizes the Exposure Draft on the financial reporting model where the GASB puts forth major changes to the current model as described in the last two chapters.

Reporting Entity

GASB Statement No. 14, issued in June 1991, defines the criteria a government must use to determine whether its reporting entity should be limited to the primary gov-

Illustration 17-21
The Financial Reporting "Pyramid"

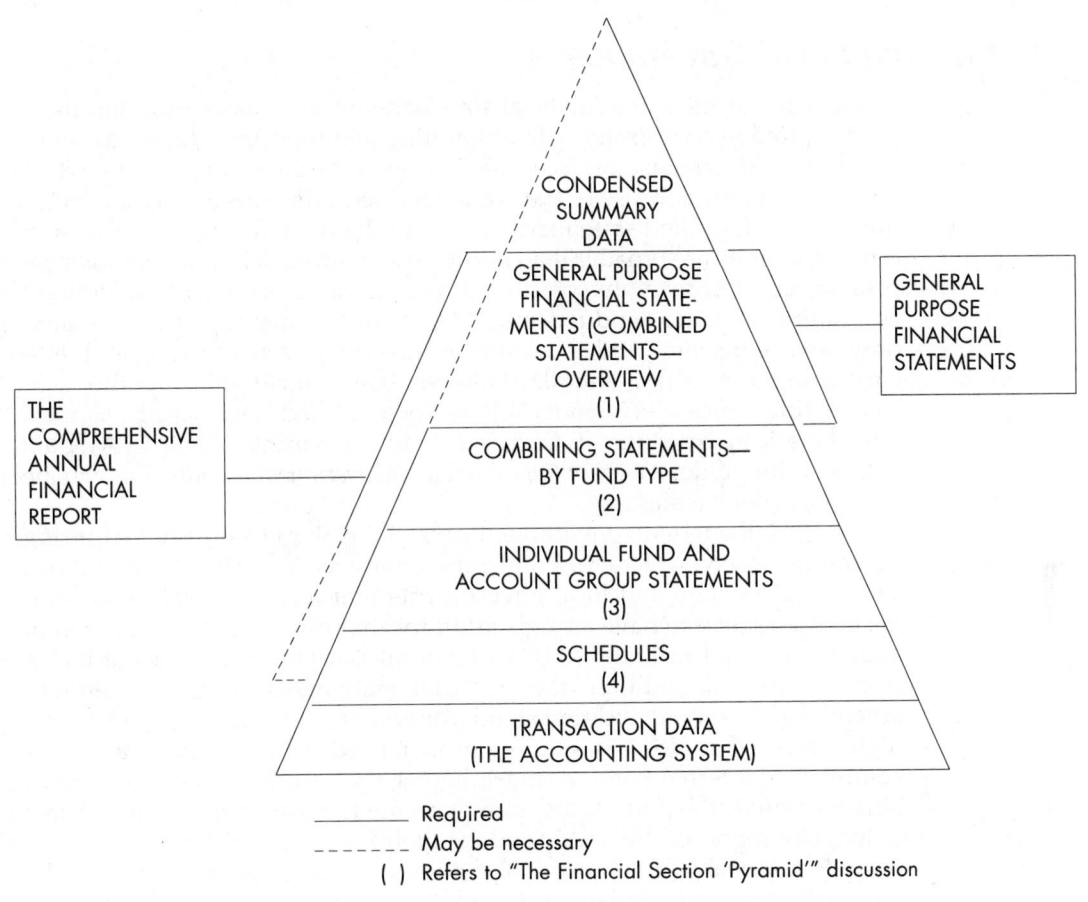

Source: GASB Codification, Section 1900.114.

ernment or whether one or more of the associated organizations (referred to as component units) are also part of the government's reporting entity. The definition of the reporting entity is based primarily on the notion of financial accountability. Financial accountability as measured by a) fiscal dependence or b) the ability of a primary government to appoint a voting majority of an organization's governing body and either be able to impose its will on the potential component unit or have the potential to receive specific financial benefit or burden. Typical component units may include authorities, commissions, boards, pension plans, development corporations, hospitals, and school districts. Most component units should be included in the financial report by discrete presentation, i.e., in one or more columns separate from the financial data of the primary government. Other component units are so intertwined with the primary government that they are blended or included with the primary government and only footnote disclosure can inform the reader of their existence.

Governments sometimes enter into joint ventures with other governments, whereby they agree to share both risks and rewards of a common activity. If a government has an equity interest in the joint venture, it should account for the investment as a long-term asset in the general long-term debt account group (or in a proprietary fund if the investment was made with proprietary resources).

The GASB currently has a project on affiliated organizations, e.g., booster clubs, fund-raising organizations, and foundations, which do not qualify as a component unit. The proposed standard would require footnote disclosure of such related entities.[16]

Audits of State and Local Governments

In order for users of the financial statements to have assurance that the statements are prepared in conformity with accounting and reporting standards set forth by the GASB, the statements are accompanied by an audit report. Most governments are audited annually because of state or federal requirements or because long-term creditors demand audited statements as part of the debt agreements. The audits of governmental units are broader than audits of a business. The *financial audit*, which is the primary audit, deals with compliance with fiscal requirements including applicable accounting standards and federal and state laws. Special *performance audits* of economy and efficiency and program results emphasize managerial effectiveness. Government auditing standards have been developed by the U.S. General Accounting Office (GAO) in its Yellow Book entitled *Government Auditing Standards.* The American Institute of Certified Public Accountants (AICPA) publishes the AICPA audit guide, *Audits of State and Local Governmental Units*17 which incorporates the Yellow Book standards.

In 1984, the federal government passed the Single Audit Act requiring audits of all entities receiving federal grants and contracts. The Single Audit Act, revised in 1996, requires state and local governments that receive $300,000 or more of *federal financial assistance* to have a single audit for that fiscal year. The act exempts governments receiving less than $300,000 of federal assistance. A single audit has two main components: an audit or the financial statements conducted under generally accepted government auditing standards and an audit of federal financial awards. A higher level of auditing is required of major federal award programs by testing for compliance, internal control, and inherent risk. Audit reports prepared under the Single Audit Act include a) an opinion on the fairness of financial statement presentation, b) a report on the study and evaluation of internal control systems' ability to provide reasonable assurance that federal programs are being managed in compliance with laws and regulations, c) a report on compliance with laws and regulations that may have a material effect on specific programs, and d) a schedule of findings and questioned costs.

Appendix

In January 1997, the GASB issued an Exposure Draft, *Basic Financial Statements—and Management's Discussion and Analysis—for State and Local Governments.* This document represents the culmination of over 10 years of discussion and debate on the presentation of a government's financial statements. If adopted, the changes will give a dramatic new look to government's financial statements. The new presentation of a government's basic financial statements is based on a *dual reporting perspective.* Adopting the dual perspective, two separate sets of financial statements will be prepared to provide different types of financial information. The GASB believes that two sets of financial statements are necessary to a) meet the diverse needs of financial statement users and b) to achieve the varied (and sometimes contrasting) objectives of GASB Concepts Statement No. 1.

---

16 GASB Exposure Draft, *The Financial Reporting Entity—Affiliated Organizations* (Norwalk, CT: Governmental Accounting Standards Board, December 1994).

17 American Institute of Certified Public Accountants, *Audits of State and Local Governmental Units*, rev. ed. (New York: AICPA, 1993), p. 29.

Unique features of the dual perspective include the following:

A fund perspective that maintains the traditional measurement focus and basis of accounting for both governmental and proprietary funds.   The financial statements under the fund perspective will look similar to those currently prepared but with two important changes. Governments will now be required to prepare separate balance sheets and statements of changes for the two fund types—governmental and proprietary. In addition, more detailed budgetary comparison statements will be required, whereby both the original and final budget are included. Moreover, information on the account groups will no longer be presented on the balance sheet. Instead, the account groups will be included as schedules in the notes to the financial statements. Fiduciary financial statements will include a statement of net assets and a statement of changes in net assets in a format similar to the new pension statements described in this chapter. A statement of cash flows for the proprietary funds will continue to be presented. Specific criteria for when fiduciary and proprietary funds can be used are also in the Exposure Draft.

An entity-wide perspective that will use the economic resources measurement focus and full accrual basis of accounting for both the government and proprietary activities.   This radically different set of financial statements will present aggregated information about the government as a whole. Instead of presenting fund data, the entity-wide statements will provide one column for all governmental activities and another for all business-type activities. A third column will be required to show component units as defined on page 17-55. Fiduciary funds would not be reported at the entity-wide perspective. The purpose of the entity-wide perspective is to provide a more comprehensive view of a government's operations and provide a longer-term perspective than is currently provided using modified accrual fund-based reporting.

Under the proposed standards, at the entity-wide perspective, governments must report all capital assets, including infrastructure assets. They must also report a charge to reflect the cost of using up capital assets (i.e., depreciation) including capital (fixed) assets of the general government. Currently, few governments report infrastructure assets. One of the more controversial requirements of the Exposure Draft is the retroactive reporting of infrastructure assets acquired in the last 25 years.

The new financial statements include a statement of net assets (balance sheet) that reports governmental and proprietary activities in separate columns and includes both long-lived assets and long-term debt as shown in Illustration A-1.

The statement of activities (comparable to an income statement) has a net program cost format. Instead of the traditional operating statement format that starts with operating revenues and then lists operating expenses, the upper portion of the statement of activities highlights program expenses. From these will be deducted the revenues that can be directly associated with these expenses. The resulting information is the net cost of a government's programs. The lower portion of the statement will present the revenues of the government at large which must be generated to finance the net program costs. A sample statement is shown in Illustration A-2. Because the entity-wide perspective uses full accrual accounting, the statement of activities will include charges for depreciation, as well as other accruals, among the expenses for each program. Therefore, this new statement will inform readers of the full cost of each governmental program. The GASB believes that this information will promote the reporting of information on interperiod equity—making it clear whether revenues of a period have covered the full cost of providing services.

A management's discussion and analysis (MD&A) will also be required.
The MD&A would introduce the financial statements by giving readers a brief, objective, and easily readable analysis of a government's financial information. An explanation of the differences between the fund and entity-wide perspectives will also be included in the MD&A. Although not required, the MD&A may also provide a detailed reconciliation between the two perspectives.

Illustration A-3 summarizes the key aspects of the dual-perspective reporting. The GASB has placed the financial reporting model as its number-one priority and expects to issue a final pronouncement to be effective in the early 2000s. The final pronouncement will likely differ somewhat from the Exposure Draft. The GASB is also deliberating the basic approach for the public college and university model.

Illustration A-1
Sample City
Statement of Net Assets
December 31, 2002

	Primary Government			Component Units
	Government Activities	Business-type Activities	Total	
Assets				
Cash and cash equivalents	$ 13,597,899	$ 10,279,143	$ 23,877,042	$ 303,935
Investments	27,365,221		27,365,221	7,428,952
Receivables (net)	12,833,132	3,609,615	16,442,747	4,042,290
Internal receivables	175,000			
Inventories	322,149	126,674	448,823	83,697
Capital assets, net (See Note 1)	170,022,760	151,388,751	321,411,511	37,744,786
Total assets	$224,316,161	$165,404,183	$389,545,344	$49,603,660
Liabilities				
Accounts Payable	6,783,310	751,430	7,534,740	1,803,332
Internal payables		175,000		
Deferred revenue	1,435,599		1,435,599	38,911
Long-term liabilities (See Note 2)	92,538,378	78,908,559	171,446,937	28,532,790
Total liabilities	$100,757,287	$ 79,834,989	$180,417,276	$30,375,033
Net Assets				
Invested in capital assets, net of related debt	90,701,684	73,088,574	163,790,258	15,906,392
Restricted for:				
Capital projects	24,715,566		24,715,566	492,445
Debt service	3,020,708	1,451,996	4,472,704	
Community development projects . .	4,811,043		4,811,043	
Other purposes	3,214,302		3,214,302	
Unrestricted (deficit)	(2,904,429)	11,028,624	8,124,195	2,829,790
Total net assets	$123,558,874	$ 85,569,194	$209,128,068	$19,228,627

Source: GASB Exposure Draft, *Basic Financial Statements—and Management's Discussion and Analysis—for State and Local Governments* (Norwalk, CT: Governmental Accounting Standards Board, January 1997).

Illustration A-2
Sample City
Statement of Activities
For the Year Ended December 31, 2002

Functions/Programs	Expenses	Program Revenues Charges for Services	Program Revenues Grants and Contributions	Net (Expense) Revenue — Primary Government Governmental Activities	Net (Expense) Revenue — Primary Government Business-type Activities	Net (Expense) Revenue — Primary Government Total	Component Units Net (Expense) Revenue
Primary government:							
General government	$ 9,571,410	$ 3,146,915	$ 843,617	$ (5,580,878)		$ (5,580,878)	
Public safety	34,844,749	1,198,855	1,369,993	(32,275,901)		(32,275,901)	
Public works	10,128,538	850,000	2,252,615	(7,025,923)		(7,025,923)	
Engineering services	1,299,645	704,793		(594,852)		(594,852)	
Health and sanitation	6,738,672	5,612,267	575,000	(551,405)		(551,405)	
Cemetery	735,866	212,496		(523,370)		(523,370)	
Culture and recreation	11,532,350	3,995,199	2,450,000	(5,087,151)		(5,087,151)	
Community development	2,919,389		2,580,000	(339,389)		(339,389)	
Interest on long-term debt	6,068,121			(6,068,121)		(6,068,121)	
Water	3,595,733	4,159,350	1,159,909		$ 1,723,526	1,723,526	
Sewer	4,912,853	7,170,533	486,010		2,743,690	2,743,690	
Parking facilities	2,796,283	1,344,087			(1,452,196)	(1,452,196)	
Total primary government	$95,143,609	$28,394,495	$11,717,144	$ (58,046,990)	$ 3,015,020	$ (55,031,970)	
Component units:							
Landfill	$ 3,382,157	$ 3,857,858	$ 11,397				$ 487,098
Public school system	31,186,498	705,765	3,937,083				(26,543,650)
Total component units	$34,568,655	$ 4,563,623	$ 3,948,480				$(26,056,552)
General revenues:							
Taxes:							
Real estate				34,168,449		34,168,449	21,893,273
Other				13,308,487		13,308,487	6,461,708
Grants and contributions not restricted to specific programs				1,457,820		1,457,820	881,763
Interest and investment earnings				1,958,144	601,349	2,559,493	22,464
Miscellaneous				884,907	104,925	989,832	
Total general revenues				51,777,807	706,274	52,484,081	29,259,208
Excess (deficiency) of revenues over expenses before special item				$ (6,269,183)	$ 3,721,294	$ (2,547,889)	$ 3,202,656
Special item:							
Gain on sale of park land				2,653,488		2,653,488	
Excess (deficiency) of revenues over expenses				$ (3,615,695)	$ 3,721,294	$105,599	$ 3,202,656
Transfers				501,409	(501,409)		
Change in net assets				(3,114,286)	3,219,885	105,599	3,202,656
Net assets—beginning				$126,673,160	$82,349,309	$209,022,469	$16,025,971
Net assets—ending				$123,558,874	$85,569,194	$209,128,068	$ 19,228,627

Source: GASB Exposure Draft, Basic Financial Statements—and Management's Discussion and Analysis—for State and Local Governments (Norwalk, CT: Governmental Accounting Standards Board, January 1997).

Illustration A-3
Essential Characteristics of Dual-Perspective Reporting

Accountability focus	Operational accountability for all governmental activities combined, all business-type activities, and all component units	Fiscal accountability for governmental fund types; operational accountability for proprietary and fiduciary fund types
Appropriate time horizon for accountability focus	Short-term and long-term	Short-term for governmental fund types; short-term and long-term for proprietary and fiduciary fund types
Appropriate Measurement Focus/Basis of Accounting for accountability focus	Economic resources/accrual	Current financial resources/modified accrual or governmental fund types; economic resources/accrual for proprietary and fiduciary fund types
Scope	All activities of the primary government and component units, except fiduciary activities	All fund types of the primary government and fiduciary component unit
Degree of detail	Summarized by category of activity (governmental, business-type, or component unit)	Detailed by fund or fund type

Source: GASB Exposure Draft, *Basic Financial Statements—and Management's Discussion and Analysis—for State and Local Governments* (Norwalk, CT: Governmental Accounting Standards Board, January 1997).

Questions

1. Discuss the similarities between a special revenue fund and a general fund.
2. Why are fixed assets, acquired with proceeds from general obligation bond issues, not permanently accounted for in a capital projects fund?
3. If a capital projects fund has authority to continue operations over several fiscal periods, why is it desirable to close its records at the end of each period?
4. Explain the necessity to introduce a deferred revenues account in the levy of capital special assessments.
5. Give the entry in the general long-term debt account group to record the issuance of bonds related to construction of general fixed assets from special assessments where the governmental unit has assumed responsibility for payment in case of default. Explain the purpose of the entry.
6. The debt service fund does not use budgetary accounts. What is the logic for not doing so?
7. When a debt service fund receives resources, it might credit Revenues (Control) or Other Financing Sources (Control). Under what circumstances would each of these credits be used?
8. What is the characteristic that determines whether an activity should be accounted for in a special revenue fund or in an enterprise fund?

9. What is the appropriate measurement focus applied to enterprise funds, and how does this cause accounting for an enterprise fund to closely resemble accounting for a business enterprise?

10. Describe two major types of interfund transfers. Under what circumstances is each used?

11. What is the difference between an agency fund and a trust fund?

12. What is the difference between an enterprise fund and an internal service fund?

13. Explain the difference between expenses and expenditures in a state and a local government.

14. Describe the difference between accounting for governmental funds and proprietary funds.

15. List and describe the nature of the four reserves in the accounting for employees' pension trust funds.

Exercises

Exercise 1.   Select the best answer for each of the following multiple-choice items. (Nos. 2, 3, 5, and 7-10 are AICPA adapted.)

1. Accounting for special revenue funds closely resembles the accounting for

   a) General funds.

   b) Capital projects funds.

   c) Enterprise funds.

   d) Agency funds.

2. In which of the following fund types of a city government are revenues and expenditures recognized on the same basis of accounting as the general fund?

   a) Nonexpendable trust.   *fiduciary fund — spend interest not princ,*

   b) Internal service.

   c) Enterprise.

   d) Debt service.

3. Revenues that are legally restricted to expenditures for specified purposes should be accounted for in special revenue funds, including

   a) Accumulation of resources for payment of general long-term debt principal and interest.

   b) Pension trust fund revenues.

   c) Gasoline taxes to finance road repairs.

   d) Proprietary fund revenues.

4. Bonds are issued at a premium by a capital projects fund. The premium should be

   a) Retained in the capital projects fund.

   b) Credited directly to the unreserved fund balance of the capital projects fund.

   c) Transferred to the debt service funds.

   d) Used to reduce the net cost of the project involved.

Modified accrual basis of acct.

5. Which of the following funds of a governmental unit recognizes revenues in the accounting period in which they become available and measurable?

	General Fund	Enterprise Fund
a)	Yes	No
b)	No	Yes
c)	Yes	Yes
d)	No	No

Dr. Encumb.

6. At the beginning of a fiscal period, encumbrances that remained at the previous year-end relating to an incomplete project in the capital projects funds generally are reinstated by crediting

   a) Fund Balance—Unreserved, Undesignated.

   b) Fund Balance—Reserved for Encumbrances.

   c) Encumbrances (Control).

   d) Expenditures (Control).

7. On June 28, 20X1, Gold City's debt service fund received funds for the future repayment of bond principal. As a consequence, the general long-term debt account group reported

   a) An increase in the amount available in debt service funds and an increase in the fund balance.

   b) An increase in the amount available in debt service funds and an increase in the amount to be provided for bonds.

   c) An increase in the amount available in debt service funds and a decrease in the amount to be provided for bonds.

   d) No changes in any amount until the bond principal is actually paid.

8. Which of the following statements is correct concerning a governmental entity's combined statement of cash flows?

   a) Cash flows from capital financing activities are reported separately from cash flows from noncapital financing activities.

   b) The statement format is the same as that of a business enterprise's statement of cash flows.

   c) Cash flows from operating activities may not be reported using the indirect method.

   d) The statement format includes columns for the general, governmental, and proprietary fund types.

9. In a government's comprehensive annual financial report (CAFR), proprietary fund types are included in which of the following combined financial statements?

	Statement of Revenues, Expenditures, and Changes in Fund Balances	Balance Sheet
a)	Yes	Yes
b)	No	No
c)	No	Yes
d)	Yes	No

10. The billings for transportation services provided to other governmental units are recorded by the internal service fund as

a) *Interfund exchanges.*

b) *Intergovernmental transfers.*

c) *Transportation appropriations.*

d) *Operating revenues.*

Exercise 2.   Select the best answer for each of the following multiple-choice items. (Nos. 3, 4, 6, and 7-9 are AICPA adapted.)

1. Resources for a capital improvement are provided by special assessments. At the start of the second year of the project, a reclassification entry in the debt service fund that debits Deferred Revenues would credit

a) *Special Assessments Receivable—Deferred.*

b) *Revenues (Control).*

c) *Unreserved Fund Balance.*

d) *Fund Balance Reserved for Special Assessments.*

2. If a governmental unit makes no guarantees regarding repayment of a capital improvement special assessment bond issue, the liability for the bonds would

a) *Not appear in the financial statements or in their notes.*

b) *Not appear in the financial statements, but would appear in the notes to the financial statements.*

c) *Appear in the capital projects funds.*

d) *Appear in the general long-term debt account group.*

3. Gaffney City's serial bonds are serviced through a debt service fund with cash provided by the general fund. In a debt service fund's statements, how are cash receipts and cash payments reported?

	Cash Receipts	Cash Payments
a)	Revenues	Expenditures
b)	Revenues	Operating transfers
c)	Operating transfers	Expenditures
d)	Operating transfers	Operating transfers

4. Taxes collected and held by Dunne County for a school district would be accounted for in which of the following funds?

a) *Trust.*

b) *Agency.*

c) *Special revenue.*

d) *Internal service.*

5. The following is a correct entry:

Construction in Progress	XXX
Investment in General Fixed Assets—	
Capital Projects Funds	XXX

The entry would be found in the

a) *Capital projects funds.*

(continued)

   b)   Enterprise funds.

   c)   General fund.

   d)   General fixed assets account group.

6.   In a government's comprehensive annual financial report (CAFR), account groups are included in which of the following combined financial statements?

	Balance Sheet	Statement of Revenues, Expenditures, and Changes in Fund Balances
a)	Yes	No
b)	No	Yes
c)	Yes	Yes
d)	No	No

7.   Clover City's comprehensive annual financial report contains both combining and combined financial statements. Total columns are

   a)   Required for both combining and combined financial statements.

   b)   Optional, but commonly shown, for combining financial statements and required for combined financial statements.

   c)   Required for combining financial statements and optional, but commonly shown, for combined financial statements.

   d)   Optional, but commonly shown, for both combining and combined financial statements.

8.   In what fund type should the proceeds from special assessment bonds issued to finance construction of sidewalks in a new subdivision be reported?

   a)   Agency fund.

   b)   Special revenue fund.

   c)   Enterprise fund.

   d)   Capital projects fund.

9.   Eureka City should issue a statement of cash flows for which of the following funds?

	Eureka City Hall Capital Projects Fund	Eureka Water Enterprise Fund
a)	No	Yes
b)	No	No
c)	Yes	No
d)	Yes	Yes

Exercise 3.   Select the best response for each of the following multiple-choice questions which refer to the transactions of Finch City. (No. 4 is AICPA adapted.)

   On March 2, 20X1, Finch City issued 10-year general obligation bonds at face amount, with interest payable March 1 and September 1. The proceeds were to be used to finance the construction of a civic center over the period April 1, 20X1, to March 31, 20X2. During the fiscal year ended June 30, 20X1, no resources had been provided to the debt service fund for the payment of principal and interest.

1. On June 30, 20X1, Finch's debt service fund should include interest payable on the general obligation bonds for

   a) 0 months. b) 3 months. c) 4 months. d) 6 months.

2. Proceeds from the general obligation bonds should be recorded in the

   a) General fund.

   b) Capital projects fund.

   c) General long-term debt account group.

   d) Debt service fund.

3. The liability for the general obligation bonds should be recorded in the

   a) General fund.

   b) Capital projects fund.

   c) General long-term debt account group.

   d) Debt service fund.

4. On June 30, 20X1, Finch's combined balance sheet should report the construction in progress for the civic center in the:

	Capital Projects Fund	General Fixed Assets Account Group
a)	Yes	Yes
b)	Yes	No
c)	No	No
d)	No	Yes

Exercise 4. Prepare journal entries to record the following events. Identify every fund(s) or group of accounts in which an entry is made.

   a) The city authorized the construction of a city hall to be financed by a $400,000 contribution of the general fund and the proceeds of a $2,000,000 general obligation serial bond issue. Both amounts are budgeted to be received in the current year. Expenditures during the current year are estimated to be $850,000. Budgetary accounts are used.

   b) The general fund remits the $400,000.

   c) The bonds are sold for 101; the premium is transferred to the debt service fund. The premium is to be used for interest payments.

   d) A contract is signed with Rollins Construction Company for the construction of the city hall for an estimated contract cost of $2,300,000.

   e) By year-end, $1,000,000 is paid against the contract with Rollins Construction Company.

Exercise 5. In 20X7, the town of Waterview authorized the construction of two concrete roadways. The public works department estimates the project cost at $400,000, $40,000 of which is transferred from the general fund to the capital projects fund. The balance will be paid for through a special assessments levy on benefiting property owners. $360,000, 4-year, 10% special assessment bonds are issued at face value, on January 1, 20X7, to finance the property owners' portion. Payments of $45,000 plus interest are made each June 30 and December 31. The bonds were issued. The town guarantees payment of the debt.

   Purchase orders totaling $80,000 are issued, and a contract is signed for the esti-

(continued)

mated $320,000 additional cost of the project. Invoices for all purchase orders total $74,000. The actual contract cost is $325,000. Liabilities for these amounts are entered. Except for $30,000 withheld on the contract until final approval, all liabilities related to the completed construction are paid. Waterview does not use budgetary accounts for these projects. Prepare entries in the capital projects fund for these events.

Exercise 6.   This exercise is based on the facts of Exercise 5 for the town of Waterview's special assessment project. Assume special assessment property owners make the required payments to the debt service fund and the debt service fund, in turn, makes the payments required by the serial bonds. Record all entries in the debt service fund and in the long-term capital debt group of accounts for 20X7.

Exercise 7.   Prepare journal entries required by a debt service fund to record the following transactions:

   a) On January 2, a $5,000,000, 6%, 10-year general obligation serial bond issue is sold at 99. Interest is payable annually on December 31, along with $\frac{1}{10}$ of the original principal.

   b) At year-end, the first serial of bonds matures, along with interest on the bond issue.

   c) The general fund transfers cash to meet the matured items.

   d) A check for the matured items is sent to First Bank, the agent handling the payments.

   e) Later, the bank reports that the first serial has been redeemed. One check for interest of $9,000 was returned by the post office because the bond owner had moved. The bank will search for the new address.

Exercise 8.   Prepare journal entries to record the following events in the City of Rosewood's Water Commission enterprise fund:

   a) From its general fund revenues, the city transferred $300,000, which is restricted for the drilling of additional wells.

   b) Billings for water consumption for the month totaled $287,000, including $67,000 billed to other funds within the city.

   c) The Water Commission collected $42,000 from other funds and $190,000 from other users on billings in item b.

   d) To raise additional funds, the utility issued $700,000 of 5%, 10-year revenue bonds at face value. Proceeds are restricted to the development of wells. *[handwritten: Assume Received cash]*

   e) The contract with the well driller showed an estimated cost of $930,000.

   f) The well driller bills its cost plus normal profit amount of $360,000 at year-end.

   g) The utility pays a $300,000 billing from the well driller.

Exercise 9.   On January 1, 20X8, Jack Kinn donated $100,000 to the city of Larkin to be set aside as a trust fund for water quality improvements made by the city. The funds were fully invested in bonds purchased at a premium with a face value of $94,000. During the year, cash received on investments was $7,500. Premiums on the bonds purchased were amortized at $600 per year. All income earned is transferred to the endowment revenue fund. A total of $6,000 was transferred to a special revenue fund to carry out the purpose of the trust. The city uses an endowment principal fund and an endowment earnings fund. Prepare the journal entries to record these transactions. Prepare the balance sheet of both funds as of December 31, 20X8.

Turn-in
12/3

Exercise 10.   Indicate into which fund a city would record each of the following transactions. (You need not make any entries.)

a) *Fixed assets are purchased with general fund cash.* GF, GFAAG

b) *Long-term serial bonds are issued to finance the construction of a new art museum. The bonds are sold at a premium.* CPF, DSF, GLTDAG

c) *The general fund transfers a sufficient amount of money to cover principal and interest requirements of a debt issue.* GF, DSF, GLTDAG

d) *The fund receiving the payment in item c makes the scheduled payment of principal and interest.* DSF, GLTDAG

e) *A special assessment project is ½ completed at year-end.* CPF, GFAAG

f) *Income is earned by the endowment principal fund and is transferred to a recipient fund, which is restricted as to its expenditures by a trust agreement.* E-E, E-P,

accrual basis

g) *Possible depreciation entries on assets are recorded.* ENT, INT, E-P

h) *The government-owned water utility issues debt to purchase new equipment.* ENT,

i) *The new city prison is completed, and there are funds left over that are transferred to the fund responsible for repaying the debt used to finance the project.* DSF, GLTDAG, CPF, GFAAG

Use the following symbols and funds for your responses:

GF	General	E-P	Endowment—Principal
SRF	Special Revenue	E-E	Endowment—Earnings
DSF	Debt Service	GFAAG	General Fixed Assets Account Group
CPF	Capital Projects		
ENT	Enterprise	GLTDAG	General Long-Term Debt Account Group
INT	Internal Service Fund		

Know for EXAM
★ Turn-in
12/3

Exercise 11.   Match the appropriate letter indicating the recording of the following transactions:

1. General obligation bonds were issued at par.   B

2. Approved purchase orders were issued for supplies.   _____

3. The above-mentioned supplies were received, and the related invoices were approved.   _____

4. General fund salaries and wages were incurred.   _____

5. The internal service fund had interfund billings.   _____

6. Revenues were earned from a previously awarded grant.   _____

7. Property taxes were collected in advance.   _____

8. Appropriations were recorded on adoption of the budget.   _____

9. Short-term financing was received from a bank, secured by the city's taxing power.   _____

10. There was an excess of estimated inflows over estimated outflows. _____

Recording of transactions:

A. Credit appropriations control.   _____
B. Credit budgetary fund balance—unreserved.
C. Credit expenditures control.
D. Credit deferred revenues.
E. Credit interfund revenues.
F. Credit tax anticipation notes payable.

(continued)

G. Credit other financing sources.
H. Credit other financing uses.
I.   Debit appropriations control.
J.   Debit deferred revenues.
K. Debit encumbrances control.
L.   Debit expenditures control.

(AICPA adapted)

Exercise 12.   Identify the letter that best describes the accounting and reporting by the following funds and account groups.

1. Enterprise fund fixed assets.

2. Capital projects fund.   _____

3. General fixed assets.   _____

4. Infrastructure fixed assets.   _____

5. Enterprise fund cash.   _____

6. General fund.   _____

7. Agency fund cash.   _____

8. General long-term debt.   _____

9. Special revenue fund.   _____

10. Debt services fund.   _____

A. Accounted for in a fiduciary fund.
B. Accounted for in a proprietary fund.
C. Accounted for in a quasi-endowment fund.
D. Accounted for in a self-balancing account group.
E. Accounted for in a special assessment fund.
F. Accounts for major construction activities.
G. Accounts for property tax revenues.
H. Accounts for payment of interest and principal on tax-supported debt.
I.   Accounts for revenues from earmarked sources to finance designated activities.
J.   Reporting is optional.

(AICPA adapted)

Problems

Problem 17-1.   Select the best response for each of the following multiple-choice questions. (Nos. 1-8 are AICPA adapted.)

1. Maple Township issued the following bonds during the year ended June 30, 20X7:

Bonds issued for the Garbage Collection Enterprise Fund that will
   service the debt $500,000
Revenue bonds to be repaid from admission fees collected by the
   Township Zoo Enterprise Fund   350,000

What amount of these bonds should be accounted for in Maple's general long-term debt account group?

a) 0   b) $350,000   c) $500,000   d) $850,000

2. On December 31, 20X9, Elm Village paid a contractor $4,500,000 for the total cost of a new Village Hall built in 20X9 on Elm-owned land. Financing for the capital project was provided by a $3,000,000 general obligation bond issue sold at face amount on December 31, 20X9, with the remaining $1,500,000 transferred from the general fund. What account and amount should be reported in Elm's 20X9 financial statements for the general fund?

   a) Other Financing Sources (Control) $4,500,000

   b) Expenditures (Control). $4,500,000

   c) Other Financing Sources (Control) $3,000,000

   d) Other Financing Uses (Control). $1,500,000

3. During 20X9, Spruce City reported the following receipts from self-sustaining activities paid for by users of the services rendered:

   Operation of water supply plant. $5,000,000
   Operation of bus system   900,000

   What amount should be accounted for in Spruce's enterprise funds?

   a) 0   b) $900,000   c) $5,000,000   d) $5,900,000

4. Through an internal service fund, Wood County operates a centralized data-processing center to provide services to Wood's other governmental units. In 20X9, this internal service fund billed Wood's Parks and Recreation Fund $75,000 for data-processing services. What account should Wood's internal service fund credit to record this $75,000 billing to the Parks and Recreation Fund?

   a) Operating Revenues (Control)

   b) Interfund Exchanges

   c) Intergovernmental Transfers

   d) Data-Processing Department Expenses

5. The following information pertains to Pine City's special revenue fund in 20X9:

   Appropriations $6,500,000
   Expenditures   5,000,000
   Other financing sources   1,500,000
   Other financing uses   2,000,000
   Revenues   8,000,000

   After Pine's general fund accounts were closed at the end of 20X9, the fund balance increased by

   a) $3,000,000   b) $2,500,000   c) $1,500,000   d) $1,000,000

6. Kew City received a $15,000,000 federal grant to finance the construction of a center for rehabilitation of drug addicts. The proceeds of this grant should be accounted for in the

   a) Special revenue funds.

   b) General fund.

   c) Capital projects funds.

   d) Trust funds.

7. Lisa County issued $5,000,000 of general obligation bonds at 101 to finance a capital project. The $50,000 premium was to be used for payment of interest. The transactions involving the premium should be accounted for in the

(continued)

a) Capital projects funds, debt service funds, and the general long-term debt account group.

b) Capital projects funds and debt service funds only.

c) Debt service funds and the general long-term debt account group only.

d) Debt service funds only.

8. In 20X9, a state government collected income taxes of $8,000,000 for the benefit of one of its cities that imposes an income tax on its residents. The state periodically remitted these collections to the city. The state should account for the $8,000,000 in the

a) General fund.

b) Agency funds.

c) Internal service funds.

d) Special assessment funds.

Problem 17-2.   (Nos. 1 and 5-8 are AICPA adapted.)

1. The following revenues were among those reported by Ariba Township in 20X4:

Net rental revenue (after depreciation) from a parking garage owned by Ariba	$ 40,000
Interest earned on investments held for employees' retirement benefits	100,000
Property taxes	6,000,000

What amount of the foregoing revenues should be accounted for in Ariba's governmental funds?

a) $6,140,000   b) $6,100,000   c) $6,040,000   d) $6,000,000

Items 2 and 3 are based on the following information:

The events relating to the City of Albury's debt service funds that occurred during the year ended December 31, 20X5, are as follows:

Debt principal matured	$2,000,000
Unmatured (accrued) interest on outstanding debt at January 1, 20X5.	50,000
Interest on matured debt.	900,000
Unmatured (accrued) interest on outstanding debt at December 31, 20X5	100,000
Interest revenue from investments	600,000
Cash transferred from the general fund for retirement of debt principal	1,000,000
Cash transferred from the general fund for payment of matured interest	900,000

All principal and interest due in 20X5 were paid on time.

2. What is the total amount of expenditures that Albury's debt service funds should record for the year ended December 31, 20X5?

a) $940,000   b) $950,000   c) $2,900,000   d) $2,500,000

3. How much revenue should Albury's debt service funds record for the year ended December 31, 20X5?

   a) $600,000   b) $1,600,000   c) $1,900,000   d) $2,500,000

4. The following assets are among those owned by the city of Foster:

Apartment building (part of the principal of a nonexpendable trust fund)	$ 200,000
City hall	800,000
Three fire stations	1,000,000
City streets and sidewalks	5,000,000

   How much should be included in Foster's general fixed assets account group?

   a) Either $1,800,000 or $6,800,000.

   b) Either $2,000,000 or $7,000,000.

   c) $6,800,000.

   d) $7,000,000.

5. The following information pertains to Grove City's interfund receivables and payables at December 31, 20X6:

Due to special revenue fund from general fund	$10,000
Due to agency fund from special revenue fund	4,000

   In Grove's special revenue fund balance sheet at December 31, 20X6, how should these interfund amounts be reported?

   a) As an asset of $6,000.

   b) As a liability of $6,000.

   c) As an asset of $4,000 and a liability of $10,000.

   d) As an asset of $10,000 and a liability of $4,000.

6. Financing for the renovation of Fir City's municipal park, begun and completed during 20X6, came from the following sources:

Grant from state government	$400,000
Proceeds from general obligation bond issue	500,000
Transfer from Fir's general fund	100,000

	Revenues	Other financing sources
a)	$1,000,000	$ 0
b)	$ 900,000	$ 100,000
c)	$ 400,000	$ 600,000
d)	0	$1,000,000

7. On April 1, 20X6, Oak County incurred the following expenditures in issuing long-term bonds:

Issue costs	$400,000
Debt insurance	90,000

   When Oak establishes the accounting for operating debt service, what amount should be deferred and amortized over the life of the bonds?

   a) $0   b) $900,000   c) $400,000   d) $490,000

8. Lake County received the following proceeds that are legally restricted to expenditure for specified purposes:

Levies on affected property owners to install sidewalks $500,000
Gasoline taxes to finance road repairs 900,000

What amount would be accounted for in Lake's special revenue funds?

a) $1,400,000
b) $900,000
c) $500,000
d) $0

Problem 17-3. Allioto County elects not to purchase commercial insurance. Instead, it sets aside resources for potential claims in an internal service "self-insurance" fund. During the year, the fund recognized $1.5 million for claims filed during the year. Of these, it paid $1.3 million. Based on the calculations of an independent actuary, the insurance fund billed, and collected, $2.0 million in premiums from the other county departments insured by the fund. Of this amount, $1.2 million was billed to the funds accounted for in the general fund and $.8 million to the county utility fund. The total charge for premiums was based on historical experience and included a reasonable provision for future catastrophe losses.

1. Prepare the journal entries in the internal service fund to record the claims recognized and paid, and the premiums billed and collected.
2. Prepare the journal entries in the other funds affected by the above.
3. If the county accounted for its self-insurance within its general fund, how would the above entries differ?

Problem 17-4. The following information pertains to Arnold Township's construction and financing of a new administration center:

Estimated total cost of project $9,000,000
Project financing:
  State entitlement grant 3,000,000
  General obligation bonds:
    Face amount 6,000,000
    Stated interest rate 6%
    Issue date . . . . December 1, 20X8
    Maturity date . . . . November 30, 20Y8

Arnold's fiscal year ended on June 30, 20X8. The following events occurred that affected the capital projects fund established to account for this project:

July 1, 20X8—The capital projects fund borrowed $250,000 from the general fund for preliminary expenses.

July 9, 20X8—Engineering and planning costs of $200,000, for which no encumbrance had been recorded, were paid to Krew Associates.

December 1, 20X8—The bonds were sold at 101. The premium is transferred to the debt service fund.

December 1, 20X8—The entitlement grant was formally approved by the state.

April 30, 20X9—A $7,000,000 contract was executed with Kimmel Construction Corporation, the general contractors for the major portion of the project. The contract provides that Arnold will withhold 4% of all billings pending satisfactory completion of the project.

May 9, 20X9—$1,000,000 of the state grant was received.

June 10, 20X9—The $250,000 borrowed from the general fund was repaid.

June 30, 20X9—Progress billing of $1,200,000 was received from Kimmel.

Arnold uses encumbrance accounting for budgetary control. Unencumbered appropriations lapse at the end of the year.

Required:

1. Prepare journal entries in the administration center capital projects fund to record the foregoing transactions.
2. Prepare the June 30, 20X9 closing entries for the administration center capital projects fund.
3. Prepare the Administration Center Capital Projects Fund balance sheet at June 30, 20X9.
4. Prepare entries needed in other funds and groups.

(AICPA adapted)

Problem 17-5.   During 20X1, Krona City issued bonds for financing the construction of a civic center, and bonds for financing improvements in the environmental controls for its water and sewer enterprise. The latter bonds require a sinking fund for their retirement. Items 1–4 represent items Krona should report in its 20X1 financial statements. For each item, determine whether it would be included in each of the funds and account groups listed below.

A. General fund.
B. Enterprise funds.
C. Capital projects funds.
D. Debt service funds.
E. General fixed assets account group.
F. General long-term debt account group.

1. Bonds payable.   _____
2. Accumulated depreciation.   _____
3. Amounts identified for the repayment of the two bond issues.   _____
4. Reserved for encumbrances.   _____

(AICPA adapted)

Problem 17-6.   You are given the following post-closing trial balance for the Special Assessment Capital Projects Fund of the city of Stone Bank as of January 1, 20X2. The project was started last year and should be completed in June of 20X2.

	Dr.	Cr.
Cash	$290,000	
Contracts Payable—Retained Percentage		$ 60,000
Fund Balance—Reserved for Encumbrances.		80,000
Fund Balance—Unreserved, Undesignated		150,000
	$290,000	$290,000

(continued)

The special assessments are collected by the debt service fund, which also makes payments of principal and interest. The city has guaranteed payment of the debt in the event of nonpayment by the special assessment property owners. The debt service fund has the following balances on January 1, 20X2:

	Dr.	Cr.
Cash	$ 20,000	
Special Assessments Receivable—Current	250,000	
Special Assessments Receivable—Deferred	250,000	
Revenue		$250,000
Deferred Revenue		250,000
Fund Balance—Reserved for Debt Service		20,000
	$520,000	$520,000

The following events occurred during 20X2:

January 2—The city adopted an operating budget for 20X2 construction activities. Expenditures are estimated at $223,400, including amounts encumbered in the prior year. Budgetary accounts are used.

January 5—Prior-year encumbrances are restored, and new encumbrances of $138,000 are recorded.

February 1—$220,000 of special assessments are collected, along with interest of $17,600. Interest of $2,400 was billed on the uncollected current assessments, which were classified as delinquent.

February 28—$115,000 was paid on outstanding special assessment bonds, including interest of $15,000.

March 14—Delinquent special assessments and interest thereon of $2,650 were collected.

May 1—Expenditures of $220,000 were vouchered to Contracts Payable. The usual 5% retained percentage was entered. The project is now complete at a total cost of $896,000.

May 10—A check for $100,000 was issued to the contractor.

Required:

Prepare journal entries to record each of the preceding events in the proper funds and groups of accounts using the following format:

Date	Fund or Account Group	Entry

Problem 17-7. Which fund or account group should be used to record the following?

GFAAG 1. A primary government's general fund equity interest in a joint venture.

GFAAG 2. Fixed assets of a governmental unit, other than those accounted for in a proprietary fund.

GLTDAG 3. A governmental unit's unmatured general obligation bonds payable.

FSF 4. Cost of maintenance for a municipal motor pool that maintains all city-owned vehicles and charges the various departments for the cost of rendering those services.

GLTDAG 5. General long-term debt of a governmental unit.

not sure 6. Deferred compensation plans, for other than proprietary fund employees, adopted under IRC 457.

agency fund →

7. Debt service transactions of a special assessment issue for which the government is not obligated in any manner.
8. Taxes collected and held for a separate school district.
9. Investments donated to the city, income from which is to be used to acquire art for the city's museum. *NON-exp. fund*

Spec. Rev, 10. Receipts from the federal government for the food stamp program.

(AICPA adapted)

Problem 17-8. The pre-closing, year-end trial balance for a capital projects fund of the city of Craig as of December 31, 20X7, follows:

	Dr.	Cr.
Cash	$ 75,000	
Investments	200,000	
Contracts Payable—Retained Percentage		$ 60,000
Revenues (Control)		16,600
Other Financing Sources (Control)		900,000
Expenditures (Control)	686,600	
Other Financing Uses (Control)	15,000	
Encumbrances (Control)	80,000	
Fund Balance—Reserved for Encumbrances		80,000
Estimated Revenues (Control)	20,000	
Estimated Other Financing Sources (Control)	950,000	
Appropriations (Control)		640,000
Estimated Other Financing Uses (Control)		25,000
Budgetary Fund Balance—Unreserved		305,000
	$2,026,600	$2,026,600

Required:

1. Prepare closing entries as of December 31, 20X7.
2. Prepare the year-end statement of revenues, expenditures, and changes in fund balance for this project that began on January 2, 20X7.
3. Prepare the balance sheet as of December 31, 20X7.

Turn-in 12/5

Problem 17-9. In response to a petition signed by the property owners of River Hills Subdivision, the city of Pierce will oversee the installation of sidewalks, curbs, and gutters in the subdivision, to be accounted for in the city's capital projects fund. Pierce reports on a calendar-year basis. Construction is estimated to cost $900,000 and will be financed by a $100,000 county grant, a $50,000 transfer from the city's general fund, and special assessments of $750,000 to be levied against subdivision property owners. One-third of the levy is to be due on February 1 of each year, starting with 20X8. The first $250,000 installment will be received by the capital projects fund directly. The remaining installments will be collected by the debt service fund and will be used to service the related bond debt. The project is to begin on January 15, 20X8, and is to take 18 months to complete. It is estimated that 70% of the work will be completed during 20X8.

To cover construction costs, a 6%, $500,000 special assessment serial bond issue will be floated on March 1, 20X8. Interest is to be paid semiannually on September 1 and March 1 by the debt service fund. One-fifth of the principal will be redeemed on March 1 of each year, starting with 20X9. Since interest earned on special assessments will offset bond interest cost, the city will not accrue interest.

(continued)

Although the special assessments will provide cash to redeem the bond principal and pay the bond interest, Pierce has pledged its full faith and credit as security for the bond obligation.

The following events happen during 20X8:

January 2—The city council adopted the annual budget for the River Hills project in the capital projects fund.

January 2—The receivables from the general fund and the county were recorded.

January 5—Special assessments were levied in accordance with the plan, with ⅓ due on February 1.

January 9—Amounts due from the general fund and the county were received.

January 10—Encumbrances for the year were recorded at $675,000.

February 1—The first special assessment installment was collected.

March 1—Bonds with a $500,000 face value were sold at 101. Except for the price, other conditions remained in accordance with the bond plan. The premium was to be transferred to the debt service fund for interest payments.

March 1—$600,000 was invested in a 5% money market account by the capital projects fund.

August 31—$10,000 for interest payment was transferred by the capital projects fund to the debt service fund.

September 1—The semiannual bond interest was paid by the debt service fund.

December 15—The contractor submitted an invoice for $600,000 that was approved for payment, except for a 10% amount to be paid on completion and acceptance of the project. Related encumbrances totaled $595,000.

December 29—$400,000 was withdrawn from the money market investment. Interest of $16,600 was received.

December 30—The contractor was mailed a check for $540,000. In addition, vouchers for $76,600 were prepared and paid for items on the project that were not encumbered.

In addition—The next assessment installment was reclassified upon special direction of the city council, and an amount equal to project expenditures-to-date was capitalized.

Required:

For each of the preceding events, prepare the journal entries for all of the funds and groups of accounts involved, using the following format:

Date	Fund or Account Group	Entry

Problem 17-10.   Prepare a Statement of Cash Flows for the internal service fund of the City of Cleveville from the following information:

Cash on hand at the beginning of the year	$ 122
Interest from investments	45
Wages and salaries paid	(3,470)
Purchases of supplies	(1,650)
Collections (for services) from other funds	6,380
Interest on long-term debt	(150)
Repayment of loans to other funds	(880)
Purchase of fixed assets	(900)
Proceeds of revenue bonds	800
Purchases of investments	(440)
Proceeds from sale of fixed assets	23
Proceeds from sale of investments	33
Loans from other funds	600

Problem 17-11.   In compliance with a newly enacted state law, Hayward County assumed the responsibility of collecting all property taxes levied within its boundaries as of July 1, 20X3. The following composite property tax rate per $100 of net assessed valuation was developed for the fiscal year ending June 30, 20X4:

Hayward County General Fund	$ 6.00
Reed City General Fund	3.00
Newbury Township General Fund.	1.00
	$10.00

All property taxes are due in quarterly installments and, after being collected, are distributed to the governmental units represented in the composite rate. To administer the collection and distribution of such taxes, Hayward County has established a tax agency fund.

Additional information:

a)   *To reimburse itself for estimated administrative expenses of operating the tax agency fund, the county is to deduct 2% from the tax collections for Reed City and Newbury Township. The total amount deducted is to be remitted to the Hayward County general fund.*

b)   *Current-year tax levies to be collected by the tax agency fund are as follows:*

	Gross Levy	Estimated Amount to be Collected
Hayward County	$3,600,000	$3,500,000
Reed City	1,800,000	1,740,000
Newbury Township	600,000	560,000
	$6,000,000	$5,800,000

c)   *In its original computation of the gross levy, Newbury Township made an error that will reduce both the gross and estimated amounts to be collected by $10,000.*

d)   *As of September 30, 20X3, the tax agency fund has received $1,440,000 in first-quarter payments. On October 1, the agency fund made a distribution to the 3 governmental units on the basis of the composite property tax rate.*

Required:

For the period July 1, 20X3, through October 1, 20X3, prepare journal entries to record the preceding transactions, using the following format:

Accounts	Hayward County Tax Agency Fund		Hayward County General Fund		Reed City General Fund		Newbury Township General Fund	
	Debit	Credit	Debit	Credit	Debit	Credit	Debit	Credit

(AICPA adapted)

Problem 17-12. Based on the following very limited information, indicate whether and how the city should report its related entity.

1. Its school district, although not a legally separate government, is managed by a school board elected by city residents. The system is financed with general tax revenues of the city, and its budget is incorporated into that of the city at large (and, thereby, is subject to the same approval and appropriation process as other city expenditures).

2. Its fixed asset financing authority is a legally separate government that leases equipment to the city. To finance the equipment, the authority issues bonds that are guaranteed by the city and expected to be paid from the rents received from the city. The authority leases equipment exclusively to the city.

3. Its housing authority, which provides loans to low-income families within the city, is governed by a 5-person board appointed by the city's mayor.

4. Its hospital is owned by the city but managed under contract by a private hospital management firm.

5. Its water purification plant is owned in equal shares by the city and 2 neighboring counties. The city's interest in the plant was acquired with resources from its water utility (enterprise) fund.

6. Its community college, a separate legal entity, is governed by a board of governors elected by city residents and has its own taxing and budgetary authority.

Problem 17-13. The following trial balance of the Employee's Retirement System Fund for Redford City was prepared by a clerk who used only balance sheet accounts in recording the events for the fiscal year ended June 30, 20X8:

Cash		$ 38,000
Due from the City		4,000
Interest Receivable		5,000
Investments, at fair value		497,000
Due to Resigned Employees		(1,000)
Annuities Payable		(3,000)
Net Plan Assets		(540,000)
		0

Balance of June 30, 20X7	$469,000
Events during 20X8:	
Amounts received from employees	32,000
Amounts received from employer	16,000
Amount due from city at year-end	4,000
Annuities paid during the year	13,000
Refunds made during the year	2,500
Annuities payable at year-end	3,000
Due to resigned employees at year-end	1,000
Investment earnings received	30,000
Accrued earnings at year-end	5,000
Difference between carrying value and	
fair value of the investments	13,500
Administrative expenses	5,000
Balance on June 30, 20X8	540,000

1. Prepare journal entries to record the events transpiring during 20X8 as they should have been recorded originally. Prepare journal entries to update the net assets.
2. Prepare a Statement of Net Assets and a Statement of Changes in Net Assets of the Employees' Retirement System Fund.

Problem 17-14.   In 20X8, a city opens a municipal landfill, which it will account for in an enterprise fund. It estimates capacity to be 6 million cubic feet and usable life to be 20 years. To close the landfill, the municipality expects to incur labor, material, and equipment costs of $4 million. Thereafter, it expects to incur an additional $6 million of cost to monitor and maintain the site.

1. In 20X8, the city uses 300,000 feet of the landfill. Prepare the journal entry to record the expense for closure and post-closure care.
2. In 20X9, it again uses 300,000 feet of the landfill. It revises its estimate of available volume to 5.8 million cubic feet and closure and post-closure costs to $10.2 million. Prepare the journal entry to record the expense for closure and post-closure care.
3. Suppose the city accounts for the landfill in the general fund. How would the above entries for 20X8 and 20X9 differ?

Problem 17-15.   The city of Danbury operates a central computer center through an internal service fund. The Computer Internal Service Fund was established by a contribution of $1,000,000 from the general fund on July 1, 20X2, at which time a building was acquired at a cost of $300,000 cash. A used computer was purchased for $600,000. The post-closing trial balance of the fund at June 30, 20X3, was as follows:

Cash	$ 120,000	
Due from General Fund	140,000	
Inventory of Materials and Supplies	80,000	
Land.	60,000	
Building	300,000	
Allowance for Depreciation—Building		$ 15,000
Computer Equipment.	660,000	
Allowance for Depreciation—Computer Equipment.		264,000
Vouchers Payable (to Outsiders)		41,000
Contributions from General Fund.		1,000,000
Retained Earnings—Unreserved.		40,000
	$1,360,000	$1,360,000

The following information applies to the year ended June 30, 20X4:
a) Materials and supplies were purchased on account for $72,000.
b) The inventory of materials and supplies at June 30, 20X4, was $65,000.
c) Salaries paid totaled $235,000, including related costs.
d) A billing from the Utility Enterprise Fund for $40,000 was received and paid.
e) Depreciation on the building and on the equipment was $6,500 and $133,000, respectively.
f) Billings to other departments for service were as follows:

(continued)

General Fund		$392,000
Water and Sewer Fund.		84,000
Special Revenue Fund.		42,000

g) *Unpaid interfund receivable balances at June 30, 20X4, were*

General Fund		$136,000
Special Revenue Funds		16,000

h) *Vouchers payable at June 30, 20X4, were $19,000.*

Required:

1. For the period July 1, 20X3, through June 30, 20X4, prepare journal entries to record the transactions in the Computer Internal Service Fund. The city uses control accounts for revenues and expenses.
2. Prepare closing entries at June 30, 20X4.

Problem 17-16.   Tyler City formally integrates budgetary accounts into its general fund. During the year ended December 31, 20X7, Tyler received a state grant to buy a bus and an additional grant for bus operation in 20X7. In 20X7, only 90% of the capital grant was used for the bus purchase, but 100% of the operating grant was disbursed. Tyler has incurred the following long-term obligations:

■ General obligation bonds issued for the water and sewer fund which will service the debt.
■ Revenue bonds to be repaid from admission fees collected from users of the municipal recreation center.

These bonds are expected to be paid from enterprise funds and are secured by Tyler's full faith, credit, and taxing power as further assurance that the obligations will be paid. Todd's 20X7 expenditures from the general fund include payments for structural alterations to a firehouse and furniture for the mayor's office.

1. In reporting the state grants for the bus purchase and operation, what should Tyler include as grant revenues for the year ended December 31, 20X7?

	90% of the capital grant	100% of the capital grant	Operating grant
a)	Yes	No	No
b)	No	Yes	No
c)	No	Yes	Yes
d)	Yes	No	Yes

2. Which of Tyler's long-term obligations should be accounted for in the general long-term debt account group?

	General Obligation Bonds	Revenue Bonds
a)	Yes	Yes
b)	Yes	No
c)	No	Yes
d)	No	No

3. When Tyler records its annual budget, which of the following control accounts indicates the amount of authorized spending limitation for the year ending December 31, 20X7?
   a) Reserved for appropriations
   b) Appropriations
   c) Reserved for encumbrances
   d) Encumbrances

4. In Tyler's general fund balance sheet presentation at December 31, 20X7, which of the following expenditures should be classified as fixed assets?
   a) No   No
   b) No   Yes
   c) Yes   No
   d) Yes   Yes

(adapted from AICPA)

Problem 17-17. A selected list of transactions for the city of Butler for the fiscal year ending June 30, 20X8, follows:

a) The city government authorized a budget with estimated revenues of $2,500,000 and appropriations of $2,450,000.

b) The city's share of state gasoline taxes is estimated to be $264,500. These taxes are to be used only for highway maintenance. Appropriations are authorized in the amount of $250,000.

c) Property taxes of $1,400,000 are levied by the city. In the past, uncollectible taxes have averaged 2% of the gross levy.

d) A $1,000,000 term bond issue for construction of a school is authorized and sold at 102. The bond premium is transferred to the debt service fund to be used for payment of interest.

e) Contracts are signed for the construction of the school at an estimated cost of $1,000,000.

f) The school is constructed at a cost of $990,000.

g) The debt service fund will need $150,000 from the general fund for estimated interest and principal payments for the year.

h) A transfer of $100,000 is made by the general fund to the debt service fund.

i) Earnings of the debt service fund amount to $3,050. Interest of $45,000 is paid.

j) Land with a fair market value of $100,000 is donated to the city.

k) The city received $205,000 in partial payment of its share of state gasoline taxes, with an additional $60,000 due from the state government in 60 days.

l) Vouchers totaling $210,000, which represent highway labor maintenance costs, are approved for payment by the special revenue fund.

Required:

For each of the events described, prepare the journal entries for all of the funds and groups of accounts involved, using the following format:

Fund or Account Group   Journal Entry

Problem 17-18.   The village of Dexter was recently incorporated and began financial operations on July 1, 20X8, the beginning of its fiscal year.

The following transactions occurred during this first fiscal year, July 1, 20X8, to June 30, 20X9:

1. The village council adopted a budget for general operations during the fiscal year ending June 30, 20X9. Revenues were estimated at $400,000. Legal authorizations for expenditures were $394,000.
2. Property taxes were levied for $390,000. It was estimated that 2% of this amount would prove to be uncollectible. These taxes were available on the date of the levy to finance current expenditures.
3. During the year, a resident of the village donated marketable securities, valued at $50,000, to the village under the terms of a trust agreement. The agreement stipulated that the principal is to be kept intact. The use of revenue generated by the securities is to be restricted to financing college scholarships for needy students. Revenue earned and received on these marketable securities amounted to $5,500 through June 30, 20X9.
4. A general fund transfer of $5,000 was made to establish an Intragovernmental Service Fund to provide for a permanent investment in inventory.
5. The village decided to install lighting in the village park. A special assessment project was authorized to install the lighting at a cost of $75,000. The appropriation was formally recorded. To finance the project, $3,000 is to be transferred from the general fund, and the balance is from special assessments.
6. Assessments were levied for $72,000, with the village contributing $3,000 from the general fund. All assessments and the village contributions were collected during the year.
7. A contract for $75,000 was let for the installation of lighting. At June 30, 20X9, the contract was completed for $75,000. The contractor was paid all but 5%, which was retained to ensure compliance with the terms of the contract. Encumbrances and other budgetary accounts are maintained.
8. During the year, the internal service fund purchased various supplies at a cost of $1,900.
9. Cash collections recorded by the general fund during the year were as follows:

Property taxes.	$386,000
Licenses and permits.	7,000

10. The village council decided to build a village hall, at an estimated cost of $500,000, to replace space occupied in rented facilities. The village does not record project authorizations. It was decided that general obligation bonds bearing interest at 6% would be issued. On June 30, 20X9, the bonds were issued at their face value of $500,000, payable in 20 years. No contracts have been signed for this project, and no expenditures have been made.
11. A fire truck was purchased for $150,000, and the voucher was approved. Payment was made through the general fund. This expenditure was previously encumbered for $145,000.

Required:

Prepare journal entries to properly record each of the preceding transactions in the appropriate fund(s) or group of accounts of Dexter for the fiscal year ended June 30, 20X9. Use the following funds and groups of accounts:

■   General fund
■   Capital projects fund

- Internal service fund
- Endowment principal fund
- Endowment earnings fund
- General long-term debt account group
- General fixed assets account group

Journal entries should be numbered to correspond with the appropriate transactions. Do not prepare closing entries for any fund.

Your answer sheet should be organized as follows:

Transaction No.	Fund or Group of Accounts	Account Title and Explanation	Amounts	
			Debit	Credit

(AICPA adapted)

Problem 17-19.   The following information relates to Dane City during its fiscal year ended December 31, 20X7:

- On October 31, 20X7, to finance the construction of a city hall annex, Dane issued 8%, 10-year general obligation bonds at their face value of $600,000. Construction expenditures during the period equaled $364,000.
- Dane reported $109,000 from hotel room taxes, restricted for tourist promotion, in a special revenue fund. The fund paid $81,000 for general promotions and $22,000 for a motor vehicle.
- 20X7 general fund revenues of $104,500 were transferred to a debt service fund and used to repay $100,000 of 9%, 15-year term bonds, and to pay $4,500 of interest. The bonds were used to acquire a citizens' center.
- At December 31, 20X7, as a consequence of past services, city firefighters had accumulated entitlements to compensated absences valued at $86,000. General fund resources available at December 31, 20X7, are expected to be used to settle $17,000 of this amount, and $69,000 is expected to be paid out of future general fund resources.
- At December 31, 20X7, Dane was responsible for $83,000 of outstanding general fund encumbrances, including $8,000 for supplies indicated below.
- Dane uses the purchases method to account for supplies. The following information relates to supplies:

Inventory	
1/1/X7	$39,000
12/31/X7	42,000
Encumbrances outstanding	
1/1/X7	6,000
12/31/X7	8,000
Purchase orders during 20X7	190,000
Amounts credited to vouchers payable during 20X7	181,000

1. The amount of 20X7 general fund operating transfers-out is _____ .

2. The 20X7 general fund liabilities from entitlements for compensated absences are _____ .

3. The 20X7 reserved amount of the general fund balance is _____ .

4. The 20X7 capital projects fund balance is _____ .

5. The 20X7 fund balance on the special revenue fund for tourist promotion is

_____ .

(continued)

6. The amount of 20X7 debt service fund expenditures is _____ .

7. The amount to be included in the general fixed asset account group for the cost of assets acquired in 20X7 is _____ .

8. The amount by which 20X7 transactions and events decreased the general long-term debt account group is _____ .

9. The amount of 20X7 supplies expenditures using the purchases method is

    _____ .

10. The total amount of 20X7 supplies encumbrances is _____ .

(AICPA adapted)

Problem 17-20.   The following information relates to Bel City, whose first fiscal year ended December 31, 20X7. Assume Bel has only the long-term debt as specified below and only the funds necessitated by the following information.

1. General fund:

	Budget	Actual
Property taxes	$5,000,000	$4,700,000
Other revenues	1,000,000	1,050,000
Total revenues	$6,000,000	$5,750,000
Total expenditures	5,600,000	5,700,000
Property taxes receivable—delinquent		420,000
Less: Allowance for estimated		
uncollectible taxes—delinquent		50,000
		$370,000

■ There were no amendments to the budget as originally adopted.

■ No property taxes receivable have been written off, and the allowance for uncollectibles balance is unchanged from the initial entry at the time of the original tax levy.

■ There were no encumbrances outstanding at December 31, 20X7.

2. Capital project fund:

■ Finances for Bel's new civic center were provided by a combination of general fund transfers, a state grant, and an issue of general obligation bonds. Any bond premium on issuance is to be used for the repayment of the bonds at their $1,200,000 par value. At December 31, 20X7, the capital project fund for the civic center had the following closing entries:

Revenues	$800,000	
Other financing sources—bond proceeds	1,230,000	
Other financing sources—operating transfers in	500,000	
Expenditures		$1,080,000
Other financing uses—operating transfers-out		30,000
Unreserved fund balance		1,420,000

■ Also, at December 31, 20X7, capital projects fund entries reflected Bel's intention to honor the $1,300,000 purchase orders and commitments outstanding for the center.

■ During 20X7, total capital projects fund encumbrances exceeded the corresponding expenditures by $42,000. All expenditures were previously encumbered.

- During 20X8, the capital projects fund received no revenues and no other financing sources. The civic center building was completed in early 20X8, and the capital projects fund was closed by a transfer of $27,000 to the general fund.

3. Water utility enterprise fund:

- Bel issued $4,000,000 revenue bonds at par. These bonds, together with a $700,000 transfer from the general fund, were used to acquire a water utility. Water utility revenues are to be the sole source of funds to retire these bonds beginning in year 2012.

Answer the following questions with a yes (Y) or no (N) in the space provided below:

1. Did recording budgetary accounts at the beginning of 20X7 increase the fund balance by $50,000? _____

2. Should the budgetary accounts for 20X7 include an entry for the expected transfer of funds from the general fund to the capital projects fund? _____

3. Should the $700,000 payment from the general fund, which was used to help establish the water utility fund, be reported as an "other financing use-operating transfer-out"? _____

4. Did the general fund receive the $30,000 bond premium from the capital projects fund? _____

5. Should a payment from the general fund for water received for normal civic center operations be reported as an "other financing use-operating transfer-out"? _____

6. Does the net property taxes receivable of $370,000 include amounts expected to be collected after March 15, 20X8? _____

7. Would closing budgetary accounts cause the fund balance to increase by $400,000? _____

8. Would the interaction between budgetary and actual amounts cause the fund balance to decrease by $350,000? _____

9. In the general fixed assets account group, should a credit amount be recorded for 20X7 in "Investment in general fixed assets—capital projects fund"? _____

10. In the general fixed assets account group, could Bel elect to record depreciation on water utility equipment? _____

11. In the general fixed assets account group, could Bel elect to record depreciation on water utility equipment? _____

12. Should the capital project fund be included in Bel's combined statement of revenues, expenditures, and changes in fund balances? _____

13. Should the water utility enterprise fund be included in Bel's combined balance sheet? _____

14. Should Bel report capital and related financing activities in its statement of cash flows in its debt service fund? _____

15. Should Bel report capital and related financing activities in its statement of cash flows in its capital project fund? _____

(continued)

16. Should Bel report capital and related financing activities in its statement of cash flows in its water utility enterprise fund? _____

Answer the following by filling in the amount in the space provided:

17. What was the amount recorded in the opening entry for appropriations?

_____

18. What was the total amount debited to property taxes receivable? _____

19. In the general long-term debt account group, what amount should be reported for bonds payable at December 31, 20X7? _____

20. In the general fixed assets account group, what amount should be recorded for "Investment in general fixed assets—capital project fund" at December 31, 20X7? _____

21. What was the completed cost of the civic center? _____

22. How much was the state capital grant for the civic center? _____

23. In the capital project fund, what was the amount of the total encumbrances recorded during 20X7? _____

24. In the capital project fund, what was the unreserved fund balance reported at December 31, 20X7? _____

(AICPA adapted)

Problem 17-21.   Port Washington's citizens authorized the construction of a new library. As a result of this project, the city had the following transactions during 20X8:

a) On January 3, 20X8, a $600,000 serial bond issue having a stated interest rate of 8% was authorized for the acquisition of land and the construction of a library building. The bonds are to be redeemed in 10 equal annual install-ments beginning February 1, 20X9.

b) On January 10, 20X8, the city made a $50,000 down payment deposit on the purchase of land, which is to be the site of the library. The contracted price for the land is $150,000, which is $40,000 below what the city esti-mated it would have to spend to acquire a site.

c) On March 1, 20X8, the city issued serial bonds having a $450,000 face value at 102. The bond indenture requires any premium to be set aside for servicing bond interest.

d) On March 10, 20X8, the city paid the remaining amount on the land con-tract and took title to the land.

e) On March 17, 20X8, the city signed a $400,000 construction contract with Rower Construction Company.

f) On July 10, 20X8, the contractor was paid $200,000 based on work com-pleted to date.

g) On September 1, 20X8, a semiannual interest payment was made on the outstanding bonds. (The general fund transferred funds to supplement the cash received from the premium in item c.)

h) On December 1, 20X8, the city issued serial bonds having a $100,000 face value at par.

i) On December 2, 20X8, the contractor completed the library and submitted a final billing of $210,000, which includes $10,000 of additional work authorized by the city in October 20X8. The $210,000 was paid to the contractor on December 12, 20X8.

j)   *Through December 10, 20X8, the city had invested excess cash (from the bond offering) in short-term certificates of deposit. The amount collected on these investments totaled $12,000.*

Required:

1. Prepare the journal entries in all fund/account groups.
2. Prepare any appropriate year-end adjusting and closing entries for the capital projects fund and the general fixed asset account group.
3. Prepare a statement of revenues, expenditures, and changes in fund balance for 20X8 for the capital projects fund.

Problem 17-22.   Ashton City was incorporated as a municipality and began operations on January 1, 20X8. The budget approved by the city council was recorded, but the cash basis was used in Ashton's books for all 20X8 transactions. Ashton has decided to use encumbrance accounting. Ashton's cash basis general fund trial balance at December 31, 20X8, is presented as follows in the preprinted worksheet found in the Text Companion section of your *Student Companion Enrichment Manual.*

Debits

Cash	$489,800
Expenditures (Control)	145,000
Estimated revenues (Control)	218,200
Total	$853,000

Credits

Appropriations (Control)	$194,000
Revenues (Control)	216,800
Bonds Payable	400,000
Premium on Bonds Payable	6,000
Budgetary Fund Balance	24,200
Fund Balance—Unreserved, Undesignated	12,000
Total	$853,000

Additional information:

Revenues	Budgeted	Actual
Property taxes	$195,200	$192,000
Licenses	14,800	15,800
Fines	8,200	9,000
Totals	$218,200	$216,800

Expenditures	Budgeted	Actual
Services	$ 80,000	$77,000
Supplies	38,000	22,000
Equipment	76,000	46,000
Totals	$194,000	$145,000

(continued)

It was estimated that 5% of the property taxes would not be collected. Accordingly, property taxes were levied to yield the budgeted amount of $205,200. Taxes of $192,000 had been collected by December 31, 20X8, and it was expected that all remaining collectible taxes would be received by February 28, 20X9.

Supplies of $8,000 and equipment of $20,000 were received, but the vouchers were not yet recorded at December 31, 20X8. Purchase orders were still outstanding for supplies and equipment not yet received, in the amounts of $2,400 and $7,600, respectively. Supplies on hand at December 31, 20X8 totaled $3,400.

On November 1, 20X8, Ashton issued 4%, 10-year obligation term bonds of $400,000 at 101½. Interest is payable each May 1 and November 1 until the maturity date. Cash from the bond premium is to be set aside and restricted for payment of interest. The bonds were issued to finance the construction of a firehouse, but no contracts had been executed by December 31, 20X8.

Required:

1. Create your own worksheet using the following format or complete the printed one found in the Text Companion section of your *Student Companion Enrichment Manual.* On the worksheet, be sure to show adjustments and distributions to the proper funds or account groups, before closing entries, in conformity with generally accepted accounting principles applicable to governmental entities. Formal adjusting entries are *not* required.

Suggestion: You may extend existing balances to proper columns without an entry. For example, Bonds Payable can be extended directly to the General Long-Term Debt column.

Ashton City
Worksheet to Correct Trial Balance
December 31, 20X8

Accounts	Trial Balance	Adjustments		General Fund	Debt Service Fund	Capital Projects Fund	General Fixed Assets	General Long-Term Debt
		Debit	Credit					

2. Prepare a Statement of Revenues, Expenditures, and Charges in Fund Balance—Budget and Actual for 20X8 for the general fund.

(AICPA adapted)

CHAPTER

18

Accounting for Not-for-Profit Organizations: Public and Private Universities

This chapter and the next detail accounting for the four major types of not-for-profit organizations. These include a) colleges and universities, b) hospitals, c) voluntary health and welfare organizations, and d) other organizations such as museums, country clubs, and religious organizations. In this chapter, the unique characteristics of not-for-profit organizations and the accounting and reporting standard-setting activity in this sector are discussed. Accounting and financial reporting for all private not-for-profit organizations is presented, followed by separate sections on accounting and financial reporting for public (governmental) and private colleges and universities. The next chapter is concerned with accounting and financial reporting for health care organizations, voluntary health and welfare organizations, and other not-for-profit organizations.

General Characteristics of Not-for-Profits

Not-for-profit activities make up a significant portion of the economy of the United States. All not-for-profit organizations provide services without the intention of realizing a profit. Such organizations are generally financed by contributions, earnings from endowments or other investments, charges for services, and government grants. External users of financial statements have common interests in assessing a) the services an organization provides and its ability to continue those services, b) its creditworthiness, and c) how managers discharge their stewardship responsibilities and other aspects of their performance.[1]

Fund Accounting

To satisfy the requirement of accounting for a diversity of resources and their use, fund accounting has traditionally been used. Fund accounting has been used to organize and manage resources for various purposes in accordance with regulations, restrictions, or limitations imposed by parties outside the institution, or with directions issued by the governing board. A clear distinction of funds that are externally restricted and those that are internally designated by action of the governing board has been maintained in the accounts and disclosed in the financial reports.

---

1 FASB Statement Nos. 117, *Financial Statements of Not-for-Profit Organizations* (Norwalk, CT: Financial Accounting Standards Board, 1993), par. 4.

The Budget

Budgets are also prepared in not-for-profit organizations. As in a commercial enterprise, the budgeting process should involve the establishment of goals, the measurement of actual performance, and the comparison of actual with projected performance to evaluate results. This process requires the input of persons who can determine what resources will become available, what the group desires to achieve with those resources, and how the resources should be applied to yield the greatest benefit. If the organization or program is well established, a useful starting point is the previous year's budget and its variances, adjusted for any changes in objectives. If the group or program is new, the preparation of an effective operating budget requires careful research to produce realistic estimates of both revenues and expenditures. Expenditures should be planned to maximize service output without producing either a surplus or a deficit. A sizable excess of revenues over expenditures implies that more or better service could be provided. A deficit may indicate the need to curtail future services, since future funds may have to be committed to cover past deficits. In accounting for not-for-profit organizations, it is not as common to find budgetary amounts formally entered into principal ledger accounts as it is in governmental accounting. Often, detailed budgetary amounts are entered directly in appropriate subsidiary records, and encumbrances representing outstanding purchase orders and other commitments for materials and supplies are entered directly in an encumbrance column in the subsidiary expenditures record. Although subsidiary records are not supported by principal ledger control accounts when this procedure is followed, some degree of control is achieved by comparing the subsidiary records with actual revenues and expenditures. If a budgetary entry is recorded, it would be similar to the one used in governmental accounting, and it would be reversed at year-end. Assuming estimated revenues exceed estimated expenditures and allocations, the budgetary entry for a governmental college or university would be

Estimated Revenues	XXX	
Estimated Expenditures (or Budget Allocations		
for Expenditures)		XXX
Unallocated Balance		XXX

Basis of Accounting

All not-for-profit organizations use the accrual basis of accounting. There are some modifications in governmental not-for-profit organizations that record expenditures for capital outlays and do not recognize depreciation. The operating statements of public colleges and universities do not report the total revenue and expenditure activity of the institution, but only that related to the current funds. The private not-for-profit organizations, particularly with the recent Financial Accounting Standards Board (FASB) guidance, use full accrual accounting. Organization-wide operating statements are expense oriented, including depreciation expense.

Development of Accounting Principles

Early development of accounting principles for nonprofit organizations was largely the responsibility of not-for-profit industry groups, including the National Association of College and University Business Officers (NACUBO), the Health Care Financial Management Association (HFMA), and the National Health Council. These industry groups, representing colleges and universities, hospitals, voluntary health and welfare organizations, and other organizations such as museums, country clubs, and religious organizations, developed manuals with accounting guidance. In response to an increasing awareness of the not-for-profit sector, the American Institute of Certified Public Accountants (AICPA) worked in conjunction with these industry groups to develop and issue four audit guides in the early 1970s. These guides have been updated and amended over the years. Applicable guides include the following:

A. For governmental not-for-profit organizations—

Audits of Colleges and Universities (May 1, 1993)
Audit and Accounting Guide: Health Care Organizations (June 1, 1996)
Audit Guide for Voluntary Health and Welfare Organizations (May 1, 1993)
Audits of Certain Nonprofit Organizations (SOP 78-10)

B. For private (nongovernmental) not-for-profit organizations—

Audit and Accounting Guide: Not-for-Profit Organizations (June 1, 1996)
Audit and Accounting Guide: Health Care Organizations (June 1, 1996)

As a result of the separate evolution of standards by each not-for-profit industry group, significant differences exist for the four types of not-for-profits in terms of fund classifications, measurement criteria, account classifications, and financial statement disclosures. The standard setters are working toward developing more consistent reporting by all not-for-profits.

Jurisdiction for Accounting and Financial Reporting

Jurisdiction for accounting and financial reporting for not-for-profit organizations is shared by the FASB and the Government Accounting Standards Board (GASB). The GASB has jurisdiction over accounting and financial reporting of governmental not-for-profits (public colleges and universities and government hospitals). The FASB has jurisdiction over accounting and financial reporting of all private not-for-profit organizations including private colleges and universities, private health care providers, voluntary health and welfare organizations, and other private not-for-profits.

New FASB Standards

In 1993, the FASB issued Statement No. 116, *Accounting for Contributions Received and Contributions Made,* and Statement No. 117, *Financial Statements of Not-for-Profit Organizations.* The issuance of these standards represents the culmination of almost 15 years of work by the FASB which began with the issuance of Concepts Statement No. 4, *Objectives of Financial Reporting by Nonbusiness Organizations* (1980). These statements make drastic changes in measurement and reporting for private not-for-profits.

These standards eliminate the inconsistent reporting practices that have existed for the various types of private nonprofit organizations and simplify the current manner of reporting. The AICPA's *Not-for-Profit Organizations* (1996) audit guide is a combined version of the previously separate college and university, voluntary health and welfare, and other nonprofit organizations guides which includes guidance for Statement Nos. 116 and 117. Similarly, the AICPA's *Health Care Organizations* (1996) audit guide now conforms to the new FASB standards.

Under the jurisdictional agreement of the Financial Accounting Foundation with the FASB and GASB, the new FASB standards apply only to private not-for-profit organizations unless the GASB specifies that they are to apply to governmental not-for-profit organizations as well. The issuance of Statement Nos. 116 and 117 creates a divergence in accounting and financial reporting for private versus public organizations. This divergence is most pronounced for public (governmental) versus private colleges and universities and is expected to continue for some time. The GASB currently has a project that addresses the financial statements to be used for public (governmental) colleges and universities. In April 1997, the GASB issued an Exposure Draft, *Basic Financial Statements—and Management's Discussion and*

Analysis—for Public Colleges and Universities, and a final standard is forthcoming. Pending adoption of a final statement from the GASB, the AICPA's *Audits of Colleges and Universities* (1993) remains the authoritative guidance for public colleges and universities. For organizations other than colleges and universities, especially hospitals, GASB standards are similar to FASB standards, as those organizations are reported in governmental enterprise funds, which generally follow FASB standards. Therefore, this text will provide a comparison of public and private college and university accounting and will present private-sector FASB guidance for all other not-for-profit organizations.

Accounting for Not-for-Profit Universities

The responsibilities of a not-for-profit university may be classified as academic, financial, student services, and public relations. Academic functions include instruction, research, and public service. The financial sphere covers the management and reporting of business and financial affairs as well as auxiliary enterprises, such as housing, food service, and student union operation. Student services include all student activities not directly classified as academic or financial, such as admissions, records, health, counseling, and publications. Public relations involves the communication and establishment of goodwill with academic and administrative staff, alumni, and the community.

The effectiveness with which a university accomplishes its objectives in these four areas depends, in part, upon the resources at its disposal. A university levies tuition fees, but these fees do not cover total operational costs. Therefore, other sources of revenue are essential. These sources include gifts, income from endowment funds, and grants from governmental units or foundations, and, for public universities, appropriations from state legislatures.

As a result of the great differences in accounting and financial reporting between public- and private-sector colleges and universities, this chapter will first present the accounting and financial statements for public colleges and universities following the guidance set forth in the AICPA *Audits of Colleges and Universities* (1993),[2] and, next, a presentation for private colleges and universities following pronouncements set forth by the FASB and adopted in the 1996 AICPA *Not-for-Profit Organizations* audit guide.[3]

Accounting for Public Universities

Traditional accounting procedures for public universities emphasize the flow of financial resources and fund accounting. College and university funds include three broad categories: current funds, plant funds, and trust and agency funds. The day-

---

2 GASB Statement No. 15, *Governmental College and University Accounting and Financial Reporting Models*, requires public colleges and universities to use either the governmental model as outlined in Chapter 16 or the 1993 AICPA audit guide model which will be described in this chapter.

3 The divergence arising in financial accounting and reporting standards under the current two-board structure is most pronounced in colleges and universities. Recent GASB statements suggest sharp differences of opinion between the two boards on many issues. For example, GASB Statement No. 8 (issued in 1988) does not require depreciation by governmental universities; Statement No. 15 (issued in 1991) allows governmental colleges and universities to follow either the governmental model or the AICPA audit guide (as amended in 1993); Statement No. 19 (issued in 1993) requires governmental colleges and universities to account for federally sponsored student financial aid in a current restricted fund; Statement No. 29 (issued in 1996) prohibits governmental colleges and universities from applying the provisions of FASB Statement Nos. 116 and 117; and GASB Statement No. 31 states that public colleges and universities that elect to follow the AICPA audit guide model should assign investment income, including changes in the fair value of investments, to funds.

to-day activities of a public university are recorded in its current funds, which consist of two self-balancing sub-funds. The *unrestricted current fund* represents amounts that are available for any current activity commensurate with the university's objectives. The *restricted current fund* accounts for those resources available only for an externally specified purpose. The segregation of unrestricted current funds from restricted current funds substantiates that the limitations placed on restricted funds by outside sources have been observed. *Plant funds* account for capital assets and for resources to be used to acquire additional capital assets or to retire indebtedness related to capital assets. Plant funds consist of several sub-groups, each of which is designed to record a certain phase of activity related to fixed assets. *Endowment and similar funds* account for endowments received. In addition, a university may employ *loan funds*, *annuity funds*, and *agency funds*. Each fund may have its own accounting records, or, if the university is large, all funds may be integrated into one record system.

The accrual basis is used in public university accounting. Operating or current funds record revenues and expenditures in nominal accounts. In the other funds, Fund Balance may be credited directly for resources received and debited directly for resource outflows. As a result, only the current funds present a statement of revenues and expenditures. The three principal financial statements for a public university are

1. The *statement of current funds revenues, expenditures, and other changes*, which provides detail on revenues, expenditures, transfers to/from other funds, and other changes in fund balances for the period.
2. The *balance sheet*, which is a stacked presentation of individual fund balance sheets indicating the financial position of each fund.
3. The *statement of changes in fund balances*, which provides a summary of activities for the period in each fund and their impact on each fund balance account.

Each of these statements is explained and illustrated at appropriate points in the discussion that follows.

University Current Funds—Unrestricted

The unrestricted current fund of a public university is similar to the general fund of a state or local government in that it accounts for current assets available to cover current operational costs and resulting current liabilities. No outside limitations apply to its resources. A public university might establish one master control account for unrestricted revenues, with details as to major sources recorded in subsidiary records. More commonly, separate revenue accounts are established, using the following three major groups of revenues:

> Educational and general revenues group, with accounts for
>> Student tuition and fees (recognized when due or billed, net of an appropriate allowance for uncollectibles)
>> Governmental appropriations (detailed as to federal, state, and local)
>> Governmental grants and contracts (detailed as to federal, state, and local)
>> Gifts and private grants
>> Endowment income
>> Other sources
> Auxiliary enterprises revenues
> Expired term endowment revenues

In the interest of full disclosure, operating revenues are recorded in these accounts. Auxiliary enterprises revenues are segregated to permit the evaluation of performance and the degree of self-support. Expired term endowment income represents dollar amounts of term endowments on which the restriction has lapsed, freeing them to become unrestricted resources.

Unrestricted current fund expenditures are the costs incurred to conduct the university's daily operations using unrestricted resources. Expenditures may be classified in a number of ways, depending on the purpose. In financial reports, the 1993 audit guide recommends classification by function for two major groupings, which are the same as the first two used to classify revenues.

> Educational and general expenditures group, with accounts for
>> Instruction (expenditures for credit and noncredit courses)
>> Research (expenditures to produce research results)
>> Public support (expenditures for noninstructional services, including conferences, seminars, and consulting)
>> Academic support (expenditures supporting instruction and public services, such as libraries, galleries, audiovisual services, and academic deans)
>> Student services (expenditures for student admission, registration, and cultural and athletic activities)
>> Institutional support (expenditures for central administration)
>> Operation and maintenance of plant
>> Student aid (expenditures for scholarships, fellowships, tuition remissions, and outright grants)
> Auxiliary enterprises expenditures

In addition to expenditures, the unrestricted current fund balance is affected by transfers. *Discretionary* or *nonmandatory* transfers, such as transfers to a loan fund or a plant fund, are transfers of unrestricted resources to other funds at the discretion of the university's governing authority. *Mandatory transfers* are required transfers of resources to other funds. Some mandatory transfers, such as amounts set aside for debt retirement and interest payment, result from binding legal contracts. Other mandatory transfers arise from the acceptance of a grant or donation that requires the university to match some or all of the amounts received. Although the source of mandatory transfers may be either unrestricted or restricted current funds, it is, more commonly, unrestricted funds.

Discretionary transfers are recorded by debiting either unrestricted current fund balance or a temporary equity account, such as Transfer to Loan Fund. The temporary equity account would be closed to unrestricted current fund balance at year-end. Mandatory transfers, however, must be recorded by debiting the account Mandatory Transfers. These transfers, which may relate to either educational and general activities or to auxiliary enterprises, are segregated on financial reports of public universities.

To illustrate the accounting process in the unrestricted current fund, assume Rogers State University (a public institution) maintains separate records for each of its funds. It uses detailed revenue and expenditure accounts recommended by the audit guide, rather than broad control accounts, and the budget is recorded formally. Encumbrance items are entered directly into subsidiary records, but no formal entries for them are made. The summarized events affecting only the unrestricted current fund are described and recorded as follows. Events affecting more than one fund are described and recorded in the multicolumn interaction matrix in Illustration 18-4 beginning on page 18-22.

Event	Entry		

B1. The following budget is approved:

Estimated revenues	$3,300,000	
Estimated expenditures	3,000,000	
Unallocated balance	300,000	

Estimated Revenues	3,300,000	
Estimated Expenditures		3,000,000
Unallocated Balance		300,000

(This is an optional entry.)

---

1. Educational and general revenue is earned or billed:

Student tuition and fees (of which $20,000 is considered uncollectible)	$1,700,000
Governmental appropriations	750,000
Private gifts and grants	250,000
Endowment income	50,000
Other income	250,000
Total	$3,000,000

(Note: Pledges are not recorded until received.)

Accounts Receivable	2,750,000	
Revenues—Student Tuition and Fees		1,680,000
Allowances for Uncollectibles		20,000
Revenues—Governmental Appropriations		750,000
Revenues—Endowment Income		50,000
Revenues—Other Income		250,000

---

2. Of the total revenues, $2,800,000 is collected, including $200 of pledges

Cash	2,800,000	
Accounts Receivable		2,600,000
Revenues—Private Gifts and Grants		200,000

---

3. Revenue billed for dormitories (an auxiliary enterprise) is $400,000, of which $20,000 is not yet received.

Cash	380,000	
Accounts Receivable	20,000	
Revenues—Auxiliary Enterprises		400,000

---

4. Purchases of materials and supplies total $400,000, of which $25,000 is not yet paid.

Inventory of Materials	400,000	
Cash		375,000
Accounts Payable		25,000

---

5. Expenditures are paid and assigned to:

Instruction	$1,050,000
Research	100,000
Academic support	150,000
Student services	200,000
Institutional support	200,000
Operation and maintenance of plant	400,000
Student aid	40,000
Auxiliary enterprises	260,000
Total	$2,400,000

Expenditures—Instruction	1,050,000	
Expenditures—Research	100,000	
Expenditures—Academic Support	150,000	
Expenditures—Student Services	200,000	
Expenditures—Institutional Support	200,000	
Expenditures—Operation and Maintenance of Plant	400,000	
Expenditures—Student Aid	40,000	
Expenditures—Auxiliary Enterprises	260,000	
Cash		2,400,000

---

6. Materials and supplies used:

Instruction	$268,000
Student services	22,000
Auxiliary enterprises	90,000
Total	$380,000

Expenditures—Instruction	268,000	
Expenditures—Student Services	22,000	
Expenditures—Auxiliary Enterprises	90,000	
Inventory of Materials		380,000

---

7. Aid is granted to students:

Remission of tuition	$140,000
Cash scholarships	35,000
Total	$175,000

Expenditures—Student Aid	175,000	
Accounts Receivable		140,000
Cash		35,000

(continued)

Event	Entry		
8. $50,000 cash contributions received.	Cash		50,000	
	Revenues—Private Gifts			
	and Grants			50,000
B2. The budgetary entry is reversed.	(If optional budgetary entry has been made)			
	Unallocated Balance.		300,000	
	Estimated Expenditures		3,000,000	
	Estimated Revenues.			3,300,000
9. The books are closed, with a separate closing entry for Auxiliary Enterprises to demonstrate the degree of success.	Revenues—Student Tuition and			
	Fees.		1,680,000	
	Revenues—Governmental			
	Appropriations.		750,000	
	Revenues—Private Gifts and Grants. .		250,000	
	Revenues—Endowment Income		50,000	
	Revenues—Other Income.		250,000	
	Expenditures—Instruction			1,318,000
	Expenditures—Research.			100,000
	Expenditures—Academic Support .			150,000
	Expenditures—Student Services. . .			222,000
	Expenditures—Institutional Support			200,000
	Expenditures—Operation and			
	Maintenance of Plant.			400,000
	Expenditures—Student Aid			215,000
	Fund Balance.			375,000
	Revenues—Auxiliary Enterprises		400,000	
	Expenditures—Auxiliary			
	Enterprises.			350,000
	Fund Balance.			50,000

University Current Funds—Restricted

For an activity to enter the restricted current fund of a public university, some limitation must exist on the resources received from an external entity. The same revenue and expenditure accounts used in the unrestricted current fund are available, but restricted current fund revenues arise primarily from governmental grants and contracts, private gifts, and endowment income. Expenditures generally are relegated to instruction, research, and student aid.

    Unless the restriction placed upon contributed resources or governmental grants is respected, these resources may have to be returned to the donor. Until they are expended properly, they should not be considered as revenue. As a consequence, expenditures govern the recognition of revenue. These resources are expenditure driven, similar to such items in governmental accounting. This situation requires the following entries in a restricted current fund:

Event	Entry	
Resources are contributed by a corporation for scholarships to minorities.	Assets Contributed	XXX	
	Fund Balance.		XXX
Expenditures are made in compliance with restrictions; revenue is recognized.	Expenditures—Student Aid	XXX	
	Cash		XXX
	Fund Balance	XXX	
	Revenues—Private Gifts and Grants		XXX

Fund Balance is increased at the time of the receipt of the resources. Revenue is not recognized until resources are expended and then in the exact amount of the expenditures. As a result, revenues will always equal expenditures in the restricted current fund.

The following events affected the restricted current fund of Rogers State University. Only one fund balance account is maintained. Data on sources, purposes, and applications of restricted resources are recorded in subsidiary records.

Event	Entry		
10. A restricted gift of $70,000 is received to assist in library operations.	Cash . . . . Fund Balance—Restricted.	70,000	70,000
11. Endowment income of $8,000 is restricted to student aid activities.	Cash . . . . Fund Balance—Restricted.	8,000	8,000
12. Of the following expenditures, all but $4,000 are paid: For library operations . . . . $67,000 For student aid . . . . 6,000 Total $73,000	Expenditures—Academic Support . . . Expenditures—Student Aid. . . . . Cash . . . . Accounts Payable.	67,000 6,000	69,000 4,000
13. Revenues are recorded to the extent of expenditures.	Fund Balance—Restricted. . . . . Revenues—Private Gifts and Grants Revenues—Endowment Income . . .	73,000	67,000 6,000
14. Federal grants for student awards through the Pell Grant program are received in the amount of $75,000. All $75,000 is distributed to qualified students.	Cash . . . . Fund Balance—Restricted. . . . . . . Expenditures—Student Aid. . . . . Cash . . . . Fund Balance—Restricted. . . . . Revenues—Government Grants and Contracts	75,000 75,000 75,000	75,000 75,000 75,000
15. A federal grant is awarded for research	Cash . . . . Fund Balance—Restricted.	100,000	100,000
16. Expenditures on the research project totaled $45,000 to date. All expenditures have been paid. Revenue is recognized to the extent that resources have been properly spent.	Expenditures—Research. . . . . Cash . . . . Fund Balance—Restricted. . . . . Revenues—Government Grants and Contracts	45,000 45,000	45,000 45,000
17. The books are closed. Since revenues equal expenditures, Fund Balance is not involved.	Revenues—Government Grants and Contracts . . . . Revenues—Private Gifts and Grants. . Revenues—Endowment Income . . . . . Expenditures—Academic Support . Expenditures—Student Aid . . . . . . Expenditures—Research.	120,000 67,000 6,000	67,000 81,000 45,000

Statement of Revenues, Expenditures, and Other Changes; The Balance Sheet; Statement of Changes in Fund Balances

The statement of revenues, expenditures, and other changes is provided by only the current funds of a public college or university since the other funds record changes in resources directly through their fund balances. This statement shows the current funds revenues by source, expenditures by function, and other changes, such as mandatory and discretionary transfers. In the design recommended by the audit guide, the statement does not attempt to show net income or net loss since this amount is not of primary concern to a not-for-profit unit. Instead, the final amount is the net increase or decrease in the unrestricted and restricted fund balances, which also is shown in the statement of changes in fund balances. The recommended form, presented in Illustration 18-1, shows columns for the unrestricted current fund, the restricted current fund, and the total.

Illustration 18-1
Rogers State University
Statement of Current Funds, Revenues, Expenditures, and Other Changes
For Year Ended June 30, 20X7

	Unrestricted	Restricted	Total
Revenues:			
Educational and general:			
Student tuition and fees	$1,680,000		$1,680,000
Governmental appropriations	750,000		750,000
Governmental grants and contracts		120,000	120,000
Private gifts and grants.	250,000	$ 67,000	317,000
Endowment income	70,000*	6,000	76,000
Other income	250,000		250,000
Total educational and general revenues.	$3,000,000	$193,000	$3,193,000
Auxiliary enterprises	400,000		400,000
Expired term endowments.	20,000*		20,000
Total revenues.	$3,420,000	$193,000	$3,613,000
Expenditures and mandatory transfers:			
Educational and general:			
Instruction	$1,318,000		$1,318,000
Research	100,000	45,000	145,000
Academic support	150,000	67,000	217,000
Student services	222,000		222,000
Institutional support	200,000		200,000
Operation and maintenance of plant	400,000		400,000
Student aid	215,000	81,000	296,000
Total educational and general expenditures	$2,605,000	$193,000	$2,798,000
Mandatory transfers for principal payment	20,000*		20,000
Total	$2,625,000	$193,000	$2,818,000
Auxiliary enterprises expenditures	350,000		350,000
Total expenditures and mandatory transfers	$2,975,000	$193,000	$3,168,000
Other transfers and additions (deductions):			
Excess of restricted receipts over transfers to revenues		$ 80,000*	$ 80,000
Transfers to other funds	$ (300,000)*		(300,000)
Net increase in fund balances.	$ 145,000	$ 80,000	$ 225,000

*Includes amounts from interaction matrix on pages 18-22 to 18-23.

Note that in the restricted current fund column the total revenues equal the total expenditures. Also note in this column the amount labeled "Excess of restricted receipts over transfers to revenues." Reviewing the entries in the restricted current fund on page 18-9, a total of $178,000 in restricted resources was received this period, but only $118,000 was expended, producing $60,000 of resources received and not expended. This item must be introduced on the statement of revenues, expenditures, and other changes in order to produce the correct net increase in Fund Balance.

An exceptionally high degree of accounting sophistication is required to interpret the statement of revenues, expenditures, and other changes in its present form. Its primary value is the detail it provides for revenues, expenditures, and transfers. However, if the primary emphasis is on resources made available (revenues) and resources applied (expenditures), a useful figure would be their difference, which is not furnished. The difference between total revenues and the sum of expenditures and mandatory transfers also is not provided, but it would have managerial value. The only net figure is the final amount of change in the fund balances. A superficial glance at the change of $145,000 in the unrestricted current fund could lead the unwary to conclude incorrectly that the fund grew by only this amount. In reality, the increase in the fund is $445,000, which is the excess of total revenues ($3,420,000) over total expenditures and mandatory transfers ($2,975,000). The discretionary transfers of $300,000 to various other funds reduced the change to $145,000.

A balance sheet for all funds, with separate, self-balancing totals for each fund is shown in Illustration 18-2 beginning on this page. A statement of changes in fund balances for all funds is presented in Illustration 18-3 on page 18-14. The balance sheet and statement of changes in fund balance will be referenced in the following discussion of other funds.

Illustration 18-2
Rogers State University
Balance Sheet
June 30, 20X7

Assets			Liabilities and Fund Balances		
Current funds:			Current funds:		
Unrestricted:			Unrestricted:		
Cash	$	463,000	Notes and accounts payable . . .	$	125,000
Due from other funds		20,000	Due to other funds		3,000
Investments		213,000	Fund balances		746,000
Receivables (net)		130,000			
Inventories of materials		20,000			
Prepaid expenses		28,000			
Total unrestricted	$	874,000	Total unrestricted	$	874,000
Restricted:			Restricted:		
Cash	$	279,000	Notes and accounts payable . . .	$	14,000
Due from other funds		20,000	Fund balances		525,000
Investments		240,000			
Receivables (net)		68,000			
Total restricted	$	539,000	Total restricted	$	539,000
Total current funds	$	1,413,000	Total current funds	$	1,413,000

(continued)

Assets		Liabilities and Fund Balances	
Loan funds:		**Loan funds:**	
Cash	$ 57,500	Unrestricted	$ 24,500
Due from other funds	3,000	Restricted	101,500
Investments	10,000		
Receivables (net)	55,500		
Total loan funds	$ 126,000	Total loan funds	$ 126,000
Endowments and similar funds:		**Endowments and similar funds:**	
Cash	$ 630,000	Due to other funds	$ 40,000
Investments	1,220,000	Fund balances:	
		Unrestricted	350,000
		Restricted	1,460,000
Total endowment and similar funds	$ 1,850,000	Total endowment and similar funds	$ 1,850,000
Annuity and life income funds:		**Annuity and life income funds:**	
Cash	$ 171,500	Life income payable	$ 1,500
Investments	286,000	Annuities payable	237,481
		Fund balances:	
		Unrestricted	218,519
Total annuity and life income funds	$457,500	Total annuity and life income funds	$ 457,500
Plant funds:		**Plant funds:**	
Unexpended:		Unexpended:	
Cash	$ 470,000	Notes and accounts payable	$ 110,000
Investments	1,240,000	Bonds payable	400,000
		Fund balances:	
		Unrestricted	200,000
		Restricted	1,000,000
Total unexpended	$ 1,710,000	Total unexpended	$ 1,710,000
Renewals and replacements:		**Renewals and replacements:**	
Cash	$ 10,000	Fund balances:	
Deposits	100,000	Unrestricted	$ 235,000
Investments	150,000	Restricted	25,000
Total renewals and replacements	$ 260,000	Total renewals and replacements	$ 260,000
Retirement of indebtedness:		**Retirement of indebtedness:**	
Cash	$ 50,000	Fund balances:	
Deposits	250,000	Unrestricted	$ 115,000
		Restricted	185,000
Total retirement of indebtedness	$ 300,000	Total retirement of indebtedness	$ 300,000

Assets		Liabilities and Fund Balances	
Investment in plant::		Investment in plant:	
Land	$ 500,000	Bonds payable	$ 2,190,000
Land improvements.	1,000,000	Mortgages payable	1,200,000
Buildings	20,000,000	Net investment in plant	$38,210,000
Equipment.	15,000,000		
Library books	5,100,000		
Total investment in plant.	$41,600,000	Total investment in plant.	$41,600,000
Total plant funds.	$43,870,000	Total plant funds.	$43,870,000
Agency funds:		Agency funds:	
Cash	$ 50,000	Deposits held for others.	$ 110,000
Investments	60,000		
Total agency funds	$ 110,000	Total agency funds	$ 110,000

Loan Funds

Loan funds are established to account for resources that are available for loans primarily to students and possibly to faculty and staff. Loan funds are revolving (self-perpetuating), with repayments of principal and the excess of interest collected over costs incurred becoming the base for additional loans. Both principal and earnings must be available for loan purposes. If only the income from a gift or grant may be used for loan purposes, the principal should not be in the loan fund but in the endowment fund.

The resources of loan funds consist mainly of gifts restricted for loan purposes and unrestricted current fund resources transferred by authorization of the governing board. Although assets are not segregated by restriction, the fund balance must reveal its restricted and unrestricted portions. In a public university, no revenue or expenditure accounts are used. Additions to the loan fund are recorded directly in the restricted or unrestricted fund balance, while expenditures and losses are deducted directly from the fund balance.

The following entries are recorded in the loan fund of Rogers State University. The loan funds are included in the balance sheet (Illustration 18-2) on pages 18-11 to 18-13 and the statement of changes in fund balances on pages 18-14 to 18-15 (Illustration 18-3).

Event	Entry		
18. A donation of $25,000 is received from an alumnus for student loan purposes.	Cash . . . . Fund Balance—Restricted.	25,000	 25,000
19. Investments carried at $5,000 are sold for $5,500. Gain is restricted.	Cash . . . . Investments . . . . Fund Balance—Restricted.	5,500	 5,000 500
20. Loans totaling $24,000 are made to students. Collections from other loans of restricted funds total $20,000 plus $1,000 of interest.	Loans Receivable . . . . Cash . . . . Cash . . . . Loans Receivable . . . . Fund Balance—Restricted.	24,000 21,000	 24,000 20,000 1,000

(continued)

Illustration 18-3
Rogers State University
Statement of Changes in Fund Balances
For Year Ended June 30, 20X7

	Current Funds	
	Unrestricted	Restricted
Revenues and other additions:		
Educational and general revenues:	$3,000,000	$175,000
Auxiliary enterprises revenues	400,000	
Expired term endowment revenues	20,000	
Gifts and bequests—restricted		70,000
Investment income—restricted.		28,000
Gain on sale of investments—restricted		
Gain on sale of investments—unrestricted.		
Retirement of indebtedness		
Expended on plant facilities.		
Total revenues and other additions	$3,420,000	$273,000
Expenditures and other deductions:		
Educational and general expenditures.	$2,605,000	$193,000
Auxiliary enterprises expenditures.	350,000	
Loan cancellations and write-offs		
Expired term endowment.		
Adjustment of actuarial liability.		
Retirement of indebtedness		
Expenditures for plant facilities		
Expenditures for plant maintenance.		
Total expenditures and other deductions.	$2,955,000	$193,000
Transfers among funds—additions (deductions):		
Mandatory principal payment	$ (20,000)	
Other transfers	(300,000)	
Total transfers	$ (320,000)	0
Net increase (decrease) for the year	$ 145,000	$ 80,000
Fund balance—beginning of the year	601,000	445,000
Fund balance—end of the year	$ 746,000	$525,000

Event	Entry		
21. Federal government monies of $30,000 restricted for student loans are received.	Cash . . . . Fund Balance—Restricted.	30,000	30,000
22. A $500 student loan made from restricted funds is uncollectible.	Fund Balance—Restricted. . . . . Loans Receivable	500	500

| | | Annuity | Plant Funds | | | |
Loan Funds	Endowment and Similar Funds	and Life Income Funds	Unexpended	Renewals and Replacements	Retirement of Indebtedness	Investment in Plant
$ 55,000	$ 120,000	$ 59,740	$ 90,000			$ 190,000
1,000		18,000	40,000	$ 5,000		
500						
	60,000	9,500				
						100,000
						290,000
$ 56,500	$ 180,000	$ 87,240	$ 130,000	$ 5,000	0	$ 580,000
$ 500						
	$ 20,000					
		$ 3,221				
					$100,000	
			$ 290,000			
				$ 50,000		
$ 500	$ 20,000	$ 3,221	$ 290,000	$ 50,000	$100,000	0
					$ 20,000	
$ 3,000	$ 150,000		$ 147,000			
$ 3,000	$ 150,000	0	$ 147,000	0	20,000	0
$ 59,000	$ 310,000	$ 84,019	$ (13,000)	$ (45,000)	$ (80,000)	$ 580,000
67,000	1,500,000	134,500	1,213,000	305,000	380,000	37,630,000
$126,000	$1,810,000	$218,519	$1,200,000	$260,000	$300,000	$38,210,000

Endowment and Similar Funds

The following types of endowment funds, each having its own fund balance account, are included in the category of Endowment and Similar Funds for a public university:

1. *Regular or pure endowments* are funds whose principal has been specified by the donor as nonexpendable. The resources are invested, and the earnings are available for expenditure, usually by the unrestricted current fund.

2. *Term endowments* are funds whose principal is expendable after a specified time period or after a designated event, at which point the resources are added to the unrestricted current fund, unless the original donor has specified some other application.

3. *Quasi-endowments* are funds set aside by the board or controlling body, usually from unrestricted current funds. Restricted current funds also may be set aside if the donor's limitations are not violated. Since these funds are discretionary, technically they do not belong to the endowment category, hence the addition to the title of "and Similar Funds."

Accounting should be detailed sufficiently in subsidiary records to demonstrate compliance with the restrictions of each endowment fund. In the balance sheet section for these funds (see Illustration 18-2), the assets are not segregated, but the fund balance section shows the endowment, term endowment, and quasi-endowment components for which separate accounts are established.

As gifts and bequests are received, either the account Fund Balance—Endowment or Fund Balance—Term Endowment is credited. Assets received as discretionary transfers result in a credit to Fund Balance—Quasi-Endowment. Gains or losses on the disposition of endowment assets are recorded directly in the appropriate fund balance account. Note that gains or losses are considered changes in principal, not income or expense, unless otherwise specified by the donor.

The resources for endowment funds are often pooled for investment purposes, with the various fund balances sharing proportionately in the outcome based on the market values of investments at the time of pooling or at specified future dates. Procedures for investment pooling are discussed in Chapter 19. Income earned on restricted endowment resources should be transferred immediately to and recorded directly in the fund balance of the restricted current fund, the loan fund, the endowment fund, or a plant fund, depending upon which fund the donor has specified should reap the benefits. Income on which there is no restriction should be transferred to and recorded directly in the unrestricted current fund, where it is credited to Endowment Income. If, for some reason, there is a delay in making the transfer, the income received should be recorded in the endowment fund, with a credit to a liability to the proper fund. The costs of managing endowment funds should be borne by the university's unrestricted current fund.

GASB Statement No. 31, *Accounting and Financial Reporting for Certain Investments and External Investment*, requires that all investments be reported at fair market value in the balance sheet. All investment income, including changes in the fair value of investments, should be recognized as revenue in the operating statement. Realized gains are not displayed separately from unrealized gains and losses.[4]

The following entries are recorded in the endowment and similar funds of Rogers State University. Transactions which involve more than one fund are shown in the multicolumn presentation in Illustration 18-4.

Event	Entry		
23. Common stock, with a market value of $60,000, and $60,000 cash are received as a pure endowment donation.	Cash . . . . Investments . . . . Fund Balance—Restricted	60,000 60,000	120,000
24. Endowment fund investments carried at $200,000 are sold for $260,000.	Cash . . . . Investments . . . . Fund Balance— Endowment	260,000	200,000 60,000
25. Investments are purchased with endowment fund cash.	Investments . . . . Cash	360,000	360,000

4 GASB Statement No. 31, *Accounting and Financial Reporting for Certain Investments and External Investment* (1997), is effective for years beginning after June 15, 1997.

Annuity and Life Income Funds

Resources may be accepted by a public university under the stipulation that periodic payments are to continue as an annuity to the donor or other designated beneficiary for an indicated time period. These resources should be accounted for in an *annuity fund* at their market value on the date of receipt. A liability for the actuarially computed present value of expected total annuity payments is recorded, with the excess credited to Annuity Fund Balance. As each payment is made, a debit is charged directly to the Annuity Payable each period and the liability is adjusted to bring it to an amount equal to the present value. For example, assume a retired administrator donated $50,000 to a university. The administrator is to receive annuity payments of $3,000 per year for life; thereafter, the principal is to be used for student aid. Assuming an estimated life of 15 years and an 8% interest rate, the present value of the annuity is actuarially computed to be $25,678. The entry to record receipt of the donation is:

Cash—Annuity	50,000	
Annuities Payable		25,678
Annuity Fund Balance		24,322

During the year, interest earned on annuity investments is added to the fund balance. At the end of the first year, the present value of the liability is adjusted by adding interest of $2,054 (8% × $25,678). The administrator is mailed a check for $3,000. Entries to record the adjustment of the liability to present value and payment to the annuitant are

Annuity Fund Balance	2,054	
Annuities Payable		2,054
Annuities Payable	3,000	
Cash		3,000

A *life income fund* is used if all income received on contributed assets is to be paid to the donor or other specified recipient for life. When the original contributed assets are recorded at market value, the corresponding credit is to Life Income Fund Balance. As income is received, a liability for its payment is established immediately.

When the annuity payments or the life income payments cease, the principal is transferred to the donor-specified fund group or to the unrestricted current fund revenue if no principal restriction exists. Also, unless otherwise specified, gains or losses on the sale of investments are treated as changes in principal and are recorded directly in the appropriate fund balance account.

Events that affected the ongoing annuity and life income funds of Rogers State University are described and recorded as follows. The balance sheet section for these funds appears in Illustration 18-2.

Event	Entry		
26. Cash of $12,000 from life income fund investments and $18,000 from annuity fund investments is received. (Separate accounts are maintained for life income cash and annuity cash.)	Cash—Life Income . . . . Life Income Payable . . . . Cash—Annuity. . . . . Annuity Fund Balance	12,000 18,000	12,000 18,000
27. A retired professor donated $100,000. The professor is to receive $6,000 per year for an estimated life of 10 years. Thereafter, the principal is to be used for student aid. The present value of the annuity is actuarially computed to be $40,260.	Cash—Annuity. . . . . Annuities Payable. . . . . Annuity Fund Balance	100,000	40,260 59,740

(continued)

Event	Entry		
28. Interest for the year on the annuity liability is recorded, 8% × $40,260.	Annuity Fund Balance	3,221	
	Annuities Payable		3,221
29. Payments are made to:	Annuities Payable	6,000	
Annuitant . . . . $ 6,000	Cash—Annuity		6,000
Life income beneficiaries 12,000			
	Life Income Payable	12,000	
	Cash—Life Income		12,000
30. Annuity fund investments with a book value of $50,000 are sold for $59,500.	Cash—Annuity	59,500	
	Investments—Annuity		50,000
	Annuity Fund Balance		9,500

If a university has a substantial amount of annuity and life income funds, two separate funds could be established, removing the necessity to identify each component of an entry. The typical financial reports of these funds would display only the financial condition (balance sheet) and the changes in fund balances (see Illustrations 18-2 and 18-3).

Plant Funds

Plant funds of public universities include four separate, self-balancing sub-groups:

1. *Unexpended plant fund* accounts for resources that are to be used to acquire properties. Such resources may be received as a gift or grant restricted to plant acquisition, in which case Fund Balance—Restricted is credited. Assets may be transferred by university authorities from the current funds or other funds, requiring a credit to Fund Balance—Unrestricted to record their receipt. When cash is expended to acquire existing capital assets, the appropriate fund balance account is debited as Cash is credited. The assets acquired are recorded in the Investment in Plant sub-group, discussed in item 4 of this list, with a credit to Net Investment in Plant. For a major construction project, a bond issue is usually floated. The proceeds and bond liability are recorded in the unexpended plant fund, preferably until the construction is completed. As work is begun, costs are debited to the Construction in Progress account. Upon completion, the total cost is transferred to the Investment in Plant sub-group, along with the related bond liability, with any difference between the two amounts recorded in Fund Balance—Unrestricted. If financing was achieved with a mortgage, the accounting procedure would be the same except for the designation of the liability as a mortgage payable.

2. *Plant fund for renewals and replacements* accounts for resources that are available to keep the physical plant in operating condition. Such expenditures seldom lead to capitalization. Resources transferred to this sub-group as a result of discretionary action by the governing board are recorded by crediting the account Fund Balance—Unrestricted. Resources received from outside sources that specified the amounts must be used for renewals and replacements are credited to Fund Balance—Restricted. When expenditures are made, the proper fund balance is debited and the cash or a liability account is credited. The amount remaining in the two fund balance accounts represents the unexpended resources available for renewals and replacements.

3. *Plant fund for retirement of indebtedness* corresponds to the debt service fund of a governmental unit. This fund accounts for the resources accumulated for the payment of interest and principal of plant fund indebtedness. Since the

liabilities are included in the Investment in Plant sub-group, payments of either interest or principal are recorded as direct reductions of the retirement of indebtedness fund balance.

4. The *Investment in Plant* sub-group controls all plant assets except those found in the endowment fund. This sub-group is similar to a combination of the general fixed assets and general long-term debt account groups of a governmental unit. Assets are acquired as a result of transfers from the unexpended plant fund sub-group, donations, and expenditures of the current funds. For a university, the costs of books and other library items are considered major outlays and are classified as plant assets. Liabilities related to the Investment in Plant are also shown in this sub-group. When principal is paid by the Plant Fund for Retirement of Indebtedness sub-group, the liability is reduced in the Investment in Plant sub-group, with a corresponding increase in Net Investment in Plant. Upon completion of a construction project whose costs were accumulated in the unexpended plant fund, the Investment in Plant sub-group debits the asset completed, credits any remaining related liability, such as Bonds Payable or Mortgage Payable, and credits the difference to the account Net Investment in Plant.

Public colleges and universities are not required to report a provision for *depreciation* of plant fund assets, but may elect to do so. The fact that depreciation need not be reported in its external financial statements does not prevent its computation and use in independent determinations of the total cost of operating the university. Such cost computations are useful in establishing charges for auxiliary enterprise services, which include dormitories, bookstores, cafeterias and restaurants, medical service, and the student union. Especially for services provided to the general public, amounts charged should include depreciation considerations, even though depreciation is not recorded formally. A part of the amount that a university receives from grants reimburses it for overhead, which should include depreciation. The only university fund in which a provision for depreciation must be entered is in the unusual case that fixed assets are part of a nonexpendable endowment fund, which must protect its principal.

Entries unique to the plant funds of Rogers State University are presented below, with an indication of which of the four sub-groups (some events affect more than one plant sub-group) is recording the event. The plant funds section of the balance sheet is shown in Illustration 18-2.

Event	Plant Fund Sub-group	Entry		
31. Stock with a market value of $90,000 is received from an art patron to finance an art gallery addition.	Unexpended Plant Fund	Investments . . . . Fund Balance— Restricted	90,000	90,000
32. A collection of first editions, appraised at $30,000, is donated to the university.	Investment in Plant	Library Books . . . . Net Investment in Plant	30,000	30,000
33. An $800,000 bond issue is sold at face value to finance a business school wing.	Unexpended Plant Fund	Cash . . . . Bonds Payable	800,000	800,000
34. Construction of the business school wing is ¼ completed.	Unexpended Plant Fund	Construction in Progress . . . . Contracts Payable	200,000	200,000

(continued)

Event	Plant Fund Sub-group	Entry
35. Restricted Earnings received on investments of: Unexpended Plant Fund . . . . $40,000 Renewals and Replacements Fund 5,000	Unexpended Plant Fund	Cash . . . . 40,000 Fund Balance— Restricted 40,000
	Renewals and Replacements Plant Fund	Cash . . . . 5,000 Fund Balance— Restricted 5,000
36. Business school contract is completed at additional cost of $640,000 and is paid in full.	Unexpended Plant Fund	Construction in Progress . . . . 640,000 Contracts Payable . . . . 200,000 Cash 840,000
37. Completed building costs are transferred to investment in plant sub-group.	Unexpended Plant Fund	Bonds Payable . . . . 800,000 Fund Balance— Unrestricted . . . . 40,000 Construction in . . . . Progress 840,000
	Investment in Plant	Building . . . . 840,000 Bonds Payable . . . . 800,000 Net Investment in Plant 40,000
38. Payment of $100,000 is made on mortgage related to completed plant.	Plant Retirement of Indebtedness Plant Fund	Fund Balance— Unrestricted . . . . 100,000 Cash 100,000
	Investment in Plant	Mortgages Payable . . . . 100,000 Net Investment in Plant 100,000
39. The cost of constructing an art gallery addition totals $250,000, financed with donor-restricted cash.	Unexpended Plant Fund	Fund Balance— Restricted . . . . 250,000 Cash 250,000
	Investment in Plant	Building . . . . 250,000 Net Investment in Plant 250,000
40. Land valued at $160,000 is donated by an alumnus.	Investment in Plant	Land . . . . 160,000 Net Investment in Plant 160,000
41. Building repairs constituting a renewal of $50,000 are paid, of which $5,000 is from restricted resources.	Renewals and Replacements Plant Fund	Fund Balance— Restricted . . . . 5,000 Fund Balance— Unrestricted . . . . 45,000 Cash 50,000

Agency Funds

Agency funds account for resources that are not the property of the university but that are held in the university's custody. An example of such resources is assets belonging to student organizations. The total amount of these resources represents a liability. As a result, there is no fund balance, and agency funds would not appear in the analysis of changes in fund balances. The balance sheet of Rogers State University, shown in Illustration 18-2, includes a section for agency funds.

Balance Sheet

The composite balance sheet in Illustration 18-2 is criticized for not giving the reader a conception of the university's total financial position. For example, Rogers State University's cash appears in 9 different places and its investments in 8, and there are 15 various fund balances. Alternative balance sheet presentations are permitted, and one would be to present a combined balance sheet with a column for each fund and, perhaps, the total. However, the audit guide cautions that "in the balance sheet, columnar fund group figures should not be crossfooted in a total column, to reflect an overall financial position of the institution, unless all necessary disclosures are made."[5] It further states that combining such items as cash into one total could be misleading since all cash is not available for discretionary spending but is, in part, restricted.

Statement of Changes in Fund Balances

The most revealing financial report for a public university is the statement of changes in fund balances. It is a statement of the university's total activities for the period. In condensed form, it reveals for each fund (except agency funds) the revenues and other additions to fund balances, expenditures and other deductions from fund balances, and transfers between funds, both mandatory and discretionary. It concludes with the net increase or decrease in each fund balance, which is combined with the beginning balance to produce the ending fund balance as shown in the balance sheet. The agency funds are excluded since they have no fund balances.

The columnar format is illustrated in the audit guide, but with the customary warning that columns should not be crossfooted unless care is taken to provide full disclosure about the restricted nature of some items. A columnar statement of changes in fund balances for Rogers State University is shown in Illustration 18-3 on pages 18-14 to 18-15.

Although most items in the statement of changes in fund balances are straightforward, a few should be noted. When the retirement of indebtedness sub-group is reduced by principal payments on plant obligations, the investment in plant sub-group is increased correspondingly. Similarly, the unexpended plant fund sub-group's expenditures for plant assets increase the investment in plant sub-group. As mentioned previously, most of the resources for payment come from the unrestricted current fund, whose fund balance was reduced when amounts were transferred to one of the plant sub-groups. When payments are actually made, there is a shifting of amounts within the sub-groups, but no additional net reduction. The other noteworthy item is that the section relating to transfers between funds is self-balancing—what increases one fund balance through mandatory or discretionary transfers reduces some other fund by the same amount.

---

5 *Audits of Colleges and Universities* (New York: American Institute of Certified Public Accountants, rev. ed., 1993), p. 57.

Multiple Effects of Transactions of a Public College or University—the Interaction Matrix

The unrestricted current and restricted current funds of a college or university are operating funds in which operating activity is recorded in revenue and expenditure accounts. Other funds are nonoperating funds in which transactions normally affecting nominal accounts are entered directly into fund balances. As in governmental accounting, transactions frequently affect more than a single fund. The matrix in Illustration 18-4 shows effects of some transactions on more than one fund.

Illustration 18-4
Interaction Between Funds

	Current Unrestricted Fund		Unexpended Plant Funds	
I(1). Cash transferred to plant fund for: Addition to plant (discretionary). Payment of mortgage (mandatory).	Mandatory Transfer for. Principal Payment .. 20,000 Fund Balance (or Transfer to Plant Fund) ..... 147,000 Cash	167,000	Cash .... 147,000 Fund Balance— Unrestricted	147,000
			Plant Retirement of Indebtedness	
			Cash .... 20,000 Fund Balance— Unrestricted ...	20,000

	Current Unrestricted Fund		Loan Funds	
I(2). The board of trustees has agreed to transfer $3,000 to the loan fund on the first day of the next fiscal year as matching money for federal grants.	Fund Balance (or Transfer to Loan Fund) ..... 3,000 Due to Other Funds	3,000	Due from Other Funds 3,000 Fund Balance— Unrestricted ...	3,000

	Current Unrestricted Fund		Endowment Funds	
I(3). The board of trustees has authorized an immediate transfer of $150,000 to the endowment fund.	Fund Balance (or Transfer to Endowment Fund).......... 150,000 Cash	150,000	Cash .... 150,000 Fund Balance—Quasi- Endowment	150,000

	Current Unrestricted Fund		Endowment Funds	
I(4). Term endowments expire. Available cash will be transferred to the current unrestricted fund.	Cash .... 20,000 Revenues—Expired Term Endowments ..	20,000	Fund Balance—Term Endowment....... 20,000 Cash	20,000

	Current Unrestricted Fund		Endowment Funds	
I(5). $20,000 unrestricted endowment income is received and will be transferred to the unrestricted current fund.	Due from Other Funds . 20,000 Revenue—Endowment Income	20,000	Cash .... 20,000 Due to Other Funds ..	20,000

	Current Restricted Fund		Endowment Funds	
I(6). $20,000 restricted endowment income is received and will be transferred to the current restricted fund. Revenue will be recognized when research expenses are incurred.	Due from Other Funds . 20,000 Fund Balance	20,000	Cash .... 20,000 Due to Other Funds ..	20,000

	Current Unrestricted Fund		
I(7). The books are closed.	Fund Balance	20,000	
	Mandatory Transfer for		
	Principal Payment . .		20,000
	Revenue—Expired Term		
	Endowments	20,000	
	Fund Balance		20,000
Note: If separate transfer accounts	Fund Balance	300,000	
were used to record discretionary	Transfer to Plant		
transfers, they would be closed	Fund		147,000
at this point.	Transfer to Loan		
	Fund		3,000
	Transfer to Endowment		
	Fund		150,000

Accounting for Private Colleges and Universities

As discussed in the previous section, FASB Statement Nos. 116 and 117 provide a major shift in accounting and financial reporting for *private* colleges and universities from the 1993 audit guide. The focus in financial reporting for private colleges and universities now emphasizes the organization as a whole. The financial statements present organization-wide totals of assets, liabilities, and net assets as well as information concerning organization-wide changes in net assets and organization-wide cash flows. Because of a shift away from a fund group focus to an organization-wide focus, there is no requirement for external financial statements to include fund group reporting. Three net asset classes—unrestricted, temporarily restricted, and permanently restricted—are used instead of fund balances. Events that were previously recorded as changes in fund balance will now be recorded as contributions, exchange transactions, capital acquisitions, or expenses. Contributions are distinguished from exchange transactions or agency relationships. Only contributions with donor-imposed restrictions affect the restricted assets. All other transactions, such as government and other awards funding research, are now considered exchange transactions and affect unrestricted net assets. Federally sponsored flow-through awards to students are accounted for as agency transactions rather than restricted asset activity.

Accounting for Contributions

With FASB Statement No. 116, private universities must now recognize contributions received and unconditional promises to give as revenues or gains in the period received. This is a significant departure from the 1993 AICPA audit guide which deferred revenue recognition until the period expenditure or expenses were incurred for the restricted purposes.

Contributions are defined by FASB Statement No. 116 as "unconditional transfers of cash or other assets to an entity or a settlement or cancellation of its liabilities in a voluntary nonreciprocal transfer. . . ."[6] Other assets include securities, land, buildings, use of facilities or utilities, materials and supplies, intangible assets, services, and unconditional promises to give those items in the future. Exceptions to the

---

6 FASB Statement No. 116, *Accounting for Contributions Received and Contributions Made* (Norwalk, CT: Financial Accounting Standards Board, 1993), par. 5. The FASB defines a nonreciprocal transfer as a transaction in which an organization receives an asset or cancellation of a liability without directly gaining value in exchange.

general recognition provision are made for contributions of services and works of art. Contributions other than services are recognized in the period received and are measured at their fair market value. Services would be recognized only if they a) create or enhance nonfinancial assets or b) require specialized skills, are provided by individuals possessing those abilities, and typically would have to be purchased if not provided by donation. Not-for-profit organizations are not required to recognize contributions of works of art, historical treasures, and similar assets if the donated items are added to collections, held for public exhibition, and preserved, cared for, and protected.

Pledges (promises to give) are divided into unconditional pledges and conditional pledges. Unconditional pledges depend only on the passage of time or the demand by the university to be collected and are recognized as a receivable and revenue in the period made. Conditional pledges depend on the occurrence of uncertain future events and should be recognized as revenue when the conditions are substantially met (i.e., the pledge becomes unconditional). An example of a conditional pledge might be a donation restricted for construction of a new building given only if the organization can raise the remaining funds through additional contributions. Pledges or other assets received subject to such conditions are recorded as refundable advances until the conditions have been substantially met, at which time revenue is recorded.

FASB Statement No. 116 states that the "present value of estimated future cash flows using a discount rate commensurate with the risks involved is an appropriate measure of the fair value of unconditional promises to give cash." Promises receivable within one year need not be discounted. An allowance for doubtful contributions should be established based on historical experience and other factors to cover any uncertainties concerning collectibility. An unconditional pledge with no donor restriction is recognized as follows:

Contributions Receivable	XXX	
Revenues—Unrestricted Contributions		XXX
Provision for uncollectible contributions	XXX	
Allowance for uncollectible contributions		XXX

Donor-Imposed Restrictions and Reclassifications

Donor-imposed restrictions have no bearing on the period in which contributions are recognized as revenue. Rather, these restrictions affect the manner of reporting contributions and related assets. All contributions received (or unconditional promises to give) are classified into one of three categories: unrestricted, temporarily restricted, or permanently restricted resources. A temporary restriction expires a) when the stipulated time has elapsed, or b) when the stipulated purpose has been fulfilled, or c) over the useful life of the donated asset. Expenditure or time restrictions require a reclassification entry to release the restriction. Gifts of long-lived assets (or long-lived assets acquired with restricted gifts of cash) with donor stipulations specifying the use of the donated asset are initially reported as temporarily restricted. The expiration (or release) of the time restriction is recorded over the useful life of the asset. Gifts of assets with no donor restrictions are classified as unrestricted. Organizations have an option to record long-lived assets acquired with donor-restricted cash as either temporarily restricted or unrestricted. If the asset is recorded as temporarily restricted, the university reclassifies a portion of the temporarily restricted amount each year as depreciation is recorded. This releasing of donor-imposed restrictions (reclassification) simultaneously decreases temporarily restricted net assets and increases unrestricted net assets in order to "match" the expenses they support (operating expenses, depreciation, etc., which decrease unrestricted net assets).

Universities also have the option to record contributions whose restrictions are met in the same reporting period as increases in unrestricted net assets, instead of increases in temporarily restricted net assets with subsequent reclassifications from temporarily restricted net assets to unrestricted net assets.

Further, if an expense is incurred for a purpose for which both unrestricted and temporarily restricted net assets are available, a donor-imposed restriction is fulfilled to the extent of the expense incurred unless the expense is for a purpose that is directly attributable to another specific external source of revenue. This provision to use restricted resources first to fund expenses is a significant change from the 1993 audit guide's provision which allows institutions to choose the source of funding—either restricted or unrestricted.

A cash contribution restricted by the donor for a specific expenditure is recorded when received.	Cash XXX	
	Revenues—Temporarily Restricted	
	Contributions	XXX
Expenses made in compliance with donor restrictions are funded by the restricted resources. Temporarily restricted net assets are released with a reclassification entry.	Expense XXX	
	Cash.	XXX
	Reclassification Out—Temporarily Restricted—	
	satisfaction of donor restrictions . . . XXX	
	Reclassification In—Unrestricted—	
	satisfaction of donor restrictions . . .	XXX

A key part of FASB Statement No. 116 is the distinction among accounting for exchange transactions, agency transactions, and contributions. Exchange transactions, that is, reciprocal transfers in which each party receives and sacrifices approximately equal value, are not considered restricted. Many transactions that traditionally had been accounted for in much the same way as contributions, for example, grants, awards, sponsorships, and appropriations, are now categorized as exchange transactions rather than contributions and accounted for as increases in unrestricted assets. Government grants which require performance by the not-for-profit organization will be accounted for as refundable deposits (liabilities) until earned. Unrestricted revenue will be earned when expenses are made in conjunction with the provisions of the grant. Other government grants, which are essentially pass-through financial aid to students, will now be accounted for as agency transactions.

Grant monies received.	Cash XXX	
	U.S. Government Grants Refundable .	XXX
Expenses incurred in conjunction with provisions of grant.	Expenses. XXX	
	Cash.	XXX
Revenue is recognized up to the amount earned by incurring above expenses.	U.S. Government Grants Refundable . . . XXX	
	Revenues—Unrestricted	XXX

Permanently restricted contributions are called *endowments*. Earnings on endowment investments are reported in the period earned as a credit to unrestricted revenue or temporarily restricted revenue depending on donor specification as to the use of the earnings. Realized and unrealized gains on endowment investments are reported as increases or decreases in unrestricted net assets unless their use is temporarily or permanently restricted by explicit donor stipulations or by law. Losses on endowment investments reduce temporarily restricted net assets to the extent that donor-imposed restrictions on net appreciation have been met before the loss occurs. Any remaining loss would reduce unrestricted net assets.[7]

Financial Statements

Financial statements prepared in accordance with FASB Statement No. 117 represent a shift away from fund reporting to an emphasis on the organization as a whole. The equity account, fund balance, has been replaced with the term *net assets.* Classification of the organization's net assets is based on the existence or absence of donor-imposed restrictions. The financial statements must display three classes of net assets: unrestricted, temporarily restricted, and permanently restricted. Changes in each of these three classes of net assets must also be reported. Reclassifications that simultaneously decrease temporarily restricted net assets and increase unrestricted net assets are reported separately.

Required external financial statements include the

1. *Statement of Financial Position* (balance sheet), which will report organization-wide totals for assets, liabilities, and net assets, and net assets identified as unrestricted, temporarily restricted, and permanently restricted.
2. *Statement of Activities,* which reports revenues, expenses, gains, losses, and reclassifications (between classes of net assets). Minimum requirements are organization-wide totals, changes in net assets for each class of assets, and all expenses recognized only in the unrestricted classification. A display of a measure of operations in the statement of activities is encouraged.
3. *Statement of Cash Flows,* with categories (operating, financing, investing) similar to business organizations.

Private college and university financial statements report expenses rather than expenditures. Further, all expenses are reported as changes in unrestricted net assets. Whereas expenditures denote outlays of resources, expenses denote "using up" of resources. Therefore, flows of resources involving outlays of cash to purchase other assets are not presented in the statement of activities but, instead, in the statement of cash flows. Depreciation is also recorded as an expense.

In 1987, the FASB issued Statement No. 93, *Recognition of Depreciation by Not-for-Profit Organizations,* which required such organizations to disclose "depreciation expense for the period"[8] as well as several other disclosures that parallel requirements of APB Opinion No. 12 issued in 1967. Land and individual works of art or historical treasures that have an extraordinarily long life were excluded from these reporting requirements. Depreciation accounting was previously required for providers of health care organizations and voluntary health and welfare organizations. FASB Statement No. 93 primarily affected universities and organizations that would normally apply standards of SOP 78-10[9] that did not use depreciation accounting.

The FASB believes that disclosure of depreciation expense and accumulated depreciation provides useful information about how a not-for-profit organization's tangible assets are wearing out. The statement requires all not-for-profit organizations to recognize the cost of using up such assets in the general-purpose financial statements.

---

7 FASB Statement No. 124, *Accounting for Certain Investments Held by Not-for-Profit Organizations* (Norwalk, CT: Financial Accounting Standards Board, 1995), standardizes not-for-profit reporting of investments. It requires that investments in equity securities with readily determinable fair market values and all investments in debt securities shall be measured at fair value. It does not apply to investments in equity securities accounted for under the equity method or to investments in consolidated subsidiaries.

8 FASB Statement No. 93, *Recognition of Depreciation by Not-for-Profit Organizations* (Norwalk, CT: Financial Accounting Standards Board, 1987), par. 5.

9 *Audits of Certain Nonprofit Organizations* (New York: American Institute of Certified Public Accountants, rev. ed., 1993).

In addition, information about liquidity must be provided. This may be accomplished by sequencing assets and liabilities according to nearness of conversion to or use of cash on the statement of financial position. Such sequencing requires cash and contributions receivable restricted by donors to investment in land, buildings, and equipment to be included in "assets restricted to investment in land, buildings, and equipment" rather than cash and contributions. Cash and equivalents of permanent endowment funds held temporarily until suitable long-term investment opportunities are identified must be included in the classification "long-term investments."

Although most not-for-profit organizations are continuing with some type of fund structure for internal management, they are no longer required to include fund information in the external financial reports. The illustrations in the body of the text in this chapter and the next assume a fund structure.[10] Accounting for events within existing fund groups is illustrated; however, financial statements without funds are presented. Disaggregated disclosure by fund groups is illustrated in the appendix to each chapter. We have provided both alternatives because SFAS No. 117 does not prescribe any one format of the financial statements so long as the minimum disclosure requirements, listed on the preceding page, are met. Therefore, fund reporting is still permitted.[11]

Colleges and universities are encouraged to develop a format for their financial statements that is most meaningful to their users. As a result, financial statement formats are expected to evolve over the next few years. Standard setters anticipate the need to monitor this development in order to determine whether limits should be placed on the flexibility allowed by FASB Statement No. 117. Models suggested by the FASB, and included in this chapter, are 1) a single column, "corporate" format and 2) disaggregation by net asset class. Colleges and universities appear to prefer the former model for the statement of financial position and the latter for the statement of activities. Illustration 18-5 on page 18-28 presents the statement of activities. Illustration 18-6 on page 18-29 presents the statement of financial position. A cash flow statement is included in Illustration 18-7 on page 18-30.

Required note disclosures include a description of the fund accounting groups and their relationship to the classes of net assets, classification of revenues, expenses, gains, losses, classification and valuation of contributions, description of accounting policies for release of donor restrictions, anticipated collection period of contributions receivables, description of collections, and detail on contributed services not meeting the reporting criteria. Note that disclosure of expenses by natural classification is suggested but not required.

Recording of both reciprocal exchange transactions and nonreciprocal contributions will change in order to provide organization-wide financial statements of assets, liabilities, net assets, changes in net assets, and cash flows. College and university administrators will have to carefully analyze the nature of each transaction to properly identify contributions and exchange transactions.

In addition, the following procedures were performed by universities implementing the new standards:

1. Adopting a policy to release restrictions for donated long-lived assets or long-lived assets acquired with restricted gifts of cash either a) immediately or b) over the useful life of the asset.

---

10 Financial statements based on net asset classification is a much different concept from fund group reporting. Many not-for-profit organizations are presenting a single-column statement of financial position with assets and liabilities reported in an aggregated basis and a multicolumn statement of activities with separate columns displaying changes in each net asset class and a total column. These formats are displayed in this chapter and the next.

11 In practice, private colleges and universities are keeping the existing fund structure. Some institutions are preparing financial statements with fund information included, while others are reporting without fund detail.

Illustration 18-5
Private University
Statement of Activities
For Year Ended June 30, 20X7

	Unrestricted	Temporarily Restricted	Permanently Restricted	Total
Changes in net assets:				
Revenues and gains:				
Tuition and fees	$ 1,700,000			$ 1,700,000
Contributions	575,000	$ 244,740	$120,000	937,740
Governmental appropriations, grants,				
and contracts	795,000			795,000
Investment income on endowment	70,000	28,000		98,000
Other investment income	251,000	45,000		296,000
Sales and services of auxiliary				
enterprises	400,000			400,000
Investment income on life income				
and annuity agreements		30,000		30,000
Net realized gains on other investments		10,000		10,000
Net realized gains on endowment	60,000			60,000
Total revenues and gains	$ 3,851,000	$ 357,740	$120,000	$ 4,328,740
Net assets released from restrictions:				
Satisfaction of program restrictions	102,000	(102,000)		0
Satisfaction of plant acquisitions				
restrictions	250,000	(250,000)		0
Satisfaction of time restrictions.	20,000	(20,000)		0
Total net assets released from				
restriction.	$ 372,000	$ (372,000)		0
Total revenues and gains and				
other support	$ 4,223,000	$ (14,260)	$120,000	$ 4,328,740
Expenses and losses:				
Educational and general:				
Instruction	$ 1,353,000			$ 1,353,000
Research.	145,000			145,000
Academic support.	217,000			217,000
Student services	222,000			222,000
Institutional support	245,500			245,500
Operation and maintenance of plant	600,000			600,000
Student aid	221,000			221,000
Total educational and general				
expenses	3,003,500			3,003,500
Auxiliary enterprises	350,000			350,000
Total expenses	$ 3,353,500	$ 0	$ 0	$ 3,353,500
Actuarial adjustment on annuity obligations . . .		3,221		3,221
Payments to life income beneficiaries		12,000		12,000
Total expenses and losses.	$ 3,353,500	$15,221	$ 0	$ 3,368,721
Increase (decrease) in net assets	$ 869,500	$(29,481)	$120,000	$ 960,019
Net assets at beginning of year	$39,299,000	$2,042,000	$834,000	$42,175,981
Net assets at end of year.	$40,168,500	$2,013,500	$954,000	$43,136,000

Illustration 18-6
Private University
Statement of Financial Position
For Period Ended June 30, 20X7

Assets:

Cash.	$ 1,494,300
Short-term investments	673,000
Accounts receivable (net of $20,000 allowance)	130,000
Contributions receivable (net of $25,000 allowance)	335,481
Inventories of supplies	20,000
Prepaid expenses	28,000
Student loans receivable.	55,500
Assets restricted to investment in land, buildings, and equipment.	1,350,000
Land, buildings, and equipment (net of accumulated depreciation of $150,000).	41,450,000
Long-term investments.	1,118,700
Endowment investments	954,000
Total assets.	47,608,981

Liabilities and Net Assets:

Accounts payable and accrued liabilities.	1,039,000
Other liabilities.	1,500
Amounts held on behalf of others.	110,000
Annuities payable.	237,481
Long-term debt	3,000,000
U.S. government grants refundable	85,000
Total liabilities.	4,472,981
Net assets:	
Unrestricted	40,168,500
Temporarily restricted.	2,013,500
Permanently restricted	954,000
Total net assets	43,136,000
Total liabilities and net assets.	47,608,981

2. Reviewing endowment funds to determine which funds meet the definitions of temporarily or permanently restricted.

3. Reviewing all funds that are presently classified as restricted to determine if expenses have been incurred that meet the restrictions.

4. Choosing a display format and deciding on the degree of aggregation in the financial statements.

5. Deciding on a method for providing information on liquidity.

6. Deciding on the level of detail to provide regarding the three classes of net assets, including whether to supply detail on the statement or in footnote disclosures.

7. *Prospectively* recording revenues and retroactively restating for all inflows—unrestricted, temporarily restricted, permanently restricted—and recording a cumulative effect in the year of adoption based on retroactive computation, or

8. Adopting *retroactively* restating opening balances of each of the three categories of net assets for the earliest year presented. Statement No. 117 does not require comparative annual financial statements but does require retroactive restatement of prior financial statements if comparative statements are presented in the year the Statement is first applied.

Illustration 18-7
Private University
Statement of Cash Flows
For Period Ended June 30, 20X7

Cash flows from operating activities:	
Student tuition and auxiliary fees	$ 2,030,000
Governmental appropriations	650,000
Research activities receipts	100,000
Interest and dividends received	308,000
Contributions received	395,000
Other receipts	75,000
Salaries and wages paid to faculty and staff	(1,935,000)
Payments to vendors for goods and services	(958,000)
Disbursements to students for financial aid	(81,000)
Payments to life income beneficiaries	(12,000)
Net cash provided by (used for) operating activities	$ 572,000
Cash flows from investing activities:	
Proceeds from sales and maturities of investments	325,000
Purchases of investments	(360,000)
Purchases of land, buildings, and equipment	(840,000)
Disbursements of loans to students and faculty	(24,000)
Repayments of loans from students and faculty	20,000
Net cash provided by (used for) investing activities	$ (879,000)
Cash flows from financing activities:	
Proceeds from issuance of notes payable	$ 800,000
Payments on long-term debt	(100,000)
Receipts of interest and dividends restricted for reinvestment	75,000
Contributions received restricted for long-term investment	200,000
Payments to annuitants	(6,000)
Receipts of refundable government loans funds	30,000
Net cash provided by (used for) financing activities	$ 999,000
Net increase (decrease) in cash and cash equivalents	692,000
Cash and cash equivalents at beginning of year	802,300
Cash and cash equivalents at end of year	1,494,300

Private University Accounting and Financial Reporting within Existing Fund Structure

As stated previously, private colleges and universities continue to use a fund structure for internal management. Outside resource providers, debt markets, contributors, and federal and state agencies also require funds-based information. Funds may be thought of as "subsidiary" accounts of the university. An important change for private universities is the reporting of revenues and expenses in all funds, not just the current funds.

A first step in implementing the FASB standards is to determine which assets in each of the funds to include in the three net asset classes. The following matrix may be helpful in comparing the fund groups and net assets classifications. Many of the funds will have more than one net asset class. This is because some transactions that traditionally have been recorded as restricted are now considered unrestricted. Under FASB No. 116, only donor-restricted resources resulting from nonreciprocal transactions will continue to be restricted. All other resources are classified as unrestricted.

Fund Group	Net Asset Class
Current unrestricted funds	Unrestricted net assets
Current restricted funds	Unrestricted net assets
	Temporarily restricted net assets
Loan funds	Unrestricted net assets
	Temporarily restricted net assets
Endowment and similar funds	Unrestricted net assets
	Temporarily restricted net assets
	Permanently restricted net assets
Plant funds	Unrestricted net assets
	Temporarily restricted net assets

To highlight the dramatic changes in accounting and financial reporting for private universities, the transactions from the public college and university example described in the previous section are recorded below, following the FASB guidance for private not-for-profits. The numbering of the events is the same for both the public and private examples. Events are marked with an * when no comparable entry is found in the public sector.

Current Unrestricted Fund.   Under FASB No. 116, most exchange transactions that affect the unrestricted net asset class will be recorded in this operating fund. Unrestricted contributions will also be recorded in this fund. Note that private colleges and universities record expenses instead of expenditures. Outflows of resources for capital asset acquisitions will not be recorded as expenditures but as an exchange of one asset for another. In addition, depreciation will be recorded in the current unrestricted funds or in the plant funds and may be allocated to the functional areas.

Event		Entry		
1. Educational and general revenue is earned or billed:		Accounts Receivable	2,750,000	
Student tuition and fees (of which $20,000		Revenues—Student Tuition and Fees .		1,700,000
is considered uncollectible)	$1,700,000	Revenues—Governmental		
Government appropriations	750,000	Appropriations		750,000
Endowment income	50,000	Revenues—Unrestricted Endowment		
Other investment income	250,000	Income		50,000
		Revenues—Unrestricted Other		
		Investment Income		250,000
* The provision for uncollectible student accounts receivable		Expenses—Institutional Support (Provision		
is considered an expense and is allocated to institutional		for Uncollectible Student Accounts		
support		Receivable)	20,000	
		Allowance for Uncollectible Student		
		Accounts Receivable		20,000
* Unrestricted contributions are pledged in the amount of		Contributions Receivable		250,000
$250,000. 10% of these pledges are assumed uncollectible.		Revenues—Unrestricted		
		Contributions		250,000

(continued)

Event	Entry		
	Expenses—Institutional Support (Provision for Uncollectible Contributions) . . .	25,000	
	Allowance for Uncollectible Contributions		25,000
2. Of the total revenues, $2,800,000 is collected, including $200,000 of pledges.	Cash	2,800,000	
	Accounts Receivable		2,600,000
	Contributions Receivable		200,000
3. Revenue billed for dormitories (an auxiliary enterprise) is $400,000, of which $20,000 is not yet received.	Cash	380,000	
	Accounts Receivable	20,000	
	Revenues—Sales and Services of Auxiliary Enterprises		400,000
4. Purchase of materials and supplies totaling $400,000, of which $25,000 is not yet paid.	Inventory of Supplies	400,000	
	Cash		375,000
	Accounts Payable		25,000

5. Expenses are paid and assigned to:

Instruction	$1,050,000	Expenses—Instruction	1,050,000	
Research	100,000	Expenses—Research	100,000	
Academic support	150,000	Expenses—Academic Support	150,000	
Student services	200,000	Expenses—Student Services	200,000	
Institutional support	200,000	Expenses—Institutional Support	200,000	
Operation and maintenance of plant	400,000	Expenses—Operation and Maintenance of Plant	400,000	
Scholarships and fellowships	40,000	Expenses—Student Aid	40,000	
Sales and services of auxiliary enterprises . . .	260,000	Expenses—Sales and Services of Auxiliary Enterprises	260,000	
		Cash		2,400,000

6. Materials and supplies used:

Instruction	268,000	Expenses—Instruction		268,000
Student services	22,000	Expenses—Student Services	22,000	
Auxiliary enterprises	90,000	Expenses—Sales and Services of Auxiliary Enterprises	90,000	
		Inventory of Supplies		380,000

7. Aid is granted to students:

Remission of tuition	140,000	Expenses—Student Aid	175,000	
Cash scholarships	35,000	Accounts Receivable		140,000
		Cash		35,000

* Services that meet the criteria of 1) creating or enhancing nonfinancial assets or 2) requiring specialized skills, provided by individuals possessing those abilities, and typically purchased if not donated. The fair market value of the services is $35,000.	Expenses—Instruction	35,000	
	Revenues—Unrestricted Contributions		35,000
8. Cash contributions are given without donor restriction.	Cash	100,000	
	Revenues—Unrestricted Contributions		100,000

Event	Entry		
9. Closing entries are prepared for the unrestricted net assets.	Revenues—Student Tuition and Fees. .	1,700,000	
	Revenues—Governmental		
	Appropriations.	750,000	
	Revenues—Unrestricted Contributions.	385,000	
	Revenues—Unrestricted Endowment		
	Income	50,000	
	Revenues—Unrestricted Other		
	Investment Income.	250,000	
	Expenses—Instructional		1,353,000
	Expenses—Research		100,000
	Expenses—Academic Support		150,000
	Expenses—Student Services		222,000
	Expenses—Institutional Support. . . .		245,000
	Expenses—Operations and		
	Maintenance of Plant		400,000
	Expenses—Student Aid		215,000
	Unrestricted Net Assets		**450,000**
	Revenues—Sales and Services of		
	Auxiliary Enterprises	400,000	
	Expenses—Sales and Services of		
	Auxiliary Enterprises		350,000
	Unrestricted Net Assets		**50,000**

Current Restricted Fund. In private universities, the current restricted fund will have both donor-restricted contributions and resources from exchange transactions, including government grants. For many universities, differentiating donor-restricted contributions as defined by FASB No. 116 from exchange transactions is very difficult.

Event	Entry		
10. A donor-restricted cash contribution is received to assist in library operations.	Cash	70,000	
	Revenues—Temporarily Restricted		
	Contributions		70,000
11. Endowment income of $8,000 is restricted to student aid activities.	Cash	8,000	
	Revenues—Temporarily Restricted		
	Endowment Income.		8,000
12. Of the following expenses, all but $4,000 are paid:	Expenses—Academic Support	67,000	
For library operations $67,000	Expenses—Student Aid	6,000	
For student aid. 6,000	Accounts Payable.		4,000
	Cash		69,000
13. Temporarily restricted revenues of $73,000 are reclassified as unrestricted when donor specifications are satisfied.	Reclassification Out—Temporarily		
	Restricted—Satisfaction of Program		
	Restrictions	73,000	
	Reclassification In—Unrestricted—		
	Satisfaction of Program		
	Restrictions		73,000

(continued)

Event	Entry		
14. Federal grants for student awards through the Pell Grant program are received in the amounts of $75,000. All $75,000 is distributed to qualified students.	See Agency Fund events and entries.		
15. A federal grant was awarded for research.	Cash . . . . U.S. Government Grants Refundable	100,000	100,000
16. Expenses for the research project totaled $45,000 to date. All expenses have been paid.	Expenses—Research . . . . Cash	45,000	45,000

Revenue is recognized to the extent that resources have been properly spent.	U. S. Government Grants
	   Refundable . . . .
	   Revenues—Government Grants and
	     Contracts . . . .
		45,000	45,000

17. Closing entries are prepared for the unrestricted net assets.	Revenues—Unrestricted Government
	   Grants and Contracts . . . .
	Reclassifications In—Unrestricted—
	   Satisfaction of Program
	   Restrictions . . . .
	   Expenses—Academic Support . . . .
	   Expenses—Student Aid . . . .
	   Expenses—Research . . . .
	   Unrestricted Net Assets . . . . . .
		45,000
		
		73,000
			
			67,000
			6,000
			45,000
			0

Closing entries are prepared for the temporarily restricted net assets.	Revenues—Temporarily Restricted
	   Contributions . . . .
	Revenues—Temporarily Restricted
	   Endowment Income. . . . .
	   Reclassifications Out—Temporarily
	   Restricted—Satisfaction of
	   Program Restrictions . . . .
	   Temporarily Restricted
	   Net Assets . . . .
		70,000
		
		8,000
			
			73,000
			
			5,000

Loan Funds.   Universities account for resources designated for student loan activity in a separate fund. This practice continues in private universities because of the large amounts of federal and state resources made available to universities for student loans. In addition, donor-restricted contributions may also specify use of the contributed resources for student loan purposes.

Event	Entry		
18. A contribution of $25,000 is received from an alumnus for student loan purposes.	Cash . . . . Revenues—Temporarily Restricted Contributions	25,000	25,000

19. Investments costing $5,000 are sold for $5,500. The gain is restricted.	Cash . . . .
	   Investments . . . .
	   Revenues—Temporarily Restricted—
	   Net Realized Gains on
	   Investments . . . .
		5,500	5,000
			
			500

Event	Entry		
20. Loans totaling $24,000 are made to students. Collections from other loans made to students total $20,000 plus $1,000 of interest. (FASB No. 116 assumes that restricted resources are used first.)	Loans Receivable . . . . Cash	24,000	24,000
	Reclassification Out—Temporarily Restricted—Satisfaction of Program Restrictions . . . . Reclassification In—Unrestricted— Satisfaction of Program Restrictions	24,000	24,000
	Cash . . . . Loans Receivable . . . . Revenues—Unrestricted Other Investment Income.	21,000	20,000 1,000
21. Federal government monies of $30,000 restricted for student loans are received.	Cash . . . . U.S. Government Grants Refundable	30,000	30,000
22. A $500 student loan is uncollectible. No provision for uncollectible loans had been previously established.	Expenses—Institutional Support (Loan Cancellations/Write-Offs) . . . Loans Receivable	500	500
* Closing entries are prepared for the unrestricted net assets.	Revenues—Unrestricted Interest Income Reclassifications In—Unrestricted— Satisfaction of Program Restrictions . . . . Expenses—Institutional Support . . . . **Unrestricted Net Assets**	1,000 24,000	500 **24,500**
* Closing entries are prepared for the temporarily restricted net assets.	Revenues—Temporarily Restricted Contributions . . . . Revenues—Temporarily Restricted Net Realized Gains on Investments . . . . Reclassifications Out—Temporarily Restricted—Satisfaction of Program Restrictions . . . . **Temporarily Restricted Net Assets**	25,000 500	24,000 **1,500**

Endowment and Similar Funds.   Colleges and universities traditionally account for permanent endowments, term endowments, and board-designated (quasi-) endowment resources in separate funds. This practice is expected to continue in private universities because external users of financial data, for example, the debt market, consider all three categories of endowments important in the lending decision. Therefore, financial reports of private universities present this information in the financial statements or in the notes.

Event	Entry		
23. Common stock, with a market value of $60,000, and $60,000 cash are received as pure endowment contributions.	Cash . . . . Endowment Investments . . . . Revenues—Permanently Restricted Contributions	60,000 60,000	120,000
* Term endowments expire, making $20,000 cash available.	Reclassification Out—Temporarily Restricted—Expiration of Time Restrictions . . . . Reclassification In—Unrestricted— Expiration of Time Restrictions. . . .	20,000	20,000
24. Endowment fund investments carried at $200,000 are sold for $260,000, and investment earnings are $40,000, of which $20,000 is temporarily restricted for research projects and $20,000 is unrestricted.	Cash . . . . Endowment Investments . . . . Revenues—Unrestricted Net Realized Gains on Endowment . Revenues—Temporarily Restricted Endowment Income . . . . Revenues—Unrestricted Endowment Income	300,000	200,000 60,000 20,000 20,000
25. Investments are purchased with fund cash.	Endowment Investments . . . . Cash	360,000	360,000
* Closing entries are prepared for the unrestricted net assets.	Reclassification In—Unrestricted— Expiration of Time Restrictions. . . . Revenues—Unrestricted Income on Endowments . . . . Revenues—Unrestricted Net Realized Gains on Endowment . . . . **Unrestricted Net Assets**	20,000 20,000 60,000	 **100,000**
* Closing entries are prepared for the temporarily restricted net assets.	Revenues—Temporarily Restricted Endowment Income. . . . . Reclassifications Out—Temporarily Restricted—Expiration of Time Restriction . . . . **Temporarily Restricted Net Assets**	20,000	 20,000 **0**
* Closing entries are prepared for the permanently restricted net assets.	Revenues—Permanently Restricted Endowment Contributions. . . . . . . **Permanently Restricted Net Assets**	120,000	 **120,000**

Annuity and Life Income Funds.   As in the example of public colleges and universities, these funds account for resources available to the college or university upon the death of the donor. Periodic payments are made to the donors for an indicated time period.

Event	Entry		
26. Cash of $12,000 from life income fund investments and $18,000 from annuity fund investments is received.	Cash . . . . Revenues—Temporarily Restricted Income on Investments	12,000	12,000
	Cash . . . . Revenues—Temporarily Restricted Income on Investments	18,000	18,000
27. A retired professor donated $100,000. The professor is to receive $6,000 per year for an estimated life of 10 years. Thereafter, the principal is to be used for student aid. The present value of the annuity at 8% is actuarially computed to be $40,260.	Cash . . . . Annuities Payable . . . . Revenues—Temporarily Restricted Contributions	100,000	40,260 59,740
28. Interest on the annuity is recorded for the year (8% × $40,260 = $3,221).	Actuarial Adjustment of Annuities Payable . . . . Annuities Payable	3,221	3,221

29. Payments are made to:

Annuitant	6,000	Annuities Payable . . . . Cash	6,000	6,000
Life income beneficiaries	12,000	Life Income Beneficiaries . . . . Cash	12,000	12,000

Event	Entry		
30. Annuity fund investments with a book value of $50,000 are sold for $59,500.	Cash . . . . Annuity Investments . . . . Revenues—Temporarily Restricted Net Realized Gains on Investments	59,500	50,000 9,500
* Closing entries are prepared for temporarily restricted net assets	Revenues—Temporarily Restricted Contributions . . . . Revenues—Temporarily Restricted Net Realized Gains on Investments . . . . Revenues—Temporarily Restricted Income on Annuity and Life Income Investments . . . . Payment to Life Income Beneficiaries . . . . Loss on Actuarial Adjustment of Annuities—Payable . . . . **Temporarily Restricted Net Assets**	59,740 9,500 30,000	12,000 3,221 **84,019**

Plant Funds.   The plant funds are one area where accounting and reporting may be simplified in private colleges and universities. The entries which follow assume one plant fund, although the sub-groups described for a public university could be retained.

Event	Entry		
31. Stock with a market value of $90,000 is received from an art patron to finance an art gallery addition.	Investments . . . . Revenue—Temporarily Restricted Contributions	90,000		90,000
32. A collection of first editions appraised at $30,000 is donated to the university. The university adopts a policy of recording contributed collections.	Library Books . . . . Revenue—Unrestricted Contributions	30,000		30,000
33. An $800,000 bond issue is sold at face value to finance a business school wing.	Cash . . . . Bonds Payable	800,000		800,000
34. Earnings received on investments are restricted for building acquisition.	Cash . . . . Revenues—Temporarily Restricted Other Investment Income	45,000		45,000
35. Construction of the business school wing is ¼ completed.	Construction in Progress . . . . Contracts Payable	200,000		200,000
36. Business school wing contract is completed at additional cost of $640,000 and is paid in full.	Construction in Progress . . . . Contracts Payable . . . . Cash	640,000 200,000		840,000
37. Completed building costs are transferred to the buildings account.	Building . . . . Construction in Progress	840,000		840,000
38. Payment of $100,000 is made on a mortgage related to the completed project.	Mortgage Payable . . . . Cash	100,000		100,000
39. The cost of constructing an art gallery addition totals $250,000 financed with donor-restricted cash. University policy is to release restrictions when assets are placed in service.	Building . . . . Cash . . . . Reclassification Out—Temporarily Restricted—Satisfaction of Plant Acquisition Restrictions . . . . Reclassifications In—Unrestricted— Satisfaction of Plant Acquisition Restrictions	250,000 250,000		250,000 250,000
40. Land valued at $160,000 is donated by an alumnus.	Land . . . . Revenues—Unrestricted Property Contribution	160,000		160,000
41. Building repairs of $50,000 are paid, of which $5,000 is from restricted resources.	Expenses . . . . Cash . . . . Reclassification Out—Temporarily Restricted—Satisfaction of Program Restrictions . . . . Reclassifications In—Unrestricted— Satisfaction of Program Restrictions	50,000 5,000		50,000 5,000

Event	Entry		
* Depreciation expense for the current period is $150,000. Depreciation expenses are allocated to operation and maintenance of plant.	Expenses—Operation and Maintenance of Plant (Provision for Depreciation)	150,000	
	Accumulated Depreciation		150,000
* Closing entries are prepared for the unrestricted net assets	Reclassifications In—Unrestricted —Satisfaction of Plant Acquisition Restrictions	250,000	
	Reclassifications In—Unrestricted— Satisfaction of Program Restrictions	5,000	
	Revenues—Unrestricted Property Contributions	190,000	
	Expenses—Operation and Maintenance of Plant		200,000
	Unrestricted Net Assets		**245,000**
* Closing entries are prepared for the temporarily restricted net assets.	Revenues—Temporarily Restricted Contributions	90,000	
	Revenues—Temporarily Restricted Other Investment Income	45,000	
	Temporarily Restricted Net Assets	**120,000**	
	Reclassification Out—Temporarily Restricted—Satisfaction of Plant Acquisition Restrictions		250,000
	Reclassification Out—Temporarily Restricted—Satisfaction of Program Restrictions		5,000

Agency Funds.   These funds account for resources held by the university on behalf of others. FASB No. 116 specifically includes federal monies that pass through the university to student recipients (Pell grants) as agency transactions. These are accounted for in the restricted current fund in public universities.

Event	Entry		
14. Federal grants for student awards through the Pell Grant program are received in the amount of $75,000.	Cash	75,000	
	Amounts Held on Behalf of Others.		75,000
All $75,000 is distributed to qualified students.	Amounts Held on Behalf of Others . .	75,000	
	Cash		75,000

Interfund Transactions.   The following are examples of interfund transactions that may be found in a private college or university. Interfund activity must be clearly marked on the financial statements and eliminated in preparing the organization-wide totals of net assets and changes in net assets.

	Current Unrestricted Fund		Plant Funds	

I(1). Cash transferred to plant fund for: Addition to plant (discretionary). Payment of mortgage (mandatory).	Unrestricted Net Assets—
	  Mandatory Transfer 20,000
	Unrestricted Net Assets—
	  Discretionary Transfer . . . 147,000
	  Cash . . . .
		
		167,000
			Cash 167,000
			Unrestricted Net Assets—
			  Mandatory Transfer .
			Unrestricted Net
			  Assets—Discretionary
			  Transfer . . . .
				
				20,000
				
				147,000

	Current Unrestricted Fund		Loan Funds	

I(2). The board of trustees has agreed to transfer $3,000 to the loan fund on the first day of the next fiscal year as matching money for federal grants.	Unrestricted Net Assets—
	  Discretionary Transfer . . . 3,000
	  Due to Other Funds . . . . . .
		
		3,000
			Due from Other Funds . 3,000
			Unrestricted Net
			  Assets—Discretionary
			  Transfer . . . .
				
				3,000

	Current Unrestricted Fund		Endowment Funds	

I(3). The board of trustees has authorized an immediate transfer of $150,000 to the endowment fund.	Unrestricted Net Assets—
	  Discretionary Transfer . . . 150,000
	  Cash . . . .
		
		150,000
			Cash 150,000
			Unrestricted Net
			  Assets—Discretionary
			  Transfer . . . .
				
				150,000

	Current Unrestricted Fund		Endowment Funds	

I(4). Expired term endowment available cash will be transferred to the current unrestricted fund.	Due from Other Funds 20,000
	Unrestricted Net Assets—
	  Discretionary Transfer . . .
		
		20,000
			Unrestricted Net
			  Assets—Discretionary
			  Transfer 20,000
			  Due to Other Funds . .
				
				20,000

	Current Unrestricted Fund		Endowment Funds	

I(5). The $20,000 unrestricted endowment income will be transferred to the unrestricted current fund.	Due from Other Funds 20,000
	Unrestricted Net Assets—
	  Discretionary Transfer . . .
		
		20,000
			Unrestricted Net
			  Assets—Discretionary
			  Transfer 20,000
			  Due to Other Funds . .
				
				20,000

	Current Restricted Fund		Endowment Funds	

I(6). The $20,000 restricted endowment income will be transferred to the current restricted fund. The restriction will be released when research expenses are incurred.	Current from Other Funds . . . 20,000
	Unrestricted Net Assets—
	  Discretionary Transfer . . . .
		
		20,000
			Unrestricted Net
			  Assets—Discretionary
			  Transfer 20,000
			  Due to Other Funds . .
				
				20,000

Appendix: Private University Financial Reports Including Funds Information

The financial statements are presented with the AICPA Audit Guide fund groups in Illustrations 18A-1 and 18A-2 (pages 18-41 to 18-43). Minimum requirements of FASB Statement No. 117 are highlighted. This fund group model was included as an alternative in the materials sent by the National Association of College and University Business Officers (NACUBO) to college and university controllers in March 1994. This model is closest to the existing model of financial statements for colleges and universities. Consequently, it may be the most understandable to those users who are familiar with the current financial statements. It may also, in certain circumstances, involve the fewest number of changes in systems and procedures to implement. If a statement of financial position and a statement of activities are presented on a fund group basis, interfund items must be identified and eliminated from the display of total assets, liabilities, and net assets. (The accounts eliminated from our examples to prepare the funds-based Statement of Financial Position and Statement of Activities include *Due to/Due from Other Funds* and *Discretionary/Mandatory Transfers*.)

Illustration 18A-1
Private University
Statement of Activities
For Period Ended June 30, 20X5

	Current Funds	Loan Funds	Endowment and Similar Funds	Plant Funds	Total
Changes in unrestricted net assets:					
Revenues and gains:					
Tuition and fees	$1,700,000				$ 1,700,000
Contributions	385,000			$190,000	575,000
Government appropriations, grants, and					
contracts	795,000				795,000
Investment income on endowment	50,000		$ 20,000		70,000
Other investment income	250,000	$ 1,000			251,000
Net realized gains on endowment			60,000		60,000
Sales and services of auxiliary enterprises.	400,000				400,000
Total unrestricted revenues and gains	$3,580,000	$ 1,000	$ 80,000	$ 190,000	$ 3,851,000
Net assets released from restrictions:					
Satisfaction of program restrictions.	$ 73,000	24,000		5,000	102,000
Satisfaction of plant acquisition					
restrictions				250,000	250,000
Satisfaction of time restrictions.			20,000		20,000
Total net assets released from restriction	$ 73,000	$ 24,000	$ 20,000	$ 255,000	$ 372,000
Total unrestricted revenues and gains and					
other support	$3,653,000	$25,000	$ 100,000	$ 445,000	$ 4,223,000
Expenses and losses:					
Education and general:					
Instruction	$1,353,000				$ 1,353,000
Research	145,000				145,000
Academic support.	217,000				217,000
Student services	222,000				222,000
Institutional support	245,000	500			245,500
Operation and maintenance of plant	400,000			200,000	600,000
Student aid	221,000				221,000
Total educational and general expenses	$2,803,000	$ 500	$ 0	$ 200,000	$ 3,003,500
Auxiliary enterprises	$ 350,000				350,000
Total expenses	$3,153,000	$ 500	$ 0	$ 200,000	$ 3,353,500
Increase (decrease) in unrestricted net assets.	500,000	24,500	100,000	245,000	869,500

(continued)

	Current Funds	Loan Funds	Endowment and Similar Funds	Plant Funds	Total
Transfers among funds—additions (deductions):					
Mandatory principal payment	$ (20,000)			$ 20,000	
Discretionary transfer—endowment income	60,000		$ (60,000)		
Other discretionary transfers	(300,000)	3,000	150,000	147,000	
Total transfers	$ (260,000)	$ 3,000	$ 90,000	$ 167,000	$ 0
Changes in temporarily restricted net assets					
Contributions	$ 70,000	$25,000	$ 59,740	$ 90,000	$ 244,740
Income on life income and annuity investments.			30,000		30,000
Endowment income	8,000		20,000		28,000
Other investment income				45,000	45,000
Net realized gains on other investments		500	9,500		10,000
Net assets released from restrictions	(73,000)	(24,000)	(20,000)	(255,000)	(372,000)
Payments to life income beneficiaries			(12,000)		(12,000)
Loss on actuarial adjustment on annuity payables			(3,221)		(3,221)
Increase (decrease) in temporarily restricted net assets	$ 5,000	$ 1,500	$ 84,019	(120,000)	**(29,481)**
Changes in permanently restricted net assets					
Contributions			120,000		120,000
Increase (decrease) in permanently restricted net assets	0	0	120,000	0	**120,000**
Net assets at beginning of year	$1,111,000	$67,000	$1,469,981	$39,528,000	$ 42,175,981
Net assets at end of year	$1,356,000	$96,000	$1,864,000	$39,820,000	**$43,136,000**

Illustration 18A-2
Private University
Statement of Financial Position
For Period Ended June 30, 20X7

	Current Funds	Loan Funds	Endowment and Similar Funds	Plant Funds	Total
Assets					
Cash	$742,000	$57,500	$164,800	$530,000	$1,494,300
Short-term investments	453,000	10,000	60,000	150,000	673,000
Accounts receivable (net)	130,000				130,000
Contributions receivable (net)	180,000		155,481		335,481
Inventories of materials	20,000				20,000
Prepaid expenses	28,000				28,000
Loans to students.		55,500			55,500
Assets restricted to investment in land, buildings, and equipment				1,350,000	1,350,000

Land, buildings, and equipment (net)				41,450,000	41,450,000
Long-term Investments			878,700	240,000	1,118,700
Endowment Investments			954,000		954,000
Total assets	$1,553,000	$123,000	$2,212,981	$43,720,000	**$47,608,981**

Liabilities and Net Assets					
Accounts payable and accrued liabilities	$ 139,000			$900,000	$ 1,039,000
Other liabilities.			$ 1,500		1,500
Amounts held on behalf of others.			110,000		110,000
Annuities payable.			237,481		237,481
Long-term debt				3,000,000	3,000,000
U.S. government grants refundable	55,000	$ 30,000			$ 85,000
Total liabilities	$ 194,000	$ 30,000	$ 348,981	$3,900,000	**$ 4,472,981**
Net Assets:					
Unrestricted	$1,114,000	$ 10,500	$ 574,000	$38,470,000	**$40,168,500**
Temporarily restricted	245,000	82,500	336,000	1,350,000	**2,013,500**
Permanently restricted.			954,000		**954,000**
Total net assets.	$1,359,000	$ 93,000	$1,864,000	$39,820,000	**$43,136,000**
Total liabilities and net assets.	$1,553,000	$123,000	$2,212,981	$43,720,000	$ 47,608,981

Questions

1. Explain the difference between a contribution and an exchange transaction. How is each recorded in a private not-for-profit organization?
2. Describe the three classes of net assets required to be reported under FASB Statement No. 117.
3. Give an example of a contribution in each of the net asset classes.
4. Distinguish between a donor restriction and a condition.
5. How might a donor-imposed restriction expire?
6. When must not-for-profit organizations recognize contributed services and contributed collection items as revenue?
7. Under what circumstances is a government grant a contribution versus an exchange transaction?
8. What choices do not-for-profit organizations have regarding display format for their financial statements?
9. What are the measurement focuses (identifying which resources are being measured) and bases of accounting (identifying when the effects of transactions or events should be recognized) used by public universities and private universities? How might the use of two measurement focuses benefit financial reporting for universities?
10. Explain the accounting for contributions (of cash, pledges, or investments that may be converted into cash) for a private university. How does this accounting for contributions differ from that of a public university?
11. Interpret the following closing entry for a public university:

Revenues—Auxiliary Enterprises	500,000	
Expenditures—Auxiliary Enterprises		480,000
Fund Balance		20,000

12. Of the various funds traditionally used in public university accounting, indicate which is probably the most complex and explain why.

13. What is included in the statement of activities of a private university?
14. Explain the major differences in accounting and financial reporting of public and private universities.
15. Explain how FASB and GASB financial reporting standards regarding reporting of depreciation differ from one another.

Exercises

Exercise 1.   Indicate (with choices a–f) how the following events are recorded in a private university:

a) Credit Contributions—Unrestricted
b) Credit Contributions—Temporarily Restricted
c) Credit Contributions—Permanently Restricted

d) Credit Refundable Deposits
e) Credit Fund Balance
f) No entry

1. Receipt of an unconditional promise to give. _____

2. Receipt of a fixed asset with donor-specified use for an outreach program. _____

3. Receipt of an unconditional cash contribution. _____

4. Receipt of cash to be used for a specific purpose. _____

5. Receipt of free accounting services. _____

6. Receipt of time of volunteers who helped with fund-raising mailings. _____

7. Receipt of an unconditional promise to give over a 5-year period. _____

8. Receipt of investments that are to be used to set up an endowment with earnings available for operations. _____

9. Receipt of a conditional promise to give. _____

10. Receipt of a fixed asset with no donor restriction. _____

11. Receipt of a cash contribution to be used next year for a research project. _____

12. Receipt of a cash contribution to be used next year for general operations at the discretion of management. _____

13. Receipt of cash as part of a government grant funding a cancer research project. A report with research results will be prepared for the government funding agency. _____

14. Receipt of a cash contribution to be used for acquisition of fixed assets. _____

15. Receipt of a permanent collection of geography maps that will be displayed to the public. _____

Exercise 2.   Indicate which of the following accounts would be used for the listed transactions in a) a public university and b) a private university.

Revenues
Revenues—Unrestricted
Revenues—Temporarily Restricted
Revenues—Permanently Restricted
Auxiliary Revenues
Transfers (or Fund Balance)
Mandatory Transfers

Auxiliary Expenses
Expenditures
Expenses
Deferred Revenue
Refundable Deposits (a liability)
Current Assets

The transactions to be classified are as follows:

a)   Pledges are received for a fund drive that is restricted for research expenditures.

b)   An allowance for uncollectible pledges for the above fund is established.

c)   Fees are collected for a seminar to be presented in the next fiscal period.

d)   Tuition for the current period is billed.

e)   An allowance for uncollectible tuition is recorded.

f)   Tuition remissions are granted to out-of-state students.

g)   Dormitory fees are billed.

h)   Salaries for union food-service workers are paid.

i)   Supplies to be used during the period are purchased.

j)   A required transfer is made to the Plant Replacement Fund.

k)   The regents meet and transfer money to the endowment fund for a stated period of time.

Exercise 3.   Record the following events that affect the unrestricted current fund of Public University, which uses the typical control accounts for its revenues and expenditures. Omit explanations.

a)   Student fees of $600,000 were assessed, of which $575,000 has been collected and $4,000 is estimated to be uncollectible.

b)   The book store operates in rented space and is run on a break-even basis. Revenues totaled $100,000, of which 80% was collected to date. Salaries of $35,000 and rent of $10,000 are paid. Other operating expenses amount to $60,000, of which $15,000 has not been paid.

c)   A mandatory transfer of $75,000 was made for a payment due on the gymnasium building mortgage.

d)   The Student Aid Committee report showed the following:

Cash scholarships issued.	$25,000
Remission of tuition	10,000

e)   A check for $10,000 and a pledge for $4,500 are received from the local medical society to cover part of the cost of research on drug effects, one of the university's educational programs. The educational programs will be conducted and paid for in the next fiscal period.

f)   The endowment fund received a check for $12,000 of interest on investments. The premium amortization on the investment is $240. The unrestricted current fund is the recipient of the income.

Exercise 4.   Record the following events that affect the restricted current fund of Public University. Omit explanations.

a) A private grant of $150,000 was received to be used exclusively for defraying costs of holding conferences on the topic of genes.

b) By year-end, $110,000 of the grant mentioned in item a) had been applied to the purpose stipulated.

c) The grant provided that amounts not awarded by year-end are to be transferred to the endowment fund. The liability to that fund is recorded.

d) An alumnus, a former athlete, contributed $20,000 to assist in the search for a basketball coach.

Exercise 5.   Record the following events that affect the loan fund of Public University. Omit explanations.

a) An alumnus donates $420,000 to establish the student loan fund. Students are charged a 5% annual interest rate.

b) Loans of $380,000 are made to students.

c) The remaining $40,000 is deposited in the university credit union, which pays a current interest rate of 7%.

d) Loans of $20,000 are repaid, plus $800 of interest.

e) Interest of $1,400 is received from the university credit union.

f) A student who had borrowed $1,000 was in a serious automobile accident and withdrew from school. The university wrote-off the loan as uncollectible.

Exercise 6.   Record the following events that affect Public University's endowment fund.

a) An alumnus donates $250,000 to the endowment fund. The cash is fully invested in bonds with a face value of $242,000 which are purchased at an $8,000 premium. The income earned is to be available for the Current Restricted Fund for curriculum improvement.

b) A check for $11,250 for interest is received. The premium amortization is $667.

c) The income is transferred to the restricted current fund.

d) The bonds are sold for $260,500.

Exercise 7.   Record the following events that affect Public University's annuity and life income funds.

a) On July 1, 20X0, J. H. Stack, Emeritus Professor of Accounting, moved out of the state. Stack donated to the university common stock with a cost basis of $50,000 and a market value of $90,000. Stack is to receive an annuity of $5,000 each year for life; at death, the securities are to be sold and the remaining cash balance is to be transferred to the student loan fund. At a 10% annual rate and a life expectancy of 12 years, the present value of the annuity payments is $34,068.

b) The stock paid $5,400 in dividends each 12-month period.

c) The annuities payable account is adjusted to present value. At year-end, a payment of $5,000 is made to Professor Stack.

d) The annuities payable account is adjusted to present value. A second payment was made a year later.

e) A month later, Professor Stack died, eliminating the liability for future annuity payments.

f) The common stock was sold for $97,000. The cash balance was transferred to the student loan fund.

Exercise 8.   Public University maintains the following active plant funds:

Unexpended
Renewals and Replacements
Retirement of Indebtedness

Indicate in which fund each of the following transactions is recorded, and make the appropriate entry:

a) A transfer of $50,000 is received from the current unrestricted fund for the purpose of funding the payment of existing debt principal.

b) The restricted current fund transfers $30,000 to be used for major repairs of university buildings. The $20,000 is spent on appropriate repairs.

c) A transfer of $200,000 is made from the unrestricted current fund to the unexpended plant fund to finance an addition to the Science Building.

d) Work on the Science addition is in progress. At year-end, costs of construction total $80,000, of which $20,000 is unpaid. The university vice-president for finance prefers that transfers to the investment in plant sub-group be made only upon completion of any project.

e) The project is completed during the next year at an additional cost of $140,000, of which $125,000 is paid.

f) Unpaid contract costs of $35,000 are paid.

g) Transfer of the Science Building addition capitalized costs is made to the investment in plant sub-group.

Exercise 9.   Record the following events that affect Public University's investment in plant sub-group.

a) A partial payment of $50,000 is made from the unrestricted current fund on the gymnasium building mortgage, which is carried as a liability in the investment in plant sub-group.

b) New gymnasium equipment costing $25,000 is purchased from the portion of the unexpended plant fund donated by a former Olympic medalist for that purpose.

c) The Science Building addition is completed at a total cost of $220,000. The contractor is paid.

d) During a celebration after a basketball victory, $2,000 of gym equipment disappeared.

Exercise 10.   Record the following events that affect the current unrestricted funds of Private University.

a) Student fees of $600,000 were assessed, of which $575,000 has been collected and $4,000 is estimated to be uncollectible.

b) The book store operates in rented space and is run on a break-even basis. Revenues totaled $100,000, of which 80% was collected to date. Salaries of $25,000 and rent of $10,000 are paid. Other operating expenses amount to $60,000, of which $15,000 has not been paid.

(continued)

c) A mandatory transfer of $75,000 was made for a payment due on the gymnasium building mortgage.

d) The Student Aid Committee report showed:

Cash scholarships issued. $25,000
Remission of tuition   10,000

e) A check for $10,000 and a pledge for $4,500 are received from the local medical society to cover part of the cost of research on drug effects, one of the university's educational programs. The educational programs will be conducted and paid for in the next fiscal period.

f) The endowment fund received a check for $12,000 of interest on investments. The premium amortization on the investment is $240. The unrestricted current fund is the recipient of the income.

Exercise 11. Record the following events that affect the current restricted funds of Private University.

a) A private grant of $150,000 was received to be used exclusively for defraying costs of holding conferences on the topic of genes.

b) By year-end, $110,000 of the grant mentioned in item a) had been applied to the purpose stipulated.

c) The grant provided that amounts not awarded by year-end are permanently restricted and are to be transferred to the endowment fund. The liability to that fund is recorded.

d) An alumnus, a former athlete, contributed $20,000 to assist in the search for a basketball coach.

Exercise 12. Record the following events that affect the loan fund of Private University.

a) An alumnus donates $420,000 to establish the student loan fund. Students are charged a 5% annual interest rate.

b) Loans of $380,000 are made to students.

c) The remaining $40,000 is deposited in the university credit union, which pays a current interest rate of 7%.

d) Loans of $20,000 are repaid, plus $800 of interest.

e) Interest of $1,400 is received from the university credit union.

f) A student who had borrowed $1,000 was in a serious automobile accident and withdrew from school. The university wrote-off the loan as uncollectible.

Exercise 13. Record the following events that affect Private University's endowment fund.

a) An alumnus donates $250,000 to the endowment fund. The cash is fully invested in bonds that are purchased at a premium. The income earned is to be available for the current restricted fund for curriculum improvement.

b) An interest check for $11,500 is received. The premium amortization is $667.

c) The income is transferred to the restricted current fund.

d) The bonds are sold for $260,500.

Exercise 14.   Record the following events that affect Private University's annuity and life income funds.

  a) On July 1, 20X0, J. H. Stack, Emeritus Professor of Accounting, moved out of the state. Stack donated to the university common stock with a cost basis of $50,000 and a market value of $90,000. Stack is to receive an annuity of $5,000 each year for life; at death, the securities are to be sold and the remaining cash balance is to be transferred to the student loan fund. At a 10% annual rate and a life expectancy of 12 years, the present value of the annuity payments is $34,000.

  b) The stock paid $5,400 in dividends each 12-month period.

  c) A payment of $5,000 is made to Professor Stack. The annuities payable account is adjusted to present value.

  d) The annuities payable account is adjusted to present value. A second payment was made a year later.

  e) A month later, Professor Stack died, eliminating the liability for future annuity payments.

  f) The common stock was sold for $97,000. The cash balance was transferred to the student loan fund.

Exercise 15.   Record the following capital-related transactions for Private University plant funds. Private University has adopted the FASB accounting and financial reporting guidance. Assume one plant fund is used.

  a) Transfers of $250,000 are received from the current unrestricted fund for the purpose of funding the payment of existing debt principal ($50,000) and building an addition to the Science Building ($200,000).

  b) Contributions of $30,000 restricted for major repairs of university buildings are received. $20,000 is spent for appropriate repairs.

  c) A partial payment of $50,000 is made on the debt principal.

  d) Work on the Science Building addition is completed with a total cost of $220,000. Unpaid contract costs total $35,000.

  e) New gymnasium equipment costing $25,000 is purchased from funds previously donated by a former Olympic medalist for that purpose.

  f) A building with a fair market value of $300,000 was donated to the university by an alumnus.

  g) Depreciation on all assets totaled $75,000.

  h) During a celebration after a basketball victory, $2,000 of gym equipment disappeared.

Problems

Problem 18-1.   Select the best answer for each of the following multiple-choice items dealing with universities:

1. For the 20X7 fall semester, Brook Public University assessed its students $4,000,000 (net of refunds), covering tuition and fees for educational and general purposes. However, only $3,700,000 was expected to be realized because tuition remissions of $80,000 were allowed to faculty members'

(continued)

children attending Brook, and scholarships totaling $220,000 were granted to students. What amount should Brook include in educational and general current funds revenues from student tuition and fees?

a) $4,000,000   b) $3,920,000   c) $3,780,000   d) $3,700,000

2. Private College is sponsored by a religious group. Volunteers from this religious group regularly contribute their skilled services to Private and are paid nominal amounts to cover their commuting costs. If Private did not receive these volunteered services, it would have to purchase similar services. During 20X6, the total amount paid to these volunteers was $12,000. The gross value of services performed by them, as determined by reference to lay-equivalent salaries, amounted to $300,000. What amount should Private record as expenses in 20X6 for these volunteers' services?

a) $312,000   b)$300,000   c) $12,000   d) 0

3. Abbott Public University's unrestricted current fund comprised the following:

    Assets. $5,000,000
    Liabilities (including deferred revenues of $100,000)   3,000,000

    The fund balance of Abbott's unrestricted current fund was

    a) $1,900,000   b) $2,000,000   c) $2,100,000   d) $5,000,000

4. The following receipts are among those recorded by Curry Private College during 20X9:

    Unrestricted gifts. $500,000
    Restricted gifts (expended for current operating purposes) . .   200,000
    Restricted gifts (not yet expended)   100,000

    The amount that should be included in revenues is

    a) $800,000   b) $700,000   c) $600,000   d) $500,000

5. In 20X7, the board of trustees of Burr Private University designated $100,000 from its current funds for college scholarships. Also in 20X7, the university received a bequest of $200,000 from an estate of a benefactor who specified that the bequest was to be used for hiring teachers to tutor handicapped students. None of the bequest has been spent. What amount should be accounted for as restricted net assets?

    a) 0   b) $100,000   c) $200,000   d) $300,000

6. The following information pertains to interest received by Beech Public University from endowment fund investments for the year ended June 30, 20X8:

	Received	Expended for Current Operations
Unrestricted	$300,000	$100,000
Restricted	500,000	75,000

    What amount should be credited to endowment income for the year ended June 30, 20X8?

    a) $800,000   b) $375,000   c) $175,000   d) $100,000

7. On July 31, 20X8, Sabio Public College showed the following amounts to be used for:

Renewal and replacement of college properties	$200,000
Retirement of indebtedness on college properties	300,000
Purchase of physical properties for college purposes, but unexpended at 7/31/X8	400,000

What total amount should be included in Sabio's plant funds at July 31, 20X8?

a) $900,000   b) $600,000   c) $400,000   d) $200,000

8. The following expenditures were among those incurred by Cheviot Public University during 20X7:

Administrative data processing	$ 50,000
Scholarships and fellowships	100,000
Operation and maintenance of physical plant	200,000

The amount to be included in the functional classification "Institutional Support" expenditures account is:

a) $50,000   b) $150,000   c) $250,000   d) $350,000

(AICPA adapted)

Problem 18-2. Select the best answer for each of the following multiple-choice items. (Nos. 1–11 are AICPA adapted.)

1. An alumnus donates securities to Rex Private College and stipulates that the principal be held in perpetuity and revenues be used for faculty travel. Dividends received from the securities should be recognized as revenues in

   a) *Endowment funds.*

   b) *Quasi-endowment funds.*

   c) *Restricted current funds.*

   d) *Unrestricted current funds.*

2. A private college's plant funds group includes which of the following subgroups?

   (1) Renewals and replacement funds
   (2) Retirement of indebtedness funds
   (3) Restricted current funds

   a) 1 and 2   b) 1 and 3   c) 2 and 3   d) none of the above

3. Funds received by a private college from donors who have stipulated that the principal is nonexpendable but that the income generated may be expended for current operating needs would be accounted for as

   a) *Contributions—Permanently Restricted.*

   b) *Contributions—Temporarily Restricted.*

   c) *Contributions—Unrestricted.*

   d) *Fund Balance Increases.*

4. The following funds were among those held by State College at December 31, 20X1:

Principal specified by the donor as nonexpendable	$500,000
Principal expendable after the year 20X9	300,000
Principal designated from unrestricted net assets	100,000

(continued)

What amount should State College classify as permanently restricted endowments?

a) $100,000   b) $300,000   c) $5   d) $900,000

5. Is the recognition of depreciation expense required for public colleges and private not-for-profit colleges?

	Public	Private
a)	No	Yes
b)	No	No
c)	Yes	Yes
d)	Yes	No

6. In the loan fund of a private or public college, each of the following types of loans would be found except which of the following?

a) Faculty
b) Computer
c) Staff
d) Student

7. In 20X2, State University's board of trustees established a $100,000 fund to be retained and invested for scholarship grants. In 20X2, the fund earned $6,000, which had not been disbursed at December 31, 20X2. What amount should State report as unrestricted investment earnings at December 31, 20X2?

a) $0
b) $6,000
c) $100,000
d) $106,000

8. On January 2, 20X2, a graduate of Oak Private College established a permanent trust fund and appointed Security Bank as the trustee. The income from the trust fund is to be paid to Oak and used only by the School of Business to support student scholarships. What entry is required on Oak's books to record the receipt of cash from the interest on the trust fund?

a) Debit cash and credit deferred revenue.
b) Debit cash and credit temporarily restricted endowment revenue.
c) Debit cash and credit temporarily restricted contributions.
d) Debit cash and credit unrestricted endowment revenue.

9. At the end of the year, Cramer Private University's balance sheet comprised $15,000,000 of assets and $9,000,000 of liabilities (including deferred revenues of $300,000). What is the balance of Cramer's net assets?

a) $5,700,000
b) $6,000,000
c) $6,300,000
d) $15,000,000

10. Financial resources of a college or university that are currently expendable at the discretion of the governing board and that have not been restricted externally nondesignated by the board for a specific purpose should be reported in the balance sheet as

a) *Board-designated current funds.*

b) *Permanently restricted net assets.*

c) *Unrestricted net assets.*

d) *Temporarily restricted net assets.*

11. Which of the following accounts would appear in the plant fund of a not-for-profit private college?

	Fuel Inventory for Power Plant	Equipment
a)	Yes	Yes
b)	No	Yes
c)	No	No
d)	Yes	No

Problem 18-3.   Record the following transactions. Identify each as a contribution or an exchange transaction, and prepare any appropriate entries.

1. Private University coordinated its annual special event with the opening of the alumni weekend. Tickets to the special event were $200 and included a buffet (cost $30), admission to the university symphony (cost $30), and a reception (cost $35). A total of 1,000 tickets was sold.

2. A local manufacturing company gave $2,000,000 to Private University to commission a study on the relationship of worker stress to chronic disease. The results of the study will be used to educate the general public.

3. Allen Corporation gave a contribution of $850,000 to Private University. Allen Corporation specifies that the gift is to be invested in perpetuity and that the income may be used by Private University to pay operating costs.

4. Local Corporation donated a building to Private College for use as new office space. The cost to Local was $75,000. The building was appraised by a professional real estate appraiser at $100,000, while another appraiser valued it at $110,000.

5. An alumna of XYZ Private College has notified the school that she will donate to the school any net proceeds in excess of $50,000 from her next novel. She stipulates that the college use her gift to buy new equipment for the writing lab.

6. Cheryl Debit, an accountant, spent Sunday afternoon at Private University sending out to alumni a mailing seeking more contributions for the building fund.

7. A very famous artist notified the local private university that she has included in her will her plans to donate all of her paintings for exhibit at the university art gallery. A copy of her will is included with her letter.

8. A grant in the amount of $400,000 from the U.S. Department of Labor and Economics was received by Private University to fund research on the impact of accounting standards. A report of research findings is to be submitted to the grantor.

9. $50,000 of U.S. government funds flow to Private University to be held for students qualifying for financial aid.

Problem 18-4.   A partial balance sheet of Greenleaf State University, a public university, as of the end of its fiscal year, July 31, 20X5, is as follows:

Greenleaf State University
Current Funds Balance Sheet
July 31, 20X5

Assets		Liabilities and Fund Balances	
Unrestricted:		**Unrestricted:**	
Cash.	$200,000	Accounts payable	$100,000
Accounts receivable (net of $15,000		Due to other fund	40,000
allowance)	360,000	Deferred revenue—tuition & fees	25,000
Prepaid expenses	40,000	Fund balance	435,000
Total unrestricted.	$600,000	Total unrestricted.	$600,000
Restricted:		**Restricted:**	
Cash.	$ 10,000	Accounts payable	$ 5,000
Investments	210,000	Fund balance	215,000
Total restricted	$220,000	Total restricted	$220,000
Total current funds.	$820,000	Total current funds.	$820,000

The following information pertains to the year ended July 31, 20X6:

a) Cash collected from students' tuition totaled $3,000,000. Of this amount, $362,000 represented accounts receivable outstanding at July 31, 20X5; $2,500,000 was for current-year tuition; and $138,000 was for tuition applicable to the semester beginning in August 20X6.

b) Deferred revenue at July 31, 20X5, was earned during the year ended July 31, 20X6.

c) Accounts receivable at July 31, 20X5, that were not collected during the year ended July 31, 20X6, were determined to be uncollectible and were written-off against the allowance account. At July 31, 20X6, the allowance account was estimated at $10,000.

d) During the year, an unrestricted appropriation of $60,000 was made by the state, to be paid to Greenleaf sometime in August 20X6.

e) During the year, unrestricted cash gifts of $80,000 were received from alumni. Greenleaf's board of trustees allocated $30,000 of these gifts to the student loan fund.

f) During the year, restricted fund investments costing $25,000 were sold for $31,000. Restricted fund investments were purchased at a cost of $40,000. Restricted fund investment income of $18,000 was earned and collected during the year. This income is restricted for an ongoing research project.

g) Unrestricted general expenses of $2,500,000 were recorded in the voucher system. At July 31, 20X6, the unrestricted accounts payable balance was $75,000.

h) The restricted accounts payable balance at July 31, 20X5, was paid. The restricted fund paid $10,000 from its investment income for costs of an ongoing research project.

i) The $40,000 due to other funds at July 31, 20X5, was paid to the plant fund as required.

j) One-quarter of the prepaid expenses at July 31, 20X5, expired during the current year and pertained to general education expense. There was no addition to prepaid expenses during the year.

Required:

1. Prepare journal entries in summary form to record the foregoing transactions for the year ended July 31, 20X6. Letter each entry to correspond with the letter indicated in the description of its respective transaction, and omit explanations. Use the following format:

		Current Funds			
		Unrestricted		Restricted	
Entry					
Letter	Accounts	Debit	Credit	Debit	Credit

2. Prepare a statement of current funds revenues, expenditures, and other changes, including a total column, for the year ended July 31, 20X6, and conclude with the fund balances at year-end.

(AICPA adapted)

Problem 18-5.   The following events occurred as part of the operations of Craig State University, a public university:

a) To construct a new computer complex, the university floated at par a $22,000,000, 7% serial bond issue on October 1, paying interest on June 30 and December 31. Accrued interest is to be transferred to the retirement of indebtedness plant fund when construction begins. Construction costs are to be accumulated in the unexpended plant fund until the unit is completed.

b) Since construction has begun, the accrued interest, which must be used to assist in meeting bond interest payments, is transferred. Payments for construction to date total $5,000,000.

c) On December 31, a mandatory transfer of $385,000 is made from the unrestricted current fund to cover the remainder of the interest due on December 31 on the bond issue.

d) The bond interest due on December 31 is paid.

e) Construction of the complex is completed at an additional cost of $17,000,000. Payment is made for $16,000,000; the balance will be paid in one year under a retained percentage agreement.

f) The cost of the complex is transferred.

g) A required transfer of $2,770,000 is made from the unrestricted current fund to cover redemption of the first serial bond of $2,000,000 plus interest.

h) Payments are made for the bond principal and interest in item g).

i) A gift of land and a building was received, appraised at $200,000 and $350,000, respectively. The state's leading industrialist made the gift on condition that the university would assume a $90,000 mortgage on the property.

j) Pledges of $100,000 to be paid in one year were received with the understanding that the funds would be used to remodel the building received in item i). It is estimated that $5,000 of the pledges will not be collected.

(continued)

k) A donor contributed $100,000 in cash for the acquisition of rare first editions for the university library. The director of the library located a collection of the first editions that was available for $160,000. The university board transferred $60,000 from the unrestricted current fund to cover the difference.

l) The first edition collection is purchased, and payment is made.

Required:

Prepare journal entries to record the events, indicating in which funds the entries are made.

Problem 18-6.   The balance sheet of Washbush Private University as of the end of its fiscal year, June 30, 20X7, is as follows:

Washbush Private University
Statement of Financial Position
For Year Ended June 30, 20X7

Assets		Liabilities and Fund Balances	
Cash	$257,000	Accounts payable	$ 40,000
Accounts receivable student tuition and. .		Deferred revenue	66,000
fees less allowance for doubtful		Long-term debt	100,000
accounts of $9,000.	311,000	Total liabilities.	206,000
		Net Assets:	
		Unrestricted	$487,000
State appropriations receivable	75,000	Temporarily restricted	40,000
Endowment investments	50,000	Permanently restricted	50,000
Property, plant, and equipment (net)	90,000	Total net assets	577,000
Total assets	$783,000	Total net assets and liabilities	$783,000

The following transactions occurred during the fiscal year ended June 30, 20X8:

a) On July 7, 20X7, a gift of $90,000 was received from an alumnus. The alumnus requested that ½ of the gift be used for the purchase of equipment for the university athletic department and the remainder be used for the establishment of a permanently restricted endowment. The alumnus further requested that the income generated by the endowment be used annually to award a scholarship to a qualified disadvantaged student. On July 20, 20X7, the board of trustees resolved that the funds of the newly established endowment would be invested in savings certificates. On July 21, 20X7, the savings certificates were purchased.

b) Revenue from student tuition and fees applicable to the year ended June 30, 20X8, amounted to $1,900,000. Of this amount, $66,000 was collected in the prior year and $1,686,000 was collected during the year ended June 30, 20X8. In addition, at June 30, 20X8, the university had received cash of $158,000 representing fees for the session beginning July 1, 20X8.

c) During the year ended June 30, 20X8, the university had collected $308,000 of the outstanding accounts receivable at the beginning of the year. The remainder was determined to be uncollectible and was written-off against the allowance account. At June 30, 20X8, the allowance account was adjusted to $6,000.

d) During the year, interest charges of $6,000 were earned and collected on late student fee payments.

e) During the year, the state appropriation was received. An additional unrestricted appropriation of $40,000 was made by the state, but it had not been paid to the university as of June 30, 20X8.

f) A gift of $30,000 cash restricted was received from alumni of the university for economic research expenses.

g) During the year, endowment investments that cost $21,000 were sold for $24,000. This includes accrued investment income amounting to $1,900. All income was restricted for programs to enhance teaching effectiveness.

h) During the year, unrestricted operating expenses of $1,800,000 were recorded. They include

Instruction.	$ 500,000
Research	400,000
Institutional support	100,000
Student aid.	100,000
Student services.	200,000
Operation and maintenance of plant. . . .	500,000
	$1,800,000

At June 30, 20X8, $60,000 of these expenses remained unpaid.

i) Temporarily restricted funds of $13,000 were spent for specified economic research described in item f).

j) The accounts payable at June 30, 20X7, were paid during the year.

k) During the year, $7,000 interest was earned and received on the savings certificates purchased in item a).

l) In honor of its 25th anniversary, Washbush Private University conducted a fund drive. Contributions of $16,000 were received. Additional unconditional pledges of $14,000 were promised for payment in December 20X8. It is anticipated that $2,000 of the pledges will be uncollectible.

Required:

1. Prepare journal entries to record the transactions. Assume fund accounting is not used.
2. Prepare a statement of activities for the year ended June 30, 20X8, using a column for each of the 3 net asset classifications and a total column.

Problem 18-7. The following events occurred as part of the operations of Kronke Private University.

a) To construct a new business building, the university floated at par a $20,000,000, 8% serial bond issued on July 1. Interest is to be paid on December 31 and June 30. In addition, contributions from the community specifically for the new building totaled $5,000,000.

b) Payments for construction to date total $7,000,000.

c) Interest payments are made on December 31.

(continued)

d) Construction of the building is completed at an additional cost of $18,000,000. Payment is made for $16,000,000; the balance will be paid in one year under a retained percentage agreement. Institutional policy is to release donor restrictions when assets are placed in service.

e) The first bond serial payment of $2,000,000 plus interest is paid.

f) A gift of land and a building was received, appraised at $200,000 and $350,000, respectively. The gift was made on the condition that the university assume a $90,000 mortgage on the property. The university assumed the mortgage.

g) Pledges with a present value of $200,000 to be paid over the next 5 years were received. The funds will be restricted for remodeling the building received in item f). It is estimated that $20,000 of the pledges will not be collected.

h) A donation of $500,000 of stock was made by a wealthy citizen. The stock cannot be sold for 5 years. After the 5-year period, the stock can be sold, and any proceeds are to be used to finance campus construction projects.

i) Dividends of $10,000 on the stock in item h) were received and were also restricted for construction projects.

j) Depreciation on the building received in item f) totaled $25,000.

Required:

1. Prepare journal entries to record these events for Kronke Private University. Assume that fund accounting is not used.
2. Prepare a statement of activities.

Problem 18-8.   The pre-closing trial balance of Park Private College has the following balances:

	Dr.	Cr.
Expenses—Instruction	1,230,000	
Expenses—Research	840,000	
Expenses—Academic Support	250,000	
Expenses—Student Services	200,000	
Expenses—Institutional Support	225,000	
Expenses—Operation and Maintenance of Plant	400,000	
Expenses—Student Aid	350,000	
Expenses—Auxiliary Enterprises Expenses	475,000	
Reclassification Out—Temporarily Restricted— Satisfaction of Program Restrictions	75,000	
Reclassification Out—Temporarily Restricted— Satisfaction of Equipment Acquisitions Restrictions	250,000	
Reclassification Out—Temporarily Restricted— Expiration of Time Restrictions	50,000	
Tuition and Fees		1,500,000
Contributions—Unrestricted		265,000
Government Appropriations, Grants, and Contracts		800,000
Other Investment Income—Unrestricted		250,000
Sales and Services of Auxiliary Enterprises		500,000

Reclassification In—Unrestricted—Satisfaction of Program Restrictions	75,000
Reclassification In—Unrestricted—Satisfaction of Equipment Acquisition Restrictions	250,000
Reclassification In—Unrestricted—Expiration of Time Restrictions	50,000
Contributions—Temporarily Restricted	200,000
Endowment Income—Temporarily Restricted	15,000
Contributions—Permanently Restricted	500,000
Net Realized Gains on Endowment— Temporarily Restricted	25,000
Unrestricted Net Assets, 1/1/X5	675,000
Temporarily Restricted Net Assets, 1/1/X5	975,000
Permanently Restricted Net Assets, 1/1/X5	2,500,000

Required:

1. Prepare closing entries for the 3 net asset classifications.
2. Prepare a statement of activities for the year ended December 31, 20X5, using a column for each of the net asset classifications.

Problem 18-9.   Using the data in Problem 18-8 and the following additional information, prepare a statement of financial position for Park Private College.

	Dr.	Cr.
Cash	275,000	
Accounts Receivable (net)	625,000	
Contributions Receivable	85,000	
Inventory of Supplies	55,000	
Student Loans Receivable	300,000	
Land, Buildings, and Equipment (net)	1,000,000	
Long-Term Investments	3,025,000	
Accounts Payable		220,000
Amounts Held on Behalf of Others		250,000
Long-Term Debt		560,000
U.S. Government Grants Refundable		100,000

Appendix Problems

Problem 18A-1.   Trial balance information for Fortune Private University is as follows for the fiscal year beginning 7/1/X5:

	Current Funds Unrestricted	Current Funds Restricted	Plant Funds	Loan Funds	Endowment Funds	Total
Cash	23,000	2,000	1,000	300		26,300
Accounts receivable	950					950
Allowance for uncollectible student tuition receivable	(75)					(75)
Contributions receivable	6,000	17,500	3,000	1,000		27,500

(continued)

	Current Funds Unrestricted	Current Funds Restricted	Plant Funds	Loan Funds	Endowment Funds	Total
Allowance for uncollectible contributions ..	(60)	(75)	(30)	(10)		(175)
Short-term investments.................	15,000	15,000				30,000
Land, buildings, and equipment			400,000			400,000
Accumulated depreciation.............			(150,000)			(150,000)
Long-term investments			100,000	10,000		110,000
Endowment investments..............					90,000	90,000
Accounts payable	(3,500)					(3,500)
Long-term debt......................			(150,000)			(150,000)
Unrestricted net assets...............	(41,315)		(103,970)	(2,290)		(147,575)
Temporarily restricted net assets:						
Accounting research study..........		(31,425)				(31,425)
Student loans...................				(9,000)		(9,000)
Purchase of buildings and equipment. ..			(100,000)			(100,000)
Periods after June 30, 20X5		(3,000)				(3,000)
Permanently restricted net assets........					(90,000)	(90,000)
	0	0	0	0	0	0

The following information pertains to the year ended June 30, 20X6:

a) Students were billed for tuition and fees of $250,000. Of this amount, $3,000 was estimated to be uncollectible.

b) A federal grant of $25,000 was received for an economic outlook study of the area. The research findings are to be summarized in a report to the government granting agency upon completion of the study.

c) Fortune Private University received cash gifts for the following purposes:

Unrestricted as to purpose	75,000
For use in future periods	20,000
For student loans	15,000
For acquisition of plant	150,000
Term endowment	5,000
Endowment in perpetuity, income restricted to use for molecular research	30,000

d) $225,000 cash was received on collection of student fees in item a).

e) The cash gifts for the term endowment and the endowment were placed in long-term investments.

f) Fortune Private University received unconditional promises to give. The payments on unconditional promises to give are due as follows:

	Currently	In Future (Present Value)	Total
Unrestricted as to purpose	4,500	2,000	6,500
For use in future periods		600	600
For accounting research	3,750	3,250	7,000
For acquisition of plant		750	750
Total.............................	8,250	6,600	14,850

g) 1% of the unrestricted and program-restricted promises to give were estimated to be uncollectible. No allowance was considered necessary on the contributions for plant.

h) A donor gave investments having a fair value of $2,000 to create an annuity trust; the related present value of the annuity obligation is $900. Upon the death of the beneficiary, the remaining trust assets are expendable for art gallery operations.

i) A local lawyer provided 5 hours of service to draw up the annuity trust agreement mentioned in item h). She did not charge for her services. She normally would charge a client $750 for consultation on a similar type of agreement. If the lawyer's services were not donated, Fortune would have hired a lawyer to draft an agreement.

j) The university received $5,000 from an individual who restricted its use to research on global warming. If the research project is not initiated within 6 months, the individual requested that the money be returned. The university has not yet undertaken the research project. Two months remain in the time period specified by the donor.

k) Investment income was received:

Yield from operating cash investments	750
Yield on endowment, unrestricted as to use	4,000
Yield on endowment, restricted as to purpose	2,000
Yield on annuity trust created this year	250

l) Payments became due on unconditional promises to give of $3,500, releasing the time restrictions. These promises, received in prior years, were not restricted to any particular purpose.

m) Equipment was purchased with $10,000 donor-restricted cash contributed in prior periods. University policy is to release restrictions over the useful life of the assets.

n) Expenses, excluding depreciation and contributed goods and services, were incurred during the year:

Instruction	100,000
Research—economic outlook study described in item b).	20,000
Research—accounting study described in item f)	15,000
Institutional support	54,000
Student aid	25,000
Academic support	22,000
Student services	18,000

o) Included in the expenses reported in item n) were $20,000, spent on an economic outlook research project financed by a grant and $15,000 for accounting research financed with private gifts.

p) Depreciation of $20,000 was recorded this year. All depreciation charges were related to plant assets acquired by donor-restricted contributions.

q) The actuarial adjustment of the present value of the annuity payable was $30 credit. An annuity payment of $150 was made.

Required:

1. Prepare the journal entries to record the above transactions for the year ended June 30, 20X6. Use the following format:

Entry Letter	Fund	Debit (Dr.)	Credit (Cr.)

2. Prepare a statement of activities for the year ended June 30, 20X6. Assume funds-based reporting is used by Fortune Private University.

Problem 18A-2.   From the information in 18A-1, prepare a statement of financial position for Fortune Private University for the year ended June 30, 20X6. Assume funds-based statements are prepared.

Problem 18A-3.   The pre-closing trial balance of Lambert Private University is as follows:

	Current Funds	Loan Funds	Endowment and Similar Funds	Plant Funds	Total
Cash.	52,500	11,550	11,000	33,500	108,550
Short-term investments	50,200	500	6,000	15,000	71,700
Accounts receivable.	34,400				34,400
Contributions receivable.	5,000				5,000
Inventories of materials	11,000				11,000
Prepaid expenses	28,000				28,000
Loans to students.		5,850			5,850
Assets restricted to investment in land, buildings, and equipment				35,000	35,000
Land, buildings, and equipment.				4,180,000	4,180,000
Long-term investments.			159,210	124,000	283,210
Endowment investments			9,540		9,540
Instruction expenses.	135,300				135,300
Research expenses	14,500				14,500
Academic support expenses	21,700				21,700
Student services expenses.	22,200	50			22,250
Institutional support expenses	20,000				20,000
Operation and maintenance of plant expenses	40,000			20,000	60,000
Student aid expenses.	24,100				24,100
Auxiliary enterprises expenses.	35,000				35,000
Reclassification out—temporarily restricted— satisfaction of program restrictions	7,300	2,400		1,000	10,700
Reclassification out—temporarily restricted— satisfaction of plant acquisition restrictions.				15,000	15,000
Reclassification out—temporarily restricted— satisfaction of time restrictions			2,000		2,000
Mandatory transfers out—principal payments.	2,000				2,000
Discretionary transfers out	30,000				30,000
Total debits.	533,200	20,350	187,750	4,423,500	5,164,800
Accounts payable	24,800			90,000	114,800
Other liabilities.			150		150
Amounts held on behalf of others.			11,000		11,000
Annuities payable.			23,200		23,200
Long-term debt				300,000	300,000
U.S. government grants refundable	5,500	3,000			8,500
Tuition and fees	170,000				170,000
Unrestricted contributions	38,500				38,500
Government appropriations, grants, and contracts	79,500				79,500
Investment income on endowment	5,000		2,000		7,000
Other investment income	25,000	100			25,100
Sales and services of auxiliary enterprises.	40,000				40,000
Contributions—temporarily restricted	7,000	2,500	5,600	9,000	24,100

	Current Funds	Loan Funds	Endowment and Similar Funds	Plant Funds	Total
Investment income on life income and annuity agreements—temporarily restricted			3,000		3,000
Endowment income—temporarily restricted	800		2,000		2,800
Other investment income—temporarily restricted				4,500	4,500
Net realized gains on other investments—temporarily restricted. .		50	950		1,000
Contributions—permanently restricted			12,000	19,000	31,000
Net realized gains on endowment—temporarily restricted			6,000		6,000
Reclassification in—unrestricted—satisfaction of program restrictions	7,300	2,400		1,000	10,700
Reclassification in—unrestricted—satisfaction of plant acquisition restrictions				15,000	15,000
Reclassification in—unrestricted—satisfaction of time restrictions			2,000		2,000
Mandatory transfers in				2,000	2,000
Discretionary transfers in		300	15,000	14,700	30,000
Unrestricted net assets—7/1/X6	107,800	3,900	1,400	260,000	373,100
Temporarily restricted net assets—7/1/X6	22,000	8,100	26,050	3,167,300	3,223,450
Permanently restricted net assets—7/1/X6			77,400	541,000	618,400
Total Credits	533,200	20,350	187,750	4,423,500	5,164,800

Required:

1. Prepare closing entries for each fund.
2. Prepare a statement of activities for the year ended June 30, 20X7, following a columnar format for each fund.

Accounting for Not-for-Profit Organizations: Health Care Providers and Voluntary Health and Welfare Organizations

This chapter discusses accounting and financial reporting for health care entities, voluntary health and welfare organizations, and other not-for-profit organizations including museums, country clubs, and religious organizations. The accounting and financial reporting presentation for all not-for-profit entities has been updated to include the recent standards for contributions and for reporting certain basic information in the general purpose external financial statements.

Accounting for Providers of Health Care Services —Governmental and Private

Advancements in medical practice and increased demand for access to health care services have led to significant growth in the health care industry. Expenditures for medical care now equal more than 10% of the gross national product. Health care entities include hospitals, clinics, continuing-care retirement communities, health maintenance organizations, home health agencies, and nursing homes. Classified by sponsorship or equity structure, health care units fall into three categories:

1. Investor-owned health care entities (or proprietary entities), which are privately owned and operated for a profit.
2. Governmental health care entities (or public entities), which are operated by a governmental unit and accounted for as an enterprise fund, such as a veterans' hospital.
3. Voluntary not-for-profit health care entities, including those with a religious affiliation, which are organized and sustained by members of a community.

Generally accepted accounting principles (GAAP) for hospitals and other health care organizations have evolved through the efforts of two industry professional associations, the American Hospital Association (AHA) and the Health Care Financial Management Association (HFMA), and the American Institute of Certified Public Accountants (AICPA). The AICPA Accounting and Audit Guide, *Health Care Organizations*, issued in June 1996, incorporates Financial Accounting Standards Board (FASB) Statement Nos. 116 and 117, described in the previous chapter. It is currently the principal source of accounting guidelines for private health care entities and governmental health care entities that choose to follow FASB standards.[1]

---

1 GASB Statement No. 20, *Accounting and Financial Reporting for Proprietary Funds and other Governmental Entities that Use Proprietary Fund Accounting* (Norwalk, CT: Governmental Accounting Standards Board, 1993) and GASB Statement No. 29, *The Use of Not-for-Profit Accounting and Financial Reporting Principles by Governmental Entities* (Norwalk, CT: Governmental Accounting Standards Board, 1997), provide guidance on the applicability of FASB and AICPA pronouncements to governmental health care organizations that use enterprise fund accounting.

A modern health care provider may be a complex entity with medical, surgical, research, teaching, and public service aspects. One very unusual element about health care operations is the manner of payment for services. A significant portion of the fees for health care service is paid by a third party, such as Medicare, Medicaid, Blue Cross, or some other insurance provider. Health care entities are reimbursed not on the basis of listed prices, but on the basis of the cost of providing services, as that cost is defined by the third-party payor. A cost determination must be made according to formulas agreed upon in the law (Medicare and Medicaid) or in the contract (other insurance providers). Cost determination requires allocation of overhead, including depreciation. Thus, not-for-profit health care organizations follow the accrual basis of accounting, permitting comparison of results with profit-oriented health care units.

With the many restrictions resulting from donations, endowments, insurance company contracts, and government regulations for reimbursement, the activities of a health care provider have traditionally been accounted for using fund accounting.[2] Health care entities employ two classes of funds:

1. General funds, which account for resources available for general operations, with no restrictions placed upon those resources by an outsider, and other exchange transactions, including resources from government grants and subsidies, tax support, and reimbursements from insurance contracts.

2. Donor-restricted funds, which account for temporarily restricted and permanently restricted resources. This class is subdivided into

   a) *Specific purpose funds, which account for donor-restricted resources temporarily restricted for current but specified operations.*

   b) *Plant replacement and expansion funds, which account for resources temporarily restricted by the donor for the acquisition, construction, or improvement of property, plant, and equipment.*

   c) *Endowment funds, which account for resources that are received to create permanently restricted endowments (whose income only may be expended) and temporarily restricted term endowments (whose principal eventually will become available for expenditure).*

   d) *Other donor-restricted funds such as annuities or life income funds, or loan funds.*

Each fund consists of a set of self-balancing accounts designed to reflect activities within its domain. Although the new FASB guidance on accounting and financial reporting represents a shift away from fund accounting to an organization-wide perspective, health care organizations are expected to continue some form of fund accounting for internal management and reporting. Some may even choose to continue to include information on funds in the external financial reports. To demonstrate the organization-wide emphasis on accounting and financial reporting, and to simplify the presentation, the following discussion assumes no fund structure. The appendix to this chapter illustrates accounting and financial reporting within the existing funds structure of a health care organization.

Classification of Assets and Liabilities

Assets of a health care provider comprise three distinct segments: current assets, assets whose use is limited, and property and equipment. Assets and liabilities are sequenced by liquidity and are classified as current or noncurrent according to GAAP.

---

2 Most hospitals have traditionally used the fund structure described in this chapter. However, other health care entities, such as health maintenance organizations, nursing homes, and home health care agencies may find it unnecessary to use fund accounting.

Assets whose use is limited include assets set aside by the governing board for a specific purpose, sometimes referred to as board-designated assets. For example, the board may authorize that $10,000 be set aside for capital improvements, which would be recorded as follows:

Cash—Limited in Use for Capital Expansion	10,000	
Cash		10,000

The limitation is internal, and, therefore, assets remain unrestricted since "restrictions" can be created only by outside sources. This segment also includes assets resulting from an operational agreement entered into by the board, such as the proceeds of a bond issue limited in use as stipulated by the bond indenture. Assets set aside to provide for self-insurance or to meet depreciation fund requirements with third-party payors belong to this segment as well.

Property and equipment include the physical properties used in operations, along with their accumulated depreciation. Current liabilities may include accounts and notes payable, deposits from patients, and advances from and amounts payable to third-party payors. Long-term liabilities may include notes, mortgages, capital leases, bond payables, and estimated malpractice costs. The net assets of the entire health care organization (which represent the difference between assets and liabilities) are divided into three classes—permanently restricted net assets, temporarily restricted net assets, and unrestricted net assets—based on the existence or absence of donor-imposed restrictions.

Classification of Revenues, Expenses, Gains, and Losses

Revenues, expenses, gains, and losses increase or decrease the net assets of a health care entity. Other events, such as expirations of donor-imposed restrictions, that simultaneously increase one class of net assets and decrease another (reclassifications) are reported as separate items. Revenues and gains may increase unrestricted net assets, temporarily restricted net assets, or permanently restricted net assets. Expenses reduce unrestricted net assets.

Revenues and expenses are considered operating if they relate to the principal activity of providing health care services. Revenues, expenses, gains, or losses from activities that are incidental to the providing of health care services or from events beyond the entity's control are classified as nonoperating.

With the desired detail incorporated in subsidiary support records, the following operating revenue control accounts are available:

1. Patient Service Revenue, the major revenue account for a hospital, in which the gross revenues earned are recorded on an accrual basis at established rates for

    a) *Routine services (room and board, general nursing, and home health care).*

    b) *Other nursing services (in operating, recovery, and delivery rooms).*

    c) *Professional services (physician's care, lab work, pharmacy, blood bank, radiology, dialysis, and physical therapy).*

2. Resident Service Revenue, the major revenue account for a nursing home or continuing-care retirement community. It records rental fees earned from residents or amortization of their advance payment of fees.

3. Other Operating Revenue, which records revenue from services other than health care provided to patients and residents. Also recorded is revenue from sales or services to persons other than patients. Thus, Other Operating Revenue would include

    a) *Revenue from educational programs, such as nursing school tuition.*

    b) *Revenue from specific purpose contributions.*

c) *Revenue from government grants to the extent that the related expenditures are included in operations. Grants that may be refundable if provisions are not met are recorded as a liability. As expenses are incurred, a matching portion of the grant is recorded from liabilities and recognized as current-period revenue.*

d) *Revenue from sales of medical or pharmacy supplies to employees or physicians.*

e) *Revenue from sale of cafeteria meals to employees, medical staff, and visitors.*

f) *Revenue from snack bars, gift shops, parking lots, and other service facilities.*

The control account *Nonoperating Revenue* records revenue not related directly to an entity's principal operations. These items are primarily financial in nature and include unrestricted and donor-restricted pledges, gifts, or grants, unrestricted income from endowment funds, maturing of term endowment funds, income and gains from investments, and gains on sales of hospital property. Investments are reported at market value with both realized and unrealized gains included as part of nonoperating revenue.

Patient Service Revenue is recorded on a gross charge basis. A third-party payor, such as Blue Cross, may reimburse a hospital on the basis of predetermined amounts that are less than the original gross charges for described services. The difference between the gross revenue and the amount expected to be collected from the third party is referred to as the *contractual adjustment*. It is deducted from the gross patient service revenue prior to preparing the financial statements. A credit is made to an allowance account in order to reduce the receivables to net expected. Also deducted from gross revenue and disclosed in the footnotes are adjustments for charitable services to indigent patients from whom collection will not be possible and courtesy allowances granted to hospital employees. The Provision for Bad Debts is reported as an expense. The objective of grouping these items is to be able to show net patient service revenue, an expense for uncollectibles, and net receivables on the financial statements.

Payments made to a health care unit by third parties include reimbursement for depreciation. Often, this portion of the payment is limited in use to replacing or adding to property, plant, or equipment. Total billings are included in revenue of the general funds to permit matching of total revenues and expenses. When collected, the specified portion is transferred to a special account with the following entry:

```
Cash—Assets Whose Use Is Limited by Agreement with
    Third-Party Payors for Funded Depreciation  . . . . . . . . . . . .    XXX
        Cash  . . . . . . . . . . . . . . . . . . . . . . . . . . . . . . . . . . . .             XXX
```

Titles given to operating expenses of a health care facility may differ, depending upon the nature of the facility's activities. With supporting details in subsidiary records, the following control accounts are common to many health care organizations:

1. Nursing Services Expense, for the cost of nursing services directly related to the patient or resident.

2. Other Professional Services Expense, for professional services indirectly related to the patient or resident, such as lab fees or pharmacy costs. Note that some hospitals combine the two accounts, Nursing Services Expense and Other Professional Services Expense, into one account labeled Professional Care of Patients Expense.

3. General Services Expense, for costs of the cafeteria, food service, and housekeeping. Where food services constitute a major cost, some hospitals prefer to segregate them into the account Dietary Services Expense.

4. Fiscal Services Expense, for admitting, cashiering, and accounting costs.

5. Administrative Services Expense, for insurance, taxes, and personnel costs.

6. Depreciation Expense, if not already allocated.
7. Interest Expense, if not already allocated.
8. Provision for Bad Debts, if not already allocated.

For example, to record salaries earned, a debit would be made to each of the first five control accounts, with subsidiary records indicating that the charge was for salaries. Expenses may be reported on the face of the statement of activities (operating statement) using either a functional presentation, such as Nursing Services Expense, or a natural classification (salaries, supplies, etc.) If a natural classification is used, health care organizations are required to disclose detail on the functional classifications in the footnotes.

Accounting for Contributions Received

Health care entities may receive gifts or donations that meet the definition of an unconditional contribution. These contributions may be unrestricted as to use or may be limited to a specific use. Unrestricted contributions are recognized at fair market value with a credit to Other Operating Revenue—Unrestricted or Nonoperating Revenue—Unrestricted, depending on whether these contributions are deemed to be ongoing major or central activities, or peripheral or incidental transactions.

Bequests and gifts restricted by the donor as to use for a) specific operating purposes, b) additions to plant, c) endowments, or d) annuities or life incomes are recorded when received at their fair market value with a credit to Revenues (other operating or nonoperating)—Temporarily Restricted or Revenues (other operating or nonoperating)—Permanently Restricted.[3] When expenditures are made consistent with the donors' stipulation, or when term endowments become available, a reclassification is made from the temporarily restricted net asset category to an unrestricted net asset category. Should resources from expired term endowments be restricted further, for example, to purchase equipment, they will remain in the temporarily restricted net asset category. Resources temporarily restricted for the purchase or construction of property, plant, and equipment are released from restriction in the period the asset is placed into service. Donor-restricted contributions in which the restriction will be met in the current period may be classified as unrestricted revenues. Some promises to give are conditional and will not be recognized until the condition is met.

Activities of health care providers are enhanced by volunteers who donate their time and abilities. Donated services must be recognized if the services received a) create or enhance nonfinancial assets or b) require specialized skills, are provided by individuals possessing those skills who are scheduled and supervised in much the same way as employees, and would typically need to be purchased if not provided by donation. Services provided by doctors, nurses, and other professionals in a health care entity may meet the above criteria. Incidental services provided by other volunteers for such things as fund raising or other activities that would not otherwise be staffed by employees would not meet the criteria. For example, most voluntary service by senior citizens, candy stripers, and others is not recorded. When an institution is operated by a religious group whose members receive token payment or no payment at all, the value of donated services should be charged to the proper expense account and credited to other operating revenue or nonoperating revenue depending on the nature of the donated services.

---

3 Prior to FASB Statement No. 116, health care organizations credited the appropriate temporarily restricted or permanently restricted fund balance account. When the donor-restricted assets were used for their intended purpose, they were recorded as a transfer or, more commonly, as a direct debit to the appropriate fund balance. The transfer was recorded in the general fund as a credit to Other Operating Revenue or Nonoperating Revenue as appropriate. Revenue recognition was delayed until expenditures were incurred. Transfers for capital purchases were not recorded as revenue, but as increases in the fund balance account of the general funds.

Donated items may also be unrestricted or restricted. Examples of donated items in a health care entity are laboratory and pharmaceutical supplies donated by drug companies or associations of doctors; donated property, plant, and equipment; and contributed use of facilities. Donated items are recognized at fair market value with a credit to Other Operating Revenue—Unrestricted or to Nonoperating Revenue—Unrestricted, depending on whether the donations constitute the entity's ongoing major or central operations or are peripheral or incidental transactions. If donated items have a donor-specified use, they may be temporarily restricted until they are used for their intended purpose. Unrestricted donations of property are recognized as Nonoperating Revenue—Unrestricted. If donations of property are donor restricted, the same entry is made but with a credit to temporarily or permanently restricted revenues.

Malpractice Claims

The current environment in relation to medical malpractice claims has caused insurance companies to dramatically raise premiums to health care providers or to limit the amount of risk they are willing to insure. To find a health care provider that is fully insured against medical malpractice losses is a rarity. Many have dropped their malpractice insurance or have adopted other approaches for protection. Some pay losses as they occur. Others establish trust funds with a trustee.

The accounting issue is to determine when the costs of malpractice claims should be recognized. An AICPA statement stipulates that:

> The ultimate costs of malpractice claims, which include costs associated with litigating or settling claims, should be accrued when the incidents occur that give rise to the claims, if it can be determined that it is probable that liabilities have been incurred and if the amounts of the losses can be reasonably estimated.4

If the health care provider is covered by insurance, the premiums applicable to the reporting period are expensed, plus an amount for estimated claim costs for the reporting period not covered by the insurance arrangement. The entry to record claim costs is

```
Medical Malpractice Costs
    (or Administrative Services Expense) . . . . . . . . . . . . . . . .      XXX
        Cash (or Unexpired Premiums) . . . . . . . . . . . . . . . . . .              XXX
        Estimated Additional Malpractice Liability . . . . . . . . . . .              XXX
```

Although hospitals report expenses on a functional basis by major program area, the medical malpractice costs are sometimes segregated from the other administrative services costs to emphasize their critical nature.

As a result of the large settlements granted in malpractice cases, some health care organizations became self-insured, establishing a trust account with an outside trustee who determines funding requirements. Two entries are necessary. The first establishes the estimated claim costs and liability:

```
Medical Malpractice Costs
    (or Administrative Services Expense) . . . . . . . . . . . . . . . .      XXX
        Estimated Malpractice Liability . . . . . . . . . . . . . . . . . .              XXX
```

---

4 Statement of Position 87-1, *Accounting for Asserted and Unasserted Medical Malpractice Claims of Health Care Providers and Related Issues* (New York: American Institute of Certified Public Accountants, March 16, 1987), par. 21.

The second entry records the contribution to the trustee:

Cash—Limited in Use Under Malpractice
  Funding Arrangement XXX
    Cash XXX

The amount in the trust account is reported in the balance sheet as an asset whose use is limited. Claims expected to be paid during the next operating cycle are classified as current liabilities, while the remainder of the liability balance is shown as noncurrent.

Whether the health care provider is covered by insurance, pays losses as they occur, or has a trust fund arrangement, the amount of the expense should reflect the best estimate of ultimate costs of malpractice claims related to incidents that occurred during the reporting period.

Illustrative Entries

To illustrate the recording of events for a hospital, the year's affairs of Columbia Hospital are summarized next. The illustrative entries employ broad categories of control accounts and natural expense classification.

Event		Entry		
1. Gross charges to patients are for:		Accounts Receivable.............	5,200,000	
		Patient Service Revenue		5,000,000
Daily patient services	$3,200,000	Other Operating Revenue		
Other nursing services............	500,000	—Unrestricted		200,000
Professional services	1,300,000			
Other nonmedical services	200,000			
Total....................	$5,200,000			
2. Estimates are made for:		Provision for Bad Debts............	22,000	
		Contractual Adjustments	380,000	
Contractual adjustments...........	$ 380,000	Allowance for Uncollectible		
Uncollectibles..................	22,000	Receivables and Third-Party		
Total....................	$ 402,000	Contractual Adjustments		402,000
3. An analysis of accounts receivable shows:		Cash........................	3,800,000	
		Allowance for Uncollectible		
Cash collected.................	$3,800,000	Receivables and Third-Party		
Contractual adjustments with		Contractual Adjustments	290,000	
third-party payors	200,000	Accounts Receivable.............		4,090,000
Uncollectible	90,000			
Total....................	$4,090,000			
4. The hospital determined that $200,000 of the services was to patients who met hospital criteria for charity care.		Charity Services	200,000	
		Accounts Receivable.............		200,000
5. Inventory purchases amounted to $700,000; payments totaled $690,000.		Inventories	700,000	
		Cash........................		690,000
		Accounts Payable		10,000
6. Drugs and supplies costing $720,000 are requisitioned.		Drugs and Supplies Used	720,000	
		Inventories		720,000

(continued)

Event	Entry		

7. Salaries earned (ignore payroll deductions) amounted to $3,000,000, of which $2,950,000 is paid.	Wages, Salaries, and Benefits . . . .
	  Cash . . . .
	  Accrued Expenses . . . .
		3,000,000	2,950,000
			50,000

8. Outside professional fees of $300,000 are paid.	Purchased Services . . . . Cash	300,000	300,000

9. Jacob Pharmaceutical Co. donated $2,000 of medicines to Columbia Hospital. Such contributions constitute a major ongoing activity of the hospital. If not donated, these medicines would have to be purchased.	Inventories . . . .
	  Other Operating Revenues—Unrestricted
	  (Contributions) . . . .
		2,000	2,000

10. Unrestricted earnings from long-term investments totaled $540,000.	Cash . . . .
	  Nonoperating Revenues—
	    Unrestricted (Investment Earnings) . .
		540,000	540,000

11. Payments are made on:
  Current installment of long-term debt . . $ 80,000
  Notes payable   200,000
  Interest expense   66,000
    Total $346,000
	Current Installment of Long-Term Debt . . .
	Notes Payable . . . .
	Interest Expense . . . .
	  Cash . . . .
		80,000
		200,000
		66,000
			346,000

12. A donor promised to give Columbia $50,000 annually for each of the next four years (recorded at present value).	Contributions Receivable . . . .
	  Nonoperating Revenues—
	    Unrestricted (Contributions) . . . . . .
		165,606	165,606

13. The hospital was recently served with a malpractice lawsuit. A prominent local trial attorney decided to assist in the defense of the hospital. Normal fees are $150 per hour. 100 total hours were devoted to the case.	Purchased Services . . . .
	  Nonoperating Revenues—
	    Unrestricted (Contributions) . . . . . .
		15,000	15,000

14. Equipment costing $110,000 is purchased for cash.	Property and Equipment . . . . Cash	110,000	110,000
15. Depreciation expense provision for the year is $400,000.	Depreciation Expense . . . . Accumulated Depreciation	400,000	400,000

16. The current portion of long-term debt is reclassified as current from:
 	
  Bonds payable . . . . $ 50,000
  Mortgage note payable   30,000
    Total . . . . $ 80,000
	Bonds Payable . . . .
	Mortgage Note Payable . . . .
	  Current Installment of Long-Term Debt .
		50,000
		30,000
			80,000

17. Professional services donated to the hospital were recognized:
  Nursing services . . . . $ 17,000
  Other professional medical services .   3,000
	Wages, Salaries, and Benefits . . . .
	  Other Operating Revenue—
	    Unrestricted (Contributions) . . . . . .
		20,000	20,000

18. A provision for medical malpractice costs of $450,000 is recorded. The hospital is self-insured.	Medical Malpractice Costs . . . . Estimated Malpractice Liability	450,000	450,000

Event	Entry		
19. A malpractice self-insurance trust at Third Bank is increased by $230,000.	Cash—Limited in Use Under Malpractice Funding Arrangement . . . . Cash	230,000	230,000
20. Third-party payor reimbursements of $250,000 are to be set aside for plant replacement.	Cash—Limited in Use by Agreement with Third-Party Payors for Plant . . . . . . Cash	250,000	250,000
21. Columbia received $50,000 cash from a donor to cover operating costs of the student nursing unit.	Cash . . . . Other Operating Revenue—Temporarily Restricted (Contributions)	50,000	50,000
22. Investment earnings are received in the amount of $75,000 restricted for cancer research.	Cash . . . . Nonoperating Revenues—Temporarily Restricted (Investment Earnings). . . .	75,000	75,000
23. $500,000 was donated to Columbia Hospital for investments in long-term securities as a pure endowment.	Cash . . . . Nonoperating Revenues—Permanently Restricted (Endowment Contributions)	500,000	500,000
24. Securities were purchased.	Endowment Investments. . . . . Cash	500,000	500,000
25. A term endowment expired. The $150,000 principal is now available for use by the hospital administration.	Reclassification Out—Temporarily Restricted—Satisfaction of Time Restrictions. . . . Reclassification In—Unrestricted—Satisfaction of Time Restriction	150,000	150,000
26. Receipts of $200,000 and an unconditional promise to give $100,000 were recorded. Gifts were to be used for operating room equipment.	Contributions Receivable. . . . . Cash . . . . Other Operating Revenues—Temporarily Restricted (Contributions)	100,000 200,000	300,000
27. Operating room equipment was purchased.	Equipment . . . . Cash	200,000	200,000
28. The AICPA audit guide requires that donor restrictions are released when the asset is placed in service.	Reclassification Out—Temporarily Restricted—Satisfaction of Plant Acquisition Restrictions . . . . Reclassification In—Unrestricted—Satisfaction of Plant Acquisition Restrictions	200,000	200,000
29. The first-year depreciation on the above operating room equipment was recorded.	Depreciation Expense. . . . . Accumulated Depreciation.	40,000	40,000
30. A $400,000 grant from a local manufacturer to be used for a patient nutritional study was received. Results of the study will be used to educate the public, not for the benefit of the donor.	Cash . . . . Other Operating Revenues—Temporarily Restricted (Contributions)	400,000	400,000

(continued)

Event	Entry		
31. Expenses were incurred for the patient nutritional study. Donor restrictions are expired to match specified expenses. A reclassification entry records the expiration of donor restrictions.	Wages, Salaries, and Benefits . . . . Drugs and Supplies Used . . . . Purchased Services . . . . Cash	25,000 10,000 15,000	50,000

	Reclassification Out—Temporarily
	   Restricted—Satisfaction of Program
	   Restrictions . . . .
	Reclassification In—Unrestricted—
	   Satisfaction of Program Restrictions .
		50,000	50,000

32. At year-end, Columbia allocates natural expenses to the functional areas based upon which program they benefited when incurred.	Nursing Services . . . .
	Other Professional Services . . . .
	General Services . . . .
	Fiscal Services . . . .
	Administrative Services . . . .
	   Wages, Salaries, and Benefits . . . . . .
	   Drugs and Supplies Used . . . .
	   Purchased Services . . . .
	   Medical Malpractice Costs . . . .
	   Depreciation Expense . . . .
	   Interest . . . .
	   Provision for Bad Debts . . . .
		1,774,000
		1,240,000
		995,000
		283,000
		791,000
			3,045,000
			730,000
			330,000
			450,000
			440,000
			66,000
			22,000

33. Closing entries. Each class of net assets is closed separately.	Patient Service Revenue—Unrestricted . . .
	Other Operating Revenue—Unrestricted .
	Nonoperating Revenue—Unrestricted . . .
	
	Reclassifications In—Unrestricted—
	   Satisfaction of Equipment Acquisition
	   Restrictions . . . .
	Reclassifications In—Unrestricted—
	   Satisfaction of Time Restrictions . . . . .
	Reclassifications In—Unrestricted—
	      Satisfaction of Program Restrictions .
	   Charity Care . . . .
	   Contractual Adjustments . . . .
	   Nursing Services . . . .
	   Other Professional Services . . . .
	   General Services . . . .
	   Fiscal Services . . . .
	   Administrative Services . . . .
	   Unrestricted Net Assets . . . .
		5,000,000
		222,000
		720,606
		
		200,000
		
		150,000
		
		50,000
			
			200,000
			380,000
			1,774,000
			1,240,000
			995,000
			283,000
			791,000
			679,606

	Other Operating Revenue—Temporarily
	   Restricted . . . .
	Nonoperating Revenue—Temporarily
	   Restricted . . . .
	Reclassifications Out—Temporarily
	   Restricted—Satisfaction of Equipment
	   Acquisition Restrictions . . . .
	Reclassifications Out—Temporarily
	   Restricted—Satisfaction of Time
	   Restrictions . . . .
		750,000
		
		75,000
			
			200,000
			
			150,000

Reclassifications Out—Temporarily Restricted—Satisfaction of Program Restrictions	50,000
Temporarily Restricted Net Assets	**425,000**

Nonoperating Revenue—Permanently Restricted Endowment Contributions	500,000	
Permanently Restricted Net Assets		**500,000**

Financial Statements of a Health Care Provider

The financial statements of a health care provider include a statement of activities which presents organization-wide totals for changes in unrestricted net assets, temporarily restricted net assets, and permanently restricted net assets. The form is straightforward, showing operating revenues minus operating expenses as an increase (decrease) in net assets from operations. The nonoperating revenue is added to this amount. Expenses are reported using functional classifications. Further information on natural classifications of expenses is suggested footnote disclosure. In practice, comparative financial statements would be presented. To conserve space, the results of only one year's activities are shown in Illustration 19-1.

Illustration 19-1
Fitale Hospital
Statement of Activities
For Year Ended December 31, 20X5

	Unrestricted	Temporarily Restricted	Permanently Restricted	Total
Revenues, gains, and other support:				
Patient service revenue (net of adjustments)	$ 4,420,000			$ 4,420,000
Other operating revenue	222,000	$ 750,000		972,000
Net assets released from restrictions:				
Satisfaction of program restrictions.	50,000	(50,000)		0
Satisfaction of equipment acquisitions restrictions	200,000	(200,000)		0
Expiration of time restrictions.	150,000	(150,000)		0
Total operating revenues, and other support.	$ 5,042,000	$ 350,000		$ 5,392,000
Expenses and losses:				
Nursing services.	$ 1,774,000			$ 1,774,000
Other professional services.	1,240,000			1,240,000
General services.	995,000			995,000
Fiscal services	283,000			283,000
Administrative services.	791,000			791,000
Total expenses and losses	$ 5,083,000			$ 5,083,000
Increase (decrease) in net assets from operations	$ (41,000)	350,000		$ 309,000
Nonoperating revenue.	$ 720,606	$75,000	$ 500,000	$ 1,295,606
Increase (decrease) in net assets.	**679,606**	**425,000**	**500,000**	**1,604,606**
Net assets at beginning of year	**4,538,000**	**879,000**	**3,560,000**	**8,977,000**
Net assets at end of year	**$5,217,606**	**$1,304,000**	**$4,060,000**	**$10,581,606**

In addition to the statement of activities, a health care organization provides a statement of financial position and a statement of cash flows. The statement of financial position, shown in Illustration 19-2, includes assets and liabilities of all funds. The sequence begins with current assets, assets whose use is limited, property and equipment, and, possibly, other assets. Also shown are the current and other liabilities of the organization and the three classes of net assets, which represent the equity of the hospital.

The statement of cash flows in Illustration 19-3 follows FASB Statement No. 95 guidance, which encourages the use of the direct method to present cash flows, although it does accept the indirect method. FASB Statement No. 117 states that the provisions of FASB Statement No. 95 also should be applied to not-for-profit health care entities amended to include among the list of cash inflows from financing activities receipts from contributions and investment income that by donor stipulation are restricted for the purpose of acquisition, construction, improving property, plant, and equipment, or other long-lived assets, or establishing or increasing a permanent endowment or term endowment.

Illustration 19-2
Fitale Hospital
Statement of Financial Position
As of December 31, 20X5

Assets:

Cash and cash equivalents	$ 735,000
Accounts and interest receivable	908,000
Inventories	81,000
Contributions receivable	265,606
Short-term investments	400,000
Assets restricted to investment in land, buildings, and equipment	445,000
Assets limited in use under malpractice funding agreement	440,000
Property, plant, and equipment (net of depreciation)	5,250,000
Long-term investments	540,000
Endowment investments	4,060,000
Total assets	**$13,124,606**

Liabilities and net assets:

Accounts payable	$53,000
Current installments of long-term debts	80,000
Accrued expenses	100,000
Notes payable	500,000
Estimated malpractice costs	640,000
Long-term debt	1,170,000
Total liabilities	**$ 2,543,000**

Net assets:

Unrestricted	**$ 5,217,606**
Temporarily restricted	**1,304,000**
Permanently restricted	**4,060,000**
Total net assets	**$10,581,606**
Total liabilities and net assets	**$13,124,606**

Illustration 19-3
Fitale Hospital
Statement of Cash Flows
For Year Ended December 31, 20X5

Cash flows from operating activities:	
Cash received from patients and third-party payors	$3,800,000
Cash received from contributions	450,000
Interest and dividends received	615,000
Cash paid to employees and suppliers	(3,990,000)
Interest Paid	(66,000)
Net cash provided by (used for) operating activities	**$ 809,000**
Cash flows from investing activities:	
Purchases of investments	$ (500,000)
Purchases of land, buildings, and equipment	(310,000)
Net cash provided by (used for) investing activities	**$(810,000)**
Cash flows from financing activities:	
Payments on notes payable	$ (200,000)
Payments on long-term debt	(80,000)
Contributions received restricted for endowment	500,000
Contributions received restricted for property, plant, and equipment	200,000
Net cash provided by (used for) financing activities	**$ 420,000**
Net Increase (decrease) in cash and cash equivalents	**$ 419,000**
Cash and cash equivalents at beginning of year	**316,000**
Cash and cash equivalents at end of year	**$ 735,000**
Reconciliation of change in net assets to net cash provided by (used for) operating activities:	
Change in net assets	$1,604,606
Adjustments to reconcile change in net assets to net cash provided by (used for) operating activities:	
Depreciation	440,000
Increase in accounts receivable	(798,000)
Increase in contributions receivable	(265,606)
Decrease in inventories	18,000
Increase in accounts payable and accrued liabilities	60,000
Contributions received restricted for endowment	(500,000)
Contributions received restricted for property, plant, and equipment	(200,000)
Increase in liability for estimated malpractice costs	450,000
Net cash provided by (used for operating activities)	$ 809,000

Accounting for Voluntary Health and Welfare Organizations

To qualify as a voluntary health and welfare organization (VHWO), two criteria must be met. First, a primary source of revenue should be contributions from donors who do not directly benefit from the organization's programs. A community symphony orchestra, for instance, would not qualify because it derives a large share of its revenue from box office receipts. Second, the program must be in the area of health, welfare, or community service, such as care for the elderly, the indigent, or the handicapped, or projects to protect the environment.

Funds

Although most contributions are made with no restrictions attached, some donations specify the purpose for which they must be expended. To segregate resources and demonstrate compliance with external restrictions, financial reports must include information on three classes of net assets: unrestricted, temporarily restricted, and permanently restricted. Many organizations will continue to further segregate resources with the use of fund accounting for internal management reporting. Whether or not funds are used, the external financial statements must report on the organization as a whole. To emphasize this organization-wide emphasis, and to simplify presentation, the illustrative entries assume no fund structure. The appendix to this chapter illustrates accounting and financial reporting for voluntary health and welfare organizations assuming the following funds structure:

1. *Current unrestricted fund*, which accounts for resources that have no external restrictions and are available for current operations at the discretion of the governing board.
2. *Current restricted fund*, which accounts for assets received from outside sources for a current operating purpose specified by the donor.
3. *Land, building, and equipment fund*, which accounts for the activity related to fixed assets.
4. *Endowment fund*, which accounts for permanently restricted endowment principal and temporarily restricted term endowments.
5. *Agency (custodian) fund*, which accounts for assets that do not belong to the organization holding them.

Accounting Principles and Procedures

The full accrual basis of accounting should be used in accounting and reporting for VHWOs if the reports are to be considered as prepared in accordance with GAAP.

The dependence upon public support for the majority of its resources influences the accounting for a VHWO. Two major categories are used to record and communicate inflows of resources: public support and revenues. *Public support* is the inflow of resources from voluntary donors who receive no direct, personal benefit from the organization's usual programs in exchange for their contributions. *Revenues* are inflows of resources resulting from a charge for service from financial activities or from other exchange transactions.

A significant aspect of accounting and reporting for VHWOs is that financial reports must show expenses on a program basis. As a result of this requirement, the costs of each program and supporting service are available, and the effectiveness with which the organization's resources have been managed can be measured.

Public Support

The following accounts are used to record receipts of assets in the public support category:

1. Contributions
2. Special Events Support
3. Legacies and Bequests
4. Received from Federated and Nonfederated Campaigns

Contributions.   Contributions received are recognized as public support in the period received and as assets, decreases of liabilities, or expenses, depending on the form of the benefits received.[5] Contributions are measured at their fair market value and reported as either unrestricted, temporarily restricted, or permanently restricted, depending on donor stipulations. Contributions also include unconditional promises to give (pledges). Therefore, unconditional promises to give must also be recognized as support in the period received. Contributions may be unrestricted or restricted for a specific purpose. Contributions that have no donor-imposed restrictions attached to them are reported as unrestricted. Contributions that have donor-imposed restrictions attached to them must be classified as temporarily or permanently restricted based on the nature of the restriction.

Cash collections that do not involve a previous promise to give are credited to the account Contributions. VHWOs also receive pledges for contributions, which are recorded at the gross amount as Contributions Receivable, with a credit to Contributions. A provision and an allowance for estimated uncollectible pledges are established based on historical collection experience. The provision for uncollectible pledges is an expense account, while the allowance is a contra-account to Pledges Receivable.

Expiration of donor-restrictions must be recognized in the period in which the restriction expires. The expiration of a restriction may be based on the lapse of time or the fulfillment of a stipulated purpose, or both. Recognition of an expiration of donor restrictions is done with a reclassification entry. Reclassifications result in an increase in the unrestricted class of net assets and a decrease in temporarily restricted net assets class. Such a reclassification increases unrestricted net assets to "match" the decrease resulting from the stipulated expense.

Temporarily restricted unconditional promises to give (pledges) are reclassified to unrestricted in the period in which the unconditional promise is received or the restriction lapses. A gift or promise to give that involves a condition is not considered a contribution until the condition is met and is, therefore, not recognized as an increase in net assets in the period in which it is received, but is disclosed in the footnotes.

Securities and other property received should be recorded at fair market value at the time of receipt. These assets are most likely to be received as temporarily or permanently restricted contributions. The donor may restrict not only the purpose but also the timing of use. If the donation is not available for use until some future fiscal period, it is recorded as Contributions—Temporarily Restricted. The amount is released from restriction (unclassified) in the period when it becomes available.

Contributed works of art, historical treasures, and similar assets need not be recognized as contributions "if the donated items are added to collections that a) are held for public exhibition, education, or research rather than financial gain, b) are protected and preserved, c) are subject to an organization policy that requires the proceeds from sales of collection items to be used to acquire other items for collections."[6]

Although organizations can choose whether or not to capitalize their collections, the choice must be applied to all collections. Capitalization may be done retroactively or prospectively.

Common to VHWOs is the donation of materials to be used in providing service or to be processed for subsequent sale. These materials should be recorded as inventory, with a credit to Unrestricted Contributions at their market value when received, provided that they are substantial in amount and a measurable value for them can be established, either by sale shortly thereafter or by appraisal. An example would be the donation of clothing or household goods to Goodwill Industries.

---

5 A contribution is defined as an "unconditional transfer of cash or other assets to an entity or a settlement or cancellation of its liabilities in a voluntary nonreciprocal transfer by another entity acting other than as an owner" (FASB Statement No. 116, par. 5).

6 *Ibid.*, par. 11.

Occasionally, a VHWO will be permitted to use building facilities rent free. In this situation, both the contribution and the rent expense should be recorded at fair rental value, usually equivalent to the amount that normally would be charged for rent. Donated fixed assets for which title is received, such as equipment or land and building, should be entered as an unrestricted, temporarily restricted, or permanently restricted contribution at market value, depending upon the donor's stipulations. Expiration of donor restrictions will occur either at the time the asset is placed in service or over the asset's useful life. Permanent restrictions do not expire.

Although the range of personal services that volunteers donate varies between organizations, these services should be recorded if they are significant and if the following criteria are met:

1. The services received create or enhance nonfinancial assets, or

2. The services received require specialized skills, are provided by individuals possessing those skills, and would typically need to be purchased if not provided by donation. (Usually, the individuals performing such services are treated in a similar fashion to employees; they have schedules, assigned duties, are supervised, etc.)

Promises to give services are also included. Recognizing contributed services that are specialized and would need to be purchased indicates to readers of the financial statements the impact these contributions have on the organization. It also indicates the need for future cash outflows in the event these services are no longer contributed.

If the criteria are met, donated services are recorded with a debit to an expense account, such as Salary Expense, and a credit to Contributions. Contributed services received that are not required to be recognized as revenues are disclosed at their fair value in the footnotes to the financial statements.

Special Events Support.   Another subdivision of the public support category covers an organization's special fund-raising events, in which the participant has the opportunity to receive something of value in exchange for a contribution. Raffles, dinners, bingo games, and bake sales are examples of special events. The gross inflow of resources is credited to Special Events Support in the fund that it is to benefit. Direct costs of the event, excluding promotional costs, are charged to Cost of Special Events. Comparing these two balances permits one to judge the effectiveness of the event. It also determines that portion of the proceeds that are contributions to the organization. If such "special events" are peripheral or incidental, they may be disclosed net of costs (which used to be the general practice), but, if they are ongoing and major activities, then gross revenue is recorded and direct costs of those activities are considered fund-raising expenses. Promotional costs, such as advertising or the salaries of employees involved in the event, are charged against fund-raising expense. The portion of the budget consumed by fund-raising expenses must also be revealed.

Legacies and Bequests.   Every VHWO hopes that its programs will be so deserving that they will encourage donors to make major contributions of personal property or real property through their wills. Since these items tend to be more substantial in amount, the audit guide recommends that such contributions be shown as a separate item of public support under Legacies and Bequests. They are entered as a credit to that account when the organization is reasonably certain of the amount to be received. Such contributions are classified as unrestricted, temporarily restricted, or permanently restricted based on donor stipulations.

Received from Federated and Nonfederated Campaigns.   The final item considered as public support is the amount received from federated (associated) and nonfederated organizations. This amount is credited to Received from Federated and Nonfederated Campaigns. An amount allocated by United Way to a health and welfare organization would be an example of support received from a federated organization. An amount raised by independent, professional fund-raising groups would be an illustration of resources received from nonfederated campaigns. Usually, contributions received from federated and nonfederated campaigns are unrestricted.

Revenues

In addition to public support, resources may be received from exchange transactions that are classified as unrestricted revenue. These resources would include the following accounts:

1. Membership Dues Revenue for dues charged members to join and use facilities or receive publications.
2. Program Services Fees for amounts charged clients for services of the organization, such as consulting, testing, or advising.
3. Sales of Publications and Supplies for proceeds from the sales of these items.

Investment transaction revenue, classified as unrestricted or restricted, could include the following accounts:

1. Investment Revenue for interest, dividends, and other earnings.
2. Realized Gain on Investment Transactions for gains from the sale or exchange of investments.
3. Net Increase (or Decrease) in Carrying Value of Investments for the unrealized appreciation (or depreciation) of investments if they are carried at market value.

Each of the items of investment transactions revenue would be recorded as unrestricted or restricted, depending on donor stipulations. Thus, the unrestricted revenue from an endowment would be recorded with a credit to Investment Revenue—Unrestricted. Restricted investment revenue is reported as temporarily or permanently restricted in compliance with the donor's wishes.

FASB Statement No. 124 requires VHWOs to carry their investments at market value.[7] Cost includes not only the total cost of purchased investments but also the market value at the date of receipt of donated investments. When there is a relatively permanent reduction in market value, the impairment to cost should be recorded. The unrealized appreciation (or depreciation) is shown separately in Net Increase (or Decrease) in Carrying Value of Investments. Realized and unrealized gains and losses on all investments are considered increases or decreases in unrestricted net assets unless restricted by donor or law.

Program and Supporting Services Costs

VHWOs exist to render service or to conduct programs. Their operating statements will not show natural expenses, such as salaries or rent, but will show the cost of each program or service the organization provides—the costs in which the general public, the contributors, and the controlling agencies are primarily interested. For example, the operating statement of an environmental protection association might show the cost of conducting a program to reduce river pollution or to provide an animal and bird sanctuary. These projects fall in an expense grouping called Program Services. The other expense grouping shown on an operating statement is referred to as Supporting Services, which includes fund-raising costs, management and general

---

7 FASB Statement No. 124, *Investments of Not-for-Profit Organizations* (Norwalk, CT: Financial Accounting Standards Board, 1995).

costs, and membership development activities for the overall direction of the organization. Management and general activities include all management, financing, and administrative activities, except for direct activities of programs or fund raising. Fund-raising activities include publicizing and conducting fund-raising campaigns; maintaining donor mailing lists; conducting special fund-raising events; preparing and distributing fund-raising materials, and other activities involved with soliciting contributions. Membership development activities include soliciting for prospective members and membership dues, membership relations, and similar activities.

Individual expenses, such as salaries or rent, are recorded in the respective natural expense accounts in much the same way that they would be recorded in the accounts of profit entities. All expenses are considered reductions in unrestricted net assets. Therefore, when expenses are recorded for purposes stipulated by donors, a reclassification of temporarily restricted to unrestricted net assets is recorded. At the end of the fiscal year, the expenses are allocated to the individual programs conducted and to the supporting services of management, fund raising, and membership development. Allocation of joint costs should be on some rational basis, such as assigning salaries on the basis of time expended, allotting rental charges on the basis of floor space, or apportioning supplies expense on the basis of consumption. However, it is not always simple to allocate costs.

The public has been deluged with informational materials that attempt to educate the reader about proper health habits to avoid disease or infection, birth control and other family planning issues, and the need to protect endangered species or the environment. Included in much of this material is a fund-raising appeal. A question arises as to whether the total cost of sending such literature should be charged to the program publicized or to fund raising, or whether it should be allocated between them. Since board members, donors, and the general public pay particular attention to the percentages of revenue consumed by administrative and fund-raising purposes, the desire to keep those percentages at a minimum is understandable.

One area of concern involves fund-raising costs being "hidden" within the program and management activities. An exposure draft issued on September 10, 1993, requires, among other things, that:

> Costs of all materials and activities that include a fund-raising appeal be reported as fund-raising costs . . . unless a bona fide program or management function has been conducted in conjunction with the appeal. If a bona fide program or management function has been conducted, the joint costs should be allocated.8

It also discusses acceptable allocation methods and lists disclosure requirements if joint costs are allocated.

Closing Entries

After all expenses have been assigned, an entry is made to close the expense accounts and charge each of the expenses to the individual programs and supporting services. For the environmental protection association used earlier as an example, the following entry might be recorded:

River Pollution Program Expense	XXX	
Animal and Bird Sanctuary Program Expense	XXX	
Management and General Services Expense	XXX	
Fund-Raising Services Expense	XXX	
Salary Expense, Supplies Expense, etc.		XXX

8 Exposure Draft, *Accounting for Costs of Materials and Activities of Not-for-Profit Organizations and State and Local Government Entities That Include a Fund-Raising Appeal* (New York: American Institute of Certified Public Accountants, 1993), par. 15.

The final closing entries close support and revenue accounts, as well as the program and services accounts, to the appropriate net asset classification. The closing entry for the Unrestricted Net Assets of the environmental protection association might be as follows:

Contributions—Unrestricted	XXX	
Legacies and Bequests—Unrestricted	XXX	
Membership Dues Revenue	XXX	
Investment Revenue—Unrestricted	XXX	
Reclassification In—Unrestricted—Satisfaction		
of Donor Restrictions	XXX	
River Pollution Program Expense		XXX
Animal and Bird Sanctuary Program Expense		XXX
Management and General Services Expense		XXX
Fund-Raising Services Expense		XXX
Unrestricted Net Assets		XXX

If the board of directors should decide to designate a specified sum of the Unrestricted Net Assets for a future program to reduce air pollution, the following entries are recorded:

Undesignated Net Assets	XXX	
Unrestricted Net Assets—Designated for		
Air Pollution Program		XXX

Similar entries to close temporarily restricted and permanently restricted accounts are the following:

Contributions—Temporarily Restricted	XXX	
Legacies and Bequests—Temporarily Restricted	XXX	
Investment Revenue—Temporarily Restricted	XXX	
Reclassifications Out—Temporarily Restricted-Satisfaction		
of Donor Restrictions		XXX
Temporarily Restricted Net Assets		XXX
Contributions—Permanently Restricted	XXX	
Legacies and Bequests—Permanently Restricted	XXX	
Permanently Restricted Net Assets		XXX

Financial Statements

Consistent with other not-for-profits, the three financial statements for VHWOs are a statement of financial position, a statement of activities, and a statement of cash flows. In addition, VHWOs must provide a statement of functional expenses.

A statement of financial position is prepared either in single-column form or with a column for each asset class. Organization-wide totals of assets, liabilities, and net assets are presented.

An activities statement can be prepared after the expense allocation entry has been recorded. It is structured with a column for each asset class and shows how effectively the organization operated during the period.

Since program costs and not the natural expenses, such as salaries, are shown in an operating statement, a summary of expenses by object-of-expense classification is provided in a separate statement. This statement of functional expenses supplements the operating statement. It presents the total of each natural expense allocated to programs and supporting services.

Day Star Activity and Respite Center serves older adults afflicted with Alzheimer's Disease or other memory impairment and their families. Day Star provides day care for clients at its day care center, which provides a respite from constant caregiving for primary caregivers. Day Star also provides limited home care for clients. The expenses that were incurred by Day Star are shown below:

Expenses:	
Salaries and payroll taxes.	$17,000
Crafts and activities	4,000
Meals on Wheels.	4,000
Office expenses.	2,000
Repairs and maintenance	1,500
Depreciation expense.	5,000
Total expenses.	$33,500

Day Star management has estimated the allocation of financial resources to organization activities and prepared the following matrix showing the allocation scheme:

	Day Care	Home Care	Management
Operating expenses	40%	35%	25%
Capital-related expenses	90	10	0

Expenses are allocated to programs and supporting services using the allocation matrix in the following manner. Then they are presented in the statement of activities.

	Total	Day Care	Home Care	Management and General
Operating expenses	$28,500	$11,400	$9,975	$7,125
Capital-related expenses	5,000	4,500	500	

Expenses also are allocated to programs and supporting services using the allocation matrix for presentation in the statement of functional expenses. The following example shows this procedure for three object-of-expense categories:

Object of Expense	Total	Day Care	Home Care	Management and General
Salaries and payroll taxes	$17,000	$ 6,800	$ 5,950	$4,250
Crafts and activities.	4,000	1,600	1,400	1,000
Meals on Wheels	4,000	1,600	1,400	1,000
Office expenses	2,000	800	700	500
Repairs and maintenance	1,500	600	525	375
Depreciation	5,000	4,500	500	
Total expenses	$33,500	$15,900	$10,475	$7,125

Illustration of Accounting for a Voluntary Health and Welfare Organization

To illustrate the recording of events and the preparation of financial reports for a VHWO, assume the People's Environmental Protection (PEP) Association, a voluntary community organization, has three programs: Valley Air Pollution, Keep Fish in the Lakes, and Flood Control. The statement of financial position of PEP on December 31, 20X6, is shown in Illustration 19-4.

Illustration 19-4
People's Environmental Protection (PEP) Association
Statement of Financial Position
As of December 31, 20X6

Assets:

Cash and cash equivalents	$ 253,500
Contributions receivable (net of $3,100 allowance)	21,500
Inventories	10,000
Short-term investments	152,000
Property, plant, and equipment (net of $16,700 accumulated depreciation)	676,000
Long-term endowment investments	253,000
Total assets	**$1,366,000**

Liabilities and net assets:

Accounts payable	$ 37,000
Notes payable	100,000
Total liabilities	**$ 137,000**

Net assets:

Unrestricted	**$ 289,900**
Temporarily restricted	**687,000**
Permanently restricted	**253,000**
Total net assets	**$1,229,000**
Total liabilities and net assets	$ 1,366,000

The following events occur during the calendar year 20X7. They are summarized to conserve space and minimize duplication. Entries are shown following each transaction. Consistent with the new FASB statements, no fund designation is recorded. VHWOs may choose to use fund accounting for donor-restricted resources, plant, and permanently restricted endowments. These are illustrated in the appendix to the chapter.

Event	Entry		
1. As a result of its fund-raising program, cash contributions of $325,000 were received. $315,000 was unrestricted, and $10,000 was restricted for valley air project operating costs. In addition, unconditional promises to give totaled $100,000, of which $80,000 was unrestricted and $20,000 restricted for acquisition of equipment.	Cash	325,000	
	Contributions—Unrestricted		315,000
	Contributions—Temporarily Restricted		10,000
	Contributions Receivable	100,000	
	Contributions—Unrestricted		80,000
	Contributions—Temporarily Restricted		20,000
2. Based on past experience, 5% of the promises to give were estimated to be uncollectible.	Provision for Uncollectible Contributions	5,000	
	Allowance for Uncollectible Contributions		5,000
3. During the year, cash was collected from some unconditional promises to give, while others were written-off as uncollectible.	Cash	95,500	
	Allowance for Uncollectible Contributions	5,600	
	Contributions Receivable		101,100

(continued)

Event	Entry		
4. A cash donation of $40,000 was received, with the donor stipulation that it be used to acquire equipment that will assist in water quality improvement.	Cash . . . . Contributions—Temporarily Restricted .	40,000		40,000

5. With the donor's approval, the $40,000 served as a partial payment on the purchase of a filter system costing $50,000. A note was signed for the unpaid balance. PEP chooses to release the donor restriction over the life of the asset.	Land, Building, and Equipment. . . . . . .
	    Cash . . . .
	    Notes Payable on Equipment . . . .
		50,000		40,000
				10,000

6. PEP received $5,000 from an individual who restricted its use to a special project within a keep-fish-in-the-lakes program. If that special project is not accomplished within six months, the individual requested that the money be returned. PEP has not yet undertaken the project. Two months remain in the time period specified by the donor.	Cash . . . . Refundable Advances	5,000		5,000

7. The following bequests were received: $100,000 unrestricted and $20,000 to be invested in an endowment whose earnings are to be unrestricted.	Cash . . . .
	    Legacies and Bequests—Unrestricted . .
	    Legacies and Bequests—Permanently
	        Restricted . . . .
		120,000		100,000
				
				20,000

8. PEP received donated goods with a fair value of $2,350. Of those donated goods, $750 is restricted by the donor for use in the keep-fish-in-the-lakes program; the remaining gifts can be used at management's discretion.	Inventories . . . .
	    Contributions—Unrestricted . . . .
	    Contributions—Temporarily Restricted .
		2,350		1,600
				750

9. PEP held a special summer event to promote its activities, the net proceeds of which were unrestricted. Gross revenues totaled $9,000, with direct costs for the event amounting to $2,000.	Cash . . . .
	    Special Events Support—Unrestricted. .
	
	Costs of Special Events . . . .
	    Cash . . . .
		9,000
		
		2,000
				9,000
				
				2,000

10. PEP uses volunteers to distribute brochures about its operations, to assist the staff with routine office work, and to make phone calls during the annual fund-raising appeal. The volunteers provided 1,000 hours of service this year. If the volunteers were not available, the tasks would either be performed by existing staff or not performed at all. PEP estimates the fair value of these services at $7.50 per hour.	No entry		
11. An annual membership to PEP is $118, permitting members and their families to use lake facilities for swimming, sailing (no motors allowed), and fishing.	Cash . . . . Membership Dues Revenue	118,000		118,000

12. The local PEP unit receives unrestricted cash of $16,000 as its share of a campaign run by its national affiliate.	Cash . . . .
	    Received from Federated and Nonfederated
	        Campaigns—Unrestricted . . . .
		16,000		16,000

13. Earnings on endowment investments total $28,000, of which $21,000 is not restricted and $7,000 is restricted to investment in equipment for flood control.	Cash . . . .
	    Investment Revenue—Unrestricted . . . .
	    Investment Revenue—Temporarily
	        Restricted . . . .
		28,000		21,000
				
				7,000

Reclassifications In—Unrestricted—		
Satisfaction of Equipment Acquisition		
Restrictions	22,000	
Reclassifications In—Unrestricted—		
Satisfaction of Time Restrictions. . . .	10,000	
Valley Air Project		132,000
Keep Fish in the Lakes Program		184,450
Flood Control Program		251,000
Management and General Services . .		29,500
Fund-Raising Services		11,000
Membership Development		2,000
Cost of Special Events		2,000
Unrestricted Net Assets.		**184,900**
Contributions—Temporarily Restricted . . .	72,750	
Investment Revenue—Temporarily		
Restricted	7,000	
Temporarily Restricted Net Assets	**56,000**	
Reclassifications Out—Unrestricted—		
Satisfaction of Program		
Restrictions		103,750
Reclassifications Out—Unrestricted—		
Satisfaction of Equipment		
Acquisition Restrictions		22,000
Reclassifications Out—Unrestricted—		
Satisfaction of Time Restrictions. . . .	10,000	
Legacies and Bequests—Endowment—		
Permanently Restricted	20,000	
Net Increase in Carrying Value of		
Endowment Investments—Permanently		
Restricted	29,000	
Gain on Sale of Endowment Investments—		
Permanently Restricted	2,000	
Permanently Restricted		
Net Assets		**51,000**

    The final entry at year-end closes the support and revenue accounts, as well as the program and supporting services expenses, into the appropriate net asset accounts. With expenses allocated to programs and supporting services, it is now possible to prepare the statement of activities (Illustration 19-5 on page 19-26). Inflows of resources from public support, revenues, and reclassification are listed first, followed by the expense totals for each program and supporting service, taken directly from the closing and allocation entries. The beginning net asset balance for each class is added, resulting in the net asset balance at the end of the period.

    Since the investments account is carried at market value, it is entirely possible that the carrying value may decrease. If this situation occurs, the account Net Decrease in Carrying Value of Investments is debited and the investments account is credited. The closing entry would credit Net Decrease in Carrying Value of Investments and debit unrestricted or permanently restricted net assets, depending on donor specifications or law.

The statement of activities of a VHWO provides valuable data on the total cost per period of each program and of supporting services. To provide the reader of its financial statements with additional information, a statement of functional expenses is included in the reports. This statement shows the allocation of each expense (salaries, rent, etc.) and reveals the cost by function of carrying on the organization's activities. The statement of functional expenses for PEP is shown in Illustration 19-6.

The statement of financial position for PEP on December 31, 19X7, is given in Illustration 19-7. The statement of cash flows shown in Illustration 19-8 includes under *financing activities* all cash inflows from contributions and investment income restricted by donor for long-term investments (or endowments) or for acquisition of fixed assets.

As is true in reporting for-profit enterprises, financial statements of VHWO would be prepared with comparative figures for the preceding year. The statements also should be accompanied by notes that would summarize significant accounting policies.

Illustration 19-5
People's Environmental Protection (PEP) Association
Statement of Activities
For Year Ended December 31, 20X7

	Unrestricted	Temporarily Restricted	Permanently Restricted	Total
Public support and revenue:				
Public support				
Contributions	$ 397,100	$ 72,750		$ 469,850
Special events (net of $2,000 direct costs)	7,000			$7,000
Legacies and bequests	100,000		$ 20,000	120,000
Received from federated and nonfederated campaigns	16,000			16,000
Total public support	$ 520,100	$ 72,750	$ 20,000	$ 612,850
Revenue:				
Membership dues	$ 118,000			118,000
Investment revenue	21,000	7,000		28,000
Net increase in carrying value of investments			29,000	29,000
Realized gain on investments			2,000	2,000
Total revenue	$ 139,000	$ 7,000	$ 31,000	$ 177,000
Net assets released from restrictions:				
Satisfaction of program requirements	$ 103,750	(103,750)		
Satisfaction of equipment acquisition requirements	22,000	(22,000)		
Expiration of time restrictions	10,000	(10,000)		
Total net assets released from restrictions	$ 135,750	$(135,750)		
Total public support and revenue	$ 794,850	$ (56,000)	$ 51,000	$ 789,850
Expenses:				
Valley air project	$ 132,000			132,000
"Keep fish in the lakes" program	184,450			184,450
Flood control program	251,000			251,000
Management and general	29,500			29,500
Fund raising	11,000			11,000
Membership development	2,000			2,000
Total expenses	$ 609,950			$ 609,950
Change in net assets	**184,900**	**(56,000)**	**51,000**	**179,900**
Net assets beginning of year	**289,000**	**687,000**	**253,000**	**1,229,000**
Net assets end of year	**$473,900**	**$631,000**	**$304,000**	**$1,408,900**

Illustration 19-6
People's Environmental Protection (PEP) Association
Statement of Functional Expenses
For Year Ended December 31, 20X7

	Total All Services	Program Services				Supporting Services			
		Valley Air Project	Keep Fish in the Lakes	Flood Control	Total Programs	Management, and General	Fund Raising	Membership Development	Total Supporting
Salaries	$200,000	$ 36,000	$ 60,000	$ 80,000	$176,000	$19,000	$ 4,500	$ 500	$24,000
Payroll taxes	30,000	5,400	9,000	12,000	26,400	3,000	500	100	3,600
Mailing and postage	50,000	10,000	20,000	19,700	49,700		200	100	300
Rent	28,000	8,000	5,000	11,600	24,600	2,000	400	1,000	3,400
Telephone	6,000	1,500	1,300	2,500	5,300		400	300	700
Research	215,000	35,000	80,000	100,000	215,000				
Professional: legal and audit	34,500	24,000	2,000	4,000	30,000	4,500			4,500
Supplies	14,450	10,100	1,450	2,900	14,450				
Provision for uncollectible contributions	5,000						5,000		5,000
Miscellaneous	5,000		2,700	2,300	5,000				
Total expenses before depreciation	$587,950	$130,000	$181,450	$235,000	$546,450	$28,500	$11,000	$2,000	$41,500
Depreciation of building and equipment	22,000	2,000	3,000	16,000	21,000	1,000			1,000
Total expenses	$609,950	$132,000	$184,450	$251,000	$567,450	$29,500	$11,000	$2,000	$42,500

Illustration 19-7
People's Environmental Protection (PEP) Association
Statement of Financial Position
As of December 31, 20X7

Assets:
Cash and cash equivalents . . . . $ 268,000
Contributions receivable (net of $2,500 allowance) 21,000
Inventories. 10,900
Short-term investments 152,000
Property, plant, and equipment (net of $38,700 accumulated depreciation) 800,000
Long-term endowment investments 304,000

Total assets **$1,555,900**

Liabilities and net assets:
Accounts payable. . . . . $ 32,000
Refundable advances 5,000
Notes payable. 110,000

Total liabilities . . . . **$ 147,000**

Net assets:
Unrestricted . . . . **$ 473,900**
Temporarily restricted **631,000**
Permanently restricted **304,000**

Total net assets **$1,408,900**
Total liabilities and net assets . . . . $ 1,555,900

Illustration 19-8
People's Environmental Protection (PEP) Association
Statement of Cash Flows
For Year Ended December 31, 20X7

Cash flows from operating activities:		
Cash received from members		$ 118,000
Cash received from contributions		402,500
Cash received from special events		7,000
Cash received from federated and nonfederated campaigns		16,000
Cash received from legacies and bequests		100,000
Cash received on a refundable advance		5,000
Interest and dividends received		21,000
Cash paid to employees and suppliers		(586,000)
Net cash provided by (used for) operating activities		**$ 83,500**
Cash flows from investing activities:		
Proceeds from sales and maturities of investments		$ 27,000
Purchases of investments		(46,000)
Purchase of land, building, and equipment		(146,000)
Net cash provided by (used for) investing activities		**$(165,000)**
Cash flow from financing activities:		
Proceeds from issuance of notes payable		$ 10,000
Receipts of interest and dividends restricted for reinvestment		7,000
Contributions received restricted for long-term investment		20,000
Contributions received restricted for investment in plant		60,000
Net cash provided by (used for) financing activities		**$ 97,000**
Net increase (decrease) in cash and cash equivalents		**$ 15,500**
Cash and cash equivalents at beginning of year		**252,500**
Cash and cash equivalents at end of year		**$ 268,000**
Reconciliation of change in net assets to net cash provided by operating activities:		
Change in net assets		$ 179,900
Depreciation		22,000
Decrease in contributions receivable		500
Increase in inventories		(900)
Increase in notes payable		10,000
Increase in refundable advances		(5,000)
Decrease in accounts payable		(5,000)
Increase in net carrying value of investments		(29,000)
Gain on sale of investments		(2,000)
Interest restricted for long-term investment		(7,000)
Contributions restricted for long-term investment		(20,000)
Contributions restricted for plant		(60,000)
Net cash provided by operating activities		$ 83,500

*$4,000 of cash at beginning of year and $5,000 of cash at year-end are included in the classification "long-term endowment investments" on the statement of financial position.

Accounting for Other Not-for-Profit Organizations

The most recent audit guide, *Not-for-Profit Organizations* (June 1, 1996), also provides accounting and audit guidance for many other organizations. Among the not-for-profit entities included in the guide are the following:

Cemetery organizations
Civic and fraternal organizations
Labor unions
Libraries and museums
Performing arts and other cultural organizations
Political parties
Private and community foundations
Private elementary and secondary schools
Professional associations
Public broadcasting stations
Religious organizations
Research and scientific organizations
Social and country clubs
Trade associations
Zoological and botanical societies

Entities that have restricted resources may use fund accounting for internal control and management reporting purposes so that they demonstrate compliance with externally imposed restrictions. Financial statements, however, report organization-wide totals for all assets and liabilities. Net assets are classified as unrestricted, temporarily restricted, or permanently restricted. Financial statements include a statement of financial position, a statement of activities, and a statement of cost flows, along with notes for appropriate disclosures of policy.

Summary Implementing FASB Statement Nos. 116 and 117

FASB Statement Nos. 116 and 117 represent the most comprehensive change in the history of financial reporting by not-for-profit organizations. The standards serve to enhance the information provided to readers of the financial statements about financial viability, financial flexibility, liquidity, cash flows, and service efforts.

Use of financial statements based on net asset classifications is a much different concept from traditional fund group reporting and requires organizations to reevaluate their current information systems. To implement the new accounting and financial reporting guidelines, organizations have to determine policies for recognition and valuation of contributions of cash, assets, and services and work toward articulation of internal information systems (fund accounting) with the new external reporting requirements.

The AICPA 1996 *Audit and Accounting Guide, Not-for-Profit Organizations,* combines previously separate not-for-profit guides—*Audits of Voluntary Health and Welfare Organizations, Audits of Certain Not-for-Profit Organizations,* and *Audits of Colleges and Universities*—in order to standardize guidance on accounting for contributions and formats of the financial statements. The AICPA 1996 *Health Care Organizations* Audit Guide also revises guidance for health care organizations to conform to the new FASB Statements. Government entities are not permitted to change their accounting and financial reporting to apply FASB nos. 116 and 117. GASB No. 29 permits not-for-profit government to continue to apply the provisions of the old audit guides as modified by applicable GASB pronouncements or change to the government model. The 1996 *Health-care Organizations* Audit Guide has specific provisions for government health-care organizations.

The FASB has two additional projects on its not-for-profit agenda: a) consolidation policies and b) service efforts and accomplishments as a means for external users to evaluate the effectiveness and efficiency of not-for-profit organizations.

Appendix: Accounting and Financial Reporting by Funds

In this appendix, the accounting and financial reporting of a health care organization and a voluntary health and welfare organization are illustrated within their respective existing fund structures. The illustrations include the same events as in the text in order for readers to compare the resulting financial statements with those assuming no funds.

Health Care Organizations

As described in the text, health care providers receive bequests, gifts, and grants that are restricted by the donor as to use for a) specific operating purposes, b) additions to plant, c) endowments, or d) annuities or life incomes. A donor-restricted fund is established for accumulating resources in each of these categories until the resources become available for expenditure by the general funds. As feeders to the general funds, donor-restricted funds are classified as temporarily restricted or permanently restricted. When the donor-restricted assets are to be used for their intended purpose, they are reclassified as unrestricted and recorded as a transfer or, more commonly, as a direct debit to the appropriate net asset account.

Specific Purpose Fund.   The specific purpose fund records donor-restricted resources available for current but specified operations as temporarily restricted contributions. When the expenditure is to be made in accordance with the donor's wishes, the temporarily restricted net assets are released from restrictions and reclassified to the unrestricted net assets. A transfer is then recorded to the general funds.

Plant Replacement and Expansion Fund.   Similarly, the plant replacement and expansion fund accounts for resources that must be used to purchase property or equipment. When an outlay for plant is made by the general funds in compliance with the wishes of the donor, a cash transfer is recorded by reducing the net assets of the plant replacement and expansion fund and increasing the net assets of the general funds. As with other not-for-profit organizations, health care organizations may choose to release the restrictions of donated fixed assets with the acquisition of the asset or over the useful life of the asset.

Endowment Fund.   The endowment fund accounts for resources that are received to create permanent endowments (whose income only may be expended) or term endowments (whose principal eventually will become available for expenditure). Revenues from permanent endowment investments are recorded as nonoperating revenues in the general fund if unrestricted or in the appropriate donor-restricted fund if restricted for specific operating or plant purposes. As term endowment funds become available for general operations, they are reclassified as unrestricted and transferred to the general fund. Should the term endowments be restricted further, for example, to purchase equipment, they are transferred to the appropriate donor-restricted fund. It is possible that use of other donor-restricted funds, such as annuity funds or loan funds, may become necessary, depending upon the activities of the organization.

Illustrative Entries for Health Care Organizations.   To illustrate the recording of events for a hospital within the current fund structure, the year's affairs of Columbia Hospital's general funds are summarized next. The illustrative entries employ the same broad categories of control accounts as the previous examples in the text. Transactions of the donor-restricted funds and transfers from the donor-restricted funds to the general funds are shown in the matrix in Illustration 19A-1 on pages 19-32 to 19-35. A funds-based statement of activities and a statement of financial position are presented in Illustrations 19A-2 and 19A-3, respectively. The required statement of cash flows cannot be presented on a funds basis and, therefore, will be the same as the one presented in Illustration 19-3 on page 19-13.

Voluntary Health and Welfare Organizations

To segregate resources and demonstrate compliance with restrictions, fund accounting is sometimes used by voluntary health and welfare organizations. As described in the text, voluntary health and welfare organizations have two current funds consisting primarily of current assets and current liabilities, a separate plant fund, and an endowment fund. Unlike health care organizations, where donor-restricted funds act as feeders to the general funds, all funds of voluntary health and welfare organizations record expenses. As a result, there are few interfund transactions compared with the other not-for-profit organizations.

The following matrix relates the funds used by most VHWOs with the "net asset" categories of the new FASB standards:

Funds	Unrestricted Net Assets	Temporarily Restricted Net Assets	Permanently Restricted Net Assets
Current Unrestricted	X		
Current Restricted.	X	X	
Land, Building, and Equipment (Plant Fund).	X	X	X
Endowment Fund		X	X
Agency (Custodial) Fund			

Current Unrestricted Fund.   The current unrestricted fund accounts are for resources that have no external restrictions and are available for current operations at the discretion of the governing board. The board, however, may place its own limitations on the fund's unrestricted net assets. In the same manner that industry appropriates retained earnings, the board of directors of a health and welfare organization may designate a portion of its unrestricted net assets for a special project. To reflect such an action, a subset of unrestricted net assets, Unrestricted Net Assets— Designated, may be displayed, provided the total amount of Unrestricted Net Assets is shown.

Current Restricted Fund.   The current restricted fund accounts for assets received from outside sources for a current operating purpose specified by the donor. The distinguishing feature between unrestricted and restricted funds is whether an externally imposed restriction exists. A contribution received by a health agency to conduct nutrition classes is an example of a restricted resource. When donor-restricted contributions are expensed, the restriction is released or reclassified to offset the expense. Specifically excluded from this fund are contributions of endowments or contributions restricted to the acquisition of plant assets, which are recorded in other appropriate funds.

Some net assets of this fund may be unrestricted; for example, grants, awards, sponsorships, and appropriations have traditionally been recorded in the restricted current fund. These may now be defined as exchange transactions in which the grantor or sponsor expects to receive something of value in return for the grant. Exchange transactions are unrestricted per FASB Statement No. 116.

Illustration 19A-1
Interaction Matrix for Fitale Hospital

Event	Specific Purpose Fund		Endowment Fund	
1–20, see descriptions on pages 19-7, 19-8, and 19-9.				
21. Fitale received $50,000 cash from a donor to cover operating costs of the student nursing unit.	Cash . . . . Other Operating Revenue— Temporarily Restricted (Contributions)	50,000 50,000		
22. Investment earnings are received in the amount of $75,000 restricted for cancer research.	Cash . . . . Nonoperating Revenues— Temporarily Restricted (Investment Earnings)	75,000 75,000		
23. $500,000 was donated to Fitale Hospital for investments in long-term securities as a pure endowment.			Cash . . . . Nonoperating Revenues— Permanently Restricted (Endowment Contributions)	500,000 500,000
24. Securities were purchased.			Endowment Investments . . . . Cash	500,000 500,000
25. A term endowment expired. The $150,000 principal is now available for use by the hospital administration.			Reclassification Out—Temporarily Restricted—Satisfaction of Time Restrictions . . . . . Reclassification In— Unrestricted Satisfaction of Time Restrictions . . . . Unrestricted Net Assets— Equity Transfer Out . . . . . Cash	150,000 150,000 150,000 150,000
26. Receipts of $200,000 and an unconditional promise to give $100,000 were recorded. Gifts were to be used for operating room equipment.				
27. Operating room equipment was purchased.				
28. AICPA audit guidance requires that donor restrictions be released when the asset is placed in service.				
29. The first-year depreciation on the above operating room equipment was recorded.				
30. A $400,000 grant from a local manufacturer to be used for a patient nutritional study was received. Results of the study will be used to educate the public, not for the benefit of the donor.	Cash . . . . Other Operating Revenue— Temporarily Restricted (Contributions)	400,000 400,000		
31. Expenses were incurred for the patient nutritional study.	Reclassification Out—Temporarily Restricted Satisfaction of Program Restrictions. . . Reclassification In— Unrestricted—Satisfaction of Program Restrictions . . . . Unrestricted Net Assets— Equity Transfer Out . . . . . Cash	50,000 50,000 50,000 50,000		

Plant Replacement and Expansion		General Fund	
		See pages 19-7, 19-8, and 19-9 for entries.	
		Cash	150,000
		Unrestricted Net Assets—Equity Transfer In		150,000
Contributions Receivable	100,000		
Cash	200,000		
Other Operating Revenues—Temporarily Restricted (Contributions)	300,000	
		Equipment	200,000
		Cash		200,000
Temporarily Restricted Net Assets—Equity Transfer Out	200,000	Cash	200,000
Cash		200,000	Temporarily Restricted Net Assets—Equity Transfer In		200,000
		Reclassification Out—Temporarily Restricted—Satisfaction of Plant Acquisition Restrictions	200,000
		Reclassification In—Unrestricted—Satisfaction of Plant Acquisition Restrictions		200,000
		Depreciation Expense	40,000
		Allowance for Depreciation		40,000
		Wages, Salaries, and Benefits	25,000
		Drugs and Supplies Used	10,000
		Purchased Services	15,000
		Cash		50,000
		Cash	50,000
		Unrestricted Net Assets—Equity Transfer In		50,000

(continued)

Event	Specific Purpose Fund		Endowment Fund	
32. Fitale allocates natural expenses to the functional areas	Nursing Services	1,774,000		
	Other Professional Services . .	1,240,000		
	General Services	995,000		
	Fiscal Services	283,000		
	Administrative Services	761,000		
	Wages, Salaries, and Benefits.		3,045,000	
	Drugs and Supplies Used. . .		730,000	
	Purchased Services		330,000	
	Medical Malpractice Costs. .		450,000	
	Depreciation Expense		440,000	
	Interest		66,000	
	Provision for Bad Debts		22,000	
33a. Closing entries—general fund.				
33b. Closing entries—specific purpose fund.	Reclassification In—Unrestricted— Satisfaction of Program Restrictions	50,000		
	Unrestricted Net Assets .		**50,000**	
	Other Operating Revenue— Temporarily Restricted	450,000		
	Nonoperating Revenue— Temporarily Restricted	75,000		
	Reclassification Out— Temporarily Restricted— Satisfaction of Program Restrictions		50,000	
	Temporarily Restricted Net Assets.		**475,000**	
33c. Closing entries—plant replacement and expansion fund.				
33d. Closing entries—endowment fund.			Reclassification In— Unrestricted—Satisfaction of Time Restrictions	150,000
			Unrestricted Net Assets.	
				150,000
			Temporarily Restricted Net Assets	150,000
			Reclassification Out— Temporarily Restricted— Satisfaction of Time Restrictions.	
				150,000
			Nonoperating Revenue— Permanently Restricted Endowment Contributions	500,000
			Permanently Restricted Net Assets	
				500,000

Plant Replacement and Expansion		General Fund	
		Patient Service Revenue—Unrestricted	5,000,000	
		Other Operating Revenue—Unrestricted	222,000	
		Nonoperating Revenue—Unrestricted	720,606	
		Reclassification In—Unrestricted—Satisfaction of Equipment Acquisition Restrictions.	200,000	
		Charity Care.		200,000
		Contractual Adjustments		380,000
		Nursing Services		1,774,000
		Other Professional Services		1,240,000
		General Services		995,000
		Fiscal Services.		283,000
		Administrative Services		791,000
		Unrestricted Net Assets.		**479,606**
		Temporarily Restricted Net Assets	**200,000**	
		Reclassification Out—Temporarily Restricted— Satisfaction of Equipment Acquisition Restrictions.		200,000

Other Operating Revenue— Temporarily Restricted	300,000		
Temporarily Restricted Net Assets	**300,000**		

Illustration 19A-2
Fitale Hospital
Statement of Activities
For Year Ended December 31, 20X5

	General Fund	Specific Purpose Fund	Plant Fund	Endowment Fund	Total
Changes in unrestricted net assets:					
Revenues, gains, and other support:					
Patient services revenue.	$4,420,000				$ 4,420,000
Other operating revenue	222,000				222,000
Total unrestricted revenue	$4,642,000				$ 4,642,000
Net assets released from restrictions:					
Satisfaction of program restrictions		$ 50,000			$ 50,000
Satisfaction of equipment acquisition					
restrictions	$ 200,000				$ 200,000
Expiration of time restrictions				$ 150,000	150,000
Total unrestricted revenues and other support. .	$4,842,000	$ 50,000		$ 150,000	$ 5,042,000
Expenses and losses:					
Nursing services.	$1,774,000				$ 1,774,000
Other professional services	1,240,000				1,240,000
General services	995,000				995,000
Fiscal services	283,000				283,000
Administrative services	791,000				791,000
Total expenses	$5,083,000				$ 5,083,000
Increase (decrease) in net assets					
from operations	$ (241,000)	$ 50,000		$ 150,000	$ (41,000)
Nonoperating revenue	720,606				720,606
Increase in unrestricted net assets	$ 479,606	$ 50,000		$ 150,000	$ 679,606
Changes in temporarily restricted net assets					
Contributions.		$450,000	$ 300,000		$ 750,000
Income on long-term investments		75,000			75,000
Net assets released from restriction	$ (200,000)	(50,000)		$ (150,000)	(400,000)
Increase (decrease) in temporarily restricted net assets	$ (200,000)	$475,000	$ 300,000	$ (150,000)	$ 425,000
Changes in permanently restricted net assets:					
Contributions.				$ 500,000	$ 500,000
Increase (decrease) in permanently restricted net assets				$ 500,000	$ 500,000
Transfers among funds—additions (deductions):					
Satisfaction of program restrictions	$ 50,000	$ (50,000)			0
Equipment acquisition	200,000		$(200,000)		0
Expiration of time restrictions	150,000			$ (150,000)	0
Total transfers.	$ 400,000	$ (50,000)	$(200,000)	$ 150,000)	0
Increase (decrease) in net assets	$ 679,606	$475,000	$ 100,000	$ 350,000	$ 1,604,606
Net assets at beginning of year	4,698,000	250,000	319,000	3,710,000	8,977,000
Net assets at end of year	$5,377,606	$725,000	$ 419,000	$4,060,000	$10,581,606

Illustration 19A-3
Fitale Hospital
Statement of Financial Position
As of December 31, 20X5

	General Fund	Specific Purpose Fund	Plant Fund	Endowment Fund	Total
Assets:					
Cash and cash equivalents.	$ 260,000	$475,000			$ 735,000
Accounts and interest receivable (net).	908,000				908,000
Inventories.	81,000				81,000
Contributions receivable	165,606		$100,000		265,000
Short-term investments	150,000	250,000			400,000
Assets restricted to investment in land, building, and equipment.	126,000		319,000		445,000
Assets limited in use under malpractice funding agreement	440,000				440,000
Property, plant, and equipment (net of depreciation)	5,250,000				5,250,000
Long-term investments	540,000				540,000
Endowment investments				$4,060,000	4,060,000
Total assets	$7,920,606	$725,000	$419,000	$4,060,000	$13,124,000
Liabilities and net assets:					
Accounts payable.	$ 53,000				$ 53,000
Current installments of long-term debt.	80,000				80,000
Accrued expenses.	100,000				100,000
Notes payable.	500,000				500,000
Estimated malpractice costs	640,000				640,000
Long-term debt.	1,170,000				1,170,000
Total liabilities	$2,543,000	0	0	0	$ 2,543,000
Net assets:					
Unrestricted	$5,217,606				$ 5,217,606
Temporarily restricted	160,000	$725,000	$419,000		1,304,000
Permanently restricted				$4,060,000	4,060,000
Total net assets	$5,377,606	$725,000	$419,000	$4,060,000	$10,581,606
Total liabilities and net assets	$7,920,606	$725,000	$419,000	$4,060,000	$13,124,606

Land, Building, and Equipment Fund (or Plant Fund). The plant fund accounts for the activity related to fixed assets, including the accumulation of resources to acquire or replace them, the liabilities related to them, as well as their acquisition, their disposal, and their depreciation. To determine the total cost of rendering service, depreciation of assets employed in providing that service must be recorded in the plant fund, with the typical depreciation entry debiting Depreciation Expense and crediting Accumulated Depreciation.

The plant fund of a VHWO may have all three net asset classes: unrestricted, temporarily restricted, and permanently restricted. Unrestricted net assets may be transfers from current funds at the discretion of the governing board. Assets acquired with unrestricted funds are unrestricted. Donor-restricted contributions specified for property and equipment are temporarily restricted. As with other not-for-profits, a VHWO may choose to release the restriction of these assets upon acquisition or over the useful life. Contributions of land are considered permanently restricted if the land cannot be sold. If no restriction exists, donated land is an unrestricted contribution.

Endowment Fund.   The endowment fund accounts for gifts or bequests with the legal restriction that the principal be maintained in perpetuity (permanently restricted) or until the occurrence of a specified event (temporarily restricted). Various conditions are possible, depending upon the desires of the contributor. Unless otherwise specified, net gains or losses on the sale of endowment fund assets are increases or decreases of the fund principal.

Endowment fund investment revenue may be restricted or unrestricted. Income is recorded directly in the fund that is to receive it. Such income not subject to any restrictions by the principal donor may be recorded directly in the current unrestricted fund as unrestricted investment revenue. If the revenue is subject to a restriction, it would be recorded as temporarily or permanently restricted in the appropriate restricted fund.

Agency (Custodian) Fund.   Agency funds of not-for-profit organizations account for assets that do not belong to the organization holding them. They often are established for payroll withholding. Custodian funds are established to account for assets received by an organization to be held or disbursed only on instructions of the person or organization from whom they were received. Flowthrough government grants are examples of this latter use of agency funds. Assets are recorded when received, along with a related liability. Only when the assets are released by the contributor will the assets be recognized as revenue in the appropriate fund.

Pooling of Investments.   If an organization accumulates substantial investments in its various funds, pooling may be advisable. Pooling of investments is the process of combining the investments of various funds into one group or pool to provide greater flexibility at lower cost and to provide diversification to spread the risk. Once pooled, individual investments lose their identity as to fund. Each contributing fund merely maintains in its investment account an amount representing its portion of the pool. Before any additions or withdrawals may be made, the market value of the total portfolio must be determined. Realized and unrealizaed gains and losses are allocated to each participating fund on the basis of its share of the total market value at the previous valuation date. The proportion of each fund's market value may be expressed in terms of units or in terms of percentages of the total. The latter method is more flexible and is used in Illustration 19A-4, which shows changes in pooled investments over a period of time.

Illustration 19A-4
Pooling of Investments

Fund	(1) Cash and/or MV of Securities	(2) Original Equity Percent	(3) (4) Total Pool December 31, 20X0 Cost	Market	(5) Mkt. Value Including $50,000	(6) Revised Equity Percent	(7) After Withdrawal of $25,000	(8) New Equity Percent
Unrestricted......	$ 36,000	20%	$ 40,000	$ 50,000	$ 50,000	16.67%	$ 25,000	9.09%
Plant..........	54,000	30	60,000	75,000	75,000	25.00	75,000	27.27
Endowment......	90,000	50	100,000	125,000	175,000	58.33	175,000	63.64
Total.........	$180,000	100%	$200,000	$250,000	$300,000	100.00%	$275,000	100.00%

Illustrative Entries for Voluntary Health and Welfare Organizations.   Entries recording the year's events for People's Environmental Protection (PEP) Association within the existing funds structure for voluntary health and welfare organizations are presented in the matrix in Illustration 19A-5 on pages 19-40 to 19-48. The statement of financial position as of December 31, 20X6, is shown in Illustration 19A-6. Closing entries are prepared for each fund. Funds-based financial statements are presented for the year ending December 31, 20X7. The statement of activities is shown in Illustration 19A-7. The statement of financial position as of December 31, 20X7, is shown in Illustration 19A-8. The statement of cash flows and statement of functional expense are not presented on a funds basis. Both statements are identical to those illustrated in the chapter.

Illustration 19A-5
Interaction Matrix for PEP

Event	Unrestricted Current Fund		Restricted Current Fund	

1. As a result of its fund-raising program, cash contributions of $325,000 were received. $315,000 was unrestricted, and $10,000 was restricted for valley air project operating costs. In addition, unconditional pledges (promises to give) totaled $100,000, of which $80,000 was unrestricted and $20,000 was restricted for acquisition of equipment.	Cash 315,000
	Contributions Receivable . . 80,000
	Contributions—
	  Unrestricted . . . .
		395,000	Cash 10,000
			Contributions—Temporarily
			  Restricted . . . .
				10,000

2. Based on past experience, 5% of the promises to give were estimated to be uncollectible.	Provision for Uncollectible
	  Contributions 4,000
	Allowance for Uncollectible
	  Contributions . . . .
		4,000		

3. During the year, cash was collected from some unconditional promises to give, while others were written-off as uncollectible.	Cash . . . . 76,500 Allowance for Uncollectible Contributions . . . . 4,600 Contributions Receivable .	81,100		
4. A cash donation of $40,000 was received, with the donor stipulation that it be used to acquire equipment that will assist in water quality improvement.				
5. With the donor's approval, the $40,000 served as a partial payment on the purchase of a filter system costing $50,000. A note was signed for the unpaid balance. PEP chooses to release the donor restriction over the life of the asset.				
6. PEP received $5,000 from an individual who restricted its use to a special project within the keep-fish-in-the-lakes program. This donation was given with the condition that, if the special project is not accomplished within 6 months, the money will be returned to the individual. PEP has not yet undertaken the project. Two months remain in the time period specified by the donor.			Cash . . . . 5,000 Refundable Advances . . .	5,000
7. The following bequests were received: $100,000 unrestricted and $20,000 to be invested in an endowment whose earnings are to be unrestricted.	Cash . . . . 100,000 Legacies and Bequests— Unrestricted	100,000		

8. PEP received donated goods with a fair value of $2,350. Of those donated goods, $750 is restricted by the donor for use in the keep-fish-in-the-lakes program; the remaining gifts can be used at management's discretion.	Inventories 1,600
	Contributions—
	  Unrestricted . . . .
		1,600	Inventories 750
			Contributions—Temporarily
			  Restricted . . . .
				750

Plant Fund			Endowment Fund		
Contributions Receivable ..	20,000				
Contributions—Temporarily					
Restricted.		20,000			
Provision for Uncollectible					
Contributions	1,000				
Allowance for Uncollectible					
Contributions		1,000			
Cash	19,000				
Allowance for Uncollectible					
Contributions	1,000				
Contributions Receivable .		20,000			
Cash	40,000				
Contributions—Temporarily					
Restricted.		40,000			
Land, Building, and					
Equipment	50,000				
Cash.		40,000			
Notes Payable on					
Equipment		10,000			
			Cash	20,000	
			Legacies and Bequests—		
			Endowment—Permanently		
			Restricted.		20,000

(continued)

Event	Unrestricted Current Fund		Restricted Current Fund

9. PEP held a special summer event to promote its activities, the net proceeds of which were unrestricted. Gross revenues totaled $9,000 with direct costs for the event amounting to $2,000.	Cash 9,000
	    Special Events Support—
	        Unrestricted 9,000
	Cost of Special Events 2,000
	    Cash 2,000		

10. PEP uses volunteers to distribute brochures about its operations, to assist the staff with routine office work, and to make phone calls during the annual fund-raising appeal. The volunteers provided 1,000 hours of service this year. If the volunteers were not available, the tasks would either be performed by existing staff or not be done at all. PEP estimates the fair value of these services to be $5 per hour.	No entry. Most volunteer services of this type do not meet criteria. This amount should be disclosed in the footnotes.		

11. An annual membership to PEP is $118, permitting members and their families to use lake facilities for swimming, sailing (no motors allowed), and fishing.	Cash 118,00
	    Membership Dues
	        Revenues 118,000		

12. The local PEP unit receives unrestricted cash of $16,000 as its share of a campaign run by its national affiliates.	Cash 16,000
	    Received from Federated
	        and Nonfederated
	        Campaigns—
	        Unrestricted 16,000		

13. Earnings on endowment investments total $28,000, of which $21,000 is not restricted and $7,000 is restricted to investment in equipment for flood control.	Cash 21,000
	    Investment Revenue—
	        Unrestricted 21,000		

14. PEP carries its investments in all funds at market value. Endowment investments are sold for $27,000. They had a cost of $20,000 and a carrying value of $25,000 in the investment account. Endowment gains are permanently restricted as specified by the donor.			
15. Additional $46,000 of investments are purchased from endowment funds.			
16. Unrestricted investments have shown no material change in market value over the year. At year-end, the market value of permanently restricted endowment investments has increased from $265,000 to $294,000. Endowment gains are permanently restricted as specified by donor.			

	Plant Fund		Endowment Fund	

Cash	7,000				
Investment Revenue—					
Temporarily Restricted . .		7,000			
			Cash	27,000	
			Investments (at market) . . .		25,000
			Gain on Sale of		
			Endowment Investments—		
			Permanently Restricted . .		2,000
			Endowment Investments—		
			Permanently Restricted . .	46,000	
			Cash.		46,000
			Endowment Investments . . .	29,000	
			Net Increase in Carrying		
			Value of Investments—		
			Permanently Restricted . .		29,000

(continued)

Event	Unrestricted Current Fund		Restricted Current Fund	

17. A lawyer provided 5 hours of service to PEP to draw up an endowment agreement. She did not charge for her services. She normally would charge a client $500 for consultation on a similar type of agreement. In the absence of the donated professional services, PEP would have hired a lawyer to draft the agreement.	Professional Services . . . . .
	  Contributions—
	    Unrestricted . . . .
		500
		
		500		

18. A special recreation building and dock costing $96,000 were purchased with unrestricted cash.	Unrestricted Net Assets—
	  Transfer Out . . . .
	  Cash. . . . .
		96,000
		
		96,000		

19. Contributions received in the prior period with the stipulation that they be used for expenses of this period are now available.			Reclassification Out—
			  Temporarily Restricted—
			  Satisfaction of Time
			  Restrictions . . . .
			Reclassification In—
			  Unrestricted—Satisfaction
			  of Time Restrictions . . . . .
				10,000
				
				10,000

20. Accounts payable and expenses were paid or established. Operating expenses related to donor-specific programs totaled $103,000.	Accounts Payable
	  (January 1). . . . .
	Salaries Expense. . . . .
	Payroll Taxes . . . .
	Mailing and Postage
	  Expense. . . . .
	Rent Expense . . . .
	Telephone Expense . . . . . .
	Research Expense . . . . . .
	Professional Services:
	  Legal and Audit . . . .
	Supplies Expense . . . . . .
	Miscellaneous Expense . . .
	  Accounts Payable . . . . .
	  Cash. . . . .
		33,000
		180,000
		24,000
		
		40,000
		23,000
		5,000
		165,000
		
		27,000
		10,000
		4,000
		31,000
		480,000
			Accounts Payable
			  (January 1). . . . .
			Salaries Expense . . . .
			Payroll Taxes. . . . .
			Mailing and Postage
			  Expense. . . . .
			Rent Expense. . . . .
			Telephone Expense. . . . . . .
			Research Expense . . . .
			Professional Services:
			  Legal and Audit. . . . . . .
			Supplies Expense. . . . .
			Miscellaneous Expense . . . .
			  Accounts Payable. . . . . . .
			  Cash . . . .
			Reclassification Out—
			  Temporarily Restricted—
			  Satisfaction of Program
			  Restrictions . . . .
			Reclassification In—
			  Temporarily Unrestricted—
			  Satisfaction of Program
			  Restrictions . . . .
				4,000
				20,000
				6,000
				
				10,000
				5,000
				1,000
				50,000
				
				7,000
				3,000
				1,000
				1,000
				106,000
				
				103,000
				
				103,000

21. Contributed goods of $1,450 were used during the year for the keep-fish-in-the-lakes program. This amount includes the $750 donor-restricted contribution in item 8.	Supplies Expense . . . .
	  Inventories . . . .
		700
		
		700
			Supplies Expense. . . . .
			  Inventories . . . .
			Reclassification Out—
			  Temporarily Restricted—
			  Satisfaction of Program
			  Restrictions . . . .
			Reclassification In—
			  Unrestricted—Satisfaction
			  of Program
			  Restrictions . . . .
				750
				
				750
				
				750
				
				750

	Plant Fund		Endowment Fund	

Cash	96,000			
Unrestricted Net Assets—				
Transfer In.		96,000		
Land, Buildings, and				
Equipment	96,000			
Cash		96,000		

(continued)

Event	Unrestricted Current Fund		Restricted Current Fund	
22. Depreciation on equipment purchased with donor-restricted contributions amounted to $22,000 for the year. (Valley air project—$2,000; Keep-fish-in-the-lakes program—$3,000; Flood control program—$16,000; Management and general services—$1,000.) An equivalent amount of temporarily restricted net assets is released from restriction.				
23. Early in the year, cash contributions for current operations were received, but they cannot be used until late in the following year.			Cash . . . . Contributions— Temporarily Restricted . . .	2,000 2,000
24. At year-end, the expenses were allocated to the various programs and supporting services.	Valley Air Project . . . . "Keep Fish in the Lakes" Program . . . . Flood Control Program. . . . Management and General Services . . . . Fund-Raising Services . . . . Membership Development . Salaries Expense. . . . . . Payroll Taxes . . . . Mailing and Postage Expense. . . . . Rent Expense. . . . . Telephone Expense . . . . Research Expense . . . . . Professional Services: Legal and Audit . . . . Supplies Expense . . . . . Miscellaneous Expense. . Provision for Uncollectible Contributions	117,000 131,700 204,000 20,500 8,000 2,000	 180,000 24,000 40,000 23,000 5,000 165,000 27,500 10,700 4,000 4,000	Valley Air Project . . . . "Keep Fish in the Lakes" Program . . . . Flood Control Program . . . . Management and General Services . . . . . . Fund-Raising Services . . . . . Membership Development Salaries Expense . . . . Payroll Taxes . . . . Mailing and Postage Expense . . . . Rent Expense . . . . Telephone Expense. . . . . . Research Expense . . . . . . Professional Services: Legal and Audit . . . . . . Supplies Expense. . . . . . . Miscellaneous Expense . . .	13,000 49,750 31,000 8,000 2,000 20,000 6,000 10,000 5,000 1,000 50,000 7,000 3,750 1,000
25. Closing entries	Contributions . . . . Special Events Support. . . . Legacies and Bequests— Unrestricted . . . . Received from Federated and Nonfederated. . . Membership Dues Revenue. Investment Revenue— Unrestricted Valley Air Project . . . . . "Keep Fish in the Lakes" Program . . . . Flood Control Program. . Management and General Services. . . . Fund-Raising Services. . . Membership Development . . . . . . Cost of Special Events . . **Unrestricted Net Assets**	397,100 9,000 100,000 16,000 118,000 **175,900**	 117,000 131,700 204,000 20,500 8,000 2,000 2,000	Reclassification In— Unrestricted—Satisfaction of Program Restrictions . . . . Reclassification In— Unrestricted—Satisfaction of Time Restrictions. . . . . Valley Air Project . . . . "Keep Fish in the Lakes" Program Flood Control Program . . . Management and General Services . . . . Fund-Raising Services . . . . **Unrestricted Net Assets** . . . . Contributions—Temporarily Restricted . . . . **Temporarily Restricted Net Assets** . . . . Reclassification Out— Unrestricted—Satisfaction of Program Restrictions . . . . Reclassification Out— Unrestricted—Satisfaction of Time Restrictions.	103,750 10,000 13,000 49,750 31,000 8,000 2,000 **10,000** 12,750 **101,000** 103,750 10,000

Plant Fund			Endowment Fund		

Depreciation Expense	22,000				
Accumulated Depreciation .		22,000			
Reclassification Out—					
Temporarily Restricted—					
Satisfaction of Equipment					
Acquisition Restrictions . .	22,000				
Reclassification In—					
Unrestricted—Satisfaction					
of Equipment Acquisition					
Restrictions		22,000			

Valley Air Project	2,000				
"Keep Fish in the Lakes"					
Program	3,000				
Flood Control Program	16,000				
Management and General					
Services	1,000				
Fund-Raising Services	1,000				
Depreciation Expense		22,000			
Provision for Uncollectibles		1,000			

Unrestricted Net Assets .	**1,000**		Legacies and Bequests—		
Reclassification In—			Endowment—Permanently		
Unrestricted—Satisfaction			Restricted	20,000	
of Equipment Acquisition			Net Increase in Carrying		
Restrictions	22,000		Value of Endowment		
Valley Air Project		2,000	Investments—Permanently		
"Keep Fish in the Lakes"			Restricted	29,000	
Program		3,000	Gain of Sale of Endowment		
Flood Control Program		16,000	Investments—Permanently		
Management and General			Restricted	2,000	
Services		1,000	**Permanently Restricted**		
Fund-Raising Services		1,000	**Net Assets**		**51,000**
Contributions—Temporarily					
Restricted	60,000				
Investment Revenue—					
Temporarily Restricted . . .	7,000				
Reclassification Out—					
Temporarily Restricted—					
Satisfaction of Equipment					
Acquisition Restrictions . .		22,000			
Temporarily Restricted					
Net Assets		45,000			

Illustration 19A-6
People's Environmental Protection (PEP) Association
Statement of Financial Position
As of December 31, 20X6

	Unrestricted Current Fund	Restricted Current Fund	Plant Fund	Endowment Fund	Total
Assets:					
Cash and cash equivalents..............	$115,500	$129,000	$ 9,000		$ 253,500
Contributions receivable (net of $3,100 allowance)	21,500				21,500
Inventories........................	10,000				10,000
Short-term investments	70,000	7,000	75,000		152,000
Long-term investments				$253,000	253,000
Property, plant, and equipment (net of $16,700 accumulated depreciation). . . .			676,000		676,000
Total assets	$217,000	$136,000	$760,000	$253,000	**$1,366,000**
Liabilities and net assets:					
Accounts payable.....................	$ 33,000	$ 4,000			$ 37,000
Notes payable.......................			$100,000		100,000
Total liabilities	$ 33,000	$ 4,000	$100,000		$ 137,000
Net assets:					
Unrestricted	$184,000		$105,000		$ 289,000
Temporarily restricted		$132,000	555,000		687,000
Permanently restricted				$253,000	253,000
Total net assets	$184,000	$132,000	$660,000	$253,000	**$1,229,000**
Total liabilities and net assets	$217,000	$136,000	$760,000	$253,000	$ 1,366,000

Illustration 19A-7
People's Environmental Protection (PEP) Association
Statement of Activities
For Year Ended December 31, 20X7

	Unrestricted Current Fund	Restricted Current Fund	Plant Fund	Endowment Fund	Total
Public support and revenue:					
Public support:					
Contributions	$397,100				$ 397,100
Special events (net of $2,000 direct costs)	7,000				7,000
Legacies and bequests.................	100,000				100,000
Received from federated and nonfederated campaigns..........................	16,000				16,000
Total public support..................	$520,100				$ 520,100

Revenue:					
Membership dues	$118,000				$ 118,000
Investment revenue	21,000				21,000
Total revenue	$139,000				$ 139,000
Net assets released from restrictions:					
Satisfaction of program restrictions		$ 103,750			$ 103,750
Satisfaction of equipment acquisition restrictions			$ 22,000		$ 22,000
Expiration of time restrictions		10,000			10,000
Total net assets released from restrictions		113,750	22,000		135,750
Total public support and revenue	$659,100	$ 113,750	$ 22,000		$ 794,850
Expenses:					
Valley air project	$117,000	$ 13,000	$ 2,000		$ 132,000
"Keep fish in the lakes" program	131,700	49,750	3,000		184,450
Flood control program	204,000	31,000	16,000		251,000
Management and general	20,500	8,000	1,000		29,500
Fund raising	8,000	2,000	1,000		11,000
Membership development	2,000				2,000
Total expenses	$483,200	$ 103,750	$ 23,000		$ 609,950
Increase (decrease) in unrestricted net assets	$175,900	$ 10,000	$ (1,000)		**$ 184,900**
Transfers among funds	$ (96,000)		$ (96,000)		-
Changes in temporarily restricted net assets:					
Contributions		$ 12,750	$ 60,000		$ 72,750
Investment income on endowment			7,000		7,000
Net assets released from restrictions		(113,750)	(22,000)		(135,750)
Increase (decrease) in temporarily restricted net assets		$(101,000)	$ 45,000		**$ (56,000)**
Changes in permanently restricted net assets:					
Legacies and bequests				$ 20,000	$ 20,000
Net increase in carrying value of investments				29,000	29,000
Gain on sale of investments				2,000	2,000
Increase (decrease) in permanently restricted net assets				$51,000	**$ 51,000**
Change in net assets	$ 79,900	$ (91,000)	$140,000	$ 51,000	**$ 179,900**
Net assets beginning of year	184,000	132,000	660,000	253,000	**1,229,000**
Net assets end of year	$263,900	$ 41,000	$800,000	$304,000	**$1,408,900**

Illustration 19A-8
People's Environmental Protection (PEP) Association
Statement of Financial Position
As of December 31, 20X7

	Unrestricted Current Fund	Restricted Current Fund	Plant Fund	Endowment Fund	Total
Assets:					
Cash and cash equivalents..............	$193,000	$40,000	$ 35,000		$ 268,000
Contributions receivable (net of $2,500					
allowance)	21,000				21,000
Inventories............................	10,900				10,900
Short-term investments	70,000	7,000	75,000		152,000
Property, plant, and equipment (net of					
$38,700 accumulated depreciation)			800,000		800,000
Long-term endowment investments				$304,000	304,000
Total assets	$294,900	$47,000	$910,000	$304,000	**$1,555,900**
Liabilities and net assets:					
Accounts payable......................	$ 31,000	$ 1,000			$ 32,000
Refundable advances		5,000			5,000
Notes payable........................			$110,000		110,000
Total liabilities	$ 31,000	$ 6,000	$110,000		**$ 147,000**
Net assets:					
Unrestricted	$263,900	$10,000	$200,000		**$ 473,900**
Temporarily restricted		31,000	600,000		**631,000**
Permanently restricted				$304,000	**304,000**
Total net assets	$263,900	$41,000	$800,000	$304,000	**$1,408,900**
Total liabilities and net assets	$294,900	$47,000	$910,000	$304,000	$1,555,900

Questions

1. Explain a hospital's rigid adherence to gross revenue determination.
2. Name the three items that are grouped in the account Allowance for Adjustments and Uncollectibles. Briefly describe the function of the account.
3. Name three different procedures that providers of health care follow to cover the cost of malpractice claims. In all procedures, what should the amount of the expense represent?
4. Name the two criteria that must be met for an entity to qualify as a VHWO.
5. Differentiate between the accounts Unrestricted Net Assets—Designated and Unrestricted Net Assets—Undesignated of a VHWO.
6. Compare and contrast accounting and financial reporting for public colleges and universities and VHWOs regarding the following issues: a) measurement focus and basis of accounting, b) presenting revenues and expenses or expenditures, c) presenting depreciation expense.
7. Differentiate between public support and revenues as sources of assets.

8. A VHWO receives a contribution of $25,000 restricted for current operations. By the end of the fiscal period, it spends $5,000 of the contribution. State the amount that is recognized as revenue, and give the journal entries to record the events.

9. Explain the logic (not the process) of pooling of investments.

10. Why does the statement of activity of a VHWO not show expenses by their natural classification, such as salary expense?

11. What is the currently recommended procedure in relation to joint-cost allocation?

Exercises

Exercise 1.

1. Inventory donated for use in a hospital should be reported as

   a) Other operating revenue.

   b) Nonoperating revenues.

   c) Additions to the unrestricted net assets.

   d) Additions to the restricted net assets.

2. Dee City's community hospital, which uses enterprise fund reporting and chooses to follow FASB guidelines, normally includes proceeds from sale of cafeteria meals in

   a) Patient service revenues.

   b) Other operating revenues.

   c) Ancillary service revenues.

   d) Deductions from dietary service expenses.

3. During 1991, Trained Hospital received $90,000 in third-party reimbursements for depreciation. These reimbursements were restricted as follows:

For replacement of fully depreciated equipment	$25,000
For additions to property	65,000

   What amount of these reimbursements should Trained include in revenue for year ended December 31, 20X1?

   a) 0

   b) $25,000

   c) $65,000

   d) $90,000

4. A hospital should report earnings from endowment funds that are restricted to a specific operating purpose as

   a) Temporarily restricted revenues.

   b) Permanently restricted revenues.

   c) Unrestricted revenues.

   d) Unrestricted revenues when expended.

5. Hospital financial resources are required by a bond indenture to be set aside to finance construction of a new pediatrics facility. In which of the following hospital net asset classes should these resources be reported?

(continued)

a) Permanently restricted.

b) Temporarily restricted.

c) Unrestricted.

d) Refundable deposits.

6. Which of the following financial statements should not-for-profit hospitals prepare?

a) Balance sheet and income statement.

b) Balance sheet, income statement, and statement of changes in financial position.

c) Statement of financial position, statement of activities, and statement of cash flows.

d) Statement of funds, statement of activities, and statement of cash flows.

7. Land valued at $400,000 and subject to a $150,000 mortgage was donated to Beaty Hospital without restriction as to use. Which of the following entries should Beaty make to record this donation?

a) Land $400,000
    Mortgage Payable   150,000
    Endowment Fund Balance   250,000

b) Land $400,000
    Mortgage Payable   150,000
    Contributions—Unrestricted   250,000

c) Land $400,000
    Debt Fund Balance   150,000
    Endowment Fund Balance   250,000

d) Land $400,000
    Mortgage Payable   150,000
    Unrestricted Fund Balance   250,000

8. In hospital accounting, restricted net assets are

a) Not available unless the board of directors removes the restrictions.

b) Restricted as to use only for board-designated purposes.

c) Not available for current operating use; however, the income generated by the funds is available for current operating use.

d) Restricted as to use by the donor, grantor, or other source of the resources.

(AICPA adapted)

Exercise 2.   A hospital has 3 revenue-controlling accounts: Patient Service Revenue, Other Operating Revenue, and Nonoperating Revenue.

a) State in general terms the type of revenue found in each controlling account.

b) Indicate into which of the three controlling accounts each of the following would be placed by using the symbols PS for Patient Service Revenue, OO for Other Operating Revenue, N for Nonoperating Revenue, and N/A if not a revenue item:

1. Tuition for entry to the nursing school   _____

2. An unrestricted gift of cash   _____

3. General nursing fees charged to patients   _____

4. Charges for physicians' care   _____

5. A restricted gift used for research on genes   _____

6. Dividends from the hospital's investments   _____

7. Revenue from gift shop sales   _____

8. Patient room and board charges   _____

9. Proceeds from sales of cafeteria meals   _____

10. Recovery room fees   _____

11. Contributions for plant replacement and expansion   _____

Exercise 3.   Record the following events of Elmwood Hospital.

a) *Patients were billed for the following gross charges:*

Room and board	$680,000
Physicians' care	220,000
Laboratory and radiology	110,000

b) *A donation of drugs with a market value of $12,000 was received from a doctor. The drugs are normally purchased.*

c) *Revenues were reported from:*

Newsstand and snack bar	$15,800
Parking lot charges	3,200
Vending machines	9,800

d) *A charity allowance of $13,000 was granted to indigent patients.*

e) *Contractual adjustments granted to patients for Medicare charges totaled $68,000.*

f) *The hospital recorded an increase in the provision of $26,000 for uncollectible receivables.*

Exercise 4.   The Pure Air Rehabilitation Hospital has the following balances that are extracted from its December 31, 20X7 trial balance:

Account	Debit	Credit
Nursing Services Expense	$230,000	
Professional Fees Expense	340,000	
General and Administrative Expense	150,000	
Depreciation Expense	90,000	
Interest Expense	13,000	
Assets Whose Use Is Limited	55,000	
Repairs and Maintenance Expense	110,000	
Provision for Uncollectible Accounts	14,000	
Contractual Adjustments	26,000	
Patient Service Revenue		$740,000
Income, Seminars		23,000
Child Day Care Revenue		15,000
Parking Fees		4,500
Endowment Income—Temporarily Restricted		120,000
Interest Income—Unrestricted		3,000
Donations—Temporarily Restricted		18,000
Gains (Distributable) on Sale of Endowments— Temporarily Restricted		56,000

(continued)

Account	Debit	Credit
Net Assets—Unrestricted (1/1/X7)		800,000
Net Assets—Temporarily Restricted (1/1/X7)..............		755,000
Net Assets—Permanently Restricted (1/1/X7)		750,000

From the above information, prepare a statement of activities for the year ended December 31, 20X7.

Exercise 5.   Alpha Hospital, a nongovernmental not-for-profit organization, has adopted an accounting policy that does not imply a time restriction on gifts of long-lived assets. For items 1 through 6, indicate the manner in which the transaction affects Alpha's financial statements.

    A. Increase in unrestricted revenues, gains, and other support.
    B. Decrease in an expense.
    C. Increase in temporarily restricted net assets.
    D. Increase in permanently restricted net assets.
    E. No required reportable event.

1. Alpha's board designates $1,000,000 to purchase investments whose income will be used for capital improvements.
2. Income from investments in item 1 above, which was not previously accrued, is received.
3. A benefactor provided funds for building expansion.
4. The funds in item 3 above are used to purchase a building in the fiscal period following the period the funds were received.
5. An accounting firm prepared Alpha's annual financial statements without charge to Alpha.
6. Alpha received investments subject to the donor's requirement that investment income be used to pay for outpatient services.

(AICPA adapted)

Exercise 6.   Ambulance Service is a not-for-profit health care provider. Prepare the reconciliation of change in net assets to net cash provided by operating activities that would accompany its statement of cash flows under the direct method for the year ended December 31, 20X6.

Decrease in net assets...........................	$ 93,000
Noncash items: Depreciation	117,000
Amortization of premium on bonds payable	22,000
Cash paid for acquisition of property...............	10,000
Payment to settle long-term note payable	63,000
Net decrease in receivables and supplies	38,000
Net increase in current payables..................	10,000

Exercise 7.   Record the following events of the Chemical Dependency Clinic, a VHWO:

    a) *Membership dues of $9,000 were collected.*
    b) *Cash contributions of $22,000 and pledges for $32,000 were received.*
    c) *It is estimated that 10% of the above pledges will prove uncollectible.*
    d) *A fund-raising dinner grossed $12,000 from the sale of 480 tickets. The catered dinner cost $15 each for the 420 people who attended, plus $200 for the rental of the dining room. Payment for these costs was made.*

e) A classic car was donated to the organization. The car has an estimated market value of $75,000. It will be the main attraction of an auction to be held in the next accounting period. The proceeds of the auction are part of the budget for activities in the next period.

f) To expand the services of the clinic, a professional fund-raising group was hired to undertake a 6-month campaign. At the end of the 6 months, the group submitted the following report:

Cash collected.	$ 70,000
Pledges (estimated 95% collectible)	30,000
Total proceeds	$100,000
Less 20% fund-raising fee (regardless of collections) . .	20,000
Net proceeds from drive	$ 80,000

Exercise 8.   Record the following events of the Mental Health Clinic, a VHWO:

a) A contribution of $10,000 was received and is to be used for the purchase of equipment, but not until an addition to the building is constructed. Construction has begun on the building.

b) Equipment costing $17,000, with a book value of $8,000, was sold for $10,000. The gain is unrestricted.

c) Depreciation of $9,000 is recorded on various plant items.

d) Equipment was purchased for $12,000, with payment due in 30 days from donor-restricted resources. Mental Health Clinic elects to release the donor restriction upon acquisition of the equipment.

e) The liability for the equipment purchased in item d) was paid.

Exercise 9.   Record the following events of Mercy Health Clinic, a VHWO:

a) In her will, a leading citizen left a bequest of $200,000 to the clinic. Stipulations were that the amount was to become the corpus of a permanent endowment. Any income received would be used first to cover any loss of principal, with the remaining revenue to be used for an educational program on mental problems. The total amount was received and invested in 8% municipal bonds purchased at face value on an interest date.

b) Three months later, half of the bond investment was sold at 101, plus $2,500 of accrued interest.

c) The remaining endowment bond investments earned $6,000. The amount is not subject to any limitations.

d) At year-end, the remaining endowment bond investments have a market value of $103,500.

Exercise 10.   Early in 20X8, a not-for-profit organization received a $4,000,000 gift from a wealthy benefactor. This benefactor specified that the gift be invested in perpetuity with income restricted to provide speaker fees for a lecture series named for the benefactor. The not-for-profit is permitted to choose suitable investments and is responsible for all other costs associated with initiating and administering this series. Neither the donor's stipulation nor the law addresses gains and losses on this permanent endowment. In 20X8, the investments purchased with the gift earned $100,000 in dividend income. The fair value of the investments increased by $240,000.

(continued)

Three presentations in the lecture series were held in 20X8. The speaker fees for the 3 presentations amounted to $140,000. The not-for-profit organization used the $100,000 dividend income to cover part of the total fees. Because the board of directors did not wish to sell part of the investments, the organization used $40,000 in unrestricted resources to pay the remainder of the speaker fees.

For items 1 through 5, determine whether the transaction should be recorded in the 20X8 statement of activities as an increase in

 A. Unrestricted net assets.
 B. Temporarily restricted net assets.
 C. Permanently restricted net assets.
 D. Either unrestricted or temporarily restricted net assets.

1. The receipt of the $4,000,000 gift
2. The $100,000 in dividend income
3. The $240,000 unrealized gain, assuming the not-for-profit's accounting policy is to record increases in net assets, for which a donor-imposed restriction is met in the same accounting period as gains and investment income are recognized, as increases in unrestricted net assets
4. The $100,000 in dividend income, assuming the lecture series is not to begin until 20X9
5. The $240,000 unrealized gain, assuming the lecture series is not to begin until 20X9

Exercise 11. The Better Life Clinic is a VHWO that has 3 main programs:

 Drug rehabilitation
 Alcohol recovery
 Weight control

Unrestricted public support received during the period was $35,000; revenues from membership services were $12,000. The following expenses and allocations to program and supporting services are shown for 20X0. Better Life elects to release donor restrictions for property, plant, and equipment over the useful life of the asset.

Distribution

Item	Amount	Drug Rehab.	Alcohol Recovery	Weight Control	Fund Raising	Gen. & Adm.
Secretarial salary	5,000					100%
Office supplies	6,000	20%	10%	10%	10%	50
Printing	8,000	10	10	20	50	10
Depreciation (all depreciation is on assets acquired with donor-restricted contributions)	4,000	20	20	20		40
Instruction	9,000	30	25	35	10	
Rent	10,000	30	20	30		20

Temporarily restricted net assets totaled $30,000 on January 1; the unrestricted net asset balance was $12,000. Prepare a statement of activities for the year.

Appendix Exercises

Exercise 19A-1.   The Health Awareness Club is a not-for-profit organization that conducts meetings and special programs dedicated to promoting better health for members of the community. Members participate in regularly scheduled classes and exercise programs. There are also a variety of community services available to the general population. During the year, various funds flow to the organization. A list of receipts follows. For each item, indicate which of the following funds records the item, and indicate the category within which the item is recorded in that fund.

Name of Fund	Category
Current unrestricted fund	Revenue—Unrestricted
Current restricted fund	Public Support—Unrestricted
Plant fund	Deferred Revenue
Endowment fund	Public Support—Temporarily Restricted
	Public Support—Permanently Restricted
	Revenue—Temporarily Restricted

The transactions were as follows:

a)   *General membership dues.*

b)   *Receipts for pancake breakfast open to public.*

c)   *Donation of equipment to be used in exercise room. Restrictions are released when assets are placed in service.*

d)   *Donation of equipment to be sold; proceeds are to be used to support education program.*

e)   *Share of federated national fund drive.*

f)   *Sale of educational books produced by the organization.*

g)   *Auction of donated services to be used to acquire additional land for expansion.*

h)   *Receipt of endowment from former president of organization.*

i)   *Income on endowment that supports youth health program.*

j)   *Pledge of $5,000 from local corporation for youth health program. The pledge is conditional, in that the organization must match the grant with funds raised from other corporate sponsors.*

Exercise 19A-2.   For the Health Awareness Club of Exercise 19A-1 above, various expenditures are recorded during the year. For each item listed, indicate the fund in which the entry would be made and the nature of the transaction. The available funds and transaction types are

Name of Fund	Nature of Transaction
Current unrestricted fund	Fund-raising expense
Current restricted fund	General and administrative expense
Plant fund	Program expense
Endowment fund	Offset to public support

(continued)

The transactions were as follows:

a) *Cost of brochures asking for donations.*
b) *Accounting services received.*
c) *Office supplies consumed.*
d) *Repair and maintenance of exercise room equipment.*
e) *Depreciation on exercise room equipment.*
f) *Costs associated with pancake breakfast.*
g) *Costs of cancer awareness program paid from donations that are restricted to this use.*

Exercise 19A-3.   On January 2, 20X9, the available cash in the following funds was placed into an investment pool:

Fund	Cash Pooled
Current unrestricted	$ 40,000
Current restricted	30,000
Plant	10,000
Endowment	20,000
Total	$100,000

During the next year, no additional cash was placed into the pool, nor was any amount withdrawn. At the end of the year, the pooled investments had a basis of $120,000, representing original contributions plus $20,000 of realized gains that remained in the investment pool. At year-end, the market value of the pool amounted to $130,000. Prepare a schedule reflecting pooling activities for the year 20X9.

Exercise 19A-4.   The characteristics of VHWOs differ in certain respects from the characteristics of state or local governmental units. As an example, VHWOs derive their revenues primarily from voluntary contributions from the general public, while governmental units derive their revenues from taxes and from services provided to their jurisdictions.

1. Describe fund accounting and discuss whether its use is consistent with the concept that an accounting entity is an economic unit that has control over resources, accepts responsibilities for making and carrying out commitments, and conducts economic activity.
2. Discuss how methods used to account for fixed assets differ between VHWOs and governmental units.

(AICPA adapted)

Problems

Problem 19-1.   Select the best answer for each of the following multiple-choice items dealing with hospitals:

On March 1, 19X8, A. C. Rowe established a $100,000 endowment fund, the income from which is to be paid to Elm Hospital for general operating purposes. Elm does not control the fund's principal. Rowe appointed West National Bank as trustee of this fund. What journal entry is required by Elm to record the establishment of the endowment?

a) Cash $100,000
        Nonexpendable Endowment Fund. $100,000

b) Cash $100,000
        Nonoperating Revenue $100,000

c) Nonexpendable Endowment Fund. $100,000
        Endowment Fund Balance $100,000

d) Memorandum entry only

2. In 20X8, Wells Hospital received an unrestricted bequest of common stock with a market value of $50,000 on the date of receipt of the stock. The testator had paid $20,000 for this stock in 20X6. Wells should record this bequest as

 a) Nonoperating revenue of $50,000.

 b) Nonoperating revenue of $30,000.

 c) Nonoperating revenue of $20,000.

 d) A memorandum entry only.

3. Cedar Hospital has a marketable equity securities portfolio that is included appropriately in noncurrent assets in unrestricted funds. The portfolio has an aggregate cost of $300,000. It had an aggregate market value of $250,000 at the end of 20X7 and $290,000 at the end of 20X6. If the portfolio was reported properly in the balance sheet at the end of 20X6, the change in the valuation allowance at the end of 20X7 should be

 a) 0.

 b) A decrease of $40,000.

 c) An increase of $40,000.

 d) An increase of $50,000.

4. Ross Hospital's accounting records disclosed the following information:

Net resources invested in plant assets (hospital
    policy is to release donor restrictions when assets
    are placed in service) $10,000,000
Board-designated funds   2,000,000

What amount should be included as unrestricted net assets?

 a) $12,000,000   b) $10,000,000   c) $2,000,000   d) 0

5. Under Cura Hospital's established rate structure, patient service revenues of $9,000,000 would have been earned for the year ended December 31, 20X7. However, only $6,750,000 was collected because of charity allowances of $1,500,000 and discounts of $750,000 to third-party payors. For the year ended December 31, 20X7, what amount should Cura record as net patient service revenues?

 a) $6,750,000   b) $7,500,000   c) $8,250,000   d) $9,000,000

6. An organization of high school seniors performs services for patients at Leer Hospital. These students are volunteers and perform services that the hospital would not otherwise provide, such as wheeling patients in the park and reading to patients. These volunteers donated 5,000 hours of service to Leer in 20X7. At the minimum wage rate, these services would amount to $22,500, while it is estimated that the fair value of these services was $27,000. In Leer's 20X7

(continued)

statement of revenues and expenses, what amount should be reported as nonoperating revenue?

   a) $27,000   b) $22,500   c) $6,250   d) 0

7. In June 20X8, Park Hospital purchased medicines from Jove Pharmaceutical Company at a cost of $2,000. However, Jove notified Park that the invoice was being canceled and the medicines were being donated to Park. Park should record this donation of medicines as

   a) A memorandum entry only.

   b) Other operating revenue of $2,000.

   c) A $2,000 credit to operating expenses.

   d) A $2,000 credit to nonoperating expenses.

8. Palma Hospital's patient service revenues for services provided in 20X8, at established rates, amounted to $8,000,000 on the accrual basis. For internal reporting, Palma uses the discharge method. Under this method, patient service revenues are recognized only when patients are discharged, with no recognition given to revenues accruing for services to patients not yet discharged. Patient service revenues at established rates using the discharge method amounted to $7,000,000 for 20X8. According to GAAP, Palma should report patient service revenues for 20X8 of

   a) Either $8,000,000 or $7,000,000, at the option of the hospital.

   b) $8,000,000.

   c) $7,500,000.

   d) $7,000,000.

9. In 20X6, Pyle Hospital received a $250,000 pure endowment grant. Also in 20X6, Pyle's governing board designated, for special uses, $300,000 which had originated from unrestricted gifts. What amount of these resources should be accounted for as part of the unrestricted net asset class?

   a) 0   b) $250,000   c) $300,000   d) $550,000

10. Cura Hospital's property, plant, and equipment, net of depreciation, amounted to $10,000,000, with related mortgage liabilities of $1,000,000. What amount should be included in the permanently restricted net asset class?

   a) 0   b) $1,000,000   c) $9,000,000   d) $10,000,000

(AICPA adapted)

Problem 19-2.   Select the best answer for each of the following multiple-choice items. Items 1 through 3 are based on the following:

The Bay Ridge Humane Society, a VHWO caring for lost animals, had the following financial inflows and outflows for the year ended December 31, 20X5:

Inflows:

Cash received from federated campaign	$680,000
Cash received that is designated for 20X6 operations	30,000
Contributions pledged for 20X5 not yet received	90,000
Contributions pledged for 20X6 not yet received	25,000
Sales of pet supplies	10,000
Pet adoption fees.	50,000

Outflows:

Kennel operations	$350,000
Pet health care	100,000
Advertising pets for adoption.	50,000
Fund raising	70,000
Administrative and general	200,000

1. In the humane society's statement of activities for the year ended December 31, 20X5, what amount should be reported under the classification of public support—unrestricted?

    a) $740,000   b) $762,000   c) $770,000   d) $825,000

2. In the humane society's statement of activities for the year ended December 31, 20X5, what amount should be reported under the classification of program services expense?

    a) $770,000   b) $450,000   c) $550,000   d) $500,000

3. In the humane society's balance sheet as of December 31, 20X5, what amount should be reported under the classification of public support—temporarily restricted?

    a) $55,000   b) $30,000   c) $25,000   d) 0

4. Arbor Haven, a voluntary welfare organization funded by contributions from the general public, received unrestricted pledges of $500,000 during 20X6. It was estimated that 12% of these pledges would be uncollectible. By the end of 20X6, $400,000 of the pledges had been collected, and it was expected that $40,000 more would be collected in 20X7, with the balance of $60,000 to be written-off as uncollectible. Donors did not specify any periods during which the donations were to be used. What amount should Arbor Haven include under public support in 20X6 for contributions?

    a) $500,000   b) $452,000   c) $440,000   d) $400,000

5. The following expenditures were among those incurred by a voluntary welfare society during 20X7:

Printing of annual report.	$10,000
Unsolicited merchandise sent to encourage contributions	20,000

    What amount should be classified as fund-raising costs in the society's statement of activities?

    a) 0   b) $10,000   c) $20,000   d) $30,000

6. Apex Inc. donated a computer to Bird Shelter, a voluntary organization. The computer cost Apex $40,000. On the date of donation, it had a book value of $25,000 and a market value of $20,000. Bird Shelter's depreciation expense should be based on

    a) $40,000   b) $25,000   c) $20,000   d) $15,000

    (AICPA adapted)

Problem 19-3. Select the best answer for each of the following multiple-choice questions. (No. 1 is AICPA adapted.)

1. In the statement of activities of a VHWO, depreciation expense should
   a) Be included as an element of expense.
   b) Be included as an element of other changes in fund balances.
   c) Be included as an element of support.
   d) Not be included.

2. Donor-restricted contributions that have been given to a VHWO for the purpose of purchasing fixed assets should be recorded as increases to
   a) Unrestricted Net Assets.
   b) Temporarily Restricted Net Assets.
   c) Permanently Restricted Net Assets.
   d) Fund Balance—Restricted.

3. The following correct entry is found on the books of a VHWO:

   Unrestricted Net Assets—Undesignated.   XXX
      Unrestricted Net Assets—Designated for AIDS Research.   XXX

   From the entry, one should conclude that the board of directors has
   a) Designated a portion of the unrestricted net assets for a future AIDS research program.
   b) Designated a portion of the restricted net assets for a future AIDS research program.
   c) Transferred resources to an AIDS research program.
   d) Directed that unused resources previously assigned to an AIDS research program be returned to unrestricted net asset classification.

4. To protect the principal of the endowment of a VHWO, unrestricted cash interest received on bond investments purchased at a premium is classified as unrestricted
   a) In an amount equal to net earnings after premium amortization.
   b) In an amount equal to the gross cash interest received.
   c) Only when the interest received equals the total premium paid.
   d) Only upon the maturity of the bonds.

5. The investments of a VHWO are pooled and carried at market value. At the end of the period, there is a decrease in total market value. The market value decrease should
   a) Not be recorded until the loss is realized.
   b) Be debited to Realized Loss on Pooled Investments.
   c) Be debited to Endowment Fund Balance.
   d) Be debited to Net Decrease in Carrying Value of Investments.

Problem 19-4. Select the best answer for each of the following multiple-choice items:

1. A nonprofit performing arts organization receives a donation that is restricted to its endowment and another donation that is restricted to use in acquiring a performing arts center. How should these donations be reported in the year received, assuming neither donation is expended in that year?

	Donation for Endowment	Donation for Performing Arts Center
a)	Contributions—Temporarily Restricted	Contributions—Temporarily Restricted
b)	Deferred Capital Additions	Capital Additions
c)	Contributions—Unrestricted	Contributions—Unrestricted
d)	Capital Additions Deferred	Capital Additions
e)	Contributions—Permanently Restricted	Contributions—Temporarily Restricted

2. Environs, a community foundation, incurred $10,000 in management and general expenses during 20X1. In Environs' statement of activities for the year ended December 31, 20X1, the $10,000 should be reported as

   a) *A direct reduction of unrestricted net assets.*

   b) *Part of supporting services expense.*

   c) *Part of program services expense.*

   d) *A contra-account to offset revenue and support.*

3. Super Seniors is a not-for-profit organization that provides services to senior citizens. Super employs a full-time staff of 10 people at an annual cost of $150,000. In addition, two volunteers work as part-time secretaries replacing last year's full-time secretary who earned $10,000. Services performed by other volunteers for special events had an estimated value of $15,000. These volunteers were employees of local businesses, and they received small-value items for their participation. What amount should Super report for salary and wage expenses related to the above items?

   a) *$150,000*

   b) *$160,000*

   c) *$165,000*

   d) *$175,000*

4. The League, a not-for-profit organization, received the following pledges:

Unrestricted	$200,000
Restricted for capital additions	150,000

   All pledges are legally enforceable; however, the League's experience indicates that 10% of all pledges prove to be uncollectible. What amount should the League report as pledges receivable net of any required allowance account?

   a) *$135,000*

   b) *$180,000*

   c) *$315,000*

   d) *$350,000*

5. Midtown Church received a donation of marketable equity securities from a church member. The securities had appreciated in value after they were purchased by the donor, and they continued to appreciate through the end of Midtown's fiscal year. At what amount should Midtown report its investment in marketable equity securities in its year-end balance sheet?

(continued)

a) Donor's cost.

b) Market value at the date of receipt.

c) Market value at the balance sheet date.

d) Market value at either the date of receipt or the balance sheet date.

6. Maple Church has cash available for investments in several different accounting funds. Maple's policy is to maximize its financial resources. How may Maple pool its investments?

a) Maple may not pool its investments.

b) Maple may pool all investments but must equitably allocate realized and unrealized gains and losses among participating funds.

c) Maple may pool only unrestricted investments but must equitably allocate realized and unrealized gains and losses among participating funds.

d) Maple may pool only restricted investments but must equitably allocate realized and unrealized gains and losses among participating funds.

7. When a nonprofit organization combines fund-raising efforts with bona fide educational efforts or program services, the total combined costs incurred are

a) Reported as program services expenses.

b) Allocated between fund-raising and program services expenses using an appropriate allocation basis.

c) Reported as fund-raising costs.

d) Reported as management and general expenses.

(AICPA adapted)

Problem 19-5. The following selected events relate to the 20X7 activities of Aires Nursing Home Inc., a not-for-profit agency:

a) Gross patient service revenue totaled $2,200,000. The provision for uncollectible accounts was estimated at $92,000. The allowance for contractual adjustments was increased by $120,000.

b) After a conference with representatives of Gold Star Insurance Company, differences between the amounts accrued and subsequent settlements reduced receivables by $60,000.

c) A grateful patient donated securities with a cost of $20,000 and a market value at date of donation of $75,000. The donation was restricted to expenditure for modernization of equipment. The donation was accepted.

d) Cash of $37,000 that had been restricted by a donor for the purchase of furniture was used this year. Aires chose to release the donor restriction over the useful life of the asset.

e) The board voluntarily transferred $50,000 of cash to add to the resources held for capital improvements.

f) Pledges of $60,000 and cash of $20,000 were received to defer operating expenses. Of the pledges, 10% are considered uncollectible. Term endowments of $10,000 matured and were released to cover operations.

g) Equipment costing $250,000 was purchased on account. Restricted resources held for that purpose will be released from restriction over the useful life of the asset.

h) The nursing home uses functional operating expense control accounts. Expenses for the year were for

Nursing services.	$1,120,000
Dietary services	230,000
Maintenance services	115,000
Administrative services	285,000
Interest	160,000
Subtotal (of which $253,000 is unpaid)	$1,910,000
Depreciation [$20,000 from assets purchased with resources in items d) and g) above]	60,000
Total	$1,970,000

Required:

1. Omitting explanations, prepare journal entries for the foregoing events.
2. Prepare a statement of activities for the year ended December 31, 20X7.

Problem 19-6.   The following nominal accounts were extracted from the December 31, 20X7 adjusted trial balance of Downs Private Hospital:

Gross patient service revenue.		$11,049,200
Research grant revenue to the extent expended		361,000
Revenue from sale of cafeteria meals to guests and employees.		108,000
Donated services of nurses and physicians (skilled services otherwise purchased).		145,000
Unrestricted gifts and grants.		100,200
Unrestricted endowment income		12,000
Gifts restricted for equipment purchase.		540,000
Donor-restricted investments for permanent endowment . .		150,000
Temporarily restricted endowment income.		25,000
Revenue from parking lot.		31,000
Revenue from vending machines		68,000
Income on investments whose use is limited by the board for capital improvements		207,000
Contributions restricted by donor for pediatric unit operations.		225,000
Reclassification in—unrestricted—satisfaction of program restrictions		125,000
Reclassification in—unrestricted—satisfaction of plant acquisition restrictions		220,000
Unrestricted net assets, 1/1/X7		625,000
Temporarily restricted net assets, 1/1/X7		825,000
Permanently restricted net assets, 1/1/X7.		2,350,000
Reclassification out—temporarily restricted— satisfaction of program restrictions.	125,000	
Reclassification out—temporarily restricted— satisfaction of plant acquisition restrictions	220,000	
Administrative services (including $30,000 malpractice cost).	112,500	
Contractual adjustments under third-party reimbursement programs	1,328,500	
Charity care	215,000	
Provision for uncollectibles	341,600	
Nursing services (including $125,000 in pediatric unit) .	6,589,100	

(continued)

Dietary services	1,511,200
Maintenance services	838,300
Depreciation and amortization	478,200
Interest expense	142,200
Loss on sale of endowment investments	5,300

Required:

Prepare a statement of activities for the year ended December 31, 20X7.

Problem 19-7.   You are provided with a summarized version of the cash account of Lakeside Hospital, a not-for-profit organization. Prepare a statement of cash flows, using the direct method, for the year ended December 31, 20X7.

Cash Account

	Debit	Credit
Cash balance, January 1, 20X7	275,900	
Cash received from: Patients	2,061,900	
Third-party payors	6,500,000	
Operation of gift shop	517,700	
Unrestricted gifts	323,500	
Contributions restricted for endowment . .	500,000	
Donor-restricted contributions for purchase of property		
and equipment	183,000	
Early repayment of long-term debt		242,300
Cash paid to: Employees		1,151,000
Suppliers		6,200,000
Providers of consultation services		800,000
Bank for interest		147,000
Contractor for purchase of property		
and equipment		501,200
Cash balance, December 31, 20X7.	$1,320,500	

Problem 19-8.   Using data from Problem 19-7 and the following additional information, prepare a reconciliation of change in net assets to net cash provided by operating activities that would accompany Lakeside Hospital's statement of cash flows for the year ended December 31, 20X7.

The following condensed statement of activities for the year ended December 31, 20X7, shows

Total operating revenues	$9,302,400
Total operating expenses	8,780,100
Income from operations	$522,300
Nonoperating revenue.	1,102,900
Excess of revenues over expenses	$1,625,200

Included in the condensed statement of activities were

Depreciation and amortization	$422,500
Noncash gifts and bequests	37,500
Increase in expense and liability for estimated	
malpractice costs	12,300

An analysis of comparative balance sheet items showed the following changes in balances during 20X7:

Increase in patient accounts receivable................	$266,300
Decrease in supplies inventory	11,800
Increase in accounts payable	10,100

Problem 19-9. Carolina Hospital's post-closing trial balance at December 31, 20X7, is as follows:

Cash	$ 370,000	
Investment in U.S. Treasury Bills.	400,000	
Investment in Corporate Bonds	500,000	
Interest Receivable	10,000	
Accounts Receivable	50,000	
Inventory.....................................	30,000	
Land...	100,000	
Building	800,000	
Equipment....................................	170,000	
Allowance for Depreciation		$ 410,000
Accounts Payable		30,000
Notes Payable		370,000
Permanently Restricted Net Assets		520,000
Unrestricted Net Assets		1,100,000
	$2,430,000	$2,430,000

Carolina, which is a not-for-profit hospital, did not maintain its books using hospital fund accounting. Effective January 1, 20X8, Carolina's board of trustees voted to adjust the December 31, 20X7 general ledger balances and to establish separate funds for the general funds, the endowment fund, and the plant replacement and expansion fund for internal control.

An audit of Carolina's accounts revealed several required adjustments:

a) *Investment in Corporate Bonds pertains to the amount required to be accumulated under a board policy to invest cash equal to accumulated depreciation until the funds are needed for asset replacement. The $500,000 balance at December 31, 20X7, is less than the full amount required because of errors in computation of building depreciation for past years. Included in the allowance for depreciation is a correctly computed amount of $90,000 applicable to equipment purchased with cash donated for that purpose. The hospital elects to release donor restrictions over the useful life of the fixed assets.*

b) *Permanently Restricted Net Assets has been credited with the following:*

Donor's bequest of cash........................	$350,000
Gain on sales of securities	50,000
Interest and dividends earned in 20X5, 20X6,	
and 20X7—Unrestricted........................	120,000
Total	$520,000

(continued)

The terms of the bequest specify that the principal, plus all gains on sales of investments, are to remain fully invested in U.S. government or corporate securities. At December 31, 20X7, $400,000 was invested in U.S. Treasury bills. The bequest further specifies that interest and dividends earned on investments are to be used for payment of current operating expenses.

c) *Land comprises the following:*

Donation of land 40 years ago, at appraised value (land is unrestricted)	$ 45,000
Appreciation in value of land as determined by an independent appraiser 5 years ago	55,000
Total	$100,000

d) *Building comprises the following:*

Hospital building completed 40 years ago when operations were started (useful life of 50 years), at cost	$720,000
Installation of elevator 20 years ago (estimated useful life of 20 years), at cost	80,000
Total	$800,000

e) *A fund drive was conducted in 20X7 to offset a possible operating loss. As of December 31, 20X7, there were unrecorded unconditional pledges of $121,000, of which 90% are likely to be collected. $75,000 of these pledges are unrestricted; the remaining $46,000 are donor restricted for cancer research.*

f) *$100,000 of the current cash balance is donor restricted for new equipment acquisition.*

Required:

Enter the post-closing trial balance on a worksheet. Use the following columnar headings with a debit and credit column for each: Trial Balance, Adjustments, General Funds, Endowment Fund, and Plant Replacement and Expansion Fund.

Enter the adjustments necessary to properly restate the general ledger account balances. Distribute the adjusted balances to establish the separate fund accounts, and complete the worksheet. Formal journal entries are not required, but supporting computations should be referenced to the worksheet adjustments.

(AICPA adapted)

Problem 19-10.   Carleton Agency, a VHWO, conducts two programs: Medical Services and Community Information Services. It had the following transactions during the year ended June 30, 20X9:

1. Received the following contributions:

Unrestricted pledges	$800,000
Restricted cash	95,000
Building fund pledges	50,000
Endowment fund cash	1,000

2. Collected the following pledges:

Unrestricted	$450,000
Building fund	20,000

3. Received the following unrestricted cash flows from

Theater party (net of direct costs)	$12,000
Bequests	10,000
Membership dues	8,000
Interest and dividends	5,000

4. Program expenses incurred (processed through vouchers payable):

Medical services	$60,000
Community information services	15,000

5. Services expenses incurred (processed through vouchers payable):

General administration	$150,000
Fund raising	200,000

6. Purchased fixed assets:

Fixed assets purchased with donor-restricted cash	$ 18,000

Carleton's policy is to release donor restrictions when assets are placed in service.

7. Depreciation of all buildings and equipment in the land, buildings, and equipment fund was allocated as follows:

Medical services program	$ 4,000
Community information services program	3,000
General administration	6,000
Fund raising	2,000

8. Vouchers paid:

Paid vouchers payable	$330,000

(AICPA adapted)

Required:

Record journal entries for the preceding transactions. Number your journal entries to coincide with the preceding transaction numbers.

Problem 19-11. The Super Senior Agency is a VHWO. The following events occurred during the year. The agency uses one control account for its fixed assets, with supporting subsidiary records.

a) Property was purchased for $200,000. A down payment of $40,000 was made from unrestricted cash, and a 14% mortgage was signed for the remainder.

b) Office furniture was purchased for $9,000 on open account.

c) A local corporation donated and installed room partitions. The value of the donated items and services was $4,000. Super Senior's policy is to release donor restrictions over the useful life of the assets to match depreciation expense.

(continued)

d) At year-end, a payment was made covering mortgage interest for one year, plus a $10,000 payment on the principal.

e) Office equipment costing $3,000, with a book value of $1,000, was sold for $1,800 cash. The gain is unrestricted.

f) Fully depreciated equipment costing $7,000 was written-off. There was no scrap value.

g) A depreciation schedule was prepared, showing annual depreciation expense of $46,000, which was recorded. Depreciation of $20,000 was for equipment donated or purchased with donated cash.

h) Two years ago, the will of an agency volunteer granted $50,000 for the acquisition and installation of theater equipment, providing the organization acquired a new building. The amount now was expended in accordance with the stipulations of the will, and payment of $50,000 was made.

i) The account payable of $9,000 mentioned in item b) was paid.

Required:

Prepare journal entries to record the preceding events.

Problem 19-12.   The June 30, 20X7 adjusted trial balances of the Bayfield Community Association for Handicapped Children follow. This association is a voluntary welfare organization.

Bayfield Community Association for Handicapped Children
Adjusted Current Funds Trial Balances
June 30, 20X7

	Unrestricted	Restricted
Cash	11,000	29,000
Bequest Receivable		5,000
Pledges Receivable	12,000	
Accrued Interest Receivable	1,000	
Investments (at cost, which approximates market)	140,000	
Endowment Investments		250,000
Accounts Payable and Accrued Expenses	50,000	1,000
Refundable Deposits	2,000	
Allowance for Uncollectible Pledges	3,000	
Net Assets, July 1, 20X6:		
Designated, Unrestricted	12,000	
Undesignated, Unrestricted	26,000	
Temporarily Restricted		3,000
Permanently Restricted		250,000
Endowment Revenue—		
Temporarily Restricted		20,000
Contributions	300,000	15,000
Membership Dues	25,000	
Program Service Fees	30,000	
Investment Income	10,000	
Auction Proceeds	42,000	

Auction Expenses	11,000			
Deaf Children's Program	120,000			
Blind Children's Program	150,000			
Management and General Services.	49,000			
Fund-Raising Services	9,000			
Provision for Uncollectible Pledges.	2,000			
Reclassification In—Satisfaction of				
Program Restrictions		5,000		
Reclassification Out—Satisfaction of				
Program Restrictions				5,000
	505,000	505,000	289,000	289,000

Required:

1. Prepare a statement of activities for the year ended June 30, 20X7.
2. Prepare a statement of financial position as of June 30, 20X7.

(AICPA adapted)

Problem 19-13. Thirty years ago, a group of civic-minded merchants in Mayfair organized the "Committee of 100" for the purpose of establishing the Mayfair Sports Club, a not-for-profit sports organization for local youth. Each of the Committee's 100 members contributed $1,000 toward the Club's capital. In addition, each participant agreed to pay dues of $200 a year for the Club's operations. All dues have been collected in full by the end of each fiscal year, which ends on March 31. Members who have discontinued their participation have been replaced by an equal number of new members by transferring the participation certificates from the former members to the new ones. Following are the Club's trial balances at April 1, 20X6:

	Debit	Credit
Cash	29,000	
Investments (at market, equal to cost)	88,000	
Inventories.	5,000	
Land.	10,000	
Building	164,000	
Accumulated Depreciation—Building		130,000
Furniture and Equipment	54,000	
Accumulated Depreciation—Furniture and Equipment		46,000
Endowment Investments	400,000	
Accounts Payable.		10,000
Participation Certificates (100 @ $1,000 each)		100,000
Unrestricted Net Assets		12,000
Temporarily Restricted Net Assets.		52,000
Permanently Restricted Net Assets		400,000
Totals	750,000	750,000

Transactions and adjustment data for the year ended March 31, 20X7, are as follows:

  a) Collections from participants for dues totaled $20,000.
  b) Snack bar and soda fountain sales amounted to $31,000.

(continued)

c)   Interest and dividends totaling $6,000 were received. This investment income is unrestricted.

d)   The following additions were made to the voucher register:

House expense	$17,000
Snack bar and soda fountain.	26,000
General and administrative	11,000

e)   Vouchers totaling $55,000 were paid.

f)   Assessments for capital improvements not yet incurred totaled $10,000. The assessments were made on March 20, 20X5, and were to be collected during the year ending March 31, 20X7.

g)   An unrestricted bequest of $5,000 was received.

h)   Investments are valued at market, which amounted to $95,000 at March 31, 20X5. There were no investment transactions during the year.

i)   Depreciation for the year is as follows:

Building	$4,000
Furniture and equipment	8,000

Depreciation is allocated to

House expense	$9,000
Snack bar and soda fountain.	2,000
General and administrative	1,000

j)   The actual physical inventory, which was $1,000 at March 31, 20X7, pertains to the snack bar and fountain.

k)   A donor contributed $10,000 to be used to acquire land for expansion.

l)   An unconditional pledge of $100,000 to be permanently restricted is received. Income is to be used to maintain the building.

Required:

1.   Prepare entries for each of the above transactions.
2.   Prepare the statement of activities for the year ended March 31, 19X7.

(AICPA adapted)

Problem 19-14.   The Caring Clinic, a VHWO, conducts two programs: Alcohol and Drug Abuse and Outreach to Teens. It has the typical supporting services of management and fund raising. Expense accounts from the pre-allocation trial balances as of December 31, 20X7 are as follows:

	Funded by Unrestricted Resources	Funded by Donor-Restricted Resources	Total
Salaries and Payroll Taxes	63,000	23,000	86,000
Telephone and Miscellaneous Expenses	10,000	2,000	12,000
Nursing and Medical Fees.	70,000	50,000	120,000
Educational Seminars Expense	46,000	20,000	66,000
Research Expense.	137,000	16,000	153,000
Medical Supplies Expense	65,000	22,000	87,000

Rent Expense.		10,000	10,000
Interest Expense on Equipment Mortgage	4,000		4,000
Depreciation Expense		20,000	20,000
Provision for Uncollectible Pledges.	26,000		26,000
	421,000	163,000	584,000

In preparation for the allocation of expenses to programs and supporting services, a study was conducted to determine an equitable manner for assigning each expense. The study resulted in the following table for percentage allocations.

Percentage of Allocations

	Programs		Supporting Services	
Expenses to Be Allocated	Alcohol and Drug Abuse	Outreach to Teens	Management	Fund Raising
All expenses (other than depreciation) financed by donor-restricted contributions	60%	40%		
Expenses financed by unrestricted resources:				
Salaries and payroll taxes.	30	20	30%	20%
Telephone and miscellaneous.	20	20	15	45
Nursing and medical fees	70	30		
Educational seminars	30	60		10
Research	60	40		
Medical supplies	90	10		
Equipment-related expenses:				
Interest.	50	10	30	10
Depreciation	50	10	30	10

Required:

1. Using a total of allocable expenses financed by donor-restricted resources, prepare a journal entry to assign those expenses to the programs.
2. With the following format, prepare a schedule to show the assignment of the allocable expenses financed by unrestricted resources to the various programs and supporting services, using the percentages provided by the problem:

Caring Clinic Allocation of Expenses
For Year Ended
December 31, 20X7

		Programs		Supporting Services	
Expense Allocated	Total Amount	Alcohol and Drug Abuse	Outreach to Teens	Management	Fund Raising

3. Using the schedule from requirement 2, prepare a journal entry to record the allocation and closing of expenses financed by unrestricted resources.
4. Prepare a journal entry to assign plant-related expenses to programs and support services.

Problem 19-15.   The Caring Clinic, a VHWO, conducts two programs: Alcohol and Drug Abuse and Outreach to Teens. It has the typical supporting services of management and fund raising. The condensed trial balances after allocable expenses have been assigned are presented as follows:

Caring Clinic
Condensed Post-allocation Trial Balances
December 31, 20X7

Debits

Assets	716,000
Endowment Assets	256,000
Alcohol and Drug Abuse Program	322,200
Outreach to Teens Program	184,100
Management and General Services	27,600
Fund-Raising Services	50,100
Cost of Special Events	18,000
Reclassification Out—Temporarily Restricted—	
Satisfaction of Program Restrictions	143,000
Reclassification Out—Temporarily Restricted—	
Satisfaction of Equipment Acquisition Restrictions	20,000
Totals	1,737,000

Credits

Liabilities	179,000
Unrestricted Net Assets	202,000
Temporarily Restricted Net Assets	196,000
Permanently Restricted Net Assets	201,000
Contributions—Unrestricted	407,000
Contributions—Temporarily Restricted	254,000
Special Events Support—Temporarily Restricted	48,000
Legacies and Bequests—Permanently Restricted	30,000
Investment Revenue—Unrestricted	13,000
Investment Revenue—Temporarily Restricted	11,000
Gain on Sale of Investments—Temporarily Restricted	8,000
Gain on Sale of Investments—Permanently Restricted	25,000
Reclassification In—Unrestricted—	
Satisfaction of Program Restrictions	143,000
Reclassification In—Unrestricted—	
Satisfaction of Equipment Acquisition Restrictions	20,000
Totals	1,737,000

Required:

1. Prepare a statement of activities in the format shown in Illustration 19-1 on page 19-11.
2. Prepare closing entries for each net asset classification.

Problem 19-16.   From the expense accounts information and allocation schedule shown in Problem 19-14, prepare a statement of functional expenses for the Caring Clinic for the year ended December 31, 20X7.

Appendix Problems

Problem 19A-1.   During the calendar year 20X7, the following events occurred at Brown Hospital, a voluntary hospital:

a) *Gross charges for hospital services were debited to Accounts Receivable. The hospital controller wishes to use separate revenue accounts for*

Room and board charges	$800,000
Charges for other professional services	300,000
Other nursing services.	150,000

b) *Estimated deductions from gross billings were as follows:*

Contractual adjustments.	$ 60,000
Charity services	18,000
Provision for uncollectible receivables.	30,000

The accounting system uses a single allowance account.

c) *Charity services accounts receivable of $15,000 were written-off.*

d) *During the year, the following contributions were received:*

From W. Brown for future acquisition of a new X-ray machine	$ 30,000
From J. Sago for an emergency fund to be used if special assistance for burn care services is required	60,000
From various sources, with no restrictions as to use.	79,000

e) *Unrestricted investment earnings from endowments totaling $23,000 have been earned and collected.*

f) *A new X-ray machine costing $35,000 is acquired with donor-restricted resources. The invoice was vouchered. Brown's policy is to release donor restrictions upon asset acquisition.*

g) *The old X-ray machine is sold for $8,000. It cost $27,000 and had a book value of $7,000 when sold. The gain is unrestricted.*

h) *The following data are provided regarding accounts receivable collections:*

Gross billings.		$980,000
Less: Contractual adjustments.		35,000
Uncollectible accounts written-off.		10,000
Cash collected		$935,000

Cash collected includes reimbursement by third-party payors for depreciation of $63,000, which must be accumulated to update facilities.

i) *Vouchers totaling $1,210,000 were issued for the following items:*

Administrative services expense	$130,000
Fiscal services expense	104,000
General services expense	225,000
Nursing services expense.	520,000
Other professional services expense	165,000
Supplies (perpetual inventory is used).	60,000
Expenses accrued at December 31, 20X6	6,000

(continued)

j)   Cash payments on vouchers payable during the year were $925,000.

k)   Supplies of $37,000 were issued to nursing services.

l)   Investments earned $7,000, all of which was received. Earnings are restricted for plant expansion.

m)   Depreciation for the year amounts to $160,000.

n)   Included in the vouchered items was a bill for burn care services of $15,000.

o)   A payment of $27,000 is made, covering $15,000 of mortgage bonds retired at face value and $12,000 for the annual interest. The hospital records interest as part of Administrative Services Expense.

p)   Endowment investments costing $50,000 were sold for $61,000. Gains are unrestricted.

Required:

Prepare journal entries to record events, using the following format:

Event	Fund	Journal Entry
a)		

Problem 19A-2.   Using the data from Problem 19A-1, prepare a statement of activities for Brown Hospital for the year ended December 31, 20X7.

Problem 19A-3.   Listed are 5 independent transactions or events that relate to a local government and to a VHWO:

a) $30,000 was disbursed from the general fund (or its equivalent) for the cash purchase of new equipment.

b)   An unrestricted cash gift of $100,000 was received from a donor.

c)   A cash gift of $40,000 was received. The use of the funds was restricted to purchase life-saving equipment. To purchase qualifying equipment, $15,000 was used.

d)   Listed common stocks with a total carrying value of $50,000 were sold by an endowment fund for $55,000 before any dividends were earned on these stocks.

e) $1,000,000 (face amount) of general obligation bonds payable were sold at par, with the proceeds required to be used solely for construction of a new building. This building was completed at a total cost of $1,000,000, and the total amount of bond issue proceeds was disbursed in payment.

Required:

1.   For each of the listed transactions or events, prepare journal entries, without explanations, specifying the affected funds and account groups and showing how these transactions or events should be recorded by a local government whose debt is serviced by general tax revenues.

2.   For each of the listed transactions or events, prepare journal entries, without explanations, specifying the affected funds and showing how these transactions or events should be recorded by a VHWO that maintains a separate plant fund.

(AICPA adapted)

Problem 19A-4.   The Caring Clinic, a VHWO, conducts two programs: Alcohol and Drug Abuse and Outreach to Teens. It has the typical supporting services of management and fund raising. The trial balances of its various funds as of January 1, 20X7, are as shown.

Debits	Unrestricted Current Fund	Restricted Current Fund	Plant Fund	Endowment Fund	Total
Cash.	$ 31,000	$ 5,000	$ 12,000	$ 1,000	$ 49,000
Investments.	120,000	23,000	45,000	200,000	388,000
Accrued Investment Revenue	6,000				6,000
Pledges Receivable	45,000				45,000
Grants Receivable	16,000				16,000
Inventories of Educational Materials	11,000				11,000
Inventories of Medical Supplies	12,000				12,000
Land, Building, and Equipment			173,000		173,000
Total	$241,000	$28,000	$230,000	$201,000	$700,000
Credits					
Allowance for Uncollectible Pledges	$ 9,000				$ 9,000
Accumulated Depreciation			$ 22,000		22,000
Accounts Payable	14,000				14,000
State Grants Refundable	16,000				16,000
10% Mortgage Payable			40,000		40,000
Unrestricted Net Assets—Undesignated	112,000		70,000		182,000
Unrestricted Net Assets—Designated for Research	50,000				50,000
Temporarily Restricted Net Assets	40,000	$28,000	98,000		166,000
Permanently Restricted Net Assets				$201,000	201,000
Total	$241,000	$28,000	$230,000	$201,000	$700,000

During 20X7, the following events related to the clinic occurred. To minimize repetition, similar events for the year are combined.

		Unrestricted	Restricted
a)	Contribution pledges received	$396,000	$162,000
b)	Estimated uncollectible pledges	20,000	6,000
c)	Cash collected on pledges	380,000	148,000
	Pledges written-off as uncollectible	18,000	5,000
d)	Investment revenue received (including accrued)	9,000	1,000
e)	Items paid:		
	Accounts payable as of January 1, 19X7	14,000	
	Salaries and payroll taxes	60,000	23,000
	Rent expense		10,000
	Telephone and miscellaneous expenses	10,000	2,000
	Nursing and medical fees	70,000	50,000
	Educational seminars expense	38,000	20,000
	Research expense	137,000	16,000
	Medical supplies (perpetual inventory is used)	71,000	29,000

(continued)

f)   The residence of a leading citizen was bequeathed in a will to the clinic. After the person's death, it was found that the building was not suitable for clinical use, and it would be sold as soon as possible. The residence was appraised at $92,000. The will stipulated that proceeds from the sale must be used to expand the clinic building. The will also provided $30,000 in cash to create a fund, the revenue from which must be devoted to an alcohol-abuse program.

g)   During the year, a dinner was held to raise additional funds for the clinic building. Gross cash proceeds were $48,000, of which $18,000 was paid for direct costs.

h)   Bids for construction of a wing for the clinic building were sought. The contract was let at a cost of $250,000. The residence received from the citizen was sold for $100,000, which was used as a partial payment on the contract, along with the net proceeds from the dinner mentioned in item g). The wing was completed. A 12%, 20-year mortgage was signed for the remaining $120,000. Caring's policy is to release donor restrictions over the life of the fixed asset to match depreciation.

i)   A grant of $16,000 from the state government, awarded last year for a special drug-abuse program, was received. The item originally was recorded as a grant receivable.

j)   At year-end, a physical inventory shows $3,000 of educational materials and $18,000 of medical supplies in the unrestricted fund and $7,000 of medical supplies in the restricted fund.

k)   Annual depreciation amounts to $20,000. $10,000 depreciation was for temporarily restricted assets.

l)   A payment of $5,000 was made against the 10% mortgage payable, and a payment of $4,000 for interest was made.

m) Plant fund investment revenue was $4,000, of which $3,000 was received. Revenue must be used for plant purposes.

n)   Endowment fund investment revenue received amounted to $16,000. There is no restriction on $10,000 of the revenue. The remaining $6,000 must be devoted to alcohol-abuse programs. Items are entered directly in recipient funds.

o) $11,000 of the contributions restricted for future periods in the Restricted Current Fund became available.

p)   The board of directors has decided to increase the Fund Balance Designated for Research from $50,000 to $90,000.

q)   Unpaid and unrecorded items in the unrestricted fund on December 31, 20X7, consist of $3,000 for accrued salaries and $10,000 for previously distributed educational brochures.

r)   Endowment fund investments costing $40,000 were sold for $65,000. The gain is unrestricted.

Required:

1.   Prepare journal entries to record the events, using the following format:

         Event   Fund   Journal Entry

         a)

2.   Prepare pre-allocation trial balances, reflecting balances immediately after the preceding entries are posted, in the same format as the trial balances at the beginning of the problem.

PART

6

FIDUCIARY ACCOUNTING

Effective estate planning continues to be an ever-increasing service provided by practicing accountants. As the value of capital markets continues to grow, more and more individuals find that their estate has increased in value. The desires of those owning an estate may be communicated through a variety of trusts or a will. It is important to properly account for the activity of an estate so that these desires are properly carried out. Furthermore, many estates are subject to an estate tax and it is important to have a basic knowledge as to how estate taxes may be minimized through gifting and the use of trusts.

Unfortunately, for a variety of reasons, a company may find that it is insolvent and unable to continue its business operations unless certain changes occur. A variety of options is available to such troubled companies. In many instances, it is possible for the company to continue operations by use of a quasi-reorganization, a debt restructuring, or a corporate reorganization. In other instances, it is apparent that the company must declare bankruptcy and liquidate its net assets. Corporate reorganizations and liquidations are subject to a number of legal requirements set forth in the Bankruptcy Code. All of these corrective actions must be accounted for according to special principles that have an effect on both the debt and equity interests in a company.

CHAPTER
20

Estates and Trusts: Their Nature and the Accountant's Role

This chapter examines the basic nature of estates and trusts and how the practicing accountant may be involved. There is a tremendous amount of complexity surrounding the legal and tax aspects of estates and trusts; therefore, this chapter provides only a broad overview.

An estate consists of the net assets of an individual at the time of his/her death. Until these net assets are completely distributed or consumed, the estate also exists as a separate, distinct entity that is governed, managed, and accounted for. Often the net assets of an estate are distributed to a trust, which also is a separate, distinct entity. The trust is an arrangement whereby assets are protected, conserved, and/or distributed by a trustee according to the terms of the trust agreement. Persons who are responsible for the management of the net assets of an estate or trust have a fiduciary responsibility. These persons, called fiduciaries, are held accountable by law and are required to prepare specialized reports that account for their actions. The role of the accountant in the preparation of these reports is discussed in this chapter.

The Role of Estate Planning

Estate planning has a primary goal of reflecting the desires of the deceased individual, referred to as the *decedent*. Proper estate planning for individuals with sizeable asset values involves income tax and gift-giving strategies. As one's wealth increases, such strategies become more important. Obviously, such planning can become extremely complex since the circumstances and desires of each individual differ. As the net assets of an estate increase in value and nature, so does the complexity of the necessary estate planning. Many attorneys and accountants specialize in estate planning, which requires special knowledge of law, taxation, and accounting. Furthermore, the Taxpayer Relief Act of 1997 contains numerous new provisions which make it the most comprehensive change to estate gift taxes since the Economic Recovery Tax Act of 1981.

As the complexity of an estate increases, so do the goals of estate planning, which should include the following:

1. Discover and clearly communicate the desires and wishes of the decedent.
2. Insure that the estate is administered or managed properly in order to satisfy the desires and wishes of the decedent.
3. Maximize the economic value of the estate's net assets.
4. Minimize the taxes that may be assessed against the assets and income of the estate.
5. Define the necessary liquidity of the estate's assets so that desired conveyances and distributions may be achieved.

6. Provide a proper and timely accounting of the activities of the estate and its fiduciary.

Communicating through a Will

Obviously, a deceased individual is not available to directly communicate his/her intentions regarding the estate. Therefore, it is critical that prior to death the person communicate through the creation of a valid *will*, a legal declaration containing directions as to the disposition of property. When an individual dies having left a will, the decedent is said to have died *testate*. The will must be presented to a *probate* court, which determines the validity of the will and identifies the fiduciary responsible for administering the will. Generally, probate law is developed by each state; therefore, it may vary significantly throughout the United States. While the Uniform Probate Code does exist, its adoption by states has been very limited.

An *inter vivos* trust is a popular way of passing property, without a will, to one's heirs and, thereby, avoiding the probate process. This type of trust is formed during one's lifetime, and property is transferred to a trust. The individual(s) making the transfer becomes trustee of the trust. Upon his/her death, a successor trustee is appointed and will have the ability to distribute the assets of the trust according to the terms of the trust.

A fiduciary responsible for the administration of a will may be named or nominated in the will. This person is referred to as an *executor* (if female, *executrix*) and, assuming he/she is able and has the desire to serve, normally will be confirmed by the probate court. If the will does not name an executor or the executor is unable to serve, the court will appoint a party referred to as an *administrator* (if female, *administratrix*). Once the will has been probated, the decedent's assets are managed by the fiduciary subject to the oversight or control of the court.

If a decedent has no will or an invalid will, the person is said to have died *intestate*. In this situation the probate court appoints an administrator and distributes the net assets of the estate according to state inheritance laws. Usually, the order of distribution is to spouse, children, grandchildren, parents, grandparents, and then collateral relations such as siblings, aunts, and uncles. In many states, if there are a spouse and children, the estate is split: one half to the spouse and one half to the children.

Identifying the Probate Principal or Corpus of an Estate

One of the first responsibilities of the fiduciary of an estate is to identify the assets of the estate. A decedent may have two types of estates. One, the *probate estate*, is described in this section and includes all of the decedent's assets passing to others by means of the will. The other estate, the *gross estate*, is the one that is used to determine the federal and state estate tax liability. The gross estate includes all assets owned by the decedent at the moment of death, regardless of whether they pass to others by means of the will, by joint tenancy, or by community property laws. These assets vary in nature and must be measured at their fair market value. The value of certain assets, such as publicly traded securities, is determined with relative ease while other assets, such as an interest in a closely held business, require independent appraisals.

The assets of the estate are referred to as the principal or *corpus* of the estate. In identifying the principal, the fiduciary must identify, or inventory, those assets that were the legal property of the decedent at the time of death. Therefore, the assets will include accrued items such as interest and rents. Items frequently comprising the estate principal include the following:

1. Cash on hand and in bank accounts.

2. Investments such as stocks, bonds, mutual funds, retirement accounts, money market funds, and survivorship annuities.

3. Accrued interest and declared dividends on the above investments as of the decedent's death.

4. Capital interests in businesses, such as closely held corporations, partnerships, and/or sole proprietorships.

5. Life insurance proceeds that are receivable by the estate, receivable by another for the benefit of the estate, or if the decedent has an ownership interest in the insurance policy. Therefore, if the decedent or the estate has an "incident of ownership," the proceeds are included in the estate.

6. Investments in real estate, including accrued rents at the date of the decedent's death.

7. Intangible assets, such as patents and royalties, including related accrued income at the date of the decedent's death.

8. Loans or notes receivable, including accrued interest at the date of the decedent's death.

9. Unpaid wages and other forms of earned income accruing to the decedent at the date of the decedent's death.

10. Personal valuables, including furniture, fixtures, jewelry, vehicles, boats, and collectible items such as coins, stamps, and artwork.

It is important to note that the preceding inventory of the principal is not reduced by the liabilities of the decedent. These obligations are recognized when they are paid or satisfied through the distribution of estate principal.

Often, it is not possible for the fiduciary to identify all of the assets of an estate initially. Those assets that are discovered subsequently must be included ultimately in the estate principal.

Exempt Property and Special Allowances.   Some state probate laws exempt certain real property from the estate principal. These assets pass directly to the designated beneficiary or joint tenant. For example, if the decedent and his/her spouse own property as joint tenants, title to the entire property passes to the surviving tenant and is excluded from the decedent's estate. A surviving spouse's interest in community property is not included in the decedent's estate. However, the decedent's interest in the property is included. Other assets of the decedent are not included in the estate principal by way of a *homestead allowance* and a *family allowance* and, therefore, are exempt from the probate process. Such assets are intended to support the family homestead and its members. Certain items of personal property (clothing, furniture, automobiles) are also exempt. However, such allowances differ significantly from state to state.

Accounting for the Inventory of a Probate Estate.   After the special exemptions and allowances for estate assets have been provided for, the fiduciary must file a report with the probate court identifying the estate principal, which consists of the initial assets transferred to the estate as well as those assets subsequently discovered. An initial accounting of the estate principal requires an entry debiting the various assets and crediting an estate principal account.

In order to demonstrate the initial accounting for estate principal, assume Jane Jacoby died on June 1, 19X7. Jane Jacoby's will names her attorney, Howard Wells, as executor of the estate. Through special exemptions and allowances, Jane Jacoby's residence, $2,000 cash, clothing, and furniture passed to her husband Walter Jacoby. Life insurance proceeds of $50,000 also were paid to the beneficiary Robert Williams, Jane Jacoby's son from a prior marriage. The remaining assets of the estate are subject to probate and are recorded as follows:

Principal Cash	81,000	
Investment in XYZ Stock	744,000	
Declared Dividend on XYZ Stock	3,000	
Investment in J&D Partnership	155,000	
Automobile	15,000	
Wages Receivable	2,000	
Estate Principal		1,000,000

An investment in Apex bonds valued at $20,000 along with accrued interest of $1,000 was discovered subsequently and is recorded as follows:

Investment in Apex Bonds	20,000	
Accrued Interest	1,000	
Estate Principal: Assets Subsequently Discovered		21,000

After recording the inventory of the estate principal, the fiduciary would submit a listing of the inventory to the probate court.

Subsequent to the initial recording of the inventory, sales or other dispositions of the assets may occur. Gains on such transactions increase the estate principal, while losses reduce principal. Continuing the above examples for the estate of Jane Jacoby, the following entries account for the sale of estate assets:

Principal Cash	165,000	
Investment in J&D Partnership		155,000
Gain on Realization of Principal Asset		10,000
Principal Cash	19,500	
Loss on Realization of Principal Asset	1,500	
Investment in Apex Bonds		20,000
Accrued Interest		1,000
Principal Cash	5,000	
Wages Receivable		2,000
Declared Dividend on XYZ Stock		3,000

Identifying Claims against the Probate Estate

The discovery and identification of claims against the decedent's estate is of equal importance to the discovery and identification of estate principal. Notification of the decedent's death is required by law, and valid claims must be identified within a prescribed period of time. The fiduciary must evaluate the validity of claims and place them in an order of priority for payment purposes. The order of priority varies from state to state; however, an example might be to observe the following order of priority:

1. Claims having a special lien against property, but not to exceed the value of the property.
2. Funeral and administrative expenses.
3. Taxes: income, estate, and inheritance.
4. Debts due the United States and various states.
5. Judgments of any court of competent jurisdiction.
6. Wages due domestic servants for a period of not more than one year prior to date of death and medical claims for the same period.
7. All other claims.

Within a class, each claim is satisfied on a pro rata basis if funds are inadequate to accomplish total payment for that class.

The following claims against the estate of Jane Jacoby are accounted for as follows:

Funeral Expenses	5,000
Administrative Expenses	3,000
Debts of Decedent Paid	23,000
Medical Expenses	7,000
Principal Cash	38,000

Tax Implications of an Estate

A major claim against the assets of an estate may result from the imposition of a federal estate tax and a state inheritance tax. An estate is considered to be a separate, distinct taxable entity during the period of administration or settlement. This period of time may not be unduly prolonged. The estate will be considered terminated after a reasonable period of time is allowed for administration and settlement. Minimizing the taxes imposed on an estate is a very complex topic and prudent estate tax planning is critical. During one's lifetime, serious consideration should be given to how various divestitures and trusts could be used to manage one's taxable estate. In addition proper planning should address the following considerations:

1. Maximizing benefits of the marital deduction.
2. Making gifts during one's lifetime.
3. Taking actions to accomplish a step-up in property basis.
4. Taking actions to benefit from a loss in property values.
5. Maneuvering with charitable deductions.
6. Planning estate liquidity.

To be protected, an estate must have a certain amount of liquid assets to pay death taxes and the probate costs of establishing the validity of the will. Otherwise, a forced sale of estate assets might result. Some form of insurance often is recommended to provide liquidity and flexibility.

Federal Estate Taxation

Significant changes regarding gratuitous transfers of property resulted from the *Tax Reform Act of 1976*. Prior to its enactment, transfers of property during the owner's lifetime were subject to the federal gift tax, while property passing as a result of death was subject to the federal estate tax. The rules and rates for these taxes were different. Most of the distinction was removed by the Tax Reform Act, which substituted a unified transfer tax, commonly referred to as the *federal estate tax*, for both life and death transfers made after 1976.

The computation of the federal estate tax may be summarized as follows:

Gross estate	XX
Less deductions allowed	– XX
Taxable estate	XX
Add post-1976 taxable gifts	+ XX
Unified tax base	XX
Tentative tax on total transfers	XX
Less tax credits	– XX
Estate tax due	XX

The starting point for the computation of the federal estate tax is the determination of the gross estate, which includes the fair market value of property owned by the decedent at date of death, regardless of the nature of the property or how it passes. Whether it is real or personal, tangible or intangible, business or nonbusiness, the property is includable. The gross estate, for tax purposes, is often greater than the estate for probate purposes due to special tax rules (for example, special rules regarding joint tenancy). The gross estate also includes transfers by the deceased during his/her lifetime in which certain rights are retained by the decedent (such as the right to enjoyment, or possession, the right to designate persons who will possess or enjoy, and of transfers which at the date of the decedent's death were subject to the decedent's power to alter, revoke, terminate, or amend the transfer).

For deaths occurring after 1997, the value of certain "qualified family-owned business interests" may be excluded from the taxable estate. Such interests include a sole proprietor's interest in a trade or business or an interest in an entity carrying on a trade or business. Certain requirements regarding value of business, percentage ownership interests, principal place of business, liquidity, nature of assets, and material participation must be satisfied in order to qualify for this exclusion.

The taxable estate is determined by subtracting the total of the following new allowable deductions:

1. Allowable expenses, such as funeral expenses and costs of administrating the estate;

2. Indebtedness against property included in the gross estate, such as a mortgage and other debts of the decedent;

3. Unpaid property and income taxes of the decedent to date of death;

4. Uninsured losses from casualty or theft of estate assets during the period of settlement;

5. Transfers to charity specified by the will; and

6. Marital deduction, which is unlimited in amount, for estate property that passes to the surviving spouse if he/she is a U.S. citizen.

The *Revenue Act of 1978* required that the taxable estate be increased by any taxable gifts made after 1976. Gifts would be taxable to the donor if their fair market value per donee for the tax year exceeded $3,000 ($6,000 for consenting spouse gifts) through 1981. For gifts after 1981, taxable gifts result if they exceed $10,000 ($20,000 for consenting spouse gifts) per donee per year. Tuition payments to an educational organization and/or medical payments made on another's behalf are not considered taxable gifts. The Taxpayers Relief Act of 1997 contains provisions to adjust the $10,000 annual exclusion for inflation. This adjustment is applicable to decedents' dying and gifts made after 1998. After taxable gifts are added to the taxable estate, the tax rates found in the *unified rate schedule* are applied to the tax base.

The tax rates on taxable estates are progressive and range from 18% to 55%. Taxable estates up to $10,000 are taxed at 18% while taxable amounts exceeding $3,000,000 are taxed at 55%. For taxable estates in excess of $10,000,000, the benefits of the graduated tax rates and the unified credit are phased out. The Unified Transfer Tax Rate Schedule is presented in Exhibit 20-1.

Exhibit 20-1
Unified Transfer Tax Rate Schedule

Column A	Column B	Column C	Column D
Taxable amount over	Taxable amount not over	Tax on amount in Column A	Rate of tax on excess over amount in Column A
			Percent
$ 0	$ 10,000	$ 0	18
10,000	20,000	1,800	20
20,000	40,000	3,800	22
40,000	60,000	8,200	24
60,000	80,000	13,000	26
80,000	100,000	18,200	28
100,000	150,000	23,800	30
150,000	250,000	38,800	32
250,000	500,000	70,800	34
500,000	750,000	155,800	37
750,000	1,000,000	248,300	39
1,000,000	1,250,000	345,800	41
1,250,000	1,500,000	448,300	43
1,500,000	2,000,000	555,800	45
2,000,000	2,500,000	780,800	49
2,500,000	3,000,000	1,025,800	53
3,000,000	. . . .	1,290,800	55

The benefits associated with the graduated rates and the unified credit are phased out for transfers of over $10,000,000.

The resulting tentative estate tax, then, is reduced by certain credits. The *unified credit* in substance results from excluding a portion of taxable estate from taxation. The maximum amount of the credit and excluded amounts are as follows:

For Decedents Dying and Gifts During	Applicable Credit Amount	Applicable Exclusion Amount
1997 (current law)	$192,800	$ 600,000
1998	202,050	625,000
1999	211,300	650,000
2000	220,550	675,000
2001	220,550	675,000
2002	229,800	700,000
2003	229,800	700,000
2004	287,300	850,000
2005	326,300	950,000
2006 and thereafter	345,800	1,000,000

The applicable credit amount corresponds with the unified transfer tax, which would be due on the applicable exclusion amount. For example, if one had a taxable estate of $675,000 in the year 2000, the unified transfer tax would be $220,550, which corresponds with the applicable credit. Additional credits against the tax due are based on state (and District of Columbia) death or inheritance taxes paid, foreign death taxes, and taxes already paid on taxable gifts made after 1976. After recognizing applicable credits, the net tax due is paid out of the principal of the estate. If the estate principal does not have adequate cash to pay the taxes, other principal assets must be liquidated in order to generate the necessary cash.

Estate Reduction with Gifts

Estate planning is essential to achieve the maximum benefit provided in the law, especially when the impact of continued inflation is considered. One simple way to reduce an estate is to make gifts annually. Through 1998, the first $10,000 ($20,000 for consenting spouse gifts) to any one person during any calendar year is excluded in determining taxable gifts. Beginning with 1998, the annual gift exclusion amount will be indexed for inflation. This is an annual exclusion. Consenting spouses who participate for 10 years in an annual gift program involving 6 recipients would be able to transfer $1,200,000 ($20,000 × 6 × 10) without incurring any gift tax, thereby preserving the full unified credit for use in their estates. Spouses also can make gifts to each other. No matter what the amount, such gifts between spouses are free of gift taxes.

One might ask, "What is the maximum total gift a husband and wife may give to one individual at one time in 1998 without incurring any tax?" For gift tax purposes, a gift made by one person to someone other than his or her spouse is considered as having been made one-half by each spouse. Each spouse is entitled to a unified credit of $202,050 (in 1998), or an exemption equivalent gift of $625,000, plus the annual $10,000 exclusion. Therefore, a husband and wife could give $1,270,000 (2 × $635,000) to one person without incurring a tax. The unified credit may be used only one time by each spouse. Once used, a unified transfer tax would be due on gifts above the annual exclusion and, eventually, on their total remaining taxable estate.

Marital Deduction

In the computation of the taxable estate, recall that a marital deduction is allowed for the value of qualifying property passing to a surviving spouse. The amount of the deduction is unlimited. No matter how large the estate, a bequest of all property to one's surviving spouse will completely eliminate federal estate taxes for the decedent. That statement is technically correct, but incomplete. It also should state that the deduction may defer estate taxes only until the death of the other spouse. At that point, it may be discovered that use of the unlimited deduction actually increased the overall estate tax. This can result because the tax rates are progressive (the higher the tax base, the higher the rates) and the effect of the unlimited marital deduction is to channel all assets into the estate of the surviving spouse.

To illustrate, assume Jane Jacoby's will stipulated that her husband Walter was to receive all of the gross estate valued at $1,550,000. Outstanding debts of $150,000 and funeral/administrative expenses totaling $50,000 are paid out of the estate. Also, assume that later in the year (assume 1998) Walter dies with the estate assets still intact. At the time of Walter's death, debts of his estate total $80,000, and $20,000 of funeral and administrative costs have been incurred. With an unlimited marital deduction, their estate tax computations are as follows:

	Jane		Walter	
Gross estate		$1,550,000		$1,350,000
Less deductions:				
Debts.	$ 150,000		$80,000	
Funeral and administrative costs	50,000		20,000	
Marital deduction.	1,350,000	(1,550,000)	0	100,000
Taxable estate		$ 0		$1,250,000
Estate tax before credits				$ 448,300
Less unified credit (available in 1998) . .				(202,050)
Estate tax due				$ 246,250

As an alternative strategy, Jane's will could have stipulated that an amount equal to the exemption equivalent ($625,000) be placed in a trust, with Walter as the income beneficiary. Such trusts are referred to as credit shelter trusts as they "shelter" a portion of the total estate from estate tax by using the credit available to each spouse. Sometimes, these trusts are also referred to as marital deduction trusts or "A–B" trusts. In any case, such trusts must meet IRS guidelines. If properly designed, the trust would not be included in Walter's estate upon his death. The remainder of Jane's net assets ($725,000) could go directly to him and qualify for the marital deduction. Now, their estate computations would be

	Jane		Walter	
Gross estate		$1,550,000		$ 725,000
Less deductions:				
Debts	$150,000		$80,000	
Funeral and administrative costs.	50,000		20,000	
Marital deduction	725,000	925,000	0	100,000
Taxable estate.		$ 625,000		$ 625,000
Estate tax before credits		$ 202,050*		$ 202,050
Less unified credit (available in 1998) . . .		202,050		202,050
Estate tax due.		$ 0		$ 0

*This amount of tax is based on the 1998 unified rate schedule for estates.

Failure to do some estate planning could cost the Jacoby family $246,250.

Valuation of Estate Assets

Fair market value must be established for assets included in an estate. Some valuations, such as the values of stocks and bonds traded on recognized exchanges, pose no problems. For other assets, such as property, jewelry, art objects, or antiques, a competent appraisal in writing should be obtained. Assets are included in the estate at their fair market value on the date of death or on an alternate valuation date, if the executor or administrator so elects. If the alternate valuation date is elected, all estate property must be valued as of six months after the decedent's death, except for property sold, distributed, or otherwise disposed of during the six-month period. Such property is valued as of the date of disposition. The alternate valuation date may be used only if it would reduce the total gross estate and decrease the estate tax liability. The alternate valuation date protects estates if there should be a significant decrease in property values during the six-month interval.

Formerly, it would have been possible for a fiduciary, knowing that there would be no estate tax to pay, to select the alternate valuation date if assets increased in value, thereby giving the heirs a higher basis for their inherited property, at no cost to the estate. To prevent this windfall, Congress took an action that permitted election of the alternate valuation date only if it would reduce the total gross estate and decrease the estate tax liability.

Congress felt it was being sufficiently generous by permitting a stepped-up basis. Recall that, to the recipient, the basis of property acquired from a decedent is market value on the date of death or alternate valuation date. That regulation may result in a step-up of basis. For example, assume Jane Jacoby held stock with a cost of $100,000. At the date of her death, it was worth $500,000 and was willed to her nephew, whose basis now becomes $500,000. A subsequent sale by him for $500,000 would result in no taxable gain. Although the value of the stock must be included in the inventory of the estate, which would be subject to the unified transfer tax only if the estate is large enough, the $400,000 gain would escape *federal income taxation* because of the step-up in basis. If Jane had sold the stock before her death, the gain would have been subject to income tax. Tax planning would suggest that, if possible, property that has appreciated substantially in value should be held as part of an estate because of the advantage of the step-up in basis. The opposite is true if there is a substantial decline in value. If Jane's stock had a value of $5,000 on the valuation date, that would become the basis to her nephew. Neither he nor the estate would derive any income tax benefit from the $95,000 loss in value. If Jane had sold the stock prior to death, benefits resulting from the deductibility of the loss for income tax purposes would have materialized.

Other Taxes Affecting an Estate

In addition to federal estate taxes, most individual states assess an inheritance tax on the value of estate assets conveyed to heirs. Unlike the estate tax, the inheritance tax is levied on the heirs rather than the estate. Certain transfers of assets are exempt while other transfers are partially exempt, depending on the amount of the transfer and the relationship of the heir. The taxable amount of nonexempt transfers is reduced further by certain deductions such as funeral and administrative expenses, debts of the decedent, and mortgages on real property.

In certain instances, an estate subsequently will generate income that is not included in the initial estate principal. The estate is viewed as a separate taxable entity. Estate income that is distributed currently and properly to a beneficiary generally is excluded from the taxable income of the estate. Therefore, the estate functions as a conduit through which the income passes to the recipient. Income passing in this manner retains the same character it had in the hands of the estate. For example, if the estate receives and distributes nontaxable income such as interest on municipal bonds, the interest remains tax free in the hands of the recipient. Normally, the beneficiary is taxed on any taxable income that he/she receives, and the estate, as a separate entity, is taxed on any income that it accumulates. Estate income taxes are assessed at the same rates as used for individual taxpayers except that the levels of income at which rates become effective are much lower for estates than they are for individuals.

Measurement of Estate Income

The tax incidence on estate income suggests the need for the estate fiduciary to distinguish between transactions affecting principal and those affecting income. Furthermore, a decedent's will may stipulate certain provisions regarding estate income that differ from those regarding principal. For example, a will might stipulate that the interest income earned on bonds subsequent to the decedent's death is to accrue to a particular beneficiary for a period of time. The recipient of the income is referred to as an *income beneficiary*, and the party ultimately receiving the principal is referred to as the *remainderman*.

If the will is not clear with respect to the measurement of income, state statutes should be applied. Many states have adopted the *Revised Uniform Principal and Income Act*, which provides guidance as to the measurement of estate principal and income. The determination of estate income does not always parallel generally accepted accounting principles (GAAP). As discussed previously, the gains or losses on the sale of estate assets is considered a component of principal rather than income. When bonds are a part of the estate at the time of death, the premium or discount on the bonds is not amortized. Generally, however, if bonds are purchased subsequently by the fiduciary, a premium is amortized whereas a discount is not amortized.

Unless the will requires it, the common procedure is not to make any charge against income for depreciation. If the decedent wishes to protect principal for the depreciation factor, there should be a statement in the will that depreciation should be charged against income and an amount equal to the depreciation should be transferred from income to principal. For the depletion on wasting assets, the general rule is that income should be charged for the depletion because of the possibility of total consumption of principal.

Settling a Probate Estate

After the debts of an estate and the applicable estate taxes have been determined and paid, the fiduciary must focus on carrying out the remaining provisions of the decedent's will as they relate to principal and income. If the decedent dies intestate, distribution of remaining estate principal is governed by applicable state law.

Distributions of Property

If a decedent dies intestate, real property is distributed according to the laws of descent of the state in which the real property is located. Personal property is distributed according to the laws of distribution of the decedent's home state, called the *state of domicile*. In general, only a spouse or blood relative may receive an intestate distribution.

In a testate situation, a distribution of real property is a *devise*, and the recipient of the property is the *devisee*. Distributions of personal property are called bequests or *legacies*, and the recipient of personal property is called the *legatee*.

A devise is usually a distribution of a specific piece of real property. In contrast, legacies may include one or more of the following types:

1. A *specific legacy* is a gift of a particular, specified thing, distinguishable from others: my 3-carat diamond ring or the twenty bottles of Romanée Conti Burgundy 1961 on the north wall of my wine cellar.
2. A *demonstrative legacy* is a gift of an amount from a specific source, with the will stipulating that if the amount cannot be satisfied from that source, it shall be satisfied from the general estate: $50,000 from several identified insurance policies. If proceeds are inadequate to meet the amount, the difference shall constitute a general legacy.
3. A *general legacy* is a gift of an indicated amount or quantity of something: $5,000 or twenty bottles of wine. However, the specific source of the payment is not designated.
4. A *residuary legacy* is composed of all estate property remaining after assigning the specific, demonstrative, and general legacies.

If the remaining estate principal, after paying debts and expenses, is not adequate to satisfy the various legacies, a process called *abatement* is followed.

Abatement requires that the legacies be satisfied to whatever extent possible in the order in which they are presented on page 20-11 (items 1 through 4). If the amount of assets designated as a general legacy is not available, the available amount is abated proportionately among the recipients. For example, assume a general legacy calls for $5,000 to be paid to each of two individuals and $2,500 to be paid to each of another two individuals and only $12,000 is available. Abatement would result in two individuals receiving $4,000 each and the other two individuals receiving $2,000 each.

In order to illustrate the accounting for the distribution of property, the earlier example regarding Jane Jacoby's estate is continued. Those events relating to Jane Jacoby's estate that were discussed previously are included as events 1 through 6 of Illustration 20-1. Events 7 through 13 of Illustration 20-1 relate to the accounting for estate income and property distributions.

The Charge and Discharge Statement

Periodically, the fiduciary will prepare a report to the court summarizing the results during the period of stewardship. This report is called a *charge and discharge statement.* The preparation of the report is simplified if a double trial balance has been prepared, since the charge and discharge statement is divided into two parts—one as to principal and one as to income. The statement for the estate of Jane Jacoby on December 31, 19X7, appears as Illustration 20-2.

In a more complex estate, each of the items in the charge and discharge statement would be supported by a schedule providing detail. For example, a supporting schedule for gains and losses on realization of principal assets might appear as follows:

Schedule of Gains and Losses on Realization of Principal Assets

	Inventory Value	Proceeds on Realization	Loss	Gain
J&D partnership	$155,000	$165,000		$10,000
Apex bonds and accrued interest	21,000	19,500	($1,500)	
Totals	$176,000	$184,500	($1,500)	$10,000

If the fiduciary had completed his/her responsibilities to the estate, all assets comprising estate principal and income would have been distributed. In this case, the charge and discharge statement would reflect zero balances as to estate principal and income. Final distributions of estate principal often are made in the form of a residual legacy and/or a trust for the benefit of designated parties. After all final distributions, the estate records are closed with the estate principal and estate income accounts serving as clearing accounts. The final distributions of the estate of Jane Jacoby, along with necessary closing entries, are recorded as events 14 through 16 of Illustration 20-1.

Summary of Items Affecting Estate Principal and Income

There are a variety of items that can affect the estate of a decedent, and the presence of a valid will certainly provides direction in this regard. The estate's fiduciary must act in a responsible manner and assume that a proper accounting of the items affecting an estate has taken place. A proper accounting will provide better management of the estate and serve as a basis for statutory reporting requirements. Today's professional accountant can support the fiduciary role by understanding the principles of estate administration and accounting. A review of the items affecting estate principal and income will help to ensure a proper accounting.

Illustration 20-1
Accounting for the Estate of Jane Jacoby

Event	Entry		
1. Recording of the initial estate inventory after special exemptions and allowances.	Principal Cash.	81,000	
	Investment in XYZ Stock	744,000	
	Declared Dividend on XYZ Stock	3,000	
	Investment in J&D Partnership.	155,000	
	Automobile.	15,000	
	Wages Receivable.	2,000	
	Estate Principal		1,000,000
2. Subsequent discovery of estate assets.	Investment in Apex Bonds	20,000	
	Accrued Interest.	1,000	
	Estate Principal: Assets		
	Subsequently Discovered		21,000
3. Sale of estate assets: J&D partnership for $165,000 cash.	Principal Cash.	165,000	
	Investment in J&D Partnership.		155,000
	Gain on Realization of Principal		
	Asset		10,000
4. Sale of estate assets: Apex bonds plus accrued interest for $19,500.	Principal Cash.	19,500	
	Loss on Realization of Principal		
	Asset	1,500	
	Investment in Apex Bonds		20,000
	Accrued Interest.		1,000
5. Receipt of accrued wages and dividends receivable.	Principal Cash.	5,000	
	Wages Receivable		2,000
	Declared Dividend on XYZ Stock		3,000
6. Payment of claims against the estate.	Funeral Expenses.	5,000	
	Administrative Expenses	3,000	
	Debts of Decedent Paid.	23,000	
	Medical Expenses	7,000	
	Principal Costs.		38,000
7. Receipt of interest on cash accounts.	Income Cash.	1,000	
	Estate Income		1,000
8. Receipt of dividend declared on XYZ stock subsequent to decedent's death.	Income Cash.	3,000	
	Estate Income		3,000
9. Distribution of specific legacy of automobile to Jacoby's nephew.	Legacies Distributed	15,000	
	Automobile.		15,000
10. Distribution of general legacy of $25,000 to Jacoby's sister.	Legacies Distributed	25,000	
	Principal Cash.		25,000
11. Distribution of specific legacy of 5,000 shares of XYZ stock to Riveredge Nature Center.	Legacies Distributed	186,000	
	Investment in XYZ Stock.		186,000
12. Payment of administrative expenses of which $100 is traceable to income.	Administrative Expenses	300	
	Expenses Chargeable Against Income. . . .	100	
	Principal Cash.		300
	Income Cash.		100

(continued)

13.	Distribution of income cash traceable to dividends received to Jane Jacoby's brother.	Distribution to Income Beneficiary . . . . . . Income Cash	3,000 	 3,000

14.	Distribution of all estate assets to the Jacoby children's trust administered by the First National Trust Company.	Principal Assets Transferred to Trust . . . . .
		Income Assets Transferred to Trust . . . . . .
		   Principal Cash . . . .
		   Investment in XYZ Stock . . . .
		   Income Cash . . . .
			765,200
			900
			
				207,200
				558,000
				900

15.	Closing of estate principal.	Estate Principal . . . .
		Estate Principal: Assets
		   Subsequently Discovered . . . .
		Gain on Realization of Principal
		   Asset . . . .
		     Loss on Realization of
		       Principal Asset . . . .
		     Funeral Expenses . . . .
		     Administrative Expenses . . . .
		     Debts of Decedent Paid . . . .
		     Medical Expenses . . . .
		     Legacies Distributed . . . .
		     Principal Assets Transferred
		       to Trust . . . .
			1,000,000
			
			21,000
			
			10,000
			
				1,500
				5,000
				3,300
				23,000
				7,000
				226,000
				
				765,200

16.	Closing of estate income.	Estate Income . . . .
		   Expenses Chargeable Against
		     Income . . . .
		   Distributions to Income
		     Beneficiary . . . .
		   Income Assets Transferred to Trust . . . . . .
			4,000
			
				100
				
				3,000
				900

The items that usually are chargeable against principal and the account debited when each item is recorded are as follows:

Item	Account Debited
Debts of the decedent incurred prior to death	Debts of Decedent Paid
Funeral and administrative expenses	Funeral and Administrative Expenses
Medical expenses	Medical Expenses
Costs incurred in probating the will	Funeral and Administrative Expenses
Final income taxes of decedent	Debts of Decedent Paid
Federal estate tax[1] and any state inheritance tax	Funeral and Administrative Expenses
Legal and other professional fees to preserve estate principal	Funeral and Administrative Expenses
Charges applicable to personal property that produces no income	Expenses Chargeable against Principal

(continued)

---

1 The Uniform Probate Code provides that where the will does not stipulate treatment of estate taxes, they are to be prorated to the recipients of estate assets on the basis of the value of the asset received relative to the aggregate value of all assets subject to tax.

Distributions of legacies or devises in a testate distribution	Legacies Distributed ⎤ often combined or ⎬ in the first Devices Distributed ⎦ account
Distributions to trusts	Principal Assets Transferred to Trust
Disposition of estate assets at a loss	Loss on Realization of Principal Assets (a gain would be credited to Gain on Realization of Principal Assets, with total proceeds on any sale of a principal asset debited to Cash—Principal)

When income cash is received, Estate Income is credited and, if the estate is large, a subsidiary ledger is maintained that details the types of income. The items for which income cash usually is disbursed and the account debited when each item is recorded are as follows:

Item	Account Debited
Expenses incurred to protect income flow	Expenses Chargeable against Income
Ordinary repairs to income-producing property	Expenses Chargeable against Income
Distributions of income cash to beneficiaries	Distributions to Income Beneficiaries
Distributions of income cash to trusts	Income Assets Transferred to Trust

Illustration 20-2
Charge and Discharge Statement

Estate of Jane Jacoby
Howard Wells, Executor
Charge and Discharge Statement
For the Period June 1, 19X7, to December 31, 19X7

As to Principal

I charge myself with:

Assets per original inventory	$1,000,000	
Assets subsequently discovered	21,000	
Net gain on realization of principal assets	8,500	
Total charges		$1,029,500

I credit myself with:

Funeral and administrative expenses	$ 8,300	
Medical expenses	7,000	
Debts of decedent paid	23,000	
Legacies distributed	226,000	
Total credits		264,300

Balances as to estate principal, consisting of:

Cash—principal	$ 207,200	
XYZ stock	558,000	
		$ 765,200

(continued)

As to Income		
I charge myself with:		
Estate income.		$4,000
I credit myself with:		
Expenses chargeable against income.	$ 100	
Distributions to income beneficiaries.	3,000	
Total credits		3,100
Balances as to estate income, consisting of:		
Cash—income		$ 900

Trust Accounting Issues

A trust is a separate, distinct entity that receives assets from an individual for the purpose of managing and distributing them over a period of time. A trust is also recognized as a taxable entity until trust assets have been distributed and the administration of the trust is completed. Trusts may be created for several reasons. It is possible that heirs to an estate currently lack the maturity, sophistication, or prudence necessary to receive substantial assets directly. Therefore, a trust is established to manage the asset for the intended heir. Trusts also provide opportunities for assets to be exempt from the probate process and, more important, taxes imposed on an estate. Finally, trusts are used as a means to convey assets to special organizations or causes, such as charities, universities, and other not-for-profit organizations. Rather than conveying estate assets directly to these organizations, a trust presents an opportunity to recognize the needs of individual heirs prior to such distributions.

Trusts may take a variety of forms. The following brief discussion of several types will serve to illustrate the various strategies for creating a trust. A *charitable remainder trust* distributes the income from trust assets to individual beneficiaries over a period of time (often for the rest of their lives) at which time the assets go to the remainderman which must be a charitable organization. Under such an arrangement, a charitable deduction is available to the *grantor* when the trust is created. Upon death of the grantor, the property is excluded from the estate, thereby escaping estate taxes. A *bypass or credit shelter trust* is designed to split assets between a surviving spouse and a trust so that the value of the marital deduction and unified credit are maximized. Generally, the surviving spouse receives income during his/her lifetime after which the trust assets are distributed to surviving children or heirs. A *qualified terminable interest property trust* (Q-TIP trust) is similar to a bypass or credit shelter trust.

Noting that trusts may be designed to accomplish a variety of purposes, they may become operative while the grantor is alive or they may be created through a will to become effective upon the grantor's death. The former type of trust is an *inter vivos*, or *living*, *trust* while the latter is referred to as a *testamentary trust*. In order to carry out the provisions of a trust, a *trustee* must be appointed. The trustee may be an individual; however, banks frequently serve as trustees. Most major banks have a trust department whose services are available for a fee.

Financial Accounting for Trusts

The accounting for a trust is very similar to the accounting for an estate. The distinction between principal and income must be maintained through the use of *trust principal* and *trust income accounts*. The trust agreement should provide direction regarding how income is to be determined. A charge and discharge statement is required periodically for both trust principal and income.

Illustration 20-3 demonstrates the accounting for various events affecting the trust established by Jane Jacoby's will.

Illustration 20-3
Accounting for the Jacoby Children's Trust

Event	Entry		
1. Receipt of distribution from the estate of Jane Jacoby.	Principal Cash.....................	207,200	
	Investment in XYZ Stock	558,000	
	Trust Principal		765,200
	Income Cash......................	900	
	Trust Income		900
2. Purchase of mutual funds with principal cash.	Investment in Mutual Fund...........	200,000	
	Principal Cash..................		200,000
3. Receipt of dividend and interest income.	Income Cash......................	5,300	
	Trust Income		5,300
4. Payment of trustee's fees and allocation to principal and income.	Administrative Expenses: Principal	400	
	Administrative Expenses: Income	200	
	Principal Cash..................		400
	Income Cash...................		200
5. Distribution of income cash to beneficiaries.	Distribution to Income Beneficiary.....................	6,000	
	Income Cash...................		6,000

To demonstrate adherence to the terms of the trust, the trustee must provide annual, confidential reports to income beneficiaries and remaindermen. For a testamentary trust, a report also must be rendered to the probate court of the county in which the will was admitted to probate. The nature of the report is dependent upon the statutory requirement of the relevant state. Generally within 30 days after the end of each year, a report must be filed that shows:

1. The trust principal on hand at the beginning of the period.
2. Changes in the trust principal during the period, such as asset acquisitions or dispositions.
3. The trust principal on hand at the end of the period, its composition, and the estimated market values of all investments.

As to trust income, the report shows:

1. The trust income on hand at the beginning of the period.
2. Trust income received during the period, detailing the sources and amounts.
3. Distributions of trust income made during the period to income beneficiaries.
4. The trust income on hand at the end of the period and how it is invested.

These requirements may be met by the periodic filing of a charge and discharge statement, provided that sufficient detail as to principal and as to income is incorporated into the report. At the time of submitting the statement to the court, many trustees prefer to close trust books to have them correspond to the annual time frame used in filing reports. Trust Principal and Trust Income are the clearing accounts used in the closing process, paralleling the procedures for closing an estate.

The trust will terminate when all trust property is distributed in accordance with the trust arrangement. For example, a trust may have been created to provide a beneficiary with income until this beneficiary reaches a specified age, at which time trust principal is released. The trustee's final report will take the same form as the periodic reports but, in addition, will itemize total distribution of trust principal and income to indicate termination of stewardship.

Questions

1. Estate planning is becoming more important to many individuals. Identify several goals of estate planning.
2. Why are the desires and wishes of a decedent easier to identify if he/she dies testate versus intestate?
3. Assuming a decedent has an investment in stocks, discuss how cash dividends and gains or losses on the disposition of stocks affect estate principal.
4. A decedent owned real estate with his spouse, and a question has arisen as to whether the property will be included in the estate of the decedent. What is the significance of owning the property as community property versus as joint tenants?
5. What is the purpose of a charge and discharge statement?
6. At what point in time are the claims against an estate recognized, and how are they satisfied if valid claims against the estate exceed estate assets?
7. Assume that an individual and her spouse have not previously made any gifts and that they wish to make a gift to their son sometime around the end of the year. Why might it be to their benefit to make a portion of the gift at the end of the current year and the balance of the gift at the beginning of the next year?
8. Is it true that federal estate taxes for a married individual may be eliminated completely by use of the unlimited marital deduction? Is the adoption of such a procedure always wise? Explain.
9. What is the logic behind the alternative valuation date not being applicable in those instances in which the total gross estate has increased in value?
10. Why are taxable gifts subsequent to 1976 added to the taxable estate in order to determine the tax base upon which taxes are assessed?
11. An estate is expected to have income that is generated by certain assets of the estate. What purpose would be served by recognizing depreciation on equipment held by the estate?
12. A decedent's will provides for the distribution of certain personal property. How does a specific legacy differ from a general legacy?
13. An estate has $180,000 of estate assets available for distribution to legatees. However, stated legacies total $220,000 in value. How is this problem resolved?
14. Someone once stated that "A trust is of value only if heirs to an estate lack maturity and/or financial responsibility." Do you agree with the statement?

Exercises

Exercise 1.   On November 1, 2000, Alice Nolan, a married woman, has been diagnosed with a terminal illness and has approximately 6 months to live. Her husband is significantly older and has been in poor health for some time. Alice has net assets with a fair market value of approximately $4,000,000. Included in the marital estate are investments in stock, life insurance policies on Alice's life naming her husband as beneficiary, corporate bonds which were purchased at a premium, and a modest timber plantation in southern Georgia. In contemplation of her death, Alice has several questions regarding how to best manage her estate and minimize estate taxes. Assume that the unified credit is $220,550 associated with an exclusion amount of $675,000 and that the annual exclusion amount for gift tax purposes is $11,000 in 2000 and $11,500 in 2001.

1. What advice would you give Alice with respect to whether or not she should dispose of certain securities which have and are expected to continue to have a market value that is less than their original cost?
2. What actions might Alice take in order to exclude the life insurance proceeds from being included in her estate?
3. Assuming that Alice has previously given $450,000 in post-1976 taxable gifts, what is the maximum annual gift that she can make to her three sisters, in total, and avoid gift taxes, assuming that her husband does not consent to the gifts?
4. Assume that the corporate bonds are to be placed in a charitable remainder trust, with her son receiving the income from the bonds for ten years and the Sierra Club receiving the remainder after that point. Why might including the amortization of the premium on the bonds as a component of determining income be advantageous to the interests of the Sierra Club?
5. If Alice's will bequests the tree plantation to her husband and the income from the plantation to her stepson, in fairness to her husband, should the income from the plantation include the effect of depletion on the timberland?

Exercise 2. Robert Wagner has become extremely ill and is doing some estate planning in contemplation of his death. Robert is married and has two minor children. It is estimated that Robert's estate would have a value of $3,600,000 and his executor would be responsible for paying $100,000 in medical/funeral expenses and $20,000 in administrative fees. In the event of Mrs. Wagner's death, it is estimated that allowable expenses of her estate would be approximately $60,000. Valid other claims against the estate are estimated to be $800,000. The estate assets are not very liquid and consist primarily of investments in stocks, bonds, and land. Mr. and Mrs. Wagner are considering establishing a trust whereby Mrs. Wagner would be the income beneficiary for the duration of her life, and the children would be the remaindermen.

1. Considering both Mr. and Mrs. Wagner, determine the minimum measure of estate assets exposed to net federal estate tax if the trust were not established. (Ignore possible homestead and family allowances.)
2. Considering both Mr. and Mrs. Wagner, determine the minimum measure of trust assets required so that there are no federal estate taxes due. (Ignore possible homestead and family allowances.) Assume that the unified credit is $220,550, which corresponds with an applicable exclusion amount of $675,000.

Exercise 3. Prior to his death, Winston Weber placed the following assets in a trust on November 15, 20X8:

Assets	Fair Market Value
Stock in Norland Medical including a $1,000 declared dividend to shareholders of record on November 1, 20X8. The dividend was paid on December 1, 20X8.	$101,000
8% Corporate bonds (face value of $200,000) including accrued interest of $7,700. Semi-annual interest was paid on December 1, 20X8. The bonds mature 23 months from the date of August 15, 20X8.	210,000

(continued)

Farmland that is leased to an adjacent landowner for a monthly rent
of $500. The lease covers a 12-month period beginning June 1, 20X8.
All monthly lease payments are due on the first of the month and have
been made when due.   240,000

Cash.   5,000

At the date of transfer to the trust, the farmland had an outstanding mortgage that was also transferred to the trust. The principal mortgage balance after the September 1, 20X8 payment was $46,937 and had the following terms: quarterly payments of $2,000 with the next payment due on December 1, 20X8, annual interest of 8% (assume each month represents a 30-day period).

Income from the trust will be paid out to the income beneficiary on the last day of each year. The calculation of income associated with the bonds should reflect the desire to preserve the corpus or principal of the estate. As trustee for the trust, prepare the necessary entries for the trust through the end of 20X8 assuming that the trust uses the cash basis of accounting.

Exercise 4. The will of Donna Kaiser, an unmarried individual, contained the following provisions regarding her estate:

a) The dairy farm located in Watertown is to be deeded to her nephew, James Quade.

b) The collection of Navajo Indian rugs is to be given to the Museum of Native American Arts.

c) Michael Kaiser, Donna's brother, is to receive $98,000 in cash.

d) Michele Kaiser, Donna's sister, is to receive all of the cash deposited in the First Bank of Watertown savings account.

e) Michele Kaiser shall receive a demonstrative legacy of $150,000 from the net proceeds of insurance policies on Donna Kaiser's life.

f) All personal effects (clothing, furniture, housewares) are to be given to Goodwill Industries.

g) All of the IBM stock is to be distributed to the World Wildlife Fund (a charitable organization).

h) All remaining assets are to be placed in trust for Donna's foster child Emily Natal.

Other claims against the estate include:

Heavenly Hands, funeral expenses.	$10,000
Attorney B. J. Wells, administrative expenses	5,000
Northwestern Mutual Life, insurance policy loans	30,000
Note due to First Bank of Watertown	20,000
Federal and state income taxes due on final tax return.	3,000
Watertown Treasurer, accrued property taxes on the farm	12,000

The inventory of Donna Kaiser's estate consists of:

Cash—checking account	$ 3,500
Cash—savings account, First Bank of Watertown	18,000
Cash—savings account, Federal Savings and Loan	73,000
Personal effects.	8,000
Navajo rug collection	49,000

Life insurance death benefit.	128,000
Watertown dairy farm	370,000
Investment in IBM stock.	220,000
Investment in U.S. treasury bonds.	20,500
Dividends declared on IBM stock	13,000

As executor of the estate, (a) explain why no federal estate taxes are due and (b) prepare a listing of all items comprising estate principal, and for each item, indicate who will receive the item and in what amount.

Exercise 5.   Jason Jackson was killed in a mountain-climbing accident in British Columbia. As Jason's trusted friend and CPA, you have been named executor of his estate and guardian to his minor child, Cody Jackson. Jason's estate consists of the following assets subject to probate:

Cash	15,000
Vacant land in Colorado	130,000
Investment in Merkt stock.	54,000
Investment in GTE stock.	13,000
Dividend declared on GTE stock.	1,000
Investment in Trident Bond Fund	40,000
Accrued interest on Trident Bond Fund.	2,000
Royalties receivable	17,000

Prepare journal entries to record the above inventory and the following events related to the estate principal and income:

a) Final medical and funeral expenses of $22,000 are paid.

b) An Individual Retirement Account (IRA) naming Jackson's estate as beneficiary and having a value of $37,000 subsequently is discovered.

c) Cash dividends of $1,000 on the GTE stock and $2,700 on the Merkt stock are received.

d) The vacant land in Colorado is sold for $150,000 less accrued property taxes of $2,000 and a broker's commission of $8,000.

e) Interest of $2,400 is received on the Trident Bond Fund, and the royalty receivable also is collected.

f) Income taxes of $4,000 on the decedent's final tax return are paid, along with $24,000 of other claims against the estate.

g) A legacy of $15,000 is paid to the High Adventure Climbing School.

h) Administrative expenses of $3,200 are paid, of which $100 is traceable to income.

Exercise 6.   Given the facts of Exercise 5, prepare the charge and discharge statement that would have resulted from the above events and prepare the entries to transfer all estate principal and income amounts to a trust for the benefit of Cody Jackson.

Exercise 7.   The estate of Marlene Johnson consists of assets having a fair market value of $308,785. As of the date of her death, the following claims exist against the estate:

(continued)

Claims Existing at Date of Death	Amount of Claim
Mortgage balance including principal and accrued interest due on personal residence with a fair market value of $200,000.	$142,580
Funeral expenses	6,300
Expenses incurred by executor of estate for administration purposes . . .	2,100
Income and estate taxes	12,400
Brokerage commissions associated with the sale of the personal residence.	16,000
A lien against the personal residence for unpaid real estate taxes	4,200
Unreimbursed medical claims for the last three months prior to death . . .	27,000
Unpaid balance of personal loan received from her brother	14,700
Unpaid balance of automobile repair expenses. A mechanic's lien has been placed on the automobile which has a fair market value of $5,000.	750
Unpaid balance of other personal expenses	3,950
Total of all claims	$229,980

Legacies addressed in the decedent's will include the following:

- $30,000 from the sale of the personal residence, after payment of mortgages, real estate taxes, and sales costs, will be paid to the decedent's brother.
- The collection of Edward S. Curtis photographs, valued at $22,000, to be given to the decedent's nephew.
- Cash of $40,000 to be divided equally among the decedent's two sisters.

Prepare a schedule, in order of priority, indicating how the assets of the estate will be disbursed.

Exercise 8.   Casey Jones died testate on May 1, 20X0. As the approved executor, prepare journal entries to record the following activities related to the estate:

   a) The assets are inventoried, and the following listing is filed with the probate court:

Cash	$ 60,000
Stock of Trains Inc.	40,000
Zip Railroad 10% bonds, interest payable March 1 and September 1, at face value (also market value)	120,000
Accrued interest on Zip bonds.	2,000
Personal and household effects	30,000
Total	$252,000

   b) Funeral expenses paid, $2,800.
   c) Dividends were declared on May 10 by Trains Inc., and the check for $800 was received on June 1.
   d) Interest on Zip Railroad bonds was collected on September 1.
   e) Half of the Zip Railroad bonds were sold on October 1 at 103 plus accrued interest.
   f) Casey was a bachelor. The will stipulates that his personal and household effects be given to his housekeeper, Karen Kay. The executor released the items to her.
   g) On December 1, the executor's fee of $3,000 was approved by the court and paid. Of the total amount, $200 is to be charged against income of the estate.

Problems

Problem 20-1. Alex Dunn, Jr., died on January 15, 20X7; his records disclose the following estate at fair market value:

Cash in bank	$ 3,750
6% note receivable, including $50 accrued interest	5,050
Stocks	50,000
Dividends declared on stocks	600
6% mortgage receivable, including $100 accrued interest	20,100
Real estate—apartment house	35,000
Household effects	8,250
Total	$122,750

Subsequent to recording the inventory of the estate, the executor discovered on July 1, 20X7, the late Alex Dunn, Sr., had created a trust fund that established his son, Alex Dunn, Jr., as life tenant and his grandson as remainderman. The assets in the fund consist solely of the outstanding capital stock of Dunn, Inc., namely, 2,000 shares of common stock. At the creation of the trust, the book value and the market value of these shares was $400,000. At December 31, 20X7, the market value was $500,000. On January 2, 20X7, Dunn, Inc., declared a $1.25 per share cash dividend payable February 2, 20X7, to shareholders of record on January 12, 20X7.

The executor's cash transactions from January 15 to January 31, 20X7, were as follows:

Cash receipts:

Jan. 20	Dividends declared		$ 600
25	6% notes receivable collected		5,000
	Interest accrued on note		58
	Stocks sold, inventoried at $22,500		20,900
	6% mortgage sold		20,100
	Interest accrued on mortgage		132
29	Real estate sold		30,250
	Dividends not previously declared		900
			$77,940

Cash disbursements:

Jan. 20	Funeral expenses		$ 750
23	Decedent's debts		8,000
25	Decedent's legacies		10,000
31	Distribution of income to widow		500
31	Property taxes assessed January 10, 20X7		1,000
			$20,250

Required:

Prepare a charge and discharge statement for the executor for the period from January 15 to January 31, 20X7.

Problem 20-2. Prior to his death, Gordon Mayer created a trust for the benefit of his two children, Gretta and Gary. At date of death, all assets of the estate and related liabilities would pass to the trust. The trust contains the following provisions:

(continued)

1. Fifty percent of the trust income in the year of the decedent's death and for the following calendar year will be paid to Gretta. Payments will be made at year-end.

2. Fifty percent of the trust income in the year of the decedent's death and for the next two calendar years will be held on behalf of Gary. The accumulated trust income, less applicable trust income taxes, will be disbursed to Gary in the month following the end of the final calendar year to which this provision relates.

3. On the one-month anniversary of the decedent's death, $200,000 will be conveyed to the Cedarburg Community Library. In the first month following the year of the decedent's death, 40% of the principal balance measured as of the prior year-end will be conveyed to St. Cecil's Community Hospital.

4. All costs associated with managing the trust's investments in stocks and bonds will be charged to principal.

5. All dividends and interest earned subsequent to the date of the decedent's death will be included in income.

6. Fees and expenses incurred by the trustee for administration purposes will be allocated equally between trust principal and income.

7. All capital improvements to maintain rental properties in good condition will be charged against trust principal.

8. All normal maintenance costs associated with rental properties will be charged against trust income.

9. The interest portion of mortgage payments on rental properties accruing after the date of death will be allocated equally between trust principal and income.

10. Depreciation will not be considered in determining trust income.

11. On November 1 in each of the two calendar years following the year of the decedent's death, $25,000 will be contributed to the Boy Scouts of America.

12. All taxes associated with the decedent's estate and final income are to be paid out of the trust principal.

Gordon Mayer died on September 18, 20X6, when his estate consisted of the following assets at fair market value: cash—$32,000; stocks and bonds—$570,000; rental properties—$1,234,000. The following additional events occurred subsequent to his death during 20X6:

a) Estate taxes in the amount of $256,000 and final personal income taxes in the amount of $27,000 were paid in 20X6.

b) Dividends and interest were received on investments in the amounts of $23,000 and $27,000, respectively. Of the dividends, $13,000 was declared as payable to shareholders of record as of September 15, 20X6. The interest received included $8,400 of accrued interest as of the decedent's death.

c) Stocks with a market value of $320,000 at date of death were sold for $335,000.

d) A new roof and siding were installed on rental properties in the amount of $134,000. Ordinary repairs on rental properties were $25,000, of which $6,700 had been incurred prior to the decedent's death.

e) Expenses associated with managing the trust's investment in stocks and bonds totaled $9,200, and the trustee's expenses were $6,000.

f) Mortgage payments on rental property totaled $94,000, of which $45,000 represented interest. Of the interest, $8,200 represented interest that had accrued as of the date of the decedent's death.

g) Gross rents of $124,000 were received.

h)   Estimated taxes of $21,434 were paid on trust income which was not distributed.

Required:

Prepare all necessary entries to record the activities of the trust subsequent to the decedent's death through the end of 20X6.

Problem 20-3.   Early in 20X0, Alex Bowe dies, leaving a gross estate of $1,400,000. He had outstanding debts of $50,000. Administrative expenses of the estate amounted to $50,000. Later that year, his wife dies, leaving an estate of $250,000 in addition to the property left to her by her husband. Administrative expenses on Mrs. Bowe's estate were $60,000.

You are provided with the following partial unified estate and gift tax table:

Exceeding (A)	Not Exceeding (B)	Tax on Amount in Column (A)	Rate of Tax on Excess over Amount in Column (A)
$ 500,000	$ 750,000	$155,800	37%
750,000	1,000,000	248,300	39
1,000,000	1,250,000	345,800	41
1,250,000	1,500,000	448,300	43

Assume that the unified credit is $220,550, which corresponds with an applicable exclusion amount of $675,000.

Required:

1. Ignoring state gift and estate taxes, determine the amount of federal estate tax on both estates if

    a)   Mr. Bowe left his total estate to his wife, exercising the unlimited marital deduction.

    b)   Mr. Bowe left his wife an estate that will equate his taxable estate with the maximum unified credit.

2. What does the estate tax computation demonstrate in relation to exercising the unlimited marital deduction?

Problem 20-4.   Maxwell Stevens, a single person, died on August 12, 20X8. His will indicated the following:

- His nephew should receive any income from the estate until such time as the estate is liquidated.
- All assets of the estate should be converted to cash in a timely manner, and the final remaining estate principal should be conveyed to Ducks Unlimited, a not-for-profit organization, with the stipulation that these funds be used for wetland preservation efforts in the state of Colorado.
- Maxwell's attorney, Janice Edquist, is to serve as executrix of the estate.

The following events occurred regarding the estate of Maxwell Stevens:

1. Various bank accounts totaling $34,000 were consolidated for estate purposes.
2. An insurance policy with a death benefit of $300,000 was discovered subsequent to death. The policy names Maxwell Stevens' niece, Cynthia Townsend, beneficiary of the policy.

(continued)

3. Stocks with a fair market value of $278,000 at date of death were sold for $267,000. Dividends on the above stocks were received in the amount of $3,400, of which $1,200 represented amounts which had been declared to shareholders of record on August 1, 20X8.
4. Bonds with a fair market value of $138,000 at date of death were sold for $143,000 including accrued interest. The accrued interest subsequent to the date of death was $850.
5. Real estate with a fair market value of $380,000 at date of death was sold for $390,000 less broker's commission of 8% and closing fees of $750. Prior to the closing on the sale of real estate, rental income in the amount of $14,500 was received and expenses (not including interest) totaling $6,550 were paid. Rental income and expenses in the amounts of $6,250 and $3,600, respectively, were traceable to the period prior to the decedent's death.
6. A land contract note on the real estate in the amount of $97,000 was paid off upon sale of the real estate. In addition to the principal amount, accrued interest in the amount of $2,550 was also paid. Of the interest, $1,230 had accrued prior to the decedent's death.
7. The following claims against the estate existed: funeral and administrative expenses, $11,200; decedent's final personal income tax liability, $3,200; and miscellaneous personal bills, $1,300.

Required:

1. Explain why the estate was not subject to any federal estate tax.
2. Assuming that the above information describes the activities of the estate and that all provisions of the decedent's will have been carried out, prepare a charge and discharge statement.

Problem 20-5.   Laurel Rose has been the executrix of her brother's estate since his death on February 1, 20X6. The following events occurred during her administration:

a) Included in the principal assets were 40, $1,000, 8% City of Pittsburgh bonds paying interest on January 1 and July 1. The bonds had a market value of 101 on February 1, 20X6. Rose sold the bonds at 103, plus accrued interest, on March 1, 20X6.

b) On March 1, 20X6, Rose purchased 50, $1,000, 5% City of Detroit bonds at 98 plus accrued interest. The bonds pay interest on April 1 and October 1. The bonds mature on April 1, 20X8.

c) On March 1, 20X6, she also purchased $10,000 (face value), 7% City of Newark bonds at 102 plus accrued interest. The bonds pay interest on June 1 and December 1. The bonds mature on December 1, 20X7.

d) On April 1, 20X6, she received a check for the interest on the Detroit bonds.

e) On June 1, 20X6, she received a check for the interest on the Newark bonds.

f) On September 1, 20X6, she sold the Detroit bonds at 101, plus accrued interest.

Required:

Prepare journal entries to record each of these events. Use the straight-line method of amortization where applicable.

Problem 20-6.   Sheri Shannon died on June 1, 20X3, leaving a valid will that named her friend, Steve Chevalier, the executor of the estate.

a)   Steve prepared the following inventory of assets, listing their market values as of June 1:

Cash.	$31,000
1,000 shares of Pal Corp. common stock	60,000
2,000 shares of BVD Corp. common stock	40,000
Rapid Transit Corp. (RTC) 8% bonds, interest payable April 1 and	
October 1, $30,000 face amount	30,300
Time-share condominium unit at Lake Tahoe, used for her	
two-week vacations	10,000
Sheri's one-half interest in the Sheri Limo Service Co.	70,000

b)   On June 15, after filing the inventory of assets with the probate court, Steve discovered Sheri's gold-coin collection that was appraised at $18,000.

c)   On June 20, a $250 check was received from Pal Corporation for dividends declared on May 10, 20X3, to owners on record as of May 30.

d)   Steve sold the time-share condominium for $14,000 on July 7.

e)   The following items were paid between June 1 and July 31:

Sheri's charge card purchases.	$1,900
Funeral costs	6,000
Lawyer's fee to probate the will	800
Cost to paint condominium prior to sale	1,100
Payment to executor approved by the court	1,700

f)   On July 5, a $15,000 check was received for Sheri's portion of partnership earnings for the quarter ended June 30. Earnings are fairly constant from one month to the next and are available for withdrawal on a monthly basis if a partner so desires. Otherwise, payments are made quarterly.

g)   Sheri's partner offered Steve $90,000 for her interest in the partnership. Steve accepted the offer and received full payment.

h)   On October 1, a check for interest was received from Rapid Transit Corp.

i)   On December 1, Steve completed Sheri's final income tax return, paying the additional tax due of $18,200.

Required:

1.   Prepare journal entries to record the events.
2.   Prepare a charge and discharge statement as of December 31, 20X3.

Problem 20-7.   You are given the following trial balance of the estate of Sheri Shannon as of December 31, 20X3. Her will stipulated that the executor should be granted $30,000 from principal cash. The remainder of the estate's principal assets and its income assets are to be transferred to Community Bank, which will act as trustee of an endowment fund. Income from trust assets shall be used for scholarships for accounting majors at a local university.

(continued)

Trial Balance

Cash—Principal	115,950	
Cash—Income	5,800	
Pal Corp. Stock	60,000	
BVD Corp. Stock	40,000	
Rapid Transit Corp. Bonds	30,300	
Coin Collection	18,000	
Estate Principal		241,700
Estate Income		5,800
Assets Subsequently Discovered		28,250
Gain on Realization of Principal Assets		24,000
Funeral and Administrative Expenses	8,500	
Debts of Decedent Paid	20,100	
Expenses Chargeable against Principal	1,100	
	299,750	299,750

Required:

1. Record the payment to the executor and the transfer of all remaining assets to the trustee.
2. Prepare journal entries to close the executor's records.
3. Prepare journal entries to record receipt of assets by the trustee. Explain why it was unnecessary to accrue the interest on the Rapid Transit Corp. bonds to the date of actual transfer.

Problem 20-8.   The probate court is dissatisfied with the procedures followed by the executor of the estate of Jean O'Brien and demands the records. The executor submits the following:

Journal Entries for the Estate of Jean O'Brien—Died, May 1, 20X6

May 8	Bank Checking Account	14,100	
	Insurance Policy at Cash Surrender Value (face of policy is $100,000 and is payable to the estate)	18,000	
	Shannon Corporation 12% Bonds (interest is payable April 1 and October 1; face value, $100,000; fair market value at date of death, $106,000; recorded at Jean's cost)	124,000	
	O'Brien Corporation Common Stock (10,000 shares of $10 par. Stock was quoted at $18 when Jean died. These shares were a gift from her father, the founder of the corporation, so I've entered them at $1, just to make a record.)	1	
	Condominium (Her condo is just like mine, which cost me $96,000 one week before she died. Her cost was $73,000.)	73,000	

(continued)

Paintings (I don't understand these, but a dealer says they are worth $25,000. They cost Jean $9,000.)	25,000	
Gain on Paintings.		16,000
Total Estate		238,101

This is a list of the assets I found so far. I made a copy of this entry and filed it with the court. I omitted a Silver Cloud Rolls-Royce, worth about $30,000. I'll keep the car instead of asking for a fee. Jean always said she wanted me to have it. She must have forgotten it when she made out her will.

9	Cash	2,000	
	O'Brien Corporation Dividend		2,000

Received a check for a dividend declared April 2 to holders of record on April 25.

June 1	Cash	100,000	
	Insurance Policy at Cash Surrender Value .		18,000
	Gain on Loss of Jean O'Brien.		82,000

This is the check from the insurance company. . . . .

5	Expenses	44,000	
	Cash		44,000

I issued checks to cover:

Funeral expenses	$ 5,100
Jean's medical bills.	300
Final income tax payments.	17,900
Jean's charges on American Express . .	700
Partial payment on estate tax. The will says it should be charged against principal, whatever that means.	20,000
Total.	$44,000

30	Expenses	25,000	
	Paintings.		25,000

Turned paintings over to Art Institute, as the will said I should do.

Sept. 10	Loss on O'Brien Corporation Common Stock.	1	
	O'Brien Corporation Common Stock		1

The will stated that the stock should be returned to the corporation, so I did it.

Oct. 1	Cash	6,000	
	Interest Received		6,000

To record check received from Shannon Corporation.

(continued)

1	Cash	90,000	
	Condominium		73,000
	Gain on Sale of Condominium		17,000

> To record sale of condo. The will says the
> proceeds should be used to establish a Jean
> O'Brien Scholarship Endowment Fund at
> State University, her alma mater.

3	Cash Turned Over to State University.	90,000	
	Cash		90,000

> I sent a check to the university for the
> scholarship endowment fund.

31	Expenses	3,000	
	Cash		3,000

> The court relieved me as executor and said
> I could not have the Rolls-Royce. This
> payment to me is to be charged to principal.
> I don't think what they did is fair to me.

Required:

1. The probate judge is disgusted with the records, terminates the executor's responsibilities, and appoints you as the replacement. Prepare a correct set of entries to date.
2. Prepare a charge and discharge statement. No supporting schedules are necessary.

Debt Restructuring, Corporate Reorganizations, and Liquidations

The principles of accounting are based on several important underlying assumptions, one of which is the going concern assumption. Since this assumption assumes that a business entity will have a long, extended life as a separate, distinct entity, valuation and classification of account balances are significantly influenced by it. For example, both the valuation of a building at depreciated historical cost, rather than net realizable value, and the classification of a building as a noncurrent asset, rather than a current asset, are in recognition of the going concern assumption. Certainly, without this assumption all assets and liabilities would be classified as current in nature.

However, over time, the going concern assumption may not hold true for all business entities. An entity may voluntarily decide to cease its business purpose. For example, a research and development (R&D) venture may cease operations at the completion of a successful or unsuccessful R&D effort. Unfortunately, a business entity also may face difficulties that cause the going concern assumption to be challenged. A business may suffer from several factors, including poor management, poor accounting controls, uncontrolled growth, loss of market share, resistance to change, government intervention, and/or a declining profit margin. Although many businesses may be able to respond to these factors in a positive manner, other businesses may become troubled or insolvent and seek corrective action. A business is considered to be insolvent if it is unable to service its liabilities, or if it technically has liabilities in excess of assets. Businesses experiencing such difficulties often are viewed as *bankrupt*, which is a state of lacking all or part of the means to service debts. This chapter focuses on several corrective actions available to a troubled or insolvent business, including troubled debt restructurings, reorganizations, and liquidations.

No business is immune from the factors that may result in financial difficulty. Large, small, young, and mature companies alike may find themselves having to cope with such difficulties. Along with the expansion of business comes the inevitable fact that some businesses may become troubled and/or fail. These difficulties are an everyday occurrence, as reflected in the excerpts from the *Wall Street Journal* shown in Exhibit 21-1.

The accounting profession is involved with troubled businesses in a variety of ways. Providing consulting services and sound financial planning and reporting, accountants may be of invaluable service in thwarting or managing the forces leading to financial difficulty. Accountants also provide an important discovery and reporting function for those businesses seeking relief from their financial difficulties.

Exhibit 21-1
Examples of Troubled Businesses

MINNESOTA MALL AQUARIUM FILES FOR BANKRUPTCY

BLOOMINGTON, Minn., (Reuters)—The owners of an aquarium built inside America's largest shopping mall have filed for protection from creditors in U.S. Bankruptcy Court, an aquarium official says.

UnderWater World at the Mall of America filed for Chapter 11 bankruptcy protection Friday in federal court in St. Paul, Minn., said Jeff Holmes, the aquarium's general manager.

The bankruptcy court filing followed news in September that Dallas-based Tarlton Aquastar, the aquarium's majority owner, had delayed $1.1 million in bond payments due March 1, then missed $1.2 million in payments due September 1.

Holmes said the attraction would remain open as it tries to restructure $21 million in debt before the next scheduled payment date in March. Attendance has been strong, he said, with 1.4 million visitors in the year ended in June.

Norwest Bank Minnesota is the aquarium's largest creditor with a secured claim of $13 million and an unsecured claim of $3.15 million.

DOW CORNING CORP.

A disclosure statement hearing is set for 11/3/97. Dow Corning has proposed a reorganization plan that provides $2.4 billion for product liability claims and $1.3 billion for commercial claims. The tort claimants' committee, which is seeking to have the district court take control of Dow Corning's Chapter 11 case, opposes the plan. The district court is expected to rule on the tort panel's bid to withdraw reference before the disclosure statement hearing.

GROSSMAN'S INC.

A disclosure statement hearing is set for 10/27/97. Under the company's proposed reorganization plan, JELD-WEN Inc. would buy a 50% stake in the company for $8.25 million. Grossman's is seeking approval to amend its $50 million debtor-in-possession credit agreement with GDI Co., an affiliate of JELD-WEN. A hearing was set for 10/9/97.

SOURCE: http://www.fedfil.com/bankruptcy/statustable.htm

DOW CORNING CORP.
BANKRUPTCY CLAIMS INFORMATION
Home Page

Individuals with any type of claim against Dow Corning Corporation ("DDC") or Dow Corning Wright Corporation ("DCWC") can learn more about their rights and responsibilities in this bankruptcy proceeding home page.

DCC has filed for protection under Chapter 11 of the U.S. Bankruptcy Code. As part of the bankruptcy process, DCC is required to provide notice to those who believe they have a claim or may have a claim in the future against the company.

Claims may arise from several sources, including commercial dealings with DCC, the use of breast implants manufactured or provided by DCC or DCWC, and the use of other long-term metal, silicone, silicone-containing implantable surgical products, medical devices and other materials manufactured or sold by DCC or DCWC. In addition to implant recipients, claimants also may include spouses and children (born and unborn) of implant recipients.

(continued)

To preserve your rights against DCC, now and in the future, you must file a claim which is received by the court-appointed docketing agent by January 15, 1997. For certain implant claimants living outside the United States, the deadline has been extended to February 14, 1997. In order to qualify for the February 14, 1997 extension, implant claimants must have continuously maintained their residences outside the United States, its territories and Puerto Rico during the period from September 15, 1996 through November 15, 1996.

If you do not file a claim form, you may lose your right to bring any claim against DCC in the future. Filing a claim form, however, does not necessarily entitle you to compensation.

Relief Procedures Not Requiring Court Action

When a business becomes insolvent or is not able to service its debts on a timely basis, there are several remedies available that do not require court approval. Since several of these remedies are discussed in intermediate textbooks, they will be only highlighted in this section. Seeking relief to financial problems outside of bankruptcy court offers several advantages. The time required to implement relief procedures is significantly less than the time required to seek relief through bankruptcy proceedings. Not requiring court action also allows the debtor's financial problems to be less public and more discreet. Knowledge of a company's financial troubles can adversely affect its ability to generate new business and acquire goods and services from vendors.

Troubled Debt Restructurings

A basic approach to resolving an inability to service debt is to seek some concessions or compromises from major creditors. A *troubled debt restructuring* is a process whereby creditors grant concessions to the debtor that they would not consider otherwise. However, both the debtor and creditor are faced with a difficult situation, and a restructuring offers the creditor the best opportunity to recover the debt, as compared to nonrestructuring alternatives.

Although not all debt restructurings qualify as troubled debt restructurings, those that do generally take several forms. Troubled debt restructurings are discussed in FASB No. 15. The most common forms of restructuring, along with the appropriate debtor accounting, are summarized as follows:

Transfer of Assets in Full Settlement:

Form: The debtor transfers assets, such as third-party receivables, real estate, and other assets, to the creditors in order to satisfy the debt either totally or partially.

Accounting by Debtor: The debtor records a gain on restructuring measured by the excess of the carrying basis of the debt, including related accrued interest, premiums, etc., and the fair market value of the transferred assets. The restructuring gain should be classified as an extraordinary item, if material. The difference between the book value of assets transferred to the debtor and their fair market value results in a gain or loss, which is not part of the gain on restructuring.

Example: Assets with a book value of $100,000 and a fair market value of $120,000 are transferred to a creditor in full settlement of a loan of $130,000 plus accrued interest of $2,000.

```
Loan Payable .................................... 130,000
Accrued Interest Payable ..........................  2,000
     Gain on Assets ...............................           20,000
     Assets .....................................          100,000
     Gain on Restructuring .........................           12,000
```

Granting an Equity Interest:

Form: Excluding existing terms for converting debt into equity (e.g., convertible debt), an equity interest in the company is granted to the creditor in order to satisfy the debt either totally or partially.

Accounting by Debtor: The debtor records a gain on restructuring measured by the excess of the carrying basis of the debt and the fair market value of the equity interest. The restructuring gain should be classified as an extraordinary item if material.

Example: Preferred stock with a par value of $20,000 and a market value of $120,000 is granted to a creditor in full settlement of a loan of $130,000 plus accrued interest of $2,000.

```
Loan Payable .................................... 130,000
Accrued Interest Payable ..........................  2,000
     Preferred Stock, at Par .......................           20,000
     Paid-In Capital in Excess of Par .................          100,000
     Gain on Restructuring .........................           12,000
```

Modification of Terms:

Form: The terms of the debt are modified in several possible ways involving interest and/or principal. Interest rates may be reduced and/or accrued interest may be reduced. The principal amount of the debt may be reduced and/or the maturity date of the loan may be extended.

Accounting by Debtor: If the total future cash payments (both principal and interest) specified by the restructuring are less than the carrying basis of the debt, a gain on restructuring is recognized. The restructuring gain should be classified as an extraordinary item, if material. After recognizing the gain, all subsequent cash payments made per the terms of the restructuring should be accounted for as a reduction of the debt payable. Therefore, no interest expense shall be recognized on the restructured debt. If the total future cash payments (both principal and interest) specified by the restructuring are more than the carrying basis of the debt, no gain on restructuring is recognized. However, interest expense is recognized between restructuring and maturity. The interest recognized should be based on an effective interest rate that equates the present value of restructured future cash payments to the carrying value of the debt.

Example A: The terms of an outstanding debt of $130,000 plus accrued interest of $2,000 have been modified as follows: payments of $60,000 per year will be made over the next two years in full satisfaction of the debt.

```
Loan Payable .................................... 130,000
Accrued Interest Payable ..........................  2,000
     Restructured Loan Payable .....................          120,000
     Gain on Restructuring .........................           12,000

Restructured Loan Payable .......................... 60,000
     Cash .....................................           60,000

Restructured Loan Payable .......................... 60,000
     Cash .....................................           60,000
```

Example B: Same situation as Example A except that the payments are $76,057 each year, which results in an effective interest rate of 10%.

Loan Payable	130,000	
Accrued Interest Payable	2,000	
Restructured Loan Payable		132,000
Restructured Loan Payable	62,857	
Interest Expense (10% × 132,000)	13,200	
Cash		76,057
Restructured Loan Payable	69,143	
Interest Expense (10% × 69,143)	6,914	
Cash		76,057

Combination Restructurings:

Form: A restructuring may involve some combination of the above restructuring features.

Accounting by Debtor: The accounting for a combination restructuring is the same as discussed above except that first, the carrying basis of the debt should be reduced by the fair market value of assets transferred and/or equity interests granted. This step does not result in the recognition of a gain on restructuring. Second, the remaining carrying basis of the debt is compared against the "modification of terms" portion of the restructuring and accounted for accordingly.

Example: Land with a fair market value of $52,000 and a cost basis of $45,000 is transferred to a creditor in partial settlement of a debt of $130,000 plus accrued interest of $2,000. The balance of the debt is satisfied by the payment of $35,000 per year for each of the next two years.

Loan Payable	130,000	
Accrued Interest Payable	2,000	
Gain on Transfer of Land		7,000
Land		45,000
Gain on Restructuring		10,000
Restructured Debt		70,000
Restructured Debt	35,000	
Cash		35,000
Restructured Debt	35,000	
Cash		35,000

As seen from the previous examples, a troubled debt restructuring may be accomplished in a variety of ways. Regardless of the method used, a formal agreement must be reached between the debtor and individual creditors. Generally, such agreements take the form of a creditor agreement or a composition agreement. A creditor agreement is used to extend the terms of a debt or make other concessions regarding future interest rates. A composition agreement is used to scale down a creditor's claims against the debtor. For example, creditors might agree to accept $0.70 per dollar of debt owed to them.

Although the above discussion of troubled debt restructuring has focused on the necessary accounting by the debtor, FASB No. 114, as amended by FASB No. 118, discusses the necessary accounting by the creditor. A creditor in a troubled debt restructuring, involving only a modification of terms of a receivable, should measure the loan receivable based on the present value of the expected future cash flows discounted at the loan's effective interest rate. As a practical matter, the creditor may measure the loan receivable at the loan's observable market price or the fair value of the collateral, assuming the loan is collateral dependent. If the measure of the impaired loan receivable is less than the recorded investment in the loan, the difference is charged to bad-debt expense and a valuation allowance is established.[1]

Quasi-Reorganizations

A corporation may not be insolvent and yet may have accumulated a relatively large deficit as a result of such problems as an excessive investment in plant assets or inventory, or management's inability to recognize and influence market demands. If management is replaced and if profits result from new policies, most state laws still will not permit declaration of dividends until the deficit is eliminated. The turnabout period and deficit elimination may take so long that the investors' interest in the company vanishes, and capital acquisition becomes difficult. To overcome such a handicap, the corporation might seek a quasi-reorganization.

Quasi-reorganization does not require court action, nor does it require the consent of creditors since creditor interests are not altered. However, the procedure is described in state laws, many of which require a quasi-reorganization to be approved by two-thirds of the stockholders. The accounting literature is not specific regarding the conditions under which a quasi-reorganization can occur. However, it was most frequently viewed as an approach which would allow for net assets to be reduced to lower market values and a deficit in retained earnings to be eliminated. The Securities and Exchange Commission has set forth specific criteria which must be satisfied before a quasi-reorganization is accepted. Furthermore, SEC Staff Accounting Bulletin (SAB) No. 78 does not allow registrants to use this procedure just to eliminate a deficit in retained earnings. Net assets must also be restated, and the net result must be a write-down in value versus a write-up.

The primary purpose of a quasi-reorganization is to eliminate a large deficit and take such action as will permit successful operations in the future. Excessive plant capacity and equipment may be sold, and remaining assets and liabilities will be revalued to reflect their fair values. For example, long-lived assets will be written down to reflect an impairment in their value.[2] Such revaluations most often increase the deficit in retained earnings. The deficit remaining after these revaluations must be reduced to zero.

It should be noted that the write-down of the assets increases the deficit, which then will be eliminated by subsequent changes in the capital structure.

The deficit is eliminated by charges against the existing paid-in capital in excess of par or stated values. If no such paid-in capital exists, it may be created by altering the capital structure and substituting stock with lower par value or lower stated value for existing shares. To illustrate the manner in which the owners' equity section in the balance sheet is revised by a quasi-reorganization, assume the following stockholders' equity:

Common stock ($10 par, 12,000 shares outstanding)	$120,000
Retained earnings (deficit)	(45,000)
Total stockholders' equity	$ 75,000

On March 1, 20X0, the stockholders approve a reduction in par value to $1. Note that such a maneuver has absolutely no effect on the proportionate interests of each stockholder.

---

1 FASB Statement No. 114, *Accounting by Creditors for Impairment of a Loan* (Norwalk, CT: Financial Accounting Standards Board, 1993).
2 FASB Statement No. 121, *Accounting for the Impairment of Long-Lived Assets and for Long-Lived Assets to be Disposed Of* (Norwalk, CT: Financial Accounting Standards Board, 1995).

The entries to record the quasi-reorganization are as follows:

Common Stock ($10 par)	120,000	
Common Stock ($1 par)		12,000
Paid-In Capital from Reduction in Stock Par Value		
(or Reorganization Capital)		108,000
To record the reduction in par value.		
Paid-In Capital from Reduction in Stock Par Value	45,000	
Retained Earnings		45,000
To eliminate the deficit.		

Immediately following the quasi-reorganization, the owners' equity section would show:

Common stock ($1 par, 12,000 shares outstanding)	$12,000
Paid-in capital from reduction in stock par value	63,000
Retained earnings (subsequent to March 1, 20X0)	0
Total stockholders' equity	$75,000

In future financial statements, retained earnings must be dated to indicate the starting point of new accumulations. The process of dating retained earnings should be continued for as long a period of time as is deemed advisable, but rarely does it exceed ten years.

Corporate Liquidations

A corporation may decide to liquidate its assets, distribute available amounts to creditors, and terminate the business. Such a liquidation may be accomplished without a formal bankruptcy proceeding through the use of a general assignment for the benefit of creditors, which generally must be agreed to by all creditors. Shareholders of the corporation receive any net assets remaining after fully satisfying the claims of creditors. Usually, assets are not adequate to fully satisfy creditor claims. In this case, creditors share according to the terms of the general assignment.

Bankruptcy Reform Act of 1978 and the Bankruptcy Code Amendments

If a satisfactory solution cannot be reached under the procedures described in the previous paragraphs, the legal proceedings for bankruptcy may be initiated. Modern bankruptcy procedures attempt to give a debtor a fresh start, unburdened by former obligations, while simultaneously accomplishing an equitable distribution of the debtor's property among creditors.

In an attempt to modernize an antiquated system existing under the Bankruptcy Act of 1898, as amended by the Chandler Act of 1938, Congress passed the *Bankruptcy Reform Act of 1978* (Title 11 of the U.S. Code), which became effective on October 1, 1979. In 1982, the U.S. Supreme Court ruled that the section of the Bankruptcy Reform Act of 1978 (hereafter referred to as the Act) giving bankruptcy judges the power to consider and rule on issues that were not directly part of the bankruptcy proceedings was unconstitutional. Under the Act, bankruptcy judges had the power to consider any issue arising in or related to bankruptcy cases. Thus, if a company had filed in bankruptcy court and another company had a damage suit against it, the damage claim could have been heard in bankruptcy court instead of in a federal district or state court. Under the Supreme Court's decision, bankruptcy judges now must limit their rulings to issues directly related to bankruptcy proceedings. In June, 1984, Congress passed a bill to overhaul the bankruptcy system. The bill limited the powers of bankruptcy judges to comply with the 1982 Supreme Court decision and created 85 new federal trial and appellate judgeships to assist with cases that spill out of bankruptcy courts. The Bankruptcy Act was amended in 1988, 1990, and, most recently, in 1994.

A bankruptcy case may be filed under one of the following operative chapters of the code:

Chapter 7: Liquidation.   A nonbusiness debtor or any business not wishing to remain in operation, except a railroad, governmental unit, bank, insurance company, or savings and loan association, may file a petition under this chapter.

Chapter 9: Adjustments of Debts of a Municipality   is not covered in this text.

Chapter 11: Reorganization.   The purpose of Chapter 11 is to allow a company (or individual) to pay a portion of its debts, discharge remaining debts, and continue in business. This chapter is used primarily by corporate or partnership debtors. Although the chapter may be used by an individual proprietor, the procedures are more cumbersome and more expensive than those of Chapter 13. Only individuals with substantial assets and liabilities resort to Chapter 11 proceedings.

Chapter 13: Adjustment of Debts of an Individual with Regular Income.   This chapter is limited exclusively to individuals, including sole proprietors, with less than $250,000 in unsecured debt and less than $750,000 in secured debt. A joint case of debtor and spouse is permissible if their combined debt does not exceed the two limitations.

There are provisions for the movement or conversion of a case from one chapter to another, such as converting an unsuccessful reorganization (Chapter 11) to a liquidation (Chapter 7). Chapters 9 and 13 of the code will not be specifically discussed in this text.

Commencement of a Bankruptcy Case

The Act states that a debtor either must be a person (individual, partnership, or corporation) residing in or having a domicile, business, or property in the United States, or must be a municipality. If a debtor initiates the action of filing a petition with the court of bankruptcy under the appropriate chapter of the Act, it is a *voluntary* case. A voluntary petition may seek relief under Chapters 7, 9, 11, or 13. Filing constitutes an *order for relief*, which represents a stay of action by prohibiting commencement or continuation of legal action against the debtor to recover a claim.

If the petition is filed by someone other than the debtor, an *involuntary* proceeding results. Such proceedings may be filed under Chapter 7 (Liquidation) or Chapter 11 (Reorganization), but not under Chapter 13, where the individual debtor is willing to make payments to creditors. Certain small businesses are allowed to use streamlined ("fast track") procedures in order to facilitate a solution to bankruptcy issues. Involuntary proceedings may not be initiated against a farmer or a charitable organization. Under Chapters 7 and 11, if a debtor has twelve or more creditors, three or more of them may file an involuntary petition, providing the total of their noncontingent, unsecured claims is $10,000 or more. If there are less than twelve creditors, one or more of them may initiate an involuntary case, but the same limit of $10,000 applies. In an involuntary case, the claims must have arisen before the order for relief was issued. The court will issue such an order if the debtor files no answer to the involuntary petition. If an answer is filed by the debtor, the court will hold a hearing, following which it will either dismiss the case, issue an order for relief, or postpone the decision pending receipt of additional information.

Corporate Reorganizations—Chapter 11

The ultimate goal of a reorganization is to restructure the debt and/or equity of a company so that the company may continue to carry on its business purpose and become a financially sound business. Unfortunately, the vast majority of reorganizations never achieve this goal. Such a reorganization often is more attractive than a debt restructuring not involving a bankruptcy proceeding because the reorganization may be more generous toward the debtor company. Generally, a reorganization reduces debt through forgiveness to a greater extent than a conventional debt restructuring. Furthermore, interest on unsecured debt is not accrued during the period of reorganization. The period of reorganization provides a company with an opportunity to delay creditors from bringing suit for delinquent debts as well as to seek protection from a variety of business risks, which may affect a company's ability to continue as a going concern. Companies have used Chapter 11 procedures to gain court protection for a broad spectrum of purposes.

Recent events have strengthened the position of those who are critical of the manner in which Chapter 11 has been manipulated. It was designed to assist those in difficulty under the conventional interpretation of indebtedness. On the docket of bankruptcy courts have been companies who have filed in order to protect themselves from mass tort litigations (Manville, with its asbestos products, and A.H. Robins Inc., with its Dalkon Shield contraceptive device), to ward off enforcement of huge judgments (Texaco), or to escape funding of pension plans (LTV Corporation). It is doubtful that Congress intended bankruptcy laws to be an umbrella of corporate protection with such serious public consequences.

Developing a Plan of Reorganization

A petition seeking a corporate reorganization may be filed voluntarily or involuntarily to seek an order for relief. Normally, the debtor remains in charge of the business, although in unusual instances, a trustee (receiver) may be appointed to take control of the company. Those unusual instances include management fraud, deceit, and/or gross mismanagement.

After the filing of the petition, the law provides that the debtor shall not be harassed by creditors or stockholders so that the debtor can devote full energy to the reorganization. For the first 120 days, the debtor has the exclusive right to file a plan of reorganization. Thereafter, a plan may be filed by any party of interest. The court appoints a committee of the creditors holding the seven largest claims against the debtor. A committee of equity security holders also may be appointed. Their primary functions are to consult with the debtor in possession (or the trustee) about the administration of the case and to assist in the formulation of a plan of reorganization.

The plan of reorganization must detail the methods and means by which it will achieve its objectives. Possible arrangements will involve eliminating some debt, reducing debt principal and/or interest, reducing interest rates, postponing payment, and exchanging an equity interest for creditor claims or exchanging a lower ranking for a higher equity interest, such as substitution of common stock for preferred stock. The plan identifies the various classes of claims (secured versus unsecured) and classes of interests (stockholders or limited partners). It indicates the claims of interests (stockholders or limited partners). It indicates the claims or interests that are not impaired, as well as the treatment to be accorded those that are impaired. A class is impaired if the plan alters its legal or contractual rights.

If a class is not impaired, it is considered to have accepted the plan. The holder of a claim or interest impaired by the plan may accept or reject it. Parties impaired are provided a description of the reorganizational plan along with a court-approved disclosure statement regarding the plan. After evaluating the plan, the affected parties must vote to approve or reject it. A plan affecting impaired creditors is approved if it is accepted by creditors representing at least two-thirds in amount and more than one-half in number of a class of claims. A plan affecting shareholders or equity interests is approved if it is accepted by holders of such interests representing at least two-thirds in amount of the allowed claims of that class.

Upon approval by the impaired parties, confirmation by the bankruptcy court is sought. Before confirmation, the court verifies that under the plan each holder of a claim or interest will receive or retain property of a value that is not less than the amount such holder would receive under a Chapter 7 liquidation. In certain instances, courts have the authority to approve the plan even though the creditors have not approved it (the cram-down provision).

Once a plan is confirmed by the court, its provisions are binding on the debtor, known as a "debtor in possession," and on all creditors and equity security holders, whether or not they accepted the plan. Confirmation vests property in the debtor company or trustee. Such property is free of all claims of creditors and interests of equity holders, except as stipulated in the provisions of the plan. Under Chapter 11, once a plan is confirmed, the payment obligation on the debtor is fixed, regardless of any subsequent increase in the debtor's net cash inflow. If the reorganization is not accomplishing its intended objectives during the period outlined in the plan, a request for modification may be submitted to the court for approval, or a request may be filed to convert to a Chapter 7 liquidation.

Accounting for the Reorganization

The accounting professional is involved significantly in providing expertise regarding corporate reorganizations. Accountants may help in the discovery of assets and liabilities or in the determination of the impact of a reorganization. Prospective information also must be generated in order to determine the effect of a reorganization plan on future operations of the company. A plan of reorganization includes debt and/or equity restructuring similar to that discussed in the earlier section of this text involving troubled debt restructurings and quasi-reorganizations.

With respect to the restructuring of debt in a bankruptcy reorganization, the principles set forth in FASB Statement No. 15 generally do not apply to a bankruptcy reorganization; therefore, a different approach is used to measure the gain or loss on restructuring involving a modification of terms. In a bankruptcy reorganization, the gain on restructuring is measured as the difference between the fair market value of the restructured consideration received (its discounted present value) and the carrying basis of the debt being restructured. In FASB Statement No. 15, the gain on restructuring is measured as the difference between the total future cash payments (both principal and interest) to be received and the carrying basis of the debt being restructured. The gain on restructuring in a bankruptcy reorganization is typically recorded as either an extraordinary item or additional paid-in capital. Recognizing the gain as a component of paid-in capital facilitates the reduction of a deficit balance in retained earnings, if appropriate as part of the reorganization plan.

The recognition of subsequent interest on the restructured debt also differs for a bankruptcy reorganization. In this case, the total interest recognized on the restructured debt is imputed at market rates and represents the difference between the fair market value of the new debt (its discounted present value using market rates) and the total of all principal and interest payments. A FASB Statement No. 15 restructuring measures the total interest as the difference between the carrying basis of the debt being restructured and the total of all principal and interest payments. Therefore, under Statement No. 15, no interest is recognized if the total of all principal and interest payments made under the restructuring agreement do not exceed the carrying basis of the original debt being restructured. Other than the above differences, the accounting principles and standards for reorganizations are applicable to both bankruptcy and nonbankruptcy reorganizations.

Companies undergoing corporate reorganizations also are required to submit to the bankruptcy court periodic reports detailing operations, cash flows, and other information that the court may request. The preparation of these statements and reports presents no unusual accounting problems. Balance sheets may distinguish between assets and liabilities existing prior to and subsequent to the approval of the reorganization or appointment of a trustee, if applicable. Generally, the books of record used to account for the company prior to reorganization also are employed during the reorganization. However, if a trustee is appointed, the trustee may elect to establish a new set of books.

If new accounting records are to be established, the assets accepted by the fiduciary are debited at their book values, with a credit to an account called X Corporation in Trusteeship. On the corporate books, the transfer of assets is recorded by debiting an account to charge the fiduciary, such as E. Schenker, Trustee. These new accounts are reciprocal and represent the accountability of the trustee.

The fiduciary is not responsible for commitments made by the corporation prior to the period of stewardship. Therefore, those liabilities remain on the corporate books. However, the courts may direct payment of such liabilities. In this case, the trustee either may directly debit X Corporation in Trusteeship or create a temporary account, such as Accounts Payable—X Corporation, which periodically is closed into the major reciprocal account. The corporation would reflect payment with a debit to Accounts Payable and a credit to the account E. Schenker, Trustee.

The usual accounting procedures are followed by the trustee to record revenues and expenses. At the end of the year or at termination of the period of stewardship, the profit or loss on the trustee's books is closed into the accountability account, X Corporation in Trusteeship. On the corporate books, net income is recorded with a debit to the trustee account and a credit to Retained Earnings, while a net loss is recorded by the reverse procedure. When control is returned to the owners, the trustee eliminates all account balances, including the X Corporation in Trusteeship balance. The corporation records these accounts and eliminates the trustee account.

While the trustee is in control, the corporation's financial story is contained partly in the records of the trustee and partly in those of the corporation. The two records must be combined in order to prepare financial statements. The following skeleton worksheet is designed to accomplish the objective of reuniting the two sets of financial information:

X Corporation in Trusteeship
E. Schenker, Trustee
Worksheet for Combined Trial Balance
for Year Ended June 30, 20X1

Account Title	Trial Balance		Adjustments and Eliminations		Combined Trial Balance
	Trustee	Corporation			
Debits: E. Schenker, Trustee		90,000		(a) 90,000	
Total Debits	500,000	420,000			
Credits: X. Corp. in Trusteeship	90,000		(a) 90,000		
Total Credits	500,000	420,000			

The worksheet begins with the trial balances of the trustee's records and the corporation's records. These trial balances should be adjusted fully before they are entered on the worksheet. Any additional adjustments discovered subsequently are entered, and the two reciprocal account balances are eliminated. The items then are combined to produce a trial balance from which financial statements may be prepared.

Corporate Liquidations—Chapter 7

The only solution for certain insolvent companies is to liquidate the assets of the company, service its debts, distribute any remaining funds to shareholders, and terminate the business. Unfortunately, corporate reorganizations frequently are not successful and ultimately result in liquidation. Commencement of a plan to liquidate may be voluntary or involuntary. Approval of the plan is subject to the same requirements as a reorganization.

The commencement of a voluntary or involuntary case under Chapter 7 (Liquidation) creates an estate that consists of the assets of the debtor, who must file an inventory of property and debts/claims identified on the following schedules:

- Real Property—at market value
- Personal Property—at market value
- Property Claimed as Exempt—at market value (the nature of exemptions varies from state to state)
- Property Not Otherwise Scheduled—at market value
- Creditors Holding Secured Claims—amount of claim and market value of security
- Creditors Holding Unsecured Priority Claims—amount of claim
- Creditors Holding Unsecured Nonpriority Claims—amount of claim

Appointment of a Trustee in Liquidation

As soon as possible after issuing the order for relief, the court appoints an interim trustee to take charge until a permanent trustee is selected, and then a meeting of creditors is called. Creditors either may elect a permanent trustee or have the interim trustee serve in that capacity. Proofs of claim are examined by the trustee, who may accept them or, if they are improper, disallow them. To be considered in the settlement, a claim normally must be filed within 90 days after the date set for the first meeting of creditors.

The debtor is required to be present at the meeting of creditors in order to be subject to examination by the creditors or the trustee and must cooperate with the trustee in the preparation of an inventory of property, the examination of proofs of claim, and the general administration of the estate. To assist the trustee, a debtor files a *statement of affairs*, consisting of answers to a series of stated questions about the identity of the debtor's records and books, transactions, and events affecting the financial condition of the debtor, including any prior bankruptcy proceedings. This *legal* statement of affairs is not to be confused with the accounting statement of affairs discussed later in the chapter.

Duties of Trustee.   The trustee shall

1. Collect and reduce to money the nonexempt property of the estate.
2. Account for all money and property received, maintaining a record of cash receipts and disbursements.
3. Investigate the financial affairs of the debtor, including a review of the forms filed by the debtor.
4. Examine proofs of claim and disallow any improper claim.
5. Furnish information reasonably requested by a party of interest.
6. Operate the business of the debtor, if any, when so authorized by the court if such operation is in the best interest of the estate and consistent with its orderly liquidation.
7. Pay dividends to creditors as promptly as practicable, with regard for priorities. (The law applies the term "dividend" to any payment made to a creditor.)

8. File reports of progress, with the final report accompanied by a detailed statement of receipts and disbursements.

Disposition of Property.   One duty of the trustee is to dispose of property, even if another entity has an allowed claim secured by a lien on the property. The claim is secured to the amount of the value of the property. For example, if a creditor has an allowed claim of $20,000, with a sole lien against real property whose market value is $30,000, the claim is fully secured. Upon realization of the property, the excess of $10,000 would be available to meet unsecured claims in the order of priority. If the creditor in the example has an allowed claim of $35,000, there is a secured claim of $30,000 and an unsecured claim of $5,000.

Priorities for Unsecured Claims.   An order of priority to receive distributions from amounts available to meet unsecured claims has been established by the Act. Each class must be paid in full or provided for before any amount is paid to the next lower class. When the amount is inadequate to pay all claims of a given class, the amount is distributed on a pro rata basis within that class. When the amount is sufficient to pay the claims of all classes, which is highly unlikely, the excess amount is returned to the debtor. The order of priority for allowed unsecured claims is as follows:

Class 1—Expenses to administer the estate. Those who administer the estate should be assured of payment; otherwise, competent attorneys and accountants would not be willing to participate.

Class 2—Debts incurred after the commencement of a case of involuntary bankruptcy but before the order for relief or appointment of a trustee. These items, referred to as "gap" creditors, are granted priority in order to permit the business to carry on its operations during the period of legal proceedings.

Class 3—Wages (salaries or commissions) up to $4,000 per individual, earned within 90 days before the filing of the petition or the cessation of the debtor's business, whichever occurs first.

Class 4—Unpaid contributions to employee benefit plans, arising from services performed up to 180 days prior to filing the petition, to the extent of $4,000 per employee covered by the plan.

Class 5—Deposits up to $1,800 each for goods or services never received from the debtor.

Class 6—Tax claims of a governmental unit. These taxes are nondischargeable (i.e., they still must be met by the debtor after the termination of the case).

Class 7—Claims of general creditors not granted priority. All remaining unsecured claims fall into this category.

For a successful case under Chapter 11 (Reorganization) or Chapter 13 (Individual), the sequence of priority also has significance. In a Chapter 11 case, the plan of reorganization will not be confirmed unless the court has determined that creditors will receive at least as much as they would under Chapter 7. The same idea is used for Chapter 13 cases, for which the Code states that the court will approve the plan only if the value of the property to be distributed on account of each allowed unsecured claim is not less than the amount that would be paid under Chapter 7.

It is important to note that although the goal of a liquidation is to discharge the debts, certain debts are not dischargeable. For example, certain taxes, fines, and/or penalties are nondischargeable.

Preparation of the Statement of Affairs

Earlier in this chapter, a reference was made to the legal statement of affairs, which consists of responses to questions regarding a debtor's financial condition. The other report with the same name is the accounting statement of affairs, which is discussed in this section of the chapter. The primary purpose of the *accounting statement of affairs* is to approximate the estimated amounts available to each class of claims. It thereby assists all concerned parties in reaching a decision as to what insolvency action is preferable. It is a balance sheet of a potentially liquidating concern rather than of a going concern. Thus, it shifts the emphasis for assets from historical cost to estimated realizable values and the allocation of proceeds to creditors and stockholders. It is important to note that the statement of affairs is based on estimated values available to creditors, and the actual values realized from the liquidation of assets may differ. Although the statement assumes a liquidation of the insolvent company, the statement also is used to evaluate the reasonableness of a corporate reorganization. Plans for a corporate reorganization will not be confirmed by the court unless creditors will receive at least as much as they would under a liquidation.

In the past, the preparation and the format of the statement of affairs have been cumbersome and confusing. Thus, a revised form is recommended, in which the statement of affairs is split into two sections, one dealing with the assets and the other with the liabilities and the owners' equity. Before the statement of affairs is prepared, however, the account balances should be adjusted fully, an income statement should be prepared, and owners' equity should be adjusted to include the net profit or net loss to date.

The asset portion of the statement of affairs identifies the assets of the liquidating entity and their book value, estimated net realizable value, and estimated gain or loss upon liquidation. Available assets are identified as follows:

1. Assets pledged with fully secured creditors,
2. Assets pledged with partially secured creditors, and
3. Free assets available to unsecured creditors.

For each asset, the net realizable value must be estimated, using whatever information is available. For example, receivables would exclude unrealizable amounts; marketable securities would be based on current market reports; and real estate would reflect current market appraisals. Some assets, such as goodwill, may have no realizable value. For each asset, the difference between realizable value and book value is entered as a gain or loss upon liquidation. The assets available to unsecured creditors also are identified on the asset section of the statement of affairs.

The liability and owners' equity section on the statement of affairs identifies the following components:

1. Fully secured creditors,
2. Partially secured creditors,
3. Unsecured creditors with priority (Class 1 through 6 creditors),
4. Unsecured creditors without priority (Class 7 creditors), and
5. Owners' equity deficiency or surplus.

In order to illustrate the statement of affairs, assume Insolve Corporation's adjusted balance sheet as of February 28, 20X2, is as appears in Illustration 21-1.

Prior to liquidation, management has decided to complete the work in process by incurring $12,000 of additional labor costs and $4,000 of additional overhead. It is expected that, upon completion, the additional finished goods can be sold for $94,000. The mortgage payable is secured by the land and building, and the bank loan is secured by the equipment. Accounts payable totaling $180,000 are secured by inventory with a book value of $180,000 and an estimated net realizable value of $160,000.

Illustration 21-1

Insolve Corporation
Balance Sheet
February 28, 20X2

Assets

Current assets:			
Cash		$ 4,000	
Accounts receivable	$ 84,000		
Less allowance for uncollectible accounts	(14,000)	70,000	
Marketable securities		20,000	
Inventories:			
Raw materials	35,000		
Work in process.	63,000		
Finished goods	124,000	222,000	$316,000
Property, plant, and equipment:			
Land		110,000	
Building		340,000	
Less accumulated depreciation—building		(158,000)	
Equipment.		290,000	
Less accumulated depreciation—equipment.		(140,000)	442,000
Goodwill (net of amortization)			48,000
Total assets			$806,000

Liabilities and Owners' Equity

Current liabilities:		
Accounts payable	$240,000	
Accrued liabilities—other	12,000	
Accrued income taxes	6,000	
Accrued mortgage interest	24,000	
Accrued liquidation expenses	13,000	
Accrued payroll taxes	14,000	
Accrued payroll (not exceeding $4,000 per person)	33,000	$342,000
Long-term liabilities:		
Mortgage payable	280,000	
Bank loan payable	200,000	480,000
Total liabilities		$822,000
Owners' equity:		
Common stock	10,000	
Paid-in capital in excess of par	40,000	
Deficit.	(66,000)	(16,000)
Total liabilities and owners' equity		$806,000

The statement of affairs for Insolve Corporation is based on assumed net realizable amounts and appears as Illustration 21-2.

Illustration 21-2

Insolve Corporation
Statement of Affairs
February 28, 20X2

Book Value	Assets	Estimated Net Realizable Value	Estimated Amount Available for Unsecured Creditors	Estimated Gain or (Loss) on Liquidation
	Assets pledged with fully secured creditors:			
$110,000	Land..................................	$130,000		$20,000
182,000	Building (net).........................	210,000		28,000
		$340,000	$36,000	
	Assets pledged with partially secured creditors:			
150,000	Equipment (net).......................	118,000		(32,000)
	Inventory			
35,000	Raw materials......................	18,000		(17,000)
63,000	Work in process (less estimated completion			
	costs of $16,000)...................	78,000		15,000
124,000	Finished goods......................	112,000		(12,000)
	Total..............................	326,000	48,000	
	Free assets:			
4,000	Cash	4,000	4,000	
70,000	Accounts receivable (net)	70,000	70,000	
20,000	Marketable securities.................	14,000	14,000	(6,000)
48,000	Goodwill............................			(48,000)
	Estimated amount available for unsecured creditors			
	with and without priority:..............		$172,000	
	Less unsecured creditors with priority		(66,000)	
	Estimated amounts for unsecured creditors without priority:			
	Net realizable amount available		$106,000	
	Deficiency (to agree with total unsecured			
	amount without priority)		68,000	
$806,000	Totals	$754,000	$174,000	($52,000)

There are several important things to note about the mechanics of the statement of affairs. First, the two major sections of the statement (Assets and Liabilities and Owners' Equity) should be completed in conjunction with each other. For example, when identifying assets pledged with partially secured creditors, the secured and unsecured amounts of liabilities to such creditors should be identified. Second, the statement is constructed to provide crossfootings as a check on the mathematical accuracy and completeness of the schedule. For example, in the asset section the book value of the assets should equal the assets' estimated net realizable value plus (minus) the estimated loss (gain) on liquidation ($806,000 = $754,000 + $52,000). In the liabilities and owners' equity section, the book value total before the owners' deficiency should equal the total of estimated secured and unsecured liabilities

Book Value	Liabilities and Owners' Equity	Estimated Secured Amount	With Priority	Without Priority
			Estimated Unsecured Amount	
	Fully secured creditors:			
$ 24,000	Accrued mortgage interest	$ 24,000		
280,000	Mortgage payable	280,000		
	Total	$304,000		
	Partially secured creditors:			
200,000	Bank loan payable	$118,000		$ 82,000
180,000	Accounts payable.	160,000		20,000
	Total	$278,000		
	Unsecured creditors with priority:			
6,000	Accrued income taxes		$ 6,000	
13,000	Accrued liquidation expenses		13,000	
14,000	Accrued payroll taxes		14,000	
33,000	Accrued payroll		33,000	
	Unsecured creditors without priority:			
12,000	Accrued liabilities—other			12,000
60,000	Accounts payable.			60,000
$822,000	Totals	$582,000	$66,000	$174,000
(16,000)	Owners' deficiency			
$806,000				

($822,000 = $582,000 + $66,000 + $174,000). Finally, the deficiency traceable to unsecured creditors without priority ($68,000) should equal the difference between the estimated net realizable value of the assets and the total of estimated secured and unsecured amounts due creditors [$68,000 = $754,000 − ($582,000 + $66,000 + $174,000)]. This deficiency represents the extent to which the net realizable value of assets is inadequate to meet the claims of creditors. Certainly, if the net realizable value of such assets exceeded the creditors' claims, the excess would be available to satisfy the claims of owners/shareholders.

Of interest to the unsecured creditors in Class 7 and the bankruptcy court is a ratio that is referred to as the dividend to general unsecured creditors. This ratio is computed as follows:

$$\text{Dividend} = \frac{\text{Net proceeds available to unsecured creditors in Class 7}}{\text{Total claims of unsecured creditors in Class 7}}$$

The dividend is an estimate of how much will be received by Class 7 unsecured creditors for each dollar owed to them, and it is expressed either in absolute amount or in percentage form.

The approximate dividend in Class 7 unsecured creditors of Insolve Corporation will be

$$\frac{\$106,000}{\$174,000} = \$0.61 \text{ on one dollar, or } 61\%$$

Preparation of Other Accounting Reports

The trustee appointed to a company in liquidation is expected to make periodic reports to the bankruptcy court regarding the activities of the trustee. In the absence of specific reporting requirements imposed by the Act, each bankruptcy court identifies the type of accounting reports to be submitted by the trustee.

Generally speaking, a court will require the trustee to provide an accounting regarding the following items pertaining to the insolvent company:

1. Unrealized assets assigned to the trustee including those subsequently discovered.
2. Assets that have been realized or liquidated.
3. Liabilities to be liquidated that have been assigned to the trustee.
4. Liabilities that have been liquidated.

Historically, the preceding information was presented in a report called the realization and liquidation account, which employed a rather cumbersome format. Currently, this information is most often presented in a worksheet format that identifies critical balances and relevant cash receipts and disbursements.

The statement of realization and liquidation differs from the statement of affairs in the following respects:

1. The statement of realization and liquidation reports the actual liquidation results. In contrast, the statement of affairs is of a pro forma nature and is based on estimated rather than actual results.
2. The statement of realization and liquidation provides an ongoing reporting of the trustee's activities and is updated throughout the liquidation process. The statement of affairs is a summary of the estimated results of a completed liquidation.

In order to illustrate the preparation of a statement of realization and liquidation, the balance sheet of Insolve Corporation, which was presented in Illustration 21-1, will be used as a starting point. Assuming the assets and liabilities contained in Insolve's balance sheet were assigned to the trustee, a statement of realization and liquidation for the period March 1, 20X2, to March 31, 20X2, is presented in Illustration 21-3. In reviewing this illustration, note that it reports actual results rather than estimated amounts, as contained in the statement of affairs. Also note that the statement reports liquidation activity to date and may be updated to reflect subsequent activity.

Illustration 21-3

Insolve Corporation
Statement of Realization and Liquidation
For the Period March 1, 20X2, to March 31, 20X2

	Assets		Fully Secured	Partially Secured	Unsecured With Priority	Unsecured Without Priority	Owners' Equity
	Cash	Noncash					
Beginning balances, assigned March 1, 20X2.	$ 4,000	$802,000	$304,000	$380,000	$66,000	$ 72,000	($16,000)
Subsequently discovered and other items:							
Assets		15,000*					15,000
Loans from officers.						20,000*	(20,000)
Additional liquidation expenses[1].					2,000		(2,000)
Cash receipts:.							
Sale of marketable securities	16,000*	(20,000)					(4,000)
Partial collection of accounts receivable	52,000	(52,000)					
Sale of equipment	124,000*	(150,000)					(26,000)
Sale of inventory[2]	134,000*	(148,000)					(14,000)
Cash disbursements:							
Partial payment of bank loan[3]	(124,000)			(200,000)		76,000	
Partial payment of accounts payable[4]	(98,000)			(135,000)		37,000	
Ending balances	$108,000	$447,000	$304,000	$ 45,000	$68,000	$205,000	($67,000)

*These amounts differ from the estimated amounts included in the statement of affairs.

1 Liquidation expenses were originally estimated to be $13,000. However, actual liquidation expenses to date total $15,000.

2 The sale of inventory consists of the following:

	Book Value	Amount Realized
Raw materials	$ 35,000	$ 18,000
Work in process (less completion costs of $18,000)	63,000	76,000
Finished goods.	50,000	40,000
	$148,000	$134,000

3 The bank loan of $200,000 is secured by the equipment, which was disposed of for $124,000 net of expenses. Therefore, $76,000 of the loan is reclassified as an unsecured liability.

4 The sale of inventory described in footnote 2 included inventory securing the accounts payable. This inventory had a book value of $135,000 and was sold for $98,000. Therefore, accounts payable with a value of $135,000 were secured only to the extent of $98,000. The unsecured portion of $37,000 ($135,000 − $98,000) is reclassified as such.

The statement also may be used to reassess the effect of a liquidation on various claims of liabilities. For example, as of March 31, 20X2, Insolve Corporation still has $447,000 of noncash assets to be realized. A statement of these assets and their newly revised estimated net realizable values follows:

Noncash Assets	Book Value	Estimated Net Realizable Value
Accounts receivable (net)	$ 18,000	$ 18,000
Inventories................................	74,000	70,000*
Land....................................	110,000	130,000
Building (net)	182,000	210,000
Goodwill.................................	48,000	0
Assets subsequently discovered	15,000	17,000
	$447,000	$445,000

*$44,000 of this amount is traceable to partially secured accounts payable.

The estimated net realizable value of noncash assets of $445,000 plus the available existing cash of $108,000 represents a total of $553,000, which would be available to satisfy liabilities and owners' equity. A tentative distribution of this total follows below:

Liabilities and Owners' Equity	Book Value	Estimated Distribution	Dividend (Payout) Percentage
Fully secured liabilities	$304,000	$304,000	100%
Partially secured liabilities:			
Book value of $45,000 less unsecured portion of $1,000	44,000	44,000	100
Unsecured liabilities:			
With priority...........................	68,000	68,000	100
Without priority:			
Book value of $205,000 plus unsecured portion of partially secured liabilities....	206,000	137,000	67
Owners' equity (deficit)	(67,000)		
	$555,000	$553,000	

Although corporate reorganizations and liquidations are significantly influenced by law, the accounting profession also may be significantly involved in the entire process. Accountants assist in the identification and valuation of assets and liabilities traceable to the insolvent company. The activities of a company involved in a Chapter 11 reorganization or a Chapter 7 liquidation must be periodically reported to the bankruptcy courts. This periodic reporting function is a major area involving the expertise of the accounting profession.

Questions

1. A troubled debt restructuring may take several forms. Identify the various forms of these restructurings.
2. Assume that debt is restructured outside of a bankruptcy reorganization. How is the amount of interest on such a restructuring recognized?
3. How does the measurement of the gain on debt restructuring differ between a restructuring which is not part of a formal bankruptcy reorganization and one that is?

4. Distinguish between a corporate reorganization and a liquidation as addressed in Chapters 11 and 7, respectively, of the Bankruptcy Reform Act.
5. How might the revaluation of a company's common stock at par value be useful in accomplishing the goal of a quasi-reorganization?
6. What are the responsibilities of a debtor under a Chapter 7 liquidation once a trustee has been appointed?
7. Under the Bankruptcy Reform Act, do all unsecured creditors share pro rata in funds as they become available? Explain.
8. Explain how the statement of affairs prepared by an accountant in a Chapter 7 liquidation differs from a statement of realization and liquidation.
9. The accounting statement of affairs contains a section identifying available assets and another section dealing with liabilities and owners' equity. Identify the categories of liabilities that are influenced by the value of free assets.
10. A creditor has a claim of $210,000 which is secured by inventory with a book value of $200,000. The inventory is sold by a broker who charges a fee of $20,000. Where does the broker's claim for her fee of $20,000 normally rank with respect to priority?
11. Various values on the statement of affairs affect the deficiency traceable to unsecured creditors without priority. Explain how the value of this deficiency is determined.

Exercises

Exercise 1. The Ames Corporation has been experiencing difficulties servicing its long-term debt which has a current balance of $620,000 including accrued interest. Ames is considering two possible alternatives to restructuring the debt. Alternative #1 would consist of conveying vacant land with a fair market value of $350,000 and a book value of $275,000 to the creditor. In addition, Ames would make two annual payments of $120,000 each. Alternative #2 would call for Ames to make five annual payments of $135,000. All payments are to be made at the end of the respective years. The market rates of interest for a 2-year and 5-year note are 10% and 12%, respectively.

1. Prepare a schedule to compare the total effect on net income of alternatives #1 and #2 related to the restructuring.
2. Discuss whether the alternative with the most favorable effect on net income provides the company with the greatest economic advantage.

Exercise 2. In an attempt to avoid liquidating the company, the management of Carter, Inc., is considering a reorganization that calls for the restructuring of $2,100,000 of debt maturing in 3 years and related accrued interest payable of $72,737. The restructuring agreement calls for monthly payments over the next 60 months, a reduction in the interest rate to 8%, and the cancellation of $200,000 of debt. The market rate of interest for such a refinancing would be 13%. In addition to the debt restructuring, management is proposing to reduce the par value of their common stock in order to generate enough paid-in capital in excess of par value to absorb a $500,000 deficit in retained earnings. The present balance of paid-in capital in excess of par value is $80,000.

1. Prepare a schedule to determine the total gain resulting from the forgiveness and restructuring of debt and the amount of future interest expense assuming (a) a nonbankruptcy approach and (b) a bankruptcy approach to the reorganization.

(continued)

2. Determine by how much the par value of common stock would have to be reduced in order to absorb the deficit in retained earnings assuming (a) a non-bankruptcy approach and (b) a bankruptcy approach.

Exercise 3. The stockholders of Vegas Corporation have authorized the company to conduct a quasi-reorganization in order to revise asset valuations and eliminate its deficit. A condensed balance sheet at October 1, 20X5, just prior to the quasi-reorganization, is as follows:

Assets		Liabilities and Equity	
Current assets	$ 400,000	Liabilities	$ 600,000
Property and equipment . .		Capital stock ($10 par). . .	2,200,000
(net)	2,000,000	Deficit	(400,000)
		Total liabilities	
Total assets	$2,400,000	and equity.	$2,400,000

Additional data:

a) Inventories have been overvalued by $80,000.

b) Plant assets have been appraised at $1,500,000.

c) Stockholders have approved a reduction in the par value of capital stock to $5 per share.

1. Prepare journal entries to record the quasi-reorganization.
2. Prepare a balance sheet for immediately after the quasi-reorganization.

Exercise 4. The creditors of the Thorel Corporation agreed to a Chapter 7 liquidation which, based on the statement of affairs, suggested that unsecured creditors without priority would receive approximately $0.60 on the dollar. The unsecured creditors are interested in determining whether the preliminary estimate still seems appropriate. The trustee was originally assigned assets of $1,480,000 and creditor claims as follows: fully secured, $670,000; partially secured, $400,000; unsecured with priority, $200,000; and unsecured without priority, $320,000. Assets with a book value of $45,000 and unsecured liabilities (without priority) of $35,000 were subsequently discovered. Assets with a total book value of $740,000 were sold for $715,000 net. Fully secured liabilities of $410,000 and partially secured liabilities of $280,000 were paid. Remaining liquidation expenses were estimated to be $30,000.

Assume the remaining assets have an estimated net realizable value as follows:

Assets traceable to fully secured creditors	$240,000
Assets traceable to partially secured creditors	110,000
Remaining assets	382,000

Determine the revised estimate of the dividend to be received by unsecured creditors without priority.

Exercise 5. Casper Blueprinting, Inc., has filed under Chapter 7 of the Bankruptcy Code. The estimated net realizable value of its assets is as follows:

Cash and cash equivalents.	$ 23,000
Accounts receivable	42,000
Inventory and supplies.	15,000
Blueprinting equipment	114,000
Furniture and fixtures.	12,000
Computer hardware and software	21,000
Delivery vehicle	14,000
	$241,000

Creditor's claims are summarized as follows:

a) Bank loan balance of $82,000 plus accrued interest of $3,000 with a first lien against blueprinting equipment.

b) Dealer-financed vehicle loan with an outstanding balance of $18,000 which is secured by the delivery vehicle.

c) Accounts payable due vendors in the amount of $21,000 and secured by the inventory and supplies.

d) A line of credit balance due of $30,000 secured by the accounts receivable.

e) Unpaid payroll and income taxes of $23,000.

f) Accounting and legal fees due in the amount of $12,000 in connection with the administration of the bankrupt estate.

g) Unpaid wages to employees totaling $4,200 ($700 represents the largest amount due any one employee).

h) Loans due shareholders of the corporation totaling $80,000.

i) Other unsecured creditors without priority in the amount of $31,000.

Prepare a schedule to show the estimated amount to be received by each major category of creditor.

Exercise 6.   Tabco Industries, Inc., has submitted to the bankruptcy courts a plan of reorganization seeking relief under Chapter 11. In order to evaluate the reasonableness of the plan, it must be evaluated against the alternative of a corporate liquidation. The following condensed trial balance and estimates of net realizable values have been prepared as of July 1, 20X9.

	Book Values		Estimated Net Realiz-
	Debit	Credit	able Value
Cash.	$ 2,000		$ 2,000
Accounts Receivable	158,000		126,400
Inventory.	74,000		60,600
Other Current Assets	16,000		12,000
Property, Plant, and Equipment (net)	420,000		440,000
Other Assets	12,000		0
Accounts Payable		$180,000	
Other Current Liabilities		134,000	
Mortgage and Related Interest Payable.		300,000	
Other Noncurrent Debt		50,000	
Owners' Equity.		18,000	
Totals	$682,000	$682,000	$641,000

(continued)

Accounts payable totaling $50,000 are secured by inventory with a book value of $50,000 and a market value of $42,000. The mortgage and the related interest payable are fully secured by land and building having a book value of $284,000 and a net realizable value of $330,000. The other noncurrent debt represents an unsecured loan from officers of the corporation. The other current liabilities, in part, include:

Unpaid wages (less than $4,000 per individual)	$ 20,000
Customer deposits (less than $1,800 per customer)..................	14,000
Real estate taxes (having a lien on the land and building)	18,000
Undeposited payroll taxes.....................................	8,000
Accounts receivable assigned (receivables are estimated to be 90% collectible)	64,000
	$124,000

The trial balance does not include $7,000 of estimated expenses to administer the liquidation.

Prepare a statement of affairs for Tabco and calculate the estimated dividend to general unsecured creditors with and without priority.

Exercise 7.   A partially completed statement of realization and liquidation is as follows:

The Rodak Corporation
Statement of Realization and Liquidation
For the Period of July 1, 20X9, to August 12, 20X9

	Assets		Liabilities				
					Unsecured		
	Cash	Noncash	Fully Secured	Partially Secured	With Priority	Without Priority	Owners' Equity
Beginning balances, assigned July 1, 20X9 ..	$12,000	$590,000	$200,000	$175,000	$54,000	$150,000	$23,000
Cash receipts: Sale of inventory	30,000	(25,000)					5,000

The following additional transactions have occurred through August 12, 20X9:

a) Receivables collected amount to $39,000. Receivables with a book value of $15,000 that were not allowed for were written off.

b) A $12,000 loan that was fully secured was paid off.

c) A valid claim is received from a leasing company seeking payment of $15,000 for equipment rentals.

d) Securities costing $18,000 are sold for $23,000, minus brokerage fee of $500.

e) Depreciation on machinery is $3,200.

f) Payments on accounts payable total $25,000, of which the entire amount was secured by the inventory sold.

g) Machinery that originally cost $85,000 and has a book value of $45,000 sold for $36,000.

h) Proceeds from the sale of machinery in (g) are remitted to the bank, which holds a $50,000 loan on the machinery.

1. Update the statement of realization and liquidation to properly reflect transactions (a) through (h).
2. Assuming the remaining noncash assets can be realized for $410,000, determine the estimated dividend to be received by unsecured creditors without priority.

Problems

Problem 21-1. Milton Company has developed a plan to restructure a major portion of its debt. The provisions of the restructuring of debt existing at February 1, 20X9, are as follows:

a) Accounts payable with a book value of $800,000 will be paid off within 2 months at the rate of $0.80 on the dollar.

b) Loans from officers with a book value of $300,000 and accrued interest of $16,000 will be satisfied by conveying land with a market value of $290,000.

c) A bank note payable with a maturity value of $1,400,000 and delinquent accrued interest of $131,237 will be exchanged for a new note. The new note in the amount of $1,480,000 will be serviced over 5 years with monthly payments reflecting a market interest rate of 12.9%.

d) An unpaid balance on the corporate line of credit of $112,000, including accrued interest, will be converted into a $100,000, 12-month note payable. Interest for the first 4 months will be waived, after which time the first of 8 monthly payments will begin bearing interest at 12%.

e) A $500,000 mortgage payable with 5 years to maturity will be refinanced over 15 years at a rate of 10.2%. In addition to the monthly payments, an initial refinancing fee of $5,000 is to be paid.

Required:

1. Prepare a schedule for management that details the estimated cash outflows over the next 6 months resulting from the debt restructuring.
2. Prepare a schedule for management that details the estimated effect on net income over the next 6 months resulting from the debt restructuring assuming

   a) The restructuring is not part of a formal bankruptcy filing.
   b) The restructuring is part of a formal bankruptcy filing.

Problem 21-2. Jensen Manufacturing, Inc., has filed under Chapter 11 of the Bankruptcy Act. At the time of filing the plan of reorganization, the company had total assets of $2,040,000 and liabilities and equity as follows:

Accounts Payable.	$210,000
Note Payable—Officer	120,000
Equipment Note Payable.	500,000
Line of Credit Payable.	360,000
Mortgage Payable	625,000
Convertible Bonds	200,000
Common Stock at Par	100,000
Paid-in Capital.	50,000
Deficit Retained Earnings.	(125,000)

(continued)

The plan of reorganization contains the following proposals:

a) *The accounts payable due vendors will be settled for $180,000, and all subsequent purchases will be on a C.O.D. basis. The payables are secured by inventory with a book value and net realizable value of $165,000.*

b) *The amount due the officer will be settled by conveying vacant land with a cost basis of $60,000 and a net realizable value of $85,000.*

c) *The equipment note is collateralized by equipment with a net book value of $410,000 and a net realizable value of $440,000. The proposal calls for servicing the debt as follows: 60 monthly payments of $10,010 including interest at 12% per annum.*

d) *The line of credit is secured by receivables and inventory which have a combined book value and net realizable value of $400,000, and the line will not be affected by the reorganization.*

e) *The mortgage will be restructured to provide for 120 monthly payments of $8,590 including interest at 10% per annum. The mortgage is secured by a building and underlying land which has a combined book value and net realizable value of $450,000 and $650,000, respectively.*

f) *The convertible bonds will be retired in exchange for a promise to make 4 annual payments of $40,000 each. The market rate for a similar loan is 11%.*

g) *The par value of the common stock will be reduced to $10,000, and the deficit will be eliminated against the additional paid-in capital.*

Required:

Before confirming the plan of reorganization, the bankruptcy court must verify that each holder of a claim or interest will not receive or retain property of a value less than the amount such holder would have received under a Chapter 7 liquidation. Calculate the minimum net realizable value of assets available to unsecured creditors—without priority which would be necessary to meet the Chapter 7 "test" referred to above. Assume that if the company were liquidated, $40,000 of liquidation expenses would be incurred.

Problem 21-3.   Given the facts of Problem 21-2, assume that the plan of reorganization was approved by the requisite number and dollar amount of holders of claims and/or interests.

Required:

Prepare a schedule which identifies each proposed element (a) through (g) of the plan and compares the income effect of the reorganization to that which would have been experienced if the reorganization plan were not part of a formal bankruptcy filing.

Problem 21-4.   Atoyo Fabricating, Inc., has not been able to service its debts adequately. The company is a family business which has been in existence for 35 years. The shareholders want to avoid liquidating the business and are seeking your help in formulating a plan of reorganization which

a) *Provides creditors with at least as much consideration as, if not more than, they would receive if the company were liquidated, and*

b) *Does not require monthly debt service in excess of $75,000.*

Information regarding the various creditor claims and possible restructuring parameters is as follows:

a) Accounts payable due vendors total $134,000. Terms are generally 2/10 net 30, and virtually all accounts are past due. Vendors with balances of $40,000 due have indicated that in satisfaction of the amount due, they would accept equal monthly installment payments bearing no less than 12% and not exceeding three months in duration. These vendors have secured their claims with inventory which has a book value and net realizable value of $55,000 and $42,000, respectively. Vendors with a balance due of $74,000 have a secured interest in inventory with a book value of $60,000 and a net realizable value of $46,000. These vendors would accept 3 monthly installment payments of $20,000 including interest at the rate of 12% in satisfaction of the amount due. The remaining payables represent unsecured amounts which would be paid $3,000 per month for the next 5 months including interest at 12%.

b) The equipment note has a balance due of $320,000 plus accrued interest of $18,000. Equipment with a book value of $280,000 and a net realizable value of $325,000 serves as collateral for this loan. The original loan had an interest rate of 11% and a remaining term of 30 months. The creditor will not agree to a change in the interest rate but will accept a revised term of 36 to 42 months in exchange for a personal guarantee of the amount due by each of the shareholders of record.

c) The note due a shareholder in the amount of $20,000 is secured by the cash surrender value of an insurance policy in the amount of $15,000 and is payable on demand. The shareholder would accept 4 semiannual payments, including interest at 12%, if the present value of these payments is equal to 120% of what would have been received if the company had been liquidated.

d) The mortgage payable of $420,000 plus accrued interest of $28,000 is fully secured by real estate with a book value of $310,000 and a net realizable value of $460,000. The original mortgage has a remaining term of 334 months and an interest rate of 9%. The mortgage company would agree to a restructuring of 360 months and an interest rate of 11%.

e) All other creditors totaling $160,000 are unsecured without priority. Management would like to propose that these creditors receive monthly payments over the next 8 months with interest at 12%. The net present value of these payments should equal 110% of what would have been received had the company been liquidated.

The book values and net realizable values of the company's assets are as follows:

	Book Value	Net Realizable Value
Cash and Cash Equivalents	$ 5,000	$ 5,000
Accounts Receivable (net)	120,000	85,000
Inventory.	145,000	100,000
Equipment (net)	330,000	345,000
Real Property (net)	310,000	460,000
Cash Surrender Values	25,000	25,000
Licensing Agreement.	30,000	10,000
Furniture and Fixtures	25,000	12,000
	$990,000	$1,042,000

(continued)

Required:

Prepare a schedule which analyzes the proposed restructuring against the goals set by management.

Problem 21-5. The past several years have been extremely difficult for Avery Manufacturing Company, Inc. During this time, the company lost significant market share and was successfully sued with respect to several product liability cases. In response to those problems, the company filed a voluntary petition to liquidate the company on May 15, 20X9, at which time the company had the following condensed trial balance:

Cash	$ 30,000	
Noncash Assets	2,958,000	
Liabilities:		
Fully Secured		$1,720,000
Partially Secured.		762,000
Unsecured—With Priority		20,000
Unsecured—Without Priority		230,000
Owners' Equity		256,000
Totals	$2,988,000	$2,988,000

The bankruptcy court issued an order of relief on June 1, 20X9. The following liquidation transaction occurred through July 15, 20X9:

a) The inventory of raw materials was disposed of as follows:

	Cost	Market Value
Returned to fully secured vendors.	$180,000	$180,000
Sold to liquidations broker	70,000	50,000
Transferred to work in process.	40,000	40,000
	$290,000	$270,000

b) Work in process with a cost prior to liquidation of $117,000 was completed with the addition of the following costs:

Raw materials per (a).	$40,000
Additional unpaid labor (individually less than $4,000).	17,000
Overhead:	
Depreciation.	1,000
Additional liabilities incurred	4,000*
	$62,000

*These debts were incurred between May 17, 20X9, and May 28, 20X9.

The finished work in process was sold for $160,000.

c) Remaining finished goods with a cost of $204,000 were sold to a liquidation broker for $154,000.

d) The company's Indiana manufacturing facility, which had a net book value of $1,240,000, was sold for $1,000,000. The $800,000 mortgage on the property and related accrued interest of $34,000 were paid off with the sales proceeds.

e) The company's warehouse with a net book value of $430,000 and an appraised value of $380,000 was assigned to the bank that held the $450,000 mortgage on the property.

f) Equipment with a net book value of $450,000 was sold at auction for $330,000. Lenders with equipment loans of $272,000, including accrued interest, received $220,000 upon sale of the equipment. Leased equipment was returned to the lessors and the company forfeited $15,000 in lease deposits.

g) Unassigned accounts receivable were realized as follows:

	Book Value	Market Value
Collected in full	$ 72,000	$72,000
Written off:		
Against a $30,000 allowance	30,000	0
In excess of allowance	14,000	0
	$116,000	$72,000

h) Assigned accounts receivable totaling $40,000 were disposed of as follows:

Collected in full	$32,000
Returned to the company with recourse	8,000

i) Expenses totaling $14,000 have been incurred by the trustee.

j) The company was just assessed another $15,000 of property taxes, which brings the total amount of taxes owed to governmental units to $35,000.

Required:

1. Prepare a statement of realization and liquidation for the period June 1, 20X9, to July 15, 20X9.
2. Determine the amount to be paid to unsecured creditors with and without priority assuming the remaining noncash assets have a net realizable value of (a) $10,000 and (b) $64,000.

   If only unsecured creditors with priority will receive a distribution, indicate which specific class of creditors will be paid.

Problem 21-6.   A creditor's committee of Carlton Company has obtained the March 31, 20X5 balance sheet shown below:

Carlton Company
Balance Sheet
March 31, 20X5

Assets

Current assets:		
Cash		$ 11,250
Marketable securities		28,750
Notes receivable	$ 10,000	
Less notes receivable discounted	10,000	0

(continued)

Accounts receivable	$ 15,000	
Less allowance for doubtful accounts	1,000	14,000
Subscriptions receivable		20,000
Inventories:		
Finished goods	$ 27,500	
Work in process	11,250	
Materials	15,000	53,750
Total current assets		$127,750
Property, plant, and equipment:		
Land and building	$112,500	
Equipment	60,000	$172,500
Less accumulated depreciation		50,000
Total property, plant, and equipment		122,500
Total assets		$250,250

Liabilities and Stockholders' Equity

Current liabilities:		
Notes payable	$ 87,500	
Accounts payable	60,000	
Salaries payable	2,650	
Property tax payable	1,150	
Total current liabilities	$151,300	
Long-term liabilities:		
First mortgage payable	$ 37,500	
Second mortgage payable	50,000	87,500
Total liabilities		$238,800
Stockholders' equity:		
Common stock, $100 par (1,000 shares authorized)		
750 shares issued	$ 75,000	
250 shares subscribed	25,000	
Total	$100,000	
Retained earnings (deficit)	(88,550)	
Total stockholders' equity		11,450
Total liabilities and stockholders' equity		$250,250

An analysis of the company's accounts disclosed the following activities through April 30, 20X5:

a) Carlton Company started business on April 1, 20X0, with authorized stock of $100 par. Of the 1,000 authorized shares, 750 were paid for in full at par, and 250 were subscribed at par, with a required 20% down payment and the balance payable upon call. All of the subscriptions receivable are due from W. Krueger, president of the company, and are fully collectible.

b) Marketable securities include the $25,000 cost of U.S. Treasury bonds valued at $23,200 and 25 shares of Groves Company common stock, costing $3,750, with a market value of $3,300.

c) The land originally cost $10,000, and the building was erected at a cost of $102,500. Of the accumulated depreciation, $30,000 is applicable to the building. The realizable value of the real estate is $75,000.

d) Notes receivable were endorsed with recourse when discounted and are expected to be dishonored. Of the accounts receivable, $3,000 are considered collectible.

e) Inventories are shown at cost. Any finished goods are expected to yield 110% of cost. If scrapped, goods in process have a realizable value of only $2,200. It is estimated, however, that the work in process can be completed by the addition of $3,000 of present materials and an expenditure of $3,500 for labor. The materials deteriorate rapidly and will realize only 20% of cost. (Use the cost completion method illustrated in the text.)

f) Equipment is estimated to have a realizable value of $12,000.

g) Notes payable include a $25,000 note to Aerotex Company and a $62,500 note to B. Williams. Aerotex holds the U.S. Treasury bonds as security for its loans. It also holds the first mortgage of $37,500 on the company's real estate, interest on which is paid through March 31, 20X5. The note payable to Williams is secured by a chattel mortgage on factory equipment. Interest on the note has been paid through March 31, 20X5. Williams also holds the second mortgage on the real estate.

h) Any expenses not specifically mentioned need not be considered. All salaries qualify for priority, including labor to complete the work in process.

Required:

Prepare a statement of affairs for Carlton Company.

Problem 21-7.   Mayne Manufacturing Company has incurred substantial losses for several years and has become insolvent. On March 31, 20X5, Mayne petitioned the court for protection from creditors and submitted the following statement of financial position.

Mayne Manufacturing Co.
Statement of Financial Position
March 31, 20X5

Assets	Book Value	Liquidation Value
Accounts receivable	$100,000	$ 50,000
Inventories.	90,000	40,000
Plant and equipment	150,000	160,000
Totals	$340,000	$250,000

Liabilities and Stockholders' Equity		
Accounts payable—general creditors	$600,000	
Common stock outstanding.	60,000	
Deficit.	(320,000)	
Total	$340,000	

Mayne's management informed the court that the company has developed a new product. A prospective customer is willing to sign a contract for the purchase of 10,000 units of this product during the year ending March 31, 20X6; 12,000 units of this product during the year ending March 31, 20X7; and 15,000 units of this prod-

(continued)

uct during the year ending March 31, 20X8; all at a price of $90 per unit. This product can be manufactured using Mayne's present facilities. Monthly production with immediate delivery is expected to be uniform within each year. Receivables are expected to be collected during the calendar month following sales.

Unit production costs of the new product are expected to be as follows:

Direct materials	$20
Direct labor.	30
Variable overhead	10

Fixed costs (excluding depreciation) will amount to $130,000 per year.

Purchases of direct materials will be paid during the calendar month following purchase. Fixed costs, direct labor, and variable overhead will be paid as incurred. Inventory of direct materials will be equal to 60 days' usage. After the first month of operations, 30 days' usage of direct materials will be ordered each month.

The general creditors have agreed to reduce their total claims to 60% of their March 31, 20X5 balances, under the following conditions:

a)   Existing accounts receivable and inventories are to be liquidated immediately, with the proceeds turned over to the general creditors.

b)   The balance of reduced accounts payable is to be paid as cash is generated from future operations, but in no event later than March 31, 20X7. No interest will be paid on these obligations.

Under this proposed plan, the general creditors would receive $110,000 more than the current liquidation value of Mayne's assets. The court has engaged you to determine the feasibility of this plan.

Required:

Ignoring any need to borrow and repay short-term funds for working capital purposes, prepare a cash budget for the years ending March 31, 20X6, and 20X7, showing the cash expected to be available to pay the claims of the general creditors and payments to general creditors and the cash remaining after payment of claims. Support the cash budget with two schedules showing collections from customers and disbursements for direct materials.

Problem 21-8.   FICO Corporation is insolvent, and its board of directors is considering several alternatives being proposed by both creditors and management. The creditors are proposing to seek an involuntary petition to liquidate the corporation. It is estimated that the assets and liabilities of the corporation as of February 1, 20X8, will have the following values:

	Book Value	Market Value
Assets pledged with fully secured creditors	$2,400,000	$2,809,000
Assets pledged with partially secured creditors	1,640,000	1,580,000
Free assets	870,000	740,000
Fully secured creditors	2,300,000	N/A
Partially secured creditors	1,640,000	N/A
Unsecured creditors:		
With priority	80,000	N/A
Without priority	1,200,000	N/A

In addition to the preceding liabilities, it is estimated that the trustee's expenses in connection with the liquidation of the corporation will be $35,000.

Management is proposing to continue operations under the supervision of a court-appointed trustee. Management's plan consists of the following:

a) Continue operations for the balance of 20X8, which would result in the following:

Sales revenue:

Collected	$1,480,000
Uncollected	210,000

Cost of sales:

Beginning inventory decrease.	60,000

Current purchases:

Paid	1,100,000
Unpaid	150,000

Selling, general, and administrative (SG&A) expenses:

Paid	80,000
Unpaid ($20,000 of Class 3 wages)	30,000

b) Accounts receivable on February 1, 20X8, of $320,000 would be disposed of as follows:

Written off	$ 30,000
Assigned as collateral of a new loan of $250,000.	290,000

c) With the exception of (b) above, all accounts receivable are considered free assets. All accounts payable are unsecured.

d) A $600,000 bank loan, which was partially secured by assets with a book value of $540,000, will be satisfied by the payment of $100,000 cash and the substitution of a new 6-month unsecured loan. The new loan calls for principal payments of $400,000 and interest payments of $24,000 based on a market rate of interest.

e) Unsecured creditors with claims of $400,000 on February 1 will accept 4,000 shares of 6.5%, cumulative, preferred stock. The preferred stock has an estimated market value of $320,000.

f) Equipment with a net book value of $640,000 will be sold for $520,000. This equipment is pledged as collateral on a $550,000 note. Holders of the note will accept the sales proceeds as payment in full. Additional equipment necessary for operations will be leased under operating leases. Applicable lease payments are included in cost of sales.

g) As of December 31, 20X8, management estimated that assets pledged with fully secured creditors will have a net realizable value of $2,750,000, assets pledged with partially secured creditors will have a net realizable value of 110% of the creditors' balances, and free assets will have a net realizable value equal to 90% of book value.

Required:

1. The board of directors of FICO Corporation has retained you to evaluate the two competing proposals. Prepare a schedule for each alternative that identifies for each category of liabilities and owners' equity: book values, assets available to satisfy claims, and dividend (recovery) percentages.
   Hint: The analysis of management's proposal should include schedules that detail the new balances for liabilities, owners' equity, and available assets as of December 31, 20X8.

2. As a common shareholder, discuss which proposal would be most attractive to you.

Index

D

E

T

Check Figures for Selected Problems

PROB.	CHECK FIGURES
1-1	Goodwill: $245,000 on Turner, $44,000 on Murray
1-2	Turner: Additional Paid-in Capital, $50,000; Retained earnings, $290,000
	Murray: Paid-in Capital, ($20,000); Retained earnings, $150,000
1-3	Purchase: Goodwill is $125,000; Purchase income is $2,500
	Pooling: Retained earnings transferred is $115,000; Pooling income is $29,000 ($20,000 direct acquisition cost is expensed)
1-4	Bond value, $311,983; Goodwill, $147,344
1-5	1. Goodwill is $80,000; 2. Allocate $125,000 on 25/75% basis to land and building
1-6	Investment in direct financing lease, $710,605; Goodwill, $382,678
1-7	Deferred tax asset, $36,000; Deferred tax liability, $74,571; Goodwill, $148,571 (gross)
1-8	1. Bargain; Allocate $1,300,000 30/30/40% to land, building, and equipment; 3. 870 added shares issued
1-9	1. and 2. Retained earnings, $585,000 (including $90,500 adjustment); 3. Reduce paid-in excess $100,000; Retained earnings, $525,000
1-10	1. Retained earnings, $1,487,500; 2. Goodwill, $886,625
1-11	1. Balance sheet retained earnings, $846,000; 2. 19X5 Net income, $330,000
2-1	Goodwill, $160,000
2-2	2. Goodwill, $240,000; 3. Minority interest, $68,000; Paid-in excess, $355,000
2-3	1. Allocate $385,000 to fixed assets
2-4	Goodwill, $63,000
2-5	1. Goodwill $200,000; 2. Balance sheet retained earnings for pooling, $550,000
2-6	Goodwill, $60,000
2-7	Balance Sheet Goodwill, $124,000; Land, $93,000; Minority interest, $50,000
2-8	2. a) Goodwill, $66,400; 2. b) Retained earnings, $1,040,000
2-9	Corrected Edward retained earnings on trial balance, $1,586,250; Reduced Edward retained earnings, $44,680 for 5% acquisition

Note: Consolidated net income refers to the controlling interest's share of combined net income.

3-1	1. Goodwill, $144,000; 3. Amortization: $4,000 depreciation, $14,400 goodwill amortization
3-2	Investment balance, $388,000; Goodwill, $40,000 (on purchase date); Consolidated net income, $169,000
3-3	Investment balance, $374,000; Goodwill, $40,000 (on purchase date); Consolidated net income, $169,000
3-4	Goodwill at purchase, $200,000; Consolidated net income, $45,000; Goodwill on balance sheet, $185,000
3-5	Consolidated net income, $95,000
3-6	Consolidated net income, $43,000; Net building on balance sheet, $735,000
3-7	Consolidated net income, $73,700; Goodwill on balance sheet, $73,800
3-8	Consolidated net income, $127,000; Balance sheet retained earnings for controlling interest, $928,000
3-9	Consolidated net income, $33,600; Goodwill on balance sheet, $30,400
3-10	Consolidated net income, $293,000; Controlling retained earnings on balance sheet, $1,602,000; Goodwill on balance sheet, $111,000
3-11	Consolidated net income, $243,650; Goodwill on balance sheet, $4,900
3-12	Consolidated net income, $374,500; Controlling retained earnings on balance sheet, $1,850,500; Goodwill on balance sheet, $640,500

3A-1   Investment balance, $388,000; Goodwill, $40,000 (on purchase date); Consolidated net income, $169,000

3A-2   Goodwill, $76,000 (on purchase date); consolidated net income, $126,400

3A-3   Goodwill, $83,000 (on purchase date); consolidated net income, $102,600

3B-1   Deferred tax expense: $10,800, current; $43,200, noncurrent; Goodwill (gross) $198,429; Special challenge: noncurrent, deferred tax expense, $32,905

3B-2   Gross goodwill on purchase date, $597,714; Minority interest, $369,400

3B-3   Gross goodwill on purchase date, $322,857; Consolidated net income, $26,233; Goodwill on balance sheet, $301,333

SA1-1   Goodwill at purchase, $32,000; NCI adjustment, $12,000; NCI share of income, $1,100; Controlling share of income, $33,600

SA1-2   NCI adjustment, $48,000; NCI share of income, $8,750; Controlling share of income, $243,650

Note: Consolidated net income refers to the controlling interest's share of combined net income.

4-1   Consolidated cost of goods sold, $7,360,000; Consolidated net income, $1,180,000

4-2   Consolidated cost of goods sold, $1,146,020; Consolidated net income, $76,740

4-3   Consolidated cost of goods sold, $809,250; Consolidated net income, $988,688; Balance sheet minority interest, $138,350

4-4   Consolidated cost of goods sold, $861,000; Consolidated net income, $206,000

4-5   Decrease in current-year depreciation, $5,750; Consolidated net income, $204,440; Minority interest on balance sheet, $53,460

4-6   Consolidated earned income on long-term contracts, $420,500; Consolidated construction in progress, $1,232,000; Consolidated net income, $146,525

4-7   Balance Sheet total for accounts and other current receivables, $385,000; Consolidated cost of goods sold, $1,607,500; Consolidated net income, $289,500

4-8   Consolidated cost of goods sold, $1,338,600; Consolidated net income, $141,295; Purchased income, $35,200

4-9   Consolidated accumulated depreciation, $137,000; Consolidated cost of goods sold, $455,000; Consolidated net income, $185,000

4-10   Same as Problem 4-9

4-11   Same as Problem 4-9

4-12   Distribute $72,000 of excess cost to building; Consolidated cost of goods sold, $187,000; Consolidated other expenses, $62,400; Consolidated net income, $75,840

4-13   Investment in Strand on December 31,19X1, $6,460,000; December 31, 19X1 retained earnings, $10,850,000

4A-1   Consolidated net income, $334,000, Consolidated ending retained earnings, $586,000

4A-2   Goodwill on balance sheet, $76,000; Consolidated cost of goods sold, $210,000; Consolidated net income, $612,700

4A-3   Same as Problem 4-9

Note: Consolidated net income refers to the controlling interest's share of combined net income.

5-1   Loss on bonds, $1,000; Consolidated net income, $806,000

5-2   January 1 loss on bonds, $2,700; Consolidated net income, $179,170

5-3   January 1 retained earnings adjustment on bonds, $15,000; Mortgage interest eliminated, $9,625; Consolidated net income, $1,499,400

5-4   March 31 gain on bonds, $8,000; Ending inventory profit, $90,000; Consolidated net income, $1,412,500

5-5   January 1 gain on bonds, $50,188; Consolidated net income, $409,812

5-6   January 1 retained earnings adjustment on bonds, $6,195; Ending inventory profit, $4,500; Consolidated net income, $123,130

5-7   Goodwill, $20,000

5-8	January 1 retained earnings adjustment on bonds, $7,023; Ending inventory profit, $6,000; Consolidated net income, $60,412
5-9	Consolidated net income, $1,021,000
5-10	Goodwill at purchase, $32,000; Accumulated depreciation on leased warehouse, $254,000; Consolidated net income, $292,400
5-11	Interest on factory lease, $7,587; Interest on equipment lease, $4,476; Consolidated net income, $154,125
5-12	Interest on machine lease, $1,417; Interest on truck lease, $3,023; Consolidated net loss, $4,081
5A-1	Interest on equipment lease, $7,939; Consolidated net income, $344,656
5A-2	none

Note: Consolidated net income refers to the controlling interest's share of combined net income.

6-1	Cash from operations, $404,500; Cash used for financing, $580,000
6-2	Cash from operations, $201,700; Cash applied to investing activities, $40,000
6-3	Cash from operations, $384,000; Cash applied to financing activities, $179,000
6-4	Consolidated BEPS = $4.83; Consolidated DEPS = $4.87
6-5	Consolidated cost of goods sold, $1,126,005; Minority interest in income, $5,582
6-6	Combined income (before deduction of minority interest) before tax, $134,000; Consolidated net income, $88,200
6-7	Combined income (before deduction of minority interest) before tax, $180,650; Consolidated net income, $120,659
6-8	Total retained earnings adjustment for deferred taxes, $5,818; Current-year adjustment for deferred taxes, $1,018; Consolidated net income, $105,706
6-9	Investor share of investee net income: 19X6, $5,500; 19X7, $5,875; 19X8, $9,687
6-10	Net investment income (before tax): 19X6, $3,250; 19X7, $4,213; 19X8, $4,300
6-11	Investment income from all investments: 19X6, $5,340; 19X7, $5,060; 19X8, $104,145

Note: Consolidated net income refers to the controlling interest's share of combined net income.

7-1	Goodwill on 20% interest, $28,000; Consolidated net income, $132,650
7-2	Goodwill: 70% interest, $20,000; 20% interest, $18,000; Investment account balance on December 31, 19X2, $412,000; Consolidated net income, $165,600
7-3	Goodwill: 20% investment, $10,000; 45% interest, $20,500; Consolidated net income, $132,950
7-4	Goodwill; 20% interest, $20,000; 60% interest, $62,000; Consolidated net income, $156,600
7-5	Purchased income, $900; Consolidated cost of goods sold, $169,000; Consolidated net income, $69,015
7-6	Purchased income, $5,000; Consolidated cost of goods sold, $1,783,000; Consolidated net income, $226,250
7-7	Gain on sale of ⅙ interest, $10,400; Loss on sale of ⅗ interest, $36,000
7-8	Correct investment account balance prior to sale, $31,900
7-9	Preferred claim on retained earnings, $16,000; Consolidated net income, $349,440
7-10	No excesses on any investments; Purchased income, $12,000; Remaining gain on bonds on January 1, $1,500; Consolidated net income, $71,040
7-11	Excess cost to equipment, $24,800; Increase in paid-in capital from retirement of preferred stock, $2,000; Consolidated net income, $43,810
7-12	Gain on sale of investment, $16,000; Consolidated cost of goods sold, $3,893,000; Consolidated net income, $861,600
7A-1	Consolidated inventory, $133,100; Retained earnings of East, $115,480
7A-2	Goodwill balance on December 31, $13,067; Encanto retained earnings, $487,217
7A-3	Retained earnings, $4,290,000
7A-4	Goodwill on purchase date, $20,000; Retained earnings adjustment on bond retirement, $1,705; Company P retained earnings, $305,135

Note: Consolidated net income refers to the controlling interest's share of combined net income.

8-1	Original goodwill: Thomas $20,000, Sand $30,000; 19X7 Thomas subsidiary income, $32,000; 19X8 total investment in Thomas increase, $26,720; Equity adjustments for subsidiary transactions, Thomas, $10,720, Sand, $4,133
8-2	Keller retained earnings adjustment $93,000; Samco adjustment to retained earnings, $87,500; Decrease to paid-in capital, $6,500
8-3	Equity adjustment for subsidiary stock sale, $1,200; Goodwill on purchase date, $42,000; Consolidated net income, $119,680
8-4	Goodwill on purchase date: 60% interest, $20,000; 4% interest, $5,520; Consolidated cost of goods sold, $1,539,300; Consolidated net income, $179,716
8-5	Gain on bonds retired, $2,100; Consolidated net income, $121,650
8-6	Consolidated cost of goods sold, $1,681,500; Consolidated net income, $155,500
8-7	Goodwill on purchase date: investment in Boehm, $33,000; Investment in Shelby, $27,380; Consolidated cost of goods sold, $1,272,000; Consolidated net income, $189,131
8-8	Consolidated cost of goods sold, $1,821,600; Consolidated net income, $149,645
8-9	Consolidated net income, $163,000
8-10	Consolidated net income, $160,510
8-11	Goodwill: 40% interest, $3,200; 35% interest, $2,300; Consolidated net income, $176,975
SA2-1	Combined price, $357,500; NCI adjustment, $17,500; NCI share of income, $14,000; Controlling share of income, $133,400
SA2-2	Decrease in retained earnings for 10% investment, $10,000; Consolidated cost of goods sold, $169,000; Consolidated net income (includes NCI share), $71,100
SA3-1	Goodwill: 70% investment, $49,000; 10% investment, $2,000
Chapter 9:	No Check Figures
10-1	1. With hedge, $252,000; 2. Recognized loss, $500; 3. $200
10-2	2. Gross profit, $188,500
10-3	2. Net effect on income of using the option, $70,750
10-4	3. Contract discount, $6,500; 4. Two-contract approach is provided
10-5	July expense, $18,962; August expense, $2,962
10-6	Assumption 1, Option C income effect, $123,000 expense
10-7	Basis of new warehouse, $1,391,440
11-1	1. $805,200
11-2	Jacklandia cumulative translation adjustment, $1,109,000; Minority interest, $2,773,500
11-3	Cumulative translation adjustment, $104,648
11-4	Cumulative translation adjustment, $1,274,400; Book value of investment, $7,674,570.
11-5	Translation adjustment, $26,571
11-6	Remeasurement gain, $877,275
11-7	2. $301,200; 4. $20,141,840
11-8	1. $111,600 remeasurement loss; 2. $45,432 debit
11-9	Tobac cumulative translation adjustment, $(3,560,637); Consolidated adjustment, $(3,560,637)
11-10	Remeasurement loss, $297,363
12-1	2nd-quarter YTD tax on cumulative effect, $25,000
12-2	B, $75,000; F, 20.77%; I, $20,100 benefit
12-3	N/A
12-4	Tax benefit on loss B, $28,550
12-5	Case B revised tax rate, 25%; 3. Tax benefit allocated to extraordinary loss, $14,529
12-6	Qt. 3 restated effective tax rate, 28.89%

12-7	Qt. 1 restated (second time) effective tax rate, 26.10%
12-8	Segment A profit, $1,646,248; Total consolidated assets, $23,328,893
12-9	All segments are reportable except battery and starter parts and tire retreading; Total consolidated pretax income, $17,200,000
13-1	Weighted average number of shares, 246,583; DEPS, $3.024
13-2	Contingent share agreement share adjustment, 13,750; DEPS, $1.763
13-3	DEPS share adjustments for agreement: B, 21,250; C, 10,000; E, 1,563
13-4	Weighted average number of shares, 840,000; DEPS, $0.665
13-5	Option #2 share adjustment, 286; DEPS, $1,880
13-6	3-month DEPS, $1.4736; 6-month DEPS, $2.564
14-1	Durand's profit: $69,905
14-2	1. Nichols, $52,682; 2. Nichols, $61,682
14-3	N/A
14-4	Jacobsen's amount due from the partnership, $188,717
14-5	Thomas's allocation of profits without Wiggins, $82,800; Purnell's allocation of profits with Wiggins, $81,267
14-6	Carson's adjusted capital, $12,600
14A-1	Net income per tax, $38,000
15-1	2. Goodwill, $20,000
15-2	2. $49,286; 4. $32,500; 6. $77,250
15-3	1. $22,000
15-4	Meyers balance, $57,640
15-5	Accept Baker's offer
15-6	Neither Janis nor Glomski would receive a distribution if the partnership were liquidated. Furthermore, Glomski would be required to contribute additional assets to the partnership.
15-7	2. Distribution A to Knapp, $16,000
15-8	Third-month balance for Barker, $24,500
15-9	First safe payment to partners: $14,257 to Nolan and $2,343 to Petersen
15-10	Part II. Aikens receives $41,500
15-11	January payment of Perry estate, $1,046
16-5	2. Debit to fund balance—unreserved, undesignated in closing entry, $52,000; 3. Total actual fund balances, June 20, 19X7, $24,000
16-6	2. Credit to fund balance—unreserved, undesignated for closing, $385,100; 3. Actual fund balance, $230,100
16-7	Debit expenditures in general fund $4,000,000; Credit unfunded pension obligation in General Long-Term Debt Account Group, $2,000,000
16-8	e) Credit to taxes receivable delinquent, $46,000; j) Debit fund balance—reserved for stores, $6,000
16-10	d) Debit to expenditures, $68,000 in general fund; Debit investment in general fixed assets in General Fixed Assets Account Group, $35,000; Debit machinery and equipment in General Fixed Assets Account Group, $80,000
16-11	c) Debit to Other Financing Uses $135,000 in general fund; e) Debit amount available in debt service fund, $135,000
16-12	2. Total general fixed assets, $6,455,00
16-13	2. Amount available in debt service funds for serial bonds on December 31, 19X7, $232,662
16-15	1. Excess of revenues over expenditures, $228, 400; 2. Total liabilities and fund equity, $462,400
16-16	b) Debit to revenues and credit to Donated Land, $27,000 in general fund; b) Debit Land in General Fixed Assets Account Group

17-4   2. Credit to Fund Balance—Unreserved, Undesignated to close, $7,600,000; 3. Total liabilities and fund balance, $8,800,000

17-6   May 1 entry: Debit to Improvements other than Buildings, $896,000 in the General Fixed Assets Account Group

17-8   3. Fund Balance—Unreserved, Undesignated in balance sheet, $150,000

17-9   Capitalized expenditures to date, $676,600 in the General Fixed Assets Account Group

17-11   Cash received by Reed City General Fund, $423,360

17-13   Net assets held in trust for pension benefits, $540,000

17-15   2. Excess of operating revenues over operating expenses in closing entry, $16,500

17-17   f) Debit to Buildings in General Fixed Assets Account Group; h) Credit Other Financing Sources in the debt service fund

17-18   4. Debit to Residual Equity Transfer-Out, $5,000 in general fund; 7. Credit Encumbrances, $75,000 in capital project fund

17-21   Capitalize total expenditures in the General Fixed Assets Account Group; Land, $150,000; Buildings, $410,000

17-22   Cash balances: General Fund, $83,800; Debt Service Fund, $6,000; Capital Projects Fund, $400,000

18-4   2. Net increase in Unrestricted Current Funds for the year, $117,000

18-5   d) Debit to Fund Balance—Restricted in Plant Fund for Retirement of Indebtedness

18-6   2. Total increase in Net Assets, $282,000

18-7   Total increase in Net Assets, $4,525,000

18-8   Total increase in Net Assets, $85,000

18-9   Total net assets, $4,235,000

18A-1   o) Debit to Reclassification Out—Temporarily Restricted, $15,000; p) Debit depreciation expense to Expenses—Operation and Maintenance of Plant, $20,000; 2. Increase in unrestricted net assets, $117,609

18A-2   Total net assets for Current Funds, $204,449

18A-3   Net Assets at end of year, $3,697,200

19-5   a) Debit to Contractual Adjustments, $120,000; h) Debit to Reclassification Out—Temporarily Restricted, $20,000; 2. Loss from operations, $48,000

19-6   Change in unrestricted net assets, $864,000; Change in Temporarily Restricted Net Assets, $445,000; Change in Permanently Restricted Net Assets, $150,000

19-7   Net cash provided by operating activities, $1,105,100

19-8   Contributions restricted for endowment, $500,000, and Contributions restricted for purchase of property and equipment, $183,000 subtracted from change in net assets to reconcile to net cash provided by operating activities

19-9   Total unrestricted net assets, $701,900; Total temporarily restricted net assets, $236,000; Total permanently restricted net assets, $400,000

19-10   6. Debit to Buildings and Equipment, $18,000; Debit to Reclassification Out—Temporarily Restricted, $18,000

19-11   g) Debit to Depreciation Expense, $46,000; Debit to Reclassifications Out—Temporarily Restricted, $20,000

19-12   1. Change in unrestricted net assets, $71,000; 2. Total net assets, $392,000

19-13   2. Change in net assets, $109,000

19-14   Total operating expenses allocated to Fundraising Services, $47,700; Total plant-related expenses allocated to Fundraising Services, $2,400

19-15   1. Change in unrestricted net assets, ($1,000); Change in temporarily restricted net assets, $140,000; Change in permanently restricted net assets, $55,000

19-16   Total expenses allocated to Alcohol and Drug Abuse, $322,200

19A-1	d) Credit to Nonoperating Revenues—Temporarily Restricted (Contributions), $30,000; Credit to Other Operating Revenues—Temporarily Restricted (Contributions), $60,000; Credit to Nonoperating Revenues—Unrestricted (Contributions), $79,000
19A-2	Change in net assets in General Fund, ($58,000)
19A-3	1. c) Debit to Equipment in Plant Fund, $15,000; 2. c) Credit to Reclassification In—Unrestricted, $15,000
19A-4	2. Total debits in Unrestricted Current Fund, $651,000; Total debits for organization, $1,793,000
20-1	Principal balance, $99,250
20-2	N/A
20-3	a) Estate tax: 0 and $330,950
20-4	2. Total charges of $1,136,250
20-5	N/A
20-6	Principal balance, $264,250
20-7	N/A
20-8	N/A
21-1	1. Cash outflows, $905,336
21-2	Total distribution to unsecured creditors under the plan of reorganization, $284,098
21-3	Item c: $50,000 bankruptcy and $0 not under bankruptcy
21-4	Consideration to be received by creditors in a liquidation is $996,661 versus $1,052,678 if a reorganization
21-5	2. b) Payment to unsecured creditors without priority, $30,000
21-6	Total to unsecured creditors without priority, $134,800
21-7	Cash balance at year-end 20X6, $75,000
21-8	1. Assets available, $5,129,000